THE ENCYCLOPEDIA
OF REVOLUTIONS AND
REVOLUTIONARIES

THE ENCYCLOPEDIA
OF REVOLUTIONS AND REVOLUTIONARIES

From Anarchism to Zhou Enlai

Martin van Creveld

Facts On File®

AN INFOBASE HOLDINGS COMPANY

Copyright © 1996 by G.G. The Jerusalem Publishing House, Ltd.
39 Tchernichovski St., P.O. Box 7147, Jerusalem 91071, Israel

Facts On File, Inc.
11 Penn Plaza
New York, NY 10001

Library of Congress Cataloging-in-Publication Data

The encyclopedia of revolutions and revolutionaries : from anarchism
   to Zhou Enlai / Martin van Creveld, editor-in-chief.
      p.   cm.
   Includes bibliographical references and index.
   ISBN 0-8160-3236-X (acid-free paper)
   1. World politics—Encyclopedias. 2. Revolutions—History—
Encyclopedias. 3. Revolutionaries—Biography—Encyclopedias.
4. Politicians—Biography—Encyclopedias. 5. Heads of state—
Biography—Encyclopedias.   I. Van Creveld, Martin L.
D21.3.E33   1996
909.08'03—dc20   95-44502

Facts On File books are available at special discounts when purchased in bulk quantities for businesses, associations, institutions or sales promotions. Please call our Special Sales Department in New York at (212) 967-8800 or (800) 322-8755.

Jacket design by Hadass Bar Yosef
Printed in Hong Kong

10 9 8 7 6 5 4 3 2 1

This book is printed on acid-free paper.

EDITOR-IN-CHIEF

MARTIN VAN CREVELD

CONSULTING EDITOR

ALAIN SILVERA

MANAGING EDITOR

RACHEL GILON

ASSISTANT EDITORS

SHMUEL HIMELSTEIN
RACHEL FELDMAN

CONTRIBUTORS

REUVEN AHARONI, Ph.D.   *Middle East*
Eretz Yisrael Studies
University of Haifa

PROFESSOR SHLOMO ARONSON, Ph.D.   *Germany*
Department of Political Science
The Hebrew University of Jerusalem

AMATZIA BARAM, Ph.D.   *Iraq*
Chairman of the Department of Middle Eastern History
University of Haifa

MENAHEM BLONDHEIM, Ph.D.   *United States*
Department of American Studies
The Hebrew University of Jerusalem

SUZANNE M.M. BURG, M.A.   *South Africa*
Somerville, MA

AVNER DE-SHALIT, Ph.D.   *Green Revolution*
Department of Political Science
The Hebrew University of Jerusalem

CLARISSA DESOUCHES, Ph.D.   *South America*
Department of History
United States International University; Universidad Internacional de México, A.C.

SILVIA ELGUERA, M.A.   *Mexico*
Division of Humanities
Autonomous Metropolitan University, Mexico

ROUBEN ENOCH, Ph.D.   *Georgia, Azerbaijan*
Editor of *Flag* (Georgian-language monthly magazine)
Israel

NAOMI FREEDMAN, M.A.   *Editorial Assistant*
Middle Eastern Studies
Williams College, MA

PROFESSOR TED FRIEDGUT, Ph.D.   *Russian History*
Department of Russian and Slavic Studies
The Hebrew University of Jerusalem

RUTH GINEO, M.A.   *Ethiopia*
Researcher in African Studies
The Harry S Truman Research Institute for the Advancement of Peace
The Hebrew University of Jerusalem

DORE GOLD, Ph.D.   *United States*
Director of the U.S. Foreign and Defense Policy Project
Jaffee Center for Strategic Studies
Tel Aviv University

AVNER HALPERN, Ph.D.   *France*
Department of History
The Hebrew University of Jerusalem

JOSEP JAFFAROV, Ph.D.   *Caucasia*
The Harry S Truman Research Institute for the Advancement of Peace
The Hebrew University of Jerusalem

PROFESSOR DAVID S. KATZ, Ph.D.   *Great Britain*
Department of History
Tel Aviv University

ASHER KAUFMAN, M.A.   *Syria*
Department of Middle Eastern Studies
The Hebrew University of Jerusalem

ANAT LAPIDOTH, Ph.D.   *Turkey*
Department of Middle Eastern Studies
Ben-Gurion University of the Negev

PROFESSOR RICHARD DE LEMOS, Ph.D.   *North America, Western Europe, Vietnam*
Chairman of the University Business and Development Committee
United States International University; Universidad Internacional de México, A.C.

BRIDGET LEVITT   *Africa*
Researcher in African Studies
Jerusalem

PHILIP GEORGE PHILIP MASILAMANI, Ph.D.   *South Asia*

Faculty of Social Sciences
University of Kent at Canterbury
Canterbury, England

MICHELLE MAZEL, M.A.   *Switzerland, Peru*

Writer and Journalist
Jerusalem

YORAM MEITAL, Ph.D.   *Egypt*

Department of Middle Eastern History
Ben-Gurion University of the Negev

VLADIMIR MESAMED, Ph.D.   *Iran*

The Harry S Truman Research Institute for the Advancement of Peace
The Hebrew University of Jerusalem

DAVID OHANA, Ph.D.   *Political Ideologies*

Historian, The Jerusalem Van Leer Institute
Jerusalem

PROFESSOR CAMILO PEREZ-BUSTILLO, Ph.D.   *Mexican History*

Department of Communication Sciences
Instituto Tecnologico y de Estudios Superiores de Monterey (ITESM), Mexico
Department of Liberal Studies
United States International University; Universidad Internacional de México, A.C.

ROHAN SAXENA, M.A.   *Indian History*

Researcher, Jerusalem

MARIO SZNAJDER, Ph.D.
Department of Political Science
The Hebrew University of Jerusalem

Italy, Fascism

ALEXANDER UCHITEL, Ph.D.
Department of History
The Hebrew University of Jerusalem

Ancient Assyria & Babylon

RAPHAEL VAGO, Ph.D.
Department of History
Tel Aviv University

Eastern Europe

PROFESSOR MARTIN VAN CREVELD, Ph.D.
Department of History
The Hebrew University of Jerusalem

Editor-in-Chief

PROFESSOR SUSANNE WAGNER DE CLEMENTI, Ph.D.
Executive Director
United States International University; Universidad Internacional de México A.C.

Mexico

DANIEL WOOL
Writer
Toronto, Canada

Editorial Writer

RONEN ZEIDEL, Ph.D.
Research Assistant
Department of Middle Eastern History
University of Haifa

Iraq

INTRODUCTION

Throughout history revolutions have been among the most important agents of change, often leading to the radical reshaping of political, economic, social and even religious institutions. Thus, already the ancient Egyptian king Tutankhamen sought to bring about a religious, cultural and social revolution in his kingdom during the fourteenth century B.C. In classical Greece there were numerous attempts to set up new and revolutionary forms of government; as to Rome, not only was it made by a revolution (the one that drove out King Tarquinius Superbus and established the republic) but its history was marked by a whole series of revolutionary events. In the modern world, the Glorious Revolution of 1688 was the first to put an end to absolute monarchical government and introduce the idea of a common law for all. The American and French revolutions brought democracy, a clear separation of the three powers and the principle of one man, one vote. On the other hand, the Russian and Chinese revolutions led to the establishment of Communist-type régimes which, in one form or another, are only now being dismantled.

In *The Encyclopedia of Revolutions and Revolutionaries* the student will find almost thirteen hundred articles about the most important revolutions in history, the people and organizations who made them and the ideologies in whose name they were carried out. Except for Australia, where there have been no revolutions, the list covers every continent. It ranges from antiquity, e.g., the Spartacus Rebellion and the revolt of Palmyra against Rome, all the way to the most recent coups and countercoups in the Middle East; and from sophisticated ideologies that have changed the world, such as Marxism, down to the slogans that have served Third World strongmen in carrying out this or that revolt.

Most revolutions erupted from below, but a few—such as Bismarck's Revolution From Above and the shah of Iran's White Revolution—came from above. Some were extremely violent, leading to the deaths of hundreds of thousands or millions of people; others, such as Gandhi's struggle for Indian independence and Czechoslovakia's 1989 Velvet Revolution, much less so. Some dissolved almost without trace, barely even affecting the fundamental structure of the countries in which they took place; others were truly epoch-making and made their effects felt not in a single country but globally. Without them civilization as we know it would have been entirely different and the pages of history, if not empty, devoid of many of their most important landmarks. Beyond these dichotomies is the fact that revolutionary ideologies and the lives of revolutionaries, as documented in this volume, often make fascinating reading. After all, few things could be more spectacular than the career of a Washington commanding the militia of Virginia at the age of twenty-two or of a Robespierre executing his enemies in the name of reason; to say nothing of the escapades of a Garibaldi carrying his wife in his arms until she died.

The first of its kind in any language, *The Encyclopedia of Revolutions and Revolutionaries* has been written by an international team of historians and scholars. It is profusely illustrated, often with rare or previously unpublished pictures especially selected from the archives and reproduced with the greatest care. It comes complete with two different indexes (one chronological, the other comprising terms not considered sufficiently important to merit entries of their own) as well as a bibliography. In it, the reader will find an important tool of reference, as well as many hours of reading about a phenomenon that has helped shape the world in which we live.

M.V.C.

A

'ABBAS, FERHAT (1899–1985) Algerian nationalist leader. Trained at the University of Algiers, 'Abbas, a pharmacist by profession, became active in public affairs in the 1930s and was several times elected to those Algerian administrative and financial assemblies to which an Algerian Muslim was eligible. At first he opposed Arab Algerian nationalism and advocated full equality for Algerian Muslims, as well as Algeria's integration in France. Disappointed by the failure of the reforms instituted by the French Popular Front government after 1936, 'Abbas gradually shifted to a more autonomist position and in 1938 founded the *Union Populaire Algerienne* (Algerian Popular Union), but his influence was limited. After serving with the French army in 1939–1940, he was also personally disappointed by the lack of equal opportunity and reward granted him by Vichy France.

After the landing of Allied forces in North Africa in November 1942, he presented a message to the French and Allied leaders, proposing a new régime of equality, full freedoms, a vaguely formulated measure of autonomy and Algerian participation in government. These demands were reformulated in February 1943 in a "Manifest," cosigned by a group of Algerian leaders. In May 1943, 'Abbas was invited to present detailed proposals, but nothing came of these talks. In 1944 he founded an organization, AMIS DU MANIFESTE ET DE LA LIBERATÉ (FRIENDS OF THE MANIFESTO AND OF LIBERTY), which was re-formed in April 1946 as the Union Democratique du Manifeste Algerien (UDMA) (Democratic Union of the Algerian Manifest), calling for an autonomous Algeria in federation with France. This was seen as a rival and alternative to MESSALI HAJJ's more extremist organization (which was known, among others and at different times as the Party of the Algerian People and the Algerian National Movement). 'Abbas was now considered anti-French and was imprisoned several times. During those years he became an advocate of full independence.

In 1956, when the armed revolt was in full swing, he escaped to Cairo, where part of the rebel leadership maintained its headquarters and joined its organization, the FRONT DE LIBERATION NATIONALE (FLN) (National Liberation Front). He played no major part in military operations, but when the FLN set up a Provisional Government of the Algerian Revolution in Cairo in September 1958, he was named prime minister. 'Abbas was, however, unable to accommodate himself fully to the policies and the leadership style of the FLN command and in August 1961 he was dismissed. He took no active part in the final negotiations of independence. In September 1962 he became president

of independent Algeria's first National Assembly. His opposition to the course the Algerian leadership was taking deepened and in August 1963 he resigned, bitterly denouncing the totalitarian, "Castroist" trends that had become dominant and the "confiscation of power" by AHMAD BEN-BELLA and his FLN associates (though he could not make that denunciation fully public). He remained in alienated opposition and without a position of power when Ben-Bella was overthrown in 1965 by HOUARI BOUMEDIENNE. In 1976 he was placed under house arrest. This, however, was later relaxed and he was able to publish, in France, several books: *Autopsie d'une guerre* (Autopsy of a war), 1980; *Le Jeune Algérien* (The young Algerian)—a collection of older essays—1981; *L'Indépendance confisquée* (Independence confiscated)—his denunciation of Ben-Bella's and Boumedienne's régimes—1984. In 1984 'Abbas was fully rehabilitated, but now, over 80 years old, he did not resume any political activity.

'ABBUD, IBRAHIM (1900–1983) Sudanese officer and nationalist, president of the Sudan 1958–1964. His ancestry is described as tribal (in differing versions). Educated at Gordon College and Military College and commissioned in 1918, 'Abbud served with the Sudan Defense Force established by the British in 1925. During World War II, he served with the Sudanese contingent in the British army in the Libyan, Ethiopian and Eritrean campaigns. When the army command was Sudanized, he became, in 1954, deputy commander-in-chief, and with the attainment of independence, commander-in-chief (1956–1964). In November 1958 'Abbud staged a coup d'état—reportedly with the encouragement of the outgoing prime minister—and became president, prime minister and minister of defense, while remaining commander-in-chief of the armed forces. His régime was conservative and oppressive and had no clear ideological orientation beyond its aspirations to stability and gradual economic improvements. In his foreign policy, 'Abbud was moderately pro-West with a growing neutralist tinge. After having suppressed several attempts to oust him, 'Abbud was toppled in October 1964 in a coup d'état led by civilian politicians and supported by some army officers. He first continued as a figurehead president, but resigned after three weeks and retired from public life.

'ABD EL KRIM (1892–1963) Berber chieftain and Moroccan anti-Spanish resistance leader. Trained as an engineer in the Spanish educational system, 'Abd el Krim became dissatisfied with the Spanish colonial administration while working in its civil service. In 1919 he returned to his Berber tribe and organized an army with the aid of his brother. In 1921, after they inflicted a defeat on the Spanish army at Anual, he founded the Republic of Rif, becoming its first and only president. The Spanish were forced to abandon their inland possessions and in 1925 el-Krim nearly succeeded in capturing Fez from the French. A combined 160,000-man French and Spanish army led by Field Marshal Pétain defeated the Berbers in 1926. El Krim was exiled to Réunion until 1947, when he settled in Egypt.

'ABD RABBUH, YASIR (1945–) Palestinian national-revolutionary leader. A native of Jerusalem, 'Abd Rabbuh started his political activity as a member of the movement of Arab Nationalists but during the sixties left it in order to join GEORGE HABASH in setting up the Popular Front for the Liberation of Palestine (PFLP). Next, in 1969, he established the Popular Democratic Front for the Liberation of Palestine (PDFLP). That organization was the first one to accept the idea of a Palestinian national authority in Gaza and the West Bank as the first stage in the establishment of a Palestinian state.

Representing the most moderate wing of the PLO, 'Abd Rabbuh has been a member of its executive committee from 1973 on. As a moderate he was able to establish ties with the Israeli left; as a near-Communist he helped YASIR ARAFAT to cement his ties with Moscow. In 1988, by which time he was in charge of the PLO's information department, he headed the Palestinian delegation during the first direct talks with the US. From then on, and even though the PDFLP split in 1991, he became more and more deeply involved in the peace talks with Israel. 1992 found him at the head of a new group, *al-Ittihad al Dimugrati al Filastine* (FIDA). In May 1994, Yasir Arafat appointed him a member of the Palestine National Authority in charge of culture and art.

ABDUH, MUHAMMAD (1849–1905) Egyptian Muslim thinker, one of the initiators and main leaders of the renaissance of Islamic thought and its reform and modernization. After the failure of the Arabi revolt in 1882, 'Abduh went into exile and published the Pan-Islamic journal *al-Urwa al-Wuthqa* (Faithful support) in Paris—together with JAMAL AD-DIN AL-AFGHANI (1839–1897), the founder of the Pan-Islamic movement, by whom he was strongly influenced. 'Abduh called for a renewal of Islamic values and their adaptation to modern life; he advocated, for instance, the abolition of polygamy. He maintained that there is no contradiction between the tenets of Islam and those of modern Western civilization and that the Islamic renaissance he advocated was the answer to Western criticism and an effective defense against the encroachment of Western values. In 1888, 'Abduh was permitted to return to Egypt, appointed a judge in the Muslim *Shari'a* courts and a member of the board of al-Azhar University and of the Legislative Council. In 1899 he was made Grand Mufti of Egypt. His ideas and writings—intensely debated by supporters and opponents—had a considerable influence on the Islamic movement and Arab nationalism.

ABDUL GHAFFAR (al-Tikriti), HARDAN (1925–1971) Iraqi officer and politician. As an air force officer, Ghaffar was, in the early 1960s, in contact with the clandestine *Ba'ath* group.

He played a leading role in the coup that overthrew the QASSEM régime in February 1963 and became commander of the air force in the *Ba'ath* régime that replaced it. When Abdul Salam 'Aref took over in November 1963, Ghaffar was appointed minister of defense, but he soon fell out with the president and was dismissed and "exiled" as ambassador to Sweden—a post which he soon left. After an officers' coup of July 1968, he became chief of the general staff and commander of the air force, and after a second coup that same month—in which the *Ba'ath* group took complete control—deputy prime minister and minister of defense, and also a member of the Revolutionary Command Council. In April 1970 he became vice-president, giving up the defense ministry. He was considered the up-and-coming man, the real power in the government. However, in the complex factional struggle within the ruling *Ba'ath* party, he ran afoul of rising strongman SADDAM HUSSEIN, who gained the upper hand and had him dismissed in October 1970 (using as a pretext his alleged responsibility for the failure of the Iraqi expeditionary force in Jordan to impose Iraq's will on King Hussein in his struggle with the PLO). Abdul Ghaffar had to go into exile. In March 1971 he was assassinated in Kuwait—it is generally assumed by agents of the Iraqi régime.

ABDUL LATIF (al-Sha'bi), FEISAL (1935–1970) South Yemeni politician. Linked from the 1950s with the all-Arab Nationalist Movement faction, he became one of the main leaders of the extreme NATIONAL LIBERATION FRONT (NLF) in the South Yemeni nationalist struggle against British rule in Aden. After the People's Republic of South Yemen attained independence in November 1967, Abdul Latif held a number of prominent government positions. In April 1969 he was named prime minister (replacing President Qahtan al-Sha'bi). Deeply involved in factional struggles, Abdul Latif was ousted in a coup in July 1969, together with his relative, President Sha'ni—reportedly because of his Arab-nationalist (as opposed to Marxist) tendencies; he was detained, and later expelled from the NLF. In April 1970 he was killed while "trying to escape."

ABDUL-RAZZAQ, 'AREF (1924–) Iraqi officer, journalist and politician. In February 1963 'Abd-Ul-Razzaq became commander of the Iraqi air force. As a Nasserist, he opposed the ABDUL KARIM QASSEM régime and later the BA'ATH PARTY, but had some affinity to the ideologically fluctuating semi-Nasserist régimes of the brothers ABDUL RAHMAN 'AREF and ABDUL SALAM 'AREF. He served the two in 1963–1964 as minister of agriculture. In September 1965, after Nasserist pressure and a reported semi-coup, he became prime minister, but was dismissed after two weeks and went into exile in Egypt. In 1966, Abdul-Razzaq was involved in an abortive Nasserist coup and detained. He was, however, released in 1967 without having stood trial. He remained a Nasserist, was sometimes consulted when the faction in power wished to form a broader united front and was again involved in a coup attempt in October 1968 and detained for some time. With the consolidation of the *Ba'ath* régime in Iraq from 1968 on, Abdul-Razzaq ceased his political activities.

ABU IYAD see KHALEF, SALAH.

ABU NIDAL see AL-BANNA, SABRI.

ADAMS, JOHN   (1735–1826) Statesman, diplomat and lawyer who became the second president of the United States, 1797–1801. Born in Braintree (now Quincy), Massachusetts, Adams could even in those very early days say that he was a fourth-generation American. After receiving his bachelor's degree from Harvard in 1755, he worked as a schoolmaster in Worcester, Massachusetts and studied law. He was admitted to the Boston bar in 1758.

His law practice led him to be active on behalf of the AMERICAN REVOLUTION. He argued against the STAMP ACT before the royal governor, but strongly disapproved of the so-called Stamp Act riots. He only grew closer to the revolutionary cause by appearing in important cases connected with it, such as the smuggling charges against JOHN HANCOCK, a prominent colonist.

In 1774, he was one of the Massachusetts delegates to the first and second Continental Congresses, becoming one of the leaders of the American Revolution. He was appointed to a committee charged with drafting the declaration of independence. Adams's greatest contribution to the declaration of independence, of which he was a signatory, was to serve as the driving force that supported and defended it through Congress.

From 1778 to 1788, Adams served his country primarily as a diplomat, taking up successive posts in France, the Netherlands and England. Returning home, he was elected vice president (1788) and reelected to this office in 1792. In 1796 he was elected president. As president, his most important achievements included the establishment of the Department of the Navy (1798) and the signing of a treaty with France (1800). In the same year he ran for a second term of office but was defeated by THOMAS JEFFERSON.

John Adams

IN A LETTER TO HIS WIFE, ABIGAIL, JULY 3, 1776

Yesterday the greatest question was decided which ever was debated in America; and a greater perhaps never was, nor will be, decided among men. A resolution was passed without one dissenting colony, that these United Colonies, are and of right ought to be, free and independent States.

AT THE SECOND CONTINENTAL CONGRESS

I have come to the conclusion that one useless man is called a disgrace, that two are called a law firm, and three or more become a congress! For ten years King George and his Parliament have called, cullied, and diddled these colonies with their illegal taxes—Stamp Acts, Townshend Acts, Sugar Acts, Tea Acts—and when we dared stand up like men they stopped our trade, seized our ships, blockaded our ports, burned our towns, and spilled our blood—and still this congress won't grant any of my proposals on Independence...

FROM AN ARTICLE IN THE BOSTON GAZETTE, 1765

Wherever a general knowledge and sensibility have prevailed among the people, arbitrary government and every kind of oppression have lessened and disappeared in proportion... Liberty cannot be preserved without a general knowledge among the people who have a right, from the frame of their nature, to knowledge... And the preservation of the means of knowledge among the lowest ranks is of more importance to the public than all the property of the rich men in the country... Let us dare to read, think, speak, and write. Let every order and degree among the people rouse their attention and animate their resolution... In a word, let every sluice of knowledge be opened and set aflowing.

LETTERS TO HIS WIFE, 1775-1776

• An ounce of mother wit is worth a pound of clergy.

• Education makes a greater difference between man and man than nature has made between man and brute.

ADAMS, SAMUEL   (1722–1803) An American revolutionary leader, signatory of the United States declaration of independence and governor of Massachusetts (1789–1793). The Boston-born and Harvard-educated Adams was one of the earliest and most effective agitators to forward the cause of American independence from Great Britain. He distinguished himself among leaders of the AMERICAN REVOLUTION, perhaps even pioneering among world statesmen, in developing new techniques for mobilizing public opinion in an age of popularized politics. Beyond propaganda, Adams was highly effective in organizing revolutionary activity on a continental scale and on a local, grass-roots level.

Adams moved into politics over a trail of business failures. One of the most disastrous of these, his erratic management of his family brewery, had left him with a moral that was to serve as one of the most persuasive tools in shaping the revolutionary mind of Americans. Power, Adams proposed, was like a drink: it was both "intoxicating by its nature" and "liable to abuse." The British ministry, he argued, was intoxicated by its new-found power of imperial government, and since the nature of power was one of encroachment, the ministry naturally proceeded to abuse its power by encroaching on Englishmen's constitutional freedoms. The first to be affected by this abuse were those on the imperial periphery and in particular the North American colonists.

Adams deftly applied his analysis to the British government of North America, highlighting acts of taxation without representation, the location of standing armies among free citizens, the exercise of power by appointed rather than elected officials and by administrative courts rather than courts governed by common law traditions. Having developed these premises, Adams went on to popularize them in a barrage of personal letters, newspaper articles, printed pamphlets and inflammatory public orations. He did so both in ad hoc forums and in the Massachusetts House of Representatives, a body in which he served from 1765 to 1774.

Adams also proved highly effective in channeling the sentiments, which he had so ably aroused, into organized public action. He was instrumental in organizing the SONS OF LIBERTY, was one of the main instigators of the unrest that erupted in the Boston Massacre and masterminded the BOSTON TEA PARTY. His activities on the continental level were no less effective. He was instrumental in organizing intercolonial "Committees of Correspondents" and in drafting the "Circular Letter" of 1768 issued by the Massachusetts House to the other colonial legislatures. Adams was also active in bringing about the First Continental Congress (1774). One of the early proponents of immediate independence, he voted for and signed the declaration of independence.

Adams, who had become something of a professional revolutionary, failed to adjust to the role of statesman and never achieved national stature in the young republic. He served in Congress only until 1781, after which he was elected lieutenant governor of Massachusetts (1789–1793) and then governor (1794–1797).

ADLER, VICTOR (1852–1918) Founder of the Austrian Social Democratic Party. Adler was born to a Jewish family in Prague. When he was four his family moved to Vienna, where the family prospered. It was thus able to leave the Leopoldstadt ghetto for a fashionable part of the city. Although he received an elementary Jewish religious education, Adler soon assimilated into German culture.

Adler studied at medical school at the University of Vienna, receiving his degree in 1881. One of his contemporaries was Sigmund Freud, with whom he once fought a duel. Adler too specialized in psychiatry at the university, but went on to devote his life to politics. In 1878 he converted to Protestantism (although his wife remained Jewish), arguing that he was severing himself from Judaism to make it easier for his children and save them from embarrassment.

In the 1870s, Adler supported Pan-Germanism, i.e., the unification of all German-speaking territories. However, in 1885, when an anti-Jewish paragraph was introduced into its program, Adler was forced out of the movement. Even as a "new" Christian, Adler was not permitted to join "*völkisch*" clubs and various societies and associations. Socialist ideology appealed to many germanized Jews and in 1886 Adler joined the Austrian labor movement. In 1888–1889 he was responsible for the establishment of the Austrian Social Democratic Party. Within the party, Adler showed remarkable talents for diplomacy in preserving the internal unity of the Austrian socialists. Politically, perhaps his biggest success was achieved when the imperial government in 1906 granted universal suffrage. He was a member of the Austrian parliament from 1905–1918 and foreign minister in the Socialist government of 1918. He died shortly after his appointment, on November 11, 1918, the day before the republic was proclaimed.

- One must have Jews as comrades, but not too many.

- The last anti-Semite will disappear with the last Jew.

- I have no vocation for quiet academic work but I am a serviceable hawker of foreign ideas—we Jews seem predestined for peddling.

- The Jews' fear of the anti-Semites is only equaled by the anti-Semites' fear of the Jews.

Victor Adler

AFAR RESISTANCE The population of Djibouti is almost equally divided between Afars and Issas. The two groups are, in fact, closely related but there is frequent rivalry. Initial intentions after independence from France (1977) were to maintain a careful ethnic balance in government and a unified political party ruled the country; however, in 1979 President Hassan Gouled, an Issa clan member, replaced this party with a new political party of his own, the *Rassemblement populaire de la progres* (RPP). The main Afar opposition groups united into an opposition movement and, in 1991, launched a full-scale insurrection. In the intervening years, many leading Afars had left Gouled's party and joined the opposition.

Since 1991, this powerful armed Afar opposition, calling itself *Le Front democratique pour la restauration de l'unite et de la democratie* (FRUD), has posed a serious challenge to the government. The Afar insurgency (mainly in the north of Djibouti) has been a major hindrance to economic development and a considerable burden on government expenditure.

AFGHANISTAN REVOLUTIONS   (1973–1979) By the early 1970s it had become clear that King Muhammad Zahir's attempts to establish a constitutional monarchy in Afghanistan were doomed to failure. Although factional movements on both sides of the political spectrum were long a feature of the Afghan political scene, the government had refused to allow them to organize into political parties. As a result the country's parliament was ineffectual, with each representative acting independently. At the same time, the student movement was causing a series of strikes which paralyzed the urban centers; some strikes produced irrelevant, even ludicrous, manifestos, but many others were sparked by the sincere desire of the organizers to be assured employment upon completing their studies. The country was ripe for a coup and several attempts were apparently organized by disillusioned political figures. Sardar Muhammad Daoud Khan, a relative of the king and a former prime minister (1953–1963), staged such a coup in 1973. Taking advantage of the king's absence—he was visiting England for medical treatment—Daoud seized the palace and declared Afghanistan a republic, with himself as president and prime minister. During his previous tenure as prime minister, Daoud had won the contempt of the devout rural masses for his declared secularism and resultant policies. Following the coup, however, he sought religious support to save the country from economic ruin and called on the government to return to its Islamic roots. Avowed leftists were dismissed from office, but Daoud also sought the support of more moderate socialists, particularly members of Babrak Karmal's *Parchan* (Flag) movement. *Parchan* cadres were organized into teams and sent to the countryside to spread the ideology of Daoud's revolution, but the result was a complete failure. In 1975, an anti-government insurgency broke out in Panjsher to overthrow "the godless, communist régime ruling in Kabul." The rebellion spread to many of the country's cities before it was finally suppressed and it was immediately followed by two failed military coups. In 1977 *Parchan* realigned itself with the more militant *Khalq* (Masses) movement, which aimed at "furthering the development of the great October Revolution in Afghanistan."

That same year, elections were called in order to create a new constitution for the country. The parliament consisted of 219 representatives elected democratically (but not by secret ballot, which was opposed by the villages) and an additional 130 members appointed by Daoud to ensure that all segments of the population were represented. But despite this attempt at a peaceful transition to democracy, the year was particularly turbulent. The new parliament took issue with much of the new constitution and Daoud found himself at odds with the country's most important foreign protector, Soviet leader Leonid Brezhnev. When the latter insisted that Western foreign advisors be forced to leave the country, Daoud responded that all foreign advisers would have to leave the country. The culmination of this tense year was the assassination of Mir Akbar Khyber, a leading *Parchan* activist, supposedly by the CIA (in fact, he was probably killed by members of the *Khalq* movement in order to promote unrest).

Khyber's funeral turned into a violent anti-government and anti-Western demonstration. Daoud attempted to curb the potential revolt by arresting the leading instigators, but this only frightened the *Parchan* and *Khalq* leadership, forcing them to

act. Within just 24 hours, Hafizullah Amin, the *Khalq*'s leading military liaison, contacted sympathetic bodies in the military and organized a coup. Because of the limited time at his disposal, his directives were often handed out as photocopies. The following day a column of tanks headed for the presidential palace. Daoud and his family were killed and Nur Muhammad Taraki, head of the People's Democratic Party of Afghanistan (PDPA) became chairman of the revolutionary council and prime minister of the new Democratic Republic of Afghanistan.

Despite Taraki's links to the Soviets, the new régime was not immediately considered Communist. On the contrary, the *Herald Tribune* described it as "democratic, Islamic, reformist, [and] nonaligned." But Taraki was a devout Stalinist, who attempted to cultivate a personality cult with himself as the "Great Leader." Civil servants from the previous régime were dismissed and often arrested and their posts were generally filled with ineffectual but loyal party cadres. *Parchan* allies in the coup were also removed from power; even Babrak Karmal, then deputy prime minister, was dismissed from his cabinet post and given an ambassadorship.

Meanwhile, Taraki proceeded with his plans to create the People's Democratic Republic of Afghanistan. He removed the green bar from the flag (green is the color of Islam), nationalized "anything worth nationalizing," limited land holdings to 15 acres and distributed the surplus to the peasantry, promoted literacy and equal rights for women and eliminated the bridal price. Many of these measures were contrary to long-established rural custom and they had already led to the downfall of Daoud as prime minister in 1963. In a short time, the countryside fell to rival anti-government militias. To improve the situation, Amin, who was not considered as threatening as Taraki, was appointed prime minister, although Taraki retained his position as the "Great Leader." This move failed to quell the unrest, which had even spread to the capital, Kabul. In 1979, American ambassador Adolph Dubs was kidnapped and killed by anti-government forces. Taraki then attempted a reconciliation with Babrak, but in need of a new scapegoat and at the behest of Brezhnev, he readied himself to depose Amin. In autumn 1979, Taraki summoned Amin to his office to relieve him of his post. Amin, however, was wary of Taraki's intentions and brought a pistol to the meeting. In the ensuing scuffle, Taraki was shot and arrested and Amin seized power.

With the country in turmoil, the Afghan Mellat, a far-right, anti-Western group attempted to stage a coup. Amin survived this challenge to his authority, but he also refused Soviet aid to suppress the rebels, thereby earning Brezhnev's contempt. In December 1979, the Soviet Union responded by invading Afghanistan. Amin was killed in the fighting and Babrak Karmal was appointed prime minister. Afghanistan's long civil war would now begin.

'AFLAQ, MICHEL   (1910–1989) Syrian political thinker, founder of the *Ba'ath* (Renaissance) party. Born in Damascus, a Greek-Orthodox Christian, 'Aflaq studied in Paris and was close to the French Communist Party. In the late 1930s he developed his own brand of revolutionary-socialist Arab nationalism, stressing the aim of immediate all-Arab unity. In the 1940s he organized, together with SALAH-UL-DIN BITAR, a group of like-minded students and young intellectuals as the Arab Renaissance (*al-Ba'ath*) Party. The party first appeared on the political scene in the Syrian elections of 1947: 'Aflaq stood as a candidate, but failed. In 1949 he served briefly as minister of education, but was again defeated when he stood for parliament. He remained secretary-general of the *Ba'ath* party when it merged in 1953 with AKRAM HOURANI's Arab Socialist party. As the party's foremost theoretician, he formulated its doctrine in his books, *The Battle of the One Destiny* (1958) and *On the Road to the Ba'ath* (1959). 'Aflaq foresaw a revolution which would create a single Arab nation and destroy all traces of internal feudalism and imperialist influences. He advocated an Arab socialism that would bring justice to the masses through social and economic reforms and that would impart political power to them.

In the factional struggles that split the party after it came to power in Syria through a coup in March 1963, 'Aflaq (with Bitar) sided with the "civilian wing," which was considered more moderate. After a 1966 coup by the "military wing," 'Aflaq left Syria. He continued leading the National (all-Arab) Command of the *Ba'ath* located in Beirut and Baghdad, to which the Syrian party no longer paid allegiance. In 1967 'Aflaq emigrated to Brazil, abandoning all political activity, but late in 1968 he moved to Baghdad to resume his leadership position. In 1970 he left Baghdad in protest against Iraq's failure to sent troops against Jordan in support of the Palestinian guerrillas, but in 1974 a reconciliation was effected and he returned to Iraq. While highly respected as an ideologue and party intellectual, 'Aflaq did not have much influence on party and state policies.

AFRICAN NATIONAL CONGRESS (ANC) Originally the South African Native National Congress, the ANC was the first nationwide African nationalist movement in South Africa, founded in 1913 by western-educated elite blacks to organize the previously scattered political activity among the blacks in the country and to address restrictions imposed on black political rights by the white South African government. The organization's petty bourgeois leadership identified with the life style and values of white society and was influenced by black Americans such as Booker T. Washington and W.E.B. Du Bois and their emphasis on emancipation through education and political organization. They saw the white régime's support of white farmers and the mine owners' need for migrant labor through limiting African land ownership to reserves (the 1913 Land Act) and restricting African residence in urban centers (the 1923 Urban Areas Act) as impediments to their political and economic development alongside the white society. The early years of the ANC were characterized by a moderate approach of petitions and deputations in support of existing rights, backed by the assumption that rationality was the key to acceptance by whites.

In 1919 the Transvaal branch of the ANC broke this pattern by organizing a passive resistance campaign against the pass laws which forced all blacks to carry passes and in 1920 a miners' strike. Both were broken by government force. The ANC then abandoned its mass action strategy and many African workers turned to the Industrial and Commercial Workers Union (ICU) to fight on their behalf. The ICU began to disintegrate in 1928 when the moderate leadership tried to expel the more militant Communist members and the ANC once again became the primary means of African political expression. At this time its younger members were calling for more radical action. President James Gumede, following a visit to the Soviet Union, favored cooperation with the Communist party. Gumede, however, lost the support of the moderate majority and was defeated in 1930. Through the 1930s, various coordinated efforts of the ANC, the African People's Organization (APO), the Cape Native Voters' Association, the South African Indian Congress (SAIC) and the South African Communist Party (SACP) failed to change government policies. Indeed, the government increased restrictions on African, Indian and Colored land rights and on their voting rights and representation. The industrial boom during World War II accelerated the urbanization of all races in South Africa, creating more favorable conditions for African political and trade union activity. Under a new president, Dr. Xuma, the ANC published *African Claims in South Africa* (1943), a proposal for a bill of rights which called for outright universal suffrage but adhered to moderate liberal principles. The war years saw the ANC's return to mass action with the formation of the ANC Youth League by OLIVER TAMBO, NELSON MANDELA and Walter Sisulu. Composed of students and young teachers who favored militant resistance to state oppression, it acted as a radical pressure group within the organization.

The 1948 victory of the National party made the doctrine of apartheid ("separateness") official State policy and began the restructuring of society along Afrikaner nationalist lines. The ANC responded by becoming more open to militant action; its 1949 conference adopted the Youth League-sponsored Program of Action to abolish racial discrimination through boycotts, strikes, civil disobedience and non-cooperation. Along these lines the ANC and the SAIC planned a program of passive resistance, the 1952 Defiance Campaign, which attracted the attention of the United Nations but then fizzled in the wake of harsh government retaliation and riots in the African townships. In 1955, the ANC, SAIC, South African Colored People's Organization and the Congress of the Democrats (a small white liberal group) organized the Congress of the People and promulgated the Freedom Charter, which included non-racial democracy, removal of discriminatory legislation, equal opportunities in education and work, redistribution of land and the nationalization of banks, mines and industry. The government arrested the groups' leaders for treason, keeping them tied up in court for the rest of the decade. In 1958, a group of ANC "Africanists" formed the Pan-Africanist Congress (PAC) to protest the multi-racial alliance which was attempting to curb the government's policies. Acute rivalry developed and the PAC attempted to out-maneuver the ANC in launching an anti-pass campaign in early 1960. This resulted in the Sharpeville Massacre, a turning point in international attention to South Africa but also an excuse for the government to ban both organizations, which continued operations underground from bases in Dar es Salaam, London, Cairo and elsewhere. In 1961 Mandela formed a new militant wing of the ANC, *Umkhonto we Sizwe* (Spear of the Nation), to begin a campaign of sabotage in the hope of forcing the white population to recognize the need for change. The government increased the powers of the security police and by 1964 many ANC leaders, including Mandela, were in prison.

Guerrilla activity increased through the 1970s. In the 1980s, changes in South Africa's international position led to negotiations by the South African government with the new Marxist régimes in Angola and Mozambique to shut down the ANC facilities in these countries. Violence escalated within the country and a state of emergency was declared. The need for a political solution was obvious, as was the inclusion of the ANC—which still had mass support in spite of the government's attempt to cultivate Buthelezi, the Zulu-nationalist head of Inkatha—as the government's negotiating partner. In 1985, the ANC and the SACP still hoped to seized power through popular insurrection, but with the collapse of the Soviet Bloc and the loss of ANC bases in Angola, negotiation seemed more realistic. President de Klerk's 1990 promise to release Mandela, unban the ANC, PAC, SACP and United Democratic Front, and begin negotiations for a new constitution, was in line with the "transition to democracy" paradigm overtaking much of the rest of the world, and seemed to pave the way for the end of apartheid. However, four years of continued violence, stop-and-go negotiations and vacillation by the government ensued as it sought to maintain control of the reform process and destabilize the ANC. With a combination of ANC-inspired internal mass action and increased international pressure, the government was forced to agree to a general election date of April 1994. The victory of Mandela and the ANC in the election was an intermediate step in the transition process which continues under the ANC's Reconstruction and Development Program. Many Africans were alienated by the lengthy negotiation process, which they viewed as serving the elite, and keeping their support remains one of the current government's challenges.

AFRIKANER BROEDERBOND (Afrikaner Band of Brothers) A South African secret society of Calvinist diehards that was and is still committed to racial segregation and Afrikaner rule. Johannes Vorster and Hendrik Verwoerd, both former prime ministers of South Africa, were prominent members of the sectarian, anti-Semitic and—in its time—pro-Nazi movement.

AFRO-SHIRAZI PARTY (ASP) Zanzibar, a British protectorate since 1890, became an independent sultanate in December 1963. There was strong opposition to the sultan both among the Arab population and the Africans (who were divided into "Shirazis" or long-term residents and "mainlanders"). In January 1964 there was an armed uprising by the Afro-Shirazi party, the sultan was deposed and a republic proclaimed. The new government signed an Act of Union with Tanganyika in April 1964, thus creating the United Republic, with the ASP leader, Abeid Karume, becoming the United Republic's first vice-president as well as chairman of the ruling revolutionary council of Zanzibar. The union was named Tanzania in October 1964. The ASP remained the official party of Zanzibar until 1977.

Karume was assassinated in 1972 and his successor, Aboud Jumbe, reorganized the Zanzibar government by extending the powers of the ASP. Despite its incorporation in Tanzania, Zanzibar retained a separate administration which ruthlessly suppressed all opposition.

A proposal to merge the TANGANYIKA AFRICAN NATIONAL UNION, the official party of mainland Tanzania, and the ASP was submitted by President Nyere in 1975 and, in February 1977, the two parties merged to form the *Chama Cha Mapinduzi* (CCM), the Revolutionary Party of Tanzania, of which Nyerere was elected chairman and Jumbe vice-chairman. The socialist-oriented CCM was the sole legal party of Tanzania from 1977 until 1992.

AGIS IV On his accession to the throne in 244 B.C., Agis, king of Sparta, sought to introduce social and economic reforms, including cancellation of debts, redistribution of lands to poor Spartans who had lost full citizenship and enlargement of the citizen body. As these revolutionary measures jeopardized the existing social order and régime, Agis's enemies managed to capture and put him to death in 242 B.C.

AGRARIAN SOCIALIST LEAGUE A Russian emigré populist revolutionary group formed in 1900 in Paris, when a number of rival factions united. The league was later one of the founding groups of the SOCIAL REVOLUTIONARY PARTY. The activity of the Agrarian Socialist League centered around publishing propaganda aimed at rousing Russia's peasants to socialist revolution. The most common theme of the league's pamphlets was "through land to freedom, and through freedom to land." The league's influence was noticeable particularly in the villages of the Central Volga and Black Earth regions of Russia. Among those prominent in the activities of the league were the eventual leader of the Socialist Revolutionaries, VIKTOR CHERNOV, and Michael R. Gots.

AGUINALDO, EMILIO (1869–1964) Philippine nationalist leader. Educated at the University of Manila, during the 1890s Aguinaldo found himself fighting against the Spanish occupation of his country at the head of a society known as the Katipunan. In December 1897 he signed an agreement with the Spaniards; in return for giving up the struggle he was given a substantial financial award and permitted to leave the country. In exile in Hong Kong and Singapore, he plotted with representatives of the US government to renew the war against Spain.

In May 1898, Aguinaldo returned to the Philippines. A month later, leading an insurrection, he proclaimed a Philippine republic with himself as its provisional president. By this time the Spanish-American War was under way and the Spaniards were losing; in December they ceded the Philippines to the US. Tensions between Aguinaldo's movement and the new American government mounted at once and, in 1899, led to the beginning of a bloody uprising. It lasted until March 1901, when Aguinaldo was captured and, in return for taking an oath of allegiance to the US, was allowed to retire to private life as well as to receive another financial reward.

In 1935, when the commonwealth government of the Philippines was established in preparation for independence, Aguinaldo ran for president but was defeated. He returned to private life, only to emerge once again when the Japanese invaded the country in 1941. During the Japanese occupation he made speeches and wrote articles against the US, even calling on General MacArthur to surrender in order to prevent further bloodshed. For these activities he was arrested after the war, held for some months, but finally released by presidential amnesty. He is remembered as the Grand Old Man of Philippine independence.

AHMAD, JALAL (1923–1969) Iranian Islamic revolutionary intellectual whose thought inspired many of the Shah's rivals. Though his family was a clerical one, Ahmad chose a Western-style education. At the age of 20 he showed an affinity for the Communist party but later joined socialist-nationalist movements. In the early 1960s, he returned to Islam by fulfilling the pilgrimage to Mecca (*Hajj*).

During the 1960s, Ahmad was noted for his writings on social and political issues. He criticized both the West and the Iranian political system, calling for a return to traditional Islam as a way to solve the country's social problems. He claimed that the rapid Westernization of Iran would deepen its dependence on the West; that Western universities trained Iranian intellectuals in nonproductive occupations, perpetuating the need for foreign advisors; and that the purchase of industrial equipment from the West led to a reliance on foreign parts and experts. He coined the term *urbazdag* ("west-toxication") to define the Iranian reality; a society blinded by the West and being pushed toward the loss of national identity. Ahmad was a member of a group of thinkers who had a major influence on the ideology of the IS-LAMIC REVOLUTION OF 1979 in its early stages, serving as a bridge between the political and the religious resistance to the Shah.

AIT-AHMAD, HUSSEIN   (1919–) Algerian nationalist, guerrilla leader and politician. Born in 1919, he was closely linked with the Berber-dominated Kabylia region. Ait-Ahmad was one of the younger members of the MOUVEMENT POUR LE TRIOMPHE DES LIBERTÉS DEMOCRATIQUES (MOVEMENT FOR THE TRIUMPH OF DEMOC-RATIC LIBERTIES) who broke away to become one of the nine "historic leaders" of the Algerian nationalists who in 1954 founded the FRONT DE LIBÉRATION NATIONALE (FLN) and began a bloody eight-year rebellion against France. He fought as a rebel leader—in his Kabylia mountains and with the rebel high command abroad, in Egypt and Tunisia—until captured by the French in October 1956 (with four other leaders, in a commercial airliner that the French forced to land). He was imprisoned in France until the 1962 agreement on Algeria's independence. In nascent independent Algeria he strongly opposed the ruling faction of AHMAD BEN-BELLA and his associates. In 1962, Ait-Ahmad went underground. He was elected in 1963 to the National Assembly, on the FLN list, and returned from exile, but soon went underground again and started militant guerrilla action against Ben-Bella's régime. He was captured in October 1964 and sentenced to death, but was pardoned by Ben-Bella. In April 1966 he escaped. In exile in France Ait-Ahmad tried to organize various opposition groups in the 1970s and 1980s, including the Party of Socialist Revolution and the Front of Socialist Forces (FFS). After the liberalization of Algeria's régime in the late 1980s, under BEN-JEDID, Ait-Ahmad returned to Algeria from his 23-year exile. He tried to build the FFS into a main democratic opposition party, strongly anti-FLN and again based mainly on Kabylia and Berber elements opposed to the growing Islamic-fundamentalist agitation. The FFS boycotted the 1990 Algerian elections and its strength has yet to be tested.

AKHENATON IV   Egyptian king of the 18th dynasty (either 1379–1362 B.C. or 1367–1359 B.C.) and revolutionary religious reformer. The son of King Amenhotep III and Queen Tiy, his original name was Amenhotep ("Amon is resting"). Ascending to the throne when he was between 12 and 14 years old and therefore under the influence of his mother, Amenhotep married Nefertiti, a princess of foreign (Asiatic) birth, who was to become his adviser and confidante.

Egypt at that time was very much dominated by a coalition between the aristocracy and the priesthood of the sun god, Amon. In order to establish his own personal rule, Akhenaton, as he now called himself, carried out a series of religious reforms during the early years of his reign that were at the same time meant to reduce the power of the aristocracy. Supported by the army, he left his capital of Thebes, where Amon's priests had traditionally ruled supreme and founded a new one in Middle Egypt under the name of Akhenaton (the Horizon of [the god] Anton) Today this place is known as El-Amarna.

During the remainder of his reign Akhenaton, while neglecting affairs of state, reformed almost every aspect of Egyptian religion. The property of all the priests and the various gods was confiscated—this may well have been the real objective of the entire exercise—and the worship of Amon prohibited. New burial customs were introduced and hymns to Aton composed which strongly resemble Psalm 104. As known to us from these hymns, the new religion was universal rather than purely Egyptian: it presented Aton as the creator of everything and everybody. He fed people and animals, gave the Nile to the Egyptians and rain to all peoples, and was responsible for the changes of day and night.

Akhenaton lived to the age of thirty and after his death the priesthood of Amon resumed its privileges. Forty years later an Egyptian text mentions him as the "the criminal." He nevertheless deserves to be remembered as a revolutionary reformer who pointed the way toward a monotheistic, universally-minded religion.

'ALAVI, BOZORG   (1905–) Iranian and left-wing revolutionary and writer. Born in 1905 in Tehran, 'Alavi studied German language and literature in Germany. He served as an instructor at the Technical School and a teacher of German at the Industrial College in Tehran. In 1936 he was accused and arrested with 53 others for planning to establish a Communist party. Following the conquest of Iran by the Allied forces in 1941, he was released from jail. 'Alavi joined the pro-Soviet TUDEH party and was associate editor of the party's newspaper, *Mardom* (The People).

When the *Tudeh* party was outlawed in the late 1940s, 'Alavi migrated to East Germany, where he served as a professor of Iranian language and literature at Humboldt University. Among his books are *Her Eyes* (1952), *The Suitcase* (1955), *Letters* (1961), *The Salaris* (1978), *Mirza* (1978) and *Demon! Demon!* (1978). He has also written a scholarly book about the Persian and German languages and literature and published a number of translations.

ALBANIA, UPRISING OF 1847   The first Albanian uprising against the Ottoman Empire, during which the spontaneous protest of peasants and mountain people produced a country-wide coordinating committee advocating nationalist sentiment (see also GJOLEKA, ZENEL; HEKALI, RAPU).

AL-BASHMIRE OMAR HASSAN AHMAD (Sudan)   see SUDAN, COUPS IN.

ALBIGENSES   A heretical sect, named after the city of Albi, which arose in southern France in the 11th century. In other parts of Europe, its members were often called the *Cathari*—the "pure ones." The sect believed in the principle of Manichaean dualism, which attempted to reconcile the belief in two distinct powers, the good and the evil, with Christian religion. The Albigenses retained the Old and the New Testaments but interpreted them allegorically, denying Jesus' corporeal sufferings and attacking the Catholic Church for its literal interpretation of the Bible. They considered such views a corruption of the faith, "the work of the Devil." For these reasons they rejected the sacraments and the liturgical role of the clergy, maintaining that the church cannot mediate between God and believer. They were opposed to the church's owning temporal property, such as lands and buildings, and receiving income. Theirs was a strict doctrine forbidding marriage and the consumption of animal products. Aware that such austerity could not be expected from the masses, they recognized two classes of the faithful—the *perfecti*—the "perfect" or "pure" ones, who received the sacrament of *consolamentum* by the laying of the hands, and the *credentes*, the "believers." Even the "believers" had to live austerely, abjuring all external signs of wealth. The Albigenses segregated themselves thus not only doctrinally but socially from Catholic society and created their own communities.

During the 12th century, the sect spread throughout southern France, its opposition to the Church establishment making it extremely popular. Repeated condemnations by Church councils and persecutions by the authorities failed to keep it down and even some of the nobility joined the sect. In 1167, the Albigenses were numerous enough to create a federation of their communities, teaching their own authorized text, the "Cathar Bible." Alarmed by their progress, the Church and the kings of France and England, Louis VII and Henry II respectively, decided to repress the movement. In 1184 a council, assembled at Verona by Pope Lucius III, dealt with the heresy and resolved to establish the Inquisition, whose function would be to investigate suspected heretics and bring them to lay trial. But these measures were ineffective and the Albigenses won even greater sympathy in the region. Some of the greater nobles even adopted an ambiguous position, which was interpreted as favoring the sect. Pope Innocent III attempted to convert the Albigenses and appointed monks, such as St. Dominic, with special missions for that purpose. The missionary activity only aggravated the situation and, in 1208, the papal legate, Peter of Casstelnau, was assassinated. The pope now decided to launch a crusade against the Albigenses and called upon the faithful of northern France to extirpate the heresy by force of arms. Led by Simon of Monfort, an army of French knights was assembled and proceeded to commit great massacres, such as that of Béziers (1208), where heretics and innocents alike perished. A coalition of southern forces, led by Peter of Aragon and Raymond VI, count of Toulouse, tried to protect the local population, but Simon won the Battle of Muret in 1213 and became the master of the province until his death in 1218. Nevertheless, the Albigenses were not entirely crushed and the French crown-prince Louis led a new crusade, which continued under his own rule (as Louis VIII) until 1226. The remnants of the Albigenses were left to the Inquisition, reorganized by Pope Gregory IX and entrusted to the new Dominican order. Bloody repression, culminating in the massacre of the Albigenses's last citadel of Montségur (1244), succeeded in stamping out the sect, but traces of the heresy remained dormant until the 14th century.

ALEXINSKY, GRIGORII ALEXEEVICH   (1879–1965) Russian Social Democrat. Alexinsky began his political life as a student organizer at Moscow University, for which he was arrested and expelled in 1902. He was active in Social Democratic activity in Moscow and St. Petersburg and was elected to the second Duma. With Lunacharsky and BOGDANOV, he founded the Forward (*Vpered*) group of Social Democrats and taught at the party school in Capri.

During World War I Alexinsky was a member of PLEKHANOV's Unity (*Yedinstvo*) faction, advocating revolutionary defense. Throughout the war he vociferously opposed Lenin's policies as playing into German hands. He emigrated to France after the so-called October RUSSIAN REVOLUTION OF 1917.

ALGERIAN REVOLUTION   When the FLN (FRONT DE LIBÉRATION NATIONALE) launched a guerrilla war for national liberation in the foothills of the Aurès mountains south of Constantine on November 1, 1954, the French were unanimous in believing that Algeria was and should remain forever an integral part of the national patrimony. A French possession since July 1830 and the home of more than a million French settlers (known as *colons* or *pieds noirs*) out of a total population of 9 million, Algeria enjoyed a privileged legal status that set it apart from the neighboring French protectorates in Tunisia and Morocco. Both of the latter had gained their independence in March 1956, after a relatively easy and bloodless struggle, whereas Algeria had for a long time been juridically incorporated into the métropole in the same way that Lorraine or Alsace, Normandy or Brittany were bound to the French republic, one and indivisible.

Subdivided into the three large departments of Algiers, Oran and Constantine, with the right of electing a slate of deputies to sit in the National Assembly in Paris, Algeria was also the oldest of French colonies since the loss of Canada in the 18th century. Thus the insurrection which erupted against French rule and the local supremacy of the *colons* assumed the character of a civil war between two peoples of different ethnic and religious heritage, both of whom claimed Algeria as their homeland and affirmed mutually exclusive rights to determine its political destiny. The protracted struggle, which had enormous repercussions not only in Algeria but also on the political fortunes of the mother country, did not come to an end until March 1962, with the signing of the Évian Agreements on the French shore of Lake Geneva. The agreements were negotiated between the FLN leader BEN-BELLA, who had spent much of the war in French captivity, and Pompidou's minister of Algerian affairs, Louis Joxe. It conceded to the Arab majority the right of unconditional independence, with only modest compensation accorded to French interests and the property rights of the settlers.

One of the reasons why the Algerian dispute defied any easy solution was because it was caught up in a worldwide movement that appeared to confirm the inevitability of decolonization. GAMAL ABDUL NASSER of Egypt, at the pinnacle of his prestige following the Suez War of November 1956, and riding the crest of a Third World crusade against the West, denounced French colonial rule as a principal obstacle to the realization of his pan-Arab dreams and supported the FLN with all the means at his disposal, including sanctuary to its political leaders. Another more intractable problem was the indecisiveness of the leaders of the Fourth Republic, who found it difficult to resist the intransigence of the settlers, especially as the settlers' cause was supported by an army still smarting from the humiliations suffered in Indochina. Even after the formation of a left-wing ministry under Guy Mollet in January 1956, France was treated to the extraordinary spectacle of a Socialist prime minister conducting a colonial war of repression against his better judgment.

After nearly four years of sanguinary and inconclusive warfare marked by savage atrocities on both sides, the Algerian impasse became the catalyst for the downfall of the Fourth Republic and its replacement by a more resolute and authoritarian régime under General de Gaulle, who came to power in May 1958 as a result of a military conspiracy hatched in Algiers. In a visit to the Algerian capital the following month, expressly designed to mark his solidarity with the *colons* and the army chiefs, the general only succeeded in raising false hopes by declaring, "*Je vous ai compris*" ("I have understood you") to the huge European crowds gathered to welcome their savior. de Gaulle, though, deliberately refused to utter the right-wing slogan, "*Algérie française,*" and began to work behind the scenes to reach a negotiated settlement along the lines of an *Algérie algérienne* with Ben-Bella and the FLN. Feeling betrayed and increasingly frustrated as French public opinion began to shift in favor of a compromise peace, extremist *colons* resorted to yet another coup, in alliance with a cabal of colonels and other junior officers in January 1960 which, after the immediate shock subsided, was quelled by Paris with little bloodshed. This was followed by a far more serious right-wing challenge to de Gaulle's authority, mounted this time by no less a personage than the former commander-in-chief in Algeria, General Raoul Salan, and his deputy, General Challe, in April 1961. Spearheaded by the OAS (The Secret Army Organization), Salan and three other senior generals took over the government in Algiers and threatened military action against metropolitan France, threatening to send parachute units to invade Paris and to seize the Elysée presidential palace itself. The crisis was so acute that the prime minister, Michel Debré, was forced to implore all Parisians over radio and television to march to Orly airport to fight back the impending attack from Algiers. In the end, only de Gaulle's enormous prestige rescued the republic from collapse. He appealed directly over the heads of the generals to the 400,000 young conscripts now serving in Algeria, commanding them to disobey orders and disarm and arrest their military superiors, thereby bringing the mutiny to an ignominious end.

The Évian accords, overwhelmingly ratified by a national plebiscite held in France on April 8, 1962, recognized Algeria as a free and independent nation and precipitated an immediate and massive exodus of virtually all its French population, most of whom settled in the south of France. Ben-Bella was proclaimed president of the new Algerian republic, but remained in power only until June 1965, when he was deposed by his own defense minister, Colonel HOUARI BOUMEDIENNE. Boumedienne established a more radical government in which he was himself President of the Council of the Revolution, dedicated to implementing the new Third World ideology of international socialism.

ALI, SALEM RUBAI   (1934? 1935?–1978) South Yemeni politician, president of South Yemen 1969–1978, schoolteacher and law student. Ali was active in the Aden nationalist move-

ment against British rule—first as a youth leader, and from 1963 within the main and extreme nationalist faction, the FRONT DE LIBÉRATION NATIONALE (NFL)—belonging to its leftist-Marxist wing, which was linked with the Arab Nationalist Movement, *Harakat al-Qawmiyyin*. When South Yemen became independent in 1967 under the NFL, Ali was suspected of factional plotting and went into exile. In June 1969 he took part in a successful coup against President QAHTAN AL-SHA'BI and his faction, and became chairman of a new presidential council, which he continued purging and reshaping in 1970 and 1971. Ali was considered pro-Chinese (as opposed to a pro-Soviet faction headed by 'ABDUL-FATTAH ISMA'IL) and during his rule South Yemen remained leftist-extremist in its international and inter-Arab policies. He gradually moderated his views and became more pragmatic, to the extent that he was later derided as "rightist"; and the rivalry between him and Isma'il grew more pronounced. This rivalry eventually led to his defeat and execution in 1978.

ALLEN, ETHAN   (1737–1789) American revolutionary. After serving in the French and Indian War (1756–1763), Allen settled in Vermont, then known as the New Hampshire Grants. The colonies of New York and New Hampshire both laid claim to the territory; in 1764, the dispute was decided in favor of New York. When the supreme court of New York ruled that all previous land grants made by New Hampshire were illegal, the settlers in Vermont formed their own militia, the Green Mountain Boys, to protect their holdings. Allen became head of this militia with the rank of colonel.

During the American Revolution, Allen and his Green Mountain Boys cooperated with the revolutionary army and took part in the conquest of Ticonderoga and Crown Point in May 1775. Four months later, he was captured during an attack on Montreal. He was released and returned to Vermont in 1777, only to find that the region's status was as yet under contention between the two neighboring states. That year, the people of Vermont declared the independent Republic of Vermont and Allen played an important role in negotiations with the British, ostensibly to incorporate Vermont as a province of Canada (there is considerable speculation that he entered these negotiations only to further Vermont's claim to statehood). He died in 1789, two years before the state of Vermont was admitted to the United States.

ALLENDE, IGNACIO   (1769–1811) Mexican independence fighter. Born in San Miguel el Grande (now San Miguel de Allende), Allende became a captain in the army. During his military years he came in contact with liberals and masons, whose views convinced him that Mexico would benefit greatly if it gained its independence from Spain. Allende organized a clandestine independence movement in San Miguel el Grande which launched an unsuccessful uprising in 1809. A new date was set for 1810. To garner greater popular support for the movement, Allende convinced the priest MIGUEL HIDALGO to participate in the uprising. After a successful uprising in Bolores, Allende organized the military during the struggle for independence that followed. Differences over military tactics caused Allende and Hidalgo to grow apart. After several defeats of the insurgent armies, Allende was captured by royalist forces in Acatita de Bajan, Coahuila. He was executed in 1811. His head was put on display in front of a building called the Alhondiga in the center of Guanajuato, a city he had defended during the uprising. The head was removed in 1821, when Allende was recognized as a hero of Mexican independence. His body was eventually buried under the Independence Monument of Mexico City.

ALLENDE GOSSENS, SALVADOR   (1908–1973) Chilean socialist leader. Born to an upper-middle-class family, Allende was trained as a physician and became one of the founders, in 1933, of Chile's Socialist party. Elected to the Chamber of Deputies in 1937, he served as minister of health from 1939 to 1942. In 1945 he entered the Senate. At the head of various combinations of Communists, Socialists and radicals, he made three unsuccessful bids at the presidency, but finally succeeded in capturing it in 1970 in spite of strong right-wing opposition. President Allende set out to reform Chilean society along Socialist lines. This included the expropriation—without compensation—of American-owned copper companies in Chile; the forced sale to the government of various privately owned Chilean companies; the establishment of peasant cooperatives; and huge wage increases which, in spite of a government imposed freeze on prices, led to rampant inflation. His policies also caused the flight of capital, decreased exports, food shortages and strikes. In spite of this, he was reelected—by an increased percentage of voters—in March 1973. However, six months later his régime was toppled by a CIA-assisted army coup and Allende, caught in the presidential palace, lost his life.

ALL FOR THE FATHERLAND PARTY   see IRON GUARD.

ALMOHADES (Al-Muwahadin)   Muslim religious movement dynasty (12th–13th centuries) in north Africa and Spain. Founded by the Berber leader Muhammad ibn Tumart, an Islamic reformer, the movement sought to restore the original values of the Muslim faith. While its ideology was not new, ibn Tumart gave it coherence and popular appeal. The refusal of the ruling Almoravides to accept his reforms led ibn Tumart to launch his movement and in 1122 declare a holy war against the Almoravides. His followers proclaimed him *Mahdi* (orthodox leader) and rallied to his campaign. After his death, his disciple, Abdul Mamun, continued the war and by 1145 had conquered Morocco and all of the Maghreb. To help the petty Muslim principalities in Spain, which were threatened by the Christian *reconquista* (reconquest), he invaded Spain in 1150 and established the Almohades rule in Andalusia. In 1172, Muslim Spain was annexed to the new empire, which pursued a policy of extreme religious fanaticism, one resented both by those Muslims who did not accept the Almohades' principles and by religious minorities, such as the Jews, who were no longer tolerated. By the end of the century, the Almohades leader, Abu Yusuf Yakub (1184–1199), had defeated the Castilian and Aragon armies, conquered Madrid and established the boundary near the Tagus river.

At the beginning of the 13th century, the Almohades began to weaken and became rather less fanatical. Their defeat by the Castilians at Las Navas de Tortosa (1212) and their territorial losses in Spain were a symptom of their weakness, which made them more dependent on the merchant class and on trade. They liberalized their religious principles and, in 1220, permitted Jewish merchants to settle in Morocco. While they succeeded in

maintaining their rule in the Maghreb, they failed to do so in Spain, where the *reconquista* reached Andalusia. In 1248, the Castilians conquered Seville and the last important stronghold of the Muslims in Spain, and became an independent kingdom and an enemy of the Almohades empire. By that time, the process of dissolution affected even the Maghreb, where local leaders in Morocco and Algeria revolted, and in the second half of the 13th century reduced the Almohades state to a small principality, one which was finally eliminated in 1296 with the creation of an independent kingdom in Morocco.

ALVAREZ, JUAN   (1790–1876) Mexican independence fighter and military figure. Alvarez participated in various independence battles against Spanish forces. His activities centered around Acapulco in the state of Guerrero. After experiencing several defeats, Alvarez organized a guerrilla movement against Spanish forces in the mountains of the state of Guerrero. His involvement in the final battle for independence in Acapulco proved decisive. In 1823, Alvarez joined Guerrero—for whom the state has been named—to oust Emperor AGUSTIN ITURBIDE. For the next 45 years Alvarez was active in the Mexican military, always siding with republican, federalist and liberal causes. From 1849 to 1853 he was governor of GUERRERO. In 1855 he was named provisional president of Mexico but resigned within a few months. He actively sought the promulgation of the reform laws which restricted church activities and power in Mexico.

AMBEDKAR, BHIMRAO RAMJI   (1891–1956) A brilliant lawyer who was instrumental in framing the Indian constitution subsequent to independence in 1947, Ambedkar was born of an untouchable family in west India and early suffered great humiliation at the hands of caste Hindus, both at school and at work. He was nonetheless so gifted that he won a scholarship that enabled him to study in the United States, Britain and Germany.

Despite his subsequent elevation to positions of great authority, Ambedkar continued to struggle for the rights of untouchables, who he believed had been betrayed by the leadership of the INDIAN NATIONAL CONGRESS. He eventually came to believe that there could be no place for untouchables within Hinduism and advocated that untouchables convert to Buddhism, as he himself did in the last year of his life. Many thousands of untouchables in the Bombay area followed his example, establishing a community of Ambedkar Buddhists that remains to this day.

'AMER, 'ABDUL HAKIM   (1919–1967) Egyptian officer and politician. 'Amer graduated from the Military Academy in 1938 and served in the War of 1948. He was one of the founders of the FREE OFFICERS that planned and mounted the EGYPTIAN REVOLUTION OF 1952 and a member of the Revolutionary Council it established. He was promoted to general and appointed commander in chief of the armed forces in June 1952. From 1954 he also served as the minister of war. In June 1967 he was considered responsible for the Egyptian debacle in the Six-Day War and resigned or was dismissed. In August 1967 he was accused of plotting a military coup and was arrested; he committed suicide in prison in September 1967.

'Amer, who came from a wealthy peasant family and had

himself acquired quite a fortune and extensive landed property (he was also involved in some questionable deals), was considered right-wing within the officers' junta, conservative in his political leanings and upper class in his life-style. He had reservations regarding the populist-socialist régime GAMAL ABDUL NASSER introduced, as well as regarding Egypt's growing alliance with the USSR and strove to enhance the leading role and special status of the armed forces and their top commander. On this account, he clashed several times with Nasser; yet his divergent tendencies never crystallized to become a rival doctrine. Until the final crisis of June 1967, he enjoyed a close personal friendship with Nasser and was considered nearest to Nasser of all the Free Officers' group.

AMERICAN REVOLUTION   Along with the French, Russian and Chinese revolutions, all of which are also covered in the present volume, the American Revolution is the one of most important events of its kind in all recorded history. As the breakup of the former Soviet Union shows, toward the end of the 20th century the world-historical trend seems to be away from giant States toward smaller ones; hence, it seems unlikely that another revolution as important as the American one will take place in the foreseeable future.

Background. The background to the revolution was formed by Britain's victory over France in the Seven Years' War (1756–1763). This victory left Canada in British hands but it also left the government at Westminster with a massive public debt (government spending had doubled during the war) which it did not know how to finance. Furthermore, the war had not put an end to the need to defend the American colonies against Spanish attempts to recapture Florida in the south and against the Indians in the west. Given that during the war itself the British parliament had voted sums for the defense of individual colonies such as Massachusetts, it seemed only reasonable to the government in London that the colonies should participate in paying for their own continued defense.

Another source of friction between Britain and the North American colonists was formed by the rights of settlement. Having taken over Canada, the British decided to assume responsibility for relations with the Indians as well. For the first time, an arbitrary line was drawn which limited the colonies' expansion; anything to the west of that line, which ran through the Appalachians, was to be handled directly by London via Quebec rather than by the American colonists. Since this included the right to trade with the native population, the loss to the colonists in terms not only of future settlement but of immediate pecuniary gain was considerable.

Things came to a head in 1763 when a new prime minister, George Grenville, took over in London and started looking for ways to reduce the government's deficit. The first measure was the Plantation Act of 1764, also known as the Sugar Act. It was soon joined by the Currency Act (1764) which withdrew from circulation the notes issued by the colonies during the war and thus forced them to rely on more expensive British money; as well as the STAMP ACT (1765), which imposed duties on all colonial commercial and legal papers, newspapers, pamphlets, cards, almanacs and dice. To make sure that these measures would in fact be obeyed, the British also set up a new chain of customs-houses as well as a special Admiralty Court to try cases arising

from them. In the eyes of the colonists, this last-named innovation meant that they would now be deprived of the right of trial by jury even though such a principle had been an accepted element in British law since the GLORIOUS REVOLUTION of 1688.

Throughout 1764–1765 the colonists protested against the new measures. Much of the diplomatic activity took place in London, where their representative, Benjamin Franklin, argued that they represented a violation of Englishmen's right to be taxed only with their consent; but there were also protests, some of them violent, in the colonies, particularly in Boston, as the most important port through which the colonies imported foreign goods and exported their own. These actions were effective and the Stamp Act was repealed only a few months after it entered into force. At the same time, however, Parliament also issued a Declaratory Act, in which it asserted its right to tax the colonists at will.

During the second half of the 1760s, friction between the colonists and the British authorities continued. Basing themselves on the distinction between internal taxes, which required consent, and external ones, which did not, the new British cabinet under Lord Charles Townsend and his chancellor of the exchequer, William Pitt, imposed a whole series of new customs duties on goods imported into the colonies. Again the result was a storm of protest, culminating in the publication of John Dickinson's *Letters from a Farmer in Pennsylvania* (1767–1768), which argued that Parliament had no power over internal colonial affairs. A movement toward boycotting British goods was also started—albeit, given Britain's industrial supremacy and the lack of manufacturing plants in the colonies themselves, it was never very effective.

By this time the debate between the colonists and the government had extended into other fields, i.e., the right of Parliament to legislate not only in matters of taxation but in general. An essay on the question, James Wilson's *Considerations of the Legislative Authority of the British Parliament,* was published in 1774; it argued that since the inhabitants of the British Empire (not only those of the American colonies) were not represented at Westminster, Parliament's authority stopped at Britain's shores. In response, the British argued that the colonists were "virtually" represented in the same way as Britain's own vote-less classes—in fact, the vast majority of the population—were.

As the debate on both sides grew more heated, Lord North took over from Townsend as prime minister in 1770. Seeking reconciliation, he promptly withdrew the duties imposed by his predecessor—all except the one on tea, which was left in force as representative of Britain's right to tax. It was, however, a question of too little too late. As the resistance movement continued to gather momentum, clashes between colonists and British troops began to take place, the most serious of which was the so-called Boston Massacre, when five civilians were killed. The troops involved were put on civilian trial. That they were ultimately acquitted reflected the brilliance of the defense, which was conducted by none other than JOHN ADAMS.

With people's minds already astir, the spark that lit the revolution was formed when Lord North sought to help the British East India Company, by giving it a monopoly on the importation of tea into the colonies. The interests of American merchants were thereby affected; on December 16, 1773 a group of Bostonians, thinly disguised as Indians, boarded a ship at anchor in the harbor and dumped some £ 10,000 worth of tea into the water. In response to this so called BOSTON TEA PARTY, the town's port was closed by the British authorities. Seeking to restore order, the British parliament disbanded the elective council of Massachusetts, replacing it with one that was appointed by the governor. The Quebec Act, also passed in the spring of 1774, joined the Mississippi Valley to Upper Canada, thus definitely putting an end to any prospect of colonial expansion to the west. **The Meeting of the Continental Congress.** Convinced that the British measures could only be met by collective action, the colonists organized a Continental Congress that met in Philadelphia in September 1774. Every state except Georgia was represented; the luminaries present included James Wilson and John Adams, whereas the Virginia delegation's instructions had been drafted by none other than THOMAS JEFFERSON. The Congress's first decision, arrived at after much debate, was to give each colony one vote regardless of wealth or population—which reflected the fact that no reliable information was available about either factor. Beyond this, opinions remained divided. While a few delegates, including James Wilson himself, were already looking forward to possible independence from Britain, the majority hesitated since they feared that once the protective hand of

the Redcoats was withdrawn, the result might be domestic disorder. In the end, the Congress confirmed the non-importation measures already taken and also called for the non-exportation of goods to Britain. This done, most of the delegates went home, hoping that some compromise would be reached.

In the event, these hopes were destined to be disappointed. When the Second Continental Congress met in Philadelphia in May 1775, the mood had turned ugly. Clashes between the citizens of Massachusetts and British troops had taken place at Lexington and Concord on April 19; the "shot that sounded around the world" proved to be the point of no return. While still paying—mainly at Dickinson's insistence—lip service to continued imperial unity with Britain, the Congress adopted a *Declaration of the Causes and Necessity of Taking up Arms* and set about raising an army under the command of GEORGE WASHINGTON. This remained on hold for a while, but the publication of THOMAS PAINE's *Common Sense* in January 1776 again brought matters to the boiling point. Faced with British intransigience, American opinion hardened. Although some 20% of the population remained loyal to the British crown, the citizens of several colonies, notably Pennsylvania, took matters into their own hands and seized power from the British Governors. Finally, on

American Star—*the leaders of the American Revolution, clockwise: G. Washington, J. Adams, J. Madision and T. Jefferson*

THOMAS JEFFERSON.   JAMES MADISON   JOHN ADAMS

July 4, 1776 the declaration of independence, written by Thomas Jefferson, was adopted.

The War of Independence. The forces that fought the American war of independence were very unevenly balanced. On the British side stood all the power of the world's largest and most experienced navy; in turn, command of the sea enabled Britain to maintain a professional land-force of 42,000 men, which was later reinforced by 30,000 German mercenaries named, after the country in which most of them originated, as "Hessians." The American forces were larger on paper—in theory the states undertook to provide almost 400,000 men, including the militias which were suitable only for local self-defense—but in practice the troops under Washington's command seldom if ever exceeded 30,000. Washington himself, like his top officers, could be considered at least a semi-professional soldier since he had gained experience during the Seven Years' War (which, in North America, was known as the French and Indian War). But this did not apply to the junior officers or the rank and file. They were people who, leading frontier lives, knew how to handle a weapon, but their understanding of military organization, discipline and tactics was far from perfect.

The first actions of what was initially a civil war inside the colonies took place in March 1776, when Washington took Boston from the British under General Howe. The Patriots were also successful in North Carolina, where British troops were defeated at Moore's Creek Bridge (February 1776); however, an attempt to capture Quebec, though it did reach the city after an incredible march through the Maine wilderness, ended in failure when the British sent in reinforcements and later pursued the colonials all the way back to Lake Champlain, where a naval action was fought. Focusing on the country between those extremes, General Howe and his brother, Admiral Richard Howe, concentrated a large fleet and 34,000 troops to capture New York; in this they were successful, and by the end of October the city was in British hands. Defeated, with his army in disarray, Washington withdrew southwest behind the Delaware. An American counterattack across the ice-ridden river on Christmas night 1776 raised his forces' morale and probably saved them from disintegration, but it did not materially change the strategic situation, since Howe remained in control of New Jersey.

The correct British strategy for 1777 would have been to drive at the heart of the rebellion in New England by means of pincer movement from the south (New York) and north (Canada). However, the moves of the two generals in command—Burgoyne in Quebec and Howe in New Jersey—were not coordinated. As the former marched south with some 9,000 men, he met with logistic difficulties as well as determined resistance on the part of the local forces. Part of his army was wiped out at Bennington on August 16, and he himself was brought to battle at Saratoga near Albany and forced to surrender on October 17; Washington, who was still far away to the south, had nothing to do with the affair.

Meanwhile Howe, possibly because he overestimated Burgoyne's ability to deal with New England on his own, had embarked his forces and taken them by sea to Chesapeake Bay. There he disembarked them and defeated Washington at Branywine Creek on September 11. Next he marched on the American capital of Philadelphia which he entered on September 25, forcing the Congress to flee. Driven to Valley Forge, Washing-

ton's forces were disintegrating owing to desertion and low morale. For him, as for the revolution, the winter of 1777–1778 was the moment when his fortunes reached their lowest ebb.

The surrender at Saratoga had, however, brought France into the conflict. Having lost Canada to the British in 1763, the French saw the colonial uprising as their opportunity at revenge and their intervention proved decisive, especially at sea. Having trained his army during the spring of 1778—the man on the job was a Prussian drillmaster, Baron Friederich Wilhelm von Steuben—Washington attacked the British at Monmouth Court House, New Jersey, on June 28, 1778 as their forces were withdrawing from Philadelphia toward New York. During the remainder of 1778 and much of 1779, the two sides skirmished in New Jersey and New York State, not, however, with decisive results, since the British remained in command of New York City and thus of a centrally-situated port that enabled them to strike both north and south.

While the war in the north (New England) and the center (New York) reached stalemate, the colonial cause suffered defeat in the south. British command of the sea, which throughout these years was almost undisputed, enabled them to land forces at will all along the eastern coast; they used this freedom to defend Savannah against the French under Admiral d'Estaing and to capture Charleston as well as Georgia. Though the British commander, General Henry Clinton, saw himself forced to interrupt his run of victories and return to New York, which was being threatened by the French under de Rochambeau, he left his subordinate, General Cornwallis, in South Carolina. Cornwallis in turn marched north through North Carolina until he reached Yorktown. There he was besieged by a combined American-French army commanded by Washington and Rochambeau; after a futile attempt at resistance, he and 7,000 men laid down their arms on October 19, 1781.

With Cornwallis's surrender, the British cause in the south was lost. Savannah was captured in July 1782, Charleston five months later, though not before the British had used both ports to evacuate thousands of loyalists and take them to Canada. New York, the last major British strongpoint, finally fell to Washington's forces in November 1783. With that, the War of the American Revolution was effectively over.

While the struggle on land was won largely by native American forces with some French assistance in the south, the story at sea was entirely different. As already noted, the British at the time possessed the world's largest and most effective navy. They used this to transport troops up and down the east coast, landing troops whenever a river-estuary offered an opportunity and military operations dictated. Though the Americans enjoyed isolated successes against this fleet, e.g., the capture of New Providence (Nassau) by Commodore Esek Hopkins in 1776—on the whole their naval efforts were mostly limited to privateering. The turning point came in 1778 when France, followed by Spain and the Netherlands, joined in the war against Britain. The latter now saw its possessions threatened not only in North America but in Gibraltar and India as well; there was even a fear that the English homeland itself might be invaded by the allies' combined fleets. All this meant that, stretched to the limit, the British had to maintain fewer ships in American waters than might otherwise have been the case. Even so, the navy, under Admiral Rodney, was able to maintain command of the North

Atlantic seaboard throughout 1779 and 1780. Only in 1781, when their other commitments forced the British to reduce their fleet and Rodney himself left the theater, did the Americans and the French reach numerical superiority. This enabled them to bottle up the British in New York, from where the latter ventured to sortie on occasion, without decisive results.

The Treaty of Paris and the Foundation of the Republic. Even as hostilities were still going on in and around North America, American and British representatives met in Paris. A preliminary peace was concluded in 1782, with Benjamin Franklin, John Adams, John Jay and Henry Laurens negotiating for the Americans; the peace became definitive in 1783. The terms of the treaty gave the US independence from Britain, with generous borders that reached as far west as the Mississippi River; other, less important, clauses confirmed Canada in British possession and gave Florida (which had been captured by the British in 1763) back to Spain. Though the treaty also guaranteed fair treatment to loyalists, in practice the promise was not kept and harsh measures, including the confiscation of property and banishment, were taken against them. Eventually, some 80,000 of them left the US for Canada, England and the British West Indies.

While the war of independence was thus being wound down, the task of establishing the republic only began. It was a question of creating a common government, common finances, a common army and other common institutions for 13 sparsely-populated colonies which hitherto had only British authority in common, and which were furthermore divided by differences of outlook between north and south, town and countryside, Protestants and the members of other religions, Federalists and Republicans. The task of building a new state *ex nihilo* was unprecedented, given that never before had men deliberately set out to create a republican government on a scale exceeding that of a single city-state or canton. Between 1783 and 1789, when the constitution was ratified (see MADISON, JAMES) and Washington elected as the country's first president (1789), the task was accomplished. For the most part it involved a series of compromises between the various interests, though eventually tending to greater centralization than was originally intended. The new country, the first in world history to base its political constitution on the idea that *all* (white) men were equal and free, was set on its way; the results are with us to the present day.

AMIN, IDI (1925–) Ex-president of Uganda. Originally an athlete and boxing champion, Amin was a British-trained professional NCO who rose to command Uganda's army after that country gained its independence in 1966. In 1971 he led a military coup that overthrew President Milton Obote and took over as Uganda's ruler, appointing himself president for life in 1976. He introduced a xenophobic policy, expelled all Asians and systematically humiliated white people. In addition he launched a campaign against minority tribes, intellectuals and opposition leaders who were killed en masse; this campaign probably cost the lives of 250,000 people.

Though regarded as a psychopath by many Westerners, Amin kept a firm grip on power and managed to survive several assassination attempts; his antics, while ridiculed by the "civilized" world, were the subject of a least some admiration by many African leaders, who would have liked to imitate his anti-impe-

rialist hysterionics but dared not. In 1976 his prestige received a grievous blow, when the Israelis landed at the Entebbe airport and set free some 100 people whom he was holding hostage as the result of a hijacking. Finally, in 1979, his régime was toppled by a force of Ugandan exiles operating from neighboring Tanzania, which crossed the border and occupied the capital of Kampala. Amin thereupon fled to exile in Saudi Arabia, where he still lives.

AMIS DU MANIFESTE ET DE LA LIBERTÉ (Friends of the Manifesto and of Liberty) A united front formed among the followers of both AHMAD MESSALI HAJJ and FERHAT 'ABBAS in 1944 in support of Ferhat's "Manifesto of the Algerian People," which advocated the establishment of an independent Algerian state through peaceful means. The organization dissolved, however, amid harsh recriminations, following the SETIF UPRISING.

AMMASH, SALEH MANDI (1924–) Iraqi officer, journalist and politician. From the 1950s one of the leading officers connected with the underground BA'ATH PARTY in that country. Ammash was imprisoned several times between 1958 and 1963 under the ADBDUL KARIM QASSEM régime. He was one of the leaders of the coup of February 1963 which overthrew Qassem and became defense minister in the new *Ba'ath*-dominated government. When that government was deposed in November 1963, he went into exile, but returned in 1966. After the first AHMAD HASAN AL-BAKR coup of July 1968, 'Ammash played a leading role in Iraqi politics. In March 1971 he lost out to SADDAM HUSSEIN for the position of president. He is rumored to have been involved in further coup attempts, but in recent years has disappeared from the public stage.

ANABAPTISTS (so called by their enemies from the Greek, meaning "rebaptizers") The term is employed in reference to a broad movement of the Reformation, contemporary with those led by LUTHER, Zwingli and CALVIN, but of a different social and religious orientation. The Anabaptists were more radical in their insistence upon a literal implementation of biblical models, e.g., refusing to allow infant baptism and insisting on adult, or believers' baptism. Essentially, the movement was an attempt to achieve moral liberation and a quest for redemption through a collective religious experience. It embodied many qualities of social protest and combined an elitist intellectual leadership with a large following of simple social background. These features, seemingly contradictory but actually of a complementary nature and belonging to the same context, may account for both the ecstatic and violent nature of the Anabaptists' experience, and for its elements of pacifism, nonresistance and social withdrawal.

Although the Anabaptists sprang up more or less simultaneously in Switzerland, Germany and the Netherlands, it was a group of young supporters of Zwingli at Zurich which set the precedent for the movement, when it performed the first ceremony of adult rebaptism on January 21, 1525. Denounced as moral and religious transgressors, its members were forced to leave the city, but began to spread the movement in the Tyrolean valleys and the Rhineland. The first doctrinal statement of the movement, the Schleitheim Confession, was published in 1527.

Direct responsibility for the spread of the movement rests

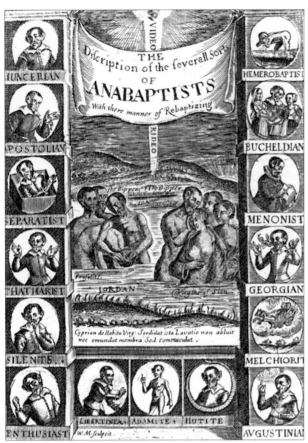

Anabaptism as the source of heresy. Title page of a pamphlet satirizing the movement, London 1645

with the early leaders, such as Conrad Grebel and Georg Blaurock. A number of successful itinerant preachers exercised a great influence in the Netherlands. Jacob Hutter was the founder of the communistic settlements in Moravia. Many of these leaders and other Anabaptists were persecuted and some were executed by Protestants and Roman Catholics alike. The fanatic cruelties and the practice of polygamy by the Anabaptists after they seized control of the city of Münster in 1534 were exploited by their enemies as evidence of the immorality of the movement. The city was recaptured by the bishop of Münster in 1535, following a 16-month siege. Immediately afterwards, Menno Simons, a Dutchman, began patient work among the persecuted Anabaptist communities of Holland and Friesland, which resulted in the removal of excessive eschatological enthusiasm in favor of pacific voluntarism.

The group has survived to the present, with the Mennonites and Hutterites following the same Anabaptist beliefs. The Baptists, too, owe a certain degree of their beliefs to the Anabaptists.

ANARCHISM Anarchism is a philosophical concept, a political belief and a social movement with the goal of a stateless society, free of legal, political or economic rule, which can be attained only through ceaseless revolutionary actions. Anarchists believe in revolutionary social change but are wary of organized political revolutions for fear that they may merely replace one authoritarian system by another. Anarchism's philosophical point of departure is that human beings are basically good and that if they are freed from compulsory laws, arbitrary rule and centralized economies, they will create humane harmony and social solidarity.

The philosophy of anarchism is quite ancient. It ranges from the biblical prophet Samuel's criticism of the monarchy, through the Greek Stoic philosopher Zeno's critique of the Platonic Republic, to the medieval Christian sects that fought both political and papal rule. However, anarchism is known mainly as a modern movement, beginning during the FRENCH REVOLUTION. The GIRONDINS reviled their radical foes, the JACOBINS, with the title "anarchists" because of their desire to continue the revolution even after Louis XVI had been deposed. The bourgeois revolution actually opposed two typical anarchist demands: decentralization and the abandonment of property. The revolution, which had begun as a rebellion against the monarchist, feudal, ecclesiastical status quo, ended up with a centralized government which established the power of the bourgeois.

The French Revolution provided images, legends and myths for the anarchist tradition of the 19th and 20th centuries, supporting the idea that political and social structures are destructible, that monarchies and aristocracies can be removed with a wave of the hand and that no constitutional structure is eternal if it is confronted by a series of violent acts.

The anarchist tradition held up for emulation the SANS-CULOTTES, who had acted against the Girondins, the Jacobins and the revolutionary dictatorship in 1793. Jacques Rous, the leader of the most violent group, the Enrages, contributed to later anarchist practice with his example of how social justice can be represented by the direct action of the masses in the streets. He and HÉBERT despaired of ROBESPIERRE and executed him with a guillotine that they themselves helped set up. In 1793, William Godwin in England published a book which was the first modern formulation of anarchism. He presented an anarchist model of small autonomous communities which share their property in a communal way. The abolishment of tyranny and of accumulated property would not take place through revolutionary action or social reform but by spreading the idea of justice and using enlightened methods to persuade individuals of the necessity of free arrangements.

Anarchism inherited several elements of the French revolution: terror as a form of political activity, republican virtue as a form of political education and conspiracy as a life style. GRACCHUS BABEUF's "Conspiration des Equax" of 1793 served as a mythic model for the 19th-century anarchists. The means Babeuf advocated and his call for the elimination of private property were anarchistic, but he believed in a strong state—a dictatorship—and the nationalization of the means of production. This was typical of the dialectics of many ideas of the French Revolution, which were anarchistic at first, yet turned statist and centralist as they succeeded and became established.

After Babeuf, FILIPPO BUONAROTTI was the prototype of the professional saboteur. He founded secret societies in Switzerland and Belgium, as well as in France after the 1830 revolution. Babeuf, Buonarotti and LOUIS AUGUSTE BLANQUI—who spent 40 of his 76 years in prison—were depicted by later generations as the personification of revolution in the 19th century.

According to James Joll, a historian of anarchism, three

myths of the French revolution became an integral part of anarchist belief: that a violent revolution is possible; that the next revolution would be a true social one and would not merely replace one ruling class by another; and that this future revolution would arrive only when a revolutionary conspiracy of devoted anarchists would arise from the existing society. From this point on, revolutions would be made not only in philosophical essays but also in the streets.

While the Enrages, Babeuf and Buonarotti provided examples of the violent revolutionary climate of anarchist terror, utopian socialists from Charles Fourier to Saint-Simon and Godwin discussed the future of society. Their ideal visions of a new world, and their image of a rational, peace-loving sort of anarchist, became part of the philosophy from which modern anarchism arose. The futurist communities of Fourier, the *phalansteries*, typified the element of cooperation. Saint-Simon criticized the revolutionaries for merely improving the mechanism of the state.

A revolutionary philosophy justifying radical change was proposed by the Young Hegelians. In the revolutionary dialectics they developed, all conflict, both political and class-based, contributes to a new synthesis of history. Max Stirner, following Feuerbach, claimed that the state would be replaced by a union of egoists and recommended violent means for realizing individual rights. The conclusion of another Young Hegelian, KARL MARX, was that the class war would end in the dictatorship of the proletariat, while PROUDHON reached anarchist conclusions instead.

It was Proudhon who provided the crucial motivation for modern anarchism. In 1840 he adopted the term "anarchism" in his essay, "What is property?" He did not believe that all rule should be abolished, advocating instead political federalism and economic "mutualism," which would restrict the authority of the central mechanisms of power through free local organizations. The ideal society requires two nonviolent revolutions: one against the present economic order and the other against the present political order. Instead of a mass revolution there must be a revolution of cells (tiny groups). At the time of the bourgeois REVOLUTIONS OF 1848 in Paris, Berlin and Vienna, Proudhon concluded, "We made a revolution without an idea."

The fathers of modern anarchism were MIKHAIL BAKUNIN (1814–1876) and Prince PETER KROPOTKIN (1842–1921). Bakunin gave anarchism a collectivist direction, claiming that the revolution must be a spontaneous mass rebellion rather than an act of a political leadership with armed forces. A military revolution would lead to a class dictatorship, an organized oligarchy and a strong state. Repression from above must be countered by terror from below—that is, propaganda through action. Bakunin's follower, SERGEI NECHAEV, came to more nihilistic conclusions: all means are legitimate for destroying corrupted states.

Wilhelm Weitling, in his book, *Guarantees of Harmony and Freedom*, combined the idea of the inevitable revolution with anarchist and Christian beliefs. As a revolutionary of the 1840s, he influenced the anarchists directly. Bakunin, whom he met in Switzerland, was impressed by Weitling's book, in which he wrote that revolutions would arise "either through harsh physical force or through spiritual power, or both. The revolutions will no longer be bloody." Bakunin thought that true revolutions are made by those who have nothing to lose. He claimed that the new ethics of revolution "can only be effectively taught among the bewildered masses swarming in our great cities and plunged into the utmost boundless misery."

Most anarchists consider themselves socialists, but since they also conceive of themselves as revolutionaries they refuse to act through parliamentary legislation or social reform. Anarchism appeared as an organized movement in Western Europe in the 1850s and 1860s. The First International (see INTERNATIONAL, FIRST), which was founded in 1864, served as a battlefield in the conflict between Marxist and anarchist groups. In 1883 the anarchists founded their own International, and its first congress was held in Amsterdam in 1907.

Kropotkin opposed the capitalist régime, advocating the founding of free Communist cells that would coordinate the means of production and consumption. This combination of anarchism and communism supported economic decentralization, which was supposed to come after the state would totally disappear in a popular revolution. From the 1880s, anarchism became more and more communistic. The Russian writer Leo Tolstoy, on the other hand, completely rejected communism, which he believed to be based on centralism, just as he rejected revolution and violence. Tolstoy's variety of anarchism was a combination of a spiritual revolution and non-cooperation with state institutions—the army, the courts and the administration. Henry David Thoreau in the 19th century, and MAHATMA GANDHI in the 20th, also favored civil disobedience over violent revolution.

In the 1880s, there was a crisis in Marxism which led to three new directions: EDUARD BERNSTEIN's parliamentary revisionism, VLADIMIR LENIN's party cadre system, and GEORGES SOREL's revolutionary violence. Sorel, a French theoretician who combined individualistic anarchism with organized revolutionary syndicalism in both France and Italy, rejected the idea of a political revolution. Instead, he advocated a permanent rebellion in the form of a proletarian general strike. He believed that revolutions stem from power and necessitate terror, while rebellions stem from freedom and necessitate violence. This philosophy of violence infiltrated the foundations of the revolutionary syndicalism advocated by fascism at the beginning of its career.

In the late 19th and early 20th centuries anarchists preached terror and the assassination of government representatives. Direct violent action replaced political and social revolution. This philosophy led to the assassination of French president M.F. Sadi Carnot in 1894, Empress Elizabeth of Austria in 1898, King Humbert I of Italy in 1900 and American president William McKinley in 1901, as well as assassinations of other figures in parliaments and public institutions.

It is thus not surprising that anarchists got the image of terrorists, although actually most anarchists were not terrorists. Anarchists' activities covered a wide range, from direct action, sabotage, political strikes and general strikes to civil disobedience, pacifism, anti-parliamentarianism and anti-patriotism. Anarchic terrorism flourished in an atmosphere of radical nationalism, a society of minorities and economic exploitation. The anarchists generally refused to organize themselves into political parties, and anarchism never became an organized mass movement like socialism. The essence of anarchism opposes organization. To spread their ideas, the anarchists made use of propaganda, demonstrations, manifestos and strikes, mainly in workers' unions. Anarchists and communists often strode arm in arm in revolutions and civil wars, but the Soviet revolution considered anarchism counterrevolutionary. Anarchist quarters in Moscow were shelled in April 1918 on orders from TROTSKY, the anarchist leaders were imprisoned and their activities were suppressed. PRIMO DE RIVERA's Spain also suppressed anarchist organizations, such as the Federacion Anarquista Iberica and Confederacion Nacional del Trabajo.

Anarchists and communists both sided with the Republicans against General FRANCISCO FRANCO in the Spanish civil war of 1936–1939, but the hostility between them led to the dissolution of their alliance, the repression of the anarchists and Franco's victory. In France and Italy, the anarchists left their stamp on revolutionary syndicalism. Anarchist unions such as the Unione Anarchica Italiana and Unione Sindicale Italiana were made illegal in the MUSSOLINI period.

Unlike European anarchism, which was associated in one way or another with revolution, American anarchism was not associated with revolution at all. From prominent figures such as EMMA GOLDMAN and ALEXANDER BERKMAN, who returned disappointed from visits to the land of the Bolshevik Revolution, to the radical students' movements in the 1960s, the American version of protest movements was always more liberal than anarchist.

ANARCHISM, RUSSIAN   The roots of Russian anarchism lie in such diverse popular and historical institutions as the nonconformist Russian religious groups, the peasant commune and the workers' cooperatives (*artel*) frequently found in 19th-century Russia. The non-Russian sources on which Russian anarchists drew included Fourier and PROUDHON, whose ideas were discussed in many of the Russian populist circles from the 1840s on. The aspect of anarchism that most appealed to young Russians was the free association of equals in a nonauthoritarian commune.

Russian anarchism developed along two main ideological lines. First was that of MIKHAIL BAKUNIN, who advocated a socialist revolution that would create a federation of free workers drawn from all sectors of the economy. Influenced by the Left Hegelian revolutionary movement in Germany, Bakunin employed the slogan: "The passion for destruction is also a creative passion." Combining his feverish lust for freedom with an inclination to conspiracy, Bakunin involved himself in every antigovernmental organization he could find, moving restlessly across all the countries of Europe, eventually promoting the idea of an international brotherhood of anarchism that would destroy all states and régimes and clear the way for the world revolution.

As opposed to Bakunin's violence and conspiracy, the strain of anarchism proposed by Prince PETER KROPOTKIN, sought to create a federation of small communes that would represent groups of producers. These ideas rose to prominence following Bakunin's death in 1876. Kropotkin, an early member of the CHAIKOVSKY CIRCLE of populists, felt that placing the means of production in the hands of the state was suicidal for society and would produce a tyranny far more dangerous than that of mere political despotism. Kropotkin's anarchism called for the socialists to live the lives of peasants and workmen, creating the example of the free commune. A third, lesser trend in anarchism was Lev Tolstoi's religiously derived creed of non-violence,

negating the state and allowing only passive resistance to evil.

Until the 1905 revolution, the Russian anarchist movement existed chiefly in exile, with its center in Geneva. From 1905 on, a growing and active movement was to be found within Russia. While most of the groups scattered throughout the Russian empire described themselves as "Anarchist-Communists," a strong anarchist-syndicalist movement, focusing on trade union organization and opposing conspiratory terror, developed in the industrial areas. Prominent among the new generation of anarchist activists was Vatslav K. Makhaysky (Volsky) whose book, *Umstvennyi rabochii* (The Intellectual Worker), in many ways presaged the ideas of MILOVAN DJILAS's *The New Class*. In the south, a particularly violent group, "the Militant International Group of Anarchists-Communists," advocated terrorism and the destruction of all existing institutions as a prelude to the creation of a new and better world. During this period the Union of Maximalists, earlier associated with the SOCIAL REVOLUTIONARY PARTY, established its own independent organization, negating parliamentarism and political parties. The Maximalists advocated a "Republic of Toilers," based on producers and communes united through a network of elected councils. Involved in bank robberies and mass terror, the Maximalists were soon hunted down by the police and the Maximalist Union lapsed between 1908 and 1917.

In 1917, the anarchist movement opposed the provisional government, supporting the BOLSHEVIKS with their slogan of "All Power to the Soviets." Anarchists were active in the many factory committees that were formed during the year and a revived Maximalist Union, led by Grigory Rivkin, Arseni Zverin and Anatoli Lamanov, played a leading role in forming the direct democracy of the Kronstadt naval base soviet. The Maximalists also appeared in other localities and accounted for close to one-third of the active anarchists. The anarchist newspaper *Stormbird* (*Burevestnik*) attained a circulation of 25,000 copies in Petrograd alone. Foreign anarchists, notably ALEXANDER BERKMAN and EMMA GOLDMAN of the USA, joined the Russian anarchists but were quickly disillusioned by the Bolshevik exercise of state power. Within six months of taking power, the Bolsheviks were suppressing anarchist activities and their criticism of Bolshevik political and economic practice. Numerous anarchists fled to Ukraine, where they tried with little success to form a united anarchist opposition. The one significant anarchist movement in Ukraine was the Revolutionary Insurgent Army of NESTOR MAKHNO. At the height of the civil war, Makhno, operating from headquarters in Gulai Pole in southeast Ukraine, cooperated with the Bolsheviks against the Whites. However, as the Bolsheviks gained the upper hand they moved to eliminate the independence of Makhno's forces and in August 1921 Makhno was defeated and forced into exile. The funeral of Prince Kropotkin in February 1921, for which numerous jailed anarchists were given a day of freedom, was the last mass appearance of anarchists until their resurgence during Gorbachev's *Perestroika*.

ANDOM AMAN   (?–1974) An Ethiopian general who was the head of the coordinating committee (the Derg) that led the ETHIOPIAN REVOLUTION OF 1974. Andom led the Derg for a short period after the overthrow of Haile Selassie, from September 9, 1974 until November 11, 1974. Andom himself was not a Derg member, but his credentials had recommended him for the job.

He was popular within the army, had behind him long years of experience in governmental affairs and, being an Eritrean, was expected to solve the Eritrean problem.

Andom represented the moderate wing within the Derg in two main areas: he sought to compromise with the Eritrean rebels and demanded fair trials for the old régime members. He also wished to reduce the 120-member Derg into a smaller group, a stand that turned the lower officers in the Derg against him. His moderate positions made him a number of enemies. In November 1974, he decided to resign and to try to gain power with the help of his supporters. On November 22, a sharply critical speech was made by HAILE MARIAM MENGISTU, the main representative of the radical wing within the Derg, against Andom and his supporters. On the same night Andom was arrested and murdered.

ANIELEWICZ, MORDECAI (1919? 1920?–1943) Commander of the Warsaw Ghetto uprising. Anielewicz was born in the slums of Warsaw. While still a youth, he joined the *Ha-Shomer ha-Tsair* Social Zionist movement and became one of its leading figures. On September 7, 1939, less than a week after the Germans invaded Poland, Anielewicz, like many of the leaders of the Zionist youth movements, fled Warsaw. He reached the Soviet-occupied area of Poland and attempted to travel to Romania, hoping to find his way to Palestine from there. Caught by the Soviet authorities, he was jailed for a short time.

Statue of Mordechai Anielewicz in Israel

> ## ANIELEWICZ'S LAST LETTER
> ### APRIL 23, 1943
>
> What happened is beyond our wildest dreams. Twice the Germans fled from our ghetto. One of our companies held out for forty minutes and the other, for over six hours... I have no words to describe to you the conditions in which the Jews are living. Only a few chosen ones will hold out; all the rest will perish sooner or later. The die is cast. In the bunkers in which our comrades are hiding, no candle can be lit for lack of air ... The main thing is: My life's dream has come true; I have lived to see Jewish resistance in the ghetto in all its greatness and glory.

After his release, en route back to Warsaw, Anielewicz visited a number of Jewish communities to gain an impression of their situation. After a short stay in Warsaw, he went on to Vilna, where many Zionist youth had concentrated. There some of them decided to return to German-occupied Poland to lead the movements' activities surreptitiously. Anielewicz also volunteered to return to Poland.

In Warsaw he organized clandestine cells, held seminars and aided the development of an underground press, to which he contributed articles. Upon receiving reports of the murder of Jews in the German-occupied areas of the Soviet Union, in the summer of 1941, Anielewicz pushed for the creation of an armed Jewish underground. The first such organization, the Anti-Fascist Bloc, was never really established and, following a wave of arrests of some of its Communist members, was dissolved.

Anielewicz went to Bedzin to help establish an armed underground, shortly before the mass deportations in Warsaw began in the summer of 1942. He returned to Warsaw to discover that only about 60,000 Jews remained and that the new armed underground organization, the Jewish Fighting Organization, was still quite weak. He set about restructuring the organization, and in November 1942 became its commander.

The first armed clashes between the Jews and the Germans occurred during the deportation drive of January 18, 1943. In a brief battle, in which many Jewish fighters fell, Anielewicz was saved by his men. The deportation ended rather quickly and the Jews of Warsaw believed it was Anielewicz's fighters who had caused the Germans to abandon their operation. Anielewicz and the armed underground's prestige rose to such a degree in the ghetto that they became its de facto leaders. Now the Jews of Warsaw feverishly built bunkers and readied themselves for armed resistance.

One the eve of the Jewish festival of Passover, April 9, 1943, the Germans began their final deportation drive in Warsaw. The armed underground reacted with all the weapons it had managed to obtain. Anielewicz commanded the fighting, which at first took place in the streets and then was confined to the bunkers. With most of his staff, he entered a bunker on 18 Mila Street. On May 8, amid the burning ruins of the ghetto, Anielewicz was killed when the bunker fell to the Germans. He is considered one of the outstanding heroes of the Holocaust. Kibbutz Yad Mordecai in Israel was named for him.

AN LUSHAN (An Lu-shan)   (703–757) Leader of a rebellion in China. Of mixed Sogdian-Turkish parentage, An served the illustrious Tang dynasty (618–907) as military commander along China's northeastern frontier. Taking advantage of the declining central power, in 755 he launched a rebellion that undermined the foundations of the empire. In 756 his forces occupied Loyang and Changan, the two capitals, and he usurped the title of emperor. He was murdered by his son in 757 and the rebellion continued under successive leaders. Although peace was restored in 763 with the help of Uighurs and other foreign forces, including Arabs, the Tang dynasty, now confined to China proper, never really recovered. Externally it was pressed by central Asian invaders and internally by lawless armies.

AN-SKI, S.   (1863–1920) Russian-Jewish revolutionary intellectual. An-ski's name at birth was Rapaport. He began his revolutionary career as a populist, reading to illiterate miners in the early 1880s in order to raise their cultural level. He was active in the SOCIAL REVOLUTIONARY PARTY, participating in emigre activities in Switzerland at the turn of the century.

From 1904 he devoted himself to literature and Jewish ethnography. In literature he is remembered for his Yiddish poem "The Oath" (*"Die Shvueh"*) which became the anthem of the Bund and for his classic Yiddish play *The Dybbuk*. An-ski headed the Jewish ethnographic expedition that collected folklore items throughout the Pale of Settlement before and during World War I.

ANTALL, JOZSEF   (1932–1993) Hungary's first democratically elected prime minister following the collapse of the Communist régime, Antall served as premier from May 1990 until his death in December 1993. A member of a prominent family of politicians, his grandfather had been secretary of state and his father a high official in the ministry of the interior who had protected Polish and Jewish refugees during World War II. Antall studied history and received his doctorate from the Eotvos Lorand university in Budapest. He worked as a secondary school teacher, librarian and archivist and from 1984 as director of the Semmelweis Museum, Library and Archives of Medical History. His academic-scientific career was shaped by his early political activity and by the Communist régime's reaction to his activism and that of many of his generation in the 1956 uprising (see HUNGARY REVOLTS AND REVOLUTIONS). At the time, Antall was the chairman of the staff of the revolutionary committee at the high school where he taught, one of the founders of the Christian Youth Federation and one of the organizers of the Independent Smallholders' party. One of the founders of the emerging Hungarian Democratic Forum (HDF) in September 1987, he played a leading role in the negotiations between the régime and the various opposition groups and in the formulation of the opposition's platform in dealing with the collapsing Communist régime. As leader of the HDF and prime minister, he led his center-right party and coalition to a controlled transition to a market economy, avoiding "shock therapy." Antall's policies focused on the deconstruction of the Communist régime's legacy, Hungary's "return" and integration in Europe, its return to na-

tional and Christian values and the fate of the Hungarian minority in the neighboring states. His line was often criticized as leaning to nationalism. When his party was rocked by events linked to the activities of extremists and anti-Semites, Antall attempted to defuse the crisis and disengaged from extremist activities. Overall, his pragmatic, noncharismatic approach led to a successful transition in Hungary and one of the smoothest processes of democratization in the former Communist Bloc. In spite of Hungary's relatively smooth transition, in the last two years his popularity was declining, as Antall was blamed for mishandling internal disputes within the ruling HDF and the government coalition and for his inability to cope with the social tensions generated by post-Communist economic and social realities.

ANTONESCU, ION   (1882–1946) Romanian soldier and statesman. Antonescu became chief of staff in 1934 and minister of defense in 1937. Dismissed after a year because of his sympathy with the fascist IRON GUARD, he became prime minister after the Vienna Award of August 1940, which ceded much of the land Romania had been granted in the aftermath of World War I. In January 1941 he savagely suppressed the IRON GUARD, whose excesses had brought the country to the brink of anarchy and civil war. The king having left the country in September of the previous year, Antonescu became a dictator and supported Germany in its Russian adventure. In August 1944 he was overthrown in a coup, put on trial, and executed in 1946 as a war criminal.

ANTONOV-OVSEENKO, VLADIMIR ALEXANDRO-VICH   (1884–1939) Bolshevik military leader. Born in a military family, Antonov-Ovseenko was enrolled in a military-engineering school but expelled for refusing to take the oath of loyalty to the czar. During the 1905 revolution he became a full-time revolutionary, organizing uprisings in various garrisons of the south. Arrested repeatedly during this period, he was ultimately sentenced to death for armed rebellion. The sentence was commuted to life in jail, but he escaped.

The years 1910–1917 were spent in exile in Paris, where Antonov-Ovseenko engaged primarily in journalistic work, working with TROTSKY and editing the newspaper *Golos* (*Voice*) with Dmitri Manuilski. He also served as secretary of the Labour Bureau of Paris in which exiled representatives of Russian trade unions worked.

In May 1917, Antonov-Ovseenko returned to Russia as a member of Trotsky's "Inter-District" group, joining the Bolsheviks with TROTSKY in July. In the Bolshevik RUSSIAN REVOLUTION OF 1917 seizure of power, Antonov-Ovseenko was among the organizers of the attack on the Winter Palace and of the arrest of KERENSKY's provisional government. In the BOLSHEVIK government he was one of the People's Commissars for military affairs and commanded the military district of Petrograd.

In the civil war of 1918–1921, Antonov-Ovseenko commanded a Bolshevik force that defeated the white general Kaledin as well as leading other operations in South Russia and Ukraine. From 1922 he commanded the political administration of the RED ARMY. As a close supporter of Trotsky, he was removed from his command in 1923 and with Trotsky's downfall was sent on diplomatic missions abroad. He was arrested and executed in the Stalin purges, but was later rehabilitated under KHRUSHCHEV in 1956.

APRIL REVOLUTION (March–April 1960) In Korean history, the revolt that toppled Syngman Rhee, only to replace him with another dictator, PARK CHUNG HEE. This was the only successful revolt in modern Korean history. Its instigators were students and it is thought to have provided an example for the STUDENT MOVEMENTS of the 1960s.

AQUINO, BENIGNO (1933–1983) Aquino, a Philippine patriot and former governor of Tarlac state, was a senator early in the presidency of Ferdinand Marcos. When Marcos declared martial law on September 23, 1972, Aquino, along with other political opponents of the régime, was jailed and later exiled. As martial law was lifted in January 1981, a coalition party nominated Salvador Laurel for the presidency and Benigno Aquino as vice-president. Marcos, however, continued to resist attempts to challenge his power, especially on the part of the Communist New People's army. Benigno Aquino was assassinated on August 21, 1983, at the Manila airport, the government claiming that a Communist was responsible. This explanation failed to satisfy the people and the assassination provoked both national and international outrage, a reaction which contributed to Marcos's fall from power and flight to the USA in 1986.

AQUINO, CORAZON (1933–) Widow of assassinated Philippine political leader BENIGNO AQUINO, ran against incumbent President Ferdinand Marcos in the elections of February, 1986. Her vice-presidential running mate was Salvador Laurel, the opposition party's presidential candidate in 1981. With no formal political background, Corazon Aquino was a symbol of opposition to the repressive Marcos régime. On February 16, the National Assembly declared that Marcos had once more won the presidency. There was, however, strong evidence of massive electoral fraud. International figures and organizations, ranging from the European Parliament through US President Reagan, accused Marcos of having stolen the election.

The result was the February Revolution, launched on February 22 by the resignation of the defense minister and the army chief of staff, both of whom called upon Marcos to resign. More than a million Filipinos took to the streets, forming a human barrier that physically halted the advance of troops and tanks. Marcos and his retinue fled the country and President Corazon Aquino, responding to the national will, dissolved the corrupt National Assembly, abolished the prime ministry and abrogated the constitution of 1973. A new Freedom Constitution was put into effect on March 26 and ratified by the constitutional commission in October and a new legislature was elected in 1987.

ARABI (URABI), AHMAD PASHA AL MISRI (1839–1911) Egyptian nationalist leader. Born of peasant parents, Arabi succeeded in being admitted to Cairo's al Azhar religious university before joining the army, where he reached the rank of colonel. From the beginning of his career he plotted against Turkish rule of his country; 1879 found him participating in the officers' revolt against the khedive, Isma'il Pasha. When the British bombarded Alexandria and took over Egypt in July 1882, it was Arabi who, having proclaimed the khedive a traitor,

organized the resistance. In September 1882, Arabi's forces were defeated at Tel el Kabir near Cairo. He himself was captured by the British and handed over to the khedive, who had him sentenced to death as a traitor. However, with British intervention he was reprieved, sent into exile, and finally allowed to return to Egypt in 1901.

ARAB NATIONAL MOVEMENT, NATIONALISM Feelings of national pride, attempts to cultivate the nation's heritage and traditions, and resistance to foreign rule have been prevalent among Arabs, as among all nations, for a considerable time. An Arab national movement in the modern sense, however—i.e., a movement based on the conception that "nations," and the Arab "nation" among them, are entitled to independence, and that States should be formed on the basis of "nations" (and not, for instance, based on religion or dynastic allegiance), and organizations with the defined aim of attaining independence and establishing an Arab nation-State (or States)—emerged only at the beginning of the 20th century.

The Arab national movement was rooted in, and preceded by, a movement of cultural and literary renaissance in the 19th century, mainly centered in the Levant (and to some degree in Egypt), strongly influenced by the penetration of Western civilization and inspired by European romantic nationalism and national liberation movements. European and American Christian missionaries also contributed significantly to that renaissance, particularly through the development of educational institutions and technical instruments (printing presses, textbooks). This national renaissance was later strongly influenced by the modernist Islamic revival movement—perhaps without fully realizing the inherent conflict between supranational Pan-Islamism and extra-religious Arab nationalism, two conceptions that parallel one another, but also overlap in some areas.

A politically motivated Arab national movement with potentially revolutionary implications began organizing in the first decade of the 20th century in the Arabic-speaking parts of the Ottoman Empire, i.e., mainly in the Fertile Crescent (the Levant and Iraq) and among students and young officers and officials from that area and the Arabian Peninsula. Egypt and Arabic-speaking North Africa were, at that time, outside the scope and target-area of incipient Arab nationalism. The organizers of the movement were influenced by the revolt of the YOUNG TURKS (1908), which, at first, seemed to open the way to a liberalized, decentralized régime.

When the new rulers of the Ottoman Empire imposed a centralist and Turkish-nationalist régime, some of the new Arab societies grew increasingly antagonistic and began envisaging full Arab independence and the dissolution of the empire; others strove for Arab autonomy within a decentralized empire. This difference coincided with the divergence described above between Islamic influences and Arab nationalist motivations; for radical Arab nationalism necessarily demanded a struggle for full independence and the abolition of Turkish rule, while Islamists were bound to be loyal to the Muslim empire, to the Ottoman sultan in his capacity as caliph—the head of the whole Islamic community. This ideological dichotomy was never fully resolved.

The Arab national movement in its initial stage consisted of various clubs or societies—such as the *Ligue de la Patrie Arabe*

(Paris, 1904); the Literary Club (*al-Muntada al-Adabi*) (Istanbul, 1909); the Decentralization Party (Cairo 1912); the Reform Committee (Beirut, 1912); *al-Qahtaniyya* (1909); the Arab Pact (*al-'Ahd,*, 1914), with its members mainly young army officers; and the Young Arab Society (*al-Fatåt*, Paris, 1911). *Al-Fatåt*, which called for full Arab independence, was perhaps the most important among these groups. In 1913 it organized an Arab nationalist conference in Paris, which is regarded as an important landmark. Members of these organizations later became prominent in the leadership of the Arab socialists. At the time they were a small group, with an active membership hardly exceeding a 100, a few hundred supporters and little influence.

An Arab insurrection arose, during World War I, from a different source: Hussein ibn 'Ali, the sharif of Mecca, of the Hashemite clan, rebelled in 1916, after preliminary contacts with the British and with their support (see ARAB REVOLT). The sharif, and particularly his sons Feisal and Abdullah, had had contacts with the Arab nationalist societies. In his exchange of letters with the British, Hussein demanded the establishment of an independent Arab State, or Arab States, in the Arabian Peninsula and the Fertile Crescent, after the dissolution of the Ottoman Empire. He obtained British support, though that support remained rather vague, envisaging a measure of British (and French) tutelage for the future Arab State(s), and was not finalized in a hard and fast agreement. The Arab nationalists in the Fertile Crescent probably sympathized with the sharif's revolt, but did not support it by a simultaneous rebellion in their countries, and only a handful of Arab officers in the Ottoman army—either deserters or prisoners who had been recruited to the cause—joined the revolt. In 1918, Prince Feisal and his troops, advancing into Transjordan and Syria as the right wing of the British and allied forces under General Allenby, were allowed to enter Damascus and establish their headquarters and an Arab administration there.

Hussein and his sons were regarded by the victorious powers as the legitimate spokesmen of Arab nationalism. Amir (Prince) Feisal represented them at the peace conference, while many of the officers from Iraq and Syria who had joined the revolt—and others who had rallied to them in 1918–1919 when they were advancing into Transjordan and Syria—became their advisers and members of the governmental bodies they set up. In 1919, a group of these officers and politicians—most of them members of the *al-Fatåt* club—created the Arab Independence party, *al-Istiqlal*. In 1919 and 1920, Syrian-Arab national congresses were organized which supported Feisal's claims and proclaimed him king of Syria (including Lebanon and Palestine), while delegates from Iraq invited his brother 'Abdullah to become king of that country.

The character of Arab nationalism in the post-World War I period was determined by the settlement imposed by the Allied powers. The Hashemite princes' design for a single Arab State, or a federation of Arab States in Arabia and the Fertile Crescent under their rule, was not implemented. Separate semi-independent States under British and French tutelage were set up instead in Iraq, Syria, Lebanon and Transjordan (with Palestine under a British mandate, to become a Jewish national home, and Hashemite rule in Arabia contested by the rising Saudi power). National movements arose in each of the States created in the formerly Turkish area, each struggling for full independence from Britain and France—sympathetic to, and supporting, each other, but separate from one another. This country-by-country fight for full independence achieved its main goal, in most cases by stages, by the 1940s and 1950s, except for the case of Palestine. By the 1960s and 1970s, all the Arab countries were fully independent and the last vestiges of foreign privileges, military bases and unequal treaties had been eliminated.

The original plans of the Arab national movement for a greater, united all-Arab entity continued to be fostered by Arab political writers and thinkers. In terms of practical politics, they survived mainly in schemes of the Hashemite rulers of Iraq and Jordan for a Fertile Crescent federation or a "Greater Syria." British backing, always suspected by the French and many Arabs, was at best partial and half-hearted and the Hashemite plans never got off the ground. These plans were, anyway, adamantly opposed by most Arab countries and particularly by Egypt, Syria and Saudi Arabia. Pan-Arab nationalism in its Hashemite version lost its relevance with the assassination of Kings Abdullah (1951) and Feisal II (1958) and the elimination of Hashemite rule in Iraq (1958).

From the 1950s, Pan-Arab nationalism appeared in new, invigorated, radical versions—postulating an all-Arab nationalism (*Qawmiyya*) that transcended the patriotism of specific Arab countries (*Wataniyya*). The shock of the Arab defeat in Palestine in 1948 was the main catalyst in that re-emergence of all-Arab nationalism. The new trends were leftist and socialist in inclination, to an extent inspired by New Left, Maoist-Castroist thought. One of these was the Movement of Arab Nationalists (*Harakat al-Qawmiyyin al-'Arab*), clandestinely organized from c. 1949–1950, at first mainly among students, e.g., at the American University of Beirut. Among its underground and never clearly identified leaders was the Palestinian GEORGE HABASH. The *Qawmiyya*, gradually moving farther left, aimed at the elimination of the conservative Arab régimes and the creation of revolutionary Arab unity; it advocated violence and terrorism against foreign interests, Israel, Arab conservatives and dissenters.

Another trend of Pan-Arab leftist-revolutionary nationalism, with a rather more elaborate ideology published in detail, was the Arab Renaissance (*al-Ba'ath*) group. This faction regarded the existing Arab States as only temporary entities, bound to be merged into a united all-Arab State—by revolutionary violence or subversion if need be. The *Ba'ath* group, at its inception mainly students and young intellectuals, cultivated ties to younger officers, particularly in the Syrian and Iraqi armies. It was these clandestine officers' cells that transformed the little club of intellectuals into a politically significant faction and enabled it first to push Syria into union with Egypt (1958), then to assist in Syria's secession from that union (1961), and finally to seize power, through military coups in Syria and Iraq (both in 1963) and, after losing power in Iraq later the same year, again in 1968. It maintains branches outside Syria and Iraq too, but except for Lebanon, these are illegal underground cells.

Pan-Arab revolutionary nationalism in the 1950s and 1960s found its strongest expression in Egyptian Nasserism and in the teachings of Libya's QADHDHAFI. The Egyptian officers' régime, in power since the FREE OFFICERS coup of 1952, under the leadership of GAMAL NASSER, turned increasingly activist in inter-Arab affairs, attempting to impose on the other Arab States a régime in its image—"Arab Socialism"—a populist-totalitarian single-party state socialism which is leftist-neutralist in international affairs. The ideology of Arab Socialism developed pragmatically, growing out of Egyptian political needs, and was never laid down as a formal, complete doctrine; and though Nasser and his aides encouraged "Nasserist" factions in other Arab countries, no all-Arab Nasserist party was ever created and rival Nasserist factions often fought each other. Even in Egypt, the régime was based on the state bureaucracy rather than on the single party (which never got off the ground). Nasserism had some affinities with Ba'athism and the Syrian Arab socialists pressed for union with Egypt, achieved in 1958, in the hope that a joint doctrine could be worked out and that the pragmatic Nasserists would accept Ba'athist ideological guidance. But after the union, the Egyptians' determination to impose their centralist single-party system and state bureaucracy on the united State soon caused a clash with the Syrian Ba'athists and led to Syria's secession in 1961.

In the 1950s and the early 1960s, Egyptian Nasserism operated chiefly through subversion, causing innumerable complaints and disputes. However, after the dissolution of the Syro-Egyptian union and the failure of all Egyptian-Nasserist attempts to topple conservative régimes and impose all-Arab unity according to Nasserist prescriptions, along with the frustration of Egypt's military intervention in Yemen (1962–1967), Nasser's all-Arab unionist fervor cooled considerably and Nasserism lost much of its momentum. After Nasser's death in 1970, Egypt's rulers abandoned revolutionary Arab socialist unionism.

Libya's Mu'ammar Qadhdhafi, in power since his military coup of 1969, developed his own version of Arab nationalism—a mass-oriented populist-totalitarian semi-socialism, fervently nationalist with strong Islamic emphasis, pressing for immediate moves toward all-Arab unity (and based, though strictly anti-Communist, on a firm alliance with the Soviet Bloc). Qadhdhafi's doctrine and policies, laid down in his "Green Book" (1976 and 1978), led him into unrelenting efforts to unite Libya with various Arab countries, coupled with subversive, even terrorist, activities that brought him into constant conflict with the very countries he wanted to merge with Libya—Egypt, Sudan, Tunisia and Morocco.

Arab nationalism, the assertion of Arab independence and power (since World War II with strong leanings to non-alignment) and the construction of modern, stable, economically and socially developed nation-States (in many cases with populist or socialist tendencies), has remained the dominant force in Arab thinking, sentiment and policy. Arab nationalism, like other independence movements, has its difficulties with the process of nation-building, the problems of régime and administration, of good government and social development. It has not completely overcome, for the sake of the nation's unity, divergences of particularist allegiances—regional, tribal and mainly communal-religious. Minority communities tend to feel a dominant first priority allegiance to their community. Many simple, uneducated Muslim Arabs hardly distinguish between "Muslim" and "Arab," instinctively regarding only a Muslim Arab as fully and really Arab. The upsurge, in recent years, of strong radical Islamic trends has added to his problem. Wide strata of the Muslim-Arab population do not, perhaps, perceive the intrinsic di-

alectic tension, and even contradiction, between extra-religious Arab nationalism and supra-national Islamism, but leaders, policy-makers and intellectuals do, and try to cope with the problem in various ways—e.g., by emphasizing the basic link between Islam and the Arab nation, the fact that Islam became a world religion through the medium of the Arabs' genius and their language and that the Arabs achieved greatness through Islam.

All-Arab nationalism, *Qawmiyya* Arab unionism, remains an aspiration, a potent emotion, a dominant ideological trend. Actually and historically, though, *Wataniyya*, the nationalism of the various Arab countries, determines policies. The two trends go side-by-side in dialectical interplay, contradicting each other and yet influencing and complementing each other. Some elements unite all Arabs, from Casablanca to the Persian Gulf, forging them into one nation; other elements make for increasing divergence and the emergence of separate Arab nations—the Egyptian, Syrian, Iraqi, Algerian, Moroccan, etc. The historically dominant trend seems to be toward growing all-Arab co-operation, but this increasing unity will result in a close alliance rather than in a move toward a federal or unionist merger. Though ideologically and emotionally the stress may be on all-Arab nationalism and many Arabs may balk at the assumption that the separate Arab States are borne by separate Arab nationals, actual Arab unity and the nationalism inspiring it are based, as the Arab League is, on the acceptance of, and respect for, the sovereignty and integrity of separate, individual Arab nation-States.

ARAB REVOLT (also **"The Revolt in the Desert"**) The uprising of Hussein ibn 'Ali, the sharif of Mecca, and his sons Ali, Abdullah and Feisal, of the Hashemite clan, against the Turkish Ottoman Empire in June 1916, during World War I. The Arab Revolt was preceded by an exchange of letters between Hussein and Sir Henry McMahon, the British high commissioner in Egypt, in which the latter promised British support for Arab independence after the war. Britain financed the Arab Revolt with £200,000 per month and supplied arms, provisions and direct artillery support; it also sent guerrilla experts, among them the legendary T.E. Lawrence ("Lawrence of Arabia"). The Arab Revolt army started with an estimated 10,000 Hijazi Bedouin, reinforced by an additional 30–40,000 semi-attached men who were recruited as needed. Its final strength is estimated to have been about 70,000 men. A number of Arab (Syrian and Iraqi) officers of the Ottoman army—either deserters or prisoners—joined the Arab Revolt, but the number involved remained very small. For a short time, the Egyptian 'Aziz 'Ali al-Masri served as chief of staff, followed by the Iraqi Nuril as-Sa'id. The rebels took Mecca with British artillery support and 'Aqaba with British naval support. Medina remained in Turkish hands, but was cut off. The Arab Revolt's main operation consisted of sabotaging the Hijaz Railway, the principal Turkish supply route to western Arabia. When the British and Allied forces, under General Allenby, advanced into Palestine and Syria during 1917–1918, the rebel army formed their right wing. The Arab army was allowed to enter Damascus first, raise the Arab flag and establish an Arab administration, semi-coordinated with the allied military administration of the occupied territories. Though this Arab government was suppressed and evicted in 1919–1920 by the French, the princes heading the Arab Revolt became the principal and recognized spokesmen for the Arab national cause at the peace conference which followed World War I. Their connection to the Arab nationalists of the Fertile Crescent was tenuous and their claims and demands were not fully realized, yet the Arab Revolt is to this day seen as the Golden Age of Arab nationalism, the cradle of Arab independence. Several of the officers of the Arab Revolt became spokesmen and leaders of the Arab socialists in the 1920s and 1930s and they continued extolling the memory of the revolt (helped by the impressive, though not quite reliable, writings of Lawrence).

ARAB REVOLT OF 1936–1939 In the mid-1930s, Jewish immigration into Palestine and the Jewish purchases of land in that country had reached unprecedented levels. The Palestinian Arabs feared that they might become a minority in the country. They therefore began to work toward achieving Arab freedom and the expulsion of the Jews.

Two political events which occurred in 1935 also had a catalytic effect: the discovery in the port of Jaffa of arms intended for the Jews and the death of Sheikh 'Izz al-Din al-Qassam. Inter-communal riots in Jaffa in April 1936 were used by radicals of the Istiqlal (Independence) party to urge the Arabs to go on strike until their national demands had been met. A countrywide network of National Committees arose to lead the strike movement. A general strike, which continued for six months, failed to force the government to change its policy toward Jewish immigration and the purchasing of land. Now the road was open for the formation of a united front of the different Arab parties, and the Higher Arab Committee—with the Mufti of Jerusalem, HAJJ AMIN AL-HUSSEINI, as president—was established in April 1936.

A month later, armed bands began to attack Jewish settlements and quarters and British government installations. Putting a voluntary end to the strike saved the Palestinians from being crushed by force. As a result, the armed bands could prepare for the second stage of fighting, which was triggered in spring 1937 when the Royal (Peel) Commission recommended the partition of Palestine.

Up to October 1938, the Arab rebels succeeded in occupying large parts of the mountainous regions. The British army, though, succeeded in gaining the upper hand and in October 1938 decided to crush the revolt by force. At the same time, the British government decided to grant the Arabs political concessions. It decided to withdraw from the partition proposal and to restrict Jewish immigration and land purchases.

The revolt was also a social protest movement, and indeed the rebels were from the lower social classes of the villages. The revolt served the Palestinian Arabs by bringing about the intervention of the Arab States in the affairs of Palestine. While the Arabs in Palestine paid a high price in terms of internal splits and feuds, they achieved their most important political victory as a result of the revolt.

ARAFAT, YASIR (1929–) Head of the Palestinian Authority in Gaza and Jericho and chairman of the PALESTINIAN LIBERATION ORGANIZATION (PLO), Arafat is the most eminent Palestinian politician and is also the generally acknowledged leader and spokesman of the Palestinian Arabs. Born in 1929, he represented a new generation: not the traditional clerical-feudal no-

bility of HAJJ AMIN AL-HUSSEINI and not the quasi-modern intellectuals such as Ahmad Shuqayri, but a representative of ultramodern activism. Arafat's personal history is shrouded in mystery, for at least two reasons. On the one hand it fits the image of the mystical but ever-present anonymous hero, whose personality is submerged in the nation, while on the other hand Arafat has something to conceal.

Arafat's real name is 'Abdul Rahman 'Abdul Ra'uf 'Arafat al-Qudura al-Husseini. His father was a merchant in Gaza, who in the 1930s lived mostly in Cairo. His mother was a daughter of the Husseini family of Jerusalem. Arafat was apparently born in Cairo and spent most of his childhood there. In the 1940s he lived primarily in Gaza. He grew up in a milieu of Palestinians even when living in Cairo, but his Arabic dialect has a distinct Egyptian influence. He spent part of the 1948 war in Jerusalem and knew 'Abdul Qadir al-Husseini, a well-known commander of Palestinian fighters against Jewish forces before the war, who died a heroic death.

In the 1950s, Arafat studied engineering at the University of Cairo. Afterwards he worked for an engineering firm in Kuwait. His main interests, though, always seem to have been militant ideologies, both Islamic-religious and Arabic-nationalist. The most definite influence on his *Weltanschauung* seems to have been the MUSLIM BRETHREN, who then flourished in Egypt.

Among the Palestinians who influenced Arafat were followers of the legacy of Sheikh 'Izz al-Din al-Qassam, in some respects a Palestinian parallel to the Muslim Brethren. Indeed, al-Qassam was the first Palestinian to become head of an underground group which engaged in terrorism. The al-Fath (see FATAH) organization, founded by Arafat, is another link in his long chain but—unlike all the others—did not peter out after a short time. Instead it became a highly developed, well-equipped establishment.

Arafat certainly has the qualifications, ambition and self-confidence of a leader, and he has always been the leader of the group around him. In the mid-1950s he was active in two Palestinian unions in Cairo. He acquired some military training from Egyptian intelligence officers. For some time he was on a mission in Germany, but gradually the idea of founding a fighting organization, very much influenced by the example of the Algerian FLN, took shape. His circle also began to publish a small clandestine paper, *Filastinuna* (Our Palestine), at first in Beirut.

Arafat was one of a group of Palestinians who attended the Palestinian National Congress of May 1964 in Jerusalem. Another was Khalid al-Hasan, Arafat's friend and cofounder of al-Fath. The latter did not participate in the congress. The existence of al-Fath was announced in public at the beginning of 1965. Its founders' names were still kept secret and at first only Arafat's nom de guerre, Abu 'Ammar, was mentioned. It was only in 1968 that Arafat's name was disclosed as a leader of al-Fath and the "official spokesman" of the organization. At that he became the foremost leader of the Palestinians and shortly thereafter the chairman of the PLO. He owed his position to the wide publicity of al-Fath's actions prior to the 1967 war and after it.

One factor of Arafat's particular success after the collapse of the Arab armies in June 1967 was his acceptance of a position of relative neutrality in inter-Arab state rivalries and in the various discussions between Left and Right. He did not dabble much in ideologies nor, for that matter, was he very good at it.

Late in 1967 Arafat, having failed to establish FATAH cells in the occupied West Bank, escaped to Jordan. There he rebuilt his organization, leading it during the head-on clash with the Israeli army at Karameh in March 1968. Later he found himself engaged in a series of heated encounters with King Hussein of Jordan. Believing that Jordan was the best place from which to start a campaign against Israel, he and his followers sought to take over power in Jordan itself. The tension between the two sides peaked in September 1970 (BLACK SEPTEMBER) when civil war broke out and the Jordanian army used force to suppress the Fatah, butchering Palestinians in their thousands. Arafat himself managed to escape to Syria. During the October 1973 war, Arafat tried to approach US leaders by sending moderate messages to the effect that the Palestinians would be willing to participate in eventual peace talks with Israel. However, Arafat and his colleagues were not invited to the Geneva Peace Conference in December 1973.

The Palestinian National Council (PNC) resolution of June 1974, calling for the establishment of a national authority in any liberated part of Palestine, paved the way for world recognition and Arafat was invited to become the first non-governmental representative to address the General Assembly of the UN. For Arafat, the invitation was the most important fruit of a diplomatic offensive that he had prepared and supervised in person.

During 1975, just one year after Arafat's diplomatic triumphs, there was a deterioration in the situation of the Palestinians in Lebanon. From his headquarters in the Fakhani district of West Beirut, Arafat urged Arab leaders to intervene in the civil war in Lebanon, a war which threatened to destroy all his achievements since the PLO's expulsion from Jordan. Lebanon had become the only country where his Fatah fedayeen could operate in relative freedom and it was important to Arafat that it remain like that. President Assad of Syria had his own reasons for wanting the Palestinians to enhance their presence in Lebanon, and with his encouragement Arafat sent his fighters to southeast Lebanon. He was now trying his hand as president of something approaching a real state within a state, the "Fatahland." This was a power base that allowed Arafat a measure of independence in facing the machinations of various Arab régimes. It also appeared to offer him new opportunities to break through the indifference of the US, the country that he most wanted to deal with. For Arafat, the advent of President Jimmy Carter seemed a hopeful development; however, he also maintained close ties with the USSR.

The summer of 1982 marked a turning point in Arafat's political life as well as in the history of the Palestinians. Due to the Israeli invasion of Lebanon in June, Arafat had to leave Beirut. His departure for Athens symbolized a deepening rift between him and President ASAD of Syria, which has persisted to this day. Instead of moving to Syria, Arafat expressed his opposition to, and disappointment with, Damascus by establishing the PLO headquarters in Tunis. After a split in the Fatah in 1983, his expulsion from Damascus by the Syrian government, fighting in Palestinian camps in Lebanon, and his second expulsion from Lebanon, he looked to Egypt and then to Jordan for support. This led him to the signature of the Jordanian-Palestinian Accords of January 1985.

As the Palestinian *Intifada* (uprising) broke out spontaneously

in December 1987, Arafat and the Tunis leadership debated how to harness it to their purpose. They found it difficult to stay abreast of the events. Watching from the outside, Arafat did not always agree with his own people inside. Even though he was opposed to some of their decisions, he was nevertheless obliged to go along with them. For example, he worried that economic pressures might abort the uprising. Arafat was quicker than most to draw the logical conclusions from the determination of the people of the territories to protest and to make sacrifices. He stated that a major new political platform should be worked out. Arafat would have to reexamine the old controversies that had dogged the PLO throughout, including its willingness to coexist with Israel in a Palestinian "mini-state" in the West Bank and Gaza. By severing the legal and administrative ties between Jordan and the West Bank in July 1988, King Hussein of Jordan accelerated the chain of events.

Arafat started jetting between Arab and other capitals in an effort to build a consensus for an independent Palestinian state. He was proposing more than a simple independence declaration; he was also anxious for the PLO to adopt a new and realistic political program. Specifically, he wanted acceptance of UN Resolution 242 of 1967, setting out Israel's right to exist in peace and security. On November 15, 1988 the great moment arrived. The PNC proclaimed the establishment of the state of Palestine. One month later, Arafat accepted Resolution 242 and renounced terrorism, thus opening the way to negotiations first with the US and then with Israel.

The PLO chairman was unanimously designated the first president of the Palestinian state by the PLO Central Council. The election of Arafat as president, however, was less important than the question of what the relationship would be between his organization, al-Fath, and the other factions or parties in the PLO. Throughout the years of the *Intifada,* Arafat personified Palestinian nationalism in the occupied territories. He also guided his representatives during 10 rounds of talks with Israel in Washington, DC. Israel's veto until then had meant that Arafat was not a legitimate partner for peace talks, but on September 13, 1993, he signed a peace treaty with Israeli Prime Minister Yitzhak Rabin.

On July 1, 1994 Arafat entered Gaza as chairman of the PNA, and since than has remained at its head, working for the establishment of an eventual Palestinian state. He was awarded the Nobel prize for peace, along with Yitzhak Rabin and Shimon Peres, for their efforts toward solving the Middle East conflict.

ARASCES AND TIRIDATES   Kings of Parthia (248/47–211/10). Arasces, leader of the Dahim tribe which revolted in 248 B.C. against the governor of Bactaria at the time of King Antiochus II (Theos) the Seleucid (261–246 B.C.), succeeded in taking control of Parthia, at the time a Seleucid province. Arasces ruled independently for two years (248–246 B.C.). In 246 B.C. he was killed and his brother Tiridates I (Tradt) came to power. Tiridates ruled over Parthia in the years 248/247–211/210 B.C. He was the founder of the Arascid dynasty (named after his brother) which ruled over what is today Armenia. Tiridates succeeded in establishing and enlarging his kingdom by taking advantage of the civil war between Seleucus II Kallinikos and Antiochus Hierax in the middle of the 2nd century B.C. After the death of Antiochus IV Epiphanes (163 B.C.), the kingdom of

Parthia went on to expand and include Mesopotamia and Medea.

ARATUS (271–213 B.C.) Ancient tyrant and social reformer. Aratus fled from his native city, Sicyon, in 264 B.C., when his father was murdered and a tyranny was established there. He was educated in Argos by his father's friends and in 251 B.C. succeeded in liberating Sicyon from its tyrant. Subsidies from King Ptolemy Philadelphus of Egypt helped Aratus solve the socioeconomic problems which troubled Sicyon, which he united with the Achaean League. Within several years Aratus became the leading statesman of the league, serving as general (*strategos*) in alternating years from 245 B.C. to his death. Aratus's policy basically aimed at three goals: liberating Greek cities from the rule of tyrants, freeing Greek cities from Macedonian rule—which was often supported by tyrants—and extending the power of the Achaean League. In 243 B.C., Aratus took Corinth from Macedonian rule by a surprise attack and united it with the Achaean League. Under the influence and pressure of Aratus, other cities joined the league, notably Megalapolis and Argos. However, faced by the growing power of CLEOMENES III, king of Sparta, Aratus changed his anti-Macedonian policy after 228 B.C. Even after the defeat of Cleomenes in 222 B.C. he supported King Philip V, thus helping him to reestablish Macedonian rule in some parts of the Peloponnesus. Yet he sensibly did not follow Philip's anti-Roman policy. In the end Aratus, the revolutionary leader, had to agree to the reestablishment of Macedonian hegemony and tyrannies in Greece in order to preserve the power of the Achaean League.

ARBENZ GUZMÁN, JACOBO (1913–1971) Guatemalan Socialist, president of Guatemala from 1950–1954. Educated in a military academy, Arbenz was a principal leader of the GUATEMALAN REVOLUTION OF 1944. As president, he instituted large-scale land redistribution, organized labor under the Communists and nationalized industry. Overthrown in 1954, he lived in exile, settling first in Uruguay and then in Cuba.

'AREF, ABDUL RAHMAN (1916–) Iraqi officer and politician, president of Iraq, 1966–1968. 'Aref was a member of the FREE OFFICERS that toppled the monarchy in July 1958. A brother of ABDUL SALAM 'AREF, he became involved in the struggle between his brother and ABDUL KARIM QASSEM. When his brother was killed in an air crash in April 1966, the Revolutionary Command Council chose 'Aref, an inoffensive compromise candidate, as president. As president—and for some months in 1967 concurrently prime minister—he followed his late brother's policies: a strongly nationalist, independent, moderately pro-Egyptian foreign policy, and an authoritarian régime of conservative state socialism at home. But he seemed to have been lacking his brother's shrewd leadership qualities. 'Aref was ousted in July 1968 by a coup headed by AHMAD HASAN AL-BAKR and Abdul-Rahman al-na'if and went into exile in England.

'AREF, ABDUL SALAM (1920–1966) Iraqi officer and politician, president of Iraq 1963–1966. Son of a Sunni middle-class Baghdad family, 'Aref was trained as a professional officer and served with the Iraqi expeditionary force in the Arab-Israel War of 1948. He was a leading member of the FREE OFFICERS that overthrew the monarchy in July 1958 and commanded the task force that took over Baghdad. As the number two member of the new régime, 'Aref was strongly Nasserist. He clearly aspired to the top leadership and soon fell out with ABDUL KARIM QASSEM, the de facto dictator of Iraq. In September 1958 he was dismissed and in November was arrested and put on trial. In February 1959, he was sentenced to death by a "Peoples Court" for plotting against the régime and planning to assassinate Qassem. The latter did not confirm the sentence and in 1961 'Aref was set free. He was one of the organizers of the coup of February 1963 (together with officers of the *Ba'ath* group) that overthrew Qassem and became president. As long as the *Ba'ath* officers were in control, his powers were only nominal, but in November 1963 he ousted the *Ba'ath* group in a bloodless semi-coup. Thereafter, he exercised real power.

As president, 'Aref at first endeavored to model his régime on a Nasserist pattern and sought a close association with GAMAL ABDUL NASSER's Egypt. In July he decreed far-reaching nationalization measures on the Egyptian model and established an Arab Socialist Union as a single party. However, 'Aref pursued these nationalization policies halfheartedly, while becoming increasingly pragmatic. He was killed in April 1966 in an air crash and succeeded by his brother ABDUL RAHMAN 'AREF.

ARGENTINA REVOLTS AND REVOLUTIONS
1890 Revolt. In 1886 Miguel Juárez Celman was elected president of Argentina. He had taken an active part in the anticlerical campaign of the previous decade and there was a great deal of Catholic anger against him. Alongside this bitterness, Argentina was then experiencing an economic recession. A large military and civilian group became aware of governmental corruption and the lower working class and labor unions were becoming increasingly disillusioned. Together the Catholics, military and proletariat concurred to form the Civic Union, which organized the revolt of July 1890. Although the first days of the revolt were seemingly successful, it was as quickly repressed—perhaps as a result of the collapse of the diversity of the members of this ad hoc union. Celman's reaction to the uprising and the criticism of his government was to resign his position, although his government remained intact.

1930 Coup. In 1892, the Radical party emerged from the Civic Union which had been responsible for the 1890 revolt against the Argentinian government. In 1896, Hipólito Irigoyen took over the position of the Radical party's leadership. He held this position until ousted in 1930.

In the elections of 1916, the Radical party won and Irigoyen became the president of Argentina. The 1922 elections, however, were won by another Radical, Marcelo de Alvear, but Irigoyen was re-elected in 1928.

Over the next two years, a number of developments led to the coup that would eventually displace Irigoyen and his government. The democratic opposition grew to fear a dictatorship from Irigoyen, while the military developed a belief that the time had come to revive the Argentinian nation, which had been subjected to the derogation of civilian governments. An additional cause for the uprising was Irigoyen's lack of knowledge in the sphere of economics and his inability to deal with the harsh economic crisis that had developed in Argentina at the time as a result of the worldwide economic depression.

The military coup which took place, with very little bloodshed, on September 4, 1930, was led by General José Uriburu and was widely supported by the civilians of Argentina. Uriburu had taken part in the 1890 revolt against President Celman and blamed its failure on the civilians' participation; now he was intent on maintaining a purely military control over the government. Uriburu had by then adopted Fascist ideas and wished to implement them in his new government by having it run by an elitist group, a plan that was rejected by many of the military revolutionaries who had joined him in the initial coup. In 1931, Uriburu succumbed to the pressures of this opposition and allowed the creation of a constitutional government.

1943 Revolt. Ramón Castillo was in office as president when World War II broke out and the Western world, along with the League of Nations, was experiencing heavy doubts as to its ability to survive Germany's might. At that time, suspicion arose that the president intended to dictate his own successor. Castillo also drew up a policy whereby Argentina would remain neutral and would protect Argentina's interests by maintaining good relations with Germany. As the United States joined in the war against the Germans, Argentinian resentment of Castillo's policy was exacerbated even further. The *Grupo de Oficiales Unidos* (GOU), a group of well-trained military officials, held that Argentina's parties were not suitable for its government, having been unable to deal with the tribulations of the past years and having lost the mainstream support of the general public, and that Argentina was lacking in military strength. On June 4, 1943, the GOU ousted Castillo and established a provisional military régime that was later (after internal conflicts between the many factions involved in the leadership) headed by Juan Perón as of 1945.

1955 Revolution. JUAN PERON was first elected as president of Argentina in February 1946 and was re-elected in 1951. He began his second administration in June 1952, but only one month after this his downfall began. The primary cause of this was the death of his wife Eva, Perón's principal link to his supporters and political advisor, and her absence led him to a succession of misjudgments in political strategies. He mishandled wage increases for his followers (the so-called *descamisados*—the "shirtless ones") and distanced himself from the Argentinian business world, from foreign economics and from the United States. In 1954 he came out against the Catholic church and in May 1955 signed a treaty with a Californian oil company regarding the exploitation of oil resources within Argentina, thereby hurting the national pride of the Argentinians.

The result was a "liberating" revolution, led by a combination of armed forces in the provinces of Argentina. Led by General Eduardo Lonardi, the revolution took place on September 16, 1955 and with it the public support for Perón disintegrated rapidly. On September 19, 1955, Perón resigned his position and left Argentina for foreign shores. The government was provisionally taken over by General Lonardi as a military dictatorship, although he claimed that his intentions were to renew constitutional government.

1962 Coup. On May 1, 1958, Arturo Frondizi, a Radicalist, was elected president of Argentina. Although beginning with a concessionary policy, Frondizi soon lost the support of the masses as he stepped on the nationalistic pride of his countrymen, beginning in December 1958 with his economic stabilization plan. As Perón had done, Frondizi arranged for the exploitation of Argentinian petroleum resources by foreign companies. This lost him the support of the diverse Argentinian parties and their followers.

While Frondizi sought the support of the military, the military it was which removed him from office. The coup was led by General Raúl Poggi, who arrested Frondizi. The government which followed was primarily a civilian administration but was guided extensively by the military.

1966 Coup. Argentina enjoyed a period of nationalist resurgence after the election of Arturo Illia of the Peoples' Radical party to the presidency. Although his domestic policies were moderate, he promptly annulled the agreements that had been made between Frondizi and various foreign oil companies concerning the exploitation of Argentina's petroleum resources, thereby moving toward the revival of Argentina's national unity. However there remained a strong element of internal dissension as Argentina still experienced inflation, financial deficits and unemployment.

In 1966 it became evident that Peronism had maintained wide-scale support. Despite the fact that there was no overwhelming dissatisfaction with the government of Illia, the military feared the possibility of Peronist victories in upcoming elections and removed Illia in a coup of June 1966. The new government, led by General Juan Carlos Onganía, did away with all political parties, imposing an authoritarian régime over Argentina that encompassed all administrative and legislative control.

1970 Coup. Onganía's authoritarian presidency suppressed the political freedom of the Argentinian people, who grew bitterly dissatisfied. The press and communications were limited by extremist censorship, leading to many violent outbreaks in 1969. Despite the growing terrorism against Onganía's régime, he refused to relax the political limitations, believing that he could uphold his power as long as he had the backing of the military. This belief, however, was contradicted as a group of military leaders approached Onganía to reform his authoritarian leadership and to reestablish the government's democracy. Onganía turned his back on this demand, whereupon the military officials ousted him from the government, replacing him with General Roberto Levingston.

1976 Coup. The exiled Juan Perón returned to his homeland in June 1973 and was elected president once again in the elections of September of that year. After his death in 1974 his second wife, who had held the position of vice-president during his lifetime, took over the presidency. Her administration was overshadowed by inflation, guerrilla activity and political insecurity. By March 1976 dissatisfaction had grown so great that she was finally put under house arrest by a military junta and her position was taken over by the leader of the group, General Jorge Rafael Videla. This government intended to rectify the economic and political situation and to undermine the guerrilla violence.

1987 Rebellion. With the election in October 1983 of civilian president Raúl Alfonsín, Argentina underwent a transformation that was to end military involvement in the government and the disruption of continuity within it. Alfonsín directed the prosecution of former leaders of the military coups and publicized his intentions to form a more stable democratic government.

Alfonsín's activism against the military injustices of the past years led to an upheaval within the military. In April 1987, an officer's rebellion took place in some of Argentina's bases. However, Alfonsín refused to be fazed by the uproar and the rebellion subsequently died down. Alfonsín did, nevertheless, order that the trials for the military human rights violations be narrowed down to commanding officers.

ARGOS REVOLUTION   In 370 B.C., civil strife (*stasis*) broke out in Argos, which had a democratic régime. The masses were instigated by a number of demagogues against the very rich citizens. The latter then attempted to overthrow the democracy. They were, however, detected, tortured and ultimately committed suicide. Thirty of the most distinguished citizens were put to death and their property was confiscated. The demagogues kept on inciting the mob, which condemned to death more than 12,000 rich men, who were then beaten to death. When the demagogues wished to stop the accusations against the well-to-do, the masses turned against them as well and all of them were put to death. It seems that most of the rich citizens of Argos were executed on this occasion. Their property was confiscated and distributed among the masses who, taking advantage of their control of the democratic institutions of the state, had decided on these measures.

ARGYLL'S REBELLION   (May–June 1685) A plot by the ninth Earl of Argyll to lead the Campbells in revolt in Scotland, in conjunction with MONMOUTH'S REBELLION in England. His 300 rebels passed through the Scottish Lowlands and marched on Glasgow, but were chased by a much stronger royal force which led to the desertion of many of his motley followers. Argyll himself was captured and summarily executed.

ARISTOGEITON AND HARMODIUS   Two young Athenians of a noble family who for personal reasons killed the Athenian tyrant Hipparchus in 514 B.C. The guards of Hippias killed Harmodius on the spot while Aristogeiton was captured, tortured and executed later on. Following the death of Hippias and the establishment of democracy in Athens, Aristogeiton and Harmodius were popularly believed to have given the Athenians equal rights in law (*isonomia*) and they were subsequently honored by annual sacrifices.

ARISTONICUS   After King Attalus III willed Pergamon to Rome on his death in 133 B.C., Aristonicus led a popular revolt against the Roman generals sent to take over the new province. Aristonicus appealed to the lower classes, including slaves who were promised their freedom and to the non-Greek population of the countryside against the well-to-do classes of the cities. Significantly, his new state was named Heliopolis ("City of the Sun"), a reference to its utopian-egalitarian character. But the revolution was also a national, anti-Roman one. Eventually Aristonicus was captured in 129 B.C. and put to death in Rome.

ARMAND, INESSA FYODOROVNA   (1874–1920) Russian feminist and revolutionary. Born in Paris, Armand was taken to Russia by an aunt when orphaned at the age of five.

In 1899, Armand joined the Moscow Society for Improving the Lot of Women and shortly after was elected its president. Her activity with this society not only heightened her consciousness of social issues but gave her a lifelong interest in the different matters affecting women.

In 1904 she joined the BOLSHEVIK wing of the Russian Social Democratic Workers party. Arrested repeatedly, she was sentenced in 1907 to exile in Siberia but succeeded in escaping to Paris, where she joined the Bolshevik emigre community, acting as liaison with the French socialists and involving herself in a school for party workers established by LENIN. She also served as secretary for the coordination of activities of all Bolshevik organizations abroad. During this period she became a devoted follower of Lenin.

In 1912, Armand returned to Russia to help organize Bolshevik activities. She was quickly arrested but once more escaped and continued her underground work, helping found and edit a legally published Bolshevik newspaper, *Rabotnitsa* (*The Working Woman*), featuring issues of particular relevance to working women.

During World War I Armand was based in Switzerland, working actively to promote Bolshevik policies denouncing the war. In April 1917 she was one of the selected group of Lenin's supporters who accompanied him on the "sealed train" back to Russia. Following the October RUSSIAN REVOLUTION OF 1917, Armand supported the Left Communists in opposing the separate peace with Germany proposed by Lenin.

Armand filled numerous important positions in the early Bolshevik régime. She was a member of the All-Russian central executive committee and chaired the Moscow region economic council. In Communist party matters she was the first director of the *Zhenotdel*, the women's section of the Russian Communist party. In this capacity she devoted considerable time and effort to the organizing of factory women. She also represented the cause of women's equality in the trade unions and in the Communist party. She died of cholera while resting in the Caucasus, after having organized and chaired an international conference of Communist women.

ARMINIUS (HERMAN)   Chieftain of the Germanic tribe of the Cherusci. Born about 18 B.C., Arminius was educated in Rome and served in the Roman army, fighting in what is today Germany under the command of the future Emperor Tiberius and acquiring Roman citizenship. However, at some point he turned against his adopted fatherland and rejoined his own people; in 9 A.D. he and his followers trapped and annihilated three Roman legions in the Teutoberger Forest, thus forcing Emperor Augustus to abandon his plans for the conquest of Germany to the river Elbe. Arminius, however, was ultimately killed by his own men in 19 A.D. During the nineteenth century he was elevated to the stature of a German national hero and a monument was built to honor him and his victory.

ARNOLD OF BRESCIA   (d. 1155) Revolutionary reformer of the Catholic church. Born in Brescia (northern Italy), Arnold studied in Paris, where he was a pupil of Peter Abelard, the French philosopher and theologian, until 1140, and one of his last supporters. After the condemnation of Abelard for heresy, he led a group of poor students at Paris and attacked personages such as Bernard of Clairvaux. Expelled from Paris by order of Louis VII, he returned to Italy, where he began systematically to attack the worldliness of the Church, maintaining that confession should be made not to a priest but by one Christian to another, that the sinfulness of a priest destroyed the value of sacraments he administered, and that the Church may not possess worldly goods or exercise temporal authority. Expelled from Brescia, he went to Rome in 1145, where he joined a local party that opposed the temporal dominion of the pope. In July 1148 he was excommunicated by Eugenius III. Retaining his popular support, he was one of the leaders of the COMMUNE OF ROME, which embodied the revolutionary trend. After the accession of Frederick Barbarossa to the empire in 1152, the commune was crushed and Arnold was arrested by the imperial army, condemned to death and delivered to the prefect of Rome, who had him executed.

ARROW CROSS   A Hungarian Fascist movement which arose in the 1930s and 1940s under the leadership of FERENC SZALASI. Calling for a restoration of Hungary's pre-World War I frontiers, the Arrow Cross adopted a violently anti-Semitic platform. The Arrow Cross was responsible for many outrages between 1935 and 1938, but the Hungarian government's arrest of Szalasi only increased his popularity. In March 1944 a German-sponsored coup overthrew the government of Admiral Horthy and put the Arrow Cross in power. In the few months it held power, the Arrow Cross was responsible for facilitating the transport of 400,000 Hungarian Jews to the Auschwitz concentration camp.

ARSALAN, SHAKIB   (1869–1946) Syrian Pan-Arab writer, poet, historian and politician, of Lebanese-Druse origin; district governor in the Ottoman Empire. Arsalan remained loyal to the sultan and joined the Arab nationalists only after World War I. In the 1920s Arsalan, mostly in exile, was active in the Syrian-Palestinian Congress, which strove to keep Pan-Arab endeavors alive, and was a leading member of its permanent delegation in Geneva. He edited the Pan-Arab weekly, *La National Arabe,* and cultivated contacts with world statesmen, including unsuccessful talks with Zionist leaders. Arsalan later exhibited near-Fascist tendencies and maintained strong ties with Italy and Nazi Germany. He also converted to Islam and drew nearer to Pan-Islamic views. Many of his numerous writings concern Islamic topics, including a detailed biography of the modern Islamic thinker, Muhammad Rashid Rida. Arsalan returned to Syria in 1937, but took no active part in Syrian political affairs. During World War II he returned to Switzerland, where he resumed his contacts with the Axis powers and called on the Arabs to collaborate with the Axis.

ARTAXIAS (or Artashes)   King of Armenia at the beginning of the 2nd century B.C. and one of the founders of the ancient kingdom of Armenia. In the battle of Magnesia in 190 B.C., the Romans defeated the Seleucid kingdom, of which Armenia was part. Two generals of Antiochus the Great (Antiochus III), king of the Seleucid kingdom, Artaxias and Zaraidres (Zareh), who were governors of two of the three districts of Armenia, revolted against Antiochus. With Roman agreement they nominated themselves as kings, Artaxias as king of Greater Armenia and Zaraidres as king of Sophene. With their combined efforts they expanded their territories by annexing neighboring territory, until they had most of historical Armenia under their control. The

two erstwhite governors may be considered as the creators of independent Armenia.

ARUSHA DECLARATION   On February 7, 1967, in the town of Arusha, Tanzania, Tanzania's president, Julius Nyerere, outlined a new type of African socialism, which became known as the Arusha Declaration. This program was accepted by the ruling party, the TANGANYIKA AFRICAN NATIONAL UNION (TANU).

Nyerere's new approach to the problems of development concentrated on economic development at the grass roots, on ordinary people and on agriculture rather than on the conventional growth sectors in the towns. According to this approach, as Africa is short of finance and as foreign capital implies foreign dominance, Africa should pull itself up by self-reliance. *Ujamaa* ("Villagization"), became the new slogan. Rural development was based not on large farms but on community villages. In this Tanzanian brand of rural socialism, the urban sector would not exploit the countryside, the educational system would serve the mass of the population rather than a privileged few and commercial banks and many industries would be nationalized.

After a severe economic decline, the government adopted more pragmatic economic measures in the mid-1980s. Although the agricultural changes introduced by *Ujamaa* were unsuccessful, the plan did provide some social benefits.

AL-ASAD, HAFEZ   (1930–) Syrian officer, president of Syria since 1971. Born in Qardaha near Lataqia, to an 'Alawi family which changed its name from Wahsh, meaning "child beast" to Asad, meaning "lion." Asad's full name translates as "the lion's guard." During his secondary school years in Lataqia, Asad became active in a student group organizing anti-French activities. Like many of his non-Sunni contemporaries, Asad quickly joined one of the secular progressive parties advocating Syrian independence. He was already active in the BA'ATH party when he attended the Air Force Academy in Aleppo in the early 1950s and became an officer. As one of 13 members of "The Military Committee" of the *Ba'ath* party, Asad participated in the coup of March 1963 that brought the party to power and became commander of the air force (promoted to the rank of *fariqu,* lieutenant-general, in 1968). From 1965 Asad was a member of the *Ba'ath* high command—both the "national" all-Arab) and the "regional" (Syrian) one. In the incessant factional struggles that rocked the Syrian *Ba'ath,* Asad sided with the "military wing" of the extreme, doctrinaire "left" which opposed the civilian faction led by MICHEL 'AFLAQ, SALAH-UL-DIN BITAR, and AMIN 'AL-HAFEZ, who were then in control. He was one of the leaders of the military wing's coup of February 1966 and became a leading figure in the régime it established, serving as acting minister of defense. However, Asad soon fell out with SALAH JADID, the top leader of the new junta, and his associates, and formed a "nationalist" faction. He also opposed Jadid's doctrinaire leftism, rejected rigid ideological definitions and preferred a pragmatic approach to political and economic issues. He opposed total identification with the Soviet Union, chafed at Syria's growing isolation within the Arab world and aimed at closer all-Arab cooperation and a stronger emphasis on the fight against Israel. In February 1969, in a bloodless semi-coup, Asad gained control of the government and party command, but accepted—reportedly on Egyptian and Russian advice—a compromise providing for a coalition which left some of his adversaries in positions of power (e.g., NUR-UL-DIN AL-ATASSI as president and prime minister). When, however, the power struggle resumed, Asad seized full control in another semi-coup in November 1970—and this time he kept power, purging and dismissing his opponents and detaining their leaders (for over 10 years, as it turned out). He assumed the premiership and became secretary-general of the *Ba'ath*. In February 1971 he nominated a "People's Council," which in turn appointed him president—a position he still holds today.

Since 1971 Asad has given Syria a régime of remarkable stability. He continued an economic policy of nationalization and a pragmatic state socialism. He established firm constitutional patterns, establishing a one-party system with regularly held elections which admit *Ba'ath*-approved independent candidates. Opposition, apart from exiled politicians, has come mainly from orthodox and fundamentalist Muslim-Sunni groups such as the MUSLIM BROTHERHOOD, which he crushed with great violence and bloodshed in 1982.

In international affairs, Asad at first entered into a close partnership with the USSR and, together with Egypt, launched the October 1973 War against Israel. Later his animosity toward Iraq led Syria into the unique position of being the only Middle Eastern Arab state (aside from Libya) to support Iran in the 1980–1988 Gulf War. In spite of his isolation, he managed to turn Syria's intervention in Lebanon into a permanent occupation of that country, whose supreme ruler he became. As the 1980s turned into the 1990s Asad, who hitherto had led the "rejectionist" anti-Israeli front, saw his Soviet supporters collapse. As a result, he has become more prepared to compromise with Israel and has proclaimed his willingness to sign a peace treaty in return for the Golan Heights lost in 1967.

AL-ASNAJ, 'ABDULLAH (1933–1981) South Yemeni and Yemeni politician. Employed in 1951–1962 by Aden Airways, Asnaj was active in the Aden Trade Unions Congress (ATUC) and became its secretary-general. In 1962 he formed and led a political wing of the ATUC, the People's Socialist party, which joined the nationalist anti-British agitation in the country and demanded the union of South Yemen with Yemen. In the mid-1960s he went into exile. In January 1966, he was one of the founders of the Front for the Liberation of Occupied South Yemen (FLOSY) and became its secretary-general. After the takeover of South Yemen by the rival NATIONAL LIBERATION FRONT (NLF) in 1967, he remained in exile and settled in North Yemen. He joined the North Yemeni government in 1971 as foreign minister and then as minister of the economy (1971–1974), and again as foreign minister (1975–1979). After he was dismissed—reportedly to please South Yemen—he continued serving as the president's advisor on foreign affairs, but lost that post in 1980. He was rumored to be linked to Sa'udi intrigues or attempted coups and to Iraqi, British and American intelligence. In March 1981 he was arrested, his immunity as a member of the Constituent People's Assembly lifted, and he was put on trial and executed.

ASSASSINS (Hashishin) Radical Muslim sect of the Ismaili faction of the Shiites. Organized to fight the opponents of the Ismailis by any means, including murder and poisoning, they al-

legedly used to fortify their spirits with the aid of hashish (hence their Arabic name, which means "users of hashish," pronounced by the French-speaking Crusaders as "assassin," which became synonymous with murderer). The sect was organized at the end of the 11th century by the Persian Ismaili leader Hasan-i Sabbah, but very soon it spread to Iraq, Syria and Egypt. When Hasan-i Sabbah died in 1124, the sect numbered thousands of adherents in several countries.

In the 12th century, the sect spread in Persia and continued to fight the Seljuks, who proceeded to massacre thousands of Ismailis. At the beginning of the 13th century the Persian Assassins became somewhat more moderate, but soon they had to fight against the Mongols and were destroyed by Hulagu Khan. At the beginning of the 12th century, the disciples of Hasan formed a powerful organization in Syria, mainly in Aleppo and Damascus. In 1126 the Damascus authorities awarded the Assassins the city of Banias, hoping to save the capital from their influence while using them to fight against the Crusaders. However, after their repression in Damascus, the Assassins preferred to surrender Banias to the Crusaders and to continue their activities against their Muslim foes. The Aleppo Assassins on the other hand, moved to Jebel Al-Summaq—the mountains between Aleppo and Homs, near the border of Antioch—where they built a stronghold. Under the leadership of Sinan ibn Salman ibn Muhammad, called Rashid a-Din, they founded a little state, which succeeded in maintaining its independence even at the time of Saladin. Under Sinan, the Assassins began to act against the Crusaders and, in 1192, two of them murdered King Conrad of Montferrat. In order to stop their activities in the Crusader states, some tribute was paid to them during the 13th century. The Mongol menace induced the Syrian Assassins to cooperate with other Muslims against the power which massacred their Persian brethren. After 1261, BAYBARS was powerful enough to make their state a protectorate and prevent their leaders from re-establishing its independence. At the end of the 13th century, the realm of the Old Man of the Mountain, as Sinan was called by his sect, was finally integrated in the Mameluke sultanate.

ASSYRIA, REVOLTS against, see BABYLON, REVOLT OF 710–689 B.C.; BABYLON, REVOLT OF 652–648 B.C.; EGYPT, REVOLT OF 671–665 B.C.; HEZEKIA, REVOLT OF; HOSEA, REVOLT OF; SIDON AND SOUTHEAST ANATOLIA, REVOLT OF.

AL-ATASSI, ADNAN (1905–) Syrian Nationalist leader. Al-Atassi was born into a landowner clan of notables which provided many leaders of modern Syria. It was centered in Homs and wielded considerable influence in all of northern Syria. When Syria had a parliamentary régime and political parties were operating, leaders of the Atassi clan were often in opposition to the mainstream nationalist movement and the Damascus government. In the 1940s and 1950s, Adnan al-Atassi and FEIDI AL-ATASSI were among the founders and leaders of the SYRIAN PEOPLE'S PARTY.

Al-Atassi came to prominence in the 1950s when he was among the founders of the People's party and minister in several governments. Accused in 1956–1957 of playing a leading role in an Iraqi-British-American plot, he was tried and sentenced to death in February 1957 (later commuted to prison for life), pardoned by Nasser in September 1960 and released into forced residence in Cairo. Nevertheless, he did not return to play an active part in Syrian politics.

AL-ATASSI, FEIDI   Syrian nationalist leader, and leader of the People's Party in the 1950s and a minister in several governments. He was accused in 1956–1957 of involvement in an alleged Iraqi-American-British plot, tried (*in absentia*, as he had fled) and acquitted. He was not further active in Syrian politics.

AL-ATASSI, HASHEM   (1874?–1960) Syrian nationalist leader, three times president of Syria. Educated in Istanbul, Turkey, Atassi served as a district governor in the Ottoman administration. In the 1920s he chaired the nationalist Syrian-Arab Congress and was for a short time prime minister of the government Amir Feisal tried to set up in Damascus. Under the French Mandate, he was one of the leaders of the "National Bloc" which fought for Syrian independence. He headed the delegation which signed the Franco-Syrian Treaty of 1936, providing for Syria's independence with certain privileges for France—a treaty that was not ratified by France and remained abortive. He was president of Syria between 1936 and 1939. In the 1940s, Atassi drifted away from the mainstream Damascus faction of the National Bloc. He took no active part in the final struggle for complete independence of 1945–1946, nor in the Syrian governments that ensued. In December 1949 he became president, but ADIB SHISHAKLI was the real, behind-the-scenes ruler and the president's powers were limited, almost nominal. When the politicians failed in their struggle with the dictator Shishakli, Atassi resigned in 1951 and began working for his overthrow. Following Shishakli's fall, Atassi returned to the presidency in 1954, but as real power was again in the hands of shifting officers' cliques, he was frustrated, resigned in September 1955, and retired from politics.

AL-ATASSI, NUR-UL-DIN   (1929?–) Syrian politician, president of Syria 1966–1970. A physician (Damascus University, 1955), Al-Atassi was close to the *Ba'ath* group. After the *Ba'ath* officers' coup of 1963, he became minister of the interior, 1963–1964; deputy prime minister, 1964–1965; and a member of the Revolutionary Council and the Presidential Council, 1964. In the struggle between rival *Ba'ath* factions, he was close to the extremist leftist "military" group, and after that faction came to power in the coup of February 1966, he was made president and secretary-general of both the "national" (i.e., all-Arab) and "regional" (Syrian) command of the BA'ATH PARTY (the wing ruling Syria). From 1968 to 1970, Al-Atassi also served as prime minister. In the struggle between the factions of HAFEZ AL-ASAD and SALAH JADID, he sided with the latter, but tried to mediate between the two. After Asad's semi-coup of 1969, Al-Atassi retained his posts as part of a compromise settlement. However, when Asad took full control in November 1970, Al-Atassi was dismissed from his three posts as president, prime minister and secretary-general and imprisoned. There were conflicting reports concerning his release. He was reportedly offered a release late in 1980, but was returned to jail or house arrest when he refused to cooperate. Apparently he was released later, but was not allowed to return to political activities.

ATATÜRK, KEMAL   (1881–1938) Founder and first president of the Turkish Republic. Born Mustafa Kemal in Salonika, Atatürk graduated from the Military Academy in Istanbul in 1905 and served in Syria, Macedonia and Tripolitania. After a brief spell as military attaché in Sofia, he distinguished himself in World War I in the Dardanelles and on the Caucasian and Palestinian fronts. Initially, he had supported the YOUNG TURKS and taken part in their conspiracies, but after the 1908 revolution he gradually became disenchanted with their policies. After the Armistice of Mudros which terminated Turkish involvement in World War I, he was recalled from Syria to Istanbul and subsequently appointed inspector of the Ninth Army in Erzurum. In May 1919 Kemal began to organize nationalist resistance to Allied plans for the dismemberment of the Turkish heartland of Anatolia and to Greek attempts to take over western Anatolia. He convened two nationalist congresses in Erzurum and Sivas in 1919 and the Grand National Assembly in Ankara in 1920. Kemal led the nationalists in the war of independence in their victorious struggle against the Allies, the Greeks and the Ottoman sultan's government. In 1923 he deposed the sultan and proclaimed the Turkish Republic.

Having received the title *Ghazi*—"Victor"—in recognition of his leadership, Kemal was elected the first president of the republic and served in this office until his death in 1938. During this period he imposed an ambitious program aimed at transforming the country into a modern, Westernized, secular state. Religious schools and religious courts were abolished and religious orders suppressed, civil and criminal law codes based on European models replaced the Muslim *Shari'a*, polygamy was

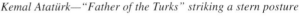
Kemal Atatürk—"Father of the Turks" striking a stern posture

outlawed, civil marriage was instituted, traditional clothing (e.g., the oriental *fez*, or hat) was banned, and the Arabic alphabet was replaced by a Latin one. For all these achievements he was given the title *Atatürk,* "Father of the Turks" in 1934.

Though he proclaimed democracy as the final goal, during his term of office only his own Republican People's party was permitted to operate. A multiparty system was introduced only after his death. Since then he has become a model for the leaders of many developing countries; in Turkey itself his ideas, known as "Kemalism," continue to serve as the ideological foundation of the state.

ATTERBURY'S PLOT   (April 1722) A Jacobite conspiracy named after Francis Atterbury (1663–1732), the Tory bishop of Rochester, England and a prominent figure among the High Church clergymen. The plan was to seize the Bank of England and to promote a rebellion and a French invasion. But the English government was warned by the French and a number of leading conspirators were arrested. Atterbury himself was banished by parliament in lieu of life imprisonment and went to join the Pretender in France. Among the conspirators was the Duke of Norfolk, but only one leader was executed. Prime Minister Walpole exploited the affair to brand all Tories as traitorous Jacobites and pushed through a tax on Roman Catholics and Non-Conformists.

AUNG GYAW, MAUNG   Burmese student-turned-martyr, killed in the anti-British protests which erupted during 1938 and 1939 in Rangoon. The unveiling of a statue in his likeness took place at a DO BAMA ASIAYON convention attended by over 4,000 Burmese.

AUNG SAN, GENERAL THAKIN   (1915–1947) Burmese nationalist leader whose political astuteness greatly facilitated the road to an independent Burma. Active in DO BAMA ASIAYON, Aung San took command of the BURMA INDEPENDENCE ARMY, the first independent Burmese army formed when Great Britain temporarily withdrew its forces during World War II. Yet when Allied victory seemed imminent, Aung San and his colleagues founded the Anti-Fascist Organization (AFO) in an to attempt to regain British favor. Through this, Aung San engineered the political survival of the high-ranking Burmese nationalist officers in the postwar era. He was able to allay conservative fears concerning communist domination of the Anti-Fascist People's Freedom League (AFPFL)—as the AFO was later called— which negotiated Burmese independence with Great Britain. Assassinated in July 1947, he did not live to see the independence of his country in 1948.

AUSTRIA-HUNGARY REVOLUTION OF 1918   see HUNGARY, REVOLTS AND REVOLUTIONS.

AUTUMN HARVEST UPRISINGS   A Chinese Communist uprising of 1927. Acting under COMINTERN directives, the Chinese Communists staged uprisings in the Hunan, Hubei, Jiangxi and Guangdong provinces in September 1927, after the break with the GUOMINDANG (GMD; Kuomintang) Nationalist forces. The idea had been to capitalize on peasant discontent during the harvest season, when landowners came to collect rent, but all the campaigns ended disastrously. For his part in the failure, MAO ZEDONG, who had been in charge in Hunan and Jiangxi, where he had recruited peasants and miners, was dismissed from the party's central committee, but he succeeded in establishing a base in southern Jiangxi with about 1,000 troops.

AVKSENTIEV, NIKOLAI D.   (1878–1943) Russian populist and a founder of the Party of Socialist Revolutionaries. Expelled for political activities from Moscow University in 1899, Avksentiev continued his studies and revolutionary activities in Germany. In 1905 he returned to Russia and was active in the Petersburg Soviet until arrested and exiled.

In 1917, Avksentiev was an executive of the Petrograd Soviet, a member of the All-Russian Central Executive of the Soviets and chair of the All-Russian Council of Peasant Deputies. In September he chaired the Democratic Conference and the pre-parliament, attempting to break Russia's political deadlock.

An active opponent of the BOLSHEVIKS, he headed the Directory in Ufa until banished by Admiral Kolchak. He then emigrated and was active in Russian circles in Paris until World War II, spending his final years in New York.

AWAMI LEAGUE   The nationalist organization which led Bangladesh to independence. A part of Pakistan until 1971, Bangladesh (then East Pakistan) was separated from West Pakistan by more than 1,000 miles of Indian territory and by ethnic and linguistic differences. Oppression by West Pakistan, particularly in economic matters, aroused resentment and resulted in the electoral victory in December 1970 of the Awami League in the national elections. The Awami League advocated a program of autonomy for the region under a new federal constitution. Since Bangladesh was more populous than West Pakistan, however, the Awami League would have dominated the Pakistani Federal Parliament. As a result, the Pakistani leadership decided to postpone the convening of the parliament. In March 1971, Bangladesh declared its independence. Pakistani President Yahya Khan then outlawed the Awami League and arrested its leader, MUJIBUR RAHMAN, provoking a civil war, Indian intervention and the ultimate defeat of the Pakistani army by the Liberation Army of East Bengal.

AXELROD, PAVEL BORISOVICH   (1850–1928) Russian Marxist ideologue and activist. Originally a member of the PEOPLE'S WILL (Narodnaya) movement, Axelrod left Russia in 1880, and was converted, along with other Narodnaya exiles in Switzerland (see LEV DEUTSCH, GEORGI PLEKHANOV, VERA ZASULICH), to Marxism. In 1883, Axelrod and Plekhanov founded the Social Democratic party. Outnumbered in the party's second congress (1903) by those rejecting his argument, Axelrod became a leading member of the MENSHEVIK party. Later he adopted an even more moderate stance, supporting the development of trade unions and parliamentary reform as opposed to revolution. He led the Liquidists from 1905, opposed the BOLSHEVIK PARTY'S rise to power and, as a result, was forced back into exile in Western Europe, where he lived until his death.

AYUTLA, REVOLUTION OF   The movement that, following Mexico's humiliating defeat in its war with the United States, forced the resignation of President Antonio Lopez de

Santa Anna in 1855. Santa Anna, elected president of Mexico for the first time in 1843 and subsequently overthrown in 1845, had been appointed generalissimo of the Mexican armed forces in 1846, at the start of the war with the United States. Disgraced by the defeat of Mexico two years later, Santa Anna went into exile in Venezuela. Recalled in 1853, he was again elected president, but in the same year proclaimed himself president-for-life.

A revolutionary group led by Melchor Ocampo and Benito Juarez offered support in 1854 to JUAN ALVAREZ, leader of a group in active rebellion in the state of Guerrero against the central government. Florencio Villareal and IGNACIO COMONFORT, fighting under Alvarez, subsequently published the later-celebrated Plan de Ayutla, which demanded that a junta composed of liberals be convened to name an interim president to replace the dictator Santa Anna. The Revolution of Ayutla garnered support in the states of Jalisco, Nuevo Leon and Guanajuato. Faced with an effective rebellion on several sides, Santa Anna resigned his office in 1855 and again went into exile, this time for almost two decades.

AZANA, MANUEL (1880–1940) The last president and head of state of the Spanish Republic at the outbreak of the civil war in 1936. After being returned to office for a second term in the wake of the electoral victory of the Popular Front in May 1936, Azana tried in vain to preserve some kind of unity among the divided factions of Spanish revolutionaries, syndicalists and anarchists, but was unable to halt the spread of domestic anarchy and at the same time check Italian and German intervention in support of General FRANCISCO FRANCO and his fascist FALANGE.

At the end of 1938, Azana made a famous heroic but unsuccessful attempt to secure French mediation to neutralize the fascist (see FASCISM) menace and to achieve the support of LEON BLUM's Popular Front government for the Spanish social revolutionaries, in order to stem the tide of European fascism. After both the French and British governments turned down his appeal because of opposition at home, Azana was easily ousted by Franco after the capture of Madrid in 1938 and had no choice but to flee to France in February 1939. There, he rejected all efforts by the die-hard Spanish Republicans to prolong the war against the invincible forces grouped around Franco. A moderate social reformer at heart, Azana in fact was a liberal constitutionalist reluctantly caught up in the great turmoil produced by the clash of the two great revolutionary ideologies of his age. He is still venerated as a hero, if not as a statesman, by the Catalans for having tried to save their revolution in Barcelona in 1934.

AZEFF, YEVNO FISHELEVICH (1869–1918) Jewish Russian revolutionary and *agent provocateur*. Azeff became active in the budding socialist revolutionary movement in Rostov, until his continued activities in the revolutionary movement came to the attention of the authorities and he was forced to flee to Germany.

Azeff settled in Karlsruhe where he studied engineering. Finding his financial resources depleted, he wrote a letter to the Ochrana, the Russian secret police, offering to sell his services as an informer against his revolutionary comrades. In 1899 he returned to Moscow, where he found a position with a general electrical-supply company. At the same time he became a prominent member of the Union of Social Revolutionaries underground.

Azeff was recognized as a leading advocate of terror as a means of liberating Russia. He often declared that "terror is the only way," but privately questioned socialist ideas. He quickly rose in the ranks of the newly-founded SOCIAL REVOLUTIONARY PARTY and was appointed to the party's first triumvirate, providing the Ochrana with invaluable information. He was also appointed leader of the Battle Organization, the militant terrorist arm of the party.

Azeff was ideologically committed to neither police nor party, refusing to give information compromising the party's leadership to the Ochrana when he realized that the 50,000 ruble award offered for that information would go to his superiors rather than to him. Furthermore, as head of the Battle Organization, he controlled the purse strings of that movement, allowing him greater financial independence than the Ochrana offered. He also felt betrayed by the police for their arrest of leading members of the party, an act that cast suspicion upon himself.

To clear himself of suspicion, Azeff took an active role in the planning and execution of the Russian interior minister, Vyacheslav Plehve, the man responsible for the Kishinev pogrom of 1903, in which 45 Jews had been murdered and hundreds more brutally beaten. The successful assassination of Plehve brought Azeff's Battle Organization to the forefront of Russian revolutionary politics. Many leading party activists were arrested as a result of information provided by Azeff to the authorities, but he managed to convince the police that he knew nothing of the details of the plot and had therefore been unable to stop it. Azeff was also instrumental in the assassination of Grand Duke Sergei, uncle of the czar and a leader of the reactionary party at court. Once again, he turned in his coconspirators while convincing the Ochrana of his inability to prevent the assassination.

After a shake-up in the police force, Azeff plotted to blow up the dreaded Ochrana headquarters in St. Petersburg. A police officer who had defected to the party informed the party leadership that an informer known by the code name of Raskin had infiltrated the higher ranks of the party. Azeff surmised that he was under suspicion and fled to Paris. He was tried in absentia by the party and sentenced to death.

Azeff moved to Germany and settled in Berlin with his mistress, Madam N., a Russian cabaret singer of German origin. The Germans imprisoned him during World War I because of his supposed revolutionary leanings. He was released from prison following the October RUSSIAN REVOLUTION OF 1917, but died soon thereafter.

AZIZBEKOV, MESHADI AZIM-BEK OGLI (1876–1918) A famous activist of the revolutionary movement in Azerbaijan and a BOLSHEVIK, one of the first Azerbaijani Marxists. Azizbekov was born in Baku, to a family of stone works laborers. He received a degree from the Baku Trade School. In 1908 he graduated from the St. Petersburg Institute of Technology. Beginning in the 1890s, he became actively involved in the revolutionary movement. In 1898 he became a member of the Russian Social Democratic Workers party (RSDRP). He returned to Baku at the end of 1904 and worked for the Baku Communist party among the Azerbaijani factory workers. He was the leader of the Social Democratic Organization, *Gummet* (Energy), created in 1904 as part of the Baku Bolshevik committee.

The revolutionary activities of Azizbekov started in the years of the RUSSIAN REVOLUTION OF 1905. In 1906, he organized workers into a civil defense corps, the Freedom Flag, which opposed the politics of the Czarist government aimed at inflaming ethnic hate among the Azerbaijani working class.

Azizbekov played a major role in spreading revolutionary ideas among the progressive part of the Azerbaijani educated class. In 1910 he was elected to the Baku City Soviet (city council), where he defended the workers' interests. In 1913–1914 he was one of the organizers and leaders of massive worker strikes.

After the February RUSSIAN REVOLUTION OF 1917, he headed the struggle of the Azerbaijani Bolsheviks to change the bourgeois-democratic revolution into a socialist one. In 1917 he was elected to the Baku Soviet of the Worker Delegates. After the October RUSSIAN REVOLUTION OF 1917, when Baku became the first city of the Transcaucasian region to proclaim the rule of the Soviet government, Azizbekov began a massive campaign among the village farmers to transfer the government control in the local counties to the hands of the Soviets. In March of 1918 he was actively involved in establishing the Soviet government in Baku. In the first Baku Soviet of the Peoples' Commissars, he held the post of regional commissar and vice-principal people's commissar for internal affairs.

After the Soviet government in Baku fell and the Turks took control of the city, Azizbekov was arrested. He was one of the 26 Baku commissars who were executed by the English on the night of September 20, 1918, 207 miles outside Krasnovodsk in Turkmenia. His remains are buried in Baku.

B

BAADER-MEINHOF GROUP A German extreme left-wing terrorist group that first attracted attention during the 1968 student riots in West Berlin. Founded by Andreas Baader (1936–1975) and Ulrike Meinhof (1934–1976), most of the members came from the upper middle class and were highly educated. The group carried out countless acts of terror in Germany as well as in other European countries; Meinhof alone was implicated in five murders before she and Baader were arrested in 1972. However, the leaders' arrests and their subsequent deaths did not put an end to the group's activities.

Incidents for which the Baader-Meinhof Group are believed to have been responsible include: the kidnapping of the OPEC oil ministers in 1975; the murder of former Italian prime minister, Aldo Moro, and the hijacking of a French airline to Entebbe, both in 1976; the kidnapping and murder of the industrial magnate, Hans Martin Schleyer in 1977; and the 1980 bombing of the Munich Oktoberfest, which claimed over 100 casualties. This last incident proved to be a turning point. During the late 1980s, several of the group's members were arrested while others relented and turned themselves in to the authorities. As a result, little has been heard of the group in recent years.

BA'ATH PARTY IN IRAQ see IRAQ, BA'ATH PARTY OF.

BA'ATH PARTY IN SYRIA see SYRIA, BA'ATH PARTY OF.

BAB (Ali Muhammad Shirazi) (1819–1850) Leader of the People's Anti-feudal Movement and armed revolts in Iran and founder of a new religious doctrine, born in Shiraz, Iran, to a merchant's family. A scholar, Bab in 1844 declared himself to be the Muslim Messiah—the 12th Imam. In its most completed form, Bab's doctrine was reflected in his book *Bayan* (Revelation), written in 1847. Bab tried to substitute his work for the Koran and the Shari'at.

Bab's doctrine, directed against feudal and clerical despotism, found overwhelming support in Iran. A wave of revolts passed through Iran which were suppressed by the Shah's régime. Bab was shot in 1850 in Tabriz, but the revolts went on until 1852.

BABEK (?–838) A great leader of a popular liberation movement in Azerbaijan in the 9th century against the domination of the Arab Abbasid caliphate. In 816, after the demise of his predecessor Javidan, Babek became the leader of the anti-Arab liberation movement in the mountain regions of South Azerbaijan, which was entirely involved in the Hurramite Rebellion. The name Hurramite comes from the term *hurram* (from Persian— "sun", "fire"). The Hurramite ideology was based on the traditions of Zoroastrism, which was dominant in this region as well as in all of Iran until the appearance of Islam. In addition, Mazdakism had a great deal of influence on the Hurramite world view. The Hurramite religion was based on the belief in two great spiritual powers which symbolized light and darkness, i.e., good and evil. The religion became the symbol of the struggle for liberation against the religion and policies of the Arabs. Islam was considered by the local population as the ideological expression of the Arab domination. The tax system which the Arabs used to collect from the farmers, totalling about half of all their produce, was met with strong resistance and intensified even more the people's opposition to the Arabs' economic policies.

Whereas, before 816, the Hurramites led by Javidan had bothered the caliphate only by sporadic resistance, after his death they became a mighty force against the Arabs under the leadership of Babek. Babek chose a very fortuitous moment for escalating the struggle. He took advantage of the infighting inside the caliphate between Caliph Mamun (809–833) and his brother Amin. During this period, the Arabs' attention was turned away from the distant northern provinces. The success of the rebellion was also aided by the fact that many local landowners joined Babek because they felt oppressed by the caliphate. In a few years, Babek managed to free all of Azerbaijan from the Arabs. After that the revolt spread to the neighboring regions. During the period from 829 to 835, the Hurramites headed by Babek were victorious over six armies of the caliphate.

Only when Caliph Mutasim (823–842) named Afshin ibn Kavus to lead the war against the Hurramites in 835 did the victory turn to the Arab side. Afshin inflicted several serious losses upon Babek. In 837 he laid siege on Babek's residence, the Badz fortress, in the Ardebill region. On August 26, after storming the fortress, Afshin's army captured and burned it down. The evidence appears to indicate that several tens of thousands of Hurramites were killed at the time. Babek was able to flee to Albania (northern Azerbaijan). There, though, he was betrayed, captured and handed over to the Arabs, who executed him in Samara in January 838.

BABEUF, FRANÇOIS NOËL (GRACCHUS) (1760–1797) Born in Saint-Quentin, Babeuf was executed, following an aborted coup d'état against the government of the French Directory, in Paris. One of the most original far-sighted political agitators produced by the FRENCH REVOLUTION of 1789, he came to be venerated by such militants as LOUIS AUGUSTE BLANQUI and Armand Barès as the founding father of a French tradition of revolutionary socialism that came to the fore in the Revolution of 1848 (see REVOLUTIONS OF 1848), in the PARIS COMMUNE OF 1871 and during the Third Republic. International communism also drew some of its inspiration from Babeuf, who is considered a genuine and authentic, although admittedly somewhat muddled, precursor of Marxism, with agrarian rather than proletarian overtones.

Babeuf's social theory and program for action rested on the principle that the social struggle, and not the liberal and political reformism associated with such democratic parties as the GIRONDINS, the JACOBINS or even the extreme left-wing Cordeliers, constitutes the real driving force of history. Starting his career as a land surveyor and notary's clerk who made his living by looking after the interests of the landed gentry in his native province of Picardy, Babeuf cast his lot with the revolution in 1789. He gravitated toward the radical Cordelier Club and then founded a populist newspaper, *Le Tribun du Peuple*. He published this intermittently while in and out of jail during the Thermidorian reaction that followed the fall of ROBESPIERRE in July 1794.

Drifting further and further away from mainstream Jacobin thought, which he came to identify with moneyed interests and middle-class values, Babeuf rejected Rousseauist attempts to bring man back to a state of nature in favor of a Communist and egalitarian society in which there would be neither rich nor poor, and each man would enjoy an equal share in all property. These ideas were set forth in the Socialist Manifesto of a new political club, the *Club du Pantheon*, which he launched after the establishment of the bourgeois-dominated Directory in 1795. They were to be put into practice through a secret society, *La Société des Egaux* (The Society of Equals), led by a body of professional and dedicated revolutionaries organized in a Leninist-type "insurrectionary committee" that would pave the way for the "final revolution." The uprising, betrayed by a double agent, was suppressed by the police in April 1796 and the trial of Babeuf in the following year, not of conspiracy, but of advocating the restoration of what had now become the legendary Jacobin constitution of 1793, was exploited by the government to discredit not only his followers but the Jacobin opposition in general. It was largely thanks to his lieutenant and young disciple, FILIPPO BUONAROTTI, a descendant of Michelangelo and ardent member of the Italian *Carbonari*, who in 1828 published *La Conspiration pour l'Egalité, dite de Babeuf*, that his ideas, known under the generic name of *Babouvisme*, became the breviary of successive generations of revolutionaries and reinforced the martyrology of the Marxist-Leninist ideology.

BABINGTON PLOT   (1586) The last straw which led to the execution of Mary, Queen of Scots. The plan was for Anthony Babington (1561–1586) to free Mary from imprisonment and to have the English Roman Catholics wait for and aid a Spanish invasion. Babington's careless letter describing the plot was intercepted by Queen Elizabeth I's spy service, organized by her minister Walsingham. Philip II's ambassador in Paris, Mendoza, was implicated, as were four Englishmen apart from Babington. The conspirators were executed in September 1586 and Mary herself was beheaded at Fotheringay on February 8, 1587.

BABU, MUHAMMAD ABDULRAHMAN   (1922–) Abdulrahman Babu was born in Zanzibar in 1922 and educated in Uganda and England. From 1957 to 1963 he was the General Secretary of the Zanzibar National party (ZNP), which stood for the rule of the sultan as a constitutional monarch and benign Arab feudalism.

The left-wing Babu was detained from 1962–1963. In 1963 he left the ZNP to found his own radical UMMA Party, which included both Arabs and Africans. On independence in December 1963, Babu became a member of the revolutionary council. In 1964 the UMMA party merged with the AFRO-SHIRAZI PARTY and Babu held various ministerial posts until 1972, when he was imprisoned following the assassination of Abeid Karume, leader of the ASP. He was released in 1978.

BABYLON, REVOLTS
Revolt of 710–689 B.C. Babylon was conquered by Sargon II in 710 B.C., but after his death at the hands of the Cimmerians in Asia Minor in 705 B.C., it rebelled. A Babylonian of the scribal family, by the name of Marduk-zakir-shumi II, became king but was soon deposed by a Chaldean chief of Bit-Yakin, Marduk-apla-iddina (Merodach-baladan of the Bible), who had ruled Babylon previously in the years 721–710 B.C.

Sargon's successor, Sennacherib, directed his first campaign against Babylon in 703 B.C. Defeated at Kish, the Chaldeans retreated to the marshes of the south and Sennacherib installed as king a Babylonian noble named Bel-ibni, who had been reared in Assyria "like a young hound." In 700 B.C., Merodach-baladan reappeared in Babylon, provoking a second Assyrian invasion. Merodach-baladan fled to Elam while Bel-ibni, who was suspected of being in compliance with rebels, was removed from the throne. Instead, Sennacherib crowned his own son, Ashurnadin-shumi, as a king of Babylon. In 694 B.C., Sennacherib organized a naval expedition against Elam. The Elamite retaliation was most painful for him: his son was captured and executed by the Elamites, who installed a pro-Elamite Babylonian, Nergal-Ushezib, in his place. Nergal-Ushezib was captured by the Assyrians six months later, but the Babylonians chose another Chaldean chief, Mushezib-Marduk, from Bit-Dakkuri, to replace him.

In 691 B.C., Sennacherib marched against Babylon for the third time. This campaign resulted in the battle of Khalule, where both sides claimed victory (as seen in the Babylonian chronicles and Assyrian annals respectively). Unable to solve the Babylonian problem in any of the traditional ways, Sennacherib decided the unthinkable—simply to destroy once and for all this ancient cultural and religious center of Mesopotamia. The siege of Babylon began in 690 B.C. and in 689 B.C. Sennacherib ordered the destruction of a dam on the Euphrates, so that Babylon was literally wiped out by the river.

The Babylonian kingdom ceased to exist for 11 years. The statue of the god Marduk was transferred to the city of Assur, where a special temple was built for his cult.
Revolt of 652–648 B.C. In an unusual arrangement of succession, Esarhaddon divided his empire between his two sons: Shamash-shum-ukin received Babylon and Ashurbanipal received Assyria proper. After the death of his father, however, Ashurbanipal concentrated all the military power in his hands and treated his brother more as a viceroy of Babylon than as an

independent king. Shamash-shum-ukin saw this as a violation of Esarhaddon's will and in 652 B.C. rebelled against his brother. The revolt was in alliance with Elam and with the Chaldean chief, Nabu-bel-shumati, grandson of Merodach-baladan.

Ashurbanipal then made a proclamation to the Babylonians, promising the preservation of their ancient privileges if they would abandon Shamash-shum-ukin. When there was no response, the war began. At first the Assyrian army was defeated by the Babylonians at Cutha. Elam, however, was politically unstable; its kings were overthrown one after another and one of them, Tammeritu II, fled to Assyria. Nabu-bel-shumati to the last minute gave the impression that he was on the Assyrian side. He even received an Assyrian auxiliary force to aid him, which he promptly took prisoner. In 650 B.C., the Assyrians invaded the Chaldean homeland in the south and deprived Babylon of its last ally. The siege of Babylon began in 650 B.C. and continued for two years. In 648 B.C., the city was taken and Shamash-shum-ukin committed suicide, setting fire to his own palace. Babylon was not destroyed this time, but lost its special status as a separate kingdom and was thereafter ruled by an Assyrian governor.

Revolt of 482 B.C. see EGYPT AND BABYLON REBELLION OF 486–481 B.C.

BACON'S REBELLION A violent 1676 seizure of Virginia's colonial government by a group of discontented settlers led by Nathaniel Bacon. The insurgents defeated the forces of the governor, Sir William Berkeley, burning down Jamestown in the process. The rebels' control over the colony was, however, only short-lived and they were soon repulsed by Berkeley's forces, Bacon succumbing to exhaustion and exposure in the course of the struggle.

The coup grew out of an unauthorized campaign launched by Bacon and a band of land-hungry settlers against the Indians occupying Virginia's northwestern boundary. The settlers' successful expedition was in direct opposition to the policy of Virginia's governor, Sir William Berkeley, who sought to stabilize relations with the neighboring tribes, notwithstanding the pressure of white colonists for fresh land. Berkeley's attempts to prevent the Baconites from occupying the Indian land led the insurgents to turn against him and his government. The insurgents' campaign, in its two phases, reflected both the economic aspirations of up-and-coming settlers and their challenge to the clique of well-established Virginians favored by Berkeley.

BAGAUDAE A name, probably of Celtic origin and perhaps meaning "fighters," used in the sources to describe farmers, serfs, shepherds and rustics in general who rose in rebellion against the rich landowners in Gaul and northern Spain. The first recorded reference to them is of c. 284 A.D., when they rose against their oppressors. They were headed by two leaders, Aelianus and Amandus. Their success made them so formidable that the emperor Diocletian appointed Maximian as commander of the province; he defeated the rebels for the time being but felt the need to improve the administration of the province. However, the difficult conditions of the rustics did not change significantly. Meanwhile, the Bagaudae continued to harass the countryside and even to attack cities from time to time and their name was used as a synonym for brigandage. Uprisings recurred frequently in Gaul in the first half of the 5th century and in

northeast Spain from 441 to 456. For a while the Bagaudae ruled Armorica, i.e., the district around the mouth of the Loire. The need to dispatch imperial armies to suppress these revolts weakened the ability of the central government to withstand the invasions of the German tribes, thus playing some part in the disintegration of the western part of the Roman empire.

BAGHDADI, ABDUL LATIF (1917–) Egyptian officer and politician. Vice-President of the United Arab Republic, 1958–1961, and of Egypt, 1962–1964. Born in 1917, he was a graduate of the military academy and a professional officer. Baghdadi, then a lieutenant colonel, was a leading member of the FREE OFFICERS who staged the EGYPTIAN REVOLUTION OF 1952 and the Revolutionary Council they established; when the officers banned all political parties and set up their own single "Liberation Organization" in January 1953, he became its inspector-general. He also chaired several purge trials of old-régime politicians. Within the junta, he was considered conservative and right-wing. In August 1957 he left the cabinet to become president of the National Assembly. He held various prominent political positions until 1964, when he was dropped as vice-president of Egypt and resigned his National Assembly post. He has not been politically active since, though as an elder statesman he is respected and sometimes volunteers advice and opinions. Baghdadi was, like other old Nasser associates, critical of ANWAR AL-SADAT's new line, especially regarding Sadat's peace treaty with Israel which he publicly denounced (jointly with three other former vice-presidents). While he seems to have accepted Egypt's growing links with the USA, he criticized the 1971 Treaty of Friendship with the USSR.

BAI LIAN JIAO see WHITE LOTUS SOCIETY.

BAKHTIAR, SHAHPUR (1914–1991) Iranian politician with Ph.D. degree in international law and political science from Paris University. In 1940, while in France, Bakhtiar was recruited to the French army for 18 months. His participation in the war against the Nazis had a great influence on his personality.

Bakhtiar returned to Iran in 1946. He was associated with the leftist Iran party. In 1951–1952 he joined MOSSADDEQ's National Front government as deputy minister of labor. After the fall of Mossaddeq in 1953 he was forced to retire from public service and continued his activities in opposition groups. He constantly criticized the shah, comparing his rule to the Nazi régime and his secret police (Savak) to the Gestapo. His subsequent arrest only increased his hostility toward the régime.

When the shah's power was shaken by a growing Islamic rebellion and US advisors counseled him to appoint a government not associated with his autocratic and corrupt régime, Bakhtiar, seen as a pro-western social democrat, was appointed prime minister in January 1979. Though he had struggled against the shah for years, he did not call for his deposition, but for a British-type constitutional monarchy.

As a modernist, secularist and liberal opposed to the influence of the Islamic clergy, Bakhtiar declined an alliance between his National Front and the Islamic opposition headed by KHOMEINI. Bakhtiar abolished the Savak and declared that Iran would no longer be the policeman of the Persian Gulf. Neither the Islamic fundamentalists nor the left accepted him, seeing him as a representative of the old régime. He was expelled from the National Front, and when the ISLAMIC REVOLUTION OF 1979 succeeded and Khomeini returned to Iran, he was dismissed—after only 38 days in power. He was arrested, but after a time was permitted to leave Iran. He settled in Paris, founded the National Resistance Movement, and was assassinated in 1991, presumably by the Iranian régime's agents.

AL-BAKR, AHMAD HASAN (1914–1982) A senior Iraqi military man and politician. Al-Bakr was born in Tikrit, Iraq, to a family of small landowners of the Begat tribe. Upon graduation from a teachers' training high school in Baghdad in 1932, he served as a primary school teacher and later joined the military academy that had been opened for cadets from middle and lower-middle class backgrounds. His military career as an officer was steady but not exceptional; in 1958 he was a lieutenant colonel. In the mid-1950s he became involved in political activity as a member of one of the groups of the FREE OFFICERS. Simultaneously, he became associated with the newly-born BA'ATH party (though he only joined the party officially as late as 1960). Following the republican revolution of July 14, 1958, he became a very central link between the two most potent pan-Arab opposition groups which sought to bring down the "secessionist" régime of General QASSEM: the civilian *Ba'ath* party and both retired and serving Nasserite army officers, the chief of these being ABDUL SALAM 'AREF.

Bakr was one of the chief planners of the first *Ba'ath* coup d'état of February 8, 1963. After the coup he became prime minister, while 'Arif was made a ceremonial president. Throughout the nine months of *Ba'ath* rule, Bakr served as a mediator between the civilian and military wings of the party, as well as between its "left" and "right" factions. In September 1963, he became a member of the regional leadership of the *Ba'ath* party and a few months later of the Pan-Arab leadership. On November 18, 1963, a severe rift between the party's "left" and "right" wings caused him to opt for a third solution, and he supported President 'Arif and his Nasserite army officers in their coup d'état which toppled the *Ba'ath* from power. After a few months of cooperation, during which he served as deputy prime minister, 'Arif dismissed him and his *Ba'ath* colleagues. In September 1964, most of the party leadership, including Bakr, were jailed for an attempted coup d'état. Upon their release a few months later, they set out anew to try to topple the 'Arif régime.

The June 1967 Arab defeat at the hands of Israel provided Bakr and his co-conspirators with a golden opportunity to agitate against the régime for its failure to give adequate military support to the Arabs. On July 17, 1968, the *Ba'ath*, together with independent army officers, assumed power in a bloodless coup d'état. Bakr led one of the army units which participated in the takeover. He then became president of the republic and chairman of the all-powerful Revolutionary Command Council. By July 30, the *Ba'ath* had rid itself of its partners, with Bakr becoming prime minister and field marshal. Bakr also held the positions of commander-in-chief of the armed forces, secretary general of the regional leadership of the party and deputy secretary-general of the Pan-Arab leadership, under MICHEL 'AFLAQ as a figurehead. Between 1973 and 1977 Bakr also served as minister of defense.

Throughout these years Bakr cooperated very closely with his young relative, the civilian party and internal security functionary, SADDAM HUSSEIN. This cooperation stemmed from mutual interdependence. Bakr needed Saddam as a watchdog against actual and potential enemies inside the party and outside of it. Saddam, for his part, even when he became the strong man in Baghdad in 1970 or 1971, could not survive on his own, because he lacked the necessary contacts with the military and sufficient support from the party old-timers and was not yet known among the Iraqi public. Thus, while Bakr needed protection, Saddam needed time. Throughout the 1970s, the two relatives effectively purged the army of politically ambitious officers and turned it into a docile tool in the hands of the party. The two relatives were also close in their approach to politics: both were pragmatists, preferring Iraqi interests over those of the Arab nation, as interpreted by traditional party ideology. Yet, on a few occasions Bakr showed more attachment to traditional party doctrine in terms of his commitment to the struggle against Israel and Arab unity. Differences, however, were minor, until the issue of Iraqi-Syrian relations came up in 1978–1979, following the Camp David accords. Whereas Bakr favored a loose federation with HAFEZ AL-ASAD's Syria, Saddam objected to it, for fear of losing his position.

On July 16, 1979, Saddam, who by then had complete control of all internal security branches and through them of the party and the army, staged a bloodless coup d'état and forced Bakr to announce his resignation due to ill health (Bakr's health was indeed somewhat shaky). A few days later, Saddam announced that he had uncovered a Syrian-sponsored plot to topple him from power and used this excuse to execute all his remaining opponents who, until then, could hide behind Bakr's back. Saddam also took advantage of this opportunity to sever ties with Damascus.

Between 1979–1982, when his death was reported, Bakr lived under house arrest and was not involved in matters of state. According to a widely-believed rumor, Bakr was murdered in 1982 by poisoning because, at a low point in his war with Iran, Saddam was afraid that the retired president might become a focus of opposition against him.

BAKUNIN MIKHAIL (1814–1876) Insurrectionist and founder of a major strain of nineteenth century ANARCHISM. Michael Bakunin was born into the landed aristocracy on his family estate, Prekhumino, in the province of Tver, northwest of Moscow. Bakunin's father chose to educate his children at home in line with the ideas of the Enlightenment thinkers who were becoming popular in Russia at that time. In 1828, Bakunin entered the Artillery School in St. Petersburg. He was dismissed, however, in 1834 on disciplinary grounds and sent to serve on the Polish frontier. He left his post the following year without receiving prior permission. Back at Prekhumino, he continued to turn against convention by objecting to his sisters' marriage engagements before leaving to study philosophy in Moscow.

In Moscow, he began an intellectual exploration of radical ideas which eventually landed him solidly on the path of activism. Bakunin frequented the intellectual circles. He developed his life-long friendship with ALEXANDER HERZEN. Bakunin soon delved into the philosophies of JOHANN FICHTE and Georg Wilhelm Hegel and in 1840 decided to travel to Berlin to finish his studies. Berlin was a center for the Young Hegelian movement and it was through his contacts there that Bakunin crossed the line between reflection and action. In 1842 he published an article, "The Reaction in Germany: A Fragment from a Frenchman," forewarning the coming revolution in Russia. The Russian embassy consequently requested his return to Russia. Upon his refusal, he was tried in absentia.

For the next several years Bakunin lived in Switzerland and Belgium, becoming increasing interested in the national liberation of the Slavic people. In Paris he met KARL MARX and PIERRE-JOSEPH PROUDHON but only fully embraced socialist ideas in 1848. In the February REVOLUTIONS OF 1848, he fought in the barricades alongside the Parisian workers. After participating in the Slavic Congress of 1848 in Prague, he wrote *An Appeal to the Slavs* in which he pressed for a federation of Slavic republics to be set up once the Austrian, German, Turkish and Russian empires had been overthrown. He declared the bourgeois to be the counter revolutionary and, betraying Slavophile sentiments, looked to the peasants as the true revolutionary force.

In 1849, he fought in the Dresden Insurrection. Captured by the authorities, Bakunin was extradited to Russia and served for six years in the infamous Peter and Paul fortress. In prison he wrote his famous *Confession to Czar Nicholas I* which has been varyingly interpreted as a repentance for misdeeds, on one extreme, and as an attempt to "educate" the czar, on the other. His revolutionary commitment, however, could hardly have been shaken. Once released to Siberia, he joined the societies of the intellectual elite of political prisoners. He also married the daughter of a Polish merchant and in 1861 escaped to England, where he rejoined Herzen.

Bakunin and Herzen's reunion was complicated by the gap that had arisen in their thinking. Bakunin's reputation in the emigré circles was still based on his position as a veteran of the 1848 revolutions and advocate of Slav independence. Yet while Bakunin had lost touch with the radical movement of Europe during his stay in Russia, Herzen had shifted to a more moderate position and perhaps was a bit overwhelmed by Bakunin's revolutionary enthusiasm. When the Polish Insurrection erupted in 1863, Bakunin abruptly left Herzen to head an unsuccessful mission to aid the rebels. Bakunin continued to correspond with Herzen throughout the rest of his life, but rather than returning to London, he decided to travel to Italy, where he frequented the liberal circles from which he recruited members for his first anarchist associations.

In the three years Bakunin spent in Italy he managed to gather a following among Italian liberals. In Naples, he founded the International Brotherhood, a secret society, whose program, "The Revolutionary Catechism," contained the first formulation of Bakunin's anarchist ideas.

Back in Geneva in 1867, Bakunin published "Federalism, Socialism and Anti-Theologism" which examined further the ideas in the Catechism. Warmly welcomed into the executive body of the liberally oriented Congress for Peace and Freedom, Bakunin and his followers broke away within a year to form the International Alliance of Social Democracy. The Alliance succeeded in establishing branches across Europe and in 1869 reorganized as local sections of the First INTERNATIONAL. In 1872, in the wake of the growing influence in the International, Bakunin broke with Marx, founding a separate anarchist International. The Marxist anarchist split in socialist thought has survived to this day.

In 1869, at the height of his influence, Bakunin befriended SERGEI NECHAEV, a young student from Moscow whose nihilistic views placed a black mark on Bakunin's record of commitment to libertarian values. When Nechaev was arrested by Swiss authorities in 1870, a manuscript entitled "Revolutionary Catechism" was confiscated. The text advocated the use of terrorist tactics and the misguided assumption that Bakunin and Nechaev cooperated fully on the work has led to the popular misconception that Bakunin shared Nechaev's nihilistic beliefs.

In 1870, Bakunin made his way to Lyon to participate in the uprising. After the fall of the PARIS COMMUNE, he returned to Switzerland and in 1873 he wrote *Statism and Anarchy*, his last major work, which sharply criticized Marx, discussed the preconditions for social revolution in Russia and described the tenets of anarchist thought. A wealthy supporter transferred the property rights of an estate over in an attempt to grant him Swiss citizenship and a safe haven for his revolutionary endeavors. This arrangement, however, misfired and in 1874 Bakunin set off to join the Italian Insurrections but did not reach Italy in time.

With the fall of the international anarchist organization, Bakunin spent his final two years in Switzerland battling bladder and kidney problems until he died in Berne.

BALABANOFF, ANGELICA (1869–1965) Of Russian origin, Balabanoff became one of the main figures of Italian socialism on the eve of World War I. She joined the Italian Socialist party after studying Marxism with Antonio Labriola at the University of Rome. MUSSOLINI met Balabanoff and greatly admired her. Through her, the future Duce became familiar with the classics of European socialism and was much influenced by her personality and thoughts. Balabanoff thought that Mussolini's views were "more the reflection of his early environment and his own rebellious egoism than of understanding and conviction; his hatred for oppression was not that impersonal hatred of a system shared by all revolutionaries; it sprang rather from his own sense of indignity and frustration, from a passion to assert his own ego and from a determination for personal revenge" (from A. Balabanoff, *My life as a Rebel*, London 1938, p. 60). In 1911, Balabanoff joined the revolutionary wing of the Italian Socialist party (PSI) and became coeditor of its organ, *Avanti*, along with Mussolini. Ideologically and politically, they parted ways with the outbreak of World War I, when she adopted a revolutionary internationalist position that rejected war. In 1915 she left Italy and became the link between the PSI and the Zimmerwald socialist antiwar movement. In 1917, she returned to Russia and joined the BOLSHEVIKS. In 1921, disillusioned with the results of the Communist revolution, she moved again, settling in Paris in 1926. Balabanoff emigrated to the USA in 1938, participating in anti-Fascist activities, always spiced by her personal and intellectual knowledge of Mussolini, and returned to Italy in 1948, where she died in 1965.

BALALA, SHEIKH SALIM KHALID (1958–) Born in Mombasa, Kenya, in 1958, Balala attended the local Islamic religious school (*Madrasa*). In 1975 he left Kenya to take part in the *Hajj* (pilgrimage) to Mecca, Saudi Arabia. He received a scholarship from the Saudi Arabian government to study Islam there. Balala went on to India to study comparative religion. In

1990, he returned to Mombasa and started preaching in the streets. His eloquence attracted large audiences. He attacked the government of Kenya, claiming that it discriminated against Muslims (who comprise about 20% of Kenya's 25 million people).

Balala became the leader of the unregistered Islamic party of Kenya. He demanded that the party be registered, but the government refused. He was frequently arrested for calling for the removal of the government and for attacking President Moi. His arrest led to demonstrations against the government, and skirmishes with the police force resulted in several casualties.

Balala's followers—mostly young, unemployed, Muslim extremists—demanded (among other things) the imposition of Muslim *Shari'a* law in the country. At the beginning of 1995, while on a trip to Germany, Balala's Kenyan passport was confiscated and he was refused re-entry into Kenya. While abroad, he continued his antigovernment propaganda.

BALBO, ITALO (1896–1940) Italian Fascist revolutionary leader, although a relative late-comer to fascism. Balbo's political origins were in the Republican party, in which he was active until 1921. It was then that he joined the Fasci di Combattimento in Ferrara, transforming his political section into a paramilitary unit, of which he became *Ras* (leader and commander). Leading his SQUADRISTI (Blackshirt Fascist militia), Balbo attacked socialists and communists in Ferrara and later in the Po valley, destroying cooperatives and party headquarters while using terrorist methods. During the MARCH ON ROME in October 1922, Balbo was appointed by MUSSOLINI as quadrumvir—one of the four leaders of the March, together with EMILIO DE BONO, Michele Bianchi and Cesare Maria De Vecchi. In 1926, Balbo entered the ministry of aviation as undersecretary and in 1929 became minister of aviation, a post he retained until 1933, developing this field and becoming internationally famous as a result of the massive Italian air expeditions he organized. In 1933, the Duce appointed Balbo governor of Libya. In this capacity he developed the North African Italian colony through infrastructural works, mainly road building and agricultural settlements. Though personally loyal to Mussolini, Balbo opposed the alliance with Germany, the Italian anti-Semitic legislation in 1938 and Italy's entry in the war. While on an inspection tour in Libya, Balbo's plane was shot down near Tobruk by Italian forces which mistook his airplane for an enemy one.

BALL, JOHN (d. 1381) Priest and social preacher. Little is known of John's early life. In 1366, while living in Essex, he was summoned before the Archbishop of Canterbury, accused of preaching the heretical doctrines of WYCLIFFE and forbidden to preach. He nevertheless continued to do so, condemning the right of the Church to own property and teaching the equality of bondsmen and gentry. In 1376 he was arrested but his popularity remained high and, in 1381, when the English PEASANTS' REVOLT broke out, he was freed and took an active part in the rebellion. Captured at Coventry, he was brought before Richard II and executed as a traitor.

BANDA, HASTINGS KAMUZU (1902–) Malawi statesman. Born in the British protectorate of Nyasaland, Banda attended a mission school for several years. In 1915 he went to South Africa and worked as a clerk in the gold mines while continuing his education. From 1928 to 1937 he lived in the United States and studied medicine. He moved to London in 1945 and there became politically active, supporting the Nyasaland African Congress. Returning to Nyasaland in 1958 as that movement's president, he spent a term in prison in 1959–1960 but emerged as his country's most important leader after it won the 1960 elections. He help negotiate Nyasaland's independence and was its first prime minister. In 1966 he became president of his country, now renamed Malawi.

BANERJEA, S. URENDRANATH (1848–1925) Indian educator, journalist and nationalist, one of the founders of the INDIAN NATIONAL CONGRESS in 1885, opponent of Lord Curzon's (viceroy in India 1899–1904) partition of Bengal in 1905. Baberjea's autobiography, *A Nation in the Making*, describes the early stages of Indian nationalism.

Toward the end of the 19th century, the first generation of Indian nationalists emerged in British India. Banerjea was a member of this early elite; an articulate political spokesman, he organized the new Indian Association in 1877. The members of the association believed that the masses, largely illiterate, were helpless and that hence only the middle class, placed between the dispossessed and the aristocracy (who spoke only for themselves), would legitimately represent all Indians.

Banerjea was a well-known figure in Indian politics for half a century. He based his politics on India's past achievements in learning, mathematics, morals, religion and even war. Banerjea toured India from his base in Calcutta, giving his views on the Indian civil service requirements, freedom of the press and representative government.

Educated in England in the latter half of the 19th century, Banerjea can be considered as a moderate compared to other nationalist leaders. His role within the Indian Association, and later the Indian National Congress, was largely that of a communicator of ideas and an organizer and collector of funds for the nationalist movement. He became one of the first of the many nationalists to go to prison, which boosted his popularity and helped mobilize support for the Indian nationalist movement.

BANI-SADR, ABOLHASSAN (1931–) Iranian politician, first president of Iran after the islamic revolution of 1979. As a student of theology, economics and sociology at Tehran University, Bani-Sadr associated with anti-shah groups such as muhammad mossaddeq's National Front. After Mossadeq's defeat in 1953, he joined various underground movements. He was arrested by the Savak secret police and in 1964 was exiled from Iran. He settled in Paris and studied at the Sorbonne, earning his Ph.D. in economics and sociology. He was active in the Union of Iranian Students. After meeting ayatollah khomeini in Najaf, Iraq in 1977, Bani-Sadr became one of Khomeini's close advisors when the ayatollah moved to Paris in 1978. He was part of a group of intellectuals (most of them anticlerical) who bridged the distance between the political opposition and the rebellious anti-shah clergy.

After the Islamic Revolution of 1979 he published a daily newspaper, Inqilab, but at first declined any official post in the government. Yet in November 1979 he was appointed minister of foreign affairs as well as minister of economics and finance.

Bani-Sadr was elected president of Iran in January 1980. Khomeini also appointed him chairman of the Supreme Defense Council. However, Bani-Sadr failed to build up a basis of support in the *majlis* (parliament). He was attacked by the radical faction of the ruling, clergy-dominated Islamic Republic party, headed by its secretary-general, Ayatollah Beheshti, inter alia for his anti-Soviet stand after the Soviet intervention in Afghanistan, his stance in the Iran-Iraq conflict, and especially his position on the American hostage crisis and his attempts to restrain the militant students.

In June 1980, Khomeini dismissed him as head of the Defense Council. A committee of inquiry found him guilty of violating the constitution and of disobeying Khomeini's orders. He escaped from Iran to France and the *Majlis* declared him unfit for the presidency, transferring his former posts to his adversaries.

In their Paris exile, he and MAS'UD RAJAVI of the MUJAHIDIN KHALQ founded, in 1981, a National Resistance Council. However, their alliance broke up when Bani-Sadr objected to Rajavi's contacts with Iraq.

Bani-Sadr continued to consider himself Iran's legal president, claiming that he enjoyed the support of the army.

Bani-Sadr is considered an important theoretician of the revolution. In three books and about fifty articles he advocated a combination of socialism and the principles of equality which characterized the beginning of Islam. He saw Islamic thinking as the framework of his beliefs. He supported the existence of a religious-clerical leadership, but rejected its actual leaders. He denounced Iran's economic dependence on the west and called for the foundation of a classless society. In his book, *My Turn to Speak* (1991), he tells the inside story of his political career and the circumstances under which it grew.

AL-BANNA, HASSAN   (1906–1949) Founder and leader of the MUSLIM BROTHERHOOD in Egypt. Born in Ismailia to a pious Muslim family, Banna graduated from the Cairo Teachers' College and became a teacher of Islam in Ismailia and Cairo schools. He regarded himself as a follower of the Islamic thinker and reformer Rashid Rida. In 1929 he founded, in Ismailia, the Muslim Brotherhood—initially an association for religious teaching that turned into a fundamentalist organization aspiring to the purification of Islam, a return to its pristine doctrine, the imposition of Islamic law and the transformation of Egypt into an Islamic state. Banna was the mentor and sole leader, the "Supreme Guide" (*al-Murshid al-'Aam*) of the Brotherhood. His simple, forceful doctrine attracted considerable support—chiefly among the lower classes, but also among some younger intellectuals, mainly students—and his frugal ways and charisma earned him much sympathy, but his organization's increasing radicalization, its subversive fanaticism and advocacy of political assassination caused the government to suppress it and drive it underground. After Prime Minister Nuqrashi was murdered in December 1948 by the Brotherhood, Banna himself was assassinated in revenge in February 1949. He was replaced as "Supreme Guide" by Sheikh Hassan Isma'il Hudeibi, but neither al-Hudeibi nor those who followed him were able to fill Banna's place as a leader. While Banna did not write a systematic exposition of his doctrine, collections of his speeches and articles have been printed several times, as well as a book of his memoirs.

AL-BANNA, SABRI ("ABU NIDAL")   (1934? 1937?–) Palestinian-Arab terrorist leader. Born in Jaffa, Abu Nidal left the emerging Israel in 1948 and grew up in Gaza. Since the 1960s he has headed a terrorist group considered the most extreme and most brutal among the Palestinian-Arab factions and guerrilla/terror gangs. Officially called "*Al-Fatah* Revolutionary Command", Abu Nidal's band appeared under various names (Black September, Black June, Black March) and in shifting links with other groups. It was kept secret even from the PALESTINE LIBERATION ORGANIZATION, with confusing disinformation deliberately spread concerning its location, operations and identity. A long list of the most brutal terrorist attacks, hijackings and assassinations—including the murder of rival Palestinian leaders—is ascribed to Abu Nidal and his group. As he refused to submit to the decisions and discipline of the PLO leadership, he and his group were reportedly expelled from the PLO in 1972 or 1974 and he was sentenced to death by the PLO. Abu Nidal and his group were reportedly hosted and supported by Iraq (until the late 1970s), and then by Syria until 1985, followed by Libya and since 1990 again by Iraq. The group's attempts to gain control of Palestinian camps in South Lebanon were defeated by ARAFAT's mainstream *Fatah* in bloody battles in 1990. There have been reports of internal rifts and power struggles inside Abu Nidal's group, but information is contradictory and confusing.

BANTE, TEFERI   (?–1977) An Ethiopian general who took part in the ETHIOPIAN REVOLUTION OF 1974. Bante was of Oromo (a Kushitic people that invaded Ethiopia during the 17th century in search for new lands) origin, a fact that he tried very hard to conceal. During the 1960s he served as a military attaché to Washington. Following Haile Selassie's overthrow he was appointed by the Derg (the provisional military administrative council) to command the second division in Eritrea. After the murder of the first chairman of the Derg, AMAN ANDOM, on November 22, 1974, Bante became the new chairman. Bante belonged to the moderate wing of the Derg and supported negotiations with the rebels in Eritrea. Following severe differences that resulted in a gun fight during one of the Derg's meetings in August 1976, Bante decided to redefine his authority and limit those of his two vice-chairmen, HAILE MIRIAM MENGISTU and Atnafu Abate. Bante also replaced all the committee heads that supported Mengistu and created a new secretarial position which had larger powers than the two vice-chairmen. On March 2, 1977, Mengistu left a Derg meeting in the middle and a group of his supporters entered the room and killed all the people present, including Teferi Bante himself.

BARAZANI, MULLA MUSTAFA   (1901–1979) Leader of the Kurdish revolt against Iraq. Joining the rebellion at an early age, Barazani spent much of the 1930s alternating between Iraqi prisons and Iranian exile; in 1943 he returned and assumed the leadership of a new rebellion. In 1945–1946 he again crossed into Iran and in 1946 commanded the army of the short-lived Kurdish Republic of Mahabad. After its collapse he escaped with a band of followers to the USSR (although he was no Communist, the

Soviet Union had supported the Mahabad republic). Barazani remained in Russia until permitted to return to Iraq after QASSEM's coup of 1958. He and his men supported Qassem against both Nasserist and Communist attempts to take over the country, but he himself was not permitted to leave Baghdad. When Kurdish hopes were disappointed by the Qassem régime and a new rebellion began fermenting, Barazani escaped to the Kurdish mountains in 1960–1961 and assumed the leadership of the renewed rebellion. Even though the military fortunes of that rebellion were declining, Iraq's armed forces were unable to liquidate it. Barazani had obtained significant aid from the shah of Iran and was able to use Iranian territory as a supply base and staging area. He also received aid, training etc. from Israel.

While Barazani's leadership remained essentially traditional and tribal, he maintained a firm alliance with political nationalist groups and formally headed the modernist-socialist Kurdish Democratic Party that had led the national struggle since the 1950s. Yet his leadership was beset by both tribal and political-factional rivalries and defections, and his rivals (such as Jalai Talabani) frequently collaborated with the Iraqi authorities. Throughout the rebellion, Barazani conducted on and off negotiations with Iraq, offering to end the rebellion for far-reaching autonomy for the Kurds. An agreement conceding a large part of Barazani's demand was reached in June 1966, but as it was not implemented the rebellion was renewed in 1968. A new agreement, even more far-reaching, was signed with the BA'ATH régime in March 1970. Again the Kurds held that it was not honestly implemented, and in March 1974 Barazani's fighters, the *Pesh Merga*, resumed battle. In March 1975, Iraq reached an agreement with Iran after which the Shah stopped his aid to the

Kurdish leader Mustapha Barazani in a smiling mood

Kurdish rebels and closed his territory to the rebels and their supplies. The rebellion collapsed and on March 20, 1975, Barazani announced its end in defeat. Barazani himself was among more than 100,000 refugees who escaped to Iran. He later went to the USA, where he died in 1979, a refugee and a broken man.

One of Barazani's sons 'Ubaid-ullah, was reported to be collaborating with the Baghdad government. Two others, Idris and Mas'ud, worked from the late 1970s to rebuild the Kurdish Democratic party and resume armed resistance, collaborating against the Iraqi régime with KHOMEINI's Iran (a rival Iranian wing of the party, rebelling against Khomeini, collaborates with Iraq). Idris died in January 1987 and Mas'ud Barazani became the main leader of the Kurdish rebels (still competing, but also frequently cooperating, with Talabani). A new rebellion, begun in March 1991, after SADDAM HUSSEIN's defeat in the Gulf war, was encouraged but not effectively aided by the USA. It was partly successful and reestablished Kurdish control over a wide area in northern and northeastern Iraq. Since June 1991, Barazani and Talabani have been negotiating with the Iraqi government for the reestablishment of an autonomic Kurdish region; so far, no agreement has been reached.

BAR KOKHBA REBELLION Jewish revolt against Rome in Judea, 132–135 A.D. The revolt was provoked by a number of edicts issued by the Roman Emperor Hadrian in the years just prior to 130 A.D. First and foremost was Hadrian's decision to build a Roman city, Aelia Capitolina, with a temple to Jupiter on the ruins of the Jerusalem temple. This enraged the Jews, who had dreamed of restoring their own temple. Hadrian's edicts also restricted the study of Jewish law and Jewish religious observance, including a ban on circumcision. Simeon bar Koziba, purportedly hailed by Rabbi Akiba ben Joseph as the messiah and given the name Bar Kokhba (Son of the Star), organized a revolt that swept the country. Jerusalem was recaptured and coins were minted, dated the year of "Jerusalem's liberation" or of "Israel's redemption."

After initial setbacks, the Romans sent a large army to Palestine—some 35,000 men—under the leadership of Gaius Julius Severus. The Romans gradually reclaimed the territory lost to Bar Kokhba, including Jerusalem. The cruel war, which lasted three and a half years and which had support for Bar Kokhba by the Jews of the Diaspora, approached its end when Bar Kokhba was besieged at Bethar, in the Judean hills. When that fortress fell, Bar Kokhba was killed. According to tradition, this occurred on the ninth of the Hebrew month of Av in 135 A.D., on the anniversary of the destruction of the two temples in Jerusalem. In addition to those who died of disease and hunger, there were said to have been 585,000 Jewish casualties of war.

The aftermath of the war saw cruel repression by Hadrian that desolated Judea, turned Jerusalem into a heathen town and imposed severe restrictions on the practice of Judaism. Though few details are available, many modern historians regard the Bar Kokhba revolt as the greatest disaster that ever befell the Jewish people until the Holocaust. Until early in the present century, however, despite many references to the leader in the Talmud, Bar Kokhba's name gave rise to few echoes. Interest in Bar Kokhba was revived by the appearance of Zionism, when he was turned into a national hero.

Tetradrachm of Bar Kokhba showing Temple façade, with the legend: 'Simeon' (i.e., Simon Bar-Kosiba = Bar Kokhba)

BAR KOKHBA, SIMEON (135 A.D.) Leader of a major Jewish revolt against Rome in Judea, 132–135. There are few reliable sources about his life and most of what is known derives from Talmudic legends of his courage and heroism and from administrative and economic documents. The name Bar Kokhba (Son of the Star) probably alludes to the messianic hopes placed in him by Rabbi Akiba; his real name appears to have been Ben or Bar Koziba, which appears on contemporary documents. After the defeat, his name was given a derogatory interpretation, son of a lie (derived from the Hebrew *kazav, "lie"*).

He had a reputation of being an autocratic and domineering ruler, requiring total obedience to his authority and total commitment to ending Roman rule of Judea and reestablishing the temple. Legend relates that in order to join his army, men were required to cut off a finger and that the rabbis, disapproving of the practice, suggested that in its place the men be required to uproot a cedar. Saint Jerome wrote that Bar Kokhba used to keep fanning a lighted blade of straw in his mouth to give the impression that he was spewing out flames. From stories such as this emerges the picture of Bar Kokhba as a driven and uncompromising leader. Another legend relates that he relied more on his own power than that of God, and that when greeted with the greeting "Gold will help" on going into battle, responded "God will neither assist nor weaken." However, there is historical evidence that he was indeed a religious man. In recent years, signed letters from him have been found in the Judean desert, addressed to one of his commanders, reminding him to separate the tithe and to provide Sabbath accommodation for visitors.

He was killed in the month of Av, according to tradition, when the Romans seized the fortress at Bethar.

BARNAVE, ANTOINE (1761–1793) One of the most prominent leaders of the FRENCH REVOLUTION during its first and more moderate phase, well before the revolution was overtaken by the rush of events and diverted into a more radical direction than

originally intended. A Protestant by birth, a lawyer by profession, Barnave was elected by his constituents in Grenoble to represent the Third Estate from the province of Dauphiné in the Estates General convened to meet in Versailles in May 1789. It was Barnave, carried away by the wave of revolutionary exuberance produced by the event, who justified the bloodshed that followed the fall of the Bastille by uttering the celebrated words, "Was this blood, then, so pure," thus making himself, like so many other early revolutionaries, an apologist of terror before he, too, became its victim.

In the debates at Versailles, Barnave emerged as the most outspoken leader of a radical faction in the Constituent Assembly and was rivalled only by MIRABEAU, who soon rallied to the conservative side as its most eloquent speaker. Barnave argued, along with his allies Duport and Lameth, in favor of the establishment of a limited constitutional monarchy composed of an assembly based on a unicameral rather than bicameral legislature, for fear that an upper chamber would promote the resurgence of the aristocracy as an obstacle to reform. But the spectacle of the embattled royal family in the wake of the aborted escape to Varennes moved him to change his mind and advocate a

Man of the people, man of the court: Barnave, 1789–1791

stronger role for the Crown as the only possible bulwark to stem the tide of revolutionary excess. It was at this point, after having been delegated by the Assembly to escort the royal couple back to Paris, that he entered into a secret correspondence with Marie Antoinette. This followed their conversation on the road back from Varennes, in a last-ditch effort to persuade the king to ratify the monarchical constitution and thereby endorse a revolutionary settlement before it could be threatened by a growing popular demand to overthrow the monarchy altogether and proclaim a republic in its place.

Following the massacre of the CHAMP DE MARS on July 17, 1791, when a petition calling for the abdication of Louis XVI, drawn up and circulated by radical elements in Paris, seemed to pave the way for things to come, Barnave played an active part in establishing the Club des Feuillants, made up of repentant constitutional monarchists like himself who were resolved to resist any further erosion of royal authority in the face of republican fervor. Arrested during the Terror as a counter-revolutionary, Barnave was brought to trial before the revolutionary tribunal, and is said to have comported himself with dignity without ever losing his composure as he tried to refute the charges brought against him by his JACOBIN enemies. The prosecution accused him of conspiring with the royal family as well as with the MARQUIS DE DAFAYETTE, the cofounder of the Feuillant club, who had then discredited his cause by defecting to the Austrians in order to restore the monarchy. Barnave was found guilty, condemned to death, and sent to the guillotine on November 29, 1793.

BARRAS, PAUL FRANÇOIS (1755–1829) A viscount under the Old Régime in France and a former officer in the elite Regiment of the Languedoc, Barras cast his lot with the FRENCH REVOLUTION after 1789 and was elected as a JACOBIN deputy to the convention, where he voted in favor of the immediate execution of the king without appeal to the people. Delegated as a "representative on mission" to the provinces to suppress royalist and GIRONDIN agitation, he participated with General Napoleon Bonaparte in the recapture and defense of the naval base of Toulon, which had opened its port to the British. Fearing for his life during the most extreme phase of the terror introduced by ROBESPIERRE's Law of Suspects, he joined hands with JEAN TALLIEN, Louis Fréron, Joseph Fouché and other moderate members of the convention in overthrowing Robespierre, SAINT-JUST and COUTHON in July 1794 and became a prominent figure in the Thermidorian (i.e., conservative) reaction that followed the Jacobin dictatorship. Again with the aid of Bonaparte, he put down the attempted royalist coup of 13 Vendémaire (October 5, 1795), which might have paved the way to a Bourbon restoration. He was instrumental in consolidating the republic, now called the Directorate, by providing it with a new constitution, the Constitution of the Year III, designed to implement a strict separation of powers between the executive and legislative branches of government.

It was during the Directorate (1795–1799) that Barras gained notoriety as the strong man of the new revolutionary régime. Based on a dual fear of democracy and dictatorship, the constitution of the Directorate restricted the franchise to the propertied classes and gave power to those who had done well out of the revolutionary settlement. Barras typified a new class of men

made up purchasers of national property (confiscated from the clergy and the *emigré* nobility), war contractors, speculators, profiteers and *nouveaux riches* who had a vested interest in perpetuating the revolution and its foreign conquests. It was Barras who arranged for the appointment of Bonaparte to command the army of Italy and also his marriage to his discarded mistress, Joséphine de Beauharnais, in 1797. In the following year, he persuaded the rest of the Directorate to give their blessing to Bonaparte's invasion of Egypt, a move that was really meant to keep the ambitious general away from Paris.

By then Barras's name had become a byword for corruption and loose living and, although he condoned the overthrow of the Directorate by accepting a large bribe on the eve of Bonaparte's coup d'état of 18 Brumaire (November 9) 1799, his reputation for venality and, excessive licentiousness excluded him from playing any further role under the Consulate and the Empire. Following the second abdication of Napoleon after the Hundred Days, Barras returned from his exile in Rome to spend the remainder of his life at his estate in Chaillot, where he finished his much-quoted memoirs.

AL-BASHIR, OMAR HASSAN AHMAD see SUDAN, COUPS IN.

BASHMIR, OMAR HASSAN see SUDAN, COUPS IN.

BASHIR, SHIHAB II (1767–1851) Lebanese Druze leader (1788–1840). Bashir was appointed emir of the Mount Lebanon Druze with the support of the prominent Jumblatt family. During his rule he made every effort to secure Mount Lebanon's autonomy from the Ottoman Empire, often alienating the leading Druze clans, including eventually the Jumblatts. Heavy taxes and land confiscations brought an end to Lebanese feudalism, but the land was redivided among Bashir's family and supporters rather than returned to the peasants. Bashir, in return for assurances of Druze autonomy in Lebanon, supported MUHAMMAD ALI's attempt to win independence for Egypt and Syria from the Ottomans. However, he acceded to Ali's demands for Druze disarmament, conscription and increased taxation, thereby losing most of his followers. In 1840, he surrendered to Turkey's British allies and was sent into exile.

BASQUE REVOLUTION Basque nationalism has gained in intensity ever since the short-lived creation of a small Basque mini-state during the SPANISH CIVIL WAR in 1936 and since the 1960s and 1970s has taken the form of a struggle for national independence, often violent and ruthless, on the part of a distinctive people of mysterious origin.

Known by the Spaniards as *Vazascondas*, a Spanish ethnic designation they have adopted to distinguish themselves from their neighbors, the Basques have been settled for centuries in the western foothills of the Pyrenees, dwelling in scattered communities on both sides of the border between France and Spain. A deeply religious people of Catholic persuasion, speaking a language unrelated to any other in the world and taking pride in traditions perpetuated in their folk tales centered around the legendary convocation of tribal councils that met twice a year around an oak tree in the town of Guernica, the Basques were swept along by the 19th-century ideology of nationalism, asserting their right to independence and self-determination in

Navarre and three other adjacent home provinces. Since the French, to say nothing of the Spanish, governments have never been willing to concede anything more than local autonomy, many Basques began supporting the terrorist tactics of a revolutionary extremist organization, whose campaign of violence in Bilbao, San Sebastien and even Madrid gained in intensity in the 1970s.

Harking back to the martyrs of Guernica, ruthlessly destroyed in an aerial bombardment by FRANCO's German allies on April 27, 1937 and commemorated by Picasso's celebrated canvas produced for the Spanish pavilion at the Paris World Exhibition in the summer of 1937, the Basques reverted to terrorist tactics in the 1970s and 1980s, notably in San Sebastien and Pamplona, after rejecting King Juan Carlos's offer of limited home rule.

BASTILLE, FALL OF THE   On July 14, 1789, the people of Paris stormed this royal fortress dominating the Right Bank working class quarter of the Faubourg Saint Antoine and thereby rescued the FRENCH REVOLUTION from an impending threat of a counterrevolution contemplated by Louis XVI, who had withdrawn from Versailles to hatch a royalist coup d'état from the safety of the Palace of Saint Cloud. The dramatic event, commemorated to this day as France's national holiday, has come to symbolize the triumph of freedom and democracy over despotism and autocracy. More significantly, the fall of the Bastille at the hands of popular insurrection "led by the people in arms" has stood out in revolutionary mythology as both a symbol and a call for action. This defining moment in the French Revolution has inspired all subsequent revolutionary movements, both in Europe and throughout the world, with the desire to emulate the French in rejecting the status quo and overthrowing old régimes in the name of human rights and popular democracy.

Under Louis XVI, the Bastille had been used as a military arsenal and fortress. But it had also gained exaggerated notoriety as a state prison as a result of pamphlets circulated in France on the eve of the revolution to discredit the *ancien régime* as the embodiment of feudalism and arbitrary rule. Thus its fall came to be interpreted as a supreme gesture of defiance against royal

The fall of the Bastille, July 14, 1789

absolutism. The attack on the fortress, whose guns were menacingly directed against the people of Paris, was precipitated by Louis XVI's decision to stifle the revolution by resorting to military force in order to dissolve the National Assembly gathered in Versailles. Inspired by political agitators to stand up for liberty and defend their lives against the threat of armed dictatorship, the crowd fought its way across an unguarded drawbridge to seize the Bastille's keep, butchered the governor and the chief representative of the Paris municipal authority—whose heads were paraded around Paris on a pike—and then set about dismantling the Bastille stone by stone in a frenzy of hatred of feudal oppression and aristocratic privilege. That task was then taken up by professional house breakers, who made a handsome profit out of the whole affair.

The episode had one immediate effect in altering the course of the French Revolution: it rescued the National Assembly sitting in Versailles from the threat of royal dissolution. But the actual events were greatly exaggerated by Jules Michelet and other 19th century French romantic historians, who tended to glorify the role of *le peuple* as the only driving force of the French Revolution. Only some 800 Frenchmen were in fact able to justify their claim to the title of "Conquerors of the Bastille," a mere handful compared to all the crowds then raging throughout Paris in search of arms. The real significance of the fall of the Bastille lies in its symbolic value. It meant that the king had lost control of Paris, and even with troops hastily called to Versailles had no chance of ever regaining it or the control of other cities in his kingdom which had followed the example of Paris in asserting their municipal autonomy. The Parisian populace, which by its rising had frustrated a royalist counterrevolution and saved the Third Estate, would henceforth control the destiny of the French Revolution.

Modern scholarship has modified this legendary event in two important respects. First, the Paris mob stormed the Bastille not to release political prisoners from its dungeons (these consisted, as it turned out, of four forgers, two lunatics and a dissipated young noble, all of them incarcerated under the notorious *lettres de cachet*), but to secure weapons to defend the capital against armed attack. In the second place, the fall of the fortress represents not the beginning of the revolution, which had been gathering momentum for the previous two years—ever since the nobles had defied royal authority—but the passing of the revolutionary initiative from the bourgeois lawyers in the Estates General to the Paris mob and its self-appointed leaders.

On July 17, the king, escorted by 50 deputies from the National Assembly in Versailles, came to Paris to receive from the hands of its newly elected mayor, the astronomer Bailly, the national cockade, which henceforth replaced the white lily flag of the *ancien régime*. The red and blue colors of the city of Paris were merged with the white of the house of Bourbon in between, to become the tricolor flag of a new revolutionary era in French history, symbolizing that Paris had reconquered the monarchy.

BATAVIAN REVOLT   SEE CIVILIS, GAIUS JULIUS.

BATAVIAN REVOLUTION   (1794–1795) From the second half of the 16th century and with only short interruptions, the Netherlands had been governed by members of the royal house of Orange who carried the title of *Stadthouder* or lieutenant-general. During the second half of the 18th century, influenced by the French example of Louis XIV and XV, William V tried to transform his position into that of an absolute monarchy and these pretensions formed the background to the appearance of the movement known as "the Patriots." Made up of an odd coalition of disaffected noblemen, wealthy bankers, artisans and shopkeepers, the movement was much influenced by the French *philosophes* and sought to move the country toward a more liberal, democratic régime. Against it stood the so-called Orangist party, mainly rurally-based, which enjoyed the support of religious people of both persuasions—Calvinist and Catholic—as well as that of the Jews, a protected minority.

The opportunity for launching a revolt finally came in 1784, when the Dutch defeat in the fourth Anglo-Dutch war (1780–1784) gave rise to widespread dissatisfaction. The province of Holland started organizing its own army, separate from that of *Stadthouder* William V. The latter thereupon panicked and fled to Gelderland. As the Estates of Holland declared that William had been deposed, the initiative passed to his wife Wilhelmina, a capable woman who was the sister of Frederick II of Prussia. Working closely with the English ambassador in the Hague, she was able to place William V's nephew, Frederick

William II, on the throne in 1786. Thereupon she arranged for a Prussian army to invade the Netherlands, scatter the Patriots—many of whom were driven into exile—and restore her husband to his former position.

The outbreak of the FRENCH REVOLUTION in 1789 gave new hope to the exiles and their friends at home. An early French attempt to invade the southern Netherlands in 1792 proved abortive; however, when French forces again crossed the border in 1794, the Patriots saw that their moment had come. As the harsh winter of 1794–1795 froze the rivers separating the southern provinces (modern Belgium) from the northern ones and allowed the French to cross, the population of the Hague rose and deposed the helpless William V, forcing him to flee to England.

Once the *Stadthouder* was no more, the Batavian Republic was proclaimed and the modernization of the country's political institutions began. Following the French model, the Patriots abolished the old system whereby power had been in the hands of the provincial estates and set up a unitary, centralized republic. They carried through a strict separation between the legislative, executive and judiciary authorities; established universal male suffrage and equality before the law and, though they did not separate state and religion, deprived the Reformed (Calvinist) Church of its position as the sole official, protected religion.

Batavian Liberty enthroned inside the Temple of the Netherlands, a contemporary print

However the republic was destined to come to an end 11 years later, when Napoleon placed his brother Louis on the Dutch throne in 1806. However, the remaining reforms instituted by the Patriots proved lasting through all subsequent changes in the form of government (from monarchy to part of the French Empire and back) and have formed the basis of the Dutch political system ever since.

BAUER, OTTO (1881–1938) Austrian socialist leader; leading theoretician of the AUSTRIAN SOCIAL DEMOCRATIC PARTY in the interwar period. Bauer was born in Vienna, the son of a wealthy textile industrialist. Like many Jewish intellectuals of his time, he joined the socialist movement. His parents were assimilated into German culture and there is no evidence that Bauer received any Jewish or religious education or indeed had any knowledge of Judaism.

Bauer's interests were broad, including sociology, history, philosophy, literature, anthropology, psychology and Marxist politics. After obtaining his law degree from the University of Vienna, he cofounded the monthly *Der Kampf* (The Struggle). This journal became a forum for socialist discussion. As a leader of the neo-Marxist school in Vienna and secretary to the Socialist faction in the Austrian parliament, Bauer presented a reassessment of the "national" question, introducing the role of nationalism into Marxist socialism. A nation, he claimed in his classic work, *Die Nationalitätenfrage und die Sozialdemokratie* (The Nationalities Question and Social Democracy) was "the totality of men united through a community of fate into a community of character."

During World War I he acted on his nationalist convictions and, unlike the more extreme socialists, not only supported the war but fought in the Austrian army and was a prisoner-of-war in Russia. In November 1918, following the collapse of the Austro-Hungarian Empire, Bauer became the first foreign minister of the Austrian republic. It was in this capacity that he strove for *Anschluss* (unification) with Germany and worked to keep the Sudeten Germans inside Austria. He resigned in July 1919 but remained a dominant force in the party. When Engelbert Dollfuss's Fascist régime came to power in 1934, Bauer took a leading part in the uprising of the workers in Vienna. He was forced to find refuge in Czechoslovakia and then Paris.

Seeing the deteriorating situation in Austria and the country's anti-Jewish decrees, Bauer abandoned his earlier views on the inevitability of assimilation. In his final article before his death in 1938, Bauer appealed to the world's conscience to save the 300,000 Jews in Austria from Nazi aggression. Bauer was an outstanding figure within the Socialist International; a prolific writer on socialist problems, opposing communism but representing the Marxist left wing within socialism.

BAYBARS (Bibars I) (1223–1277) Mameluke sultan of Egypt and Syria. Born in Caucasia, Baybars was sold into slavery at an early age and taken to Egypt. There he entered the corps of slave soldiers, or Mamelukes, and rose to become its commander. Having commanded the Egyptian vanguard at the battle of Ayn Jalud (1260) in which he defeated the Mongols, he revolted against the sultan, Sayf al-Dain Kutuz, and took over power himself. As sultan, he was able to extend his rule both over Syria and over parts of Saudi Arabia.

BAZARGAN, MEHDI (1905–) Iranian politician and first prime minister (1979) of the AYATOLLAH KHOMEINI's Islamic régime. Born in Tabriz in 1905 to a well-known family of merchants, Bazargan graduated with a degree in thermodynamic engineering from Paris University. He began his revolutionary career in the 1940s as a deputy minister in MUHAMMAD MOSSADDEQ's radical government (1951–1953) and as chairman of the Committee for Oil Nationalization. During the 1950s he was also general manager of the Tehran Water Board and dean of the Tehran University Technical College.

After Mossaddeq's fall in 1953, Bazargan was active in anti-shah groups, such as the revived National Front, in the early 1960s. In 1961 he founded his own Iran Liberation (or Freedom) Movement. He was also among the founders of the Human Rights Association in 1977. Bazargan was arrested several times.

During the course of the IRANIAN REVOLUTION OF 1979, Khomeini appointed him prime minister, namely the head of a transitional government composed mainly of members of the National Front and of Bazargan's Liberation Movement. Bazargan was also appointed to the central committee of the ruling Islamic Republic party and was in charge of labor affairs in the Council of the Islamic Revolution. His appointment was an expression of Khomeini's appreciation of his personal integrity, Islamic fervor and his struggle against the Shah. It was not a mandate for his faction, and the real power remained in the hands of Khomeini, the Council of the Islamic Revolution, the Revolutionary Guards and the clergy. Bazargan tried to resign in March and August 1979 in protest against the closing of newspapers, the banning of party activities and mass executions. However, only on November 5, 1979, a day after the seizure of 62 American hostages, did Khomeini finally accept his resignation.

Bazargan was allowed to continue expressing moderate opposition to the new régime—the only politician to be granted such freedom. In 1980 he was elected to the *majlis* (parliament), where he continued to criticize the government, calling, for example, for an end to the Iran-Iraq war. He was, however, restricted, frequently harassed and forbidden to maintain an active organization or publish a newspaper. In 1984 he refused (or was not permitted) to run again for the *majlis*, and in 1985 the régime prevented him from presenting his candidacy for the presidency. Since 1986, when he was barred from setting up an Association for the Nation's Sovereignty and Freedom, he has been heard of only on occasion.

BAZAROV (RUDNEV), VLADIMIR ALEXANDROVICH (1874–1939) Russian economist and philosopher. Born in Tula, Bazarov went on to study in Moscow University, where he was arrested for revolutionary activity and expelled in 1892. After years of alternate exile and political involvement, he emigrated to Berlin in 1901, where he was one of a group attempting to unify the quarreling factions of the Russian Social Democrats. For some years he was a BOLSHEVIK, but found the movement's outlook philosophically incompatible with his own concept of socialism. In 1917, he was one of Maxim Gorky's group and wrote for the newspaper *Novaya zhizn*, espousing the MENSHEVIK internationalist view. At the time of the Bolshevik seizure of power, Bazarov called for a broad socialist coalition and the immediate convening of the long-promised constituent assembly.

In 1922, Bazarov began work for the State Economic Planning Commission, where he became well known for his views on the gradual development of industry and the primary accumulation of capital through development of Russia's agricultural sector. Although arrested in 1930 and imprisoned for a year and a half on charges of counterrevolutionary activity, Bazarov was never tried. After his release he lived in Moscow, translating philosophical texts until his death of natural causes.

AL-BAZZAZ, ABDUL RAHMAN   (1913–1973) Iraqi nationalist and jurist; a Sunni Muslim born in Baghdad. A fervent nationalist, Bazzaz was detained in 1941, after the defeat of the RASHID 'ALI KILANI régime, for his anti-British and pro-German attitude. From 1955, he was dean of the Baghdad Law College. In 1957, he was arrested for Nasserist anti-régime activities which helped precipitate the IRAQ REVOLUTION OF 1958. After the July revolution, Bazzaz was among those pushing the new régime toward Nasserist politics and in 1959 was arrested for his suspected involvement in a Nasserist plot. After ABDUL KARIM QASSEM's fall in 1963, Bazzaz held several prominent government positions, becoming prime minister in 1965. He tried to restore civilian-political rule and thus soon fell out with the army officers really in control. After the *Ba'ath* coup of July 1968, Bazzaz was arrested for plotting with the western powers. He was released in 1970 and went into exile to England, where he died in July 1973.

BEBEL, AUGUST   (1840–1913) German socialist leader. Bebel began his long political and parliamentary career as a Saxon, anti-Prussian, Marxist labor leader. He then accepted the reality of a united, undemocratic Germany in order to transform it gradually to a free socialist society. Bebel and WILHELM LIEBKNECHT were the founding fathers of the Social Democratic party of Germany (SPD), which united various socialist organizations and amended some original, radical programs adopted at the Gotha Conference of 1875 in an endeavor "to obtain the free state and the Socialist society—by all legal means." Bebel's role was crucial in maintaining the party's core and spirit when the party was declared illegal by Chancellor V. Bismarck. In 1890, the SPD managed not only to survive but to defeat Bismarck's anti-socialist laws at the polls—the only legal avenue allowed to it. Bebel did not use this victory to openly challenge the bourgeois society, as he defined it. Instead, he pursued a parliamentary legal course, related in his view to the Marxist maxim of the unavoidable growth and weight of the industrial proletariat, while ignoring MARX's revolutionary phase as such. Consequently, he was regarded as a typically moderate socialist bureaucrat. He generated severe criticism from the Left, as well as from the Right, for being a "revisionist" (i.e., moderate, reform) Social Democrat.

BEER HALL PUTSCH OF 1923   The name given to Hitler's gamble in attempting to assume power in Munich and to force the German far right to overthrow democracy in Germany. The Putsch, or coup of 1923 resulted from a general crisis in Weimar, Germany. The Ruhr region was occupied by the French and hyperinflation was destroying the entire German middle class; socialist and Communist coalitions ruled Saxony and Thuringia, the former directly assisted by Moscow, which seemed to have justified a separate Bavarian, ultra-rightist government. The measures taken by the central government in Berlin and by local army commanders against the Communist ministers elsewhere had not yet been repeated in Bavaria itself, an inaction which led to the resignation of the socialist ministers from chancellor Stresemann's central government. The steps taken against the Communists, and the end of the Communist threat mainly in Saxony, made the Bavarian conservatives drop a plan secretly conceived beforehand not just to maintain a separate régime in their federal state, but to unite the whole German far right and overthrow the Weimar Republic. Hitler's Nazi party was a part of that conspiracy, but he was not its one and only leader. A loose far-right organization—of which Hitler was just the political leader, not the military commander—was formed and expected a signal from the Bavarian army to march on Berlin. The Bavarian government, though, retreated from the march, once satisfied with the defeat of the Communists and the resulting resignation of the socialists from Stresemann's cabinet. Hitler then decided to march on his own, ordering his SA (*Sturmabteilungen*), with the support of some other far-right units and with General Ludendorff marching in the front, to force the hand of the Bavarian conservative government, whose members he took prisoner and held in a beer hall. He trusted them not to flee, which, however, they did. The government then ordered the riot police to open fire on Hitler's men. This was on November 9, 1923. Hitler fled but was arrested and convicted to five years' "fortress arrest" at Landsberg. The lessons he learned from this failure were profound: first, not to allow his SA to be subordinated to the military command of other far-right but less reliable organizations; second, not to allow it to march alone against the armed might of the State; third, not to trust conservative, or any, allies, but to blackmail and gain effective control over them; fourth, to undermine conservative power by becoming an independent, yet flexible "voice of the young, the simple front soldiers" and generate an opaque but radical anti-establishment message. All of these later helped him on his way to seize power.

BEGIN, MENAHEM   (1913–1992) Israeli prime minister, leader of the Jewish underground movement, the IRGUN ZVAI LEUMI, during the British mandate over Palestine, proponent of Revisionist Zionism (a strongly nationalist approach which opposed the Zionist mainstream as too moderate), and Nobel Peace Prize recipient. Born in Brest-Litovsk, Poland, to an ardent Zionist family, at the age of 15 Begin joined the Zionist youth movement, Betar, which advocated the immediate establishment of a Jewish state in Palestine.

By 1939 Begin had become the Betar commissioner (head) in Czechoslovakia and later the Betar chief in Poland, where he played a major role in expediting the illegal immigration of Jews to Palestine. After Poland was invaded in 1939, Begin and a few members of his family escaped to Vilnius, then under Soviet rule. The Soviets arrested him in 1940 for his Zionist activities and sent him to a Siberian concentration camp. His eight-year sentence was commuted when ADOLF HITLER invaded Russia. He was allowed to join the Polish force formed by General Wladyslaw Anders and sent by the Allies to the Middle East. In 1942 he made his way to Palestine, where he became the Betar chief in Jerusalem. From 1943 he commanded the Irgun Zvai Leumi (the National Army Organization)—known as the

Irgun—an extremist and paramilitary underground aligned with Revisionist Zionist factions. In 1944, the Irgun declared war on the British forces in Palestine and Begin planned and executed a guerrilla campaign against them.

In 1946, Begin ordered the bombing of the King David hotel, in which 91 persons (Britons, Jews and Arabs) were killed. His most controversial act, however, came in early 1948 when the Irgun, together with the even more militant Stern Group, carried out an operation in the Arab village of Deir Yassin, during which large numbers of Arabs were killed. For the Palestinians, this action became a symbol of Jewish ruthlessness.

When the mandate of the British government in Palestine ended and DAVID BEN-GURION proclaimed the independence of the State of Israel in May 1948, Begin and his group emerged from the underground.

With the establishment of the State of Israel, Begin founded his parliamentary party, *Herut* (Freedom). His policy was one of extreme nationalism with some religious emphasis, and included, in principle, the claim to a Jewish state "on both sides of the Jordan," opposition to socialist trends and the primacy of the State. He remained in the opposition on other issues as well, initially representing only a small minority of voters.

As the 1950s and 1960s wore on, Begin began to acquire respectability, especially between 1967 (just prior to the Six Day War) and 1970, when he served as minister without portfolio in a government of national unity. In 1977, the *Likud* rode to power for the first time in the national elections.

A few months after the election, at the initiative of ANWAR SADAT, Begin hosted the Egyptian president in Jerusalem, in what became the first official step in the process that led to the signing of a peace treaty between the two countries in March 1979. For his efforts in the peace process, he won the 1978 Nobel Peace Prize jointly with Sadat.

In 1982, Begin ordered the invasion of Lebanon. The war turned out to be a terrible failure for Israel. As it dragged on Begin was deeply affected by the growing roster of Israeli casualties. Within a year his wife died and Begin resigned from public life in September 1983. Thereafter he lived as a recluse in his own home. He wrote two books, *White Nights*, on his experiences in Soviet prison camps, and *The Revolt*, on his fight against the British.

BELARUS PEOPLE'S FRONT (BPF—Adradzhenne) A broad-based political (revolutionary) movement for the national regeneration of Belarus based on the principles of democracy and humanism, the development of culture and the achievement of real political independence. It has been active since 1988. Its political activities include participation in election campaigns and mass actions, analysis of the national economic situation, proposed alternative programs, as well as cultural and educational work. Its leader, Zenon Pozdniak, began work in the ranks of the Stalin's Victims Memorial Historical Educational Society (*Martirolog Balarusi*). The movement's constituent congress took place in June 1989 in Vilnius. It adopted a program which spoke of the necessity of abolishing the Communist party's monopoly and of establishing a multiparty system in Belarus. In addition, the congress proposed that different forms of property ownership be legalized, that the Byelorussian republic be integrated into the European economic structure and that only

the Byelorussian language be recognized as the state language.

In 1989–1994, the BPF undertook numerous environmental actions, attempted to create workers' strike committees and a Belarus Army Union, and initiated legislative innovations in the Belarus parliament. It developed close ties with the people's front movements in the ex-USSR states of the Baltics, Ukraine and Moldova and has representatives in Poland, the USA and Canada. At the same time, most of the BPF's activities have been no more than declarative. Its ideas and slogans have been voiced primarily by nationalist intellectuals, but have not been supported by the major part of the population. The BPF opposes any union with Russia. It regards Moscow as the chief opponent to Belarus national independence and the main culprit responsible for the deep economic, political, cultural and ecological crises in Belarus. The BPF has proposed the creation of a Baltic Black Sea Union, to include Belarus, Latvia, Lithuania, Estonia and the Ukraine, but without Russia. The BPF supported national regeneration and demanded the rapid nationalization of Belarus (the so-called "Belorusizatsia"). The national minorities in Belarus—the Russians, Ukrainians, Poles, Jews and others, have not supported the Front.

In July 1994, in the first Belarus presidential election, Alexander Lukashenko, a strong opponent of the BPF, received 80% of the votes. Lukashenko promised to continue the course of Belarus regeneration, but at the same time to reconstruct the traditional economical and cultural ties with its neighbors, above all Russia, which had been broken earlier.

BELINSKY, VISSARION GRIGORYEVICH (1811–1848) Radical Russian literary critic and philosopher. Like many of his contemporaries, Belinsky's radicalism was influenced heavily by German philosophy. Hegel, Fichte and Schelling all helped form his outlook. His Hegelian acceptance of the régime of Nicholas I brought him into bitter conflict with HERZEN. Belinsky was expelled from Moscow university in 1832 for criticizing the institution of serfdom in a play that he wrote. He gradually became more radically critical of the czarist régime, moving to left Hegelian positions.

By 1842, Belinsky had adopted the then-popular outlook of Fourierist socialism and had acquainted himself with the entire spectrum of French socialist thought based on psychological and moral foundations. His political and philosophical explorations initiated the wave of western radical thought that held sway in Russian circles through the 1840s, in opposition to the romantic Slavophilism then resurgent in nationalist circles. At the same time Belinsky had established himself as a radical literary critic, evaluating literature principally from the standpoint of its social commitment.

In 1847, Belinsky went with BAKUNIN to Paris to seek opportunities for practical political activity but, unlike Bakunin, Herzen and a multitude of other Russian revolutionaries, Belinsky felt himself stifled and cut off when outside Russia and hastened back, despite Bakunin's warnings that nothing but arrest and exile awaited him in Russia. His death at the age of 36 saved him from the czarist police repression that accompanied the REVOLUTIONS OF 1848 in Europe.

BELLUM SOCIALE (War of the Allies) Revolt of the Italian allies of Rome (91–87 B.C.). Rome had extended its rule over

Italy in the 5th to the 3rd centuries B.C. by defeating the various city-states and tribes of the peninsula. In some cases it annexed the vanquished states and bestowed Roman citizenship upon their citizens. In most cases, however, separate treaties were signed with the Italian city-states and tribes, which maintained their autonomy but had to provide Rome with military assistance in its wars and to refrain from attacks against other Roman allies. These Italian allies helped Rome overcome the Hannibalic crisis and provided it with the military manpower it needed for the conquest of the provinces. These allies eventually became exasperated with the growing interference of Rome in their internal affairs and the discrimination against their soldiers, notably in the distribution of booty seized in the wars overseas. From the Gracchan period on, they gradually realized that the solution to their problems was to attain Roman citizenship, even at the expense of losing autonomy. When in 91 B.C. an attempt to enfranchise them was selfishly defeated in Rome, they rose in rebellion, aiming at setting up a separate Italian confederacy. The Roman army suffered several defeats in the ensuing war and it was only after bills were passed to confer on the allies Roman citizenship that Rome was able to subdue those who had persisted in the revolt.

BELOBORODOV, ALEXANDER (1891–193?) Bolshevik revolutionary activist. Beloborodov joined the BOLSHEVIK faction in 1908 and in the RUSSIAN REVOLUTION OF 1917 was active in the Ural mountain region. As chairman of the regional soviet, he was in charge of arrangements for the guarding of the czar and his family, and ultimately, for their execution in the city of Ekaterinburg. In 1918 he was elected a member of the central committee of the Russian Communist party. During the civil war he was deputy commissar for political affairs in the RED ARMY, working under LEON TROTSKY. After the civil war he was appointed people's commissar for internal affairs. As a supporter of Trotsky, Beloborodov was removed from positions of responsibility. He disappeared in the purges of the 1930s and was executed in one of the prison labor camps.

BENARIO, OLGA (1908–1942) Jewish-German Communist revolutionary. Born in Munich, Benario joined the Communists in 1923. She met and fell in love with OTTO BRAUN, with whom she moved to Berlin and joined the red fortress of the German left. During her stay in Berlin she registered with the police under the assumed name of Frieda Wolf Behrendt. She was also known as Olga Sinek and Eva Kruger. As she gained notoriety within the Communist organizations and the German police, she was thought to be involved in carrying out Braun's secret orders and both were imprisoned in Germany. After her release from jail, she aided in Braun's liberation. The two then moved to the Soviet Union, where both worked for the COMINTERN. In Moscow, she was ordered to take charge of LUIZ CARLOS PRESTES's security upon his return to Brazil, after a three-year stay in the Soviet Union. They left Moscow in December 1934. As part of the scheme, they were to pose as a newly wed Portuguese couple on their way to Peru for their honeymoon. They travelled from France with false passports, under the assumed names of Antonio Vilar and María Bergner Vilar. Luiz Carlos Prestes and Olga Benario became real-life husband and wife and as such arrived in Brazil. The *Intentiona Comunista*, a re-

volt initiated by Prestes, was quickly suppressed and both Luiz-Carlos and Olga were imprisoned. Against the constitutional decree that prohibited the deportation of any foreign woman pregnant by a Brazilian man, Olga, known at that time as María Prestes, was deported to Germany by order of President Vargas. As María Prestes had no criminal record in Brazil, her deportation was seen as a vengeful act against her husband. Prestes's daughter was born in the German prison of Barnimstrasse on November 27, 1936. Thanks to the international campaign headed by Prestes's mother and sister, the young girl was released to her grandmother's care while Olga Benario remained in prison. She was transferred to Lichtenburg concentration camp, then to Ravansbrück. She was executed in the gas chamber of Bernburg in 1942.

BEN-BARKA, MEHDI (1920–1965) Moroccan nationalist leader and politician. One of the younger leaders of the *Istiqlal* Party, Ben-Barka served as chairman of the Consultative Assembly (1956–1959) that preceded the establishment of elected representatives and legislative bodies in Morocco. Within the Istiqlal, he headed a leftist faction opposed to the traditional leadership. In 1959, he seceded with his faction and founded the *Union Nationale des Forces Populaires* (The National Union of Popular Forces). Accused of involvement in subversion and plots, he soon went into exile in France. In 1963–1964 he was tried in absentia and sentenced to death, though the king later pardoned him. In October 1965, Ben-Barka disappeared in France and it was generally assumed that he had been abducted and murdered by the Moroccan secret services, though his body was never found. The "Ben-Barka Affair" caused a grave crisis in French-Moroccan relations for several years.

BEN-BELLA, AHMAD (or sometimes **Muhammad**) (1916? 1918?–) Algerian politician and leader of the nationalist revolt, president of Algeria 1963–1965. Ben-Bella emerged as a nationalist leader after World War II. He served in the French army during the war and received both the Croix de Guerre and the Médaille Militaire. Following the abortive uprising of 1945 in which over 100 Europeans were killed, he resigned and entered local politics. He was soon forced underground and joined the MOUVEMENT POUR LE TRIOMPHE DES LIBERTÉS DÉMOCRATIQUES (MTLD) led by AHMAD MESSALI HAJJ, which advocated full independence for Algeria. Discouraged by the failure of legal methods, he soon began advocating armed struggle and set up, with a group of like-minded associates, BELKACEM KRIM, Muhammad Khidr and HUSSEIN AIT-AHMAD, an underground "*Organisation Speciale*" for that purpose, thus breaking with Messali and the MTLD. In 1950 he was arrested and sentenced to seven years' imprisonment. He escaped in March 1952 to Cairo and established there the headquarters of the groups preparing an armed revolt. In 1953 his *Organisation Speciale* turned into a *Conseil Revolutionnaire pour l'Unite et l'Action*, out of which emerged the FRONT DE LIBÉRATION NATIONALE (FLN) in 1954. When the FLN began an armed revolt in November 1954, Ben-Bella was its most prominent leader. In October 1956, when Ben-Bella was flying from Morocco to Tunis, the French secret services arranged for the pilot to land at Algiers and arrested Ben-Bella and four other rebel leaders, including Khidr and Ait-Ahmad. While Ben-Bella was in prison in France and could no longer

Ben Bella (in a civilian suit) receives a hero's welcome in Algiers

lead the rebellion, his colleagues kept his place in their leadership bodies and managed to consult him; he was named, for instance, deputy premier in the FLN's provisional government of 1958 and 1961.

Ben-Bella was released in March 1962, following a French-Algerian agreement and cease-fire. In September 1963 he was elected president in a referendum, as the only candidate, nominated by the FLN.

Ben-Bella's harsh policies and his suppression of opposition leaders with a proud FLN fighting record caused much unrest and dissatisfaction. In June 1965 he was overthrown by his associate and protege HOUARI BOUMEDIENNE and imprisoned. His confinement was eased from 1979, after Boumedienne's death, and in October 1980 he was released. He refused, however, to associate himself with the régime in power and soon went into voluntary exile in France, where he co-founded various opposition groups in exile—adopting an increasingly Islamic and pro-Libyan line. These groups, factionally split, did not have much impact on political realities in Algeria. In 1982 he co-founded an "International Islamic Commission for Human Rights." After the liberalization of Algeria's régime by President CHADLI BEN-JEDID, Ben-Bella returned to Algeria in September 1990. Taking an extreme militant line, he has since endeavored—apparently with very limited success—to rebuild a party of his own and a position of influence.

BEN-GURION, DAVID (1886–1973) Israeli statesman and first prime minister of the State of Israel. Born David Green in Plonsk, Russia, Ben-Gurion received a traditional Jewish education and acquired his interest in Zionism from his father. As a boy he organized the *Ezra* society to promote the study of Hebrew and Zionist ideology. Between 1904 and 1906 he worked as a teacher in Warsaw and became involved in Labor Zionist politics, attending the first conference of the Labor Zionist movement, *Poale Zion*, in Poland in 1905. He was involved with Jewish self-defense during the 1903 pogroms and from

then on recognized the need for Jewish power. In 1906 he took a decisive step when he immigrated to Palestine in the second wave of Zionist immigration, from whose ranks came the founding fathers of modern Israel. He worked at first as an agricultural laborer in Galilee, but continued his political activity.

After the 1908 revolution of the YOUNG TURKS in Turkey, Ben-Gurion prepared himself to take part as a representative of the Jewish community of Palestine in the Turkish parliament. For that purpose he enrolled at Istanbul University to study law and spent two semesters there, but the outbreak of World War I cut short his studies.

He returned to Palestine and a few months later was expelled by the Turkish government for subversive Zionist activities. He went first to Alexandria and then to the United States (May 1915). He advocated the establishment of a Jewish legion in the British army to help liberate Palestine from the Turks and joined the legion when it was formed in 1918, arriving in Palestine in June in British army uniform.

Even before his release from the army, he brought about a partial unification of the labor movement in Palestine by establishing the *Ahdut ha-Avodah* party. In 1920, he was one of the founders of the *Histadrut*, the General Federation of Trade Unions, heading it as secretary general from 1921 to 1935. From then until his retirement in 1963, he was the leading figure in the Jewish community, participating in all Zionist congresses as a member of the elected assembly and as a leader of his party. In 1930, he achieved another dream by further uniting the Labor party with the creation of *Mapai*, the dominant party in the Jewish community and Israel from its establishment until 1977.

David Ben-Gurion

Ben-Gurion's Zionist socialism called for the gradual creation in Palestine of the economic, industrial, agricultural, educational, military and cultural infrastructure on which the future Jewish state would be built, led by the labor movement. He called for national control over natural resources and public utilities, stressed socialist education and advocated massive immigration. In the 1930s he met with a number of leading Palestinian Arabs but failed to reach any significant agreement with them. While calling for the creation of a strong Jewish defense force, he also realized the need to maintain working relations with the British government as long as the Jewish community was small and relatively weak vis-à-vis the Arabs.

Elected to the Zionist executive in 1934, the following year he became the chairman of the Jewish Agency, the international representative arm of the World Zionist Organization and headed that body until 1948. Together with Chaim Weizmann and Moshe Sharett, he led the struggle for the creation of a Jewish state. In 1937, he supported the partition plan of the British royal commission, arguing that even a sliver of Jewish sovereignty would help to rescue the growing number of refugees fleeing from Nazi Germany. In 1939, he participated in the round table conference in London, convened to decide the future of Palestine. When the conference failed, the British government issued the May 1939 white paper limiting Jewish immigration to Palestine and all but banning the sale of land to Jews there. When World War II broke out, Ben-Gurion coined the phrase, "We shall fight the white paper as though there was no war, and we shall fight the Nazis as though there was no white paper." During the war, he was involved in political and diplomatic work in London, New York and Washington, and attended the Baltimore Conference which called for the creation of a Jewish commonwealth after the war. In 1945, he visited the Holocaust survivors in camps in Germany and became convinced of the absolute necessity of the immediate establishment of the Jewish State.

He pushed for an activist anti-British policy of resistance and for illegal immigration to Palestine in the face of British restrictions. In 1946, he took over the defense portfolio of the Jewish Agency and began to prepare the underground army, the HAGANAH, for the coming inevitable struggle for independence, acquiring heavy weapons in Europe and the United States.

In March 1948, he was named chairman of the People's Executive and in this capacity he proclaimed the independence of the State of Israel on May 14, 1948, becoming its first prime minister and defense minister. He was the key figure in the military and political moves during the Israeli war of independence. His leadership was fundamental in bringing about an Israeli military victory and the firm foundation of the country's independence. He guided the country for the next 15 years (with a two-year respite), in which Israel received and absorbed over a million immigrants, forged its diplomatic position in the world, entrenched its economy and expanded its settlements and trade.

Ben-Gurion stressed the concept of *mamlahiyut* (statism), which called for the state to take over institutions and functions which had been the responsibility of political parties in the prestate era. His government created the unified Israel Defense Forces subservient to the civilian authorities, banning all private armies. Under him, the government established a state school system, a state labor exchange, a social security system and a nonpolitical civil service. Ben-Gurion fought for a democratic constitution and for a reform in the country's electoral system but failed to achieve either.

In foreign policy, he espoused strong ties with the west. He also signed an agreement with West Germany for reparations and later forged close military ties with France. Between late 1953 and early 1955 he remained in retirement in the Negev Kibbutz of Sde Boker. Recalled to office in view of the deteriorating military situation, he led Israel into the October 1956 Sinai campaign together with Britain and France. In a swift military campaign, Israel occupied Sinai but was forced to withdraw under Soviet and American pressure. Nevertheless the campaign gave Israel a decade of relative tranquility and a stronger and more confident army and country, making it a factor to be reckoned with in the Middle East. It failed however within the Middle East.

Domestic politics marred Ben-Gurion's final days in office. He resigned in June 1963, feeling that his colleagues had betrayed him. In 1965, he split *Mapai* when he created the breakaway *Rafi* party. The party won 10 seats in the 1965 Knesset elections and after the Six-Day war returned to *Mapai*—but without Ben-Gurion. Ben-Gurion advocated withdrawal from all the territories taken in the war, except Jerusalem and the Golan Heights, in return for real peace.

BEN-GURION ADDRESSING THE KNESSET (JULY 3, 1950)

The motives at work in the Jewish immigration to the Land of Israel in all generations, including our own, have been many and varied. Longings for redemption, ancient memories, religious feelings, love of homeland and above all, distress—economic, political and spiritual distress. With the foundation of the State, a new factor has been added whose strength will continually increase; the power of appeal and attraction embedded in the State of Israel. The pace and scope of the return of the exiles will in no small measure depend on our ability to augment this appeal and turn the State of Israel into the center for the realization of the longings of the nation and for the satisfaction of its material and spiritual needs.

BEN-JEDID, CHADLI (al-Sadhili) (1929–) Algerian officer and politician. President of Algeria since 1979. Born in eastern Algeria into a peasant family, Ben-Jedid received no higher education. According to French reports never confirmed by Algerian sources, he served in the French army in the early 1950s. He joined the FRONT DE LIBÉRATION NATIONALE (FLN) forces of the armed revolt in 1955 and rapidly rose in rank, soon being named a colonel. In 1961 he was appointed to the general staff of HOUARI BOUMEDIENNE's rebel army in Tunis and from 1962 was a member of the Revolutionary Council. In the factional struggles of 1962–1963 he supported Boumedienne and AHMAD BEN-BELLA and was named commander of the Constantine region.

From 1963–1964 he commanded the Oran region and, while supporting Boumedienne, ruled it with a strong hand as his personal fief for 15 years. He took no part in ideological debates or factional struggles.

When, after the death of Boumedienne in December 1978, the struggle for the succession seemed to be deadlocked, Ben-Jedid emerged as the army's candidate and a generally acceptable compromise. Nominated by the FLN as the single candidate for the presidency, he was elected in February 1979 in a referendum.

While he made no major changes in Algeria's policies of state socialism and radicalism, Ben-Jedid fostered the influence of technocrats, de-emphasized ideological-doctrinal elements and relaxed Algeria's régime, ending the monopoly of the FLN and gradually legalizing rival political parties. In recent years, Ben-Jedid has faced increasing difficulties as the economic situation deteriorated (serious unrest was suppressed in October 1988 with bloody violence) and both Berber nationalism and Islamic fundamentalism rose.

BEN YAIR, ELAZAR One of three main principal leaders who led the GREAT JEWISH REVOLT against Rome in 66–73 A.D. A member of a family of freedom fighters that had its origins a century earlier—one of his ancestors had opposed Herod the Great—he and his followers captured the fortress of MASADA during the early days of the revolt, massacring the Roman garrison there. They remained at Masada until, seven years later, they were besieged by the Roman army which had by that time completed the reconquest of the rest of the country. Elazar commanded his followers until it was clear that they could no longer fight.

To avoid being captured by the Romans he exhorted them to die by their own hands, and 960 men, women and children—including Elazar himself—did in fact commit suicide rather than submit. The contents of Elazar's speech as reported by Josephus—who admits to not having been present—have led some modern historians to cast doubt on the veracity of the tale. However, during the excavations of Masada which were held in the 1960s a potsherd bearing Elazar's name came to light, indicating that the story almost certainly had some basis in fact.

CONCLUSION OF ELEAZAR BEN YAIR'S SPEECH BEFORE THE MASADA MASS SUICIDE

● Our hands are still at liberty and have a sword in them; let them be subservient to us in our glorious design; let us die before we become slaves under our enemies, and let us go out of the world, together with our children and our wives, in a state of freedom....

● Let us make haste and instead of affording the Romans so much pleasure as they hope for in getting us under their power, let us leave them an example which shall at once cause their astonishment at our death and their admiration of our resolution.

BERISHA, SALI (1944–) Albanian democratic leader. Originally trained as a cardiologist, Berisha was a member of the ruling Albanian Workers' party until 1990, when mass protests forced President Ramiz Alia to introduce democratic reforms. In 1991, Berisha co-founded the Democratic party, which ran for the people's assembly in Albania's first free elections. Because of government gerrymandering, the Albanian Workers' Party, reconstituted as the Socialist party, won the election, but continued protests forced the Albanian government to call new elections the following year. In 1992, Sali Berisha was elected president of Albania.

BERKMAN, ALEXANDER (1870–1936) US anarchist. Born in Vilna (Vilnius) in what was then part of Russia, Alexander Berkman emigrated to the United States in 1888. He became a member of the Pioneers of Freedom, one of the first Jewish anarchist groups founded by Russian immigrants and later joined the German anarchist movement. Together with EMMA GOLDMAN, he led the anarchist movement in America.

In 1892, in Homestead, Pennsylvania, Berkman shot and attempted to kill the director of the local steelworks, as a protest against the treatment of the workers during a strike. Although he only wounded the director, he was sentenced to 22 years imprisonment and was released after 14 years. He renewed his association with Emma Goldman and, during World War I, was convicted of engaging in propaganda against conscription and of obstructing the draft. He was again sent to prison and upon his release in 1919 was deported to the USSR.

Berkman could not reconcile BOLSHEVIK philosophy with his libertarian principles and was disappointed with the Bolshevik régime. In 1922 he left the Soviet Union for Germany and in 1925 moved to France.

Berkman's publications include *Prison Memoirs of an Anarchist* (1912), *The Kronstadt Rebellion* (1922), *The Bolshevik Myth* (1925), *The Anti-Climax* (1925) and *Now and After: the ABC of Communist Anarchism* (1929). In 1936, he committed suicide in Nice.

BERNSTEIN, EDUARD (1850–1932) German socialist propagandist and political theorist. Born in Berlin, one of 15 children of a Jewish railroad engineer, Bernstein first worked as a junior employee of the S. & L. Rothschild Bank in Berlin. He was moved politically toward socialism by the events of the time, particularly the economic crisis of the early 1870s, which reinforced his belief in the fragility of capitalism, and by the speeches of German radical and socialist leaders following the 1870 Franco-Prussian war. In 1872, he joined the Marxist wing of the labor movement.

Bernstein formulated the basis of a democratic socialism that suited the changing conditions of capitalist society. He was the first German socialist to challenge the fundamental economic assumptions on which MARX's model of revolution was based and he questioned the concentration on the final goal of socialism at the expense of the means and the method by which it was to be achieved.

Bernstein left Germany following the enactment of Bismarck's anti-socialist laws and made his base in Switzerland, where he became editor in 1881 of *Der Sozialdemokrat*, which was the official organ of the underground exiled Social Democratic Party

(SPD). Although the paper was published in Zurich, it was then smuggled into Germany.

At the request of Bismarck, Bernstein was expelled from Switzerland in 1888. He moved to London, where he continued the publication of the periodical until 1890. In this period he was much influenced by the Fabian Society in England, which advocated a gradualist development of socialism. Here he published his main work, *Evolutionary Socialism* (1899; English translation, 1909). In 1901, Bernstein returned to Germany to become the theoretician of the revisionist school of the Reformist labor movement. He rejected Marx's theory of an imminent collapse of capitalist society, pointing out that the middle class was not declining, the peasants were not sinking, crises were not growing larger and mass misery was not increasing. He argued that the prospects for lasting success lay in steady advancement rather than mass upheaval.

In 1902, Bernstein was elected a member of the Reichstag, sitting until 1906 and again from 1912 to 1918. During World War I he sided with the Independent Socialists protesting against war and militarism. From 1920 to 1928 he sat in parliament as a Social Democrat.

Bernstein became alarmed by Hitlerism and the rise of the right-wing National Socialist party but was powerless to prevent its advance. He died in 1932, six weeks before Hitler's accession to power. His memoirs, *My Years of Exile*, appeared in 1921 (see also MARXISM).

BETANCOURT, ROMULO (1908–1981) Venezuelan politician. A left-winger who organized antigovernment demonstrations during his student days, Betancourt was exiled between 1928–1936 and 1939–1941, at which time he returned to found the Democratic Action party. In 1945 this party came to power and Betancourt, now president, initiated a series of social reforms. Again exiled following a coup in 1948, he returned in 1958 and was again elected president, retaining this office until 1964. He worked for the industrialization of Venezuela. After 1964 he lived in exile for eight years, returned in 1972 and ran unsuccessfully in the 1973 elections.

BIERUT, BOLESLAW (1892–1956) Polish Communist leader of poor peasant origin. Bierut was a member of the Communist party from its inception in 1918. In that year he fled to the Soviet Union and spent the years 1926–1933 on COMINTERN assignments. Jailed in Poland for seven years during a mission, he escaped to Moscow with the outbreak of World War II, was active in organizing the Communist underground and was one of the founders and leaders of the Soviet-promoted Polish Workers' party (the CP). 1944 found him among the top leadership of the Krajowa Rada Narodova (Homeland National Council), the pro-Communist led resistance formation. He was regarded by the west as a pawn of Stalin, in contrast to GOMULKA, and was characterized by Anthony Eden as a "rat."

In the first postwar years, a power struggle developed between Bierut and Gomulka, the latter having the upper hand for a time until 1948, when Gomulka was removed and replaced by Bierut. In 1947–1952 Bierut was president of the republic, premier from 1952–1953 and First Secretary of the Polish Workers' party from 1954. He died in Moscow of heart failure in March 1956, the shock of Nikita Khruschev's revelations at the 20th Party congress evidently being too much for him to deal with.

A loyal Stalinist, Bierut was a lifelong true believer, even in the hard times when Stalin decimated and eliminated the Polish Communists. Yet after Stalin's death in 1953 he was eager to join the growing bandwagon leading to de-Stalinization.

BIKO, STEPHEN (1946–1976) African activist and founder of the BLACK CONSCIOUSNESS MOVEMENT. Biko was born in Kingwilliamstown, Cape Province, South Africa, and attended primary and secondary school locally before starting at the Bantu Education Department-run Lovedale Institute in Alice, which he left shortly for the Roman Catholic Marianhill in Natal. He attended medical school at the University of Natal Non-European section in Durban, where he founded the South African Students' Organization (SASO) with Barney Pityana. SASO was intended as a black alternative to the multiracial but white-dominated National Union of South African Students. Biko's early writings on the philosophy of Black Consciousness appeared in his SASO Newsletter column "I Write What I Like" (published in Britain as part of a collection by the same name shortly after his death). SASO eventually expanded into the Black People's Convention (BPC) in 1972, to bring Black Consciousness to the masses. Biko left school in 1972 and began to work for Black Community Programs (BCP), a grassroots community development organization in Durban, until he was banned by the South African government in March 1973 for his SASO activities. Restricted to Kingwilliamstown, he founded the Eastern Cape Branch of BCP and worked as branch executive until his banning order was expanded in 1975 to prevent him from working for the organization.

In spite of the banning order, Biko continued to lead Black Consciousness activities; during 1975, Kingwilliamstown became a center for the movement. He was arrested and detained for 101 days in 1976 under Section Six of the Terrorism Act, which permitted unlimited detention in solitary confinement, but was released without being charged. In January 1977, he was elected honorary president of the BPC by a national planning meeting (he was not allowed to hold office because of the banning order). Then, in August, he was detained again and died in detention on September 12, of what an official inquest revealed to be brain injuries from beatings, though the cause of death was initially given as "hunger strike." His death drew global attention to the South African government's use of torture and murder against black activists. Five weeks later, all Black Consciousness organization branches were banned and many of its leaders arrested. The movement never recovered, but many of its members joined the AFRICAN NATIONAL CONGRESS or Pan-Africanist Congress (PAC) in exile. Moreover, the ideas of Black Consciousness inspired a new militancy, particularly among black youth, which could be tapped into by the ANC and other organizations operating underground.

While Biko is best known outside South Africa because of his death, his leadership in the Black Consciousness Movement was instrumental in carrying mass action against apartheid forward to another generation, after the banning of the ANC and the PAC in 1960. His approach was a psychological one, the idea being that blacks had been subjugated for so long that they could only liberate themselves if they were "conscientized," learning to assert themselves and overcome their sense of defeat at the hands of the whites. He emphasized grassroots involvement and the necessity of a unified approach, with all oppressed peoples confronting the oppressors together; the term "black" in Biko's usage referred to Indians and Coloreds as well as Africans. Black Consciousness had a theological element, drawn from (American) Black Theology. Biko advocated extracting the westernizing elements from Christianity, which had been brought to Africa as part of the colonizing process, and viewing Christ as an agent of the oppressed. Often accused of promoting separatism or "reverse apartheid," Biko emphasized that while the goal was a nonracial society, blacks needed to create a forum in which they could express their needs and desires independently from the domination of whites, however sympathetic some whites might be. The role of the white liberals was to reeducate their fellow whites, not to attempt to speak for or organize the blacks. The ideas of Black Consciousness appealed greatly to South African blacks, and while the movement may have been organizationally weak, these ideas were strong enough to galvanize militant activity, as the SOWETO RIOTS of 1976 demonstrated. Had Biko lived, the South African government feared that he might be a major unifying force of black action in South Africa.

BITAR, SALAH-UL-DIN (1912–1980) Syrian politician. Born in Damascus to a prominent family, Bitar studied physics at the Universities of Damascus and Paris and worked as a teacher. In 1940, together with MICHEL 'AFLAQ, he founded, among Syrian and Arab students and intellectuals in Paris, a leftist-nationalist Pan-Arab party, *al-Ba'ath al-'Arabi* (Arab Renaissance), and became editor of its organ, *al-Ba'ath*. When the *Ba'ath* group became a political party of growing importance in the late 1940s and the 1950s, Bitar was one of its chief leaders. In 1954, after the overthrow of ADIB SHISHAKLI, Bitar was elected to parliament. In 1956–1957 he was foreign minister and worked, with his BA'ATH PARTY associates, for the union of Syria and Egypt. When that union—the Union of Arab Republics (UAR)—was established in 1958, Bitar became minister of national guidance in the government of the UAR. He resigned in 1959, when GAMAL ABDUL NASSER began curbing the influence of the *Ba'ath* leaders and drove them into opposition. In 1961, after Syria's secession from the UAR, Bitar lost his seat in the elections. After the *Ba'ath* officers' coup of 1963, Bitar became prime minister and foreign minister. As the *Ba'ath* government increasingly turned into a military régime, with the civilian politicians and ideologues losing whatever influence they had, Bitar had to step down late in 1964 in favor of General AMIN-'AL-HAFEZ; he also lost his position in the *Ba'ath* party high command. With the decline of Hafez, Bitar briefly became prime minister in January 1966, but was overthrown in a February 1966 coup in which the *Ba'ath* leftist "military" faction seized power. He was arrested, but escaped to Lebanon. He was expelled, together with 'Aflaq, from the *Ba'ath* party—i.e., from the faction now ruling Syria. In his Lebanese exile, Bitar was not active in the rival wing of the *Ba'ath* controlled by 'Aflaq and linked with the Iraqi *Ba'ath*. He later moved to Paris and dissociated himself from both wings of the party. In 1969 he was sentenced to death in absentia by a Syrian court, but in 1971 he was pardoned. In the late 1970s he briefly returned to Syria, but, finding cooperation with the AL-ASAD régime impossi-

ble, he soon left again for Paris, where he became the rallying point for various dissident groups in exile. Bitar was assassinated in Paris in July 1980—allegedly by the Syrian secret service according to an anti-Syrian *Ba'ath* spokesman.

BLACK CONSCIOUSNESS MOVEMENT Originated as a student movement responding to the "separate development" policies of the South African government, under which the black homelands or Bantustans would be developed into separate satellite states to the white nation of South Africa, the movement was inspired by the black power movement in the USA and the radical writings of FRANTZ FANON. The term "black" was used in an innovative way to refer to all non-whites—Africans, Indians and Coloureds—in order to forge a common identity among oppressed groups in South Africa, and the movement did succeed in engendering cooperation between these groups.

In 1969, STEPHEN BIKO and Barney Pityana founded the all-black South African Students' Organization (SASO) as an alternative to the multiracial but white-dominated National Union of South African Students (NUSAS), with Biko as its first president, succeeded after one year by Pityana. SASO's aims were to provide a means for non-white students to make known their grievances and to establish the identity, needs and aspirations of the non-white NUSAS members.

By 1972, the Black Peoples' Convention (BPC) was founded as the political wing of the Black Consciousness Movement; it was the closest thing blacks had to a national political party ever since the 1960 banning of the AFRICAN NATIONAL CONGRESS and the PAN-AFRICANIST CONGRESS. As the political goals of the movement began to come to the fore, the government responded with oppressive measures. In 1973, Biko, Pityana and six other Black Consciousness leaders were banned by the South African government. A banning order confined its target to a particular magisterial district (in Biko's case, Kingwilliamstown) and prohibited him or her from speaking in public, attending any gatherings except church services, being quoted in the press or any publication, having visitors in the home, or meeting with more than one person at a time. In spite of this, the movement continued to grow. Black Community programs became one of the primary focuses of activity. Through starting and supporting local home industries and health clinics, such as the Zanempilo Clinic founded by Biko outside of Kingwilliamstown in 1975, it was hoped to build grass root support for Black Consciousness by showing what blacks were capable of doing even under the prevailing system.

The government crackdown against Black Consciousness intensified and in 1975, when SASO and the BPC tried to organize pro-FRELIMO rallies to celebrate the liberation of Mozambique, 30 movement leaders were rounded up and detained. The so-called trial of Black Consciousness began in January 1975, and of the 13 charged nine were eventually convicted. The June 1976 Soweto uprising became a massacre when security forces opened fire on a demonstration of African and Colored school children protesting the use of Afrikaans as the medium of instruction in non-white secondary schools. Though not organized by the Black Consciousness Movement, the uprising may have been inspired by its rhetoric. The government responded with further detentions under the new Internal Security Act, which effectively prevented movement leaders from channeling the momentum started by the uprising. Also in 1976, Mapetla Mohapi became the first member of the Black Consciousness Movement to die in detention (earlier, Ongkopotso Tiro had been killed by a parcel bomb while in exile in Botswana and Nthuli Shezi had been pushed in front of a train). Biko was also detained but was released at the end of 1976. He was detained again in August 1977 and died in detention three weeks later, the cause of death revealed by an inquest to be brain injuries.

Biko's death in prison drew worldwide attention to the South African government's use of torture and murder in its dealings with black opposition groups. Shortly thereafter, in October 1977, all Black Consciousness organizations were banned. The movement was never able to recover from this and many of its members joined the African National Congress (ANC) or the Pan-African Congress (PAC) in exile. In the wake of this suppression, a number of local civic organizations developed in the townships that provided organizational networks for generally local, spontaneous demonstrations in the early and mid-1980s. However, there was no effective, legal replacement for the movement to provide a united militant opposition within the country until the ANC, PAC and other organizations were unbanned in 1990.

BLACK DRAGON SOCIETY Ultra-nationalist Japanese society founded in 1900 by Uchida Ryohei. The organization sought to promote Japanese expansion in east Asia, especially at the expense of Russia, and reached its peak during the Russo-Japanese War of 1905. Later it supported SUN YAT-SEN and the CHINESE REPUBLICAN REVOLUTION OF 1911, hoping that that revolution would lead to diminished Western influence and open the door to Japanese infiltration of China.

BLACK FLAGS Late 19th-century Chinese guerrillas, remnants of the TAIPING and Panthay rebellions, who infiltrated northern Vietnam and aided the Vietnamese resistance to the French. In 1882 the Chinese encouraged the Black Flags to attack the small French force in Hanoi and the French commandant was killed. With the outbreak of the Sino-French war (1883–1885), the Chinese co-opted the Black Flags.

BLACK HAND Serbian terrorist organization founded in 1911 and led by Colonel DRAGUTIN DIMITRIJEVIC. Several Serbian cabinet ministers were also members. The society used terrorism and assassination in order to try to achieve the annexation of all southern Slav territories within the Austrio-Hungarian Empire to Serbia. In June 1914, a Black Hand assassin, GAVRILO PRINCIP, shot and killed the Austro-Hungarian heir to the throne and his wife, sparking off World War I. The society later tried to direct Serbia's war policy. In 1917 the society was disbanded.

BLACK MUSLIMS (Lost-Found Nation of Islam in the Wilderness of North America; or Nation of Islam) An extremist Afro-American movement established in 1930 and invigorated in the 1960s, which espouses an ideology of Black Nationalism and extreme separatism. Notwithstanding its revolutionary ideology and racist polemics, the movement has distinguished itself in intensive religious and welfare activities at the grass roots level within the Afro-American community.

The Nation of Islam was founded in Detroit by a local peddler, Wali Fard (or: Farrad, Farad), cast by his followers as an incarnation of God, Allah. Fard was succeeded, in 1934, by his disciple, Elijah Poole, appropriately renamed Muhammad, i.e., Allah's prophet. In its beginnings the movement recast MARCUS GARVEY's legacy of Black Nationalism, formulated in the 1920s, into a radical militant platform flavored by Islamic religious substances.

Social unrest and the emergence of the civil rights movement in the early 1960s gave the Black Muslims a significant boost. The two most significant spokesmen in bringing the movement's message to the fore of Afro-American consciousness in the period were MALCOLM X and Muhammad Ali, the latter the Olympic, and then world, heavyweight boxing champion. In 1963, Malcolm X fell out with Elijah Muhammad. Muhammad adhered to the original tenets of Black Separatism and Nationalism while Malcolm X developed a more universal platform of protest, preaching black activism in the context of broader revolutionary changes in the American economy and politics. He left the movement a year later, and the Nation of Islam was implicated in his assassination in 1965.

The Black Muslims' constructive work in rehabilitating prisoners and their creative agricultural and industrial projects for improving economic conditions of the Afro-American minority brought them wide support in the course of the 1970s and 1980s. The Black Muslims' separatist ideology, calling for Afro-American self-determination and their racist teachings directed against Jews, made many see the movement, over the years, as a dangerous incendiary one. Yet it preaches obedience to the laws and its record has been one of peaceful, constructive, religious and communal reform.

BLACK PANTHERS A militant Afro-American organization established in Oakland, California, in 1966 to promote black liberation. The Black Panthers blended an extreme version of Black Nationalism with Marxist ideas. Their major activities, however, focused on developing self-reliance and cohesiveness within the Afro-American community rather than confronting America's majority groups.

The movement was founded by two young Afro-American militants, Huey P. Newton and Bobby G. Seale. Their early acts of establishing a quasi-military organization to defend Afro-Americans against police violence and staging an armed protest near California's capitol brought the movement instant national exposure. The publicity helped the movement spread rapidly to other major urban centers and to establish itself as a symbol of black militancy. Schism and disharmony within the movement and suspicion of serious crimes committed by its leaders led to the movement's rapid demise in the early 1970s.

BLANC, LOUIS (1811–1882) Born in Madrid, a scion of the noble Pozzo di Borgo Corsican dynasty on his mother's side. Blanco was a noted French socialist thinker and militant, vehemently but unjustly ridiculed by KARL MARX as a muddled and sentimental "Utopian Socialist," and held responsible for many of the failures of the REVOLUTIONS OF 1848. Along with the Comte Henri de Saint Simon, Robert Owen and Charles Fourier, Blanc's ideas shaped the thinking of the first romantic generation of socialist enthusiasts whose illusions came to grief with the shattering experience of 1848. These ideas were set out in his most famous book, *The Organization of Labor* (1839), which became an instant best seller during the July Monarchy. Blanc argued that political reform was the only means to achieve social reform and that the government should acknowledge and promote the workman's "right to work" (he was the first writer to coin that revolutionary slogan) by setting up state-run *ateliers nationaux* or "national workshops" designed to compete freely with private enterprise in accordance with the prevailing economic theory of *laissez-faire, laissez-passer*. His ideas were received with widespread enthusiasm by the French workers suffering from the social distress and economic hardships produced by the excess of an unregulated economy during the "Hungry Forties." However, they were thoroughly discredited during the revolution of 1848 because of the way there were implemented and deliberately distorted, under the guise of the so-called "social workshops" established by his bourgeois detractors, who controlled the government of the Second Republic between March and June of 1848. Far from implementing Blanc's ideas of state intervention in the labor market, these state factories were in fact conceived as a system of welfare relief for indigents and derelicts. Their abrupt dissolution by decree on June 22 immediately precipitated the bloody insurrection of June 1848, which brought to an end the great dream of social revolution. Escaping to London after 1849, Blanc did not return to France until the fall of the Second Empire in September 1870, but was careful to keep his distance from the PARIS COMMUNE. He nevertheless campaigned for the separation of Church and State, the introduction of an income tax and the granting of a general amnesty for all the members of the commune still living in exile. Two of his other books, *A History of Ten Years* and *History of the French Revolution*, are still highly regarded by French leftists.

After having voted in 1875, as a deputy in the Versailles parliament, for the creation of the bourgeois Third Republic, Blanc died in Cannes in 1882.

BLANQUI, LOUIS AUGUSTE (1805–1881) A perfect example of the revolutionary enthusiasm produced by all the social turbulence and political instability which beset France from the revolution of 1830 (see REVOLUTIONS OF 1830) to the establishment of the Third Republic in 1875, Louis Auguste Blanqui became a legend in his own lifetime as the most notorious conspirator and full-time revolutionary agitator to haunt the streets of Paris. He had abandoned his law studies in the 1820s to launch a secret society, the *Société des Familles*, originally an offshoot of the Italian CARBONARI, and the first of many such underground conspiratorial cells which he never ceased to envisage as the spearhead of a large-scale social and atheist revolution.

Son of a member of the French Revolutionary convention of 1792 and the brother of the socialist economist, Jérôme-Adolphe Blanqui, Blanqui played a leading part in no fewer than four revolutions: the July 1830 Paris Insurrection, known as "The Three Glorious Days," that brought about the fall of Louis Philippe's Orleanist monarchy; the two populist revolutions of February and June 1848 (see REVOLUTIONS OF 1848), which established and then discredited the short-lived Second Republic (1848–1851); the overthrow of the Second Empire in July 1870; and, finally, the PARIS COMMUNE of 1871, for which

Blanqui was venerated as a secular saint by Communists of succeeding generations. As a result of all his activities, Blanqui spent no fewer than a total of 33 years of his life in prison under four different political régimes. He thus came to be known in revolutionary and working-class circles as *l'Enfermé* or "the imprisoned one," a martyr to the cause of the "Republic, one and indivisible," fighting to the death against all its betrayers as well as its traditional detractors and enemies from the Right. An ascetic but passionate militant for the cause of freedom, Blanqui never failed to accept any opportunity to join every available conspiracy against the tyranny of the Church and the power of the rich. He was also an indefatigable polemicist and prolific journalist, the editor of a weekly, later a daily, *Ni Dieu Ini Maître* ("Neither God nor Master"), which he launched with the assistance of two other Communard disciples, Edouard Vaillant and Emile Eudes, in November 1880. He remained till the end an unrepentant anticlerical and a resolute opponent of all forms of authority. Most historians regard him, however, not so much as a forerunner of Marxist socialism but as a vestigial remnant of a recurring cycle of JACOBIN idealism bequeathed to the 19th century by the FRENCH REVOLUTION OF 1789. On January 5, 1881, his coffin was escorted by a cortege of 100,000 socialists and freethinkers to the Père Lachaise, in a grandiose ceremony matched in its pomp and circumstance only by the return of Napoleon's ashes in 1836 and the funeral of Victor Hugo in 1885. In that same year, a famous memorial designed by the sculptor Dalou, paid through donations from a public subscription, was erected on his tomb. It was inscribed with an epitaph from the *Internationale*, originally written at the height of the Paris Commune of 1871 and commemorating the exploits of this incorrigible rebel.

BLOODY SUNDAY In Russian history, the incident that marked the violent stage of the RUSSIAN REVOLUTION OF 1905. On January 22 (January 9, old style) a massive demonstration took place in St. Petersburg by industrial workers, led by the priest GEORGES GAPONE. The demonstrators hoped to present their demands for reform to the czar himself, and for that purpose they marched to the Winter Palace. Though the czar was not, in fact, present in the city, the chief of security—his uncle Grand Duke Vladimir—panicked and ordered the police to fire on the demonstration which, until that point, had been peaceful enough. When the result of the shooting, perhaps 100 dead and many more wounded, became known, the unrest spread from St. Petersburg throughout the main cities of Russia.

BLÜCHER, VASILY KONSTANTINOVICH (1889–1938) Chief Russian military adviser to Chinese Nationalist forces between 1924 and 1927. Of peasant origin, Bluecher was an outstanding military leader during the RUSSIAN REVOLUTION OF 1917. Sent to China by the COMINTERN to assist CHIANG KAI-SHEK'S forces, he became senior military adviser at WHAMPOA MILITARY ACADEMY and was of inestimable value to the NATIONAL REVOLUTIONARY ARMY. After the Nationalist (GUOMINDANG)-Communist rupture in July, 1927, Blücher and other Soviet advisors were dismissed. He stayed to participate in the planning of the CHINESE COMMUNIST PARTY'S (CCP) NANCHANG UPRISING and left China in August of that year. Though he was subsequently raised to the rank of marshal in the Soviet army, in 1938, on

Stalin's personal orders, Blücher was arrested and died in prison.

BLUM, LEON (1872–1950) First Jewish and socialist prime minister of France. Born in Paris to an old Alsatian family, Blum was prodigiously gifted from youth. After brilliant studies at the law faculty in Paris, he earned a reputation as a poet and author, publishing *En lisant: Réflexions critiques, Au théâtre* (4 vols.; 1905–1914), *Marriage* (1907) and a work on Stendhal (1914). In his essay on marriage, Blum daringly recommended that young women should enjoy as much freedom as young men and advocated trial marriages.

From 1896 to 1919, he served in the government as a legal advisor in the council of state and rose to become master of requests. The Dreyfus affair and his friendship with the socialist leader, JEAN JAURŇS, drew him to politics and the French Socialist party. He became a deputy (member) in parliament for the Socialist party in 1919 and after the Communists split off from the party, applied himself to reorganizing the socialist movement so successfully that he soon became one of its leaders. In 1921, he founded the socialist daily, *Le Populaire*. Although his party made gains in the 1932 elections, Blum refused to cooperate with the Radical Socialists.

When 1934 riots revealed a serious threat of FASCISM in France, Blum took the lead in regrouping the leftist factions and established the Popular Front of Socialists, Radical Socialists and Communists. The front obtained a majority in parliament in June 1936 and Blum became prime minister. Confronted by strong opposition and many social problems, Blum's government worked quickly at making good on its promises by introducing daring reforms, such as a 40-hour work week, paid vacations and nationalization of war industries and of the Bank of France, all these within a few weeks of taking office.

Blum was aware of the problems facing France's national defense in the light of German rearmament. When Great Britain refused to help the republicans in the SPANISH CIVIL WAR, the French government adopted a similar policy of non-intervention, which was criticized by the left. By nature, Blum tended toward conciliation. In June 1937, defeated in parliament after a right-wing campaign tinged with anti-Semitism, Blum resigned. He served as vice-premier in the subsequent Popular Front government and was premier for nine months again in March 1938.

In 1938 Blum founded the Socialist Committee for Palestine. He accepted Chaim Weizmann's invitation to participate in the first meeting of the enlarged Jewish Agency in Zurich in 1929.

At the beginning of the German occupation of France in 1940, the Vichy government had Blum arrested and accused him of having supported the war. In 1942 he was brought to trial at Riom and conducted to a brilliant defense, which led the authorities to suspend his trial. At the trial he noted that at the beginning of his political career he had been accused of being a pacifist, but that, because he had tried to maintain the military capacity of France, he was now being accused of being an advocate of war.

Blum remained in prison and was then sent to a concentration camp in Germany, from which he was freed by the American army in 1945. Upon his return to France, he resumed his political activities. In December 1946 he formed a Socialist government that lasted only one month. He was again deputy prime minister in 1948. He is regarded as one of the great figures of French and international socialism. In Israel, a kibbutz, Kfar Blum, was named after him.

BOCCHINI, ARTURO (1880–1940) Trained as a lawyer, Bocchini entered the Italian civil service in 1903, specializing in police work within the framework of the ministry of interior affairs. In the Fascist (see FASCISM) period, he rose rapidly in the ranks of the police, becoming prefect of Brescia in 1922. There he established close links with Alfonso Turati, the future general secretary of the Fascist party—PNF. After assuming the prefectures of Bologna and Genoa, Bocchini was appointed chief of police by MUSSOLINI in September 1926 and remained at this post until his death in 1940. In charge of Mussolini's personal security and of infiltrating the ranks of the anti-Fascists, Bocchini created a special branch of "political police," which in 1930 became the *Organizzazione Vigilanza Repressione Antifascismo* ("Watch and Repression of Antifascism Organization"), better known as OVRA. This organization, considered essential for the existence of the totalitarian Fascist state, developed a wide network of informants and collaborators within and outside Italy, infiltrating and cracking opposition organizations such as the Communist party, *Giustizia e Liberta* ("Justice and Freedom"), anarchist groups and Slovenes. It brought thousands of members of the opposition to trial in a Special Court, and many were condemned to long prison terms and even to death. The OVRA was also in charge of informing Mussolini, and later Galeazzo Ciano, Italy's foreign affairs minister and the Duce's son-in-law, of dissension within the Fascist ranks, a role which acquired importance with the Italian invasion of Ethiopia in 1935 and the Italian intervention in the SPANISH CIVIL WAR in 1936. Though he was not ideologically committed to the cause, Arturo Bocchini's contribution to fascism as a civil servant and technocrat was of great importance.

BOGDANOV (MALINOVSKY), ALEXANDER (1873–1928) Philosopher and economist. Bogdanov was among the founders of the BOLSHEVIK faction of the Social Democratic Workers party of Russia, but in 1907 disagreed with LENIN on participation in the Duma and as a result left the Bolsheviks. At this time he attempted a philosophical adaptation of MARXISM, introducing to it ideas from Mach and Avenarius. Bogdanov, together with Maxim Gorky, then formed the Forward (*Vpered*) group, and helped found a school for revolutionary party workers in Capri. He maintained his opposition to parliamentary participation, calling for the Social Democratic deputies in the Duma to submit to party dictate or resign.

From 1913, Bogdanov turned more and more to philosophical and social research, working on a science of universal sociocultural organization under the name of Tectology. During World War I he served as an army surgeon. In 1917 he opposed the Bolshevik slogan of "All Power to the Soviets," fearing that it would lead to a civil war between the peasants and the urban workers. He also cast doubt on the idea that a socialist revolution in Russia would spark workers' revolutions throughout Europe. Bogdanov advocated a democratic republic as a long-term transition toward socialism, emphasizing his theme that societies were determined not only by economic factors but by cultural and educational development as well. He founded the Russian Proletarian Cultural and Educational Society (*proletkult*) as a step toward realizing his theories of sociocultural organization.

Throughout 1917, Bogdanov opposed Lenin as authoritarian and opposed the idea that concentration of the economy in the hands of the state would speed the transition to socialism. From 1923 he devoted himself to research in the field of blood transfusion, dying of complications resulting from a self-administered transfusion.

Bogdanov's writings included the *Short Course* (1896) and the two-volume *Course* (1910)—both standard expositions of Marxist economics—his series, *Tectology* (1913–1922), and other philosophical and political works.

BOGROV, DMITRI (1887–1911) Russian revolutionary. Son of a well-known Jewish attorney in Kiev, Bogrov became an anarchist in 1906, having entered revolutionary activity while still in high school. Early in 1907 he became a paid agent of the political police, the *Okhrana*, first in Kiev and later in St. Petersburg. Bogrov was hanged in September 1911 after fatally wounding Prime Minister Stolypin at the Kiev opera house in the presence of the czar. It is not known to this day whether he was acting on behalf of the revolutionaries or the police.

BO GU see QIN BANGXIAN.

BOLÍVAR, SIMON (1783–1830) Venezuelan soldier and statesman; champion of South American independence. Bolívar was born in Caracas, Venezuela, to one of the most influential families in the city. An early influence on him was Simon Rodríguez, an eccentric and freethinking tutor who introduced the boy to the teachings of Jean-Jacques Rousseau, Voltaire and similar thinkers.

Bolívar joined the local militia, where he attained the rank of second lieutenant. In 1799, he traveled to Spain to join an uncle. There, he continued his education and received an introduction to life at the royal court. His uncle's arrest and imprisonment in 1802 aroused a contempt for monarchy that Bolívar bore throughout his life.

He returned to Venezuela in 1807. The country was then aflame with growing nationalist ferment, particularly as a result of the abortive attempt at that time of Francisco de Miranda to achieve independence from Spain. Groups of conspirators met clandestinely to promote the cause of independence, among them Bolívar. In 1810, Governor Vincente de Emparáan was deposed and a ruling junta of local patriots was formed. Despite his lack of formal military experience, Bolívar was appointed a lieutenant colonel of the infantry militia. Bolívar set out to London to gain backing for the rebels. He met Miranda there and convinced him to return to South America to lead the independence movement.

A national congress was called in 1811 to draft a constitution for the new state. Although he was not a delegate, Bolívar played an active role in its deliberations. In his first recorded political address, he proclaimed, "To hesitate is to perish." Independence was declared on July 5, 1811. Bolívar joined the army commanded by Miranda, but the two soon drifted apart. When, Miranda decided to negotiate an armistice with Spain, abandoning independence, Bolívar betrayed him to the Spanish.

Escaping to neighboring New Granada (now Colombia), Bolívar issued his famed Cartagena Manifesto, in which he blamed South American disunity for Venezuela's final defeat.

Bolívar fought six major battles against the Spanish and became known as El Liberator (the Liberator) after his conquest of Mérida. On August 6, 1813, he led his troops into Caracas. A nominal local government was established, but Bolívar, assuming the role of commander-in-chief, became virtual dictator of the country.

Royalist troops eventually forced Bolívar to flee to Jamaica. For the next three years, his base of operations was in Haiti. In 1816 he led 250 men to Venezuela. Despite their lack of weapons and supplies, they won several decisive victories against royalist troops, in the process gaining massive local support. Bolívar's army grew considerably; by 1817, he was able to move his headquarters to the provincial capital of Angostura.

With General Francisco Santander, Bolívar set out on a long, hazardous march to New Granada during the rainy season, succeeding in capturing Bogotá. In December 1819 Bolívar declared the formation of the Republic of Colombia, comprising Venezuela, New Granada and Quito (present day Ecuador), the latter yet uncaptured at the time of his declaration. Proclaimed president of Greater Colombia, Bolívar reconquered Venezuela after the Battle of Carabobo (June, 1821). In 1822 he liberated Ecuador. In 1823, after deliberations with JOSÉ DE SAN MARTIN, Bolívar entered Peru.

Simon Bolivar

That year, Bolívar organized the first conference of the newly independent states of former Spanish America, held in Panama. Colombia, Mexico, Peru and the Central American states met together in what was to become the Organization of American States. Bolívar was even offered the crown in recognition of his contribution to South American independence, but he rejected the offer in favor of a republican system of government. He was appalled by growing regionalism and nationalist trends among the new countries that portended the end of his dream of a united continent.

Bolívar's final years were marked by misfortune. He survived an assassination attempt, only to witness the slow breakup of the Colombia Federation and war between Colombia and Peru. In 1829, his home province of Venezuela declared itself independent. Bolívar settled on a ranch in Santa Marta, where he contracted tuberculosis and died.

LAST TESTAMENT OF SIMON BOLÍVAR

● Colombians!

● You have witnessed my efforts to establish liberty where tyranny once reigned. I have labored unselfishly, sacrificing my fortune and my peace of mind. When I became convinced that you distrusted my motives, I resigned my command. My enemies have played upon your credulity and destroyed what I hold most sacred: my reputation and my love of liberty. I have been the victim of my persecutors, who have brought me to the brink of the grave. I forgive them.

● As I depart from your midst, my love for you tells me that I should make known my last wishes. I aspire to no other glory than the consolidation of Colombia. You must all work for the supreme good of the union: my people, by obeying the present government in order to rid themselves of anarchy; the ministers from their sanctuary, by addressing their supplications to heaven; and the military, by using their swords to defend the guarantees of organized society.

● Colombians! My last wishes are for the happiness of our native land. If my death will help to end party strife and to consolidate the union, I shall go to my grave in peace.

BOLIVIAN REVOLUTION OF 1952 In 1951, VICTOR PAZ ESTENSSORO, who had escaped Bolivia following the bloody 1946 uprising against the National Revolutionary Movement (MNR), was elected to the presidency in abstentia. When the incumbent régime denied the presidency to Paz, the country rose up, miners struck and the then-recently initiated agricultural development program ground to a halt. One result was rampant inflation. Economic problems produced national unrest, but it was the rebellion of the miners which ignited a full-scale revolution

in 1952. This in turn led to the restoration of the MNR to power and Paz Estenssoro to the presidency.

BOLSHEVIK PARTY Founded in 1903 as a result of the split in the Social Democratic Workers party of Russia at its second congress. In August 1917, the Bolshevik (literally "majority men") party was renamed the Communist Party of Russia (Bolsheviks), and with the formation of the Soviet Union it became the Communist Party of the Soviet Union (Bolsheviks). Only in October 1952, at the 19th party congress, did it drop the title Bolshevik from its official name, in accordance with a suggestion from Stalin, who explained that no more Mensheviks (literally "minority men"—see MENSHEVIK PARTY) existed in the USSR.

At the time of the party's founding, the Bolsheviks differed from the Mensheviks chiefly in their insistence that each member of the party be under the discipline of a local branch of the party and that party members be "professional revolutionaries," devoting their full efforts to the cause of political revolution. The central and unitary structure of the party was also an issue at the second congress, causing the Jewish BUND and other national minority groups of Social Democrats to leave the party and establish their own national Social Democratic parties. These defections left the Bolsheviks as the majority.

The chief architect of the Bolshevik party was VLADIMIR LENIN, who sought an organizational structure suitable to revolutionary activity under the conditions of an autocratic régime. In a letter explaining his concept, Lenin likened the party to an orchestra in which the conductor has full knowledge and control of each instrumentalist's capacities and performance. He insisted on a compact central committee that would have full control over the ideological and operational content of the party's central newspaper, in addition to maintaining contact with party branches through a network of agents of the central committee. The fullest exposition of his concept of the Bolshevik party is contained in his 1902 essay, "What Is to be Done." The organizational principles of Bolshevism were based on Lenin's concepts, under the name of "Democratic Centralism." This code consisted of four elements: all party executive personnel and bodies were to be elected; all elected bodies were to report periodically to those who elected them; all decisions and actions of lower party bodies were subject to the approval of higher party bodies; all party members were bound to active support and implementation of all party decisions. Thus the democratic elements of election and reporting were made subject to the hierarchical discipline of the party.

Elections in the lower bodies were only considered valid if the higher bodies approved the results. Thus delegates to local, regional or national party congresses could only be elected if the superior executives (whose actions the delegates were to discuss and judge) approved of their views. In this manner, the democratic elements were vitiated and "a circular flow of power" was created. This in turn formed the basis of a self-perpetuating leadership.

As the party developed, it included several additional elements in its ideology. A central part of Bolshevik ideology was the insistence on "dictatorship of the proletariat" in the period immediately following the revolution. This category, originated by FERDINAND LASALLE, and marginal to KARL MARX'S and FRIEDRICH

ENGELS's concept of socialism, led directly to the single-party régime that developed in Soviet Russia. In addition, the seizure of power by armed uprising and civil war as a prominent component of revolution both became central points in Bolshevik thinking as a result of the RUSSIAN REVOLUTION OF 1905. Finally, there came the use of the party and its professional revolutionary cadres as an instrument of the transformation of society in a country lacking the developed working class deemed necessary in orthodox Marxism for the construction of socialism. For Lenin, political power was both a necessary and sufficient condition for the creation of socialism, and the Bolshevik party, as developed in his theory and practice, was the instrument that would both attain and make use of political power to this end.

Lenin's single-minded centralist approach evoked considerable criticism in other socialist groups, both in Russia and abroad. Both reformers such as KARL KAUTSKY and Marxist revolutionaries such as ROSA LUXEMBURG saw in Lenin's system the triumph of extreme Jacobinism and neglect of those democratic elements seen by the more moderate socialists as fundamental to socialist society. At the time of the Bolshevik seizure of power, Lenin's "shortcut of history"—the attempt to build proletarian socialism in a peasant country—was a focus of criticism. Despite these criticisms, democratic centralism remained the basic organizational principle, not only of the Communist party but of the USSR, from Lenin's time up to the Gorbachev reforms of the late 1980s.

BONCH-BRUEVICH, VLADIMIR D. (1873–1955) Russian Communist revolutionary. Son of a Moscow land surveyor, Bonch-Bruevich was exiled from the city for four years while still a teenager because of revolutionary involvement. After his exile he wrote, edited and distributed illegal literature to workers until 1896, when he emigrated to Switzerland to study science. After a brief sojourn in Canada to study the customs of the Dukhobor sect he returned to revolutionary work, joining LENIN'S BOLSHEVIKS in 1903. He worked on *Pravda* from its 1912 inception, and in 1917 was an editor of the Petrograd Soviet's *Izvestiia*.

During the summer and autumn of 1917, Lenin used Bonch-Bruevich's summer home in Finland as a hiding place. In the October RUSSIAN REVOLUTION OF 1917 he was a member of the Petrograd military revolutionary committee and later military commissar of the Smolny district in Petrograd, in which the Bolshevik party headquarters were situated. As secretary of the first Soviet government, he drew up the December 1917 decree nationalizing the banks. After the revolutionary period he continued his research into Russian religious sects and eventually became the director of the Moscow Museum of the History of Religion and Atheism.

BOOTH'S RISING (August 1659) The failure and resignation of OLIVER CROMWELL's son Richard gave new hope to the defeated royalists in England, who planned an uprising under Sir George Booth (later Lord Delemere: 1622–1684). The plan was for naval support to be forthcoming by Montagu and for James, Duke of York (later King James II) to invade England with French support. Booth captured Chester on August 19, 1659, but was easily defeated by General Lambert and imprisoned in the Tower of London.

BORODIN, MICHAEL (Mikhail Markovich Gruzenberg) (1884–1951) Chief Soviet adviser to the GUOMINDANG (Chinese Nationalist party; GMD) (1923–1927). Born to Jewish parents in Latvia, Borodin was associated with the BUND (Jewish socialist organization) in 1900 and in 1903 joined the BOLSHEVIK faction of the Russian Social Democratic Party in Riga. Under the name Berg, he lived in the US from 1907 until 1918. After returning to Russia, he served the COMINTERN as an underground agent, using various aliases, in Spain, Mexico, the United States and England. A dynamic and highly intelligent organizer with a commanding presence, Borodin won SUN YAT-SEN's confidence when he arrived in Canton in October 1923. He helped shape the GMD's militant ideology and prepare the ground for the Nationalist Revolution. During that period, he was one of the most influential men in China. After the GMD-CCP (CHINESE COMMUNIST PARTY) rupture in 1927, he returned to the Soviet Union. He was arrested in 1951 and died in a Siberian prison camp.

The face of the Comintern: Mikhail Borodin

BOSTON TEA PARTY "Boston Harbor a tea-pot this night" was the battle cry of a band of American patriots, disguised as Indians, who approached Boston Harbor's waterfront on December 16, 1773. Amidst a large turnout of Bostonians as spectators, the patriots tossed into the water 342 chests of tea, worth 10,000 English pounds, which were the property of the imperial East India Company. This colorful incident constituted one of the most significant landmarks on the colonists' road to open rebellion.

It was the Tea Act, issued by parliament in 1763, which had stirred the pot so lively. Intended merely to support the faltering company by granting it a monopoly on tea distribution in colonial markets, the Tea Act was considered by North American colonists as intended to reassert parliament's right to tax the colonies through regulating imperial commerce. The colonists not only resented the tax but also disputed parliament's right to levy it under the English constitution and considered the act an infringement of their liberties as Englishmen. Consequent to the passage of the act, as ships laden with East India tea reached North American sea ports, local activists prevented the landing of their cargoes. In Massachusetts, Governor Thomas Hutchinson ordered that the ships were not to leave harbor before they unloaded their chests of tea. The patriots, masquerading as Indians, helped accomplish precisely that.

The first violent act of the American colonists, which became known as the Boston Tea Party, demonstrated the significance of the imperial laws of commerce and their constitutional implications in widening the gap between the British North American colonists and the mother country. Although local, the episode reflected deep-seated discontent of almost continental scope against the imperial ministry and the policies it promoted.

BOUDICCA   Wife of the king of the Iceni, a Celtic tribe which inhabited East Anglia and which was on good terms with Rome when the Emperor Claudius began the conquest of Britain. After the death of her husband in 60 A.D., Roman agents maltreated Boudicca and her daughters. The Iceni then rose in rebellion under the leadership of Boudicca. They sacked Colchester, Verulamium (St. Albans) and London and defeated a Roman army. When the insurgents engaged the govenor Suetonius Paulinus in battle, they suffered a complete defeat and Boudicca soon committed suicide.

BOUMEDIENNE, HOUARI   (1927–1978) Algerian officer and revolutionary. Born Muhammad Boukharouba in the 'Annaba (Bone) region of eastern Algeria, the son of a farm laborer, Boumedienne was later said to have studied Arabic literature in universities in Tunis and Cairo (the latter in the famed Al-Azhar University). He stayed on in Cairo working as a teacher. It was here that he met AHMAD BEN-BELLA and other leaders of the incipient Algerian revolt. In 1954 he joined their FRONT DE LIBÉRATION NATIONALE (FLN) and soon became one of the revolt's commanders. In 1955 he landed in western Algeria with a group of rebels and soon headed the rebel formations in the Oran region. He later returned to FLN headquarters (now in Tunis), became a member of the revolutionary council set up in 1956 and in March 1960 was appointed chief of staff of the rebel army. After the French-Algerian agreement of 1962, he led that army into Algeria. When tensions between the guerrillas inside Algeria and the "regular" rebel army entering from Tunisia led to armed clashes, Boumedienne firmly insisted on the primacy of the regulars. He also became involved in factional struggles, vigorously backing Ben-Bella. In July 1962 he was dismissed by the FLN Prime Minister Ben-Khedda, but, firmly backed by Ben-Bella, ignored this order, marched into Algiers and imposed the rule of his army and Ben-Bella's fac-

tion. When Ben-Bella set up the first government of an independent Algeria in September 1962, Boumedienne became his defense minister, and from September 1963 deputy prime minister, but tensions developed between the two men. In June 1965 Boumedienne overthrew Ben-Bella in a coup and imprisoned him. In his 13 years as head of state, he consistently maintained Algeria's state socialism and alliances with the Soviet Bloc. While Boumedienne had little charisma, his leadership, strengthened by purges and political assassinations, was unquestioned until his death in December 1978.

From terrorist to statesman: Boumedienne with the Kuwaiti minister of oil, 1975 in their first meeting

BOURGUIBA, AL-HABIB   (1903–) The most prominent leader of Tunisian nationalism, who led Tunisia to independence, president of Tunisia 1957–1987. Born in Monastir, Tunisia, Bourguiba studied law in France and began practicing as a lawyer. He was active in the nationalist movement represented by *Destour* (the Constitution Party). In 1934 he was among a group of younger activists who seceded from the party, dissatisfied with its traditional leadership and lack of vigor, and founded the NEO-DESTOUR party, which soon became the chief spokesman of Tunisian nationalism.

Bourguiba was imprisoned in 1934–1936 and again from 1938. He was released in 1942 by the German occupiers of Tunisia. His official biographers are silent about his relations with the Germans after his release; he seems to have collaborated with them to some degree, but this has not been fully clarified. In 1945 he escaped renewed French surveillance and harassment and went to Cairo, where the nationalists of the three Maghrib countries established their headquarters. In 1950 he went to France to negotiate Tunisia's independence, but when these talks failed he was again arrested. He was released but kept under surveillance until the final negotiations on Tunisia's independence, 1954–1955. During those years Bourguiba had to face more extremist elements within his movement—both the guerrillas fighting an armed struggle, and a faction of the *Neo-Destour* led by his rival, Saleh Ben-Yussuf—but he won out.

After Tunisia attained partial independence in 1955 and full independence in March 1956, Bourguiba was elected president of the Constituent Assembly in April 1956. For three decades he was the supreme leader of Tunisia, endeavoring to give the country a modernist, moderate, liberal, pro-western shape. He abolished polygamy, restricted the rule of Islamic law and made the secular institutions of the state supreme. As his rule became oppressive and his senility obvious, his succession was for years Tunisia's major problem. He was deposed in November 1987 in a coup headed by Zein-al-'Abedin Ben-Ali, who became president. Bourguiba was permitted to retire and has since been living in isolation and under strict surveillance.

BOUTEFLIKA, ABDEL AZIZ   (1937–) Algerian politician. Bouteflika first achieved prominence as a ruthless executioner during Algeria's struggle for independence; in 1962 he became the new country's minister of sport and later (1963) its minister of foreign affairs. He was president of the UN General Assembly (1974). His vitriolic attacks on western imperialism have made him into something of a Third World hero.

BOXER UPRISING   An anti-foreign and specifically anti-Christian movement, composed mainly of peasants, including many adolescents, that flared up in the Shandong province in 1898 and drew China into war with a number of foreign powers in 1900. The secret society Yihequan, whose name was roughly translated by Westerners as "Righteous and Harmonious Fists," or simply "Boxers," conducted a set of rituals which, it claimed, made its adherents impervious to foreign bullets. Spirit-possession was the path to invulnerability. The Boxers called upon a popular deity and went into a trance when the spirit possessed them. Essentially, this was an instance of mass shamanism rooted in popular culture and religion, fueled by resentment of the foreign incursion into China. In the villages, foreign missionaries and Chinese Christians, both protected by foreign gunboats, were highly visible symbols of imperialism. The Boxers hoped to frighten the "foreign bandits" out of the country by first massacring Chinese converts. Thus, the number of Chinese killed by Boxer bands far exceeded the number of foreign victims (less than 250, mostly missionaries, many of whom were killed in Shanxi in June–July 1900). Political and economic conditions combined to set off the movement in Shandong, a traditional hotbed of heterodox sects. In 1897, Germany seized a concession in Shandong as recompense for the murder of two

German Catholic priests. The Chinese rage was accelerated the following year, when the flooding of the Yellow River brought misery to millions of homeless peasants. Purported to have originally been anti-dynastic as well as anti-foreign, by September 1899 the Boxers' aim was to "Support the Qing dynasty and destroy the foreigners." Expelled from Shandong by a new governor in December, the Boxers ran wild in the metropolitan province of Zhili, where officials were more hospitable. In June 1900, Boxer bands entered Beijing and stopped an international relief force of over 2,000 troops from reaching the capital. The empress dowager, misled into believing that the foreigners wanted her replaced, co-opted the Boxers and ordered imperial forces to resist the foreigners. On June 20, the German minister was killed and the legations were besieged, and the next day China declared war on the foreign powers. However, powerful regional leaders realized that China had no hope of winning and tried to limit the damage. They ignored the war declaration and enforced peace. These realistic officials informed foreign governments that "rebels" had seized power in Beijing and had launched an "unauthorized" war. This limited the war to the north and created the fiction of the Boxer "rebellion," which was convenient to both sides. An international relief force of some 20,000 troops from seven countries liberated the legations on August 14, and the empress dowager and the emperor fled Beijing in disguise the next day as allied troops began looting the capital. The troops were later joined by a German force that engaged mostly in punitive expeditions that terrorized north China for six months. The Boxer Protocol, signed in September 1901, imposed a crippling indemnity upon China.

A boxer being beheaded

BRAUN, OTTO (Chinese pseudonym, "Li De")   (1900–1974) Military adviser to Chinese Communists. Born in Germany, near Munich, Braun served in the Austro-Hungarian army during World War I, was captured by the Russians and joined the RED ARMY after the October RUSSIAN REVOLUTION OF 1917. He was active in the German Communist movement in 1919, was arrested and imprisoned but escaped in 1928. Sent to the Soviet Union by the German Communist party, he studied at the Frunze military academy, and in 1932 the COMINTERN sent him to China to act as a military adviser to the Chinese Communists. In 1933 he went to Ruijin, capital of the Chinese Soviet Republic in Jiangxi, and played a major role in planning Communist military strategy. Accused of "left-adventurism" and "dogmatism," he was held responsible for the change from guerrilla tactics to positional warfare that forced the Communists to retreat to the north. He became the only westerner to participate in the entire LONG MARCH, but with the ascendancy of MAO ZEDONG in January 1935 Braun lost his influence, becoming a mere observer. He stayed in Yan'an, the new Communist capital, until 1939, when the COMINTERN ordered him to return to the Soviet Union, where he spent the war years. In 1953 he settled in the German Democratic Republic and died in East Berlin in 1974.

BRAZIL COUPS, SECOND REPUBLIC, 1930

GETULIO VARGAS, governor of the state of Rio Grande do Sul and presidential candidate against Dr. Julio Prestes, became dictator of Brazil in October 1930 following a coup that year. In 1931 he declared a moratorium on the service of foreign debt and adopted a program of destruction of crop surpluses. However this resulted in a large deficit for the government.

In the summer of 1932, an 83-day revolution was initiated in Sao Paulo to protest against the delay in returning to constitutional government. The revolutionary army was well equipped and its defeat came only after the defection of one of its leaders. However all was not lost, for in July 1934 a strongly nationalistic constitution was promulgated. In essence, this constitution aimed at the improvement of the social and economic conditions of the citizens. It decreased the privileges of foreigners and gave women the right to vote and hold public office. In 1937, in response to national unrest, Vargas was elected president under this constitution.

BRAZILIAN REVOLUTION OF 1889

On April 13, 1831, Dom Pedro de Alcántara was named second emperor of Brazil. During his reign, Brazil became one of the best-governed countries. By 1870, he had even allowed the spread of republican ideas. Dissatisfaction arose among the Catholics, because the emperor had chosen to take the Masons' side in the quarrels between these two groups between 1873 and 1875. Discontent also existed in the military because of the punishment meted out to certain officers for having criticized the government. Plantation owners who had been impoverished by the loss of their slaves also joined the enemies of the emperor. By the middle of 1889, the viscount of Ouro Prêto was requested to form a new government, under which suffrage was increased, religious freedom was established and import duties lowered. However, these reforms did not suffice to decrease the dissatisfaction of the military. On November 15, 1889, Deodoro da Fonseca seized control of the main government departments and arrested the members of the government. The same evening, the republic of Brazil was proclaimed by a decree published in the name of the army, navy and the nation and Dom Pedro and his family were exiled. A provisional government was appointed under the leadership of Deodoro Da Fonseca.

BRECHT, BERTOLT

(1898–1956) German poet and dramatist. Brecht was at first an a political, rebellious, somewhat cynical expressionist poet, but later he adopted sharp social revolutionary views, tending to communism, although he never joined the party. A poet, satirist and a great theater director first, he and the composer Kurt Weil won international attention with a Ger-

Bertolt Brecht during a rehearsal of his play, Mother Courage

man version of the Beggar's Opera, known ever since as *Die Dreigroschenoper* (The threepenny opera, 1928). In this work, which was highly modern but still a popular theatrical-musical, Brecht sought to expose western, and any bourgeoise society as a mixture of crime, sex and greed, controlled by the legendary "Mack the Knife." Later Brecht developed his "theatrical alienation theory," rejecting the Aristotelian principles of drama, which were supposed to lead the public to catharsis by identifying with the drama's relevant heroes. Brecht sought to make the viewers detest, reject and study his heroes in contempt or disillusion, leading toward political awakening. In this he revolutionized the theater, but also achieved two opposing goals in Germany itself—some were alienated to the opposite redirection, having sensed Brecht's' Communist credo, and some—all over the world—liked and identified with his detested or otherwise problematic heroes, such as *Mutter Courage* (Mother courage, 1941).

In Brecht's direct, and some less direct theatrical attacks on Nazism as a product of wild running capitalism such as *Der Jasager/Der Neinsager* (He who said yes/He who said no) and *Die Massnahme* (The measures taken), as well as *Der aufhaltsame Aufstieg der Arturo Ui* (The resistible rise of Arturo Ui, 1941.) Brecht demonstrated a doctrinaire simplistic view of Nazism and its success. At the same time he maintained his own version of hate and disapproval of the western, especially American way of life. He lived for a while in the United States and became highly respected in the English-speaking world due to the latters' tradition of literary satirical criticism and English opening to radical social criticism. A "cultural hero" in the west, Brecht returned to East Berlin in 1949, where he founded and directed his Berliner Ensemble. A play by Guenther Grass, criticizing Brecht's indifference toward the uprising of the East Berlin workers in 1952, was ignored worldwide due to Brecht's standing as a "revolutionary art hero." A recent scholarly biography blamed him for plagiarizing the texts of most of his major theatrical works from his mistresses and for a rather Stalinist personality.

BRESHKO-BRESHKOVSKAYA, KATERINA   (1844–1934) Russian Communist revolutionary, known widely as "The Little Grandmother of the Revolution." The daughter of serf-owning gentry, Breshkovskaya took part in all phases of the Russian revolutionary movement, from populism through revolutionary terror, to revolution and the turbulent politics of postrevolutionary emigration. Her first activity for the betterment of society was based on religious beliefs. In the years immediately following the emancipation of the serfs, she organized educational and community welfare work for the peasantry. Frustrated by the autocracy's restrictions, she moved to Kiev in 1871, where she founded a socialist commune with her sister and a friend, conducting educational activities among the young people of Kiev. Here she also came into contact with the ideological debates that raged in the populist movement (see POPULISM). It was at this time that she became convinced of the efficacy of terror in the revolutionary movement.

Breshkovskaya was among those who went TO THE PEOPLE in 1874, where she was arrested after several months of activity among the peasantry. After four years of detention she was one of the defendants in "The Trial of the 193," and had the dubious distinction of being the first woman sentenced to exile with hard labor.

Allowed to return to European Russia in 1896, she continued her revolutionary work and was active in founding the Party of Socialist Revolutionaries. She utilized her international reputation, raising money for the revolutionary movement during lecture tours abroad. She hastened back to Russia to take part in the RUSSIAN REVOLUTION OF 1905 and in 1907 was arrested and condemned to lifelong exile. During this exile she was aided by ALEXANDER KERENSKY, with whom she forged a close political alliance and personal friendship. Upon her return to Petrograd after the February RUSSIAN REVOLUTION OF 1917, she supported Kerensky and the provisional government that he headed from July to November. She was active against the BOLSHEVIK seizure of power, first while in Russia, where she supported Socialist Revolutionary efforts to oppose the Bolsheviks, and later after emigration to Czechoslovakia, where she died at the age of 90. Her memoirs were published in an English edition entitled *Hidden Springs of the Russian Revolution: Personal Memoirs of Katerina Breshkovskaya* (Stanford: Stanford University Press, 1931).

BRISSOT, JACQUES PIERRE   (1754–1793) One of the most vigorous and effective orators, journalists and parliamentarians produced by the FRENCH REVOLUTION, Brissot is chiefly renowned as the leader of the radical party—or more appropriately, the faction—called the GIRONDINS, known at the height of its power between 1791 and 1793 as the Brissotins. He was a re-

lentless champion of the emancipation of the black slaves in the French Caribbean sugar colonies and a publicist and pamphleteer of enormous verve and talent.

Born in modest circumstances in the cathedral town of Chartres, the son of a restaurant owner, he started his career as a lawyer's clerk and joined the underworld of literary hacks and political pamphleteers. He preferred to call himself Brissot de Warville after buying an estate by that name at the end of the *ancien régime*. He·made his way to London, where he earned a precarious living turning out scurrilous broadsides against Marie Antoinette. In 1788, he visited the American colonies after the war of independence, where he wrote admiringly and perceptively about its revolution and democratic society. His radical views drew him naturally to the zealous enthusiasts of the Third Estate, and when the revolution broke out he tried to steer it in the direction of a European crusade for the rights of man. By the end of 1789 he had broken away from the faction around the MARQUIS DE LAFAYETTE, which secretly supported the claims of the Duke d'Orléans to replace his cousin Louis XVI on the throne, and became a national celebrity by founding *Le Patriote Français*, the most radical of the revolution's early newspapers. Condemning all parties as factional and disruptive of the main ideas of the revolution, Brissot argued that there could only be one revolutionary party, the party of *Les Patriotes*.

Even before 1788, Brissot had launched the *Société des Amis des Noirs*, calling for the abolition of slavery, and was now able to lobby the legislative assembly to declare the emancipation of slavery in France, the first country ever to do so. After the king's aborted flight to Varennes on June 21, 1791, Brissot led a campaign calling for his abdication, voted with the majority of the assembly in favor of the execution of Louis XVI and took an increasingly radical line in arguing that the revolution could only survive by spreading its ideas to the Rhineland, Italy and the Austrian Netherlands.

Elected a deputy for Paris in 1791, Brissot played a major part as a member of the PARIS COMMUNE in organizing the popular demonstrations of the Champs de Mars, which called for the replacement of the monarchy by a republic. When re-elected to the revolutionary Convention in 1792, he used all his energies, this time as a deputy for his home department of the Eure et Loir, to provoke Austria into hostilities. Brissot calculated that war would expose the king as a traitor and pave the way to a revolutionary republic; the royalists predicted that military defeat would undermine the revolution and thereby restore the king to his former power.

It was as the undisputed leader of the Brissotins in the newly elected convention that Brissot reached the peak of his influence. In the period immediately before and during the first tumultuous year of the revolutionary Convention, the Brissotins were virtually in control of the course of the revolution. The life and death struggle between his party and ROBESPIERRE's JACOBINS, both in and out of the convention, which the Jacobins finally won on June 2, 1793, by encouraging the mob leaders of the SANS-CULOTTES to expel Brissot and 30 other Brissotins from the convention hall, has tended to obscure that fact that Brissot was a true believer in a radical and more humane revolution than any of his adversaries and that his ideas were more noble and virtuous than the narrow ideology of Robespierre, who believed that revolutionary virtue could only be imposed by means of the reign of terror, not by popular enthusiasm and reformist zeal.

What Brissot stood for were the same ideas of liberty and progress so eloquently put forward by his Girondin political ally and revolutionary mentor, the Marquis de Condorcet, the great Enlightenment philosopher who was proscribed with him on June 3. Forced to go underground by the Jacobins, Brissot tried to escape across the frontier to Geneva but was caught. He was sent to the guillotine after a one-week mock trial, on October 31, 1793, having devoted the five months he spent in prison to writing his memoirs and a defense of the Brissotin ideology of the revolution.

BRISSOTINS   see GIRONDINS.

BRITISH UNION OF FASCISTS (BUF)   An organization founded by Oswald Mosley in 1932; in 1933 it adopted the Black Shirt and the Fascist (see FASCISM) salute. In 1933–1934 it created many incidents by holding meetings in which hecklers were beaten up, and by staging marches through the largely Jewish East End of London. In 1936 the Public Order Act virtually killed the movement, but in the late 1960s a successor organization, the so-called National Front, became active once again.

BROWN, JOHN   (1800–1859) A fanatic American abolitionist who first preached, then attempted, "to purge this land with blood." Born in Corrington, Connecticut and raised in Hudson, Ohio, Brown was an early convert to the cause of radical abolitionism. In 1855, the shifty ne'er-do-well Brown settled in Ossawatomie, Kansas, with his five sons. Kansas, just recently opened to settlement, was torn between Free-Soilers and pro-slavery settlers. In retaliation for a pro-slavery attack on the free city of Lawrence, Brown together with four of his sons and two sympathizers launched a raid on pro-slavery settlers along Pottawottamie Creek, brutally killing five men and boys.

Extreme abolitionists in the North cheered on "Brown of Ossawatomie," spurring him on to a more comprehensive and dangerous act in his violent anti-slavery crusade. Backed by financial support from a number of respectable northern abolitionists, Brown conceived a plan for arming Southern slaves and inciting them to open rebellion against their masters. Part of his plan was to establish a stronghold in northern Virginia to which slaves from all over the South would flee and from which they would be dispatched to spread insurrection throughout the slave states.

On the night of October 16, 1859, Brown led a force of 21 heavily armed men in an attack on the federal arsenal in Harpers Ferry, Virginia. Among the raiders were a number of runaway slaves and three of Brown's sons. After storming into the compound, Brown and his force were counter-attacked by local militia forces and a contingent of federal troops commanded by Robert E. Lee. After two days of siege, the insurgents surrendered. Brown was tried and convicted on charges of conspiracy, treason and murder.

Influential northern ideologues, reformers and journalists raised a choir of eloquent pleas to spare the life of the man who had rebelled against the law of the land out of adherence to a "higher law." The appeals, which in essence argued the legitimacy of rebellion even in a democracy governed by law, were of

no avail and John Brown was then hanged on December 2, 1859.

The American South was shocked by the condoning of insurgence in northern public opinion no less than by the raid itself. Before the second anniversary of Brown's raid, it would be the South that would illustrate the legitimacy of rebellion in American politics.

BRUMAIRE, COUP D'ÉTAT OF   This name, corresponding to the "misty" or "foggy" month of November in the calendar of the FRENCH REVOLUTION, designates the bloodless military coup d'état on November 9 and 10, 1799 that overthrew the Directorate that had governed France since 1795 and replaced it with the Consulate under General Bonaparte. Unlike previous coups, such as Vendémiaire, Germinal or Prairial which had punctuated the stormy history of the Directorate, Brumaire was conceived and carried out not through the independent action of mob orators and the SANS-CULOTTES but by a political conspiracy. Its leader was Abbé Sieyès, the chief conspirator; he himself hand-picked Bonaparte, who had just returned from Egypt on October 9, as the plotters' "sword," when his first choice, General Joubert, was inopportunely killed at the battle of Novi in northern Italy.

The plot went through two phases and took two days to accomplish, but not without a snag that made it necessary to resort to force. On the first day, 18 Brumaire, TALLEYRAND was able to neutralize the five Directors in the Luxembourg Palace in Paris by bribing Barras, the strong man of the régime, and persuading two others to resign or withdraw from office. On the second, the two legislative houses of parliament, the Council for the Five Hundred and the Council of the Ancients, which had been hastily convened from Paris to sit in the Orangerie of the Palace of Saint Cloud in fear of a false rumor of an impending JACOBIN coup, solemnly reaffirmed the legitimacy of the republic and swore their loyalty to the constitution. When General Bonaparte, at the head of his guards, was invited by his brother, Lucien, who had taken the chair for that extraordinary session, to enter the chamber and harangue the deputies, he was greeted with cries of "Outlaw, Outlaw!" and stabbed in the face. He lost his nerve and fled outside. As the council's own guard hesitated, Lucien emerged and saved the day, appealing to Bonaparte's soldiers to rescue their general from the dagger of the assassins inside and clear out the deputies from the Orangerie. Talleyrand, who had master-minded the coup from the nearby country home of his then-current mistress, the English actress Mrs. Simmons, then invited the small band of plotters to dinner.

Thus ended the revolution's first 10 years of experiment in parliamentary government. Though Bonaparte had only a handful of supporters, he emerged victorious. Overriding parliament, Brumaire was approved by a national plebiscite which made possible four years of authoritarian rule under Bonaparte as First Consul, at first for 10 years, then for life. In 1804, Bonaparte was proclaimed emperor under the name of Napoleon.

BRUTUS, LUCIUS IUNIUS   The hero who, according to Roman tradition, in the 6th century B.C. expelled the last Etruscan king of Rome, Tarquinius Superbus. It was the latter's tyrannical rule which made the monarchy something loathed by Rome from then on. Brutus exploited the rape of the noble LUCRETIA by the son of the king and her subsequent suicide to instigate the people to rise against the tyrant. He instituted liberty and the annual office of two consuls, each with equal powers, thus establishing the Roman Republic in 509 B.C. Many of the stories concerning Brutus are certainly legendary. Some constitutional and religious regulations may have been ascribed to him because he allegedly executed his sons when they conspired to restore the monarchy in Rome. Brutus found his death in war against the Etruscans, who supported the exiled king.

BRUTUS, MARCUS IUNIUS A Roman nobleman born about 85 B.C., Brutus spent most of his career maneuvering uneasily between the rival factions of Julius Caesar (who at one time took Brutus' mother, Servillia, as his mistress) and Gnaeus Pompeus, whom he supported in the civil war of 49 B.C. In spite of this political agility and his habit of lending money at 48% annual interest, he somehow managed to gain a reputation for marble-like integrity.

By 45 B.C. Brutus was working closely with Caesar, who treated him like a son. It therefore came as a great shock to Caesar when he joined the conspirators against him. Citing Caesar's alleged desire to found a monarchy in Rome, the conspirators surrounded him and stabbed him to death on the Senate floor, on the Ides of March (March 15).

Caesar's last words as he fell—"*et tu Brute*" ("You too, Brutus?") have gone down in history. Brutus himself had to flee from Rome when Caesar's deputy Marc Antony turned the population against him and his fellow conspirators. Brutus waged war against Antony and Caesar's heir, Octavian. At the Battle of Philippi, in 42 B.C., he was defeated and took his own life.

BUKHARIN, NIKOLAI IVANOVICH (1888–1938) One of the leaders of the BOLSHEVIK PARTY and among its leading economic theorists, Bukharin was born into a middle-class Moscow family and began the study of economics at Moscow University. In 1906, under the influence of the revolutionary events of the period, he left university to join the Bolshevik underground. Elected to the Bolshevik committee of Moscow in 1909, he was twice arrested in 1909 and again in 1910. He left Russia in 1911, eventually becoming involved in Bolshevik activity in Cracow. He helped edit the party newspaper, *Pravda*, and at LENIN's request assisted STALIN in the preparation of his 1913 essay, "Marxism on the National and Colonial Question." In 1915 and 1916, Bukharin differed sharply with Lenin in his analysis of imperialism and his approach to national self-determination, differences which found expression in his book, *Imperialism and World Economy*, completed in 1915.

Deported by the Austrian authorities at the outbreak of World War I, Bukharin travelled through Scandinavia and settled in New York in 1916, editing a Marxist newspaper, *Novyi Mir* ("New World"). He returned to Russia after the February RUSSIAN REVOLUTION OF 1917, resuming his activity in Moscow as a member of both the city committee and the regional bureau. In December 1917, he for a short time assumed the editorship of *Pravda*, resigning to lead the fight of the LEFT COMMUNIST faction, which advocated revolutionary war instead of Lenin's proposed separate peace with the Germans. As leader of the Left Communists, Bukharin advocated the most radical policies of War Communism (1918–1921), such as the centralizing of all economic functions in the State. Many of these policies were

explained in his 1920 work, written together with Yevgenii Preobrazhensky, *The ABC of Communism*. He resumed his editorship of *Pravda* in July 1918, continuing in this position until 1929. From 1934 to 1937 he was editor of the central government newspaper, *Izvestia*. Simultaneously he was active in the Communist International, rising to chair its executive in 1926.

During the New Economic Policy (1921–1926), Bukharin became a supporter of moderation, looking to peasant prosperity to provide the capital surplus necessary for the socialist industrialization program. In this period he joined Stalin in fighting TROTSKY, KAMENEV and ZINOVIEV. Once the latter were defeated, Stalin turned against Bukharin. He was tried and executed as a Trotskyist. As part of Khrushchev's de-Stalinization, Bukharin was absolved of all criminal charges, but his political rehabilitation was only made public officially in 1987, when Mikhail Gorbachev referred to Bukharin as one who, despite having made some political errors, had rendered great service to the Communist party.

BULGARIA, COMMUNIST TAKEOVER AND COLLAPSE

Communist Takeover of 1944. The Communist takeover of Bulgaria in 1944 was swift and well planned. With the backing of the Soviet forces in September 1944, the Fatherland Front, composed of leftist elements and including the Communists who had 8,000 members, took power. Holding the top ministries of justice and the interior, they proceeded to remove, by "salami tactics," the opposition forces, most notably the Agrarian Union. The Union's leader, Nikola Petkov, was arrested in the parliament and executed in 1947 for plotting to overthrow the régime. By August 1945, the democratic opposition withdrew from the Front in protest at the Communist-initiated terror. Purges in the government apparatus and the army assured the victory of the Fatherland Front in rigged elections in 1945 and 1946, although the opposition still managed to gain some 30% of the votes in 1946. The Communists also moved to "unite" with factions of parties that were undermined and split by Communist tactics. A plebiscite in September 1946 abolished the monarchy, yet another step on the road to a complete takeover. The execution of alleged war criminals removed numerous potential opponents to the régime and spread further terror. Following the removal of the opposition and the rift with Yugoslavia, Communist leader GREGORI DIMITROV, who had spent the war years in Moscow, moved to purge the Communist party. Thus in March 1949, Traichko Kostov, the "internal" leader of the party, who had spent the war years in Bulgaria, was purged. He was hanged in late 1949, having been charged with being a foreign agent. Dimitrov's death in July 1949 and the violent purges within the Communist party that year closed the first chapter in Bulgaria's postwar history.

Communist Collapse, 1989–1990. The Gorbachev type of reforms were never really carried out by the Bulgarian Communist leadership, although some ambitious reform plans were proposed but never implemented. In their last years in power, the Communists increased their assimilatory pressures on the large Turkish minority, a last ditch attempt to gain some legitimacy by using a nationalist card, a tactic not unknown to Communist régimes. Dissidence emerged slowly and cautiously, and by the beginning of 1989 there were several opposition groups, one of them significantly called The Discussion Club for the Support of *Perestroika* and *Glasnost*. An independent trade union movement as well as an enviromental one, the *Ecoglasnost*, indicated the emergence of opposition which, although not united in its initial phases, was on a clear collision course with the régime. The fleeing of some 300,000 Turks in wake of the nationalist pressures and public demonstrations in late October 1989 represented a clear challenge to the régime. As in some other East European countries, internal pressure was built up within the Bulgarian Communist party (CP) to save the régime by removing the top leadership and embarking on a reformist road. The Bulgarian Communist leader, ZHIVKOV, was removed on November 10, 1989 as the result of an internal coup within the party leadership led by Foreign Minister Petur Mladenov. The latter recognized the desperate economic situation, referred to the country as being "on the verge of cardiac arrest," and promising far-reaching democratization and reforms. It was not popular power that toppled the régime; mass demonstrations for radical changes took place some two months after Zhivkov's downfall and not before it. Unlike the case in Czechoslovakia, there was no "Bulgarian Havel," but only some younger apparachiks attempting to save the régime. Only a week after the internal palace revolution did the Union of Democratic Forces, a loose organization of some 15 opposition groups, emerge and challenge the restructured Communist party, which was renamed the Bulgarian Socialist party in April 1990. Several new political parties emerged, some of them based on the parties that had been removed by the Communists in the late 1940s, such as the Bulgarian Agrarian National Union. In fact, Communist power did not collapse, but rather shifted into the hands of a reformist group, which itself underwent several internal changes, disengaging itself from the unpopular practices identified with the long Zhivkov era. Having won the June 1990 elections with 47% of the votes, power—albeit unstable and challenged by the opposition—remained in the hands of the Bulgarian Socialist party. It could still count on the votes, especially in the rural areas, where the party organization handled the masses as in the Zhivkov era. Bulgarian democrats considered the November 1989 events as an "unfinished revolution," in contrast to the Polish, Czechoslovak and Hungarian cases.

BUND Also known as the Jewish Bund, its full name was the General Union of Jewish Workers in Lithuania, Poland and Russia. Toward the end of the 19th century the emancipation of the Jews from the old ghetto, combined with the rise of modern nationalism and anti-Semitism, confronted educated European Jews with an unprecedented challenge, since they could neither communicate with their traditional parents nor integrate into the Gentile world. Against this background, many of them saw revolutionary socialism, with its emphasis on secular internationalism, as the solution; here, at last, was a movement which would allow them to integrate into the modern world.

Against this background, the Bund was founded in Vilnius in 1897 by a small group of Jewish workers and intellectuals and rapidly developed into the most effective organization of its kind in Czarist Russia. Demanding the end of discrimination against the Jews as well as a socialist revolution in Russia, the Bund clashed with LENIN, who claimed that there was no room among socialists for a separate Jewish organization. Its leaders

thereupon walked out of the second congress of the Russian Social Democratic party (1903) and, from that point on, they generally supported the MENSHEVIKS. In 1920, the organization split. One wing joined the BOLSHEVIKS, who had seized power in Russia three years earlier. The other, led by Rafael Abramovich, insisted in retaining its separate identity and was soon suppressed. Outside Russia, though, the Bund continued to be active until the beginning of World War II.

BUNKE, TAMARA (TANIA) (1946–1967) Best-known as "*Tania la guerrillera*," a young woman of German origin (the daughter of German Communists who had emigrated to Argentina, where she was raised) and a citizen of the German Democratic Republic (GDR), who fought and died as a member of the guerrilla expeditionary force in Bolivia commanded by ERNESTO CHE GUEVARA during 1966–1967. Bunke was the chief go-between used by the Cubans for organizing a support network for the Bolivian effort in neighboring Argentina and arrived in La Paz, Bolivia on November 18, 1964, under the name of Laura Gutierrez Bauer, where she played an important role in organizing the preliminary stages of the Bolivian expedition.

She also served as the link between the incipient guerrilla force commanded by Che and the French revolutionary, scholar and journalist Regis Debray, who arrived in Bolivia from Cuba in early March 1967, with the mission of "informing the outside world" of Che's presence there. Bunke died in combat at the Vado del Yeso ambush of one of the detachments of the guerrilla forces by Bolivian infantry on August 31, 1967, while crossing the Rio Grande river together with six other guerrilla combatants. In the cemetery of the Bolivian town of Vallaegrande, near the site of the murder of Guevara by Bolivian soldiers after his capture, close to the airfield, "lies the body of 'Tania', the beautiful girl guerrilla who died with nine others on 31 August after being treacherously led into an ambush in the Rio Grande."

"Tania" quickly became a symbol of the incorporation of women into revolutionary struggles throughout the world and became the name used by Patricia Hearst after her bizarre conversion to the cause of her kidnappers of the Symbionese Liberation Army in northern California in 1974.

BUONAROTTI, FILIPPO MICHELE (1761–1837) Professional French revolutionary of Italian origin. Born in Pisa of a noble Florentine family and a graduate of the University of Pisa's law faculty, Buonarotti became Gracchus BABEUF's chief lieutenant in the 1796 Paris Conspiracy of the Equals, which failed in its immediate objective to overthrow the directorate and replace it with a Communist régime dedicated to establishing social and economic equality. His account of that conspiracy, published in two volumes in Brussels in 1828, gave it the status of a great republican legend which inspired successive generations of revolutionaries, until the fall of the PARIS COMMUNE in 1871 and well beyond, into the early years of the Third Republic. Transformed into a secular gospel designed to bring about the ultimate triumph of an aborted revolution locked in deadly combat against the forces of reaction and religious obscurantism, under the long shadow cast by Napoleon's military despotism in both France and abroad, Buonarotti's work was adopted as the most famous textbook for apprentice revolutionaries throughout the 19th century, as they tried to re-enact the great accomplishments of the FRENCH REVOLUTION and bring down the walls of all the other Bastilles still standing in the way of reform.

Buonarotti's *Conspiration de l'Egalite dite de Babeuf* was both a vindication of Jacobinism as the immediate precursor of communism and a reaffirmation, at least in the opinion of some of his disciples, of the doctrine of Marxist socialism as the wave of the future. Both MARX and ENGELS, for instance, paid tribute to his paramount importance as a transmitter of the ideas of the Enlightenment and the French Revolution and hailed his vindication of the aims and purposes of *Bobouvisme* as an important ingredient in their own Communist ideology.

Buonarotti's communism, however, was essentially conceived in moral rather than economic terms. It glorified ROBESPIERRE's 1794 Republic of Virtue as an inspiring example for all true believers to emulate but showed little understanding of the proletariat as a revolutionary force, which even such a social theorist as the Comte de Saint-Simon, scornfully dismissed by Marx as a "Utopian Socialist," recognized as the most vital factor in his doctrine of material progress.

A born conspirator and skillful propagandist, Buonarotti helped to create the great revolutionary movement of the 19th century that spread beyond France to Italy, Belgium and the Rhineland, to fuse the ideas of the French Revolution with the struggle for national unification and self-determination in western and central Europe. This brought him into contact with the Italian CARBONARI and its French counterpart, the Charbonnerie, as well as Mazzini's YOUNG ITALY. All of these were directly inspired, both in theory and practice, by his own underground organization, the *Sublimes-Maîtres-Parfaits*, a secret society run along Masonic lines, with the goal of training a revolutionary elite in using masonry as a facade for various plots and conspiracies.

Forced into exile throughout most of his life, first in Geneva then in Brussels, Buonarotti gained enormous prestige as the heir and successor of Babeuf, and shaped the ideas of a new generation of revolutionaries such as LOUIS AUGUSTE BLANQUI and Armand Barbès, who followed his example by establishing a network of revolutionary clubs and secret societies to bring down the bourgeois monarchy of Louis Philippe.

BURMA INDEPENDENCE ARMY (BIA) A Burmese nationalist organization led by THAKIN AUNG SAN in 1942. It was able to organize 23,000 men and seize power temporarily, between the withdrawal of the British and the arrival of the Japanese.

BURMESE COUP (1962) In the years following its independence, Burma suffered from severe ethnic and social problems. The economy was stagnant, corruption was rampant and separatist insurgencies threatened to tear the country apart. Faced with chaos, President U Nu decided in 1958 to hand power to a caretaker government headed by General Ne Win. Ne Win proved to be a particularly capable ruler. Although he adhered to Burma's democratic constitution, he was able to bring an efficient military apparatus into the daily life of the country. The cost of living dropped, crime was practically eliminated and squatters in Rangoon, most of them refugees from the rural areas, were peacefully resettled in newly-established suburbs. In

many instances, Ne Win adopted harsh policies with the various rebel movements, but he also expressed willingness to acquiesce to some of their objectives and even persuaded the hereditary leaders of two important groups, the Shan and the Kayah, to relinquish some of their traditional powers. By 1960, the date set for Burma's return to democracy, the country seemed to be recovering from the troubles of the previous 12 years.

In that year's elections, U Nu and his Clean-AFPFL (Anti-Fascist People's Freedom League) won a clear majority of the votes. Soon after assuming the presidency, however, it became clear that many of his election promises could not be fulfilled. He had promised to nationalize industry, but this was opposed by both the local business community and by foreign companies operating in Burma. He had planned to make Buddhism the official state religion, but this was contested by the Karen, Chin and Kachin ethnic minorities and by the Arakan Muslims. On the other hand, his attempts to renege on this promise sparked riots among Buddhist monks in the capital. He had offered the Mon and Arakanese Muslims their own states within Burma's federal structure, but this only exacerbated simmering ethnic tensions among them and among other ethnic minorities. In 1962 U Nu resigned, realizing that his attempts at reform had been a failure.

The political vacuum was filled by Ne Win. In March 1962, he seized power and established a revolutionary council to govern the country. This council consisted of 17 members—15 from the army and one each from the navy and the air force. Later, when describing the objectives of his coup, Ne Win explained that democracy had "failed to serve [Burma's] socialist development." Outlining his régime's program in the *Burmese Way to Socialism*, Ne Win again set about finding solutions for the country's problems: ethnic and religious distinctions and a disproportionate power structure. Unlike many other countries, the Burmese never placed particular value on wealth. Instead, they valued political power and the way in which power was then distributed among the population was asymmetrical. In effect, the Burmese revolution differed from so many other socialist revolutions in that its stated purpose was to remedy social rather than economic inequalities.

Of course, the working classes remained "the vanguards and custodians of the revolution." The vast landholdings of the Buddhist monasteries were redistributed among the peasantry, but this was also intended to put an end to the preferred status of Buddhists over members of other religions. Under Ne Win, students and civil servants were forced to engage in physical labor, in a clear move away from westernization. As for ethnic factionalism, Ne Win used the army as a "unifying superstructure" in which members of different groups were forced to intermix. Later Ne Win organized the Burmese Socialist Program Party (BSPP) as the country's sole political party, another factor aimed at unifying the disparate elements of the population. In 1973, he provided Burma with a new constitution, uniquely suited to his own brand of socialism.

Nevertheless, Ne Win's policies failed to achieve their goals. He had forced the Indian minority out of the civil service and the overseas Chinese out of commerce, but he failed to provide capable replacements from among Burma's own indigenous population. Foreign governments and investors were wary of his enforced isolation of Burma and the local population demanded the restoration of basic civil liberties such as freedom of expression. In 1987, with civil war again looming, Ne Win resigned. Two new governments, one led by a civilian, Maung Maung, failed to restore order, and in September of that year General Saw Maung seized control of the the government. Free elections were held in 1990, but as of this writing the military has refused to hand over power to the elected government.

BURR, AARON (Burr Conspiracy)   Aaron Burr, one of the most enigmatic of American politicians during the early Republic period, was acquitted of charges of treason by a controversial decision of John Marshall's Supreme Court in 1807. Yet much evidence suggests that Burr, who had served as vice-president during Thomas Jefferson's first term (1801–1805), had master, minded and attempted a rebellion through which he and his confidants would gain control over territories extending to the west of the Mississippi river. Burr apparently expected to establish in the territories he would either remove from nominal US control or conquer from the Spaniards a separate political entity supported by one of the great European powers of the time.

Earlier in his career, Burr was accused by Alexander Hamilton, a long-time rival, of conspiring to have the New England and Middle Atlantic states secede from the Union. In the most famous duel in American history, Hamilton would pay with his life for incurring Burr's wrath. Still, however disloyal in his public career, Burr demonstrated exemplary life-long devotion to his disabled wife and to their only child.

BYELORUSSIAN PEASANTS-WORKERS GROMADA (Society)   In 1925–1927, a revolutionary left-wing organization that arose in West Byelorussia (Poland) with the aim of first achieving self-determination and then joining the USSR. Its main leaders were B.A. Tarashkevitch, S.A. Rak-Mikhailovsky, and P. Metla; its main publications were *Thzinbelarusa* (Byelorussian life) and *Narodnce Delo* (People's duty).

Demanding reforms such as national equality for Byelorussians in Poland, the party made use of its leaders' parliamentary immunity to carry out its activities. These activities were considered sufficiently dangerous for the Polish government to become alarmed; in 1927 *Gromada* itself was banned and 400 of its leaders and activists arrested and sentenced in a series of show trials. The remaining activists, driven underground, joined the West Byelorussian Communist party, only to find themselves declared traitors by the COMINTERN (1939) and suppressed for the second time when STALIN's forces occupied eastern Poland in 1939.

BYELORUSSIAN REVOLUTIONARY GROMADA (Society)   (1902–1918) A revolutionary organization that rose in west Byelorussia. Its leaders were Ivan and Anton Lustkevitch, A. Pashkevitsch and A. Burbis. Claiming to represent the Byelorussian working people, the leaders saw themselves as the chief promoters of anti-czarist agitation in the country. They maintained close links with similar parties in neighboring countries.

In 1906, having gained wide support among the Byelorussian peasantry, the *Gromada* broadened its aims to include an autonomous Byelorussian state with its capital at Grodno. During World War I, the German occupation on the one hand, and the outbreak of the RUSSIAN REVOLUTION OF 1917 on the other, enabled the leaders to maneuver between the two sides. The result, though, was a split between liberals and left wingers. The former, who wanted to set up a democratic régime, ended up by being forcibly suppressed. The latter created the Byelorussian Communist party and, from that time on formed an integral part of the COMMUNIST PARTY OF THE SOVIET UNION.

BYELORUSSIAN REVOLUTIONARY ORGANIZATION   (1922–1923) A left-wing revolutionary organization whose objective was to detach west Byelorussia from Poland and join it to the rest of Byelorussia which, at that time, was part of the USSR. In 1923 it dissolved itself, joining the West Byelorussian Communist party. This did not prevent its leaders and activists from being rounded up and liquidated by STALIN after he annexed east Poland in 1939.

BYELORUSSIAN SOCIALIST-REVOLUTION PARTY   (1918–1924) A peasant-based revolutionary movement that did not content itself with Byelorussian "autonomy" inside the Soviet Union but instead sought to achieve independence and to unite with Lithuania. Another source of conflict with the COMMUNIST PARTY OF THE SOVIET UNION was their differing views about the respective role of workers and peasants; the latter, after all, constituted 90% of Byelorussia's population. Thus to talk of a Peasants' party was, in the eyes of the Byelorussian leaders, pure nonsense.

The end of the Polish-Soviet war (1921) terminated the dream of Byelorussian independence. Some of its activists were arrested by the Soviet government and exiled to Poland; others fled to the west (especially Czechoslovakia) from which they attempted to carry on the struggle. In 1924, those who had remained in the USSR dissolved the Byelorussian Socialist-Revolution Party. However, this did not save them from being liquidated by STALIN during the late 1920s and 1930s.

C

CABRAL AMILCAR see PARTIDO AFRICANO DA INDEPENDENCIA DA GUINÉ E CABO VERDE (PAIGC).

CAI AO (Ts'ai Ao) (1882–1916) Chinese revolutionary. Born in Hunan to a prosperous peasant family, Cai had a good classical education before attending a modern school, where he absorbed progressive influences. After studying in a Japanese military academy, he held various military posts in China. He joined the CHINESE REPUBLICAN REVOLUTION OF 1911 and became military governor of Yunnan. In 1916 he was one of the key army leaders in the successful campaign against Yuan Shikai's plan to become emperor. After Yuan's death in June, Cai was appointed governor of Sichuan, but he died of cancer soon afterward.

CAI HESEN (Ts'ai Ho-sen) (1895–1931) Chinese Communist. Born in Hunan, Cai was MAO-ZEDONG's classmate at the First Normal School in Changsha and became his close friend. He was active in a work-study program in France, where he arrived in 1920 with a group of Hunanese students. While in France he became a Marxist and an admirer of the Soviet model, which he advocated for China. His letters and translated articles influenced Mao and other students at home, and in France he laid the foundations for a branch of the CHINESE COMMUNIST PARTY (CCP). Expelled from France in 1922, he returned to China and was elected to the CCP central committee. He became editor of the party's monthly journal and head of the central committee's propaganda department. He spent the year 1926 in Moscow as a delegate to the COMINTERN. Sent to Hong Kong in 1931 as secretary of the party's Guangdong-Guangxi branch, he was arrested by the police and extradited to Canton, where he was executed.

CAI TINGKAI (Ts'ai T'ing-k'ai) (1892–1968) Chinese military leader. Son of a Guangdong peasant, Cai joined the army at an early age, participated in the CHINESE REPUBLICAN REVOLUTION OF 1911 and, after studying in the Canton Military Academy, became a regimental commander in the National Revolutionary army.

In 1932 he achieved international fame when the 19th Route army, of which he was field commander, resisted the Japanese attack on Shanghai for more than three months. In 1933 he participated in the Fujian Revolt against CHIANG HAI-SHEK. Although he held nominal posts in the Chinese army during the Sino-Japanese war, he remained critical of the GUOMINDANG (Kuomintang), and after the establishment of the People's Republic he held various high offices, the last of which was the deputy chairmanship of the national defense council.

CAI YUANPEI (Ts'ai Yüan-p'ei) (1868–1940) Chinese revolutionary and educator. Born in Zhejiang, Cai received the highest degree in the traditional civil service examinations, but after the failure of the 1898 reform movement, abandoned an official career and combined an admiration of Russian nihilism with educational and anti-Manchu revolutionary activities. A four-year stay in Germany (1907–1911) included study at Leipzig University that aroused his interest in western, and especially Kantian, philosophy. He joined the CHINESE REPUBLICAN REVOLUTION OF 1911 and served briefly as minister of education in the first republican cabinet, but soon became disillusioned with politics. It was as an educator and advocate of freedom of thought that he made his great contribution to modern China. As chancellor of Beijing University (1916–1926), he encouraged the intellectual ferment that made that institution the center of the MAY FOURTH MOVEMENT.

CALLES, PLUTARCO ELIAS (1877–1945) Mexican revolutionary and president. After Francisco Madero's takeover of the Mexican presidency in 1913, Calles organized a military brigade in Sonora. He was the first leader in northern Mexico to rise against the presidential takeover of VICTORIANO HUERTA (1914). Serving under the command of another revolutionary commander, ALVARO OBREGON, Calles became military commander of Hermosillo. In 1915, under the presidency of VENUSTIANO CARRANZA, Calles was named governor of Sonora. As governor, Calles battled Francisco "Pancho" Villa's (see VILLA, PANCHO) troops in that state. From 1919 to 1920 he was minister of industry and commerce under Carranza and in 1920, after Carranza's assassination, became minister of war under Huerta's presidency. During Obregon's presidency, Calles was in charge of the ministry of the interior from 1920 to 1923. From 1924 to 1928 he was president of Mexico. Calles instituted a variety of anti-clerical restrictions, which led to Catholic uprisings throughout Mexico known as the CRISTERO REVOLUTION. His policies were all of a nationalist bent, with a special emphasis on socialized education. Still politically active under the presidencies of Portes Gil, Ortiz Ribi and Rodriguez, Calles was accused of antigovernment activities by President CARDENAS, who had been Calles's disciple. In 1936, Calles was expelled from Mexico. In 1941, he returned to Mexico, where he died of a bladder disease in 1945.

CALVIN, JOHN (1509–1564) French theologian and religious leader, the second greatest leader of the Reformation, after LUTHER. Born in Noyon, northeast of Paris, to a father who was an apostolic notary, Calvin was destined for an ecclesiastical career and at 11 was given a small church benefice and received a tonsure. In 1523 he was sent to study theology in Paris. Although not ordained, he seemed to be on the way to become a priest, but in 1528, at his father's suggestion, began to study law at Orleans. Moving to Bourges (1529), Calvin became influenced by Protestant ideas at a local circle of students dominated by the German Melchior Wolmar. However, he did not yet break with Roman Catholicism and his first published work, a Latin commentary of Seneca's *De Clementia* (1532), which displayed a great deal of humanist erudition, had little to do with the religious issue.

Calvin's espousal of the Reformation took place late in 1533, while he was on a visit to Paris. Forced to flee persecution, he found refuge in Angoulême, where he met the old Lefèvre d'Etaples, a prominent scholar and humanist. He then returned to Noyon (1534), resigned his benefices and was briefly imprisoned. In the same year, the appearance of many Protestant placards in Paris resulted in a wider wave of persecution. Soon, the level of persecution intensified and his brother was executed, forcing Calvin to flee to Basle (1535). It was there that the first edition of his *Christiannae Religionis Institutio* (Institutes of the Christian religion) appeared in March 1536. Later, this exposition of Calvin's religious doctrine was twice enlarged and masterfully translated into French by the author (1541; 1560). But already in its first form it revealed a superb quality of intellectual clarity and systematic thought. Proceeding from the assumption that mankind was in a state of wickedness, the consequence of Adam's fall, and that man had no free will of his own, Calvin concluded that salvation was predestined and the result of God's grace alone. The volume reduced the sacraments to two: baptism and the Lord's supper, and gave them a largely symbolic meaning. While denying that transubstantiation took place at the Eucharist, Calvin contended that Christ was spiritually present and communicated his virtue to the faithful.

While passing through Geneva in July 1536, Calvin accepted the invitation of Guillaume Farel, who had been laboring for years to reform the city, and stayed on as a preacher and professor of theology. He soon became the leading personality in the city, and persuaded the council of government to adopt various severe regulations. But his attempt to establish control over morals aroused opposition and, in 1538, he was ordered to leave. For the next three years he headed a French congregation at Strasbourg, where he befriended Bucer (Butzer), a leading German Protestant reformer. There he wrote a number of theological tracts and his famous reply to Cardinal Sadoleto (1539), in which he defended the Reformation. In 1541 he represented Strasbourg at the Diet of Regensburg. That year, he married Idelette de Bure, a widow with three children, who died eight years later.

A change of government in Geneva brought Calvin an invitation to return (September 1541). This time, his plans for a theocratic régime were carried through and, by a series of periodically-approved ordinances, he established a church government that increasingly tightened the supervision over the private lives of the citizens. Calvin's complicated system, which included four classes of officers—pastors, doctors, elders and deacons—was assisted by laymen informers who admonished and reported the sinners, and by the consistory, a tribunal of morals which wielded the right of excommunication. Resistance to this system flared up periodically. Not only were many persons prosecuted for heresy, adultery and blasphemy, in which confession was frequently extorted by torture, but there were a sizable number of cases which ended with death sentences and public executions, among them the burning for heresy—after he denied the trinity—of Michael Servetus (1553). Other forms of punishment were public recantation and exile. Nevertheless, in the last 10 years of his life, Calvin became the supreme authority in Geneva and imposed a moralistic code of behavior, which prohibited loud singing and dancing, indecent dress and drunkenness.

At the same time, Calvin made Geneva the most important European Protestant center of his time. He gave shelter to English refugees and inspired the spreading of his doctrines in France and the Netherlands. He continuously preached and wrote and, in 1559, founded the Geneva Theological Academy, which was headed by his closest supporter, Theodore Beza. A strong personality leading a simple austere life, Calvin emphasized the values of discipline, hard work, thrift and strict morality. Carried to the New World by the English Puritans, his teachings had a bearing on the consolidation of the national ethics of the mightiest modern capitalistic state.

Jean Calvin, young man in a hurry

CAMBODIA (KAMPUCHEA), 1970 COUP On November 7, 1953 as a result of Norodom Sihanouk's earlier announced "Crusade for Independence," Kampuchea became an independent state. So revered was Prince Sihanouk that his birthday, which falls two days later, is celebrated as Kampuchean Independence Day. Sihanouk organized his own party, which won 82% of the vote in the September 1955 elections. Until he was ousted in 1970, Sihanouk retained both popularity and supremacy in the domestic arena. In foreign affairs, he denounced the Communist insurgency active elsewhere in Southeast Asia and moved closer to the United States. One result was increased KHMER ROUGE guerrilla activity against his government.

In January 1970, Sihanouk left Kampuchea, ostensibly on a medical visit but actually in an attempt to pressure Hanoi into withdrawing support from the Khmer Rouge. On March 17, a coup led by Lon Nol and Sirik Matak deposed Sihanouk in his absence. He then accepted asylum in Beijing, continuing to head the Kampuchean government in exile until 1975.

CAMBRIDGE CONSPIRACY (1415) An English plan to murder Henry V on the eve of his departure at Southampton to invade France, and to replace him with Edmund de Mortimer, Earl of March. The main conspirator was Richard, Earl of Cambridge (a grandson of Edward III), the brother-in-law of the intended new king. The other chief conspirators were Sir Thomas Grey and Henry Lord Scrope of Masham, themselves related to unsuccessful traitors to Henry IV. March, though, revealed the conspiracy to Henry V, who had the three rebels beheaded.

CANEK'S REVOLT In 1761, 1,000–1,500 Yucatec Mayans in the Mexican town of Cisteil rose up against the Spanish, under the leadership of Jacinto Canek, an itinerant prophet. While the revolt was quelled within a few weeks and Canek cruelly executed, it had interesting international implications. In 1761 Britain and Spain were at war, and the possibility of British encouragement may have induced Canek to foment his revolt at that time. Whatever the case, it is probable that arms were smuggled to Canek from neighboring British Honduras.

CANTON UPRISING (December 1927) Chinese Communist revolt. After the rupture of its coalition with the GUOMINDANG (GMD), the CHINESE COMMUNIST PARTY (CCP) followed COMINTERN instructions and undertook a series of ill-fated uprisings beginning in August 1927 (NANCHANG, AUTUMN HARVEST UPRISINGS). Attempting to justify his Chinese policy, STALIN urged the CCP to attack Canton and other major cities where strong proletarian support was anticipated. Accordingly, on December 11, Red Army forces led by YE TING and YE JIANYING captured Canton. Their Canton commune lasted only a few days. On December 13, GMD troops recaptured the city, inflicting heavy losses on the CCP and its sympathizers. This was the last of the CCP uprisings in 1927 and the most disastrous. Some 200 party cadres and over 2,000 soldiers were killed, along with five Russians from the Soviet consulate who were captured and executed. The Canton Uprising marked the high point of direct Soviet Russian involvement in the Chinese Communist revolution. After the defeat, the CCP began to pursue a more independent course, emphasizing the rural option that had been cultivated by MAO ZEDONG. Complete independence from the Comintern and final abandonment of the policy of urban insurrection would still require several years.

CANUDOS REVOLT OF 1896 The Brazilian Canudos revolt of 1896, although regional, would become a conflict of state sovereignty and became known throughout Brazil. It was born out of a seemingly insignificant incident. Antônio Conselheiro, rec-

ognized all over the north of Brazil for building innumerable churches, bought a quantity of wood from the town of Juàzeiro, a quantity which it could not provide. Conselheiro let it be known that his followers were to invade Juàzeiro. A 100-strong state troop was sent to this town. The idea was to invade the town of Canudos before the invasion of Juàzeiro itself took place. Conselheiro's followers surprised the state troops in Uaua, but were unable to obtain a victory. The official count was of a 150 dead from Canudos. The state troops returned to Juàzeiro, where an even larger army was formed from both state and national troops. The national army was faced with unending guerrilla tactics by the Canudo forces but finally obtained victory because of the military equipment which they had and which the Canudos lacked.

CAPITOLINUS, MARCUS MANLIUS Of a patrician family, consul in 392 B.C. and a hero of Roman legend. It was Capitolinus who allegedly saved the Capitol of Rome from capture. Awakened by the cackling of the sacred geese, he prevented the Gauls from taking the citadel and threw them from the Tarpeian Rock. However, this hero was soon involved in a social crisis in Rome, for the Gallic sacking of Rome caused many poor peasants to suffer debt and become bondsmen of their creditors. By paying the debts to those bondsmen, Capitolinus obtained the support of the plebs, which he may have attempted to exploit to enhance his personal position. At any rate, he was accused of trying to establish tyranny in Rome and executed in 384 B.C., by being thrown from the same Tarpeian Rock.

CARBONARI (Charcoal Burners) In Italian history, an early 19th-century group that advocated liberal and patriotic ideas. The origins of the Carbonari are unknown; possibly they were an offshoot of the FRENCH REVOLUTION in France. The first Carbonari lodges seem to have made their appearance in southern Italy around 1800. In the name of Italian independence, they opposed Joachim Murat, the French marshal whom Napoleon had made king of Naples, and by 1814 their influence had spread northward into the Marches and Romagna. By this time they had turned from a liberal society into a predominately patriotic one. Opposing Austrian rule of the peninsula, their aim was a sovereign Italian state, though they could never agree among themselves as to what form it should take.

The members of the Carbonari came primarily from the upper classes, i.e., the nobility, professionals and small landowners as well as government officials. Like other secret societies of the time, they developed colorful rituals such as initiation ceremonies, symbols, secret greetings, etc. The movement peaked during the years immediately after 1814; in 1820 it spearheaded a rebellion against the Bourbon kings of Naples which, however, was suppressed. In 1831 it organized revolts in Bologna, Parma and Modena, only to have these suppressed by the Austrian army. Thereupon the movement largely disappeared. Many of its ideas were taken over by GIUSEPPE MAZZINI and his YOUNG ITALY movement and carried over into the Italian RISORGIMENTO, or national rebirth movement.

CARDENAS, LAZARO (1895–1970) Mexican populist and nationalist politician. A tax collector and jailer, Cardenas fought against both VILLA and Zapata during the Mexican revolution

(1911–1917). A protege of PLUTARCO ELIAS CALLES, he became governor of Michoacan (1928) and then secretary of war (1933). From 1934 to 1940, he was the Mexican president as the head of the National Revolutionary Party (PNR). During his time in office Cardenas carried out land reform, restructured the PNR to include four sectors: the agricultural, the labor, the military and the popular sectors, and renamed the party the Mexican Revolutionary Party (PRM). Cardenas nationalized Mexico's petroleum industry and formed the national petroleum company, PEMEX. His nationalist policies endeared him to the Mexican populace while alienating him from the US From 1942 to 1945 he was again secretary of war.

CARLISM In Spanish history, a revolutionary movement of Catholic-conservative character whose aim was to overthrow the liberal monarchy established after the end of the Napoleonic Wars. Active during the 1820s, the movement was led by, and named after, Don Carlos, younger brother of King Ferdinand VII of Spain. After the latter's death the movement rose in revolt (1833–1839) but was defeated with the aid of French troops. Thereafter the Carlists, representing the extreme right, remained active in Spanish politics.

CARNOT, LAZARE (1753–1823), known as "Le Grand Carnot" or "The Organizer of Victory," Carnot was a French mathematician and military engineer who became a legend in his day as the most outstanding military strategist in the Revolutionary Convention that ruled France between 1792 and 1794. Elected by the parliament, along with the *coventionnels* such as ROBESPIERRE, COUTHON and SAINT-JUST, to become a member of the JACOBIN dictatorship known as the COMMITTEE OF PUBLIC SAFETY, Carnot immediately distinguished himself by the vigorous and efficient way he was able to mobilize national resources and channel popular energies to promote the cause of the revolution against its enemies.

This took the form of the *levée en masse,* or levy in mass, a system of universal conscription introduced by the Committee of Public Safety in August 1793, which had the effect of revolutionizing modern warfare. It introduced the novel and far-reaching idea that in time of emergency the state had the right to command the services of all its citizens, and enabled France to throw into battle massive military formations against which the older professional royal armies fielded by Austria and Prussia were clearly outclassed. This modern concept of the citizen-army, totalling more than a million men under arms by the end of 1794, transformed the idea of war from a struggle between armies into a conflict between whole nations, regimented and equipped for battle. Carnot's organization of the military draft, carried one step further by the Directory in its law of conscription passed in September 1798, laid the groundwork for the military dictatorship of Napoleon.

CARRANZA, VENUSTIANO (1859–1920) Mexican soldier and politician. A landowner's son, Carranza held the positions of local deputy, senator and interim governor of Coahuila from 1898 to 1908. Along with the state legislature of Coahuila, Carranza refused to recognize the presidency of VICTORIANO HUERTA, a refusal officially stated by Carranza in the Treaty of Guadelupe. This treaty stipulated that Carranza would be the interim presi-

dent of Mexico once the capital city was in the hands of his rebel forces. In 1914, Carranza established his government in Chihuahua.

In a later declaration Carranza announced the principles underlying Mexico's revolutionary battle: to fight against the abuses of those in power; to eliminate the military forces of the federal army; to implement democracy in Mexico; to foment the well-being of workers; to emancipate in economic terms all peasants by redistributing land; and to punish and hold the Catholic clergy responsible for its political involvement. In August 1914 the Teoloyucan Agreements were signed and Carranza's forces occupied Mexico City. Although he declared himself the Head of Mexico, Carranza refused the title of interim president. Displeased with the election of Eulalio Gutierrez as interim president, he established a separate government in Veracruz. After several victories of Carranza's constitutionalist forces, he moved his government back to Mexico City in 1915. In 1917, after the civil war, he organized the constitutional Congress and called for presidential elections, which he won as the head of the Liberal Constitutionalist party. Faced with political opposition from northern states, he was overthrown in an armed uprising in 1920 and was forced to take flight. Betrayed by his own military, Carranza was assassinated that same year. In 1942, his remains were buried at the Monument of the Revolution in Mexico City.

CARRERRA, JOSE MIGUEL (1785–1821) Chilean revolutionary leader. During the revolt against Spain, Carrerra was the leader of the *exal tados,* or radicals, whose aim was the achievement of immediate independence. In 1811, he mounted a coup against the junta that had led the revolt and assumed power in Chile. Two years later he was deposed by O'HIGGINS, but in another coup (1814) regained control of the revolutionary forces. Defeated by the Spaniards, Carrerra fled first to Argentina and then to the United States, in an attempt to enlist aid against Spain. Returning to Argentina in 1816, he was not allowed to continue into Chile. Frustrated, he mounted several coup attempts against the government in Buenos Aires, until finally betrayed and shot by his own men.

CARRIER, JEAN BAPTISTE (1756–1794) French revolutionary politician. Carrier carried out to excess the anticlericalist policies of the JACOBIN government of the COMMITTEE OF PUBLIC SAFETY by the way he decided to root out Catholicism in the western province of Brittany, particularly in the Atlantic seaport of Nantes and the royalist region of the Vendée. Born of bourgeois stock in Aurillac, Carrier began his revolutionary career in the FRENCH REVOLUTION by becoming Aurillac's public prosecutor. In 1793, he was elected by his district to the republican Convention, where he led a vigorous attack against the GIRONDINS. As a lawyer, he was also instrumental in laying the groundwork for setting up the revolutionary tribunal which executed summary justice against the enemies of the Jacobin republic. Sent as a representative mission (deputies from the convention were delegated as commissars to control the provinces) to put down the revolt of the Vendée, Carrier ruled in Nantes as a virtual proconsul in the name of the Paris Convention and gained national notoriety for his *noyades* of February 1794, drowning several boat loads of royalists, Catholics and Girondins in the Loire. ROBESPIERRE was revolted by his behavior. Carrier was arrested during the Thermidorian reaction and sent to the guillotine amid public revulsion for his deeds.

CASSIUS, LONGINUS GAIUS A Roman nobleman who fought under Pompey at the Battle of Pharsalus (48 B.C.) and after his defeat was pardoned by Julius Caesar. Cassius, however, organized the conspiracy against Caesar and was among those who stabbed him on the floor of the Senate. Forced to flee Rome, he took his own life in 42 B.C. after the conspirators' defeat at the hands of Antony and Octavian. Shakespeare's Caesar said of him:

> ● Let me have men about me that are fat,
> ● Sleek headed men and such as sleep o' nights.
> ● Yonder Cassius has a lean and hungry look,
> ● He thinks too much; such men are dangerous.

CASTELAR Y RIPOLL, EMILIO (1832–1899) Spanish revolutionary. A republican and a liberal, Castelar was a professor of history at the University of Madrid, where he achieved fame by his attacks on the monarchy. He participated in an abortive republican rising of 1866, was arrested and sentenced to death. However he escaped from prison and made his way to France. After the revolution of 1868, however, he returned and in 1873 became leader of the newly established Spanish republic.

In 1874, Castelar was ousted from office by his own republican friends, who opposed his moderate policies, and when a military coup overthrew the democratic régime later in the same year he went into exile. Subsequently, however, he returned to Spain, re-entered parliament and remained active in politics as well as writing numerous novels and works on history.

CASTE WARS The Mexican Caste Wars, a set of indigenous revolts which began in Yucatan in 1847–1848, are considered the only successful rebellion of indigenous peoples against colonial powers and their successors in the Americas. Beginning during the armed conflict between Mexico and the USA, the Caste Wars lasted until 1854, with sporadic guerrilla resistance continuing until 1901. The conflict in the state of Yucatan, which spread to the territory of Quintana Roo, was regional and concerned differences between indigenous Mayans and non-Mayans (the latter including mixed-blood Ladinos). The Mayans suffered mistreatment by Ladinos and even more serious mistreatment on the part of people claiming purely European descent.

To understand the roots of the Caste Wars, one must also understand that at the time of the Mexican war of independence (1810–1821), Mexico had five distinct racial classes or castes: Creoles, also called *gente decente* ("decent people"), were a white minority consisting of the sons and daughters of Spaniards, who took advantage of the return of the Spaniards to Europe to remain in Mexico as the ruling class; Ladinos or Mestizos, people of mixed European and Indian blood, who felt superior because of their lighter skin color, when compared to the Indians; Mulattos, few in number, of mixed European and African descent; Pardos, a relatively sparse African-Indian mixture, mostly from the state of Tabasco, were descendants of several hundred African ex-slaves; Indians, largely Yucatec Mayans in the Yucatan—these were at the bottom of the scale.

The Caste Wars began with frontier Mayans burning many Ladino properties and with the massacre of large numbers of non-Mayans following the execution of Manuel Antonio Ay, one of the Mayan leaders, on July 26, 1847. The Indians said they burned as the Ladinos had taught them and killed whites as the whites had killed Mayans. Military forces were unable to suppress the uprising and by the end of May 1848, with more than three-quarters of the Mayan population in revolt, the rebels had gained control of 80% of the Yucatan peninsula. The Church tried to intervene but also failed, and the bishop fled to Havana.

The Indians wanted relief from oppressive taxation by Church and State and promised to burn no more if the commandant at Merida surrendered. For reasons yet undetermined, when but a short distance from Merida, the Mayans began to retreat. Dissension among them began to appear in late 1848, but the struggle continued into the mid-1850s. With the religious movement called "*cruzob*," or the "cult of the talking cross," the revolt became a guerrilla war. An autonomous Mayan state established in the southern Yucatan peninsula remained essentially independent until 1902.

CASTILLO ARMAS, CARLOS (1914–1957) President of Guatemala. With the resignation of President Jorge Ubico in 1944, Guatemala seemed poised for a transition to democracy. A short-lived revolutionary triumvirate, which seized power in 1944 with the backing of students, along with the nascent labor movement and some of the younger members of the military, ensured the democratic election, in 1945, of Juan Jos Arvalo as president. Various reforms introduced by Arvalo and his sucessor, Jacobo Arbenz Guzman, were instigated by the left-wing alliance that had brought them to power and aimed at ending foreign, particularly American, economic exploitation of the country. Opposed to these reforms was the Movimiento de Liberacion Nacional (MLN), a militant right-wing group supported by conservative elements such as the Catholic church and major landowners.

In 1950, under the leadership of Castillo Armas, the MLN made an abortive attempt to prevent Guzman from assuming the presidency. Castillo Armas fled to Honduras, from where he maintained contacts with his conservative backers in Guatemala and the American state department, in order to organize an "army of liberation" to depose Guzman. In 1954, senior Guatemalan military leaders informed Guzman that they would not defend his government from MLN invasion, forcing him to resign and enabling Castillo Armas to assume the presidency. He immediately suspended or obstructed all reform programs, thereby intensifying right-wing and American interests in the country. He was assassinated by a palace guard in 1957.

CASTRO (RUZ), FIDEL (1926–) Cuban revolutionary. Born the illegitimate son to a farmer in eastern Cuba, Castro attended various Catholic boarding schools before studying law at Havana University. At the university he became interested in politics; in 1948 he was charged with assassinating another student leader, but the charge was never proved. In 1952, he stood for election to parliament as a candidate of the left-wing Cuban People's party, only to face disappointment as the elections were cancelled by President Carlos Prio Socarras.

In 1953, Castro participated in an attack on the Cuban military, was arrested and sent to prison. Released in 1955, he went to Mexico where, along with his brother Raul, ERNESTO CHE GUEVARA and a few others he set up an organization whose aim was to topple the corrupt, US supported government of Fulgeno Batista. By this time he had read the Marxist classics and had become a convinced Communist, a position which he still appears to hold. In December 1956, the group returned to Cuba and opened guerrilla warfare in Oriente province, where Castro had been born. Support for the régime crumbled and on December 31, 1958 the rebels entered Havana after Batista had fled.

As Cuba's ruler—which, under various titles, he has been for the last 40 years—Castro carried out a variety of reforms. Establishing an authoritarian one-party régime, he confiscated foreign-owned businesses as well as the most important home-owned means of production, redistributed land among the peasants, expanded the people's access to health services and education and proclaimed the right (and obligation) of every citizen to be employed. These left-wing reforms, which naturally led to a pro-Soviet orientation in foreign affairs, made him a thorn in the eye of the US. Beginning about 1960, the American government made many attempts to topple him, first by organizing an invasion of the island and then, when that failed, by means reportedly of several abortive assassination attempts.

Castro in turn attempted to export his revolution. Not only has he been accused of involvement in the murder of President

The clothes were different, the ideology the same: Fidel Castro with Nikita Khrushchev, 1961

Kennedy—though the accusations have never been proved—but he sent his associate Guevara to fight in the jungles of Bolivia. When the attempt to rouse that country's peasants failed, he provided Cuban troops to assist other Marxist revolutionaries around the world, most notably in Angola in 1976. On the whole, however, these attempts were not successful. During the 1980s, the second oil crisis, the withdrawal of Soviet economic support and the continuing American embargo all but bankrupted Cuba. President of Cuba since 1976—prior to that time he was prime minister— Castro still hangs on to power, a sad testimonial to yet another idealistic revolution gone sour partly on its own account and partly because of the opposition that it met on the part of the most powerful country on earth.

CATILINE, LUCIUS SERGIUS A turbulent patrician born in 108 B.C., who twice failed in the elections for the consulate (64, 63 B.C.), the highest office in Rome. Heavily indebted and embittered, Cataline conspired to take the government by force, seeking and obtaining wide support with the slogan of *tabulae novae*, the abolition of debts. Frustrated and impoverished aristocrats, dispossesed veterans, people who had lost their properties in the civil wars of the 80s and indebted artisans and shopkeepers joined him. His leading supporters were sent to incite the population in several parts of Italy, while he himself plotted to assassinate the consul Cicero, his archenemy, in Rome. The latter, however, discovered the plot and induced the Senate to proclaim a state of emergency. Cataline left Rome to take command of his army in Etruria. Several ringleaders who remained in Rome hoping to carry out the plot were arrested by Cicero and, after a decision of the Senate, were put to death. Early in January 62 B.C., Catiline's forces were annihilated in battle and he himself fell fighting. The contemporary Roman historian, Sallust, wrote a monograph on the conspiracy, an illustration of the moral degeneration of Roman society and, in particular, of the corruption of the aristocracy.

CATO STREET CONSPIRACY (1820) Arthur Thistlewood (1770–1820) and about 20 followers planned to murder the English cabinet and take over the government. One of their number was a government agent and they were arrested in a hay loft at Cato Street, Marlebone, London, on February 23, 1820, at the eleventh hour. Thistlewood and four others were hanged and five others transported.

CEAUSESCU, NICOLAE (1918–1989) Secretary-general of the Romanian Communist party (1965–1989) and president of Romania (1974–1989), the last Stalinist dictator in Eastern Europe, the oldest of 10 children born into a poor peasant family. Ceausescu joined the youth branch of the Communist movement at the age of 14, a fact used as a myth during the years of his unlimited personality cult. Active in the party, he was jailed for illegal activity before and during World War II. His rise after 1944 was a rapid one, first as secretary of the Union of Communist Youth, then as deputy minister of agriculture and after 1950 in charge of the political section of the army as deputy minister of the armed forces. This was followed by two years— 1952–1954—as head of the *Orgburo*, in charge of the party's organization, a crucial position for the ambitious young careerist. From late 1955 he was a full member of the Politburo and 10 years later, with the death of Gheorghiu-Dej, he was elected party leader, a position which he held until his execution on December 25, 1989. Between 1965–1989 he held all the major posts in the country, as president, chairman of the defense council and supreme commander of the armed forces and chairman of the supreme council on socioeconomic development. He pursued a line of nationalist communism, placing Romania's national interests, as defined by him, above Romanian loyalty to the Soviet and world Communist line. Innovative in foreign policy, Ceausescu moved to a "partial alignment" within the socialist system, often openly critical of the Soviet Union. In internal affairs he instituted a harsh socioeconomic régime, which caused an almost total collapse of the country's economy by 1989 and demoralized the population, although foreign debts were repaid. Repressive measures against the population, including the Hungarian minority, intensified, and the régime lost whatever sympathy it had for its independent line. His personality cult and the placement of his wife and family members in top positions further alienated the outside world and his country. When he refused to introduce reforms he was toppled in December 1989, in a move that combined a palace coup with mass agitation against the régime.

CENTRAL ASIA REVOLT OF 1916   A revolt in central Asia occasioned by the Russian czar's edict of June 26, 1916 mobilizing the population for service in the Russian army. The revolt was facilitated by the worsening economic situation in the Russian empire's central Asian region owing to World War I

The revolt began on July 4, 1916 in Khojand (contemporary Tajikistan). It soon spread throughout Uzbekistan, Turkmenistan, Kazakhstan and Kirgizia. The rebels attacked Russian military units located in central Asia and police staffs, set the administration houses on fire, destroyed the enlisted persons' records, etc. They also dealt with usurers and landlords. The rebels' activities were particularly prevalent in Kazakhstan's Turgai district, Turkmenistan's southern regions and in Uzbekistan's Jizzakh district. In some regions the leadership of the revolt fell into the hands of the Muslim clergy and assumed a nationalist and anti-Russia character.

Russian troops were sent out against the rebels and the revolt was cruelly suppressed. Thousands of the rebels were captured and executed without trial and their properties were confiscated. However, the revolt did upset the Russian authorities' plans: instead of the 250,000 they had planned on, they could only mobilize 120,000 persons. Fearing a massacre, thousands of the participants in the revolt fled to Iran, Afghanistan and western China.

CHAADAYEV, PYOTR YAKOVLEVICH (1794–1856) Russian dissident philosopher. As a youthful officer in an elite guards regiment, Chaadayev took part in the war against Napoleon in Russia and abroad. He came under the influence of the Decembrists and the spirit of freedom that suffused Pushkin's writings. At the same time he absorbed non-Orthodox religious influences and developed an attitude of admiration for the political and social developments in Western Europe. From 1823 to 1826 he traveled in Europe and was thus saved from arrest as a member of the Decembrist Northern Society. Even so, he was detained and interrogated when he returned to Russia.

Chaadayev's first public notice came from his *Philosophical Letter*, published in 1836. Here he attacked not only Russia's governmental system and the institution of serfdom, but also Russia's entire history, casting doubt on the nation's future existence. All of literate Russia debated this essay, while the Moscow journal that printed it was closed, the editor sent into Siberian exile and the censor who had approved publication was dismissed. Czar Nicholas I, still nervous after the DECEMBRIST REVOLT, reacted by having Chaadayev declared insane and subjected to a year of daily police and medical surveillance.

Chaadayev was given his freedom only after revising his thoughts in the *Apology of a Lunatic*. He took up residence in Moscow, where his reputation for having suffered for the cause of intellectual freedom drew visitors from both the Russian aristocracy and foreign intellectuals. Although he openly continued his admiration for West European institutions, he expressed no identification with Russian radicalism, hewing to ideas that may be described as romantic conservatism. Not a believer in socialism, he nevertheless predicted its advent in Russia—not because it was a correct social system, but because its opponents offered such an evil alternative. In 1849, he deplored the revolutionary chaos of Europe and expressed support for Russian intervention against the revolutions. Two years later he wrote the authorities a strong letter rejecting HERZEN's praise of him and declared loyalty and support for the czar, whom he described as an instrument of divine will. At the same time, he explained to his intimates that one must save one's own skin. Thus, nominally a free man, Chaadayev lived out his life as a prisoner of Russia's political environment.

CHAIKOVSKY CIRCLE   Followers of Nikolay Vasilyevich Chaikovsky (1850–1926), who in 1871 assumed the leadership of a group of students organized by MARK A. NATANSON after Natanson's arrest. The Chaikovsky Circle combined the search for an ethical base of social revolution with a sense of the duty owed by the educated to the masses. It demanded both individual activism and a fusing of one's life, through the group, with society. Non-dogmatic, the Chaikovsky Circle attracted large groups of students to its educational and propaganda activities, which it based largely on legally published works. Prince PETER KROPOTKIN is only one example of the outstanding figures whose careers were influenced by the Chaikovsky Circle. The Circle was the source of the 1874 TO THE PEOPLE movement.

CHALCO REBELLION   In 1868, just after Mexico had been liberated from French occupation, a peasant rebellion broke out in Chalco, east of Mexico City. The rebellion had been planned in the village of Acuatla early in the year, and on February 2 a proclamation was issued calling for an uprising against the owners of large estates in Chalco. The first and second attempts at armed resistance were put down by government forces, but by 1869 the uprising had expanded over a much larger area. The rebellion did not succeed in any direct sense, but many landowners, bankrupted by the conflict, were forced to put up their lands for sale.

CHAMP DE MARS   Literally, the "Field of the God of War," located on the Paris left bank adjacent to the École Militaire and in the vicinity of les Invalides, this area became France's major public forum, where national holidays commemorating the FRENCH REVOLUTION were celebrated after 1790. The venue for holding national pageants glorifying the revolution was moved to arches of triumph begun by Napoleon in the Carousel in the Louvre and the Champs Elysées, but these had not yet been completed by the end of the Empire in 1815.

Although nothing could match the storming of the Bastille as the defining moment in the mythology of the French Revolution, the total destruction of every scrap of masonry that comprised that symbol of the *ancien régime* made it necessary to shift the focus of revolutionary symbolism to this large park built and designed by the architect Gabriel, who had in 1780 built the right bank Place (which changed its name in 1789 to Place de la Concorde) to serve as a huge parade ground for the École Militaire. It soon became the capital's main amusement park and was the site from which the physicist Charles flew his first air balloon in 1783 to Billancourt.

On July 14, 1790 more than 300,000 "patriots" gathered from all over France to the Champ de Mars to celebrate the anniversary of July 14, for what was called the Fête de la Fédération, glorifying the unification of all 80 of the country's départements under the aegis of Paris, which replaced Versailles as the nation's capital. TALLEYRAND, bishop of Autun under the *ancien régime*, assisted by 300 priests, celebrated mass at the Altar of the Nation and the joyous crowd joined the MARQUIS DE LAFAYETTE, commander of the National Guard, in swearing an oath of loyalty to the new constitution.

Things went awry during the following year's celebration of the Fête de la Fédération. This time a turbulent crowd, protesting against the both the king's treachery and the government's connivance in retaining him on the throne despite his aborted escape to Varennes on June 21, signed a petition on the Altar of the Nation calling for his abdication and demanded a republic by hoisting the red flag for the first time. The massacre of the Champ de Mars, at the cost of 50 dead who became the first martyrs of the republic, further widened the gulf between the SANS-CULOTTES and the bourgeois mayor of Paris, the academician Bailly, who had no choice but to proclaim martial law and turn to Lafayette and his National Guard to crush the demonstration. Bailly himself was to pay the ultimate price for having ordered the massacre. Two years later, at the height of the terror, he was condemned to death for his part in the fusillade of 1791. For this special occasion, the guillotine was transferred from its usual location, the Place de la Concorde, to the Champ de Mars. Bailly was ordered to re-assemble it on the site of the Altar to the Nation. As he marched to his death, bareheaded and with his shirt collar open in a cold November drizzle, the revolution's most celebrated astronomer began to shiver. A sans-culottes yelled: "*Tu trembles, Bailly.*" Bailly replied gently: "*Jai froid, mon ami.*"

On June 8, 1794 the Champ de Mars was transformed by the premier pageant master of the revolution and the empire, the painter Jacques Louis David, into the site for the celebration of the Feast of the Supreme Being. A glorious mountain, made of not too durable plaster, was erected to replace the Altar to the Nation, adorned by statues of nymphs and virgins also made of plaster. The deputies of the Convention were seated, along with, laid out on tiers below them, a choir and orchestra of more than 3,000 singers and musicians recruited from sans-culottes delegations and from all the Paris theaters and operas. The assembled crowd joined in singing the first eight stanzas of a hymn of invocation to the revolutionary deity. ROBESPSIERRE, dressed in a sky blue tunic and powdered wig, solemnly presided over the magnificent performance. Less than two months later he was sent to the guillotine.

CHAMULA REBELLION In 1868, according to legend, three green stones fell from the sky near Tjazaljemel, in the Mexican state of Chiapas. According to this legend, the stones, which had been placed in a wooden box, began to talk, telling the Chamulans to rise up and reclaim their heritage. Taking the CASTE WARS of Yucatan, in which he had fought, as his cue, Ignacio Galindo joined forces with local leaders to organize an army. The root cause of the rebellion was landlessness, as the Criollos (people of European ancestry) in mountainous highland Chiapas held most of the cultivatable terrain, leaving the Chamulans to farm impossibly steep slopes. The Chamulans assaulted the city of San Cristobal and held it for a time in 1869, but the leaders and their principal followers were massacred in the reprisals which came shortly thereafter.

CHANG CHUEH   see ZHANG JUE.

CHANG HSIEN-CHUNG   see ZHANG XIANZHONG.

CHANG HSIU   see ZHANG XIU.

CHANG KUO-T'AO   see ZHANG GUOTAO.

CHANG LO-HSING   see ZHANG LOXING.

CHANG LU   see ZHANG LU.

CHANG PING-LIN   see ZHANG BINGLIN.

CHANG T'AI-YEN   see ZHANG TAIYAN.

CHANG WEN-T'IEN   see ZHANG WENTIAN.

CHAO KUANG-YIN   see ZHAO KUANGYIN.

CHARETTE DE LA CONTRIE, FRANÇOIS DE   (1763–1769) Charette was the most celebrated of the legendary heroes of the Vendée Revolt in Brittany, who led the resistance against the FRENCH REVOLUTION's efforts to impose by force the new political and social order enshrined in the principles of 1789. Charette's Rebellion brought to a head the struggle between the centralization of revolutionary government in Paris on the one hand and the yearning for local self-government and home rule manifested by many provinces still loyal to the *ancien régime* on the other.

Born in the port town of Couffé in the Vendée, the most traditional and conservative part of Brittany south of the Loire, Charette was naturally drawn to the navy which, unlike the new model army forged for the revolution by the genius of the minister of war, LAZARE CARNOT, remained a stronghold of royalist sentiment and Catholic loyalties. Instead of going to sea, Charette resolved to resist the imposition of JACOBIN rule in Brittany by launching a local peasant revolt in Machécoul in 1790.

Machécoul became the catalyst of the Vendée peasant revolt, which no French régime was ever able to contain until Napoleon neutralized the Catholics by signing the concordat with the pope in April 1802. Republican revolutionary mythology as well as royalist memories, however, regard General Hoche, who was to die prematurely in 1797 after a failed invasion of Ireland, as the man who subdued the Vendée.

After an abortive siege of Nantes, Charette was forced to sign a truce, the Pacification of La Jaunaye, in February 1795, with the expeditionary force sent by Paris under General Lazare Hoche. He was, however, encouraged to resume the fight when a British squadron came to fan the flames of the counterrevolution by landing a French army of royalist émigrés under the Comte d'Artois, the brother of Louis XVI, in Quiberon harbor. The landing was defeated by Hoche, who also earned the credit and the glory of capturing Charette. Charette was brought in chains to Nantes and executed by a firing squad on March 29, 1796, which is still marked as a day of mourning in the Vendée.

CHARLES ALBERT OF SAVOY (1798–1849) King of Sardinia. As heir to the throne of Sardinia and Piedmont, Charles Albert participated in the Napoleonic Wars against Austria. He returned to Turin in 1814, only to find that he despised the reactionary attitudes of the royal court. He apparently played some role in the 1821 uprising in Piedmont which forced King Victor Emmanuel I to abdicate the throne in favor of his brother Charles Felix, but, as presumptive heir to the throne and since Charles Felix was abroad, Charles Albert was appointed regent. His youthful flirtation with liberalism was realized when he succumbed to liberal pressure and adopted a new constitution modeled on the liberal Spanish one. The constitution was quickly renounced by Charles Felix, prompting an uprising throughout the country. Charles Albert was exiled to the garrison of Novara but soon made his way to Florence, where he had a political turnabout. In 1823, he went to war against the Spanish, thereby angering his liberal-minded countrymen who courted the Spanish régime and sought to introduce Spanish-style liberalism to Italy.

Charles Albert assumed the throne of Sardinia in 1831. Despite his disappointing political about-face, Italian liberals expressed the hope that he would once again display the political open-mindedness that he had shown as regent. Evidence of this is attested to in a letter by GIUSEPPE MAZZINI, the leader of the Italian nationalists, to Charles Albert, urging him to be the "Italian Napoleon" in the battle for Italian unification. To their chagrin, Charles Albert was a disappointment. He ignored Mazzini's challenge, allied himself with Austria and suppressed local liberals and members of the CARBONARI. Nevertheless, Charles Albert did abolish all remaining feudal privileges and promoted economic development in the country; in 1837 he established a unified legal code for the discontiguous regions of his kingdom.

Charles Albert turned against Austria in 1840, although critics charge that he was more interested with increasing his own prestige than with the campaign for Italian unification, which was being hindered by the Habsburgs. In 1848, he enacted a supposedly "liberal" constitution, although in fact he retained real power for himself by having ministers responsible to him alone rather than to parliament. He was supportive of the Milanese attempt to break with Austria (the Five Days of Milan) and himself went to northern Italy to fight against the Habsburgs. After two defeats,

however, Charles Albert abdicated the throne and went into exile in Portugal, where he soon died. Modern historians are divided as to whether Charles Albert actually furthered the cause of Italian unification or, by his political indecisiveness, actually hindered it.

CHARTISM 19th century British reform movement. Although the Reform Bill of 1832 expanded the electorate considerably, there were still some 4 million British workers who possessed neither the wealth nor the property qualifications to vote. Originating in 1837–1838—a time of great economic hardship owing to high unemployment and the effects of the Poor Law Amendment Act of 1834—Chartism was the first working-class movement in British history to assume national rather than merely local importance. The injustice of being unable to vote had sparked numerous protest groups throughout the country, one of which, the Working Men's Association of London (founded in 1836) would achieve national fame as the spokesgroup for the disenfranchised classes. In 1837, William Lovett, a disciple of Robert Owen and a founder of the Working Men's Association, published the organization's charter, consisting of six points: universal manhood suffrage (Lovett also supported women's suffrage, but this was rejected as impractical at the time), secret ballots, an annual parliament, equal electoral districts, no property qualifications for members of parliament and salaries for members of parliament. This charter received wide acclaim and its supporters became known as Chartists.

Originally, members of the Chartist movement such as Henry Vincent sought to realize their objectives by petitioning members of parliament: these were known as moral-force Chartists. Others, such as JOHN FROST and the physical-force Chartists, called for more violent means. Meanwhile, FEARGUS O'CONNOR, a physical-force Chartist and editor of the movement's newspaper, *The Northern Star*, called for the resettlement of workers in their own rural communities. These disparate opinions illustrate the true problem faced by the Chartist movement: a lack of competent leadership.

Although in its early years the movement seemed capable of achieving its aims, the leadership was often arrested as a threat to national security. In May 1839, some of the physical-force Chartists and their followers moved to Birmingham, where riots broke out and where Lovett was arrested. Radicalized by these events, the remaining Chartists returned to London in July and submitted their demands to parliament, only to see them summarily dismissed. Some of the movement's leaders thereupon resorted to force, organizing a rising at Newport; it was swiftly suppressed and the leaders banished to Australia. Frost, in fact, is believed by some historians to have brought England to the brink of civil war by his actions.

The failure of armed force caused the remaining Chartists to change their tactics. Focusing on propaganda, they mobilized widespread support and in 1842 were able to present parliament with a second national petition, this time with no fewer than 3 million signatures attached to it. Once again parliament rejected it. By then the movement had lost its momentum. Rather than adhere to its original agenda, various Chartist-aligned movements emerged, such as Chartist churches and temperance societies. By the 1850s, as the country's economic situation improved, Chartism disappeared as a political force in Britain.

CH'EN CHIONG-MING see CHEN JIONGMING.

CHEN DUXIU (Ch'en Tu-hsiu) (1879–1942) Chinese Communist leader and journalist. Born to a wealthy Anhui family, Chen passed a civil service examination at the age of 17 after receiving a classical education. He undertook modern studies, including English and French, in a Hangzhou academy and then in Japan (1902 and 1906). According to some reports, between 1907 and 1910 he spent time in France and became an ardent admirer of French culture and its revolutionary political tradition. He joined the CHINESE REPUBLICAN REVOLUTION OF 1911 and the 1913 revolt against Yuan Shikai. By this time, he had acquired experience as a teacher and journalist.

His rise to fame began in Shanghai in 1915, when he founded the monthly, *New Youth* (*Xin Qing-nian*, *La Jeunesse*), and fired the opening shots of what was to become a major onslaught against the traditional Chinese society and values. Chen warned that unless animated by a new, dynamic, individualistic spirit, China was doomed to oblivion. He argued that democracy and science epitomized the modern, creative spirit of the west and that Confucianism and the entire structure of traditional culture and beliefs were antithetical to these life-giving values. Chen's radical views struck a responsive chord among Chinese students and intellectuals and in 1917 CAI YUANPEI, chancellor of the influential Beijing University, appointed Chen Dean of Letters, a position that augmented his influence. He continued to edit *new youth*, and its influence and circle of readers increased.

However, his faith in the west was severely shaken when the Paris Peace Conference supported Japan on the Shandong issue (see MAY FOURTH MOVEMENT). Chen joined the student demonstrators and in June 1919 was arrested and sent to prison for almost three months. Upon his release, he resigned his university post and moved to Shanghai, where his yearning for dramatic action began clouding his former advocacy of democracy and individualism. The October RUSSIAN REVOLUTION OF 1917 and MARXISM, with its claim to being "scientific," became new objects of admiration and in 1920 he began planning the establishment of a Communist party in China. He was in Canton in July 1921 when the party was formally established in Shanghai, but the delegates accepted most of his policy and organizational proposals and elected him secretary of the central committee. His discussions with HENDRICK SNEEVLIET in Shanghai determined the CHINESE COMMUNIST PARTY's (CCP) relationship with the COMINTERN. In 1922, he and other CCP members reluctantly accepted the Comintern directive to accept SUN YAT-SEN's conditions for a united front, and they joined the GUOMINDANG (Kuomintang) as individuals and submitted to its authority. Chen attended the Comintern's Fourth Congress in Moscow (November–December 1922) and retained leadership of the CCP until August 1927, when the Guomindang purged the Communists. He became the scapegoat for a party debacle (see AUTUMN HARVEST UPRISINGS) that had resulted mainly from obeying Moscow's directives. In August, an emergency conference removed Chen from the party leadership and replaced him with QU QIUBAI. In addition to political defeat, around this time Chen also suffered a personal tragedy. Two of his sons were executed for Communist activities during the anti-Red terror of 1927.

Chen still retained some influence in the party, but was expelled in 1929 after criticizing its subservience to the Comintern.

In 1932, after a brief and disappointing experience as a Trotskyite (see PENG SHUZHI), he was arrested, and in 1933 was sentenced to 15 years imprisonment. He rebuffed Guomindang overtures but was released in 1937 when the outbreak of the Sino-Japanese war induced the Guomindang government to declare a general amnesty. While supporting the united front against Japan, he shunned political activity and spent his final years in relative obscurity. His last writings reflect a renewed faith in the democratic values that had once inspired him. He wrote that even a socialist society should emulate Western democratic practices such as parliamentary government, the guarantee of civil rights, protection of opposition parties and free elections. He criticized the Stalinist dictatorship and warned against dogmatic ideologies that stifle individualism.

Long excoriated as a "right opportunist" and "capitulationist" by CCP historians who even obscured his leadership role in the May Fourth movement, Chen has recently been posthumously rehabilitated and hailed as one of the outstanding historical figures of modern China and the world socialist movement. However, Chinese communism, especially during its Maoist phase, bore little of Chen's influence. He was more of an orthodox Marxist and more cosmopolitian in outlook than LI DAZHAO and Li's disciple, MAO ZEDONG. Nor did he share their faith in the peasantry's revolutionary potential. In many ways, Chen's views resembled those of PLEKHANOV and the Russian MENSHEVIKS.

CH'EN, EUGENE (Chen Youren) (1878–1944) Chinese revolutionary, lawyer and publicist. Born in Trinidad (British West Indies) to Cantonese immigrants, Ch'en qualified as a barrister and in 1911 moved to London. There he met SUN YAT-SEN, who persuaded him to use his legal talent on behalf of China. He arrived in China in 1912 and served briefly in the newly-formed republican government, and then edited an English-language journal, the *Peking Gazette*. He became Sun Yat-sen's foreign policy adviser and spokesman in 1922 and after Sun's death was associated with the left-GUOMINDANG (GMD). Capable and articulate in opposing imperialism, he played a major role in foreign affairs, scoring a diplomatic triumph for the GMD in 1927 when he secured the return of British concessions in Hankow. After the 1927 purge of the Communists, he left for Moscow and stayed in Europe until 1931. He joined movements against CHIANG KAI-SHEK, including the FUJIAN REVOLT, and refused to serve in Chiang's government during the war. He was in Hong Kong when it was occupied by the Japanese, who later moved him to Shanghai. A staunch nationalist, he resisted Japanese blandishments to join the puppet régime of WANG JINGWEI.

CHENG CH'ENG-KUNG see ZHENG CHENGGONG.

CHÉNIER, ANDRÉ DE (1762–1794) The most celebrated poet of the FRENCH REVOLUTION who sang the praises of its early glories and enormous promise in such poems as "*Les Bucoliques*," "*Les Idylles*" and "*Néère*," but was eventually revolted by its JACOBIN excesses and, at the age of 32, only two days before the Thermidorians overthrew ROBESPIERRE, was sent to the guillotine as an enemy of the people.

Born in Constantinople, the son of the French consul to the Ottoman Empire, the young Chénier rallied with enthusiasm to the French Revolution, returned to Paris to launch the *Société de*

89, wrote many articles for *Le Journal de Paris* and rallied to the constitutionalist Feuillant Club founded by Lafayette. His moderate political views aroused the displeasure of the Jacobin government and he was arrested and imprisoned in the prison of Saint Lazare in March 1794. It was there that he wrote his most celebrated poem, "*La Jeune Captive*," dedicated to the ravishing Aimée de Coigny, who became his mistress in prison. His brother, Marie Joseph, a prominent member of the Convention who was André's political adversary and celebrated as the composer of revolutionary hymns written to the story of the SANS-CU-LOTTES, tried in vain to save his life. In "*Néère*," reprinted in most anthologies of French lyrical poetry, he foretold his own fate and that of the revolution he had welcomed.

CHEN JIONGMING (Ch'en Chiong-ming) (1878–1933) Chinese revolutionary and warlord. Educated in both classical and modern styles, Chen engaged in anti-Manchu and social reform activities in his native province of Guangdong before the CHINESE REPUBLICAN REVOLUTION OF 1911 and held political and military posts in the province afterward. He joined the anti-Yuan Shikai campaign (1913) and backed SUN YAT-SEN's constitution protection movement in Guangdong (1918). In 1920, his forces captured Canton and Sun appointed him provincial governor. Chen preferred rehabilitating his native province rather than pursuing Sun's risky plan for a northern expedition and in 1922 this policy difference led him to open rebellion. Sun fled to Shanghai, but the following year Chen himself was driven from Canton and two years later his army was completely routed by GUOMINDANG (Kuomintang) forces. As a regional militarist, Chen was considered a warlord, but of an unusually enlightened type. He instituted reforms and attracted progressive intellectuals.

CHEN SHAOYU see WANG MING.

CHEN SHENG (Ch'en Sheng) (d. 209 B.C.) Chinese rebel. In 209 B.C., a year after the death of Shi Huang-di (the First Emperor and founder of the Qin dynasty—221–206), Chen and his follower, WU GUANG, led a revolt of frontier guards that spread rapidly in what is present-day Anhui and Henan. The revolt, triggered by exactions of forced labor, heavy taxation and harsh punishments, was suppressed, but it ultimately led to the overthrow of the Qin dynasty. This was one of the first recorded peasant revolts in Chinese history.

CH'EN TU-HSIU see CHEN DUXIU.

CHEN YOUREN see CH'EN, EUGENE.

CHEN YUN (Ch'en Yun) (1905–1995) Chinese Communist leader. Born in the Shanghai area in Jiangsu, after finishing primary school Chen worked as an apprentice and clerk for the *Commercial Press* in Shanghai. Active in the MAY 30TH MOVEMENT of 1925, he joined the CHINESE COMMUNIST PARTY (CCP) that year. In 1927, after the CCP-GUOMINDANG (GMD) split, he engaged in labor agitation in Shanghai. He joined the Jiangxi CCP base (soviet) in 1931, was elected to the CCP central committee (CC) in 1934 and participated in part of the Long March (1934–1935). He supported MAO ZEDONG at the Zunyi conference (January 1, 1935), after which he was sent to Shanghai for clandestine party

work and then to Moscow, where he joined the CCP delegation to the COMINTERN. In 1937, he returned to the new CCP headquarters in Yan'an to head the CC's organization department and in 1944 was vice-chairman of the office for financial and economic matters in the northwest base area. He was elected to the Politburo in 1945. After the defeat of Japan in 1945, he held important political and economic posts in Manchuria. In 1948, he was elected chairman of the All-China Federation of Trade Unions. After the establishment of the People's Republic of China (PRC) in 1949, he assumed major responsibilities in the economic sector and was the first minister of heavy industry (1949–1950). In 1954, he was named senior vice-premier of the State Council and was acting premier when ZHOU ENLAI was absent in 1955 and 1956. In 1956 he became vice-chairman of the CC and a member of the Politburo's Standing Committee. In the early 1960s he worked with Zhou Enlai, LIU SHAOQI and DENG XIAOPING to repair damage wrought by the disastrous GREAT LEAP FORWARD (1958–1959).

Frowned upon by Mao Zedong, who considered him a "rightist," Chen became inactive after 1962. During the Cultural Revolution (1966–1976—see GREAT PROLETARIAN CULTURAL REVOLUTION) he was removed from all leading posts except membership in the CC. In 1978, he was restored to the Politburo and to the vice-chairmanship of the CC and became first secretary of the Commission for Inspecting Party Discipline. Chen played a leading role in purging the CCP of Cultural Revolution influences. Although loyal to Deng Xiaoping, he felt Deng was moving too fast in removing centralized economic control. In 1987, he was elected chairman of the CC's Advisory Commission and helped plan the program to rein in inflation in 1988. Until his death in 1995, he was considered the most influential opponent of the prevailing free-market policies.

CHERNOV, VIKTOR MIKHAILOVICH (1866–1952) Founder of the Russian SOCIAL REVOLUTIONARY PARTY in 1902. After the RUSSIAN REVOLUTION OF 1917, Chernov returned to Russia and became minister of agriculture. In 1918 he was made president of the Constituent Assembly. After that body was dissolved by the Bolsheviks (see BOLSHEVIK PARTY), he became their opponent. From 1924 he lived in exile, where he wrote *The Great Russian Revolution* (tr. 1936).

CHETNIKS The term derives from "ceta" in Serbian, a company of guerrilla fighters. Such groups, which have a long tradition in various Balkan rebellious activities, emerged in Serbia during the first Serbian revolution of 1804, when the "Chetniks" were irregular bandit groups operating against Turkish rule. In the Balkan wars and in World War I, Chetnik irregular units were used effeciently by the Serb army for guerrilla warfare. In World War I they raided German lines, disrupted enemy communications and spread panic and confusion. From 1921 on, a Chetnik Association for Freedom and Honor of the Fatherland was active in interwar Yugoslavia, promoting Serb nationalist causes. However the term "Chetniks" is most associated with the anti-Communist units led by General Staff Colonel Draza Mihailovic during World War II. The Chetniks were active after Yugoslavia's collapse in April 1941, but were destroyed as a fighting force by TITO's partisans by mid-October 1944. Loyal to the London-based government in exile, they enjoyed western support until the beginning of 1944. Their prime targets were the partisans, which led them into a complex policy of cooperation with the German and Italian occupiers while claiming to advance Allied strategy in the Balkans. Their vision of the revival of a strong anti-Communist Serbian-dominated Yugoslavia drove them into a desperate civil war against the leftist forces. Mihailovic was executed in 1946, in spite of Western pleas. Since the break-up of Yugoslavia in 1991, Serb units in Bosnia and Croatia have adopted Chetnik symbols and have been branded by their opponents simply as "Chetniks," evoking images of banditry and of attempts at Serbian hegemony.

CHIANG KAI-SHEK (Jiang Jieshi) (1887–1975) Chinese revolutionary and nationalist leader. Chiang, son of a Zhejiang salt merchant, attended a Chinese military academy (Baoding, 1907) and Japanese military academies (1908–1911). He joined the TONGMENGHUI in 1908, met SUN YAT-SEN in 1910 and fought in the Shanghai area during the CHINESE REPUBLICAN REVOLUTION OF 1911 and the CHINESE REVOLUTION OF 1913. He joined Sun in Canton in 1918 and served on the staff of CHEN JIONGMING's Guangdong army. In 1919 he maintained close ties with the Green Gang, a powerful Shanghai secret society, and in 1920 he rejoined Sun in Guangdong. His steadfast support of Sun during Chen Jiongming's revolt in 1922 cemented their relationship and the following year, when Sun returned to Canton, Chiang became his chief of staff. But the big boost to his career was his appointment as chief of the study mission that Sun sent to Moscow after his agreement with the Soviets. During his stay in the Soviet Union (September–November 1923), Chiang met TROTSKY and other of-

ficials. As one of the few professional soldiers whose loyalty to Sun was unquestioned, Chiang became indispensable to the Kuomintang (GUOMINDANG—GMD). He was appointed commandant of the WHAMPOA MILITARY ACADEMY in 1924 and forged permanent relationships with many cadets who later comprised the Whampoa clique. After Sun's death in 1925, Chiang was not a major contender for political leadership, but dominated the military and retained the confidence of its Soviet advisers. The latter rated him as the most capable of the GMD officers and noted that he was studying Napoleon in Japanese (the only foreign language he knew). In July 1926, he was named supreme commander of the National Revolutionary army and launched the NORTHERN EXPEDITION. But his relations with the CHINESE COMMUNIST PARTY (CCP) had worsened, and in April 1927, after capturing Shanghai and Nanjing, Chiang brought the entente to a bloody end with the indiscriminate execution of Communists and suspected sympathizers in Shanghai. BORODIN and other Soviet advisers were sent home. Later in the year, Chiang married Soong Meiling, younger sister of Sun Yat-sen's widow and a member of one of the most influential families in China. In 1928, Beijing fell to the Northern Expedition and Chiang became head of a national government that was established in Nanjing.

However, China was still not united. Chiang had to contend with regional militarists, GMD factionalism and the growing power of the CCP in south-central China. Moreover, Japanese aggression, beginning with the seizure of Manchuria in 1931, severely handicapped Chiang's unification efforts. Choosing to buy time by placating the Japanese, Chiang concentrated on the Communist threat and continued with the encirclement campaigns

Chiang Kai-Shek as dictator of Taiwan, 1976

that had started in 1930. German advisers and material assistance strengthened his army, and by 1934 a decimated Red Army had been forced to retreat to the northwest. Meanwhile, public opinion clamored for ending the civil war and for resisting Japan. In December 1936, while Chiang was on an inspection tour in Xi'an, nationalist officers detained him and demanded that he form a united front against Japan. Held captive for two weeks, Chiang's release was secured through the mediation of the Communists who, with Moscow's strong concurrence, felt that Chiang was the best candidate for rallying the nation against the Japanese. Chiang apparently agreed to the united front, and upon his release was hailed as a national hero.

In July 1937, Chiang spoke for the nation when he refused to accept the demeaning conditions that Japan demanded for settling the incident at Lugouqiao (Marco Polo bridge). Fighting spread in north China and in August the undeclared Sino-Japanese War broke out in full fury in Shanghai. In September, the GMD and CCP agreed on a joint war effort under Chiang's military leadership. Shanghai fell in November after a heroic but costly three-month stand and in December frustrated Japanese troops went on a rampage in Nanjing. Tortured and butchered with unbelievable barbarity, more than 200,000 civilians fell victim to what became known as the "Rape of Nanjing." As the Japanese advanced, Chiang's army tried to resist but was outgunned and outmaneuvered by an enemy that bombed defenseless cities and engaged in chemical and bacteriological warfare. The national government had in the meantime moved to Hankou, where in March 1938 an Extraordinary GMD Congress elected Chiang leader with a title equivalent to that which had been Sun Yat-sen's. He now had veto power over all party decisions. Later in the year, the government relocated to Chongqing in the southwest. The war now became more of a holding action as the Japanese consolidated their positions along the railway lines of eastern China. GMD and especially CCP guerrillas continued to harass them, but Chiang never expected to defeat Japan on his own. Exercising dominant power through control of both party and army, he dug in and waited for the internationalization of the conflict, which he presumed would not only humble Japan but ensure postwar GMD supremacy. He diverted troops to contain the Communists, and the shaky alliance ended with the clash known as the New Fourth Army incident in January 1941.

When the US joined the conflict after Pearl Harbor (December 7, 1941), Chiang's international status rose immediately and in July 1942 he was named supreme commander of allied forces in the China theater, which included Indochina and Thailand. Added prestige came in 1943 when Chiang, who was named Chairman of the Republic of China in October, participated in the Cairo Conference and China was recognized as one of the four "great powers." American aid, however, also brought American criticism for what was considered Chiang's preference for protecting his personal position at the expense of the war effort. In October 1944, Chiang succeeded in persuading Washington to dismiss his chief critic, General Joseph Warren Stilwell, who had been commander of US forces in the China-Burma-India theater and concurrently chief of staff to Chiang.

Japan's surrender (September 1945) raised the curtain on the GMD-CCP showdown. American mediation failed to prevent civil war. After gaining initial victories, Chiang overextended his lines and lost Manchuria in November 1948. Ably led and with considerable popular support, the Communists swept through north China and on January 21, 1949 Chiang resigned from the presidency of the republic. At the end of the year, when CCP forces were closing in on southwest China, he flew to Taiwan. There he resumed the presidency of the republic in March 1950, with the support of more than 2 million civilians and soldiers who had fled from the mainland.

Taking personal responsibility for the mainland debacle, Chiang renovated the GMD. Under his rule, Taiwan, which benefited from US assistance after Chinese intervention in the Korean War in October 1950, made remarkable economic progress. His son, Chiang Ching-kuo, who became president in 1978, worked toward greater political democratization.

Critics have emphasized Chiang Kai-shek's authoritarianism, including Fascist inclinations, and his view of Communism as a purely military problem while neglecting social-economic sources of discontent. However, there is no denying his patriotism and personal integrity, and his unfailing commitment to the realization of nationalist goals. Under his leadership, the republic made great strides toward recovering national rights and created the framework for an effective national government. Even the CCP now acknowledges the crucial role his army played in resisting Japan for eight years. But the war diverted attention from pressing internal problems and left Chiang more vulnerable to the Communist challenge.

CHIANO CHUNG-CHENG   see CHIANG KAI-SHEK.

CHILE, COUPS IN   The 1920 presidential elections in Chile were indecisive and not one of the presidential candidates received the required majority of votes. The congress finally chose Arturo Alessandri as president, but the senate consistently refused to cooperate with him. The economic problems due to the decreased export of nitrates, copper and wool exacerbated the situation and made it necessary to take strong economic measures. In 1924, an income tax was adopted in order to increase the government's revenue. The newly elected congress, favorable to the president, voted a pay increase for the armed forces. However, increasing tension and dissatisfaction among the military, caused by Alessandri's refusal to devalue the national currency, forced him to resign. His resignation was not accepted by the congress but he was given a six-month leave of absence. On September 10, 1924, he left the country. A military junta headed by General Luis Altamirano assumed the government but was overthrown because Altamirano had failed to carry out reforms he had promised. A new junta was appointed and Alessandri was invited to return. He again assumed the presidency on March 20, 1925. In July 1927, General Carlos Ibáñez del Campo was inaugurated as president of Chile.

CHICHERIN, GEORGI VASILEVICH   (1872–1930) Bolshevik (see BOLSHEVIK PARTY) politician. Scion of an aristocratic family, Chicherin worked at the Czarist foreign ministry before going abroad and joining the MENSHEVIKS. Returning to Russia in January 1918, he joined the Bolsheviks and later the same year was appointed Soviet People's Commissar for Foreign Affairs succeeding TROTSKY. His most important achievement in that post was to conclude the Treaty of Rapallo with Germany in 1922. He held his post until 1930, when he resigned because of ill health.

CHIGIRIN CONSPIRACY In 1877, a group of young populist revolutionaries, including the future Social Democrat LEV DEUTSCH, succeeded in organizing several hundred peasants of the Ukraine into an armed militia to seize landowners' estates there. They claimed to be emissaries of the czar, playing on the widespread peasant belief that the landowners had frustrated the czar's intention to give all the land over to the peasantry at the time of the emancipation. Although the uprising was quickly crushed by the Russian army, it had a widespread shock effect, convincing populist activists that the peasants could be organized for revolution.

CHILUBA, FREDERICK JACOB TITUS (1943–) Chiluba was born in the Copperbelt of Northern Zambia on 30 April, 1943. After completing his education, Chiluba began to occupy himself with social issues and workers' rights. He was the central figure in trade union activity in Zambia for many years and became the head of the Zambian Congress of Trade Unions, the umbrella organization of Zambian Trade Unions.

At the beginning of 1991, Chiluba was elected leader of the Movement for Multiparty Democracy (MMD), which had been founded in 1990 and was at the time the only non-governmental political organization in Zambia. It was not originally a party, for Zambia's leader, KENNETH KAUNDA had forbidden the formation of political parties except for his own United National Independence Party (UNIP).

Zambia's first ever multiparty political elections took place in October 1991 and Chiluba won a landslide victory, defeating Kaunda, who had ruled Zambia since independence from Britain in 1964. On 2 November 1991, Chilaba became Zambia's new president.

Chiluba, a Protestant, is a member of the United Church of Zambia and a deeply religious man.

CHINESE REVIVAL SOCIETY see HUG XING HUI; XING ZHONG HUI.

CHINA see under individual entries.

CHINESE COMMUNIST PARTY (CCP) MARXISM, socialism and anarchism were among the foreign ideas that evoked interest in early 20th-century China, but it was only after World War I that Marxism received serious attention there. Under the impact of the RUSSIAN REVOLUTION OF 1917 and the MAY FOURTH MOVEMENT, leading intellectuals, notably CHEN DUXIU and LI DAZHAO, organized socialist study groups in 1919. In May 1920, members of different revolutionary persuasions, encouraged by the COMINTERN agent, Gregor Voitinsky, decided to establish a Communist party. The First National Congress in July 1921, consisting of 12 delegates representing 57 members, marked the CCP's formal inauguration. Guided by the Comintern doctrine which held that "half feudal, half colonial" China could not envisage an immediate proletarian revolution, the CCP was enjoined to actively support the national revolutionary movement, including bourgeois democrats, in the struggle against foreign imperialism and domestic "feudalism," while at the same time preparing an independent proletarian movement for the future struggle against the bourgeoisie. This was the policy that produced the first Koumintang (GUOMINDANG—GMD)-CCP united front (1923–

1927). The CCP, whose members had to join the GMD as individuals, played a subordinate role in the united front, much to the dissatisfaction of its leaders. They nevertheless obeyed Moscow's instructions that the party meet SUN YAT-SEN's conditions for collaboration. The CCP played an active role in the first stage of the NORTHERN EXPEDITION. Its membership, consisting mainly of urban workers, was close to 60,000 in 1927, when CHIANG KAI-SHEK's purge left it in shambles. Driven from the cities, the CCP turned to the countryside and organized armed insurrection. After several ill-fated uprisings—NANCHANG, AUTUMN HARVEST and CANTON—in 1927, MAO ZEDONG, leading a force of a 1,000 men, established the first Communist base at Jinggan mountain (Jinggangshan) in southern Jiangxi, near the Hunan border.

Political and military power now stemmed primarily from the peasantry. Attracting poor peasants with land distribution and terrorizing others, the CCP created scattered soviets and Red Army units in the hinterlands of south-central China. Official party leadership, however, rested with "returned students" and other proteges of Moscow who worked underground in Shanghai until they joined the CHINESE SOVIET REPUBLIC in December 1931. Earlier, in December 1930, Chiang Kai-shek had launched his first encirclement campaign. The fifth, beginning in October 1933, forced the CCP to undertake the Long March and relocate in northern China. On the way, at the Zunyi conference in January 1935, Mao was elected chairman of the Politburo and assumed supreme leadership. This marked the triumph of the CCP rural base over its urban center and the ascendancy, for the first time, of a leader who lacked prior endorsement from Moscow.

During the Yenan phase (1936–1945), which included the second CCP-GMD united front during the Sino-Japanese war (1937–1945), CCP power grew exponentially. Appealing to nationalist sentiments and moderating its agrarian policies, the party mobilized peasants in anti-Japanese guerrilla warfare. By 1945, party membership had soared to 1,210,000. During the postwar struggle, the highly motivated and battle-hardened CCP forces drove the GMD from the mainland and established the People's Republic of China (October 1949), with Beijing as the new capital.

Under Mao Zedong's leadership, the CCP unified China for the first time in over 30 years, asserted its independence, both from the west and the Soviet Union, and launched it on the road to modernization and industrialization. But Mao's policies exacted a heavy and needless loss of human lives. About 2 million landlords were executed during the land-reform campaign, and the disastrous GREAT LEAP FORWARD (1958–1959) took an even heavier toll. Veteran revolutionary comrades criticized Mao's economic policies and in 1966 he lashed back and subjected the party and the nation to the horrors of the GREAT PROLETARIAN CULTURAL REVOLUTION. After his death in September 1976 the party tried to shift most of the blame on the "Gang of Four," but Mao's image was irremediably tarnished and party prestige had plummeted.

Since the historic 3rd plenary session of the 11th Central Committee (December 1978) and the leadership of DENG XIAOPING, the CCP has rejected Maoist radicalism and embraced a "reform and open door" policy that has catapulted China into the front rank of world economic powers. In pursuit of the "Four Modernizations" (referring to the modernization of industry, agriculture, science and technology, and national defense) the CCP has abandoned collectivism and postponed the socialist stage. Yet, while encouraging private enterprise and foreign investment, the party still claims to take "Marxism-Leninism and Mao Zedong Thought" as its guide to action and declares that its ultimate goal is the creation of a Communist social system. This may reflect the faith of Deng and other veteran revolutionaries, but with everyone, including the party cadre, pursuing wealth, the ideological message could become irrelevant. The CCP, which began with 57 members, now has 57 million. However, given the new priorities of the Dengist era, it may have to redefine its mission. In the meantime, it retains a monopoly of political power.

Like its totalitarian Soviet prototype, the CCP directs and supervises the parallel state administration. Power is concentrated at the top and flows down. National congresses, now usually held every five years (the last, the 14th, was in 1992) elect the central committee (CC) which in turn elects the Politburo, whose Standing Committee is the highest decision-making authority. Through its Central Military Commission, the party controls the army, the world's largest. The general secretary of the CC is the leading party official. (A new title, party chairman, was created for Mao Zedong in 1943, but was abolished in 1982.) Since 1989, Jiang Zemin has been general secretary. The paramount leader is still Deng Xiaoping, who holds no official title.

CHINESE COMMUNIST REVOLUTION The antecedent causes of the revolution which brought the Communists to power in 1949 can be traced to the mid-19th century. An internal systemic crisis (see TAIPING REBELLION) had combined with foreign invasion to launch China on an unsteady course toward modernization accompanied by tumultous upheavals (e.g., TAIPING REBELLION, BOXER UPRISING and the CHINESE REPUBLICAN REVOLUTION OF 1911). While traditional society was being transformed during a period of political disintegration, the impact of the MAY FOURTH MOVEMENT and the inspiration of the BOLSHEVIK Revolution led to the formation of the CHINESE COMMUNIST PARTY (CCP) in 1921. This was the first step in a protracted revolutionary process that can be divided into five stages: 1) formative phase; 2) first united front; 3) agrarian-based revolutionary war; 4) second united front; 5) full-scale civil war.

Formative phase. (1921–1923) Dominated by intellectuals, the CCP extended its influence to the emergent labor movement (see DENG ZHONGXIA) and began organizing peasants (see PENG PAI). The Second Party Congress (1922) voted to join the COMINTERN and the Third Congress (1923) accepted Comintern (i.e. Leninist) strategy that gave temporary priority to the national revolution ("anti-feudal, anti-imperialist"). In practice, this required acceptance of subordinate status under the GUOMINDANG (GMD) in the joint nationalist effort. It also reflected Moscow's determination to gear the Chinese revolution to its own national interests.

First United Front. (1924–1927) At The First National Congress of the reorganized GMD (1924) Communists were given key positions in the senior party, more than their numbers warranted. Furthermore, they dominated the GMD labor and peasant bureaus and helped bring the masses into the nationalist movement. GMD members lacked the young Communists' dedication to radical reform and their enthusiasm for working within the lower reaches of society. The CCP and its adjunct, the Socialist Youth Corps (later renamed Communist Youth Corps) recruited students whose social responsibilities had been awakened by the May Fourth Movement. A Communist headed the GMD peasant bureau, and Communists conducted classes that trained field workers for the rural areas. Similarly, the Communists had more experience in organizing labor and more taste for strike activity. Though China was still an overwhelmingly agrarian society, World War I had stimulated the growth of Chinese industry, especially in the major port cities. Communists led the All-China Federation of Trade Unions (founded in May 1925) which represented 540,000 workers. Conditions of factory work throughout China, reminiscent of the worst evils of early European industrialization, provoked militant responses, particularly against the foreign owners who controlled much of China's modern industry. The 19th-century unequal treaties had given foreigners special rights (e.g., extraterritoriality, low tariffs) which were enforced by foreign gunboats. Thus Communists could inject an anti-imperialist component in their labor agitation. It was this fusion of labor issues and anti-imperialism that in 1925 fueled a year-long, nationwide series of strikes, boycotts and demonstrations that came to be known as the MAY 30TH MOVEMENT. On May 15, a Japanese foreman killed a Chinese worker during a strike. Although this led to anti-Japanese demonstrations, the British became the chief target and the movement derived its name from what happened on May 30: British-led police in Shanghai's International Settlement fired upon demonstrators, killing 13. In response, anti-British demonstrations flared up elsewhere, especially in the Canton-Hong Kong region. On June 23, demonstrators in Canton clashed with Anglo-French forces defending foreign consulates in Shameen Island and 52 Chinese, including students and cadets from the WHAMPOA MILITARY ACADEMY, were killed. The reaction to the "Shameen massacre" intensified antiforeign agitation, especially against Britain, the major imperialist power. The strike and boycott against Hong Kong, which did not end until October 1926, crippled Britain's south China trade and virtually paralyzed the colony's economic activity.

The surge in anti-imperialist sentiments strengthend both the GMD and the CCP. However, the latter, which dominated the movement, gained much more. It also had considerable success in the countryside, where exhorbitant rent and taxes and a highly unequal distribution of land facilitated peasant mobilization. By June 1926, total membership in peasant associations was close to one million. Communist success in tapping popular sources of discontent now posed a threat to conservative GMD elements, who in any case were always suspicious of CCP ties to Moscow. Nationalism had brought the two parties together. The issue of social revolution drew them apart. The final rupture came during the course of the NORTHERN EXPEDITION.

By early 1927 one wing of the National Revolutionary army, dominated by the left-GMD and Communists, had captured Wuhan in central China and made it the new capital of the nationalist government that had been established in Canton in 1925. Another force, led by CHIANG KAI-SHEK, was pushing toward Shanghai and Nanjing in the east. South-central China, where Wuhan's influence predominated, witnessed the largest rural upheaval since the Taiping Rebellion. Communists had encouraged peasant uprisings but could not always contain their violence. Revolution now provoked counterrevolution. The rift in nationalist ranks, reflecting a power struggle as well as conflicting ideologies, deepened. Wuhan had political legitimacy but Chiang had superior military forces and struck first. On April 12 Shanghai was the scene of a brutal purge of Communists and their labor sympathizers. A few days later the slaughter was repeated in Canton, the other stronghold of the labor movement. The Communists, following Moscow's lead, kept faith with the left-GMD, but two months later were expelled from Wuhan. By the end of the year party membership would be less than 10,000. Nevertheless, the Communists still had a core of dedicated young leaders who had gained valuable organizational and military experience. Moreover, they were now free of the ambiguous relationship with the GMD, and as they regrouped in the countryside, objective conditions would enable them to assert more freedom from Moscow.

Agrarian-based Revolutionary War. (1927–1937) Driven underground in the cities, the Communists now adapted their strategy and, tactics to the rural environment. They established soviets and, what was most important for their survival and future victory, they created a party army and became adept at waging guerrilla warfare. In a sense, this was a return to the traditional pattern of anti-dynastic rebellion. At first, however, Moscow prodded the CCP into undertaking a series of reckless military ventures that began with the Nanchang and Autumn Harvest uprisings and ended with a disastrous attack on Canton (December 1927), all of which crippled the already weakened Communist movement. Next came a period of conflict over leadership and strategy, compounded by contradictory directives from the Comintern. While acknowledging the peasant "content" of the revolution, Moscow still demanded that it be led by the urban proletariat. The 6th CCP Congress (June–July 1928) was held in Moscow. QU QIUBAI, condemned as a "putschist" and "left deviationist," was replaced as general-secretary by XIANG ZHONGFA, though actual power was held by LI LISAN and his collaborator, ZHOU ENLAI. In line with Comintern directives, Li tried to foment urban insurrection. When he failed, it was his turn to be condemned as a "putschist," and in 1931 leadership passed to Moscow's proteges known as the "returned students" (see WANG MING and QIN BANGXIAN). This was last known instance of direct Soviet interference in the internal affairs of the CCP. But the shifts in leadership in the underground headquarters in Shanghai were a sideshow. The real retrenchment and recovery of Red power was in the hinterland. Mao Zedong, who in February 1927 had advocated relying upon peasant insurrection, established the first Communist base at Jinggangshan in southern Jiangxi in October. In April 1928, ZHU DE and his forces joined Mao and formed the alliance that would eventually lead the Communists to victory. The combined force was named the 4th Red Army, with Zhu as commander and Mao political commissar. Enemy pressure forced abandonment of Jinggangshan and in 1929 they established a new base at Ruijin, further south in Jiangxi, near the Fujian border. This became the central Soviet base. It was a more defensible area and enabled the Communists to expand their power through a radical policy of land distribution often accompanied by violence.

Besides the three soviets in the Jiangxi region, others were in Hubei-Henan-Anhui (under ZHANG GUODAO), west Hubei-Hunan (under HE LONG), and north Shaanxi, where GAO GANG was active. By early 1930, these areas provided the Red Army with some

60,000 troops in 13 units. The Communists gained some respite while Chiang Kai-shek was preoccupied fighting regional militarists and GMD dissidents, but in December he was free to launch a major assault against the Jiangxi Soviet areas. This was the first of his encirclement campaigns and was easily repulsed by the Red Army. The 2nd encirclement campaign (February–May 1931) ended in disaster for the GMD. The Communists took 20,000 prisoners and expanded their territory. Chiang took personal command of the 3rd campaign starting in July and was making headway until he called it off when the Japanese invaded Manchuria (September 1931). Again enjoying a respite, the Communists expanded the territory of the central Soviet base, and its population rose to almost 2,500,000. In December, the First All-China Congress of Soviets, meeting in Ruijin, proclaimed the establishment of the CHINESE SOVIET REPUBLIC and set up a Central Soviet Government headed by MAO ZEDONG. ZHU DE was named chairman of the Revolutionary Military Council, which had over-all control of the Red Army, and whose strength reached 200,000 with 150,000 rifles. In an effective propaganda ploy, the Chinese Soviet government declared war against Japan in April 1932. However, despite the growing Japanese menace, Chiang Kai-shek committed the bulk of his forces against the Communists.

For his 4th encirclement campaign (June 1932–February 1933), Chiang mobilized 500,000 troops and scored successes against other soviet areas but became bogged down in Jiangxi. Trouble with the Japanese along the Great Wall forced him to abort the campaign. However, when a truce was declared in the north, he started the 5th encirclement campaign in November 1933. Chiang and his German advisers resorted to a new strategy. By combining economic blockade with military attacks and by luring the Red Army (now over 300,000 strong) into switching from guerrilla tactics to positional warfare, they inflicted heavy losses on the Communists and drastically reduced the territory under their control. In the summer of 1934, the central Soviet area faced annihilation. Its army was down to 130,000 and its territory was less than a fifth of what it had been in 1932. In October 1934, the Communists made the agonizing decision to evacuate Jiangxi and break out to the northwest in what became known as the LONG MARCH.

On the way, the CCP leaders held a conference in Zunyi (Guizhou province) in January 1935 and elected Mao Zedong chairman of the Politburo. This was the first time the party had chosen a leader who had not previously been endorsed by Moscow, and thus represented a further step away from foreign tutelage. It was also a victory for Mao's strategy of guerrilla warfare. In December, when Mao's force reached north Shaanxi and linked up with existing soviets, the CCP issued a call for a united front against Japan. This was in accord with the Comintern's appeal for a global united front against fascism. It was also in accord with a growing popular demand for resisting Japan and ending civil strife. Then, in December 1936, Chiang Kai-shek found himself held captive by Chinese troops, originally from Manchuria, who preferred fighting Japanese to annihilating Communists. Communist mediation (see ZHOU ENLAI) secured his release. GMD-CCP hostilities now ceased and the way was cleared for the second united front.

Second United Front. (1937–1945) In August–September 1937, after six months of negotiations and two months after the opening shots of the Sino-Japanese war (July 7), agreements on the united front were made public. The Communist motives were quite clear. Their forces had been practically decimated, down to about 30,000 men, including the survivors of the Long March, existing local forces and new recruits. A period of respite and retrenchment was an absolute necessity. At the same time, a refusal to halt civil war would have clashed with national interests that demanded an all-out effort against the Japanese. This was not just an attempt to win popular, non-Communist, support—which it did—but it also reflected the nationalist feelings of the Communists themselves. And finally, the international situation (SPANISH CIVIL WAR, Rome-Berlin Axis and the German-Italian-Japanese Anti-Comintern Pact) and the danger facing the Soviet Union demanded a concerted effort against imperialism and fascism. GMD conditions did not affect Mao's basic concern, which was to hold on to territory and build an army. The changes he made were nominal: the Soviet régime became the Shaanxi-Gansu-Ningxia Border Region and the Red Army became the Eighth Route Army (later changed to Eighteenth Group Army). In return, the GMD allowed the CCP to set up liaison offices in several important cities, to publish the *New China Daily* and to send representatives to two advisory bodies. The Nationalist government also started sending monthly subsidies (terminated in 1940) to help defray the expenses of the so-called reintegrated territories and army. In addition to the Eighth Route Army, the GMD also authorized the formation of a second Communist force, the New Fourth Army, composed mainly of survivors in Jiangxi and Fujian who had not joined the Long March. They numbered about 10,000 and were assigned to east China. Thus, at the start of the Sino-Japanese war, the CCP controlled only part of north Shaanxi, where it had established its capital at Yan'an in December 1936. The party and army numbered about 40,000 each. But the next eight years witnessed a spectacular increase in CCP power and left it in a favorable position to contend for the mastery of China.

Several factors account for the Communist success. First of all, during the war as a whole, about 70% of the Japanese forces engaged the Nationalist army under the GMD. This was especially true of the first two years of the war, when the Japanese directed their main effort in eastern and central China. This enabled the Communists to expand their bases in north China and to infiltrate behind the Japanese lines. By 1940, the CCP had grown 20 times larger (to 800,000) and the army five times larger (to 500,000). Communist growth far exceeded that which had been authorized by the GMD. The united front, which had been shaky from the start, practically came to an end when a series of local conflicts led to the New Fourth Army Incident in January 1941 (see YE TING). However, mutual restraint prevented civil war, though the nationalists tightened the blockade of the north that had begun in 1939.

The crucial development during this period was that in the areas under its control the CCP succeeded in mobilizing popular support. This was achieved through a moderate land reform program that, after eliminating glaring inequalities in landownership, concentrated on rent and tax reductions and in promoting cooperatives and mutual-aid teams. Villagers, who were encouraged to become literate, were given a share in determining their destiny by participating in meetings, peasant associations and elections. They engaged in production drives that enabled the

border regions to survive a blockade by 400,000 nationalist troops. They joined militias and self-defense forces as well as regular army units. Though manipulated by the CCP, the "New Democracy" that it promoted gave peasants more political rights than they had ever enjoyed in the past. These political and socioeconomic policies, no less than anti-Japanese nationalist sentiments, drew mass support for the Communists. Also, university and high school students were attracted to Yan'an, where they underwent indoctrination in the party's schools and academies, and then served as cadres in the border regions and in the army. Thought-reform campaigns weeded out "unorthodox" thinking and ensured that an expanding party would also be highly disciplined. Though the Red Army provided the indispensable shield, any evaluation of the Communists' success cannot discount the organizational aptitude that helped them harness mass support. This combination of military and political prowess enabled the border regions to withstand fierce Japanese attacks from 1940 to the end of 1943. By 1944, when Japanese pressure had eased, the Communists were once more expanding. At the end of the war they had 18 base areas in north and central China, an army of close to one million, and party membership of 1,200,000. (About one-third of the soldiers were also party members.) The weapons had now been forged, and would be employed in full force in the postwar struggle for power.

Full-Scale Civil War. (1946–1949) On August 11, 1945, in anticipation of the Japanese surrender, Chiang Kai-shek ordered all Communist troops to hold their positions. Mao Zedong and Zhu De refused, and the race began to take over Japanese-held territory north of the Yangtze. Three days later, when Japan formally surrendered, Chiang immediately invited Mao Zedong to Chongqing for discussions. In principle they agreed on unification and the establishment of democratic rule. Mutual distrust, however, prevented implementation. The Communists refused to withdraw from all their base areas and continued to advance. Most GMD troops were in the south, and the Americans transported about 500,000 of them to the coastal areas by air and sea. Chiang ordered Japanese troops not to surrender to the Communists and to recover territory that had been lost to them. As contention over control of north China threatened to erupt into civil war, the United States sent General George C. Marshall to mediate. Marshall, who arrived in late December 1945, was able to effect a cease-fire in January. A Political Consultative Conference was convened to work out peace plans and the formation of a coalition government. While at this time both sides may have preferred a peaceful solution, neither had sufficient faith in the other to make the necessary compromises. The truce first broke down in Manchuria, and on June 30, when the period for another truce expired, the mediation effort faltered. With both sides hardening their positions, Marshall's mission became practically impossible and he left in January 1947.

During this first phase of the civil war (1946–1947), the GMD captured most of the cities, including Yan'an, while the Communists retreated and resorted to guerrilla war. In July 1946, the Communist forces were renamed the PEOPLE'S LIBERATION ARMY (PLA). At this time, on paper at least, the nationalists possessed overwhelming superiority. They had 2,500,000 troops—double that of the CCP—and more and better arms and equipment. They had the advantage of considerable American assistance in supplies, and an American military advisory group was set up in

March 1946 to help develop their armed forces. Some of their forces had already been trained and equipped by Americans during the war. Altogether, from August 1945 to early 1948, the United States aid to Nationalist China was over 2 billion dollars. The Communists, on the other hand, had no navy or air force, and depended largely on captured enemy stock for heavy weapons. As guerrilla fighters, they seemed incapable of surviving the large-scale battles that were in store for them. The little help they received from the Russians in Manchuria was in no way comparable to US aid to the GMD. Actually, in 1945, as Mao Zedong recalled bitterly, Stalin wanted the CCP to cooperate with Chiang Kai-shek and not engage in civil war.

Yet, beneath the surface the picture of GMD formidability changes radically. The burden of resisting the Japanese onslaught had been mostly theirs and had left them tired and dispirited. In contrast to the ideologically motivated and disciplined Communist forces, the ordinary nationalist soldiers, who had been forcibly recruited and often abused by their officers, lacked a strong incentive to continue to fight. Upper ranks were still riddled by the regional jealousies and factionalism that had hampered the war effort. Nor did Chiang and his generals display sound strategic sense in committing so many forces to Manchuria and major cities. In 1936, General Marshall had warned him that though the Communists were retreating, their forces were intact, and before leaving he told Chiang that he doubted whether the GMD could destroy the Communists through military means.

It was in the non-military sphere, however, that the GMD's inadequacies were most glaring. It had never tackled the agrarian problem aggressively and the wartime government was even less inclined to deal with rural inequalities. In the civil war, therefore, the GMD not only lacked the support of the peasants—over 80% of the population—but often encountered their hostility. The situation in the cities was hardly better. Inflation, which had plagued Chongqing during the war, erupted into hyperinflation. Workers went on strike and students and intellectuals, who were inclined to blame the GMD for the civil war, promoted peace movements that were violently repressed. In general, a war-weary population resented the GMD insistence upon waging another war in their already devastated country.

In the second year of the civil war (1947–1948), the above-mentioned factors came into play as the Communists mounted a counteroffensive. In Manchuria, PLA forces led by Lin Biao began a series of campaigns in September 1947, and by mid-1948 had achieved strategic superiority. In the third and final year (1948–1949), the PLA completed its sweep of Manchuria (November 1948) and turned south. Beiping fell on January 31. Meanwhile, the decisive Huai-Hai campaign (November-January) in northern Jiangsu was coming to a close. Each side had deployed about 500,000 troops, but the PLA had the logistical support of 2 million peasants. DENG XIAOPING headed the coordinated Communist effort which ended in disaster for the Nationalists, who lost their entire force (300,000 taken prisoner and the rest as casualties). This had been the last Nationalist stand north of the Yangtze. The PLA crossed that potential defense line in April and entered Shanghai in May. In the autumn the PLA took over the southwest and, except for minor pockets of resistance, the war on the mainland was over. On October 1, Mao Zedong proclaimed the establishment of the People's Republic of China.

Beijing, formerly called Beiping, then became the new capital.

CHINESE NATIONALIST REVOLUTION (1923–1928) Nationalist campaign to unify China. In 1923, SUN YAT-SEN's Nationalist party—GUOMINDANG (GMD)—started planning a northern drive to unify China, which had been divided among regional militarists (warlords) since 1916. Strengthened by the united front (1923–1927) with the CHINESE COMMUNIST PARTY (CCP) and Soviet Russian assistance, the GMD consolidated its hold on Canton, establishing a "national government" and a NATIONAL REVOLUTIONARY ARMY (NRA) in June 1925. The drive north (NORTHERN EXPEDITION) began in July 1926 with CHIANG KAI-SHEK as commander in chief. As GMD and CCP organizers and propagandists won popular support from workers and peasants and numerous warlord contingents were absorbed, the NRA advanced rapidly. Wuchang, the Hubei capital, fell on October 10, the 15th anniversary of the CHINESE REUBLICAN REVOLUTION OF 1911, the anti-dynastic upheaval that had given birth to the Chinese Republic and which had erupted there. By then the middle Yangtze valley was in Nationalist hands. After heavy fighting, Jiangxi was captured in November and in December the Nationalists controlled seven provinces, with a total population of about 170 million.

In early 1927, fissures were evident in Nationalist ranks. The left GMD and the CCP dominated the new government established in Wuhan and pursued more vigorous anti-landlord and anti-imperialist policies. Spurred by anti-imperialist agitators, including the CCP leader, LI LISAN, Chinese mobs stormed into British concessions in Hankou and Jiujiang. Wuhan's foreign spokesman, EUGENE CHEN, scored a major diplomatic triumph for the Nationalists when the British surrendered the Hankou concession in February 1927 and their enclave in March 1927. Meanwhile, Chiang Kai-shek, increasingly identified with the right GMD, was based in Jiangxi, poised for the attack on Shanghai. The International Settlement there had the greatest concentration of foreigners and was the hub of British financial interests. The militant Shanghai labor movement, dominated by the CCP, staged mass rallies and demonstrations and armed workers led uprisings against the local warlords in order to facilitate Chiang Kai-shek's advance. The British, fearing a repetition of the Hankou takeover, sent naval and military reinforcements. A total of 40 foreign warships and 16,000 troops was on hand to protect the major bastion of imperialism in China. Negotiations with Chiang Kai-shek eased their fears. On April 12, his forces, with foreign concurrence, joined local anti-Communist elements in a bloody purge of the CCP and labor organizations in Shanghai. Three days later the "white terror" was extended to Nanjing, which Chiang had chosen for the new Nationalist capital. Earlier, in March, when NRA troops first entered Nanjing, they attacked foreign consulates, killing several foreigners. A retaliatory bombardment by British and American warships claimed a large number of Chinese lives. The Nanjing Incident was one of the rare occasions when anti-imperialist furor provoked the killing of foreigners. On the whole, the NRA was highly disciplined and, unlike warlord armies, showed concern for the civilian population. Enjoying tremendous popular support, the Nationalist Revolution had taken over central China in less than a year and was halfway to Beijing. But the coalition with the CCP, which had made a considerable contribution to the revolution's success, came to an end.

For several months, the left-GMD in Wuhan cooperated with the CCP in opposing Chiang Kai-shek. In July, however, the left-GMD also broke with the CCP and later rejoined Chiang Kai-shek. After regrouping in Nanjing, the NRA resumed its drive north in March 1928. On the way, the most serious clash with foreigners occurred in Shandong. In May, after a minor skirmish had apparently been settled amicably, an impetuous Japanese officer took retaliatory action against Jinan and the vicinity. Thousands of Chinese troops and civilians were killed during three days of fighting. The Jinan Incident inflamed anti-Japanese feelings but Chiang Kai-shek exercised restraint and resumed the northern campaign. In June, the NRA captured Beijing ("northern capital"), renaming it Beiping ("northern peace").

The Nationalist government was formally inaugurated in its new capital, Nanjing, on October 10, 1928, the 17th anniversary of the 1911 Revolution. The republican government was now reorganized according to Sun's original plan. The GMD inaugurated a period of one-party rule, ostensibly to carry out a program of political tutelage prior to establishing full constitutional government. By the end of the year the new government, headed by Chiang Kai-shek, had gained general international recognition.

Nanjing's actual power, however, was narrowly circumscribed by regional militarists, co-opted during the rapid advance of the NRA. In purging the left, the GMD lost some of its own revolutionary vigor and ties with the peasant masses. The real stronghold of the Nanjing government was in the better-developed eastern seaboard, in commercial centers like Shanghai. The GMD itself became increasingly militarized, seeking military solutions to problems rooted in socioeconomic distress. The CCP, thriving in the countryside, proved difficult to defeat militarily. Yet whatever chance the GMD had for subduing its enemy and modernizing China according to Sun Yat-sen's vision of a more equitable society was seriously impaired by the Japanese invasion, beginning with the conquest of Manchuria in 1931 and finally erupting into full-scale war during 1937–1945 (see also GUOMINDANG; CHIANG KAI-SHEK; CHINESE COMMUNIST REVOLUTION).

CHINESE REPUBLICAN REVOLUTION OF 1911 In the 19th century, internal and external pressures weakened the Qing (Manchu) dynasty (1644–1912), eventually leading to its collapse and the end of China's 2000-year-old imperial system. In part, internal troubles were symptomatic of the downward phase of the dynastic cycle that describes the life-span of most Chinese dynasties. According to this pattern, Chinese dynasties, like all hereditary institutions, eventually lose their initial vigor and administrative efficiency. As central control slackens, the literati-bureaucratic elite, known as gentry families, augments its private economic interests at public expense. As tax collectors, landowners and usurers, gentry families squeeze the peasantry—the vast majority of the population—and at the same time deprive the imperial treasury of revenue, which in turn leads to neglect of public works and increased vulnerability to natural disasters. In the end, the dynasty falls victim to peasant uprisings or foreign invasions or a combination of the two. The cycle starts all over again when a new dynasty restores a viable balance between imperial needs, gentry affluence and peasant subsistence

However, the 19th century internal crisis was not merely administrative, but also systemic. As a result of the early efficiency of Qing rule and other factors, the Chinese population had been rising at an unprecedented rate since the 18th century. By 1850 it was well over 400 million, narrowing the gap between productive capacity and population. The long-term solution—science and industrialization—required accommodation to ideas and institutions that clashed with the Sino-centric, Confucian order.

In addition, China had to contend with the western imperialist invasion. In the Opium war (1840–1842) Britain brought an end to China's self-imposed exclusiveness. For the next half century foreigners dictated a series of unequal treaties that deprived the Chinese empire of territory and sovereign rights. The west also brought ideas and techniques that undermined tradition.

As alien conquerors, the Manchus faced an additional problem. Though they delegated power to Chinese officials and had ruled in exemplary Confucian fashion for 150 years, the ethnic issue had never disappeared entirely. It flared up when they appeared unable to repel foreign invaders and alleviate domestic distress. In a way, the Manchus became scapegoats for what was essentially the inadequacy of the traditional order. Paradoxically, as non-Chinese rulers whose claim to the "Mandate of Heaven" derived from their adherence to Confucianism, they were more stubbornly orthodox than a native dynasty might have been when faced with the unprecedented threat of the industrialized west.

The popular response to the 19th century crisis was a rise in peasant turbulence and secret society uprisings, heavily tinged with anti-Manchuism. The TAIPING REBELLION (1850–1864), the most destructive civil war in world history, almost toppled the dynasty. The elite response was gradual modernization, at first limited to the military sphere. Nevertheless, new ideas, stemming from missionaries, foreign-controlled treaty-ports like Hong Kong and Shanghai, translations of foreign writings and from the government's own limited efforts, provided the impetus for an elitist reform movement in the last decade of the century. China's defeat by Japan (1894–1895), long despised as an inferior replica of the Celestial Empire, sent shock waves through elitist circles. It also encouraged the imperialist scramble for concessions in 1898 that seemed to portend the breakup of China. Though supported by the young emperor, Guangxu (1871–1908), an attempt at radical institutional reform, heavily influenced by the Japanese model, was aborted by conservatives led by the empress dowager Ci Xi, (1835–1908), in September 1898, just 100 days after it was launched.

SUN YAT-SEN's first revolutionary organization, XING ZHONG HUI (Society to Restore China's Prosperity), formed in Hawaii in 1894, represented the emergence of a new elite—non-gentry but foreign-educated. Anti-Manchu and republican-oriented and harnessing traditional secret society fighters and overseas Chinese money, Sun tried to seize Canton in 1895 and took advantage of the BOXER UPRISING in 1900 in the north to stage another attempt. While Sun tried to revive revolution from abroad, the Boxer disaster finally induced the Qing dynasty to launch a serious reform program. For the first decade of the 20th century the dynasty was in the unfortunate position of a traditional regime whose belated reforms generate more radical demands. Modernization, inspired in part by the Japanese model, created new interests and demands that could not be contained within the traditional political setting. Modern entrepreneurs, intellectuals and army officers sought changes that rulers could not accommodate without jeopardizing their own prerogatives. The modern Chinese press, developing since the 1890s, resonated with nationalist themes. Social Darwinist ideas, first introduced into China toward the close of the 19th century by Yan Fu (1854–1921), pioneer translator and interpreter of western thought, aroused fears for China's survival. A backward China, writers warned, would be the next victim of the predatory imperialism enveloping the globe. The strongest voice sounding the alarm was that of Liang Qichao (1873–1929). The foremost Chinese publicist of his time, Liang had been a disciple of Kang Youwei (1858–1927), leader of the ill-fated 100-day reform of 1898. Since then in exile in Japan, Liang exerted a powerful intellectual influence, introducing western political thought to young Chinese.

The most important of the government's post-Boxer reforms—and ultimately the most crucial for its own fate—was educational modernization, also inspired by the Japanese model. At home, new schools nurtured radical ideas, while experience in Japan—where thousands were sent at government expense—sharpened students' awareness of China's low status in the world and bred contempt for the officials who had sent them and who, by doing so, had admitted the inadequacy of their own traditional learning. In 1903, the 18 year old ZOU RONG, educated in modern schools in China and Japan, published the seditious tract, *The Revolutionary Army*. Distributed in hundreds of thousands of copies that reached Chinese readers throughout the world, it became the most famous of revolutionary writings. Zou's highest priority was anti-Manchuism: "If we wish to resist foreign aggression, we must first purge the internal evil."

In 1905, reverberations from Japan's stunning victory in the Russo-Japanese war (1904–1905), the first modern Asian triumph over a European power, accelerated official Chinese reform and also encouraged revolutionaries. In a war waged largely on Chinese soil, the Japanese demonstrated that modernization was the key to successful resistance to the west. The Japanese example prompted the Manchu court to take steps toward establishing constitutional government. The concession, however, was greeted with suspicion and provoked demands for faster political reform. In a dramatic illustration of the widening gap between imperial authorities and revolutionary nationalists, a student threw a bomb at the delegation of imperial commissioners embarking upon a study tour of foreign governments.

The RUSSIAN REVOLUTION OF 1905 also encouraged Chinese revolutionaries. That same year the Chinese government decided to abolish the traditional examination system, the main prop of the age-old Confucian political system. This gave a further impetus to modern education. More students went to Japan where, by 1906, they numbered over 10,000 and supplied recruits for revolution. At home, officially encouraged chambers of commerce articulated the interests of local merchants and strengthened the trend toward regionalism, which was also a vehicle for an anti-imperialist, "rights recovery" movement. Although it was not indifferent to nationalist sentiments and made efforts to resist imperialist incursions, the central government, threatened by foreign gunboats and saddled with foreign loan and indemnity payments, could not satisfy popular demands. The 1905 anti-American boycott, led by merchants and students protesting the renewal of discriminatory immigration laws, was indicative of popular nationalism. Pressured by the Americans, the government helped end the boycott.

In addition to its failure to satisfy the new urban elite, the official reform program antagonized the peasant masses. As taxpayers and tenants, peasants bore the financial burden of reform but derived no visible benefits. New schools and overseas education mainly served gentry families, who also dominated newly created local self-government institutions. Long deteriorating as a result of land hunger, rural conditions worsened as a side effect of urban economic development. With commercial opportunities attracting gentry to the cities, absentee landlordism became more prevalent and hardened the conditions of tenancy. Modern domestic industry and foreign imports hurt village handicraft industries, the traditional supplement to agriculture. At the same time, peasant recruits to the new armies were infected by revolutionary propaganda and increased migration to the cities exposed them to nationalist agitation. Though growing, industry could not absorb all the refugees from village poverty. Traditional artisans and manual laborers resented the machines that displaced them and the foreigners who introduced the machines. Economic and nationalist issues combined to provoke strikes against foreign firms, which had won the right to engage in manufacturing in treaty ports after the Sino-Japanese war (1894–1895). Anti-foreign, including anti-missionary, incidents mounted. Blaming the Beijing government, the foreign powers resorted to gunboat diplomacy, provoking nationalist anger against them and the dynasty they intimidated. Thus, by 1905, powerful nationalist sentiments, affecting all strata of Chinese society, inevitably focused on the easiest target—an alien dynasty that appeared unable to defend Chinese sovereignty. Though growing in frequency and scope, most anti-dynastic outbursts were spontaneous or hastily conceived.

In August 1905, a better organized revolutionary threat took shape with the formation of Sun Yat-sen's TONGMENGHUI (revolutionary alliance) (TMH) in Tokyo. Formed through an amalgamation of Sun's Cantonese-based XINGZHONGHUI, now moribund, with HUAXINGHUI and GUANGFUHUI, from the middle and lower Yangtze provinces respectively, the TMH drew upon the overseas students representing most Chinese provinces. With a formal organizational apparatus headed by Sun and an ideology and program for action, it was China's first modern-type political party. Anti-Manchuism, republicanism and a moderate socialism provided the ideological content that was largely Sun's contribution, later to become famous as his Three Principles of the People. He also worked out a nine year timetable for the full implementation of representative government after achieving military victory. Not all of Sun's ideas were fully endorsed by his colleagues. Yet his seniority as an anti-Manchu conspirator, his reputed access to overseas Chinese funds and connections with foreigners—especially Japanese—made his leadership acceptable. Winning foreign sympathy was important for avoiding imperialist intervention, which was the common fear of potential rebels who remembered the fate of the Taipings. During the first few years, while Sun was usually abroad raising money among overseas Chinese, his comrades spread the revolutionary message in the TMH monthly, *Min Bao* (*People's Report*). They also debated with reformist adversaries, whose journal, *Xin Min Cong Bao* (*New People's Miscellany*), was edited by the redoubtable Liang Qichao. Bitter enemies of the empress dowager, Liang and his mentor, Kang Youwei, still supported the young emperor and were committed to constitutional monarchy under the Manchus.

While in Japan, Liang became more radical. Despite his anti-Manchu predilections, he feared that revolution would invite foreign intervention and that in any case China was not yet ready for republicanism. Nevertheless, the revolutionary option attracted many of his former disciples. In 1906, while the journalistic duel was going on in Japan, peasants and miners launched a desperate rebellion in the Hunan-Jiangxi border (Ping-Liu-Li) area in south-central China, the same region where MAO ZEDONG would build a guerrilla base some twenty years later. Secret societies, assisted by students—including some who had returned from Japan—supplied the leadership of what was called "The Revolutionary Vanguard of the Southern Army of the Chinese National Army." Around 20,000-strong, poorly armed and lacking a clearly defined political program, the rebels nevertheless tied down government troops from four provinces for a month before being repressed. Brutal reprisals took thousands of lives. The Ping-Liu-Li Uprising was a further demonstration of the potential for revolution. It also revealed that uprisings would be futile if not sustained by better organized forces.

In 1907–1908, the TMH went into action, undertaking six unsuccessful uprisings in southern China from Hanoi, led by HUANG XING. Sun Yat-sen had expected but did not receive French assistance. In most of these attempts, the TMH depended upon secret society (Triad) fighters. However, in its next failed enterprise, at Canton in 1910, it enlisted defecting soldiers, a strategy that would later prove successful. In April 1911, Huang Xing led another Canton uprising. Well-funded and based upon dissident army units and student members, it failed when prematurely disclosed by the assassination of a Manchu general. Frustrated by successive defeats, SONG JIAOREN and other TMH leaders questioned Sun's leadership. Abandoning Sun's Cantonese orientation, they shifted the emphasis to their own home province in the middle Yangtze.

Meanwhile, the Manchu government had been forced to make more concessions. In August 1908 it had outlined plans for constitutional rule, scheduling implementation in nine years. In October, dynastic leadership had been weakened by the death of the young emperor and the empress dowager in November 1908. A two-and half year old infant sat on the throne, while the best of Chinese officials who had guided China through the crises of the 19th century were passing from the scene. Their most capable successor, Yuan Shikai (1859–1916) was dismissed in 1909. That year, the convening of provincial assemblies spurred demands for a faster retreat from absolutism. In 1910, the newly-formed National Assembly—half of its members chosen by provincial bodies dominated by merchants and gentry and half chosen by the throne—forced the Manchu court to schedule parliamentary government for 1913. Still under pressure from constitutionalists, who were not necessarily revolutionaries, the Manchus agreed to replace the Grand Council, which they had dominated, with a cabinet. Though too weak to resist demands for reform, the imperial family hesitated to share power. The cabinet it unveiled in May 1911 was packed with incompetent Manchu nobles, thus striking a blow at the

imperial family's credibility and Chinese ethnic pride. The critical test of the new leadership came soon and it was found wanting.

During the summer, Chinese entrepeneurs had been agitating against the government's plan to nationalize a projected railway network (Huguang railways) connecting the Yangtze valley with the south. Since indigenous capital was lacking, the government had to accept a foreign consortium loan to finance the project. A Railway Protect League was formed to protest losses to local investors and the mortgaging of Chinese resources to foreign imperialists. Demonstrations led to riots, joined by masses who had other, numerous, grievances against the authorities. In September, after troops killed rioters, Sichuan, China's largest province, was in disorder. Troops were shifted from Hubei, in the central Yangtze, the area now targeted by the TMH.

Rather than the TMH, however, a local group that had recruited soldiers from the modern military (New Army) took the initiative at Wuchang, the Hubei capital, on October 10, the day subsequently celebrated as the anniversary of the CHINESE REPUBLICAN REVOLUTION OF 1911. Unlike previous aborted risings, this one was sustained and spread because various strata in Chinese society who, not all for the same reason, wanted an end to Manchu rule. Since no well-known leader was initially present at Wuchang, LI YUANHONG, a brigade commander, was pressed into service as military governor of Hubei. On October 11, he proclaimed the province part of the "Chinese Republic." At the end of the month TMH leaders arrived, including Huang Xing, who took command of the revolutionary forces even though he was subordinate to Li. In desperation, the Manchu court recalled Yuan Shikai, giving him command of all imperial forces, the strongest of which were personally loyal to him. In November, the court met demands for constitutional government and named Yuan premier as well. Hard fighting led to a stalemate on the Wuhan (Wuchang, Hanyang, Hankow) front, while other provinces began opting for independence, usually led by provincial militarists and assemblies which were concerned with keeping the masses under rein. By December, all the southern, central and northwestern provinces had declared independence.

Sun Yat-sen was abroad when he heard news of the Wuchang uprising. While in Europe he wired revolutionary leaders that either LI YUANHONG or Yuan Shikai would be acceptable to him for presidency of the future republic. What prompted Sun to forgo an all-out struggle on behalf of himself and the TMH was the fear, earlier voiced by Liang Qichao, that a prolonged civil war would invite foreign intervention. This fear of the foreign powers, whose bankers controlled Chinese finances and whose warships patrolled Chinese waters, was a distinguishing characteristic of the 1911 Revolution. Both revolutionary and imperial forces were scrupulous in avoiding injury to foreign lives and property. The revolutionaries promised to honor payments on foreign debts and respect foreign privileges if the powers refrained from aiding the Manchus. Actually, the fear was mutual. Foreign diplomats were relieved that this was not another Boxer Uprising. They agreed to let the revolution run its course without helping the Manchus. But they would be interested in the choice for new head of state.

When Sun Yat-sen returned at the end of December, he was elected provisional president of the Chinese Republic in Nanjing. However, he immediately notified Yuan Shikai that he would resign in his favor if Yuan declared allegiance to the republic. Yuan, the favored candidate of provincial leaders and the foreign powers, particularly the British, did his part and negotiated the Manchu abdication on February 12, 1912. Sun resigned the next day and the Nanjing assembly elected Yuan in his place. On March 10, he was inaugurated in Beijing, not in Nanjing—which the revolutionaries had preferred as capital of the republic. Yuan, however, insisted that his presence in the traditional capital was required in order to keep his troops in line. This foreshadowed the troubles with Yuan that would lead to the CHINESE REVOLUTION OF 1913.

Though it did not control the revolution or seize power, the TMH had achieved its primary objective: the overthrow of the Manchus and the end of dynastic rule. But no viable political system was put in place. The fate of the republic now rested with Yuan Shikai and the militarists. Soon it would be realized that the 1911 Revolution was not *the* Chinese revolution but only a transitional phase in the long transformative process required for achieving a truly modern and stable Chinese polity and society. What form it will eventually take is still open to question. (See also NATIONALIST REVOLUTION; CHINESE COMMUNIST REVOLUTION.)

CHINESE REVOLUTIONARY PARTY (CRP—Zhonghua Gemingdang)   After the failure of the CHINESE REVOLUTION OF 1913 against Yuan Shikai, SUN YAT-SEN and his followers continued the anti-Yuan struggle from Japan, where in 1914 they formed the CRP. Feeling that both the GUOMINDANG—GMD and its predecessor, TONGMENGHUI (TMH) had not been sufficiently disciplined, Sun insisted that CRP members swear loyalty to him personally and be fingerprinted. Some former followers, including HUANG XING, objected and refused to join. The CRP resembled both traditional secret societies and the Leninist model which Sun was later to admire. Sun revived the TMH's democratic and socialist slogans but omitted the principle of nationalism, since the TMH version of nationalism had emphasized anti-Manchuism, an objective that had been attained in the CHINESE REPUBLICAN REVOLUTION OF 1911. In 1915, Japan threatened China with the notorious 21 demands and became the main target of Chinese nationalism. Sun, on the other hand, solicited Japanese aid in his obsession to remove Yuan Shikai. The CRP participated in the campaign that frustrated Yuan's attempt to revive the monarchy and which led to his downfall in 1916. In October 1919, when nationalist feelings intensified as a result of the MAY FOURTH MOVEMENT, Sun reconstituted the GMD and the CRP came to an end.

CHINESE REVOLUTION OF 1913   A Chinese Nationalist party (GUOMINDANG—GMD) revolt against Yuan Shikai. After the 1911 revolution which had established the Chinese republic, friction developed between Yuan and the Guomindang, successor to the TONG MENG HUI, which had been the largest revolutionary organization. Yuan, as president of the republic, used authoritarian methods to curb parliamentary powers. After leading the GMD to victory in elections in the winter of 1912–1913, its parliamentary leader, SONG JIAOREN, was assassinated in April. Though Yuan was implicated, a consortium of foreign banks granted a loan to his government, which was forced to mortgage Chinese revenues. When the GMD protested that Yuan had vio-

lated the provisional constitution by not securing parliamentary approval, he dismissed the GMD military governors in June. In July, a GMD general started what was called the "second revolution," in which seven provinces declared independence. Poorly armed and lacking popular support, the revolt collapsed in September. SUN YAT-SEN and his GMD followers attempted to continue the anti-Yuan struggle under the banner of the CHINESE REVOLUTIONARY PARTY, organized in Japan in 1914. Meanwhile, Yuan assumed dictatorial powers. His death in 1916, after failing to establish a new dynasty with himself as emperor, left China divided by regional militarists (the warlord period, 1916–1928).

CHINESE SOVIET REPUBLIC   On November 7, 1931 (the 14th anniversary of the BOLSHEVIK Revolution) the CCP convened the First All-China Congress of Soviets at Ruijin in Jiangxi province and proclaimed the establishment of a Chinese Soviet Republic, based on the principle of "the democratic dictatorship of the proletariat and peasantry." Its central executive Committee elected a council of people's commissars, with MAO ZEDONG as chairman. Mao was reelected in January 1934 when the second congress met at Ruijin, but in October 1934 the Ruijin government was dissolved when the LONG MARCH began (see CHINESE COMMUNIST PARTY; CHINESE COMMUNIST REVOLUTION).

CH'IN PNAG-HSIEN   see QIN BANGXIAN.

CHOU EN-LAI   see ZHOU ENLAI.

CHRISTOPHE, HENRI   (1767–1820) Fighter for Haitian independence; king of northern Haiti. Christophe, a liberated slave, was born on the Caribbean island of Grenada to *giffe* (mixed black and mulatto) parents. Little is known about his life prior to the Haitian Slave revolt of 1800, although he apparently travelled in the United States, where he absorbed a sense of revolutionary fervor. Christophe took an active role in the Haitian antislavery rebellion of 1791, thereby coming to the attention of the revolt's leader, TOUSSAINT L'OUVERTURE, who appointed him a commander in his army. Christophe so distinguished himself in this role that Toussaint L'Ouverture's successor, Jean-Jacques Dessalines, appointed him general in 1802.

Christophe participated in the conspiracy that led to the assassination of Dessalines in 1806. Although as commander of the northern region of Haiti he expected to succeed Dessalines, Christophe's succession was challenged by the southern commander, Alexandre Pétion. For 14 years the two men waged an inconclusive civil war, resulting in an unofficial partition of Haiti. Pétion established a republican government in the south; Christophe, a staunch autocrat, declared himself King Henri I of Haiti in the north.

Under the guidance of his prime minister, Baron de Vastey, Christophe was a successful but unpopular monarch. A policy of forced labor revived the stagnant coffee and sugar trade, enriching both king and country. Although great sums were spent on a massive building campaign, which included the royal palace and the fortress of La Ferrire, most of the government's income was spent on developing an educational and cultural infrastructure. Independent Haiti was regarded by Christophe as a unique opportunity for blacks to prove themselves capable of living as free men. Yet Christophe's oppressive measures and his conflict with

Pétion aroused increasing discontent among his subjects. Threatened with a coup d'état, Christophe committed suicide.

> We will make rapid strides towards civilization. Let them dispute, if they please, the existence of our intellectual facilities, our little or no aptness for the arts and sciences, while we reply to these with irresistible arguments, and prove to the impious by facts and examples that the Blacks, like the Whites, are men, and like them are the works of a Divine Omnipotence.

CHU CHIH-HSIN see ZHU ZHIXIN.

CH'Ü CH'IU-PAI see QU QIUBAI.

CHUNGHUA KOMINGTANG see ZHONGHUA GEMINGDANG.

CHU TE see ZHU DE.

CHU YÜAN-CHANG see ZHU YUANZHANG.

CIVILIS, GAIUS JULIUS In early Dutch history, the scion of a noble family of the Batavian tribe in what is now Holland. Having served as an officer in the Roman army, the one-eyed Civilis was arrested in 68 A.D. on suspicion of mutiny, sent to Rome in chains, but released. Back in his home country, in 69 A.D. he incited his fellow Batavians to revolt against Rome and succeeded in enlisting the aid of two other Germanic tribes, the Frisii and the Chatii. The rebellion was squashed by Rome some time after 70 A.D. Civilis himself surrendered and his subsequent fate is unknown.

Originally little but a local chieftain, Civilis was later transformed into a Dutch national hero. The solemn ceremony in which he and the rebels swore to conquer or die, as described by the Roman historian Tacitus, became the subject of a famous painting by Rembrandt.

CIVIL WAR, ENGLISH (1642–1648) The hope of King Charles I of England (1625–1649) to rule without parliament and to make himself an absolute monarch led to an endless number of grievances, which only piled up without resolution over the years. The king was supported by the Anglican church and the least developed areas of England furthest from the center. Support for the parliament, on the other hand, came from the trading classes, London and the south and east of England, which were much more economically developed. One important grievance was Ship Money, which in 1635 was altered from being a tax levied on ports alone to a charge on the entire country. A prominent country gentleman, John Hampden, refused to pay and was convicted in court, becoming the first public martyr for opposition to the crown. Charles's decision to implement the English Book of Common Prayer in Presbyterian Scotland in 1637 led to a galvanization of public opinion against him and the following year a Solemn League and Covenant was signed for the defense of more radical Protestants. The invasion of Scottish forces in the First Bishops' War (1639) gave Charles no choice but to summon parliament (1640), which insisted on dealing with their grievances before discussing the main issue of national defense.

The so-called "Short Parliament" was dismissed after a few weeks, but further disturbances with the Scots led to parliament being summoned once again. The Scots in the Treaty of Ripon (1640) demanded that the English pay for the occupation of their own northern counties until peace was secured. The "Long Parliament" took the opportunity to dilute royal authority, impeaching both the most prominent member of the king's council, the Earl of Strafford, and the Archbishop of Canterbury, William Laud. It also abolished the courts of Star Chamber and High Commission, which had been notorious for arbitrary justice. Eventually the king could no longer accept these attacks on his office and, having failed to arrest the five leading members of the House of Commons in January 1642, withdrew from London and began to organize an offensive attack against the parliamentary authority. In August 1642, he set up the royal standard and declared war on his own parliament. The first battle at Edgehill (October 23, 1642) was a draw and the king's better-trained and experienced forces initially won the day. But the parliamentary army regrouped and reorganized according to more up-to-date continental models, and its Eastern Association became a new standard in English military achievement. Armed with a Solemn League and Covenant (1643) of immense symbolic value, the parliamentary forces won a great victory at Marston Moor (July 2, 1644), which gave them full control of the north of England. The king was decisively defeated at Naseby (June 14, 1645) and surrendered to the Scots the following year, being handed over to parliament in January 1647. A second civil war began and ended in 1648, which only sealed the king's fate.

The more radical parliamentarians ejected the moderates in "Pride's Purge," by which 96 members of parliament were not allowed to take their seats and the remaining Rump Parliament voted to bring the king to trial. Charles rejected the authority of the court, which condemned him to death without his participation in the proceedings. Charles was executed on January 30, 1649, paradoxically for treason against the king.

CLASSICUS, JULIUS Commander of a Treveri cavalry unit in the army of Vitellius. In 69 A.D. Classicus remained loyal to Rome and fought against Civilis; the following year, however, he joined the revolt against Rome. In 70 A.D. he was defeated by Cerialis, but continued service with Civilis. His subsequent movements are unknown.

CLEISTHENES (6th century B.C.) An Athenian statesman of the noble family of the Alcmaeonids, who began his career by cooperating with the tyrant Hippias. After he and the other Alcmaeonids were exiled by the tyrant, Cleisthenes managed to persuade the Spartans to overthrow the Athenian tyranny. This feat was achieved by the Spartan king Cleomenes, who expelled Hippias and his supporters in 510 B.C. Shortly afterwards a struggle for power developed between Cleisthenes and another aristocratic faction. Despite the intervention of Cleomenes who tried to establish an oligarchy, Cleisthenes won the day by appealing to popular support and carrying out important reforms. The Athenian state was reorganized and ten local tribes, each composed of three units (*trittyes*) from the interior, the city and the coastal regions, superseded the four old ethnic tribes. The smallest administrative-political units were the *demoi*, that is, the villages, townships and urban wards. Everyone who lived in a *demos* at the time of the reform was registered as an Athenian citizen. Cleisthenes thus enlarged the citizen body of the Athenian state and broke the power of the aristocracy, which was based on the organization of the old ethnic tribes. He instituted a new Council of State (*boule*) of 500 members, 50 from each tribe, and is credited with several other laws. The new institutions remained in force for generations, forming the basis for the other democratic developments, and Cleisthenes is generally believed to have created Athenian democracy.

CLEOMENES III   Born in 260 B.C. to one of the two royal families of Sparta, Cleomenes ascended the throne in 235 B.C. He adopted the social-political ideas of AGIS IV under the influence of his wife, the latter's widow. An able general, he won victories against Aetolia and the Achaean League in 229–227 B.C., following which he seized absolute power in Sparta, slaying and expelling his opponents among the great land owners. He then carried out a social-political revolution in Sparta: debts were cancelled, the lands of the rich confiscated and plots of land were distributed to the poor and unprivileged, who thereby received Spartan citizenship. Cleomenes also revived the traditional Spartan education and simple way of life, thus restoring the constitution of the legendary legislator Lycurgus. The number of citizens now increased to several thousand (instead of 700 before the revolution), all of whom could be enlisted to serve in the Spartan army. Cleomenes used his formidable power to expand Sparta's rule in the Pedoponessos at the expense of the Achaean League, whose leader, ARATUS, then made an alliance with Antigonus Doson, king of Macedonia. Cleomenes was decisively defeated at Sellasia (222 B.C.) and fled to Egypt, whereupon his reforms were abolished. He committed suicide in 219 B.C., after his failure to stir up a revolution in Alexandria.

CLOOTS, JEAN BAPTISTE DU VAL DE GRACE, BARON OF   (1755–1794) Nicknamed "The Friend of Humanity." A Prussian revolutionary born in the duchy of Cleves in the Rhineland, Cloots made his way to Paris on the eve of the FRENCH REVOLUTION of 1789 and espoused its cause with the passionate fervor of a neophyte who set out to proclaim its virtues in the name of all mankind. Drawn into the orbit of the JACOBIN Club well before the election of the Convention in May 1793, he is chiefly remembered in revolutionary mythology for the grandiloquent address he drafted in the name of the popular masses "Against all the despots of the world."

Cloots went about professing his mission as "The Orator of all Mankind" in revolutionary circles and preached the revolutionary gospel that the purpose of the French Revolution was to overthrow the twin evils of "throne and altar" in all the rest of Europe, in the name of human progress. The Legislative Assembly elected him an honorary French citizen, in the same way that it also elected THOMAS PAINE, GEORGE WASHINGTON, Jeremy Bentham and others to underline the fact that the French Revolution was the harbinger of world revolution.

Elected as a deputy to the French Convention of 1793, he joined the ranks of other extra-parliamentary agitators such as DANTON, CAMILLE DESMOULINS and the poetically self-named FABRE D'EGLANTINE, and gradually gravitated toward the left-wing Club des Cordeliers, where he gained notoriety for his radical anticler-

icalism and populist enthusiasm. His fanaticism and revolutionary fervor went even further than ROBESPIERRE's radicalism. Ostracized by the Jacobins and tainted by his association with the SANS-CULOTTES faction which went under the name of the *Hébertistes*, he was sent to the guillotine in the great terror purge of April 1794.

CODREANU, CORNELIU ZELEA   (1899–1938) Romanian Fascist (see FASCISM) leader. Graduating from a military academy in Moldavia, Codreanu attended the University of Iasi, where he founded the NATIONAL CHRISTIAN ANTI-SEMITIC LEAGUE. In 1927 he founded the infamous LEGION OF THE ARCHANGEL MICHAEL, from which the IRON GUARD arose. He was personally responsible for numerous political assassinations, including that of liberal Prime Minister Ion Duca. In 1938, he was arrested under the authoritarian régime of King Carol II and killed while supposedly trying to escape.

COHN-BENEDIT, DANIEL   (1943–) Jewish German-born student leader. While a student at Nanterre, Paris, Cohn-Benedit emerged as the sharp-witted inspiring leader of the MAY REVOLUTION of 1968 which almost toppled de Gaulle. Known as Danny the Red, Cohn-Benedit rejected what he called Stalinist filth (i.e., Moscow State Communism) and was influenced by MAO ZEDONG and CHE GUEVARA. He resigned from the student leadership after the 1968 revolt, claiming he did not want to become the subject of yet another personality cult.

COLLINS, MICHAEL   (1890–1922) Irish nationalist who fought in the EASTER UPRISING. An MP in the SINN FEIN government (1919–1921), Collins was one of the chief rebels against the English government, although in December 1921 he was one of the signatories to the Anglo-Irish treaty. The repudiation of this agreement sparked the civil war in Ireland, and 10 days after becoming leader of the new transitional government he was assassinated by a group of Republicans.

COLONELS' COUP (Revolution of April 21, 1967)   Right-wing military coup in Greece. The uncertain political situation in Greece in the 1950s and 1960s, coupled with rapid modernization and westernization, led to unrest among certain factions in the Greek military establishment. After winning the 1964 general election, Prime Minister Georgios Papandreou initiated reforms aimed at modernizing the educational system and made overtures to the left by releasing most of the remaining prisoners from Greece's civil war (1947–1949) and thawing relations with the eastern bloc. Papandreou's son, Andreas, who wielded considerable influence in the new government, was under investigation for alleged ties with *Aspida* (the Shield), a clandestine group of left-leaning army officers suspected of conspiring to sieze power. Papandreou himself posed a personal threat to the military by attempting to take over the ministry of defense and, supposedly, to purge the army of far right elements.

On April 21, 1967, Colonels Georgios Papadopoulos and Nikolaos Makaresos and Brigadier Stylianos Pattakos staged a coup that overthrew Papandreou. Styled the Revolution of 21 April, 1967, the stated objective of the revolt was to preclude a Communist takeover of Greece and "to defend Helleno-Christian civilization from western and secular influences" by a "rebaptism in the wellsprings of ancestral tradition." At first a civilian puppet government was installed, but after a failed countercoup initiated by King Constantine, Papadopoulos had himself declared prime minister.

Although the government introduced harsh measures against the population aimed at curbing resistance, this only furthered the general atmosphere of discontent with the new régime. Half a million Athenians attended the funeral of Georgios Papandreou in 1968, signaling not only support for the deposed premier but disapproval of the government in power. By 1973, student protests had erupted throughout Greece and an abortive naval mutiny intimated that even the army had not been totally purged of antigovernment elements. Papadopoulos was overthrown by Dimitrios Ionnidis, head of the dreaded military police, but this only ignited further civilian protests. An attempt to win public support by bringing about *enosis* (unification) with Cyprus failed when the army refused to cooperate. Finally, in July 1974, the military régime collapsed and civilian rule was restored.

COMINTERN Also known as the Third, or Communist, INTER-NATIONAL; an organization set up in Moscow in March 1919 to promote worldwide revolution. This was a centralized organization with very strict admission rules and various Socialist parties (e.g., in Italy) broke up over the question of membership. When it became clear, early in the 1920s, that there was no imminent revolution outside Russia, the Comintern was turned into an instrument of Soviet foreign policy and into an auxiliary in the power struggle within the Soviet leadership itself. In 1927, Comintern policies resulted in a serious defeat for the CHINESE COMMUNIST PARTY; in 1933, the organization dug a grave for the German Communists when it refused them permission to ally themselves with the Social Democrats to stop Hitler's rise to power. In 1943, the Comintern was dissolved as a gesture of goodwill toward Russia's wartime allies.

COMITÉ REVOLUTIONNAIRE D'UNITÉ ET D'ACTION (CRUA—Revolutionary Committee of Unity and Action) An Algerian nationalist organization established by the ORGANISATION SPECIALE (SPECIAL ORGANIZATION) to coordinate an armed struggle for Algerian independence. It was dominated by MUSTAFA BEN BOULAID and AHMED BEN-BELLA. The CRUA met on October 10, 1954, when it changed its name to the FRONT DE LIBÉRATION NATIONALE and set a date for the commencement of the ALGERIAN REVOLUTION.

COMMITTEE OF PUBLIC SAFETY The central organ of government under the first French Republic, which was proclaimed during the most radical phase of the FRENCH REVOLUTION in September 1792. The committee, representing the executive branch of the newly elected revolutionary convention, filled the political vacuum created by the collapse of France's first experiment in constitutional monarchy that had come to an end with the outbreak of war and the revolution of the SANS-CULOTTES in August 1792. In the face of the national emergency and a domestic crisis of unique intensity, the committee was granted sweeping ad hoc executive powers by the sovereign and unicameral convention on April 5, 1793, for the sole purpose of waging war against the enemies of the revolution, both at home and abroad. It soon found it necessary, however, on the basis of

a wide measure of support from the JACOBIN majority, to stifle all domestic opposition by imposing a one-year Reign of Terror, from July 1793 to July 1794. This year marked the most climactic phase in the decade of revolution and was only brought to an end when the committee's three most radical members, ROBESPIERRE, COUTHON and SAINT-JUST, were overthrown and executed following the coup d'état of Thermidor (1794)—a date which corresponds with the Year III of the revolutionary calendar that the committee introduced to usher in the new Reign of Virtue. Originally consisting of nine members co-opted by the convention on a rotating monthly basis, the committee was at first dominated by DANTON and his friends, Barère and Cambon, and shared executive power with the Committee of General Security. The mounting pressures of war transformed the Committee of Public Safety into the instrument of Jacobin dictatorship. As it launched a life and death struggle against the GIRONDIN revolt raging in two-thirds of the provinces, it also paved the way to the increasing dictatorship of Paris over the rest of France as well. In July 1793 its membership was enlarged to 12, the legendary "Twelve who Ruled" of revolutionary lore, who exercised collective authority in the name of the convention and stayed in power with little opposition for a whole year. These included such ruthless revolutionaries as Robespierre, Couthon, and Saint-Just and newcomers such as Lindet, Jean Bon Saint André, Hérault de Séchelles and the "Grand Carnot," the "Organizer of Victory"; as well as two extremists, Billaud Varenne and Collot d'Herbois, who often pushed their colleagues in a socialist direction. Rarely has France possessed such a strong and vigorous government, still theoretically responsible to the legislative chamber yet capable of carrying out and enforcing resolute and independent policies of its own with wide public support in the capital and certain Jacobin provinces. The committee's new composition and the pressures of war and civil strife that challenged the survival of the republic from day to day had the effect of transforming a body of 12 ordinary deputies into a remarkably efficient war cabinet dedicated to defending the republic, "One and Indivisible," from the *ancien régimes* of Europe and of consolidating the gains of the revolution against the forces of counterrevolution at home. Its actions were inspired by a dedication to keep the revolution's ardor alive against all odds, so that the committee's French name of *Salut Public*, which designates national salvation as well as national security, gives a more accurate and authentic sense of the loyalties it was able to command as well as the hatreds it inspired among its enemies and detractors. Saint-Just, its most fanatic and visionary member, predicted its downfall when he declared in June 1793, after the country had turned down his revolutionary *Ventôse* decrees, "*La Révolution est glacée*" ("The Revolution is frozen"). The ambiguities of the form of totalitarian democracy the committee tried to adopt illustrate one of the recurring dilemmas of revolutionary ideology in theory and practice, but also served as a guide and a warning to Marxist revolutionaries in the following century. The committee operated on the principle that the mind and conscience of Jacobinism represented democracy in its purest form. Since the people, according to strict revolutionary doctrine, were incapable of ever exercising tyranny on others, let alone on themselves, the committee could legitimately claim to be speaking in the name of direct democracy exercised by the sovereign convention and delegated to the committee as its sole executive. It was therefore free to act without restraint on behalf of the general will and the good of revolution. This could thus justify the creation of a revolutionary police state that would force the people to be free and spread the values of civic virtue among all the citizens mobilized by the revolution.

COMMUNEROS In 1520–1521, an uprising of the cities of Spanish Castile against the rule of their new king, Charles I (Emperor Charles V). The background to the revolt was the opposition by the towns, and specifically the lower middle classes made up of small merchants and artisans, to the attempts of the aristocracy to monopolize urban government. A contributory cause was the arrogance and corruption of Charles's non-Spanish councillors, whom he had recently introduced from Burgundy. At the time the revolt broke out, Charles himself was away in Germany. Accordingly, the task of suppressing it fell to the Castilian grandees who mobilized their private forces in the name of the king, defeated the rebels at the battle of Villalar (April 1521) and finally retook Toledo in October of the same year. When Charles returned to Spain in 1522, the revolt had for all practical purposes been crushed; it only remained for him to decide whom among the surviving ringleaders to execute and whom to pardon. Of the rebels' objectives—tax cuts, curbs on the power of the aristocracy and a greater voice in municipal affairs for the middle classes—none was achieved. On the contrary, the failure of the communeros movement marked the unequivocal establishment in Castile of the alliance between Crown and nobility which, in essence, was to last until the time of the French Revolution.

COMMUNISM A revolutionary doctrine, which at one time ruled approximately one-third of the earth's inhabitants, according to which society—as directed by the state and not the private individual—should be the owner of all economic, and hence political, power. Though the variants of communism are extremely numerous, its basic tenets as formulated by KARL MARX and, above all, VLADMIMIR ILYICH LENIN may be summarized as follows: First, all history is the reflection of the ways in which economic production, and hence the distribution of wealth, has been organized in different times and places; on this foundation rests everything else. Second, the organization of society into classes is the most important result of all systems of production that have hitherto existed, and history is essentially the story of the struggle between these classes. Third, given the fact that capitalism is the most important mode of production in modern times, the class struggle has crystallized in the form of a war between the bourgeoisie, which owns the means of production, and the proletariat which, though it does not own anything, does the actual work and produces all wealth. Fourth, owing to laws that are inherent in the capitalist process of production itself, the number of bourgeois owners is destined to fall as that of the proletarians grow. Finally, the growing disproportion between owners and workers—exploiters and exploited—makes it both possible and necessary to carry out a violent revolution that will put an end to capitalism. Indeed it has been the objective of communism to bring about just such a revolution and, after it, a new society in which the organized proletariat will take the means of production out of private ownership and use them for its own purposes rather than those of the capitalists.

Antecedents to Communist ideology, in the form of programs planning for the communal ownership of social wealth, can be found from Plato's *Republic* on. The Jewish Essenes, Jesus Christ, Thomas Moore, the 16th-century ANABAPTISTS, some political leaders during the FRENCH REVOLUTION and several early 19th-century "utopian" writers have all been represented as early, or proto-Communists. Modern communism, though, originated with Karl Marx who, together with FRIEDRICH ENGELS, published the *Communist Manifesto* in 1848. Social Democratic parties, with their program based more or less on Marxist ideas, began appearing in many European countries from about 1875 on; after 1890 there began to emerge differences between maximalists and minimalists, i.e., those which demanded the violent overthrow of the existing order and those which were prepared to live within it or at any rate commit themselves to gradual, parliamentary reforms rather then revolution. The first true Communist party was founded in 1903 by Lenin, whose followers left the Russian Social Democratic party and were known as BOLSHEVIKS. In 1918–1919, following the RUSSIAN REVOLUTION OF 1917 and the Bolshevik seizure of power, most European Socialist parties split. Those which were willing to accept Moscow's leadership and join the Third International (see INTERNATIONAL, THIRD) were henceforward known as Communists, whereas those which rejected the Soviet leadership and were, by this time, more or less reconciled to working within the existing order, were known as socialists.

Apart from a short-lived revolution in Hungary (1919), communism between the world wars did not succeed in gaining power anywhere outside Russia. In Italy and the countries of Eastern Europe (the Baltic states, Poland, Hungary, Romania and later Greece) it was outlawed by right-wing or Fascist régimes. In Germany, the Communist party became the country's third largest by 1930, and cooperated with the National Socialists (Nazis) in bringing the Weimar Republic to an end. This party was eradicated by barbaric means, only to be revived after 1945. In France the Communists, in an effort to stem the Fascist menace, entered a so-called Popular Front Government under Leon Blum in 1938–1939. In Spain, Communists and Socialists together governed the country from 1939, fought and lost the civil war, and were suppressed by General FRANCISCO FRANCO. In Britain there was a Communist party from 1920 on, but it never achieved any degree of influence.

In 1944–1948, communism was exported to most of the countries of Eastern Europe (Poland, Czechoslovakia, Hungary, Romania, Bulgaria, Albania, East Germany) at the tip of "liberating" Red Army bayonets and often against considerable resistance. In Yugoslavia, a native Communist movement under JOSIP BROZ TITO gained power in 1945. In Greece, a Communist movement fought and lost a civil war between 1944 and 1949. In West Germany, a Communist party existed but had little influence. In France, for three decades after World War II the Communists regularly polled 20–25% of the vote, only to see their influence wane from 1978 on. In Italy the situation was similar; there, too, the retreat began during the early 1980s. The Communist parties of Portugal and Spain were outlawed by Salazar and Franco respectively, and while they did reemerge after the end of dictatorship in 1974 and 1976, they remained in opposition. As has been said, in the last quarter of the 20th century in the rich western countries communism had been outflanked by hedonism which, at long last, had reached virtually all classes and resulted in the society of mass consumption.

The developing world, though, was a different matter. In Latin America and Asia, communism first emerged during the 1920s; in Africa the same happened from 1945 on. Hardly any of the countries in these regions possessed large-scale industry or a well developed bourgeoisie; therefore, as indeed had already happened to some extent in Russia (and in marked contradiction to communism's original ideological tenets), the various movements that appeared in them were often based not on the urban proletariat but on the rural peasant-masses. The first developing country to become Communist was China, where a Communist party had been founded in 1921 and came to power in 1949, after fighting first the GUOMINDANG, then the Japanese and finally the Guomindang again. In both Korea and North Vietnam, Communist governments came to power during the period 1945–1954; in 1975–1980, South Vietnam and Afghanistan followed. Laos and Cambodia saw the establishment of Communist régimes in 1975. Cuba became Communist in 1959, Chile in 1970; by that time there was hardly any Latin American country which did not have Communist guerrillas fighting on its soil. During the 1960s, many newly independent African countries also set up one-party régimes and adopted extreme left-wing social and economic policies, although in the end few of them described themselves as outright Communists.

As was their professed aim, wherever Communist régimes came to power they nationalized the principal means of production, including land, mines, factories, banks, insurance, transportation and telecommunications. All these were taken over by the state which, from this time on, ran them by means of its own employees; in most places only small-scale enterprise was left in private hands. In every Communist country, the state bureaucracy was, in turn, watched over and directed by the Communist party which, claiming to act in the name of the working class, assumed overall control. The members of the former ruling elites were thrust aside, their possessions expropriated and, in some cases (e.g., Russia and China) they themselves were killed. Having seized power by legal or illegal means, Communist parties tried to make sure of keeping it by declaring themselves the sole legal ones. They took over the public media, imposed censorship over all ideas except for their own, and abolished the liberal freedoms of assembly, expression, thought and movement.

Considered as a worldwide movement, the power of communism probably peaked in 1975–1980, when the countries that professed to be Communist—or else, like Ethiopia and Somalia, were so far on the left that they were indistinguishable from Communist régimes—included over one-third of the world's population. Meanwhile, though, the movement had become much too widespread to remain the monolithic, tightly disciplined "vanguard of the proletariat" envisioned by Lenin. Probably the first serious split took place in 1956 when NIKITA KHRUSCHEV, at that time secretary general of the Soviet Communist party, delivered a speech that denounced the crimes of JOSEPH STALIN (hitherto considered the greatest Communist leader after Lenin) and shocked many believers as well as unbelievers. In the late 1950s and early 1960s there followed the Soviet-Chinese split. It left the Communist world divided between a comparatively moderate Soviet Bloc which was prepared to live with the west and a considerably more radical China which, at least in

words, was prepared to carry on with the task of bringing about world revolution. Both sides engaged in violent denunciations of each other and, in 1969–1970, even came close to going to war against each other. The Soviet invasion of Czechoslovakia in 1968, while successful in its goal of preventing that country from reforming itself and keeping it within the Communist Bloc, put off many people who had previously been sympathetic to the Communist cause. Throughout these decades, the very success of communism in spreading its message in many countries all over the developing world was a source of weakness as well as strength because, adapting themselves to local conditions, there were now almost as many different forms of communism as there were states.

Then the tide turned. Already in 1973, Chile, where a brutal coup had overthrown the government of SALVADOR GOSSENS AL-LENDE, had become the first country to remove a Communist government. That, however, proved to be a swallow that did not summer bring; the real turning point came in the mid-1980s. A new Soviet leader, Michael Gorbachev, took over power in the Soviet Union. Pressed by his country's growing economic and technical backwardness vis á vis the west, he cautiously set to dismantle some of the stifling state controls that had led to it. Soon, however, the trickle became a flood and he found himself carried away by the flood. Partly because of his reforms, partly because of the impact of the war which the Soviet Union had fought and lost in Afghanistan (1981–1989), the world's oldest and strongest Communist régime started coming apart at the seams. An attempt in the summer of 1991 to launch a coup and restore the situation failed; from that time the USSR disintegrated, as its parts, including Russia itself, became separate countries and, in near-desperate economic situations, struggled to set up western-style parliamentary governments.

The collapse of the Soviet Union was followed by that of communism in its east European satellites, all of which reformed themselves between 1989–1991. The results of decades of Communist domination now stood there for all to see; mostly these took the form of poverty, technological backwardness and, in places, extreme damage to the environment and even a declining life expectancy of the population. Except for a few diehards, the spectacle took away communism's last adherents in the developed countries as well as in most developing ones. As of this writing, in 1994, only one country, namely Cuba, remains truly Communist. All the rest have either committed themselves to a market economy based on private property and capitalism or, in a few cases such as China (and, most recently, Vietnam), to rapid capitalist development under the continued tutelage of a Communist party. Communism, without a doubt the greatest revolutionary movement of all time, has failed for the time being, nor does a credible successor appear on the horizon. Yet many of the circumstances that originally led to communism, such as extreme and widespread poverty, exploitation and class warfare still persist. Should market economies fail to solve or at least to alleviate these problems, as seems likely to happen in many countries, then in one form or another it may yet return.

COMMUNIST LEAGUE OF LONDON A clandestine organization of German Communists that operated in England from 1847 to 1852. The origins of the Communist League of London can be traced to the socialist German emigrés in Paris in the

1830s, who organized themselves into the *Bund der Kommunisten* (Communist League). In 1836, an extremist faction split from the League, calling itself the *Bund der Gerechten* (League of the Just). By 1840, many of the Bund's members had relocated to London, where they formed the German Workers' Educational Association, later known as the Communist Workers' Educational Society.

After attending a meeting of the Society in 1845, FRIEDRICH ENGELS convinced KARL MARX to participate in their activities. Marx was impressed by the society and convinced them to coordinate their activities with other, like-minded groups: the result was the Communist League. In autumn 1847, the league published the first (and only) issue of *The Communist Journal*. This publishing venture was unexceptional except that blazoned across the banner was the slogan, "Proletarians of all lands, unite!"

At the second congress of the Communist League, Marx impressed the participants with his call for class war to resolve the plight of the workers. His passionate oratory prompted the organizers to ask him to compose a platform for the movement. The result was a 23 page pamphlet, published in Brussels in 1848: *The Communist Manifesto*.

Shortly after the appearance of Marx's *Manifesto*, revolutions broke out in France and Germany. Many of the German emigrés left London to take part in the uprisings and the Communist League, which never had more than 100 or so members, gradually disappeared. It was disbanded in 1852, but it had already made its mark on world history by commissioning the writing of the *Communist Manifesto*.

COMMUNIST PARTY OF FRANCE (PCF)   Founded in 1920 by the left wing of the Socialist party, with which it broke over the question of joining the COMINTERN, the PCF did not gain any considerable following until 1936. At that time it gave its support to the Popular Front, without, however, joining the government under LEON BLUM, in an attempt to stem the rising tide of FASCISM. During World War II, the party was driven underground by the Vichy government but managed to survive and to set up a resistance movement that fought the German occupation forces throughout the war. The party gained 25% of the vote in 1945 and participated in the government till 1946. From then on it continued to attract 20–22% of the vote until the mid-1980s. During the early 1970s it became, officially at least, committed to Euro-communism. Its leader, Georges Marchais, though, continued to be regarded by many as a crusty old Stalinist, cast in the same mold as his immediate predecessor, Waldeck-Rochet, and the PCF's founding father and World War II leader, Maurice Thorez. It was Thorez, who remained in exile in Moscow throughout the war, who claimed all the credit for the PCF's resistance record and masterminded its comeback after the liberation in 1944.

Following the election of François Mitterand to the presidency in 1976, with the Communists and Socialists jointly committed to carry out a platform along socialist lines called the Common Program, Mitterand decided to call snap elections in 1977 for a new National Assembly that would consolidate his personal triumph as sole leader of the left in the Elysée Palace. The parliamentary results were a landslide victory for Mitterand's second term and saw the almost total eclipse of the Communist party by its Socialist allies and rivals. Thus, its traditional support of one in four of the French electorate dwindled and finally collapsed, as the Communist illusion was steadily eroded by social conditions and the course of events, both at home and abroad. The electoral success of such populist parties as Jean Marie Le Pen's *Front National* and the end of the cold war contributed to the demise of the party, although its candidate in the first round of the 1995 race for the presidency against Mitterand's right-wing successor, Jacques Chirac, could still rely on a hard-core of party loyalists and left-wing sympathizers.

But the PCF had always really been a state of mind rather than a political party. From the 1940s until the backlash against the 1968 student revolt, it had been a pole of attraction for all of France's left-wing intellectuals and represented a protest vote in defiance of the status quo. The PCF has been aptly compared by Annie Kriegel, one of its leading intellectuals, to Dante's Inferno, made up of three concentric circles: an outer ring of 5 million voters and revolutionary sympathizers who always voted as far left as possible, an inner circle of 300,000 card-carrying party stalwarts and only a handful of apparatchik bosses and militants at the center, controlling the party from the PCF headquarters at the Place Stalingrade in Paris.

COMMUNIST PARTY OF GERMANY   see LUXEMBURG, ROSA.

COMMUNIST PARTY OF GREECE   Founded in 1918, the party took part in parliamentary life during the 1920s and 1930s but was driven underground in 1936 by General Metaas, after an abortive attempt to organize a general strike. It nevertheless survived, organized an effective guerrilla campaign against the Germans in 1941–1944, and from 1945 until 1949 fought a civil war in order to wrest power from the royalist government. Defeated and outlawed, it nevertheless continues to be a major force in Greek political life. It was made legal again after the fall of the military régime in 1974.

COMMUNIST PARTY OF HUNGARY   Founded in 1918, the party almost immediately staged an uprising and seized power for four months. Under its leader, BELA KUN, Hungary was proclaimed a Soviet republic. Driven underground by the Whites under Admiral Horthy, the party reemerged after World War II and, supported by the Soviet occupation forces, seized power in 1948 even though it had polled less than 20% of the vote in the 1945 elections. During the 1956 revolt (see HUNGARY, REVOLTS AND REVOLUTIONS—1956 UPRISING), the party virtually disintegrated and had to be reconstructed on a much narrower basis.

The newly reorganized party engaged in a gradual dialogue with the people, relaxing some of the means of control over the population and engaging in a more rational and flexible economic and social policy. The Hungarian Socialist Workers' Party (HSWP) endorsed and supported the Soviet clampdown on the PRAGUE SPRING OF 1968, but there were signs that the party leadership had reservations over its continued loyalty to the Moscow line. However, through the years Secretary-General Janos Kadar's more open line gradually lost its appeal, not only by occasional tough policies toward opponents but because of the growing opposition and pressure toward more significant reforms. A reformist wing, influenced by Gorbachev's *perestroika*, emerged after 1985. In May 1988, Kadar was removed (officially, he resigned) and the party entered into its last phase, in which dialogue with the emerging opposition began, with conservatives attempting to stop the process of reform. Reformists such as Imre Pozsgay pushed for a line which in fact led to the end of the one-party régime. After bitter debates, the HSWP reversed its attitude toward the character of the 1956 Revolution and in June 1989 the leaders of that time, who had been executed, were reburied in an almost symbolical act in which the Communists buried their past. In bitter debates within the party, as the demise of the régime was clear, the Communists shed their Marxist-Leninist revolutionary character and in October 1989 the HSWP dissolved itself. Its heir, the Hungarian Socialist Party led by Gyula Horn, acclaimed Western-style democratic socialism and returned to power following the 1994 general elections. A small conservative wing reorganized itself, remaining loyal to the "Leninist ideals," but was pushed by the electorate into the fringes of political life.

COMMUNIST PARTY OF INDONESIA   see INDONESIAN COUP.

COMMUNIST PARTY OF ITALY (PCI—Partito Comunista Italiano)

Founded at the Socialist Party of Italy—PSI—Congress of Livorno in January 1921, the Communist party of Italy was led by ANTONIO GRAMSCI of the *Ordine Nuovo* (New Order) socialist section and Amadeo Bordiga, of the abstentionist section of Italian socialism. The PCI adhered to the Leninist principles of the Third International (see INTERNATIONAL, THIRD) and declared itself a revolutionary party. The PCI was declared illegal by the Fascist (see FASCISM) régime in 1926 and in 1927 Gramsci and other Communist leaders were prosecuted and sentenced to long jail terms. The PCI went underground and refused to cooperate with the socialists. In the 1930s, changes in the policies of the Third International, related to the anti-Fascist front established to defend the Spanish Republic against fascism, brought about cooperation between the PCI and other Italian anti-Fascist political organizations in Italy and abroad. PCI members led the partisan anti-Fascist struggle in those parts of Italy occupied by the Germans on September 8, 1943.

In 1944, PALMIRO TOGLIATTI, the leader of the PCI, returned to Italy from the Soviet Union and imposed the "new party" line of cooperation with democratic forces interested in the establishment of an anti-Fascist régime in postwar Italy. The PCI was a major actor in the CLN—*Comitato di Liberazione Nazionale* (Committee of National Liberation) and in the first postwar Italian democratic governments. The realities of the cold war brought about the expulsion of the Communists from the government by the Christian Democratic prime minister, Alcide De Gasperi, in 1947. In spite of this, the PCI cooperated in the enactment of the Italian republican constitution of 1948. In the 1950s, the revelations about STALIN's atrocities and the harsh repression of the Hungarian revolt in 1956 by Soviet troops brought about the formulation of the "Italian way to socialism" that finally developed into Eurocommunism. Renouncing the principles of the dictatorship of the proletariat and the abolition of private property and adopting Gramsci's theoretical formulations about cultural hegemony and the role of civil society, the PCI, under the leadership of Enrico Berlinguer, tried to reach a

historic compromise with the Christian Democrats. This attempt failed in the 1970s, in spite of considerable electoral gains for the PCI. In the 1980s, a decline in voter support and the disintegration of the Communist régimes in Eastern Europe and later in the Soviet Union brought about reforms that transformed the PCI, under the leadership of Achille Occheto, into the *Partito Democratico della Sinistra* (PDS—Democratic Party of the Left) of declared liberal democratic vocation, and provoked the secession of *Rifondazione Comunista* (Communist Refoundation), a smaller group still holding old Communist beliefs. The failure of the PDS in the March 1994 elections brought about the election of Massimo D'Alema as party leader.

COMMUNIST PARTY OF KAMPUCHEA   see KHMER ROUGE.

COMMUNIST PARTY OF POLAND

Founded in 1918, the party was outlawed a year later and shifted its base to the USSR. During the 1930s, it suffered heavily from Stalin's purges. In 1944, two organizations, the Polish workers' party in occupied Poland and the Union of Polish Patriots on Soviet soil, joined to form the Committee of National Liberation. Supported by the Red Army, this group seized power in 1945 and won the 1948 elections.

The Polish United Workers' party (PUWP), the official title of the Communist party (CP), underwent severe crises after the Polish October of 1956. Originally, the party enjoyed some popularity but it gradually degenerated and changed leaders as GOMULKA, GIERECK, Kania and Jaruzelski consecutively tried to solve the deepening political, social and economic crisis in the country. Polish communism had no clear aims aside from clinging to power, and the emergence of Solidarity in 1980–1981 presented the gravest crisis to the régime. Jaruzelski's controversial régime, oscillating between a hard line and some flexibility, rocked the PUWP bitterly. The Gorbachev reforms accelerated the internal debates within the party, as a reformist wing tried to save the party by introducing reforms and easing the means of control over society. The party rapidly entered its reformist phase, as it attempted to save its rule by engaging in a dialogue with the relegalized Solidarity movement in April 1989. Leadership changes within the party strengthened its reformist character, but for Polish Communists it was clear that the only way out of the crisis was to exit from the political scene. In January 1990, after hundreds of thousands of members had left, the last party congress decided on the party's disbanding. The party split in two or even three factions, as the mainstream emerged as the Social Democracy of the Polish Republic. The new (Communist) party, adhering to a social democratic line, won the 1993 elections at the head of a leftist coalition.

COMMUNIST PARTY OF THE SOVIET UNION

Founded in 1898 as the Social Democratic Workers' Party of Russia, the Communist party traces it lineage through the 1903 split into MENSHEVIKS and BOLSHEVIKS. The latter, led by VLADIMIR LENIN, adopted the name of the Communist Party of Russia (Bolsheviks), in 1918 and, with the founding of the Union of Socialist Soviet Republics in 1922, assumed the name of the Communist Party of the Soviet Union (Bolsheviks)—CPSU. The designation "Bolshevik" was finally dropped in the year 1952, since, it was claimed, there simply were no more Mensheviks in existence.

The organizing principle of the CPSU was "Democratic Centralism." This consisted of the following elements: all party officials, from the highest to the lowest, are elected by the body that they head; all higher party bodies are responsible for supervision of the party organizations below them; all party bodies periodically report to their electors; all party members are required to take an active role in implementing party decisions. While there is clearly a democratic element in the elected nature and accountability of all the party bodies, the second element, instituting a hierarchy of veto power over lower decisions, to a large extent curtailed this. Higher party committees were charged with approving the list of candidates for delegates to those conferences and congresses that would have as their principal task the reelection of those same committees. Thus there was what has been called "a circular flow of power." No party organization's decisions were considered valid until reviewed and approved by a higher authority. LENIN also postulated a highly centralized ideological control, in which a small and politically homogeneous leadership would publicize party priorities through a central party newspaper and would maintain direct control over local committees by means of emissaries. Conspiracy was also an element in the Communist party's organizational credo, and up to the first RUSSIAN REVOLUTION OF 1917 it maintained an underground apparatus and operated largely through various emigré centers in Europe. After taking power in the October 1917 revolution, the Communist party moved steadily toward a single-party rule, an element that had not been present in the party's prerevolutionary ideas. At the end of the civil war, the 10th party congress added the final organizational characteristic to the Communist party, in the form of a resolution barring intra-party factions. While individual expressions of opposition to party policy were nominally tolerated, any action to gain adherents to such an opposition was punished as factionalism.

Following Lenin's death in 1924, a succession struggle was waged, in which JOSEPH STALIN succeeded in dominating the Communist party apparatus and pushing out his rivals, namely TROTSKY, BUKHARIN, ZINOVIEV and KAMENEV. Eventually he had all of them executed. In the aftermath of the succession struggle, Stalin instituted purges that destroyed the incumbents of all institutions of Soviet society, including those in the party, the army and the secret police, as well as those in science, culture and administration.

Following Stalin's death in 1953, a process of "de-Stalinization" took place, in an attempt to reinvigorate a party apparatus largely paralysed by a fear of purges. This culminated in Nikita Khrushchev's "secret speech" at the 20th CPSU congress in 1956, in which Stalin's crimes against veteran party members were denounced, and the resolution of the 22nd Congress in 1961 to remove Stalin's body from the Red Square mausoleum, where it had been enshrined alongside Lenin. With this announcement that CPSU policies were not endowed with infallibility, an opening was created for the emergence of ideological differences within the international Communist movement. Originally proposed as a democratic "polycentrism" in the determination of Communist policies in the world, this debate led to an open schism in international communism, with the CPSU leading one side and the Communist party of the People's Republic of China leading the other.

Inside the USSR, the policy of making all responsible positions in the economy and society dependent on the party authorities' approval, the system known as *nomenklatura*, created a situation in which educated persons wishing to advance their careers joined the party. Thus, while the near-20 million party members represented only about 11% of the population aged 18 and over in the USSR, among males aged 40 and over with a higher education, i.e., the population from which most of the administrative elite would be drawn, 30% were party members. Such careerist motivations stood in contradiction to traditional Communist party values. The Communist party had always held to the principle of being a vanguard elite rather than a mass party and those joining it were subject to a year of candidacy, the recommendations of veteran party members, and an ideological examination before being admitted to full membership. In Article 6 of the 1977 USSR constitution, the de facto Communist party monopoly on political and administrative power was given legal status. The article not only defined the CPSU as the "leading and directing force of Soviet society," but stated that Communist party members were to constitute "the inner nucleus of all organizations, whether state or public, determining the formation and implementation of Soviet policy, both domestic and foreign."

During the years that Leonid Brezhnev was secretary-general of the CPSU (1964–1982), the slogans "trust in cadres" and "stability of cadres" brought about the aging and corruption of Communist party functionaries, an erosion of ideology and a loss of public authority. All of these processes complicated the economic, social and political difficulties that were growing in the USSR and the East European Communist régimes. When Brezhnev's death in November 1982 was followed within two and a half years by the deaths of his two aged and ill successors, the need for change in the organization and activity of the CPSU was apparent.

The period of change instituted in March 1985 by Mikhail Gorbachev was centered around reform of the CPSU. Gorbachev's stated aim was to re-ideologize the party, making it an authoritative leader of public opinion and replacing the administrative and political monopoly that the party had enjoyed. Ideological and bureaucratic opposition from within the upper and middle echelons of the party stalled Gorbachev's reforms, and he gradually reduced the party's power, culminating in the March 1990 amendment of Article 6, ending the CPSU's monopoly on politics.

In the days following the abortive August 1991 putsch against Gorbachev, the parliament of the Russian Federation declared all Communist party property nationalized and banned all activity, central or local, of the CPSU in Russia. While declaring himself opposed to such a sweeping ban, Gorbachev declared the central bodies of the CPSU disbanded and resigned as secretary-general. In the following months, almost all the remaining republics of the USSR followed Russia's lead and banned the Communist party. Since the collapse of the Soviet Union, Communist parties, whether renamed or under their old names, have been widely relegalized and several have returned to power or form the main parliamentary opposition in their republics.

COMMUNIST PARTY OF SPAIN (Partido Comunista de España) Founded in 1921, the Communist party of Spain was banned under the authoritarian régime of PRIMO DE RIVERA but reemerged after the establishment of the republic in 1931. From 1936 it formed part of the Popular Front government. Following the government's defeat in the three-year SPANISH CIVIL WAR (1933–1936), the party's leaders went into exile in France, the Soviet Union and Latin America. Although the party was suppressed and outlawed during the FRANCO era (1936–1975), it re-emerged following the dictator's death. The Spanish Communist party is currently trying to convince voters that it is no longer committed to Stalinism but can be considered a democratic force in Spain. Together with other, smaller Communist factions and renegade socialists it formed the United Left, a political bloc that garnered just under 10% of the Spanish vote in the 1993 elections. Despite denials by the party's leadership that in wake of *perestroika* the party was emerging as a democratic socialist force in Spain, in some areas the party's traditional hammer and sickle symbol was replaced by that of the United Left.

COMONFORT, IGNACIO   (1812–1863) Mexican liberal and president. Comonfort distinguished himself with his military ability, fighting at the side of Mexico's President Santa Anna against President Anastasio Bustamante in 1832. From 1834 to 1846, Comonfort held various political positions both at the local and state levels. In 1847, Comonfort headed Mexico City's defense against the North American invasion. In 1854 Comonfort, together with JUAN ALVAREZ, fought against Santa Anna (who had been brought back from exile to resume the position of Mexico's president) on behalf of the liberal cause. Once Santa Anna had been defeated, Alvarez was named president and Comonfort became minister of war. Comonfort replaced Alavarez in 1855 upon the latter's resignation. In 1857, Comonfort was elected president and oversaw the implementation of a new, liberal constitution. He appointed BENITO JUAREZ to head the supreme court, which tacitly gave Juarez vice-presidential powers. That same year Comonfort was ousted by Felix Zuloaga, who annulled the constitution. After a short exile in the US, Comonfort returned to Mexico to defend his country against the French invasion. Comonfort lost his life during a battle against the French and against conservative forces near Celaya in 1863.

CONDÉ, LOUIS II DE BOURBON   (1621–1686) French aristocrat and rebel leader. The scion of one of the most important noble families in France, Condé received an excellent education at the hands of the Jesuits as well as engaging in the usual aristocratic pursuits of horsemanship and the chase (of both deer and women). Serving in the army of King Louis XIII, he quickly rose to the rank of general; on January 19, 1643 it was he who, commanding the French, won the battle of Rocroy and thereby put an end to Spain's status as the greatest power of the time.

After Rocroy, Condé—now recognized as the foremost French general of his age—continued serving in the army. In 1649 he led the royal forces in the siege of Paris, which had rebelled; however, such was his arrogance in disobeying the orders of Cardinal Mazarin, who at that time acted as regent (for King Louis XIV, who was a minor) and the real ruler of France, that the latter had him, his brother and his brother-in-law arrested. When the three of them were set free after 13 months' incarceration, they promptly rebelled. Going to the estates in southeastern France, they gathered around them a faction of noblemen who were dissatisfied with Mazarin's attempts to impose absolutist government. Six years were spent in fighting Mazarin in the name of the nobility's privileges, during which Condé and his associates did not even hesitate to ally themselves with France's greatest enemy, Spain. However, in 1658, at the Battle of the Dunes, Condé 's forces were defeated. He now made his way to Paris where Louis XIV, his minority over, was just assuming power. He succeeded in re-entering the king's good graces and, back in strict harness, continued serving him as one of the greatest generals France has ever had.

CONFÉDÉRATION GÉNÉRALE DU TRAVAIL (CGT)   To this day France's most powerful trade union federation, the *Confédération Générale du Travail* (General Confederation of Labor), was founded in Limoges in 1895. It became the most radical revolutionary working class movement during the Third and Fourth Republics and remains organized labor's chief standard bearer in the Fifth Republic. In 1921, it was seriously challenged by the defection of its Communist wing, which broke away to form the more radical CGTU (*Confédération Générale du Travail Unifieé*), a rupture which was a mirror image of an even deeper cleavage in the mainstream French Socialist party founded in 1905 by JEAN JAURES. Nevertheless the CGT continued to gain ground, mostly among unskilled and semi-skilled workers, reaching a membership of more than 2 million between 1906 and 1909, when the Radical Prime Minister Georges Clemenceau managed to crush a wave of violent strikes and industrial unrest orchestrated by a virulently anti-bourgeois CGT.

The CGT had originally succeeded in winning the decisive support and dedication of the revolutionary left as a result of the Dreyfus Revolution (i.e., the political changes brought about by the Dreyfus case), which culminated in 1902 with the formation of Emile Combes's Radical cabinet. The electoral gains made by a political coalition of Republicans, Radicals and Socialists, who had championed the civil rights of Captain Dreyfus after 1898, in the name of social justice and labor reforms, had the effect of putting wind into the sails of the CGT, universally perceived by most revolutionaries as a major force for achieving working class solidarity with the moral and political support of the Dreyfusard intellectuals.

The CGT was deeply divided from the outset on a single tactical issue, debated by its intellectual elite in moral and philosophical terms: the proclamation of the general strike as a revolutionary gesture, which would serve as a catalyst for triggering off the socialist revolution in one single and violent stroke. The general strike was advocated as the CGT's only moral raison d'être by the anarcho-syndicalist supporters of GEORGES SOREL. Reformist and more gradualist strategies were put forward by a moderate wing, which stood for a pragmatic working alliance with other revolutionary forces in order to retain the CGTs credibility. The syndicalists and anarchists finally prevailed in 1906 with the adoption of the general strike in the platform of the Charter of Amiens. This was due to the widespread impact of the idea of the myth of the general strike laid down by Sorel in *La Révolution Dreyfusienne* and *The Reflections on Violence*, the latter a collection of essays edited in 1908 by his follower Daniel Halévy, a Dreyfusard intellectual. The victory of LEON BLUM's Popular Front in 1936 produced a reunification of the CGT and the CGTU at the Congress of Toulouse, raising its membership to 5 million workers. It achieved its greatest triumph for the working class in the Matignon agreements, signed with a Popular Front government confronted by a spate of wildcat strikes, widespread but nonviolent industrial agitation and the occupation of factories by workers' soviets. The Matignon agreements included paid holidays, which had far-reaching social consequences, and an average 12% wage hike across the board. Leon Blum also conceded the right of collective bargaining in return for the syndicalists' pledge to repudiate the threat of direct action against the bourgeois state. Outlawed under the Vichy régime, the CGT has been under Communist leadership since the liberation of France in August 1944, but has been forced to share its exclusive prestige with labor or other trade union federations, such as the Socialist FO (*Force Ouvrière*), the moderate CFDT (*Confédération Française Démocratique du Travail*), the Catholic CFTC (*Confédération Française des Travailleures Chrétiens*) and the white collar CGC (*Confédération Générale des Cadres*).

CONGO-BRAZZAVILLE, COUPS (1968, 1977) The prowestern Abbé Fulbert Youlou, first president of Congo after its independence from France in 1960, resigned in August 1963 and a new government was formed under Alphonse Massamba-Débat. This government was the first major departure from colonial policy in central Africa and indicated an increasingly marked swing toward "revolutionary" policies. A new constitution was drawn up and a party—the *Mouvement national de la révolution* (MNR), founded on Marxist-Leninist principles—became the sole political party (1964).

In the following years, there was tension between the MNR and the army, and the charismatic paratroop commander, Captain Marien Ngouabi, emerged as the dominant figure in Congolese politics. In August 1968, Ngouabi seized power in a military coup. In January 1969 he became president and, in December of that year, a new Marxist vanguard party, the *Parti congolais du travail* (PCT), replaced the MNR. In January 1970 the country was renamed the People's Republic of the Congo (instead of the Republic of the Congo). A new militia was organized along Chinese lines.

However, tribal tension, disagreements over political ideology and power struggles within the political elite led to continuing instability, and there were unsuccessful coup attempts in 1972 and 1973. In March 1977, after several failed attempts on his life, Ngouabi was assassinated. The assassination was said to be the work of supporters of ex-president Massamba-Débat, who was immediately arrested, tried and executed.

On April 3, 1977, Colonel (later Brigadier-General) JOACHIM YHOMBI-OPANGO, former chief of staff of the armed forces, was appointed head of state. Yhombi-Opango was anti-left and had opposed the left-wing critics of Ngouabi's régime. Yhombi-Opango improved relations with the USA and France, but his régime inherited severe economic problems and came into conflict with the left wing of the PCT.

In February 1979, faced with a collapse in support, Yhombi-Opango surrendered his powers to a provisional committee appointed by the PCT. In March 1979, the president of this committee, Colonel (later General) Denis Sassou-Nguesso, was appointed president of the republic and chairman of the PCT's central committee. Nguesso was a follower of Ngouabi and a long-time rival of Yhombi-Opango.

CONNOLLY, JAMES (1868–1916) Irish revolutionary leader. A nationalist and a Marxist, Connolly founded the Irish Socialist Republican party and during World War I commanded an Irish Citizen Army against the British. Following the abortive EASTER RISING (April 1916), he was caught and hanged. He figures in two famous poems by W.B. Yeats, *Easter 1916* and *The Rose Tree*.

CONSULATE, THE The constitutional régime of the Year VIII of the FRENCH REVOLUTION, which replaced the constitution of the Republican directorate by the coup d'état of 18 Brumaire (November) 1799. The new constitution was drafted by the ABBÉ SIÉYÈS, a veteran of the revolution's constitutional monarchy of 1790, with crucial revisions made by his fellow conspirator, General Bonaparte, after the coup had accomplished its purpose of destroying the ineffective republic originally proclaimed in the Year I. The Consulate remained the form of government in force until Bonaparte modified it in the spring of 1802 and replaced it altogether with the proclamation of the empire in May 1804.

As originally conceived by Siéyès, executive power was to be shared by three consuls—Siéyès, Bonaparte and Roger Ducos—serving for a 10-year term, but his draft was modified by Bonaparte to make the other two subordinate to himself as First Consul. Subsequent modifications, always approved by popular plebiscite, appointed Bonaparte Consul for life with the right to nominate his successor. The legislative bodies were essentially consultative, indirectly chosen by the First Consul and ultimately responsible to him. Real power was wielded by Bonaparte acting through a national plebiscite. This régime, like its successors, the First and Second Empires under Napoleon III, has been called a form of plebiscitary democracy.

It was under this kind of enlightened despotism that France was able to bring to an end a decade of wars against the first and second coalitions of all the major powers of Europe and even sign the Peace of Amiens with England, consolidate its sway over the satellite countries in the Low Countries and the Rhineland and the sister republics set up in northern Italy, lay the basis for what became the Napoleonic Code, which effectively guaranteed the gains of the revolution, and reconcile Catholic opinion by negotiating the Concordat with the pope in April 1802. On December 2, 1804 the pope would be brought to Paris to crown the Emperor of the French in Notre Dame cathedral.

CONTINENTAL ARMY In June 1775, after the first military engagements with British troops in Massachusetts, the Second CONTINENTAL CONGRESS resolved to establish a continental army. The army, common to the colonies in revolt, was intended to supplement the state militias. It was to be funded by bills of credit redeemable by the colonies. Congress named George Washington, a veteran of colonial wars on the Virginia frontier, as commander in chief of the army, and he was installed in Cambridge on July 3, 1775.

Through eight years of war, Congress failed to provide the Continental Army with a stable flow of supplies or with reliable payment for its soldiers. Nor did it succeed in arranging for a continuous supply of manpower to fill the ranks thinned by death, injury and desertion, or with capable commanders for its regiments. The Continental Army's numbers fluctuated between lows in the 4,000s and an all-war high of 17,000. Yet notwithstanding the difficulties, Congress did persist in the effort and backed Washington as the army's commander in chief throughout the war.

The army's performance was in kind: it lost more battles than it won, but it persisted and ultimately emerged victorious in the overall contest. In the aftermath of the revolutionary war, the continental army would form the nucleus of the young republic's standing army.

CONTINENTAL CONGRESS The First Continental Congress in what was to become the United States of America in 1774 and the Second Continental Congress from 1775 up to the official adoption of the American declaration of independence in 1776, were the de facto revolutionary government of a nation in uprising.

The First Continental Congress convened in Philadelphia on September 5, 1774, for the purpose of modeling a common response to the Coercive Acts legislated by the British parliament. The congress, with delegates representing 12 of the 13 future states, issued a series of official statements, including a declaration of rights and grievances, addressed to the king, the people of Britain and its fellow colonists. It also resolved to pass on to the colonies a number of recommendations which implied active resistance to British authority. Among these was a recommendation to the colonies to establish militias and to enforce economic sanctions against Britain. Congress went as far as to adopt the Suffolk resolves, which advised Massachusetts to form an independent government. The final act of the First Continental Congress was a resolution to convene again on May 10, 1775.

When the Second Continental Congress convened, on schedule, military engagements between Massachusetts colonists and the forces of the mother country had already taken place in Lexington and Concord and the Congress faced the specter of an all-out war. Indeed, the Congress gradually assumed the role of coordination and leadership of an armed revolt in the making. In that capacity, it created the CONTINENTAL ARMY, commissioning its commanders, and attempted, not always successfully, to raise troops as well as sufficient funds for their provisioning.

Paralleling its management of the escalating military conflict, the congress maintained an official exchange of declarations with the British authorities in an attempt to reach a peaceful settlement. The Congress persisted with its efforts at appeasement until May 1776, when it authorized the colonies to establish popular governments in place of governments founded on royal authority. On July 2, the Congress voted for independence and on July 4, 1776 it legislated itself into legitimacy by adopting the declaration of independence.

The Second Continental Congress directed the American military effort until the successful conclusion of the war. It also governed the states' common affairs, including the adoption of the Articles of Confederation in 1781.

CONVENTION The national government of France which presided over the course of the FRENCH REVOLUTION during its most climactic phase, from the fall of Louis XVI on August 10, 1792 to the fall of ROBESPIERRE in July 1794. Elected in a climate

of national crisis which expressed the free will of a people waging war against foreign and domestic enemies of the revolution, the Convention is generally regarded as the embodiment of revolutionary democracy in action. This depends, of course, on what is meant by democracy and revolution. In fact, the Convention operated on the basis of a constitution which concentrated power in the hands of a unicameral legislative body elected by universal manhood suffrage and exercised national sovereignty through its own standing committees, thereby conforming to a principle favored by the apostle of modern democracy, Jean-Jacques Rousseau, but directly challenged by Montesquieu's alternative argument in favor of the separation of powers as the only safeguard against the despotism of liberty. Although nine out of ten French voters had not taken the trouble to go to the polls, the Convention was the first parliament in history to be elected on the basis of direct popular democracy, only vagrants, actors and women being excluded from the vote.

The Convention began its task by abolishing the monarchy and, to symbolize the opening of the new era for all mankind, it resolved to date its decrees from the Year I of the Republic, which was solemnly proclaimed on September 22, 1792. From the very beginning, its life was disrupted by an open and dramatic conflict between the two factions it had inherited from its predecessor, the dissolved monarchist Legislative Assembly, the GIRONDINS and the JACOBINS. The Jacobin faction became known as the Mountain, based on the highest tiers its members occupied in the assembly hall of the Manège or Riding School in the Tuileries Palace. The former, known as the Brissotins—so named because of their most energetic leader (see BRISSOT, JACQUES PIERRE)—assumed the same commanding position in the Convention they had held under the king and were the party of a war à outrance against the crowned heads of Europe. The majority, holding a middle of the road position and sitting in between the two and known as the *Marais* or Marsh, was eventually won over to the Jacobins after the elimination of the Girondin party in June 1793 transformed the constitution into a tool of Jacobin dictatorship. The Jacobin leaders, ruling by means of the Jacobin Club in Paris which met daily on the Rue Saint Honoré and the Convention's COMMITTEE OF PUBLIC SAFETY sitting in the Tuileries, controlled the two organs of power. They gave France the most effective democratic government it has ever known, enabling it to wage all-out war against most of Europe while at the same time succeeding in crushing the Catholic and Royalist Vendée as well as the *fédéré* revolt which the Girondins had been able to keep alive in two-thirds of the French provinces.

The Jacobin dictatorship of Paris was exercised in the name of direct democracy along the lines laid down by Rousseau's general will. The *Contrat Social* had defined the general will as the will of the people, one and indivisible, the mainspring of civil society, incapable of committing any act of tyranny. The Convention tried, against enormous odds, to lay the basis of the revolutionary reign of virtue even if this meant resorting to a reign of terror to wipe out the errors and corruption of the *ancien régime*. That was the theory. In practice it was also compelled by circumstances beyond its control and, above all, by the pressures of war, to share democratic power with the independently elected PARIS COMMUNE, the elite of the SANS-CULOTTES and a militant wing of *sectionnaires* claiming to represent the people as the real voice of democracy. Challenged, on the one hand, by DANTON,

DESMOULINS and the *Indulgent* faction to the right and, on the other, by a radical but amorphous coalition of *Hebertistes* and *Enragés*, de-Christianizers and other extra-parliamentary factions and pressure groups from the left, the Convention was finally purged of its Jacobin elements in the coup d'état of Thermidor, carried out in great secrecy in July 1794. After dismantling the government and the repressive apparatus of the Revolutionary Tribunal and abolishing its own executive arm, the Committee of Public Safety, the Thermidorian majority in the Convention, representing the moderate and now chastened interests of the Marsh of September 1792, adopted the new constitution of the DIRECTORATE in 1795, Year III. Under this new system of parliamentary government resting on a strong legislature and a weak executive responsible to the two chambers, France tried one again to reconcile liberty with order without sacrificing the gains of the revolution.

CONVENTION PEOPLE'S PARTY   The Convention People's Party (CPP) was founded in 1949, in what was then called the Gold Coast, by Dr. KWAME NKRUMAH. It demanded immediate self-government from the British and was more radical than the United Gold Coast Convention (UGCC)—founded in 1947 by the lawyer Dr. J. B. Danquah—of which Nkrumah had been the secretary.

The general election of 1951 was won by the CPP and in the following year Nkrumah became prime minister. Subsequent elections in 1954 and 1956 were also won by the CPP. On March 6, 1957, the Gold Coast became independent and was renamed Ghana. It was the first British dependency in sub-Saharan Africa to attain independence under majority rule.

Nkrumah espoused "African socialism"—a mixture of nationalism, vaguely-defined "socialism" and "Africanity" i.e., solidarity with other developing countries. Ghana maintained close links with the USSR and its allies while remaining economically dependent on western countries.

In 1957, opponents of the CPP united to form the United Party (UP) led by Dr. Kofi Busia. The government introduced repressive measures, in particular the Preventive Detention Act (1958), which allowed the imprisonment of opponents without trial for five years. Ghana became a republic in July 1960, with Nkrumah as executive president. From 1957 onwards Ghana progressed toward being a one-party state, and in 1964 this was legalized with Ghana becoming, in official terms, "a socialist single-party state."

Following widespread discontent at the country's economic difficulties and at alleged corruption within the CPP, Nkrumah was deposed by the army and police in February 1966. The CPP was abolished and replaced by a National Liberation Council, which comprised four army and four police officers.

CORDAY, CHARLOTTE DE   (1768–1793) A young enthusiast dedicated to the noblest ideals of the FRENCH REVOLUTION, who championed the GIRONDIST faction against its sworn enemy the JACOBINS, at the height of their struggle for supremacy in 1793. Corday became an instant martyr to her cause when, on July 13, 1793, she plunged a butcher knife into the heart of Jacobin journalist and orator JEAN PAUL MARAT as he lay in his bath to treat a skin ailment, a scene depicted in a famous painting by David.

Corday, a scion of a Norman gentry family descended from the dramatist Corneille, who had been brought up on the views of Jean Jacques Rousseau and the Abbe Raynal, had been appalled by the ruthless proscription of BRISSOT and 50 Girondist deputies from the hall of the Convention as a result of the intervention of the mob—an act of violence she ascribed to the instigation of Marat's newspaper. At her trial she made an eloquent plea in justification of tyrannicide during times of revolution. She was sent to the guillotine on July 17, 1793.

COSGRAVE, WILLIAM THOMAS   (1880–1965) Irish politician. An early member of the SINN FEIN, Cosgrave fought in the EASTER RISING of 1916 and was sentenced to life imprisonment. Released after a year, he helped to establish the new Irish parliament and government in Dublin in 1921. A relatively unknown figure until then, he became prime minister in 1922 and held the post until 1932, earning considerable unpopularity because of high taxation and a conciliatory policy toward Great Britain.

COSTA, ANDREA   (1851–1910) Italian socialist. As a student in the University of Bologna, Costa was drawn to the anarchist philosophy of MIKHAIL BAKUNIN. He participated in several meetings of the First International (see INTERNATIONAL, FIRST) and founded two journals, *Fascio Operaio* (1871) and *Martello* (1874). After a short prison term for plotting a revolt in Romagna, he emigrated to Paris, where he came under the influence of the Russian socialist Anna Kuliscioff and converted from anarchism to socialism. Before returning to Italy in 1880, he issued a famous letter, *Agli amici di Romagna*, in which he described his political metamorphosis; this letter played an important role in the spread of socialism throughout Italy. That same year he founded the *Rivista Internazionale de Socialismo* in Milan and in 1881 he began publishing a new journal, *Avanti!*, in which he outlined his socialist philosophy. The following year he became the first socialist elected to the Italian chamber of deputies, but it was only in 1892, at the Congress of Genoa, that the Italian Socialist party, then called the *Partito dei Lavoratori Italiani*, was founded. At the congress, and later during the siege of Milan (1898), Costa called on socialists throughout Italy to pool their resources and cooperate. Costa's integrity, popularity and pivotal role in Italian politics was recognized shortly before his death. In 1908, he was elected vice-president of the chamber of deputies.

COUTHON, GEORGES AUGUSTE   (1755–1794) One of ROBESPIERRE's most loyal associates on the COMMITTEE OF PUBLIC SAFETY which governed the French republic at the height of the FRENCH REVOLUTION from 1793 to 1794. Along with his junior partner, the JACOBIN fanatic SAINT-JUST, Couthon formed part of the hard core triumvirate in the Committee of twelve deputies of the CONVENTION which sought to establish a radical democratic dictatorship in its name.

Born in the central province of Auvergne, Couthon took up law in Clermont Ferand and was elected to represent his district as a deputy to the legislative assembly in 1792 and again to the Convention which replaced it the following year. A short, stocky and severely crippled man whose lameness confined him to a wheel chair, he was the most idealistic and devoted champion of Jacobin revolutionarism and followed the logic of his doctrines to the bitter end. Sent as a 'representative on mission' to crush a

GIRONDIN insurrection in France's second capital, Lyons, he suppressed it with quiet efficiency but refused to obey orders to raze the city to the ground. As a result, he was relieved of his mission and replaced by a more ruthless colleague on the Committee of Public Safety, Collot d'Herbois.

Before returning to Paris, he issued a series of decrees to implement radical changes both in the Lyonnais and the adjacent *département* of the Pûy-de-Dome, requisitioned grain to feed the capital and imposed a capital levy on the rich. Along with Collot and Saint-Just, he was also responsible for passing the notorious law of 22 Prairial in April 1793, by which the Convention suspended the civil liberties of the revolution's political enemies to expedite the work of the revolutionary tribunal. Despite his reputation as a mild and sensible man, it was Couthon who assisted Robespierre in eliminating the moderate Dantonists and the radical Hébertists at one fell swoop in April and could still contend in June that the revolution could only survive by destroying yet more enemies, whom he foolishly refused to name, thereby causing panic within the ranks of the convention.

His infirmities restricted him to speaking mostly at the Jacobin Club more easily accessible to his cumbersome wheel chair than the convention hall across the Rue Saint Honoré, but he remained a staunch supporter of Robespierre's policies, sharing his vision of a Republic of Virtue—and also ultimately sharing his fate. Along with Saint-Just and Robespierre, he was declared an outlaw by the Thermidorians following the overthrow of the Committee on July 9, and all three were executed together in the same *fournée* (batch) after a summary trial on July 28, 1794. The executioner had to make several attempts to chop his head off his crippled body and then displayed his head from the four corners of the platform to the cheering crowd.

COXEY'S ARMY A diminutive, picturesque army of unemployed workers that staged a symbolic American revolution. In the spring of 1894, Coxey's Army of laborers launched a six-week march from the west coast to Washington DC. This was a period of severe depression following the panic of 1893, and the army of unemployed workers intended to represent a "living petition" to Congress for relief legislation.

The originator of the protest was Jacob Sechler Coxey, a self-made businessman and quarry owner who intended the attack of his "army" on Washington to draw attention both to the plight of the workers and to his own scheme for solving it. The plan had two planks: a large issue of inflationary legal-tender currency and a national initiative, to be funded by the new issues, for building and improving roads and other infrastructural work. Coxey believed that his plan would help bring about immediate relief by creating jobs and would invigorate long-term recovery by improving the conditions for sustained economic growth.

The march of the industrial army was certainly highly successful as a publicity stunt, but no more. Coxey's march brought a total of only 500 men to Washington rather than the 100,000 who were expected, while affiliated marches from other points in the west added to the march a mere 1,200 protesters. The entire episode was thus not exactly classifiable as a rebellion: the army was figurative, the march was no more than a simple parade, and fittingly, Coxey, the rebel leader was promptly arrested and jailed in Washington based on police charges of carrying banners and of stepping on the Capitol's grass.

CRISTERO REVOLUTION The Cristero revolution took place during 1926–1929 in Mexico; its rallying cry was "*Viva Cristo Rey*." The anticlerical government of President CALLES had declared that all Church buildings were state property and enacted laws suppressing Church activity. On July 24, 1926, Mexican prelates effectively went on strike, suspending all religious services and calling for an economic boycott on the part of the faithful. As the Cristero uprising erupted in August, soldiers killed priests, raped nuns and looted churches. In retaliation, Cristeros executed captured federal soldiers, entered schools and killed "atheistic" teachers and, in April 1927, burned a train bound for Guadalajara.

The Cristero revolution was primarily a peasant rebellion, resulting in an alliance between the Catholic Church and peasants. It was not just a religious war: the peasants were also fighting for their lands, because foreign oil companies favored making Article 27 of the 1917 Mexican constitution, dealing with land reform, nonretroactive.

Under their flag, the Cristeros were directed to kill those who they believed were opposing the Church. One of their targets was the president-elect chosen to succeed Calles, General ALVARO OBREGON. Fifty thousand peasants were then fighting against the government in the states of Jalisco, Colima, Michoacan, Zacatecas and Nayarit.

A conspiracy against Obregon was launched in the house of "Madre Conchita" (Maria Concepcion Acevedo), a Catholic nun. She had been in charge of a convent in a southern suburb of Mexico City until it was closed during the government's campaign against the Church. Madre Conchita planned the assassination of Obregon, which was carried out by a fanatic artist named Jose de Leon Toral during an open-air banquet in a restaurant called "La Bombilla" ("The Little Bomb") in July, 1928. While Toral was executed, Madre Conchita's death sentence was later commuted to 20 years in prison.

After the Church condemned the assassination, Calles, with the mediation of Catholic officials in the USA and United States Ambassador Dwight Morrow, reached an agreement with it, ending his ideological campaign against the Church, enabling churches to reopen, permitting the return of exiled clergymen and allowing religious instruction within churches. The result was the termination, in 1929, of the three-year long church strike and of the Cristero revolt.

CROIX DE FEU, LES (Cross of Fire) A right-wing and proto-Fascist organization of French World War I veterans founded in 1927 by Count François de La Rocque de Severac, a retired lieutenant-colonel with a gift for mob oratory and organizing party discipline. Originally restricted to veterans who had earned the Croix de Guerre in combat (hence its name), it opened up its ranks to all ex-servicemen in 1931 to become a mass movement against socialism and internationalism, with a peak membership of 260,000 by 1934.

The *Croix de Feu* shared the same ideology of integral nationalism, anti-Semitism and rabid hostility to parliamentary democracy exhibited by CHARLES MAURRAS's *Action Française* and other extra-parliamentary leagues dedicated to overthrowing the Third Republic. These *ligues* ranged all the way from the *Action Française*'s paramilitary offshoot, the *Camelots de Roi* and Pierre Taittinger's *Jeunesses Patriotes*, to the *Solidarité*

Française and the Francisites, all of them inspired, in one way or another, by the victory of fascism over parliamentary democracy in MUSSOLINI's Italy.

The *Croix de Feu* played a major part in the bloody Paris insurrection of February 6, 1934, which almost succeeded in toppling the republic and was subsequently dissolved by the Popular Front government under LEON BLUM, which came to power in 1936. De La Rocque's reaction was to transform his movement into a political party, the *Parti Social Français* (PSF), with the aim of coming to power by electoral methods. This move, which has obvious analogies with HITLER's Nazi (see NATIONAL SOCIALIST PARTY) movement, was tantamount to acknowledging the failure of the revolutionary agitation of the leagues by the biggest and most powerful of them. The PSF, with a membership of almost 3 million, was able to reach out to an even larger audience by means of a lively newspaper, *Le Petit Journal*, which was widely read by the petty bourgeoisie, which regarded communism as a greater threat than FASCISM. Discredited because of its association with Vichy and its half-hearted policy of collaboration with the Germans, the PSF was disbanded at the liberation after World War II. De La Rocque, who had inconsistently supported the Resistance and suffered deportation to Germany in 1942, escaped trial in 1945 on the grounds of failing health.

CROMWELL, OLIVER (1599–1658) From an undistinguished background of middling Huntingdon farmers, Cromwell came under Puritan influence at Sidney Sussex College, Cambridge, which he left only a year after his father's death. At some point in his mid-thirties he underwent a sudden conversion to Calvinism. He had been elected to parliament in 1628, where he sat for a year, but when he returned to that institution in the Short and Long Parliaments he was a changed man. He proved himself to be a natural leader and parliamentarian, earning a reputation as a fighter for the rights of the small landowners. When the civil war began, he proved himself to be a natural military man, organizing a regiment of cavalry, taking part in the reorganization of the Eastern Association and playing a major role at the important battle of Marston Moor (1644). Within a year he was second in command in the army and a major figure in the trial and execution of the king in 1649, succeeding Fairfax as commander in chief of the army in 1650.

Cromwell spent a year in Ireland (August 1649–May 1650), during which he wiped out the Irish resistance to the new régime. His work there ensured the settlement of English Protestants in Ireland and the permanency of the Irish problem in British life and politics. Cromwell was also instrumental in defeating King Charles II at Dunbar (September 3, 1650) and in eliminating the Royalist Scots as a military force in the succeeding months. Although the most important figure in England, he was troubled by the need to set up a framework for representative government which would simultaneously express the demands of the "godly" people and not hinder the achievement of his political policies. His most original idea was the organization of a representative body based on godly churches instead of on geographical districts. This "Barebone's Parliament" met in the latter part of 1653, but soon came to quarrel about tithes and other mundane matters and was forcibly dissolved by Cromwell himself. The "Instrument of Government" (December 16, 1653), a written constitution, made Cromwell Lord Protector and gave

him an official status as political leader. His increasing dictatorship lost him many supporters, especially his reaction to continuing Royalist plots by dividing the country into military districts and placing them under the rule of major-generals. These military dictators were abolished by the "Humble Petition and Advice," a further written constitution, which allowed the Protector to name his successor and choose the members of his council. Yet even his refusal of a crown did little to endear him to important sectors of the ruling groups. His death in 1658 showed how much the republic was dependent solely on him: his son Richard lasted for barely six months and the generals were compelled to ask the executed king's son, Charles II, to take the throne.

Oliver Cromwell as the Savior of England

CUBA, REVOLTS AND REVOLUTIONS
1933 Revolt. General Gerardo Machado y Morale was inaugurated as president of Cuba in 1925. His presidency was characterized by strong repressive measures by the government against the rebellion which had been brought about by economic and financial crises. In response to the request by Machado to extend his presidential term, the congress changed it to six years. Machado's intention to rule as a dictator led to several revolts. On August 12, 1933, Machado was overthrown by the Revolt of the Six Sergeants, led by Sergeant Fulgencio Batista y Zaldivar. A period of disorder followed. Dr. Miguel Mariano Gómez y Arias was elected president in January 1936 but impeached in December of that same year. The vice-president, Federico Laredo Bru, then occupied the executive office. President Fulgencio Batista was inaugurated on October 10, 1940.

1959 Revolt. Ramón Grau San Martín was elected president of Cuba in June 1944. His administration was characterized by continuous strikes and a plot to assassinate him. Grau San Martín was succeeded by Carlos Prío Socarrás, elected in June 1948, who was in turn overthrown by a military uprising led by Batista in 1952. General Batista assumed the powers of chief of state on March 11, 1952, just one day after the uprising. On July 26, 1953, a young lawyer named FIDEL CASTRO led an attack on the army barracks of Santiago de Cuba. He was arrested and sentenced to 15 years in prison but let free 11 months later as a result of Batista's general amnesty decree. Batista was once again reelected in 1954. Castro landed in the province of Oriente in 1956 and carried out guerrilla warfare against the government forces in the hills of that province until March 17, 1958, when he declared total war on the Batista régime. The presidential election of 1958 was won by Andrés Rivero, with Batista's backing. However, by January 1959 the Batista administration collapsed and Manuel Urrutia was named provisional president. On January 8, 1959, Castro made his triumphant entrance into Havana. In July 1959, Osvaldo Dorticós Torrado replaced Urrutia and Fidel Castro assumed the office of prime minister, becoming president in 1976. Castro still rules Cuba.

CULPEPER'S REBELLION The 1667 seizure of power in the Albermarle region in North Carolina, the United States, by a group of settlers led by John Culpeper and George Durant. The insurgents had been stopped by the acting governor and customs collector, John Miller and his coterie, from exporting tobacco in a manner which evaded the duties stipulated by the navigation laws. Culpeper and his frustrated supporters jailed Miller and members of his council, took control of the machinery of government and managed the affairs of the colony for more than a year.

Both Miller, who had succeeded in escaping from prison, and Culpeper himself subsequently traveled to England in an attempt to gain support for their conflicting claims to the government of the colony. Culpeper, charged in court with treason, was acquitted, after pleading that there was no regular government in Carolina at the time he seized power. Thus, while in a strict legal sense the episode may not have constituted a revolt, in practice it was no less than a violent usurpation of legitimate power.

CULTURAL REVOLUTION   see GREAT PROLETARIAN CULTURAL REVOLUTION.

CUZA, ALEXANDER Early Romanian Fascist and leading anti-Semite. One of the founders of the first Romanian socialist journal, *Dacia*, in 1883, Cuza later turned to radical nationalism and anti-Semitism, heading the NATIONAL CHRISTIAN ANTI-SEMITIC LEAGUE while a lecturer at the faculty of law at the University of Iasi. After breaking with CORNELIU CODREANU, his National Christian party won considerable support in the interwar period.

CYRUS THE YOUNGER, REVOLT OF (401 B.C.) Cyrus was the younger son of Darius II. In 408 B.C. he was appointed as supreme commander of Persian armed forces in Asia Minor with the extraordinary title *karanos*, above the local satraps. He saw himself as a legitimate heir of his father since, according to the Persian custom, not the elder son inherited the throne, but the

son who was born when his father was already king. When Darius II lay dying at the beginning of 404 B.C. Cyrus came to Babylon, but when he arrived his father was already dead and his elder brother Arshak had been crowned as king under the throne name of Artaxerxes II. Cyrus was accused by Tissaphernes, satrap of Caria and his subordinate, of plotting against the new king and was arrested. With the help of his mother, Parysatis, however, he was cleared of all charges, released and returned to Asia Minor.

Soon after his return Cyrus began to hire Greek mercenaries under the pretext of conducting a war against Pisidian tribes, but with a secret intention of overthrowing his brother. There was no shortage of men since in 404 B.C., the great Peloponnesian War had just ended and many professional soldiers from both sides were ready to serve anyone for a profit. By 401 B.C., Cyrus hired 13,000 soldiers. Their commander was Clearchus (a Spartan), and Xenophon, an Athenian writer who later wrote an account of this campaign, was among them.

In the Spring of 401 B.C., Cyrus left Sardes and marched east toward Cilicia, where he obtained a large amount of money needed to pay his mercenaries from the local vassal king Suenesius. At Issus, Cyrus received some reinforcements from Greece and proceeded to the so-called "Cilician Gates"—the heavily fortified passage to Syria. Artaxerxes II ordered Abrocomus, who assembled a large army in Syria for the invasion of Egypt, to defend this passage, but he failed to arrive in time. Cyrus entered Syria unopposed and there revealed to his army the true purpose of the expedition.

Both armies finally met near a village, Cunaxa, about 90 km. from Babylon. According to Greek authors, Cyrus had 13,000 Greek mercenaries, 40,000 Persian infantry and 30,000 cavalrymen, and Artaxerxes had 400,000 soldiers. However, once again Abrocomus was late to join the battle, which took place on September 1, 401 B.C.

Clearchus, with the Greek mercenaries, commanded the right wing; Arieus, commander of Persian troops, was on the left wing; and Cyrus himself took command of the center. On the other side Tissaphernes commanded the lift wing, opposite Clearchus, and Artaxerxes was in the center. Sickle-bearing chariots which were riding in front of the king's army caused no harm to the Greeks, who let them go through their lines and then charged in close formation. Tissaphernes's troops fled from the battlefield and Persians around Cyrus began to prostrate themselves in front of him as in front of a king. At this point Cyrus, with 600 horsemen, attacked Artaxerxes and wounded him in the chest, but immediately afterwards he himself was killed by a Carian soldier. After the death of Cyrus his Persian troops fled, but the Greeks continued to advance until sunset.

In the morning both sides claimed the victory, but with Cyrus dead the continuation of the war lost any purpose. Clearchus proposed to make Arieus king, but the latter declined the offer. Royal messengers demanded that the rebels lay down their arms, but they refused. After several days of negotiations, Tissaphernes promised them safe passage back to Greece. The rebels retreated to Opis, only to find there a fresh Persian army which had arrived from Media to cut their retreat. Clearchus tried to offer his troops to the king for the suppression of a rebellion of Amyrtaeus in Egypt, and Tissaphernes invited him and other Greek officers for negotiations in his headquarters. When the Greeks entered Tissaphernes's tent the junior officers were killed on the spot and the senior officers were arrested and later beheaded. Arieus with his Persian troops crossed over to the king.

Thus the Greeks found themselves in the heart of the Persian Empire, without allies, without their own commanders, without clear knowledge of their location and between two Persian armies preventing their advance or retreat. Yet in this hopeless situation they did not lose heart. They elected new commanders (Xenophon among them), and decided to break through on their own in an attempt to reach safety. In their retreat, known as the "March of the 10,000" (8,600 out of 13,000 returned), they marched through Assyria, Kurdistan and Armenia, and finally reached the Black Sea near Trapezus.

CZECHOSLOVAKIA, COUPS

Communist Takeover of 1948. The Communist coup of February 1948 completed the process that began with the last phases of Czechoslovakia's liberation at the end of World War II. American troops approached Prague, but the greater part of the country was liberated by the advancing Red Army. The London-based government-in-exile led by President Benes agreed to the formation of a Communist-led goverment, which emerged with the Kosice Program in 1945. In this, the Communists held the important posts of interior, agriculture, education and information, along with a strong base in the National Security Corps. The Communist build-up following the advance of the Soviet troops was swift and efficient, as party leaders KLEMENT GOTTWALD and RUDOLF SLANSKY proceeded to lay the groundwork for the takeover of the country. Benes's talks with STALIN in March 1945 took place at a time when the Communists were already in control of top positions of the emerging Slovak, Czech and federal structures. Communist influence grew as "mass" organizations created and controlled by the Communist party (CP) undermined the country's democratic institutions. From 50,000 members at the end of the war, party membership grew to 1.4 million by the end of 1947. In the first postwar elections in May 1946, the Communists won 38% (more in the Czech area, less in Slovakia) and emerged as the largest political formation, after having successfully discredited but not eliminated opposition forces. The Communists received widespread support from peasants who benefited from the distribution of German lands. The agrarian opposition, the Agrarian party, was not allowed to take part in the elections. The new coalition government was led by Klement Gottwald, with the participation of centrist and leftist parties such as the Czech People's party, the National Socialists and the Slovak Democratic party. Soviet pressure to refuse the invitation to participate in the Marshall Plan in 1947 brought tension between the Communist ministers and Foreign Minister Masaryk, who, it seems, was pushed to his death from his office window in March 1948. The power struggle accelerated by the end of 1947, as Czechoslovakia was the only state in Eastern Europe where the Communist takeover had not yet been completed, in spite of the Communists dominating the most vital institutions. The showdown came in February 1948, when a Communist-initiated government and a constitutional crisis led to the threat of use of force by the Communists, as the armed Workers' Militia prevented any attempts to oppose by force the final Communist push. The one-party régime was born unopposed, as the Communists proceeded to remove and delegitimize the other political formations such as the Social Democrats, who "united" with the Communists in June 1948. President Benes, who died of a broken heart in September 1948, was yet another victim of the Communist takeover. (See also PRAGUE, SPRING OF.)

The Velvet Revolution of 1989. The collapse of the Communist régime took place against the background of the growing crisis of legitimacy in which the Communists found themselves as the Gorbachev reforms showed their impact in Eastern Europe. As the country was not in an acute economic crisis, the conservative HUSAK leadership felt that reforms could be mild, gradual and less damaging to the party's grip on society than the Soviet model. The opposition centered around a group named Charter 77, led by intellectuals, some of whose members, like VACLAV HAVEL, had spent years in jail for their convictions, and around the Catholic church, especially in Slovakia. The Communist party, led by Milos Jakes, who had replaced Husak at the end of 1987, refused to conduct a dialogue with the emerging opposition groups, which had not yet received mass support. The Jakes leadership removed some of the older hard liners, as the régime tried to pay more lip service to the ideals of reform, without, however, really implementing it. In January 1989, Havel was re-arrested and sentenced to jail along with several colleagues and the opposition became more vocal and visible, targeting the "soft spots" of the régime, especially the human rights aspects. Rapid changes within the party and the government leadership during 1989 indicated that the more the Communists tried to save face by "internal democratization" and promises of reform, the more rapidly they lost control. The Communist collapse took place in spite of the fact that no effective, well-coordinated opposition emerged until the very end, when the Civic Forum and its Slovak counterpart, the Public Against Violence, were formed to take control of the country. A series of huge public rallies and strikes, in which improvisation and clumsy Communist provocations played a major role, brought the régime to lose control. The masses demanded democracy, human rights and the downfall of the régime and rejected further promises of reforms which came too late. The Civic Forum's leadership formulated its program for a new Czechoslovakia as the Communist party and the government waited for the opposition to provide a final coup de grace, which came at the end of November, when in several rapid and dramatic moves the National Assembly revoked the articles guaranteeing the CP's leading role. Gustav Husak resigned as president, the hero of the Prague Spring, ALEXANDER DUBCEK became chairman of the National Assembly and Vaclav Havel was elected president as of January 1, 1990.

D

DAN, (GURVICH) FYODOR (1871–1947) MENSHEVIK journalist and political leader. Dan began his revolutionary activity with the St. Petersburg Union of Struggle for the Liberation of the Working Class in 1894. Two years later he was arrested and exiled for three years, emigrating to Berlin in 1901. His activity in Berlin was both journalistic and political. He was active in preparing the second congress of the Social Democratic Workers' Party of Russia. He later became prominent in the Menshevik wing of the RSDRP, and from 1906 was a member of its central committee, responsible for matters of party organization.

He returned to Russia in 1913 and was arrested as a revolutionary with the outbreak of World War I. In 1915, he was drafted as an army doctor. He served in Siberia, where he was able to maintain contact with other exiled socialist leaders.

In March 1917, Dan returned to Petrograd, joining the group advocating "revolutionary defencism." He was elected deputy chair of the All-Russian Executive of the Soviets in June 1917. Following the seizure of power by the BOLSHEVIKS in October 1917, Dan joined the Menshevik Internationalist leader, MARTOV, in advocating a broad socialist coalition and political freedom for all socialist parties. In 1921, with the final outlawing of Menshevik activity in Soviet Russia, Dan was arrested and went into exile in early 1922.

In exile, Dan served on the editorial board of the newspaper *Socialist Courier* (*Sotsialisticheskii vestnik*). He continued to hope for the democratization of the USSR, a position that gradually brought him into conflict with his emigre colleagues. In 1940 he left Europe for New York, where he edited his own newspaper, *New Path* (*Novyi put*). Shortly before his death in New York he published *The Origins of Bolshevism*, legitimizing the Bolshevik régime as the force that had realized socialism in Russia.

D'ANNUNZIO, GABRIELE (1863–1938) A major and prolific Italian poet and writer of theater plays in Italian, French and Latin. D'Annunzio, an eccentric public figure, was also well known for his military exploits and political adventures. By the end of the 19th century, he had read NIETZSCHE and was influenced by the German philosopher's ideas. In 1897, he was elected to parliament as a representative of the extreme right. In 1900, he aligned himself with the extreme left of the Socialist party of Italy and later joined the nationalist ranks. His amours, literary fame and political career made D'Annuzio one of the most striking personalities of his time. In 1914, D'Annunzio eloquently drew crowds into the pro-war camp. He volunteered

for army service, performed many heroic deeds, was wounded, lost an eye in the war and was decorated for his actions in various occasions. Popular as an hero both of culture and war, he was able in September 1919 to attract a large group of veterans in order to occupy the town of Fiume (see FIUME, MARCH ON) in Yugoslavia for Italy, against the will of the allies and of the Italian government. By this act, D'Annunzio was, according to his view, awarding his country what it had rightfully won through its war sacrifices. In Fiume, D'Annunzio inaugurated a modern political style intended to incorporate the masses into politics through theatrical speeches, ritual acts, political displays and choreography. This was the inauguration of a new political style later to be adopted by MUSSOLINI and FASCISM. D'Annunzio, with the assistance of ALCESTE DE AMBRIS and his national revolutionary syndicalist theories (see SYNDICALISM), drafted the Carnaro Charter—Fiume's constitution—of a corporative character, which was later declared by the Fascists as the political model for the Fascist state. Mussolini heralded D'Annunzio's ideas in Italy but retained part of the funds collected for Fiume, since he saw in Gabriele D'Annunzio a dangerous rival for the leadership of the Fascist movement. The failure of the Fiume experiment, at the end of 1920, brought about D'Annunzio's retirement from politics to the Vittoriale degli Italiani, a luxurious villa on the banks of Lake Garda. D'Annunzio supported fascism and in 1924, on the occasion of the signature of the treaty with Yugoslavia that awarded Fiume to Italy, the Italian king awarded the poet-soldier the title of Prince of Monte Nevoso. The collected works of D'Annunzio were published in 49 volumes in 1937 and the writer was named president of the Royal Academy.

DANTON, GEORGES-JACQUES (1759–1795) French revolutionary, born in the small village of Acris-sur-Aube, about 100 miles from Paris. Danton's family was originally of peasant stock but through hard work had reached the level of petit-bourgeois. Raised in the countryside, Danton remained attached to the soil and the land. He was a coarse man, with a tendency toward bluntness that verged on the shocking. When he gained power, he ruled without the self-discipline and cool detachment mastered by more practiced aristocrats. He was, for a while, the most popular figure of his time, undoubtedly charming and persuasive, if also volatile and often unpredictable. He was also somewhat shocking to look at. His face was pockmarked and it bore the scars of being trampled by pigs in the barnyard as a boy and mauled by the horn of a cow whose udders he had been sucking. It was said that "It would be easier to paint the eruption of a volcano than the features of this great man."

At age 13 Danton was sent to be educated by Oratorian priests, a particularly open-minded, scientifically-oriented sect that inspired in Danton a love of learning, although he was described as a generally lazy student whose innate brilliance appeared only in sudden bursts.

After his education was over, his family met with the priests to determine the further course of his life. It was decided, much to the young Danton's pleasure, that he was to study law. He set out for Paris in 1780 with almost no money and managed, through the sheer force of his personality, to be taken on as a lawyer's apprentice, although he lacked the necessary experience.

During this time he met and fell in love with Antoinette Charpentier, the daughter of the owner of a cafe he frequented. He borrowed money to set up a law practice and married Antoinette two days later. The practice thrived and he took to signing his name d'Anton as if he were an aristocrat. The couple lived somewhat pretentiously, entertaining frequently and often finding themselves stretched financially beyond their means.

They lived in the Cordeliers district of Paris, inhabited by students, printers, journalists and other unmonied intellectuals. The district became a hotbed of dissent in the early days of the FRENCH REVOLUTION of 1789, its name becoming synonymous with the Cordeliers movement, of which Danton became the first president, following a heroic attempt to protect JEAN MARAT, another revolutionary journalist, from arrest. Danton then joined the GIRONDINS, a movement that, along with the JACOBINS, took power in the heat of revolution. They formed a government, the legislative assembly—of which Danton was not officially a part—and plotted to overthrow the monarchy.

Danton became minister of justice in the new government and was in part responsible, although it is unclear to what degree, for the September Massacres, one of the bloodiest revolutionary purges of the general population. He rallied the nation with the cry "Everything belongs to the country when the country is in danger."

After the massacres, it became impossible for Danton to realign himself with the moderate faction of which he had originally been a part. He had always been a realist, and as the revolution took on a life of its own, political distinctions and groups to which one belonged became increasingly changeable and unclear. Danton was no longer a Girondin or Cordelier; in fact they became his enemies. He was also not a Jacobin but clearly a part of the self-interested and bloody power struggle that characterized the Terror.

Shortly after Danton officially became part of the government, personal tragedy struck. He went away for two weeks and returned to discover that his beloved wife had died, leaving him with two young sons. His own downfall can be traced, in part, to Antoinette's death. Always immensely popular with the public and famed for his ability to whip up public emotion, he became unable to sustain the level of stamina that had catapulted him to power. The Jacobins and their leader, MAXIMILIEN ROBESPIERRE, grabbed the reins and held on firmly and brutally. The Girondins, whom Danton saw as the true voice of republicanism, were being slaughtered. Danton became physically and emotionally exhausted and made what can now can be seen as his fatal mistake. Claiming illness, he retired for a short while to the countryside to regain his strength. However, in leaving the seat of power for just a brief time he gave his enemies considerable leeway to conspire against him. He returned to find himself accused of plotting to reinstate the monarchy. Danton's revolution, his "war to elevate French people," ended in 1794 when he was tried and imprisoned for crimes against the revolution. His execution marked the height of the Terror, one of the most violent periods in French history. On the scaffold he said to the executioner, "You must show my head to the people. It is worth showing."

DARIUS I, GENERAL REBELLION AGAINST (522–520 B.C.)

On September 29, 522 B.C., Darius and six other conspirators killed King Bardiya (referred to in Greek sources as Smerdis or Mardos), son of Cyrus the Great, and seized the Persian throne. Darius claimed that the deposed king was an imposter named Gaumata the Magus. Regardless of whether Darius had deposed the king or an imposter, his coup was perceived as usurpation throughout the empire and provoked a general uprising of almost all satrapies, with the exception of the countries west of the Euphrates. Darius himself described his struggle against the rebels in a rock inscription in Behistun, in which he claimed that he had suppressed all of them during a single year.

Immediately after the coup, Elam and Babylon rebelled. In Elam, Assina proclaimed himself king, but his uprising was quickly quelled by troops faithful to Darius. In Babylon, Nadintu-Bel, who claimed to be the son of the last Babylonian king, Nabonidus, assumed the royal name of Nebuchadnezzar and was recognized as king on October 3, 522 B.C. Darius himself led his army to Babylon and the rebels were defeated in two battles—on December 13 on the Tigris and on December 18 on the Euphrates. Nadintu-Bel fled to Babylon, where he was taken prisoner and executed. While Darius remained in Babylon, rebellions broke out in Elam again as well as in Media, Armenia, Parthia, Hyrcania, Sagartia, Margiana, Arachosia and Persia itself.

Martiya, a Persian, proclaimed himself king of Elam under the Elamite name Imanish, but was seized and killed by the Elamites themselves. In Media, Fravartish (Phraortes) claimed to be Khshathrita (king) of the Median royal house of Cyaxares. He was supported by Armenia, Parthia and Hyrcania. Darius sent his generals to quell these rebellions: Vidarna (Hydarnes) to Media and Dadarshish and Vaumisa to Armenia, while his father, Vishtaspa (Hystaspes), was in command in Parthia and Hyrcania. Vaumisa engaged with the rebels on December 31, 522 B.C. at Izala, in what had formerly been Assyrian territory, while Vidarna attacked Marush on January 12, 521 B.C. and Vishtaspa attacked Vishpauzatish on March 8, 521 B.C. Darius himself arrived in Media and won a decisive victory on May 7 of that year at Kundurush, but Fravartish escaped to Raga in eastern Media. Dadarshish fought two battles in Armenia—on May 21 at Zuzahya and six days later at Tigra, but the struggle for Armenia and Parthia continued. In Armenia, the rebels were crushed by Dadarshish on June 21 at Uyama, and a few days later by Vaumisa at Autiara. Meanwhile, Darius arrived in Parthia and defeated the rebels on July 12 at Patigrabana. Fravartish was finally captured during the same month and was executed in the Median capital of Ecbatana.

In Sagartia in western Media, Chissatakhma also claimed to be a king of the house of Cyaxares. Darius sent Takhmaspada against him, who defeated the enemy in battle. Chissatakhma was captured and executed at Arbela. In Margiana, central Asia, Frada had proclaimed himself king. He was defeated by Dadarshish, the satrap of neighboring Bactria, on December 10, 522 B.C.

The most serious threat to Darius was posed by the rebellion in Persia proper, where Vahyazdata proclaimed himself king under the name of Bardiya. The war against him began in Arachosia, in eastern Iran, where Vivana fought the rebels on December 29, 522 B.C., finally defeating them on February 21, 521 B.C. Darius's troops, led by Artavadiya, entered Persia, where they engaged in battle on May 25 at Rakha. Vahyazdata was finally defeated and captured on July 16 at Parga.

Thus, by July 521 B.C. the most dangerous uprisings among the Iranian satrapies had been quelled by Darius, but already on August 16 the same year Babylon rebelled for the second time.

Detail from the Treasury building in Persepolis, depicting a royal receiption. King Darius is shown seated on his throne

Arakha the Armenian claimed to be Nebuchadnezzar, son of Nabonidus. Darius sent Vindafarna (Intaphernes), one of the conspirators who had killed Bardiya, against him and Babylon was taken on November 27. This was the last rebellion included by Darius in his account of victories achieved in a single year (actually 14 months), but in 520 B.C. Elam rebelled for the third time under the leadership of Atamaita. This rebellion was suppressed by Gaubaruva (Gobrias), another conspirator against Bardiya.

In the Behistun inscription, Darius also mentions rebellions in Sattagydia, Scythia and Egypt, but says nothing about their suppression. The uprisings of Sattagydia and Scythia were probably connected to the rebellions in neighboring Arachosia and Margiana. As for Egypt, conquered by Cambyzus in 525–522 B.C., the only source which mentions a rebellion against Darius is a very late Greek author, Polyaenus, who claims that Darius gave the Egyptians 100 talents of silver for the purchase of a new sacred bull for Apis and the Egyptians, impressed by this gesture, brought their uprising to an end. According to Egyptian sources the old Apis died on August 31, 518 B.C.

Darius's success should probably be explained by the gradual transformation of the Persian popular militia (*kara*) into a standing army during the wars of conquest of Cyrus and Cambyzus. This army lost its connection with the local population and became loyal only to its military commanders.

DARRÉ, RICHARD WALTHER (1895–1953) nazi agrarian expert. Darré was born in Belgrano, Argentina, and moved to Germany as an agrarian dreamer, where he tried to maintain and enhance German peasantry and prevent urbanization at its expense. This reactionary revolution was widely accepted by many followers of the German far right, but the Nazi party did not endorse it as its sole aim. Darré was made the Nazi party's agrarian adviser in 1930 and head of the SS's own Race Office–the embryo of the future SS Race and Settlement Main Office, which was in charge of German colonization of East European territories. Darré gave the SS its concept of "a new nobility created from blood and earth," and became minister of food supply in 1933. He forced German peasantry to join a Nazi-controlled organization, but during World War II lost all his offices due to an alleged dispute on war policy. Darré was sentenced after the war to seven years in jail but was released in 1950.

DAVIS, ANGELA (1944–) Black American revolutionary leader. Davis studied under HERBERT MARCUSE at the University of California but was dismissed from her post as professor of philosophy in 1969 owing to the fact that she was a member of the Communist party. In 1970 she was suspected of complicity in the kidnapping from the courtroom of a young black revolutionary, George Jackson, during which incident the judge had been killed. Davis then went into hiding, was arrested, tried and acquitted in one of the most celebrated trials of the century.

DE AMBRIS, ALCESTE (b. Licciana Nardi, 1874–1934) Italian revolutionary syndicalist leader. An early member of the Italian Socialist party, De Ambris abandoned his law studies in favor of political activism. In 1898, escaping trial in Italy, he emigrated to Brazil, where he organized Italian immigrant workers and founded *Avanti*, a socialist weekly that provoked the wrath of the local landowners. Facing trial again, De Ambris's return to Italy was made possible by an amnesty. In Italy, he joined the revolutionary syndicalist (see SYNDICALISM) wing of the Socialist party and became involved in the organization of general strikes, as secretary of the Parma Chamber of Labor. It is in this period that he began the publication of *L'Internazionale*, a paper that would become the carrier of the ideas of direct action, syndical organization and the mythical revolutionary general strike, trying to combine the ideologies of KARL MARX and GEORGES SOREL. De Ambris, as a syndical leader, organized the Parma agrarian general strike lasting from May 1 until June 24, 1908. The failure of the strike drove him to exile in Switzerland, in order to avoid capture and trial, and to a revision of his revolutionary syndicalist theories. While he opposed the Italian conquest of Libya in 1911, in the summer of 1914 he proclaimed a new theory about "revolutionary war." According to it, Italy had to join the war on the side of France and Britain in order to stop the reactionary powers—Germany and Austria—and to open revolutionary possibilities for its people. After the war, De Ambris proclaimed a national syndicalist theory that combined the fulfilling of national and social needs, and provided MUSSOLINI and the Fascists with their first political programs. At the end of 1919, he joined D'ANNUNZIO at Fiume and designed a constitutional project for Italy that D'Annunzio made public as the *Carta del Carnaro*, the political model of the Regency of Fiume. This document, later cited by the Fascists as the model for their Corporative State, was Mazzinian revolutionary in nature and provided a political framework for modernization along the lines of national syndicalism. Disillusioned by the turning to the right of Mussolini and Italian FASCISM, De Ambris left Italy for exile in September 1923, for the third and last time. In France, he published anti-Fascist articles and received an offer from CURZIO MALAPARTE to return, join the Fascist ranks and become minister of the corporations, which he refused. De Ambris died in exile in 1934.

DE BONO, EMILIO   (1866–1944) Italian Fascist revolutionary leader. A military officer who had served in the Italo-Turkish war and in World War I, De Bono joined the Fascist (see FASCISM) ranks in 1921. His links with the military led to his being appointed as a quadrumvir—one of the four leaders appointed by MUSSOLINI to lead the MARCH ON ROME—together with Italo Balbo, Michele Bianchi and Cesare Maria De Vecchi. After Mussolini's nomination as prime minister, De Bono was appointed director general of public security and, a short time afterwards, the first commander of the Fascist militia. His task in controlling the most violent and intransigent elements in the *squadri*—Fascist squads—was difficult, and when, in June 1924, a group of those murdered Giacomo Matteotti, one of the main leaders of the anti-Fascist parliamentarian opposition, De Bono was accused of complicity in the murder. Acquitted of all charges a year later, he was rewarded with the governorship of Tripolitania, especially since during the long months of pressure in prison he had consistently refused to implicate other Fascists. In 1928, Mussolini appointed De Bono minister of the colonies. It was in this position that he formulated the future policies that led to the Italian invasion of Ethiopia in October 1935. De Bono himself, as high commissioner for East Africa, led the Italian invasion, which proceeded at a slower pace than Mussolini wished.

This led to his replacement by his rival, Pietro Badoglio. De Bono was promoted to the rank of marshal and relegated to ceremonial functions. In July 1943, De Bono voted in favor of DINO GRANDI's motion in the Great Fascist Council to remove Mussolini. In October 1943, he was arrested for his part in the coup against Mussolini, brought to Verona to stand trial, found guilty and executed.

DEBRAY, JULES REGIS   (1942–) French revolutionary. A Marxist philosopher, Debray wrote *Castroism; the Long March of Latin America* (1965). In 1966 he became a history professor in Cuba and a leading spokesman of the New Left. In 1967, Debray joined CHE GUEVARA in his guerrilla campaign in Bolivia. Captured, tortured and sentenced to 30 years in prison, Debray was released in 1970 and returned to France. In 1977 he wrote a book on President ALLENDE of Chile.

DECEMBRIST REVOLT   On December 14, 1825, some 3,000 Russian soldiers and sailors refused to swear allegiance to the new Russian czar, Nicholas I, and raised the cry, "Constantine and Constitution!" They were demanding that the previous czar's brother take the throne and call a constitutional assembly, ending 200 years during which autocracy was one of the formal principles of the Russian state. Badly organized and without unified leadership, this first Russian revolution was quickly crushed. Five of its leaders were hanged and others jailed and exiled.

The moving spirits behind this rebellion were young nobles influenced by the ideas of the FRENCH REVOLUTION and alienated by the reactionary politics of Alexander I, the previous czar. Some of the Decembrist leaders had been educated in European universities, while others had served in the Russian armies that had defeated Napoleon and had themselves felt the influence of new social and political currents in Western Europe. Within Russia, they had absorbed the moral and political critique of Russia's backwardness expressed in the works of the nascent intelligentsia: Pushkin, Griboyedov, Radishchev and others. They were also evidently influenced by the egalitarian values of the Masonic order, founded in Russia during that period. Over a period of 10 years preceding the Decembrist revolt, a series of secret organizations served as centers for the recruitment of supporters and the elaboration of a social blueprint for Russia.

Two rather different programs were developed by the Decembrist leaders. NIKITA MURAVEV, leader of the "Northern Society," drew up a "Russian Constitution" that included the emancipation of the serfs, the rule of law and the equality of all citizens. At the same time, the document emphasized private property rights, specifically those of the landowning classes, and set property qualifications for voting and for being elected. The "Russian Truth" expounded by PAVEL PESTEL, of the "Southern Society," had clear JACOBIN influences. It called for a provisional dictatorship to rule during the transition from autocracy and included expropriation of land for the benefit of the freed serfs. Pestel's plan also included the incorporation of neighboring lands into the Russian state and the assimilation of their peoples.

The mythology of the Decembrist rebellion, with wives faithfully accompanying their exiled husbands on the wearying journey into Siberian exile, and the ideologies of the different Decembrist leaders, influenced later generations of Russian revolutionaries.

DECLARATION OF THE RIGHTS OF MAN AND CITIZEN

This revolutionary declaration was devised as the guiding principle of the FRENCH REVOLUTION and as the preface to the French constitution of 1791. It was enacted by the French National Assembly on August 26, 1789. The declaration was meant to be applicable not only to revolutionary France but to all peoples in perpetuity. It invalidated the rights of kings to rule France and granted "inalienable rights," including: the proposition that all men were equal; people were sovereign; the people had a right to vote and make laws through their chosen representatives; personal freedom and the freedoms of speech, the press and the religion; the protection of personal property and due process under the law.

Depending on the source, either the MARQUIS DE LAFAYETTE or Count SIEYES is credited with putting this document together. Historians also disagree as to the origins of the document. Some believe the United States declaration of independence was the major influence. Others believe the predominance of ideas can be traced to English principles. Others point to the Calvinistic doctrine, while yet other experts feel that Rousseau's *Social Contract* was the applicable source. The declaration was the primary source used by many of the European countries during the 19th century in their push toward the adoption of civil and political rights and sounded the death knell to the autocratic rulers in Europe.

DE LEON, DANIEL (1852–1914) US socialist leader. De Leon was born in the Caribbean island of Curaçao. which was first colonized by the Dutch and had a long-established Jewish community. Having been brought up in Curaçao, where slavery was the main source of income until it was abolished in 1863 (when De Leon was 11), De Leon, even as a child, was acutely aware of the social injustices surrounding him.

Upon the death of his father, De Leon went to Europe to continue his education. He received the degree of Bachelor of Philosophy from the University of Leyden and, upon moving to the United States in 1872, had a distinguished career at the Columbia Law School, where he became a lecturer on Latin American diplomacy (1883–1889).

While still at Columbia, he was drawn to the labor movement. He joined the Knights of Labor in 1883, during a period of intense strikes and struggles in labor organization, and emerging as a strong leader of the labor movement was not looked upon very favorably by the Columbia University administration. After not being appointed to a promised professorship, De Leon left Columbia and dedicated himself to the labor movement. In 1890, he became a member of the Socialist Labor Party, upon which he had a dominating influence for the following two decades in his various capacities as nationwide public speaker and, especially, through his editorship of the newspaper, *The Weekly People* (later, *Daily People*). As editor of the journal from 1892 until his death, he stamped his personality on the party. He also ran for public office as a Socialist candidate on several occasions; in 1891 he ran for the govenorship of New York State. He wanted to create a labor movement that would include unskilled workers and would constitute a political revolutionary force. A group of leading Jewish socialists left the party in reaction to his policies and in 1899 MORRIS HILLQUIT and his colleagues withdrew in protest against his radicalism. De

Leon has been blamed for the attempts to establish an authoritarian rule over his party through personal invective, the expulsion of opponents and control of the press.

With the consonancy of the rival Socialist Party of America, Dr. De Leon began to re-evaluate standard social democratic theory, believing that the simple voting of the socialist party—and so the proletariat—into power would not be enough. Proletarian economic power was essential to force the capitalists to accept the electoral success. Otherwise the capitalists would lock the workers out of the factories and starve them into political submission. In 1905, he gained the control of Industrial Workers of the World (IWW). When he and his followers were expelled in 1908 by extremists, he organized the rival IWW, but it did not flourish.

While he was sharply criticized during his lifetime, De Leon is recognized today as the father of "American Marxism." His works were appreciated by international socialist leaders of the stature of VLADIMIR LENIN.

DEMOCRATIC FRONT FOR THE LIBERATION OF PALESTINE (DFLP) Palestinian nationalist movement. The DFLP was founded in 1969 by Naif Hawatmeh as a splinter group of the Popular Front for the Liberation of Palestine (PFLP). Since its formation, the movement has been in opposition to the mainstream Palestinian nationalist movement, headed by YASIR ARAFAT and the PALESTINE LIBERATION ORGANIZATION (PLO). Unlike most Palestinian organizations, it believes in a scientific-socialist solution to the Palestinian-Israeli conflict and rejects the idea of a West Bank-Gaza Palestinian state. Nevertheless, it was also the first group with grassroots support to call for coexistence with Israel and its members have been engaged in dialogue with left-wing Israelis since the 1960s.

The DFLP rejects the declaration of principles that formed the basis of the peace accord between the Palestinians and Israelis and has said that it will boycott elections in the Palestinian autonomous region. At the same time it has said that it will protest if no elections are held or if the elections are conducted undemocratically.

DENG XIAOPING (Teng Hsiao-p'ing) (1904–) Chinese Communist leader. Deng was born to a Sichuan landlord family. By the time he was 16, he had completed middle school and a year-long preparatory course for overseas studies. His political consciousness, like that of so many of his generation, was aroused by the MAY FOURTH MOVEMENT. He spent five years in France (1920–1925), working in a factory in Lyon and engaging in political activity among Chinese students. In 1924 he joined the French branch of the CHINESE COMMUNIST PARTY (CCP). Called home during the first CCP-GUOMINDANG (GMD) united front (see CHINESE COMMUNIST REVOLUTION), he stopped in Moscow for several months of intensive training. In China, the party assigned him to propaganda work with the military. After the united front collapsed (1927), Deng joined the Communist underground in Shanghai and in 1929 was sent to the southwestern province of Guangxi to help organize a guerrilla movement. When the Guangxi position became untenable, Deng and his comrades fought their way through to the central Soviet base in Jiangxi in 1931. He then served the Red Army in various propaganda and organizational roles and further developed his talent

for political-military work. He also began a close relationship with MAO ZEDONG, supporting him during intra-party struggles and accompanying him on the LONG MARCH (1934–1935). During the Sino-Japanese war (1937–1945), Deng was political commissar of the Eighth Route Army's 129th Division, which engaged the Japanese in north China. At the CCP 7th party congress (1945) he was elected to the central committee (CC) for the first time. During the civil war he served with the Second Field army and participated in the crucial Huai-Hai battle. After the establishment of the People's Republic (1949) he rose rapidly in the political hierarchy: vice-premier in ZHOU ENLAI's cabinet (1952); membership in the State Planning Committee (1952–1954); finance minister (1953–1954); secretary-general of the CC (1954); membership in the CCP Politburo (1955); membership in the six-man standing committee of the Politburo and general secretary of the CCP (1956). Thus at the age of 52, relatively young for CCP leaders, Deng reached the top echelon, specializing in party discipline and economic planning.

In the early 1960s, however, Deng joined Mao's critics. This marked him for attack during the Cultural Revolution (see GREAT PROLETARIAN CULTURAL REVOLUTION). Denounced as the "number two person in authority taking the capitalist road" (his ally, LIU SHAOQI, was "number one"), Deng was dismissed from his offices and publicly humiliated. Self-criticism, including repentance at having ignored Mao and Mao's thought, was to no avail. In late 1966, Red Guards drove him through the streets of Beijing wearing a dunce-cap. His family also suffered: his eldest son, a physics student at Beijing University, jumped out of a fourth-story window to escape Red Guard tormentors. He broke his spine and was denied medical treatment. Later, Deng was permitted to nurse him, giving him sponge baths and massaging his legs. He has remained a paraplegic.

In 1973, two years after LIN BIAO's demise and after the worst phase of the Cultural Revolution, Deng began a slow ascent from the depths of degradation. Zhou Enlai needed him to help restore political and economic order. He was reinstated as a vice-premier, returned to the Politburo in 1973 and took an active role in international affairs, addressing a special session of the United Nations in 1974. The following year, while Zhou Enlai's moderates still had the upper hand, Deng became first vice-premier of the government, vice-chairman of the party and chief of staff of the military. Zhou's death (January 8, 1976) led to the return of the radicals and a second purging of Deng, now labeled an "unrepentant capitalist roader."

Mao's death (September 9, 1976) paved the way for Deng's second rehabilitation and gradual assumption of supreme power. In 1977 he was restored to his previous positions and began building support for the repudiation of radicalism that would be authorized at the 3rd plenum of the 11th CC (December 1978; see CHINESE COMMUNIST PARTY). Since then Deng's program of "reform and open door" has transformed the face of China. The stigma attached to making money has been removed, giving free rein to peasant proprietors and urban entrepreneurs. Deng has personified the new opening of China to the outside world, He visited Japan in 1978 to sign the Sino-Japanese Treaty of Peace and Friendship and traveled to the US in January, a month after normalization of diplomatic relations.

Though unprepossessing in appearance (only five feet tall) and lacking a flair for dramatics, Deng has a forceful personality. Determination, intelligence and political shrewdness enabled him to climb to the top. Adroit at neutralizing both doctrinaire leftists and "bourgeois liberals," he has not hesitated to use brute force when deemed necessary (the Tiananmen Massacre, June 1989). Yet, on the whole he has responded to deep-felt needs of the Chinese people. What they fear most is chaos, and Deng, having been twice victimized by Maoist extremism, seems to ensure it will not reappear. Like Zhou Enlai and unlike Mao Zedong, Deng spent years abroad and learned first-hand the meaning of modernization. But while economic liberalization has raised the general standard of living, there is a shadier side to the Dengist era: repression of civil rights, growing disparities in wealth, bureaucratic corruption and nepotism, of which Deng himself has been accused.

By 1980, Deng began grooming potential successors and in 1988 he resigned from all official positions, the last being chairmanship of the government military commission. (It is said that the only title he now holds is chairman of the Chinese Bridge Association. Addiction to bridge was one of the personal "crimes" for which he was excoriated during the Cultural Revolution.) Despite advanced age and growing infirmity, he is still China's paramount leader, and despite his pragmatic style Deng probably still believes that in principle, if not in practice, communism is attainable.

DENG YANDA (Teng Yen-ta) (1895–1931) Chinese revolutionary. Born in Guangdong, Deng studied at a military primary school and joined the CHINESE REPUBLICAN REVOLUTION OF 1911. He served as a GUOMINDANG (GMD) army officer, helped organize the WHAMPOA MILITARY ACADEMY (1924) and was an important commander in the GMD's military campaign to unify China (NORTHERN EXPEDITION; 1926–1927). A staunch advocate of AGRARIAN REVOLUTION and collaboration with the CHINESE COMMUNIST PARTY (CCP), Deng broke with the GMD after its purge of the Communists (1927). He also criticized the CCP for its subservience to Moscow. Returning to China in 1930 after traveling abroad for three years, he tried to organize a third party. GMD authorities arrested him on charges of treason and executed him in 1931.

DENG YINGCHAO (Teng Ying-ch'ao) (1904-1992) Chinese Communist leader. Deng was born in Nanning (Guangxi) to a Henan family. Her father, who had been a magistrate, died when she was a child and Deng was brought up by her mother, who worked as a medical practitioner and teacher. She attended school in Beijing and Tianjin from 1913 to 1920 and then taught in a primary school. While studying at a normal school in Tianjin, she joined ZHOU ENLAI and others in leading students during the MAY FOURTH MOVEMENT. Active in organizing women's groups, she joined the Communist Youth League and the CHINESE COMMUNIST PARTY (CCP) in 1925 and headed the women's section of the Tianjin CCP. That year she moved to Canton to serve on the Guangdong-Guangxi regional CCP committee and was also secretary of the women's section. Zhou Enlai had in the meantime returned from abroad and they were married in 1925. After the CCP split with the GUOMINDANG (GMD) in 1927, the two worked in the CCP underground headquarters in Shanghai before joining the Jiangxi guerrilla base in 1932. One of the few women to participate in the grueling LONG MARCH

(1934–1935), Deng was active in women's organizations during the Sino-Japanese war (1937–1945) and joined Zhou in representing the CCP at the GMD wartime capital of Chongqing. In 1945 she was elected an alternate member of the CCP central committee (CC). After the establishment of the People's Republic of China (PRC) in 1949, she held various posts in women's organizations and in the National People's Congress. She was elected to full membership in the CC and survived the Cultural Revolution (see GREAT PROLETARIAN CULTURAL REVOLUTION) (1966–1976). A prominent political figure in her own right, after Zhou's death in 1976 she continued to rise in the party hierarchy and was a strong supporter of DENG XIAOPING. She was elected to the Politburo in 1978 and named second secretary of the CCP Central Commission for Inspecting Discipline. In 1983 she was elected chairperson of the Chinese People's Political Consultative Conference, a united-front body that includes non-Communists as well as Communists. She was a major spokesperson on the Taiwan issue.

DENG ZHONGXIA (Teng Chung-hsia)   (1897–1933) Chinese revolutionary. Born to a wealthy Hunan family, Deng studied at Beijing University. Influenced by LI LAZHAO and the MAY FOURTH MOVEMENT, Deng became one of the early Chinese converts to MARXISM and a leader of the labor movement. He was the CHINESE COMMUNIST PARTY (CCP) representative on the Canton-Hong Kong strike committee (1925; see CHINESE COMMUNIST REVOLUTION). In 1933, while working in the Shanghai Communist underground and engaged in anti-Japanese activity, Deng was arrested by police in the French concession. He was extradited to Nanjing and executed by GUOMINDANG (GMD) authorities.

Deng Yingchao, 1926, a year after her marriage to Zhou Enlai

DESAI, MORAJI   (1896–1995) Indian elder statesman and devout Hindu. Introduced to politics by MAHATMA GANDHI, Desai fought for self rule against the British. He was deputy prime minister during the rule of Indira Gandhi (1967–1969) but resigned in protest against her policies. She had him jailed despite his age, but he survived 18 months in prison. He was prime minister from 1977 to 1979.

DESMOULINS, LUCIE CAMILLE SIMPLICE   (1760–1794) French politician, orator and publicist. Desmoulins stands out as the quintessential symbol of both the glory and tragedy of the FRENCH REVOLUTION of 1789. His career and the way it ended illustrate the dreams and dilemmas of many another revolutionary who came in his wake and followed his example. Born of a well-to-do provincial bourgeois family from the area of Guise, steeped in the classics and the writings of the *philosophes*, a lawyer by training and profession, he was an eloquent public speaker who, against enormous odds, was able to overcome his stutter.

Desmoulins rallied with all his heart and soul to the cause of the French Revolution in the fervent hope that it would bring about the emancipation of France and all mankind. Unfortunately, he discovered through bitter experience that the course of revolution, like the double-faced Roman God Janus whose symbolic character had captivated his imagination as a schoolboy, displays, on the one hand, the face of Virtue and, on the other, the face of Terror.

A graduate of the prestigious lycée Louis le Grand in Paris, where he formed a lifelong friendship with his fellow schoolmate ROBESPIERRE, the young Camille thrust himself into the revolutionary fray by publishing a now lost pamphlet, *La Philosophie au Peuple Francais.* This outlined a blueprint for popular sovereignty and direct democracy, along the lines laid down by his childhood idol Jean-Jacques Rousseau, the guiding spirit of his generation of revolutionaries.

What really brought him into the limelight, however, was the conspicuous role that he played in the capture of the Bastille on July 14, 1789. Desmoulins was the orator who inspired a large crowd milling about the gardens of the Palais Royal on that day to express its defiance against monarchical authority by mounting an attack against the notorious royal fortress dominating Paris, in order to arm themselves against what was perceived to be Louis XVI's impending coup d'état against the National Assembly sitting in Versailles. Although historians now agree that the rioters were in fact acting largely out of fear and were seeking to defend Paris from an armed attack, contemporaries were quick to hail Desmoulins's victory as one of the crucial turning points in the history of the revolution.

After first gravitating toward the COMTE DE MIRABEAU and his moderate circle of constitutional monarchists, Desmoulins changed his mind and veered sharply to the left to link his fortunes with the Cordeliers Club, the most radical of Parisian revolutionary factions dominated by the great figure of GEORGES DANTON, whose warm and gregarious personality made a strong impression on his own vibrant personality. Hailed by his fellow JACOBINS as a journalist of great verve and talent, Desmoulins became the key figure in presenting a positive vision of the revolution to the rest of Europe by editing, from October 1789 to July 1791, the Revolution's most widely read newspaper, *Les*

Révolutions de France et de Brabant. The paper had an enormous impact in spreading the gospel of 1789 beyond France's national borders, first to the Low Countries, then throughout the Rhineland and in northern Italy.

The last and most dramatic phase of Demoulins's life was associated with the excesses of the terror, but also with its immediate prelude, the Paris insurrection of August 10, 1792, which marked the downfall of the monarchy and the proclamation of the republic, "one and indivisible." Following the leadership of Danton, Desmoulins played a major role in exploiting the armed attack against royal authority to discredit the moderate GIRONDINS who, after the dissolution of the legislative assembly, still seemed able to retain control of a working majority in the revolutionary CONVENTION, the new parliamentary body elected in 1793.

The final twist to Desmoulins's dramatic career as a revolutionary came with the climactic year 1794, the most eventful in a decade of revolution. As his patron Danton ceased to play a leading role in the terror and came increasingly under attack from the radical Hébertists and their SANS-CULOTTES allies, Desmoulins took the decision to put himself behind a daring campaign calling for the relaxation of the terror and a return to revolutionary normalcy. First with the tacit approval of Robespierre, then with the open support of Danton, he launched, in yet another of his newspapers, *Le Vieux Cordeller*, a devastating attack on the network of spies and informers which, in the name of the revolution, was in fact turning France into a police state of unprecedented terror. In the end, however, Robespierre and a majority of the republic's governing COMMITTEE OF PUBLIC SAFETY decided to withdraw their support from Desmoulins's pleas for clemency and resolved to eliminate in one bold stroke both Danton's supporters and the radical Hébertists, in two successive purges in March and April 1794, against what today would be called the right- and left-wing deviationists from the Jacobin party line. On April 13, 1794, Desmoulins, along with Danton and the other moderates, was found guilty of conspiring against the state and sent to the guillotine. His adored wife, Lucille, who had pleaded in vain with Robespierre to spare his old schoolmate's life, followed him to the gallows.

DEUTSCH, LEV (1855–1943) Russian-Jewish revolutionary activist. Deutsch began his revolutionary career in 1874 with the populists (see POPULISM) in the Ukraine. In 1877 he organized a peasant militia to expropriate landed nobles in what was known as the "Chigirin Conspiracy." Two years later, he joined GEORGI PLEKHANOV, Pavel Axelrod and VERA ZASULICH in the "Black Repartition." In 1880 he fled Russia and in 1883 in Switzerland helped form the first Russian Marxist organization, the "Group for the Emancipation of Labor." In the controversy over a "People's Will" leaflet urging Russians to intensify the 1881 wave of anti-Jewish pogroms and turn them into a general social revolution, Deutsch took the stand that while socialism meant national and religious equality, it would be inconvenient for the moment to try and explain this to the Russian masses, as their reaction would be to claim that the revolutionaries had not only murdered the czar, but were also defenders of the Jews.

Arrested in Germany in 1884, he was returned to Russia and sentenced to 16 years imprisonment with hard labor. This was the basis for his autobiographical *Sixteen Years in Siberia.* His

escape from Siberia after 13 years earned him fame among the Russian emigrés whom he rejoined. Deutsch was once more jailed in Russia in 1906, having returned to take part in the 1905 revolution. After his release, he emigrated, first to Europe, then to New York, where he edited a socialist newspaper, *Svobodnoe slovo* (Free Word).

In the 1903 split of the Social Democratic Workers' Party of Russia, Deutsch sided with the MENSHEVIKS, together with all his earlier colleagues. Returning from America after the February 1917 revolution, Deutsch was active with Plekhanov in the *Yedinstvo* (Unity) group which tried to unite Russian Social-Democrats against what they saw as a "premature" socialist revolution. He also joined Plekhanov in supporting Russia's participation in World War I. Following the October RUSSIAN REVOLUTION OF 1917, Deutsch ceased political activity, devoting himself to editing and publishing Plekhanov's literary and publicistic heritage.

DE VALERA, EAMON (1882–1975) Irish nationalist and statesman. De Valera was born in New York City to a Spanish father and an Irish mother. His father died when he was only three and his mother returned to Ireland. He completed a degree in mathematics at University College, Dublin, and for a time taught mathematics at schools in Dublin.

Fascinated with the revival of Ireland's native language, De Valera joined the Gaelic League in 1908. As yet uninvolved in nationalist politics, he supported the Irish Parliamentary party, a moderate group advocating self-rule. In 1913, the Gaelic League, along with several other nationally-minded groups, including SINN FEIN, merged to form the Irish Volunteers, a vociferous alternative to the Parliamentary party. One of these groups was the Irish Revolutionary Brotherhood (IRB), a republican movement dedicated to armed struggle in attaining Irish independence.

The IRB gained rapid ascendancy over the other groups. De Valera was drawn to its uncompromising principles and participated in the abortive EASTER RISING of 1916 as a battalion commander, defending Boland's Mill in Dublin. His cunning military strategy was responsible for over half the British casualties and he was sentenced to death, commuted to life imprisonment only because of his American citizenship. A prison strike he organized in 1917 led to his release that same year by the new British government, intent on making a goodwill gesture to the Irish.

At that time, Irish representatives were negotiating terms for a home rule scheme to exclude the predominantly Protestant north. De Valera rejected this and attended a rival SINN FEIN congress, demanding total independence. One month after his release, he was elected to the British parliament but refused to take his seat, for that would have implied acceptance of British rule. He was also elected president of Sinn Fein and of the Volunteers. Accused in World War I of collaborating with the Germans, De Valera was returned to prison in England in 1918. While in prison, he was re-elected to parliament on behalf of Sinn Fein, his party winning 73 of the 105 seats allotted to Ireland.

The Sinn Fein delegates still at liberty chose to form their own parliament, the Dail. After De Valera managed to escape from Lincoln prison using a master key he received baked in a cake, he traveled in disguise to the United States. Upon return-

De Valera inspecting the Irish Republican Army, 1922

ing to Ireland in 1920, he was elected president of the "republic" proclaimed by the Dail.

The British government now regarded De Valera as a moderate leader with whom it could negotiate its proposal that the north be separated from the south. At the same time, IRISH REPUBLICAN ARMY militants took advantage of a British truce to import arms in case of rebellion. The negotiations with Great Britain led to the founding, in 1922, of the Irish Free State as a British dominion. Six Protestant counties were excluded from the Irish Free State. Unwilling to compromise on the unity of the island, De Valera rejected the treaty and resigned in order to form a provisional republican government. The treaty's ratification moved the fledgling Irish Free State toward civil war.

A provisional government was indeed formed by De Valera and the *Cumann na Poblachta* (League of the Republic). Although advocating a peaceful resolution to the crisis, De Valera joined the republican revolutionaries as a soldier in the civil war which flared between the factions. He was arrested by the Free State government in 1923 but was released the following year. He now abandoned armed struggle in favor of political activism, to form the Fianna Fail (Soldiers of Destiny) party and was elected to the Dail in 1927.

As a result of the 1932 elections, Fianna Fail formed the government, with De Valera (popularly called "Dev") as prime minister and foreign minister. That year, his international reputation was confirmed by his presidency of the League of Nations Council, and in 1938 he presided over the League of Nations Assembly. At home, he abolished the oath of allegiance to the British crown and suspended payment of annuities due to Britain, leading to an economic war between the two countries. In 1937 he sponsored a new constitution, changing the name of

the Irish Free State to Eire (Ireland), the constitution to apply in it "pending the reintegration of national territory." In September 1939 he declared the country's neutrality in World War II. He was the only world leader to offer condolences to Germany on HITLER's death. After the war, support for his party seesawed. He was defeated in 1948 but again served as prime minister from 1951 to 1954 and from 1957 to 1959, when he resigned to become president, serving until he was 91 in 1973.

DEVEREUX, ROBERT, EARL OF ESSEX   (1567– 1601) A courtier and close friend of Queen Elizabeth I of England, Devereux had a string of military adventures to his credit but suffered the constant opposition of the powerful Cecil faction at court. In 1599 he was sent to put down O'NEILL'S REVOLT in Ireland, but after concluding a truce he returned to England without permission. After being imprisoned and released, he led a half-hearted rebellion. He was captured and executed for treason.

DIAZ, PORFIRIO   (1830–1915) Mexican revolutionary turned president. A mestizo (half caste) of humble origin, Diaz studied for the priesthood but joined the army during the war against the US (1846–1848). That proved to be the beginning of a distinguished military career, during which he also managed to acquire a degree in law. Having fought against the French in 1861–1867, Diaz resigned his command and returned to his native province of Daxaca. However, during the 1870s he reentered politics, conspiring first against President benito juarez and later against President Sebastian Lerdo de Tejada. In 1876, he was forced to flee to the US but returned soon after and, having defeated the government forces, seized power and was formally elected president in May 1877.

As his country's ruler for almost 40 years—except for 1880–1884 he was continuously in office until 1911—Diaz instituted strong authoritarian government. His attempts to improve the economic situation by attracting foreign capital were successful at first, but after 1900 decline set in. In 1911, faced by a military revolt led by FRANCISCO MADERO, he resigned and left Mexico for exile in Paris, where he died.

DIGGERS   In English history, a small group of extremist social revolutionaries associated with the PURITAN REVOLUTION of the late 1640s. Driven by straitened economic circumstances on the one hand, and by the revolutionary pamphlets of Gerard Winstanley and William Everard on the other, the Diggers held that the revolution had been fought not just against the king but against the landlords as well. They thus sought to establish a community that would work the land in common and share its products. The authorities, greatly alarmed, took legal action against them and also instigated mob violence; after holding out for almost a year, the Diggers were dispersed.

DIMANSTEIN, SIMON   (1886–1937) Russian Communist. Dimanstein was born in the Byelorussian (now Belarus) town of Vitebsk to a devoutly religious Jewish family. He studied in a Hassidic yeshiva (Talmudic academy) and received ordination from a leading Talmudist of the day. At the same time he studied Russian and became active in the revolutionary movement. In 1904 he joined the BOLSHEVIK PARTY of Vilna, but was soon arrested for distributing propaganda to Jewish workers. He managed to escape, first to Minsk and then to Riga, but was arrested again in 1908 and sentenced to six years' hard labor in Siberia. He escaped again in 1913 and made his way to France, where he spent several years in exile.

Returning to Russia following the RUSSIAN REVOLUTION OF 1917, Dimanstein was appointed to positions that were often nominally minor but in fact gave him major influence in Lithuania, the Ukraine and Turkistan. Thus, he was appointed director of the Institute for National Minorities. Dimanstein also attempted to bring the message of communism to the Jewish masses by translating LENIN into Yiddish.

As an expert on minority issues, Dimanstein cooperated closely with Stalin in the early days of the revolution, even serving as his assistant. Following STALIN's rise to power, however, his influence decreased. He dropped from sight during the great purge of 1936 and is believed to have been executed in 1937.

DIMITRIJEVIC, DRAGUTIN   (1876–1917) Serb colonel, the Serbian general staff's chief of intelligence and founder of the BLACK HAND. Known also as Apis the Bee, he is believed to have been responsible in part for the 1903 assassination of Serbian King Alexander Obrenovic as well as of Archduke Francis Ferdinand, an act which triggered the outbreak of World War I in 1914. An indefatigable plotter against his own as well as foreign governments, he was finally arrested and shot by order of Prime Minister Pasi in 1917.

DIMITROV, GREGORI MIKHAILOVICH   (1882–1949) Bulgarian Communist leader. Dimitrov became famous when, during a COMINTERN mission to Berlin in 1933, he was arrested and accused of being responsible for the engineering of the Re-ichstag fire. After a brilliant defense, he was extradited to the USSR and later became prime minister. In 1947–1948 he was involved in the plans for a Balkan federation until forced to desist by STALIN. Dimitrov later died while under medical treatment in the USSR.

DIRECTORATE, THE   (in French, *Le Directoire*, sometimes rendered as the Directory) The name given to the executive branch of government, and hence by extension to the régime, set up after the Thermidorian reaction during the FRENCH REVOLUTION. It followed the coup of Thermidor in July 1794 which overthrew the JACOBIN dictatorship of the COMMITTEE OF PUBLIC SAFETY, and was replaced by the coup of Brumaire in November 1799, which introduced a more authoritarian Consulate with General Bonaparte as First Consul. By French standards, the régime of the Directorate (1795–1799), born out of one coup and destroyed by another, marks an endurance record during the decade of revolution. The five directors, who were jointly responsible for the conduct of the republic's affairs in the face of a Jacobin resurgence from the left and royalist conspiracies on the right, tried their best to steer a middle course of the *juste milieu*, both at home and abroad. This was only made possible by resorting to the army, which replaced the SANS-CULOTTES and Hebértistes of the Convention. The army finally intervened in Brumaire in 1799 to put an end to this revolutionary experiment.

DISSENT (Soviet Union)   Term used as a generic designation for all those groups that sought to live by principles other than those laid down by the Communist party of the Soviet Union. In Russian, such persons were referred to as *inakomysliaiu-shchye*—"those who think differently." Such persons or groups existed throughout the history of the Soviet régime. Small and local dissident groups of students and political activists are known to have existed briefly in the 1950s and early 1960s, but the phenomenon of dissent became organized, public and of politically significant proportions between the mid-1960s and the opening of the Soviet system by 1987. In that year, dissidents such as Sergei Kovalev, Sergei Grigoryants and Anatoly Shcharansky were freed, censorship of the media was abolished and there was no longer a need for conspiratorial dissent.

The dissent movement in the Soviet Union was made up of a number of independent movements that cooperated on the basis of their common defense against the Soviet authorities but were often in disagreement and even in conflict regarding the priorities of reform of the Soviet system and the tactics and strategy to be followed. There were movements for religious freedom (Baptists, Pentecostalists, Lithuanian Catholics); for national, cultural and political rights (Ukrainians, the Baltic peoples, Jews, Germans, Armenians, Crimean Tatars and Russian nationalists); for political reform, social justice and human rights (the Helsinki Group, independent trade unions, the Democratic Movement, Women's rights, the Independent Peace Movement); and a host of widely differing individual, transitory and socially marginal ideas (Esperanto, Hari Krishna, homosexuals and lesbians, punk culture, neo-Fascists, etc.).

From the mid-1960s on, when the dissent movement first surfaced in public with petitions protesting the 1966 trials of the Soviet writers Andrei Sinyavsky and Yulii Daniel, through the mid-1970s, some 2,000 activists could be identified as having signed petitions or directed open letters on political democratization and human rights to institutions in the USSR or abroad. Almost all of these were members of the intelligentsia: writers, scientists, university-trained persons in the humanities, social sciences and technical fields. Only in the free trade union movement was there a significant component of workers. The national and religious dissent movements, by their very nature, encompassed a broader cross section of society. The number and variety of dissent movements, each led by its own mentors, makes the naming of all dissident leaders impossible, but the most widely known in the movement for human rights were the academic Andrei Sakharov, the writer Alexander Solzhenitsyn, the historian Roy Medvedev and his brother Zhores, Pyotr Yakir and Pavel Litvinov.

The varied expressions of dissent are recorded in the phenomenon of *samizdat*—self-publishing. Since the Soviet régime jealously guarded its monopoly on the press and on all media of public expression, those holding different ideas could only communicate them through the writing and transmission of uncensored thought outside the institutionalized channels of communication. Thus a network of hand-typed or photographed manuscripts sprang up. A typewriter, some carbon paper and a ream of onion-skin paper, or a camera and a home darkroom plus a large measure of civic courage and dedication were all that were needed to produce a *samizdat* book, essay, manifesto or newspaper. The "press-run" of such creations sometimes reached into the thousands, as copies were re-copied and spread and the audience for the best-known of these creations ran into more than 10,000 readers. The public willing to read and pass on these publications was clearly much broader than that willing to take the effort and risk of producing *samizdat* or of signing protest petitions. The apogee of *samizdat* creation was *The Chronicle of Current Events*, which began its publication in 1968 in conjunction with the UN Year of Human Rights and evaded all attempts of the Soviet authorities to prevent its publication for nearly ten years, during which nearly 70 editions were produced and distributed within the USSR. The Chronicle acted as a clearing house for information on violation of human rights throughout the country, carefully cross-checking the accuracy of information, avoiding entrapment in the rumor mill that was so active within the Soviet Union. In many cases the Chronicle was the only source of publication of arrests and trials affecting the smaller national and religious dissent movements. The success of the Chronicle was based on a conspiratorial structured support network for the passing on of information and the acquisition of paper, as well as the actual typing and distribution. The editorial board was extremely secretive and was renewed approximately every second year as members were arrested.

Between the conspiratorial anti-régime protests of dissidents and conformist passivity lay a semi-dissident culture that operated legally in the "gray areas" between conformism and conspiracy, an area that changed with the changing outlook of the régime. Many prominent figures, such as the poet Evgenii Yevtushenko, charted a zig-zag course, often conformist but at times clearly critical if not dissident. This culture consisted of theater, journalism, film and art and, above all, bards whose songs contained ambiguous messages of criticism in satirical form, exposing topics excluded from the official culture: crime, anti-Semitism, alcoholism, official corruption and the régime's hypocrisy. Preeminent among the bards were Vladimir Vyssotsky, Bulat Okudzhava, Yulii Kim and Alexander Galich. The latter were particularly popular among the youth of the USSR in the mid- and late 1960s and those of their creations that were not printed or issued on recordings were copied on recorded tape and distributed in what became known as *magnitizdat*, from the Russian *magnitophon*—a tape recorder. Their importance lies in their ability to reach a broad audience of youth, even among solidly establishment sectors of the population. Even after the collapse of the Soviet Union, the songs of these bards retained a broad popularity.

The dissent movement, a "parallel society" that stood apart from the official norms of the régime, has, since the collapse of Communist party rule in the former Soviet Union, provided the public norms and moral leadership that are the foundation for educational, cultural and political reforms in many of the former Soviet republics.

DJAPARIDZE, PROKOFIY APRASIONOVICH (1880–1918) One of the foremost activists of the BOLSHEVIK PARTY, whose party code name was Alyosha. Djaparidze was born in the village of Sherdomet in the Kutaissi region. He studied at the Tiflis Teachers' Institute, from which he was expelled for participating in illegal Marxist youth clubs. In 1898 he joined the Tiflis organization of the Russian Social Democratic Workers party (RSDWP) and became closely acquainted with JOSEPH STALIN and other revolutionaries. In August of 1900, Djaparidze participated in organizing and conducting a mass strike of the Tiflis railroad workers led by Stalin. After the strike Djaparidze was arrested, spent 11 months in prison (in the Metechsk Castle) and was sent out to the Kutaissi region. In 1901–1904 he continued his revolutionary activities in the Kutaissi Social Democratic Organization and later was part of the Caucasus Union Committee of the RSDWP led by Stalin.

In 1904 he was sent to Baku, where he became part of the Baku Bolshevik Committee. At the same time he was the party organizer of the biggest oil-producing region of Balahan. In December of 1904 he was one of the leaders of the all-Baku workers' political strike. In 1904, along with AZIZBEKOV and others, he organized the Social Democratic Group *Gummet* for political work among the Azerbaijani factory workers. In 1906, along with SHAUMYAN, he arranged for the publication of the Bolshevik newspaper, *The Baku Worker*. In 1908 Djaparidze was arrested, but the Union of Oil Production Workers soon achieved his release. In 1909, Djaparidze conducted political work in Tiflis and Baku, where he was arrested. In 1910 he was forbidden to live in the Caucasus for five years, and in June of that year he was sent to Rostov-on-the-Don. In March 1911, at a meeting of the Don Committee of the Communist party, he was arrested again and exiled for three years to Velikiy Ystyug (the Vologod region). In 1914, Djaparidze returned to Tiflis and participated in the underground work of the Bolshevik organization. In the middle of 1915, he was arrested once again and exiled to the village of Kamenka in the Enisy region, from where he shortly escaped back to Tiflis. From there he was directed to Trapezund, where, under the name Baratov, he conducted revolutionary work among the soldiers of the Czar's army.

After the February RUSSIAN REVOLUTION OF 1917, Djaparidze came to Baku and, along with Shaumyan, Azizbekov and others, headed the revolutionary struggle.

In September of 1917, Djaparidze led an all-Baku workers strike. In March and April of 1918 he was part of the Committee for the Revolutionary Defense which supervised the struggle against the Musavat party and was part of the Baku Soviet People's Committee as commissar for internal affairs, while continuing to be chairman of the Executive Committee of the Baku Soviet. During the days of serious food shortages, he was assigned to be the commissar of provisions. After the fall of the Soviet government in Baku, he was arrested by the English, transported to Krasnovodsk, and on the night of September 20, 1918 was among the 26 commissars who were executed. Later his remains were transported to Baku.

DJILAS, MILOVAN (1911–1995) Yugoslav Communist politician, once heir-apparent to Communist leader JOSIP BROZ TITO. Born in Montenegro, one of seven children, his life was marked by war, revolution, conquest of power, disappointment and banishment.

Djilas joined the Communist underground opposition to the Yugoslav monarchy while studying law in Belgrade. In 1933 he was arrested and sentenced to three years in prison; this happened to be the same jail where, 20 years later, he would spend time as a victim of the Communist régime, even though he was one of its leaders. Released after that first imprisonment, Djilas first met Tito in 1937 and in 1938 became a member of the central committee of the Communist party of Yugoslavia and one of Tito's closest aides.

During the Axis occupation of 1941–1945, Djilas was a member of the supreme headquarters, with the rank of lieutenant general; as such he played a major part in the guerrilla war against the occupation forces. For a time he commanded the partisan forces in Montenegro. His reputation at the time was that of a charismatic, ruthless and ascetic commander. Among other things, he was responsible for negotiating local truces with the Nazis, dealing with the advisors sent to the partisans by the British and negotiating with STALIN for aid.

Following Yugoslavia's liberation in 1944–1945, Djilas ruthlessly persecuted the defeated enemies of the partisans. In 1948 he was elected a member of the Politburo and put in charge of the "agitation-propaganda" (AGITPROP) department. This post gave him total control over the country's media and effectively made him into Yugoslavia's number two man directly after Tito.

After the break between Yugoslavia and the Soviet Union in 1948, Djilas emerged as the chief denouncer of Stalinism and its practices and was branded by Moscow a top "revisionist." However by the end of 1953 a clear metamorphosis was becoming evident: he denounced the rigid one-party system that Tito had installed and called for reforms that would save the régime from total collapse. Thereupon his fall from grace was rapid. Stripped of all his functions, in 1954 he was given a three-year sentence of strict confinement. The publishing of his book, *The New Class*, which was smuggled to the west and eventually translated into 60 languages, dealt a devastating blow to the "high priests of Communism," who should be nailed to "history's cross of shame." It earned him a further sentence from which he was freed in 1961 and placed on parole. While on parole he published another book, *Conversations with Stalin* (1962), in which he branded the Soviet leader "history's greatest criminal"

but also pointed to his own party's errors. This earned him another jail sentence from which he was freed in 1966. Forbidden to publish or leave the country, he became a non-person but continued writing, ultimately publishing the *Memoirs of a Revolutionary* (1973). He was equally vehement in his denunciations of the post-Communist nationalist régime of Slobodan Milosevic; to the end he remained faithful to the idea of a democratic Yugoslavia as the only way of dealing with the country's complex ethnic problems. By the time he died, though, Yugoslavia had already disintegrated, and his passing received little official attention.

The face of protest; Djilas after a hunger strike

DO BAMA ASIAYON A Burmese nationalist organization founded on July 4, 1933 by middle-class youth attempting to direct the peasants and workers toward a struggle for independence. This organization provided the impetus for future leaders of Burma such as Thakin Nu, THAKIN AUNG SAN and THAKIN SOE to engage in political activities. In 1938, the predominantly Marxist All Burma Students' Union took over *Do Bama Asiayon*, splitting the movement. While participating in general elections, Do *Bama Asiayon* advocated extra-parliamentary measures, including participation in anti-British demonstrations and in the formation of an independent provisional government. Adopting a populist policy which appealed to the peasants, the organization also attempted to organize the oil field workers, in the process achieving widespread political mobilization (see also AUNG GYAW, MAUNG).

DOBROLIUBOV, NIKOLAI ALEKSANDROVICH (1836–1861) Russian revolutionary. Son of one of the most respected and cultured clergymen in the Nizhny Novgorod region,

Dobroliubov was sent for his education to a seminary and later to a teachers' training school. These sharpened his natural bent for examination of universal moral problems. Pursuing a higher education in history and philosophy in St. Petersburg, he was attracted to a group of students influenced by the example of the Decembrists and of dissident radicals after them. In 1855, the group published a leaflet attacking Russia's political system.

An ardent socialist at the age of 20, Dobroliubov was invited to join the editorial staff of the radical journal *Contemporary (Sovremennik)* as chief literary editor. Here he wrote prolifically for five years, exercising a tremendous influence on the younger generation, particularly as regards the need for a spiritual regeneration of the intelligentsia as a precondition for bettering the life of Russia's downtrodden population. He urged the intelligentsia to explore the social injustice that lay behind crime and poverty rather than seeking bureaucratic solutions of more efficient police and more jails. In particular, he preached the doctrine of self-help; education toward broad democratic participation in political reform. His comments on Ostrovsky's comedies (1859) and on Goncharov's "Oblomov" (1859) remain classics of Russian social criticism, urging the obligation of personal effort to a better society.

Dobroliubov developed tuberculosis and travelled to Italy seeking a cure, but returned to Russia where he died at the age of 25, nine months after the emancipation of the serfs.

DODASHVILI, SOLOMON (1805–1836) Georgian philosopher and journalist, one of the leaders of the 1832 conspiracy in Georgia of the nobility. In 1827, Dodashvili graduated the philosophy-jurisprudence department of the St. Petersburg University, where he shared the most progressive Russian ideas, those of the Decembrists, that greatly influenced the formation of his outlook. After returning to Georgia in 1828, he edited a newspaper there. The literary section of the newspaper played a significant role in promoting national ideas within Georgia.

Among the leaders of the 1832 Nobility Conspiracy, Dodashvili was the one with the most extreme ideas. He stood for abolition of the monarchy and serfdom and the establishment of a republic. He considered universal education a mandatory condition for the better future of the country. Following the failure of the conspiracy, Dodashvili was transferred to Viatka in Northern Russia, where he died of tuberculosis.

Dodashvili's ideas exerted great influence on the formation of the Georgian national movement and the outlook of generations to come.

DOMINICAN REPUBLIC, 1930 COUP Until 1930, the history of the Dominican Republic had been marked by endless disturbances, revolutions and general chaos. In February 1930, in what at first looked simply like another coup, the commander of the national guard, General Rafael Leuidas Trujillo Molina, overthrew President Horacio Vasquez and assumed power himself. The coup in question proved to be a turning point in the history of the republic since Trujillo, working through various members of his family, was able to provide stability and rule the country until he was assassinated in 1961.

DONG BIWU (Tung Pi-wu) (1886–1975) Chinese Communist leader. Born to a "landless gentry" family in Hubei and educated in both classical and modern studies, Dong participated in the chinese republican revolution of 1911, joined the tongmenghui, and supported sun yat-sen's post-revolutionary efforts. In 1917, he received a law degree from Tokyo Law College. The may fourth movement convinced him of the need to mobilize the masses, and he became a founding member of the chinese communist party (CCP) in 1921. When the first guomindang-CCP united front collapsed (1927), he fled abroad and studied at Lenin University in Moscow (1928–1932). He joined the Jiangxi soviet (1932) and participated in the long march (1934–1935). At Yan'an, he headed the Communist party school and later served as liaison officer with the Guomindang (GMD). In 1945, he was the only Communist delegate to the San Francisco UN conference. As an elder statesman, after the founding of the People's Republic (1949), Dong held important party and governmental posts, e.g., senior vice-premier, president of the Supreme People's Court, membership in the CCP central committee and Politburo, and vice-chairman of the People's Republic (1959).

DRAHOMANOV, MYHAILO (1841–1895) Ukrainian historian and ethnographer. Born in Poltava, Drahomanov graduated from Kiev University and took up a teaching post there. In 1876 he was dismissed and exiled for his advocacy of national cultural autonomy for the Ukraine. As head of the Ukrainian Federalists, a moderate socialist party, he was one of the most influential political theorists of the Ukraine before 1917. His creed was based on the concept that freedom and socialism could only be realized together, and that a "community of free communities," allowing each nation its own expression, was the best structure for a multicultural society. His emphasis on Ukrainian national interests caused friction with the Russian emigrés in Geneva.

Drahomanov remained in exile in Switzerland and Bulgaria to his death. He taught history, engaged in ethnographic research, particularly in the realm of Ukrainian folk culture and was a central figure in the Ukrainian emigré press, editing the Ukrainian-language socio-political journal, *Hromada (Society)*.

DUBCEK, ALEXANDER (1921–1993) Czechoslovak Communist reformer, as First Secretary of the Czechoslovak Communist party (CzCP), Dubcek was the leader and hero of the PRAGUE SPRING OF 1968. Born in Slovakia, he worked as an apprentice machine fitter and later as a skilled worker in the Skoda works during World War II. From 1939 on he was a member of the CzCP. Active in the Slovak resistance in 1944, he entered into full party activity in 1944, spending the mid-1950s in further political education in the Soviet Union. From 1958, he was a member of the central committee of the Slovak CP and Deputy of the National Assembly, and between 1963–1968 was the highest ranking party leader in Slovakia. In January 1968 he was unexpectedly appointed as successor to the hardliner Antony Novotny, as First Secretary of the CzCP. His personal modesty and style immediately made him popular, although he had been largely unknown to the public until then. Though he never renounced his Marxist faith, he promoted "socialism with a human face" and led the political-intellectual "Spring of Prague." Up to the Soviet invasion of August 1968 he believed that the Soviet leadership understood his positive aims of reforming the Communist system. His reform program was based on deep Marxist and humanist values, on the perception that the system would be workable if only the Communist party adopted internal restructuring and pluralism. He promoted the reforms as the only true option for the victory of socialism and claimed that the reforms did not endanger the régime. Following the Soviet invasion of August 20–21, 1968, he was arrested briefly and then released, remaining as First Secretary of the party until April 1969. Expelled from the party in 1970 by the HUSAK leadership, he found employment with the Slovak ministry of forestry and became a non-person until 1989, when he allied himself with VACLAV HAVEL, becoming chairman of the federal parliament and leader of the Slovak Social Democratic party. He was opposed to the break-up of Czechoslovakia, but his moral voice faded as he was associated with attempts to reform communism in a public atmosphere that had no need for reform Communists. He died in November 1993 as a result of a car crash, a tragic death after a tragic attempt to reform communism.

DUC D'ORLÉANS   see ORLÉANS, PHILLIPPE, DUKE OF.

DUMOURIEZ, CHARLES FRANCOIS DU PÉRIER (1739–1823) French general and politician, an early example of general-politicians produced by the FRENCH REVOLUTION of 1789, who sought to combine their positions in the army with political intrigue, not unlike Hoche, Pichegru, Bernadotte, MURAT and most notably Napoleon Bonaparte himself. Dumouriez can be seen as a modern precursor of 20th-century military strongmen who rose to power as a result of the forces released by revolution and counterrevolution.

Following a successful career of political intrigue, including various secret diplomatic missions under the *ancien régime* as the protege of Choiseul, chief minister under Louis XV, Dumouriez cast his lot with the cause of the revolution and soon gravitated to the circle of Lafayette, the Comte de MIRABEAU and other politicians belonging to "the committee of thirty," a secret revolutionary faction in the pay of the Duc d'Orleans, who was conspiring to force the abdication of his cousin Louis XVI in order to seize the throne in the name of the revolution. Promoted to lieutenant general by his GIRONDIN friends in 1791, he became Louis XVI's minister of war and foreign affairs and virtual head of the Girondist war cabinet appointed in March 1792.

Forced into resignation along with his ally Roland and the other Girondin ministers as a result of the declaration of war in April, he immediately took personal command of the Army of the North in the national emergency posed by the creation of a formidable coalition of Austrians and Prussians. He won the two great battles of Valmy in September and Jemappes in November 1792, thus opening the way for the liberation of the Austrian Netherlands (the Low Countries) from the Habsburgs. Not unlike his political ally, Lafayette, who betrayed the revolution by going over to the Austrians, Dumouriez also began contemplating a defection: first to the Prussians, then to the Austrians. During the dramatic months that followed the fall of Louis XVI and the proclamation of the JACOBIN republic in September, he opened peace talks with the enemy. He compounded his treachery with a scheme that would have restored Louis XVI to the throne by marching his army against Paris. At the same time, he conspire to carve out a military fiefdom for himself out of a new state to be created out of Belgium and Holland, a

scheme that was in fact implemented under the restored House of Orange at the Congress of Vienna in 1815.

His plans were aborted after his invasion of Holland was halted and checked at the battle of Neerwinden of April 5, 1793, he himself having dramatically arrested the deputies who had been sent by the CONVENTION to arrest him. He finally deserted to the Austrians in April 1793, almost one year to the day after the outbreak of the great revolutionary war he had himself launched, and rallied unequivocally to the counterrevolution. He refused an invitation to return to France during the Bourbon restoration and spent the rest of his life in exile in England.

DUPONT DE L'EURE, JACQUES CHARLES   (1767–1855) A prominent magistrate who sat in the parliament of Normandy under the *ancién régime*, Dupont de l'Eure rallied to the FRENCH REVOLUTION in the summer of 1789 and became a deputy in the Constituent Assembly after the Estates General convened by Louis XVI in Versailles in May 1789 resolved to draft a new constitution to embody the principles of the revolution.

A distinguished constitutional lawyer, Dupont de l'Eure helped to draft the first constitution of the revolution and was dismayed to see it overthrown in September 1792 by the revolutionary convention which, in defiance of democratic principles, delegated its full powers to the JACOBIN dictatorship of the COMMITTEE OF PUBLIC SAFETY. He again had a hand in drafting the constitution of the DIRECTORATE in 1794 and 1795 and was elected to his home district of the Eure to sit as a deputy in its lower house, the Council of the Five Hundred, which was dissolved by General Napoleon Bonaparte in the coup d'état of Brumaire in November 1799.

Under the Empire, he became a member of the legislative assembly, earning the gratitude of the emperor, who nominated him to the chamber of deputies which was hastily convened during the Hundred Days. Dupont de l'Eure was among a handful of deputies who voted for the succession of Napoleon II, the emperor's son, after Napoleon's second abdication of 1815.

He later played a part in the July 1830 revolution as a member of its first government, along with his old friend Lafayette, and also rallied to the republicans who tried to established a conservative republic after the February 1848 Revolution (see REVOLUTIONS OF 1848).

DUVALIER, FRANCOIS   (1907–1971) Haitian political leader. Trained as a physician, Duvalier rose through his country's health service and also contributed to the daily *Action Nationale* by writing articles on black nationalism and voodoo as the twin pillars of Haitian culture. From 1948 he was minister of public health; however, when a military coup under Paul E. Magloire overthrew President Estime in 1950, Duvalier left the government and started working for the American Sanitary Mission in Haiti.

By 1954, Duvalier had become the leader of the opposition to Magloire and was living underground. In December of that year he and his followers organized a coup that led to Magloire's resignation.

During the succeeding three years, Haiti had six different governments; finally, in December 1957, Duvalier himself was elected president. Once in power, he reduced the size of the army, set up his own private paramilitary organization in the form of the Tontons Macoutes or Bogeymen, and moved steadily toward an absolute dictatorship based on police intimidation and voodoo ritual. Known as "Papa Doc," he remained in office until his death in 1971, when he was succeeded by his son, Jean-Claude Duvalier, nicknamed "Baby Doc."

DU WENXIU (Tu Wen-hsiu) (d. 1873) Chinese Muslim rebel. Taking advantage of the TAIPING REBELLION, Muslims in the southwest province of Yunnan rose in revolt in 1855. In 1856, Du established an Islamic kingdom, called Pingnan ("Pacification of the South"), in western Yunnan and took the title of Sultan Suleiman. Arms and ammunition from Burma helped prolong the revolt, sometimes called the Panthay Rebellion, from the Burmese term for "Muslim." Millions perished before the revolt was crushed. In 1873, when his capital, Dali, fell, Du committed suicide.

DYBENKO, PAVEL Y. (1889–1938) BOLSHEVIK political and military leader. Dybenko joined the Bolsheviks in 1912, while in the Russian navy. In July 1917 he was imprisoned for helping lead the Kronstadt naval garrison in the "July Days" riots. His successes in bringing the sailors of the Baltic fleet over to the Bolshevik side in the October RUSSIAN REVOLUTION OF 1917 led to his appointment as people's commissar for the navy in the first Soviet government.

During the civil war he commanded an army in the Ukraine. In 1921, he headed the command of the Kronstadt garrison, after the suppression of the anti-Bolshevik revolt there. Later he was involved in military training, particularly in the field of artillery.

Dybenko was executed in the Stalinist purges, and served as the prototype of the Bolshevik sailor in Koestler's *Darkness at Noon.*

DZERZHINSKY, FELIKS EDMUNDOVICH (1877–1926) Soviet Communist politician. A member of the Social Democratic Party's Central Committee from 1906, Dzerzhinsky was exiled to Siberia but escaped after the February RUSSIAN REVOLUTION OF 1917 and in October voted with LENIN in favor of a Bolshevik uprising against the provisional government. He was rewarded by being made head of the Cheka (the All-Russian Extraordinary Commission for Combatting Counterrevolution and Sabotage), or secret police, and in this capacity waged a ruthless campaign of terror against the new régime's opponents.

Dzerzhinsky was commissar of transport (1921) and chairman of the council of the national economy (1924). At the same time, Dzerzhinsky headed the central committee's subcommittee for party discipline, which was a post he used in order to help STALIN exterminate his opponents.

E

EASTER RISING In Irish history, a rebellion against British rule that took place on Easter day, April 24, 1916, and was defeated. The leaders of the insurrection were Patrick Pearse and Tom Clarke; the organization which they headed was the Irish Republican Brotherhood, itself part of the so-called Irish Volunteers. In addition, there was the so-called Irish Citizen Army, whose membership consisted largely of Dublin workers.

Originally the plan was for the uprising to be national in scope. However, security was extremely lax; everybody in Dublin—as well as the British, through their intelligence service—knew what was coming. When the British succeeded in intercepting a consignment of German arms earmarked for the rebels, the leaders of the Brotherhood outside Dublin cancelled whatever moves they had been planning. However, the Irish Volunteers and the Irish Citizen Army went ahead on their own. With a total force of about 1,700 men, they rose and seized the Dublin Post Office as well as several other strategic buildings.

While Pearse read a proclamation on the founding of an Irish Republic, British troops arrived on the scene. Using artillery, they easily recaptured the post office as well as other buildings and, after about a week of fighting in the streets, restored order. Pearse and 14 other leaders of the uprising were court-martialled and hanged in Dublin Castle. In retrospect, though, the incident proved perhaps the most decisive single event in Ireland's long struggle for independence from Britain. It showed the British that, no matter what, their rule would not be accepted by the people. Negotiations were thus resumed almost immediately after World War I ended, although these were still accompanied by a guerrilla campaign. When the Irish Free State was founded in December 1921, its first prime minister, EAMON DE VALERA, was the senior survivor of the Rising.

EAST TIMOR UPRISING In 1974, in the wake of the Officers' Coup (see PORTUGAL, REVOLTS AND REVOLUTIONS IN—1974

Irish rebels barricading themselves in Dublin's streets during the Easter Rebellion

OFFICERS REVOLUTION) and the establishment of democracy in Portugal, that country offered self-determination to its colonial possessions, among them East Timor in the Indonesian archipelago. The islanders were divided as to what they should choose. The two main political parties, the *Frente Revolucionário de Este Timor Independente* (Revolutionary Front for an Independent East Timor—FRETILIN) and the *Uni o Democrática Timorense* (Timorese Democratic Union—UDT) both favored independence, although the UDT supported the gradual transfer of powers and the formation of a Portuguese Community of former colonies, while FRETILIN demanded immediate self-rule. There were also several smaller groups, most notably the AS-SOCIAÃO o Popular Democrátic Timorense (Timorese Popular Democratic Association—Apodeti), which favored integration into Indonesia. By 1975, FRETILIN and the UDT had formed a fragile coalition, aimed at achieving independence within five to ten years.

By autumn, however, the coalition broke down, and the UDT, fearing that FRETILIN would take advantage of the tense situation in order to seize power, engineered a coup of its own. Fighting immediately broke out between the warring factions and the Portuguese withdrew from the capital, Dili. The UDT was then repulsed from Dili, but it reorganized in the Indonesian half of the island (West Timor) and declared itself in favor of integration.

For some time, FRETILIN's leadership expected the Portuguese to return to the island and reestablish order; until then, they set about forming their own provisional government. Finally, by late November 1975, it became apparent that the Portuguese had no intention of returning and FRETILIN declared the independent Republic of East Timor. Nine days later, Indonesian troops invaded the island, backed by the UDT and APODETI: East Timor was incorporated into Indonesia in 1976. Meanwhile, FRETILIN supporters retreated to the countryside, where they carried out an armed struggle against the occupation. The results were disastrous. Despite world condemnation, Indonesia took the harshest measures against the insurgents, often violating their human rights in the most brutal fashion. In 1981, for instance, during *Operasi Keamanan* (Operation Security), they used human shields when attacking FRETILIN strongholds.

According to some estimates, about 200,000 people were killed in the civil war, one-third of the country's population before independence. But no one can be certain as to what really happened during the uprising. East Timor is geographically remote and the Indonesian authorities imposed a clamp-down on press reports from the island.

Although the rebellion seems to have been quelled, there are still simmering issues that might cause it to flare again. In 1989, Australia and Indonesia signed the Timor Gap Zone of Cooperation treaty, agreeing to jointly explore and exploit the rich crude oil deposits in the territorial waters of East Timor. Again in 1991, the country seemed on the brink of war after Indonesian police opened fire on a memorial service in the capital of Dili, killing some 200 protesters. Portugal has made persistent calls on the Indonesian government to recognize East Timor's independence and the United Nations has debated the East Timor question on numerous occasions, but there seems to be no solution in the offing.

ECUADOR, COUPS IN

Independence Struggle of 1845–1890. In 1845, a new constitution was adopted in Ecuador, in which liberal and anticlerical ideas were endorsed. The president's term was set at four years. Vincent Romón Roca was elected president, but the country plunged into revolution because of the radical legislature. Revolution, would last until 1860. In 1850, a coup brought Diego Noboa to the presidential seat. New constitutions were drawn up in 1851 and 1852. The latter one provided for the expulsion of the Jesuits and the abolition of slavery. José María Urbina was elected president in 1852 and four years later Francisco Robles. The country was in chaos, Peru blockaded Guayaquil and General Guillermo Franco, who was in command there, was forced to sign away the sovereignty of the province of Azuay to Peru. General Flores and General Gabriel García Moreno joined forces. Together they defeated Franco and recaptured the port of Guayaquil. General Flores retired and García Moreno was elected president of Ecuador in 1861, under yet another constitution.

Jerónimo Carrión was elected president in 1865 but difficulties with the Congress and with García Moreno forced him to resign in 1867. Two years later, García Moreno was again elected president of Ecuador. In order to perpetuate himself in power, he amended the constitution, providing a six-year presidential term and allowing for his immediate reelection. Despite strong opposition from liberals and anticlericals, García Moreno was reelected in 1875. His 14 years of direct or indirect power ended on August 6, 1875, when he was assassinated. There followed 20 years of anarchy and constant presidential changes.
Revoltution of 1905. General Leónidas Plaza Gutiérrez ruled the country peacefully from 1901 to 1905. His successor, Lizardo García, was overthrown by a revolution in 1905. In January 1906, Eloy Alfaro became president again. A new constitution was written, providing a four-year term for the presidency as well as the direct vote of the people. There would be no immediate reelection of the president, a bicameral legislature was to be installed and education would be in the hands of laymen. Alfaro was inaugurated in 1907. Liberal opposition forced him to resign in 1911. He left the country but was persuaded to return. He was assassinated the following January.
Upheavals of 1912–1940. Anarchy and rapid presidential changes followed the assassination of Alfaro in Ecuador. Leónidas Plaza Gutiérrez was again elected president. His successor, Gonzalo Córdoba was deposed in 1918 and there followed a period of government juntas, constantly being changed, in power. In 1926, the army named Dr. Isidro Ayora president of Ecuador. A new constitution was established in 1929 and Dr. Ayora was again elected to the executive seat. The world economic crisis resulted in criticism of Ayora. He resigned in 1930. Colonel Luis Larrea Alba became president and a new era of revolutions and strikes followed. Federico Páez was elected in 1935, but opposition to his harsh economic measures against left-wing activists caused his resignation in 1937 and Alberto Enríquez assumed the presidential seat.

EGMOND, LAMORAAL (1522–1568) Flemish nobleman, early leader of the REVOLT OF THE NETHERLANDS against Spain. A famous general, Egmond commanded the forces of Emperor Charles V, the Holy Roman Emperor, in their victory over those of Henry II of France at St. Quentin in 1557; in 1559, Charles's son Philip II made him chief executive of the provinces of Flanders and Artois as well as a member of the council of the Netherlands that governed the county as a whole.

However, Egmond and other leading noblemen resisted the absolutist tendencies of Philip's government and his tendency to rely on Spaniards as his deputies in the Netherlands. While maintaining "loyal" opposition and taking an oath of allegiance to the king, Egmond withdrew from the council of state and went to his own country of Flanders, where he severely suppressed a Calvinist uprising. Failing to see the danger when Philip's new commander, the Duke of Alba, arrived in the Netherlands, Egmond remained in the country and was arrested and executed as a rebel. His execution, with that of his comrade FILIPS VAN MONTMORENCY HOORNE, marked the real beginning of the 80-year struggle that ultimately led to the emergence of the Netherlands as an independent country.

EGYPT, REBELLIONS, REVOLTS AND REVOLUTIONS
Egypt and Babylon Rebellion of 486–481 B.C. Darius I began preparations for the invasion of Greece in 489 B.C., but was interrupted by a rebellion in Egypt in October 486 B.C. In November 486 B.C. Darius died, leaving the problem of rebellious Egypt to his successor, Xerxes. The rebellion was suppressed by Xerxes only in January 484 B.C., and Egypt was severely punished by him. The property of many temples was confiscated, the Xerxes was not crowned the Egyptian Pharaoh, and this country became one of the regular satrapies of the Persian Empire.

Now Xerxes was ready to proceed with the preparations for the Greek expedition, but already in Tammuz (June–July) 484 B.C. Babylon rebelled, under the leadership of Bel-shimani. Though this rebellion was quelled in two weeks, Babylon rebelled again in August 482 B.C., this time under the leadership of Shamash-riba. The Second Babylonian uprising was more successful since the main Persian army was already in Asia Minor on its way to Greece. Xerxes dispatched Megabyzus (Bagabukhsha) against the rebels. The siege of Babylon continued for seven months and the city was taken in March 481 B.C. As in Egypt the punishment was severe, the temple of the Babylonian national god Marduk, Esagila, was plundered, and the golden stature of Marduk himself was taken to Persepolis, though, contrary to widespread view, Esagila was not destroyed or closed. From 481 B.C. Xerxes ceased to be called "King of Babylon," but was called only "King of Countries."

Thus, both Egypt and Babylon lost their special position within the Persian Empire as separate kingdoms united with Persia by the person of the king, but became regular satrapies. However, if for Egypt this was only the beginning of its long struggle for independence from Persia, for Babylon the rebellion of Shamash-riba was the last attempt to overthrow a foreign rule in the long history of this country. The rebellions of 486–481 B.C. in Egypt and Babylon gave Themistocles time to complete an Athenian naval program that was initiated in 487 B.C.—before the Persian invasion.

Revolt of 671–665 B.C. King Esarchaddon of Assyria conquered Lower Egypt in 671 B.C. and Takharqa, king of Egypt of the 25th Ethiopian (Nubian) dynasty, retreated to Upper Egypt. Unlike later conquerors of this country, Esarchaddon was not crowned as an Egyptian Pharaoh, but transformed Egypt into an Assyrian province ruled jointly by Assyrian officials and 20 local princes. His conquest was short-lived, however, and after his departure from Egypt Takharqa returned and drove the Assyrians out of the country. In 669 B.C., Esarchaddon prepared a new expedition to Egypt, but died on his way at Kharran.

Esarchaddon's successor, Ashurbanipal, assisted by 22 kings of Syria and Palestine, invaded Egypt shortly after his ascension. Takharqa was defeated, driven out of Memphis and fled to the Egyptian Thebes (Biblical No-Amon). This time the Assyrian army followed him to this ancient capital of Upper Egypt. Takharqa abandoned Thebes and crossed the Nile. However, while Ashurbanipal occupied Thebes, or on his way back, the news of a conspiracy between Takharqa and 20 princes of the Delta reached him. The conspirators were arrested and deported to Assyria, but one of them, Necho, prince of Sais, was forgiven and appointed as Assyrian viceroy of Egypt. This meant abandonment of Esarchaddon's policy of direct rule over Egypt.

In 665 B.C., Takharqa died and his nephew Tanut-Amon invaded Egypt, again driving the Assyrians and their Egyptian collaborators out of Memphis. In his second Egyptian expedition, Ashurbanipal took Memphis and marched to Thebes again, this time destroying the city. With this episode, Nubian involvement in Egyptian affairs came to an end.

By 655 B.C., Necho's son, who bore the Assyrian name of Nabu-shezibanni, with the help of Carian and Greek mercenaries (according to Herodotus), became an independent ruler under the Egyptian name of Psammetichus I. His successors, the Egyptian kings of the 26th dynasty, tried to conceal their origin as collaborators with foreign conquerors, and the Assyrian conquest of Egypt was never mentioned in Egyptian historiography.

Rebellion of 460–454 B.C. This rebellion was initiated in the western Egyptian delta by a Libyan—Inarus, son of Psammetichus—in 460 B.C. Later he was joined by Amyrtaeus of Sais. The rebels soon took control of the entire delta and northern Nile valley, but Memphis and upper Egypt remained under Persian control. The Persian satrap of Egypt, Achemenes, brother of Xerxes I and uncle of King Artaxerxes I, was defeated and killed by the rebels in the battle at Papremis in 460 B.C.

After this victory, Inarus asked for help from Athens. In 459 B.C., the Athenians sent Egypt a navy of 200 ships. Athenian ships entered the Nile and destroyed a Persian fleet, then the combined forces of Athenians and the Egyptian rebels took Memphis. The remnants of the Persian garrison, together with Persian civilians and loyalist Egyptians, retreated to the White Wall citadel.

The siege of the White Wall continued until 456 B.C., when Artaxerxes I sent Megabyzus (Bagabukhsha), satrap of Syria, to Egypt with a large ground force and Phoenician fleet. The Athenian fleet was completely destroyed and Memphis retaken by the Persians. Inarus, with the remnants of his supporters and Athenians, fled to the island of Prosopitis in the western delta.

In 454 B.C., the Persians succeeded in connecting the island to the mainland and invaded it with their ground forces. Inarus capitulated and only a small group of Athenians succeeded in escaping to Cyrena. Meanwhile, a reinforcement of 50 Athenian ships reached Egypt unaware of the fate of their compatriots there. They were attacked by the Persians from land and sea and destroyed.

Thus, after four years of rebellion, the Persians regained control of Egypt. Only Amyrtaeus remained independent, hiding in the marshes of the western delta. Megabyzus was recalled to Syria and Arsames (Arshama), grandson of Darius I, was appointed as the new satrap of Egypt.

Rebellion of 404–342 B.C. Darius II died in March 404 B.C. and according to Manetho was the last Pharaoh of the 27th Persian dynasty. After him Amyrtaeus II, descendant of Amyrtaeus I of Sais, who had maintained a pocket of resistance in the western delta after the rebellion of Inarus, established his own 28th dynasty. Egypt was lost to Persia for 60 years and was reconquered only in 342 B.C., 10 years before the Macedonian invasion.

The Jewish garrison of Elephantine in Upper Egypt remained loyal to the Persians until 401 B.C., when Artaxerxes II sent Abrocomus with a large army from Syria against Egypt, but it was during this year that the revolt of CYRUS THE YOUNGER began and this force was diverted to fight against the more dangerous enemy. Thus, by 400 B.C. all of Egypt was under the control of Amyrtaeus. In 399 B.C., he was overthrown by Nepherites I of Mendes, founder of the 29th dynasty. It was probably during his reign that the Jewish garrison of Elephantine was finally dissolved.

In 393 B.C., Achoris, son of Nepherites I, became Pharaoh. In 385–383 B.C., the Persians made an attempt to reconquer Egypt but Achoris took the initiative and even seized Tyre, the central base of the Phoenician fleet in the eastern Mediterranean. The successors of Achoris, Psammuthes and Nepherites II, ruled only for one year and four months, and in 380 B.C. Nectanebes I of Sebennytus founded a new, 30th dynasty. In 373 B.C., a large Persian army under the command of Pharnabazus invaded Egypt, but after initial successes it retreated with great losses.

In 362 B.C., Tachos, son of Nectanebes I, inherited the throne of Egypt. He planned to conduct an offensive war against Persia in Syria and Palestine. For this purpose he hired 10,000 Athenian mercenaries under the command of Chabrias and 1,000 Spartans led by the aged Spartan king Agesilaus. In order to finance this army, Tachos confiscated the property of Egyptian temples and introduced new taxes. In response to these measures, even though Tachos conducted a successful offensive in Syria, Egypt rebelled against him, under the leadership of his nephew, Nectanebes II. Chabrias remained loyal to Tachos, but Agesilaus supported the rebels. When the situation became hopeless for Tachos, he fled to Persia, while Chabrias and the mercenaries returned to Athens. Meanwhile, a new rebellion had been launched in Mendes in the delta, against Nectanebes II. This time Agesilaus remained loyal to him and the rebellion was suppressed, but Nectanebes II had to abolish the reforms of Tachos and quit his offensive against Persia.

Artaxerxes II died in December 359 B.C. and his son Ochus became king under the name of Artaxerxes III. In 350 B.C., he made his first attempt to invade Egypt but in 349 B.C. Sidon and other Phoenician cities rebelled with Egyptian support. In 346 B.C., Nectanebes II sent Mentor from Rhodus with 4,000 Greek mercenaries to Sidon, but in the next year Tennes, king of Sidon, together with Mentor, betrayed the rebels and helped the Persians to take the city. In 344 B.C., Artaxerxes III hired 64,000 Greek mercenaries in Thebes, Argos and Asia Minor and sent them in 343 B.C. against Egypt. Nectanebes II met this army at Pelusium with 60,000 Egyptians and 20,000 Greek mercenaries. Mentor, who had served Nectanebes II earlier, disclosed to the Persians the plan of the fortifications of Pelusium, but the siege of the city continued until the Persian seaborne attack in the delta. Nectanebes II had to retreat in order to defend Memphis, but his Greek mercenaries crossed over to the enemy and in 342 B.C. the Persians conquered Memphis and the rest of Egypt. Nectanebes II fled to Nubia, where he remained as an independent ruler until 341 B.C.

Egypt Revolutioln of 1952 (July 1952 Revolution). On July 23, 1952 a group of Egyptian military officers, the FREE OFFICERS, successfully launched a military coup in Egypt. Over a relatively short period of time, the officers established a régime that was fundamentally different from those which had existed in Egypt since the early 19th century. The political, economic and social upheaval in the country—which included increased Arab nationalism and the promotion of Arab civilization, and which coincided with the military coup—was evidence of much more that a military coup and the outbreak of a large-scale revolution. During the 1940s, Egypt was in financial and political straits. Moreover, the social rift between the wealthy upper class that often associated with the royalty, the destitute lower class and the groups of immigrants, had widened. This internal turmoil was manifested in increased acts of violence, distorted parliamentary processes and a lack of public regard and faith in the corrupt royal house and in the existing political parties. The continued presence of the British military in Egypt only suppressed the tense reality.

During the first stage of the coup, the Free Officers did not adopt any strong ideological stand. Their goals and priorities were yet undefined. Their central aim was to bring down the monarchical régime, which to them was a symbol of their country's hardships, and to achieve the removal of the remaining British troops in Egypt. These two goals were indeed carried out within two years, but by then the revolutionary rulers had extended their domestic and foreign aspirations.

A direct result of the coup was the militarization of the bureaucracy and the government, specifically on the senior levels. After the coup had been carried out, a Revolutionary Command Council (RCC) was established. This was made up of 13 revolutionary leaders and soon became the executive arm of the government and ultimately the State's central power. Major-General MUHAMMAD NAGIB was elected Egypt's first president and some months later also became the country's prime minister. His colleague—and later foe—Lieutenant Colonel GAMAL ABDUL NASSER, was deputy prime minister and minister of interior, although he gained most of his power through his position as chairman of the RCC. ABDUL HAKIM 'AMER, a confidant of Nasser, was elected commander in chief. During the summer and fall of 1952, the RCC ordered a complete purge of the military and government. During this time, ministers, top military officers and their confidants were discharged from their positions. Already at this stage, the foundations were being set for authoritarian rule in Egypt.

As the Free Officers took over the different governmental posts, the new rulers had to deal with many internal and external challenges. Within Egypt a struggle developed between the revolutionary government and various political and economic opposition powers, the latter headed by the principal wealthy landowners and the Wafd party. An abortive attempt was made to integrate the MUSLIM BROTHERHOOD in the new government, but this merely led to long-lasting hostilities. The officers felt their aspirations to throw off the former régime and its characteristics were threatened by the Muslim Brotherhood and the other oppositional factors. The revolutionary rulers fought the political and economic opposition with legislation and open suppression. In January 1953, all parties were disbanded and all political activism beyond the government was outlawed. A year later, the government declared the Muslim Brotherhood an illegal organization and the majority of its leaders were arrested. Isolated attempts were made to demonstrate against these steps, but these were suppressed with an iron hand.

At the same time, the new government began a program of agrarian reform. Large tracts of agricultural land were confiscated from wealthy landowners and reallocated to farmers who owned no fields. In the name of social justice the officers, most of whom belonged to the lower middle classes, requested that the foundations of the political-economic elite be dismantled. Thus, the fact that agrarian reform was relevant to the day-to-day lives of millions of peasants in Egypt was utilized as a channel of achieving legitimacy. In retrospect, however, the achievements of the agrarian reform were minimal, as compared to the expected results.

The monarchy having been abolished, Egypt was proclaimed a presidential republic on July 18, 1953 and Muhammad Nagib was installed as president. This reform, alongside the many domestic challenges in Egypt, was carried out in the shadow of a power struggle between President Nagib and the president of the RCC, Nasser. The personal conflict between the two was a reflection of the internal dispute among the new régime's leaders regarding the revolution's goals and their fulfillment. Nagib supported reinstatement of a civilian government and opposed the manner of contending with the social and political powers of Egypt. The Muslim Brotherhood made an abortive attempt on Nasser's life, and this led to the RCC's and Nasser's decision, with the support of 'Amer's army, to oust Nagib (November 14, 1954), put him under house arrest, declare Nasser president and escalate the struggle against the Muslim Brotherhood and other rivals of the officers' government. At this point, these opposition movements were regarded as enemies of the revolution.

In its foreign relations, the government had to navigate its way with caution against the background of the cold war which dictated the international relations of that period. From the first, the leaders of the revolutionary government had to formulate a stand concerning a large number of foreign issues, including the government's policy regarding the Great Powers, the Arab countries and the conflict with Israel. However the continued presence of British forces in Egypt constituted the issue of the highest priority in the agenda of foreign affairs. Considering themselves the representatives of Egyptian nationalism, the officers wanted to oust the long-standing British presence in Egypt as quickly as possible. An agreement that was finally reached with Britain (October 19, 1954) gave evidence of increased Egyptian independence. The agreement provided for British forces to be removed from Egypt within 20 months. The British base on the Suez Canal would be activated only in a case of emergency, the canal would be declared an international passage and Sudan's status would be left to the Sudanese people to determine. Late in 1954, after the agreement between Britain and Nasser succeeded in restraining the ruling forces, a new stage in the July Revolution began. Over the following 16 years, Nasser's personality was the primary factor in Egypt's policy-making. His charisma as an Arab and Egyptian leader became increasingly influential in Egypt and outside. Two guiding factors shaped his domestic and external policies: a view of Egypt as the heart of the Arab nation, and the struggle against imperialism. The government then undertook the development of a collective national consciousness—which was essential to the revolutionary society and government—and pressed home the importance of a struggle against imperialism. To Nasser, Egypt, given its status and heritage, was meant to play a leading role in such important struggles. Accordingly, the régime in Cairo differentiated between revolutionary régimes that were to be supported and those that were "reactionary" and imperialist, which were to be suppressed. Among the latter were included the sovereign rulers of most Arab countries, western countries and Israel. The Nasserist movement supported those groups that wished to eliminate the reactionary parties in the Arab countries, against the backdrop of the development of a "cold Arab war" and the escalation of tension between Egypt and the western countries.

The nationalization of the Suez Canal, Nasser's success in maneuvering his country into achieving political gains during the Suez Crisis (July 1956–March 1957), the abortive attempt to unite Egypt and Syria (February 1958–September 1961) and Egypt's involvement in the war with Yemen were all milestones in the Nasserist attempt at realizing the leader's vision. However, the failure of economic reform and of the attempt to shape 'Arab socialism' in Egypt, the unsuccessful 'export' of revolutionary values and Nasserism to the Arab world, and mostly Egypt's defeat in the 1967 war, overshadowed the Egyptian government's attempts to maintain the policies identified with the July Revolution. From this point on, Egypt's internal and foreign affairs were pragmatic and almost totally free of its previous ideology.

This tendency away from revolutionary fervor and toward pragmatism persisted and increased after Nasser died (September 28, 1970) and MUHAMMAD ANWAR AL-SADAT was appointed president of Egypt. Moreover, the government developed a philosophy that differentiated between its commitments to the July Revolution and its values, and its dissociation from some of the Nasserist policies. Thus, the first half of the 1970s was characterized by de-Nasserization among various factions, which was encouraged somewhat by the government. During the presidencies of Sadat and Mubarak, his successors since 1981, this led to the government's abandonment of socialism for a more liberal economy. The party politics system was renewed and even some of the Muslim Brotherhood activities were permitted. A policy that worked in the interests of mainstream Egyptian nationalism was implemented; this took the place of attempts to force revolutionary ideas on "reactionary" Arab countries, to rely on Soviet support, to lead a struggle against western imperialism and to conduct an armed struggle against Israel. Egypt reestablished ties with other Arab sovereignties such as Saudi Arabia and Jordan, improved its relations with the United States and the western countries and, in March 1979, became the first Arab state to sign a peace agreement with Israel.

Over the past few years only a minority of Egyptians have

defined themselves as Nasserist, wishing to maintain the original principles of the July Revolution and Nasser's policies. The revolution's failure and its leader's downfall are explained by the Nasserists as a result of poor social and economic preparation. On the other hand, the factions that had been undermined during Nasser's presidency—the Wafd Party, the Muslim Brotherhood and those affected by the economic reforms—have been revived. They see in the failed revolution and Nasser's policies an expression of messianic ideas that had no function in Egypt's welfare. Although the last two decades have witnessed a public debate regarding the July Revolution, its ideas and the means by which it was carried out, the Egyptian government and many public sectors still see the July Revolution as a symbol of the establishment of greater and independent Egypt.

EHRENBURG, ILYA GRIGORIEVITCH (1891–1967) Soviet writer. Of Jewish origin, Ehrenburg was arrested for revolutionary activity before emigrating to Paris in 1911. He returned to Russia in 1917 and went through the civil war. After another period abroad, he returned home in 1941. A prolific writer of fiction and Communist propaganda, he was one of Soviet Russia's most effective literary spokesmen during and after World War II. He is remembered for his exhortation of the Red Army in 1945 to kill all Germans.

In 1954 he wrote *The Dawn*, a title which has become synonymous with the period of de-Stalinization that began with the dictator's death and lasted until about 1966. Another well-known work of his was *The Fall of Paris* (1948), for which he was awarded a Stalin Prize. He wrote his memoirs in six volumes (tr. 1962–1967).

EISNER, KURT (1867–1919) German socialist, journalist and statesman. Eisner, born in Berlin, was the son of a Jewish merchant with a lucrative business in military accessories and decorations. In Marburg, he studied literature and philosophy at Hermann Cohen's Neo-Kantian school. Here he developed his own thoughts, combining Kant with socialism. In 1892 he published his first book, *Friedrich Nietzsche and the Apostle of the Future*. Between 1892 and 1893 he held a position as a journalist for the *Frankfurter Zeitung*. Eisner moved back to Marburg to write for various Berlin newspapers, but a criticism of the Kaiser, entitled *Ceasar Mania*, landed him in prison for nine months. Although his jail term disqualified him for a position he had been offered at Marburg University, his notoriety led to his appointment as editor of the Social Democrats' newspaper, *Vorwärts*. He worked in Nuremberg from 1907 to 1910, and in Munich from 1910. However when, in August 1914, he used his column to criticize German aggression, he lost his job. He became known as somewhat of an eccentric who wandered around Munich with a knapsack of books or provisions on his back.

In 1916, at a tavern in Munich, he founded a weekly discussion group with an antiwar slant. Although the authorities took little notice of this activity, he soon had audiences of some 100 listeners. At least part of the attraction was evidently his own outlandish appearance, an affected look of etherealism. In 1917 he joined the Independent Social Democratic Party and became its leader.

In 1918 he was arrested as a leader of the antiwar strikes and imprisoned for eight and a half months without trial or charge,

but was released following the protest of socialists in the Reichstag. He took a leading role in the bloodless revolution which overthrew the Bavarian monarchy and proclaimed the Bavarian Republic. In the new government, he was appointed both prime minister and foreign minister. He pressed for internal security, unity among the Socialist factions in Bavaria and social and economic reforms, expressing his views in *Die Neue Zeitung*. In February 1919 he was assassinated by a right-wing fanatic, but not before he had published a series of documents purporting to prove German responsibility for the outbreak of the war. His collected works were published later that year.

EMPIRE, FRENCH It was under the Empire that Napoleon Bonaparte, proclaimed emperor of the French by popular acclamation in May 1804, ruled revolutionary France until his first abdication in April 1814 in the palace of Fontainebleau, south of Paris. Following his return from exile in the island of Elba in March 1815 and the ensuing adventure of the Hundred Days, his second more decisive defeat at the hands of Wellington at the battle of Waterloo in Belgium led to his second abdication in June 1815 and the second restoration of the Bourbons under Louis XVI's brother, Louis XVII.

It is important to stress the fact that Napoleon was crowned by the pope in December 1804 in Notre Dame Cathedral, not as 'Emperor of France,' which would have signified the affirmation of territorial sovereignty over the realm along the lines of the claims made by the deposed Bourbon kings, but as 'Emperor of the French,' implying that his power rested on the sovereign will of the people who had endorsed his title through a national plebiscite. Plebiscitary democracy, much favored by Bonapartists as an instrument of revolution, was revived by his nephew, Napoleon III, who ruled the Second Empire from 1852 to 1870.

The First Empire's great historical achievement was to have consolidated the gains of the FRENCH REVOLUTION at home and spread its principles to the rest of the world by extending French dominion through most of Europe, including Poland—re-created by Napoleon as the Duchy of Warsaw—and Russia west of the Urals. Its guiding principle at home was epitomized by Napoleon's hand-picked cabinet, the Council of State, which he charged with the task of safeguarding the Empire's constitution. Addressing the council as it began its deliberations on drafting the great Napoleonic Code that remains the law of France to this day, Napoleon urged it to devise a code that would graft the revolutionary settlement onto the laws and traditions of the *ancien régime* by declaring: "From Clovis to the COMMITTEE OF PUBLIC SAFETY, I embrace it all."

The French Empire or 'Le Grand Empire,' which at its peak in 1811 stretched all the way from the old Hanseatic port of Lubeck on the Baltic to the toe of Italy and including the Dalmatian coast, placed under one of Napoleon's marshals a satellite kingdom in the Iberian Peninsula, while his brother, Joseph, was given the throne of Spain, another brother, Louis, was made king of Holland, and the third, Jerome, was elected king of Westphalia in central Germany. This was too precarious a structure to outlast the genius of a Corsican adventurer condemned as a usurper by all the crowned dynasties of Europe. Equally flimsy and ephemeral were a string of client states or dependencies such as the Kingdom of Naples under Marshal Murat and

Napoleon's sister, Caroline; the north Italian satellites of the Cisalpine and Ligurian republics and the Helvetic republic in Switzerland. By the operation of the classical European balance of power, the Congress of Vienna was able in 1815 to put an end to Napoleon's dream of becoming a new Alexander or a new Caesar and redrew the map of Europe by restoring the principle of legitimism and bringing Bourbon France back to peaceful habits.

More lasting than the Empire's European hegemony were the reforms that were carried out in France to place the principles of the revolution on a firm and permanent footing. Acting as an enlightened despot and bypassing the weak and ineffective legislative bodies by acting through a highly centralized bureaucracy, Napoleon consolidated the legacy of 1789 in the famous code that bears his name. Not the least virtue of the Civil Code is that its 2,281 articles can be conveniently printed in a small book that can easily be carried to the four corners of the world. Other lasting reforms, such as an educational system geared to the bourgeois lycées at the secondary level and to a network of the *grandes écoles*, the *Ecole Normale* and the *Ecole Polytechnique*, to mold the bourgeois elite created by the revolution, and a highly centralized administration controlled by the minister of the interior through the *préfets* at the local level, testify to the enduring legacy of the First Empire.

Sportsman, ladies' man, best friend one could have: the young Friedrich Engels studied liberal and revolutionary writers

ENGELS, FRIEDRICH (1820–1895) Social scientist, writer, philosopher and revolutionary who, along with KARL MARX, was the progenitor of modern COMMUNISM. Engels was born in Barmen, Prussia, to a moderately liberal family with strong Protestant religious beliefs. His father owned a textile factory in Barmen and was a partner in another plant in Manchester, England. From the time he was 18 years old, Engels worked in the family business, studying liberal and revolutionary writers in private during his early apprenticeship in business management.

Hegelian philosophy particularly intrigued Engels. He became an agnostic and began publishing his writings under the pseudonym Friedrich Oswald. In 1841 he served in an artillery regiment in Berlin, where he attended university lectures and meetings of The Free, a young Hegelian group. After being discharged from the army in 1842, Engels met the Jewish journalist MOSES HESS, who then considered communism the logical extension of Hegel's theories.

Engels was forced to leave Germany because of his revolutionary views. He spent much of his time in England. During the day he was a successful businessman in his family's cotton plant; at night he studied the economic and political situation of Britain's work force. He also wrote about communism and attended meetings of radicals. Generous, robust, with a vast capacity for words and a good sportsman to boot, during his young days he was something of a ladies' man; later, rejecting the institution of marriage, he lived with Mary Burns, an uneducated working-class Irish woman.

Having met each other for the first time in 1844, Engels and Marx began writing together, attacking moderate Hegelians and socialists who opposed revolution. Engels introduced Marx to the study of economics, and later endorsed his philosophy of a materialist (economic) interpretation of history, according to which religious, cultural and social values are all determined by economic factors. In their 40 years' cooperation, Engels always played second fiddle to Marx, and in fact it was only for this reason that their friendship lasted.

In 1847, at the second congress of the COMMUNIST LEAGUE, Engels and Marx were commissioned to write a statement on Communist philosophy, *The Communist Manifesto*, that would contain a complete theoretical and practical party program. They completed a German version in January 1848; a French translation appeared in the months between the revolution in France of February 1848 and the insurrection there in June (see REVOLUTIONS OF 1848). During that time Engels returned to Germany, where revolution had also broken out, and he and Marx published a Communist daily disguised as a democratic newspaper. When the revolution failed, they returned to London to reorganize the Communist League. Engels supported himself, Mary Burns, Karl Marx and Marx's wife and children with earnings from his family's business, in which be had become a partner. In 1852, the Communist League was dissolved following the trials of Communists in Cologne. Twelve years later, a more broad-based, less radical socialist group, called the International Workingmen's Association, was set up.

In 1863 Mary Burns died. Engels later lived with her sister, Lizzy, finally agreeing to marry her as she lay on her death bed. In 1869 he sold his partnership in the family business, receiving enough from the sale to sustain himself for the rest of his life and provide a modest annual income to Karl Marx. Engels contributed toward the first part of Marx's *Das Kapital*, and edited the next two volumes after Marx's death in 1883.

Of Engels's other writings, his *The Condition of the Working Class in England* (1844) is a pioneering work of social science. Addressing economic matters, he wrote *Anti Dühring* (*Herr Dühring's revolutions in science*; 1878), *Socialism, Utopian and Scientific* (1882), *The Origins of the Family* (1884) and *Private Property and the State* (1884). An excellent journalist and polemicist, he helped popularize Marx's ideas while refusing to take credit for himself. By the time he died in 1895 he had become the grand old man of German socialism in particular and, together with Marx, was on his way to being accepted as the patron saint of communism.

ENGLISH PEASANTS' REVOLT   (1381) After the Black Plague devastated Europe, the English Statutes of Laborers (1351) froze laborers' wages in order to save the feudal system. This statute's unpopularity contributed to 26 years of sporadic peasant violence in protest against the strict feudal system. The English poll taxes of 1377 and 1380 increased the violence, which culminated in the Peasants' Revolt of 1381.

The first five months of 1381 were marked by an increase in peasant violence against the nobles of the feudal manor. By June a rebellion had broken out in many places around Kent and Essex. The peasants of Kent declared themselves the rulers of Canterbury, Maidstone and Rochester. They seized all of the countryside, taking families as hostages, and blocked pilgrims on their way to prayer at Canterbury. Soon, leaders such as Thomas Barber and Jack Straw in Essex and Geoffrey Lister in Norfolk met up with the most influential leader of the rebellion in Kent, WALTER (WAT) TYLER.

As the angry masses reached the outskirts of London, they communicated with one another across the Thames river. By June 12 they had reached East London, coopting many artisans and city workers to their ranks. The revolt was not aimed at the boy king, Richard II, himself, but was aimed more at his uncle and counselor, John of Gaunt, Duke of Lancaster.

After entering the city itself, the rioters burned the Savoy palace of John of Gaunt, the Temple, and the building of the Knights Hospitallers at Clerkenwell. The violence also turned on foreigners, some of whom were beaten and murdered. Most of the rioters did not loot and steal but instead inebriated themselves on wine and violence. That night, the city of London burned. The next morning, the king set up a makeshift meeting with some of the rioters at Mile End. After negotiating an agreement with the king, some rioters went home. However not all of the revolt's participants were present at the meeting, and many now took advantage of the king's absence and stormed the Tower of London. They seized the lord chancellor, Archbishop Sudbury; the lord treasurer, Robert Hales; and other ministers, and took them to Tower Hill. There they were tried, found guilty and immediately beheaded. That night, the city of London was in turmoil.

On Saturday morning, a conference was set up by the king at Smithfield Square. The king met with the self-proclaimed leader of the rebellion, Wat Tyler. Visibly drunk and disrespectful, Tyler had not come to negotiate but to make even more serious demands on the king, including the abolition of the feudal system and a reduction of the church's authority. However, Tyler

was dragged from his horse and stabbed to death in the king's presence. The morale of the rebellion quickly drained, and London would soon be deserted.

As soon as the rebellion dissipated in London, the king renounced all promises and concessions he had ·made to the rebels. In the meantime, however, the revolt had spread through much of the south, east and midlands of England. A total of 10 counties and their major population centers were in the hands of the revolt for a few days. The peasants wanted to destroy any and all of the feudal records which bound them to the land. One observer said, "They punished by beheading each and all who were acquainted with the laws of the country. . . . They were eager to give old records to the flames and lest any should for the future make new ones they put all such as were able to do so to death."

The revolt was quelled ruthlessly by the nobles, knights and aristocracy of the countryside. They quickly hanged or beheaded anyone involved. A proclamation was later released excusing anyone who had acted illegally in destroying the revolt.

The disjointed, bloody uprising which took place in England in 1381 was similar to many such rebellions which took place throughout late-medieval Europe (such as the JACQUERIE PEASANT REVOLT in France). These movements were indicative of a disenchanted peasant class that lashed out against the social and economic order of the day. New poll taxes, the stagnation of the Hundred Years' war with France and the reassertion of an antiquated feudal system all contributed to the revolt in England. One of the slogans of the revolt (later to become a slogan for many revolts all around Europe) was, "When Adam dug and Eve span, who was the gentleman?"

ENVER PASHA   (1881–1922) Turkish military and political leader. Born in Istanbul, Enver graduated from the Military Academy and, as a professional officer, played an active part in the events in Macedonia leading to the 1908 revolution of the YOUNG TURKS. He served as military attache in Berlin and returned to fight against the Italians in the Tripolitanian war in 1911. In January 1913, Enver led a coup which brought down the Liberal party then in power in Istanbul. Together with TALAT PASHA and KEMAL PASHA he then formed a triumvirate that ruled Turkey until 1918. Having become a military hero by recapturing Edirne (Adrianople) from the Bulgarians in the Second Balkan war in 1913, Enver was promoted to the rank of general and appointed minister of war. With strong Pan-Turkish and pro-German inclinations, he was instrumental in bringing about Turkey's entry into World War I as an ally of Germany. During the war he led the Ottoman Third army in an disastrous campaign on the Russian front. After the armistice he was tried and sentenced to death; he fled to Berlin and then to Russia and Turkistan, where he intrigued against the new Kemalist Turkey and took part in a Muslim nationalist insurrection, in the course of which he was killed.

ERITREAN PEOPLE'S LIBERATION FRONT (EPLF)
Movement seeking independence, or at least autonomy, for Eritrea from Ethiopia, founded in 1958. It was succeeded by the Eritrean Liberation Front (ELF), which began an armed struggle in September 1961. A reformist group separated from the ELF in 1970 and formed the Eritrean People's Liberation Front

(EPLF). A Marxist-Leninist party, the EPLF enjoyed support from both Christians and Muslims (between whom Eritrea is almost equally divided). The EPLF maintained an army, the Eritrean People's Liberation Army (EPLA), which waged guerrilla war against the Ethiopian government.

After the fall of Ethiopian president MENGISTU HAILE MARIAM, the EPLF succeeded in taking control of Eritrea and formed a provisional government in May 1991. Eritrea was granted independence on May 24, 1993, with the EPLF forming a provisional government. At independence, many of the EPLF's rival political organizations declared their support for the transitional government. The secretary-general of the EPLF, Issaias Afewerki, is currently the head of state of Eritrea.

ETHIOPIAN PEOPLE'S REVOLUTIONARY DEMOCRATIC FRONT (EPRDF)

Ethiopian revolutionary movement. The EPRDF was founded in 1989 as a coalition of six revolutionary armies dedicated to overthrowing the Marxist régime of Colonel MENGISTU HAILE MARIAM of Ethiopia. The movement is dominated by the Tigray People's Liberation Front (TPLF) and includes the Ethiopian People's Democratic Movement (EPDM), uniting various Amhara antigovernment forces; the Oromo People's Democratic Organization, representing the Muslim Oromo population of Ethiopia; several other ethnic movements; and various Eritrean nationalist groups under the umbrella of the ERITREAN PEOPLE'S LIBERATION FRONT (EPLF). In May 1991, the EPRDF took the Ethiopian capital, Addis Ababa, and established a revolutionary government with Meles Zenawi at its head.

Zenawi's political involvement dates from his days as founder and head of the Marxist-Leninist League of Tigray. Nevertheless, to organize his coalition of revolutionary partners he abandoned Marxist dogma and promised a free market economy, democratic elections, the rule of law and self-determination for Eritrea and those ethnic groups which so desire. Eritrea did, in fact, gain independence; however critics of Zenawi's régime claim that he has reneged on many of his other promises, threatened the unity of Ethiopia by his policy of ethnic redistribution of lands and created an oligarchic government.

L'ETOILE NORD AFRICAINE (NORTH AFRICAN STAR)

The most radical of Algerian nationalist groups, established in the 1920s. The organization demanded land redistribution and universal suffrage. Led by AHMAD MESSALI HAJJ, its populist socialist program influenced the ideology of the FRONT DE LIBÉRATION NATIONALE (FLN). The organization was banned in 1929, but resurrected as the Parti du Peuple Algerien in 1937.

ETHIOPIAN REVOLUTION OF 1974

In 1974, the ruler of Ethiopia, Emperor Haile Selassie, and his pro-western, feudalist régime were overthrown. The previous 11 years had been marked by growing opposition to Haile and his régime. In particular, there were annual student riots from 1965 onward. Among the issues raised by the students were land reform, corruption among senior officials and sharply rising prices.

The failure of the government and administration to deal with the country's problems was compounded by a serious drought in the Tigre and Wollo provinces in 1972–1974. What made things worse was that the famine only became public knowledge in Ethiopia because of international publicity.

In February 1974, there was a wave of strikes and mutinies in most units of the armed forces. After a series of revelations of financial manipulations, Haile Selassie was finally deposed on September 12, 1974. He died 11 months later, while still in detention.

Haile Selassie's régime was replaced by a Provisional Military Administrative Council (PMAC), popularly. known as the Derg (committee). The PMAC, composed of 120 soldiers, saw itself as the vanguard of the Ethiopian revolution and, under the influence of left-wing intellectuals returning from abroad, opted for a socialist mode of government. Major (later Lieutenant-Colonel) MENGISTU HAILE MARIAM emerged as the most influential member of the Derg.

On December 20, 1974, Ethiopia was officially declared a socialist state. More than 100 companies were nationalized or partly taken over. The most important reform was in March 1975, when all rural land was nationalized, followed by urban land four months' later. Tens of thousands of students were sent to the countryside on a national campaign for development, to carry out health and literacy education and to help organize land reforms. Peasant associations were set up. The "villagization" program brought together several villages or single units. However, these developments adversely affected agricultural development and state farms proved—as elsewhere—to be inefficient. The resettlement of famine victims was ill-organized, and up to one million people died in the disastrous drought of 1984–1985.

The 1974 revolution also led to a change in Ethiopian foreign policy. Ethiopia turned away from the west, expelled the US military advisory mission and signed a treaty of friendship and cooperation with the USSR. Close relations were also developed with Cuba, which provided substantial military assistance in the war with Somalia (1977–1978). There were also close contacts with the German Democratic Republic (GDR) and other Eastern European states and with the Marxist-Leninist People's Democratic Republic of Yemen (PDRY).

EUTHYDEMUS

King of Bactria (modern Afghanistan) from 235 to 200 B.C. Born in Magnesia, he was probably a governor under the king of Bactria, Diodotus II. He rebelled against this king, killed him, took his throne and reigned over Bactria, uniting its various parts into a powerful kingdom. In 208 B.C. he was attacked by the Seleucid King Antiochus III (the Great) and forced to retreat to his capital Bactra (possibly Balkh in northern Afghanistan). After a siege of two years, a peace treaty was signed and Euthydemus was recognized as an independent ruler of Bactria. Later he attacked Parthia and seized the provinces of Arachosia, Aria and Sogdiana, thus consolidating his kingdom.

EZLN see ZAPATISTA NATIONAL LIBERATION ARMY.

F

FABRE D'ÉGLANTINE, PHILIPPE FRANÇOIS (1750–1794) A poet born in the southern town of Carcassonne, France, Fabre added the name Églantine to this common name after winning a literary prize in the Floral Games in Languedoc. He won a modest reputation as the author of light verse, comedies and songs, such as *Il pleut, il pleut, bergère*. Carried away by the idealism of the FRENCH REVOLUTION, he rallied to the radical Club of the Cordeliers, where he became the protégé of GEORGES DANTON and CAMILLE DESMOULINS. His chief claim to fame was to have devised the new revolutionary calendar introduced by the CONVENTION in October 1792 and which remained France's only official calendar until well into the EMPIRE. An attempt to restore it during the PARIS COMMUNE of 1871, which was resolved to revive the great days of the 1792 convention and the insurrectionary Commune of the Revolution, was voted down.

Since modern history, it was universally believed, began with the new régime that was ushered in by the Convention and not with 1789, Year I of the revolutionary calendar began on September 22, 1792, to mark the proclamation of the republic, "One and Indivisible." Fabre d'Églantine invented poetic names such as Vendémiaire, Fructidor, Ventôse, Brumaire and Germinal to correspond to each of the new months. These were now divided into thirty days in order to conform to the decimal system already in force, with five 'sans culottides,' or national holidays, added on at the end of each year. Sundays, holidays and saints' days were replaced by a week consisting of 10 days, designated as a 'décade,' so that the republic allowed only three days of rest per month instead of the more frequent traditional weekends. Nothing could have revolutionized the common man's sense of time and place more than such a drastic change in public spirit and culture.

Fabre d'Églantine was unable to resist the temptations of speculation opened up by the war economy. Much to the dismay of his friend ROBESPIERRE, dubbed 'The Incorruptible,' he was caught up in the scandal of the East India Company, lumped together with the party of the Indulgents led by his mentor Danton, and sent to the guillotine with the whole batch of Dantonists in April 1794.

FAISAL I SEE FEISAL I.

FALANGE The name adopted by the mainstream Fascist (see FASCISM) party in post-Republican Spain, founded in 1933 through the initiative of strong man Jose Antonio Rivera (1903–1936), the son of the first Spanish dictator in modern times, General MIGUEL PRIMO DE RIVERA. The elder de Rivera had seized power to bolster a faltering monarchy, based on middle-class support and with a Fascist style dictatorship, in September 1923. The transfer of power had been accomplished at the behest of King Alfonso XIII himself in the face of widespread agitation for Catalan and Basque separatism, mounting Communist and anarchist threats and a resulting paralysis in Spain's fledging parliamentary system. The Falange was later revived and transformed by FRANCISCO FRANCO into the only political party tolerated in Spain following his own seizure of power in 1937 and throughout his dictatorship. It maintained unchallenged prestige and authority until the restoration of the Spanish monarchy under Prince Juan Carlos on October 30, 1975, a transfer of power carried out with the blessings of Franco himself at the end of his life and leading to the creation of today's constitutional Bourbon monarchy.

Although the Falange's ideology was inspired in large part by the example set in the early 1920s by the triumph of BENITO MUSSOLINI's *fasces* (or Fascist paramilitary units) in Italy under the monarchy, Jose Antonio's Spanish version of fascism tried quite naturally to stress his country's indigenous nationalism and traditional royalism over populist or internationalist socialist currents in the ideological make-up of his exclusivist and quasi-Fascist party with a distinctive Spanish character. The implementation of his program provoked the resistance of a united "popular front," grouping together Spanish republicans, socialists and anarcho-syndicalists in the course of the chaotic situation resulting from the outbreak of the civil war and Antonio was executed in Alicante on November 20, 1936.

It was in the course of the second phase of the civil war, beginning in 1937, that General Franco and his military clique, after having invaded the Spanish mainland from their military outposts in the offshore Spanish colonies, was able to expand the Falange movement into what now became the mainstream Fascist party officially known as the Traditional Spanish Falange. Its platform fused a modified version of fascism, now the prevailing ideology of the political régimes in both Nazi Germany and Fascist Italy, with a residual form of Spanish Catholicism and old-fashioned conservatism to create an amalgamate political ideology called corporatism. As a result, from 1936 until July 1942 the Grand Council of the Falange formally replaced Spain's moribund parliamentary system as the main legislative and deliberate body of the nation and was dedicated to the purpose of legislating the framework of a corporatist state along Italian lines. The consolidation of Franco's power as the undisputed leader—

el Caudillo—of the new Spanish state is regarded by historians as the counterpart of the Fuhrer principle in Germany or Mussolini's assumption of the title of *il Duce* in Italy.

Internal dissensions among the Fascist factions within the Falange and the necessity of trimming the sails of Spain's foreign policy to the needs of positive neutralism during World War II enabled Franco to free himself of its bosses, whose power had declined almost completely by the time of the restoration of the monarchy in 1975 which introduced Spain's present constitutional monarchy.

FANON, FRANTZ (1925–1961) Revolutionary writer and activist. Fanon was born in Martinique to an upper-middle class family and educated at the private lycée in Fort-de-France. He joined the Free French army in 1944 and served on the European front. His military service earned him an education in France where, studying psychiatry in Lyons, he mingled with leftist and Trotskyite students and remained politically active. He completed his degree in 1951 and returned briefly to Martinique, where he found the political and professional climate too stifling to remain.

Returning to France, he began his residency in Saint Alban under Tosquelles, whose sociotherapy approach greatly influenced him and supported his political thinking. His later shift from psychiatric practice to political action was based on assumptions about human relations derived from his work at Saint Alban. Other influences at this time were the existentialists of postwar France, especially Sartre, Heidegger, Kierkegaard and Jaspers. LENIN, MARX and TROTSKY were his chief political influences. It was during this period that he turned to writing. *Black Skin, White Masks* (1952), a sketch of the psychology of colonization, with philosophical roots in Hegel and Sartre, arose out of questioning whether or not normal relations were possible between blacks and whites. Fanon saw the relations between blacks and whites, or colonizer and colonized, as part of a rigid system which determined their relations.

After moving to Algeria to practice psychiatry, Fanon became involved in the ALGERIAN REVOLUTION. He joined the FLN (FRONT DE LIBÉRATION NATIONALE) in 1956. Until his death, he served the revolution in the capacity of editor, political essayist, representative of the provisional government and ambassador at large in Africa. He was based in Tunis, the headquarters of the FLN press, and continued to develop his study of colonialism, emphasizing an aspect that many had ignored: the human consequences of a system that determined the limits of people's actions. In *A Dying Colonialism* (1959), he examined the internal psychic effect of the confrontation between the French and Algerians, as well as the network of relationships fixed by the colonial system—the "psychology of colonization." One major factor he studied was the lack of communication between the colonizers and the colonized and the impact this had on their relations. Revolution transformed individuals as well as the relations between them. This book marked Fanon's transition between focusing on psychiatric problems to a commitment to more direct political action.

Fanon traveled to Mali and Ghana in 1960, following consultation with the provisional government regarding FLN policy in Africa. During this time he learned that he had leukemia. After returning from Mali, he travelled to the USSR for treatment and then back to Tunis. Following his death in 1961, he was buried in Algeria. His death was mourned greatly in both Tunisia and Algeria. His contribution to the revolution, including the role he had played in spreading word of the revolution to the rest of Africa, was acknowledged in *el Moudjahid,* the newspaper of the FLN, which described him as an African and Algerian intellectual.

Before his death, Fanon completed *The Wretched of the Earth* and consulted with Sartre on writing an introduction. This was his most important political work, providing an analysis of the political development of the Third World. Yet the book was mainly publicized for its treatment of the question of violence, which Fanon felt was the only way to gain international attention. Fanon also argued against the tendency to imitate Europe. His fear was that a Muslim bourgeoisie would replace the colonialists without restructuring Algerian society. He also believed that the army would better supervise the growth of socialism than would the bourgeoisie and it would not be susceptible to the materialistic corruption of the latter. He felt that the African leaders of postcolonial states became parasitic "intermediaries" between metropolitan capitalists and the oppressed masses, perpetuating neocolonial relations, and he emphasized the revolutionary potential of the peasantry. His concerns led him to be more sympathetic to the National Liberation Army (ALN) toward the end of his life and to participate in the political education of ALN cadres—the ALN was a combination of intellectuals and peasants, contrasted with the more bourgeois and opportunistic FLN.

In subsequent years, Fanon's intellectual and political contribution to the revolution was called into question by the independent Algerian government, possibly in an attempt to reenforce its authentic Algerian nature and to distance itself from policies it chose not to pursue. However, Fanon's influence extended well beyond Algeria—in Africa his analysis of colonialism and the need for violent struggle were welcomed, less so his criticism of the neocolonialist bourgeoisie. His ideas also had an impact on the black liberation movement in the United States (in particular the BLACK PANTHER PARTY) and the Palestinian resistance organizations.

FARINACCI, ROBERTO (1892–1945) Italian Fascist (see FASCISM) revolutionary leader. A telegraph operator in the railways, Farinacci joined the Socialist party and in the summer of 1914 became the leader of the interventionist agitation in Cremona. Immediately after the war—during which he spent a year of service at the front—Farinacci joined MUSSOLINI and was one of the founders of the *Fasci di Combattimento* at Piazza San Sepolcro on March 21, 1919. Immediately afterwards he became the *Ras*—leader of the Fascist squad—of Cremona and made much use of verbal and physical violence against the "Reds" and all those who opposed fascism. In 1921, he was one of the 35 Fascists elected to parliament and later became an important figure in the Fascist militia. Farinacci was seen as a revolutionary Fascist proclaiming the need for a strong state dominated by the Fascist party and in favor of the labor masses, while at the same time profoundly nationalist and anti-Communist. Appointed secretary general of the Fascist party at the beginning of the Fascist dictatorship in 1925, Farinacci undertook the revolutionary "Fascistization" of Italy, with a mixture of political activism and terrorism. The need for normalization and the fact that Mussolini's personal grip over the state had been strengthened, caused Farinacci to be dropped from the leadership of the party in 1926. He then devoted his energies to attempting to stop the normalization of fascism. In 1938, Farinacci was able to give free rein to his anti-Semitism within the framework of the new Fascist racial policies. He also sided with Italy's entry into World War II as Germany's main ally. During the puppet Salo Republic (see ITALIAN SOCIAL REPUBLIC) set up by the Germans for Mussolini, Farinacci collaborated with the Germans. He was caught and executed by a partisan squad while trying to escape to Switzerland in April 1945.

FASCISM   One of the most important modern revolutionary political ideologies, movements and régimes. The word *fascio* is related to the Latin *fasces*, a bundle or group of rods with an axe carried by the Roman lictors as a symbol of consular authority. In modern Italy, *fascio* is used to denominate political groups or associations, such as the *Fascio di Combattimento* (Combat Fascio), founded by BENITO MUSSOLINI at the Piazza San Sepolcro meeting on March 21, 1919. The political movement led by Mussolini adopted the name Fascism, and similar political groups in Europe and elsewhere, combining radical nationalism with certain brands of anti-Marxist socialism, productivism, state-controlled corporativism and the aesthetization of politics, were included in the same category or perceived of themselves as Fascists.

The Fascist ideology was elaborated intellectually well before World War I, within the framework of a cultural revolution that rejected materialism, rationalism, positivism, humanism and the political heritage of the FRENCH REVOLUTION as anti-natural and decadent. Politically, this could be synthesized in the rejection of liberal democracy and its socialist alternatives as unworkable options, basically opposed to human and social nature. At the end of the 19th century, French and Italian intellectuals such as GEORGES SOREL, Gustave Le Bon, Henri Bergson, Vilfredo Pareto, Gaetano Mosca and Scipio Sighele had elaborated theories that stressed the antirational and antimaterialist nature of social life. Pareto's theories about the need for elite circulation as immanent to the exercise of power; Sorel's ideas about proletarian violence as the motor of history and as an alternative to bourgeois domination and decadence; Le Bon's definitions of the crowd as an irrational social actor; and Bergson's perception of the need for a vital drive to fulfil personal, social and historical goals all combined with NIETZSCHE's vision of the role of the will and the opposition between rational calculation and heroic values.

Revolutionary syndicalist circles in France and Italy, looking for a workable theory of revolution to replace Marxist historical materialism that, by the end of the 19th century, has not produced the expected changes, found in this formula and in the revision of Marxist economic theory a response to their plight. By revising MARX's theory of value in terms of neoclassic and hedonistic economic theory, the revolutionary syndicalists were able to change the basic categories of class warfare from proletarian versus bourgeois into a productionistic confrontation between the producers and the parasites. Internalizing Sorel's political vision of the mobilizing myth of the revolutionary general strike led by workers' syndical elites, the Italian revolutionary syndi-

calists learned, through a process of trial and error, about the limits of working-class solidarity. Another telling point was the nonrevolutionary character of the socialist elites associated with the Italian Socialist party—PSI. Breaking away from the PSI and the CGL—the General Confederation of Labor—which was linked to it, the revolutionary syndicalists tried to provoke the revolution through agrarian general strikes of the Po valley in 1907 and 1908. The leadership was convinced of the power of the mobilizing myth and of the weakness of socialism. It was while searching for the right formula for revolution that the Italian revolutionary syndicalists and their French counterparts confronted the leaders and activists of nationalism.

In both countries, the nationalists were looking for ways to cope with the results of the industrial revolution, i.e., to find a way to integrate the masses into their movement. In France, at the beginning of the second decade of the 20th century, revolutionary SYNDICALISM and radical nationalism met intellectually through Sorel's cooperation with the circles around *L'Action Francaise*, its nationalist and anti-Semitic *L'Independance*, and the publication of *les Cahiers du Cercle Proudhon*. Although in Italy the parallel phenomenon manifested itself through *L'Idea nazionale* and later *La Lupa*, the circumstances and results were different. Enrico Corradini, one of the main figures of Italian literary and political nationalism, cooperated in these intellectual and publicistic enterprises. He also elaborated a theoretical framework for the solution to the problem of poverty, the massive Italian emigration resulting from the latter and the lack of colonies and imperial developmental opportunities. His theory served as a bridge between the goals of the revolutionaries, coming from the ranks of syndicalism, and the nationalists, occupied until then more in literary and intellectual exercises than in practical policies. Corradini claimed that Italy was a proletarian nation confronting bourgeois imperialism. In his scheme, socialism and nationalism came together to solve the problems of the nation and the poor. Being mainly proletarian, and as such emigratory and deprived of colonies, Italy could, according to Corradini, only solve its social and national problems through international war against the bourgeois and imperialist nations, thereby acquiring colonies.

These ideas did not produce immediate political results, but the polemics around Italian intervention in Libya and the ensuing war against Turkey produced further developments in revolutionary syndicalist thought. The proletariat was being abandoned as the subject of history in favor of a new subject, the nation. The mobilizing myth related to the proletariat was dumped too: the general strike could not stop the enthusiastic Italian masses from following the national flag marching toward Cirenaica and Tripolitania. A new myth combining nation and revolution developed: the myth of the revolutionary war.

In the summer of 1914, when Italy did not enter the war, DE AMBRIS and the rest of the revolutionary syndicalist leadership were the first in the revolutionary left to raise the flag of interventionism in the name of the revolution. In October 1914, they formed the *Fascio Rivoluzionario d'Azione Internazionalista* to promote Italian intervention in World War I. Michele Bianchi, later to be one of the Fascist quadrumviri of the MARCH ON ROME in 1922, was made general secretary of the *Fascio*. *Pagine Libere*, the revolutionary syndicalist review, became the organ of this movement. Important revolutionary syndicalist leaders, many of whom would later become leading Fascists, were its leaders: Filippo Corridoni, Angelo Olivetti, Massimo Rocca, Cesare Rossim and others.

Mussolini, deeply influenced intellectually and personally by the revolutionary syndicalist leaders, left the neutralist PSI in November 1914 to join the ranks of leftist interventionism that also included Mazzinian republicans. In December 1914, the former *Fascio* changed its name to *Fascio d'Azione Rivoluzionari* (the Revolutionary Action Fascio), and began an intense interventionist campaign in which Mussolini's newspaper, *Il Popolo d'Italia*, played a central role. In May 1915, Italy entered the war on the side of France and Great Britain. Believing themselves to be on their road to revolution, the members of the *Fascio Rivoluzionario* closed ranks behind the government and fully supported the war effort. Thus, it is possible to claim that already before World War I the ideological elements that would reform the soul of fascism after the war had already been fully developed.

Military and political participation in the war helped the interventionists learn about the power of the state and the psychological and social impact of life at the front. The way the military was organized was very much in keeping with the political activism and heroic perceptions of the leftist interventionists: solidarity, self-sacrifice, austerity, efficiency and unity of action, all qualities nonexistent in the quagmire of liberal democratic decadence. At the end of the war, the possibility of imposing military models and values on politics became a reality within the polarized confrontation between the left and the right during 1919–1920. Unemployment, social unrest, unfulfilled political promises and the menace of a Soviet-style revolution characterized the year in which fascism was founded by Mussolini. Ideologically, the future Duce was highly dependent on DE AMBRIS, Lanzillo, Panunzio, Olivetti and other revolutionary syndicalists, who in the interim, through the myth of revolutionary war, had internalized nationalist principles into their vision of revolution and had become national revolutionary syndicalists.

The first political programs of fascism as a movement were clearly leftist, demanding the creation of a republic; workers' rights and their representation in industrial management; anticlericalism; expropriation of church property; and the expropriation of land, mines, transport means and undue war profits. In the beginning, the Fascist movement was mainly urban and attracted leftist interventionists, futurist nationalists and veterans. It was clearly anti-socialist, despising the social democratic ideals of reform, and at the same time anti-Soviet, claiming that a Russian-style revolution in a poor country such as Italy would result in widespread hunger and chaos. The lack of electoral success of the Fascist movement in the national elections of October 1919, when not a single Fascist candidate was elected to parliament, reinforced the activist manifestations of the *squadrismo*—Fascist squads. These violent groups were initially composed of veterans of the *arditi* (special forces of the Italian army in the war) willing to fight against the socialists in the cities and villages—and created the image of socialism as the common enemy of the Fascists, the conservatives and the nationalists.

While in 1920 Mussolini and fascism still held the revolutionary ideals and programs of leftist interventionism, the occupation of the factories in the industrial belt of Italy in August–September 1920 changed things. The political compromise that Giovanni Giolitti, the prime minister, imposed on all sides did not satisfy anyone, deepening the feeling of crisis. Landlords and factory owners felt betrayed by Giolitti and the liberal democratic state that allowed the socialists to gain access to the management of industries, thus curtailing the principle of private property. The owners' class looked to Fascist activism and violence as the only way to stop a socialist revolution. Revolutionary socialists felt betrayed by the compromise reached and were on the verge of splitting the ranks within the socialists.

To complicate matters, in September 1919, the warrior-bard GABRIELE D'ANNUNZIO had marched with his legionnaires into Fiume in order to annex it to Italy. Mussolini and the Fascists supported this move. In September 1920, d'Annunzio enacted the *Carta del Carnaro* as the political constitution of the Regency of Fiume but also as a future political model for Italy.

At the end of 1920, fascism began enjoying the support of landowners and industrialists, as well as the tacit acquiescence of the police and military authorities in its terror campaign against the socialists. Italy entered a period of quasi-civil war from which it would exit only with Mussolini's accession to power after the March on Rome at the end of October 1922.

The Fascists now moved to the right, but this had ideological and political costs. Many left-wingers and revolutionaries abandoned the movement and began opposing it. The programs and ideological declarations of its leaders became more centrist, and Mussolini negotiated with the nationalists and the liberals as the elections of May 1921 approached. He also began to talk in terms of imperialism and national expansion. *Squadrismo* was the dominant feature of fascism in this period, in spite of its acceptance of the rules of parliamentarian politics. In the elections of 1921, the Fascists succeeded in sending 35 of their candidates to parliament. The seeming incoherence of the Fascists' approach, in running candidates for the parliament while at the same time trying to undermine it in every way possible, can be interpreted as a two-pronged tactic to attain power. Creating a situation of violence that could be solved only by the Fascists in power on the one hand, and participating actively in the political life on the other, was the way Mussolini eventually attained power "legally." The *squadri* leaders—ROBERTO FARINACCI, ITALO BALBO, DINO GRANDI and others, were the immediate destroyers of existing legality, trying to bring down what fascism saw as a senile parliamentarian liberal democracy.

Abandoning their former revolutionary programs, the Fascists in 1922 expressed their belief in actions. Their goal was to govern Italy for its own good, the means being violence and politics.

At the end of October 1922, the March on Rome was staged. The Fascists and their nationalist allies were a small political minority in society as well as in parliament. Resolute action by the government of Luigi Facta or by the king against them would probably have disbanded the Fascist columns marching on Rome. They were no match for the army and the royal guards. But the king refused to impose a state of siege and instead called upon Mussolini to form the government. This represented the first compromise between the Fascists and the traditional ruling classes of Italy. Although the Duce formed a minority government, the Fascists slowly dismantled the democratic liberal state, persecuted their political enemies and, in 1925, after having survived politically the crisis resulting from the assassination of the socialist leader Giacomo Matteotti by Fascist thugs in June 1924, Benito Mussolini established a Fascist dictatorship over the country. Through censorship, the opposition press was silenced. The Fascists controlled parliament and the government and they began persecuting their political enemies and sending them to jail or into exile.

From this period onwards, the Fascists attempted to organize Italy as a totalitarian and corporative state. The totalitarian spirit of fascism found its basis in the philosophy of Giovanni Gentile, which stressed a social unity of opinion, will and inspiration to create a homogeneous community of consensus about thought and actions. Totalitarianism was mentioned by Mussolini for the first time in his January 5, 1925 speech about the Fascistization of Italy. The kind of mobilization techniques used by the Fascists—the use of a multiplicity of organizations regulating social, syndical, cultural and professional life—and many symbolic acts—parades, marches and ceremonies—combined with a widespread effort to imbue the population with Mussolini's political doctrine and to close the public sphere to discussion and debate, thereby contributing to the creation of the image of a totalitarian state. The limits to Fascist totalitarianism were defined by the compromises the *Partito Nazionale Fascista* (National Fascist party—PNF) and the state assumed vis á vis the monarchy, the church, the military and the industrialists. These sectors continued to enjoy relatively high degrees of autonomy within the Fascist state, in spite of the totalitarian spirit recognized by it.

In 1926 and 1927, the Fascists assumed control of the labor market through legislation inspired by ALFREDO ROCCO's brand of nationalist authoritarian corporativism. The aim was to discipline production and the goal was partially achieved by prohibiting strikes and lockouts, subjecting labor disputes to the obligatory arbitration of state courts, the creation of a ministry of corporations administered by the theoretician Giuseppe Bottai, and the enactment of the *Carta del Lavoro* (Labor charter).

In 1929, the Fascists solved the historical dispute between Italy and the Catholic Church by signing the Lateran Pacts. The PNF grew in numbers, from more than about 600,000 members in 1927 to more than 6 million in 1939, but the party was subordinated to the needs and goals of the Fascist state.

In 1932, in his article in the *Italian Encyclopedia* on fascism, Mussolini could claim control over the political forces, the moral forces and the economic forces, resulting in the existence of a Fascist corporative state. Under slogans such as *credere, obbedire, combattere* (believe, obey, fight) and *Mussolini has empre ragione* (Mussolini is always right), the Fascists created the image of having revolutionized Italian society. The reality was less clear, with the traditional social forces still very powerful. Indeed, the Fascists' penetration of the social fabric was sometimes more formal than real.

Economic development was greatly hampered by the world economic crisis of the 1930s. The State reacted by the creation of the *Istituto di Ricostruzione Industriale*—IRI (Industrial Reconstruction Institute)—to support failing industries and reduce the massive unemployment in the country. Nevertheless, the general standard of living declined.

In 1935, Fascist Italy attacked and conquered Ethiopia and in 1936 it intervened in the SPANISH CIVIL WAR, strengthening ties with the second Fascist state in Europe, national socialist Germany. The Rome-Berlin Axis was established and formalized through the Steel Pact of May 1939.

Paralleling this, the corporatization of Italy proceeded onward. In 1930, the National Council of the Corporations was established. In 1934, the Italian society was organized into 22 mixed corporations of owners and workers, representing the main sectors of production. These corporations all had parliamentary representation. In 1938, the lower chamber of parliament, elected on the basis of a territorial system of representation, was replaced by the Chamber of Fasces and Corporations, in which most of the members were elected or nominated by the corporations. Thus Mussolini could claim, at least formally, to have organized Italy as a Fascist Corporative State.

Mussolini's intervention in international politics added to the image of a dynamic Fascist Italy projecting its influence and ideology beyond its national borders and thus created an image of power. Italy joined World War II on the German side in June 1940. Its military victories were rare, its defeats numerous. The Italian empire, created after the conquest of Ethiopia, disintegrated under the British onslaught. By 1943, Italy had lost all its possessions in Africa; was entangled in ferocious wars against Greek, Yugoslav and Albanian partisans; had lost many divisions in the Soviet Union and most of its fleet; and the Allies were landing in Sicily and would later land on the Italian mainland.

On the night of July 24–25, 1943 the Fascist Grand Council, led by Dino Grandi, deposed Mussolini with the acquiescence of the king and the army. Sent to prison, Mussolini was rescued from the Gran Sasso in September 1943 by the Germans, flown to Munich and brought back to Italy to establish the ITALIAN SOCIAL REPUBLIC, popularly known as the Republic of Salo. This was to be a satellite state of Nazi Germany that claimed to have returned to the Fascist revolutionary origins of 1919.

The RSI—*Republica Sociale Italiana* (Italian Social Republic)—proclaimed itself as antibourgeois, antimonarchical and anti-Semitic, but was unable to carry out the programs that the Fascist Republican party decided upon at the Verona Congress of November 1943. It had to cooperate with the German economic war effort by augmenting production through discipline and coercion, thus creating a contradiction between its practices and its pro-worker revolutionary declarations. It had to take into consideration the Catholic roots of the population, in spite of its anticlericalism.

German military policies dominated the Salo Republic, and the Fascists, subordinated to the Germans, cooperated in the German anti-partisan campaigns and Jewish deportations to the death camps in Eastern Europe. This was the culmination of the Fascist racial policies that had begun in 1938 with the enactment of the Italian racial laws.

The advancing allied armies reduced the territorial control of the Salo Republic to a small area around Milan, and in April 1945 the second Italian Fascist state ceased to exist, after Mussolini's flight, capture and execution.

FATAH *Al-Fath*, literally "the conquest" (the name is a reverse Arabic acronym of *Harakat al-Tahrir al-Filastini*—the Movement for the Liberation of Palestine).

Al-Fath is the oldest, largest and most influential of the

Palestinian resistance groups. It is, in a sense, the historical heir to the Arab Higher Committee which fought the British during the 1930s and 1940s. *Al-Fath* was established toward the end of the 1950s by YASIR ARAFAT (then a student at Cairo University), KHALIL AL-WAZIR (ABU-JIHAD), SALAH KHALAF (ABU IYAD) and Faruq al-Qaddumi (Abu Lutf). This leadership was collegial. These men have remained leaders ever since *al-Fath*'s inception, although their dominance has been challenged from time to time. They share the same sociological, educational and career backgrounds. Their shared experiences in the 1948 war (Israel's war of independence), in student politics and in insurgent activities have produced a cohesiveness that has remained intact, and the *al-Fath* leadership has remained remarkably stable. *Al-Fath*'s titular leader is Arafat.

By calling *al-Fath* a movement rather than an organization, its founders attempted to include as many Palestinians as possible. Because of its size, its policy of recruiting from all segments of Palestinian society, and its self-proclaimed mission of embodying Palestinian national aspirations, the *al-Fath* membership covers a wide spectrum of ideological and social orientations. The ideological basis of *al-Fath* was left deliberately weak in order to prevent factions and splits. *Al-Fath* as a whole is conservative in comparison with other Palestinian organizations, and has a large number of Islamic Arab nationalists. It nevertheless has a powerful socialist wing. The result has been a certain amount of ideological confusion and inconsistency. Although *al-Fath* stresses its secular character, Muslims form the majority of its Palestinian recruitment base, and Muslim religious motivations are clearly apparent in *al-Fath*. This confusion has been exploited by *al-Fath*'s opponents within and without the Arab world. Arafat has been accused both of being a tool of the MUSLIM BROTHERHOOD and of being subservient to ABDUL NASSER.

Part of this confusion stems from the fact that two contrasting Arab ideological movements influenced *al-Fath*'s development and structure: the Islamic right—as, for example, the MUSLIM BROTHHOOD in Egypt; and the Arab nationalist left—including the Algerian FRONT DE LIBÉRATION NATIONALE and the Syrian BA'ATH. While the Muslim Brotherhood dominated the first decade of *al-Fath* in the 1950s, the Algerians and Syrians provided the military and organizational capability of *al-Fath* operations in the 1960s. In this sense, *al-Fath* itself represents in microcosm the tensions and conflicts which have been convulsing the Middle East—for example, the conflict of western secular values and their organizational output versus Islamic values and their organizational consequences. The organizational split within *al-Fath* between rightist and leftist factions is one source of *al-Fath*'s proclaimed nonideological, nonpolitical stance, as well as its attitude of noninterference in the affairs of Arab governments left or right.

From the start, *al-Fath* emphasized the military thrust of its movement as carried out by its military arm, *al-'Asifa* ("the storm"). The first military operation was carried out on January 1, 1965, and this day was proclaimed as its founding day. After the Arab defeat in the 1967 war, *al-Fath*, representing the "Activist" *Fida'i* trend, was considerably strengthened as an alternative to the PALESTINE LIBERATION ORGANIZATION (PLO). On July 1968, *al-Fath* joined the PLO's principal bodies and was shortly in a dominant position in the PLO. Finally, during February

1969 it took over the PLO leadership. The *al-Fath* leader, Yasir Arafat, became chairman of the PLO executive committee.

Al-Fath's military doctrine was based to a large extent on Chinese and North Vietnamese principles of guerrilla warfare. *Al-Fath* stressed the primacy of Palestinian interests and the role of a national armed struggle for Palestinian national liberation.

However, *al-Fath* did not escape internal splits. Thus, the most active separatist group is Black June, a splinter group formed in 1976. It is headed by Abu Nidal (SABRI AL-BANNA), *al-Fath*'s former representative in Iraq. The Black September group, on the other hand, was created by *al-Fath* itself in 1971, in response to Jordan's repression of the PLO in 1970. It was headed by Salah Khalaf (Abu Iyad) and constituted a kind of "special force" for particularly difficult tasks.

The Syrian-backed Abu Musa revolt within *al-Fath* against Arafat's authority was of great significance. This revolt broke out in May 1983 in response to the nomination, by the supreme command, of several officers to head the *al-Fath* troops in eastern Lebanon, in an area controlled by Syria. *Al-Fath* fighting units gave in to the insurgents and Arafat and his followers were pushed to Tripoli, Lebanon.

The agreement between Israel and the PLO which was signed in 1994 gave *al-Fath* members the opportunity to take over most of the important positions in the Palestinian Authority which was established in the Gaza Strip and Jericho. Arafat, as head of the authority, has recruited most of the police and security personnel from the cadres of *al-Fath* members.

FEDAYAN-E KHALQ ORGANIZATION (FKO) Founded in Iran in 1965 among students as an underground organization, the main task that the FKO set itself was the overthrowing of the Iranian shah by a left-wing national democratic revolution. Having begun an armed struggle against the shah's régime in the early 1970s, the FKO became very popular among students, young members of the intelligentsia and workers until the 1979 Islamic Revolution. On the eve of the Islamic Revolution of 1979 (see IRAN, REVOLTS AND REVOLUTIONS), the FKO had over 5,000 fighters and nearly 50,000 followers—the number is said to have reached 300,000 during the revolution itself. FKO armed groups played a decisive role in the 1979 revolution in Tehran.

Before the February armed revolt and immediately after its victory, the FKO heads expressed their support for KHOMEINI's political course. However they repeatedly claimed the right to freedom for their activities. After the government took measures directed against the left wing in August 1979, the FKO leadership decided to stop supporting the clerical authorities.

At present, the FKO's activities are underground. Its political and strategical goals are to struggle against the theocratic régime, to abrogate the reactionary laws that have reduced Iran's citizens' freedoms, to turn the land over to the peasants, to liquidate the large landlords' ownership of land, to establish democracy, etc. Since 1983, the FKO headquarters have been located outside of Iran. The FKO's organs are *Kar* (*Labor*, inside Iran) and *Aksariyat* (*The Majority*, outside of Iran). At present, the bulk of the FKO membership and activists live in Western Europe and the USA.

FEDAYAN ISLAM A militant, fanatically right-wing, Iranian organization, founded in 1946 and inspired by the medieval AS-SASSINS order. In 1950–1951, the Fedayan Islam cooperated with the right-wing religious leader AYATOLLAH ABUL QASSEM KASHANI in a campaign against the shah and in favor of oil nationaliza-tion. In March 1951, members of the Fedayan Islam assassi-nated Prime Minister Razmara, who had publicly opposed na-tionalization. Following the assassination, MUHAMMAD MOSSAD-DEQ became prime minister and oil was nationalized. In June 1951, cooperation between the Fedayan Islam and Kashani was halted, and Kashani formed his own terrorist organization. After the restoration of the shah's power, brought about by General Zahedi's coup of 1953, the Fedayan Islam was suppressed. This, however, did not prevent some of its members from assassinat-ing Prime Minister Hassan Ali Mansur in 1965. Following this murder, the authorities once again took measures against the or-ganization, this time succeeding in liquidating it. However, more than a decade later, many of the leaders of the Fedayan Is-lam played a prominent role in the Islamic Revolution of 1979 (see IRAN, REVOLTS AND REVOLUTIONS).

FEDAYEEN *Fida'iyin* (in classical Arabic, *Fidai'yun*; singu-lar, *Fida'i*) literally, "those who sacrifice themselves," originally in the defense of Islam, nowadays in defense of their nation. Originally this term was applied to members of certain Shiite schismatic sects of the 8th century. Later it was generalized to designate warriors stationed along the borders of Islamic states, whose duty it was to defend the Islamic community from hostile invaders. As such, it was a term of great honor. Today, *Fida'iyin* is the term Palestinians use in reference to themselves as mem-bers of the resistance, a term which involves emotional and moral connotations.

Since 1948, the Gaza Strip has always been the main source of hostile action against Israel. The numerous refugees in this area constitute a frustrated population for which such activities have been a major outlet of pressures and tensions. Up to 1955, actions within Israeli territory involved theft and personal dam-age. These were mostly individual affairs, independent of any organized movements.

However, toward the mid-1950s, the Egyptian government in-troduced a commando group called the Fedayeen, which ini-tially numbered some 700 men. Sabotage against Israel was en-couraged and was carried out under the authority of Egyptian Intelligence. The model consisted of small three to four men squads infiltrating into Israel, causing material damage, and then returning to their base or crossing over to Jordan. Often, those returning from Jordan to the Gaza Strip would also launch other operations on the way back home.

At first, the Israeli response was essentially defensive. More soldiers, mainly from the border police established in 1950, were sent for detection and ambush operations along the bor-ders. With the emergence of Fedayeen terrorism, small Israeli units carried out retaliation operations beyond the border against villages that served as bases for the Fedayeen. Such a case was the Qibyah operation in mid-October 1953. In 1955, Israel offi-cially adopted the position that the neighboring countries would be held responsible for Fedayeen infiltration from within their borders.

The Sinai Campaign, in October 1956, ended the attacks by the Fedayeen. Israel invaded the Gaza Strip and destroyed the

Fedayeen bases. In the mid-1960s, however, Fedayeen raids be-gan again, this time at the initiative of the new Palestinian na-tionalist movements, mainly *al-Fath* (FATAH), which repeated the motto that Fedayeen (guerrilla) action was strategic rather than tactical.

FEDER, GOTTFRIED (1883–1941) Nazi economic spokesman and exponent of the "Leftism of the Right" in post-World War I Germany. Feder was a popular, rather well-known plebeian speaker arguing against "interest slavery," and achieved some prominence in the late teens of this century. He was in-vited to speak before the rightist *Deutsche Arbeiter-partei* (DAP) of Anton Drexler, which eventually became HITLER's Nazi party. After the collapse of Hitler's BEER HALL PUTSCH of 1923, Feder joined Drexler as a more moderate member of the party's central committee, emphasizing a pseudo-socialist and ultra-nationalist social revolutionary program, free of the mili-tary inclinations of the Stormtroopers (SA) and concentrating on political work. Feder called for the creation of nationalist labor unions (*VönischeKampfgewerkschaften*, VKG) affiliated with the Nazi party, and an opening to the Left in order to compete with the Socialist and Communist parties for the votes of urban labor. Hitler hesitated, because this plan blurred his clear anti-Semitic and racist priorities by fighting capitalists—Jews and non-Jews alike. Hitler further feared that unionization would de-centralize the party, and wanted the SA to regain a prominent role in its campaign to assume power. Feder was finally pushed aside, holding the nominal title of chairman of the party's eco-nomic council. Feder supported the strategy of GREGOR STRASSER, the very able party general manager and "Leftist" planner, of a coalition with the conservatives. He saw this as necessary due to the unrest within the SA and the party's impatient mood, fol-lowing its stagnation and eventual electoral losses late in 1932. Feder tried to convince Hitler to adopt a clear, positive program, because even though he had mobilized all the far right votes, he had lost heavily among floating voters. Hitler refused to listen, and in fact was made chancellor—his permanent pre-condition for a coalition—because the conservatives believed that he was weakened enough to be softened for their purposes. Feder then vanished into oblivion.

FEISAL I, IBN HUSSEIN (1885–1933) King of Iraq, 1921–1933. Born in Taif, Hejaz, the third son of Sharif (later King) Hussein of the Hashemite dynasty, Feisal grew up in Is-tanbul, where his father lived in exile. He returned to Hejaz with his father in 1908, when Hussein was appointed Amir of Mecca. On the eve of World War I he established contact with the ARAB NATIONALIST MOVEMENT in Damascus. When, in Hejaz in 1916, his father launched the ARAB REVOLT OF 1916–1918, Feisal took command of the Northern Army which harassed Turkish forces in guerrilla operations, and from 1917 advanced northwar into Transjordan as part of General Allenby's British and Allied forces. Feisal and his contingent were allowed to enter Damas-cus on October 1, 1918 and assume control of inner Syria in the name of Arab nationalism, under the supervision of the Allies' provisional military administration.

In March 1920, Feisal was proclaimed king of Syria. How-ever, French forces soon clashed with troops of Feisal's régime and forced him to abdicate. British Colonial Secretary Winston

Churchill then secured for Feisal the kingdom of Iraq, and in August 1921 he was proclaimed king there. He remained on the throne until his death in September 1933.

FICHTE, JOHANN GOTTLIEB (1762–1814) German philosopher. Fichte was born to an artisan family in the Kingdom of Saxony. He studied in Jena and Leipzig, and became a major link between Emanuel Kant's revolutionary philosophy and modern German and European nationalism. Fichte tried to bridge the gap originally opened by Kant between practical and theoretical philosophy, and between nature and metaphysics. The issue was how to grasp the working of the supernatural in the natural—a problem Kant thought man's mind cannot resolve. Fichte tried to solve it by arguing that we explain things from within natural laws and, on the other hand, "according" to them. He emphasized the Kantian principle of practical reason over pure, or theoretical, reason by creating an unconditioned "highest principle," the "absolute self," which creates itself as such and determines its nature accordingly. The "non-self" or the world are created and divided by the "self" in such a way that moral activities can overcome the dualism of subject-object in the experimental world. Fichte thus gave the individual the right to function as the one who determines morality in such a way that moral actions are able to assume a highly, individually reasoned, nationalistic character.

The French occupation of Berlin in 1806 drove Fichte toward a militant, morally grounded German nationalism. His "Eighth Speech to the German Nation" combined the individualistic principle of the absolute self with the moral obligation to belong to the nation, the seeming non-self, which rises above the individual and gives it its real meaning. National society is hence the source and the framework for the development of the individual, and the society's liberation is provided by national education. Fichte was a very important theorist of 19th-century nationalism and was rediscovered as such by German intellectuals—including some who joined the Nazis—after World War I, except that the majority, as Fichte himself, were free of racist or social-revolutionary ideas justifying a Darwinian war with the "inferior."

FIFTEEN REBELLION (1715) In 1707, the Act of Union finally joined Scotland with England as a single kingdom. This event, as well as Scottish unhappiness with the Hanoverian king who occupied the throne at Westminster, formed the background to the Fifteen Rebellion (which became known as such in reference to the year in which it too place). Its leaders were King James I—"the Old Pretender"—who had been deposed in 1688 and who lived in exile in France, and the Scottish Earl of Mar. When the latter raised the standard of revolt at Perth, James returned from abroad and took over nominal command; however, they were unable to attract support in other parts of the country such as Devonshire, and their forces were defeated at the battle of Sheriffmuir (November 13, 1715). Thereupon both the Pretender and the earl fled, leaving their troops to be dispersed by the English General Cadogan.

While these events were going on, English Jacobites rose in Northumberland, where they were joined by Scottish rebels. Their joint forces were defeated at Preston (November 13, 1715), which signalled the end of the Fifteen. The English government's decision to treat the rebels with a modicum of leniency, and especially not to dismantle the Scottish clan system, left the basis of discontent intact and enabled it to reemerge for the last time exactly 30 years later.

FIFTH MONARCHY MEN An extremist group of religious radicals during the English civil war and interregnum (the latter half of the 17th century). The group believed that mankind was on the verge of the destruction of the fourth monarchy—Rome, including the Roman Catholic Church—as depicted in the Book of Daniel. According to this plan, Jesus himself would appear on earth to usher in the divine fifth monarchy, whereupon he would rule on earth for 1,000 years. Their beliefs were very widely held during this period, but what made them different was their willingness to help prepare for the Second Coming with specific and radical measures. The Fifth Monarchy Men had significant support in the parliamentary army and were a thorn in the government's side until Venner's Rebellion (January 1661), which was their last active effort to prepare the mundane world for the coming of the Messiah.

FIGNER, VERA NIKOLAYEVNA (1852–1942) Russian revolutionary populist. While studying medicine in Zurich, Figner became a socialist and returned to Russia before graduation to work as a nurse and conduct populist propaganda in Samara. In 1879 she became a member of the executive of the PEOPLE'S WILL party, participating in preparations for the 1881 murder of Czar Alexander II and a year later for the assassination of a general. The wave of arrests that followed these actions destroyed the executive committee. Only Vera Figner remained free and in Russia, but she was finally captured by the police and in 1884 condemned to death. The sentence was commuted to life imprisonment at hard labor and she spent 20 years in the cells of the Shlisselberg fortress. Released, she spent 10 years in the emigration that she had always opposed. In 1915 she returned to Russia, where she wrote her seven-volume memoir, *Records of a Life's Work*, and was active among former political prisoners. She is buried in the Novodevichy cemetery in Moscow.

FIRST INTERNATIONAL see INTERNATIONAL, FIRST.

FIUME, MARCH ON Fiume was the port of the kingdom of Hungary, located in the northeastern corner of the Istrian Peninsula in the North Adriatic sea. At the end of World War I, the inner city was populated by an Italian majority while the outskirts and neighboring villages had a clear Slav—Slovene and Croat—majority. The Italian poet and war hero, GABRIELE D'ANNUNZIO, leading an army of veterans, occupied Fiume in September 1919. This was in clear contravention of the agreements between the Allies, which provided for Fiume to be transformed into a Free City. The Italian government of Nitti opposed D'Annunzio's capture of Fiume and his intention to impose Italian sovereignty on the area, but parliamentarian instability did not allow for military action against the bard-warrior and his legionnaires. Next, D'Annunzio organized the Regency of Carnaro, waiting for the opportunity to integrate it into Italy or to use it as a springboard to march on Rome, destroy liberal democracy and impose his own political style and ideology. Fiume became a focus of revolutionary activities, attracting not only Italian nationalists, socialists, revolutionary syndicalists, Fascists, republicans and anarchists but also revolutionaries from Ireland, India, Egypt, Albania and other nations, who together constituted the League of Fiume. This organization was created in order to act in concert against the League of Nations; the policies of Wilson; France; Great Britain; the Kingdom of the Serbs, Croats and Slovenes (later to become Yugoslavia); and the spirit of Versailles, which was regarded by D'Annunzio as a plutocratic club of bourgeois and imperialist countries. D'Annunzio, styling himself *Comandante*, ruled Fiume for over a year, while planning to take over other Italian cities in the eastern Adriatic. Attacking rationalism, materialism and bourgeois decadence, the Comandante rejected the Treaty of Versailles as "decrepit, obtuse, deceiving, betraying and cruel," while exalting Fiume as the place of "youth, beauty, daring and newness." In his new political style, especially in the astonishing theatrical speech-dialogues between the charismatic leader and the mass, we see a precursor of FASCISM. Solidarity and union were fostered through the use of multiple symbols: uniforms, flags, oaths of allegiance, marches and insignia all created a special kind of political mass-theater, in which traditional social and political criteria did not function. In Fiume, the population was politically mobilized through the massive use of symbols of a historical, religious and cultural nature and of mythical appeal. The rejection of the elective representation principles of liberal democracy in favor of direct political participation were coupled with the rejection of both capitalism and socialism as principles of economic and social organization. In September 1920, D'Annunzio enacted the Charter of Carnaro as the constitution of the Regency of Fiume and intended it as a framework of the future political model for Italy as well. Largely influenced by the revolutionary national syndicalist ideas of ALCESTE DE AMBRIS, who meanwhile had become secretary of the Comandante's cabinet, the charter presented a model based on principles that internalized the aesthetic vision of modern politics invented by D'Annunzio. The highly revolutionary model envisioned by De Ambris and D'Annunzio was declaratively adopted by fascism as a framework for the Italian Corporatist State, although even a superficial examination will show profound differences between De Ambris's Mazzinian corporatism—meant to free society by erasing economic inequality and social differences—and ALFREDO ROCCO's Fascist model, which was highly hierarchical and totalitarian. Fiume did not prosper as a political project, and during Christmas of 1920 the Italian government of Giovanni Giolitti took advantage of favorable political circumstances to remove D'Annunzio and his legionnaires. In November 1920 the Treaty of Rapallo declared Fiume a free city, and in 1921 it began functioning as such. At the end of 1922 the Fascists in the city destabilized it, creating the need for further negotiations. In January 1924, the Pact of Rome gave Fiume to Fascist Italy in exchange for Italian recognition of Yugoslav claims to Susak and Port Baros. Fiume was liberated by Yugoslav partisans in 1945, becoming part of Yugoslavia.

FIVE PECKS OF RICE BAND   Chinese faith-healing sect that revolted in the western province of Sichuan in 184 A.D. First led by ZHANG XIU, the "wizard shaman," and then by ZHANG LU, the name of this Daoist cult derived from the practice of collecting five pecks of rice from families of those who had been cured. Finally quelled in 215, this revolt, together with that of another Daoist sect, the YELLOW TURBANS, helped speed the downfall of the Later Han dynasty (25–200).

FLN   see FRONT DE LIBÉRATION NATIONALE.

FLORES MAGON, RICARDO   (1873–1922) Mexican revolutionary and anarchist. First arrested in 1892 for protesting against the PORFIRIO DIAZ administration, Flores Magon became known for his vociferous opposition to government as such. In 1893, Flores Magon published *El Democrata*, which was banned within three months of publication. Later, together with his brother Jesus, he formed the Regeneration group, which led to the brothers' arrest. In 1903, Diaz banned all publications by the Flores Magon brothers and Ricardo together with his brother Enrique moved to the United States. In the US, Ricardo and other liberals published their program for the Liberal party. The program delineated socioeconomic and political reforms with a socialist tinge. US Ambassador Thompson labeled the Flores Magon brothers anarchists and accused them of fomenting revolutionary sentiment in Mexico. The US government in turn sentenced Ricardo to a 36-month prison term. By 1910 and after various confrontations with government, he had come increasingly under anarchist influences. His ideals began to focus on land distribution rather than on political change. His stated theme was "Land and Liberty." Although he refused to side with FRANCISCO MADERO, he encouraged his followers to take advantage of the Maderista movement. With recognition from the international anarchist movement, Flores Magon signed a declaration in support of the October RUSSIAN REVOLUTION OF 1917. As a result, he was once again arrested in the US. In 1922 and on the verge of blindness, he died in a Texas jail. His body was returned to Mexico.

FLYNN, ELIZABETH GURLEY   (1890–1964) American socialist orator, who at the age of 16 joined the industrial workers of the world and became its most notable female activist. A field organizer and circuit speaker from 1907 on, her autobiography, *The Rebel Girl*, provides a vivid account of the movement and its major personalities. In 1927 she joined the Communist Party and was imprisoned in 1952 under the Smith Act. Upon her release she wrote her second book, *The Alderson Story: My Life as a Political Prisoner*, and agitated forcefully in the defense of others persecuted during the McCarthy era.

FORTY-FIVE REBELLION   (1745) The Young Pretender, Prince Charles Edward Stuart ("Bonnie Prince Charlie"), landed in Scotland on 23 July 1745, hoping that the war between England and France would distract the attention and engage the forces of the British government in London as he undertook to take the British throne by means of a rebellion. His father, the Old Pretender (the son of James II, who had been deposed in 1688) was proclaimed king at Perth, and Charles's rebel forces entered Edinburgh on September 16, 1745. They continued their way toward London, reaching Carlisle on November 17 and Derby on December 4, having already passed through Manchester. Yet despite these early successes, the Pretender's forces dwindled to only 5,000 men, and with help from the French not forthcoming, he reluctantly began his retreat, withdrawing all the way to Inverness, finally to be defeated by Cumberland at the epic battle of Culloden (April 16, 1746). The Young Pretender fled to France on September 20, and Cumberland began a ruthless program of repression, not only of Scottish political ambitions, but of the Highland chiefs and of Scottish culture itself.

FORUHAR, DARIUS   (1928–) Iranian politician, leader of the Iran National Party. Born in Tehran, Foruhar studied law in Isfahan and Tehran. While practicing law, he was one of the founders of the Pan-Iran Party and later of the Iran National Party; both of these groups joined the NATIONAL FRONT OF IRAN coalition supporting MUHAMMAD MOSSADDEQ against the shah, 1951–1953. After Mossaddeq's fall in 1953, Foruhar continued backing the National Front, now half-underground as an opposition group. He was arrested several times and spent a total of 15 years in jail. After the Islamic Revolution of 1979 (see IRAN, REVOLTS, REVOLUTION), while the National Front was still half-permitted to function, he served for some months as minister of labor in MEHDI BAZARGAN's government. Foruhar was one of the many candidates for the presidency in 1980, but not a prominent one, and failed to attract a significant share of the vote. Under the Islamic régime, he could no longer be politically active.

FOUQUIER-TINVILLE, ANTOINE QUENTIN   (1747–1795) The most notorious magistrate responsible for expediting revolutionary justice during the French Reign of Terror. A man of peasant origins, Fouquier-Tinville was born in the northern town of Saint Quentin, briefly articled to a notary and then made his way to Paris to seek his fortune with the outbreak of the FRENCH REVOLUTION. He led an obscure life as lawyer until the JACOBINS came to power. In 1793, in an effort to avoid a recurrence of the wanton violence of the September massacres perpetrated by the Paris mob which had spread terror by taking the law into its own hands, the CONVENTION established a special revolutionary tribunal in Paris to judge political criminals, ranging all the way from emigrés to insubordinate generals like DUMOURIEZ and unruly mob leaders. In March 1793, the Convention appointed Fouquier-Tinville as the court's public prosecutor.

Under Fouquier-Tinville, the revolutionary tribunal became a shortcut to the guillotine. Suspending legal procedures, he expedited trials by curtailing preliminary hearings and public deliberations, repeatedly interrupted testimony, confided privately to the jury and judged for himself the degree of complicity of the accused. These procedures were carried out at the behest of the Convention, anxious to expedite multiple trials and eliminate such political enemies as the GIRONDINS or the royalists, extending later to DANTON and the Indulgents and Hébert and the *Enragés*. The 22 Girondin deputies arrested in June were tried en bloc, for instance, and Madame du Barry, the Duke of ORLÉANS, ANDRÉ CHÉNIER and hundreds of others were all sent to the guillotine without the slightest regard for due process or the rights of the accused.

When the Jacobin law of 22 Prairial did away with civil liberties totally, Fouquier-Tinville found it even easier to distort the judicial process and give free rein to his political animosities. Such political prisoners as DANTON and CAMILLE DESMOULINS were sent to their deaths without the slightest pretence to a fair hearing. After the fall of ROBESPIERRE and the dismantling of the COMMITTEE OF PUBLIC SAFETY in Thermidor, it was Fouquier Tinville's turn to stand trial before a brand new revolutionary tribunal. Accused of vindictiveness and violence before a less than impartial jury, he was sent to the guillotine in May 1795 and his decapitated head was then displayed to a cheering crowd from every corner of the scaffold.

FOURTH INTERNATIONAL   see INTERNATIONAL, FOURTH.

FRANCO, FRANCISO BAHAMONDE   (1892–1975) Spanish general and politician, more accurately described as a general-politician typical of so many other junta-style 20th-century dictators who used FASCISM as a revolutionary principle of action, Franco became his country's *el Caudillo* (supreme leader) and undisputed chief of state from 1937 until his death. Franco's revolutionary and conservative régime, based on the ideology of corporatism, in effect came to an end when the Caudillo on July 22, 1969 nominated Prince Juan Carlos to succeed him as king and thereby restored Spain's old Bourbon royal line.

Born in the northern province of Galiciainto to a family of naval officers, Franco decided to become an army cadet, graduated from the Toledo military academy and then served mostly in Spanish Morocco from 1910 to 1927, where he assisted General Jose Sanjurjo in subduing sporadic revolts launched by 'ABD EL KRIM in the Rif mountains in northern Morocco. Promoted to lieutenant-general and then transferred to the Saragossa military school, he soon earned the political sympathy of right-wing circles for his suppression of the Asturian miners' strike and their embryonic Communist revolutionary movement in October 1934.

Rising to the rank of chief of the general staff in 1935, then appointed military governor-general of the Canary Islands, he took the initiative of leading his forces across to the mainland on July 18, 1936 in order to challenge the elected socialist government in Madrid, a military intervention that is usually regarded as marking the beginning of the SPANISH CIVIL WAR which raged from 1936 to 1939. On October 1, 1936, he was proclaimed both commander in chief of the nationalist anti-Loyalist forces and head of the Spanish State by a military junta in Salamanca. Germany and Italy were quick to recognize his quasi-Fascist government in November, but it was not until the fall of Barcelona and the conclusion of the civil war three years later that Great Britain and France extended their recognition in February 1939. President Roosevelt waited until his capture of Madrid in April 1939, however, to establish diplomatic relations.

Franco's brand of FASCISM transformed the Spanish state into a corporatist state. His ideas were largely inspired by the Fascist precedent set by MUSSOLINI in Italy: it was based on a single political party, the FALANGE, with himself acknowledged as both party leader and chief of state. Political opposition and social protest were severely curtailed and the press, unions, student organizations and so on placed under strict state control. Above all, provincial autonomy was ruthlessly suppressed.

With the outbreak of World War II, Franco decided to pursue a policy of neutralism. Despite a futile effort by HITLER following the fall of France to persuade him to join the ranks of the Axis powers at a famous meeting held in Hendaye on the

Franco-Spanish border on October 23, 1940, Franco succeeded in preserving Spanish neutrality in the same manner that President Inonu guarded Turkish neutrality at the other end of the Mediterranean.

Although condemned by the western powers in the postwar period because of his unfashionable Fascist ideas, Franco skilfully managed to further strengthen his power base by having himself proclaimed Caudillo for life in July 1947 until he could find a way of settling the matter of a royalist restoration. His refusal to bring Spain into line with western democracy by liberalizing its institutions and modernizing its economy had the effect of arousing domestic opposition from students, the liberal professions and even the Church, which had been a major pillar of the Fascist state. But it was especially the Basques and the Catalans from Barcelona who were the most vociferous in their opposition. Although the US under Eisenhower's presidency continued to lend him its support during the cold war, Spain was universally condemned by both East and West. Finally, on July 29, 1975 Franco decided to nominate Prince Juan Carlos, grandson of Alfonso XIII, to succeed him. On October 30, 1975, the monarchy was officially restored as Franco lay on his death bed. Not unlike his contemporary Iberian dictator, Antonio de Oliveira Salazar of Portugal, Franco resisted political change for as long as possible in his own lifetime. The régime of both dictators was protracted, but was followed in both cases by the triumph of democracy.

FREEMASONRY   Freemasonry is one of the most important and fascinating organizations in the democratic industrialized western world, but the quantity of academic research dealing with it is surprisingly limited. The history of freemasonry in England and the United States is still terra incognita to a large extent. One reason for this is that the masonic organizations, which exist to this very day, are careful to keep their records far from prying eyes. Only French freemasonry has made public those documents that relate to the period up to World War II.

French freemasonry is an organization whose unique character has enabled it to survive for over two centuries, while maintaining a high level of involvement in the process of the democratization of the western world. This unique and widespread involvement in the sociopolitical affairs of the country has taken place under the cover of a masonic "philosophy" of a mystical nature, masonic symbolism and a religious cult. This masonic cover is more or less common to freemasonry the world over and gives it its universal character. The nature of freemasonry's political activities differs from country to country and confers on each national masonic organization its own specific nature. French freemasonry in this respect underwent more far-reaching modifications than its sister organizations in England and America.

There exist two theories to explain the origin of the term "freemason." One claims that this is a shortened version of the title "freestone mason" given in the 15th century to the builders of English cathedrals, who decorated building stones with Catholic motifs. The other interprets the term as coming from "franc-mason," which was in use in England in the 14th century to denote a "free mason," i.e., one who had the right to move about freely, a right which the builders of the cathedrals needed in order to move from one building site to another. On every site there was a lodge next to the cathedral, in which the masons could rest and keep their tools. At the head of the lodge stood the master mason. Contemporary masonic customs have their roots in the norms developed around the medieval masonic lodge, which today is called operative freemasonry. Apprentices are accepted into the "companionship" of the freemasons in a special secret ceremony, with the aim of ultimately obtaining the degree of master mason.

In 1717, four London lodges decided to establish a federation or Order (in France: *obediance*), the Great Lodge of England, which is till considered to be the most senior institution among world freemasonry. It is nearly certain that the four founding lodges did not consist of professional masons but that the intellectuals who used to meet in them used the customs of professional freemasons in order to obtain a legitimacy for their activities. A committee was formed whose task was the formulation of a constitution for the order. This constitution is known to this very day by the name of the committee chairman, the Presbyterian minister James Anderson. The constitution made joining the order conditional on the candidate's belief in one of the accepted religions, without forcing any particular religion on him. The Anderson Constitution was published in 1723. Nine years later, Benjamin Franklin published it in America and it appeared in France and Germany in 1736 and 1741 respectively. By 1771, the Great Lodge of England encompassed no fewer than 1,200 lodges.

In Paris, the first lodge was opened in 1726 by supporters of the House of Stuart who had escaped to France from Cromwell's England. A few years later, some Protestant lodges were founded, which counted among their members high French and English officials, including Montesquieu. In 1771, there were already some 500 lodges in France. English traders and government officials also spread freemasonry during the 18th century into central and southern Europe. During the 1770s, the masonic lodges in England, France and the rest of Europe were places of *sociabilité,* in which were nurtured close relations among people of disparate occupations, people who spent their time in the intellectual discussion of new social and political ideas. These lodges tended to have an increasing indifference toward the religious denomination of their members, since the significant disputes were among the supporters of such advanced ideas as empiricism, deism and liberalism rather than among the champions of the various religions. Catholics, Protestants and Jews found here a common ideological denominator and moved away from their coreligionists.

In America, from the beginning of the 18th century masonic activities took place under the auspices of England and France. In 1730, the Great Lodge of New York, New Jersey and Pennsylvania was founded. Benjamin Franklin belonged to a masonic lodge in Philadelphia and published the Anderson Constitution as part of his activities there. In 1733, the Great Lodge of Boston, whose influence reached down to South Carolina, was founded. Until 1787, American freemasonry grew rapidly due to the presence of numerous sailors and merchants who populated the lodges of the port cities and even founded new ones. Unlike Europe, in which the masonic lodges served as the meeting place of a minority which rejected religious fanaticism and aspired to develop a liberal secular culture, in America freemasonry was indifferent to its members' religion, but required them to be religious. To this very day, one cannot become a freemason in the United States if one does not have a religious faith of one kind or another. On the other hand, freemasonry was racist and would not accept blacks as members. The liberal tendencies of American freemasonry drew to it the leaders of the AMERICAN REVOLUTION, with GEORGE WASHINGTON, Benjamin Franklin, Lafayette, and ROCHAMBEAU among its active members.

At first, the masonic lodge was composed of "apprentices" and "companions," whose activities were regulated by the master of the lodge. Later, from 1740, there arose in England a new cult which used the motif of the death of Hiram, the architect of King Solomon's Temple, as the basis for the creation of a new rank of Master. This new symbolic freemasonry consisted of three ranks, with the head of the lodge being a "Venerable." The initiation ceremony also became more theatrical and included the use of swords, seclusion in a dark room and a ceremony of purification by means of the four elements: fire, water, air and earth. Also added was an entire new hierarchy of "superior grades" in keeping with the imaginary history of freemasonry, which supposedly described events in freemasonry's past, beginning with the ancient Orient and the Middle East, through Greece and Rome and on up to the 18th century.

France. The central institution of the leadership of French freemasonry was founded in 1773, due to the efforts of the nobleman de Luxemburg. This institution received the name *Grand Orient de France* and consisted of a number of committees, among which the most important was the *Grand Loge de Couseil,* which in fact served as the governing body of the Grand Orient and was directed successfully by de Luxemburg and his assistants, drawn from the circles of the liberal nobility. The Grand Orient cultivated the cult of the Grand Architect of the Universe, but it was not the only one to do so. In addition to the Grand Orient there existed other orders, the best known of which, *La Grande Loge de France*, continues to function to this day. The latter order fostered what it called *le rite écossais ancien accepté* (the Ancient Accepted Scottish Rite). Despite the fact that the Grand Orient was not a source of great intellectual innovations during the period of the Enlightenment, some of its lodges did much to disseminate it. The lodge of the Nine Sisters (*Les Neuf Soeurs*) in particular was active in that sphere. Founded in 1776, it made membership conditional on the applicant having solid credentials in the intellectual world of the Enlightenment. One of its more illustrious members was Voltaire.

On the eve of the FRENCH REVOLUTION, the Grand Orient consisted of more than 700 lodges. Altogether at the time of the revolution there were between 25,000 and 50,000 freemasons in France in several orders, but their influence on the revolution was very limited. As individuals, masons as such played many prominent roles in the institutions and the events of the revolution, but the Grand Orient as an organization as such played no part in it, if one discounts the fact that it served as the model for the movement of the different provincial JACOBIN clubs which clustered around the "Mother Club" in Paris. During the Napoleonic era, freemasonry was part of the establishment and was used for the purpose of controlling social groups whose wealth had accumulated as a result of the revolution. Toward the end of the 1820s, revolutionary tendencies increased among members of freemasonry and some lodges formed terrorist groups on the model of the Italian CARBONARI.

As the revolution of July 1830 did not result in the establishment of a republic, it became clear to a considerable proportion of the French republicans that while it was possible to attain a victory by violent means and to take over the government, there was no guaranteeing that the new régime would be republican. Ten years of learning their lessons convinced them that only a reformist policy was capable of bringing about the republicanization of the political system. As a result, the masonic orders were recognized as a fitting vehicle for the dissemination of republican ideas and values throughout society. The advantage of freemasonry, in the eyes of the republican camp, was in its being a rather well-developed democratic and federative organizational framework spread over most of the country. Therefore the masonic lodges could become centers of democratic propaganda and political activities which, despite their great geographical dispersion, would not become isolated and retain mutual connections through central institutions residing in Paris.

During the first half of the 1840s, some of the lodges did indeed develop into political clubs which debated progressive sociopolitical theories, mostly of a socialist character. The aim was to devise a coherent republican philosophy with the power to unify the entire republican camp around an overall reformist policy. The only idea which passed the hurdle of the debates and was unanimously accepted by all republican freemasons was the idea of "sociabilité and association." The intellectual and organizational potential inherent in this phenomenon grabbed the attention of the freemasons, who decided to turn it into the main means for bringing about the democratization of the French political system. Once the idea of sociabilité took hold among the masonic lodges in 1845, it became the main force behind the process of democratization of France. The idea aided freemasonry in developing two important instruments for shaping a democratic political system, i.e., regional masonic congresses and the model of positive leadership. These two, under suitable historical circumstances, made it possible for the freemasons to found republican volunteer organizations and to organize them as the social basis of a democratic régime. When the latter's very existence was in danger, the freemasons helped these organizations to launch their first political party, the Radical party, as a bulwark against the danger posed to the régime from its enemies.

The regional masonic congresses were founded in western France in 1845, as a solution to the inability of the smaller towns to maintain political clubs on their own. Within two years, these congresses had become regional platforms for republican political discussions, with parliamentary rules of debate and balloting. They spread to the midi and to northeastern and northwestern France. This rapid development was arbitrarily put to an end by Louis-Phillippe, and the suppression of the masonic congresses movement drove many freemasons to lead the revolutionary movement. Freemasonry paid the price, after the fall of the Second Republic, of having the Grand Orient subordinated to a dictatorial régime. The liberalization permitted by Louis-Napoleon in the 1860s created a relatively free political environment which made it possible to return to the idea of sociabilité and to revive the masonic political clubs within the lodges.

The masonic orders were banned by the Vatican for acting as agents of the new liberalism, which threatened to limit the influence of the Holy See. The masonic lodges reacted by proposing to hold an anti-council at the same time as the Vatican's council. The freemason movement of Lyon opposed this proposal, because it considered it a potential step toward another revolution, the anti-council's purpose being to mobilize freemasonry for an open confrontation with Louis-Napoleon. At any rate, these lively masonic political activities drew the attention of political innovators such as Léon Gambetta and Jean Macé.

Macé, with the aid of freemasonry, developed the model of positive leadership during the second half of the 1860s. He did this while setting up the *Ligue de l'Enseignement.* Macé had joined freemasonry in order to learn its organizational methods, (based on the principle of sociabilité and association) and to apply them to society-at-large through the *Ligue de l'Enseignement.* Thus the *Ligue* becoming a nationwide voluntary organization with a structure and aims similar to those of freemasonry, but without the masonic symbolism and mysticism, which were replaced by the pedagogical ideas of the *Ligue.*

The model of positive leadership emphasized the personal initiative that the founder of the voluntary organization must show. He publishes his concept in the press and personally takes upon himself most leadership tasks during the formative period, while agreeing to act according to the democratic rules of his organization. These rules consist basically of respecting the ideological, functional and economic autonomy of the basic groups within the national federation. The model thus calls for the relations between leader and follower to be based on rationalism and to be free of dogma, be it military, ideological, religious or any other. This gave freemasonry a formula for influencing society-at-large through the creation of organizations similar to the *Ligue de l'Enseignement.*

Macé was also involved, together with other freemasons of the League for Education, in renewing the activities of the congresses in the period after the REVOLUTION OF 1848. The first renewed congress was held in Metz in the year 1869. By 1882, the ramifications of the Franco-Prussian war, the PARIS COMMUNE and the US Civil War had faded and the Congress of the Federation of the Lodges of eastern France renewed its activities. By the end of the century, five more annual congresses had come into being, comprising the rest of the federations of the Grand Orient. The agenda of the masonic congresses movement was identical to the national political agenda, as interpreted by the republican camp. On this basis, close ties were formed between the parliament, the government and the masonic congresses. These ties meant that the masonic movement was involved in the process of legislation.

It is conceivable that the system of ties so formed and supported by a growing number of voluntary and professional organizations could have continued its existence undisturbed, but the Dreyfus Affair changed this state of affairs. It was interpreted by freemasonry and by the republican movement as a mortal threat to the democratic régime. In the face of this threat, the congresses and the model of positive leadership were activated, in concert, to form an additional line of defense for democracy, in the form of the Radical party. During the final quarter of the 19th century, this model continued to develop and served as the main instrument in the establishment of the Radical party, which was founded in 1901. The Radical party thus came into being as a result of the confluence of the historical processes which had created the movement of regional masonic congresses, the voluntary and professional organizations and the model of positive leadership.

The French freemasons thus played a crucial role in the long democratization process of France, contributing to the strengthening of the democratic North Atlantic sphere that included the USA and England.

FREE OFFICERS   The name adopted by the military officers who took part in the military coup in Egypt on July 23, 1952. Historical circumstances, only in part related to this group, effected the process that led to its formulation. The years between the two world wars were marked by nationalist tension and by a struggle to increase independence from Britain, which had ruled in Egypt for many decades. Widespread disappointment developed at the attempt at forming a liberal government and at Egypt's limited independence, coupled with dissatisfaction at the faltering economy and the widening gap between the poor majority and the wealthy minority. These factors had formed the background to a new agreement between the Egyptian and British governments in 1936, under which Egypt's independence was increased, although a British military and economic presence still remained.

One outcome of the Anglo-Egyptian agreement was greater Egyptian access to the military academy. This now enabled members of families which were not part of the elite classes to also become officers in the Egyptian army. Thus, among those accepted into the academy were some individuals who would later carry out the Egyptian Revolution of 1952 (see EGYPT, REVELLIONS, REVOLTS AND REVOLUTIONS) as military officers. GAMAL ABDUL NASSER, ANWAR AL-SADAT, KHALED MUHYI-UL-DIN and ZAKARIYYA MUHYI-AL-DIN were among those drafted into the new group at the military academy, and these regularly discussed issues related to the social and governmental future of Egypt. Like most of their contemporaries, these young officers were imbued with nationalism and intent on reinforcing their country's independence and finding a solution to its socioeconomic straits. Already at this early stage, it was evident that the members of this group identified with a number of parties and held different ideologies. However, their common denominator was their understanding that the monarchical rule under Farouk was cut off from society and did not act to satisfy its needs.

As internal pressures intensified during World War II, especially in 1942, Nasser began to expand the group of officers with whom he shared his thoughts regarding the burning national issues of the day. At the same time he and his company began forming ties with opposition factions, including the MUSLIM BROTHERHOOD, and this involved cautious underground activity.

Egypt's defeat in the war against Israel in 1948 left the Egyptian army disillusioned, especially Nasser and his group. Late in 1949, this led Nasser and a number of officers to form a foundation committee named the Free Officers. Within this framework, the members discussed the possibility of reforming the government in Egypt, although at first no concrete plans were made to carry out a military coup. Their activities focused on drafting more officers into the organization and orchestrating contacts with various opposition factions in Egypt.

The internal disorder of Egypt in 1951–1952, especially the burning of Cairo during the riots of January 26, 1952, spurred the Free Officers to debate the possibility of carrying out a military coup that would remove the reins of government from King Farouk. Most of the officers having remained out of the public eye, they approached Major-General MUHAMMAD NAGIB, who had already criticized the government's policies, to stand as their leader. The Free Officers competed for the leadership of the Egyptian army's officers' club (December 27, 1951), and when Nagib attained this position he was opposed by King Farouk's representative. During the first few months of 1952, in reaction to increased agitation and instability, representatives of the Free Officers held secret talks with the United States embassy in Cairo, learning from it that Washington would not disapprove of an internal reform in Egypt.

On July 22, 1952 the Free Officers found that their activities had been discovered by the government, which was planning to take measures against them. At this point Nasser and his confidants decided to take preventive action. In the early hours of the next day, the Free Officers carried out a military coup. It was a bloodless coup d'etat and was completed with almost no resistance. Three days later, King Farouk and his family went into exile and a new chapter in the history of Egypt began. Upon seizing power, the Free Officers established the Revolutionary Command Council (RCC), which was run by members of the Free Officers. The revolutionary régime was, in fact, stabilized by placing most of the Free Officers members in key roles. During its first years in government, the Free Officers were an object of widespread admiration in Egypt and a model for a number of officers' associations in other Arab countries.

FRELIMO see FRENTE DE LIBERAÇÃO DE MOÇAMBIQUE.

FRENCH REVOLUTION The chain of events which was eventually to culminate in the French Revolution began unfolding in August, 1786. It was in that month that Charles Calonne, Louis XVI's minister of finance, announced that the country was facing bankruptcy. The only way to ameliorate the situation was through a more equitable distribution of the tax load. This, however, necessitated a thorough economic and political reform and, to a certain extent, a reform of French society. On the eve of the revolution, France was under the rule of an absolute monarchy: the king held in his hands the power, the authority and the right to undertake reforms. Calonne did manage to convince Louis XVI that it was imperative to make some radical changes. This, though, was not sufficient, as the king never managed to overcome the power struggles which were so characteristic of the cabinet. Calonne's success in convincing the king aroused the opposition of both the cabinet and the *parlements,* which constituted the major opposition to the king. The *parlements* were "sovereign" courts of appeal which controlled the 13 judicial provinces of France.

The participation of the *parlements* in the legislative process was guaranteed by the requirement that for a bill of law to go into effect it had to be registered in the *parlements'* records. The *parlements* had the right to amend the law by means of "remonstrances" sent to the king. The *parlement* of Paris and those of the provinces had a long history of opposition to royal legislation, but on the eve of the 1789 revolution they lacked the

strength to stand up to a forceful cabinet with a clearly defined policy. It may therefore be assumed that they were incapable of constituting an obstacle to reforms. But reforms were not even considered before 1786.

The crux of Calonne's reform was the introduction of a land tax to be levied on produce at harvest time, at a uniform rate from all Frenchmen. Other steps included in the reform proposal were the abolition of internal customs, the abolition of forced labor or the *corvée* and an easing of the governmental control of the grain trade. The reform was to be financed by means of funds which the government hoped to raise with the support of a new body, the Assembly of Notables, by means of which Calonne meant to bypass the opposition of the *parlements.* However, even though its members had been appointed from among the Three Estates, the Assembly evinced a stubborn resistance to the reforms of Calonne. Nor did his replacement by de Brienne, Archbishop of Toulouse, make the desired impression on the Assembly, which proceeded to transform its opposition into a demand for convening a national assembly of the Estates General, arguing that the latter was the only body with the authority to ratify an overall tax reform. Eventually the Assembly of Notables was dismissed and de Brienne made preparations for implementing Calonne's reforms. Meanwhile, the economic crisis and the government's inability to deal with it had become a topic of public debate, highlighting the government's weakness in the face of crisis.

The *parlement* of Paris refused to ratify the tax reform bill and called for convening the Estates General. In response, Louis XVI expelled the *parlement* from Paris and shut down the political clubs and societies, whose number had greatly increased at that time. That conflict came to an end only after Calonne's reforms were repealed and a royal pledge given that the Estates would be convened in 1792. The *parlements* of the provinces now joined in opposing the king and in demanding that the Estates be convened. The government attempted to break their resistance by disbanding them and establishing an alternative judicial system. The *parlements* remained steadfast in their opposition and also succeeded in gaining the support of public opinion throughout France. But it was neither the parliamentary opposition nor public opinion which brought about the breakdown of the *ancien régime,* which had reached the end of the line at the end of August, 1788, due to its inability to deal with the problems of the economy.

Until 1788, the bourgeoisie did not by-and-large oppose the nobility and the *parlements.* It was only the demand for convening the Estates General and the attendant struggles concerning its composition and the procedures for taking votes at its sessions that invested sudden importance in a minority which had been opposed to the *ancien régime.* This minority could now make itself felt thanks to the increasing prevalence of a norm of public activity, in which political clubs, discussion groups and masonic lodges played a key role. By the end of the 18th century, public opinion, molded by these groups, had become a major factor, encompassing elements of both the nobility and the bourgeoisie. The central issue in which it played a role was the support given by the bourgeoisie to the aristocracy in the latter's fight against despotism and for the establishment of liberal representative institutions which would enable the taxpayers to participate in the formulation of the national budget. It was only during the debate over the character and modes of action of these proposed institutions that the bourgeoisie began to formulate a class consciousness, mainly with regard to the role it was to play within a political system based on the assembly of the Estates General.

In September, 1788, it became clear that the decision of the Paris *parlement* to hold the Estates General according to the protocol of 1614 meant that the number of representatives of the Third Estate would constitute only one-third of the total number of representatives and that votes would not be on a personal basis but by considering the vote of each Estate as a whole. In response, a well-synchronized campaign was launched by a political club whose members were mostly noblemen and which met at the house of Adrien Duport. Among its members were parliamentary deputies, clerics, members of the royal court, bankers, academics, lawyers and journalists—in short, representatives of the intellectual elite of Paris. The aim of the club's propaganda campaign was to convince the bourgeoisie of the need to convene the Estates General under new rules of procedure, which would fit its intended role as the initiator of radical reform in France. The campaign was a definite success, the government deciding to double the number of representatives allotted to the Third Estate, although still leaving undecided the issue of the voting system. In response, in January 1789 EMMANUEL SIEYES published the revolution's most well-known pamphlet, *What is the Third Estate? (Qu'est-ce que le Tiers État?)*, in which he claimed that as long as the nobility and the clergy refused to grant political rights to the Third Estate and to pay taxes, they

The Declaration of the Rights of Man, 1789

could not be considered part of the nation. Sieyès called on the representatives of the Third Estate in the *Estates General* to demand that balloting be on a personal basis and to bring all parliamentary activity to a halt until this demand was met. This parliamentary stratagem was eventually carried out to the letter.

The elections to the Estates General took place in March and April, 1789. At the same time, the assemblies of electors at all levels were to prepare "grievance lists" (*cahiers de doléances*) for the consideration of the Estates General. The grievance list of the Third Estate, prepared in part according to examples circulated by Parisian political clubs, was the first collective political expression of the bourgeoisie. Most of the assemblies called for introducing the personal ballot at the Estates, uniform taxation, making the right to hold public office available to anyone with the required qualifications irrespective of class, turning the Estates General into a permanent institution with the exclusive right to ratify taxation, protecting the rights of the individual and establishing democratic councils at the local level. Most grievance lists did not contain demands to abolish the feudal system, confiscate Church property or abolish the monarchy and the aristocracy. These demands only turned up later, during the months of May, June and July 1789. The main point of contention with the two upper Estates was the issue of the personal ballot. All three Estates, though, were in general agreement on the subject of establishing a constitutional monarchy which would respect the individual and his personal and political rights.

The Estates General convened at Versailles on May 4, 1789, at a time of unrest among the lower classes caused by the rise in the price of bread. On the advice of Sieyès, the Third Estate refused to proclaim itself a legally constituted assembly and to begin its deliberations, pending the other Estates' agreement that all three Estates together would ratify the membership of the representatives. Thus the assembly reached a dead end in June. In the meantime, Louis XVI began moving army units into Paris, the price of bread continued to rise and rumors were spreading concerning the obstacles which were being put in the way of the Estates General by the nobility. On June 10, 1789, Sieyès proposed inviting the representatives of the other Estates to jointly ratify the legitimacy of their representatives and, in case his call remained unheeded, to have the Third Estate do so even without their consent. With the ratification of this proposal by an overwhelming majority on June 17, the Third Estate had turned itself into a national assembly.

Thus it transpired that the bourgeoisie became revolutionary and began taking legislative steps to change the system of government. Among the clergy, there developed a tendency to go over to the Third Estate, and the latter accordingly decided to call its assembly the *Assemblée Nationale*. This constituted a message to Louis XVI to the effect that he was no longer the sole ruler of France. In response, the king locked the hall in which the deliberations of the Third Estate took place. The Third Estate, on June 20, moved the deliberations to a nearby tennis court and pledged, in the presence of some clergymen and nobles who had gone over to its side, that it would not disperse until a constitution was ratified. A week, later the nobles and the clergy joined the Third Estate, making the existence of the National Assembly into a legally binding fact.

The *Palais Royal* had been a center of political activity for some years before the Estates General convened. In July, its cafes were dominated by "the patriotic party," a loose extra-parliamentary grouping which supported the representatives of the Third Estate in the Estates General. On July 12, the leaders of the party organized a popular demonstration whose causes were a protest against the concentration of military and police forces in Paris, rumors to the effect that the city was being purposefully starved and the dismissal of Finance Minister Jacques Necker, who had become the hero of the Third Estate. The purpose of the demonstration was to force the king to stop opposing the parliamentary work of the National Assembly. About 6,000 people marched to the royal palace and besieged it. On the following day there began a hysterical search for food and arms. All flour warehouses and armories were broken into and looted. On July 14, the mob reached the Bastille and captured it, believing that it contained a great quantity of arms.

The level of violence at this event was rather low, but it was enough to instill terror into the hearts of the representatives of the Third Estate in the electoral councils of the districts of Paris. They decided to set up a municipal guard which they called the National Guard. This was subordinated to an elected committee which had received a vote of confidence from the inhabitants and in effect took control of the city. Finally, Louis XVI took his soldiers out of Paris and annulled the dismissal of Necker. The National Assembly had won and its deputies took over the government of France and of Paris. The same thing occurred in all the other cities of France. The old city councils were dismissed and units of the National Guard were set up to keep the peace.

In 1789, peasants constituted over 80% of the population of France. Until that year they had remained passive, but the elections and the composition of grievance lists encouraged them to take the law into their own hands when their expectations were not met, and to force the National Assembly to accept their demands. News of a disappointing nature which reached them from the Estates General in Versailles made the peasants suspicious and impatient. Rumors from Paris began to circulate in the countryside to the effect that there was an "aristocratic plot" to foil the reforms with the help of "bandits." These rumors gained credence with the appearance of nomads, beggars and migrants who roamed the rural roads. The peasants were afraid that the aristocracy might exploit these people to bring about a premature harvesting of the grain so that they, the peasants, would starve. The uprising of June 12 brought the panic to a peak and caused "the Great Fear." After the peasants, who were already organized and armed against any attempt to rob them of their crop, realized that the robbers were non-existent, they went on to attack hundreds of castles, some of which were burned down.

On August 11, 1789, the National Assembly granted a legal basis to the Great Fear by abolishing all feudal duties and levies, aristocratic, provincial and municipal privileges, Church taxes and the sale of jobs in the civil service. That evening, therefore, the political system which had existed up to that moment became the *ancien régime*. The new, revolutionary régime which took its place was given a legal basis in the law abolishing feudalism and in the DECLARATION OF THE RIGHTS OF MAN AND CITIZEN. It dealt mostly with the ways to prevent the arbitrary rule of a despotic king. The introduction stated that the main cause of governmental corruption lay in ignorance, indifference and contempt for human rights. The body of the declaration condemned the monarchy's arbitrary rule, which infringed on the rights to freedom, property, security and protection against opposition. The means for protecting these rights were to be institutions representing national sovereignty and the rule of law. Thus the declaration gave expression to the political consensus which had already been evident in the grievance lists. The only article which aroused serious debate was the one dealing with the freedom of worship. The clergy expressed its opposition to the proposed wording and succeeded in passing a quite intolerant version. With this one exception, the declaration reflected faithfully the philosophy of those who had made the revolution, i.e., property owners who were interested less in social issues and more in ensuring that a dictatorial régime would not once again cause widespread disorder. The Declaration of the Rights of Man and Citizen gave constitutional legitimacy to a new political culture based on organized public action as a way of participating in determining the character of the state. The justification for this belief was moral, founded on the contention that men are born, and remain, free having equal rights.

Louis XVI, though, had the authority to veto legislation. He used his authority to prevent the ratification of the legislation concerning the abolishment of feudalism and the Declaration of the Rights of Man and Citizen. At the same time, he reinforced the guard around his palace at Versailles, an act which was condemned by the electoral councils of Paris and by the press. The possibility of famine and the military threat convinced the electoral councils that it was imperative to bring the king to Paris from Versailles, in order to free him from the stranglehold of his court and so that he would be able to solve all the problems facing the nation. On October 5, a procession of women, accompanied by many men, set out toward Versailles. This mass demonstration had the effect of compelling the royal family to set out for Paris together with wagons loaded with flour. The events of October proved once again that direct action taken by the Parisian masses could affect French politics at the national level. The major loser was Louis XVI, who had no choice but to confirm the legislative reforms. But the status of the National Assembly also weakened in comparison to the growing strength of the Parisian popular movement.

The Constituent Assembly now turned its attention to administrative reform. The local government was reorganized and the *département* became the administrative division at the top of the hierarchy. The new administrative system worked well because it was run by people who were elected in fairly democratic elections: about 4.3 million Frenchmen had the right to vote. This constituted about two-thirds of the adult male population and was higher than the proportion of voters in England and the North American States. In order to overcome the deepening economic crisis, the Constituent Assembly decided on March 17, 1790 to sell to the public the land which had belonged to the Church and which had been expropriated in 1789. It was also decided to use this property as security for an issue of paper currency, called *assignats*. The value of that currency soon dropped rapidly and caused economic problems which persisted throughout the revolutionary period. The nationalization of Church property also required turning the clergy into civil servants. The members of the Constituent Assembly therefore demanded that the Church be subordinated to the State. This was done through the ratification of the Civil Constitution of the Clergy on July 12, 1790, which stated that priests and bishops would be elected by the citizens and would have to pledge an oath of allegiance to the civil constitution. This oath was the cause of one of the deepest cleavages in the revolution and granted the counterrevolution a broad popular base.

The opponents of the 1789 revolution began to act in an organized manner after the emigration of the Comte d'Artois, the Condé and Polignac families and others. Within France, counterrevolutionary activities began in the Toulouse area, based on antirevolutionary and anti-Protestant Catholic organizations which were unified within the framework of a Catholic national guard. The first stage of the counterrevolution ended in failure, but the regular pattern of its activities was determined at that time: an uprising based on an alliance between foreign forces and French rebels. The composition of the rival camps was not determined by class or profession, but by the social interests of various groups in the population and by the positions taken by the local elite. In some areas, the opposition to the civil constitution had, by the first half of 1791, become a mass movement which applied terror against the revolutionary clergy.

In the years 1789–1790, the "patriots" also set up several organizations which, together with a fitting ideology which was developed by them, became important tools in their struggles. One such organization was the National Guard, which played a key role in suppressing riots from 1790 on. Although only "active citizens," i.e., those who paid enough taxes to have obtained the right to vote, were eligible to serve in it, about three-fourths of its manpower consisted of petty merchants and artisans. The majority of the officers corps, which was elected, was of bourgeois origin, and nearly every member of the Jacobin clubs joined the guard. Unlike the National Guard, the JACOBINS established a network of clubs throughout France which were in constant contact with one another. The network was founded by the radical representatives of Brittany to the Estates General, who would gather regularly at a certain coffee house in Versailles in order to discuss upcoming votes in the Estates. After a time they set up, together with other representatives, a club which played an important role in preparing the parliamentary debate which preceded the abolition of feudalism. After the events of October, the Breton Club made the former Jacobin monastery in Paris its regular meeting place and so the Jacobin club which came into being functioned as the headquarters of the radical party, led by BARNAVE, Duport and, to a lesser extent, ROBESPIERRE and others. It became the model for others and in the spring of 1791 there were more than 900 such clubs throughout France.

In addition to the Jacobin clubs, there appeared in some of the large towns a number of *sociétés populaires,* which constituted a reaction to aristocratic propaganda and the ferment caused by the civil constitution of the clergy. From September, 1790, such clubs existed in every one of Lyon's 32 electoral districts, or *sections.* These sent their representatives to the "central club," whose task it was to coordinate the struggle against the counterrevolution. In some of the *sociétés populaires,* the number of registered members reached 3,000 per club, as compared to about 40 members in a typical Jacobin club. The *sociétés populaires* of Paris were particularly active and some of them joined forces with the *Club des Cordeliers* which, from its inception in April 1790 led, in concert with radical journalists such as JEAN-PAUL MARAT, the opposition against the Paris city council; the National Guard commander, the MARQUIS DE LAFAYETTE; and discrimination against civilians.

A power struggle developed between the Paris municipality, the *sections* and the headquarters of the National Guard. The ideological basis of the struggle was the issue of representative democracy versus direct democracy. The theories of direct democracy which had been developed at the *Club des Cordeliers* influenced the entire sections movement. The sovereignty of the *sections,* the accountability toward them of the National Assembly deputies, the mutual assistance the *sections* gave one another, the right to revolt, the right to hold a plebiscite, etc.— all these SANS-CULOTTES doctrines could be found in the speeches and articles of the leaders of the *Club des Cordeliers* and in the radical press in 1790. True, they enjoyed the widespread support of artisans and laborers, but they were developed by bourgeois intellectuals such as DANTON, DESMOULINS, BRISSOT and MARAT.

The *sections* constituted the kernel of the opposition to the bourgeoisie which had made the revolution of 1789, but until the king's flight to Varennes on June 21, 1791, unanimity ruled and the power base of the revolution remained firm. The capture of the king on his return to Paris aroused a new dispute in the Constituent Assembly and among the French people. Though the king was removed from the throne and the National Assembly appropriated to itself the functions of the legislative and judicial branches of government, it refused to indict him and to deprive him of his crown. In response, the *Club des Cordeliers* organized a campaign of collecting signatures in the CHAMP DE MARS on political petitions which contained a somewhat ambiguous demand for the establishment of a republic. The National Guard was sent to disperse the demonstrators and the event turned into a massacre, but this act of repression succeeded in paralyzing the popular movement for an entire year.

The Legislative Assembly convened in October 1791. It consisted entirely of new deputies. Despite their conservative leanings, there gradually developed among them distinctively terroristic tendencies, the origins of which can be traced to the pressure applied by the antirevolutionary clergy and its supporters. The patriots saw the issue of the clergy as bound up with that of the emigré noblemen. At the end of 1790, about 6,000 officers had deserted from the army and joined the military forces of Prince de Condé in Koblenz. For that reason, the patriots saw in the declaration of war of August 27, 1791 a real threat, despite the fact that it was meaningless in practical terms. The solution to the problem of the antirevolutionary clergy and the military threat posed by the emigrés was thought to be a preventive war. Brissot was the leader of the prowar deputies of the Legislative Assembly, who were concentrated mostly in the Girondist party. He claimed that a war would strengthen the character of the people and purge it of the tendency to surrender to despotism. Among the Jacobin clubs could also be found some supporters of war, but Robespierre was opposed to it, because he thought that the officers corps could not be trusted. His, though, was a lone voice.

The Legislative Assembly declared war against the kings of Austria and Prussia, in April and June 1792 respectively. The first defeats brought about a state of turmoil among the members of the sections of Paris, who began to call themselves *sans-culottes* so as to stress their popular character. The Girondins passed a law in the Assembly concerning the concentration of 20,000 volunteers of the National Guard, called *Fédérés,* in Paris for its defense. The National Assembly also announced a state of emergency (*la patrie en danger*) and ordered the local authorities and the *sections* to hold continuous sessions. At the same time, the stream of protests against the king, sent from *départments*, municipal councils and clubs, grew ever stronger and the *Fédérés* unit of Marseilles, the largest such unit, arrived in Paris. The inactivity of the assembly and the Jacobins moved the radicals of the *Club des Cordeliers* to seize power in Paris. On August 20, the *Fédérés*, together with the National Guard of Paris, attacked the soldiers of the king's palace guard. The king fled from his palace and took refuge in the building of the National Assembly. In this *Journée,* the number of casualties was higher than in any other so far during the revolution.

While in the west of France a peasant resistance movement against general mobilization was gaining ground, a power struggle for the control of France was developing between the Paris municipality and the Legislative Assembly. On August 20, the Prussian army invaded France and the Paris municipality ordered all "suspects'" of treason to be disarmed. It was in this atmosphere of counterrevolution, treason and defeat that the massacre of September 1792 broke out, a massacre which constituted the climax of a phenomenon which had had its beginnings in the provinces. It lasted five days, during which the mob killed between 1,100 and 1,400 prisoners. However, on September 20, the French army won a victory over the Prussians at Valmy and then invaded Savoy and crossed the Rhine. The atmosphere of fear which had begotten the massacre was no more.

Under the influence of the war and the abolition of the monarchy, the revolution underwent a process of democratization. During the months of August–September 1792, a constant stream of delegations entered the building of the National Assembly in order to express their confidence. Women prepared clothing and bandages, volunteers built fortifications around Paris and the men, some of them without arms, left for the front. Still, not all Frenchmen joined the revolution. In the west, the general mobilization caused riots and thousands of young men joined the ranks of those opposed to the revolution.

The national assembly which was elected in August 1792 received the appellation of the National Convention (*Convent*). It ruled France until November 1795 and its influence continued to be felt through its acts of legislation until 1798. The CONVENTION restrained the opponents of the revolution, proclaimed the First Republic on September 22, 1792, defeated the European coalition and prepared the way for future conquests. But the methods it used were violent. It failed to solve the problems of the economy and persecuted the clubs and the s*ans-culottes*. The social structure of the Convention gave expression to the transition from the world of the king's servants, the *parlements* and the academies of the old provinces to the lively world of clubs, the National Guard and a revolutionary administration dominated by lawyers. Until June 2, 1793, the main split which characterized it was between Brissot's Girondist party and the *Montagnards*, led by Robespierre, Danton and Marat. "The mountain," or left, voted in a more consistent manner, thanks to its control of the Jacobin club, which acted as a party leadership. The Girondins were less unified since their strength lay with a number of *salons*, the most prominent of these being that of Mme.

Roland. They had a tendency to engage in small talk and gossip at the expense of making plans for acting in concert. The majority of the deputies of the Convention, including the center, supported a number of common political items: an aggressive foreign policy aimed at abolishing the old political system in Europe, upholding the sanctity of private property and maintaining a free trade in grain.

Beyond that, there was profound disagreement. The Girondins believed that the left would countenance, or even encourage, massacres and uprisings in order to establish a dictatorship or to consolidate the hegemony of Paris over the provinces. The left was of the opinion that the Girondins were antirevolutionary monarchists. An important initial victory of the left was the sentencing to death of Louis XVI, who was executed on January 21, 1793. This enhanced the power of the left in Paris, in the provinces and among the Jacobin clubs and *sociétés populaires.*

The escalation of the war gave an added impetus to the counterrevolution and the number of people it managed to mobilize grew. The immediate cause was the drafting of 300,000 men into the army. This brought about a wave of riots by draft dodgers in the west and north of France, and the Convention was forced to centralize the administration and make use of systematic repression. South of the Loire, in the *Vendée militaire*, a counterrevolutionary army led by noblemen, clerics and peasants captured all the towns and murdered many republicans. This occurred at the same time as the army's defeats in the north and a mutiny which broke out among the ranks. The economic problems also cropped up once more and the popular movement in Paris again demanded maximum prices, in particular a maximal price for bread.

Economic difficulties, civil war in the west, military defeats and the treacherous acts of generals, were all explained as the result of conspiracies which justified the use of terror. The practical application of the terror was through the establishment of a revolutionary tribunal by the Convention and revolutionary committees by the *sections* and the municipalities. On April 6, 1793, the COMMITTEE OF PUBLIC SAFETY (*Le comité de Salut Publique*) was set up. It became the de facto government and was granted the authority to take all steps necessary to protect the country. The committee passed a law which made it possible to execute armed rebels within 24 hours and unlimited authority was given to "deputies on mission" sent to the *départments* to conduct the general mobilization.

The crisis had the effect of purging the Convention of the Girondist party. This was done by the army, without the intervention of Robespierre and Danton. In fact, there was never any real threat to the rule of the *Montagnard* party in the Convention. Furthermore, the ratification of the Convention of 1793 weakened the moral base of the federalist movement, since inherent in the act was a declaration of loyalty to the rule of law on the part of the Convention. But the situation in Toulon, which signed an agreement with the British navy, and also in Lyon and Marseilles was different. In these towns a real rebellion occurred, which was considered treasonous, particularly following the military setbacks in the *Vendée* and on the northern and eastern fronts. It was this multifaceted crisis that provided the impetus for having Robespierre join the Committee of Public Safety.

Robespierre called for uniting the nation behind "a single will," by which he meant not the dictatorship of one man, but rather mobilization of the nation's total energies and resources for the attainment of a well-defined objective. But the problem was that he also counted the bourgeoisie among the enemies of the people and allied himself exclusively with the representatives of the artisans and the workers, the *sans-culottes*.

Following the failure of Danton's attempts to reach a peace agreement with some of France's enemies, only partial successes on the federalist front, setbacks on the *Vendée* front and along the border and the attacks of Marat, Hébert and Roux on the Committee of Public Safety, the Convention was also infected with war fever and announced a general mobilization on August 23, 1793. The law required bachelors aged 18 to 25 to be inducted into the army. The laws of "Maximum" were passed for like reasons and were not merely the result of *sans-culottes'* pressure. Its purpose was to prevent the country from going bankrupt and to ensure continuing supplies to the army.

On September 4–5, 1793, the Jacobin club organized a mass demonstration in front of the Convention in order to demand the removal of aristocrats from the army and the establishment of a revolutionary army. The *sections* and *sociétés populaires* were also invited. The Convention gave in to this pressure and ordered the setting up of the revolutionary army, the arrest of suspects and priority to the Terror. It was the Jacobins, not the *sans-culottes*, who planned the demonstration. The demand of the *sans-culottes* to arrest all aristocrats as suspects and to purge the army of them was not accepted. The revolutionary committees were not given a free hand to deal with suspects and they were subordinated to the government, not the sections. Robespierre and Danton, while supporting the demonstration, strove to institutionalize the *sections* and to limit the number of sessions that they held. Thus it was that on September 5 the Jacobins succeeded in keeping the *sans-culottes* in line and to limit their direct democracy.

On September 9, Lyon fell to the government army and in December Toulon fell to the guns of Napoleon. The provincial rebellion was thus put down. On the northern and northwestern fronts the French forces were victorious and halted the Prussians, Austrians and British. In December, the monarchist army (*Chouans*) of the *Vendée*, which took refuge in Brittany, was also defeated after some hard fighting. Thus the way was open to the Terror of 1794 (Year II of the Republic).

Terror as a system of repression was the result of the conflict between revolution and counterrevolution, which persisted throughout the revolutionary period. Robespierre, Saint-Just and others of the Committee of Public Safety spoke throughout Year II of the need to strengthen the *virtu,* which meant purging society as it was of corruption and constructing a new one. Despite this, the terror was in general aimed at the opponents of the revolution and did not have noticeably class-specific tendencies. The activities of the revolutionary tribunals were aided by the revolutionary army, and in particular the revolutionary committees. The latter were set up in March and April, 1793, and their main sphere of activity was based on the Law of Suspects of September 17, 1793, which made it possible to arrest those suspected of dictatorial and federalist leanings and of opposition to democracy.

By the end of December, 1793, the *Montagnard* party had al-

ready taken significant steps toward saving the republic, not the least of them being the victories of the army on both internal and external fronts. Within the party there began to be heard voices calling for putting an end to the terror and the issue aroused acrimonious debates which made it impossible to convert the country from a state of emergency to one of peace. Danton was the most prominent of those who supported ending the terror. To his mind, the terror was an emergency measure and not a system of government. The criticism leveled by Danton and his followers against the *Montagnards* was aimed at the "dictatorship of the committee." Robespierre attempted to reach a compromise by defining the revolutionary government as one that enjoyed extraordinary powers but was not extremist in its methods. He failed. Danton was executed and his moderate party lost its influence (April 5, 1794).

As a result of this struggle, the Committee of Public Safety became the government. This was an important step on the way to institutionalizing the terror, which received its final approval on October 10, 1793, when the government declared itself revolutionary until peace was attained. The *sans-culottes* movement was the main victim of the Jacobin dictatorship and when the city council and the revolutionary committees were directly subordinated to the Committee of Public Safety, they completely lost the basis of their existence. Thus the *sans-culottes* movement came to an end as an autonomous entity.

The Jacobin dictatorship was freed from the challenge of the popular movement which had contributed to its rise to power. But its inability to hold on to this power was not the result of a fall in its popularity but rather because of internecine disputes. The quarrel which broke out with the Committee of General Security, second in importance only to the Committee of Public Safety, and the tensions which existed within the latter, eroded the standing of Robespierre. Finally, the victory over Austria of June 26, 1794 and the French invasion of Belgium made a crucial contribution to this downfall, because despite the fact that these events lessened the needed for the terror as a system of emergency government, Robespierre insisted on viewing the republican régime as the incarnation of private and public morality. In fact, he declared that there was no connection between military success, which after all was the primary aim of the laws of March–April, 1793, and the abolition of the terror.

After Robespierre addressed a direct call to the Convention to purge the Committee of Public Safety and the Committee of General Security, the members of these committees reacted quickly, and on the 9th of Thermidor (July 27, 1794) arrested him and his followers. The Convention won in its confrontation with Robespierre because it was stronger than any of its individual members. This enabled it to act through the *sans-culottes* organizations, the National Guard and the revolutionary committees. On the 10th of Thermidor, i.e., the next day, Robespierre and his followers were tried and executed. The terror came to an end and the revolution began sliding toward the Bonapartist dictatorship. The attempts of the Convention to deal with the economic crisis by abolishing price controls failed. The expenditures of the war had brought about high inflation and the prices of basic commodities rocketed. The economic collapse of 1794 caused extreme poverty and the appearance of bands of robbers in the provinces. The central government showed signs of disintegration. In the midi, there were increasing demonstrations of support for the antirevolutionary clergy and resistance to the general mobilization. During 1794, a movement began into the forests, where gangs formed to become the power base of the monarchist peasants. These turned into a strong antirevolutionary movement and managed to paralyze the activities of the government in the rural areas. The Convention was not able to deal with the problem through army units, since these were busy in the Low Countries. Instead, it tried to solve the problem by moderating the law of general mobilization and its anticlerical policies. This helped to bring about a cease-fire.

The riots which occurred on April 1 and May 20, 1795 proved that public opinion had changed following the fall of Robespierre. The demands were more moderate and were not accompanied by calls for drastic steps. The *Journées* of Prairial (June, 1795) were part food riots and part armed insurrection. They were accompanied by the demand to arrest deputies of the Convention and to put into effect the constitution of 1793. During the two days that the affair lasted, guns were placed opposite the Tuilleries gardens but in the end the crowd dispersed without a battle. In response, additional members of the *Montagnard* party were arrested and army units attacked the Faubourg Saint-Antoine and dismantled the barricades there. Many were executed and even more were imprisoned. This was the end of the *sans-culottes* movement, whose remaining activists went underground.

The suppression of the uprising of Prairial nearly put an end to the journées as periodic uprisings in Paris which so typified the revolution. In the end the army proved victorious, but using it to suppress a popular movement showed the extent to which the government depended on it. During 1795, the disintegration of the authority of the central government accelerated throughout France. As a part of the "White Terror," the remnants of the Jacobin establishment were persecuted and Jacobins who were in prison were murdered by gangs of killers with monarchist leanings. On the other hand, the situation along the fronts improved and France signed peace treaties with Prussia, the Netherlands and Spain. Only with England did a state of war still exist. The uprising of the monarchist peasants, financed and aided by the monarchists, was put down by General Auch. The stability thus attained enabled the Convention to formulate the constitution of 1795, which drastically limited the right to vote and to be elected and practically left the middle classes, which had led the revolution from the beginning, with no chance of sending any representatives to the National Assembly.

Out of fear of a Jacobin dictatorship, the new constitution provided for an extreme separation of powers. The legislative branch consisted of two houses, the Council of Five Hundred and the Senate. The former had the authority to initiate and pass legislation, while the Senate could only offer amendments. The executive branch consisted of a five-member *Directoire* (Directory or DIRECTORATE) elected by the Council of Five Hundred. The Directory could neither initiate, formulate nor veto legislation. It could only suggest an agenda for the legislative branch. It also had no authority to determine the size of the budget or to declare war. It had to be content with managing external relations, supervising the armed forces, carrying out the law and appointing cabinet ministers. The constitution aspired above all else to prevent any resurgence of Jacobinism. This it did by banning the activities of political clubs.

In August 1795, the Convention passed a series of laws which ensured that two-thirds of the incumbent deputies would retain their seats in the new Convention. The results of the elections proved that the electorate was not opposed merely to the *Montagnard* party, but to the members of the legislature in general. The "laws of the two-thirds" caused an uprising in October 1795, during which seven *sections* rebelled. Napoleon was one of the officers sent by the Directory to put down the uprising. The attack of the forces of the *sections* was stopped with cannon fire and the National Guard was put under the command of Napoleon. This was the second time that the army had saved the republic and protected its weak government, which had lost its control over the departments and was unable to prevent the disintegration of public administration caused by the attacks of antirevolutionary gangs active in the west and the midi. The Directory aimed its greatest military efforts against the gangs that operated in the west, where there was the possibility of an English landing by sea. A force of 100,000 men was therefore concentrated in that area, under the command of General Auch. On July 16, 1795, he put down the uprising by means of brutal acts of murder and robbery. At the same time, Napoleon had his first successes on the Italian front, although the soldiers he led were barefoot, starving and dressed in tatters. The loyalty of these units to the brilliant young general only increased when the soldiers' pay, which did not arrive on time from Paris, was exchanged for allowances from his private account.

In addition to the wars inside the country and abroad, the Directory also waged a struggle against the Jacobin movement, which was reawakening. The "conspiracy of the equals" of BABEUF served as a good opportunity. In 1795, Babeuf came out against the principles of private property and proposed abolishing the free market system entirely. In their place he wanted to establish a bureaucratic communism which would manage industry and agriculture and market their products on an egalitarian basis. The transition to this kind of communism was to be accomplished through the nationalization of the property of the dead. Thus both private property and poverty were supposed to disappear after a single generation. Babeuf's communism was to come to power thanks to the activities of a small leadership and a revolutionary avant-guarde. The repressive measures of the Directory pushed the Jacobins into Babeuf's camp. In 1795, the number of members in the neo-Jacobin Pantheon club, which supported Babeuf, reached 3,000. Other clubs opened in Paris as well and in other towns. Napoleon reacted by closing the Pantheon and by proclaiming that expression of support for the constitution of 1793 constituted treason.

In response, Babeuf founded a revolutionary committee, whose function it was to prepare the revolution and to put the constitution of 1793 and communism into effect. The police arrested Babeuf and his supporters and began an operation aimed at the final liquidation of the Jacobin movement. They proceeded to arrest hundreds of patriots who had no direct connection with the activities of Baubeuf and held a public trial. Thanks to the pressure of the press, only Babeuf himself and one of his followers were executed (May 17, 1797), while the majority of those arrested were set free.

Along with the military victories in Italy and on the internal front, England continued in its efforts to destabilize France internally by financing the activities of monarchist gangs and the election campaigns of pro-monarchy candidates. The elections which took place in March 1797 brought into both houses of the legislature a rather large monarchist party. This was a sign that the bourgeoisie, the landowners and the wealthy had become alienated from the Convention, which made desperate efforts to gain the support of these elites while banning all organized political activities. On September 4, the triumvirate (BARRAS, Reubel and la Revellier) made an attempt at halting the successes of the monarchists and purged the second Directory, the houses of parliament and the central and local public administration of monarchists. These steps were temporarily successful. From a legal point of view, the Third Estate had become the nation. The republic had managed to survive and the economy showed some improvement, but the second Directory proved incapable of stabilizing itself.

During the election campaign of 1798, the Directory led a propaganda campaign against the monarchists and the Jacobin clubs. Because of the "red peril," it even announced a partial state of emergency. These steps, however, did not stop the establishment of scores of clubs in the provinces and in Paris, called *cerceles de la constitution*. These circles, although lacking a main headquarters, maintained contact through the Jacobin press. They called for the democratization of the public administration, progressive taxation, aid for the soldiers, governmental prevention of starvation and free education. The Directory perceived as a danger the possibility that the urban workers would once again participate in the political process, with an attendant return of the terror and of attacks against property. The Jacobins won about one-third of the seats in the Council of Five Hundred, but most of them were expelled following a purge conducted by the Directory on May 11, 1798. The government also closed their clubs and newspapers

These measures of repression made it possible for the Directory to stabilize its rule. However, its inability to withstand the pressures put on it by merchant suppliers to the army for imperial conquest brought about its downfall due to the disintegrating national economy. The war against the second European coalition was renewed and at the same time an expeditionary force was sent to Egypt under the command of Napoleon. The administration of the conquered lands absorbed a great deal of money from the people, money which found its way into the pockets of the generals and the soldiers. The corruption of the administration of the conquered lands, together with Napoleon's disastrous expedition to Egypt (1798) and the completion of the conquest of Italy, made it clear that the Directory had lost control over generals who loathed the civilian government.

Napoleon landed in southern France on October 9, 1798. One reason for the warm welcome he received had to do with the victories of the French army in Europe and the hopes which were entertained that Napoleon would gain a decisive victory over the coalition armies. But the more important reason was that Napoleon symbolized the great victories of 1792. In the army, Napoleon's popularity sprang from a widespread feeling that the military had been betrayed by society and had become the last bastion of the real revolution. Napoleon also had the support of the intellectuals and the political elites which aspired to establish a liberal government. However, only a small minority of the Jacobin party supported his *coup d'état*. It took place on the morning of 18 Brumaire (November 9, 1799) and began

with the proclamation of two decrees by the Senate, one ordering the removal of both Assemblies to Saint-Cloud and the other appointing Napoleon as the commander of Paris. The Council of Five Hundred dared express its opposition to Napoleon's appointment, but this opposition melted under the threats of the military. The supports of both houses of parliament elected him, along with Sieyès and Roger Ducos, as members of the Provisional Consulate. A committee was appointed to formulate a new constitution and to purge the Council of Five-hundred of the opponents of Napoleon. The First Republic had come to an end, and with it ended the French Revolution.

The First Republic collapsed because it lacked the political means to solve the contradictions between the government and the legislature and because it failed to overcome the crises which racked the political elites. The inability of the political system to insulate itself from the violence of the mobs was an expression of its failure to establish a democratic régime of the kind that existed in England and the United States. Its breaking point occurred during the short period between the victory which the Committee of Public Safety had gained under the leadership of Robespierre in 1794, and his overthrow and execution. Robespierre's failure was the result of a combination of errors made by all the actors in the political arena. He erred by not agreeing to a gradual easing of the emergency regulations instituted during the period of the war. His parliamentary opponents erred when they rejected his demand to be recognized as leader of the state with executive authority. They were unwilling to give him and his government a freedom of action which today every democratic government enjoys and to be satisfied with their right to legislate and to review the government's action.

This debate concerning the separation of the government from the National Assembly took place at a difficult moment, in which the revolutionary administration was still suffering from battle shock and was thus unable to maintain an unhurried discussion which could have ended in compromise and mutual agreement. Robespierre believed that without a solution to this conflict it was not possible to return to everyday routine. On the other hand, the members of the National Assembly were concerned lest Robespierre, as head of state, use against them the means of terror which he had applied against the enemies of the revolution during the period of the war. Thus it was that the pressures of war and the inability of the political system to extricate itself quickly from battle shock and to stabilize a democratic political system based on separation of powers and human and civil rights made inevitable its slide toward the Bonapartist dictatorship. It was only 75 years later that French public opinion managed to develop a stable consciousness of a democratic régime which was free of the violent revolutionary myth and of the fear lest the separation of powers bring about a dictatorship. The Third Republic was the embodiment of this new political culture.

FRENCH STUDENT REVOLUTION The name given to a student uprising in France, culminating in May and June 1968. It was characterized by a spontaneous paroxysm of student fury and discontent, directed, in the first instance, against the archaic conditions and rigid curriculum of the French educational system and the lack of job opportunities for graduates in a stagnant economy marked by unemployment for youngsters with college degrees. It soon spread, however, beyond the universities and high school *lycées*, to coalesce into a wider and seemingly irresistible movement of popular protest against the arrogance and complacency of the Fifth Republic, as the latter prepared to commemorate its 10th anniversary. The leading editorialist of the prestigious Paris daily *Le Monde* gave a historical resonance to the joyful revolution unleashed by the students, by recalling Lamartin's famous words on the eve of the 1848 revolution (see REVOLUTIONS OF 1848) that "France is bored." To other observers, it brought to mind Wordsworth's lines on the fall of the Bastille, "Bliss was it in that dawn to be alive, but to be young was very heaven." For a few outrageous weeks that summer an astonished world watched in anxious disbelief as a motley assortment of young students and workers joined forces with a broad cross-section of French men and women from every walk of life to challenge all forms of authority—political, economic and social—and only narrowly missed the chance of toppling de Gaulle's régime.

What in the end proved to be a glorious but abortive revolution, still designated by the French euphemism *les événements* or "the events" (corresponding in spirit to what the 1960s' counterculture used to call a "happening"), began with an outburst of student indignation over curricular changes imposed by the education minister on the brand-new campus of Nanterre in the northern suburbs of Paris. Student agitation and rhetorical vio-

French students' revolutionary poster, 1968; the promised "long struggle" proved to be short-lived

lence, mobilized by DANIEL COHN-BENEDIT (known as "Danny the Red") and his insurrectionary organization, labelled the "22 March Movement," spread like wildfire to other provincial colleges, schools and universities, reaching its peak on May 3, with the outright seizure and occupation of the Paris Sorbonne, which was noisily and dramatically converted into a populist Student Commune open to all men and women of good will in open rebellion against the status quo. A terrified rector appealed to the authorities. The police responded with brutality. In the wake of bloody street skirmishes which erupted on the night of May 10–11, "the Night of the Barricades," the students and their local sympathizers, re-enacting the ancient rites and rituals of Parisian revolution, proclaimed the independence of the Latin Quarter in the name of "student power" and appealed to the rest of the country to follow their example. The workers were the first to respond with a sporadic wave of sit-in strikes of unprecedented proportions, far more extensive and disruptive than anything ever seen before, even surpassing the heady days of the Popular Front. By May 20, more than 7 million workers, almost the entire French labor force, had laid down their tools, bringing the country to a standstill and virtually paralyzing the whole economy. Industry and commerce, public services and utilities, transportation, the mails, the telephones and telegraph service, the state-run media and the schools, all came to a halt, as the country—gripped by a wave of romantic euphoria spreading into every nook and cranny of society—decided to celebrate a national holiday in sympathy with the beleaguered students.

The government's reaction was at first hysterical, then conciliatory. The unions seized the opportunity to negotiate the so-called Rue de Grenelle labor agreements with Prime Minister Georges Pompidou, leading to salary increases of at least 12% across the board, as well as a drastic reduction in working hours. The labor unrest did not, however, subside, as the rank-and-file workers, organized in Soviet-style strike committees, rebelled against union discipline, disavowed any settlement made in their name with the bourgeois order, and reaffirmed their solidarity with the intransigence of the students, as work stoppages and wildcat strikes continued to spread throughout the country. The crisis came to a head when de Gaulle, who had refused to cut short a state visit to Romania, tried to stem the growing tide of anarchy by a television appearance on May 24, in which he promised a national referendum on workers' participation in industry and educational reforms to appease the students. His performance, the worst in his career, had the effect of intensifying the social turbulence and opening the way to a political crisis of unique intensity. Following a mammoth popular rally of 800,000 demonstrators gathered at the Left bank Place Denfert-Rochereau, two notable opposition leaders, Mitterand and Pierre Mendès-France, long-standing adversaries of orthodox Gaullism, came forward to propose the creation of a provisional government under the aegis of the Left. The Communists, who had so far stood on the sidelines, denouncing the radical students and workers as Trotskyites, anarchists and Maoists, now decided to jump into the fray and demanded that de Gaulle step down from office.

Suddenly, when all was lost and the régime seemed clearly on the verge of collapse, the general cancelled his weekly cabinet meeting and left Paris by helicopter on May 29 for an unknown destination. It was assumed he had gone to his country retreat in

Lorraine to announce his resignation. Instead, as was revealed only later, he had secretly flown to West Germany to reassure himself of the support of General Massu and the French army chiefs stationed in the Rhineland. The next day he reappeared in Paris, and in a theatrical volte-face which took everyone, including his own disheartened supporters, by surprise, he delivered the most vigorous and eloquent speech of his career, recalling his famous appeal from his London exile on June 18, 1940, that France was determined to continue the war against Hitler. This time, speaking only on radio, he presented the country with a clear and unequivocal choice: either communism or Gaullism. Declaring his resolve never to resign under pressure and his readiness to resort to military force if necessary, he declared that he would postpone the referendum, dissolve the National Assembly and call for fresh elections to determine the real mood of the silent majority. Inspired by his charismatic leadership, the electorate, growing weary of the rampant anarchy and groping for a practical way to return to normalcy, seemed prepared to ratify his decision and give him a clear mandate to remain at the helm. A monster rally orchestrated by André Malraux and gathering an estimated million Gaullist sympathizers at the Place de la Concorde—clearly outnumbering the leftist rally the month before—was interpreted as indicating a profound change in the national mood. In the elections, which began on June 23, the Gaullist party led by Pompidou scored a resounding victory over all the combined parties of the left, routing the Socialists and Communists in particular, and gaining for the first time in the history of the Republic an absolute working majority in the National Assembly. This was Pompidou's finest hour and singled him out for the succession to the presidency of the Fifth Republic in June 1969, when de Gaulle finally stepped down.

FRENTE DE LIBERTAÇÃO DE MOÇAMBIQUE (FRELIMO) Formed in 1962 by the merger of three existing nationalist parties: the *União Democrática Nacional de Moçambique* (UDENAMO), the Mozambique African Nationalist Union (MANU), and the *União Africana de Moçambique Independente* (UNAMI). The president of this united movement was Dr. EDUARDO MONDLANE. When Mondlane was assassinated in February 1969, SAMORA MACHEL became head of FRELIMO.

FRELIMO maintained a sizeable armed force, by guerrilla standards, and had an effective and politically astute leadership, although it controlled only a small portion of territory.

Following the Portuguese coup of April of 1974. FRELIMO demanded full independence for Mozambique. It faced no challenge from the Portuguese settlers in Mozambique, who were politically just as alienated as the Mozambicans by the administration in Lisbon.

A transitional government, with Joaquim Alberto Chissano as prime minister, was formed and led the country to independence on June 25, 1975. The FRELIMO leader, Samora Machel, became the republic's first president.

In 1977, FRELIMO reorganized itself from a relatively broad grouping into a "Marxist-Leninist vanguard party" and declared that its broad goal was a socialist Mozambique. The government nationalized virtually all land, transport and communications, as well as private medicine, schools and legal practices. Great emphasis was placed on education.

Samora Machel died in a plane crash, under suspicious cir-

cumstances, in October 1986, and Joaquim Chissano, then minister of foreign affairs, was appointed president of FRELIMO by the party's central committee.

At the 5th party congress, in July 1989, fundamental changes in FRELIMO's political and economic philosophy were announced. The party abandoned its exclusive Marxist-Leninist orientation and agreed to extend the right of membership to religious believers and property-owners. In 1990 a new constitution provided for the introduction of a multiparty system, and the country's name was changed from the People's Republic of Mozambique to the Republic of Mozambique.

FRIENDS OF THE MANIFESTO AND OF LIBERTY see AMIS DU MANIFESTÉ DE LA LIBERTÉ.

FRONDES, THE   (1648–1653) A cycle of civil wars punctuated by Spanish invasions that spread throughout France during the minority of Louis XIV. At the time the country was ruled by the queen regent, Anne of Austria, widow of Louis XIII, and her chief advisor, Cardinal Mazarin (a Sicilian by birth and also her lover).

The causes of the war, named in derision after the French word for the sling or catapult used as a toy weapon by Paris street urchins, were related to the frivolous interests and petty ambitions of the royal court, the princes of the blood and the parliament of Paris. As usual in France during a royal minority under the precarious regency of a foreign queen mother, the nobles and parliament seized the occasion to reassert their rights and privileges against a weakened centralized government and did so in the name of provincial liberties and local immunities.

The civil war consisted of a tangled web of urban riots, peasant insurrections, coups d'état at court and Spanish incursions launched across the frontiers. It was dominated, however, by two major forces: the revolt of the parliaments (1648–1649) and the Fronde of the Princes (1650–1653). Mazarin was finally able to bring to an end the squabbling by capitalizing on the national revulsion against domestic anarchy and the humiliation of foreign intervention in order to re-assert the royal authority of a young and ambitious king.

By the time of his death in 1661, Mazarin had established a solid foundation for the creation of what was to become Louis XIV's absolute monarchy: a national yearning for order even at the price of sacrificing liberty; a nobility so thoroughly cowed into submission as to become a servile appendage of the royal court at Versailles; rebellious and unruly parliaments, which had so badly fumbled their legitimate right to resistance that they were now hopelessly discredited and restricted to carrying out their judicial functions instead of playing their part, as in England, in the legislative process of the realm; and the Bourbon monarchy itself, largely as a result of the creation of the splendor and magnificence of Versailles and the treaties of Westphalia (1648) and the peace of the Pyrenees (1659), reaching the pinnacle of its power without any domestic opposition or the threat of any rivalry from the rest of Europe.

FRONT DE LIBÉRATION NATIONALE (FLN) An Algerian nationalist organization, founded underground c. 1954 by a group of young activists dissatisfied with the leadership of MESSALI HAJJ and other established nationalist leaders and their parties (the *Mouvement pour le Triomphe des Libertés Démocratiques*—MTLD and the *Parti Populaire Algérien*—PPA). The younger group held armed struggle to be unavoidable and resolved to prepare for it. It formed an *Organisation Secrète* (or *Spéciale*) for that purpose in the early 1950s and later seceded from the MTLD and formed the *Comité Révolutionnaire pour l'Unité et l'Action* (CRUA), which transformed itself in 1954 into the FLN, led by AHMAD BEN-BELLA, BELKACEM KRIM, HUSSEIN AIT-AHMAD, Muhammad Khidr and others, with headquarters in Cairo and later Tunis. In November 1954, the FLN opened the armed struggle against France. It established a strong guerrilla force which developed into a full-fledged army and also claimed the political leadership of the country. It led an unrelenting armed struggle for over seven years and finally achieved Algeria's independence in 1962.

During the 1960s, the FLN conducted and won an internal-factional struggle over the formation of independent Algeria's institutions. It established itself as the country's single party, dominating the government and providing all leading functionaries. In the process, it eliminated all rival groups and also "purged" and ousted all factions within the FLN that opposed Ben-Bella's dominant group. The FLN has remained in that ruling position throughout the 33 years of independent Algeria. Its leadership and its congress determine the candidate for the presidency and all candidates for the national assembly, whereas the elections are in reality plebiscites to endorse prepared lists.

FRONT DE LIBERATION QUEBECOIS A Canadian separatist group formed in the early 1960s and aimed at achieving the independence of French-speaking Quebec from English-speaking Canada. In 1970, demanding the release of separatist prisoners, its members kidnapped and then murdered Labor Minister Pierre Laporte, compelling Prime Minister Trudeau to impose six months of martial law. Since then, having entered mainstream politics, the group's terrorist activities have generally subsided, although the cause of Quebec separatism is still ardently pursued by the *Parti Québécois*.

FROST, JOHN (1784–1877) British advocate of CHARTISM. Trained as a tailor, Frost was influenced by the writings of THOMAS PAINE and was an avid pamphleteer in his own right, calling for electoral reform and relief for the rural poor. He joined the Chartists in 1838 and generally identified with the more moderate wing of the movement. At the same time, he

also called for more violent measures in response to governmental suppression of the movement.

The arrest of working class leaders in 1839 prompted Frost, together with William Jones and Zephaniah Williams, to organize a mass protest outside the Newport hotel where the Chartist leaders were being held. Some 30,000 people were expected to participate in the demonstration. However, when the day arrived, only Frost and about 3,000 followers actually showed up. The group marched on the hotel, which was guarded by 28 soldiers. A shot was fired and in the ensuing melee some 20 people were killed and 50 were wounded. Frost fled the site but was arrested shortly after. At his trial it was argued, possibly with some basis, that he actually intended this demonstration to be the first stage of a countrywide insurrection that would topple the government and establish a republic with Frost as president. In 1840 he was sentenced to death, but the sentence was later commuted to deportation to Tasmania. Frost returned to Britain in 1856, but from then on took little part in further political activities.

FRUNZE, MIKHAIL VASILEYVITCH (1885–1925) Russian soldier. An early revolutionary, Frunze was exiled to Siberia in 1914 but returned after three years to take part in the RUSSIAN REVOLUTION OF 1917. In that year he led the revolution in Byelorussia, then commanded the BOLSHEVIK army that defeated the Whites under Admiral Kolchak and General Wrangel. A brilliant soldier with distinctly modern ideas, he succeeded TROTSKY as commissar for war in 1925 but in the same year succumbed to the effect of an operation forced on him by STALIN. The Soviet Union's central military academy is named after him and justly so, insofar as he was the founder of Soviet military science.

FUJIAN REVOLT A rebellion against Chinese Nationalist government in 1933. In November of that year, opponents of CHIANG KAI-SHEK, including CAI TINGKAI, established a People's Revolutionary government in Fuzhou and called for the overthrow of the GUOMINDANG (GMD) government. They advocated more liberal, democratic policies and firmer resistance to Japan. EUGENE CH'EN served as foreign minister. Expected support from other anti-Chiang forces, including the Communists, failed to materialize and the revolt collapsed in January 1934.

FUKIEN REVOLT see FUJIAN REVOLT.

G

GAIUS SEMPRONIUS   see GRACCHUS, GAIUS SEMPRONIUS.

GALEN   see BLÜCHER.

GANDHI, MOHANDAS KARAMCHAND (MAHATMA)

(1869–1948) Indian political and spiritual leader. Born in Porbandar, the capital of a small principality in Gujarat, western India, where his father was chief minister, Gandhi grew up in a pious Hindu household. There, he took the doctrine of *ahimsa*—refraining from harming any living being—for granted; it was later to constitute an integral part of his personal philosophy of social and political action.

After studying law in London (1888–1891), Gandhi was unable to make a living as a lawyer in India. He lived there for two years before sailing to Natal, South Africa, to work for an Indian firm. Journeying by train from Durban to Pretoria, Gandhi, despite his elegant western dress and manner, was expelled from his first-class carriage at the insistence of a white passenger, who objected to sharing it with an Indian. In later years, he consistently designated this as the single most important formative experience of his life; it moved him to assert his dignity as an Indian and a man in a country where apartheid laws rendered him and his fellow Indian immigrants second-class citizens.

Gandhi soon became recognized as a leader of the South African Indian community, staying on to fight for its interests even after his original work was completed. His trip was to have lasted a few months; he remained in South Africa for 21 years.

Founding the Natal Indian Congress, Gandhi organized demands for improved civil rights for the thousands of Indians living in the then-crown colony, most of whom were indentured laborers. In 1899, stressing duties as well as rights, he argued that as citizens of the British Empire, Indians should help defend Natal during the Boer War, and formed an 1,100-man Indian volunteer ambulance corps.

His opposition to the Transvaal government's 1906 registration ordinance, which required all Indians over the age of eight to be fingerprinted and carry an identity card, marked Gandhi's first use of strategies based on his principle of *satyagraha* (literally "truth-firmness," or passive resistance). His religious convictions had led him to a complete disavowal of violence, but he still received a jail sentence for organizing a boycott of the registration process and for the peaceful picketing of registration centers.

While in prison, he read Henry Thoreau's *On Civil Disobedience*, which asserts the individual's right to ignore unjust laws

and refuse allegiance to a government whose tyranny has become unbearable. The book inspired him to oppose the 1913 decision by the Transvaal government to close its borders to Indians. Thousands of floggings and hundreds of jailings could not break the nonviolent movement and, in the face of international condemnation of its heavy-handed retaliatory measures, Jan Smuts's government engineered a compromise agreement with Gandhi. Gandhi eventually sailed back to India in 1914.

Hailed as "Mahatma" ("Great-Souled") by Rabindranath Tagore, Gandhi played only a minor role in Indian politics until 1919, when he organized nonviolent protests against the Rowlatt

Gandhi, described by Winston Churchill as a "half naked fakir," leaving 10 Downing Street after meeting Prime Minister MacDonald in 1931

Act, which sought to repress agitation for Indian independence. The British authorities' response was nowhere more brutal than in the northern Indian city of Amritsar, Punjab, on April 13, 1919, where some 1,500 unarmed and nonviolent protesters were shot by troops, almost 400 being killed. Shocked and horrified, the Indians intensified their calls for independence from the British.

Following this incident, Gandhi was quickly recognized as the undisputed leader of the Indian nationalist movement. He succeeded in transforming the INDIAN NATIONAL CONGRESS from a superannuated body of anglicized Indian gentlemen into a genuinely representative mass organization, using it as the launching pad for a campaign of nonviolent noncooperation against British rule. To the dismay of many of his colleagues, he called off the successful campaign in 1922, when outbreaks of violence convinced him that his followers did not fully understand the importance of the nonviolence principle. He was arrested shortly thereafter, but was released due to ill health after serving three years in jail.

Convinced that self-sufficiency was an essential prerequisite for successful Indian self-government, he called for a boycott of British goods and a return to the wearing of rough homespun cotton clothing; he himself spent an hour each day at a spinning wheel and homespun soon became the official uniform of nationalist political leaders. In 1930, he marched to Dandi on the Gujarat coast and collected sea salt, in defiance of the government monopoly on the manufacture and sale of salt. The wave of civil disobedience that this action triggered resulted in 60,000 arrests, including that of Gandhi himself. However, the British government was eventually forced to acknowledge Indian nationalist aspirations. The man Winston Churchill had derided as a "half-naked fakir" traveled to London to negotiate with the British government; but the negotiators did not yield a deadline for British withdrawal from India, to which Gandhi had aspired.

Even after he left the Indian National Congress in 1934, he remained the spiritual leader of the nationalist movement and the Indian people, exerting considerable practical and moral influence. His principles led him to staunchly refuse to approve Indian support for the British war effort. Meanwhile, his 1942 call for the British to "Quit India" led to his imprisonment and that of the entire Congress leadership. Five years later, in August 1947, India became an independent state.

Gandhi had consistently struggled against a separation of the subcontinent into two states, a Hindu state and a Muslim state. The decision had nevertheless been taken, and India was divided into India and Pakistan. The sectarian bloodbath that followed the partition claimed one million lives. Gandhi spent the night of the independence celebrations in Calcutta, where his presence successfully prevented the communal violence that had flared elsewhere. When violence did finally erupt there, Gandhi, 77 years old and in poor health, expressed his intention of fasting until the fighting had completely stopped. He had fasted before to achieve spiritual or political ends, but never before had his life been so clearly at risk; 72 hours after he had begun his fast, hostilities ceased.

In January 1948, Gandhi arranged a truce in the riot-torn capital, Delhi, after fasting for five days. At the end of the month he was assassinated by a Hindu fanatic at one of his own prayer meetings. He died with the words "*He, Ram*" (O! God) on his lips. Thousands of tributes were made to him and many were strongly moved by JAWAHARLAL NEHRU's representation of him as "that light that represented the living, the eternal truths, reminding us of the right path, drawing us from error, taking this ancient country to freedom."

The initiator of the 20th century's struggles against colonialism, racism and violence, Gandhi has also been an influential symbol of the moral and spiritual resources of developing countries. His theory and practice of nonviolent direct action sparked the immense growth of nonviolent protest throughout the world.

Among the writings of Mahatma Gandhi are *Hind Swaraj* (1909) and his autobiography, *The Story of My Experiments with Truth* (1927–1929).

GAO GANG (Kao Kang)   (1902–1954) Chinese Communist leader. A native of Shaanxi, Gao studied in a military academy and joined the CHINESE COMMUNIST PARTY (CCP) in 1926. After the split with the GUOMINDANG (GMD) in 1927, he helped form peasant guerrilla units. In 1935, he was one of the leaders of the Shaanxi-Gansu soviet, which was joined by MAO ZEDONG and the remnants of the LONG MARCH later in the year. Gao had high standing in the Yan'an Communist régime (see CHINESE COMMUNIST REVOLUTION) and after 1949 was the leading party and government figure in the northeast (Manchuria). In 1952, he was appointed head of the newly-formed state planning committee, charged with directing the first five-year plan (1953–1957). Gao returned to Beijing in 1953 but dropped from view the following year. Later it was reported that he had committed suicide in February 1954 after being accused of "anti-party activities." His unpardonable crime may have been an attempt to use his Soviet connections in a CCP power struggle. This was the first purge of a major CCP and government figure in the People's Republic.

GAPONE, GEORGES APOLLONOVITCH   (1870–1906) Russian priest, revolutionary and secret police agent. As chaplain of the St. Petersburg prison, Gapone, who was a brilliant speaker, was recruited by the Czarist secret police *Okhrana* to found a workers' movement that was originally supposed to be pro-Czar. Gradually, however, he began to take his role as a workers' representative seriously and in January 1905 organized a giant demonstration of 100,000 people who picketed peacefully in front of the Winter Palace in St. Petersburg while carrying the Czar's icons. The police opened fire, thereby sparking off the RUSSIAN REVOLUTION OF 1905. Gapone himself fled abroad, later returning to his post as an *Okhrana* spy. He was finally hanged as an *agent provocateur* by his fellow revolutionaries.

GARANG, JOHN   (1945–) Colonel Dr. John Garang de Mabior was born in Sudan in 1945 and educated in Tanzania and the USA, where he studied in the military academy and at Iowa University. He obtained a Ph.D. in economics.

Garang worked as a research assistant at Dar-es-Salaam University from 1969–1970, before joining the *Anya Nya*—southern Sudanese rebels fighting against the government.

In March 1972, the Addis Ababa Agreement was signed between the Sudanese government and the southerners. This agreement gave autonomy to the southern region of Sudan. After this, Garang served in the Sudanese army in a variety of senior posts, including battalion commander and deputy director of military research. He also lectured in the department of rural economy of the University of Khartoum (1982–1983).

In 1983, President Nimeri of Sudan reneged on the 1972 agreement and imposed *Shari'a* (Islamic) law on the Christian and animist population of southern Sudan. Garang then formed the SUDAN PEOPLE'S LIBERATION MOVEMENT (SPLM), with the aim of abrogating the *Shari'a* and turning Sudan into a secular state with autonomy for the south.

GARIBALDI, GIUSEPPE   (1807–1882) Italian soldier and revolutionary, romantic hero of the fight to unify Italy. Garibaldi was born in Nice to a pious mother who hoped that her mellow-voiced, sweet-tempered child would become a priest. However young Garibaldi had no such desire. Not an intellectual, he studied only what interested him and often escaped from his studies to go hunting or fishing. He became a seaman like his father, sailing the Mediterranean and Black seas for 10 years. An Italian revolutionary's tales of efforts to create a unified, republican Italy fired his interest and indignation.

Garibaldi asked GIUSEPPE MAZZINI, the leading advocate of the Italian struggle for freedom, how he could help the cause and was told to enlist in the Piedmont navy and, by spreading propaganda, foster a naval mutiny that would spark a republican revolution. The plot failed, Garibaldi escaped to France and Piedmont condemned him to death. He was thrilled to read the newspaper stories that appeared afterwards (newspaper reports always embellished his exploits, giving him great pleasure).

Garibaldi now sailed for Uruguay, as Mazzini had no other work for him. He stayed in South America for 12 years between 1836 and 1848, fighting in its wars of independence. He also met Anna Maria Riviero da Silva (known as Anita), a married woman, who ran off with him, rode beside him on his campaigns (jealously reluctant to let him out of her sight), bore his children and married him after her husband's death. Garibaldi's hazardous wartime adventures taught him invaluable skills, ranging from conducting guerrilla warfare and riding a horse, to rounding up and slaughtering livestock to feed his men, or using a poncho as a shield against the elements.

Accounts of Garibaldi's exploits made him famous in Italy, where a new pope, Pius IX, had been elected in 1846. Garibaldi dreamed of saving Italy in the name of Pius's spiritual leader-

Garibaldi entering Naples, 1859

ship, with an army of Italian soldiers that he would train. Pius, though, never responded when he offered his military services. News of the 1848 revolutions sweeping through Italy excited Garibaldi, and he and his army of 85 men, two cannons and 800 muskets left South America for Italy, where his arrival was greeted with much enthusiasm but few volunteers. Rejected by Piedmont because of his republicanism and lack of formal military training, Garibaldi marched to Milan, where he joined forces with Mazzini. He fought two battles against the Austrians in Milan before being forced, heavily outnumbered, to retreat to Switzerland, convinced more than ever that Italy's future lay in independence and unity.

Garibaldi was drawn to an increasingly radical Rome, from which Pius had fled after an insurrection in 1848. Although elected to the Roman assembly, Garibaldi was a poor politician and was impatient with parliamentary procedure. The assembly disregarded his demand for the immediate establishment of an independent Roman republic. Disgusted, he returned to soldiering, in which capacity he was the mainstay and inspiration of Rome's defense against French forces fighting to restore papal rule. The administrative incompetence of the short-lived republic which was established forced its army to retreat before a superior French force. The republic's failure caused a great rift between Garibaldi and Mazzini. Garibaldi refused to surrender to the French. During the retreat from Rome his wife Anita died. His international reputation for heroism and patriotism preceded him into his second exile, from 1849 to 1854, to the United States and later Peru.

Piedmont's prime minister, Count Camillo Benso di Cavour, thought he could make use of Garibaldi, and allowed him to return in 1854. Cavour wanted to create an independent Italy ruled by the conservative constitutional monarchy of Piedmont. Public association with Garibaldi could channel republican fervor—that might otherwise turn to revolution—into support for a war to unify Italy. However, it could also make Cavour's careful statesmanship seem a cover for revolution and alienate Piedmont's foreign allies. Cavour solved this problem by making Garibaldi a major-general in a volunteer corps rather than in the regular army. Despite Piedmont's unsuccessful war against Austria in 1859 to gain Italian liberation, Garibaldi was an honored hero.

Garibaldi was romantically involved with several women after Anita: Mrs. Roberts, an English socialite who lionized him; the wealthy Madame Schwartz, who wanted the rights to publish his memoirs; and his housekeeper, who gave birth to a daughter. His marriage in 1860 to Giuseppina, the daughter of the Marchese Raimondi, lasted only a few hours before he left her, having learned she had a lover. It took another 20 years for the marriage to be annulled so that he could marry the peasant woman Francesca Armosino, with whom he had lived since 1866.

Piedmont made use of Garibaldi even though it found him a distinct an embarrassment, publicly disavowing him while at the same time secretly supporting his military campaigns which greatly increased its territory. Conservatives were afraid of his socialist ideas and many in the military were jealous of his victories. The church disliked Garibaldi because of his ambition to take Rome (which Cavour thwarted, fearing adverse international reaction), because he evacuated monasteries and convents to house his soldiers and because he was a freethinker.

Garibaldi's greatest military exploit was his leadership of the expedition of "the thousand heroes," in which his army, the Red Shirts, freed Sicily in May 1860 and then conquered Naples in September, defeating the kingdom of the two Sicilies. In 1861, Victor Emmanuel was proclaimed king of Italy. In the war of 1866, Garibaldi again commanded the Red Shirts in Tyrol. He was not with the Italian forces that finally took possession of Rome in 1870, but later that year fought for the French in the Franco-Prussian war. Garibaldi outlived both Cavour and Mazzini. He spent his last years on the island of Caprera where, crippled by old wounds and rheumatism and visited frequently by admirers, he wrote two novels.

GARVEY, MARCUS (1887–1940) Black nationalist and separatist; self-proclaimed first president of the provisional government-in-exile of Africa. Garvey was born in Saint Ann's Bay, Jamaica. A leading campaigner for social reform on the island, he helped organize a printers' union strike in 1907, which demanded higher wages. Appalled by the state of black laborers in Jamaica, he traveled to Central America, where he found the situation on the large banana plantations no better. He returned to Jamaica in 1912, only to set out again shortly thereafter, this time bound for London. There he met several prominent African nationalists, among them Duse Muhammad Ali of Egypt, who became his spiritual mentor. Garvey was also deeply influenced by Booker T. Washington's *Up From Slavery*, a book that would change his life. Washington's call for black self-sufficiency captivated Garvey, and he brought Washington's message back home with him to Jamaica in 1914. There he founded the Universal Negro Improvement Association (UNIA), with the intention of starting an agricultural and industrial school not unlike Washington's own Tuskegee Institute.

Garvey's notions of black pride differed from those of his hero, however. Under the slogan "One God, One Aim, One Destiny," he advanced the causes of black ownership of business and the liberation of Africa from colonialism and its resettlement by the black diaspora; he also advocated black racial purity and total social separation. Having reached the conclusion that he was only marginally effective because of Jamaica's relative isolation, Garvey relocated to Harlem, New York City, in 1916. He founded a newspaper, *The Negro World*, and quickly began attracting adherents to the UNIA. Within two months, membership in the UNIA had risen to 2,000 in New York alone. By 1919 there were 30 branches across the United States as well as branches in Latin America, the Caribbean and Africa.

Garvey began realizing his own ideas by establishing a shipping company, the Black Star Line, to sail between New York and the Caribbean. In 1920, he organized the First UNIA International Congress. 25,000 delegates from around the world filled Madison Square Garden to hear Garvey speak. At the fourth congress, Garvey was declared head of state of the provisional government-in-exile of Africa. A campaign to raise 200 million dollars for a resettlement program in Liberia failed when the Liberian government, under pressure from Britain and France, banned UNIA supporters from settling in the country.

Garvey's luck continued to decline. Even his personal appeal could not undo the harm done to his movement by the radical direction he was taking. In 1925, he was charged with mail

fraud because of the methods used by him to sell the stock of his floundering shipping company and sentenced to five years in the Atlanta penitentiary. He received a presidential pardon in 1927, but had to leave the United States. In 1928 he journeyed through Europe, trying to gain support for the establishment of an independent black state in the former German African colonies. Garvey returned to Jamaica, only to find that the local branch of the UNIA had broken away from the American UNIA. Although he made occasional statements in support of black causes, the most notable being his condemnation of Ethiopian emperor Haile Selassie for fleeing the invading Italian troops, Garvey's importance in the world political scene declined rapidly. After several unhappy years in Jamaica he returned to London, where he died. In 1964 his body was returned to Jamaica and buried in Kingston with full honors.

Garvey was a dreamer whose elaborate plans seemed destined to failure. He was scoffed at by such leading African Americans as W.E. Du Bois of the National Association for the Advancement of Colored People (NAACP) and publisher Robert S. Abbot. At the same time, Garvey's contribution to the welfare of black men and women around the world is undeniable. He was the first to urge them to take pride in their identity as a distinct ethnic group. Future African leaders such as Ghana's KWAME NKRUMAH stated that Garvey played an important role in the development of their own philosophies of political independence and Pan-Africanism.

> Where is the Black man's government? Where is his king and kingdom? Where is his president, his army, his navy, his men of big affairs? I could not find them, and then I declared, "I will help to to make them !"
>
> **Marcus Garvey**

GE LAO HUI (Ko Lao Hui—Society of Brothers and Elders) A Chinese secret society. Probably an offshoot of the TRIAD SOCIETY, it grew rapidly during the latter half of the 19th century, when social unrest led to the proliferation and political activation of numerous secret societies. Under various names, it became the most extensive and influential society, particularly in central, north and west China, and participated in the CHINESE REPUBLICAN REVOLUTION OF 1911. ZHU DE is said to have been associated with the Ge Lao Hui, which was courted by Communist leaders during the 1930s.

GENERAL STRIKE In theory, an attempt to bring national life to a halt through the cessation of work in all industries. In the last years of the 19th century, GEORGES SOREL and the Syndicalists (see SYNDICALISM) came to regard the general strike not merely as an economic weapon in the hands of the working class, but also as the best possible method by which it would be possible to bring down the existing order. Famous general strikes in the 20th century included Italy (1904), Russia (1905, where it helped force the Czar to grant a constitution), Sweden (1909), Germany (1920, where it brought about the failure of a right-wing coup), Britain (1926) and France (1938 and 1968). In the 1970s it was used most often in Italy; in the North American continent, by contrast, it is virtually unknown, though there have been a few attempts to organize general strikes on a regional basis (Seattle and Winnipeg, 1919; San Francisco, 1934).

GEORGIA, REVOLTS AND REVOLUTIONS

Imereti-Guria (Western Georgia) Uprising. (1819–1820) A popular uprising against the colonial policy of the Russian Czars. After the establishment of Russian rule in western Georgia, all the social strata were dissatisfied: the farmers—who had to pay new taxes; the nobility—who lost a considerable part of their rights; and the Church—which was no longer able to manage its properties as it wished. This dissatisfaction grew significantly following a June 1819 decision by the Russian government to undertake a so-called Church reform, which translated into the imposition of higher taxes. This overall dissatisfaction was transformed into armed resistance. The uprising began in Imereti and soon spread to Guria as well. The temporary success of the rebellion impelled the government to resort to the severest measures. Additional troops were deployed in Imereti and Guria, and by the end of July 1820 the resistance groups had been defeated. Several of the revolt leaders emigrated, 10 were hanged and others were exiled. Notwithstanding the government's success in suppressing the uprising, its Church reform was not undertaken in the form in which it had initially been planned.

Conspiracy of 1832. A conspiracy of Georgian nobility against the Russian colonial régime. The Georgian princes and the nobility were unable to come to terms with the loss of independence and their privileges as the result of the annexation of Georgia by the Russian Empire (1801), and dreamed of the restoration of national sovereignty. A secret organization of the nobility was formed in 1825 with a charter—*Acti Gonieri*—and program which aimed to restore independence under the terms of the Russian-Georgian Treaty of 1783 (complete freedom in internal affairs while under Russian auspices in the international arena) and the establishment of a constitutional monarchy in Georgia. The conspiracy was predicated on the people as a whole joining the struggle when the nobles gave the word. December 20, 1832 was set as the date of uprising but on December 9 the conspiracy was betrayed. The leaders and participants were exiled for various periods of time. The ideas behind the conspiracy exerted a great deal of influence on the formation of the national liberation movement in the following decades.

Guria (Western Georgia) Uprising of 1841. An anti-servitude and anticolonial uprising. The reasons for dissatisfaction were the growth of the feudal system and colonial oppression and increases in the state taxes. The dissatisfaction was intensified by the arbitrary behavior of the local military and civil officers. The actual grounds for the insurrection were a new law which required taxes to be paid in cash rather than kind. Farmers without money organized armed gangs to fight the government forces. Some of the nobility joined the revolt and one of their members, A. Shalikashvili, became a leader of the uprising. The rebels seized almost all of Guria and attacked the administrative center, Ozurgeti. Regiments of the regular army were sent to suppress the rebellion. In the crucial battle, more than 60 farmers were killed and 50 leaders were captured. Shalikashvili was sent to Siberia, but others who had been involved were soon released in order to avoid further uprisings.

Samegrelo Uprising. (1856–1857) An uprising against social oppression in a large western Georgian province. In the 1850s, Samegrelo still retained a certain degree of formal autonomy within the Russian Empire. Attacks by Turkish gangs devastated the province and made the life of the peasants unbearable. The farmers found it ever more difficult to bear the increasing burden of taxes. At first, these farmers began to express dissatisfaction verbally, but eventually this was transformed into an armed uprising that spread throughout Samegrelo in the fall of 1856. The leader of the 20,000 participants in the revolt was Utu Mikava, a blacksmith. In 1857, the rebels seized the administrative center of Samegrelo, Zugdidi. They presented the Russian government with an eight-clause demand that included banning the arbitrary imposition and collection of taxes, abolishment of the trade in serfs, etc. The farmers were promised that their demands would be met, but soon new higher taxes were imposed. The uprising was therefore renewed. In response, the government resorted to severe measures. Following bloody battles from August through November 1857, the uprising was defeated and 41 of its leaders were exiled. The Russian government abolished Samegrelo's autonomy as a result of the uprising.

Revolution of 1905–1907. A part of the so-called 1905–1907 Russian Bourgeois-Democratic Revolution (see RUSSIAN REVOLUTION OF 1905). All the social, economic and political contradictions that characterized the Russian empire of the early 20th century, and which brought about the formation of a revolutionary situation, were present in Georgia as well. In addition to these conditions, the Georgians were subject to national oppression, and this, too, intensified the popular dissatisfaction in the region. The masses in Georgia were led by the local political parties. The largest of these was the Social Democratic party, which preached revolutionary ideas among the workers and farmers in almost every part of the region. The Socialist Federalist party, which stood for the unity of all the social strata and enjoyed the support of the Georgian intellectuals, also propounded revolutionary ideas. Thus, the Georgian workers and peasantry joined the struggle of their Russian counterparts at the very beginning of the 1905 revolution. As a response to the events of Bloody Sunday (January 9, 1905), a political struggle began in Tbilisi, the capital of Georgia. The farmers, on their part, expressed their support by boycotting the local representatives of the Czarist régime. A punitive expedition was sent to Georgia and martial law was introduced. In response, the farmers formed local revolutionary committees, assuming power in a number of regions. These committees had their own armed force—the Red Squads. The intellectuals, hoping to achieve national independence, joined the struggle of the workers and the farmers. Georgian society was especially outraged when, on August 29, 1905, the police stormed a meeting hall and shot at the participants. The Georgian workers and farmers also took part in the all-Russian political strike of October 1905. Revolutionary committees were formed that seized power. Representatives of the BOLSHEVIK group within the Social Democratic party called upon the people to engage in an armed uprising. The Georgian MENSHEVIKS, in contrast, did not support resorting to such extreme measures. They considered forced concessions obtained from the government to be a revolutionary success in itself. The struggle went on even after the government announced its Manifest of October 17. A so-called Caucasian Bureau was formed to lead the uprising and a military-technical commission was established to train and arm the fighting squads of the revolution. On December 12, the rebels seized the Tbilisi railway station and its neighboring districts. Bloody battles took place on December 15–24 in the streets of Tbilisi as well as in other regions of Georgia, where people tried to stop the military. The insurrection in Tbilisi was defeated by government forces with artillery support. After the failure of the December uprising, the rebellion began to subside in all of Russia and Georgia, although isolated battles still took place, accompanied by terror. By 1907, the government had managed to crush the revolution completely. Years of severe reaction followed the 1905–1907 revolution.

February 1917 Revolution. A democratic revolution, part of the February RUSSIAN REVOLUTION OF 1917. In early 1917, there was no revolutionary situation in Georgia itself. Moreover, due to government attempts to suppress any information on the events in Petrograd, those living in Georgia only found out about these events at a much later time. A revolutionary mood started to overwhelm Georgia on March 4, with festive meetings and demonstrations in Tbilisi, the capital. The MENSHEVIK party formed a new governing body and it's leader, NOE ZHORDANIA, was elected the chairman of the Tbilisi Workers' Soviet. Soon the soldiers in the area formed their own Soviet, where Socialist Revolutionaries (known in Russia as *Essers*) took control. The provisional government handed power in the area to a special committee, but the Soviets nevertheless retained the real power. Despite some discussions between the different political parties, the issue of national sovereignty did not arise at this stage.

Abkhazia Armed Uprising of 1918. An uprising in 1918 to establish Soviet rule in Abkhazia. After the October RUSSIAN REVOLUTION OF 1917, MENSHEVIKS were in charge of the Abkhazian Soviets. The BOLSHEVIKS, extremely disturbed by this, vigorously preached their ideas among masses. Meanwhile they began preparing for an armed uprising, the planning of which was inspired by the Abkhazian Bolshevik leaders Eprem Eshba, Nestor Lakoba, IVANE (MAMIA) ORAKHELASHVILI and Giorgi Atarbegov. The uprising began in Gagra in March 1918. On April 9, the Bolsheviks entered the capital, Sukhumi, declared Soviet rule and began socialist reforms. The revolutionary committee under the leadership of Eshba was declared the supreme governing body. The committee was to be in charge of defense as well. It kept in touch with the Soviet government of Russia and directly with LENIN, but due to the complicated situation on the civil war fronts, it was unable to receive assistance from Moscow. The Transcaucasian Sejm sent a military force to suppress the uprising. The local opponents of the Soviet régime joined the force, and together they defeated the outnumbered Bolsheviks in a decisive battle on May 17. Menshevik rule was established in Abkhazia, although isolated fighting continued until the final suppression of the uprising.

GERMAN DEMOCRATIC REPUBLIC (GDR)
Communist Takeover and Establishment of the GDR. The proclamation of the GDR on October 7, 1949 in the Soviet occupation zone of Germany symbolized both the fate of postwar Germany, divided into two states, and the completion of the eastern zone's Communist takeover. In the period of the Anti-Fascist Democratic Order between May 1945 and October 1949, the foundations for a German Communist state were laid by the hard core German Communists of the Ulbricht Group, named after the party leader, WALTER ULBRICHT, who returned from Russia in order to carry out the process of the postwar communization of

the Soviet occupation zone, once the division of Germany into occupation zones became clear. A rapid process of de-nazification proved in the long run to be more efficient against potential enemies, as small time Nazi cronies changed their line and became loyal members of the Communist movement. Four political parties were allowed to function: the Communist Party (KPD), the Social Democrats (SPD), the Christian Democratic Union (CDU) and the Liberal Democratic Party of Germany (LLPD), which in August 1945 formed the Anti-Fascist Democratic Bloc, the only political umbrella formation allowed to function. Communist penetration into the other parties started early, and by April 1946 the Communists and the Social Democrats united in the Socialist Unity Party (SED) that ruled the GDR until its collapse in November 1989. The united party was clearly dominated by the Communists, and the agreement on parity between the two was never really implemented. The fusion of the SPD with the Communists eliminated any contacts between the SPD in the Western sectors and the Soviet-dominated zone. Mass front organizations built up by the Communists representing economic and social sectors of the population, trade unions, youth and women's movements further undermined the other remaining parties' effective functioning and advanced the process of the Communist takeover. Changes in the economic life of the Soviet zone represented clear steps in the Communist takeover, as the economy, including agriculture, was nationalized and socialized. The "revolution in the land" prepared the way for the later collectivization of the peasants and their levelling into a rural working class, along with the urban proletariat. The Soviet model of a "workers' and peasants' state" was rapidly pushed into German society in the Soviet occupation zone, as differences between the two parts of Germany were becoming evident and hopefully, from a Communist viewpoint, also irreversible. Likewise, religious life was regulated in a way that reflected the Communist attitude toward the churches, by disconnecting religious ties between the two Germanys' religious establishments. In 1949, when the two German states were officially established, the GDR's population was well indoctrinated into the "progressive" and "anti-Fascist" legacy of that specific area of Germany (as opposed to the "imperialist warmonger" Western Federal Republic), as the groundwork for the future theory of a German socialist nation was prepared.

Communist Collapse of 1989. The ruling elite of the GDR rejected any experiments with Gorbachev-type reforms, as it correctly realized the paradoxical situation of the artificial German Communist state—the more it introduced market reforms and capitalism, the less chances it would have to survive as a separate state. The raison d'être of the GDR was in its Marxist uniqueness and not in its becoming a second German capitalist state. Thus, ideological purity was seen as a safety valve against the spiritual and physical survival of the Berlin Wall. The ruling Socialist Unity Party's policy was aimed at justifying its national Communist line, to stress the alleged successful performance of the economy and the society's cohesion. Along with strategic considerations on the importance of safeguarding the socialist régime, the Honecker leadership presented a defiant line: an ideological dogmatism which was based, among others, on the mutual need between a strong Soviet power and a strong socialist GDR. As the Soviet régime entered its stage of reforms and collapse, the GDR system was bound to follow, in spite of the tough rejectionist SED line. In a quest for legitimacy, the Honecker régime adopted features which fostered a "socialist German nationhood," a pragmatic line that was gradually infused into Marxist ideology. The penetration of East German society through the appeals of the West German success, the various strategies adopted by the opposition and the alternative "areas of freedom" which the churches, especially the Protestant ones, provided, shifted the régime into a constant offensive-defensive which only further eroded its standing. Reformists within the ruling party were slow to appear, but gathered power with the spiraling process of collapse, symbolized by a massive exit of East Germans asking for asylum in Eastern European states, especially Hungary, which opened its borders to Austria. Mass demonstrations in October and early November brought the régime to the brink as a new party leadership attempted to introduce some reforms. Its main achievement was the opening of the borders, the speeding up of the collapse in face of the masses who repudiated the very existence of the Communist régime and of the GDR. The opening of the Berlin Wall on November 9, 1989 broke the final spell of the GDR, and the attempts by a reformist government and party leadership to exit in a dignified manner were rejected by the people. The GDR collapsed "into the arms of West Germany," as one observer noted, and the rapid process of reunification was under way. On January 29, 1990 a "government of national responsability" took control until the elections that were held in March, which formalized the old order's collapse.

GERMANIAS, UPRISING OF   (1519–1520) The Germanias, or Christian brotherhoods, of Valencia and Mallorca in Spain, were made up mostly of members of the urban lower class and guilds. In 1519–1520 they rose in armed rebellion, their aim being to secure a greater voice in municipal government and a reduction of taxes. As the revolt spread, it soon became out of hand and turned into riots against the Muslim population; this cost it the support of such members of the middle classes who had originally chosen to join the uprising. Their desertion enabled the royal governor, Diego Hurtado do Mendoza, to retrieve the situation and destroy the forces of the Germanias in October 1521. The upshot was reprisals, in which over 800 rebels were sentenced—mostly to fines and confiscations—for the "crime of Germanias and popular union." Only in December 1524 did all resistance came to an end, whereupon a general pardon was issued.

GERMAN REVOLUTION OF 1918   see LUXEMBURG, ROSA.

GERO, ERNO   (1898–1980) Hungarian Communist leader. Born in Budapest, Gero joined the Communist party in 1918 and was active in the revolution led by BELA KUN the following year. When that failed, he escaped to Germany but later returned clandestinely to Hungary, where he edited a Communist underground newspaper. Gero lived in Soviet Russia for a time and was in Spain during the civil war, apparently guiding the Catalan Communists. He returned to Hungary in 1944 with the Russian army and was soon occupying leading positions in that country. From 1956 to 1966 he was deputy prime minister and a member of the Politburo, a key personality in governing Hungary. In 1956, when MATYAS RAKOSI fell victim to the anti-Stalinist

movement in Moscow, Gero was appointed first secretary of the Communist party. His rule was short and unpopular; he introduced harsh measures to try to counter the revolution, but was swept aside during the heady 10 days of liberation from Russian domination. He was deposed and fled the country, reportedly in one of the Russian tanks he had summoned to restore the Communist autocracy.

Prevented from returning to Hungary, Gero lived for a number of years in the USSR. He was allowed to return to Hungary in 1962, although he was expelled from the Communist party. Thereafter, he remained quietly in retirement.

GERSHUNI, GRIGORY   (1870–1908) Russian populist (see POPULISM) revolutionary terrorist. Trained as a pharmacist, Gershuni devoted his adult life to revolutionary politics. In 1898 he organized the Workers' Party for the Political Liberation of Russia in Minsk. Arrested in 1900, he secured his release by persuading the czarist chief of police, Zubatov, of his willingness to be part of the latter's police-sponsored trade unionism. In 1901–1902, he was influential in recruiting populist groups in Russia to join the newly-formed Party of Socialist Revolutionaries. Gershuni headed the party's military organization, organizing the assassination of prominent officials. Captured in 1903, he was tried and sentenced to death. When the sentence was commuted to life imprisonment at hard labor, Gershuni escaped, making his way across China and the United States, appearing at the Socialist Revolutionary congress in Europe in February 1907, where he demanded intensification of the party's terror campaign. He died of tuberculosis in Switzerland.

GHADR PARTY   An organization of expatriate Indian nationalists centered in the USA. Founded around 1910 by Har Datal, a visiting professor of philosophy at Stanford University, it drew most of its support from immigrant Sikh farmers in the San Joaquin valley and Indian students at the University of California at Berkeley.

The organization produced a revolutionary newspaper, *Ghadr* ("Mutiny" or "Revolution" in Urdu), and in 1915 made an abortive attempt to send guns and guerrilla soldiers to India. *Ghadr* party activists hoped that the arrival of their forces would trigger a spontaneous uprising among the Indian masses. However the British had successfully infiltrated their movement and the attempt, sponsored by the German government, foundered. The German involvement resulted in *Ghadr* party leaders being tried in America in 1918 for having compromised American neutrality in the early years of the war. The movement subsequently folded and never recovered, but had served as an important training ground for Sikh and Untouchable nationalist activists and remains a great source of pride to the expatriate Indian nationalist community in the USA.

GHEORGHIU-DEJ, GHEORGHE   (1901–1965) Romania's Communist leader between 1948–1965. Born in Barlad of a family of Bulgarian origin, Gheorghiu-Dej was an early activist of the Communist movement while working in the national railways and one of the leaders of the major waves of workers' strikes of 1932–1933. Sentenced to 12 years in prison, he escaped from detention and helped reorganize the small Communist party (CP) on the eve of the August 1944 coup in which

Romania joined the Allies. During the Communist takeover, he became a cabinet minister as well as leader of the CP until his death. By 1952 he held the dual posts of prime minister and party secretary. A cunning politician, he engineered a series of purges in 1952 and got rid of all real or alleged opposition. A "home Communist" who removed Moscovites, he was a Stalinist in his style but very much wary of STALIN and his heirs.

After 1956, Gheorghiu-Dej gradually initiated Romania's national communism, most strongly manifested a year before his death in April 1964 by the so-called Declaration of Independence, in which Gheorghiu-Dej asserted Romania's special road. Rejecting Soviet pressures for stronger economic and political integration, he initiated closer ties with the west and a brief form of glasnost in the early 1960s. A person with some charisma, a non-intellectual if not actually anti-intellectual, he left no impact on Marxist thought, albeit a strong one on the practical side of the enforcement of communism, on the elimination of former colleagues and on pragmatic shifts in policies.

GHOSE, SRI AUROBINDO (1872–1950) Indian nationalist and mystic. Originally educated at a Christian school in Darjeeling, northeast India, Ghose was sent to England for further schooling; there, he proved himself a talented linguist and went on to study at Cambridge. On his return to India he occupied a series of professorial posts in Baroda and Calcutta. At this time he also became interested in yoga and in Indian languages and philosophy, and entered intensive studies in classical Sanskrit.

Between 1902 and 1910, Ghose was deeply involved in the Indian freedom movement, actively proselytizing for forceful resistance to British rule. His activities earned him two years of imprisonment, whereupon he fled to the French enclave of Pondicherry in southeast India. There he withdrew from active politics and founded an *ashram* (spiritual center), wherein he expounded his theories of spiritual evolution to ever-growing numbers of followers from India and abroad. Today he is better remembered for his spiritual than for his political activities.

GIAP, VO NGUYEN (1912–) Military commander to HO CHI MINH. He is regarded by many experts as one of the two or three greatest military strategists of the 20th century. Born in Quangbinh province, he earned a doctorate in law from the University of Hanoi in 1937. Giap was a member of the Indochinese Communist party until 1939, when it was banned. He then went to China and, in 1945, returned to Hanoi with a Vietminh army to liberate the city from the Japanese.

A military genius, Giap commanded the Vietminh, which boasted a world-class infantry, against the French. When the French commander, Navarre, drastically underestimated Giap's ability to resupply his Vietminh troops, the Frenchman set a "trap" at Dien Bien Phu. Giap turned the tables by using a "secret weapon"—2,000 bicycles reinforced with extra supports—so that peasants could carry and push up to 500 pounds each through the rough terrain leading to Dien Bien Phu. This was about twice what an elephant could carry and five times the amount of an average man. He defeated the French and Dien Bien Phu fell on May 7, 1954.

Giap used his mastery of guerrilla warfare to command the guerrilla forces in Vietnam against the South Vietnamese and the United States in the 1960s. It was he who was the mastermind of the Tet offensive in 1968. Vo Nguyen Giap retired in 1982.

GIERECK, EDWARD (1913–) Polish Communist politician. Giereck spent most of the interwar period in France, the Communist party being illegal in pre-1939 Poland. He worked for the Belgian Resistance during World War II. In 1948, he returned to Poland and by 1959 had risen to membership of the Politburo. As the party's leading expert on economic questions, he became one of Poland's top leaders, succeeding GOMULKA in 1970 as First Secretary of the party. He remained in power until September 1980, when he resigned due to ill health, unable to cope with the crisis generated by Solidarity's emergence and the social and economic crisis in which the régime found itself.

GIRONDINS One of the two major groups of deputies, inaccurately designated as parties, during the FRENCH REVOLUTION who confronted each other in a titanic struggle for power during the most climactic phase of the revolution from 1791 to 1793. The political duel between the Girondins and JACOBINS had widespread repercussions both at home and abroad. It caused the outbreak of war in all of Europe and precipitated civil war between Paris and the rest of the country, known as the federalist reaction against the Jacobin dictatorship of ROBESPIERRE and THE COMMITTEE OF PUBLIC SAFETY.

Unlike the radical Jacobins, whose power and prestige was based on a wide network of revolutionary clubs under the control of the great Jacobin Club in Paris, the Girondins were a loosely organized faction of like-minded radical deputies who gathered informally at meals in theater lobbies or in such salons as Mme. Roland's or the Marquis de Condorcet's. This coterie never became a political party in any formal sense, not even voting as a separate bloc in the assembly. It was closely in touch, however, with the political sentiments of the independent-minded provinces, as opposed to the Jacobins who converged on Paris as their main political base and formed an alliance with the PARIS COMMUNE and the leadership of the SANS-CULOTTES. Since many, but by no means all, of their leaders came from the southwestern region of the Gironde with its capital at Bordeaux, they have passed into history as the party of the Girondins. During the revolution, this clique of left-wing activists was called the BRISSOTINS, after their most prominent member, JACQUES PIERRE BRISSOT, who himself came from the Loire region.

Again, unlike the Jacobins, the Girondins tended to be starry-eyed idealists, swept along on the crest of a wave of revolutionary romanticism inspired by Jean-Jacques Rousseau's *Emile* and typified by the revolutionary zeal of Brissot, Roland de la Platière and his lovely wife Manon and the sentimental orator Pétion—who declared that he always followed his darling Liberty (*Liberté, Liberté chérie*) as his lode star. The Girondins argued that the revolution made it possible to regenerate mankind along the rational lines laid down by their principal philosopher, Condorcet, championing the sectional interests of the bourgeoisie—not only out of a selfish class interest in laissez faire, as their Marxist enemies had contended, but because they believed that only a free market could consolidate the great gains made by the revolution.

On April 20, 1792, they threw the gauntlet at the rest of Europe by declaring war against "the King of Austria and Hungary," proclaiming to the world, as a Girondist manifesto put it, that this was waged as "a war of Peoples against Kings." By the beginning of 1793, they had gone one step further by recklessly rushing into war with England, Holland, Prussia and Spain, thus starting a cycle of war, revolution and civil war which was to prove to be their undoing. The initial "rush on Europe," however, soon led to military setbacks and diplomatic reverses, the defection of their chief generals, DUMOURIEZ and the MARQUIS DE LAFAYETTE, to the enemy and, by exposing their inability to adapt the revolution's free trade policies to a war economy, laid bare their incompetence and made them vulnerable to Jacobin attacks.

Fearful of the Jacobins' appeal to the mob, the Girondins bungled in their first attempt to arrest Robespierre and DANTON and were themselves outmaneuvered and overthrown by a *sans-culottes* attack on the convention hall on June 2, 1793. By the following October, Brissot and all their leaders had been sent to the guillotine. Condorcet and other Girondin fugitives were hounded out of hiding and killed or, like THOMAS PAINE, managed to make their way abroad.

The Girondins stood out for their faith in preserving parliamentary democracy and constitutional liberties at any price, a difficult balancing act to carry out in the best of times but even harder during a time of revolution. They were also dedicated to upholding the principles of the free market despite the urgency of war, a policy which set them further and further apart from the *sans-culottes*. The Jacobins were prepared to compromise with their principles in order to form a tactical alliance with the Paris mob. They were therefore able to destroy their political rivals, set the revolution aflame through the Reign of Terror, defend it from the rest of Europe and also crush the Girondin-inspired federalist revolt against the Jacobin dictatorship of Paris. This was to have far-reaching consequences on the course of the revolution and also shaped its legacy for all other revolutions to come.

GJOLEKA, ZENEL   Leader of the mountain people in the ALBANIAN UPRISING OF 1847.

GLADIATORIAL WAR   (73–71 B.C.) Revolt of gladiators and slaves during the period of the Roman Republic. Fights of gladiators (derived from the latin word *gladius*, "sword") were first held in Rome in 264 B.C. Usually, gladiatorial combats formed part of funeral rites. The gladiators were prisoners of war, condemned criminals, slaves or even freemen who volunteered to fight for a fee. Gladiators were trained in special schools. In 73 B.C., SPARTACUS, a Thracian gladiator, escaped with over 70 fellow gladiators from the gladiatorial schools in Capua to establish a base at Mount Vesuvius. When word of this reached Rome, the *praetor* Publius Varinius was sent with three thousand troops to subdue the rebellion. After Spartacus defeated Varinius unexpectedly, he appealed to the slaves of Rome to reclaim their freedom. Numerous slaves joined Spartacus, and at the height of his power he had an army of 70,000 men. With such a force, mainly comprised of Thracians, Celts and Germans, he gained extraordinary victories over the Roman armies, including those of the consuls of 72 B.C. Spartacus's army secured considerable control of southern Italy. His fellow leader, Crixus, separated with a large following, only to be crushed by a Roman army that same year. Spartacus chose to

lead his men northward, hoping that upon reaching the Alps they would return home as free men. When they arrived in Cisalpine Gaul, however, his followers refused to disperse, demanding to march on Rome itself. Spartacus realized that even if they were to seize power, his undisciplined men would be incapable of maintaining it. He thus led them back to southern Italy and tried to cross the Strait of Messina to Sicily, but was not able to acquire the necessary ships. In 71 B.C., his entire army was finally destroyed by Marcus Crassus, who had six legions, Spartacus himself falling during the fighting. Those who were captured alive, 6,000 in number, were crucified, and Pompey, returning from Spain, executed those who had managed to flee. Although Spartacus did not bring about any change in the institution of slavery in Rome—and perhaps did not even intend to do so—he remains a legendary figure, inspiring revolutionary leaders and capturing the imagination of subsequent generations. Modern attempts, notably by MARX and his followers, to attribute to Spartacus social-revolutionary ideology are baseless.

GLEICHSCHALTUNG   A critical step in the Nazi revolution, *Gleichschaltung* stood for the elimination of Weimar Germany's political structure and institutions toward the creation of a new political system. Starting with the purging of the relatively independent civil service and with the progressive elimination of the traditional Prussian *Reichsstäate* (law-based state), the Nazis abolished the Weimar Party system and destroyed the Federal system which had existed in Germany since 1867.

The term *Gleichschaltung* has been translated as "putting into the same gear," but it could as well be rendered as "equalizing" or "streamlining." In reality, it meant the destruction of traditional and democratic German, Prussian and local institutions by abolishing their humanistic, Christian and rational-traditional ethos. However, *Gleichschaltung* also meant the centralization of power in Hitler's own hands and the removal of many constitutional restraints that might have stood in his way. It left the country subject to a large number of Nazi personalities and institutions, all of whom received their power from Hitler and many of whom actively competed with each other.

Legally speaking, the most important measure leading toward *Gleichschaltung* was the so-called "Enabling Act" of March 23, 1933. While promising not to infringe either on parliamentary rights or on those of the states (*Laender*) comprising Germany, it gave Hitler's government four years in which to operate without constitutional restraints.

However, the Nazis very soon broke their promises. The first to be "equalized" was the civil service. The Law for the Restoration of the Professional Civil Service of April 7, 1933 abolished all limits upon the authority of superiors, who demanded complete political reliability from their subordinates. It also introduced racial and anti-Semitic discrimination into the civil service, including all institutions of higher education in Germany.

Next came the legal system, which was undercut by the introduction of concentration camps operating on the basis of emergency decrees that largely suspended human rights. Meanwhile, the judiciary was infiltrated by Nazi lawyers. The legal system itself soon became an arm of the Nazi Party, and in 1942 Hitler was formally empowered to remove judges at will.

In the spring of 1933 the old political parties were abolished, and by the law of July 14, 1933 the Nazi party became the only legal faction in Germany. Attempts to reestablish other parties became illegal and subject to punishment.

As a further part of *Gleichschaltung*, the state parliaments (*Landtage*) were effectively neutralized early in 1933, when their work became subject to commissioners appointed by the central government; next, on April 7, 1933, they were abolished. Henceforward Germany's ancient, half-way autonomous states became simply administrative districts of the Third Reich.

The process of "streamlining" labor organizations and trade unions, of middle-class associations and of farmers and agricultural workers, was completed by late 1933, when all of them were absorbed into Nazi-controlled armed forces. Yet when President Hindenburg died in August 1934 and Hitler took his place as Fuehrer and Reichschancellor, the Wehrmacht, too, was made to swear an oath of allegiance to him personally. As to the industrialists, after a few of them had been terrorized by the SS during the early days of the Nazi régime, they sank into political oblivion. Instead, they concentrated on making as much money as possible out of rearmament and, later, the war itself.

Finally, media and arts were also "streamlined" to fit the demands of the totalitarian state. A propaganda ministry under JOSEPH GOEBBELS was established, with separate departments for press, radio, film, music, painting, literature, etc. In art, too, Hitler's taste was turned into supreme law. Among other things, this meant that modern art was rejected as *entartete Kunst* ("degenerate art"). By such means, *Gleichschaltung* not only led to the destruction of Germany's cultural traditions but also to their recasting in the Nazi leadership's own spitting image.

GLORIOUS REVOLUTION   (1688) King James II of England was not only a Roman Catholic in a Protestant country but also contemptuous of public sensibilities in constantly using his powers to allow other Catholics to play a full role in government. The birth of a son seemed to spell the ultimate triumph of Rome, so seven prominent politicians made overtures to William of Orange to come to England and replace the king. James refused French help and thereby lost his throne, being forced to flee (not without English connivance, for the English were happy to see him go quietly) in what was described in a legal fiction as his abdication. The English parliament thereby declared the throne vacant and chose William and Mary as their monarchs. The new rulers for their part approved a bill of rights which made their concessions law. The Glorious Revolution effectively destroyed the notion of divine right, and made the monarchy dependent on both parliament and the established church.

James, for his part, refused to give up the throne without a struggle, and landed in Ireland in March 1689. William for his part exempted non-Anglican Protestants from certain legal penalties and succeeded in making the struggle against James even more clearly confessional. He also pardoned all those who had supported the deposed king in the past. Having prepared the way, William could thus go to Ireland himself, and defeat James II at the Battle of the Boyne (July 1, 1690), forcing the former king to flee to France. At the same time, William pacified Scotland, which was still holding out against taking the oath of allegiance to the new monarch. At the Massacre of Glencoe (February 13, 1692) a group of soldiers killed the MacDonald clan

chieftain and thus signaled the subjection of Scotland to the English king.

GLYN DWR REBELLION   (1400–1409) A personal dispute between Owain Glyn Dwr (c. 1359–c. 1416), a Welshman educated in London and trained at court, and Lord Grey of Ruthin, escalated into a general Welsh rebellion emphasizing native traditions and attempts to alleviate a repressive economic situation. In 1404, Glyn Dwr declared himself Prince of Wales, convened a parliament and allied himself with the kings of France and Scotland and the Irish princes. However, it was impossible to hold out against the English without French aid. Unfortunately for him, the aid was insufficient and by 1408 he was on the run, eventually disappearing. Despite the devastation he caused to Wales, his cause remained popular, at least on the symbolic level.

GOBIND SINGH see GOVINDSINGH.

GOEBBELS, PAUL JOSEPH   (1897–1945) Nazi minister of propaganda. Goebbels was the son of a poor and pious Catholic family of laborers from the Rhineland town of Rheydt. Goebbels's childhood was apparently tainted by his physique: one of his legs was a clubfoot and eight centimeters shorter than the other, causing a pronounced limp. However, his physical handicap was compensated for by his intellect.

Goebbels was rejected by the German army in World War I because of his handicap. Like many German youths of his time, after Germany's defeat he turned to radical politics. At first he was attracted to socialism, and he remained an advocate of the socialist platform of the National Socialists until late in his career. Upon completing his doctorate in literature and philosophy at the University of Heidelberg, he planned to become a writer.

Goebbels joined the Nazi Party in 1924 and found work as managing editor of a biweekly journal published by GREGOR STRASSER, leader of the party in northern Germany. Goebbels's reputation as a party spokesman now grew rapidly; his rich baritone voice and expressive hands made him an ideal orator. Goebbels's passionate advocacy of Nazism was noted by ADOLF HITLER, and he was appointed *Gauleiter* (district party leader) of Berlin in 1926, with the task of winning the capital over to Nazism.

Goebbels's activities in Berlin brought the fledgling party to national prominence. In 1928 he was made the Nazi Party's propaganda chief. Among the techniques he adopted were the use of blazing red posters (to contrast with the stark Berlin walls); the creation of the myth of Horst Wessel (one of the early Nazi Party members who had been killed in a political quarrel in 1930) as a larger-than-life hero; and debates held against recordings of political opponents (instituted when Chancellor Heinrich Bruning "refused" to debate with Goebbels—in fact, he was not asked). Goebbels organized heroic funerals for party men who had actually been killed in brawls. It was he who arranged to have Hitler flown around the country for innumerable speaking engagements. All this time Goebbels dreamed of the possibility of planning and controlling radio broadcasts. Like Hitler, he believed that the spoken word was far more effective than the written word.

After Hitler swept into power in January 1933, Goebbels was

appointed minister of popular education and culture—a new ministry that reached into every aspect of German life. In this capacity, his often-insipid articles now appeared almost daily, and newspaper censorship became the rule.

He was the father of modern propaganda in the totalitarian state (a term that he coined); it was his theory that the greater the lie, the greater the chance that it would be believed. On May 10, 1933 he instigated the public burning of "un-German" books. He was now able to take control of the radio, which he made into a powerful weapon, internally and internationally. Always a fan of the cinema, Goebbels encouraged the development of a Nazi film industry whose productions, though mostly banal, included such propaganda masterpieces as the anti-British *Ohm Kruger*, the anti-Semitic *Jud Süss* ("the Jew Süss") and *The Eternal Jew*.

Goebbels's house was a popular retreat for leading Nazi politicians, especially Hitler. However, Goebbels was also a noted womanizer who enjoyed the company of young actresses. One such affair, with the Czech actress Lida Barova, was only broken off at the insistence of Hitler. Hitler was infuriated by the many crises in Goebbels's marriage to Magda Quandt, which was portrayed to the public as an ideal marriage.

Until the end of the war, Goebbels believed in Hitler's infallibility. Even as the Allies encircled Berlin, Goebbels remained with Hitler, spending the final days in his bunker under the chancellery. On the day after Hitler's suicide, unwilling to allow his children to survive the fall of the Reich, Goebbels had them poisoned. He and his wife then left the bunker and committed suicide; his charred remains were identified by Russian troops a few hours later.

GOLDMAN, EMMA (1869–1940) US anarchist. Born in Kovno (Kaunas), Lithuania, Goldman became conversant with revolutionary ideas in St. Petersburg before moving to the United States in 1886. Initially, she worked in a clothing factory in Rochester, New York, where she became involved with the German socialists, and later at a corset factory in New Haven, Connecticut. In 1887, the trial and execution of four anarchists accused of exploding a bomb that had killed seven policemen in Chicago's Haymarket square motivated her to join the anarchist movement.

On moving to New York City in 1889, she met ALEXANDER BERKMAN, who became her sometime lover and lifelong companion. During the Homestead Strike in 1892, guards of the Carnegie Steel Company shot several steel strikers. Goldman and Berkman felt that the company president, Henry Clay Frick, was responsible for the strikers' death and plotted to kill him. After his attempt on Frick's life failed, Berkman was imprisoned for 14 years. Goldman led the anarchist cause during these years. A spellbinding orator, she delivered lectures in German, Russian, Yiddish and English. In 1893, she was imprisoned for seven months for inciting a riot in New York City. In 1901, she was even accused of inspiring Leon Czolgosz to shoot President William McKinley.

Her best-known publication was a monthly magazine that she founded in 1906 entitled *Mother Earth*. It appeared for 11 years, coedited by her and Berkman after he was released from prison. An early feminist, she also traveled throughout the United States lecturing on behalf of birth control and women's rights.

She noted that "everything within a woman that craves assertion and activity should reach its fullest expression." In 1916, she was imprisoned for violating laws that prohibited the distribution of birth control information.

In 1917, during World War I, she and Berkman were jailed for two years for opposing the draft. As a result of the Red Scare in the United States that followed the RUSSIAN REVOLUTION OF 1917, they were deported to Russia in 1919. In her work, *My Disillusionment in Russia* (1924), she described their unhappiness with the new Russian government. Two years after their arrival she and Berkman left as exiles without a country. Goldman later married a Welsh anarchist and ultimately settled in the south of France, where she wrote her autobiography, *Living My Life* (1931). She died in Canada and was buried in Chicago, near the graves of the anarchists of the Haymarket riot.

FROM THE EMMA GOLDMAN OBITUARY, CIRCULATED BY ASSOCIATED PRESS, MAY 14, 1940

Emma Goldman, apostle of philosophic anarchism and of "voluntary communism," was born in Russia, spent 33 years of her life in the U.S. fighting for her ideals, for which she suffered imprisonment, and was an incorrigible revolutionist to the end.

She was deported from the U.S. in 1919 for obstructing conscription, fled in 1921 from Soviet Russia, where she had hoped to find the realization of her social dreams but found only disillusionment, and saw her ideals defeated again in the civil war in Spain, in which she took an active part. In the social history of the United States she wrote a chapter all her own, and in the history of the worldwide revolutionary movement of her time she made a place for herself beside that of her teacher, Peter Kropotkin.

After fighting for a generation against what she considered the ills of the social system in the U.S., she opposed Lenin and Trotsky because she believed them guilty of betraying the socialist ideal by establishing what she denounced as the new despotism. Her experience in Russia confirmed her in her belief that all government was wrong, and that the new society for which she stood could be established only on the basis of anarchism, through the free cooperating of the masses.

GOMULKA, WLADYSLAW (1905–1982) Polish Communist leader. Born in Austrian Galicia, Gomulka became active in left-wing politics while still in his teens and at the age of 21 joined a Communist trade union. During the 1930s he was arrested several times for his Communist activities; 1939 found him defending Warsaw as a member of a workers' battalion. During the German occupation, he was active in the underground Polish Workers' Party rising to become its secretary in 1943.

After Poland was liberated by the Red Army, Gomulka occupied powerful positions as deputy prime minister of the provisional government and was also in charge of the so-called regained territories, i.e. those taken over from Germany. October 1948 found him a member of the Central Committee of the Polish Communist Party, but he was immediately accused of opposing the socialization of agriculture and of pursuing a "nationalist" line. A power struggle followed, and Gomulka was purged by his Stalinst opponents. Held in protective custody from 1951 to 1954, he reemerged in October 1956 and, after a dramatic chain of events, found himself Party leader.

As a ruler of Poland from 1956 to 1970, Gomulka tried to introduce what he called "the Polish way to socialism." While remaining loyal to Moscow, he instituted limited reforms, especially in agriculture; these, however, were abandoned during the late 1960s after a wave of unrest swept the country. In 1970, he was challenged within the Party by a nationalist faction led by MOCZAR on the one hand and by a conservative faction led by GIERECK on the other. Deposed, he is remembered as the anti-Stalinist of 1948 who returned in triumph in 1956 and later failed to cope with Poland's problems.

GORDON RIOTS   (June 2–9, 1780) Lord George Gordon of England, a strange Protestant nobleman who would end his days as a convert to Judaism, instructed his Protestant Association to oppose the Roman Catholic Relief Act which had been passed in 1778. On June 2, 1780, Gordon presented a petition to parliament to this effect. He was escorted by crowds of supporters. By the evening this crowd had turned into a mob, attacking houses, churches, prisons and breweries. Troops were called out, but only after a number of days did they manage to regain control. By then it was too late to prevent the massive damage and looting which had gone on in London.

GÖRING, HERMANN WILHELM   (1893–1846) Nazi leader; founder of the Gestapo and the Luftwaffe (German air force). Göring was born to a wealthy family on the fringes of the German aristocracy. An unexceptional but robust student who preferred mountain climbing and hunting in the Bavarian Alps to studying, he was sent to a military academy, where he excelled. In World War I he served as a reconnaissance pilot, winning several medals and citations, and was awarded the Iron Cross First Class for downing an enemy airplane with his pistol. In 1915, he joined the squadron of Manfred von Richthofen, the Red Baron, and even commanded the squadron for a short time after Richthofen's death. In the course of the war he won Germany's highest honor, *Pour le Mérite*, awarded to individuals showing acts of outstanding courage in battle.

With the collapse of Germany, Göring was left penniless. The terms of Germany's surrender proscribed maintaining an air force and, like so many of his compatriots, Göring was hard-pressed to find work. He spent some time in voluntary exile in Denmark and Sweden, where he found work as a pilot. Returning to Germany, he was attracted to the Nazi party and admired ADOLF HITLER who, in turn, recognized the value of a decorated war hero to his party and offered him command of the party's private army, the SA. Göring joined Hitler during the abortive BEER HALL PUTCH in Munich in 1923. When the troops turned on the demonstrators, Göring was shot in the groin.

After spending some time in Austria, Italy and Sweden, he returned to Germany in 1927. Hitler had already achieved national renown and Göring, who had many connections among the nobility and industrialists, was sent to Berlin to secure financial support for the party. He persuaded Hitler to have him represent the Nazi party in the Reichstag in 1928. Although Hitler was at first skeptical, he admitted that Göring was both well-connected and personable, and one of the few party members who could win the support of bankers and industrialists. His social skills were unmatched by any of the Nazi leaders, and his military reputation won him entrance into many important houses in Germany, where he was referred to as Hitler's "ambassador."

Göring was appointed president of the Reichstag in 1932. As the highest-ranking Nazi in the country, he was instrumental in bringing Hitler to power by showing total disregard for parliamentary procedure. When Hitler was appointed chancellor in 1933, Göring received several cabinet posts. In 1933 he became prime minister of Prussia and commissioner for aviation.

As Hitler's top henchman, Göring was in large part responsible for carrying through the National Socialist Revolution. It was Göring who formed the instrument of terror known as the Gestapo; and it was also Göring who was probably responsible for setting the Reichstag fire that cleared the way to dictatorship. Finally, in August 1934, it was Göring who, presiding over the so-called "Night of the Long Knives," orchestrated the liquidation of ERNST RÖHM and his followers among the SA leadership. In 1935 he was appointed commander of the Luftwaffe.

Göring became economic minister in 1936. He amassed considerable wealth and built up an enormous art collection through looting and theft. He was responsible for the confiscation of Jewish property in 1937 and for a time was in charge of the Nazi anti-Jewish policy. He was opposed to war as a threat to Germany's economic recovery and sought to avoid the invasion of Czechoslovakia and Poland. Only when war in Poland was inevitable did Göring put his air force's full potential into battle. On the day World War II broke out, Hitler appointed Göring field marshal and his heir.

The early years of the war saw Göring's prestige soar, but

• Naturally the common people don't want war... but after all it is the leaders of the country who determine the policy, and it is always a simple matter to drag the people along, whether it is a democracy or a fascist dictatorship, or a parliament, or a communist dictatorship. Voice or no voice, the people can always be brought to the bidding of the leaders. That is easy. All you have to do is to tell them that they are being attacked, and denounce the pacifists for lack of patriotism and exposing the country to danger. It works the same in all countries.

• Guns will make us powerful; butter will only make us fat (usually misquoted as "guns instead of butter").
Hermann Göring

when the Luftwaffe was unable to quell Britain and protect Germany from Allied air attacks, Göring lost Hitler's approval. While retaining his title, others took away his power and he spent the final years of the war in semi-retirement on his large estate. When defeat was certain, he believed that Hitler had become incapacitated and declared himself Führer, an act for which he was stripped of his rank and expelled from the party.

Göring was captured by the Allies and brought to trail at Nuremberg. He was one of the few defendants who did not deny responsibility for the régime's atrocities and, as the leading defendant in the proceedings, seemed, to many observers, to relish having finally attained his goal of succeeding Hitler. Göring was sentenced to death, but two hours before he was to be hanged he poisoned himself in his cell.

GOTTWALD, KLEMENT (1896–1953) Czechoslovak Communist politician. Gottwald helped found the Czechoslovakian Communist party and served on its central committee from 1925. In 1935, he was made secretary of the COMINTERN. Living in Moscow during World War II, he returned to Czechoslovakia in 1945 to become deputy prime minister under Benes and in 1946 became prime minister and Communist party chairman. In 1948 he led a coup, after which he also took over as president and transformed Czechoslovakia into a Soviet-type state by means of a series of large purges and spectacular show trials.

GOVIND SINGH (1668–1708) The tenth in the line of gurus, or spiritual leaders, of the Sikhs. It was Singh who transformed this Punjab-based religious sect into a radical warrior people which violently opposed Muslim hegemony in that region. He also established many of the practices and customs that characterize the Sikhs to this day, including the obligatory wearing of the five Ks: *Kesh* (long hair and beard), *Kungha* (hair-comb), *Kuchcha* (shorts), *Kara* (iron bangle), and *Kripan* (sword).

GOWON, YAKUBU (1934–) Nigerian politician. Having chosen a military career, Gowon attended the Sandhurst Military Academy in Great Britain. He was absent from Nigeria in January 1966 when a coup brought a military junta to power, but he was chosen by the new leadership to be the country's chief of staff. Following a second coup in June of that year, Gowon became head of state. He was unable to restrain the growing ethnic tensions then plaguing the country, which culminated in the massacre of Ibo in the northern region and the secession of the predominantly Ibo in the eastern region as the Republic of Biafra in 1967. His "police action" to restore national unity lasted from 1967–1969 and resulted in over one million deaths.

After the successful reincorporation of Biafra into Nigeria, Gowon adopted a policy of reconciliation with the Ibo secessionists and promised to restore civilian rule in Nigeria by 1976. In 1974, however, he proclaimed that the target date was no longer feasible, sparking nationwide discontent. He was deposed in a bloodless military coup in 1975, while attending a meeting of the Organization of African Unity in Kampala, Uganda. Rather than return to Nigeria, he chose to pursue academic studies in Great Britain, completing a doctorate in political science in 1984. He denied having participated in a failed countercoup in 1976, intended to restore him to power. Gowon now resides in Lomé, Togo.

GRACCHUS, GAIUS SEMPRONIUS Roman social reformer active during the second half of the second century B.C. As TIBERIUS GRACCHUS's younger brother, Gaius served on the latter's agricultural board for the redistribution of land. In 123 and 122 B.C., he was elected Tribune and reenacted his brother's reforms as well as a variety of other measures which were designed to weaken the power of the ruling senatorial oligarchy. One law reaffirmed the principle that the death penalty should be endorsed by the *comita centuriata* (assembly of Roman citizens). Several laws strengthened the *Equites* (citizens whose property was worth at least 400,000 sesterces) at the expense of the senate, giving them the right to serve in the army courts, from which the senators were barred. A corn law gave citizens wheat at a relatively low price. Other laws eased military service, renewed the distribution of land and gave work to citizens. The considerable popular support which he had garnered waned when, in another measure aimed at weakening the Senate, he sought to extend civil rights to Rome's Latin allies. Fighting broke out between the supporters of Gaius Sempronius and those of the Senate which, in 121 B.C., led to his death. He left behind him the *Lex Frumenteria*, a law under which the Roman Republic undertook to feed the urban masses, who were thereby freed of the need to work for a living and became a ready tool in the hands of any demagogue.

GRACCHUS, TIBERIUS SEMPRONIUS Roman social reformer active during the second half of the second century B.C. Born some time between 169 and 164 B.C. to well-known and respected Patrician (i.e., aristocratic) parents, he entered upon the usual Roman military-political career for a man of his class. After serving in Spain, he took the unusual step, for a Roman nobleman, of having himself elected Tribune in 133 B.C. In this office, he introduced a bill to distribute small plots of land to poor citizens, thereby solving the social problems caused by the dispossession of small farmers and the growth of the proletariat; as propertied citizens, the new settlers would be qualified for military service. Tiberius took the unprecedented step of deposing Octavius, his colleague in office, who had vetoed the bill, which was soon passed. The opposition now included not only possessors of public land, soon to lose their possessions and those who feared the rise of the political power of Tiberius, but also those who regarded his methods as constitutionally dangerous. His candidature to be reelected Tribune to complete the agrarian reforms was interpreted as an attempt to consolidate a personal rule. Tiberius' opponents accused him of aiming to establish tyranny, and he and many of his supporters were lynched on the Capitol by a mob led by senators. His socioeconomic reforms were abandoned. His murder—the first of its kind to take place in the Republic for centuries—became the starting point for a series of civil wars which, 100 years later, resulted in the disintegration of the Roman Republic and the establishment of the Roman Empire in its stead.

GRAMSCI, ANTONIO (1891–1937) The main theoretician and one of the founding fathers of the Italian Communist party. Gramsci was very much influenced by his crippled childhood in his native and poverty-stricken Sardinia. He entered the University of Turin in 1911, joined the Socialist party (PSI) and began writing for its newspaper, *Avanti*. By 1917, Gramsci was already secretary of the Turinese section of the Italian Socialist party and in 1919 he began publishing, with PALMIRO TOGLIATTI, Umberto Terracini and Angelo Tasca, the weekly *L'Ordine Nuovo*. Adhering to the principles of LENIN and the Third International (see INTERNATIONAL, THIRD), Gramsci helped to found the Italian Communist party (PCI), seceding from the Socialist party at the Livorno Congress in January 1921. In 1922, Gramsci went to Russia and worked in the Third International, then moved to Austria in 1923 and, after having being elected to parliament, returned to Italy in May 1924 to confront FASCISM. From the earliest years of the PCI, Gramsci labored hard to create a viable political structure for the party while fighting the extremist line of its leader, Amadeo Bordiga. His opposition to MUSSOLINI and fascism led to his arrest in November 1926 and to a sentence of 20 years in prison, as decreed by a Fascist Special Tribunal for the Defense of the State. Defeated and ill, Antonio Gramsci did not surrender and organized seminars on political thought in jail, collecting his thoughts in his *Prison Notebooks*. It was in this phase that Gramsci reevaluated the Marxist concepts of politics, law, culture and morals—the superstructure—which he regarded just as vital to the revolutionary process as the economic relations of production—the infrastructure. He elaborated on the theory of the cultural hegemony to be achieved by the revolutionary forces in a war in which civil society would slowly be conquered by a historical bloc of progressive forces and ideas. According to Gramsci, only by achieving cultural hegemony could the left move into the stage of socioeconomic revolution, in which political power would be assumed as the final act. As a neo-Marxist, Gramsci contributed to the left-wing perceptions of post-industrial European societies that would characterize Eurocommunism in the 1970s and 1980s. Trying to build a bridge between agricultural and industrial workers, he also dealt extensively with the problems of southern Italy. Gramsci's health deteriorated and he was transferred to a hospital prison. Under international pressure, his sentence was reduced but he died in April 1937, leaving an intellectual heritage that influenced Italian communism after World War II.

GRANDI, DINO   (1895–1988) Italian Fascist (see FASCISM) revolutionary leader. After acquiring a degree in law, Grandi joined the *Fasci di Azione Rivoluzionaia* (Fasces of Revolutionary Action), which represented the interventionist left, in November 1914. In World War I he served with distinction in the ranks of the Alpine troops, attaining the rank of captain. He joined the Fascist camp in 1920 as a Mazzinian syndicalist, and in 1921 was elected to parliament and appointed as regional secretary of the Fasci in Emilia Romagna. Grandi's revolutionary perception of FASCISM as a new national democracy led him to oppose MUSSOLINI's policies of making peace with the socialists and of the transformation of the Fasci from a movement into a political party. In the MARCH ON ROME, Grandi was the chief of staff of the *quadrumviri*. In 1924, he was reelected to parliament and served as vice-president of the Chamber of Deputies. In 1925, after a brief period at the ministry of interior affairs, Grandi was appointed undersecretary of foreign affairs and in 1929 he became minister of foreign affairs. His policies were realistic and geared to weaken France and make possible the creation of an Italian colonial empire without provoking a European war. This was to be achieved by taking the middle ground

between the French and German positions. In 1932, Mussolini took over the direction of foreign policy and appointed Grandi ambassador to London. There he was very active and successful in reducing sanctions imposed on Italy as a result of the invasion of Ethiopia in 1935. He became the architect of the Italo-British rapprochement in 1937 and was responsible for the central role Mussolini played in the Munich conference in September 1938. Back in Italy, in 1939 Grandi was appointed minister of justice and then president of the Chamber of Fasces and Corporations. Grandi was against Italy joining the German side of World War II. In 1940 he was sent, with other ministers, to fight in the Italian invasion of Greece. It was he who called the meeting of the Fascist Grand Council that deposed Mussolini on July 24–25, 1943. Tried at the Verona trials by the Fascists of Mussolini's puppet Salo Republic (see ITALIAN SOCIAL REPUBLIC), Grandi was condemned to death in absentia. He was acquitted by the High Commission of Expurgation of Fascism, emigrated to Brazil and returned to Italy in the 1950s. He died in Bologna in 1988.

GREAT JEWISH REVOLT   see JEWISH REVOLT.

GREAT LEAP FORWARD   (1958–1959) A Massive Chinese campaign for increasing production. Disappointed with Soviet-style economic planning, MAO ZEDONG envisioned a rapid Chinese road to socialism and industrialization by substituting zeal for technical competence and human will for capital investment. The key to the success of this scheme was the commune. Chinese peasants, organized into some 24,000 self-sufficient collectives, each with about 22,500 people, were mobilized in a frenzied drive to increase agricultural and industrial production, the latter including primitive smelters for iron and steel. This unrealistic policy, combined with natural disasters for three consecutive years (1959–1961) and Moscow's abrupt termination of assistance in 1960, produced one of the worst famines in Chinese history.

The Chinese themselves admit that 16 million died; others report a much higher death toll. The disaster evoked direct criticism of Mao within the party hierarchy for the first time since the 1930s.

GREAT PROLETARIAN CULTURAL REVOLUTION (1966–1976) A massive, violent campaign to renew revolutionary fervor in China. Facing covert opposition in the CHINESE COMMUNIST PARTY (CCP) after the disastrous consequences of the GREAT LEAP FORWARD (1958–1960), MAO ZEDONG turned to the "masses" in an effort to restore his personal authority and combat " revisionism." There was also an ideological dimension to this power struggle. Arguing that contradictions would continue to plague society even after the establishment of socialism, Mao felt that continuous or permanent revolution was necessary in order to prevent the restoration of capitalism. He believed that the essential teaching of Marxism was encapsulated in one sentence: "To rebel is justified." His antiparty campaign first took the form of a socialist education movement in the early 1960s, and in January 1965 for the first time he designated party leaders who were taking the "capitalist road" as the target of the movement. In November, the opening shots of the cultural revolution were fired when a newspaper article attacked the vice-major of Beijing. JIANG QING, Mao's wife, who is said to have inspired the article, would soon emerge from political obscurity to join LIN BIAO, defense minister from 1959, in the forefront of Mao's most faithful disciples. In early 1966, Mao escalated his attack against "capitalist-roaders" within the party, and in May he had the Politburo issue a circular that gave him supreme leadership of the incipient cultural revolution. In August, a meeting of the party's central committee, packed with Mao's supporters, gave its blessing to the Great Proletarian Cultural Revolution. Since most of the party still opposed him, Mao relied upon the revolutionary masses, including teenagers organized into Red Guards, who made their first appearance at a gigantic rally in Beijing on August 18. With LIN BIAO in charge, the PEOPLE'S LIBERATION ARMY (PLA) supplied the logistics for Red Guard activities. During the next few months, 11 million Red Guards appeared at rallies and were then dispersed throughout the country in order to use an "iron broom" to sweep away "old ideas, culture, customs and habits of the exploiting classes," and to "smash all kinds of monsters and freaks who were attempting to subvert the proletarian dictatorship." This was essentially a license to destroy cultural artifacts and abuse and physically attack party leaders and anyone else considered tainted with "rightism." Intellectuals were prime targets. Possession of foreign books, foreign clothing, or even foreign-style haircuts was sufficient to provoke attack. Mass hysteria engulfed Mao's youthful admirers. Printing presses worked overtime to supply millions of copies of Mao's writings, including 350 million copies of *Quotations from Chairman Mao Zedong,* commonly referred to as *The Little Red Book.* "Big-character" wall posters carrying the latest revolutionary message appeared throughout the country. Red Guards issued instructions via radio, and semiliterate villagers were told whom they had to fight. Most universities were closed, as educational and other institutions were paralyzed.

Based upon the Red Guards, other revolutionary rebels and the PLA, the course of the cultural revolution was not preplanned. Although the immediate object—the purging of Mao's party opponents, notably LIU SHAOQI and DENG XIAOPING—was achieved by 1968, disorder had reached anarchic proportions. Maoists fought with each other as well as with suspected "revisionists." Mao realized that he had unleashed forces beyond his control and in 1968 authorized the PLA to restore a semblance of order. Revolutionary fervor further abated in 1971, when it was announced that Lin Biao, who had been designated to be Mao's successor, had died in a plane crash after allegedly plotting a coup. Some foreign observers feel that the cultural revolution ended in 1969, when the convulsive phase was over, but for most Chinese normalcy did not return until Mao's death in 1976 and the subsequent removal of Jiang Qing's clique (the "Gang of Four"). Ten years of turmoil which brought death and suffering to millions of Chinese ended the cult of Mao Zedong. It also ended CCP infallibility. Since then the party has been judged by its performance.

GREEK COLONELS' COUP see COLONELS' COUP.

GREEK REVOLT (Greek War of Independence) (1821–1829) Most of the area generally known as Greece came under Turkish rule after the fall of Constantinople in 1453. For three

centuries thereafter the country was relatively quiet, albeit with occasional uprisings by bandits, some of which were supported by foreign powers, particularly Russia. The last such revolt broke out in the Peloponnese in 1770 and took the Ottomans nine years to suppress. Its causes were religious grievances, financial oppression on the part of the local Turkish governors and possibly a desire for independence or at least autonomy on the part of the Greek aristocracy, all with a strong admixture of Russian meddling.

The events of 1776–1789—first the AMERICAN REVOLUTION, then the FRENCH REVOLUTION—did not go unnoticed in Greece. Greek urban residents dreamed of emulating western democratic and liberal achievements; conversely, liberals in many countries—particularly in England and France—were not adverse to aiding Greece against the "unspeakable Turk." More aid, though motivated by considerations of foreign policy rather than any noble sentiments, came from the courts of Vienna and St. Petersburg. Both of them hoped to expand in the Balkans at the Porte's expense, and both provided Greek revolutionaries with asylum as well as some money and aid.

The standard of revolt was raised for the first time by Bishop Germanos at the monastery of Hagia Lavra, in the Peloponnese,

The Greek Revolt, which began in 1821, as it appeared in Western eyes (painting by Delacroix, 1828)

on March 25, 1821. The rebels quickly took control not only of the Peloponnese but of Crete and much of central Greece, including Athens and Thebes; however, after 1825 a stalemate prevailed as the Ottomans were able to suppress attempted revolts in Thesally, Macedonia and Mount Athos. By that time, two different Greek revolutionary governments were in existence and they were quarrelling furiously with each other. The ensuing chaos enabled the Ottoman governor of Egypt, MUHAMMAD ALI, to send his son Ibrahim at the head of a large army. It landed in the Peloponnese, took control of most of the peninsula and recaptured the key position of Saloniki in April 1826.

At the time Saloniki fell, it seemed that the revolt was doomed and that the reoccupation of central Greece by Ottoman forces was only a question of time. However, the western powers intervened. Their navies fought the Battle of Navarino (October 20, 1825), annihilating the Ottoman fleet. Next, Czar Nicholas I of Russia also intervened, and his forces, advancing through Romania and Bulgaria, threatened Constantinople. In the Treaty of Adrianople (September 14, 1829) the Turks capitulated and Greek independence was recognized as a fait accompli.

GREEN REVOLUTION The term "revolution" is usually used in political science to refer to a régime's overthrow or to political violence leading to a radical change of program or to a new régime, but the "green" revolution is of a very different kind.

One way in which the Greens are revolutionary is that the Green parties and Green politics cannot be categorized as the politics of either left or right. Indeed, Green parties define themselves as standing neither on the left nor on the right, but in front. This is for two reasons: first, their form and style, and second, their ideology. By no means can the Green parties be described as a new version of any old parties. They form umbrella organizations for various groups which unite in order to change the system, through decentralized and democratic activities, mass demonstrations and extra-parliamentary, unconventional activities.

Their style is always informal. They believe that democracy implies the abolition of the distinctions between politicians and the general public. This implies informal dress, simple, straightforward language, the abolition of pompous rhetoric, and rotation (including, sometimes, those elected to offices transferring part of their salaries to the party's fund).

As for the Greens' ideology, it combines diverse ideas, e.g., anti-nuclear energy, women's liberation, a holistic life and sustainable development. But there are two common principles: first, that democracy implies participation, with priority to decisions at the grassroots-level over the "elite" level, and the abolition of the system in which a professional minority governs in a paternalistic manner; and second, post-materialism—the public and political debate should concentrate on the abolition of divisions between races, sexes and nations, on social responsibility, friendship, education, life-style and public atmosphere, rather than on issues which derive from and reflect the greediness of our current society. The main sphere in which this greediness is manifested is our relationship with the environment, and therefore this relationship should be radically transformed into a system of respect and harmony rather than exploitation.

On this point, the Greens differ from many other parties, in that they do not think that the "environmental" problems are technical and hence better technology will offer the right solution. Rather, they believe that these problems originate in a warped consciousness which is inspired by current politics. Since the democratic system is legitimized by economic success and its ability to achieve "economic prosperity," politics centers on materialistic progress. The byproduct, though, is the degradation of our social and existential conditions and spiritual impoverishment. Rather than conducting our lives according to economic utility, we should think of our economical activities as restricted by environmental and spiritual needs.

Thus the earth itself becomes the guide for politics and social life. As Sara Parkin, one of the founders of the Green party in the UK claims, Green politics is about "abandoning our obsession with ourselves, and putting the Earth into the center of all the models and plans we make for our personal and collective activities." Following this, Andrew Dobson, in his book *Green Political Thought*, derives principles for politics from what Greens find in nature: from diversity they derive toleration and pluralism, from interdependence—equality, from longevity—tradition. To this one can add that from ecology itself Greens derive the idea that societal structures are multi-dimensional "webs of dynamic systems" rather than hierarchically arranged organizations which can be reduced to their individual components.

A combination of this new style with the new ideology is that politics is not regarded as a profession, first because professional politicians tend to be affected by the way they live within a closed circle of politicians, and second, because the target of professional politics is to control and to win more power rather than to bring about sustainability, the latter being based on interrelatedness. The Greens therefore oppose politics which considers governments to be the main instrument to bring about change. They regard politics in a much broader perspective, according to which activities outside the formal political arena are preferable socially and spiritually to activities within the formal institutions. The Greens thus put forward a serious challenge to the current political system, because they call for the end of movement politics in its traditional meaning. As the German activist Petra Kelly put it, the Greens are an "antiparty party."

However, Green politics is revolutionary in another aspect, i.e., its search for moral grounds which cannot be found in any of the other currents of thought and parties. This is the biocentric outlook, which regards all species as equal, morally speaking. This is not a conservative challenge to the anthropocentric attitude typical of the revolt against the centrality of God, but rather an "enlargement of reason to more comprehensive and hence more efficient means of analysis."

Putting the Earth and its needs in the center of human thought, as the Green would advocate, implies a radical change in human policies. Rather than leading their lives according to the anthropocentric view, the Greens believe that humans should realize that all their social and personal goals will be better achieved if they conduct their lives according to what the human being is: one species among others, within a system of ecosystems. Politics therefore encompasses matters of relationships between human beings and animals, rivers, trees, etc., based on new environmental ethics.

Thus the Greens' perspective on social issues is novel and distinct, both in the role it gives to the Earth and to social control of technology, and in the sort of questions that the Greens ask, such as who we are and what it means to be human, what nature is, and what the place is of humans within their context, i.e., the environment. The Greens want us to rethink not only the way we live but also the way we perceive ourselves, from our everyday life at home—what we eat, what we read, the cultural events we enjoy—to the global politics of our time.

GRIFFITH, ARTHUR (1872–1922) Irish politician. Coming from a poor background, Griffith became editor of various political newspapers that put forward passive resistance as the way to Irish independence from British rule. In 1902 he founded the SINN FEIN movement and in 1914 opposed Irish participation in Britain's World War I war effort. He took no part in the EASTER RISING OF 1916, but this did not save him from being imprisoned by the British then and again in 1918–1919 and 1920–1921. In 1919–1920 he acted as head of the self-proclaimed Irish Republic during the absence of DE VALERA; in 1922 he became his country's president, but he died soon thereafter.

GRINEVITSKY, IGNATY (1855–1881) Russian populist terrorist. A one-time engineering student, Grinevitsky joined PEOPLE'S WILL and was one of the four persons selected to throw bombs at Alexander II. His outward mildness and quiet bearing had earned him the underground name of Pussycat. On March 1, 1881 he threw the nitroglycerin bomb that killed the czar, and he fell victim to the explosion, dying the same night in hospital without revealing his identity to the police. A fatalist, Grinevitsky wrote on the eve of his death, "Alexander II must die... He will die, and with him we, his enemies, his executioners will die too. How many more sacrifices will our unfortunate homeland demand of its sons before it is freed?"

GRIVAS, GEORGIOS THEODOROS (1898–1974) Greek Cypriot revolutionary leader. During World War II, Grivas was in charge of an anti-German resistance group that operated in Athens. Returning to his native Cyprus after the war, he organized the *Ethniki Organosis Kipriakou Agonos* (EOKA), the National Organization of Cypriot Struggle, in order to achieve his country's independence from Britain and lead it into union with Greece. Together with Archbishop MAKARIOS, who led the political arm of the movement, he waged a terrorist campaign against Britain until independence was achieved in 1961.

Next, however, Makarios and Grivas fell out. Whereas the former was elected as president of the republic, the latter continued his struggle for union with Greece (known as *enosis*) and in 1971 became a fugitive in his own country. In 1974, in the midst of an attempted coup whose purpose was to bring about the long sought after union, Grivas died. Meanwhile, however, the coup had led to a Turkish invasion of Cyprus. As a result, the island was divided between the Greek and Turkish communities and union with Greece became a more remote possibility than ever.

GRUZENBERG see BORODIN, MIHAL.

GUANG FU HUI (Kuang Fu Hui) (Restoration Society) A Chinese revolutionary organization. Dedicated to the overthrow of the Qing dynasty, the Guang Fu Hui was founded in Shanghai in 1904 and was active in the lower Yangtze valley provinces of Zhejiang, Anhui and Jiangsu. Consisting mainly of young intellectuals led by CAI YUANPEI, the organization planned to overthrow the Manchus with the help of local secret societies. Most of its members left it and joined the TONGMENGHUI (TMH) in 1905, but the organization continued to exist and attempted a revolt in its own name in 1907. In 1910 it opposed SUN YAT-SEN's strategy for the TMH, and was reorganized in Tokyo under the leadership of ZHANG TAIYAN. After loosely cooperating with the TMH during the CHINESE REPUBLICAN REVOLUTIONOF 1911, the party died out soon afterward.

GUATEMALAN UPRISING (1944–1945) During the worldwide depression of the 1930s, Jorge Ubico y Castaneda embarked on what was to become a 14-year dictatorship of Guatemala. He encountered no serious opposition until late spring 1944, when nonviolent public demonstrations were staged by workers and professionals demanding the right to organize. Ubico's main support came from the landed aristocracy, who expected the suppression of dissent and movements for social change, toward which end the president had not hesitated to use violent means. Shocked by the opposition he unexpectedly experienced in 1944, Ubico resigned on July 1, turning over power to General Frederico Ponce Vaides. Ponce proceeded to institute a few reforms but was ousted by the same dissident groups in mid-October, opening the way for Juan Jose Arevalo's victory in the presidential election of December 1944. Arevalo took the oath of office on March 15, 1945 as president of Guatemala.

GUENTHER, HANS FRIEDRICH KARL (1891–1968) The foremost racial "expert" of the NAZI party, Guenther supplied "scientific evidence" for the Aryan theory of racial supremacy and of Jewish inferiority. His research was simplistic, utterly false and distorted, but it seemed to have given German nationalistic romanticism a scientific base. As such, it was adopted by HITLER and implemented by the SS and other racist-oriented agencies of the Third Reich. Guenther held high academic positions at Jena, Berlin and Freiburg until the end of the Nazi régime.

GUERRERO, VINCENTE (1782–1831) Mexican revolutionary leader. A career officer, Guerrero led the uprising against Spain in the southwestern highlands from 1810 on. In 1815, when the execution of JOSE MARIA MORELOS left the revolution without a leader, he took command and, along with AGUSTIN DE ITURBIDE, successfully fought the Spaniards until independence was achieved in 1821.

In 1829, Guerrero led another revolt, this time against his own government, and became president of Mexico. However, he lasted less than a year in office before he was overthrown and executed by General Santa Anna.

GUERRILLA WARFARE Throughout history, one of the main instruments by which rebels and revolutionaries have sought to achieve their aims has been guerrilla warfare. Such warfare is at least as old as the Chinese commander and military writer Sun Tzu, who laid down its principles around the year

350 B.C. Since then there has probably not been a decade where these principles were not applied by one people or another against its rulers, oppressors or conquerors.

Unlike conventional war, guerrilla warfare is waged without a regular army, without heavy weapons, and without fronts or lines of communication: its aim, initially at any rate, is to disrupt and intimidate rather than to conquer. Throughout history, lightly armed guerrillas have stood a chance only in terrain that afforded natural obstacles—such as mountains, forests or swamps—or else in densely populated cities, where the crowds themselves provided cover. Constantly in need of food, shelter, information and fresh recruits, guerrilla fighters cannot succeed unless they obtain the support of the population—which they usually do by a combination of terror and the promise of national, social and economic reforms to be instituted after the achievement of victory. Often too weak to inflict much physical damage, guerrilla warfare relies on military operations mainly for their political and propaganda effect; hence it is absolutely vital to coordinate military, political and psychological strategy, in order to achieve the best possible results overall.

The first stage in a guerrilla campaign usually consists of isolated acts of terrorism directed against individuals such as government officials, tax collectors, etc. Next a campaign of disruption is launched, aimed not so much at achieving destruction per se as at demonstrating the government's inability to control the country and maintain order. Relying on "hit and run" tactics, stealth and surprise, never standing up to confront superior forces but always concentrating against inferior ones, guerrillas then start attacking isolated outposts, lines of communication and convoys. Provided these measures are successful, the third stage is to create a permanent base in some inaccessible part of the country and use it for the construction of more or less regular forces. By this time, subversion and propaganda will—hopefully for the guerrillas—have brought a large part of the population, as well as at least some of the members of the government's armed forces, over to the guerrilla side. At the right moment the guerrillas will have to leave their shelter and, exposing themselves to the hazards of regular warfare, launch the final push. In the entire course of a guerrilla campaign, nothing is as critical as the timing of that push; should it be premature, the chances are that the regular forces, relying on their superior organization and equipment, will make short shrift of the insurgents.

Historically speaking, some of the more important uprisings that made extensive use of guerrilla methods were the HASMONEAN REVOLT against the Seleucid monarchy (168–164 B.C.); many of the revolts against Rome, including that of SERTORIUS and the BAR KOKHBA REVOLT OF 132–135 A.D.; and the 13th-century Albigensian Revolt. The 14th century JACEQUERIE made use of guerrilla methods before it was brutally suppressed by the French nobility. Any number of revolts in China also used these methods. Early modern Europe saw occasional guerrilla campaigns being waged against the Spanish and French monarchies in particular; however, the modern history of guerrilla warfare starts with the AMERICAN REVOLUTION which, in its early stages, was waged along classical guerrilla lines and ended up by demolishing British rule in the colonies. In 1808–1809, the example of the American colonists was taken up by the Spanish people who fought against the Napoleonic occupation of their coun-

try and, within five years, succeeded in making it virtually ungovernable. Other peoples which resisted Napoleon by similar methods included the Russians in 1812 and the inhabitants of Tyrol, both with considerable success.

During the 19th century, following the introduction of the different modern means of transport and communication such as railways and telegraphs, guerrilla warfare all but disappeared from the more advanced countries. This was not so in other parts of the world; as Europe expanded into Asia and Africa during the century between 1815 and 1914, its armies very often encountered local resistance in the form of guerrilla warfare. This was usually crushed by the most brutal means. Examples are the suppression of the Algerians (along with the Tunisians and Moroccans) by the French, of the New Zealand Maoris and Afrikaners (Boers) by the British, of the Philippine Malay by the Americans, and of the inhabitants of Southwest and Southeast Africa by the Germans. On the other hand, the 19th century also witnessed several cases where revolutionary guerrilla warfare was successful. Good examples are the GREEK REVOLT against Turkey which took place in 1821–1829 and the Mexican revolt against the attempt of Napoleon III to put a foreign prince, Maximilian of Habsburg, on the throne.

During World War I, the British-assisted ARAB REVOLT made use of guerrilla warfare and assisted in the overthrow of the Ottoman empire. The British were, however, soon to see the instrument turned against them; in 1919 a guerrilla campaign broke out in Ireland and, within three years, brought that country independence from Britain. This success did not go unnoticed, and gave the signal for any number of uprisings in other colonized countries in the era before World War II, including Syria, Palestine, Egypt, Iraq, Northern India (present-day Pakistan) and Morocco. Though all of these were eventually suppressed, some with extreme brutality, the old self-confidence with which the colonial powers had carried out their dirty work was gone.

From 1939 on, the German and Japanese conquests gave rise to another wave of guerrilla wars. By this time, the position of the guerrilla in the eyes of the "civilized" world had entirely changed: instead of being considered criminals and bandits who deserved to be exterminated, the anti-Nazi and anti-Japanese insurgents were considered heroes deserving of applause as well as support in the form of arms and money. The first effective guerrilla movement to emerge was the one led by JOSEPH TITO in Yugoslavia. It was followed by outbreaks in Russia, Greece, Poland, France and northern Italy. There were also generally less effective similar movements against the Japanese in Burma, Indonesia and the Philippines. By 1945, there was scarcely a country that had been occupied by an Axis power which did not boast a guerrilla uprising, large or small. Many of them were not just nationalist but Communist, promising to bring about not merely national liberation but social revolution as well.

World War II over, the western victors would dearly have liked to put guerrilla warfare to rest. Encouraged by the Soviet Union, however, it refused to disappear and instead was adopted by different colonial peoples as a means of carrying out their revolts against the various imperialist occupiers. In 1947–1948, the first countries to free themselves of colonial rule were India and Israel. In 1949, a prolonged guerrilla campaign in China reached its climax, overthrowing the GUOMINDANG government and establishing a revolutionary Communist régime. Next came an uprising against the Dutch in Indonesia as well as the Communist-instigated revolt of the Vietnamese people against the French. This was followed by a large number of uprisings during the 1950s, many of them accompanied by vicious guerrilla campaigns that sought to expel the imperialists even as they promised to establish a new social and economic order. Within less than 20 years from the end of World War II, the European empires, which had taken centuries to construct, were giving way in face of these revolts and found themselves in the final stages of decay and dissolution.

In 1965 the Americans, attempting to establish a democratic South Vietnam, were confronted by a Communist-led revolutionary guerrilla war. Over the next eight years the Americans suffered 55,000 casualties (not counting the wounded) and invested 150 million dollars in an effort to defeat their opponents, only to be soundly defeated themselves. No sooner had the Americans withdrawn from Indochina in 1975, than a revolt overthrew the Salazar régime in Portugal and enabled the last colonies of all, Angola and Mozambique, to achieve their freedom. With that it appeared to many that the era of modern guerrilla uprisings had come to an end, but that belief was to prove premature. The potential of guerrilla warfare as a revolutionary instrument for the liberation of peoples who were oppressed or regarded themselves as oppressed had by no means exhausted itself. From South Africa to the Philippines, and from the Spanish Basque country to Tibet, campaigns based on guerrilla principles continued to be waged in numerous parts of the world.

In 1979 the Soviet Union, at that time considered by many the world's strongest military power, invaded Afghanistan. Here the Soviet troops, too, were confronted with a guerrilla campaign. Ten years and 13,000 dead later, not only did the Red Army pull out of Afghanistan but, its credibility in ruins, had to stand by helplessly as other parts of the Soviet empire broke away and established their independence. With that, the floodgates were opened. As of the beginning of 1995 there were some 30 guerrilla campaigns, large and small, being waged worldwide. The majority continued to take place in Third World countries, including Latin America, where this form of war has always been endemic.

However, some were being fought in what until the end of the 1980s had been known as the Second, or Communist, World: nor is there any reason to believe that the revolutionary potential of so-called First World, or developed countries is spent, and that they are in principle immune to its ravages. As the end of the second millennium approaches, it is clear that guerrilla warfare in its various forms—ranging from sporadic terrorist acts to full-scale insurgency—continues to form a powerful instrument with revolutionary potential that few if any established states can afford to ignore. Either they find ways to put an end to it or, sooner or later, it will put an end to many of them.

GUEVARA, ERNESTO (CHE) (1928–1967) Latin American revolutionary. Ernesto Guevara de la Serna (he legally adopted the name Che in 1959) was the eldest child of a left-leaning, middle-class family in Buenos Aires, Argentina. As a young medical student he spent many vacations travelling across South America, where he was appalled by prevailing socioeconomic conditions and became convinced that only the violent over-

throw of existing régimes could remedy the situation. After receiving his M.D. degree in 1953, he was advised to make his way to Guatemala, where the new government, headed by JACOBO ARBENZ GUZMAN, had adopted a progressive social platform. The collapse of the régime the following year in a CIA-sponsored coup made a strong impression on him and later helped Guevara formulate his revolutionary philosophy. The role of the military in the coup taught him that, for a revolution to succeed, it was necessary to destroy pre-existing military institutions, whereas peasant complacency had shown that it was vital to mobilize and arm the masses. Finally, he believed that American intervention had proven that the United States was the foremost threat to the revolution.

Following the coup, Guevara worked in Mexico as a doctor. Among his first acquaintances there were RAUL CASTRO and FIDEL CASTRO, who were forming an expeditionary force to depose the reactionary régime of Fulgencio Batista in Cuba. Guevara was immediately impressed by the Castros and joined the force as a doctor. They embarked for Cuba in November 1956. Guevara landed—three days late—with 82 comrades at Belic, Oriente Province on December 2. His small force was immediately ambushed by troops loyal to Batista. Only 17 participants survived and Guevara was wounded. By 1957, however, he had been promoted to major for his exceptional organizational abilities; in one province he established a bakery, an arms shop and a clandestine radio station within a few days of his arrival. He was instrumental in the capture of the Las Villas Province and served as coordinator between Fidel Castro's forces and other rebel groups.

On December 29, Batista sent a trainload of troops to recapture the Oriente Province. In a pitched two-hour battle, Guevara captured the train. Two days later Batista fled Cuba; on January 2, 1959 Castro entered Havana. Guevara was granted Cuban citizenship and later appointed to several prominent positions, among them president of the National Bank of Cuba and minister of industry.

Despite the dramatic success of the CUBAN REVOLUTION of 1959, Guevara soon realized that the consensus generated by victory would become strained as revolutionary socioeconomic reforms gained momentum. He therefore supported a complete transformation of the existing agricultural structure on the island along socialist lines and promoted the Rebel Army as the vanguard of the people—the only instrument capable of mobilizing the masses and bringing about social revolution.

After a diplomatic stint abroad, Guevara returned to Cuba to implement the industrialization and nationalization of the banks. He feared economic dependence on the United States, which he blamed for Cuba's underdevelopment and encouraged trade links with the Soviet Union and the Communist Bloc. Having failed, however, to create an industrial base on the island, he began promoting Communist camaraderie in the creation of the "new socialist man." Everyone, he believed, should be a guerrilla, combatting imperialism, illiteracy, underdevelopment and reformism. Guevara's idealism angered many of Cuba's supporters, including the Soviet Union. He was instrumental in arranging the deployment of Soviet missiles in Cuba, and traveled extensively, advocating the establishment of a Third World Union. Cuba, he claimed, was the stepping stone for the spread of revolution to the western hemisphere.

In March 1965, Guevara delivered his last public address, sparking rumors of a quarrel with Castro. Even Castro was unsure of his whereabouts until October of that year, when he received a letter from the Congo stating that, "other ills of the world demand my aid." Guevara returned to South America, where, he contended, the conditions were ripe for revolution. While most Communist parties rejected him, he established a guerrilla base in Santa Cruz, Bolivia. On October 8, 1967, the camp was attacked by the Bolivian army. Guevara was captured and shot dead.

Although he had failed to gain mass support, Che Guevara is still idolized by contemporary revolutionary groups. His writings, the most notable of these being *Guerilla Warfare* (1960), are important manuals for revolutionary movements today.

GUILD SOCIALISM   In British history, a socialist (see SOCIALISM) movement that was influential mainly during the period 1900–1920. Based on works by Arthur Penty (*The Restoration of the Guild System*, 1906) and George Hobson (*National Guilds*, 1912–1913), guild socialism was akin to SYNDICALISM, in that it wanted capitalism to be destroyed by the direct action of the working classes. However, unlike other brands of socialist theory, guild socialism did not think in terms of the means of production being taken over by the State, even a "Workers' State"; rather, its ideologues wanted to see industry run by "guilds" which would represent the workers of a specific industry on a national scale. The guilds would be responsible for the welfare of their workers, regardless of whether or not they were employed at any particular time; they were to be democratically governed, and the state was to retain a role in fixing national objectives.

Though democratic and socialist, guild socialism thus bore an unmistakable resemblance to the corporate state advocated by FASCISM; both sought to organize the economic activity of individual types of industry on a national scale and both wanted the guilds, or corporations, to carry social and cultural responsibilities beyond the strictly economic sphere. Fascism, however, triumphed in many countries, whereas guild socialism declined after 1920.

GUINEA-BISSAU INDEPENDENCE CABO VERDE   see PARTIDO AFRICANO DA INDEPENDENCIA DA GUINÉ E CABO VERDE (PAIGC).

GUINEAN INDEPENDENCE   The sudden independence of Guinea (Conakry) in 1958 had a domino effect on the rest of colonial French West Africa and led all the other French colonies in the region to declare their independence within just four years.

In 1946, Félix Houphouet-Boigny (later president of Côte d'Ivoire) and other native leaders in French West Africa organized the *Rassemblement Démocratique Africain* (African Democratic Organization; RDA) to bring about the reform of the colonial system. The following year a local branch of the RDA, the *Parti Démocratique de Guinée* (Democratic Party of Guinea PDG;) was formed in Guinea by AHMED SEKOU TOURE a greatgrandson of the great Malinke warrior-king Samori Toure and the local head of the CONFÉDÉRATION GÉNÉRALE DE TRAVAIL (General Confederation of Labor; CGT), the colony's labor union.

Toure differed from the other political leaders of Guinea at the time. He detested the ethnic divisions that threatened to tear the colony apart and believed that the diverse tribes of Guinea could form a nation-state united by bonds of worker solidarity and Islam. "At sunset," he would say, "when you pray to God, say that each man is a brother and that all men are equal." His organizational and oratory skills, coupled with the country's sudden economic growth (and the resultant benefits for the working classes he represented), made Toure the most popular politician in the colony and a viable candidate for the president of the Territorial Assembly in the 1954 elections. Fearing that this would lead to their downfall, the ethnic parties overcame their differences and formed the "Bloc" to defeat Toure at the polls. The election was certainly corrupt and Toure was defeated at the polls, but this only enhanced his popularity. In the municipal elections of 1956, he was elected mayor of Conakry, the capital, and in 1957 the PDG won 56 of the 60 seats in the Territorial Assembly. Toure was now vice-president of the Government Council.

In this capacity, Toure began to implement a complicated program to end the country's ethnic divisions. First, he abolished the traditional chieftaincies, thereby restructuring the national power bases. He then introduced a policy whereby members of one ethnic group would administer and govern other ethnic groups: for instance, the constituencies dominated by the Malinke were represented by members of the Fula tribe in the Territorial Assembly, and the local administration was run by civil servants from various other tribes. It was Toure's hope that, in this way, people would begin to refer to themselves as Guineans, rather than as Fula, Malinke, Susu, etc.,

Meanwhile, in France, the Algerian crisis was reaching a head and Charles de Gaulle was recalled to the premiership. De Gaulle believed that French society was in need of restructuring, and called a plebiscite in France and the colonies to approve his new constitution, the constitution of the Fifth Republic. De Gaulle was determined to see his constitution approved and warned the colonies that if they rejected it, France would cut off all ties and leave them on their own. Encouraged to do so by Houphouet-Boigny, almost all French African leaders approved of the new constitution; only Toure hesitated, declaring, "We prefer poverty in freedom to riches in slavery." Behind Toure was KWAME NKRUMAH, whose own country, Ghana, had become the first European colony to gain independence just one year earlier.

Toure did not believe that de Gaulle would really carry out his threats. In a discussion with a British journalist, he asked: "How can a mother abandon her children?" But when Guinea became the only colony to vote "No," France immediately withdrew from the country. Within days, all aid was halted and virtually all French administrators left the country, taking with them even files, office furniture and their telephones. The newly independent Republic of Guinea was forced to start its existence with nothing in hand.

In the coming weeks, other western nations refused to help Guinea. Desperate, Toure turned to Russia, which offered an immediate loan of £12 million and technical advisors. To the west, it seemed that Guinea had joined the Soviet Bloc, and this only increased their hesitancy to deal with Toure. Nkrumah, too, offered financial aid and the option of merging with Ghana in the spirit of Pan-Africanism; Toure accepted the former but

balked at the latter, not wanting his country to come under Accra's rule. For three years, however, Guinea was entirely dependent on Russian aid, and the country gained the reputation of
being Africa's first Marxist state.

There was little truth to these allegations. Toure was indeed a
Marxist, but he was an African Marxist, whose political ideology was uniquely suited to the special conditions of his country.
During the 1961 Teacher's Plot, for instance, children reported
being told by their teachers that the country must choose to
align itself with either the East or the West. Toure responded by
expelling the Soviet ambassador as an accomplice to the conspirators. Actually, Toure's political ideology centered on the
concept of the *Parti-état* (Party-State): "the people command
the party [the PDG], and the party commands the people."

Toure ruled Guinea with a strong hand till his death in 1984.
In many ways his régime failed to fulfill the promise of the early
years. Throughout the 1960s, there were numerous plot attempts
and purges, and thousands of political opponents were jailed in
the 1970s. Nevertheless, Guinea provided a model for African
nationalists. Under Toure's guidance, it showed how a nation-
state could be molded out of diverse, often rival ethnic groups.

GUNPOWDER PLOT (November 5, 1605) A conspiracy to
blow up the British houses of parliament and King James I, led
by Robert Catesby, in an attempt to bring the Roman Catholics
to power. Other conspirators included Robert Winter, John
Wright and Guy Fawkes, all of whom were Catholics. They
stored 30 barrels of gunpowder in a cellar under the House of
Lords in March 1605 and waited patiently until the opening of
the next session of parliament, when the king, Commons and
Lords would be assembled. Francis Tresham, who was to have
helped lead the rising, worried about the safety of his Catholic
kinsman Lord Monteagle, and warned him in an anonymous letter. Monteagle immediately brought the note to Robert Cecil,
the king's intelligence officer, and subsequent investigation led
to the arrest, red-handed, of Guy Fawkes on November 5, 1605.
The conspirators were executed (1606) and harsher laws enacted to enforce existing measures.

**GUOMINDANG (GMD; Kuomintang; Chinese Nationalist
Party)** Chinese nationalist revolutionary party. After the CHI-
NESE REPUBLICAN REVOLUTION OF 1911, SUN YAT-SEN's revolutionary
organization, TONGMENGHUI, became an open political party in
the newly-formed republic. In August 1912, it absorbed several
minority parties to form the Guomindang (GMD). Though national elections held in December 1912 and January 1913 gave
it a parliamentary majority, it was denied the fruits of victory by
the republic's provisional president, Yuan Shikai. Yuan's autocratic style, including his suspected implication in the assassination of the GMD's parliamentary leader, SONG JIAOREN, provoked
GMD leaders to attempt a "second revolution" (the CHINESE REV-
OLUTION OF 1913) which was easily suppressed by September.
Sun and some loyal followers regrouped in Tokyo to form the
Zhonghua Gemingdang (CHINESE REVOLUTIONARY PARTY) in 1914.

In October 1919, Sun reactivated the GMD in the wake of the
nationalist, anti-warlord ferment led by students and intellectuals (see MAY FOURTH MOVEMENT). The first national congress of
the GMD (January 1924) confirmed Sun's alliance with the Soviet Union and the admission of Communists (the CHINESE COM-

MUNIST PARTY—CCP) to the GMD. It also added a radical twist
to Sun's Three Principles of the People, taking a strong anti-imperialist stance and appealing to workers and peasants. Sun's
death in March 1925 left the party without an authoritative
leader but with a commitment to realize Sun's plans for China.
How to interpret his ideas was to be disputed among all
claimants to his mantle, including the CCP. At first, senior followers of Sun (WANG JINGWEI, HU HANMIN, LIAO ZHONGKAI) provided collective leadership, while CHIANG KAI-SHEK, though low
in the party hierarchy, gained power as the head of its military
arm.

Despite intraparty dissension and growing friction with the
CCP, in 1926–1927 the GMD retained sufficient unity and revolutionary momentum to enable its NATIONAL REVOLUTIONARY ARMY
to march north, defeating or coopting local warlords and capturing Shanghai and Nanjing. The first united front collapsed in
April 1927, when Chiang purged the Communists (see CHINESE
COMMUNIST REVOLUTION). In June, Chiang completed the northern
expedition by taking Beijing and renaming it Beiping ("northern
peace"), since the capital of the republic was now Nanjing
("southern capital"). As chairman of the State Council, Chiang
filled the role of president of the republic.

For the next two decades, the GMD tried to rule China
through a single-party government. In 1928, it claimed the military phase of the national revolution had ended and the period of
political tutelage was to begin. According to Sun Yat-sen's plan,
during this period the national government would assist local
units in developing self-government capabilities, and after a few
years the entire nation would be able to enjoy constitutional
self-rule. Sun's three-stage blueprint for achieving democracy
was probably overambitious and impractical, but it nevertheless
reflected his basic commitment to democracy. Whether the
GMD under Chiang Kai-shek retained that commitment is questionable: it failed to take adequate measures to train people in
self-government and did not declare the end of tutelage until
1948, on the eve of the Communist takeover. However, even under the best of conditions it would have been difficult to prepare
a nation of close to 500 million people, mostly illiterate, for democratic government. As it was, objective circumstances seriously impeded the tutorial function. Internally, the Nanjing
régime was threatened by military insurgencies and externally
by Japanese invaders. This reinforced the GMD's inherent tendency toward militarization.

The power of the central government was narrowly circumscribed. At the outset it had direct control of only five provinces
located in the middle and lower Yangtze valley. Most of China
remained in the hands of semi-independent militarists only
nominally allied to the GMD. In addition, Nanjing was challenged by the CCP's Red Army. Thus Chiang Kai-shek gave
highest priority to national integration and continued to do so
after Japan invaded Manchuria in 1931 and advanced into north
China. He retained the policy of "first pacification, then resistance" until 1937. During that time the GMD made considerable
progress in building a national governmental framework and bureaucracy in Nanjing and in reducing, though not entirely eliminating, the influence of regional militarists. It gained a partial
recovery of China's sovereign rights, e.g., tariff autonomy and
reduction of foreign concessions. There was also economic
progress, particularly in the eastern seaboard provinces under

direct GMD control. It was here that modernization, led by a western-trained elite, was most noticeable. These gains were offset by the eight-year Sino-Japanese war (1937–1945) in which over 20 million Chinese were killed and the greater portion of the modern economy destroyed. GMD forces bore the brunt of the Japanese onslaught and, despite their often inept management of the war effort, made a significant contribution to the Allied victory. It has been estimated that one-quarter of the Japanese killed in *all* theaters were killed in China. Yet the war sapped the GMD's strength and facilitated the Communist takeover.

Objective conditions notwithstanding, the GMD, as Chiang himself later admitted, cannot be absolved entirely of blame for loss of mainland China. After 1928, the party lost its revolutionary vigor and links to the masses. It suppressed peasant associations and crippled independent labor unions. Though the party claimed over 3 million members in 1945, it was not tightly-knit but fractured by various cliques professing loyalty to Chiang. Based upon the Leninist organizational principle of "democratic centralism," the party's rule became increasingly authoritarian but too weak to be considered totalitarian. The military, especially the officers comprising the Whampoa (see WHAMPOA MILITARY ACADEMY) clique, provided the basis of Chiang's control of the party. By 1938, Chiang's hold over the party, army and government made him a virtual dictator. Besides forfeiting the countryside to the Communists, the GMD came to alienate a large number of intellectuals who resented authoritarian rule.

However, after regrouping in Taiwan in 1949, Chiang and several million followers did what they were unable or unwilling to do at home. In Taiwan, which it calls the Republic of China (ROC), the GMD combined land reform and industrialization to produce remarkable economic growth and a high standard of living. Despite the loss of its UN seat to the People's Republic of China in 1971 and severance of relations with its closest supporter, the US, in 1979, the ROC economy has continued to flourish. This has been achieved under coercive GMD rule, which was relaxed only recently. Chiang Kai-shek's son and successor to the presidency, Chiang Ching-kuo, started the liberalization process during his tenure (1978–1988). It has been accelerated by Lee Teng-hui, president since 1988. Lee, the first Taiwan-born GMD leader, symbolizes the transition of power from the mainland old-guard to the Taiwanese, ethnic Chinese whose ancestors had migrated from the China coast in previous centuries and who comprise the vast majority of the island's population. Under the mainlanders' monopoly of power, the Taiwanese had been second-class citizens. The ROC is still far from a model democracy, but martial law was fully lifted in 1989 and opposition parties can now participate in elections. What is still not permitted is advocacy of Taiwanese independence, since the ROC, like the People's Republic, contends there is only one China, of which Taiwan is an integral part. Though Chiang Kai-shek's dream of reconquering the mainland has long faded, the ROC is not without influence there. It is a leading exporter to, and investor in, the People's Republic, and serves as a model for modernization that contrasts favorably with the Communist version. Given Taiwan's success story and revelations of the darker side of Chinese communism, scholars are now inclined to take a more sympathetic view of the GMD's earlier struggle to unify and modernize China.

GURU GOVIND SINGH   see GOVIND SINGH.

GUZMAN, JACOBO ARBENZ   see ARBENZ GUZMAN, JACOBO.

GWINNETT, BUTTON   (1735–1777) Born in Gloucester, England, this American patriot originally was an exporter to the American colonies. He came to Charleston, South Carolina and bought a plantation on St. Catherine's Island in Georgia. He was an early revolutionary and a member of the Continental Congress which developed the principles of the AMERICAN REVOLUTION and guided the American war of independence. He was one of the signers of the declaration of independence in 1776. He was killed in 1777 in a duel with General McIntosh over who was to command the revolutionary troops from Georgia.

H

HABASH, GEORGE (1925–) Palestinian-Arab guerrilla or terrorist leader and politician. Born in Lydda, Palestine, a Greek-Orthodox Christian, Habash graduated in medicine from the American University of Beirut. After the Arab-Israel war of 1948 he settled for some years in Amman. In the 1950s, he was one of the founders and the ideological mentor of the ARAB NATIONALIST MOVEMENT (ANM; *Harakat al-Qawmiyyin al-'Arab*)— an extreme nationalist, Pan-Arab group, largely underground, whose leaders were never publicly identified, that opposed the established Arab governments and increasingly adopted Marxist-Maoist doctrines. In 1969, Habash was a cofounder of the Popular Front for the Liberation of Palestine (PFLP), an extremist guerrilla or terrorist formation strongly influenced by and connected with the ANM. The PFLP, of which Habash has remained the leader, advocates all-out guerrilla war against Israel and opposes a political solution involving compromise.

Habash is a bitter rival of the mainstream PLO (PALESTINE LIBERATION ORGANIZATION) politics led by YASSER ARAFAT, cooperates only partly in their joint roof organization (he boycotted the PLO Executive and Central Council from 1974–1975 to 1981 and again from 1984) and does not submit to its discipline. In 1970, his organization staged several brutal hijackings of foreign civilian airlines, holding the passengers hostage, and continued such operations even after the PLO, in the mid-1970s, decided to discontinue them. Habash is also thought to have triggered the bloody clashes that erupted in 1970 between PLO guerrillas in Jordan and the Jordanian government. Relations between Habash and the governments of the Arab states, including those hosting him and his group, have always been difficult. For some years GAMAL ABDUL NASSER of Egypt sponsored and protected him, hoping to cultivate his group as a "Nasserist" faction, but the alliance soon fell apart. The same held true, in the late 1960s, for the *Ba'ath* government of Syria; despite ideological elements common to the *Ba'ath* and the ANM and PFLP. Doctrinal-factional disputes and Habash's refusal to submit to the guidance and discipline of any government made a full alliance impossible. Habash was even detained for some time by Syria in the late 1960s.

Since the 1970s, Habash has resided mostly in Syria, but relations remain reserved and the alliance partial. Habash did not fully join the Syrian-instigated intra-PLO rebellion against Arafat and his faction in 1983. Though he continues to reject Arafat's leadership, he is, in contrast to the Syrian-guided rebels, prepared to negotiate with him, and maintains, together with NAIF HAWATMA and his Popular Democratic Front for the Liberation of Palestine (PDFLP), a middle position between the rebels and Arafat's faction. Habash cofounded, with the PDFLP and some other groups, an anti-Arafat Democratic Alliance within the PLO in May 1984. In March 1985, he joined with the pro-Syrian National Alliance in forming a new Palestine National Salvation Front (this time without his ally Hawatma). In an April 1987 reconciliation he rejoined the PLO National Council and Executive, but remained a focus of opposition to the Palestine National Council's decision of November 1988 to accept a Palestinian-Arab state in *part* of Palestine and in peaceful coexistence with Israel. He announced, however, that he would abide by the decision of the majority. Despite Habash's intense, high-pressure activity, his PFLP has remained a small group and his influence is limited.

HABYARIMANA, JUVÉNAL (1940–1994) Habyarimana was born in Rwanda and educated in Zaire. He served in the Rwandan army, being promoted to lieutenant colonel in 1967 and later to major general.

Tension between the Hutu and their former overlords, the Tutsi ethnic groups, has been fierce in Rwanda since at least the 1950s and there were massacres in 1963. Again in 1972–1973, conflict threatened to break out between the two groups. At that time, Habyarimana was minister of defense and head of the national guard. In July 1973, he led a bloodless coup against the president, Grégoire Kayibanda (Rwanda's first president and also a Hutu). Habyarimana proclaimed the Second Republic and established a military administration.

He promised, however, to end military rule and return the country to civilian government within five years. In July 1975, on the occasion of the second anniversary of the creation of the Second Republic, Habyarimana announced the formation of a new party, the *Mouvement révolutionnaire national pour le développement* (MRND), intended to include both soldiers and civilians. The principal objective of the new party was to eradicate regional and ethnic hatreds and to promote rural development.

A new constitution was approved in December 1978 to return the country to civilian rule. The MNRD was reaffirmed as the sole legal party, which it remained until 1991. Habyarimana was reelected president in 1978, 1983 and 1988. In April 1992, he relinquished his military titles and functions in accordance with a new constitutional provision forbidding participation in the political process by the armed forces.

In October 1990, Rwanda was invaded by the exiled Tutsi-dominated *Front patriotique Rwandais* (FPR). The conflict continued throughout 1991–1992 and thousands were killed or displaced. A dialogue between the government and the FPR started in May 1992. There was a cease-fire and then violence broke out again. In February 1993, another cease-fire was followed by a peace accord signed formally in August 1993 between President Habyarimana and the FPR leader in Arusha, Tanzania.

On April 4, 1994, however, Habyarimana was murdered, together with the president of neighboring Burundi. This led to the renewed outbreak of civil war between the Tutsis and Hutus.

AL-HAFEZ, AMIN (1920? 1921?–) Syrian officer and politician. President of Syria 1963–1966. Aleppo born, Hafez was a noncommissioned officer in the French-Syrian "Special Forces" and in 1947 graduated from the Syrian army's military academy. A veteran member of the *Ba'ath* Party group of officers, Hafez, after the *Ba'ath* took power in the coup of March 1963, was recalled from his post as military attache in Argentina to become deputy prime minister and minister of the interior in the SALAH UL-DIN BITAR cabinet. He soon emerged as the most prominent leader of the new régime. In July 1963 he became Chairman of the Revolutionary Council, i.e., de facto head of state, a post he retained when in May 1964 that body was reshaped as a Presidential Council. In the factional struggles within the ruling *Ba'ath* group, Hafez, though trying to stay above the factions and keep the régime united, gradually became identified with the "civilian" faction of MICHEL AFLAQ and Salah-ul-Din Bitar, which was considered more moderate and "rightist." In August 1965, he ousted SALAH JADID, the head of the extremist "military faction," from his post as chief of staff.

In February 1966, Hafez was overthrown by a coup of Jadid's military faction, wounded and imprisoned. He was released in June 1967 and went into exile in Lebanon. There he took part in efforts to organize the ousted wing of the *Ba'ath*. In 1968, his faction joined a National Progressive Front of several groups opposed to the Syrian régime. As his *Ba'ath* wing retained control of Iraq, he moved, with 'Aflaq and others, to that country. Hafez has remained in Iraq, as a member of the leadership of the pro-Iraqi *Ba'ath* wing, He remains involved in anti-Syrian activities on behalf of the Iraqi régime and the "National Alliance for the Liberation of Syria," a loose coalition of anti HAFEZ-AL-ASAD factions.

HAGANAH Hebrew for "defense." Jewish underground organization established in 1920 to defend Jewish life, property and honor in Palestine. Its establishment followed Arab riots, particularly in the Jewish quarter of Jerusalem, and the British failure to defend the Jews there.

From its inception, the *Haganah* was closely linked with the labor federation *Histadrut*. In 1931 seceding members of the *Histadrut* founded a rival body, later known as the IRGUN ZVAI LEUMI (IZL).

Originally, each Jewish settlement was responsible for its own defense under the general supervision of the *Haganah* high command. However, after the massacre of the Jews of Hebron in 1929, its organization became more centralized. It organized smuggling and storing of arms; later it manufactured many of its own weapons. During the Arab 1936–1939 disturbances, the emphasis was on defense of settlements. Members of the *Ha-*

ganah joined the supernumerary Jewish police set up by the government. Gradually, a more activist policy was adopted and Arab guerrillas were attacked in their own bases

In World War II, the *Haganah* ordered its members to join the British Army. Meanwhile, a crack unit known as *Palmah* was formed and assisted in operations against Vichy-French Syria and Lebanon. Several *Haganah* members parachuted behind enemy lines in Europe to conduct various operations and also to help the Jews in occupied Europe. At the end of the war, *Haganah* members serving in the British army in Europe smuggled Jews to the European coast. From there, the *Palmah* transported them to Palestine, running the gauntlet of the British blockade of Jewish immigrants.

In 1946–1947, when the struggle in Palestine intensified, the *Haganah*, despite repressive British measures, became more active in armed resistance (mainly in smuggling Jews into Palestine and related activities), sometimes in cooperation with the IZL. This struggle was one of the factors that led to the establishment of Israel in 1948.

By the end of 1947, the *Haganah* comprised 25,000–30,000 men and women. It formed the nucleus of the armed forces which fought during the initial stages of the Israeli war of independence and from it evolved the Israel Defense Forces (IDF). The *Haganah* was dissolved in 1948 upon the establishment of the independent State of Israel.

HAITHAM, MUHAMMAD 'ALI (1940?–) South Yemeni politician, prime minister and member of the Presidential Council in 1969–1971. A school teacher, Haitham was active in the nationalist movement of Aden and South Yemen and a member of the central committee of its leading organization, the NATIONAL LIBERATION FRONT (NFL). When South Yemen became independent in 1967, Haitham was named minister of the interior and, after a 1970 coup, became prime minister. In the factional struggles that ensued, Haitham was considered right-wing, too close to tribal interests, and linked to Saudi Arabia. He also ran afoul of ABDUL-FATTAH ISMA'IL, then the strong man of the régime. He has since been living in Egypt. In 1975 and 1976, unsuccessful attempts were made to assassinate him. In his exile, he organized and headed political groups trying to operate against South Yemen's Marxist régime.

HALE, NATHAN (1755–1776) The "martyr spy" of the AMERICAN REVOLUTION. Soon after the Battle of Lexington, Hale joined the revolutionary army with the rank of lieutenant. He served with distinction in the siege of Boston and in 1776 was promoted to captain. That year, General GEORGE WASHINGTON called for volunteers to spy on the British positions in Long Island. Disguised as a school master, Hale made a successful survey of British troops there and drew detailed maps of British positions. He was captured before he could reach the American lines, supposedly after a cousin, Samuel Hale, informed on him. Hale was hanged the following day. Before he died, he made a brief speech defending American independence and ending with the words from the play *Cato* by Joseph Addison—a play very popular among American patriots at the time—"I only regret that I have but one life to lose for my country."

HANCOCK, JOHN (1737–1793) Prominent Massachusetts

merchant, revolutionary leader and governor, who penned the first and most prominent signature on the United States declaration of independence.

Hancock had amassed his fortune in the service of the merchant house of his uncle, Thomas Hancock. He joined the firm after graduating from Harvard in 1754 and inherited it 10 years later. By 1765, he was both the richest man in Boston and one of its boldest radicals. This combination, which appeared to indicate outstanding self-sacrifice and subordination of economic interest to principle, endowed him with great prestige and prominence in the revolutionary movement. Hancock's intellectual prowess, political acumen and later, military ability, did not necessarily match expectations.

Hancock, who was strongly influenced by SAMUEL ADAMS and associated with him in revolutionary activities, was elected to the Massachusetts general court in 1769, and then named head of the Boston Committee of Patriots in 1770. Subsequently he served as president of the Massachusetts provisional congress (1774–1775), and of the second Continental Congress. He was, however, thwarted by Congress in his ambition to become commander of the CONTINENTAL ARMY and resigned his position of president of the Congress in 1777. Hancock's blundering command of Massachusetts militia contingents in a Rhode Island campaign would prove the wisdom of his fellow congressmen in preferring Washington. In 1780 Hancock was elected Massachusetts's first governor, and except for the two years centering on SHAYS'S REBELLION served continuously in that position for nine terms. In 1788 Hancock ably presided over the state convention that ratified the constitution.

HANI, CHRIS   (1942–1993) South African activist and Communist Party leader. He was born in Sabalele, a small, poor village in the Transkei, South Africa. His experience growing up in such an environment fueled a lifelong commitment to improving the conditions of the rural poor. He joined the AFRICAN NATIONAL CONGRESS (ANC) in exile after it was banned in 1960 and did not return to South Africa until the ANC was unbanned in 1990. By then he had risen to the rank of chief of staff of *Umkhonto we Sizwe* (MK, The Spear of the Nation), the ANC's military branch.

After his return to South Africa, Hani was one of the most popular of the younger generation of African leaders. His leadership in MK guaranteed his popularity among the militant youth, and he played this up by making it known that he was opposed to the suspension of armed struggle, even suggesting that it might be resumed. After WINNIE MANDELA, Hani was seen as one of the main advocates to continue the policy of ungovernability if the whites did not respond quickly enough. He also drew on a tribal power base, spending much of his time in the Transkei rallying support from his Xhosa kinsmen. The ANC's regional committee was filled with his protégés, and he even made allusions to the Xhosa chiefs of the past by holding court in Umtata, capital of the Xhosa homeland.

Hani's prominence in the South African Communist Party (SACP), unbanned at the same time as the ANC, also insured his popularity among the blacks, as well as trepidation among the whites. The South African government had dispensed its share of anti-Communist propaganda during the cold war, and when the SACP had shown itself to be a strong ally to black workers, it became the first opposition group to be banned. Communists were favored by the South African blacks because the whites spoke out against them and also because of the Party's alliance with the ANC. This alliance was strengthened during the exile years by the Soviet Union, which supplied military training, weapons and scholarships to the ANC. When the newly-unbanned SACP announced the names of 22 of its leaders in July 1990, Hani was one of nine who were also on the ANC's National Executive Committee, which then numbered 37, indicating the degree to which the SACP-ANC alliance had been maintained.

Hani was a popular speaker among the township blacks and developed a strong constituency among the angry young men with little education and few prospects for gainful employment. After the exceptionally violent months following the beginning of talks with the government, Hani's views toward the effectiveness of violence as a response to the reluctance of the white government to cede power changed. During a nationwide strike in August, 1992, Hani spoke publicly against the danger of violence and was anxious to show that blacks could protest without bloodshed. He declared before the strike that the days of violent response to the government's foot-dragging were over. He was considered to be the best hope for redirecting the violent energies of his constituency toward more productive activities. Shortly before his death, he originated the idea of a peace corps serving under the auspices of the National Peace Accord to involve the unemployed youth in community development and to provide them with rudimentary training to improve their chances of employment, as a means to bring an end to township violence. He felt that controlling violence and socioeconomic development needed to occur simultaneously in order to be effective.

Hani was generally considered to have the largest following in the ANC after Mandela and to be the most likely successor in the event of Mandela's retirement or death. In the July 1991 ANC conference, in which 2,000 delegates met for five days to elect the leadership, Hani received the most votes of any of the candidates standing for membership in the National Executive Committee. This indicated the strength of the hard-liners in the ANC, even though the moderates won the top five leadership positions. In 1992, Hani accepted the position of secretary-general of the SACP offered to him by JOE SLOVO and others. This decision appeared to make little sense if Hani was aiming to head the ANC, but one possible explanation was that he was being held in reserve as the leader the people would turn to if the ANC compromised itself by conceding too much to the whites.

Shortly after a breakthrough in negotiations in February 1993, in which the ANC and the government agreed in principle on a five-year transition during which a multiparty cabinet and parliament would share power following a general election (the Government of National Unity of which Hani had been a chief sponsor), Hani was assassinated by a Polish immigrant member of the Fascist Afrikaner Weerstand Beweging (AWB; Afrikaner Resistance Movement). His assassin had conspired with Clive Derby Lewis, a British-born parliamentarian of the Conservative Party, and both were eventually sentenced to death. Hani's assassination rocked South Africa. Over 70 people died in the outbreak after his death, and more than 2 million people attended 85 rallies to mourn him. At his funeral, MANDELA referred to

Hani's insistence that the weapons reported stolen from an air force base earlier had actually been taken for use in covert operations; one of these guns had killed Hani.

Hani's assassination was clearly an attempt to derail the negotiations process; the white extremists preferred anarchy to the possibility of black rule. In this, it backfired. Worried that the country could be plunged into outright civil war, the negotiating parties pushed forward and within a short time had set a date for South Africa's first democratic elections.

HASMONEAN REVOLT The Hasmonean revolt in Judea was precipitated by the religious persecution which was declared by the Seleucid King Antiochus IV Epiphanes in 167 B.C. and was basically a popular rising of the Jewish countryside against the Hellenizing Jews and their Seleucid supporters. The Hellenizing party had previously persuaded the king to transform Jerusalem into a Greek city named Antioch, in which the citizens would be Hellenized Jews. This Hellenistic reform was resented by Jews faithful to Jewish law. Tension rose also high among the Hellenizers because of personal rivalry between the two contenders for the office of high priest, which evolved into open war. Infuriated by his failure to take Egypt in 168 B.C. because of Roman intervention, Antiochus considered the civil strife as a rebellion. He garrisoned Jerusalem, banned the practice of the Jewish religion and turned the temple into a sanctuary of Zeus. Active resistance was started by the priest Mattathias of the house of Hasmon, who slew the king's men and Jewish collaborators when they tried to introduce the cult of Zeus in his native town of Modi'in. Under the command of Judas Maccabeus, Mattathias's son, the rebels engaged in GUERRILLA WARFARE and later even regular battles. Thanks to his victories on the battlefield, Judas was able to recapture Jerusalem and to purify and rededicate the Temple in 164 B.C. The Hellenizing Jews found refuge in the citadel (Akra), which was manned by the king's troops. Judas and his brothers led military expeditions to Transjordan and Galilee to save the Jews living there from the attacks of the neighboring peoples. Before his death, in 164 B.C., Antiochus IV cancelled the persecutions and offered amnesty to all Jews who laid down their arms before a certain date. Judas, however, aimed now at liberating the Jews from foreign rule altogether. In 162 B.C., King Antiochus V and his chief minister Lysias attacked Judea and Judas was defeated, but the foreigners were forced to leave the country because of urgent needs at home. They nevertheless affirmed the right of the Jews to exercise their religion freely. This did not end the internal struggle between the nationalists and the Jews loyal to Jewish law against the Hellenizers, who were now on the defensive. Although Judas had been defeated and killed in battle in 160 B.C., his brother Jonathan eventually took control of Judea and was recognized as high priest by the Seleucid king in 152 B.C., the Hellenizers losing all ground. Complete liberation was achieved in 141 B.C. when Simon, Jonathan's brother and successor, took the Akra.

HATEM, ABDUL-QADER (1917–) Egyptian officer and politician. Hatem graduated from the military college in 1939 and from the staff college in 1952 and also obtained degrees in political economy (B.A., London, 1947), political science (M.A., Cairo, 1953) and information (Ph.D., Cairo). He was one of the FREE OFFICERS who staged the coup of July 1952 and became GAMAL ABDUL NASSER's assistant for press and information. In 1957, he retired from the army with the rank of colonel and became active in political life.

From 1966–1971 he held no government position, owing to the factional struggles within Nasser's ruling group. He was several times considered, in the 1970s, a candidate for the premiership, but did not attain that office. Apart from numerous articles, Hatem wrote or edited several books on matters of information and propaganda.

HATTA, MOHAMMAD (1902–1980) Indonesian nationalist and political leader. Born on the island of Sumatra, Hatta was aware of Dutch colonial excesses in Indonesia while still a child, and he was a member of the nationalist League of Young Sumatrans. Later, as a student in the Netherlands, he joined the *Perhimpunan Indonesia* (Association of Indonesia) and contributed to its nationalist journal, *Indonesia Merdeka*. In 1927 he joined the League Against Imperialism and Colonial Oppression, and he was arrested by the Dutch authorities for "incitement to revolt." Hatta's arrest sparked a new anticolonial campaign in both Indonesia and the Netherlands, but his defense speech, later published as *Indonesia Free*, caused such a stir that he was acquitted. Hatta returned to Indonesia in 1932 and joined Sukarno's Partai Nasional Indonesia (PNI; INDONESIAN NATIONALIST PARTY), a political organization that strove to foster political awareness among the masses and bring about the end of the country's class society. He was firmly convinced of the inherent evil of colonialism, and argued that "Colonial relationships remain dominated by irreconcilable differences." Hatta was also a staunch advocate of NONCOOPERATION in all dealings with the Dutch: although he did not support violence, he believed that "The alien Dutch ruler will never voluntarily free the rich colony from the Netherlands." His political activities led to his arrest in 1934, along with SUKARNO, the founder of the PNI, and other activists. Exiled to Boven Digul, New Guinea, he was released in 1942, shortly before the Japanese occupation of the archipelago.

Hatta opposed the Japanese occupation of Indonesia, claiming that "Indonesian youth would rather see Indonesia sink to the bottom of the sea than have it ruled by a foreign power." In 1945, immediately after the Japanese were expelled from the island, he and Sukarno declared the independent Republic of Indonesia and began ruling the country as a diumvirate (the *Dwi Tunggal*), with Sukarno as president and Hatta as vice-president. However, this unilateral declaration of independence was not recognized by the Netherlands, which attempted to reoccupy its former colony. During the ensuing civil war, Hatta was captured by the Dutch, but he was consequently released so that he could chair the Indonesian delegation of the 1949 Round Table Conference in the Hague. As a result of the conference, the Dutch government conceded to Indonesian independence and withdrew its troops from the country.

Sukarno and Hatta ruled jointly until 1956, when Hatta suddenly announced his retirement. Officially, he claimed that he never planned to remain in office for more than a few years, but it soon became apparent that he opposed Sukarno's ban on political parties and the policy of *gotong royong*, or decision through consensus, the final pillar of the *Penta Sila* political ideology that had guided Indonesia since independence. Nevertheless, Hatta was subtle in his criticism of Sukarno: "Hopefully, the spirit of the Five Pillars, which is alive again and seethes in the hearts of the Indonesian people, can restore the political movement of the Indonesian nation to a straight course toward implementation of the aims of the Indonesian revolution, which were ignored by the Proclamation of August 17, 1945." Politically, Hatta forged his own unique synthesis of devotion to Islam and to socialism. He supported the nationalization of land, water and natural resources as well as of all means of production, claiming that "Socialism is sanctioned by God."

In 1967, Hatta planned to launch a new political party, the *Gerakan Demokrasi Islam Indonesia* (Indonesian Islamic Democratic Movement), but his plans were hindered by Suharto. From then until his death he lived in retirement and refused to participate in Indonesian politics.

HATUM, SALIM   (?–1967) Syrian Druze officer. As the head of Syria's commando units, at first with the rank of major and then colonel, Hatum was linked with the underground group of *Ba'ath* officers. In February 1966 he took a leading part in the coup that brought to power the "military" and extremist faction of the *Ba'ath* under SALAH JADID. Later, however, he plotted with the ousted *Ba'ath* civilian faction and reportedly also with Jordan's secret services. In September 1966 he attempted another coup and, when that failed, escaped to Jordan with some of his supporters. In June 1967, during the Six-Day War, he suddenly returned to Syria—to put himself, as he said, at the service of the army; but the régime maintained he had come to overthrow it, put him on summary trial and executed him in June 1967.

HAVEL, VACLAV   (1936–) Author, playwright, president of the Czech Republic. Born in Prague, Havel studied at the technological institute, having been barred from studying history and philosophy at the university because of his "bourgeois" origin. After 1960 he began a career in the theater. He was active in the PRAGUE SPRING OF 1968, a founding member and spokesman of the Charter 77 movement and the author of many essays on the totalitarian system and dissent. In 1979, he was sentenced to four and a half years in prison for his involvement in the human rights movement, an experience which he documented in *Letters to Olga* (1988). In November 1989 he was one of the leading members of the Civic Forum, and with the collapse of the régime was elected president of the Czechoslovak Republic. Following the separation of the state's two parts, he was elected President of the Czech Republic. His OPEN *Letters–Selected Writings* (1965–1990), published in the West in 1991, portrays his moral philosophy and his attachment to his country and his nation's values, as an integral part of European civilization. Vaclav is a strong supporter of democratic values, of ethnic coexistence and regional cooperation, and has been a vehement opponent of totalitarian and anti-democratic thought and practice. He is often described as a philosopher by inclination, a moralist by conviction and less a politician.

HAWATMA, NAIF   (1934–) Palestinian-Jordanian guerrilla or terrorist (depending on one's viewpoint) leader. A Greek-Catholic Christian born in al-Salt, Jordan, Hawatma is a Marxist-Maoist. He was active in the extremist ARAB NATIONALIST

MOVEMENT (AMN—*al-Qawmiyyun al-'Arab*) in the 1950s and 1960s and in the Popular Front for the Liberation of Palestine (PFLP) that grew out of it after 1967, and headed its left wing. In 1969, Hawatma seceded from the PFLP and set up his own organization, the Popular Democratic Front for the Liberation of Palestine (PDFLP), in constant leftist opposition to YASIR ARAFAT and the mainstream of the PALESTINE LIBERATION ORGANIZATION (PLO).

HAYWOOD, WILLIAM (BIG BILL) DUDLEY   (1869–1928) Revolutionary US labor leader and founder of the IWW (Industrial Workers of the World, 1905), who advocated violence in forwarding the cause of laborers and their unions.

Haywood was born in Salt Lake City and as a child began working in the local copper mines. He joined the Western Federation of Miners in 1896 and, advocating militant positions, became the federation's leader. After federal troops had crushed a mining strike in Colorado in a bloody confrontation, he sought to establish a national organization that would effectively protect the rights of miners and other unskilled laborers. The IWW that grew out of these efforts adopted a militant stance, in line with Haywood's advocacy of "a little sabotage in the right place at the proper time." The alleged militancy of the "Wobblies," coupled perhaps with one-eyed Haywood's imposing appearance, made him a prime suspect in the murder of a conservative governor of Idaho. While "Big Bill" was ultimately acquitted, he remained identified with agitation for violence and was expelled, in 1912, even from the Socialist Party. In 1918 he was convicted of sedition and in 1921, jumping bail, fled to the Soviet Union. He died there in 1928.

HEAVEN AND EARTH SOCIETY   see TRIAD SOCIETY.

HÉBERT, JACQUES   (1757–1794) French extreme left journalist and mob orator. Hébert was the most prominent populist agitator produced by the political turmoil and social upheaval unleashed by the FRENCH REVOLUTION. He gained enormous notoriety at the height of the terror as the editor of a scurrilous and satirical paper, *Le Pére Duchesne,* which he founded in the wake of the national emergency following the outbreak of war. His vigorous press campaign had the effect of giving a radical twist to the course of the revolution. As the self-appointed spokesman of an extremist faction bringing together a motley assortment of anarchists, anticlerical fanatics and dissidents of all stripes designated at the time as the *Enragés* (the Wild Ones—although more commonly known to historians as the party of the Hébertistes), he was able to forge a working-class coalition in favor of a campaign championing populist and anti-Christian causes. The fact that he was also able to gain wide support in the Paris underworld of financiers, speculators in assignats and war profiteers, earned him the contempt of the incorruptible ROBESPIERRE and the hard line JACOBINS.

An activist from the very outset of the revolution, Hébert naturally gravitated to the most radical of the political clubs, the Cordeliers, which was then dominated by the Tribune of the People and hero of the Parisian resistance against the Prussians, GEORGES DANTON. But Hébert soon broke away from his rival and resolved to maintain his distance from mainstream political life. He drew instead on the extra-parliamentary rage of the

SANS-CULOTTES and showed great skill in directing their anger against aristocrats, the clergy and the bourgeois *nouveaux riches*. These enemies of the revolution were relentlessly ridiculed in a steady stream of obscene and virulent articles published in *Le Pére Duchesne*. Couched in a mock popular argot style, *Le Pére Duschesne* has served as the inspiration for a French genre of political satire still represented in such contemporary political weeklies as *Le Canard Enchaîne*.

Hébert's fame and prestige spread even further after the mob sacked the Tuileries on August 10, 1792. The eruption of the crowd as an independent force in the revolution gave him the chance to strengthen his power base among the activist elite of the *sans-culottes*. In particular, he proved able to win over the loyalty of the popular clubs which had sprung up in the working-class electoral wards (the *sections*) by distributing free bread vouchers through a network of Hébertise party thugs and ward captains. At the same time, he could still rely on the moral support of JEAN-PAUL MARAT's *L'Ami du Peuple* and the material help provided by Chaumette, the PARIS COMMUNE's public prosecutor, who had access to the military arsenals of the capital. It was thanks to the light artillery furnished by Chaumette that the two of them were able to penetrate into the hall of the CONVENTION in the great public demonstration of June 1793 and obtain the arrest of its leading GIRONDIN deputies.

The peak of Hérbert's influence was reached during the Great Terror of 1793. The chaos produced by military setbacks suffered at the hands of the Austrians and the panic caused by the Girondin revolt in the provinces provided the raw material for extremists and fanatics from all sides of the radical left. Exploiting this pervasive malaise through his newspaper, Hérbert launched his greatest campaign of general denunciation by fanning the flames of social distress and political discontent. The popular hysteria aroused by an alleged counterrevolutionary plot was now directed against Robespierre and the JACOBIN leadership. Especially repellent to Robespierre were the wild pretensions of Hébert's anti-Christian cult, *Le Culte de la Deèsse Raison,* a bizarre grass-roots evangelical faith which challenged the state-sponsored Jacobin religion of the Supreme Being.

Finally, in the spring of 1793, Robespierre decided to crush the left-wing deviationists. Both the right- and the left-wing opposition were eliminated at one fell swoop by incriminating their leaders. In two successive purges prepared in great secrecy and swiftly carried out in April and May 1793, the COMMITTEE OF PUBLIC SAFETY ordered the execution, first of Hébert and the Hébertistes, and then of Danton and the *Indulgents* who had pressed for a relaxation of the terror and the suppression of *Enragé* fanaticism. Robespierre and the Jacobin leaders were to be executed in their turn in July, leaving the way open to the Thermidorians to reverse the acceleration of radicalism and set the clock back to the original principles of the revolution of 1789.

Marxist revolutionary theory has condemned Hébertism as left-wing deviationism, a dangerous temptation which is to be resisted by the proletariat at all costs. Lumped together with the anarchist ideas put forward by PROUDHON and BAKUNIN in the mid-19th century, the legacy of Hébertisme amounted to no less than MARX's bête noire, since it could divert the working class from its revolutionary vocation and transform it into a lumpenproletariat attracting the dregs of society.

HEHE REBELLION   The Hehe state was founded in southern Tanganyika (now part of Tanzania) in the 1840s. The Hehe bravely resisted the Germans under their great warrior chief, Mkwawa. A military expedition sent by the Germans in 1891 was routed, with many German deaths.

After a long war, the Hehe capital was captured by the Germans in 1894. Mkwawa escaped and was hunted for four years, until he committed suicide to avoid capture. The Hehe military organization was broken up.

HEKALI, RAPU   Peasant leader of the ALBANIAN UPRISING OF 1847.

HE LONG (Ho Lung)   (1896–1969) Chinese Communist military leader. Born in Hunan, He was induced to follow a military career by his father, a poor but locally prominent army officer. He led a peasant uprising in 1916 and gradually built a force of several thousand before joining a warlord army, where he became a regimental commander. In 1926 he joined the GUOMINDANG's military campaign to unify China (NORTHERN EXPEDITION). In 1927, when the first united front collapsed (see CHINESE COMMUNIST REVOLUTION), he was a leader in the Communists' NANCHANG UPRISING on August l, joined the Communist party (CCP) in September, and subsequently became one of the main builders of the Red Army. During the LONG MARCH, his forces finally reached the northern Shaanxi base in October 1936. In 1937, he was appointed commander of one of the three divisions comprising the EIGHTH ROUTE ARMY and played a prominent role in Communist military successes. In 1945, he was elected to the CCP central committee, and after 1949 he held high governmental positions. In recognition of his military achievements, he was awarded the rank of Marshal of the People's Republic of China in 1955. In 1956, he was reelected to the central committee and elected to the Politburo. He died in June 1969 while being persecuted by the LIN BIAO clique during the GREAT PROLETARIAN CULTURAL REVOLUTION.

HELOTS, REVOLT OF   The helots of Sparta had been subjugated by the Dorian invaders by the 10th century B.C., together with the majority of the population of Messenia (western Peloponnesus), which was conquered in the 8th and 7th centuries B.C. The helots belonged to the state, but each one was assigned to a Spartan citizen whose plot of land he had to cultivate and to whom he owed personal services. The helots were sometimes conscripted to serve in the army. The Messenian helots tried to revolt on various occasions, notably in 464 B.C., after an earthquake, and again during the Peleponnesian War between Sparta and Athens (431–404 B.C.). Helped by the Theban general Epaminondas, the Messenians recovered their independence in 369 B.C. Many other helots were set free by NABIS.

HENRY, PATRICK   (1736–1799) One of America's most prominent revolutionary leaders and orators. His remarkable political career was marked by extreme vacillation to and from a staunch nationalist position. The constants of his political thought were best represented in his oratory and, in particular, in his most memorable phrase: "Give me liberty or give me death." The dominance of the idea of liberty provides the key to Henry's ambiguity on the nature of American nationalism.

Patrick Henry was born in Hanover County, Virginia, in 1736. After failing as a planter and a shopkeeper, he entered the legal profession and became a highly successful lawyer. In his most celebrated case, the Parsons Cause series, Henry argued that the king, by exceeding his constitutional powers in his acts in Virginia, had forfeited his claims to authority over the colony. Henry's subsequent shift from Virginia law into colonial politics was a natural progression.

Early in the STAMP ACT crisis, he distinguished himself as one of the most militant spokesmen and activists in the cause of American liberty. He played an important role in convening the first continental congress. In its sessions, he was one of the most ardent supporters of united colonial action against British rule, and a major force in defining national independence as the colonists' overall goal.

Henry resigned from the second congress in 1776 to assist in organizing and commanding the fledgling Continental army. However, he left the army after being superseded in his command. Shortly thereafter he was elected free Virginia's first governor, an office to which he was subsequently reelected twice. He was also elected as a delegate to the constitutional convention, but he refused to attend. From his Virginia vantage point, a more perfect union of the states was distasteful; indeed, an infringement of his cause célèbre—liberty. Henry's harsh criticism of the constitution as drafted, a document which he considered an affront to "the spirit of Republicanism," and his demands to limit the powers which it conferred on the national government, were highly instrumental in the introduction and ratification of the Bill of Rights.

Even after the adoption of the Bill of Rights, Henry refused to support Washington or to join the federalist administration. It was only a decade after the ratification of the constitution that his fears that a strong central government would endanger liberty finally subsided. In 1799, he was elected to the Virginia house of delegates on a Federalist ticket. Henry died before taking his seat as a Federalist.

HERZEN, ALEXANDER IVANOVICH   (1812–1870) Russian philosopher and journalist. Often called the father of Russian POPULISM, Herzen received an education in science at the University of Moscow. His first conflict with the authorities came in 1834, when he was briefly exiled to Vyatka for participating in a radical discussion group in which he expressed admiration for the DECEMBRIST rebels. In 1847, enriched by an inheritance from his father, he emigrated to Europe, where he followed the advent and failure of the REVOLUTIONS OF 1848 first with enthusiasm, then with despair—the despair compounded by the dissolution of his marriage.

Settling in London in 1852, he developed an antiviolent, humanist-Christian philosophy. From 1855 to 1862, together with his lifelong friend NIKOLAI OGAREV, he published Polyarnaia zvezda (North star) and from 1857 to 1867, the fortnightly journal Kolokol (The Tocsin). The latter, written almost solely by Herzen and Ogarev themselves, was smuggled into Russia, eventually attaining a circulation of thousands of copies. It assumed particular importance as the almost sole source of uncensored social thought in Russia. This was particularly so in the years leading up to the 1861 emancipation of the serfs, when numerous government officials, and even the czar, were said to consult its views of reform. Herzen's vigorous critique of the shortcomings of the emancipation and his support of the 1863 Polish rebellion undermined his popularity and influence in Russian establishment circles. In addition, his growing opposition to revolutionary violence put him out of step with the rising generation of radical populist youth in Russia.

Herzen's intellectual credo was based on the supremacy of man's freedom and the independence of the individual personality. His socialism wore a human face, derived in part from humanist Christianity and in part from classical liberal ideas. Never an admirer of mid-19th-century Europe, he looked romantically to the Russian village as a model of human relations, of mutual aid and support, and as a possible cradle of a native Russian socialism that would avoid the human degradations of European capitalist society.

HESS, MOSES   (1812–1875) German socialist, forerunner of Zionism, who provided a socio-philosophical basis for Jewish nationalism. Born in Bonn, he received an Orthodox Jewish upbringing in the home of his grandfather; his parents had moved to Cologne, where his father established a sugar refinery. At the age of 14, when Hess's mother died, his father brought him to Cologne to train him for a business career. The young man proved to be unsuitable for business, however, preferring to immerse himself in messianic visions and philosophical books, especially those of Spinoza and Hegel. He was self-taught, except for a few terms at the University of Bonn between 1837–1839.

At age 25, Hess published his first book, *The Sacred History of Mankind by a Young Disciple of Spinoza* (1837). He clothed his philosophic views in Christian symbols, grouping his division of human history under the headings of God the Father, God the Son and God the Holy Ghost. In his second book, *The European Triarchy* (1841), he advocated the reconstruction of the social and political order into a European federation on a socialistic basis, under the leadership of the three powerful states of Prussia, France and England. In such a united Europe, Jews would be permitted to make their patriotic contribution. He pleaded for the Jews' right to marry Christians so as to facilitate the process of merging both groups into a higher synthesis. He himself practiced what he preached and married a Christian prostitute, which he saw as an attempt to redress social injustice.

Hess made major contributions to socialist theory. He both collaborated and differed with KARL MARX and other radicals. In the columns of the first socialist daily, *Rheinische Zeitung*, which he help to found and edit, he gave expression to his political views. His humanitarian socialism was ultimately ridiculed by Marx and FREIDRICH ENGELS in the *Communist Manifesto*. His Jewish origins were not overlooked by his friends and his opponents; he was even dubbed "the Communist Rabbi Moses." Without abandoning his faith in socialism, his thinking gradually began to concentrate on the Jewish question.

In *Rome and Jerusalem* (1862), a pioneering classic of Zionism, he confessed that he had long been estranged from the Jewish people, but that he had come to realize that they could never be an organic part of other peoples, since Jews were a separate nationality, linked by unbreakable bonds to their ancestral heritage and to the Holy Land that had first fashioned them. As a nation, Jews had once made important contributions to humanity. They could do so again if they were reconstituted as a nation on their ancient soil. There the vision of Jewish sages and prophets, of transforming the individualistic, capitalistic system into a socialistic, messianic system could be realized by the founding of Jewish cooperative communities. Preparations for the resumption of a normal Jewish national existence had to be made by agitating for national alertness, by gathering financial resources for the moment when a favorable opportunity would present itself, and by establishing a network of Jewish settlements north of the projected Suez Canal and throughout the area between the Mediterranean and the Jordan. His book had no immediate repercussions, but 40 years after it was written Theodor Herzl read it and noted in his diary, "What a noble exalted spirit. Everything that we tried is already in this book."

Hess's last years were concentrated on socialist activity, and he cooperated closely with FERDINAND LASSALLE. He lived mostly in Paris and at his request was buried in a Jewish cemetery near Cologne. His remains were transferred to Israel in 1961, and buried next to the Sea of Galilee.

HEZEKIAH, REVOLT OF   (705–701 B.C.) Sargon II was killed in a battle against the Cimmerians in 705 B.C. in Asia Minor, his sudden death provoking a general uprising of various peoples subject to Assyrian rule. Vassal kings of Phoenicia and Palestine: Luli, king of Sidon; Sidqia, king of Ashkelon; and Hezekiah, king of Judah rebelled, and the people of Ekron overthrew their king, Padi, and handed him over to Hezekiah, who was probably a leader of the rebellion. The rebels concluded an alliance with Shabako, king of Egypt, of the Ethiopian (Nubian) dynasty.

In 701 B.C. Sennacherib, successor to Sargon II, marched with his army to suppress the rebellion. Luli fled overseas and Ethba'al was installed on the throne of Sidon. Sidqia was captured and deported with his family to Assyria and a new king with an Assyrian name, Sharru-lu-dari, was installed in Ashkelon. Sennacherib entered Judah, besieged Jerusalem and captured 46 towns (Lachish among them). Hezekiah carefully prepared for the siege and provided Jerusalem with its water supply through an underground tunnel.

Two eloquent descriptions of this siege have survived in the Bible and in an Assyrian account of Sennacherib's third campaign. Despite attempts by some scholars to dissociate them, both probably reflect to the same event, but from the opposite points of view. According to the Assyrian account, Hezekiah, closed in Jerusalem "like a bird in a cage," paid 30 talents of gold and 800 talents of silver; his daughters and concubines were taken to Assyria; his kingdom was reduced and parts of it were given to the loyal kings of Ashdod, Ekron and Gaza; Padi was released and reinstalled in Ekron, but Hezekiah himself, in contrast to the other rebels, remained on his throne. The Biblical account includes speeches of the Assyrian cup-bearer delivered "in the Jewish language," trying to persuade the Jerusalemites to surrender and of Isaiah the prophet who encouraged the king. It tells about the miraculous destruction of the Assyrian army by "the angel of the Lord," but the payment of talents of gold and silver is also mentioned.

HIDALGO Y COSTILLA, MIGUEL   (1753–1811) Mexican revolutionary priest in the MEXICAN REVOLUTION OF 1810, considered to be the "Father of Mexico." The son of a Creole estate

manager, Hidalgo's studies for the priesthood at the Jesuit College de San Francisco Javier were disturbed by the proclamation of King Charles III of Spain banning the Jesuits from Mexico. He continued his clerical studies at the College of San Nicolás Obispo, but also found time to learn local Indian languages and read the proscribed revolutionary literature of France. After his ordination in 1778, Hidalgo served as rector of the college until a scandal over mismanagement of funds led to his resignation.

In his new position as curate of the village of San Felipe, Hidalgo came under the constant scrutiny of the Inquisition. Not only had he abandoned the spiritual welfare of his parishioners in favor of their physical well-being, but he was rumored to have abandoned important church dogma. In fact, he had questioned the Virgin Birth and the authority of the pope and had even taken a mistress to flaunt his rejection of celibacy. His home was modeled after fashionable French salons, and a theater and orchestra were organized. Among his close friends was a liberal cavalry captain, IGNACIO ALLENDE, with whom he organized a revolutionary society under the guise of a literary club. Together they established a newspaper, *El Despertador Americano*, and signed the first proclamation outlawing slavery in the New World.

Foremost on their minds were plans to overthrow the Spanish régime and declare Mexico's independence. A coup was planned for December 8, 1810, but by September news had leaked out and the Spanish army came to arrest the conspirators. When, on September 16, Hidalgo and Allende discovered that they were about to be arrested, they decided to act immediately. Hidalgo ran to the church and rang its bell, summoning his parishioners to what they assumed was mass. Instead, he exhorted them to revolt.

Here Hidalgo issued his renowned *Grito del Dolores* (Cry of Dolores), inciting the peasant masses to a defensive war against the Spanish. Adopting the Virgin of Guadalupe, a humbly dressed Indian icon, as his standard, Hidalgo attracted a growing mob of peasants. The entire local militia of San Miguel joined the rebels in their assault on the provincial capital of Guanajuato. The mob, now numbering almost 100,000 men, raged out of control, pillaging the towns on the road to Guanajuato.

Hildalgo reached Mexico City on November 1, 1810. Allende encouraged him to invade the city, but Hidalgo realized that the revolutionary fervor of his supporters had waned. After several days' hesitation, he turned north to Morelia (present-day Guadalajara), where he was chased by Spanish troops. His retreat was fatal. To Allende, it seemed that Hidalgo's bloated ego bordered on insanity. As the self-proclaimed "Captain General of America," Hidalgo insisted upon being addressed as "Serene Highness." Finally, Hidalgo was removed from his command and installed as a figurehead.

In January 1811, the Spanish caught the rebels en route to the United States. The rebels were routed and Allende and Hidalgo captured. Allende was executed immediately and Hidalgo was taken in chains to Chihuahua, to face the Inquisition. Although he recanted, he was defrocked and sentenced to death by firing squad. His decapitated head was placed in a cage and suspended from the Guanajuato granary as a warning to all future insurgents. It remained there until 1821.

September 16, the anniversary of *Grito del Dolores*, is now the observed as principal national holiday of Mexico, celebrating as it does the achievements of a man who died 10 years before the country's independence.

HILL, JOSEPH (JOE) HILLSTROM (1879–1915) Joe Hill's distinction as a labor leader derived mainly from the popularity of the labor songs he wrote. His subsequent fame in labor circles and in popular culture was also due to the popularity of a song, this time a ballad of an execution that transformed Joe Hill into a union martyr.

A few years after his immigration from Sweden as Joseph Hillstrom, Joe Hill became active in the Industrial Workers of the World (IWW). His efforts focused on organizing strikes among west coast dockside workers in the early 1910s. The labor songs he wrote were, however, his main contribution in spreading the message and promoting the cause of radical labor unionism. Hill was convicted in 1914 in a Utah murder, on the basis of circumstantial evidence. Almost two years of appeals and an intensive public opinion campaign were in vain and he was executed in November 1915. "The copper bosses killed you Joe," lamented the most famous ballad associated with this would-be revolutionary.

HILLQUIT, MORRIS (1869–1933) US socialist. A Jew, born Moishe Hillkowitz in Riga, Hillquit's father was a factory owner who enrolled his son in a non-Jewish secular school. At age 15 Hillquit already saw himself as a socialist, following many other secular Jewish students of the time. With the decline in his father's fortunes, the family emigrated to the United States in 1886 and settled in New York. Hillquit was drawn to East Side Jewish radical circles and on his 18th birthday joined the Socialist Labor party, soon becoming one of its active crusaders against anarchism.

After graduating from New York Law School, Hillquit and his brother opened a successful law practice, often representing unions. In 1899 he was one of the leaders of the right-wing opposition faction of constitutional socialists, which split from the Socialist Labor Party in protest against the radical leadership of DANIEL DE LEON. This led in 1900 to the foundation of the Social Democratic Party, which in turn evolved into the Socialist Party, of which Hillquit was the outstanding ideologist and tactician. Hillquit was now a major figure in the American socialist movement, in which he took a centrist position between the revolutionary left and the reformist right.

After World War I broke out in 1914, Hillquit used his energies to keep the party intact and to launch an aggressive antiwar crusade. He published a peace platform that blamed the war on European capitalists and imperialists and sought to keep the United States out of the war. Running for Congress in a New York district, he was only narrowly defeated. He was now more prepared to cooperate with other antiwar organizations and was a founder of the People's Council for Democracy and Peace. In 1917, he ran for mayor of New York and attracted a broad coalition of support in his unsuccessful bid, in which he received 22% of the votes.

After the war, he represented American Socialists in the Second International (see INTERNATIONAL, SECOND). From 1920 he campaigned against American Communists, regarding them as a harmful alien import. Until the 1930s he dominated his party's international relations and in 1929 was elected chairman of the national party. At this time he took a more cautious attitude, seeking to soften socialism so as to make it more palatable to the American people. His model was now the British Labor party, which was achieving electoral success in Britain. His views roused the ire of LENIN, who called him a social traitor and excluded him from membership in the Third International (see INTERNATIONAL, THIRD). Hillquit continued to anger the left-wingers with his cautious attitude to strikes, his agreement to government-dictated arbitration agreements and his indifference to democratic reform within the unions. Throughout this period he ran for Congress and for mayor of New York, only to succumb eventually to tuberculosis, from which he had long suffered.

Hillquit wrote *From Marx to Lenin* (1921), a critique of the non-Marxist aspects of Bolshevism, and his autobiography, *Loose Leaves from a Busy Life* (1934).

HIMMLER, HEINRICH (1900–1945) Reichsfuehrer SS—head of the Nazi terror mass murder and internal security organizations. Himmler's father was a teacher at the Bavarian king's court and later a schoolmaster in Landshut. The son internalized his bid for discipline and social hierarchy and even though he adopted several Catholic traditions, pursued them in his own way following the earthquake of November 1918. He combined them with vulgar Darwinism and Germanic romanticism, hypernationalism and a sense of radical power politics typical of the new, revolutionary, extreme right in Germany. A typical anti-Christian "scientific" interest existed in his mind, along with respect and admiration toward the order of the Jesuits, whose history he studied as best he could.

While in his teens, Himmler joined a variety of youth organizations, among them one that preached "Blood, Earth and Sword" and emphasized the "revival of the German peasantry." Later, he joined the army as a 17-year-old volunteer and supposedly served in the front as a cadet between December 1917 and December 1918. He then joined several "Freikorps" but in fact studied agriculture and graduated from the technical college in Munich in 1922. In 1923, Himmler participated in HITLER'S BEER HALL PUTSCH. In 1925 he became the secretary of GREGOR STRASSER, the propaganda and later organization chief of the Nazi party. He then met Hitler and became his loyal servant by first informing him about Strasser's rather independent activities. This initial secret police-like function catapulted Himmler to high party positions and to the role of deputy commander of the SS—Hitler's bodyguard, which was also entrusted with ensuring the future racial elite of the Third Reich.

Having been appointed Reichesfuehrer SS in 1929, Himmler combined various superstitions, such as magnetism, astrology, racism, the revival of ancient Germany history and the selection of the "fit" with considerable organizational skills—particularly in selecting people—and relentless ambition. Opportunity came his way after the Nazi seizure of power in 1933. From then on his goal was to infiltrate Germany's police and possibly its judiciary as well. On his way to uniting Germany's entire police and security system under his own command he displayed clear goals, great political skill and, when necessary, patience. Meanwhile he institutionalized the first concentration camps, using them to torture (and sometimes kill) those unfortunate enough to become inmates and to terrorize those who remained outside.

Thanks to his position as Reichesfuehrer SS, the recruitment of able subordinates and the establishment of controlling ties with the state and party elites (it was his practice to appoint persons whom he wanted to cultivate as honorary SS members), Himmler was able to achieve his goals by stages. First he was appointed chief of the Munich police, then of the Bavarian police and finally deputy minister of the interior and head of the German police (1936). By then he already possessed a secret intelligence service of his own, the SD, which held a monopoly in his sphere. Under Himmler's supervision, the SS established a number of "research" organizations that supplied him with the means and justification for the eventual murder of "racial" enemies such as Jews and gypsies as well as the mentally deficient.

During World War II, it was Himmler's SS-SD police units which were responsible for the first mass murders in the occupied territories of Eastern Europe; later those murders were institutionalized in several death centers. His own role in this largest crime in history was that of an organizer, sometimes initiator, and faithful interpreter of Hitler's initiatives and explicit orders. Later during the war Himmler became minister of the interior, commander of the home army and for a short while even commanded an army group. Towards the end he tried to disguise his crimes and trade some remaining Jews with the western Allies. This caused Hitler to dismiss him from all his posts. Having failed to establish his credentials with the west, Himmler put on a disguise and attempted to escape. Captured by the British, he managed to commit suicide before his identity was established.

HINNAWI, SAMI (1898? 1904?–1950) Syrian officer and nationalist. In August 1949, as a colonel, he staged a coup against President HUSNI ZA'IM, executed both Za'im and his prime minister, al-Barazi, and appointed himself chairman of the Revolutionary Council and chief of staff. He allowed political activity to resume and in November 1949 held elections. He was close to the People's Party (*Hizb al-Sha'b*) and encouraged its participation in the government. He initiated closer relations with the Hashemite kingdoms, Jordan and especially Iraq, and was suspected of planning a union of Syria and Iraq. Hinnawi was deposed, in another coup, by ADIB SHISHAKLI in December 1949, and arrested, but he was soon released and allowed to leave for Beirut. There he was murdered in 1950—reportedly in revenge for the killing of al-Barazi.

HITLER, ADOLF (1889–1945) German dictator, born in Branau, Austria, the son of Alois Schicklgruber. Hitler's mother was 23 years younger than Alois, worked for the Hitler family as a maid during Alois's second marriage and bore him two stillborn children before becoming his third wife. She pampered and indulged Hitler, her first living child, against his father's wishes. His father sternly disapproved of Hitler's poor performance in school. Lazy, undisciplined and convinced that his gift for drawing meant he was an artistic genius, Hitler refused to study anything else and left school at 16 without a diploma following his father's death.

Claiming that his artistic temperament made regular work hours uncongenial, Hitler refused to get a job. He was shocked and bitterly disappointed when, at 18, he failed to be accepted to the Academy of Fine Arts in Vienna. Rejected also by the school of architecture, he soon ran through his inheritance from his parents and a government orphan's allowance and was reduced to sleeping in doorways, municipal shelters and on park benches. He supported himself by begging, various odd jobs, painting advertisements and copying picture postcards, but preferred reading newspapers, discussing politics (dominating every discussion and screaming with rage if contradicted) and concocting get-rich-quick schemes.

The foundations for Hitler's political and social ideas were laid during his five years in Vienna, when he became anti-Semitic and an extreme German nationalist. His interest in the supernatural led him to the *Ostrara* movement, which combined occultism with anti-Semitism, presenting a vision of the world as a struggle of the noble white race against its beastlike inferiors (advocating the inferiors' sterilization, deportation and murder), and took a swastika as its symbol.

Strong feelings of German nationalism and an increasing distaste for the multinational Austro-Hungarian empire prompted Hitler's move to Munich in 1913. He immediately volunteered for the German army when World War I broke out, and found there the sense of security and identification he had hitherto lacked. Now obsessively clean, he spent hours trying to remove every speck of dirt and trace of body odor. He was a good sol-

Hitler delivering a speech on February 3, 1935, Berlin, Germany

dier, serving well as a courier, receiving several decorations including the Iron Cross for bravery, and achieving the rank of a corporal. Temporarily blinded in a gas attack, he was in a hospital when he heard of the armistice. At that time he decided to enter politics.

Hitler remained in the army after the armistice but refused to participate in the revolutions that broke out in Germany. When the revolution in Bavaria was overthrown by reactionaries, Hitler supplied them with information about revolutionary sympathizers. The new government used Hitler to infiltrate civilian radical groups, which landed him in a small meeting held by the anti-Semitic German Workers' Party in 1919. Finding himself in agreement, he was moved to give a speech of his own advocating a greater Germany that was so persuasive that he was invited to become a member of the party's steering committee. Six months later he left the army to devote himself to the party, which, revitalized by his genius for propaganda and oratory, changed its name to the *Nationalsozialistische Deutsche Arbeiterpartie* (NATIONAL SOCIALIST GERMAN WORKERS PARTY)—the Nazi party. In 1921 he became its chairman and the Nazis began to take on some of the trappings for which they later became famous: Hitler acquired the title "*Unser Führer*" (Our Leader), instituted the *Heil!* greeting (later, Heil Hitler!), and designed the Nazi flag—a black swastika on a blood-red background.

When the Munich BEER HALL PUTSCH of 1923 turned into a complete failure, Hitler, bitterly disappointed and sure that his political career had ended, threatened to commit suicide. He recovered in time to use his trial as a public forum to advertise his goals. His skilled oratory, combined with extensive newspaper coverage, gained him international fame. Sentenced in 1924 to five years' imprisonment in a fortress, he used his lenient prison conditions to dictate the first volume of his book, *Mein Kampf* My Struggle).

Mein Kampf spelled out Hitler's plans for Germany's future— inclusion of all German-speaking areas into Germany, conquest of vast territories to the east, avenging the humiliation of Germany's defeat, wiping out communism and getting rid of the Jews, whom he saw as inferior parasites responsible for Germany's defeat. Repetitious and boring, the book sold poorly until Hitler became dictator and made possession of a copy obligatory.

By the time Hitler was released (after serving only nine months of his sentence), Germany had stabilized its economy through currency reform, established friendly relations with the rest of Europe and outlawed the Nazi party. Having decided that power could be achieved through legal means, Hitler persuaded Bavaria's prime minister to lift the ban. The Great Depression in fact led to the rise of his party. Playing on the fear in Germany of the Communists, Hitler was appointed chancellor of a minority government in January 1933 and in August 1934 also became head of state under the title of Fuehrer.

Unlike other revolutionaries, who do not implement their radical ideas after taking power, Hitler's career, in his Promethean attempt to establish "a new order," first in Germany and then the rest of Europe (if not the world), had just begun. The first two years he spent consolidating his power. This he did by banning all other political parties, destroying the trade unions, eliminating local and provincial elections, turning the Reichstag (parliament) into "the world's best paid choir" (not being allowed to vote, all it ever did was to sing the two national anthems), and

---

● The great masses of the people will more easily fall victims to a big lie than a small one.
● The one means that wins the victory over reason: terror and force.
● The efficiency of the truly national leader consists primarily in preventing the division of the attention of a people and in concentrating it on a single enemy.

From *Mein Kampf*

● Mankind has grown strong in eternal struggles and will only perish through eternal peace.
● Success is the sole earthly judge of right and wrong.
● The first essential for success is a perpetual and regular employment of violence.

Adolf Hitler

Adolf Hitler is a bloodthirsty guttersnipe, a monster of wickedness, insatiable in his lust for blood and plunder.

Winston Churchill

---

killing opponents (as well as many of his own former comrades) who seemed too radical to him or incarcerating them in concentration camps. He also started the process of "eliminating" the Jews by introducing discriminatory legislation against them. The result of these and other measures was a totalitarian dictatorship which, save for that of STALIN in the USSR, had no parallel in world history.

Next, Hitler turned his attention toward foreign policy. He reintroduced conscription, vastly increased the armed forces, marched his troops into the Rhineland which had been demilitarized since World War I, and in 1938 annexed Austria as well as parts of Czechoslovakia. In March 1939 he destroyed what was left of that country, but by this time his sabre rattling and professed expansionism had thoroughly alarmed the world. When he turned to Poland as his next victim, he found himself faced by an Anglo-French coalition which, in spite of many hesitations, firmly opposed him.

On September 1, 1939, having just concluded a non-aggression treaty with the Soviet Union which guaranteed that he would not have to fight a two-front war, Hitler gave the order for his armed forces to invade Poland. During the next six years he exercised supreme command, at first winning spectacular successes but then, from 1942 on, suffering one defeat after another as his enemies—which by now included the United States and Soviet Union as well as Britain—fought back. Both his initial victories and subsequent defeats served to make him more and more radical; he implemented the mass execution of civilians in Poland in 1939 and the extermination of the Jews, first by shooting and then by gas, in 1941. By the time Germany had been defeated, the number of his victims, including those who were deliberately starved to death in Russia but excluding the troops who fought for or against him, ran into the tens of millions.

Yet, when Hitler dictated his so-called *Political Testament* in

April 1945, the only thing he regretted was not having been radical enough. By that time Germany's impending defeat was certain, with most of the country overrun and the Soviets fighting their way into Berlin. On April 30, 1945, having just married his long-time mistress Eva Braun and had her take poison, Adolf Hitler put a gun to his mouth and shot himself.

HO CHI MINH (1890–1969) Vietnamese revolutionary and political leader, born Nguyen That Thanh in Annam, central Vietnam. His father, a minor government official, was dismissed from his job for activities against the French colonial régime. Ho grew up a committed anticolonialist, the first of his many pseudonyms being Nguyen Ai Quoc (Nguyen the Patriot). After working as a teacher in his home district, he began traveling in 1911, working as a kitchen hand aboard a passenger liner and later on the staff of the Carlton Hotel in London. Toward the end of World War I he settled in France, where he became a member of the French Socialist party. At the 1920 Tours party congress he sided with the leftist faction, which split off from the socialist mainstream to join the Third International (see INTERNATIONAL, THIRD). As a founding member of the French Communist party, he often criticized it for its lack of interest in the colonial question.

Ho was recognized early on as a gifted theoretician and polemicist. He edited *Le Paria* (The Outcast), a monthly anticolonialist journal, and in 1923 was chosen to study in Moscow at the Communist University of the Toilers of the East, set up by the Russian authorities as a training center for Asian Communists.

In 1925, the Soviet authorities entrusted him with the task of promoting Communist revolution in Indochina. While acting as translator for MICHAEL BORODIN, the official Soviet adviser to SUN YAT-SEN's nationalist GUOMINDANG in Canton, China, Ho devoted most of his energy to recruiting and training young fellow-Vietnamese expatriates for an anticolonial uprising. He founded the Association of Revolutionary Annamite Youth and was the forerunner of the Indochinese Communist party of 1930, which in turn spawned the Vietnam Workers' party.

After leaving China in 1927, Ho embarked on an extensive and often dangerous mission throughout Southeast Asia, disseminating Marxist teachings, establishing Communist organizations, and advocating armed resistance to colonialism in Malaya, Siam (now Thailand), the Dutch East Indies (now Indonesia) and Indochina. With the failure of the 1940 uprising against the French in Indochina, he was forced to flee to southern China, where the League for the Independence of Vietnam—commonly known as the VIET MINH—was set up at a congress in Kwangsi in 1941. Ho now took the nom de guerre with which he achieved international fame, Ho Chi Minh ("He who Enlightens").

With World War II raging in Europe, the fall of France to the Axis forces in 1940 allowed the Japanese to establish their authority in Vietnam—using the existing French administrators—by setting up Emperor Bao Dai as their puppet in the southern capital of Saigon. In 1944, Ho and his close associate, VO NGUYEN GIAP, organized Viet Minh strongholds over a wide area of northern Vietnam, leaving them well placed to take advantage of the power vacuum that was created when, in 1945, the Japanese arrested the French administration. Within a month of

Japan's surrender to the Allied forces in August 1945, the Viet Minh, in alliance with other nationalist groups, formed a provisional Vietnamese government based in Hanoi. Ho announced the creation of an independent Democratic Republic of Vietnam by virtue of his position as prime minister, foreign minister and president of the new administration. Echoing the sentiments of the American declaration of independence, he declared: "All men are born equal: the Creator has given us inviolable rights, life, liberty and happiness."

Following the Indochina war, the Viet Minh gained control over the whole of northern Vietnam in 1954. The international community recognized the Vietnamese right to self-determination through the Geneva Agreement of 1954, which provided for the establishment of a demarcation line between northern and southern Vietnam until free elections could be held to choose a representative national government.

Those elections never took place. Frightened that free elections might result in a Communist victory, the United States prevailed upon Bao Dai to appoint Ngo Dinh Diem, an antiCommunist, to rule South Vietnam. In response, the North Vietnamese government undertook the training of southern Vietnamese Communists, the VIET CONG, who then infiltrated the south to encourage insurrection.

As early as 1955, Ho had surrendered his premiership of North Vietnam, but his appointees and disciples continued to fill the key places in the North Vietnamese administration—so his influence remained significant. Small and seemingly fragile, he dressed simply and lived austerely. He was widely revered as a patriot and liberator and as the elder statesman of the Vietnamese revolution. Even the increasingly repressive and totalitarian nature of a poor, isolated and embattled North Vietnamese régime propped up by Chinese food aid and Soviet arms could not undermine the popularity of "Uncle Ho," as he was known by the people. When North Vietnamese troops finally captured Saigon in 1975, it was renamed Ho Chi Minh City in his memory.

HO LUNG see HE LONG.

HONG XIUQUAN (Hung Hsiu-chüan) (1814–1864) Leader of the TAIPING REBELLION in China. Hong was born to a peasant Hakka family in Guangdong. (The Hakka were a sublinguistic community that had migrated from north China centuries earlier and were frequently at odds with native Cantonese.) Though Hong showed an aptitude for learning and both he and his family hoped that he would pass the civil service examinations and achieve the prestigious literati status, he never succeeded. In 1837, after failing in his third attempt, Hong fell into a trance or "twilight-state" for about 40 days, during which he saw visions. His illness, probably psychotic, changed his personality: he assumed a dignified, solemn manner and would often severely scold others for what he considered to be immoral behavior. In 1843, after failing to pass the examinations for the fourth time, he looked at a Christian missionary tract he had received in 1836. It included translated portions of the Bible, sermons on some of the texts, and admonished readers to believe in God and Jesus Christ, to obey the Ten Commandments and never to worship devils. At the time he had paid little attention to the pamphlet. Now, after studying it carefully, he believed that in his visions he had seen God and Jesus Christ, and that he himself was God's younger son, the new Messiah, whose mission it was to defeat evil and bring about God's rule on earth. Blending Judeo-Christian themes with ancient Chinese ones, Hong began creating his own religion and baptized relatives and friends. In 1847, he went to a mountain area in southern Guangxi where a disciple had formed the God Worshippers Society, consisting of several thousand followers—mostly peasants and miners. The Hakkas, who predominated in the movement, benefited from the protection it provided against non-Hakka enemies. The movement gradually grew, attracting poor peasants, bandits and other disaffected elements. While preaching and smashing idols in the villages, Hong began using the term, "Taiping" (great peace). In 1850, the rebellion started when government forces sent in to crush the movement, which had grown to dangerous proportions, were repulsed. Though religious in origin, the movement took on a political dimension when Hong included the Manchus among the demons he felt obligated to destroy. Yet Hong was primarily a religious mystic who lacked essential leadership qualities. It was only because he had able lieutenants who handled organizational and military matters that the movement could become as powerful as it did. In January 1851, after a decisive victory over imperial forces, Hong declared the formation of a new dynasty, the Taiping Tianguo (Heavenly Kingdom of Great Peace), assuming for himself the title of Tian Wang (Heavenly King).

The Taiping forces, fueled by religious fanaticism, anti-Manchuism and peasant discontent, then embarked upon a remarkable march north that took them through the Yangtze valley and Nanjing, where they established their capital in March 1853. While their make-shift army, led by untrained but gifted military leaders, kept defeating imperial forces, internecine fighting broke out in 1856. Hong's behavior was megalomanic and seclusive, and his court, rife with corruption, began resembling that of a decadent Chinese dynasty. The entire movement started losing its initial vigor. Nevertheless, led by a brilliant commander, Li Xiucheng, the Taipings remained a formidable threat for a number of years. The end came in 1864. Hong Xiuquan died in June and Nanjing fell in July.

HOORNE, FILIPS VAN MONTMORENCY (1524–1568) Dutch nobleman and early leader in the REVOLT OF THE NETHERLANDS against Spain. A general and statesman who had served Emperor Charles V of the Holy Roman Empire, Hoorne sat on the council of state when the emperor's son, Philip II of Spain, took over in 1556. Together with his colleagues, WILLIAM THE SILENT and LAMORAAL EGMOND, he opposed the centralizing tendencies of the new king as well as his preference for Spanish advisers over native ones. Politically he stood in the middle; unlike Egmond (who persecuted the Calvinists in his province of Flanders) he pleaded for religious toleration, and unlike William the Silent (who early on decided on armed resistance against Spain) he hoped to avoid an open breach. His moderation did not avail him and in December 1567 he was imprisoned on the orders of the new Spanish governor, the Duke of Alba. Six months later Hoorne's and Egmond's execution, which took place in Brussels, marked the real beginning of the revolt.

HOSEA, REVOLT OF In 732 B.C. Tiglath-Pileser III, at the request of Ahaz, king of Judah, attacked the kingdom of Israel (called by the Assyrians *Bit-Humriya*—"the House of Omri"). He installed Hosea (called by the Assyrians Ausi) on its throne as an Assyrian vassal king in place of Pekah, overthrown by his own people. Tiglath-Pileser III died in 726 B.C. and Hosea rebelled against his successor, Shalmaneser V, relying upon Bocchoris, king of Egypt (called Sigor in the Septuagint and So—after his capital, Sais—in the Hebrew Bible). Shalmaneser V besieged Samaria and, according to the Bible and the Babylonian chronicle, took it in 722 B.C. He died in the same year and his successor, Sargon II, claimed the victory for himself, but he probably only deported the Samarian population to Media and resettled Samaria with the deportees from the Babylonian city of Cutha.

HOURANI, AKRAM (1914–) Syrian socialist and journalist, vice-president of the United Arab Republic (UAR, Egypt-Syria), 1958–1959. Born in Homs, Syria, Hourani was active in various nationalist organizations. During World War II he went to Iraq and reportedly participated in groups preparing and assisting RASHID 'ALI KILANI's seizure of power in 1941. In 1943 and 1947 he was elected to parliament, profiling himself as a campaigner for agrarian reform and a defender of the oppressed tenants against the big landlords. For some time he edited a newspaper, *al-Yakza*. In 1948 he volunteered for service with AL-QAWUQJI's "Army of Deliverance" against emerging Israel and saw action in Galilee. In 1949 Hourani supported three successive military coups—holding prominent positions in the government of each. In 1949–1950 he belonged to a loose "Republican Bloc" in parliament, but in 1950 founded his own party, the Arab Socialist party. That party merged in 1953 with the *Ba'ath* party and Hourani became, with MICHEL AFLAQ and SALAH-UL-DIN BITAR, one of the top leaders of the united Arab Socialist *Ba'ath* party. He fell out with the political leadership and went into exile in Lebanon. In 1954, however, after ADIB SHISHAKLI's fall, Hourani returned and was reelected, becoming president of the parliament in 1957. He was one of the architects of Syria's union with Egypt. Together with his *Ba'ath* colleagues, though, he soon became bitterly critical of the new Egyptian-dominated régime and its chief leader, GAMAL ABDUL NASSER, and late in 1959 he resigned. After Syria's secession and the disbandment of the UAR in 1961, Hourani opposed the *Ba'ath* party's efforts for a renewed federal union with Egypt. He left the party and, elected in December 1961 on his own local Homs list of candidates, tried to reestablish his Arab Socialist party. During the *Ba'ath* officers' coup of March 1963 he was arrested, and when released went into exile to Lebanon. He has not returned to Syria since, but has been cultivating his faction in exile, as a potential alternative to Syria's military *Ba'ath* régime, joining, since 1968, with various like-minded factions in an exiled National Progressive Front.

HOXHA, ENVER (1908–1985) Albanian Communist leader. At the age of 22, Hoxha went to France to study and became involved in revolutionary politics. Returning to Albania in 1936 as a teacher of French, he conducted study groups on MARXISM and COMMUNISM. In 1939, when Albania was occupied by the Italians, Hoxha became provisional secretary of the Albanian Communist party, which in 1941 changed its name to the Albanian

Party of Labor. During World War II, Hoxha led the national liberation front and by the end of 1944 had liberated almost the whole of Albania without outside help. In October 1944, he became president of the Albanian provisional government and commander in chief of the army, in addition to leading his party. In 1946–1953 he also held the portfolios of defense and foreign affairs.

Under Hoxha's leadership, Albania sided with the USSR in condemning TITO's government in Yugoslavia. In December 1961, Albania broke with the USSR over the de-Stalinization taking place in the latter and sided with China against "Soviet revisionism." In 1978 Hoxha accused MAO ZEDONG of ulterior motives in his relations with Albania and relations remained strained until 1983. At the time of his death in April 1985, Hoxha was negotiating cooperation agreements with neighboring Yugoslavia, but still stubbornly maintaining an independence that kept his régime one of the most closed and xenophobic in the world.

HRUSHEVSKY, MYHAILO   (1866–1934) Ukrainian historian and national leader. Hrushevsky taught at the University of Lvov until his advocacy of Ukrainian national rights led to his exile from Ukraine in 1894. In Austria, he began work on his 10-volume *History of the Ukraine* (1903–1936). Returning to the Ukraine in 1906, he helped establish the Ukrainian Scientific Society and led the Progressivist party. Exiled at the outbreak of World War I, he returned to Kiev after the February RUSSIAN REVOLUTION OF 1917 to preside over the Ukrainian National Rada. With the BOLSHEVIK conquest of power he emigrated, returning in 1924. He devoted himself to the Ukrainian Academy of Sciences, though his work and he himself were repudiated before his death.

HSAYA SAN REBELLION   (1930–1932) A widespread rebellion of over 10,000 Burmese peasants, ostensibly sparked by British tax laws and restrictions on bamboo and timber use. The rebellion triggered anti-Chinese riots and hostilities between the Burmese and the Indians, both of which were to characterize later violent outbursts of discontent.

HSIANG YÜ   see XIANG YU.

HSING CHUNG HUI   see XING ZHONG HUI.

HUA HSING HUI   see HUA XING HUI.

HUANG CHAO (Huang Ch'ao)   (d. 884) Chinese rebel. A native of Shandong, Huang led a peasant rebellion that hastened the end of the already weakened Tang dynasty (618–907) (see AN LUSHAN). In 875 Huang, who was a wealthy salt smuggler and a frustrated candidate in the civil service examinations, joined a rebellion led by another salt smuggler, Wang Xianzhi, and assumed leadership of the rebellion when Wang was killed. While voicing egalitarian slogans that attracted peasants, the rebel leaders represented the new middle-class of landlord-merchants and entrepeneurs who resented government restrictions on private business. After raising havoc in the north, Huang's forces swept through south China (878–879), sacked the rich commercial city of Canton and returned to the north. In 880

they captured the eastern capital, Loyang, and in 881 the main capital, Changan, forcing the emperor to flee. Huang proclaimed himself emperor of a new dynasty. Aided by Turkish troops, imperial forces drove him from Changan in 883. His death in 884 ended the rebellion, but from that time onward Tang emperors were mere puppets manipulated by regional military leaders.

HUANG HSING   see HUANG XING.

HUANGPU   see WHAMPOA MILITARY ACADEMY.

HUANG XING (Huang Hsing)   (1874–1916) Chinese revolutionary leader. Born in Hunan, Huang was the son of a school teacher, received a traditional education and in 1892 passed the first stage of the civil service examinations. In 1897 he began studying at the Liang-Hu (Hunan-Hubei) Academy in Wuchang (Hubei province) which reflected the educational policies of the reformist governor-general, Zhang Zhidong. After graduating in 1902, he was among the students chosen for normal-school training in Japan, where he joined radical, anti-Manchu students and evinced a special interest in military training. Huang returned to China in 1903 and accepted a teaching post in Changsha. Dismissed by the school authorities for spreading revolutionary propaganda among the students, Huang formed the revolutionary organization, HUA XING HUI, in December. When their planned uprising in 1904 was aborted, he fled to Japan, but returned to Hunan in early 1905 for another attempt. When this too failed, he took refuge in Japan and gained prominence among Chinese student revolutionaries and Japanese sympathizers.

Huang met SUN YAT-SEN in July 1905 and was instrumental in inducing his fellow-Hunanese to join Sun in forming the TONGMENGHUI (TMH). Sun became chairman and Huang second in command. Sun was the party's ideologue and fund-raiser and Huang its military strategist. He commanded most of the TMH armed uprisings in China and was an early advocate of trying to subvert government troops rather than relying solely upon secret society fighters. On April 27, 1911, Huang won fame as leader of a daring but unsuccessful attempt to capture Canton. He himself was wounded and 85 comrades, including some of the best-educated returned students from Japan, were killed. The uprising has been commemorated as the "Three Twenty-nine Revolution," since according to the traditional calendar it occurred on the 29th day of the 3rd lunar month.

Huang was in Hong Kong when the CHINESE REPUBLICAN REVOLUTION OF 1911 erupted in Wuchang on October 10. He arrived in Hankou on the 28th and became commander in chief of the revolutionary army. Fierce fighting during the last week of November resulted in setbacks for the revolutionaries. Some criticized Huang but others claimed his stubborn resistance against superior forces had gained time for uprisings in other provinces. By that time over 10 provinces had declared independence of imperial rule. With LI YUANHONG in charge of defending Wuchang, Huang left for Shanghai, arriving on December 1. The following day the revolutionaries captured Nanjing. As the Wuchang front stabilized and as cease-fires went into effect, the revolutionaries started discussing leadership of a provisional government. A deadlock ensued between supporters of Li Yuanhong and Huang. This was resolved by the arrival of Sun Yat-sen, who was elected provisional president in Nanjing on December 29.

Huang was appointed minister of war and played a dominant role in domestic policy during the period of the provisional government, until Sun Yat-sen resigned in favor of Yuan Shikai in March and the capital was shifted to Beijing. In 1913, when relations worsened between Yuan and the republicans, now organized as the GUOMINDANG, Huang was reluctant to subject China to another civil war and preferred a political solution. Nevertheless, when the CHINESE REVOLUTION OF 1913 ("second revolution") erupted in July, he took command of forces in Nanjing. Realizing that defeat was inevitable, he left for Japan at the end of the month. When Sun Yat-sen reorganized his followers into the Zhonghua Gemingdang (CHINESE REVOLUTIONARY PARTY) in Tokyo in 1914, Huang balked at Sun's demand for an oath of personal loyalty, considering it a violation of the spirit of the republican revolution. He left for the United States and did not return to China until June 1916, soon after Yuan Shikai's death. He had in the meantime reconciled his differences with Sun, who had dropped the demand for personal obedience. On October 10, the 5th anniversary of the outbreak of the 1911 revolution, Huang fell ill and died three weeks later.

HUA XING HUI (Hua Hsing Hui) (Society for China's Revival)
A Chinese revolutionary organization. Founded by HUANG XING in December 1903, it was a mainly Hunanese organization, most of whose members came from literati families. Most had either studied in Japan or would do so later. Although it began with about 30 members, it hoped to accomplish its aim of overthrowing the Manchu (Qing) dynasty by coopting local secret societies such as the GE LAO HUI. In 1904, its plan to capture the provincial capital, Changsha, failed. In 1905 it joined with other revolutionary groups in Tokyo to establish the TONGMENGHUI (TMH). Former members of Hua Xing Hui played leading roles in the TMH and the CHINESE REVOLUTION OF 1911.

HUERTA, VICTORIANO   (1845–1916) Mexican military figure and president. Huerta was distinguished initially by his military ability, battling both the Maya of Yucatan and the Zapatistas in Morelos and in Guerrero under the presidency of POR-FIRIO DIAZ. During MADERO's presidency, Huerta continued with military activities and successfully defeated insurrections against Madero. Dissatisfied with some of the changes instituted by Madero, Huerta eventually joined the rebel forces led by Felix Diaz, nephew of the deposed dictator Diaz, against Madero. Huerta ousted Madero in a military coup, which was supported by the US government and its ambassador to Mexico, Henry Lane Wilson. Although President Taft had accepted Huerta, the newly elected US President Woodrow Wilson failed to recognize Huerta's government and intervened militarily in Mexico in 1914. Together with Chile, Argentina and Brazil, the US forced Huerta to resign and established a provisional government for Mexico. In 1916, Huerta, imprisoned in the United States for his connections with German spies, died of cirrhosis of the liver.

HU HANMIN (Hu Han-min)   (1879–1936) Chinese revolutionary leader. Born in Guangdong to a family with a literary, bureaucratic background, Hu received a classical education, earning an advanced degree in the civil service examinations in 1900. In 1904 he went to Japan to study at the Tokyo Law School and graduated in 1906. He joined SUN YAT-SEN'S TONG-MENGHUI (TMH) shortly after it was formed in 1905 and became Sun's devoted follower. While studying law, he was an editor and major writer for the TMH organ, *Min Bao* (*People's report*). He participated in the CHINESE REPUBLICAN REVOLUTION OF 1911 and became the first military governor of Guangdong (1911–1913). After Sun died in 1925, Hu gradually lost influence, despite his senior rank in the GUOMINDANG (GMD) central executive committee (CEC). He first quarreled with his former comrade, WANG JINGWEI, and then broke with CHIANG KAI-SHEK in 1931. While Hu was in Europe in 1935, the GMD reelected him to the CEC, but he died in Canton before assuming the post. Hu's main contribution to the TMH and early GMD was as an ideologue, especially as an expositor of Sun's Three Principles of the People. Though a strong anti-Communist, Hu was among those responsible for arousing interest in MARXISM in 1919. He applied Marxist analysis to explain the economic origins of imperialism but rejected the class-conflict concept.

HUNGARY, REVOLTS AND REVOLUTIONS
1848 Revolution. The "Springtime of Nations" in Hungary was influenced by the French and Italian revolutions and the parallel stirrings in Vienna. Through peaceful means and mass demonstrations, the reformers demanded civil rights, the emancipation of peasants and independence from Austria. These were far-reaching demands that could have been met if the liberal revolution had been successful in Austria itself. Under the leadership of LAJOS KOSSUTH, Hungary proceeded with an anti-Habsburg line, yet one that did not satisfy the national demands of nation-

The end of a revolution; Hungary 1849

alities living under Hungarian control. The national poet, Sandor Petofi's patriotic and romantic nationalism, fueled popular support for revolutionary ideals. In April 1849, Hungary was declared a republic with a liberal constitution and Kossuth proclaimed as governor-president of an embattled state that at first drove out the Austrians from Hungarian territory. The new régime was opposed by its own nationalities, chiefly the Croats, and by the Austrian reactionary régime which requested and received the support of Russia. Faced with internal strife within the leadership of the young republic, imperial Russian troops crushed Hungary after a series of bitter campaigns. However, for Hungarians the struggle for independence and national rights remained the main legacy of the spring of 1848, its spirit revived in some of the ideals of the 1956 uprising.

Communist Revolt of 1919. The first Soviet republic outside Russia was established in Hungary in March 1919 and lasted for 133 days. The Hungarian socialist revolution in some ways followed a pattern similar to the Russian one. With the collapse of the Austro-Hungarian monarchy in late October 1918, a democratic-bourgeois republic headed by Mihaly Karolyi was established. The new régime acted under almost impossible conditions, coping with a grave economic crisis and with the dislocation of hundreds of thousands of Hungarians in the country and from the areas that had been lost to the various newly born successor states. Nationalist groups were organizing to oppose by force the forthcoming harsh conditions of peace and the occupying Allied forces. The extreme left, led by BELA KUN and composed mainly of returning prisoners of war from Soviet Russia and encouraged by LENIN, formed the Hungarian Communist party (CP) and prepared for a BOLSHEVIK style of takeover. The unification of the Social Democrats and the Communists boosted their bargaining power, as Hungary was presented with a tough Allied ultimatum on the conditions of peace. On March 21, 1919, a new Communist government took control and declared Hungary a Soviet Republic. BELA KUN, the leading figure, was the People's Commissar for Foreign Affairs. The short lived Communist régime pursued a radical social line of land reform and nationalization of private property, reinforced by "revolutionary justice" which alienated the upper and middle classes.

Internal dissent was not the main reason for the collapse of the short-lived Soviet Republic. It was the defeat of the Hungarian Red Army by forces encroaching on Hungary, especially the Romanian ones from the east. Patriotic slogans were used by the Kun leadership and attempts were made to link up with the embattled Russian Red Army fighting in the civil war. "White" Hungarian forces led by Admiral Nicholas Horthy gave the régime its final blow, and "White Terror" replaced the "Red Terror."

Fascist Takeover of 1944. In March 1943, the Germans occupied Hungary and forced the regent, Admiral Nicholas Horthy, to accept a more pro-German government in the face of Horthy's attempts to negotiate with the Allies. Hungary, the "reluctant satellite," was given to understand that there was no alternative to a loyal pro-Nazi line. Mass arrests of anti-Germans took place; in May 1944, the deportation of some 600,000 Jews of the country began and was completed in three months. As Horthy proceeded with his attempts to strike a deal with the Allies, especially in the wake of Romania's renunciation of its ties with the Axis on August 23, 1944, the Germans intensified their pressure on Hungary. The Germans thwarted Horthy's attempts and

in October imposed a régime of the extreme radical-right ARROW CROSS, led by FERENC SZALASI. It was at this late stage of the war that Hungarian Nazism came to power, by a German-engineered takeover. The main body of the Hungarian army remained loyal to the new régime, but the Hungarian state in fact ceased to function as the central government and authority was in the hands of extremist Arrow Cross gangs, whose five-month reign of terror against "disloyal elements to the nation"—especially Jews—was one of the darkest periods in modern Hungarian history. The Arrow Cross proved to be loyal to the German Reich to the bitter end. As Soviet troops advanced into Hungarian territory in September 1944, a provisional government was formed which concluded an armistice with the Allies. The Szalasi régime collapsed with the complete liberation of Hungary, and the leaders of the régime were executed in 1945–1946.

Communist Takeover. (1949) Hungary's one-party régime was born with the fusion between the Communists and the Social Democrats in March 1948, when the Stalinist phase began. The takeover encompassed several stages, starting with the country's liberation in April 1945. In the first provisional government formed in December 1944, the Communists participated in the united Hungarian National Independence Front, along with other parties such as the Social Democrats, the Smallholders and the National Peasants party. The Communist leaders were mainly "Muscovites" who had spent the war years in the Soviet Union. Their leader, MATYAS RAKOSI, acted swiftly to speed up the "process of democratization" in the shadow of the Soviet military presence. The Communists introduced popular reforms, such as land reform, in their struggle against the opposition. In this struggle the powerful political police, led and controlled by the Communists, played a very useful role. In the first free general elections in November 1944, the Smallholders received 51% of the vote and the Communists only 17%. In the new coalition government, the Communists intensified their struggle for power by focusing on the Smallholders party. In view of the bleak outlook concerning Hungary's future borders at the Paris Peace Conference, the Communists used patriotic slogans and hinted at Moscow's goodwill toward Hungary if the "democratization" of the country were to be speeded up. The Communists inititiated several government crises, aiming at a showdown with the Smallholders and at the same time attempted to attract "progressive" elements to their ranks. In June 1947, Premier Ferenc Nagy resigned and left the country, at a time when the Communists were already in control of the police and government apparatus. The premier's departure under pressure was preceded by Communist provocations and the arrest of Smallholder deputies, who were accused of conspiracy against the state. In August 1947, the Communists and their allies emerged as the largest group, as the victorious powers signed the Paris Peace Treaty returning Hungary to its 1937 borders. A rapid transformation of society was already underway, as the Communists proceeded to ameliorate economic conditions. The last clampdown on the opposition followed after the elections. The Communist pressure on the other parties intensified, this time focusing on the Social Democrats. In 1948, it was the turn of the Roman Catholic church to be targeted, in yet another major move in the country's "communization." On August 20, 1949, Hungary became a "People's Republic" with a Soviet-type constitution officially promulgated.

1956 Uprising. In October 1956, intellectual opposition and mass stirrings following the impact of the 20th congress of the Communist party in the Soviet Union turned into a full-scale mass demonstration that became an uprising against the régime. Demanding the removal of all elements linked to the discredited Rakosi-Gero leadership associated with the old line, a new government and party reshuffle took place, led by IMRE NAGY and Janos Kadar, as the party leaders attempted to introduce radical reforms. Within days, postwar political parties banned by the Communists reemerged, the Church under the leadership of the newly released Cardinal Mindszenty reestablished its role in society and the Communist régime was on a path of total collapse as the Communist party lost control and authority. Imre Nagy's attempts to form a coalition government which would eventually led to Hungary's leaving the Warsaw Pact and the emergence of a multiparty system led to the formation of a Soviet-supported leadership under Janos Kadar. As units of the Hungarian army joined the armed revolutionary forces, the Soviet army invaded on November 4 to reestablish control and install the Kadar-led group. The Kadar government and party leadership took control in what was termed a defeat of the "counter-revolutionary Fascist Horthyist" forces. Imre Nagy and his close followers were executed in 1958, to be reburied with full honors in June 1989 by the Communist régime on the verge of its own total demise.

The legacy of 1956 remains multifaceted, as leftist, conservative and right-wing opinions have conflicting views of their role and perspectives at the time of the events. During its last period in power, the Communist régime recognized the "popular and mass" character of the events of that time, and after 1989 leading activists who had been jailed in the aftermath of 1956 emerged in the new post-Communist elite, including President Arpad Goncz and his first prime minister, Jozsef Antall.

Communist Collapse of 1989–1990. The Hungarian transfer of power was perhaps the smoothest and best planned in Eastern Europe. With opposition among dissidents evident ever since the mid-1980s, the Hungarian Socialist Workers' party was torn between emerging reformist factions, for a time led by the popular politician Imre Pozsgay and hard-liners who attempted to thwart more drastic Gorbachev-type of reforms. By May 1989, the aging party leader Kadar had been removed and retired, the leading victims of the 1956 uprising had been rehabilitated and reburied with full honors and a younger generation of pragmatists had taken control. A new reformist government led by Miklos Nemeth declared the separation of party and state; meanwhile the dialogue with the emerging opposition, determined and coordinated to topple the sinking régime, took a new turn. While pursuing a reformist line, it was clear to the reform Communists that in fact they were dismantling the one-party state and that a multiparty system was rapidly developing. The last

Scenes from the Hungarian Uprising; Stalin cast down

congress of the ruling party took place in October 1989, and in the first free democratic elections in June 1990 the centrist Hungarian Democratic Forum emerged victorious with 24% of the votes.

HUNG HSIU-CHÜAN see HONG XIUQUAN.

HUSAK, GUSTAV (1913–) Czechoslovak Communist leader and statesman. Born near Bratislava, Husak was trained as a lawyer and engaged in illegal Communist activity from 1932 on. During World War II he was one of the top Communist party leaders; after it ended he led the Slovak party and occupied important government posts. In 1951, during the party purges, he was arrested and sentenced to a life term as a "bourgeois-nationalist." He was freed in 1960 and, after having spent three years as a construction worker, reemerged in top posts in the Slovak Communist party.

After the abortive PRAGUE SPRING of 1968, Husak was put in charge of the "normalization" process imposed by the Soviet Union. He remained in his post as party chairman until December 1987 and as the Czechoslovak president until December 1989, when the Communist régime collapsed. His drab tone and style, conservative to the very end, showed very little change from the early 1970s on, and it was not only when Gorbachev visited Prague in 1987 that Husak admitted the need for some reforms.

HUSAYN, SADDAM The president of Iraq, the commander in chief of its armed forces and the secretary-general of the Iraqi-led faction of the *Ba'ath* party since July 1979. Saddam Hussein al-Nasiri was born on April 28, 1937 in the tiny village of 'Uja, near Tikrit, to a poor peasant family of the Beigat tribe, a member of the Abu-Nasir tribal federation. Until he was two or three years old, the child grew up at the home of his maternal uncle, the nationalist army officer Khayr Allah Talfah. He then returned to his mother, who by then was married to his paternal uncle, Hajj Ibrahim. When he was 10 years old, defying his parents' wishes he left 'Uja for Tikrit to attend primary school. In 1955 he moved to Baghdad for his secondary school education. There he joined the Ba'ath party in 1957.

Following the successful military coup d'état that toppled the monarchy on July 14, 1958, the *Ba'ath* party challenged the ruling dictator, General ABDUL KARIM QASSEM, over his rejection of unification with Egypt and Syria (the United Arab Republic). On October 7, 1959, Hussein and a few other *Ba'ath* young men made an unsuccessful attempt on Qassem's life. Hussein managed to escape, crossing the border into Syria, where he became a hero and was promoted to full membership by the party's leader MICHEL AFLAQ. He then moved to Egypt, where he stayed as a protege of Egyptian President GAMAL ABDUL NASSER. He was deeply impressed by the authoritarian-charismatic leadership of the Egyptian leader.

In February 1963, following a successful *Ba'ath* coup d'état against Qassem, Hussein traveled to Baghdad, where he became active as a middle-level party official. In November, the party lost power to General ABDUL SALAM 'AREF, and within a few months Hussein and other senior *Ba'ath* activists were imprisoned. In 1966 he escaped from prison and on July 17, 1968 participated in a successful coup d'état that toppled the régime. By

then Hussein was already the single most powerful security chief within the *Ba'ath* party, even though his name was known only to the senior membership.

In November 1969, Hussein became deputy chairman of the Revolutionary Command Council (RCC) and vice-president. At the time, the president, chairman of the party's regional leadership, prime minister and commander in chief of the armed forces was General AHMAD HASAN AL-BAKR. Until July 1979, seemingly serving his president loyally, Hussein gradually eliminated all of the party's rivals, but also his personal rivals within the party, real and perceived. From the early 1970s he was the real power behind the president. His most important contribution to foreign policy was shifting the main emphasis from Pan-Arab to Iraqi interests. On the ideological level, he embarked on the creation of a particular Iraqi national myth, based on Islamic as well as pre-Islamic Mesopotamian history. In July 1979, he forced Bakr to resign, declared himself president and executed many of the régime's luminaries whom he suspected of disloyalty.

Some 15 months after he became president, Hussein, whose international and socioeconomic policies until then had been extremely cautious, lost his restraint and attacked AYATOLLAH KHOMEINI's revolutionary Iran. Initially he intended to conquer the oil-rich province of Khuzistan-Arabistan and bring about the downfall of the Islamic régime in Tehran. Having realized that his offensive had failed and that his troops were stranded, he changed tack and announced that he was ready for a cease-fire and peace agreement. Khomeini rejected these conditions and made his own demands and the war lasted for eight years.

During the war Hussein, again revealing the cautious side of his personality, adopted very pragmatic policies. He improved relations with east and west, as well as with the conservative Arab régimes whose economic and strategic support he needed desperately. He showed signs of moderation over the Arab-Israeli conflict and he made every effort to rely on fortifications and fire power in the battlefield, thus avoiding heavy casualties to his army. Finally, in 1983, he started using chemical weapons against the Iranian troops. In 1988 he extended this use to his own civilian population, when he poisoned a number of Kurdish settlements. By the spring of 1988, these methods started to show results. In July, the Iranian army was pushed from all Iraqi territories and showed signs of total disintegration. Khomeini had no choice but to accept a cease-fire which he defined as "poison."

Following the cease-fire, the régime itself aroused very high expectations in Iraq for economic recovery and prosperity, but the reality was dismal. As a result of the war, Iraq owed its non-Arab debtors at least 40 billion dollars, with an equal sum owed to its Arab conservative backers. Oil prices were depressed, Arab aid nearly dried out and the economy was in shambles. Unemployment reached staggering proportions, price hikes were unparalleled and the public started complaining. On the international arena, however, developments looked promising to the Iraqi president. Arab frustration at the slow pace of the Arab-Israeli peace process created the psychological infrastructure for Iraq to become the new all-Arab hero. This possibility was made even more real by the fact that Iraq still retained a million-strong army and its military industry was able to produce missiles with chemical warheads that could reach Israel.

The decline of the USSR was interpreted by Hussein as an opportunity. In the first place, he offered Iraq as the new protector of the Arabs, replacing the Soviets. Second, as he saw it, an attack on oil-rich Kuwait would no longer be seen by the west as a Soviet scheme but, rather, as a local skirmish. In his contacts with the American diplomatic community a few days before the occupation of Kuwait, Hussein's impression was that the US, even though it would clearly be angry, would still not go to war for Kuwait. Therefore, following the invasion he offered the USA something he believed it could not turn down: an undisturbed flow of oil from the Gulf at the price of $25 per barrel, in return for recognition of his control over Kuwait and a status of "the Policeman of the Gulf."

Having realized that the USA was unable to accept these terms, Hussein was still convinced that, despite full UN support, it would not dare go to war due to its "Vietnam complex." Thus he annexed Kuwait, and to prevent war he resorted mainly to threats. He also offered a compromise, but his offer was highly unrealistic. When the actual fighting started on January 17, 1991, the Iraqi president still believed that, after having been bled white the American troops would stop in their tracks and start serious negotiations. This way Hussein allowed the USA to achieve its overt and covert agenda, i.e., the liberation of Kuwait and the crippling of his war machine and strategic infrastructure.

Seen from the American viewpoint, however, the war ended before it could destroy the Republican Guard. This mistake was compounded by permission given to the Iraqi army to use its helicopter gunships. As a result, Hussein was able to put down massive uprisings in March–April 1991 in the Shiite south and Kurdish north. As in previous cases, when finding himself in danger, Hussein showed his remarkable ability to cut his losses, regroup his forces and go on the offensive. Since the end of the Gulf war on February 28, 1991, while making a number of mistakes, the Iraqi president has still managed to control his countrymen through a combination of extreme coercion and limited economic benefits. He supervised the reconstruction of the war-racked infrastructure sufficiently to allow the economy to function at a minimum level, and he made sure that each citizen under his political control would get some 50%–60% of his needs in calories through a government-sponsored food coupon system. In his speeches, Hussein often manipulated intercommunal suspicions and fears when promising that, if his régime was toppled, Iraq would turn into a Lebanon or would be "Balkanized." Bearing in mind that, between 1988 and 1991, Hussein's troops killed between 100,000–200,000 Kurds and between 30,000–100,000 Shiites, such predictions sounded to many Sunni Arabs as credible. Thus, even those people who wanted him out of power—and there were a great number in post-Gulf War Iraq—still had something to lose: food rations and, despite the alarming rate of crime and official corruption, a minimum level of law and order. Saddam Hussein has also managed to harness to his service family and tribal forces. At least since 1979, most of the important positions within his internal security apparatus and the senior military command have been in the hands of his family, tribe (abu-Nasir), region (Tikrit), and the Sunni Arab community of Iraq, in this order of preference. In addition, he managed to co-opt a number of Shiite personalities and Shiite and Kurdish tribal leaders who bound their fate with

his régime. These measures explain the fact that, despite his defeat in the war, the extensive war damage and an ongoing international embargo since August 1990, as of the summer 1995 Saddam Hussein was still in power.

HUSS, JAN (1369?–1415) Czech cleric and the most important forerunner of the 16th-century reformation in central Europe. Born to a peasant family in about 1369, he entered the University of Prague around 1390, took his Master's degree in 1396 and, in 1398, began teaching there. Having been ordained, he quickly acquired a reputation as a preacher at the Bethlehem Chapel in Prague (1402). That year he was made rector of the university. At this time Huss came under the influence of WYCLIFFE, whose ideas were introduced into Bohemia by Jerome of Prague, a friend of Huss. Huss began to criticize the moral conduct of the clergy. He also translated Wycliffe's writings into Czech. Popular with his own countrymen, he was increasingly attacked by the non-Czech faculty and students of the university, who incited Archbishop Zbynek of Prague to take measures against him. However, in 1409, a royal decree of King Wenceslaus gave the Czech nation control over the university, causing the German students to leave and making the university a Wycliffe stronghold. Soon the Archbishop forbade Huss to preach and, early in 1411, he was excommunicated by Pope John XXIII, who also put Prague under an interdict.

In 1412, Huss denounced the papal legate who came to Prague to promote the sale of indulgences. The affair caused a public riot, and the king made Huss leave Prague with his followers and take refuge with some Czech nobles. He then wrote his main work, *De Ecclesia* (*On the Church*), wherein, following Wycliffe, he advocated the purification of the Catholic Church. Having been granted a safe-conduct by Emperor Sigismund, he left in October 1414 to appear before the Council of Constance, to answer charges brought against him. However when he arrived at Constance he was put under arrest, and at his trial of June 1415 he was not allowed to speak in his own defense. Refusing to make a public recantation, he was burnt at the stake on July 6, 1415.

In Bohemia, his execution provoked vehement protests against the conduct of the council and the breach of faith by the

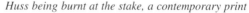

Huss being burnt at the stake, a contemporary print

emperor. Huss was declared a national hero, and his followers began to drive out Catholic priests, to renounce the authority of Rome and to launch the movement known as the Hussite Wars (1420–1436). Though the Hussites were ultimately defeated, their founder continues to be regarded as the father of the Czech nation.

HUSSEIN, KAMEL-UL-DIN (1921–) Egyptian officer and politician, vice-president of Egypt 1961–1964. Hussein graduated from the Military College in 1939. Reportedly a member of, or close to, the MUSLIM BROTHERHOOD, he served with the volunteer force it organized to help the Palestine Arabs in early 1948, before Egypt's regular forces entered the war. In 1952, as a major, he was one of the FREE OFFICERS who toppled King Farouq and his régime. He figured prominently in GAMAL ABDUL NASSER's government but eventually fell out of influence because of his right-wing Islamic sympathies. Hussein became a staunch opponent of Sadat, and particularly his peace policy toward Israel in 1978. While he holds no position of institutional influence, he has remained, under Mubarak's régime, a potential rallying point of opposition.

HUSSEIN, SADDAM see HUSAYN, SADDAM.

AL-HUSSEINI, HAJJ (MUHAMMAD) AMIN (1893? 1895?–1974) Palestinian-Arab politician and religious leader. During World War I, Husseini served as a junior officer in the Turkish army. After the British and Allied forces took Palestine in 1917–1918, he was recruiting officer for Amir Feisal's army of the ARAB REVOLT, and later an official in the provisional British military government. At the same time he became active in nationalist organizations and in agitation. He was president of the Arab Club (al-Nadi al-'Arabi) in Jerusalem, one of the two main associations of nationalist youth, which saw Palestine as part of an all-Syrian unity. He incited and headed anti-Jewish riots in April 1920 and was tried in absentia by a military court and sentenced to 10 years imprisonment, but he escaped. In August 1920 he was pardoned by the high commissioner.

In March 1921, the Mufti of Jerusalem, Kamel Husseini, Husseini's stepbrother, died and in May 1921 the high commissioner appointed Husseini as Mufti. The position of Mufti was one carrying much prestige and spiritual and social influence, but no actual power. Husseini soon added another post with greater power potential. When the British Mandatory government in December 1921 decreed the creation of a five-member Supreme Muslim Council, to be indirectly elected in accordance with Ottoman procedure, elections were held in January 1922 and Husseini was elected president of the council. His chairmanship of the council gave Husseini much power. He used this to advance his clan's and his faction's influence and to fight his opponents among the Palestine Arabs, the Zionists, the National Home policy of the Mandate and the government. He fostered the Muslim character of Jerusalem and the position of its two great mosques, and injected a religious character into the struggle against Zionism. This was the background of his agitation concerning Jewish rights at the Western ("Wailing") Wall that led to major disturbances in August 1929.

From the late 1920s, Husseini became the most important political leader of the Palestinian Arabs. Husseini's politics were hard-line and extremist. In April 1936, he formed an Arab Higher Committee and became its chairman. As such, he was the chief organizer of the ARAB REVOLT OF 1936–1939 as well as mounting internal terror against Arab opponents. In October 1937, he was dismissed by the government from his position as president of the Supreme Muslim Council, which was disbanded, while the Arab Higher Committee was outlawed. He escaped to Lebanon and Syria, where he continued to direct the Palestinian-Arab rebellion. In 1939 he travelled to Iraq, where he was close to RASHID 'ALI KILANI and the pro-Nazi Iraqi army officers and assisted them in their revolt in 1941. When that revolt was put down, Husseini escaped to Italy and Nazi Germany, where he was welcomed as a leader of anti-British Arab nationalism, received by ADOLF HITLER and accorded an honored position. He aided the Nazi war effort as a propagandist, mobilizing Muslim public opinion throughout the world and recruiting Muslim volunteers for the German armed forces from Bosnia and Yugoslavia.

After the war, Husseini was detained by the French army but escaped and in June 1946 went to Egypt. He was not allowed to return to Palestine, but was appointed by the Arab League to be chairman of the renewed Arab Higher Committee it set up for the Palestinian Arabs (JAMAL AL-HUSSEINI actually headed the committee, but its presidency was kept "vacant" for Husseini). He began organizing the final struggle of the Palestinian Arabs against partition and the emergence of a Jewish state.

After the Arab defeat of 1948, Husseini tried to form a "Government of All Palestine" in Egyptian-occupied Gaza, but that body failed to gain any influence over the course of events and was dissolved after a few years of a shadow existence. Husseini, still residing in Cairo, established an alternative residence in Beirut and in 1959 went to live there permanently. He endeavored to revive the Arab Higher Committee and to continue sabotaging the Jordanian annexation of the Arab part of Palestine, namely the West Bank, but the committee, and Husseini's own influence, continuously declined, particularly after the foundation of the PALESTINE LIBERATION ORGANIZATION (PLO) in 1964 (which Husseini and his Higher Committee opposed). Husseini spent the last decade of his life as a respected refugee, hardly involved in political affairs and with no influence over them.

AL-HUSSEINI, JAMAL (1892? 1894?–1982) Palestinian-Arab politician, educated at the Anglican St. George School in Jerusalem and the American University of Beirut, where his medical studies were interrupted when World War I broke out in 1914. After the war, Husseini served in the British military administration, as an official in the health department and assistant to the governors of Nablus and Ramla. From 1921 to 1934 he was secretary to the Arab Executive headed by his uncle Mussa Kazim Husseini, and in this capacity joined, inter alia, a delegation sent to London in 1930 for negotiations. In 1928–1930 he was concurrently secretary of the Supreme Muslim Council headed by HAJJ AMIN AL-HUSSEINI. After the disintegration of the Arab Executive, he organized the political framework of the Husseini faction, the Palestine Arab Party, founded in 1935, appeared as editor of its organ al-Liwa', and represented it on the Arab Higher Committee set up in April 1936 to lead the ARAB REVOLT OF 1936–1939. He was the right hand of its chairman, HAJJ AMIN AL-HUSSEINI. When the Higher Committee was outlawed and some of its members arrested in October 1937, he escaped. In February 1939 he was permitted to head the Palestinian-Arab delegation to the London Round Table Conference, despite an outstanding arrest warrant. In 1940–1941 he was active among Palestinian-Arab exiles in Iraq and supported RASHID 'ALI KILANI's anti-British revolt. When that revolt in 1941 was put down, he escaped to Iran, but was caught by the British and detained in Rhodesia. He was released in late 1945—a measure that led his faction to agree to the establishment of a new Arab Higher Committee, though he himself was still barred from Palestine.

In February 1946, Husseini was permitted to return to Palestine, assume the leadership of his party and set up a new Higher Committee. From 1946 he led the Arabs of Palestine toward vi-olent armed resistance to the partition of the country and the foundation of a Jewish state. For that purpose he organized paramilitary youth squads, *al-Futuwwa*. During the Arab-Israel war of 1948, he was in Cairo, Damascus and Beirut, endeavoring to direct the Palestinian-Arab fighting forces, but he and his party and his Higher Committee failed in their efforts to maintain their leadership. After the defeat, Husseini was foreign minister in the abortive "Government of All Palestine" set up in Gaza in September–October 1948. He continued his efforts in exile to keep alive the Higher Committee, but had little success. He later went to Saudi Arabia and joined its service as a senior adviser, while in fact retiring from political activity. Husseini wrote many articles and also two political novels, *On the Hajaz Railway* and *Thurayya*.

I

IBANEZ, CARLOS DEL CAMPO (1877–1960) Chilean soldier and revolutionary. A professional soldier who had reached the rank of colonel in 1924, Ibanez took part in the military coup that ousted President Alessandri Palma in that year. From then until 1931 he effectively controlled Chile, first as minister of war, then as minister of the interior and finally (1927–1928) as president. His term of office however, coincided with the Great Depression and popular discontent forced him to resign and flee to Argentina.

In 1937 and 1939 Ibanez unsuccessfully attempted to stage a military coup so as to return to power. Defeated in the elections of 1942, he actually did manage to make a comeback, at the head of an arch-conservative coalition in 1952. By then, however, he had shed his former Nazi ties, and his régime, lasting until 1958, brought Chile a measure of effective if authoritarian administration and some economic growth.

IONIAN REVOLT By the 8th century B.C., the Ionians, a segment of the Greek people, had emigrated to the Aegean islands and the western coast of Asia Minor, where the region colonized by them was known as Ionia. Their states were Miletus, Ephesus, Phocaea, Chios and Samos. These Greek city-states of Asia Minor were conquered by Persia between the years 546–544 B.C. As a result, the city-states were ruled by pro-Persian tyrants and had to pay tribute. In 499 B.C., Aristagores, the tyrant of Miletus, instigated the Ionians to revolt against Persia. He renounced his own tyranny, thus setting an example for the expulsion of the tyrants from the other city-states. In addition to the widespread discontent with the rule of the tyrants, the commercial competition of the Phoenicians—who were favored by Persia—may have been a contributory motive for the revolt. The rebel Ionians established a league to direct the war against Persia and the league issued federal coinage. The rebels, however, received little support from the Greeks of Greece itself: but 20 ships from Athens and 5 ships from Eratria. Sparta, the strongest city-state, refused to cooperate. In 498 B.C., the rebels burned down Sardes, the seat of the Persian governor of Ionia, and in 497 B.C. defeated a Phoenician fleet off Cyprus. The revolt of Greek cities spread from the Bosphorus to Cyprus. However, the rebel cities failed to act in harmony. The Persians recovered Cyprus and were able to form a strong fleet consisting of Phoenician, Cypriot and Egyptian ships. In 495 B.C., the Ionian fleet, depleted by the desertion of several major cities, was defeated at Lade. Miletus was captured and sacked in 494 B.C. and in a short time Persian rule was restored throughout the western coast of Asia Minor. Persia, however, renounced its policy of supporting tyrants and the Ionian Greek-cities were allowed to form democratic régimes.

INDEPENDENCE SOCIETY see ZI LI HUI.

INDIAN MUTINY (1857) The Indian mutiny broke out on May 10, 1857 at Meerut, a garrison town in northern India situated some 50 miles east of Delhi. While the catalyst for its outbreak was the introduction into the Indian army of the new Enfield rifle, the cartridges of which were rumored to be greased with a mixture of cows' and pigs' lard (anathema to both Hindu and Muslim soldiers), its underlying causes were political, social, religious and military, for the policies pursued by the British were seen by Indians as threatening the very fabric of their society and culture.

While British Governor General Dalhousie implemented the annexation of the lands of many of India's princes, thus managing to disaffect some of the most powerful Indians in the land, his administration's reforms in the spheres of education, family law and transportation were executed without consultation with the native population and engendered fears on the latter's part of a breakdown in the traditional caste system. Meanwhile, British-condoned criticism by Christian missionaries of the Hindu religion aroused suspicion that attempts would be made to force conversion to Christianity.

Perhaps the most significant single factor leading to the mutiny was the discriminatory treatment faced by the sepoys, the Indian soldiers who formed the vast majority of the rank and file of the Indian army. Their salaries were far lower than those of their British counterparts in the armed forces, and even the most senior among them were often forced to serve under extremely junior British officers. At the same time they constituted over three-quarters of the army's total manpower of 233,000. Resentful of their inferior position vis-á-vis the British, they were also the only group of Indians with the organization and wherewithal to manifest their frustration in action that could threaten British rule.

When Indian soldiers refusing to use the new Enfield cartridges were jailed, other Indian troops revolted, killing their officers and marching on Delhi. The mutineers initially enjoyed considerable success: there were no European troops in Delhi and the local garrison joined them in proclaiming Bahadur Shah II (the aged Mughal emperor who had long been no more than a puppet of the British) as emperor of Delhi.

The mutiny rapidly spread through northern India, with Delhi, Cawnpore and Lucknow becoming the main foci of the conflict. The mutineers were hampered by the absence of support from any more than a handful of Indian princes, the indifference of the majority of Indian civilians and their own lack of any coherent plan of campaign.

However, it was only with considerable difficulty that the British managed to reassert control, with the help of Sikh, Gurkha and southern Indian troops who had remained loyal to the colonial power. Acts of cruelty and vengeance were legion on both sides as Delhi was recaptured (and Bahadur Shah II executed) on September 14, 1857 and Lucknow just 11 days later. It was left to fresh British troops under the command of Generals Sir Colin Campbell and Sir Hugh Rose to complete the mopping-up operations by July 1858, at which time the mutiny was declared over.

Despite having failed, the mutiny signaled significant changes in India. It marked the transfer of the administration from the East India Company to the British crown, while a proclamation was issued promising amnesty, religious toleration and an end to the annexation of princely states. The British came to understand that they could not ride roughshod over the sensibilities of their native subjects, while Indian nationalist aspirations were whetted for the first time.

As Indians came to be better represented within the administration and its bureaucracy, the post-mutiny period also saw the evolution of an educated Indian middle class, which was to form the backbone of the leadership of the nationalist movement in succeeding decades. A clear turning point in the history of British-Indian relations had been reached and negotiated.

INDIAN NATIONAL CONGRESS The largest and most important of India's nationalist political institutions was founded by an Englishman, Allan Octavian Hume, in 1885, holding its first session (attended by 71 representatives) in Bombay. Its protagonists originally declared that it would serve to strengthen the position of the British Empire in India. The organization was therefore looked upon favorably by the British administration, which regarded it as a useful and harmless barometer of educated middle-class Indian opinion. Early congress members had considerable faith in and admiration for the British and their political principles and institutions, subscribing to the view that such was the occupiers' fairmindedness that Indian grievances only needed to be brought to their attention in order to be alleviated.

This faith soon proved to be misplaced. British government inaction in the face of congress demands for reforms in education and the legal system and, most importantly, for an expansion of self-government, led to the emergence of a radical wing within the congress, led by individuals such as Tilak, Ghose and Lala Rajpat Rai. It was they who prevailed at the 1905 congress session, at which a motion was passed demanding that India have a government that was "autonomous and absolutely free of British control." By 1916 the congress and the MUSLIM LEAGUE had united in demanding self-government. The 1918 Montagu-Chelmsford reforms (enshrined in the 1919 Government of India Act), which provided for direct popular representation in the legislature and established partial provincial autonomy, were rejected by Congress's now ascendant nationalists, and in 1920 MAHATMA GANDHI inspired the congress to declare complete self-rule (*purna swaraj*) as its aim, a goal to be pursued through a

Indian mutineers taken by surprise by British lancers

policy of nonviolent non-cooperation with the government of India. Congress had finally evolved a sanction that it could effectively use against the occupier.

Under Gandhi's leadership, the congress gained popular support as never before, further broadening its non-sectarian appeal by joining forces with the Muslim KHILAFAT MOVEMENT (led by the Ali brothers) and, in the wake of the Turkish decline after World War I, by striving to preserve the caliph of Turkey as the spiritual leader of the Muslim world. It was during this period that it definitively shed its genteel, middle-class image and became a genuine radical nationalist movement with a nationwide membership crossing class and caste barriers.

The non-cooperation movement won widespread backing from across the Indian social spectrum. Using and transforming traditional Indian forms of dissidence such as the *hartal*—a type of strike—Gandhi skillfully used his South African experiences in organizing mass nonviolent direct action to create a uniquely Indian form of revolt.

British retaliation became brutal, however, and Gandhi called off the movement when reports of violence from the Indian side began to emerge. However, the congress's agitation against the occupation continued and the 1929 session declared that complete Indian independence was its goal. 1930 saw the launching of the civil disobedience movement, which aimed at paralyzing the government of India by the mass nonviolent performance of specific illegal acts. Gandhi and other prominent congress leaders were imprisoned, only to be released as the British sought to negotiate with their unruly colonial subjects. However, the truce was short-lived, with Gandhi being reimprisoned just three weeks after returning from the abortive 1931 Round Table Conference in London.

Due to outbreaks of violence, civil disobedience was again called off on two further occasions, but the period of World War II revealed the extent to which Britain was dependent upon Indian manpower and resources to achieve its regional war aims and the degree to which it was prepared to use oppressive measures against Indian nationalist organizations in order to ensure the requisite cooperation.

By 1945, Britain was financially exhausted by the exigencies of the war effort, and its domestic public elected a Labour party administration that was far more amenable to Indian independence and increasingly convinced of the impracticality of retaining control of colonial possessions. Independence was achieved on August 14, 1947, albeit the congress's jubilation was somewhat muted by the partition (demanded by JINNAH's Muslim League) of the subcontinent into Muslim Pakistan and Hindu India.

With JAWAHARLAL NEHRU as the first prime minister of an independent India, the congress became the ruling party of independent India, a position it has sustained, despite internal disputes, splits and brief periods in opposition, until today.

INDONESIAN COUP (1965) In the years following independence, the government of Indonesia's President SUKARNO became autocratic and authoritarian. His political orientation grew increasingly leftist and he allied himself with MAO ZEDONG and Communist China. Although most political parties were officially disbanded, one party, the *Partai Komunis Indonesia* (Indonesian Communist Party; PKI) became disproportionately in-

fluential in national politics and was considered a natural ally of Sukarno's own *Partai Nasional Indonesia* (INDONESIAN NATIONALIST PARTY; PNI) The culmination of Sukarno's policies was his decision to withdraw Indonesia from the United Nations in protest at China's exclusion and his proposal to arm the workers. The latter in particular caused considerable concern among the military, which feared that this was an attempt to undermine its power base.

In 1965, Sukarno intercepted a document from the British ambassador to the Foreign Office in London stating that, "It would be well emphasized once more to our local friends in the army that the strictest caution, discipline, and coordination are essential to the success of the enterprise." Although the document was probably a forgery, Sukarno was convinced that a military coup was inevitable. But he had little time to respond to these supposed threats. In the summer of 1965 he became seriously ill and the country began to brace itself for the uncertainty of the post-Sukarno era. Both the PKI and the military regarded themselves as the most logical candidates to succeed Sukarno and both groups organized themselves accordingly.

The first to act was the PKI, which had extensive contacts in the army and particularly the air force. Claiming that a cabal of military leaders was planning to overthrow Sukarno, it had troops loyal to the PKI kidnap and kill eight leading generals. Other troops occupied strategic objectives in Jakarta and took Sukarno into protective custody. The coup's leadership believed that Sukarno would be sympathetic to its objectives, but if he proved hostile it had given orders to dispose of him as well.

Perhaps the greatest mistake of the coup's leadership was its failure to dispose of all the members of the army's high command. In the ensuing anarchy of the coup, a lesser known general, Suharto, realizing what was actually taking place, staged a countercoup and seized power for those divisions of the army still loyal to Sukarno. He defeated the rebel divisions in the capital and seized Jakarta's radio station, forcing the PKI leadership to flee. Despite his differences with the army, Sukarno then granted Suharto a mandate to restore order.

Meanwhile, the public was outraged at the PKI's attempt to seize power. Mobs stormed the party's headquarters and killed known Communists in the streets. They also vented their anger at ethnic Chinese, who, they believed, were behind Indonesia's alliance with Peking. Within days, mob violence spread to the country's other islands: by the year's end an estimated 200,000 people had been killed. Even Sukarno was not immune to this anti-Communist sentiment. Although he remained the head of state, he had a falling-out with Suharto and his influence dropped sharply. Despite numerous appeals to the public, he was unable to curb the violence.

The unrest in Indonesia lasted for one and a half years. Finally, in March 1967, Sukarno was forced to resign from office amid widespread student protests. Suharto was sworn in as acting president and the PKI was disbanded. Ironically, although Sukarno was deposed, his *Penta Sila* (Five Pillars) has remained the basis of Indonesian political ideology until the present.

INDONESIAN NATIONALIST PARTY (Partai National Indonesia; PNI) An Indonesian political party, founded in 1926 by AHMED SUKARNO, a former Javanese engineer and charismatic orator. The party's objectives were to gain mass support for Indonesian independence from Dutch colonial rule. Although the archipelago had been inundated with independence movements since the turn of the century, these were mostly limited to an intellectual following. Only one, the Sarekat Islam, had succeeded in gaining mass support for its conservative Islamic platform. The PNI differed from the Sarekat Islam by believing in the fusion of socialist and Muslim ideologies. "Can Islam, a religion, cooperate in facing the colonial forces with nationalism, which is primarily concerned with the nation, and with MARXISM, which is based on the philosophy of materialism?" asked Sukarno. "We say with firm conviction: Yes, it can be done." Sukarno explained that "True Islam has some of the characteristics of socialism.... Muslims should not forget that Marxism's materialist interpretation of history can often serve them as a guide when they are faced with difficult problems of economics and world politics." As for the west, Sukarno was emphatic: "To me, both the [American] declaration of independence and the Communist Manifesto contain undying truths, but the west does not permit a middle road."

In its struggle for independence, the PNI adopted the policy of non-cooperation with the Dutch colonial authorities. Because this was considered sedition, the party leadership, including Sukarno and MOHAMMAD HATTA, were arrested and exiled to the remote island of New Guinea. They were released shortly before the Japanese conquest of Indonesia in 1942 and succeeded in obtaining Japanese support at least in principle to Indonesian independence. In fact, the Japanese authorities actually promoted the use of Bahasa Indonesia as the archipelago's official language and formed an indigenous militia, both of which were important elements of the PNI's platform: the latter also played an important role in the country's struggle for independence, which was declared by Sukarno and Hatta immediately after the Japanese withdrawal from Indonesia in 1945. After four years of fighting, the Netherlands conceded Indonesia's independence and the PNI became the country's leading political party.

In the post-independence era, the PNI's ideology, and indeed the entire country's ideology, was based on the *Penta Sila* (Five Pillars): belief in one God, in the justness of the human race, in Indonesian unity, in social justice and in guided democracy resulting from *gotong royong*, or decision through consensus: government decisions were to receive the unanimous support of all of the people's representatives. Sukarno's insistence on the final pillar was a point of contention between him and the democratically-minded Hatta. In 1956, Hatta resigned his post as deputy prime minister and went into voluntary retirement. In the ensuing years, the PNI became increasingly aligned with the PKI (*Partai Komunis Indonesia*; Indonesian Communist party), until that party was destroyed following the abortive coup in 1965.

INTELLIGENTSIA The concept of the *intelligentsia* in Russia draws from the French 18th-century "intelligence," and embodies a critical, rationalist independence of thought. The father of the Russian intelligentsia is generally held to be Alexander Radishchev, who in 1790 published his essay "A Journey From St. Petersburg to Moscow," giving an unvarnished account of living conditions in Russia.

Throughout the 19th century, educated Russians eagerly debated ideas regarding the perfection of the state and society.

Their views embodied a broad range of approaches, from the conservative and nationalist Slavophiles to the anarchists. Their common denominator was the urge toward perfection and the merciless examination of all existing institutions.

In the historiography of Russia there are differing views of the Russian intelligentsia. The majority view regards the radical intelligentsia as having been an important force in moving Russia toward reforming its autocratic institutions (see e.g., Franco Venturi, *Roots of Revolution*). A differing view (e.g., the work of Richard Pipes on the Russian Revolution) regards the intelligentsia as having been chronically discontented, detached from reality and extremist. In this view, the intelligentsia were responsible for having frustrated all moderate measures of reform and were therefore ultimately responsible for the Bolshevik revolution (see RUSSIAN REVOLUTION OF 1917).

In the Soviet period, the definition of intelligentsia was changed from the classical concept of the conscience of society to the idea of persons performing technical tasks demanding higher education. The Soviet intelligentsia was thus seen as a broad stratum of society employed chiefly in intellectual labor. In this sense, the Soviet intelligentsia is often pointed out as the middle class in Soviet society, a force for stability devoted chiefly to maintaining its own social and economic status. The importance of this stratum in the eyes of the authorities was its role as a necessary component in the attainment of technological progress that would enhance the Soviet Union's economic well-being and international security.

During the post-Stalin period, however, the original concept of intelligentsia reappeared in the dissident movement of independent critical thinkers, personified by such figures as Andrei Amalryk, Andrei Sakharov, Alexander Solzhenitsyn and Vladimir Bukovsky. Though relatively few in numbers, their laboriously reproduced polemics and literary creations are thought to have spread to an audience numbered in the tens of thousands in all corners of the Soviet Union. As critics, they were repressed by the Soviet authorities, undergoing much the same treatment as their 19th-century predecessors.

INTERNATIONAL name of four successive organizations, viz: **First International.** The formal title was The International Working Men's Association—a revolutionary socialist organization established during a mass meeting in London on September 28, 1864. Most of the founders were French and British union leaders. Though KARL MARX, who lived in London at the time, did not participate in the meeting that created the organization, he was elected to the general council and soon came to play a leading role in its deliberations. Structurally, the International was made up of individual members in various countries and also of trade unions which were affiliated to it en bloc. Its supreme body was the congress, which met in a different city each year and laid down general policies. A general council, elected by the congress, was permanently based in London and looked after the International's day to day business.

Though the number of its members probably never exceeded 20,000, at the time of its foundation the International excited widespread fears as a secret workingmen's organization ready to rise in revolution and seize power in various countries. It did in fact support strikes and demonstrations all over Europe. After the suppression of the PARIS COMMUNE, Marx, as one of the

International's leaders, wrote a flaming pamphlet in its defense, thus earning himself instant fame. However, the organization's ranks were soon torn by dissension between the followers of various leaders. Besides Marx, who always insisted on the nature of the International as a centralized, disciplined organization, there were the views of AUGUST BLANQUI—which tended toward conspiracy—and those of MICHAEL BAKUNIN, who was an anarchist and opposed any sort of central authority, including that of Marx, to say nothing of the milder, reform-minded ideas of PIERRE-JOSEPH PROUDHON. In 1881, to prevent the supporters of Bakunin from taking over the general council, FRIEDRICH ENGELS, representing Marx, suggested that the International move its headquarters to New York. This proved to be its death blow and the organization languished and died.

Second International. Also known as the Socialist International, a workingman's organization founded in Paris in 1889. Regarding itself as the successor to the First International, it differed from the latter in that it did not accept individual members but only trade unions and national parties. Its structure was, accordingly, fairly decentralized, and indeed it was only in 1900 that it even established a permanent executive, the International Socialist Bureau, whose seat was in Brussels. Still, by 1912 the International was represented in every European country as well as in the United States, Canada and Japan. Its total membership was said to have stood at no fewer than 12 million members.

Unlike the First International, the Second stood for gradual evolution toward socialism and in 1896 it even expelled those of its members, i.e., the anarchists, who demanded the violent overthrow of existing society. Still, the organization's reformist stance was never clear cut. Throughout the first decade of the 20th century it was interested primarily in preventing a situation whereby, as a consequence of war, workers of various countries would have to fight each other. Accordingly, in 1907 it adopted a resolution, proposed by LENIN and ROSA LUXEMBURG, which threatened revolution in case war did break out.

As it was, World War I confounded the expectations of both moderates and revolutionaries. The majority of workingmen in every country forgot their socialist principles and went to the front cheerfully enough to slaughter one another. A minority of leaders—albeit a growing one—met in Zimmerwald, Switzerland, in 1915, denounced the war and insisted on immediate peace without victory, annexations or reparations. By then, most socialists were supporting their various countries' war effort to the hilt and were thus no longer international. Those who remained internationally-minded, on the other hand, were drifting away from socialism to revolutionary communism.

These divisions led to the effective disintegration of the International as an organization. It was reestablished in 1951, this time as a roof for socialist parties, but by this time it had long lost any revolutionary character.

Third (Communist) International. Also known as the COMINTERN, the "Third International" had been proposed by Lenin at the outset of World War I, when the various Socialist parties of Europe each supported their own governments, effectively terminating the Second (Socialist) International. Of the 54 delegates and observers, representing 19 different socialist organizations, who attended the founding conference of the Comintern in March 1919, only five came from outside Russia. In addition to proposing a program of revolutionary mass action against all

capitalist governments, the conference condemned the reconstituted Socialist International as a "tool of the bourgeoisie," and called upon the working classes of all countries to press for recognition of Soviet Russia and to condemn the foreign intervention in the Russian civil war. GRIGORY ZINOVIEV was elected Chairman of the Comintern Executive.

At its second congress (July–August 1921), the Comintern adopted its "Twenty-One Conditions" for membership, which included having only one party in any country, that party to be named "The Communist Party of...." The 21 conditions made the Comintern into a centralized, Leninist organization. The Comintern also organized international bodies of trade unions, peasants, youth, etc., to spread Communist principles and influence.

Through the 1920s and 1930s, the Comintern maintained a discipline that included purges of various parties' leaderships, as tactics changed regarding relations with other socialist and non-socialist parties. A case in point was the Comintern's order to the CHINESE COMMUNIST PARTY in 1927 to dissolve itself and have its members join the GUOMINDANG. In many cases, the pressures on the member parties reflected political tensions within the Communist party of the Soviet Union (e.g., the quarrel between Stalin and Trotsky). In Germany, at the beginning of the 1930s, the Comintern instructed the German Communist party to regard the Social-Democratic party as its chief opponent rather than the National Socialists. Only after the rise of Hitler and his destruction of the German Communists was the "Popular Front" tactic adopted.

At the outbreak of World War II, Russia was an onlooker by virtue of the Nazi-Soviet Non-Aggression pact signed on August 23, 1939. The Comintern denounced the war as "an imperialist conflict," and until the Nazi attack on the USSR all Comintern affiliates opposed the war in their various countries. With the formation of the Grand Alliance against the Axis powers, the Comintern began to support the war. In June 1943, in the context of relations between the Soviet Union, Great Britain and the United States, the Comintern was dissolved, and in its place a Communist Information Bureau—the Cominform—was established, headed by a Soviet official, Boris Ponomarev, as an agency to collect and disseminate information among the Communist parties. In September 1947 the Cominform was restructured and its headquarters located in Belgrade (later in Bucharest and Prague). Though the Cominform never presented itself as the "single world Communist party" that the Comintern claimed to be, it operated in similar fashion, organizing leadership purges of its member parties and expelling TITO's Yugoslavia in mid-1948.

Throughout its existence, the Comintern maintained its own journal, *The Communist International*, published in a large number of languages. In 1947, the Cominform began to publish a newspaper, *For a Lasting Peace! For a People's Democracy!* edited by a Soviet journalist, Pavel Yudin, which later became the periodical journal *Problems of Peace and Socialism*. True to Comintern traditions, both of these were Soviet-controlled and disseminated in a large number of languages. The latter continued publication from Prague until the collapse of the Communist régime in 1989.

Fourth International. An organization of Trotskyite factions first proposed during the 1920s and finally established in 1931, after the victory of the Nazis in the elections of September 1930 convinced LEON TROTSKY that something had to be done. Throughout the 1930s, the organization held congresses in which it advocated its goals, ranging from moderate improvements in working conditions to the violent overthrow of capitalism. During the same period, however, many of its leaders were liquidated by the agents of STALIN, culminating in the murder of Trotsky himself, which took place in 1940. Thereupon the organization disintegrated. Attempts to rebuild it after World War II failed owing to divisions among its leaders, even though Trotskyite groups remained active in many countries and maintained loose links with each other.

IRA   see IRISH REPUBLICAN ARMY.

IRAN LIBERATION MOVEMENT   A political movement formed by AYATOLLAH MAHMUD TALEGHANI and MEHDY BAZARGAN in April 1961. Soon after foundation, the Liberation Movement joined the Iran National Front. The main goal proclaimed by the Liberation Movement in its official statement was consolidation and strengthening of the National Front and devotion to the Iranian people's religious, national and social needs. From the beginning of its political activity, the Liberation Movement called for a positive neutralist foreign policy and for the establishment of a "legal power" by means of free elections all over the country. Its leaders aspired to ensure total freedom to all the Iranian people and waged an ideological war against the shah's régime. The movement favored a full alliance with the anti-régime 'ulama' (council of scholarly men) and even with the Iranian clergymen, who opposed even the shah's few positive reforms in agriculture and industry.

After the bloody disturbances in June, 1963, the leaders of the opposition were arrested and the Liberation Movement was officially banned. Nevertheless, its members continued to hold secret meetings in Iran's largest cities. In 1965, the Liberation Movement formed an autonomous bloc together with the National party and the Socialist Society. They called the new alliance the Third National Front, and disseminated propaganda among Iranian students in Western Europe and North America. The Third National Front tried to establish a fruitful relationship with clerical leaders in exile, especially with the AYATOLLAH KHOMEINI in Iraq.

In comparison with all the other political organizations affiliated with the Iran National Front, the Liberation Movement played the most decisive role in the Islamic Revolution of 1979 (see IRAN, REVOLTS AND REVOLUTIONS). It established close links with Ayatollah Khomeini and successfully won to its side a number of intellectuals and radical technocrats. After the Islamic revolution, the activists of the Liberation Movement obtained key positions in the provisional government formed by their leader, Mehdy Bazargan.

IRAN PARTY   An Iranian, left-wing revolutionary organization. Founded in 1943, at which time the country was occupied by British and Soviet troops, its objective was to restore Iranian sovereignty both inside and outside its borders.

Finding its main support among intellectuals—students, technocrats and government employees—the Iran party always had an anti-western orientation. In 1949 it joined MOSSADDEQ's Na-

tional Front; in 1953 it took part in the coup of that year and later played a prominent role in the struggle for the nationalization of Iran's oil.

After the shah's restoration, both the Iran party and the National Front were banned until the early 1960s. Only then was the party allowed to resume its political activities. For a year after KHOMEINI's seizure of power in 1979 it played a prominent role in the government, with its secretary-general, SHAPHUR BAKHTIAR, serving as prime minister. However, the alliance with Khomeini did not last and in the early 1980s the party disappeared.

IRAN, REVOLTS AND REVOLUTIONS

1953 Coup. An armed coup on August 19, 1953 led by retired General F. Zahedi. Following this, the National Front government headed by MUHAMMAD MOSSADDEQ undertook decisive steps directed at the nationalization of the Iranian oil industry. The National Front promoted the speedy adoption of a law nationalizing Iran's oil. The law envisaged the nationalization of the British-Iranian Oil Company and an immediate transfer of its property to the Iranian people. On April 29, 1951, the Iranian parliament confirmed Mossaddeq as prime minister. However, when attempting to implement the law, Mossaddeq's government was involved in a direct confrontation with England and the USA, and Mosaddeq was eventually toppled in August 1953.

Islamic Revolution. On February 10–11, 1979, the Islamic Revolution unfolded in Iran. The revolution was facilitated by a worsening economic situation in the second half of the 1970s, the non-implementation of agricultural reforms, and a growing westernization of the country that was unacceptable to the majority of Iranians. The destruction of fundamental moral traditions and distinctive cultural values had created a vacuum that was filled by Islam. The clergy, opposed to the monarchy, called for the establishment of an Islamic republic and won the overwhelmingly endorsement of the Iranian masses. Vigorous reaction to the imposed modernization took the form of a major political struggle for democratic freedom and rights.

From January 1978, strong antigovernment demonstrations spread throughout Iran. The protesters demanded freedom for political prisoners, improvement of economic conditions for the masses and the restoration of all the provisions of the constitution.

On February 1, 1979, the day that KHOMEINI returned to Tehran, the Temporary Committee of Islamic Revolution was founded, and this body became the real power in the country. Meanwhile, the Islamic revolutionary guards, as well as the members of the left and left-radical alignments, armed themselves. As a result of the armed revolt, the monarchy was overthrown on February 10–11. On April 1, Iran was officially proclaimed as an Islamic republic. The new constitution was approved by a referendum on December 2–3, 1979. On January 25, 1980, the first presidential elections took place, and elections for the parliament (*majlis*) were held during March–May.

The new government declared Iranian withdrawal from CENTO (the Central Treaty Organization, consisting of Turkey, Iran, Pakistan and Great Britain), the cancellation of a number of military and civilian treaties with the US, the annulment of its agreement with the international oil concessions, termination of its unpublicized relations with Israel and stoppage of oil deliveries to western countries and racist régimes.

After the clergy consolidated its position, Iran turned its attention toward important socioeconomic developments, agricultural reform, the nationalization of foreign trade and cultural reforms. The Iranian leadership sought and obtained overwhelming support for the Islamization of Iranian society or the so-called Islamic Cultural Revolution. The Islamic Cultural Revolution began on June 5, 1980, when all the schools of higher learning were closed for an indefinite period. The Cultural Revolution then spread to the mass media: periodicals, radio, television and cinema.

Khomeini demanded a radical change in the activities of the mass media, claiming that they had had a great detrimental effect upon Islam during the shah's reign. Many journalists were dismissed. The screening of foreign films and the possession or sale of most video cassettes was prohibited. The primary and secondary school curricula were radically revised. The Koran and the *Shari'a* (basis of Muslim law) became the main subjects of the school curriculum. The effects of the Cultural Revolution were visibly reflected in the status of women. It became their duty to wear special clothing which covered almost all of their bodies. Iranian women were also restricted in their choice of profession, males and females had to be educated separately, polygamy and temporary marriage were permitted, etc.

"Exporting" the Islamic Revolution became one of the main principles of Iran's foreign policy. It was defined as the "sacred duty and direct obligation" of all Iranians. This was based on Khomeini's opinion that the main task of Muslims is to lay the foundation for a world Islamic state that will be able to exercise decisive influence on world policy. The idea of "exporting" the Islamic Revolution to other countries was enshrined in the Iranian constitution and was adopted as part of state policy.

Tehran's drive toward "exporting the Islamic revolution" caused political instability in some quarters of the Islamic world, especially in the Persian Gulf region. A 1981 coup attempt in Bahrain, antigovernment demonstrations by Shiites in Saudi Arabia and Hizbullah activities in Lebanon were all strongly linked to Iran's "export"-promotion activities. In conformity with its policy, the Tehran government has offered support for various separatist and illegal organizations such as the Supreme Assembly of Islamic Revolution in Iraq, the Oman Islamic Front, 'Ad-dava in Kuwait and the Moro National Liberation Front in the Philippines.

IRAQ, BA'ATH PARTY OF   The *Ba'ath* party was introduced into the Iraqi intellectual and political scene during the second half of the 1940s. Its first members and emissaries were Syrian students. Roughly at the same time, Iraqi students who were studying in Syria and Lebanon joined the party there.

During 1948–1949, the party began to grow. It also started to attract high school students with Pan-Arab and mildly socialistic convictions. These had become disillusioned with the *Istiqlal* party's inaction and "bourgeois parliamentarism" and objected to the internationalism of the Communists and their support for the establishment of the State of Israel. Still, by the end of 1949 the party numbered only a few score people, almost exclusively middle- and lower-middle-class Baghdad-based students.

The early 1950s saw greater expansion, when new five-member "cells" (*khalaya*) were formed. By 1953, the party issued its first newsletter. During the first half of the 1950s, students who graduated from the Higher Teachers College moved to teaching positions and started proselytizing among their own high-school students.

In 1951, Fu'ad al-Rikabi, a Nasiriyya-born Shiite engineering student in Baghdad, assumed the chairmanship of the organization. The membership then numbered around 50, but in the next year it doubled and in 1955 had reached 289. In 1952, the Iraqi party was recognized by the party center in Damascus as a "branch" and a year later it established its military bureau, thus inaugurating its activity among army personnel.

Even though the party was popular mainly among young Sunni-Arab activists, many Shiite youth were also attracted to its political activism, social message and, not least important, its non-sectarian ideology. Educated and secular Shiite Arabs were captivated by the promise of a united Arab society stretching from Iraq to the Atlantic Ocean, where religious creed would be of no significance and Sunni-Shiite equality would thus be absolute.

The July 14, 1958, coup de'etat of the FREE OFFICERS under General ABDUL KARIM QASSEM, which toppled the monarchy, catapulted the party into prominence and resulted in great expansion in its ranks. Within a few months membership swelled from a few hundred to a few thousand. This was also when the party established close ties with a number of Sunni Pan-Arab army officers.

The *Ba'ath* influence within the army's officer corps was enhanced by the fact that most officers had been alienated by Qassem's support for the Communists and his decision to remain at arm's length from GAMAL ABDUL NASSER's Egypt. Following the suppression of a Pan-Arab revolt in Mosul in March 1959 and the execution of a number of Pan-Arab officers in October of the same year, the *Ba'ath* party made an unsuccessful attempt on Qassem's life. Among the would-be assassins was a young junior member, SADDAM HUSSEIN al-Nasiri al-Tikriti. Following the attempt, the régime cracked down on the party until it managed to completely freeze its activity in Iraq. The Pan-Arab leadership in Syria accused *Ba'ath* Secretary-General Rikabi of acting without authorization when he ordered the assassination and he was expelled. After a brief period of decline, the party cadres were regrouped and many who had fled to Syria returned.

On February 8, 1963, the *Ba'ath* engineered a bloody military coup de'état, killing Qassem and many of his officers, followed by thousands of Communists, real and perceived. The new *Ba'ath* régime, however, lasted only some nine months.

As a result of internal divisions, the party tore itself apart. One faction, led by the new secretary-general, the Sunni 'Ali Salih al-Sa'di, advocated radical socialistic reforms. Others (a "rightist" group led by the Shiites Talib Shabib and Hazin Jawad and a "centrist" one, based mainly on army officers like Prime Minister AHMAD HASAN AL-BAKR and supported by Secretary-General MICHEL 'AFLAQ in Syria), strongly objected to any economic policy that would jeopardize the support of the army officers and the middle-class.

Due to total chaos in the various government branches, the economy started to disintegrate. As a result of the mass murder of Communists by the large and unruly National Guard militia, the régime lost crucial Soviet support.

On November 18, 1963, the titular president, General Abdul

Salam 'Aref, with the help of a few *Ba'ath* army officers and activists but mainly of Nasserite officers, took over. A few months after the party's downfall, those party officials who had collaborated with 'Aref were sacked and in September 1964 they were jailed when a coup d'état, prepared by the *Ba'ath*, was exposed.

More than four years elapsed until the party could again stage a coup d'état. These years were dedicated to slow clandestine reorganization that necessitated a high degree of secrecy and compartmentalization. This was the reason for the ascendency of the young Saddam Hussein, the party's security chief, to a position of great power, a change noticed, however, only by a very few. As he himself described it, the conclusions he drew from the failure of 1963 were that next time no divisions should be allowed within the ranks of the party and the army had to be domesticated to become a docile tool in the hands of civilian party activists. During the little-known years between the party's downfall in 1963 and July 1968, most of the Shiite senior activists were ostracized, tortured or killed by the 'Aref régime or left the party of their own volition.

In the middle and lower echelons, however, Shiite membership in the party, albeit far smaller than before, still remained substantial. During those years not only did the Sunni element become more prominent than ever, but its members from the town of Tikrit, north of Baghdad, became particularly central.

The relatively lax rule of ABDUL RAHMAN 'AREF (1966–1968), the blow to the régime's prestige as a result of Iraq's poor performance in the Six-Day war of June 1967 and economic difficulties, created a suitable environment for renewed *Ba'ath* political activity. On July 17, 1968, military forces under two *Ba'ath* officers and with the aid of the non-*Ba'ath* commanders of key units in and around the capital, surrounded the presidential palace and forced 'Aref to resign. In a second bloodless coup d'état, on July 30 of that year, *Ba'ath* militiamen led by Saddam Hussein arrested and exiled Abdul Rahman Na'if and Ibrahim al-Da'ud, the two most important non-*Ba'ath* army officers who had helped the party to power. Since then Iraq has been ruled by the *Ba'ath* party alone.

Between 1968 and 1979 the president, chairman of the party's regional leadership, prime minister and commander in chief of the armed forces was General Ahmad Hasan al-Bakr. His chief lieutenant, and since the early 1970s the "strong man" in Baghdad, was his distant cousin, Saddam Hussein. Both hailed from Tikrit and from the tribal federation of Abu Nasir. Bakr needed Saddam's security skills and extreme ruthlessness to eliminate all opposition and Saddam needed his elderly relative in his dealings with the senior army officers and in order to bestow on the régime a semblance of public respectability.

Saddam Hussein's first step as chief of security in the new régime was to purge the army of some 2,000 officers suspected of disloyalty to the party. From that time on the army was put under the close surveilance of a number of security bodies and gradually became a tame tool in the hands of the political leadership. At the expense of efficiency, loyalty rather than professionalism became the most important criterion for promotion. Within the civilian party organization, too, Saddam Hussein carried out continuous purges. Under the guise of eliminating subversive elements within the party and its enemies from without, he managed to eliminate all his personal opponents inside the Iraqi *Ba'ath* Party. It did this by using the notorious party inter-

nal security apparatus, the Special Bureau (*al-Maktab al-Khass*).

Following the 1968 coup d'état, the party started to expand its membership, with a quantum leap after Saddam Hussein became president in 1979. In 1968, there were no more than a few thousand members and supporters. By the late 1980s there were 1.6 million, with a much smaller hard core of full members numbering 30,000–40,000. The massive expansion meant major organizational changes.

Since 1968, the party has been in control over all unions: workers, peasants, students, youth, women, teachers, lawyers, etc. Membership, at least at the lowest echelon of the party, is a necessary condition for promotion in all government and public institutions and even for acceptance to certain university faculties. The mass membership has meant a tremendous influx of Shiites into the lower echelons of the party (Kurds were not forced to join). It also meant, however, that the party was awash with people who were ambivalent, sometimes hostile toward it, and others who joined out of sheer opportunism. At the highest echelon of membership, selection is much more careful, but there is evidence that many full members are not very dedicated. This fact was exposed during the March 1991 uprising (*intifada*) in the Shiite south and the revolt in the Kurdish north. In both cases, senior party activists fled to Baghdad and left the provinces to the revolutionaries.

On July 16, 1979, Saddam Hussein removed his elderly predecessor from power and placed him under house arrest until he died, possibly having been murdered, in 1982. By early August 1979, a large number of very senior party members whom the new president suspected of disloyalty to him personally had been executed under the pretext of a plot which they had allegedly prepared in collaboration with Syria's HAFEZ AL-ASAD.

During the 1990s, party history was intimately connected with the Iran-Iraq war (1980–1988). Party members were assigned numerous duties. Many of them in the ranks of the party militia—the Popular Army (*al-jaysh al-sha'bi*)—were sent to the battlefield or performed security and policing duties in their respective governorates or both. Party members disseminated the party's views among the public, including an unprecedented cult of personality around the president. During the Iran-Iraq war, the party lost most of its autonomy and became an obedient tool in the president's hand. This development was reflected, amongst other things, in the ease with which the president made arbitrary political, strategic, economic, social and even ideological decisions, changing party doctrine at will according to the changing circumstances. There were even many cases when budgets for party branches were slashed. At the same time, however, much authority was delegated to many individual members, giving them the power of life and death over the population.

Following the *Intifada,* in which party branches were burnt down all over the Shiite south and the Kurdish north and hundreds of party activists who did not flee were massacred, the president himself castigated the party for having lost touch with the masses and its members for forsaking their posts and showing very poor fighting spirit. The president further dealt his ruling party a blow when he turned to a great number of tribal sheikhs to support the régime, rewarding them with money, lands and arms, and bestowing great honor upon them. Many party members saw in it a betrayal. Muted protests were sounded in the Iraqi press, but to no avail. In the same fashion, members of the president's extended family and retired army officers were given key administrative positions at the expense of party activists, notably positions as governors. Between mid-1991 and late 1992, the party held a number of high-level congresses in which its problems were discussed in great detail, and since 1993 there is some evidence that party organization, activity and morale have been resuscitated somewhat. However, the crisis is not over: while the party is expected to fight corruption and enforce law and order in practically every realm, including actions in crime prevention and price control, it itself often comes under the régime's media attacks for official corruption and mismanagement. Worse still, at present the party's senior echelon is faced with a major dilemma: its members are expected to protect and uphold the rule of the president and his extended family who, at the same time, continuously undermine their own autonomy and authority.

IRAQ, REVOLUTION OF 1958

Iraq, which from the 16th century until the end of World War I had consisted of a number of provinces under Ottoman rule, became a British mandate in 1921. In 1933 the country became formally independent; in 1948 British troops were pulled out and a new treaty of alliance with Britain was signed. In 1955, Iraq joined the Baghdad Treaty and thus became part of the west's anti-Soviet alliance system in the Middle East. The treaty was widely regarded as obsequious and as a step away from the remainder of the Arab world which, at that time, was increasingly dominated by left-wing ideologies spreading from Egypt, where GAMAL NASSER had taken power in the previous year. Dissatisfaction with the treaty, plus widespread corruption inside the government itself, provided the background to the 1958 coup.

The leaders of the coup were Brigadier General ABDUL KARIM QASSEM and his close collaborator, ABDUL SALAM 'AREF. Toward the mid-1950s, they and a number of fellow officers set up a FREE OFFICERS organization, modeled on the Egyptian one and professing a similar left-wing, secular, anti-imperialist, anti-Israeli revolutionary ideology. The opportunity for a revolt was provided in the summer of 1958, when hostilities broke out between Israel and Jordan. Under cover of moving to the aid of Jordan, Qassem and 'Aref were able to get an army brigade into Baghdad and, on July 14, used it to carry out their coup. The leading members of the royal house, including King Feisal and his son, were executed. Prime Minister Nuri al-Sa'id fell into the hands of a mob as he was trying to escape and was lynched. As head of the Free Officers, Qassem formed a cabinet under his own chairmanship. He also appointed himself minister of defense and commander in chief of the armed forces. Meanwhile 'Aref became minister of the interior and deputy commander of the armed forces.

Under the new constitution which was promulgated by the revolutionaries, Iraq became a republic in which power was shared between the cabinet and a so-called "sovereignty council" consisting of three members; in reality, though, these arrangements merely served a thin veil to cover Qassem's dictatorship. The next few years saw Iraq moving away from its previous alliance with the west into a more pro-Soviet stance. Domestically, many of the country's old economic elite had their property expropriated and parts of the Iraqi economy (including

oil, which provided over 90% of all foreign currency income) were nationalized. Qassem and 'Aref could not agree on whether Iraqi affairs or Pan-Arab ones should be given priority, and it was against this background that the latter was dropped from the government. In February 1963, he and part of the army, supported by the Iraqi *Ba'ath* party (see IRAQ, BA'ATH PARTY OF), organized another revolt, killing Qassem and assuming power themselves.

Arabs of the world, unite: poster from the Iraqi Revolution, 1958

IRELAND, REBELLIONS see IRISH REBELLIONS.

IRGUN ZVAI LEUMI (IZL)

A Hebrew term meaning "National Military Organization." Know commonly by its acronym, IZL, this was an underground defense and resistance organization in Palestine. It was founded before the establishment of the State of Israel by Jews in response to the 1929 Arab riots in that country against Jews.

Reacting to further Arab disturbances which broke out in April 1936, the IZL adopted an activist policy, contrary to the HAGANAH policy of *havlagah* (self-restraint). On November 14, 1937, Arab buses were fired at, marketplaces were bombed and individual Arabs killed. At the same time, the IZL also engaged in bringing illegal immigrants from Europe to Palestine. Following the publication of the 1939 White Paper by the government of Great Britain which imposed limitations on Jewish immigration to Palestine, the IZL launched a series of attacks against British institutions and installations and assassinated officers of the Central Investigation Department (CID) accused of torturing IZL detainees.

Upon the outbreak of World War II, the IZL ceased its anti-British activities and encouraged its members to enlist in the British army and participate in the war against Nazi Germany. IZL commander David Raziel (1910–1941) was killed during a British commando raid in Iraq. In November 1943, MENAHEM BEGIN was appointed the new IZL commander and on February 1, 1944 declared a revolt against Britain, accusing that country of betraying the Jewish people. Over the following four years, members of the IZL attacked scores of British installations, army camps, police stations, government offices—mining roads and railways and sabotaging British targets in Europe was well.

After the British Labour government came to power in 1945 and failed to change the 1939 White Paper policy, the IZL participated in the Hebrew Resistance Movement along with the Haganah and LEHI. On July 26, 1946, the Government Secretariat and British army headquarters were greatly damaged in an IZL attack on the King David Hotel in Jerusalem.

The IZL rejected the UN partition plan of 1947 and continued its operations against the British and reprisal attacks against the Arabs without any coordination with the Haganah. The large number of Arab deaths in the IZL-led attack on Deir Yassin became another cause célèbre between the organized Jewish community in Palestine and the dissidents. The IZL's attack on Jaffa led to a mass exodus of Arabs. The IZL, which according to its own statistics numbered 5,000 on the eve of the establishment of the state, officially disbanded on June 1, 1948, two weeks after the declaration of Israel's independence.

IRISH REBELLIONS

Rebellion of 1641. The removal of the Earl of Strafford led to great expressions of Irish resentment of the settlement of English Protestants in Ireland. On October 23, 1641, the Gaelic Irish in Ulster rose and massacred thousands of English and Scots, being joined by the end of the year by the Roman Catholic nobility. The English parliament, meanwhile, was too suspicious of King Charles I to vote him an army which would be used against the Irish right then and against themselves later. The Irish were therefore free to organize a supreme council to govern Ireland (May 1642), and to hold a General Assembly which met in October. The Irish rebellion was not subdued until OLIVER CROMWELL was sent there in 1649–1650.

Rebellion of 1798. The Society of United Irishmen, founded in 1791 by Wolfe Tone, gradually became more revolutionary in the last years of the century. It hoped to have help from the French to achieve independence, and indeed a French fleet with 15,000 troops did land in Ireland in December 1796. Bad weather, though, forced it to retreat. Leaders of the United Irishmen were arrested in March 1798 while plotting to capture Dublin, and the movement soon took on a religious fervor. The rebellion was most prominent in County Wexford. By October, Tone was captured and the rebellion defeated.

IRISH REPUBLICAN ARMY (IRA)

An organization created in 1916 to fight for Irish independence from Britain. Considered the military arm of the SINN FEIN movement, in 1919–1921 it fought an effective guerrilla war against the British. When the latter gave in and agreed to establish the Irish Free State in part of Ireland, the IRA split. One wing, known as the "Regulars," accepted the settlement and laid down its arms; the other, known as the "Irregulars," refused to do so, claiming that victory remained incomplete so long as the province of Ulster, too, was not included within the Irish State. In the civil war that broke out between the Irish government and the Irregulars (1922), the latter were defeated.

Though outlawed in 1931 by Irish Prime Minister EAMON DE VALERA, the IRA did not cease to exist. Instead it continued to recruit and gather arms and, in 1938–1939, launched a fresh wave of attacks on British targets. Embarrassed by these attacks, the Irish government in Dublin took harsh repressive measures,

including provisions for internment without trial and the execution of five IRA leaders. However, even persecution in its own homeland did not cause the organization to dissolve. For 20 years after 1945 it continued to launch isolated attacks without making any headway or, indeed, gaining much support for its actions.

In 1968 the situation changed. Angry over discrimination in voting, housing and employment, Ulster's Catholic population gave growing support to the IRA. Financial support came from the Irish community in the US and arms from some radical Arab countries such as MUAMMAR GHADHDHAFI's Libya. Thus encouraged, the IRA was able to recruit new members and launch a renewed terrorist campaign, although the organization split once again—this time between the "Official" wing, which was committed to political change, and the "Provisionals" or Provos, with their emphasis on violence. The latter on their own proved strong enough to carry on their struggle for 26 years. The most spectacular single moment of terrorism came in 1979 when Queen Elizabeth's cousin, Lord Mountbatten, was killed when a bomb wrecked his fishing boat. During the entire period, approximately 3,000 people have been killed, including perhaps 300 terrorists, 1,000 members of the security forces and 1,700 civilians.

In the autumn of 1994, responding to hints by British Prime Minister John Major that a political settlement might be possible, the IRA agreed to a cease-fire. From that time on its activities have been confined to the negotiating table; should an agreement fail to emerge, however, there is little doubt that sooner or later either the IRA itself or some successor organiza-

Irish youth wearing a gas mask during the 1969 "troubles"

tion will renew the armed struggle for an Irish independence.

IRON GUARD A Romanian Fascist movement that arose in the period between the two world wars. The successor of the LEGION OF THE ARCHANGEL MICHAEL, the Guard was established in 1930 and emphasized rabid nationalism, religious mysticism, virulent and often violent anti-Semitism and the Volkist belief that the peasant represented the acme of all creation. Engaging in political terrorism and mobilization in the countryside, the movement attracted the support of the peasantry and the urban lower-middle class. After liberal Prime Minister Ion Duca ordered the dissolution of the movement and massive arrests in late 1933, he was shot. In 1937 the Guard (renamed the All for the Fatherland Party) captured 16.5% of the vote in the national elections. Its leader, Corneliu Zelea Codreanu, was arrested and killed in prison in 1938. In 1939, the Guard assassinated Prime Minister Calinescu but claimed enough political support to participate in the government in 1940.

Under its new leader, HORIA SIMA, the Guard launched an uprising in September 1940, forcing King Carol II to abdicate. In a bloody battle for control of the country waged against ION ANTONESCU and his army supporters, the Guard murdered many of its enemies and several thousand Romanian Jews before it was suppressed in January 1941. Though Antonescu later claimed leadership of the Guard, which in this sense continued to govern Romania until 1944, its real leaders had fled to Nazi Germany, where these "idealists" were held hostage to ensure Antonescu's compliance.

ISLAMIC REVOLUTION see IRAN, REVOLTS AND REVOLUTIONS.

ISMA'IL (AL-JAWFI), 'ABDUL-FATTAH (1936? 1938?–1986) South Yemeni politician, president of South Yemen 1978–1980. Of North Yemeni origin, Isma'il was employed in the 1950s in Aden by the British Petroleum Company and was active in the NATIONAL LIBERATION FRONT (NLF), the most extremist among the various underground nationalist groups; by 1964 he was considered one of its chief leaders, in charge of its political and military/terrorist activities, and heading its leftist-Marxist wing. When South Yemen attained independence in November 1967, Isma'il held numerous high-ranking positions in the government, bringing his Moscow loyalist faction into power between 1978 and 1980.

A constant factional struggle brought Isma'il into growing conflict with 'ALI NASSER MUHAMMAD, and in April 1980 Isma'il was forced to resign the presidency and go into exile. He spent the next five years in the USSR. The Soviet Union apparently mediated between the factions, and in 1985 Isma'il was allowed to return, and his supporters were restored to party and government positions. However, factional tensions increased during 1985, climaxing in January 1986; a coup d'état staged by Isma'il and his faction led to bitter, confused fighting and the overthrow of 'Ali Nasser Muhammad. While the coup itself succeeded, Isma'il himself was killed (in 'Ali Nasser Muhammad's version—executed).

ITALIAN SOCIAL REPUBLIC (Republicia Sociale Italiana) Known popularly as the Republic of Salo, as MUSSOLINI resided in the village of Salo on the banks of Garda Lake, not far from Verona, this existed between September 1943 and April 1945. Controlled by the Germans, the Social Republic's founding nucleus consisted of Pavolini, FARINACCI, Preziosi and Ricci, all extremist Fascists (see FASCISM) who had taken refuge in Germany after Mussolini's deposition and imprisonment in July 1943. In September of that year, the Duce was rescued from prison in a German commando action and evacuated to Germany, where he agreed to recreate a Fascist state in the parts of Italy occupied by the German army. The new Fascist régime was pledged to return to the ideological origins of fascism in 1919.

The main instruments of power in the Salo Republic were the Republican Fascist party led by Alessandro Pavolini and the Fascist Militia commanded by Renato Ricci. The return to the leftist and revolutionary origins of fascism was enunciated in the 18 points of the Verona Manifest, approved by the renewed Fascist party on November 15–16, 1943. These points included the abandonment of the corporatist ideals and structures in favor of radical social legislation and a national confederation of labor to insure the workers' rights. The Verona Manifest also included crude anti-Semitic and racist articles meant to please Nazi Germany, its patron power.

The realities of the Italian Social Republic were harsher than its plans and ideals. The Republican National Guard of Ricci terrorized the countryside in search of anti-Fascists and fully cooperated, together with other Fascist militia formations, in the persecution and deportation of Jews by the Germans. Its declared pro-labor policies stood in direct contradiction to the demands that the Germans made of the industrialized northern Italy in the framework of their war effort, and were thus inoperative. Thus, the return to the revolutionary origins of fascism remained merely declarative in nature, never to be carried out as policy.

The Social Republic established a special Fascist court that tried and condemned the "traitors" of July 24–25, 1943 who had deposed Mussolini—Ciano, DE BONO, Marinelli and Gottardi. Anti-partisan operations increased during 1944, and Mussolini tried vainly to reach a separate peace with the Allies and to open his government to collaboration with non-Fascists. The advancing allied armies had by April 1945 reduced the Italian Social Republic to no more than a small stretch of land around Milan. The republic collapsed with Mussolini's flight on April 25, 1945.

ITURBIDE, AGUSTIN DE (1783–1824) Mexican independence fighter and first emperor of Mexico. Iturbide first distinguished himself in his military capacity, fighting at the side of HIDALGO, in favor of Mexican independence. In 1821, Iturbide and VICENTE GUERRERO, a fellow revolutionary leader, signed the Plan of Iguala, which called for the conservation of Roman Catholicism, independence and union, and a constitutional monarchy in Mexico. The plan was accepted by Viceroy O'Donoju, and Iturbide was named first emperor of Mexico in 1822. In 1823, he abdicated and fled into exile. He returned to Mexico and was executed for treason the following year.

IZL see IRGUN ZVAI LEUMI.

J

AL-JABERI, SA'DULLAH (1892–1947) A Syrian nationalist from his youth, Sa'Dullah was one of the leaders of the National Bloc under the French mandate. He was arrested several times during the years of struggle in the early 1930s. He served as a minister in several governments of the National Bloc in 1936–1939, in the brief period of movement toward full independence in the late 1930s. After the National Bloc returned to power in 1943, he was twice prime minister—in 1943–1944 and 1945–1946. In between, in 1944–1945, he was president of the National Assembly.

JABOTINSKY, VLADIMIR (ZE'EV) (1880–1940) Zionist leader; founder and head of the Revisionist movement in Zionism; author. Born in Odessa, Jabotinsky received a Jewish and general education and at a young age mastered Hebrew. He was early attracted to journalism and literature. Upon completing his high-school education he traveled to Berne and later to Rome, where he studied law and served as a correspondent for Odessa newspapers. Upon his return to Russia in 1901, he embarked on a journalistic career and began to take part in local Zionist activity.

When World War I broke out, Jabotinsky covered the front lines for the liberal Moscow newspaper *Russkiya Vedomosti*. In 1915 he reached Egypt and began to advocate, together with Joseph Trumpeldor, the creation of a Jewish army that would fight with the Allies against the Turks and help liberate Palestine. Later he continued this campaign in England and in Russia. His efforts were crowned with success when Britain set up the 38th Royal Fusilliers Battalion, in which Jabotinsky served as an officer in Palestine in 1918. He remained there and, while still in uniform, took part in local politics and served as the commander of the Jerusalem defense during Arab riots in April 1920. For this he was tried and sentenced to 15 years of hard labor. Released after a few weeks in Acre prison, he went to London and participated in the July 1920 Zionist conference there. A year later he was elected a member of the Zionist Executive, the highest body of the World Zionist Organization, and engaged in Zionist work in England and in Palestine. He resigned from this post early in 1923, in protest over what he considered the openly pro-British policy pursued by Chaim Weizmann, president of the World Zionist Organization. Two years later, in Berlin, he established the Revisionist movement.

His brand of Zionism stressed political work and action designed to lead to the early establishment of a Jewish state on both banks of the Jordan river. He opposed the 1922 partition of Palestine that led to the establishment of Transjordan. He called upon the Zionists to issue a clear-cut definition of their goals, and demanded unrestricted mass immigration to Palestine instead of the gradualist policy accepted by the official Zionist leadership. At the time he also began to develop his ideas about the need to build a Jewish fighting force for any eventuality. He opposed the Marxist idea of class warfare and thought that Palestine should be built through the efforts of private capital and private enterprise, thereby clashing with the dominant Labor movement in Palestine.

As president of the Revisionist and *Betar* (Revisionist youth) movements, he traveled around the world, but his largest following was among Polish Jewry, whose impending destruction he foretold long before the Holocaust. The gap between Jabotinsky and the official Jewish leadership in Palestine grew. He was barred by the British mandatory government from living in Palestine, especially after he advocated a policy of active defense and retaliation against Arab terrorists following the 1929 riots. In 1934 he entered into an agreement with DAVID BEN-GURION to ease the tensions between the Revisionist and Labor movements in Palestine, but a majority of the Labor membership refused to ratify the agreement. A year later he seceded from the World Zionist Organization. He established and headed the New Zionist Organization, the main preoccupation of which in the late 1930s was to evacuate as many Jews as possible from Eastern Europe to Palestine, through illegal immigration if need be. During the ARAB REVOLT OF 1936–1939 in Palestine, he called for an end to the policy of self-restraint practiced by the official Jewish underground, HAGANAH, and was instrumental in establishing the activist Palestine underground, the IRGUN ZVAI LEUMI (IZL), which he directed from overseas. That body began a series of retaliatory actions against Arabs and the British in Palestine. In 1937 he appeared before a British royal commission and spoke against the proposed scheme to partition Palestine, his opposition being based both on ideological grounds and on his feeling that the proposed size of the Jewish state would not be large enough for the 1.5 million Jews that would need to be evacuated from Eastern Europe. On the eve of World War II Jabotinsky was living in Paris; he later moved to London. He attempted to pressure the Polish and Romanian governments into pushing Britain to revise its immigration policies, but his efforts were unsuccessful. His last struggle was to bring about the creation, once again, of a Jewish army within the framework of the British army, to fight the Nazis. He died near New York and was buried there. According to his wishes, his remains were reinterred in 1964 on Mount Herzl in Jerusalem by the government of Israel in a state ceremony.

Jabotinsky was a prolific author in Hebrew, Russian and English. His best-known work was the biblical novel, *Samson the Nazirite* (1926), written in Russian (and used as the basis for the Hollywood film, *Samson and Delilah*). He translated Poe's "The Raven" and Dante's *Inferno* into Hebrew and the poems of Chaim Nahman Bialik from Hebrew into Russian.

JACOBINS, RUSSIAN Violent uprisings against the authorities had periodically marked Russian life for several centuries, but the philosophy of a revolutionary dictatorship transforming society by force, imported from France in the theories of the DE-CEMBRIST, PAVEL PESTEL, emerges full-blown as a reaction to the suppression of the REVOLUTIONS OF 1848. In the manifesto *Young Russia*, written in 1862, Peter Zaichnevsky first coined the slogan, "He who is not with us is against us, and all means are used in destroying an enemy." Both HERZEN and BAKUNIN, each from his own particular viewpoint, criticized *Young Russia* as un-Russian and anti-popular. The theory of Jacobinism in Russia was further elaborated by PETER TKACHEV and by SERGEI NECHAEV, who added the element of a small and conspiratial leadership to the idea of revolutionary dictatorship. Their ideas influenced the organization of the *Narodnaya Volya* (PEOPLE'S WILL), in its campaign of personal terror against czarist officials. LENIN was often accused of succumbing to Jacobin influences in his scheme of party organization. In 1903 GEORGI PLEKHANOV aroused controversy and opposition in the Social Democratic Workers' party of Russia when he proclaimed that "the safety of the revolution is our supreme law!" This saying was cited by Lenin when he disbanded the Constituent Assembly in 1918.

JACOBINS, FRENCH The most radical political faction during the FRENCH REVOLUTION, particularly associated with ROBE-SPIERRE and the COMMITTEE OF PUBLIC SAFETY during the terror of 1793–1794. Originating with the Breton club, an informal gathering of deputies from Brittany elected to sit in the Third Estate in Versailles in May 1789, the Jacobins came to dominate the course of events during the most climactic phase of the revolution: the period stretching from the election of the revolutionary convention in September 1793 to the fall of Robespierre, SAINT-JUST and COUTHON.

The Jacobin Club, or Society of Friends of the Constitution, received its name from the club's premises in Paris, the former Dominican monastery of Saint Roch located on the Rue Saint Honoré in Paris, right across from the CONVENTION in the royal palace of the Tuileries. (Dominican monks were popularly known as Jacobins because their order was dedicated to Saint Jacques.) As the revolution gained momentum with the outbreak of war against Austria and Prussia in April 1792, a network of provincial Jacobin clubs affiliated with the Parisian Jacobins also sprang up in all of the major French cities and towns. Claiming to represent the revolutionary conscience and the legacy of 1789 against the forces of counterrevolution and clerical reaction both at home and abroad, they usurped the powers of local government and administration to become the instruments of Jacobin centralization and dictatorship at the local level. Jacobin power ultimately rested, however, with the Convention, the first revolutionary body in European history ever

elected according to the principle of universal manhood suffrage. The Jacobins, usually known as the Mountain because of the high seats their members occupied in the chamber, waged a titanic struggle against their enemies, the GIRONDINS, whom they finally eliminated with the support of the Parisian SANS-CULOTTES as the reign of terror spread from the capital to the rest of the country. Under pressure from the PARIS COMMUNE or city hall, dominated by the left-wing Cordeliers club and a growing wave of popular agitation fomented by extra-parliamentary elements known as the *Enragés* (Wild Ones), the Jacobins were forced to adopt a more populist revolutionary program, going well beyond the bourgeois interests they had originally championed. Suppressed as a political force during the Thermidorian reaction and the Directory (Directorate) and made largely superfluous by the centralized despotism of the Consulate and the Empire, Jacobinism survived as the most enduring legacy of the revolutionary tradition. What held the Jacobins together, however, was less class interest than a common democratic ideology directly derived from the writings of Jean-Jacques Rousseau, especially *The Social Contract* and its assertion that nothing should be allowed to stand in the way of the general will. The Jacobins' ardent republicanism and revolutionary fervor have inspired countless disciples to emulate their deeds in the belief that democracy was, in fact, a substitute religion and that the reign of terror was only a prelude to the reign of virtue.

JADID, SALAH (1929–) Syrian officer and politician. An Alawi born in Lataqia, Jadid became a professional officer. In the 1950s he joined a clandestine cell of the leftist Pan-Arab SYRIAN BA'ATH PARTY and soon began playing a leading role in it. He was among those who prepared and staged the coup of March 1963 that brought the *Ba'ath* to power in Syria. After the *Ba'ath* group won in a bitter factional struggle with the Nasserists, Jadid became chief of staff later that year. In an intra-*Ba'ath* factional struggle in 1964–1965, Jadid headed the military faction, which was more extreme-leftist and doctrinaire in its political orientation than the civilian faction. When the civilian and more moderate wing, led by MICHEL 'AFLAQ, SALAH-UL-DIN BITAR and AMIN AL-HAFEZ won out, Jadid temporarily lost his post. In February 1966, in a coup, he ousted the ruling faction and installed his military faction in the Syrian government and army as well as in the Syrian-regional *Ba'ath* command.

In the new régime he established in 1966, Jadid took no formal post in either the government or the army but contented himself with the position of deputy secretary-general, leaving the position of secretary-general to NUR-UL-DIN AL-ATASSI. In reality, Jadid was the strong man of Syria for over four years. His policy was doctrinaire and leftist both inside Syria and in regard to foreign relations. Syria's increasing isolation within the Arab world caused by Jadid's policies was one of the reasons for the widening of a split within the *Ba'ath*. Parts of his own military faction, led by Defense Minister HAFEZ AL-ASAD, coalesced in a "nationalist" faction and turned against Jadid in February 1969. Asad, in a bloodless semi-coup, gained control of the government and the party command but accepted a compromise: a coalition in which the Jadid group kept some important posts. In 1970 Asad, in a second semi-coup, seized full control. Jadid and his associates were dismissed and detained for over 10 years. Jadid was released in 1983. Ever since, he has been kept under close surveillance and has not been allowed to play any role in public or political life.

JADIDISM (from the Arabic *jadid*—"new") A widespread movement in the early 1900s for the national liberation and progress in Turkistan (contemporary Uzbekistan and Tajikistan). Jadidism appeared on the heels of various Pan-Islamic and Pan-Turkic trends in the countries of the Muslim east in the late 1800s–early 1900s, spreading to Turkistan and Bukhara. The Jadidists tried to find a compromise between Islamic traditions and the European conception of modernization. The Jadidists' program of state government was essentially similar to European models of constitutional monarchies. From the Jadidists' point of view, Islam is capable of using western models of management technology and economic progress for the strengthening of Muslim government. This kind of modernization, unlike that of Western Europe, was not directed against religious foundations, but it was impossible to realize such programs as long as Turkistan was ruled by Czarist Russia.

The Jadidists opened many schools based on their new pedagogical principles. For the first time the students studied secular subjects, and the Jadidists prepared a number of textbooks for such schools. They propagandized the ideas of the Turkistan peoples' national liberation from Russian rule, with the goal of establishing real national independence.

The head of Jadidism in Turkistan, Mahmudkhoja Behbudi (1874–1919) and his disciples (Fitzat, Hamza, Abdulla Kaderi, Chulpan, Aini, Ajzi, Taballo, etc.) established a new system of people's education, a national press in the Uzbek and Tajik languages and local theater groups. The Jadidist activities were confronted by Islamic fundamentalists, who in 1918 organized massive terror against the supporters of Jadidism. The Jadidist press consisted of approximately 10 periodicals.

JALLUD, ABDUL-SALAM (1940/1? 1943?–) Libyan officer and politician. Colonel Qadhdhafi's chief associate and Libya's "number two" leader under various official designations. A professional officer commissioned in 1965, Jallud, then a captain, took part in Qadhdhafi's coup of September 1, 1969. Since then Jallud has held numerous government posts, including prime minister in 1992.

Jallud has been the architect of much of Libya's foreign relations, particularly in regard to the USSR, where he has been a frequent visitor since 1972.

JAMAL-AD-DIN AL-AFGHANI (1839–1897) Famous Muslim theologian, founder of Pan-Islamism and the Muslim Reformation. Afghani lived in India, Iran, Iraq and Turkey. His works regarded pan-Islamic ideas as revealing "overwhelming Muslim solidarity." He called for the setting up of a common Muslim state in the form of a caliphate. His Pan-Islamic concept was used by the rulers of the Ottoman Empire, with the sultan of Turkey considered the head of all the Muslims until 1924. Afghani appealed for the rebirth of Islam in its primal purity, with a division of political and clerical powers.

Afghani's activities favored the development of a national liberation movement in the Middle East. Under his leadership, for the first time a secret society was founded in Iran that criticized the shah's policy and demanded immediate reforms, liquidation of the absolute monarchy and adoption of a constitution. Afghani was the first to suggest the concept of Islamic socialism and tried to combine early Islamic principles with western democratic ideals.

JAPANESE RED ARMY The name sometimes given to a small group of militant Japanese students who participated in a number of violent terrorist activities in the 1970s. Its political program and ramifications remained unclear. Though predominantly directed against the Japanese government, some of these activities were carried out abroad in conjunction with other extremist groups. Among the operations attributed to the Japanese Red Army are the hijacking of a Japan Airlines plane to North Korea (1970), a massacre carried out by Kozo Okamoto at Tel Aviv airport (1972) and the takeover of the American embassy in Kuala Lumpur (1975). The group allegedly planned an attack at the Seoul Olympics (1988) modeled on the Munich massacre.

JACQUERIE Peasant uprising in 14th-century France. The term derived from Jacques, a name commonly associated with French peasants. The revolt broke out in 1358 in northeastern France in reaction to the social and economic changes which the nobility had imposed upon the peasants following the Black Death. However, it was also connected with the difficulties France was experiencing after its defeat at the Battle of Poitiers (1356). New taxes had to be raised and it was the peasants who were most heavily burdened. The nature of the Jacquerie uprising was extremely violent. Under its leader, Guillaume Cale, the rebels attempted to attack Paris, expecting to join in the burghers' revolt headed by Etienne Marcel. The Jacquerie only succeeded in uniting the nobility and the burghers, and as a result the revolt was cruelly crushed.

JAURÉS, JEAN (1859–1914) French socialist leader. The most vibrant and eloquent French socialist leader and orator of his day, Jaurès broke ranks with his Marxist comrades to defend the principle of human rights, by throwing himself into the Dreyfus Affair in protest against a blatant case of miscarriage of justice. He went on to become the founder and leader of France's first parliamentary socialist party, the SFIO (*Section Française de l'Internationale Ouvrière*), of which François Mitterand's Socialist party of the 1980s was the residual legatee. Born of a bourgeois family in the southern town of Castres near Toulouse, he graduated first in his class at the Ecole Normale Supéieure in Paris, where he was won over to socialism and Dreyfusism by the school librarian, Lucien Herr, who perceived these two movements as part and parcel of the same struggle to achieve social justice. Not unlike LEON BLUM, Charles Péguy and other famous *normaliens*, who made the same transition from being passionate defenders of Captain Dreyfus's innocence to championing the cause of socialism, Jaurès always believed in a specifically French form of socialism shaped by the JACOBIN legacy of the FRENCH REVOLUTION, and remained suspicious of the arid dogmas of MARXISM, rejected as an alien doctrine of little relevance to the real needs and aspirations of the French working class. He was nevertheless forced to conform, against his better judgment, to the Socialist International's ruling, adopted at the 1905 Amsterdam congress, that prohibited socialist participation in "bourgeois coalitions," thereby depriving himself of the chance of ever holding any cabinet office during the Third Republic. Instead, he proved to be remarkably effective as a leader of the *Délégation des Gauches*, a parliamentary steering committee made up of a coalition of Radicals, Radical-Socialists and his own SFIO, in implementing progressive legislation under the premiership of Emile Combes and Clemenceau (both of them Radicals), most notably the separation of Church and State which was enacted in December 1905.

Besides being an anticlerical, Jaurès was also an ardent pacifist who strenuously campaigned against excessive nationalism and warmongering and argued in favor of the creation of a "Citizens Army" to replace national conscription. He made a last ditch attempt to prevent the outbreak of hostilities in a famous speech he gave at the International Socialists' Congress in Brussels on July 28, 1914, imploring his German fellow socialists to avert war by voting against mobilization in the Reichstag, a defining moment in the saga of international socialism vividly evoked in the final chapters of Roger Martin du Gard's novel, *Les Thibault*. Jaurés was assassinated on his return to Paris by a French fanatic nationalist as he sat in a café on July 31, 1914. As the leading editorialist of *l'Humanité*, founded by Lucien Herr and other Dreyfusards in 1904 (which was taken over as the official organ of the French Communist party following the breakup of a unified French socialist party in the early 1920s), he was responsible more than anyone else for promoting a generous and humane brand of socialism that won many earnest supporters to his party. He also found the time to become a first-rate historian, chiefly remembered as the author of *A Socialist History of the French Revolution*, published posthumously in eight volumes, 1922–1924 and as editor of the *Histoire Socialiste: 1789–1900* (12 volumes, 1900–1908) which demonstrated, by means of systematic scholarship, that it was possible to reconcile the socialist mystique with the Jacobin tradition.

JEFFERSON, THOMAS (1743–1826) One of the founding fathers of the United States and its third president. A brilliant thinker and writer, Jefferson was the main author of the American declaration of independence. He also served as governor of Virginia, ambassador to France and secretary of state. But above all, the soft-spoken contemplative Virginia patrician was a revolutionary.

While the revolutionary nature of Jefferson's statesmanship on the eve of American independence is self-evident, his political opposition to the Federalist government of the early republic may be considered at least as revolutionary. Indeed, to many conservative minds his organizing an opposition faction, or party, represented an act of insurgence and his ascendancy to the presidency on a democratic-republican platform was commonly referred to as "a real revolution of 1800." Jefferson himself considered his election "a real revolution in the principles of our government," comparable in significance only to the AMERICAN REVOLUTION of 1776. But it was beneath the surface of politics and statesmanship that Jefferson's nature as a revolutionary was most apparent; his original, path-breaking ideas and his free creative thinking conditioned his revolutionary leadership in affairs of state.

Thomas Jefferson was born on Virginia's western frontier in 1743 to a land-owning, aristocratic family. He attended the College of William and Mary and thereafter read law and joined the Virginia bar in 1767. The brilliant young lawyer was an instant

hit in provincial politics. He was elected to the House of Burgesses in 1769 and became identified with the struggle to defend the rights of the colonists from British oppression. In 1774 he published the *Summary View of the Right of British America*. It was a brilliant fusing of Enlightenment ideas concerning the natural rights of man, a liberal and optimistic assessment of societies' ability to regulate themselves and a hard-headed analysis of political structures and constitutional rights. The pamphlet received immediate recognition and popularity. Shortly after its publication, Jefferson was elected a delegate to the Continental Congress and was named a member of the committee charged with drafting a declaration of independence.

The declaration, which in its final form was Jefferson's text with minor revisions, applied the theory of the rights of man to the political situation in the colonies, based on a forceful exposition of the British Crown's infringement of the colonists' political, legal and constitutional rights. In one of the few changes made in the original draft, a clause which applied the tenet that "all men are created equal" to American slavery was stricken out. The contrast between the profound idealistic ideas of the revolutionary movement and social reality appeared too obvious in this case. Jefferson's personal life exemplified the same painful contrast: notwithstanding his lofty ideas as to inalienable human rights, he was a slave-holder and not a very benevolent one at that.

After independence, Jefferson returned to Virginia's legislature

Thomas Jefferson

and led its liberal wing. He was elected governor in 1779 and served the colony in that position for two terms. In 1783 he joined the American delegation in Europe and succeeded Benjamin Franklin as minister to France. There he experienced his second uprising, this time as a sympathetic eyewitness to the FRENCH REVOLUTION. At the time, America was entering the process of effecting thorough-going changes in its structure of government through framing a constitution. Jefferson made his contribution to the remaking of American government through an intensive correspondence with James Madison, father of the constitution. In 1789, he joined the new administration, under the constitution, as secretary of state. However, within the cabinet Jefferson became a strong opponent of the policy of concentrating power in the national government through broad construction of the constitution and of encouraging manufacturing and commerce at the expense of the agricultural sector. In 1791, he began organizing opposition to Hamilton's policies and in 1793 he resigned from the cabinet to organize the opposition in earnest.

The elections of 1796 pitted JOHN ADAMS as representative of the Federalist government against Thomas Jefferson, now leader of a democratic-republican opposition. Adams won and Jefferson, as vice-president, developed a coherent platform in opposition to Federalist ideas and policies. On that platform he was elected president in 1800, in what was widely considered to be the onset of a second American revolution.

Through two terms in office, however, Jefferson's staunch opposition to a strong central government was considerably diluted. The famous statement he had made upon election: "we are all Republicans, we are all Federalists," which was originally meant to appease his worried opponents, turned out to be a statement of policy. His presidency represented a convergence of his liberal ideas with Federalist precedents and policies. In the purchase of Louisiana (1803) and the Embargo Act he demonstrated his conversion to the Hamiltonian ideas of the necessity of a strong central government.

After his second term in office, Jefferson returned to Monticello, the Virginia estate he had designed. He dedicated himself to a contemplative life and to the building and development of the University of Virginia. He died on the 50th anniversary of the declaration of independence, on July 4, 1826.

JEROBOAM (I) BEN NEBAT

(–901 B.C.) The first king of the divided kingdom of Israel after the death of King Solomon (c. 908 B.C.). A member of a noble family of the tribe of Ephraim, Jeroboam served in Solomon's administration and was in charge of a labor force that fortified Jerusalem. According to the Greek translation of the Bible, he returned to his native city of Zeredah where he planned a rebellion against King Solomon. For this purpose, he assembled a force of 300 chariots. Spiritual support came from the prophet Ahija the Shilonite, who tore Jeroboam's robe into 12 pieces, giving ten of them to Jeroboam to symbolize the 10 tribes that were to be torn from Solomon's kingdom and put under his—Jeroboam's—rule. However, the rebellion was defeated and Jeroboam was forced to flee to Egypt. There he was given asylum and even became the son-in-law of Pharaoh Shishak (Sheshonk).

When Solomon died, his son and successor, Rehoboam, was confronted by a popular demand for the reduction of taxes. After the demand was refused, 10 tribes rose and appointed Jeroboam as their king. He set up the independent kingdom of Israel—as opposed to that of Judea, which continued to be governed by Rehoboam—and took various steps to make the division permanent. These included the construction of a new capital at Shechem (Nablus) and the adoption of various new festivals. His own reign lasted for 21 years and the dynasty that he founded survived until 720 B.C., when it was destroyed by the Assyrians under King Sargon.

JEWISH DEFENSE LEAGUE (JDL)

Right-wing organization of American Jewish militants. In the late 1960s, the Jewish community of New York was beginning to feel threatened by the rise of the Black Power movement. Elderly Jews living in poor neighborhoods were frequently targeted in anti-Semitic attacks; although most of these Jews were poor themselves, they were identified by young African Americans as slum landlords and exploiters of the city's black community. The Jewish establishment, which had overwhemingly abandoned the poor neighborhoods for Manhattan and the suburbs, seemed aloof to the problems of the Jewish poor and made few practical efforts to ameliorate the situation.

To some Jews, however, the rise of anti-Semitism could no longer be tolerated. Inspired by American radicalism and Israel's stunning victory in the Six Day war, they began talking about the need to reassert Jewish pride and to take actions to protect immediate Jewish interests. Among the most vocal advocates of Jewish self-defense was MEIR KAHANE. Raised in a Revisionist (right-wing) Zionist household, he had completed a degree in international law and received rabbinic ordination. While serving as the rabbi of a small congregation in the borough of Queens, he was confronted with the increase in anti-Semitic hooliganism on an almost daily basis, and decided that it was time for Jews to fight back. In 1968 he founded the JDL, an organization of young Jews committed to using physical force to protect their interests.

Kahane's stated objective won him the whole-hearted support of many Jews, but particularly the young, who sought a Jewish means of expressing their fashionable radical politics, and the elderly, who required immediate assistance. Most, however, condemned his methods, which involved leading gangs of Jewish toughs in street confrontations against gangs of young African Americans, many of which were wrongly targeted. Kahane was a sensationalist, who employed almost any means to achieve his ends. For instance, in a newspaper advertisement aimed at soliciting funds and new recruits, he showed a picture of young Jews armed with chains and iron bars. "Is this any way for good Jewish boys to act?" asked the caption. Many of his followers were involved in scuffles with the police, but this only hardened their resolve by evoking images of anti-Semitic oppression at all levels of power.

As the JDL grew, Kahane became involved in even larger Jewish issues, such as the Arab-Israel conflict and, particularly, freedom of emigration for Soviet Jews. His methods in dealing with these issues were even more spectacular than those he employed on the streets of Brooklyn and Queens. He organized protests both outside and inside performances of the Bolshoi Ballet, he released frogs in the offices of several of his opponents (intended as a parody of the 10 plagues, which he promised to bring upon them), and he harassed the families of Soviet diplomats, believing that this would win him, and therefore his objectives, extensive press coverage.

By the early 1970s, the Jewish leadership of the United States had become virulently opposed to the JDL and its supporters and labelled Kahane a madman and a racist. Meanwhile, Kahane began speaking openly of the "specter of anti-Semitism" that loomed over the United States. Finally, in 1971, he emigrated to Israel, where he later founded the KACH movement. But for several years Kahane shuttled between Jerusalem and New York and remained the head of the JDL in both countries. JDL activities continued, but without Kahane's charismatic leadership and full-time attention to the movement's needs, the American movement slowly reverted to its original objectives: the protection of Jewish interests in poor neighborhoods. Kahane's increasing involvement in right-wing Israeli politics only furthered the rift between JDL and its leader, and by 1976 Kahane was removed as head of the JDL.

The JDL still survives in New York and other urban centers in the United States with sizeable Jewish populations. Its activities, however, cannot be compared to those of the movement's heyday under Kahane, and consist mainly of patrolling Jewish neighborhoods and organizing an occasional demonstration on behalf of Israel.

JEWISH REVOLT (66–73 A.D.) Rome took direct control of Judea in 6 A.D. after the deposition of Archelaus, Herod's son. Most of the governors sent to rule the province were cruel, rapacious and indifferent or even hostile to the religious sensitivities of the Jews. In the recurrent conflicts between the Jews and Greeks in the cities of mixed population, especially Caesarea, they sided with the Greeks and severely punished the Jews. Although the order of the emperor Caligula to set up his statue in the Temple was not ultimately carried out due to the timely murder of the emperor in Rome, the danger could not be forgotten by the Jews. Oppressed, plundered and occasionally massacred by the hostile governors and their troops—mostly recruited from the Greek population of the province—the Jews were provoked to fight back against their oppressors and to regain their freedom. Jewish zealots had quite early developed the ideology that Roman rule was unacceptable on religious grounds. Added to this, expectations for messianic deliverance had risen high. In addition, social and economic polarity tore apart the Jewish society. The governing class, including the high priests, was hated by the poor, low classes. A considerable number of the well-to-do who had collaborated with the Romans fell victims to the attacks of the patriotic *sicari*, whose name was derived from the fact that they used *sicae* (daggers) to assassinate their enemies. Things came to a head under Gessius Florus (64–66 A.D.), the worst of all the procurators of Judea. He plundered the Temple's treasury, sacked Jerusalem and let his soldiers massacre the population. Even Jews with Roman citizenship were crucified. At last, the masses of Jerusalem rose against him and he retreated to Caesarea. The revolt against Rome was openly declared by the decision taken to cease the daily sacrifice to the emperor. Those who advocated loyalty to Rome, mainly the high priests and well-to-do persons, were persecuted and killed and the Roman garrison was annihilated. Jerusalem was finally liberated from Roman rule in the summer of 66 A.D.

When the news spread throughout in the country, fighting broke out between Jews and Greeks, each side massacring members of the other wherever it had the upper hand. Cestius Gallus the governor of Syria, marched on Jerusalem with some 35,000 troops but failed in the siege of the city and the rebels routed his army as it retreated. A government for the conduct of the war was set up, initially made up of men of the upper classes. Commanders were appointed to take charge of the defense of Jerusalem and every one of the districts of the country. The only attempt the rebels made to extend the territory under their control, by attacking Ascalon, ended in disaster. From then on they were content with strengthening the fortifications of the country. The emperor Nero then appointed Vespasian, an experienced general, to subdue the rebellion. He concentrated his army, some 60,000 troops, in Ptolemais in the early spring of 67 A.D. His first aim was to recover Galilee, which was under the command of Josephus son of Matthias, the author of the history of the revolt (in his *The Jewish War*). As Josephus did not dare face the Roman army on the battlefield, the war turned into a series of sieges. It took Vespasian some fifty days to take the major fortress of Jotapata, commanded by Josephus himself. Josephus surrendered to the Romans after the capture of the city. Gamla, the major fortress in Gaulanitis, was also taken after strong resistance, and all the other forts and towns of Galilee, Gaulanitis and Samaria were taken easily by the Romans by the end of 67 A.D.

The zealots of Jerusalem and the party of John of Gischala, who escaped to the capital, suspected the leaders of the revolution of pro-Roman tendencies. Helped by the Idumaean Jews, the extremists gained the upper hand and destroyed their opponents, mostly high priests and well-to-do persons. Vespasian took advantage of this civil war to subjugate the various districts encircling Jerusalem. The death of Nero and the ensuing Roman civil war halted his attack on the Jewish capital. Vespasian was proclaimed emperor in July 69 A.D. and became occupied with preparations for taking control of Italy and the other parts of the empire. The conduct of the war was thus left to his son Titus. The rebels in Jerusalem, divided into three factions led by John of Gischala, Simon Bar-Giora and Eleazar son of Simon respectively, unfortunately used the respite to fight each other, destroying war materials and stores of grain. Titus began the siege a few days before the Passover festival of 70 A.D., having under his command some 65,000 men: legionnaires, auxiliary troops and contingents of friendly kings. The defenders, who according to Josephus amounted to 23,400 men, were divided and weakened even before the beginning of the siege. The fugitives from all parts of the country who had taken refuge in Jerusalem worsened the situation, for famine soon played havoc in the besieged city. Even so, it took Titus almost five months to conquer the city, for the defenders fought back stoutly and devoutly expecting, to the very end, to be delivered by God. In the end, Titus had the Temple set on fire, the city destroyed and the survivors sold into slavery. The Jews were not allowed to return to Jerusalem, in which a Roman legion was stationed. The remaining fortresses of the rebels were captured over the next three years.

JEWISH REVOLT UNDER TRAJAN (115–117 A.D.) A series of furious Jewish revolts swept several provinces of the eastern Roman Empire while the emperor Trajan was engaged in the conquest of Mesopotamia (Iraq) in 115 A.D. The first to rise were probably the Jews of Cyrene and the revolt then spread to Egypt,

Cyprus and Mesopotamia. The Jews massacred their enemies, the Greeks, maltreated atrociously those captured, destroyed temples of the heathen and won successes even against regular Roman troops. The reported number of victims—hundreds of thousands—and the atrocities are certainly exaggerated and yet they reveal the fury of the Jewish rebels. Although the causes of the revolts are not clear, the Jews may well have been motivated by messianic aspirations and the long hatred between them and the Greeks. In Mesopotamia, the last region to revolt (116 A.D.), the Jews joined a general uprising against the Roman conquest. Trajan employed the best of his generals to subdue the rebels, who were eventually annihilated ruthlessly. The Jewish communities of Cyrene and Egypt were depleted, no Jews were allowed to enter Cyprus and in Mesopotamia the Moor Lucius Quietus, a distinguished general in the service of Trajan, extinguished the rebellion with much ferocity. He was also sent to Judea to quell an upheaval that had arisen there in 117 A.D. Apparently from then on the second legion was stationed in that province.

JIANG QING (Chiang Ch'ing) (1914–1991) Chinese Communist, widow of MAO ZEDONG. Born in Shandong, Jiang Qing suffered greatly as a child. Impoverished and beaten by a brutal father, she and her mother fled home, and at age 14 she joined an underground theater troupe in Shandong. She later became an actress in Shanghai, using the name Lanping. She appeared in plays and films, mostly in bit parts, but also in a few larger roles. She claimed to have joined the CHINESE COMMUNIST PARTY (CCP) in Qingdao in 1932. She arrived at the Communist capital, Yan'an, in 1937, and in 1938 began living with Mao even before he had divorced his second wife. Party officials opposed the marriage but gave their approval on the condition that she keep out of politics. For the most part the condition was met. However, in the 1960s, as Mao prepared to attack his critics in the party, she became increasingly active and in 1966 emerged as one of the leaders of the Cultural Revolution of 1966–1976 (see GREAT PROLETARIAN CULTURAL REVOLUTION). As a member and leader of the notorious "gang of four," she epitomized the viciousness and brutality of the Cultural Revolution. She was deputy chairman of the Cultural Revolution's leadership group, served on the Politburo and supervised literature and the arts.

In October 1976, one month after Mao's death, Jiang Qing was arrested. By this time she had earned the reputation that made her one of the most hated figures in modern Chinese history. Brought to trial in 1980 along with other members of the "gang of four," she faced her accusers defiantly, never renounced her Maoist views, and claimed that she had only carried out the chairman's orders. She was sentenced to death but this was commuted to life imprisonment. In 1984 she was released from custody in order to receive medical treatment. There were rumors that she was suffering from throat cancer. On June 14, 1991 the official Chinese news agency announced that she had committed suicide on May 14.

JIANG JIESHI see CHIANG KAI-SHEK.

JIBRIL, AHMAD (1935? 1937?–) Palestinian-Arab guerrilla or terrorist organizer. Born in Yazur near Ramla, Palestine, Jibril left his home with his family in 1948, among other Palestinian refugees. He grew up in Jordan and Syria and until 1958 served in the Syrian army, attaining the rank of captain. In the 1960s he began organizing groups to attack Israel, and in 1967 his group joined the Popular Front for the Liberation of Palestine (PFLP) led by GEORGE HABASH. In 1968, however the PFLP split and Jibril seceded, forming his own organization, naming it PFLP—General Command. This group, even more extremist than the PFLP in its policies and terror methods, is small, tightly knit and kept secret even from the leadership of the PALESTINE LIBERATION ORGANIZATION (PLO). It has perpetrated some of the worst terrorist attacks against targets both in Israel and in foreign countries (including daring ventures such as an attack by fighters flown in by hang gliders in November 1987). Jibril also became known for a deal in May 1985, in which Israel granted him the release of 1,150 detainees and convicted prisoners in exchange for three Israeli soldiers he had captured.

In intra-PLO politics, Jibril and his group form a most extremist faction, opposing YASIR ARAFAT and the mainstream leadership. In 1983, he joined a Syrian-supported armed rebellion of dissident PLO-FATAH squads against Arafat and his men in Lebanon that expelled the latter from east Lebanon and Tripoli, and from 1984/85 he adhered to a "National Alliance" and a "National Salvation Front" of anti-Arafat groups within and without the PLO. In 1987, Jibril and his groups were suspended—and according to one version expelled—from the PLO. Though Jibril did not fully accept Syrian "guidance" and discipline, most of the time he was hosted and tolerated in Syria, where he still is as of this writing. In the late 1980s he reportedly developed strong links with Iraq and Iran.

JINNAH, MUHAMMAD ALI (1876–1948) Indian revolutionary and founder of Pakistan. Born in Karachi to a Muslim family, Jinnah went on to practice law in Bombay, where he developed a thriving practice. Influenced by the burgeoning nationalist sentiment among the educated Indian middle classes, he joined the INDIAN NATIONAL CONGRESS, then led by moderate leaders such as Dadabhai Naoraji and Gopal Krishna Gokhale, and was elected to the Central Legislative Council from a Muslim constituency in Bombay in 1910. Although he could not be considered a typical Indian Muslim (he did not speak Urdu, the primary language of the Muslim community in India, drank alcohol and favored elegantly tailored suits over the homespun cotton garb that was to become almost de rigueur among the nationalist leadership), Jinnah retained a strong consciousness of the problematic position of the minority Muslim population within a predominantly Hindu India. In 1913 he joined the MUSLIM LEAGUE which had been founded just seven years earlier, and by 1916 had become its president.

Jinnah, with the cooperation of the congress, championed the establishment of separate Muslim electorates and weighted representations for Muslims in those provinces where they constituted a minority. His break with the congress resulted from his opposition to GANDHI's noncooperation movement, which eventually foundered in the mid-1920s. Thereafter, Jinnah was increasingly preoccupied with the problem of securing the rights of India's Muslims in any future settlement with the British granting Indian home rule. He feared that the Muslims would be subjugated to the Hindus in any such agreement. The word "Pakistan" (Land of the Pure) had been coined by Choudhri Rahmat Ali in 1933 to designate those northeastern Indian provinces that contained a Muslim majority. Jinnah had the establishment of Pakistan adopted as the Muslim League's official aim in 1940.

His western tastes and manners notwithstanding, Jinnah was a charismatic speaker and motivator of the Muslim masses. As the time for the British withdrawal neared, direct action by Muslims throughout the majority Muslim provinces made the partition of India into two separate states ever more probable, despite strong opposition to this move on the part of the congress leadership; Gandhi in particular saw partition as a recipe for disaster and a betrayal of the non-sectarian principles he espoused. Jinnah, now gravely ill, nonetheless managed to see his dream for an independent Pakistan fulfilled in August 1947, and briefly served as the new nation's first president until his death in 1948. By that time, the degree of turmoil, death and destruction engendered by the population movements precipitated by partition had become fully apparent.

JOFFE, ADOLF ABROMOVICH (1883–1927) Russian revolutionary and diplomat of the early years of Soviet Russia. Joffe was born in Simferopol, and originally joined the MENSHEVIK party. He was befriended by LEON TROTSKY when they were both living in Vienna. He helped Trotsky edit the Viennese *Pravda* and organized the smuggling of the paper into Russia. Joffe was arrested and imprisoned by the czarist authorities in 1912, but was released following the first RUSSIAN REVOLUTION OF 1917, and in July 1917 joined the BOLSHEVIK party.

In April 1918, Joffe was appointed Soviet ambassador to Berlin. In 1920 he led the Russian delegation to the peace talks with Poland. In late 1922 he traveled to the Far East to strengthen Soviet influence in that region of the world. Joffe continued to be closely allied to Trotsky and was part of the opposition to JOSEPH STALIN and the ruling triumvirate after VLADIMIR LENIN's death. He was also ambassador in Vienna (1923–1924) and Tokyo (1924–1925). By early 1927 he was gravely ill, but was refused permission to travel abroad for medical treatment—even at his own expense. Stalin subjected him to increasing harassment, and he shot himself in the Kremlin as a protest against the expulsion of Trotsky and MAXIM LITVINOV from the party.

Joffe's funeral was attended by thousands, even though it had not been announced. It marked Trotsky's last public appearance in Russia.

JOFFE, MARIE   Second wife of ADOLF JOFFE (a Russian revolutionary and diplomat of the early years of Soviet Russia). Having married him in 1918, Marie worked as an editor and secretary for BOLSHEVIK publications and publishing houses. In 1929 she protested TROTSKY's expulsion from the COMMUNIST PARTY OF THE SOVIET UNION at a general editorial meeting. She was arrested, exiled and later sent to a labor camp. She was only rehabilitated and allowed to return to Moscow after the 22nd party congress in 1957. She then learned that the couple's son, born in 1919, had died in 1937. She emigrated to Israel in 1975 and wrote a book about her experiences, published in English as *One Long Night.*

JONES, JOHN PAUL   (1742–1792) American naval hero of the AMERICAN REVOLUTION, whose indomitable courage and bril-

liant seamanship won him the title of "Father of the US Navy." Jones was born John Paul, son of a gardener in Scotland, where he inherited the doggedness and cavalier attitude that were to serve him well at sea. Jones received his first command at the age of 21, of a small merchant vessel, the John, earning a reputation as a harsh master. In 1773, Jones killed the ringleader of a mutiny. To escape punishment, he traveled incognito to Virginia and attached "Jones" to his name.

The impending American Revolution, however, brought him out of quiet obscurity. In 1775, he received his first commission as a lieutenant of the frigate *Alfred*, the first ship to fly the continental flag. He quickly achieved several resounding victories for the fledgling US navy. Given command of the *Ranger*, the most notable event of his first cruise was the capture of the *Drake*, the first British naval ship captured by the Continental navy. He then received an old and slow refitted merchantman named the *Bonhomme Richard*, which won an unlikely victory over the *Countess of Scarborough* and *Serapis*.

Returning to America in 1787, he was awarded a gold medal by Congress for his valor and service, but still had no place in an America at peace. In 1788, he received an offer to command a fleet for the Russian navy against the Turks. However, a scurrilous rumor that he had violated a young girl hastened his unceremonious return to France in 1789. In 1792, the US government appointed him commissioner to Algiers, but before the letter detailing the appointment reached him he died, prematurely aged by his years at sea.

JOSELEWICZ, BEREK   (1768–1809) Polish patriot. A Jew and a native of Kretinga in western Lithuania, Joselewicz originally worked in commerce and entered the service of Vilna's prince-bishop. While on a business trip to Paris in 1789, he was drawn to the new ideals of the FRENCH REVOLUTION; these made him a natural ally of the Polish liberals, who favored Jewish emancipation, and of their leader, TADEUSZ KOSCIUSZKO. Under the menace of a third and final partition of their country, the Poles decided to take up arms against their chief oppressors, Catherine the Great of Russia and Frederick William II of Prussia. Some Jews, aware of Kosciuszko's libertarianism, joined the insurrection that he launched in March 1794.

Following the expulsion of Warsaw's Russian garrison, Kosciuszko took the momentous step of granting Joselewicz permission to organize a separate Jewish cavalry regiment, appointing him colonel of the "Jewish Legion." In an appeal for volunteers, printed in Yiddish on October 1, 1794, Joselewicz urged his fellow-Jews to "be like lions and leopards so that, with God's help, we may drive the enemy from our land." Mostly poor youths with no military experience, the 500 idealistic Jews who answered his call brought their own horses and had the rest of their equipment supplied by Warsaw's Jewish community. Ordered to defend the largely Jewish suburb of Praga, Joselewicz and his men fought back when seasoned Russian troops under the formidable Count Alexander Suvorov attacked this forward position on November 4. Their bravery notwithstanding, only Joselewicz and 20 other legionaries survived the battle, hewing their way through the Russian lines. Praga's civilian population was then massacred by Suvorov's infuriated Cossacks. Joselewicz was killed 15 years later, while leading two squadrons of the Polish army in a battle against Austrian forces.

The end of the revolution: the execution of Mexico's Emperor Maximillian, 1863

JUÁREZ, BENITO PABLO   (1806–1872) Mexican leader. Born in San Pablo Guelatao near Oaxaca, Mexico, the son of poor Zapotec Indians, Juárez was orphaned at age three and left to the care of an uncle. In 1829, he enrolled at the Oaxaca Institute of Arts and Sciences, studying law and science. Three years later he became a member of the state legislature. Always driving himself, he was admitted to the Mexican bar in 1834 and began his practice immediately. He often represented poor Indians with legal problems and found himself becoming involved in politics as a strong supporter of liberal views. In 1842 he was appointed a civil court judge and in 1844 his liberal, anticlerical tendencies became evident when he resigned his position of government secretary, refusing to punish those who had not paid their Church tithes.

By the age of 37, with the improvement of his social and economic position, he was finally able to marry the daughter of a well-known family.

In 1846, conservatives lost their hold over Oaxaca's state government, and Juárez, together with Luis Fernando del Campo and Jose Simeon Arteaga, took over the government. He played an important part in the Federal Congress responsible for mortgaging ecclesiastic properties required to finance Mexico's war with the United States (1846–1847). From 1847 to 1852 he held the position of interim, and then fully-elected, governor of Oaxaca. His administration focused on education expansion, improved agricultural and mining practices, and the emancipation of women. Due to disagreements with President Santa Anna, Juarez was exiled.

In the US he joined other exiles, most notably JUAN ALVAREZ and IGNACIO COMONFORT, to plot the overthrow of the military dictator. They launched the Mexican revolution of 1855 and established the first liberal régime in Mexico. It took a bitter war, lasting until 1861, before Juárez's conservative opponents were finally defeated. The government was practically bankrupt and Juárez's solution—a two-year moratorium on payment of all foreign debts—was not approved by foreign creditors, with the result that the French ultimately conquered Mexico, installing Maximilian, an Austrian prince, as emperor of Mexico.

In 1867, the United States finally induced the French troops to withdraw from Mexico and Juárez triumphantly returned to Mexico City. The most prominent personality in Mexico during the turbulent period of 1856 to 1872, Juárez brought Mexico out of feudalism and welded the country into a democratic republic.

JULY REVOLUTION   King Charles X's (1824–1830) desire to restore the French monarchy to its previous power, his passionate belief that his enemies were sinful—which led to the readmission of the religious orders and clergy, especially the Jesuits, who had been banished during the FRENCH REVOLUTION of 1789—and his ceaseless pressure to restore the privileges of the aristocracy, caused fervent opposition by the public and in parliament.

Charles replaced whatever moderate counselors he still had, and appointed the Prince de Polignac his chief minister. Polignac was a hard-line supporter of Charles's policies, and parliament reproached the king by appointing a minister of its own choosing. Charles retaliated by dissolving parliament, but the new elections showed an even greater opposition to Polignac.

To deal with the situation Charles, in July 1830, issued the Ordinances of St. Cloud, a series of abhorrent proclamations, which, among other things, dissolved the newly elected parliament before it met, deprived most of the electorate of their vote and suspended freedom of the press. The response was immediate. The protest was led by the writer Adolphe Thiers, who was supported by printers and journalists, and proved only a precursor of the events that followed.

The revolutionary fever was very much alive in Paris and it did not take much time for the mob, under republican leaders, led in part by the general MARQUIS DE LAFAYETTE and the statesman Jacques Laffitte, to seize the Hôtel de Ville where the municipal government was housed. Notre Dame and some significant arsenals and guardhouses were also occupied. The opposing soldiers were disheartened and had no food since the rebels had also captured the military bakeries. The situation was grave, a fact not realized by Charles and Polignac.

Events then moved swiftly. After only three days of fighting Paris was in rebel hands. Charles offered to dismiss Polignac and rescind his ordinances, but it was too late. On July 30 Thiers, who had conveniently returned from the country, had the walls of the city plastered with posters supporting Louis Phillipe, Duke of Orleans, head of a younger branch of the Bourbon house, who, because of his family's revolutionary history, was sure to appeal to the middle and lower classes. However, he was not well known and it was not until the next day, when he embraced Lafayette and received from him the French tricolor, that his reception was guaranteed. Charles was forced to abdicate and flee to England. The French legislature elected Louis Philippe—the "Citizen King"—to the monarchy, under the condition that he rule as a constitutional monarch.

JULY 1952 REVOLUTION   see EGYPT, REBELLIONS, REVOLTS AND REVOLUTIONS.

K

KACH Right-wing Israeli political movement. *Kach* was founded as a political party in 1976 by Rabbi MEIR KAHANE, the founder of the JEWISH DEFENSE LEAGUE. The party adopted an extreme right-wing platform, which included the institution of religious law in all aspects of day-to-day life, the annexation of all territories occupied by Israel in the Six-Day war, and the expulsion of Arab residents from the occupied territories and Israel proper.

In many ways, *Kach* served as a gadfly in the Israeli political scene. Even the most right-wing parties considered it to be a fanatical fringe element, barely worthy of attention. For 10 years it failed to win a single seat in the *Knesset* (Israel's parliament), despite the movement's vocal propaganda apparatus. Nevertheless, it did cause other rightist groups to adopt a harder line toward the Palestinian issue (one group, *Moledet* [Homeland], which advocates the transfer of the Palestinian population of the West Bank and Gaza, is represented in the *Knesset* and has even been represented in the government), and *Kach* members or supporters (Kahane himself consistently denied engaging in any illegal activities) participated in a number of violent acts against Palestinians and left-wing Israelis. *Kach* received national prominence in 1984, when Kahane was finally elected to the *Knesset*. He used his new-found parliamentary immunity to further his political agenda, this despite numerous suspensions and a news boycott of his activities. Furthermore, it seemed that in the next elections *Kach* would increase its parliamentary bloc to as many as six seats. In response, the *Knesset* passed a law disqualifying avowedly racist parties from running in national elections. In the following elections, *Kach* was banned from participating.

The loss of parliamentary respectability seemed to be the death knoll for *Kach*. Although it claimed hundreds of thousands of supporters from all segments of Israel's population, it was unable to mobilize them. The small core group was often imprisoned and Kahane himself spent time in jail for inciting racial hatred. In November 1990, while collecting funds, Kahane was assassinated in New York, allegedly by an Islamic fundamentalist. His death signalled the break-up of *Kach* into two rival movements: a core group, led by Baruch Marzel, and a smaller faction, *Kahane Hai* (Kahane Lives) led by Kahane's son. The split was based mainly on personality feuds within the movement and had little to do with ideology.

In 1994 a *Kach* supporter, Dr. Baruch Goldstein, entered the Cave of the Patriarchs in Hebron and opened fire on a group of Palestinian worshippers, killing 29. Although Goldstein acted independently, his attack was regarded by the Israeli government as a direct result of *Kach*'s fervently anti-Arab ideology. Both *Kach* and *Kahane Hai* were declared illegal, and the leadership of both movements was placed in administrative detention. The leadership has since been released, but the ban on their activities, as well as the close scrutiny of the Israeli police, seems to have put an end to both groups as viable movements in the Israeli political spectrum.

KAGANOVICH, LAZAR MOISEYEVICH (1893–1991) Soviet Communist Party and government official. Born into a poor Jewish family near Kiev, Kaganovich began working as a shoemaker while still a youth. In 1911, he joined the BOLSHEVIKS and began organizing strikes. By 1924, he was a member of the Bolshevik central committee and in 1925 was appointed to head the Communist Party of Ukraine. In 1930, he became a member of the Politburo and First Secretary of the Moscow party organization, retaining the latter position until 1935. In 1934, at the 17th Communist Party congress ("The Congress of Victors") he was elected chairman of the party control commission and bore major responsibility for the blood purge that began in December of that year.

Together with his party posts, he also served as commissar for heavy industry and for transport in the Soviet government and played an important role in organizing the war effort during World War II. In 1947, he briefly resumed his post as head of the Communist party in Ukraine. After STALIN's death he was a member of the central committee's presidium (Politburo) and first deputy chairman of the Soviet council of ministers. In June 1957, he took part in an abortive attempt to depose Nikita Khrushchev. He was stripped of his party and government posts and sent to manage a cement plant in the Urals. Retiring on pension, he returned to Moscow, where he lived until his death.

KAHANE, MEIR (1932–1990) Rabbi and Jewish activist, founder of the JEWISH DEFENSE LEAGUE (JDL) and KACH movement. Born in Brooklyn as Martin David Kahane, he was the son of a rabbi. A member of the Revisionist Zionist youth movement, *Betar*, Kahane first got into trouble with the police at the age of 15 when he smashed the windows of the car carrying visiting British Foreign Secretary Ernest Bevin, in protest against the British mandatory policy on Jewish immigration to Palestine. He estimated that he spent a total of three years in US prisons as the result of his various acts.

Kahane was ordained an Orthodox rabbi and obtained a law

degree from New York University. He served for a time as a synagogue rabbi in Queens and as editor of the Brooklyn-based *Jewish Press.*

During the 1960s he founded the Jewish Defense League in New York; it did not eschew the use of violence, including bombings, adopting the motto "Never Again"—no repeat of the Holocaust. Its activities included self-defense operations in urban areas (especially Brooklyn) where Jews felt threatened, and harassment of Soviet activities in New York as a protest against the Soviet anti-Jewish policy. Kahane is also claimed to have been an FBI undercover agent during the 1960s, using the name Michael King.

He moved to Israel in 1971, claiming that only in Israel can one live a full Jewish life and avoid assimilating non-Jewish values, but also possibly to avoid further entanglement with United States law authorities after receiving a five year suspended sentence. In 1976 he founded a movement, *Kach,* in Israel, the main platform of which was the expulsion of the Arabs from Israel and the re-making of the country as a non-democratic State based on Jewish instead of secular law. Standing for the *Knesset* (parliament), he eventually obtained a seat in 1981. His four years there were stormy and his behavior led to a number of suspensions. In 1988, the *Knesset* passed a resolution barring parties with a racist policy from standing for election; Kahane's party was subsequently disqualified. Kahane himself was condemned by almost the entire gamut of organized Jewry.

In 1990, Kahane was assassinated in New York at a gathering of his supporters. The Egyptian-born, naturalized American who was tried for his murder was convicted of weapons offenses, but, in a verdict which surprised many, was not convicted of the murder itself.

Kahane wrote, among others, *The Jewish Stake in Vietnam* (coauthored by Meir Kahane, Joseph Churba and Michael King, 1967); *Never Again (1970); Letters from Prisons* (1974); and *They Must Go* (1980).

KALINOVSKY, KONSTANTIN (KASTUS)   (1838–1864)
Byelorussian patriot and revolutionary hero, thinker, leader of a revolutionary rebellion of 1863–1864 in Byelorussia and Lithuania. His family, while of noble stock, was landless and penniless. Graduating in 1860 from St. Petersburg University, Kalinovsky returned to Byelorussia and took part in the revolutionary movement there. In 1861, in Grodno, he united a group of local intellectuals and arranged ties with the people involved in the revolution in Vilna. He rallied peasants to the struggle against the landlords and the czar. He was assisted by companions from Moscow and St. Petersburg, from whom he received arms. In 1862–1863, Kalinovsky published a newspaper entitled *Muzhitskaya Pravda* (The Truth of the peasants). At first it appeared in Byelorussian and called for resistance to the oppressors of the Byelorussians. Kalinovksy strongly criticized the reform of 1861 as an open fraud committed by the czar and the landlords. He propagated the idea of a democratic republic in Byelorussia and defended the right of the Byelorussians to their national liberty, independence and development of their culture.

Kalinovsky idealized the peasants movement. He demanded liberty of conscience for all, and personally preferred the United church over the Greek Orthodox church. He led the radical wing of the Vilna Committee which prepared for armed revolt against

the czar. The revolt was suppressed and Kalinovsky was arrested on February 9, 1864, sentenced and executed.

KAMENEV, LEV BORISOVICH   (1883–1936) Russian revolutionary and Soviet leader. Born Lev Rosenfeld in Moscow to a Jewish father, Kamenev studied law at the University of Moscow and joined the Russian Social Democratic party. Following his arrest for antigovernment agitation, he fled to Paris in 1902 and became a confidant of VLADIMIR LENIN. In spite of his prior arrest, he soon returned to Russia and joined the BOLSHEVIK PARTY.

Still using the name Rosenfeld, he moved to the Georgian city of Tiflis, where he headed the revolutionary movement. In Tiflis he assumed the Russian name Kamenev, meaning "Man of Stone." Although he was a man of little personal ambition, he was well connected to other leading revolutionaries; his wife, Olga Bronstein, for example, was LEON TROTSKY's sister. In Tiflis, he befriended JOSEPH STALIN and possibly introduced him to Lenin.

In 1908, Kamenev moved to Switzerland. There, as coeditor with Lenin of *Proletarii* and *Socialdemokrat,* two important party papers, he drew attention for his lucid and expressive writing. Although Lenin had sent him back to St. Petersburg in 1914 to oversee the progress of the Bolshevik faction in the Duma (Russian parliament), his reputation as a writer had preceded him and Trotsky called on him to edit his own party newspaper, *Pravda.*

Upon the outbreak of World War I, Kamenev opposed Lenin's policy of supporting Russia's defeat as a means of hastening the revolution. Despite this nationalist stance, for which he was later suspected of being an agent of the Okhrana (the Russian secret police), he was exiled to Siberia for the course of the war, only returning to Petrograd during the general amnesty granted by the provisional government following the RUSSIAN REVOLUTION OF 1917. In the capital, he renewed his ties with Stalin, with whom he directed the revolt.

Kamenev was generally noted for taking a cautious approach to the revolution. With GRIGORI ZINOVIEV, he opposed Lenin's plans for a coup d'état to replace the provisional government, supporting instead the establishment of a wide coalition of all socialist parties. Lenin was so enraged by this that he demanded Kamenev's and Zinoviev's expulsion from the party. Trotsky, in his *History of the Russian Revolution,* later commented on Kamenev's moderation: "Kamenev grasped better than most Bolsheviks the general ideas of Lenin, but he grasped them in order to give them the mildest possible interpretation in practice."

The years 1920 to 1925 mark the pinnacle of Kamenev's power. After mending his breach with Lenin, he was appointed chairman of the Moscow Soviet, deputy chairman of the Council of Peoples' Commissariats, and editor of *Pravda.* Following Lenin's death, Kamenev, together with Stalin and Zinoviev, formed a triumvirate that governed Russia. The main rival to the triumvirate's power was Trotsky, whom they opposed wholeheartedly. Only later did Kamenev and Zinoviev join Trotsky in opposing Stalin. Stalin attempted to rid himself of Kamenev, first by sending him as ambassador to Fascist Italy in 1926, and then, in 1927, by having him expelled from the party and exiled to the Urals.

Stalin used the 1934 assassination of Politburo member Sergei M. Kirov as grounds for the great purges of 1936. Kamenev was sentenced to death in a show trial in which he "admitted" to participating in a Trotskyite plot to assassinate all members of the ruling Politburo. Some have suggested that Stalin's motives in ridding himself of Kamenev were primarily anti-Semitic. Stalin himself denied this, saying, "We are fighting Trotsky, Zinoviev and Kamenev, not because they are Jews but because they are Oppositionists."

KANU   see KENYA AFRICAN UNION.

KAO KANG   see GAO GANG.

KAPP PUTSCH OF 1920   A military-rightist attempt to overthrow the Weimar republic, which failed due to a general strike. The originators of the *putsch* were the military free corps operating in and outside Germany. These troops, mostly monarchist and anti-republican, put down an ill-prepared Communist rebellion in Berlin early in 1919 and fought the BOLSHEVIKS in the Baltic states. Finally the Western Allies ordered their disbandment, whereupon their regular army commander, General Walter v. Luettwitz, and a conservative east Prussian official, Wolfgang Kapp, conspired to overthrow the socialist government unless it accepted their demands. These were: new elections, the cessation of the policy of troop reduction ordered by the Allies, the dismissal of the legally elected government and the creation of a cabinet of experts. The president of the republic, Friedrich Ebert, and his minister of war, Gustav Noske, flatly refused and called upon the regular army to stop the rebels' free corps from marching on Berlin. The army's actual chief of staff, General Hans v. Seeckt, refused to open fire on comrades in arms, whereupon the legal government left Berlin to Stuttgart and the capital fell into Kapp's and Luettwitz's hands. Ebert's socialist government called upon the workers to strike against the illegal government, which had no idea how to function in the vacuum created by the general strike. Soon they abandoned their hollow power, and the Kapp Putsch became the source of a legend, namely that organized labor could defeat any rightist attempt to destroy the republic.

KARAKHAN, LEV MIKHAYLOVICH   (1889–1937) Armenian revolutionary and Soviet diplomat. As a high school student, Karakhan took part in anti-czarist demonstrations, joining the Social Democrats in 1904. He studied law in St. Petersburg from 1910 to 1915, but was exiled for antiwar agitation.

Returning to Petrograd after the February RUSSIAN REVOLUTION OF 1917, he was elected to the city Duma as well as to the executive of the Petrograd Soviet. In October 1917, he was a BOLSHEVIK representative on the Soviet's military revolutionary committee.

Karakhan's diplomatic career began as secretary to the Russian delegation at the Brest-Litovsk peace talks. Later, he served as ambassador to Poland, China and Turkey, and as the Soviet foreign office's premier specialist on Asia. He was executed in the STALIN purges as a former associate of TROTSKY.

KARELIN, APPOLON ANDREEVICH   (1863–1926) Russian revolutionary. A populist during his high school and univer-

sity days, Karelin was arrested repeatedly and exiled. Escaping to France, he formed the Brotherhood of Free Communists, an anarchist-Communist group, in 1905. In 1917, he returned to Russia as a follower of KROPOTKIN, but supported the October RUSSIAN REVOLUTION OF 1917, working in the system of soviets and leading the Federation of Communist Anarchists. As other anarchists, he opposed the repressive bureaucracy of the Soviet régime. His followers were jailed and his organization declared illegal in the early 1920s. Karelin himself died a natural death.

KARUME, ABEID   see AFRO-SHIRAZI PARTY.

KASAVUBU, JOSEPH   (1910–1969) Congolese nationalist leader. A priest by training, Kasavubu worked as a teacher, entering the Belgian civil service in 1942. Throughout the 1940s and 1950s he took part in nationalist activities as head of *Abako*, a cultural and political group based on the Bakongo tribe. *Abako* won the municipal elections at Leopoldville in 1957, enabling Kasavubu to play a major role in the negotiations which led to the creation of an independent Zaire in 1960. He became prime minister under President PATRICE LUMUMBA. Kasavubu opposed Lumumba's pro-Soviet line and the two engaged in a campaign of mutual recrimination until Kasavubu ousted Lumumba with the aid of the army. In November 1965, Kasavubu was overthrown by MOBUTU, after which he retired to his farm, where he lived until his death.

KASHANI, AYATOLLAH ABUL QASSEM   (1881? 1885?– 1962) Iranian Islamic cleric and politician, a member of the Islamic religious hierarchy hostile to the shah and his establishment, and particularly to foreign (i.e., British) intervention. Born in Tehran, Kashani was raised in Iraq, where he resided until the end of World War I. In the late 1940s he encouraged the establishment of the FEDAYAN ISLAM, a radical extremist group that did not recoil from assassinating key establishment leaders.

In 1947, Kashani was arrested and sent into forced exile in Qazvin until the end of that year. Following a failed attempt on the shah's life in February 1949, he was again arrested and exiled to Lebanon. In June 1950 he was allowed to return. He was elected to the *majlis* (parliament) and in 1950–1951 supported the radical MUHAMMAD MOSSADDEQ'S NATIONAL FRONT and his election as prime minister. In 1952, Kashani was elected president of the *majlis*, but he soon fell out with Mossaddeq (who was too leftist-secularist for his taste) and was ousted from the presidency of parliament in July 1953. He thereupon joined the opposition and contributed to Mossaddeq's fall in August 1953. Despite this brief collaboration with the shah's policies, Kashani, in his opposition to the shah and his governments, continued fostering extremist Islamic organizations like the *Fedayan Islam*. He was a predecessor and mentor of the AYATOLLAH KHOMEINI.

KAUNDA, KENNETH DAVID   (1924–) Zambian statesman. A qualified teacher, Kaunda entered politics in the late 1940s and rose to lead the Northern Rhodesian African National Congress in 1952. In 1957 he founded a breakaway group, the Zambian African National Congress, and was imprisoned by the British when it was banned. In 1960 he was elected president of the United National Independence Party which, together with the African National Congress, won the elections of 1962. In January 1964 he became prime minister of Northern Rhodesia; in October of the same year he became first president of Zambia—as Northern Rhodesia had been renamed by then—a position he still maintains.

KAUTSKY, KARL   (1854–1938) German socialist ideologue and politician. Kautsky was born in Prague and became a prominent Social Democrat party (SDP) member in Vienna, as editor of the important publication *Die Neue Zeit* (*The New Time*) and as FRIEDRICH ENGELS's secretary (1881). Kautsky was regarded as a major interpreter of MARXISM but gave it a milder, reformist rather than radical-revolutionary accent. He formulated the SPD's official party program, which remained valid for decades and which was known as the Erfurt program, in 1891. In his manifesto, Kautsky laid down the theoretical foundations to the strategy—previously adopted by AUGUST BEBEL—of socialist ascendance by parliamentary means, through the growth, education and self-consciousness of the organized German proletariat. Upon the outbreak of World War I, Kautsky joined the pacifist Independent Social Democratic party of Germany (USPD) but was vehemently opposed to the revolutionary pacifists such as ROSA LUXEMBURG. After Germany's defeat, he was a member of the new ruling cabinet for a while but then returned to the SPD and formulated its program of 1922 along anti-revolutionary and anti-BOLSHEVIK lines. He further opposed mass strikes—seemingly the sharpest weapon of organized labor—and thereby generated vehement criticism by the far Left. In 1933, Kautsky left Germany for Vienna and Holland and dedicated most of his time to writing history and to the study of socialist opposition to FASCISM. Kautsky was the archetype of a doctrinaire, dry and unimaginative German Social Democrat, whose enormous theoretical output and central ideological position influenced the whole socialist movement for decades.

KAVTARADZE, SERGO   (1885–1971) Georgian revolutionary and statesman. Kavtaradze joined the Russian Social Democratic Workers' party in 1903 and was active in its Imereti and Samegrelo—western Georgian provinces—committees. He graduated from the law school of the St. Petersburg University and remained in St. Petersburg to be active in the local BOLSHEVIK organization. In 1915–1916 he was one of the leaders of a Bolshevik organization in Tbilisi and was arrested several times. In 1918, Kavtaradze became the chairman of the executive committee of the Vladikavkaz Soviet. In 1920 he was appointed an advisor to the Russian mission in Georgia. After the establishment of Soviet rule in Georgia, he held the post of the deputy chairman of the Revolutionary Committee and that of minister of justice. In 1920 Kavtaradze became the chairman of the government. In 1924–1927 he served as a deputy of the general prosecutor of the Soviet Union. The party expelled him from its ranks for being an active member of a Trotskyite organization. In 1940 he was acquitted. He held various diplomatic posts until his retirement in 1956.

KEDROV, MIKHAIL S.   (1896–1941) BOLSHEVIK military and police official. Expelled in 1899 from his medical studies at Moscow University, Kedrov joined the Social Democrats in 1901 but spent most of his years in prison and exile until his

emigration to Switzerland in 1912. It was there that he completed his medical studies. He served as a military physician in the Russian army from 1916, resuming active political life in 1917.

In November 1917, Kedrov was appointed deputy commissar for war, supervising the demobilization of the Imperial Russian army. He was head of RED ARMY internal security during most of the civil war and later headed the forced labor section of the Internal Commissariat. During the New Economic Policy (NEP) years he was active in economic planning and later as a supreme court prosecutor. He was arrested as a Trotskyite in April 1939 and executed two years later.

KEMAL (JAMAL) PASHA   (1872–1922) Turkish officer and one of the chief leaders of the YOUNG TURKS. Kemal graduated from the Cadet School and the War Academy in 1861 and served in Macedonia and Thrace. As a young officer, he joined underground groups preparing a rebellion, known as the "Committee of Union and Progress." After the revolution of 1908, he became a member of the military government. He later served as governor of the Adana and Baghdad provinces, head of the security forces and minister of public works.

After a shortlived counterrevolution in 1913, Kemal staged a coup, together with ENVER PASHA and TALAT PASHA that reinstated a government of the Young Turks. He became military governor of Istanbul, minister of naval affairs and, together with Enver and Talat, in fact ruled Turkey during World War I. Following Turkey's defeat in World War I, he escaped to Germany, Afghanistan, and later Tiflis, where he was assassinated in 1922 by an Armenian nationalist. His *Memoirs of a Turkish Statesman* was published in 1922 in Munich and London.

Kemal Pasha, the Turkish governor, here shown inspecting German aircraft during World War I

KENYA AFRICAN UNION (KANU) Founded in 1960. The transitional constitution of that year had given Africans overwhelming superiority in the legislative council and legalized national political parties. The African members of the council formed KANU and the former president of the Kenyan African Union (KAU), James Gichuru, was appointed acting president.

The KAU was a nationalist organization, founded in 1944, demanding African access to white-owned land. The movement comprised the educated elite of several tribes and commanded little popular support except among the Kikuyu. In 1947, JOMO KENYATTA became president of the organization. In 1953, Kenyatta was imprisoned for alleged involvement in MAU MAU activities, and the KAU was banned.

Following his release from prison in August 1961, Kenyatta assumed the presidency of KANU. Unlike the KAU, KANU was a nation-wide party, and it led Kenya to independence in 1963.

Between 1969–1982, Kenya was a de facto one-party state. In June 1982, this situation was legalized and Kenya became a de jure one-party state. This lasted until 1991 when, in December of that year, the constitution was amended to legalize a multiparty political system. However, KANU still has an overwhelming majority and is currently the ruling party in Kenya. It has been led by President Daniel arap Moi since the death of Kenyatta.

Kikuyu women suspected of assisting terrorists being removed to a concentration camp during the Kenyan uprising

KENYATTA, JOMO (1894–1978) African nationalist and first leader of independent Kenya. A member of the Kikuyu tribe, Kenyatta's original name was Kamau wa Ngengi. From an early age he was assigned the duty of looking after his family's livestock. He also often accompanied his grandfather, revered as a prophet and magician, on his travels around Kikuyuland. At about age 13 Kenyatta left home for the Church of Scotland mission, where he received treatment for a spinal disease and remained for five years, studying and assist-

ing with the first translation of the New Testament into Kikuyu.

On being baptized, he changed his name to Johnstone Kamau. In 1914 he moved to Nairobi, where he began working as an interpreter at the Supreme Court, and later as an inspector of water supplies, a post that gained him status among Africans. He adopted the name Kenyatta from *Muibi wa kinyata*, the name of a beaded belt he wore. He soon became involved in politics, joining the Young Kikuyu Association. In 1928 he was elected general secretary of the KIKUYU CENTRAL ASSOCIATION (KCA) and edited the party newspaper, in it formulating the African case against exclusive European occupation of the Kenya Highlands.

Kenyatta visited London in 1929 and again in 1931 on behalf of the KCA. Interested in communism, he made a four-month visit to Russia in 1933, returning to London, where he worked as an assistant in phonetics and taught Kikuyu at London University. He represented Kikuyu grievances against colonialism and campaigned for his people's right to self-determination, by presenting petitions to government officials and voicing his opinions in the British press. He studied social anthropology under Bronislav Malinowsky at the London School of Economics, publishing his thesis in 1938 in the form of a book, *Facing Mount Kenya*, which, as well as being a pioneering work of anthropology, was also a perceptive criticism of British colonialism.

Through the Workers' Educational Association, Kenyatta lectured on Kenya and imperialism and met his second wife. With the outbreak of World War II, the couple moved to a small village in Sussex, where Kenyatta worked as a farm laborer, adopting the forename "Jomo" from the nickname "Jumbo," which the villagers called him on account of his stature. In 1945, he helped to form the Pan-African Federation and the following year organized the fifth Pan-African Congress in Manchester.

Leaving his English family behind, Kenyatta returned to Kenya in 1946, where he was made president of the KCA—by now banned by the British—and of the KENYA AFRICAN UNION (KAU), and campaigned for independence through peaceful means, emerging as a much loved national figure.

In 1952 he was arrested by the colonial authorities and charged with managing MAU MAU, the violent nationalist movement opposing colonialism. Although no evidence was found linking him to this cause, he was nonetheless convicted and imprisoned at Lokitaung. His arrest sparked off bloody rebellion and unrelenting pressure for his release, until he was finally freed in 1961.

In 1962 he was elected to the legislative council, becoming Kenya's first prime minister in May 1963, and then president upon the declaration of Kenya as a republic in December 1964.

As a proponent of African socialism, Kenyatta believed that traditional tribal values of individual responsibility and cooperation within the extended family could serve as a model for the governance of and organization within the nation-state. Under the slogan of *Harambee* (pulling together), he called upon all Kenyans, regardless of race or tribal affiliation, to cooperate in developing Kenya. Under his government, black Kenyans were allowed rights to purchase land that had formerly been reserved exclusively for whites, improvements were made in education, the economy grew rapidly and agriculture, industry, and tourism were expanded. Overcoming tribal rivalries, Kenyatta refrained from using violence to achieve stability.

Kenyatta was instrumental in forming the East African Community in 1965, which operated mainly as a customs union between Kenya, Uganda and Tanzania. After General IDI AMIN's coup in 1971, Kenyatta's mediation was crucial in avoiding a war between Tanzania and Uganda

Toward the end of his life, Mzee or Father of the Nation, as Kenyatta was fondly known, confined himself largely to ceremonial duties.

Kenyatta addressing a rally

KERENSKY, ALEKSANDER FYODOROVICH (1881–1970)

Born in Simbirsk, Russia, son of a school principal, Kerensky graduated in law from St. Petersburg University in 1904. His career as a revolutionary began in the SOCIAL REVOLUTIONARY PARTY. He gained prominence as a defense lawyer in political cases and as the investigator of the massacre of 170 striking gold miners in Siberia. He was elected a deputy to the Fourth Duma in 1912.

In the first provisional government, formed following the February RUSSIAN REVOLUTION OF 1917, Kerensky served as minister of justice, the only Socialist to join the government. Later, he served as minister of war and prime minister. Noted in this period for his passionate, almost hysterical oratory, he was dubbed "Persuader-in-Chief." Successive provisional governments failed to achieve peace or alleviate Russia's economic crisis, and Kerensky was overthrown in October 1917 by LENIN's BOLSHEVIKS.

Kerensky fled to Europe, where he remained active in anti-Bolsheivk politics until World War II. In 1940 he left Paris for New York, where he occupied himself with writing and lecturing until his death.

KETSKHOVELI, VLADIMIR (LADO) (1876–1903)

Georgian professional revolutionary, one of the founders of a Social Democratic Leninist organization in Georgia. Ketskhoveli enrolled in the religious seminary of Tbilisi in 1891, where he joined an illegal group of students. He was expelled in 1893 for organizing a student strike. Afterwards he studied at the Kiev religious seminary and was once again expelled and even arrested for revolutionary activities in 1896. In 1897, he returned to Georgia and joined *Mesame Dasi*—a Social Democratic organization. In 1900 Ketskhoveli arrived in Baku, assigned the task of organizing Leninist committees and an illegal printing-house. In September 1902 he was arrested and transferred to the Tbilisi prison, where he went on propagandizing revolutionary ideas among prisoners. In July 1903, Ketskhoveli led a prisoners' strike and was eventually killed by a prison guard. His death was marked by demonstrations by Social Democrats in Tbilisi and Baku.

KHALAF, SALAH ("ABU IYAD") (1930? 1933?–1991)

Palestinian-Arab politician and guerilla/terrorist organizer. Born in Jaffa, Khalaf left his home with his family for Gaza, along with other Palestinian refugees, when Israel became independent in 1948. He studied at a Cairo teachers' college and worked in Gaza schools. In the 1960s Khalaf was among the organizers of the FATAH guerrilla/terror group which from 1969 became the dominant faction in the PALESTINE LIBERATION ORGANIZATION (PLO). In the 1970s and 1980s he emerged as one of the two or three top leaders of *Fatah* and one of YASIR ARAFAT's chief associates. He was a member of *Fatah*'s Executive Council, but, as primarily a "military" man, was not on the PLO Executive. Khalaf was co-responsible for most of *Fatah*'s military/terrorist operations. He was also rumored to be in charge of several secret branches of *Fatah* for special operations, such as the launching of Black September—or at least of one section of that group (in which more extremist, dissident elements soon became dominant). Khalaf's image was that of a hard-liner. In the late 1980s, however, he seemed gradually to become more moderate. He fully supported Arafat's new policies proclaimed in November 1988, opting for a political and diplomatic solution of the Palestinian-Arab issue and the future peaceful coexistence with Israel by a Palestinian state in part of Palestine. He was therefore hated by the more extremist groups within and without the PLO, the more so as he was thought to be in charge of the mainstream's violent suppression of dissident groups (such as Abu Nidal's men [see AL-BANNA, SABRI] in south Lebanese camps in 1990). Khalaf was seen by many as a possible successor to Arafat as PLO chairman. He was assassinated in January 1991 at his headquarters in Tunis by bodyguards identified by the PLO as Abu Nidal's men. Khalaf published his life story and views in a book, *Palestinien sans Patrie* (Palestinian without a country) in 1978, ghostwritten by the French journalist Eric Rouleau.

KHALIL, 'ABDULLAH (1888? 1892?–1970)

Sudanese officer and nationalist. Prime minister of Sudan (1956–1958). Khalil served in the Egyptian army (1910–1924), and in the Sudanese Defense Forces from their establishment in 1925 until his retirement in 1944 as a brigadier-general, the first Sudanese to attain that rank. In 1945 he founded the Nation party (*Hizb al-Umma*) which advocated independence for Sudan (as opposed to union with Egypt) and was closely linked to the MAHDIYYA sect's leadership. After the attainment of independence on January 1, 1956, his own *Umma* party gradually gained political control. Khalil followed a moderate, conservative, pro-western policy. He was overthrown by General IBRAHIM 'ABBUD's military coup of November 1958, and retired. In 1960–1962 he was suspected of subversive activities against the 'Abbud régime and was put under house arrest. He may have had some influence on the formation of the National United Front that overthrew 'Abbud in October 1964, but did not resume an active political role.

KHALKHALI (SADEQI), MUHAMMAD SADEQ (1926–)
Iranian Islamic cleric and politician. Born in Khalkhal (eastern
Azerbaijan region), Khalkhali studied theology in Tehran and
Qom. He has written books and articles about both religious and
secular issues.

In the late 1940s, he was affiliated with the radical FEDAYAN
ISLAM organization, and since the early 1960s was a follower of
AYATOLLAH KHOMEINI. He went into hiding following the execution of the Fedayan Islam's leaders in 1956, and was later arrested several times after Khomeini was exiled from Iran in
1963.

Following the Islamic Revolution of 1979 (see IRAN, REVOLTS
AND REVOLUTIONS), Khalkhali for a few years headed the Islamic
Revolutionary Court which tried members of the shah's régime,
and the Anti-Drug Islamic Revolutionary Court; he became
known for his cruel sentences, sending hundreds to the gallows
(the "Hanging Judge"). He was a founding member of the
Tehran Council of Militant Clerics. Khalkhali was elected to the
majlis (parliament) for three terms from 1980 and was a member of its foreign affairs committee. He belongs to the radical
extremist faction advocating an unrelenting struggle against
counterrevolutionaries. In May 1991, according to unconfirmed
reports, a writ was issued for his arrest and trial for illegal executions, embezzlement and corruption.

KHAMENEI, AYATOLLAH SAYYID 'ALI (1939–) Iranian
religious leader, president of Iran 1981–1989, supreme spiritual
leader since June 1990. Born in Mashhad to a family of Islamic
clerics, Khamenei studied theology in Najaf, Iraq, and returned
to Qom, Iran, in 1958 to study under the Ayatollahs Borujerdi,
Ha'eri and KHOMEINI, obtaining a degree in Islamic jurisprudence and the title of *Hojat-ul-Islam* (a lesser rank than ayatollah). He took part in the WHITE REVOLUTION (1962–1963) and
was arrested, but later resumed activities against the government. For some time he cooperated with the leftist-Islamic MU-
JAHIDIN KHALQ. He co-founded an organization of militant clergymen. Khamenei reportedly received guerrilla training in
camps of the PALESTINE LIBERATION ORGANIZATION (PLO) in
Lebanon.

In 1978, Khamenei joined Islamic activists in Mashhad, and
after the February Islamic Revolution of 1979 (see IRAN, REVOLTS
AND REVOLUTIONS), was among the founders of the Islamic Republic Party (IRP). A leading member of the Tehran Militant
Clergy Association and the Foundation of the Oppressed, he
held a variety of political posts. In 1980 he was elected to the
majlis (parliament).

In June 1981, while speaking in a Tehran mosque, he was
wounded by a bomb set off by the *Mujahidin Khalq* and his
right hand was paralyzed. In September he was elected general
secretary of the IRP, a day after his predecessor, Muhammad
Javad Bahonar, was assassinated. One month later he was
elected president of the party by a 95% majority of the popular
vote. After Khomeini's death in June 1990, he was named
Khomeini's successor as supreme spiritual leader. While continuing Ayatollah Khomeini's fundamentalist Islamic policies,
Khamenei is considered more pragmatic and moderate. He has
written several books in Persian, including *The Role of Muslims
in the Liberation of India, The General Outline of Islamic
Thought in the Qur'an, Life of Imam Sadeq, From the Depth of*

Prayers and *The Waiting*. He has also translated a number of
western books into Persian.

KHAN, ABDUL GHAFFAR (1890–1988) Also known as
Badshah Khan and "the Frontier Gandhi," the most significant
20th-century leader of the Pathans, a martial Muslim ethnic
group inhabiting northwest India (now Pakistan) and
Afghanistan. Khan joined the Indian nationalist movement in
the wake of the British government of India's 1919 Rowlatt Act
and went on to join the KHILAFAT MOVEMENT (an organization
dedicated to strengthening ties between Indian Muslims and the
Turkish caliphate), whose North-West Frontier Province committee he was soon elected to lead.

Khan was profoundly affected by his meeting with MAHATMA
GANDHI and JAWAHARLAL NEHRU in 1929 and joined the *Khudai
Khidmatgar* (Servants of God) movement in his native state.
This nonviolent organization agitated for nationalist goals while
seeking to awaken Pathani political consciousness. Thanks to
Khan, it enjoyed close ties with the INDIAN NATIONAL CONGRESS,
on the central committee of which he served for many years.

Although Khan opposed the partition of India, he decided to
remain in his native state, where he continued to campaign non-
violently for Pathani rights to autonomy and self-determination.
His activism earned him a total of over 30 years in jail.

AL-KHATIB, AHMAD (1927? 1928? 1930?–) Syrian politician. A teacher by profession, Khatib was active in the SYRIAN
BA'ATH PARTY, and in the 1960s became a member of the party
leadership, though he never joined the first echelon. He also
headed the Syrian Teachers' Union. In December 1965 he became a member of the Presidential Council—for three months,
until the March 1966 coup of the military faction. When HAFEZ
AL-ASAD, in a November 1970 coup, deposed the president, government and party leadership and became prime minister,
Khatib was appointed president, in a provisional arrangement
not submitted to a referendum. In February 1971, when Asad
decided to take the presidency himself, Khatib stepped down.
He then became president of the newly-appointed National Assembly ("People's Council") and a member of the *Ba'ath* "regional" (Syrian) command. In December 1971 he was appointed prime minister of the newly created "Federation of
Arab Republics" (Syria-Egypt-Libya) which never materialized.

KHIABANI, MUHAMMAD (1880–1920) One of the leaders
of the National Liberation Movement in Iran and head of the
Democratic party in Iranian Azerbaijan. Khiabani was born in
Khamne into a merchant's family. During 1905–1911, he
played a decisive role in the opposition to the shah and gradually became one of the leaders of the democratic movement. He
was an active participant in the 1908–1909 Tabriz revolt. After
the founding of the Azerbaijan Democratic party in 1917, he
became its leader. The party's program demanded political and
democratic freedoms and autonomy for the people of Iran's
Azerbaijan. In April 1920, Khiabani led the Tabriz revolt which
seized power in Iranian Azerbaijan. In June 1920, an Azerbaijan government was formed in Iran by Khiabani, who realized
the need for reforms in the economy, culture and education. In
September 1920, however, the troops of the central Iranian

government captured Tabriz. Khiabani was brutally killed. To this day, his name is respected by Iranians.

KHILAFAT MOVEMENT   Led by the Ali brothers, Muhammad and Shaukat, and by Abul Kalam Azad, the *Khilafat* movement was established in India in the early years of the 20th century to strengthen ties between Indian Muslims and the Turkish caliphate that represented their spiritual leadership. It reflected Indian Muslims' growing fear of being marginalized in Indian society and it openly encouraged religious militancy.

The Ali brothers agreed to align the Khilafat movement with GANDHI's nonviolent noncooperation movement in exchange for the latter's espousal of the Khilafat cause, thus bringing the full weight of the INDIAN NATIONAL CONGRESS behind Khilafat demands. However, the Khilafat's credibility as an expression of Indian nationalism was weakened by the 1920 *hijrat* (the departure of 18,000 Indian Muslim peasants to Afghanistan on the grounds that India was a land of apostates) and the 1921 Moplah rebellion (in which south Indian Arab-Muslims attacked their Hindu neighbors). With the abandonment of noncooperation in 1922, the Khilafat was fatally weakened, and it finally collapsed with Kemal Atatürk's abolition of the caliphate in 1924.

KHMER ROUGE   On April 17, 1975 the Revolutionary Army of Kampuchea captured the Cambodian capital, Phnom Penh, and declared the founding of a Democratic Kampuchea that would usher a new era; the day was marked as the first day of Year Zero. The Communist Party of Kampuchea (PKK, or *Khmer Rouge*) had struggled for 24 years to overthrow successive Cambodian governments. After the revolution's success, the "radical egalitarian" theories of the *Khmer Rouge* plunged Cambodia into what one critic called an "autogenocidal revolution." Out of 7.3 million Cambodians alive on that fateful day in 1975, less than 6 million lived to welcome the Vietnamese army at the end of 1978, when it invaded and occupied the country. A larger percentage of the population was decimated during this "popular" revolution than in any other of the 20th century.

In 1951, the PKK was founded in opposition to Prince Norodom Sihanouk's hierarchic, bureaucratic government. After nine years of political foment, the party's leadership, under POL POT, Ieng Sary and Son Sen, fled to the hills for fear of imprisonment. It was during this period that the insurgency began and the party made contact with other Communist parties in China and Southeast Asia.

Violence first erupted at the beginning of 1967, when peasants in the Samlaut District of Battambang Province rioted against the district's civil administration. Pol Pot quickly called off the violence, but soon after that, the PKK attacked a government post at Bay Damran, near Battambang City. With that, the Revolutionary Army of Kampuchea, with about 4,000 men, began a systematic armed struggle against Sihanouk's civil administration. By the end of the month, the party had targeted and killed village chiefs throughout the country. The next two years saw the PKK mount a full-scale revolt against Sihanouk, while American involvement in the war in neighboring Vietnam escalated.

In spite of Prince Sihanouk's declaration in 1968 of neutrality, by 1970 he had tacitly permitted the North Vietnamese to use eastern Cambodia as a staging ground for attacks against the American troops in South Vietnam. Meanwhile the PKK had amassed an army of approximately 15,000 men and continued to recruit followers in the North Vietnamese occupation zone of eastern Cambodia. In response, the United States and South Vietnam invaded eastern Cambodia and supported a military coup against Sihanouk.

General Lon Nol, the coup leader, took over the Cambodian government (now called the Khmer Republic), receiving military assistance from the United States. He allowed the United States to drop more bombs on eastern Cambodia between 1970 and 1973 than had been dropped in all of World War II. The bombing rendered nearly 80% of the area's land unarable. Their government's own support for the destruction of the eastern part of the country radicalized the Cambodian population and the Khmer Rouge, swelling their army to 40,000 men and women.

During the first half of the 1970s, the Khmer Republic maintained its power in Phnom Penh and a few scattered cities, while the countryside succumbed to civil war and US bombing. Indeed, the American military and economic assistance provided to the Khmer Republic was the only factor maintaining Lon Nol's corrupt, inefficient government.

As the North Vietnamese gradually filtered out of Cambodia after the spring of 1972, and as the United States Congress declared the bombing of Cambodia illegal in 1973, the conflict between the Khmer Rouge and the Khmer Republic increased. Brigades were being formed in the Revolutionary Army of Kampuchea, and by February 1974 there were more than 175 battalions.

Prince Norodom Sihanouk, who had been exiled to China, backed the PKK's struggle against Lon Nol and the Khmer Republic. With the PKK receiving China's support and an imminent victory for North Vietnam in the Vietnam war, the United States Congress terminated all military assistance to Cambodia in early 1975. The PKK's army, now numbering up to 60,000, decided to besiege the capital, Phnom Penh. It succeeded in February 1975 when it blockaded the Mekong River to prevent supplies from reaching the city.

All Americans were evacuated from the country on April 15; two days later Democratic Kampuchea was proclaimed. However, it was not until September 1977 that Pol Pot, prime minister and party secretary of Democratic Kampuchea, spoke of the post-victory period and the role of the PKK in the revolution. He stated that it was a period of "Socialist revolution, Socialist construction and defense of Democratic Kampuchea." For more than a year until then it was not clear what the revolution's ideology had really been.

In the wake of the Communist revolution, the party leadership, lacking a trained, educated cadre, decided to "reconstruct" an "egalitarian" Cambodian society from "ground zero." In order to establish this revolutionary order, it deliberately increased the country's diplomatic isolation and emptied all the major urban centers (even Phnom Penh, which had had a population of up to 3 million). Out of fear of contamination from anything "western" or "elite," the government proceeded to kill all the educated officials and supporters of Cambodia's previous régimes. The country's situation deteriorated as the Khmer Rouge forced people to cultivate the "killing fields" and ruled as a totalitarian régime.

The revolution's ideology quickly became clear: absolute independence and self-reliance, continuation of totalitarian rule over the country, an economic "agrarian" revolution and a social revolution of Khmer values. The national anthem of Angkar, as the government was known, reflected these revolutionary ideals:

> The red, red blood splatters the cities and plains of the Cambodian fatherland.
>
> The sublime blood of the workers and peasants,
>
> The blood of revolutionary combatants of both sexes.
>
> The blood spills out in great indignation and a resolute urge to fight.
>
> 17 April, that day under the revolutionary flag
>
> The blood certainly liberates us from slavery.

The country slipped into a state of massive human suffering. After Democratic Kampuchea began a crusade against ethnic minorities, including the Cham and Khmer-Vietnamese, and after military excursions into Vietnamese territory by Cambodia, the Vietnamese government decided to invade. Occupying the country in less than a month, the Vietnamese set up a puppet régime on January 7, 1979. The Khmer Rouge were forced back into guerrilla warfare along the Thai-Cambodia border, and the horrors of Democratic Kampuchea were revealed to the world. However, 10 years later the Vietnamese withdrew and the Khmer Rouge, emerging from the jungle, continued its campaign of terror while at the same time holding talks regarding the possibility of gaining the government.

KHODZHAYEV, FAYZULLA (1896–1938) Uzbek BOLSHEVIK revolutionary. Influenced by the *Jadidist* (Innovators) movement against religious conservatism, this son of a wealthy Bukharan family became a founder of the underground radical Young Bukhara movement.

In 1918–1919 he was the movement representative in Moscow. In September 1920 the Bolsheviks conquered Bukhara and Khodzhayev headed the revolutionary committee ruling the area. The Young Bukharans then joined the Bukharan Communist party.

With the admission of Uzbekistan to the USSR in 1924, Khodzhayev became chairman of the Council of People's Commissars, holding the post until his arrest as a Trotskyite in 1937.

KHOMEINI, AYATOLLAH SAYYID RUHOLAH MUSSAUI (1900–1989) Iranian Muslim-Shiite spiritual and political leader of the Islamic Revolution of 1979 (see IRAN, REVOLTS AND REVOLUTIONS). Born in Khomein in the Isfahan region to a clergyman who was murdered when Khomeini was five months old, at the age of six he knew the Qur'an by heart. In 1917 he began studying theology with his brother, the Ayatollah Murteza Rasandideh, and from 1921 he studied in Qom, Iran. He completed his studies in 1926 and began his career as an Islamic cleric. He soon gained a reputation as a brilliant teacher of theology.

In the early 1940s he published his first book, *The Key to Secrets*, and continued to teach at the Greater Fayzieh seminary. Khomeini was drawn into Islamic political activities, e.g., campaigns against a law which allowed non-Muslims to run for local councils and women to vote. That law was cancelled, but the shah's reforms, known as the WHITE REVOLUTION, caused further protests from the clerical leadership. After harsh measures to suppress dissent, the protests escalated, from about March 1963, into a violent anti-shah movement. After the death of the top Shiite leader, Ayatollah Borujerdi, in 1962, Khomeini succeeded him. He was arrested and was exiled in 1964, moving to Turkey and then to Iraq, while directing the struggle against the shah from his exile.

It was during the years of exile that Khomeini's image, as it was to become known to the world, crystallized. Beetle-browed and unsmiling, with a white beard, he lived off figs and yogurt, spent hours each day in prayer and meditation, and abstained from sexual intercourse. In 1977 he started calling himself "Imam"—the highest, most sacred appellation for Shiite Islam, not applied to anyone for many centuries—and ordered an escalation of the Islamic revolution. The Iraqis considered his activities dangerous and expelled him. In 1978 he was granted refuge in France and set up headquarters near Paris. The shah's régime collapsed in late 1978–early 1979 and Khomeini triumphantly returned to Tehran in February 1979 and took over the supreme leadership of Iran. At first, he set up a provisional government headed by MEHDI BAZARGAN. The following month, Khomeini proclaimed the foundation of the Islamic Republic, which would be based on the ideology of pure Islam as interpreted by

Khomeini returning to Iran during the Revolution of 1979

him and his followers, and which would provide remedies to all of society's ills. The republic would be led by the masters of Islamic religious law and jurisprudence (*Wilayat al-Faqih*). According to Khomeini's book, *Hokamat-e-Islami* (Islamic governance), of 1970, the clerical leaders, whom he saw as the legitimate rulers, should guide the affairs of state (e.g., lay down guidelines for the country in their Friday sermons). A new constitution reflecting these principles was endorsed by plebiscite in December 1979. Khomeini himself was the undisputed "Savant Guide" (*Wali Fagih*) or "Revolutionary Leader" (*Rebber*), above the institutions of state and government.

As Imam, Khomeini was the ultimate arbiter of all issues in doubt or dispute: the constant factional wrangle between hardliners and "moderates" within the new political and religious establishment, the division of powers between the various government institutions and councils of Guardians and of Experts, and the problem of determining his successor. In June 1981 he dismissed President ABOLHASSAN BANI-SADR (he formally "guided" Parliament to vote him unfit) and saw to it that the new head of state would be a man fully loyal to him. Attempting to export his Islamic revolution, he ruled Iran with little internal threat for 10 years.

KHRUSHCHEV, NIKITA SERGEYEVICH   (1894–1971)
Soviet Communist leader. Born into a poor peasant family in the Kursk region of Russia, Khrushchev grew up in the Donbass settlement of Iuzovka in the Ukraine where his father mined coal, first to augment the family income in the winters and later as a profession. Khrushchev was apprenticed in a mine equipment factory where he learned technical trades and grew up with a working class consciousness.

In March 1917, his fellow workers elected him a delegate to the regional soviet, where he met LAZAR KAGANOVICH, who was to be his first political patron and whose style of administration Khrushchev copied. In January 1918, Khrushchev joined the BOLSHEVIKS and enlisted as a political commissar in a Red Guard regiment, serving in the civil war. Returning to Iuzovka, he enrolled in the Workers' Faculty (*Rabfak*) where he gained a higher technical education. During this time he was the Communist party secretary of the *Rabfak*.

After graduation, Khrushchev served as Communist party organizer of a district near Iuzovka until coopted for party work, first in Kharkov under Kaganovich and later in Kiev. In 1929 he enrolled in the Bauman Technical Institute in Moscow, where he again served as Communist party secretary of his class. In 1931 he was elected party secretary of the Bauman district and by 1935 had risen to First Secretary of the Moscow region party committee. In this capacity, he supervised the beginnings of the Stalinist purges in the party.

In 1938 he became First Secretary of the Communist party of the Ukraine, carrying out the purge of the party and implementing the annexation and Sovietization of West Ukraine at the end of 1939. During this period, Khrushchev became a candidate and then later a full member of the Politburo.

From 1941 to 1945 Khrushchev was a political commissar in the Red Army, serving on the southwest front in Ukraine and at Stalingrad. After the war he once again served as Communist party chief of the Ukraine, except for a brief period during which Kaganovich was sent from Moscow and Khrushchev be-

came head of the Ukrainian government. This was a difficult period of rebuilding Communist party control, putting down a Ukrainian nationalist insurgency in western Ukraine and reviving a ruined economy. Toward the end of 1949 Khrushchev returned to Moscow as a secretary of the central committee.

In the succession to power after STALIN's death in 1953, Khrushchev became senior secretary of the central committee and in September was officially named First Secretary. He then proceeded to oust his competitors in the Politburo, pushing through a policy of repudiating many of Stalin's policies—both domestic and foreign—as well as of the dead dictator himself. In doing so, Khrushchev claimed to be returning to the "Leninist principles" which he said he had absorbed in the early years of the revolution. While Khrushchev's reforms included a measure of cultural and political reform within the Soviet Union, he harshly repressed Polish and Hungarian attempts to determine their own political courses. His policies included an improvement in the food supply and housing for the consumer sector and mass mobilization of citizens on a volunteer basis for everything from agricultural settlement in northern Kazakhstan and western Siberia to weekend campaigns of cleanup and beautification in rundown housing projects. In addition, he mobilized citizens into government and Communist party affairs, partly as a realization of "the withering away of the state" and partly to overcome political and bureaucratic resistance to his reforms.

In October 1964, Khrushchev's Politburo colleagues, with the support of the party and government apparatus, deposed him from his party and government posts, sending him into retirement. Khrushchev's revenge was to dictate memoirs that were later published outside the Soviet Union. Several of his reforms presaged the *perestroika* of the Gorbachev régime.

The genial face of Communism: Nikita Khrushchev, 1959

KIKUYU CENTRAL ASSOCIATION (KCA) The Kikuyu Central Association was founded in 1924 in Kenya. It continued the radical trend in Kenyan African politics but was limited to one tribe, the Kikuyu.

The Kikuyu Central Association demanded power for the educated Kikuyu elite, who objected to the established tribal institutions that cooperated with the British. Its aims were the release of land confiscated by the British, and civil rights for the Africans, including the right to associate and form organizations. It demanded the appointment of one paramount chief for the whole Kikuyu tribe, improvements in health services and freedom to grow coffee. It also wanted the use of the Kikuyu language in official correspondence. It opposed self-rule under the whites and also objected to the federation of east Africa. The association also fought European missionary attempts to stop female circumcision.

KILANI, RASHID 'ALI (1892–1965) Iraqi politician. Prime minister 1933, 1940, 1941. Born in Baghdad, scion of a leading Muslim Sunni family, Kilani graduated from the Baghdad Law School. After serving briefly as a judge, he soon became active in politics. He first joined the government in 1924 as minister of justice and then minister of the interior (1925–1928). In 1931 he co-founded the nationalist *al-Ikla' al-Watani* (National Brotherhood) party which rejected the terms of the Anglo-Iraqi Treaty of 1930. In 1933 he became prime minister for the first time, for half a year. He then served as minister of interior in 1935–1936 and in December 1938 became Chief of the Royal Cabinet.

Strongly nationalist and anti-British, Kilani saw World War II as an opportunity to complete Iraq's independence by fully emancipating it from British influence. He was at first cautious and hesitant as to the means to oust Britain and deny it the facilities which Iraq was obliged, under the Treaty of 1930, to put at its disposal. The ex-Mufti of Jerusalem, HAJJ AMIN AL-HUSSEINI, then in Baghdad, encouraged him, and the group of anti-British and pro-German colonels then de facto ruling Iraq behind the scenes (the "Golden Square"), saw him as a potential instrument of its policies and projected him into the premiership in March 1940, with the help of some of the older politicians of other factions. In January 1941 he had to cede the premiership because of factional intrigues, but in April 1941 he was reinstated as prime minister in what amounted to a semi-coup by the colonels. In the grave crisis that followed—an attempt to deny facilities and services to the British that led to military operations against Britain, a call for German help, the dismissal and replacement of the pro-British Regent and a purge of his supporters and the Hashemite-loyal and pro-British political establishment—Kilani was little more than a puppet. When his rebellious government and its forces were defeated by the British at the end of May, he fled with those who had placed him in power. He went to Germany, where he served the Nazi war effort as a leading Arab collaborator and propagandist.

After the war, Kilani lived as an exile in Saudi Arabia and Egypt. After the Iraqi coup of July 1958 he hoped that ABDUL KARIM QASSEM'S revolutionary régime would turn Pan-Arab-nationalist and Nasserist and offer him an honored place among its leaders, so he returned to Iraq in September 1958. His hopes were, however, soon disappointed and he was also concerned by what he saw as the "leftist" turn of the new régime. He became involved with Nasserist plotters, or gave his name to their attempts, and was arrested. In July 1959 it was announced that he had been sentenced to death in a secret trial in December 1958. He was, however, granted a reprieve and in July 1961 was released from prison. He played no further part in public life.

KING, MARTIN LUTHER JR. (1929–1968) Martin Luther King Jr. was the most prominent leader in the American civil rights movement in the 1950s and 1960s. Together with MAHATMA GANDHI, he served as one of the world's most influential models of the effectiveness of nonviolent means in achieving revolutionary ends.

Ironically, King's nonviolent campaign was viewed, on the one hand, by conservative opponents as insurgence while on the other hand his revolutionary achievements did not prevent continuous criticism by extremists of his alleged conformity and compliance. A more tragic irony was the striking contrast between King's gospel of non-violent disobedience and the extent of the violence that was directed against him: he was beaten, jailed, his house bombed, his life threatened time after time and then violently taken by an assassin in 1968.

King was born in Atlanta, Georgia, in 1929. He attended Morehouse College in Atlanta, then the Crozer Theological Seminary in Pennsylvania and Boston University. From the latter institution he received a Ph.D. in theology on the strength of a dissertation which subsequently became controversial. In 1954, prior to completing his degree, he was installed as a Baptist pastor in Montgomery, Alabama.

Shortly after his installation, Montgomery became the site of a major civil rights controversy, focusing on race segregation in the public transport system. Rosa Parks, a civil rights activist, was jailed for disobeying the local law of segregation in buses and the Afro-American community responded by boycotting the public transport system. The young minister became the leader of a nationally publicized campaign, as president of the Montgomery Improvement Association. In the aftermath of the struggle, the Supreme Court ruled Alabama's segregation laws unconstitutional and King emerged as a civil rights leader of national stature.

His next move was to spread the cause and the tactics of his Montgomery campaign throughout the South. In 1957, he was active in the founding of the Southern Christian Leadership Conference (SCLC) and was named its president. Under King's leadership, the organization campaigned for full implementation of Afro-American voting and political rights, for the eradication of social segregation in the South and for full social equality in the North. In the course of this struggle, the young leader perfected his theory of active, but not violent, resistance to discrimination.

With all his efforts to spread protest through SCLC activities in the early 1960s, it was the rank and file of the Afro-American community which ignited mass-protest activities. King, however, gave his blessing to organizations more extreme than his own, such as the Student Non-Violent Coordinating Committee, the real leaders of the great marches and sit-ins, the most notable of which took place in Atlanta (1960), Albany, Georgia (1961–1962) and Birmingham (1963). But it was King who organized the most notable expression of mass protest of the period: the march on Washington on August 28, 1963. The march, which drew 250,000 protesters to the capital, culminated in a mass convention at the foot of the Lincoln Memorial. From the steps of the memorial, King delivered his most memorable and eloquent plea for equality and justice—the "I have a dream" oration.

This Washington march was the most effective testimony to the effect of nonviolent mass action to further the civil rights cause. Its profound effect was represented in the legislation of the comprehensive Civil Rights Acts of 1964. King's role in the protest movement received international recognition by his being awarded the Nobel Peace Prize that same year. Yet the international recognition did not reflect King's faltering position in the protest movement. His moderation was coming under increasing criticism from more radical leaders such as MALCOLM X and Stokely Carmichael. Moreover, the support and sympathy he had formerly received from the Kennedy administration had gradually eroded and finally turned into overt hostility. King's public criticism of America's involvement in Vietnam and his "poor people's campaign" for an economic reordering of priorities and for profound change in social welfare policies brought him into conflict with the Johnson administration and in particular with J. Edgar Hoover and his FBI.

It was a lone assassin, James Early Ray, who ended King's life in 1968. His martyrdom and the void he left in the leadership of the Afro-American community and the civil rights campaign put the opposition to, and criticism of, Martin Luther King in proper perspective. A retrospective tribute to his achievements was the 1986 proclamation of his birthday as a federal holiday.

Martin Luther King leading a protest march

KIRALY, BELA (1912–) Hungarian soldier, politician and historian. A graduate of the elite Ludovika military academy and a general staff officer, Kiraly crossed over to the Soviet side in 1944, abandoning a rapid career in the Hungarian military hierarchy. In 1951, as commander of the military academy, he was arrested for "antistate conspiracy" and sentenced to death. Freed in 1956 before the Hungarian revolution, in October he became the head of the national guard and in fact headed the military opposition both as commander and as the head of security in the short-lived revolutionary government suppressed by the Soviet invasion of November 4, 1956. He then left for Austria and in 1957 settled in the United States, obtained a Ph.D. from Colum-

bia, led several Hungarian organizations in exile and became a prolific writer and editor of academic studies related to Hungary's and Eastern Europe's fate. After the demise of the Communist régime in Hungary in 1990, he returned home for a brief career as a nonparty politician. Later, disappointed by the realities of post-communism, he moved back to the US.

KIS, JANOS (1943–) Leading Hungarian dissident in the later stages of the Communist régime, philosopher, social critic and politician. Educated in philosophy at the University of Budapest, in 1973 he was expelled from the Institute of Philosophy of the Hungarian Academy of Sciences, and prohibited from publishing. For a while he worked as a free-lance translator and later became one of the early founders and leaders of the democratic opposition to the Communist régime. In 1981 he became editor of the influential *samizdat* publication, *Beszelo*. His main theme was the need for organization outside the Communist system, as the régime is unable to reform itself. Kis became one of the top influential intellectual voices criticizing the régime, building up the liberal opposition. In 1988–1989 he served as visiting professor at the New School for Social Research, New York. After 1988 he continued to hold leading roles, including that of spokesman of the SzDSz (Alliance of Free Democrats), and president of the party. Among his publications are *For a Democratic Alternative* (1989, in English) and *Do We Have Human Rights?* (1986).

KO LAO HUI see GE LAO HUI.

KOLLONTAY, ALEKSANDRA MIKHAILOVNA (1872–1952) Soviet revolutionary, author and diplomat. A general's daughter, Kollontay became a revolutionary in 1908 and lived abroad until 1917. In 1920 she opposed the government's attempt to take over control of the trade unions but was defeated by LENIN. She later served as ambassador to Norway (1923–1930) and Sweden (1930–1945), where she took part in negotiating the Finnish-Russian armistice of 1944. She is remembered as an advocate of free love, on which she wrote extensively, and one of her lovers is reputed to have been STALIN.

KOREA, SOUTH, 1960–1961 COUP OF In the presidential elections of March 1960, Syngman Rhee, president of the Republic of Korea from 1948, announced another victory for himself. Opponents of his régime claimed that the elections had been rigged and even the normally supportive US government condemned the increasingly repressive measures of what had become an authoritarian régime. In the APRIL REVOLUTION, Korean students took to the streets to demonstrate against Rhee and on April 26 the president resigned. The National Assembly thereupon reduced the office of president to a largely ceremonial position. In a special election held in July, Chang Myun's Democratic party won by a large margin. The economy continued to deteriorate, however, and there were further demonstrations. Chang Myun had been prime minister for less than a year when, on May 16, 1961, a coup engineered by high-ranking military officers and led by Major General PARK CHUNG HEE succeeded in setting up an interim military government. The 1962 constitution ratified shortly thereafter reestablished a strong civilian presidency.

KOSCIUSZKO, TADEUSZ ANDRZEI BONAWENTURA

(1746–1817) Polish nationalist statesman and soldier. Born into a noble family in the village of Mereczowszczyno, Kosciuszko early developed a fierce love for his native country and a wish to see it free from foreign domination. He opted for a career in the army, beginning his military education in the Warsaw Corps of cadets, where he specialized in military architecture and the construction of fortifications. Outstandingly talented, he was chosen to go to Paris to further develop his skills as an architect and draftsman. In 1772, during his absence, Austria, Russia and Prussia cooperated in a tripartite partition of Poland.

Kosciuszko returned to Poland in 1774, but was forced to flee the country two years later to escape the wrath of General Josef Sosnowski, with whose daughter he had unsuccessfully attempted to elope after being engaged as her art teacher. He traveled to America, where he was inspired by the aims and ideals of the AMERICAN REVOLUTION. He sympathized with the country's desire for sovereign statehood, and offered his services to the US forces in their war against Britain. Between 1778 and 1780 he was able to put his theoretical training to practical use, supervising the fortification of the West Point military academy. He later served as an engineer and cavalry officer, and by war's end had risen to the rank of brigadier general, being granted US citizenship in recognition of his contribution to the country. Despite having acquired a substantial estate in the United States, as an ardent Polish nationalist he chose to go back to his homeland, which continued to suffer the depredations of the land-hungry great powers that surrounded it.

On his return in 1784, Kosciuszko was unable to secure a position in the Polish army due to his association with antimonarchist elements, and was reduced to living in near-poverty on his small country estate, awaiting the opportunity to participate in the struggle to reassert Poland's independent statehood. At this time, he demonstrated his liberal convictions by freeing his own serfs from part of their villein duty, despite the additional hardship this caused him.

The institution of liberal reforms in Poland in 1789 coincided with the FRENCH REVOLUTION and heralded Kosciuszko's return to military service, assisted by the patronage of his old sweetheart, Ludwika Sosnowski, who was now married to the influential Prince Lubomirski. Kosciuszko rose to fame in Poland through his spirited leadership of Polish troops opposing Catherine the Great's Russian forces, the latter having invaded Poland in 1792 in an effort to suppress the reformist constitution adopted there in 1791. However, despite his defeat of the invading forces at the Battle of Dubianka, he was unable to resist the Russians' superior forces indefinitely. Catherine's troops completed the occupation and, with King Stanislaw II forced to renounce his reform program, Kosciuszko went into exile in France, from where he plotted insurrection to restore Polish sovereignty.

The Polish Uprising of 1794 (see POLAND, REVOLTS AND REVOLUTIONS), which Kosciuszko returned to lead and organize, enjoyed great popular support but was hampered by a lack of adequate weapons in the face of well-equipped professional opponents. Kosciuszko nevertheless managed to inflict a defeat on the Russians at Raclawice, with a force consisting largely of hurriedly-recruited peasants brandishing a motley assortment of agricultural implements. Later, leading the defense of a besieged Warsaw, he was able to enlist the aid of the civilian population in resisting the enemy by building defensive earthworks. Even during such a period of crisis, he found time to institute liberalizing reforms: his Polaniec Proclamation declared Poland's long-indentured serfs free. Despite the desperate heroism of his Polish men, Kosciuszko was for a second time faced with having to bow to superior might; the defeat of Poland's nationalists at Maciejowice and Kosciuszko's capture signaled the collapse of the rebellion and the final partition of Poland.

Released from the Peter-Paul fortress in St. Petersburg in 1797, Kosciuszko was unable to realize his deep-seated desire to live to see a free Poland. After his death, his remains were transferred to Cracow Cathedral, where they were buried alongside those of Poland's kings.

KOSSUTH, LAJOS

(1808–1894) Hungarian statesman, patriot and revolutionary hero. Kossuth's family was of old noble stock but landless and penniless. Graduating in 1821 from a Calvinist law school, he practiced law and served as a junior official in his native country between 1824 and 1832.

In 1832, Kossuth was sent by his employer, Countess Andrassy, to the National Diet in Pozsany to appear as a substitute delegate for one of her relatives. At the Diet, Kossuth was captivated by the liberal ideas of Hungary's new reformers, who aimed to overthrow the absolutist system under which Hungary was ruled from Vienna. It was in this atmosphere that he developed his own liberal and nationalist program. Although not entitled to participate in Diet debates, he devised his own method of influencing Hungarian politics by issuing bulletins of the Diet's meetings. These bulletins were not verbatim reports but overt political messages which were circulated throughout Hungary. They were greeted with instant success. In 1836, after the end of the Diet session, Kossuth was invited to report on Hungary's county assemblies. However, he was no longer protected by parliamentary immunity. Judging him seditious, the authorities sentenced him in 1837 to four years in prison. Freed three years later, he became editor of *Pesti Hirlap* (Pest News) and created Hungary's first political newspaper. His articles and political radicalism angered the authorities, who eventually engineered his dismissal from the newspaper.

Kossuth attempted to continue his struggle through other means, and sought to create several associations for the development and protection of Hungary's industry, with the aim of achieving greater economic independence for the country. Although doomed to failure, his associations allowed him to maintain a public profile as a populist hero. In 1847 he was elected to the Diet at Pozsany as leader of the National Opposition. Inspired by the French and Italian REVOLUTIONS OF 1848, the Hungarian reformers conducted a bloodless revolution in March of that year. They demanded and received civil rights, emancipation of the peasantry, the abolition of privilege, and independence from Austria. Kossuth, with his legal knowledge and fiery oratory, played a decisive role, and when, in April, Hungary was granted a separate government, he was appointed minister of finance in Hungary's first constitutional cabinet.

Kossuth intensified his anti-Austrian campaign. His principles were liberal, but his nationalism was opposed to the fulfillment of the ambitions of the Slavic, Romanian and German minorities in Hungary, and he was particularly resented in Croatia. When the Austrians encouraged the Croat army to prepare to move against Hungary, Kossuth became head of the Hungarian Government of National Defense. Before the advance of the Austrians, his government withdrew to Debrecen, where he organized the brilliant spring campaign that drove the Austrians out of Hungary. In April 1849, the Hungarian parliament declared Hungary an independent republic and acclaimed Kossuth governor-president.

Victory was, however, short-lived. Russian troops intervened in favor of Austria and Kossuth was forced to resign the government to General Artur Gorgey, his arch-rival. Two days later, Gorgey surrendered to the Russians and Kossuth fled to Turkey. He visited England and the United States and was received as a champion of liberty. However, he could not raise official support for his cause. Returning to western Europe, he spent the rest of his life in impoverished exile, plotting a new revolution in Hungary, after having refused an offer of amnesty in 1890. He died in Turin, Italy. His body was returned to Budapest and he was buried in state. After his death, Kossuth remained a popular hero, his name forever linked with Hungary's struggle for national independence and civil rights.

Kossuth calling his fellow-Hungarians to arms

KOSTOV, TRAYCHO (1897–1949) Bulgarian Communist leader. Born in Sofia, Kostov was active in the Communist movement from the 1920s on. Involved in various underground activities, known as an excellent organizer and a purger of "leftist deviationists" within his own party, he was jailed and later exiled by the interwar government.

Returning from exile in the Soviet Union, between 1944 and 1949 Kostov climbed rapidly in the party hierarchy, reaching the highest position of First Secretary of the Bulgarian Communist party. His decline began in March 1948, and in March 1949 he was removed from all party and government posts. A victim of the Stalinist purges, he was accused of "nationalist deviation" and of being a police agent of the previous régime. At his trial he denounced his "confession," but this did not save him from

being executed in June 1949. From 1978 on, as part of the process of de-Stalinization, he was gradually rehabilitated and his *Selected Works* were published.

KOUNTCHÉ, SEYNI (1931–1987) A Nigerian soldier, Kountché received his military training in Mali, Senegal and France. He was chief of staff of the Nigerian army from 1973–1974 and in 1974 was promoted to lieutenant colonel.

The drought of 1969–1974 and the falling world price for ground nuts—Niger's main export—caused a catastrophic economic situation in the country. There were accusations of corruption and food-hoarding at the highest government levels. In April 1974, Kountché led a coup which overthrew President Hamani Dion, who—together with his *Parti progressiste nigérien* (PPN)—had ruled Niger since independence from France in 1960. After the coup, stocks of food were found in the homes of some of Dion's ministers.

Kountché became the new president of Niger and set up a Supreme Military Council (CMS), which he headed, to rule the country. The military government's main preoccupation was planning economic recovery and rooting out corruption in public life. Good relations with France, which Dion had favored, were maintained, but the USA became Niger's principal donor.

From 1981 onwards, Kountché gradually began to increase civilian representation in the CMS. In 1982, preparations were made for a constitutional form of government. In 1983, Kountché appointed a civilian prime minister but was himself promoted to major general. In November 1987, after a year of ill-health, Kountché died, aged 56.

KOXINGA see ZHENG CHENGGONG.

KRASIN, LEONID BORISOVICH (1870–1926) Russian revolutionary electrical engineer and diplomat. While studying engineering at the St. Petersburg Technical Institute, Krasin also studied MARXISM and engaged in revolutionary agitation. For this he was arrested and exiled several times in the 1890s. He joined the Social Democratic Workers' party of Russia when it was founded in 1898. From 1900 to 1904 he was engaged in engineering work in Baku, but simultaneously organized revolutionary propaganda, constructing and operating a BOLSHEVIK clandestine press.

From 1905 to 1908 he designed and supervised the installation of St. Petersburg's electrical system. During this period, as a member of the Bolshevik central committee, he participated in planning an armed revolutionary uprising against the autocracy. As a reputable engineer, he was also LENIN's liaison to affluent circles contributing to the Bolsheviks, while at the same time organizing the controversial Bolshevik campaign of bank robberies to finance party work. Jailed briefly in 1908, he emigrated to Berlin where he worked for the Siemens company, returning to Russia in 1913 as director of its St. Petersburg affiliate.

During World War I Krasin adopted a patriotic stance, leaving the Bolsheviks. He was active in a war industries commission and became a director of an arms plant and a bank. After the Bolshevik seizure of power in October 1917, Krasin rejoined the party. He negotiated the economic terms of the Brest-Litovsk Treaty, organized military supply during the civil war and served as People's Commissar for Trade and Industry. In

1919, he negotiated the peace treaty between Soviet Russia and Estonia. In 1921, as head of the Soviet economic mission in London, Krasin negotiated a British-Soviet trade agreement, and participated in the Genoa Conference, marking Soviet Russia's re-entry into the international community. After a brief stint as People's Commissar for Foreign Trade he served as Soviet ambassador in Paris and then London, where he died.

KREMER, ARKADI (1865–1935) Polish-Jewish revolutionary. Born in Vilna, Kremer became a revolutionary while studying mathematics and engineering in St. Petersburg. After a period of arrest and exile he returned to Vilna in 1890 and became one of the prominent Marxists. He played a central role in the creation in 1897 of the General Jewish Workers Alliance of Lithuania, Poland and Russia—the BUND. As Bund representative, Kremer was one of nine Marxist delegates who created the Social Democratic Workers' party of Russia in Minsk in March 1898. Imprisoned briefly in the autumn of 1898, Kremer emigrated, serving in Europe as emissary of the Bund's committee abroad. He returned to Russia in 1905, to serve in the Petrograd Soviet and to lead Bund activities. Arrested in 1907, he ceased to be a professional revolutionary although he remained an active Bund member. He emigrated to France in 1912 and remained there throughout World War I and the revolutionary period in Russia. Only in 1921 did he return to Poland, where he taught mathematics and was active in Bund affairs until his death.

KRIM, BELKACEM (1922–1970) Algerian nationalist. After serving in the French army during World War II, Krim returned to his native Kabylia province, Algeria, and joined the MTLD (MOUVEMENT POUR LE TRIOMPHE DES LIBERTÉS DÉMOCRATIQUES— Movement for the Triumph of Democratic Liberties), traveling extensively throughout the countryside to promote Algerian independence. The MTLD was then split into two wings: the PPA (*Parti du Peuple Algerien*—Algerian People's Party), a political organization, and its paramilitary affiliate, the OS (ORGANISATION SPECIALE—Special Organization), comprised mainly of MTLD members who believed that armed revolt was necessary to expel the French from the country. Krim belonged to both factions; he became a fugitive in 1947 after being sentenced to death in absentia for assassinating a forest ranger.

As renegade leader of the OS in Kabylia, Krim scored some spectacular successes against the colonial authorities. He operated in both urban and rural settings, destroying roads, cutting phone lines, ruining European crops and eliminating informers and collaborators. The government always responded with harsh reprisals, but Krim and his followers always escaped before the French arrived. The civilian population was usually punished for these acts of terror, but this only embittered them further against the French and made them more supportive of the nationalists' objectives. This policy was imitated by other provincial leaders of the OS and was later adopted by the FLN (FRONT DE LIBERATION NATIONAL—National Liberation Front).

Despite its successes, internal dissension at the leadership level was threatening the unity of the MTLD. In 1954, Krim and eight others became the "historic leaders" of a new group, CRUA (COMITÉ RÉVOLUTIONNAIRE D'UNITE ET D'ACTION—Revolutionary Committee of Unity and Action), founded as a result of these tensions. As leader of his native Kabylia province, he participated in a series of clandestine meetings held from March to October 1954, during which it was decided to take up arms against the French. The rebellion was scheduled to begin at 1 a.m. on the morning of November 1, All Saints Day. Immediately before the revolt began, the CRUA was divided into two parallel organizations: the FLN, a political organization, and the ALN (*Armée de Liberation Nationale*—National Liberation Army), its military wing.

The National Council of the Algerian Revolution was formed in August 1956, with Krim as a full member; he was also one of five members of the secret *Comité de Co-ordination et Execution* (CCE—Committee of Coordination and Implementation). It was in this capacity that he helped mastermind the Battle of Algiers, a year-long terrorism campaign that shook the colonial capital in 1956–1957. He then fled to Cairo with the CRUA leadership, where they declared the provisional government of the Algerian republic. Krim served in several capacities in this government—as minister of war, foreign affairs and the interior. In 1962, he led the Algerian delegation to the Evian conference, where the French agreed to Algerian independence. He succeeded in winning many major concessions from the French, including the abandonment of a partition proposal; this staved off French support for the creation of two states, one Arab and one Berber, and fostered the formation of an Algerian national, rather than an Islamic Arab state. Krim also made several concessions, including the continuation of a French military and nuclear presence in Algeria.

After independence in 1962, the tasks of nation-building seemed beyond the capacity of the divided FLN elite. Krim opposed BEN-BELLA's ruling coalition and in 1965 found himself accused of plotting to overthrow Algerian strongman HOUARI BOUMEDIENNE. Although these charges remained unsubstantiated, a weak opposition movement, the MDRA (*Mouvement Démocratique de Renouveau Algerien*—Democratic Movement for Algerian Renewal), did coalesce around him. Sentenced to death, Krim fled to Europe, where he was assassinated in 1970, apparently by agents of the Algerian secret service.

KRONSTADT REBELLION (March 1921) Early in 1921, hunger and harsh labor regulations imposed by the BOLSHEVIK government led to unrest among the population of the Soviet town of Kronstadt on the Gulf of Finland. There was an uprising among the sailors of the naval base there—who three and a half years earlier had played a decisive role in bringing the Bolsheviks to power—demanding economic reforms as well as political freedom and civil rights. A force led by TROTSKY crushed the rebellion with much bloodshed. However, the revolt had the effect of persuading the Bolsheviks that the time had come to relent, whereupon the New Economic Policy (NEP), which allowed a limited amount of capitalism, was introduced.

KROPOTKIN, PETER (1842–1921) Russian geologist and founder of anarchist communism. Born in Dmitrov, near Moscow, Kropotkin was the son of a high-ranking officer, a descendant of the princes of Kiev. He was educated in the Corps of Pages, the most exclusive military school in Russia, on the recommendation of Czar Nicholas I. His academic brilliance won him the honor of serving as the personal page of Czar Alexander II for a year.

Yet status was not enough for the young Kropotkin. In 1862 he left for Siberia where, despite his family's disapproval, he elected to join the unfashionable regiment of the Mounted Cossacks. In Moscow he had acquired liberal views and he hoped that in Siberia he would be able to participate in the political reforms which had followed the emancipation of the serfs in 1861. His inspection of Siberia's penal system, a duty assigned to him by the governor of Transbaikalia, awakened him to the inhumanity of autocratic government. Through his acquaintance with the political prisoners, he began to acquire more radical ideas and was introduced to PIERRE-JOSEPH PROUDHON's *Economic Contradictions*.

Siberia also provided him with the opportunity to pursue scientific inquiries, which built him a reputation as a well-respected geographer. The execution of Polish prisoners who had attempted to escape to the Chinese coast finally induced him to resign from the army in 1867 and he headed toward St. Petersburg, where he registered in the university. However, his sense of social injustice pursued him. In 1871, when he was offered the secretaryship of the Russian Geographic Society, he refused the position in favor of a revolutionary career. In 1872, he left for Switzerland to join the growing community of Russian political exiles who had gathered there.

In Switzerland, Kropotkin mixed with the followers of both KARL MARX and MICHAEL BAKUNIN who had established branches of the First INTERNATIONAL. His meeting with James Guillaume and the anarchist watchmakers of the Jura finally converted him to anarchism, and in 1874 he set off for St. Petersburg again to advance the anarchist cause. He frequented the CHAIKOVSKY CIRCLE, the leading populist group, and disguised as the peasant Borodin took up residence in working-class quarters. He was, however, arrested and spent two years in the Peter-Paul fortress until his daring escape from a military hospital landed him back in Europe.

Kropotkin resided for the most part in Switzerland, until the Russian ambassador requested his expulsion shortly after the assassination of Alexander II in 1881. During this period, he became one of the most renowned figures in the international anarchist movement. These were his most active years, and he edited two journals, *L'Avant Garde* and *Le Revolte*, the latter becoming the most influential anarchist organ since Proudhon's *Le Peuple*. At the height of his radicalism in 1880, Kropotkin wrote, "Permanent revolt by word of mouth, in writing, by the dagger, the rifle, dynamite . . . Everything is good which falls outside legality." In later years, he retracted such views.

In 1881, Kropotkin moved to France, where anarchism had sown strong roots among the Lyon workers. Two years later Kropotkin was arrested on charges of having incited strikes which had resulted in a riot among the miners of Montceau. Finally in 1886, pressure exerted by such impressive figures as George Clemenceau and Victor Hugo obtained his release. He left for England, where he remained until the RUSSIAN REVOLUTION OF 1917.

In England, Kropotkin led a quiet life of research and writing. Shaken by the anarchist assassinations of the last two decades of the 19th century, he reverted to the principles of the Chaikovsky Circle, emphasizing the value of the written word and rejecting the use of the dagger. His home became a meeting place for a wide range of intellectuals and English radicals, including George Bernard Shaw, Tom Mann, and Ford Madox Ford. He attended the functions of the Royal Geographical Society and had a reputation for personal integrity.

Although he had first advocated his theory of anarchist communism at the Jura congress in 1880, it was in England that he published his major works propounding this concept and extending anarchism from a political principle to a philosophy of ethics with a sound basis in scientific theory. His major works include *The Conquest of Bread* (1892), *Fields, Factories and Workshops* (1899) and *Mutual Aid* (1902). When war broke out in 1914, however, his support for the Allies alienated most of his anarchist comrades.

Kropotkin, like Proudhon and Bakunin before him, advocated a revolution which would result in a stateless society, and upon returning home in 1917 he refused to join the provisional government. Once the Bolsheviks seized power, Kropotkin, whose fame protected him from the persecution suffered by other Russian anarchists, met with VLADIMIR LENIN and vocalized his criticism of Bolshevik policies. His death in 1921 left the Russian anarchist movement unprotected against the harsh repression of the Soviet government. Yet Kropotkin's anarchist communism continued to inspire movements throughout the world and he remains today one of the most highly regarded anarchist thinkers.

KRUPSKAYA, NADEZHDA KONSTANTINOVNA (1869–1939) LENIN's wife. A revolutionary from girlhood, Krupskaya was exiled in 1898 and married Lenin in Siberia. From 1900–1917 the couple lived abroad, where Krupskaya helped found the BOLSHEVIK PARTY and worked for the party newspaper, *Iskra*. After the February RUSSIAN REVOLUTION OF 1917 they returned to Russia, where Krupskaya specialized in educational affairs. In 1923 her relations with STALIN deteriorated and in 1924 she urged Lenin to remove him from the post of party secretary-general. After Lenin's death, she joined the opposition to Stalin but disassociated herself from it in 1926, after which she took no further part in the struggle for power. She did, however, continue as a member of the party's central committee (until 1927) and as vice-commissar for education (until 1939).

KRYLENKO, NIKOLAI VASILIYEVICH (1885–1938) Soviet military and political personality. Son of a political exile, Krylenko was a student rebel leader in the RUSSIAN REVOLUTION OF 1905. He majored in history and philosophy and later studied law. In World War I he was conscripted and was arrested for organizing BOLSHEVIK antiwar propaganda. In November 1917, Krylenko was included in the commissariat of war and appointed commander in chief of the armed forces, charged with achieving an armistice.

From 1922 to 1931, as state prosecutor, he organized the first show trials. In 1932 he was appointed people's commissar of justice for the RSFSR and in 1936 for the USSR. He was arrested in the purge of 1937 and shot without a public trial.

KUANG FU HUI see GUANG FU HUI.

KU KLUX KLAN An American white supremacist racist organization which, originating in 1866, was given its present form in 1915. Boasting such bizarre titles as "Dragon" and

"Wizard" and using three drops of Jesus' blood as their symbol, clansmen have specialized in illegal action against Negroes, e.g., tarring and feathering, lynching and raping. The organization reached its greatest power during the early 1920s, when it had an alleged 4–5 million members and was a powerful factor in southern politics; during the 1930s, however, its power declined after one of its leaders was convicted of corruption and second-degree murder. The organization again attracted attention in the early 1960s, when it took part in the fight against the civil rights movement, and in 1978 when its leader visited Britain in order to establish a branch there, playing a game of hide-and-seek with Scotland Yard. Though at present possessing few members and little influence, the Ku Klux Klan clearly represents the frustrations of a white minority of psychopaths in America and would consequently appear to be in no danger of disappearing.

KUN, BELA   (1886–1937) Hungarian Communist leader. Born in a small Transylvanian town, the son of a storekeeper, Kun was educated in Kolozsvar (Cluj). Kun joined the Hungarian Social Democratic Party in 1902, working first as a journalist, then as a clerk and later as the manager of the Kolozsvar Worker's Insurance Fund. He was discharged from this job for misconduct. Kun joined the Austro-Hungarian army in 1914 and was captured by the Russians in 1916. In Russia, he joined the BOLSHEVIK PARTY and helped it organize the revolutionary movement among prisoners of war in the Tomsk camp. He met VLADIMIR LENIN in St. Petersburg in 1917. From March 1918, Kun was leader of the Hungarian group in the Russian Communist Party and edited its newspaper. From May of that year he was chairman of the International Federation of Socialist POWs. He participated in the victory over the Moscow counterrevolutionaries, fought on the Perm front and organized the international units of the RED ARMY.

In November 1918, Kun returned to Hungary, founded the COMMUNIST PARTY OF HUNGARY and its organ, *Voeroes Ujsag* (*Red Newspaper*), and wrote pamphlets. His fiery speeches led to his arrest, and he was severely beaten by the police in February 1919. However, he continued to direct the preparations for proletarian revolution from jail, and elaborated a scheme to unite the Social Democratic and Communist parties. He was liberated from prison on March 21, 1919, the day the Hungarian Soviet Republic was proclaimed, and was immediately appointed Commissar for Foreign and Military Affairs, that is, virtual leader of the government.

Calling his régime "the Dictatorship of the Proletariat," Kun nationalized banks, large businesses and estates. Ruthlessly suppressing opposition, he eliminated moderate elements in the government and exploited the wave of popular nationalism that swept the country. He created a Red Army that reconquered territory that had been lost to the Czechs and Romanians, and overran Slovakia.

However, the reaction to his régime came quickly. Soviet help failed to arrive. The peasants were alienated by the decision that private estates should be nationalized rather than distributed among them. Food distribution broke down. After initial successes, the army refused to fight, leading to its defeat at the hands of the Romanians.

Within a few months, the proletarian dictatorship fell and Kun

emigrated to Austria, where he was taken into custody and held for a short time in an asylum for the insane. He then traveled to the Soviet Union, where he was elected an executive member at the Third Congress of the Communist International, serving from 1921 to 1936 and playing a leading role in the reorganization of the Hungarian Communist Party. In connection with this work, he returned to Vienna illegally in 1928, was discovered, jailed, and then sent back to Russia. He was also active in strengthening several other Communist parties. Finally, in 1937, he was arrested during the Stalinist purges, accused of Trotskyism and executed.

At the end of World War II, when Hungary came into the Soviet orbit and Hungarian Stalinists surviving in Russia returned to organize the Communist party, Kun's name and the 1919 proletarian dictatorship became taboo. It was only after the Hungarian Uprising of 1956 (see HUNGARY, REVOLTS AND REVOLUTIONS) that he was rehabilitated. His collected writings and speeches were first published in Hungary in 1958.

KUOMINTANG see GUOMINDANG.

KURDISH REVOLT IN IRAQ   A long-term revolt with many vicissitudes, continuing from the 1920s to the present, of the frustrated national aspirations of the Kurds ever since the fall of the Ottoman Empire after World War I.

Both the European superpowers and the local Iraqi governments made promises for autonomy to the Kurds in the 1920s, yet none were fulfilled. The Barazani family led the Kurdish national movement and by the early 1940s MUSTAFA BARAZANI, who founded and headed the Kurdish Democratic party, became the leader of the Kurdish national struggle.

In the 1960s, the Kurdish revolt was on the ascent. The attempts of the Iraqi régimes to suppress the unrest were only partly successful due to the Kurds recovering financial support from Iran and Israel. The Iraqis, on their part, founded irregular Kurdish units, supported parties from tribes opposed to the Barazani family and encouraged factions like that of Jalal Talabani, who became the leading opponent to Mustafa Barazani.

During the years of the revolt, negotiations continued intermittently with the different Iraqi governments, the goal being to bring about a Kurdish-Iraqi reconciliation on the basis of a certain degree of autonomy to the Kurds. In June 1966, an agreement was formulated by the Iraqi prime minister, Bazzaz. Its failure, however, brought on a full-steam renewal of the revolt.

In the 1970s, a similar pattern took place. In March 1970 an agreement was achieved, more far-reaching in its definition of autonomy for the Kurds than the one of 1966. It recognized the Kurdish people as one of the two nations coexisting in the Iraqi state. Yet, by March 1974, the date by which the agreement was supposed to be implemented, the two sides had not reached agreement over several details, such as fixing the borders of the autonomous region. The Iraqi government one-sidedly implemented the agreement, using Kurdish collaborators and anti-Barazani factions. The revolt then rose up strongly in 1974 but collapsed in 1975, when the Iranian shah stopped the aid he had been giving the rebels. The guerrilla units were dismantled and the Kurdish leaders, including Mustafa Barazani—who died in exile in the United States in 1979—managed to escape.

In the late 1970s, the sons of Mustafa Barazani tried to revive the revolt. This attempt later gained various successes due to the aid Iran gave the Kurdish rebels after the Iraq-Iran war broke out in September 1980. This aid symbolized a turning point in the Kurdish struggle, because on the one hand the Kurds assisted an enemy of the State and were branded as traitors of the Iraqi State and, on the other hand, the Iraqi *Ba'ath* régime was helped by a foreign country—Turkey—to suppress the Kurdish revolt. In crushing the revolt, the Iraqi authorities even used chemical weapons in March 1988 against Kurdish villages.

The Gulf War in 1991 and the defeat of Iraq provided another chance for the Kurds to achieve their national objectives. The United States encouraged Kurdish elements to revolt against the Iraqi régime. This uprising and the parallel intervention of the allied forces created a safe haven for Iraqi Kurds. Yet, the Kurdish question in Iraq has not been solved and more rounds in the Iraqi-Kurdish struggle have been predicted.

KURDISH WORKERS PARTY   see PKK.

KUSKOVA, EKATERINA   (1869–1958) Russian revolutionary publicist. Kuskova began her revolutionary activity as a youth and joined the student rebels who stirred up the peasantry during the 1892 famine. She became a Marxist while studying midwifery in Moscow and, after having been arrested and exiled, emigrated in 1894.

In Berlin, Kuskova was active among the Social Democrats, adopting a "legal-Marxist" position which favored the views of the German Social-Democrat EDUARD BERNSTEIN. During an evening of ideological discussion, Kuskova jotted down her basic outlook and this was later published as the "Credo" Program, expressing the so-called "Economist" approach. This stated that workers should gain organizational experience and ideological consciousness through participating in the fight for economic rights before being introduced to the struggle for political democracy and socialism.

In the period of the RUSSIAN REVOLUTION OF 1917, Kuskova was briefly associated with the Constitutional Democratic party, helping to organize its activities. She was active in the liberal press and worked for women's rights and consumer cooperatives. In 1917, she was politically active as a liberal independent. Exiled in 1921 by the BOLSHEVIK government for her criticism of it, she lived in Switzerland until her death.

L

LAFAYETTE, MARIE JOSEPH MARQUIS DE (1757–1834) French aristocrat who distinguished himself during both the AMERICAN REVOLUTION and the FRENCH REVOLUTION. The scion of an ancient, immensely rich, aristocratic family, Lafayette arrived in Philadelphia in July 1777. Fighting under GEORGE WASHINGTON, whom he befriended, Lafayette distinguished himself at the Battle of Brandywine and later at Barren Hill. Early in 1779 he returned to France to drum up support for the revolutionaries; in April 1780 he was back in America, this time as the commander of an expeditionary army 6,000 men strong. Commanding in Virginia, he brought about the surrender of General Cornwallis at Yorktown and thus was able to play a decisive role in bringing about American independence.

Returning to France in 1784, Lafayette made himself conspicuous as the leader of the so-called liberal-aristocratic faction, a small coterie of noblemen that advocated religious toleration and the abolition of the slave trade. The outbreak of the French Revolution in 1789 found him a member of the States General; though himself a nobleman, he supported the demands of the Third Estate and later wrote the first draft of the Declaration of the Rights of Man and of the Citizen. As commander of the National Guard, in October of the same year he saved King Louis XVI and his wife from the fury of a mob that had invaded Versailles and brought them in safety to Paris, where they became hostages of the revolution.

Having thus far supported the revolution, Lafayette, fearing for his own property and that of the members of his class, started turning against it in 1790 when it became radicalized. In July 1791 he ordered his troops to fire on a mob that demanded the abdication of the king, killing or wounding approximately 50 persons. Renouncing his position as commander of the Guard, he took over command of an army at Metz and was actively plotting against the National Assembly at the time the monarchy was overthrown in August 1792.

Having saved himself from being accused of treason by defecting to the Austrians, Lafayette returned to France in 1799 and settled down to a private life. During the Restoration he was a member of the Chamber of Deputies (1814–1824) and in 1824–1825 visited the United States, where he was given a hero's welcome. July 1830 found him once again commanding the National Guard. Six months later he retired.

LAMARTINE, ALPHONSE-MARIE-LOUIS DE PRAT DE (1790–1869) France's most famous Romantic poet, but also a revolutionary statesman and politician who played a crucial part in the overthrow of the July Monarchy in February 1848 (see REVOLUTIONS OF 1848) and its dramatic aftermath. Born to an old Franche Comte aristocratic family from the Burgundian town of Macon, Lamartine grew up in the bucolic atmosphere of one of his parents' many estates. Under the influence of his father, a royalist who had been imprisoned during the FRENCH REVOLUTION, he was at first drawn to Legitimism and the intellectually rigid Catholicism he had imbibed in the Jesuit college of Bellay, even serving for a while in the royal bodyguard of Louis XVIII. But his political sympathies soon moved him in the direction of liberalism and Utopian socialism. After having tried out a career in the diplomatic service which took him to Naples and Florence and making a famous voyage to the Holy Land, he was elected as a liberal deputy to the Orleanist chamber in 1833. By then, his *Meditations Poetiques* and other collections of verse had made him France's most eminent poet, his country's equivalent of Byron, earning him a seat at the French Academy and the plaudits of the young Romantic generation. His vindication of the republican cause that had inspired the "Great Revolution," commemorated in his book on the GIRONDINS, caused a sensation in 1847 and made him the idol of the revolutionary left. In an arresting phrase uttered in a speech that he delivered before the chamber of deputies, he was able to recapture the malaise that had spread throughout the land on the eve of the outbreak of the February revolution when he declared that "France is bored."

With the proclamation of the Second Republic, in which he played a conspicuous and highly dramatic role, he became the hero of the Paris crowd and was placed in charge of the foreign ministry in the provisional government of the Second Republic. His refusal to sanction French intervention on behalf of the Polish revolution and his failure to mediate the recurring disputes between Republican and Socialist members of his cabinet shifted national attention to the social conflicts spreading throughout Paris, which he proved incapable of controlling. A lofty but not too practical view of the new society and his repeated speeches on the public good and the ideals of justice and liberty, at a time of acute social distress, were scarcely enough to contain the class tensions that were to tear the republic apart with the eruption of the June Days of the revolutions of 1848. Rather than withdraw from politics like the rest of the Republican intellectuals, Lamartine decided to run for president but was barely able to win more than 1% of the national vote against Louis Napoleon in 1849. He soon retired to private life and to more travel abroad.

An eloquent public speaker and phrase-maker of genius, Lamartine was the very embodiment of the high hopes raised throughout the rest of Europe by the example set by the Paris revolution in February 1848. Its Romantic zeal and universal appeal are admirably recaptured in his words: "When France sneezes, Europe catches cold." Reassuring his colleague LEDRU-ROLLIN, who as minister of the interior in the provisional government of the Second Republic had decided to take the gamble of introducing universal suffrage, Lamartine consoled himself with the words, "*Vox Populi, Vox Dei:* We must leave something up to Providence." Alexis de Tocqueville, another intellectual who succeeded him as foreign minister in 1849, saw in Lamartine a striking example of the French phenomenon of the intellectual in politics.

LAND AND LIBERTY (Zemlya I Volya)   Russian revolutionary political party founded in 1876 by MARK A. NATANSON, former leader of the CHAIKOVSKY CIRCLE, and Alexander D. Mikhaylov, a future leader of the PEOPLE'S WILL, in the wake of the failure of the TO THE PEOPLE movement. It used the name of a group founded 14 years earlier by radical populists which had soon petered out. The first program of Land and Liberty, formulated about demands that its members believed could be realized in the immediate future, included all land to be given to the peasants, self-determination for all national minorities and village self-government. This program also called for arousing the nation against the autocracy through revolutionary propaganda, but left the future form of government and questions of political norms and institutions to be determined by the people.

Under pressure from the young intelligentsia and the growth of industrial capitalism in Russia, a new program was adopted in 1878. Its opening declaration was, "Our ultimate economic and political ideal is anarchy and collectivism." In this program, the emphasis was on a tightly-knit revolutionary association seeking support among workers and intellectuals as well as among the peasants for the speediest possible overthrow of the autocracy. The use of terror was adopted as an instrument of vengeance against brutal régime officials and particularly against police spies and movement renegades, breaking with the earlier opposition to political violence. The emphasis on political activity, was, however, on having a presence in provincial towns and rural centers, where the population might be educated by personal example as well as by propaganda. Among the prominent populists taking part in the activities of Land and Liberty were VERA FIGNER and GEORGI PLEKHANOV. Despite the dedicated energy of its members, the party's activities were quashed by the political police and by 1879 it had no rural cells operating in any part of the Russian empire. Following VERA ZASULICH's famous attempt on the life of General Trepov, the incidence of political assassinations rose steadily until World War I, becoming a major consideration in both governmental and revolutionary politics.

Programmatic principles notwithstanding, it was only the central circle in St. Petersburg that was a closely organized camaraderie of perhaps 20 members. Other regional and local groups or individuals adhered to the party on a basis of loose association for cooperation in specific projects. The total number of adherents was probably never more than 200, only a cou-

ple of dozen of which established themselves briefly in villages. At the same time, the party's underground press printed the party's two main publications in editions of 3,000 copies each and some 400 young people took part in the first open demonstration organized by the party at the Kazan Cathedral on December 6, 1876.

The transition to violence was completed at the June 1879 Voronezh congress of the party, which decided to resolve differences of opinion regarding its political tactics, long-term objectives and above all the use of revolutionary terror. Here, in addition to changing the party's name to The People's Will (*Narodnaya Volya*), a program was adopted calling for political terror to overthrow the autocracy and not simply as an instrument of retribution. This terror was to be directed by a conspiratorially organized executive committee. The overthrow of the régime was to be followed by an elected constituent assembly to determine the nature of the new order. The question of terror split the party irretrievably. Plekhanov and his supporters left to form their own group and, with the changing of the name and division of the party's meager assets on August 15, 1879, Land and Liberty ceased to exist.

LANDAUER, GUSTAV   (1870–1919) German socialist-anarchist, philosopher, essayist. Born in Karlsruhe to a prosperous Jewish family, he was educated in literature, philosophy and the social sciences at several universities in Germany and Switzerland. While still a student at Berlin, he participated in radical and socialist activities.

At age 21 he obtained a post as editor of *Der Sozialist*, a journal which advocated changes in the political system and a reorganization of society more extreme than that advocated by the Social Democratic Party. Soon the mild-mannered, soft-spoken Landauer emerged as a major theoretician of anarchism. In 1893 and 1899 he was imprisoned for propagating subversive causes. In his thirties, he popularized the works of PETER KROPOTKIN, whose anarchist views resembled his own. Contributing to the fin de siécle anarchist subculture, he gave a modern rendering of the medieval German mystic Meister Eckhart. He translated Bernard Shaw, Oscar Wilde, Walt Whitman and Debendranath Tagore from English. He collaborated with the German writer, Fritz Mauthner, in the critique of language as an inadequate expression of thought and joined with the Jewish scholar and philosopher Martin Buber in efforts to forestall a possible world conflict. However, World War I erupted before a conference they had planned could take place.

Drawn to the theater as an artistic medium of communal expression, Landauer lectured to receptive audiences on William Shakespeare, lectures which were collected posthumously in two volumes (1923). Though not a Zionist, he advocated the establishment of workers communes, such as later found realization in socialist kibbutzim in Palestine.

During the revolutionary upheavals that rocked Central Europe after World War I, a Bavarian soviet republic came into existence for a few months. Its leader, KURT EISNER, invited Landauer to join the government as minister of public relations. After the collapse of the Communist régime following the assassination of Eisner, Landauer was captured and shortly thereafter taken from prison by reactionary officers, brutally tortured and trampled to death by their iron-shod boots. His last words to his killers are reported to have been: "To think that you are human!"

LARGO, CABALLERO FRANCISCO (1869–1946) Spanish socialist leader. Of working-class origin, Largo joined the Socialist party in 1894 and soon distinguished himself as a trade-union activist. He played a leading part in organizing the general strike of 1917 in Spain and was sentenced to life imprisonment; however, in 1918 he was released following his election to parliament. Throughout the 1920s and early 1930s he remained active in Spanish politics, moving steadily to the left. After the elections of 1936, he became prime minister and led the republic during the civil war against FRANCO and the FALANGE. Forced to resign in 1937, he went to live in France, was interned by the Germans in Dachau during World War II, but survived and finally died in exile.

LASHEVICH, MIKHAIL (1884–1928) BOLSHEVIK military and political leader. A member of the Russian Social Democratic Workers party (RSDRP) from 1901, Lashevich was a Bolshevik from the time of the faction's formation. Conscripted into the Russian imperial army in World War I, he served as a sergeant and was twice wounded in action. After the February RUSSIAN REVOLUTION OF 1917, he became a member of the "soldiers' section" of the Petrograd Soviet and later of its military revolutionary committee.

In October 1917, Lashevich accompanied TROTSKY on the crucial mission of persuading the garrison of the Peter-Paul fortress to support the Bolsheviks. He also commanded the operation seizing the State Bank, the treasury and other key points. During the civil war, Lashevich commanded a number of armies on various fronts, helping defeat Yudenich opposite Petrograd and Denikin and Kolchak in the east, as well as participating in the war against Poland. He was a public critic of the policy of incorporating professional experts from the old régime into the RED ARMY and other Soviet institutions. Regarding the use of the czarist generals, he said, "We will squeeze them like lemons and then discard them." This was the first of a series of disagreements with Trotsky over military policy.

Appointed a member of the Presidium of the Leningrad Soviet, Lashevich became a member of the Communist party central committee in 1923. As a close associate of ZINOVIEV, he was demoted to candidate status in 1925, and a year later banished and sent to manage the Chinese Eastern railway in Harbin. He died by his own hand in August 1928.

LASSALLE, FERDINAND (1825–1864) German socialist and founder of the German labor movement. Lassalle was born in Breslau, Germany (today Wroclaw, Poland). His father was a well-to-do Jewish merchant and town councilor who had germanized the family name from Lassalle to Lassal and supported the German enlightenment. After attending a business school in Leipzig, Lassalle went to the University of Breslau, where he fell under the spell of the Young Hegelians. He studied philosophy, history and philology. His diaries and letters from this period show his romantic and melodramatic views. To widen his horizons and perhaps also to avoid expulsion on political grounds, he continued his education in Berlin. It was at this time that he visited France (1845–1846), where he met and became friendly with the German poet Henrich Heine. Heine was engaged in a battle with his family regarding a pension and Lassalle enthusiastically joined forces to help him. While in France, Lassalle reverted to the original family name spelling.

In 1846, Lassalle found another cause to champion; that of Countess Sophie von Hatzfeldt. Under the laws of the time, she was unable to obtain a divorce despite her husband's mistreatment of her. Lassalle threw himself into the case with typical enthusiasm. For eight years he waged legal battles on her behalf until she was awarded her divorce, garnering much publicity and renown for himself in the process and achieving his own financial independence when the countess granted him a permanent annual income in 1854.

Before that, in 1848, Lassalle had moved to Dusseldorf, where he had taken part in the revolution of that year (see REVOLUTIONS OF 1848) and was eventually imprisoned for six months for fomenting violence. His justification of his actions, printed in 1849, enhanced his fame. During the early 1850s, Lassalle and KARL MARX were in regular correspondence as Lassalle sought to help Marx in various practical ways. However, the differences between the two were too deeply rooted for their association to continue. Lassalle was a lamboyant political personality and a financially secure frequenter of Berlin literary salons; these qualities helped him to secure the support of the working classes in the 1860s, but drove a wedge between himself and Marx, the stateless refugee writing in poverty-stricken exile. The growing differences in their political and philosophical doctrines were too great to be bridged. FRIEDRICH ENGELS had despised Lassalle almost from the outset, referring to him as a "greasy Jew."

Lassalle's reputation was greatly enhanced by the publication of his work on the Greek philosopher Heraclitus and his dramatic epic, *Franz von Sickingen* (1858). He was now a lion of Berlin society. His understanding of the need for style in politics, as much as his political aims and views, even attracted Otto von Bismarck. It was also of great use to him in disseminating his ideas for integrating the workers into a united and strong Germany. Arousing the political awareness of German Workers, he organized an army of workers to agitate for universal suffrage. In 1863, he founded and was elected first president of the ADAV (*Allgemeiner Deutscher Arbeiterverein*—General Association of German Workers), the first workers political party in Germany. The ADAV became the channel through which Lassalle disseminated his political ideas. Its members idolized their authoritarian and charismatic leader.

In 1864, Lassalle embarked on what was to be his last love affair (which inspired George Meredith's *Tragic Comedians*). Having proposed to a lady in Switzerland, he claimed that her family disapproved of him because of his Jewish origins and offered to be baptized. He then challenged her father and her former fiancé to a duel. The fiancé accepted and Lassalle was shot dead at their encounter. He was buried in the Jewish cemetery in Breslau. Paradoxically, it was this romantic, ambitious and grandiose personality, who had promised his fiancée that he would one day enter Berlin as president of the German republic in a chariot drawn by six white horses, who had through his hard work and political insight laid the foundations for the future German Socialist Democratic Party.

LATSIS, MARTIN (1883–1938) Latvian BOLSHEVIK. Born of a peasant family, Latsis became a schoolteacher before joining the Social-Democratic party of Latvia in 1905. He then became a professional revolutionary, wandering across the Russian empire. In 1916, he escaped from exile in Siberia and joined the Petrograd Bolshevik committee. In the first Bolshevik government following the October RUSSIAN REVOLUTION OF 1917, he was on the executive of the commissariat of the interior as well as of the Cheka, the All-Russian Special Commission for Fighting Sabotage, Speculation and Counterrevolution.

Throughout the civil war, Latsis held posts with various Cheka bodies, in which he became known for his rigid extremism. He was the author of the policy and procedures manuals of that institution, enunciating the aim of wiping out the entire property-owning class. In his view, "innocent" and "guilty" were class terms rather than judicial matters.

During the NEP (New Economic Policy) period, Latsis held several leading industrial positions in the salt industry, the coal industry and agriculture. From 1932, he directed the institute of economics named after PLEKHANOV. He was arrested in the 1937 purge wave and executed a year later. His name has since been cleared of all wrongdoing.

LAVOISIER, ANTOINE LAURENT DE (1743–1794) France's most celebrated chemist during the Age of the Enlightenment. Lavoisier's experimental work, culminating in his *Traité de la Chimie* published on the eve of the FRENCH REVOLUTION in 1789, was regarded as a vindication of the scientific revolution ushered in by Newtonian physics.

Lavoisier rallied to the revolution with the conviction that the new era would be an instrument of progress and would advance the cause of science for the welfare of all mankind. In 1790, he was appointed to the newly created bureau of weights and measures charged with converting France to the decimal system, but his most notable achievement was to make the French manufacture of gunpowder at the *Salpetrière* (the Saltpeter factory in Paris) the most productive and efficient in Europe, thereby assuring the superiority of France's revolutionary armies over their enemies in the war of the First Coalition. The great and decisive victory of the battle of Valmy on September 20, 1792 has been largely credited to the quality of the powder and grapeshot used by General Kellerman's artillery as compared to the Duke of Brunswick's forces.

Unfortunately, as he was linked to the GIRONDINS and found it hard to conceal the fact that he had served as a Farmer General under the *ancien régime*, Lavoisier suffered the same fate as BRISSOT and other enemies of the state when ROBESPIERRE came to power with the intention of wiping out all opposition to Jacobinism. Lavoisier was sent to the guillotine along with the rest of the GIRONDINS, the Duke of Orléans—now called Philippe Egalité—and a shrieking Mme. Du Barry, whose only crime was to have been Louis XV's favorite mistress, on May 8, 1794. Robespierre's friend, CAMILLE DESMOULINS, justified killing France's greatest scientist when he declared in a speech at the Jacobin Club, *"Les Dieux on soif"*—"The Gods are thirsty."

LAVROV, PETER (1823–1900) Russian populist thinker associated with the Narodniki (Populist see POPULISM) movement. Born into the Russian gentry in 1823, Lavrov was educated at home until 1838, when he was sent to the Mikhailovskii artillery school, an elite military academy. In 1842, he elected to remain at the school as a science teacher rather than serve in the army. Between 1858 and 1861 he won acclaim within the Russian INTELLIGENTSIA by virtue of his philosophical works, *Sketch of a Theory of Personality, Essays on Questions of Practical Philosophy* and *Three Talks on the Contemporary Significance of Philosophy*. The harsh repression of the student unrest of 1861 and 1862 radicalized his views. Influenced by the utilitarian principles of John Stuart Mill, the ethics of PIERRE-JOSEPH PROUDHON, and the left Hegelian concept of historical development, Lavrov quickly established himself within Russian populist tradition, drawing criticism from such eminent figures as Nicholas Chernyshevski and DMITRI PISAREV. In 1866, he was arrested and sent into internal exile after the crackdown on Russian radicals following an attempt on the life of Alexander II. He managed, however, to continue publishing articles and in 1868 his *Historical Letters* brought a new elitist idea into populism. Lavrov argued that the people's welfare could only be achieved through the formation of a party comprised of the intellectual elite. This idea was later adopted by VLADIMIR LENIN and attests to the influence of non-Marxist ideas on Leninist thought.

In 1870, Lavrov escaped with the assistance of young radicals (see LOPATIN, GERMAN) and spent the remainder of his life writing for Russian emigre journals. Between 1873 and 1876 he edited *Forward*, the most widely circulated journal of the period. During the last decades of his life he committed himself to supporting the revolutionary vanguard within Russia. When the Narodniki movement split between moderates and radicals, despite his call for unity he eventually sided with the terrorist arm, the PEOPLE'S WILL, and edited its overseas journal between 1883 and 1886. Before dying of a stroke in 1900, he endorsed the program of the League of Agrarian Socialism, an organization which preceded the formation of the SOCIAL REVOLUTIONARY PARTY.

LEDRU-ROLLIN, ALEXANDRE-AUGUSTE (1807–1874) French revolutionary statesman, Republican orator and publicist who held the key ministry of the interior in the provisional government of the Second French Republic proclaimed by the Paris Revolution of February 1848 (see REVOLUTIONS OF

1848). It was in that position that he took the initiative for organizing elections to the new assembly by means of universal manhood suffrage. A neo-JACOBIN in the great tradition of the First Republic of 1792, he justified his action by invoking the example of the democratically elected CONVENTION which had rescued the 1789 revolution from its enemies. Ledru-Rollin's leap in the dark had disastrous results for French democracy. The elections produced a conservative and royalist assembly that resisted radical reforms. A second assembly, even more reactionary in spirit, was in turn overthrown by Louis Napoleon in the coup d'état of December 2, 1851. A national plebiscite held on December 14 overwhelmingly ratified Napoleon's action, thereby endorsing the violation of democratic and republican institutions in the name of a Bonapartist form of plebiscitary democracy.

Ledru-Rollin's career as a revolutionary is instructive. The rising hope of the Republican opposition under the ORLEANS monarchy, he founded *La Reforme* in 1834, which became the most vociferous organ for radical change along republican lines. Out of the chaos of the February revolution he was appointed, along with LAMARTINE and five others, to the provisional government of the new republic. To pacify Paris without arousing the hostility of the conservative and Catholic provinces proved to be beyond his abilities. Following the bloody sequel of the June Days of 1848, when the bourgeois republic took the decision to crush the Paris proletarian revolution, Ledru-Rollin's brand of revolution stood revealed as hollow and irrelevant rhetoric. When the conservative government of the Second Republic, with Louis Napoleon elected as its president, violated its own principles by sending a force under General Oudinot to overthrow MAZZINI's Roman Republic, Ledru-Rollin's supporters could stand it no further. Contrary to the wishes of their leader, they staged a futile attempt at revolution on June 13, 1849, which had no popular support. It was easily quashed by the government and Ledru-Rollin was forced to flee abroad.

LEFT COMMUNISTS   In Soviet history, a group which, in 1917–1918, opposed LENIN's determination to make peace with the Central Powers, insisting that the war should go on. In their opinion, Russia was too underdeveloped to build socialism by itself; hence it was necessary to carry on revolutionary war in order to spark off revolution in other countries, which would then in turn extend a fraternal helping hand to the USSR.

In domestic affairs, the group, led by NIKOLAI BUKHARIN, insisted on greater participation by the workers in the economy. Although the group actually commanded a majority within the BOLSHEVIK PARTY in January 1918, its proposals for the continuation of the war were defeated at the 7th party congress which ratified the Peace of Brest-Litovsk with Germany. In June 1918, the Soviet government nationalized all large industrial enterprises; the Left Communists regarded this as a vindication of their demands in domestic affairs and subsequently dissolved themselves.

LEGION OF ARCHANGEL MICHAEL   Fascist (see FASCISM) predecessor of the Romanian IRON GUARD. Founded in June 1927 by CORNELIU ZELEA CODREANU and fellow students of the NATIONAL CHRISTIAN ANTI-SEMITIC LEAGUE (LANC), the Legion's first move was to establish a journal, *Land of Our Forefathers*, which attracted a readership of a few thousand following the publicized trial of the LANC leadership. Organized into "nests" of up to 13 individuals and inspired by Russian Narodniki (Populist) ideas, the Legion established work camps in the countryside, building roads, schools and churches. Bearing the icon of Saint Michael and with its members dressed in green shirts, the movement captured widespread peasant support before Codreanu changed its name to the IRON GUARD.

LEHI   Hebrew acronym of *Lohamei Herut Yisrael* (Fighters for the Freedom of Israel), an underground resistance group in pre-state Israel referred to as the "Stern Gang," after its founder, Avraham Stern.

Lehi was formed by breakaway IZL (IRGUN ZVAI LEUMI) members in 1940 in the aftermath of the IZL decision to cease its attacks against the British administration. The *Lehi* manifesto was contained in a document entitled "The 18 Principles of Renaissance." In it, Stern defined the mandatory authority as an alien ruler who had to be expelled from the Jewish homeland, characterizing Zionism as the movement for the redemption of the Jewish people. *Lehi*, in a revolutionary posture, adopted tactics of personal terror and direct action, committing acts of political assassination, most notably that of Lord Moyne in Cairo in 1944. *Lehi* viewed the Arab problem as being exacerbated by British imperialist intrigues and advocated a solution to the Arab-Jewish conflict based on a population transfer. *Lehi*'s diplomatic efforts during 1940–1941 were directed at Italy and Germany in the belief that anti-British aid would be forthcoming. In addition, it was hoped that these contacts would ease the situation of European Jewry. A *Lehi* emissary did meet with a German Foreign Office representative in Beirut but was informed that Germany supported Arab nationalism. In mid-June 1941, Stern met HAGANAH leader Yitzhak Sadeh (1890–1952), who was seeking recruits, but declined since he saw no quid pro quo in this cooperation.

Stern was shot dead by the Central Investigation Department (CID) officers in Tel Aviv in February 1942, and a replacement triumvirate command was eventually organized comprising Nathan Yellin-Mor, Israel Eldad and Yitzhak Shamir.

Lehi carried its attacks abroad and struck at targets in London. Three of its members were sentenced to hanging; two were executed in Cairo in 1945 and another blew himself up in the Jerusalem prison in 1947.

A fundamental political orientation promoted by *Lehi* was the neutralization of the Middle East. After World War II, approaches were made to the Soviet Union and other Eastern Bloc countries, and a Bulgarian Communist delegation met with *Lehi* in Tel Aviv in 1947.

Lehi disbanded in May 1948 and most of its members enlisted in the IDF (Israel Defense Forces). In Jerusalem, it preserved a separate status until it was outlawed after the assassination of UN Mediator Count Bernadotte in September 1948. Like the IZL, *Lehi* too ran a list in the first *Knesset*, the Fighters' List, which obtained a single seat. Service in *Lehi* was eventually granted official recognition, which entitled its members to army service pensions.

LEISLER REBELLION   The Leisler rebellion in colonial

New York (1689–1691) had it origins in two sets of circumstances: political upheaval on an imperial scale and deep social strains at the local level. When news of the GLORIOUS REVOLUTION of 1688 in England reached New York, the militia was called up to strengthen the defense of Manhattan. In June 1689, members of the militia took control of Fort James in the name of William and Mary, the new monarchs. They were led by the testy Captain Jacob Leisler, a long time opponent of the dominant Anglo-Dutch landed elite. Once in control of the city, Leisler assumed the title and powers of acting governor of the colony.

In March 1691, the new royal governor, commissioned by William and Mary's new régime, arrived in New York, but Leisler refused to surrender the government. A short contest was enough to defeat Leisler, whose power had eroded considerably through two years of misrule, an abortive military campaign against Canada and constant strife with the entrenched social powers. Leisler was tried for treason and hanged in May 1691, however, the sentence was annulled posthumously in 1695. For many years thereafter, New York politics would be marked by continuous struggle between Leislerian and anti-Leislerian factions.

LENIN (ULYANOV), VLADIMIR ILICH (1870–1924)
Founder of the Russian Communist Party (Bolsheviks) (see COMMUNIST PARTY OF THE USSR) and organizer of the October RUSSIAN REVOLUTION OF 1917 in which the BOLSHEVIKS seized power. Lenin was born in Simbirsk (today Ulyanovsk) where his father was first a teacher of physics and mathematics and later superintendent of schools for the province. In 1887, his older brother, Alexander, was arrested and later executed for involvement in a plot against the life of the czar. In Communist hagiography this event is cited as decisive in turning Lenin away from the revolutionary terror prominent at the turn of the century and toward Marxist political revolution.

Graduating from the Simbirsk gymnasium with a gold medal in 1887, Lenin enrolled in the faculty of law at the University of Kazan, but after a few months was expelled and banished from the city for participation in student demonstrations. Lenin persisted, and in 1891 earned a law degree as an external student from the University of St. Petersburg. Following first contacts with the revolutionary INTELLIGENTSIA in the Volga towns of Samara and Kazan, he settled in St. Petersburg in 1893, joining a Marxist-oriented circle, and writing his first published essay, a polemic against the populist movement's peasant-centered approach to revolution.

In 1895, Lenin traveled to Europe and made the acquaintance of GEORGI PLEKHANOV, father of Russian MARXISM, and his Group for the Liberation of Labor. Returning to Russia, Lenin, together with others of his revolution-inclined friends, founded the St. Petersburg Union of Struggle for the Liberation of Labor. Within a few months the group was discovered by the police and Lenin was among those arrested. He spent 14 months in jail and then, in 1897, was banished for three years to Siberia. The following year he was joined in exile by his fiancée, NADEZHDA KRUPSKAYA, whom he then married. During this period he wrote intensively, publishing his first major research work, The Development of Capitalism in Russia, in which he argued that Russia was rapidly becoming a capitalist and industrial society, and

therefore the industrial working class was the key to political revolution.

In 1900, he joined the revolutionary emigrés and, together with Plekhanov, MARTOV, POTRESOV and VERA ZASULICH, founded the Social-Democratic newspaper Iskra (the Spark). In 1902, in preparation for the second congress of the Social Democratic Workers Party of Russia (SDWPR), Lenin published one of his most important works, What is to be Done? in which he set forth the basic concepts of the Leninist party—a centralized, conspiratorial organization of professional revolutionaries—as necessary for leading the working class to revolutionary action in the conditions of autocratic Russia. Paraphrasing Archimedes, Lenin claimed, "Give me a party of professional revolutionaries, and I will turn Russia upside down!"

The 1903 second congress of the SDWPR, held in Brussels and London, led to a split between the majority (Bolsheviks) and the minority (MENSHEVIKS). The split was with regard to organizational matters, with Lenin insisting on the disciplined, centralized control that he had set forth in his essay. Lenin's BOLSHEVIK PARTY, despite repeated attempts at unification of the Social-Democratic movement, remained a distinct political entity, and in 1918 adopted the name the Russian Communist Party (Bolsheviks). When the "minority" Mensheviks, led by Martov and Plekhanov, proved to be a majority in the party, Lenin left the editorial board of Iskra, and early in 1905 founded a rival newspaper, Vpered (Forward), published, like Iskra, in Switzerland and smuggled into Russia.

The outbreak of the RUSSIAN REVOLUTION OF 1905 caught Lenin in Switzerland, and like many of his emigré colleagues he hastened to return to Russia to participate in the growing waves of popular discontent. Throughout the year of 1905 he maintained his polemic against the Mensheviks and against all compromise with the autocracy. He therefore called on his Bolsheviks to boycott the first elections to the consultative assembly granted by the czar, the Duma. He also supported an attempted armed uprising in December 1905 in the Krasnaya Presnya district of Moscow. The uprising was quashed by soldiers using artillery, with great loss of life and destruction of property. Lenin drew two major conclusions from what he regarded as the failure of the 1905 revolution. The first was that a socialist revolution would have to be accomplished by an armed uprising, and from that time on the Bolsheviks paid great attention to obtaining weapons and forming armed workers groups, as well as to conducting propaganda within the armed forces. The second conclusion was the refuting of conventional Marxist wisdom that made a successful socialist revolution in Russia conditional on a prior "democratic revolution," in which the propertied classes would take power from the autocracy and open the society both to political democracy and to socioeconomic development during which a strong working class could be formed. As a substitute, Lenin proposed the "Revolutionary-Democratic Dictatorship of the Proletariat and Peasants." This scheme, which became basic to LENINISM, proposed the seizure of power by the workers not for the creation of a socialist régime, which he acknowledged would be premature in Russia, but for the establishment of the "democratic" régime, which, Lenin claimed, the propertied classes of Russia were too weak and cowardly to establish for themselves. The inclusion of the peasantry, led by the proletariat, was a result of the 1905 events in which peasant revolts

Lenin addressing a crowd on Sverdlov Square, May 5, 1920, with Trotsky and Kamenev beside him

The same scene (retouched under Stalin), minus the presence of Trotsky and Kamenev in a later publication

had been more widespread and more violent than those of the workers—a natural phenomenon in a country that was 90% peasant and suffered widespread and increasing poverty.

The repressions that soon curbed the modest democratic gains of the 1905 revolution forced Lenin into emigration once again. In 1906, he moved to Finland and a year later back to Switzerland. Until 1917 he was to roam in exile, directing the underground activities of his "professional revolutionaries" largely by courier and by his smuggled newspapers. In May 1912, the Bolsheviks were able to begin publishing a party newspaper, *Pravda*, within Russia. Lenin, chafing at the difficulties of communication from afar, had by this time relocated to Cracow, then part of the Austro-Hungarian empire, near the borders of Russia. There he was arrested by the Austrian authorities with the outbreak of war, and quickly deported to Switzerland.

From Switzerland, Lenin fought against those socialists who supported their countries' war efforts, calling for the workers to "turn the imperialist war into a civil war." At the socialist conferences in Zimmerwald in September 1915 and Kienthal in April 1916, Lenin proposed the above slogan, as well as calling for the establishment of a third socialist International (see INTERNATIONAL, THIRD) to replace the existing International. Lenin remained in a minority at both conferences. During this period he wrote and published his work, *Imperialism, the Highest Stage of Capitalism*, derived from the work of the British economist, J.A. Hobson, dealing with what he saw as the inevitable clash of capitalist countries in their competition over resources and markets throughout the world. In April 1917, following the overthrow of the czar, the establishment of a provisional government and the spread of workers, soldiers' and peasants' soviets across the Russian empire, Lenin and a number of other revolutionaries returned to Russia in a sealed train, permitted to cross Germany by the German government.

Upon his arrival in Petrograd, Lenin published his "April Theses," declaring the then-radical aim of accomplishing a socialist revolution in Russia by turning the soviets into organs of state power. He refined the Bolshevik program down to the slogan of "Peace, Land and Bread," and by a combination of organization and propaganda turned what had been an unpopular marginal splinter group into a party controlling a majority in the workers

organizations of Petrograd and Moscow. This was all the more remarkable since between the beginning of July and late October Lenin was in hiding in Finland, accused by the provisional government of being a German agent and of having attempted an armed uprising.

On October 25 (Julian calendar; November 7 by the Gregorian calendar), in coordination with the assembling of the Second All-Russian Congress of Soviets, Lenin's Bolsheviks, spurred on by his insistence on immediate action, overthrew the provisional government and set up a "government of the Soviets," a one-party government boycotted by the other socialist parties in protest against the military seizure of power. Despite internal and external pressures, Lenin clung firm to his principle that the key element in any revolution is the control of state power and insisted that all coalition partners accept Bolshevik control on the basis of the Soviet government established at the second congress. Because he had decreed the immediate apportionment of land to the peasants by local peasant committees, Lenin gained the support of the Left Socialist-Revolutionaries, led by MARIA SPIRIDONOVA, removing the stigma of a single-party government. However, when Lenin overcame stiff resistance in his own party and signed the Peace of Brest-Litovsk with Germany, ceding large tracts of territory and paying Germany reparations, the Left Socialist-Revolutionaries quit Lenin's government, attempted to sabotage the peace by a wave of terror against German representatives and, on July 6, 1918, attempted an armed insurrection.

In its first weeks, the new "Soviet of People's Commissars" nationalized the banks, established a monopoly of foreign trade and established a short-lived Workers' Control in industry, nationalizing those large enterprises in which the owners either opposed the workers committees or attempted a lockout. During the period of the intervention and civil war (June 1918–March 1921), when both domestic and foreign enemies attempted to overthrow the Bolshevik government, Lenin instituted the policy of War Communism which involved the mobilization of all resources for the war effort.

This policy included compulsory mobilization for the army or for labor, widespread rationing of food, clothing, fuel and other necessities, administrative allocation of housing, requisitioning of grain and other supplies and nationalization of heavy industry. During this period Lenin also implemented his proposals from the period of World War I, presiding over the establishment in March 1919, of the Third (Communist) International, a body intended to spread the Communist revolution throughout the world. As part of its organizational code, the Communist International demanded of its members that they organize their parties according to Lenin's model as set forth in *What Is To Be Done?* The COMINTERN, as it was known, was disbanded in 1943, when the USSR was allied with Great Britain and the US in the war against Nazi Germany.

In March 1921, the Soviet régime was confronted with workers strikes in Petrograd, peasant uprisings and resistance to the continued requisitioning of grain, and finally by an uprising of the Kronstadt garrison under the slogan, "Long Live the Soviets, Down with the Bolsheviks!" In addition to forceful suppression of this opposition, Lenin urged the adoption of the New Economic Policy (NEP) which gave the peasants greater latitude in raising and marketing their crops, and allowed private trade and private enterprise in light industry and manufacture, while maintaining the state's control of finance, foreign trade and heavy industry. At the same time, political groupings other than the Bolsheviks were declared illegal and a rigorous discipline was imposed within the Bolshevik party.

Throughout 1921 Lenin was engaged in the discussions regarding the political reorganization of the territories held by the Soviet régime. Ultimately, he proposed the form of an ethno-federal union preserving the identities of the national minorities within constituent units of what became the Union of Soviet Socialist Republics (USSR). This was in contrast to the unitary state with limited non-territorial autonomy for minorities, proposed by STALIN. Faced with the problem of resurgent Russian dominance in what was essentially the successor to the multinational Russian empire, Lenin adopted the dialectical approach that the minorities' search for national identity had to be satisfied and they had to be granted some measure of equality and self-determination before they could progress to a supra-national proletarian-Soviet identity. After the declaration of the USSR on December 30, 1922, Lenin's policy was implemented in a hierarchy of national territories that eventually represented 53 of the Soviet Union's ethnic groups.

Lenin, overstrained by four years of tension, and weakened by a wound incurred in 1918 when one of the Socialist Revolutionaries attempted to assassinate him, suffered a stroke in May 1922, a second, more serious stroke in December and a third in May 1923 that deprived him of his powers of speech. During his two-year illness he dictated two of his last major works, "How We Should Reorganize the Workers' and Peasants' Inspectorate" and "Better Fewer but Better." Both of these essays discuss the bureaucratic distortions appearing in the Soviet administration. In addition, Lenin dictated a political testament weighing the merits and shortcomings of all those who might succeed him as leader of the Communist Party, and a harsh letter, condemning Stalin for rudeness to Krupskaya.

On January 21, 1924 Lenin died. He was embalmed and placed in a glass casket within a granite mausoleum on Red Square by the Kremlin walls. His tomb became a pilgrimage site and his body an object of veneration much in the manner of saints of the Russian Orthodox church. Thus began a cult of Lenin that was nurtured throughout Soviet culture and in some measure has even survived the collapse of the USSR.

LENINISM   Three distinct features may be distinguished in the contribution of VLADIMIR ILYICH LENIN to revolutionary theory.

First was his system of party organization, based on strong central control, and the demand that ideological unity be achieved, by splits and purges if necessary, to eliminate any deviation or compromise. This messianic insistence on a single truth, elaborated in a series of publications in 1902–1903, marked the history of the Communist movement. It found expression not only in the theory and practice of the COMMUNIST PARTY OF THE SOVIET UNION, but in the rules of the Communist International.

The second feature was Lenin's belief that the necessity to seize political power in a revolutionary situation takes precedence over any other consideration. Thus, Bolshevism was marked by a tendency to " hurry and take shortcuts," believing that once political power was secured, whatever social conditions were missing (in Russia, this meant the development of productive industry and the growth of a large proletariat) could be created, thus bringing socioeconomic reality into line with revolutionary theory.

The third feature of Leninism was its reliance on armed uprising as the key to power. Following the failure of the RUSSIAN REVOLUTION OF 1905 and the repression of the workers movement, Lenin adopted a strongly militarized outlook and vocabulary. Influenced by the thinking of Clausewitz, he preached the use of civil war as a means to political ends. The successful accession to power of the BOLSHEVIK PARTY in October 1917 was largely due to military units and armed workers formations directed by the Military Revolutionary Committee of the Petrograd Soviet, chaired by LEON TROTSKY.

LEPIDUS, MARCUS AEMILIUS   (– c. 77B.C.) A Roman statesman of noble family who, as consul in 78 B.C., agitated to renew the sale of cheap corn, recall exiles and restore the powers of the tribunes of the plebs, which had been reduced under the dictatorship of Sulla in 81 B.C. Lepidus was given Gaul as a province and established contact with the rebellious SERTORIUS in Spain. When it was reported, in early 77 B.C., that Lepidus was marching on Rome, the senate proclaimed a state of emergency and declared him a public enemy. Defeated by the senate generals, Lepidus fled to Sardinia, where he soon died. The survivors of the revolt joined Sertorius.

LEVELLERS   The most extreme democrats in OLIVER CROMWELL's army, who advocated a more widespread franchise, religious toleration and republicanism. While initially sympathetic to their demands, Cromwell was forced to crush them in the interest of unity after their mutiny of November 1647. Their last stand was in May 1649, after which time their influence declined and almost disappeared.

LIAO ZHONGKAI (Liao Chung-k'ai)   (1877–1925) Chinese revolutionary. Born into a Cantonese family in San Francisco where his father was in business, Liao received his early education in the US. In 1893, he accompanied his mother to Hong Kong and in 1902 began studying political economy at Waseda

University in Tokyo. He met SUN YAT-SEN in 1903, became his devoted disciple, and in 1904 was sent on a secret mission to Tianjin. In 1905 he joined the TONGMENGHUI (TMH) leadership and also headed the Chinese student association in Japan. Sun, who was strongly influenced by Henry George, had Liao translate part of George's *Progress and Poverty*, which appeared in the first issue of the TMH organ, *Min Bao* (People's report), in 1905. In 1909, after receiving a degree in economics at Chuo University, Liao returned to China, passed a special examination for overseas students, and was given an adminstrative post in Manchuria.

When the CHINESE REPUBLICAN REVOLUTION OF 1911 erupted, he served as financial adminstrator in HU HANMIN's military government in Canton. He participated in the 1913 revolution (the "second revolution") against Yuan Shikai, joined Sun in exile in Japan and served on the staff of Sun's Zhonghua Gemingdang (CHINESE REVOLUTIONARY PARTY) established in Tokyo in 1914. Liao subsequently followed Sun Yat-sen in his attempts to revitalize the revolution. He joined the top echelon of the GUOMINDANG (GMD), specializing in financial administration and stressing the socialist component of Sun's economic philosophy. Impressed by the Bolshevik revolution (see RUSSIAN REVOLUTION OF 1917), Liao became one of the architects of Sun's alliance with the Soviet Union and the CHINESE COMMUNIST PARTY. After Sun's discussions with the Russian diplomat, ADOLPH JOFFE, in 1923, Liao accompanied Joffe to Japan and apparently worked out details of the alliance. In 1923 he became governor of Guangdong and minister of finance and helped organize the GMD along Leninist lines after the party's reorganization in 1924. He was the party's representative at the WHAMPOA MILITARY ACADEMY, active in the party's military campaigns in Guangdong and in the anti-British strikes and boycotts associated with the MAY 30TH MOVEMENT of 1925. Given his tremendous influence in the party and his closeness to Sun Yat-sen, Liao was regarded as a possible successor when Sun died in March 1925. He was also a leader of the GMD left wing. His assassination in August 1925 has been attributed to the party's right-wing elements.

LIBER, MARK (Mikhail Goldman) (1880–1937) Polish-Jewish political leader. Liber entered the revolutionary movement as a youth, following two older brothers active in Social Democratic circles. He first made his mark in the Jewish BUND, where in 1901 he championed its stand on Jewish national, as well as civil, rights. As a Bund spokesman, he was active at the second congress of the Social Democratic Workers Party of Russia in 1903. From 1905 to 1918 he was a member of the Bund Central Committee.

In 1917, while still a member of the Bund leadership, he allied himself with the Mensheviks (see MENSHEVIK PARTY) FYODOR DAN and IRAKLI TSERETELI in the executive committee of the Petrograd Soviet. He supported the coalition of socialists and liberals in the provisional government throughout 1917. When the Bolsheviks (see BOLSHEVIK PARTY) seized power, Liber strongly opposed all cooperation with them as detrimental to the cause of socialism, losing his leading influence in both the Menshevik party and the Bund.

In 1920, at the end of the civil war, Liber returned from the Ukraine to Moscow, where he held a minor governmental position in economic administration. From 1922 he was part of a small Menshevik underground in Soviet Russia. He was soon arrested and was executed in 1937.

LIBERIAN CIVIL WAR President William Tolbert of Liberia was assassinated on April 12, 1980, in a military coup led by Master Sergeant (later General) Samuel Doe. Doe suppressed political opponents and mismanaged the economy.

In December 1989, civil conflict broke out, with armed insurrection by rebel forces in the northeastern border region of Nimba. The rebels were members of a hitherto unknown organization, the National Patriotic Front of Liberia (NPFL), led by Charles Taylor, a former government official sought on corruption charges. The armed conflict between the Liberian army and the rebels developed into a conflict between Doe's ethnic group, the Krahn, and the local Gio and Mano tribes. There were numerous atrocities on both sides.

In 1990, the NPLF advanced on the capital, Monrovia. A breakaway faction of the NPLF, led by Prince Yormie Johnson, succeeded in taking control of parts of Monrovia. In August 1990, foreign nationals and diplomatic staff were evacuated.

Also in 1990, Amos Sawyer, leader of the Liberian Peoples' party (LPP) became president of an interim government of National Unity (IGNU). The Economic Union of West African States (ECOWAS) tried unsuccessfully to negotiate a cease-fire. In August 1990 it sent in forces to try and enforce peace.

Johnson's rebel faction, later known as the Independent National Patriotic Front of Liberia (INPFL), captured Doe and tortured him to death in September 1990. In spite of a peace agreement signed at Yamoussoukro, Côte d'Ivoire, in October 1991, fighting continued and, in October 1992, the INPFL launched an offensive against the ECOWAS forces (called ECOMOG), largely made up of Nigerian soldiers. As a result, ECOMOG abandoned its previous peace-keeping stance, for a more direct confrontational role.

LIBYA, REVOLUTION OF 1969 An Italian colony from 1911, Libya was conquered by the British in World War II. In December 1951 it became the first country to be created by a resolution of the United Nations, with Idris, the leader of the dominant Senussi tribe, elevated to the throne. At that time the country was a barren desert whose inhabitants numbered under 2 million, mostly illiterate bedouin. However, during the 1950s it gained international importance as a huge American air base was constructed and vast reserves of oil discovered.

King Idris's régime was reactionary, clericalist and obscurantist. During the 1960s it met with opposition on the part of a group of "Free Officers," who modeled themselves on the group of that name in Egypt, the leader being Colonel MU'AMMAR QADHDHAFI. Qadhdhafi was just 29 years old when he and his fellow conspirators deposed King Idris in September 1969 and proclaimed a socialist Arab republic modeled on GAMAL ABDUL NASSER's Egypt.

The goals of the revolution were set forth in Qadhdhafi's *Green Book* which, published in three parts between 1975 and 1979, described a kind of Arab utopia combining Islam with social justice. Under his rule, Libya nationalized the British and American oil companies that operated in its territory. Qadhdhafi played a major role in leading the Organization of Petroleum

Producing Countries (OPEC) to increase its prices by a factor of four between 1972 and 1974. The added revenues were used by Libya to purchase vast amounts of Soviet arms which, it later turned out, the Libyans were unable to maintain and were left to rust in the desert. In 1981, Libya's attempt to export its revolution to neighboring Chad (and gain valuable raw materials in the process) was defeated by French troops. From the mid-1980s on, the main manifestations of its continuing "revolution" have been numerous acts of terrorism committed all over the world against Jewish, Israeli, British and American targets as well as the régime's own opponents in exile. As Qadhdhafi's oil revenues declined during the late 1980s, his revolutionary ardor cooled. He and his régime do, however, remain a thorn in the side of the international system.

LI DAZHAO (Li Ta-chao)　(1888–1927) Born to a Hebei peasant family and orphaned at an early age, Li was brought up by his grandfather, a petty merchant and landlord, who provided for his education at a private village school. The grandfather also arranged for Li to be married at the age of 11 to the daughter of a local peasant family. A modest inheritance from his grandfather enabled Li to begin modern studies at a prefectural school in 1905. In 1907–1913 he majored in political economy at the Beiyang College of Law and Political Science in Tianjin. This was a modern, Japanese-influenced institution where Li also studied Japanese and English. Despite his sympathy for SUN YAT-SEN, after the revolution Li was inclined to support Yuan Shikai but soon became disillusioned with him as well. In 1913, he began studies in Tokyo's Waseda University and was introduced to a wide range of western philosophers, including Henri Bergson and Ralph Waldo Emerson. He returned to China in early April 1916 to join the conservative constitutional opposition to Yuan Shikai. However, after Yuan's demise in June, opportunistic politicians and warlords continued to make a mockery of the republic. The following year Li's political ideas changed sharply.

He lost hope in parliamentary democracy and opted for revolution as the only solution for China. He became associated with CHEN DUXIU and the new culture movement (see MAY FOURTH MOVEMENT) in late 1917, and in January 1918 joined the editorial board of Chen's influential monthly, *New Youth*. In February he joined Chen at Beijing University, where he served as chief librarian and later (1920) as professor of history, economics and political science. Though the two worked together closely, their revolutionary convictions developed along different paths. In their pre-Marxist phases, both attacked traditional society and its values, but Li felt that cultural change alone was insufficient and sought immediate political action. Furthermore, unlike Chen, who until 1919 pinned his hopes on the west, Li found another source for China's salvation. He was the first important Chinese intellectual to proclaim support for the Bolshevik revolution (see RUSSIAN REVOLUTION OF 1917). In July 1918 he wrote that the Russian revolution had universal significance and presaged the dawn of a new age, in which China could share. He also wrote that in turning its relative backwardness into an advantage by the release of "surplus energy for development," Russia served as a model for China. His more famous article, "The Victory of Bolshevism," appeared in the November issue of *New Youth*. This was around the time Mao Zedong arrived in

Beijing. Li employed him as a library assistant and became his mentor in MARXISM.

Having acclaimed the Bolshevik revolution and its new social order, Li now began studying its doctrinal basis more carefully. In May 1919 he edited a special issue of *New Youth* devoted almost exclusively to Marxism, including the first part of his own article, "My Marxist Views." Thus Chinese Communist historians consider him China's first Marxist. In the meantime the anti-imperialist May 4 ferment, in which Li participated, made Chen Duxiu and other intellectuals more receptive to the Communist message. In 1920, Li organized a Marxist study group in Beijing, met the newly-arrived COMINTERN representative, GREGORY VOITINSKY, and sent him to Shanghai with a letter of introduction to Chen. With Voitinsky's help, Chen and Li began organizing Communist nuclei in Shanghai and Beijing respectively. Li's students, ZHANG GUODAO and DENG ZHONGXIA, established links with north China railroad workers. The stage was now set for the formal inauguration of the CHINESE COMMUNIST PARTY (CCP), which took place in Shanghai in July 1921. Academic duties prevented Li from attending, while Chen, too, who was busy in Canton, was not present, but they are considered cofounders of the CCP. Li was elected to the CCP central committee at its 2nd national congress in July 1922.

Li was active in the united front (1923–1927) with the GUOMINDANG (GMD). In August 1922 he was the first CCP member to join the GMD, and was elected to its central executive committee at the 1924 party congress. That year he also attended the 5th Comintern congress in Moscow. In 1926, Li and fellow Communists controlled the GMD in Beijing, but repression by local warlords forced them to take refuge in the Soviet embassy compound. Li continued to direct party activities in north China until April 6, 1927, when forces under the Manchurian warlord, Zhang Zuolin, raided the compound. On April 28, Li and 19 of his comrades were executed by strangulation.

Li's influence survived. A less orthodox Marxist than Chen Duxiu, he injected voluntarist, peasant-oriented ("populist") and strong nationalist strains in Chinese communism. Li's ideas laid the foundation for MAO ZEDONG's sinification of Marxism.

LI DI　see BRAUN, OTTO.

LIEBKNECHT, KARL　(1871–1919) German socialist politician. In 1907, Liebknecht's antimilitarist writings led to a conviction for high treason; released, he entered the Prussian Lower House in 1908 and the Reichstag in 1912. A left-wing Social Democrat, he was one of the few deputies who refused to support the government at the outbreak of World War I. Imprisoned from 1916 to 1918, he was released just in time to take part in the German Revolution of November 1918, when he and ROSA LUXEMBURG left the Social Democratic party to found the League of SPARTAKISTS. An uprising in Berlin (January 1919) failed, however, and in its wake Liebknecht was killed by right-wing troops while being taken to prison.

LIEBKNECHT, WILHELM　(1826–1900) German socialist revolutionary leader. A lawyer by profession, at an early age Liebknecht developed socialist ideas. His work, however, took him to Switzerland, with the result that he missed the Paris Revolution of February 1848 (see REVOLUTIONS OF 1848). Returning to

Baden, Germany, just as the revolution there was being suppressed by Prussian troops, he was arrested, released eight months later and expelled to Switzerland. From Switzerland he made his way to England, where he was to remain from 1849 to 1862 and where, along with KARL MARX and FRIEDRICH ENGELS, he was active in the COMMUNIST LEAGUE.

In 1862, having been granted an amnesty by the Prussian government, Liebknecht returned to Berlin. He continued his socialist activities as a writer and, along with AUGUST BEBEL, founded the German Social Democratic party in 1869. In 1870–1871 he and Bebel opposed the war against France. As a result he was arrested for "treasonable intentions," tried and sentenced to two years' imprisonment. After his release, Liebknecht continued to lead the Social Democratic party. However, by this time he had shed his early conspiratory inclinations and hoped to achieve socialism primarily by means of worker education.

LIEUTENANTS' REBELLION   A political-military movement in Brazil which from 1920 to 1935 sought to remove the old republic and force the termination of the political power in the hands of the agro-export minority. Known by the name of the Lieutenants' Rebellion, its members were lieutenants, lower rank military men and civilians. Three uprisings were led by these men: in 1922, 1924 and 1930. The group's program included the secret ballot, war against administrative corruption and electoral fraud, true political representation, freedom of thought and press, the reestablishment of the equilibrium among the three powers and limitation of presidential powers, increased autonomy for the judiciary and state centralization. Among the best known members of the group was LUIZ CARLOS PRESTES, who separated himself from this movement when he joined the Communist party of Brazil.

LI HSIU-CH'ENG   see LI XIUCHENG.

LI LISAN (Li Li-san)   (1899–1967) Chinese Communist leader. Born in Hunan, the son of a village teacher, Li studied at the Changsha First Normal School, where he became acquainted with MAO ZEDONG, though the two never became friends. He went to France in 1919 as part of the work-study program. In 1921, he joined ZHOU ENLAI and others in Paris, where they organized the Communist Youth party, soon to be part of the CHINESE COMMUNIST PARTY (CCP). Expelled from France because of participation in a demonstration protesting a French loan to the Beijing warlord government, Li returned to China and joined the CCP in December 1921. Li's forte was labor agitation. In Hunan and Jiangxi, Li, together with LIU SHAOQI and Mao Zedong, organized a series of strikes, most notably at the Anyuan mines and on the Canton-Hankou railroad in September 1922.

In 1925, Li led labor strikes that were part of the anti-imperialist MAY 30TH MOVEMENT (see CHINESE COMMUNIST REVOLUTION) and headed the newly-organized Shanghai General Labor Union. Threatened with arrest in September, he was sent to Moscow to attend conferences of the COMINTERN executive committee and the Red International Federation of Trade Unions. Returning to China in 1926, Li filled high posts in the labor movement and was elected to the CCP central committee and Politburo at the 5th CCP congress in 1927. His own father had

in the meantime become a victim of the peasant fury that the CCP had incited but could not always contain. Though armed with a letter written by his son, the elder Li was executed in his home county after being branded a "village boss and bad gentry." After the GUOMINDANG broke with the CCP in April 1927, Li participated in the ill-fated NANCHANG UPRISING of August 1 and in December became head of the Guangdong CCP.

The 6th CCP congress, held in Moscow in 1928, reelected him to the central committee and Politburo. Though Xiang Zhongfa was nominal head of the party, Li became its dominant figure. The "Li Lisan line," confirmed by a central committee meeting in Shanghai in 1929, called for armed urban insurrection. Boasting that "China needs a LENIN and China needs me," Li dismissed the peasant movement as a mere side-current in the revolutionary wave. Zhou Enlai supported him; Mao Zedong opposed him. The RED ARMY under PENG DEHUAI succeeded in capturing Changsha at the end of July 1930 but could only hold it for a few days. In September, the CCP assessed the damage wrought by the "Li Lisan line" and removed him from the Politburo. He never regained political influence. Sent to Moscow for "self-examination," he remained there for the next 15 years. Pleading guilty to charges of "deviationism," he was sent to the Lenin Institute for indoctrination in 1931.

The 7th CCP congress (1945) elected him in absentia to the central committee. After returning to China in 1946 he worked in Manchuria, and from 1949–1951 was minister of labor in the People's Republic. He subsequently held only minor posts. Victimized by the Cultural Revolution (see GREAT PROLETARIAN CULTURAL REVOLUTION), he died in June 1967. He was rehabilitated posthumously in 1980.

LIN BIAO (Lin Piao)   (1907–1971) Chinese Communist military leader. Born into a small landowning family in Hubei, Lin became interested in socialism while studying at middle school and in 1925 joined the CHINESE COMMUNIST PARTY (CCP). In 1926 he studied at the WHAMPOA MILITARY ACADEMY, joined the NATIONAL REVOLUTIONARY army and became platoon leader in YE TING's regiment during the NORTHERN EXPEDITION to unify China. After the GUOMINDANG (GMD)-CCP rupture in April 1927, Lin joined the CCP's August 1 NANCHANG UPRISING. Despite his young age, Lin rose rapidly in the RED ARMY, attracting the attention of its commander, ZHU DE. At the CCP's Jiangxi base, beginning in 1930, Lin distinguished himself in engagements resisting GMD encirclement campaigns. He commanded the 1st Army corps in the epic LONG MARCH (1934–1935), and in 1936 was appointed head of the Red Army Academy in Yan'an, the new CCP capital. When the second GMD-CCP united front was formed in 1937, he commanded the 115th Division in the CCP's EIGHTH ROUTE ARMY. In September 1937, he gained fame when his forces annihilated a Japanese brigade at Pingxingguan (north-eastern Shanxi), giving the Communists their first victory in the Sino-Japanese war (1937–1945). He was wounded in 1938 and sent to the Soviet Union for medical treatment, staying there for three and a half years.

Returning to Yan'an in 1942, he became MAO ZEDONG's deputy at the CCP party school. In 1945, the 7th CCP congress elected him to the central committee. In October he went to Manchuria to command the Northeast Field army and head the local CCP and civil government. While in Manchuria, Lin received equipment the Russians had taken from the Japanese. After GMD forces scored early gains, Lin counterattacked in 1947, winning complete control of Manchuria the following year (see CHINESE COMMUNIST REVOLUTION). Reorganized as the 4th Field Army with Lin serving as both commander and political commissar, his forces moved south, capturing Tianjin and Beijing on the way (January 1949).

With the establishment of the People's Republic on October 1, 1949, Lin filled several high positions in the government, party and military. Although units of his 4th Field Army spearheaded China's intervention in the Korean war in October 1950, it is not certain whether he himself was in command. In 1955, he was made a Marshal of the People's Republic, an honor shared by nine other Communist commanders. That year he was also elected to the CCP Politburo, and as a vice-chairman of the central committee, was an ex officio member of the Politburo's standing committee, the CCP's highest organ. He was now the sixth ranking member of the CCP. In 1959 Lin became minister of defense, replacing PENG DEHUAI, who had criticized Mao's GREAT LEAP FORWARD (1958–1959) and neglected military modernization. In order to defeat his party opponents, Mao needed the support of the army. With Zhu De inactive and Peng Dehuai in disfavor, he relied upon Lin. In the 1960s, Mao built up the prestige of his protege and that of the People's Liberation Army (PLA), which now became the main vehicle for glorifying and disseminating the thought of Mao Zedong (MAOISM). In September 1965, Lin was chosen to make a major policy statement—"Long Live the Victory of the People's War"—at the celebrations of the 20th anniversary of the victory over Japan. He was now hailed as the authoritative expositor of Mao's doctrines. That he was also Mao's designated successor became clear at the early August 1966 meeting of the CCP central committee meeting that launched the turbulent phase of the Cultural Revolution (see CHINESE COMMUNIST REVOLUTION). Lin replaced Liu Shaoqi as Mao's second in command and "closest comrade-in-arms." On August 18, he stood at Mao's side during the first rally of the Red Guards and became Mao's flag-bearer in the Cultural Revolution. The new party constitution issued at the CCP 9th congress in 1969 confirmed Lin's status as Mao's designated successor. Two years later he disappeared from view. The public had to wait an additional two years for an ostensibly detailed explanation.

The official version, released at the 10th CCP congress in August 1973, stated that Lin had died in a plane crash in Mongolia on September 13, 1971, while trying to escape to the Soviet Union after having allegedly plotted to assassinate Mao. The CCP central committee now expelled him posthumously from the party. In 1981, a special tribunal of China's highest judicial body decided Lin had been the "prime culprit in the counterrevolutionary clique." Nevertheless, the Lin Biao episode, including his alleged plot and even the manner of his death, still provokes conjecture.

LIN PIAO   see LIN BIAO.

LI SHIMIN (Li Shih-min)   (597–649) Chinese rebel and later emperor. In 617 Li urged his father, LI YUAN, to rebel against the Sui dynasty (589–618). Aided by Turkish allies, they captured the capital of Changan and in 618 Li Yuan became emperor of the Tang dynasty (618–907). In 626 Li Yuan, known as Gao Zu, abdicated in favor of Li Shimin, after the latter had eliminated two of his brothers, including the eldest—the heir-apparent. Li Shimin, known in history as Tai Zong, unified and expanded the Chinese empire to include present-day Xinjiang, Tibet and Mongolia, but failed to conquer Korea. He introduced administrative reforms, encouraged scholarship and helped make the Tang a "golden age" in Chinese history.

LI TA-CHAO   see LI DAZHAO.

LI TE   see BRAUN, OTTO.

LITVINOV, MAXIM   (1876–1951) Russian revolutionary and Soviet diplomat. The son of Jewish parents, he was born Meir Moseevich Wallach in Bialystok, where he had his early schooling. Attracted to socialist ideas from his teens, he joined the Russian Social Democratic Party in 1898. He was arrested in 1901 and exiled. In 1902 he escaped to Switzerland, where he first met VLADIMIR LENIN and fell under his spell. The following year he infiltrated back into Russia and took part in the RUSSIAN REVOLUTION OF 1905. After its failure, he spent the next 12 years in exile in France and Britain, working closely with Lenin. A few days after the Communist RUSSIAN REVOLUTION OF 1917 he was appointed the Soviet agent in Britain, but was arrested by the British for propaganda activities and exchanged for the leader of the British expedition to Russia, Robert Bruce Lockhart.

Between 1921 and 1939, Litvinov served as deputy foreign minister and foreign minister of the Soviet Union and was active in disarmament negotiations. His policy was to ensure the growth of the Soviet Union and to remove threats of war.

After Russia entered the League of Nations in 1934, his chubby figure became well known in the halls of the League in Geneva, where he pleaded the cause of collective security (saying "peace is indivisible") and world disarmament. In 1933, he headed the Soviet delegation that negotiated with President Franklin D. Roosevelt the resumption of diplomatic relations with the United States. A fervent anti-Nazi, he urged the League of Nations to plan collective resistance against Nazi Germany. He resigned shortly before the signing of the 1939 German-Soviet nonaggression pact and was replaced by VYACHESLAV M. MOLOTOV. After the outbreak of World War II he returned to duty and, when Germany invaded Russia, in June 1941, he was appointed ambassador to the United States. His excellent command of the English language and his vast diplomatic experience made him a popular figure in Washington, where he served until 1943. At that time he was appointed deputy commissar of foreign affairs, but retired later that year.

LI TZU-CH'ENG   see LI ZICHENG.

LIU BANG (Liu Pang)   (247–195 B.C.) Chinese rebel and later emperor. Born in present-day Jiangsu, Liu, who was of peasant origin, became a village official and in 209 B.C. joined XIANG YU's rebellion against the Qin dynasty (221–207 B.C.). In 206 B.C., Xiang defeated the Qin forces and divided the empire among his generals, giving Liu Bang the title King of Han. The two then struggled for control of the empire. Liu emerged victorious and in 202 B.C. declared himself emperor, calling his dynasty Han, with his capital at Chang'an (modern Xi'an). The Han dynasty, divided into the Former Han (202 B.C.–9 A.D.) and the Later Han (25–220), had enduring significance for Chinese civilization. Its political forms and patterns of thought influenced succeeding dynasties, and even today Chinese still call themselves "men of Han." One of the few peasants to found a Chinese dynasty, Liu was able to prepare the ground for the Han achievement by coopting scholar-officials. He is best known by his posthumous title, Gao Zu ("High progenitor").

LIU PANG   see LIU BANG.

LIU SHAO-CH'I   see LIU SHAOQI.

LIU SHAOQI (Liu Shao-ch'i)   (1898–1969) Chinese Communist leader. Born into a small landowning family in Hunan, Liu attended a village primary school, graduated from Changsha's First Normal School in 1919, and became infused with the nationalist fervor of the MAY FOURTH MOVEMENT. Like many other students, he planned to join the work-study program in France and began studying French. In 1920 his plans changed. In Shanghai he joined the Socialist Youth Corps organized by the COMINTERN agent, GREGORY VOITINSKY, who recruited him for study in the Soviet Union. He arrived in Moscow in 1921 to attend the newly-formed Communist University of the Toilers of the East and joined the Moscow branch of the CHINESE COMMUNIST PARTY (CCP). He was among the first CCP members to have studied in the Soviet Union. Returning to China in 1922, Liu proved to be a skillful labor agitator and helped organize strikes of miners and railroad workers led by LI LISAN. He was among leaders of the anti-British labor agitation and boycott of 1925–1926 that became known as the MAY 30TH MOVEMENT (see CHINESE COMMUNIST REVOLUTION) and was active both in Shanghai and Canton.

When the combined GUOMINDANG (GMD)-CCP forces marched north in 1926, Liu helped organize labor support in the Wuhan area and led the mass movement that forced the British to relinquish their Hankow concession in 1927. That year, the 5th CCP Congress elected him to the central committee. When the GMD-CCP coalition collapsed in April, Liu continued to work in the Communist underground in various "white areas" including Shanghai, Hebei and Manchuria.

Undertaking secret tasks for the CCP, Liu was out of the limelight but constantly exposed to danger. In 1929, he was arrested and imprisoned briefly in Fengtian (Mukden; Shenyang) after leading a labor struggle at a cotton mill. In 1930, he went to Moscow to attend a meeting of the Red International Federation of Trade Unions and stayed there for a year. In 1931, he became an alternate member of the Politburo and head of the CCP labor bureau. By 1932 it had become too dangerous to work in GMD-controlled areas, and Liu joined the CCP Jiangxi base and participated in the LONG MARCH (1934–1935) that brought the RED ARMY to the northwest. On the way, he supported MAO ZEDONG's leadership at the Zunyi conference (January 1935). Between 1936 and 1939 he headed CCP regional bureaus in north and central China, organizing anti-Japanese resistance. Returning to Yan'an, the CCP capital, in 1939, he delivered a major address at the Institute of Marxism-Leninism entitled "On the Self-Cul-

tivation of Communists" (better known as "How to be a Good Communist"). Printed in the CCP organ, *Liberation Daily*, this was Liu's first publication under his own name and became a catechism in the CCP thought-reform campaigns targeted at non-proletarian CCP members (actually, the majority), who needed to cultivate a proletarian consciousness. Liu filled an essential role in consolidating Mao Zedong's power in Yan'an. In 1941, he served as political commissar to the reconstituted New 4th Army after its clash with GMD forces in January (see YE TING). Returning to Yan'an in 1943, he became vice-chairman of the CCP military council, headed by Mao Zedong. Liu was now part of the CCP inner circle, its authority on organizational, urban and labor matters, and a major theoretician. His record as a dedicated and effective revolutionary was unblemished. At the 7th CCP congress in 1945, he was chosen to submit the report on the revised party constitution that enshrined the thought of Mao Zedong (see MAOISM) as the CCP's guiding doctrine. Liu was now elected to full membership in the Politburo. In August 1945, at the end of the Sino-Japanese war (1937–1945), he filled in for Mao at Yan'an when the chairman went to Chongqing to negotiate with CHIANG KAI-SHEK. In 1947, during the GMD-CCP civil war (1946–1949), he presided over the conference on agrarian policy that determined the CCP's land-reform program in areas it controlled.

After the Communist victory in 1949, Liu became second-ranking vice-chairman of the newly established People's Republic, behind ZHU DE, the first vice-chairman, and Chairman Mao. But Liu, rather than the aging Zhu De, was being groomed to succeed Mao. Accorded numerous high positions, he issued important policy statements covering domestic and international issues and consistently lavished praise on Mao, crediting him personally for the achievements of the revolution. When Mao decided to relinquish the chairmanship of the People's Republic in April 1959, Liu was elected to succeed him and was designated Mao's "closest comrade in arms." Mao remained CCP chairman. Publicly, Liu endorsed Mao's GREAT LEAP FORWARD (1958–1959) but was deeply involved in the retrenchment process that followed and tried to exercise a moderating influence. For this circumvention of Mao's policies, he was later to pay a heavy price. In the meantime he remained Mao's designated heir, was an active head of state, received foreign dignitaries and traveled abroad, including a trip to Moscow in 1960.

As the Cultural Revolution (see GREAT PROLETARIAN CULTURAL REVOLUTION) of 1966–1976 gathered force, it focused on Liu. In August 1966, LIN BIAO superseded him as Mao's heir apparent and "closest comrade in arms." Liu, though still head of state, was downgraded to number eight in the CCP hierarchy. In October the central committee forced him to write a self-criticism, allegedly admitting to recent and past errors. He was the principal target of Red Guard posters, but official organs still referred to him obliquely as the "No.1 man in authority taking the capitalist road," "China's KHRUSHCHEV," and various other epithets. It was only in October 1968 that the Central Committee identified him by name, dismissed him from all posts and pledged to "continue to settle accounts with him and his accomplices for their crimes in betraying the party and the country." Liu and his family were subjected to indignity and torture. In October 1969 he was flown to a maximum security prison in Kaifeng. He died of pneumonia in November.

Liu's real "crime" had been his effort to tone down Mao's frenetic, heaven-storming approach to China's problems and to seek more rational, pragmatic solutions. In 1980, the post-Mao leadership restored his good name.

LI XIANNIAN (Li Xien-nien) (1909–1992) Chinese Communist leader. Born to a poor Hubei peasant family, Li had some village schooling and then worked as a carpenter. In 1926, he was a peasant activist during the Nationalist revolution and joined the CHINESE COMMUNIST PARTY (CCP) in 1927. After the CCP-GUOMINDANG (GMD) split in 1927, he joined the CCP guerrilla base (Soviet) in the Hunan-Hubei-Anhui region (see ZHANG GUOTAO) and served as a political commissar during the LONG MARCH (1934–1935), though his unit went west into Xinjiang and did not join the northern Shaanxi base until 1937. Active in guerrilla fighting during the Sino-Japanese war (1937–1945), Li was elected to the CCP central committee in 1945. After the establishment of the People's Republic of China (PRC) in 1949, he served as CCP and government leader in Hubei until 1954, when he was appointed minister of finance in Beijing. In 1956 he was elected to the CCP Politburo. As one of the few leaders who remained in office during the Cultural Revolution of 1966–1976 (see GREAT PROLETARIAN CULTURAL REVOLUTION), he helped ZHOU ENLAI keep the economy from falling into complete chaos. Elected to the Politburo's Standing Committee in 1977, he also became vice-chairman of the CC, a post that was eliminated in 1982. In 1983 he was elected chairman of the PRC, a prestigious but largely ceremonial position, which he held until 1988, when he was replaced by YANG SHANGKUN.

LI XIUCHENG (Li Hsiu-ch'eng) (1823–1864) Chinese rebel commander. Li was born to a poor peasant family in Guangxi. An uncle taught him to read, but from the age of 10 he had to help work the land. In 1851, the family's impoverished existence induced him to leave home and join the TAIPING REBELLION (1850–1864), which had erupted in his native province. He rose rapidly in the ranks of Taiping fighters to become their foremost military leader. Untainted by the corruption and vice that infected the Taiping leadership, Li led a model peasant army and was an able and just administrator as well as a military genius. In 1859 he was given the title Loyal King. He became the mainstay of the rebellion and was largely responsible for its prolongation. In 1863 the Heavenly King, HONG XXIUCHUAN, rejected his advice to retreat from Nanjing, the Taiping capital. It fell in 1864 and Li was executed.

LI YUAN (Li Yüan) (565–635) Chinese rebel and later emperor. A native of Shanxi, Li was an official under the Sui dynasty (589–618), and at the urging of his son, LI SHIMIN, revolted in 617 and in 618 became the first emperor of the Tang dynasty (618–907). Known as Gao Zu, he abdicated in 626 in favor of Li Shimin, who was mainly responsible for unifying the empire.

LI YUANHONG (Li Yüan-hung) (1864–1928) Chinese revolutionary leader. Born to a Hubei military family, Li received naval training, participated in the Sino-Japanese war (1894–1895) and then embarked upon an army career. He was sent to Japan several times between 1897–1902 to study military modernization. In 1906, he became a brigade commander in the modernized Hubei army, which by 1911 had become heavily infiltrated with revolutionary sympathizers. In the absence of well-known leaders when the revolution erupted unexpectedly on October 10, mutinous soldiers forced Li, the senior army officer present, to head the revolutionary régime established in Wuchang (see CHINESE REPUBLICAN REVOLUTION OF 1911). At first reluctant, Li became more committed to the revolution as it spread to other provinces. He was elected to the provisional vice-presidency of the republican government established by SUN YAT-SEN in Nanjing in January 1912 and retained the title when Yuan Shikai succeeded Sun in March. Li had little to do with Yuan's increasingly dictatorial régime, nor was he on good terms with the GUOMINDANG (GMD) opposition.

When Yuan died on June 6, 1916, Li succeeded him to the presidency. Lacking a personal army, he was unable to defend constitutional government against warlord interference. He resigned in 1917 but resumed the presidency in 1922, hoping that the militarists' power could be curbed. His hopes were not realized and he was forced to resign again in 1923. A sincere advocate of parliamentary government, there was no place for him in the era of warlord politics that fragmented China from 1916 to 1928.

LI ZICHENG (Li Tzu-ch'eng) (1605?–1645) Chinese bandit rebel. A Shaanxi native skilled in horsemanship and archery, Li served in the Ming army and in 1630 joined one of the many bandit gangs that were roaming northwest China. The Ming dynasty (1368–1644) had long been debilitated by peasant unrest fueled by excessive taxation. By the 1620s, a weak central government, dominated by eunuchs, was constantly pressed by rebel bands composed of peasants and mutinous soldiers, who often controlled entire provinces. Shaanxi, struck by a famine in 1628, was particularly turbulent. This was the setting that gave Li his opportunity. Attracting peasants with egalitarian slogans and even enlisting a few scholars, he enlarged his sphere of conquests and in April 1644 took Beijing, the Ming capital. The last Ming emperor committed suicide. Though Li proclaimed himself emperor of a new dynasty, Shun, his triumph was short-lived. While rebels had been raising havoc within China, the Manchus, a much more formidable and better organized force, were poised to breach the Great Wall and conquer China from the northeast. Aided by a Ming commander, WU SANGUAI, the Manchus took Beijing in June and established the Qing dynasty (1644–1912). Li fled west and then south. Though the new dynastic rulers were foreigners, they had already adopted Chinese-type bureaucratic rule in their Manchurian homeland. Most Chinese literati, whose cooperation was essential for governing the empire, thus felt the Manchus had a better claim to legitimacy than a native Chinese bandit. Li's rapacity also cost him peasant support. In the summer of 1645 he was killed by villagers while on a raid in search of food.

LOLLARDS The name given to the followers of JOHN WYCLIFFE and to the English religious dissenters of the 15th century. The Lollards revolted against the Church hierarchy and emphasized redemption through faith. They rejected a number of Catholic doctrines, including transubstantiation, favoring the preaching and reading of the Bible. Persecuted under the *De haertico comburendo* (On the Burning of Heretics) statute of

1401, many Lollards were made to recant. Others, though, continued as an underground movement, persisting in small enclaves throughout the 15th century. Their adherents were mainly town laborers and artisans. While the movement probably contributed to the acceptance of the Reformation in England, it was certainly not a decisive factor in this.

LONG MARCH (1934–1935) Epic Chinese Communist trek from the southeast to the northwestern frontier. A year-long, 9,660-kilometer (6,000-mile) journey on foot while fighting better-armed GUOMINDANG (GMD) forces and overcoming natural hazards, the Long March is the great saga of the CHINESE COMMUNIST REVOLUTION. It began as a desperate, improvised attempt to break through CHIANG KAI-SHEK's 5th encirclement campaign, launched in October 1933. Aided by German advisers and employing about 800,000 troops, Chiang had augmented his military offensive with a stringent economic blockade. Lured into costly positional warfare, the RED ARMY took heavy losses. After nine months the territory of the Chinese Soviet republic was drastically reduced. Food supplies were running low. In August 1934, a vanguard detachment made a preliminary breakthrough. On October 16 the main body, the 1st Front Army under MAO ZEDONG and ZHU DE, abandoned the Jiangxi base and headed west. Two weeks after they left, Moscow sent a radio message authorizing the move. Mao's younger brother was one of the guerrilla fighters who stayed behind to delay the advancing GMD army. He was killed in action several months later.

Of the roughly 100,000 who began the march, 85,000 were soldiers, most less than 24 years old. The 15,000 non-combatants, mostly cadres, included 35 women. Initially the plan was to relocate in Hunan and join HE LONG's 2nd Front army. Expecting a relatively short march, they took along cumbersome items like sewing machines and printing presses, but no adequate maps. However, Chiang Kai-shek had anticipated their move and blocked it. In December, his forces engaged the Communists in a fierce, five-day battle on the Xiang river in northern Guangxi. The 1st Front Army survived, but at a tremendous cost, losing nearly two-thirds of its strength. The Communists now changed their plan. They headed west and invaded Guizhou, taking Zunyi easily in January 1935. While they rested, the Politburo held the historic meeting that made Mao Zedong supreme leader of the CHINESE COMMUNIST PARTY (CCP). Mao, given the newly created post of chairman of the Politburo, insisted upon returning to mobile warfare. Heavy equipment, which had previously bogged them down, was abandoned. The slogan issued at the Zunyi conference, "Go north to fight the Japanese," finally gave the soldiers a sense of direction. The plan now was to join ZHANG GUODAO's 4th Front Army in Sichuan for a northward thrust into Shaanxi. Plans were changed again when the enemy barred the way into Sichuan and forced Zhang Guotao to retreat further west. Zigzagging and retreating until they could force a way open, the Communists entered Sichuan through Yunnan. In May they crossed the raging waters of the Dadu river, in what was one of the most daring exploits of the entire march. Pushing further north they reached the Great Snow Mountains on the Sichuan-Sikang border, scaled peaks of over 10,000 feet and suffered severely from frost and starvation. In June, they met Zhang Guodao in northern Sichuan. Disputing Mao's authority, Zhang wanted to go

west and establish a base in Sikang and a link with the Russians through Xinjiang. Mao favored going north to Shaanxi, site of the last remaining Chinese soviet. The two went their separate ways with their respective armies. Plunging ahead, Mao's force had to endure another ordeal, the crossing of the treacherous morass known as the Grasslands, where nights were so cold they had to sleep standing back to back in pairs or groups of four. No new source of food was available. Hunger became acute. Finally, on October 19, 1935, they reached Wuqi in northern Shaanxi, where local comrades welcomed them. The Long March for the 1st Front Army was over. In 1936, Zhang Guodao's and He Long's forces would join them at their new capital, Yan'an.

Less than 10,000 of the original 100,000 made it to the end. The rest had either died or deserted. The survivors had crossed 11 provinces, and rivers, mountains and swamps. They had weathered enemy fire, including aerial bombardment, sickness and starvation. Babies born on the march were either given to peasants or abandoned. Even Mao's wife, already pregnant when they started, handed over her newly-born daughter to a peasant couple. No trace of the child was ever found.

A monument to human endurance and determination, the Long March ensured the survival of the Communist revolution under the leadership of Mao Zedong. It enabled the CCP to regroup, expand and take full advantage of the Sino-Japanese war (1937–1945).

LOPATIN, GERMAN (1845–1918) Russian populist educator and revolutionary. Lopatin's political outlook was formed by contact with Ishutin's terrorist "Organization" in St. Petersburg. Here he learned sympathy for the people of Russia along with a rejection of the group's terrorist tactics, which he regarded as a folly that would only increase repression. In 1867, he took part in creating The Society of the Ruble, with the aim of recruiting dedicated youth to teach in the countryside and at the same time to gather and disseminate information regarding the living conditions of the peasants. Earlier, he had helped publish and distribute I. A. Khudyakov's *Old Russia,* noting that although it was only a small book intended for the lower school grades, "in expert hands it could say many things which are most unwelcome to the censor."

Arrested and exiled in 1868, he fled abroad, becoming a member of the General Council of the First INTERNATIONAL, a friend of MARX and ENGELS and translator of the first volume of *Das Kapital* into Russian. In February 1870, he organized the escape of PETER LAVROV from his exile in Vologda province and two years later he unsuccessfully attempted a similar rescue of Nicholas Chernyshevsky. The combination of his literary, organizational, and educational work won Lopatin a reputation among the most active revolutionaries of the 1870s and 1880s.

In February 1884, having re-embraced terrorism, he joined the PEOPLE'S WILL, helping the movement reunite after its radical younger members had rebelled against the executive committee. In October 1884, in the midst of preparing an assassination attempt against Count Dmitry Tolstoy, the reactionary minister of the interior, Lopatin was arrested and condemned to death. On his person he had not only two dynamite bombs but lists of People's Will members and supporters and codes used by the movement. A wave of arrests followed across the country, putting an end to the movement's resurgent activity. Lopatin's sentence was commuted to life imprisonment and he was confined in the Schlusselberg fortress until the RUSSIAN REVOLUTION OF 1905.

LUCRETIA In Roman tradition, a beautiful Roman woman renowned for her virtue, who was raped by Sextus, son of King Tarquinius Superbus. Unable to endure life, she informed her husband, Tarquinius Collatinus, of the event and subsequently committed suicide. The enraged people rose under LUCIUS IUNIUS BRUTUS and expelled the king and his family, thus bringing the monarchy to an end and leading to the founding of the Roman Republic.

Lucretia, by Lucas Cranach the Younger

LUDDITE RIOTS (1811–1816) Industrial disturbances in England caused by textile workers who feared for their jobs during a period of economic troubles ultimately caused by the Napoleonic War, and exacerbated by laws which forbade unionization and which fixed wages and conditions of apprenticeship. The riots began in Nottinghamshire during March 1811, where textile workers under the banner of the quasi-mythical Ned Ludd, King Ludd or General Ludd, systematically destroyed machinery used in the industry, including power looms and shearing machines. The troubles spread to Derbyshire, Leicestershire, Cheshire and Yorkshire. The government managed to eradicate the disturbances only after a number of years of severe repression, including making the destruction of textile machinery a capital offence. Outbreaks of Luddism continued until 1816.

LUMUMBA, PATRICE HEMERY (1925–1961) Congolese nationalist leader. A member of the Batetela tribe, Lumumba was educated in mission schools and later worked for the post office. In 1958 he helped found the All African People's Conference in Accra, which launched an abortive uprising against the Belgians in the Congo. There he developed more radical views after meeting such personalities as KWAME NKRAMAH. He fled, returned and was imprisoned by the Belgians. In 1960, however, he was released in order to take part in the negotiations for Congolese independence, where he canvassed for a unitary state. He became the first prime minister of Zaire, as the Congo had been renamed, in June, 1960 but was immediately faced with a crisis as Katanga, under Moise Tshombe, declared its independence and threatened the integrity of Zaire. He called in UN troops, who restored order in Zaire but refused to restore secessionist Katanga. Lumumba then appealed to the USSR and the Eastern Bloc countries for help in preserving Zaire under a single government but was dismissed in September 1960 by the cautious and conservative President JOSEPH KASAVUBU. Placed under house arrest, he escaped to Katanga where he was murdered under mysterious circumstances in February 1961. Although not a solid left-winger, Lumumba at the time came to symbolize the desire to free Africa of US political domination.

LUTHER, MARTIN (1483–1546) German religious leader, leader of the Reformation. Born in Eisleben, Saxony, Luther was the second son of a successful miner from Thuringia. At 13 his father sent him to school at Magdeburg for a year, then to Eisenbach for three years (1498–1501). Luther then entered the University of Erfurt, where he studied philosophy and received a master's degree in January 1505. Revealing marked intellectual ability, he was intended by his father to became a lawyer. Narrowly surviving death in a thunderstorm, Luther abruptly gave up his legal studies and vowed to become a monk. To this end, he entered the monastery of the Observantine Augustinians at Erfurt (July 1505). Ordained a priest in 1507, he was shortly afterwards recommended as an instructor to the newly-founded University of Wittenberg. He arrived there in 1508, and lectured on ethics while continuing his studies of divinity. In 1509 he returned to Erfurt and, in 1510, was sent by his order to Rome, where he spent the winter months without betraying any concern about the secular court of Pope Julius II. He returned to Wittenberg in 1511 and, in 1512, received a doctorate in theology and became a professor of biblical studies at the university, a post he held continuously until his death. His exegetical lectures of 1515–1516 on Paul's Epistle to the Romans, and those of 1516–1517 on Galatians, were beginning to attract the attention of students and fellow lecturers. At the same time he acquired experience as a preacher and, from 1515, he served as vicar of his order, a post that entailed the supervision of 11 monasteries.

Luther's religious crisis probably stemmed from his anxiety for his own salvation, and consequently his tendency to approach theological problems directly, rather than from a speculative approach, in the then-current scholastic fashion. He surmounted personal doubts by forming his own interpretation of crucial passages in the New Testament, and devised the concept of Justification by Faith which became a cornerstone of his theology. Yet it is doubtful whether Luther's inner crises would have had such resounding effect, had he not also intuitively known that the time was ripe for a new spiritual message. The appearance of the seller of indulgences, Johann Tetzel, in the vicinity of Wittenberg supplied the necessary stimulus for action and prompted Luther to draw up his famous 95 Theses, which he pinned to the doors of Wittenberg's Castle Church on November 1, 1517. Here he challenged not only the sale of indulgences, but also the actual authority of the Church to remit sins. To him, guilt, repentance and pardon were entirely dependent upon the sinner's change of heart and God's forgiveness. Although the theses were presented as a challenge to a disputation (which never took place), they immediately aroused tremendous interest. They quickly spread throughout Germany, making the name of Luther a household word, while the sale of indulgences suffered a sharp decline.

Denounced to Rome as a heretic, Luther entered into a controversy with several conservative opponents, among them Johann Eck and the Italian Dominican Silvestre Mazzolini. He was summoned to Rome, but the summons was changed to an appearance before the papal legate Cajetan at Augsburg. This meeting, in October 1518, changed nothing and Luther, who enjoyed the protection of Frederick III (the Wise) of Saxony, returned to Wittenberg. In December, Karl von Miltitz, a personal emissary of Leo X, likewise failed to persuade Luther to issue a retraction. Meanwhile, public opinion in Germany and elsewhere was becoming increasingly favorable toward Luther, who

was revealed as a competent and incredibly prolific publicist. In July 1519, he took part in a crucial disputation with Eck at Leipzig, where for the first time he publicly announced that popes and general councils were not infallible.

Luther's break with Roman Catholicism culminated in 1520, when he published his three famous treatises. The first, *An den christilchen Adel deutscher Nation* (To the Christian nobility of the German nation), called upon the German princes to reform the Church by their own initiative. It attacked the celibacy of the clergy, pilgrimages, the veneration of saints, religious orders and the authority of the pope. The second, *Von der babyloninischen Gefangenschaft der Kirche* (On the Babylonian captivity of the Church), rejected the old sacramental system, allowing only baptism and the Eucharist. The third, *Von der Freiheit eines Christenmenschen* (On the liberty of the Christian man), had a more devotional tone, and elaborated on the liberation of the Christian man by inner faith, contrasting this with the obligation to perform good works. These treatises, especially the first two, were written in a vehement style and language which themselves barred any attempt at reconciliation. On June 15, 1520, Leo X published the bull *Exsurge domine* which cited Luther's heretical ideas and gave him 60 days to recant. Luther responded by burning it, and, on January 3, 1521, the Pope issued another bull, *Decret romanum pontificem*, which excommunicated him.

Summoned to appear before the Diet of Worms (April 17–18, 1521), Luther lived up to the great test by remaining faithful to his beliefs before Emperor Charles V. As a declared heretic he could have been placed under the imperial ban and liable to be put to death. But the Elector of Saxony arranged to have him seized and taken to a place of hiding, Wartburg Castle near

Martin Luther, ordained as a priest in 1507, preaches his revolutionary beliefs to his followers

Eisenbach, and there he spent the next 10 months (May 1521–February 1522). His sudden disappearance gave rise to all kinds of rumors and caused widespread indignation at his possible assassination by the emissaries of Rome. While Luther was in hiding, his followers, especially in Wittenberg, began openly to abandon the old religious ways. Priestly celibacy was discarded, monks and nuns left their convents and churches were cleansed of pictures and images. Luther, who was in communication with the outside, encouraged these changes in his letters and pamphlets. In Wartburg, he also began his translation of the Bible into German, first rendering the New Testament from the Greek. The whole work, including the Old Testament translated from the Hebrew, was published in 1534 and exercised a profound influence on the formation of the German language.

Luther returned to Wittenberg in March 1522 in order to put a stop to the accelerating pace of religious reforms, which were becoming a threat to the civil order. He abolished the private mass, confession and fasts, but made the changes gradual, slowly introducing liturgical innovations. He did not involve himself in the Knights' War (1522–1523), but condemned the popular rebellion against constituted authority in the PEASANTS' WAR (1524–1525). When he failed to mediate between the peasants and the Elector of Saxony, he composed the harsh pamphlet of May 1525, *Wider die mördischen und röubishcen Rotten der Bauern* (against the murderous and thieving peasant bands). Written under the impression of reports he had received about the brutalities of the rebels, the pamphlet called for their merciless extermination by any horrible means. Immediately after the suppression of the rebellion, he married a 26-year old former Cistercian nun, Katherine von Bora. Eventually he settled into a comfortable life as the head of a large family which included five children and several destitute relatives, though this did not lessen his tremendous activity. He appreciated his wife and consulted her frequently.

The Diet of Speyer (1526) resulted in the first conditional recognition of the Reformation. From here on, the struggle for the survival of Protestantism in Germany was carried mainly by the subscribing secular rulers. Luther on his part became more concerned with the unity of the movement, which by then had split into several major factions. His meeting with Zwingli and others at the Colloquy of Marburg (1529) only sharpened their differences. In 1530, unable to attend the Diet as he was still formally under the imperial ban, he let Philipp Melanchthon, a fellow-theologian who shared his views, take his place, approving the latter's Augsburg confession which later became the most important exposition of Lutheran principles. His own Schmalkaldic Articles (1537) reiterated his differences with Roman Catholicism. Remaining always in close rapport with the Protestant princes, he gave his consent in 1539 to the bigamous marriage of Philip of Hesse, signing a document to that effect together with Melanchthon and Martin Bucer, the latter a leading light of the Reformation in Strasbourg. Luther's last years were passed in ill health and incessant work. He became more flexible on theological matters, and continued to labor for unity in the midst of growing dissension among his followers. He died in Eisleben during a journey in mid-winter to arbitrate an inheritance dispute between the counts of Mansfeld.

Luther was the author of a massive body of works, mostly small treatises and pamphlets. Of special interest are his replies to Erasmus and Henry VIII of England, his hymns and his *Tischreden*, conversations at table which his students recorded. As a preacher, he possessed a great command of language and ready metaphors which aroused the enthusiasm of his listeners. But he could be harshly abusive toward his opponents, and became gradually more intolerant of such groups as the Anabaptists and the Jews. Indeed, his vulgar outburst against the Jews, uttered in his later years, is frequently cited as the precursor of modern German anti-Semitism. Although he remained to the end of his life bound by the narrow cultural horizons of his early youth, his personality is still eminently relevant to the present age. Few troubled souls in the entire history of mankind found courage such as Luther showed to confront their society with moral means alone, and to effect such decisive changes.

LUTHULI, ALBERT JOHN (1894–1967) Black South African leader. A founder and president of the AFRICAN NATIONAL CONGRESS which fought apartheid, Luthuli was deprived of his chieftainship in 1952. He was one of the accused in a treason trial of 1956, but was released a year later and banished to his farm in 1959. In March 1960 he publicly burned the pass which each black was required to carry, and called for a day of mourning in protest against the Sharpeville massacre of blacks, committed by the South African police. He was awarded the 1960 Nobel Prize for Peace. He wrote *Let My People Go* (1962). Luthuli died after being hit by a train.

LUXEMBURG, ROSA (1871–1919) Jewish-Polish German revolutionary, thinker and activist. Growing up in Russian-dominated Poland, Luxemburg suffered from a birth defect that made her limp; on one occasion she described herself as "a heap of rags." At an early age she became involved in revolutionary activities and in 1889 was force to leave for Zurich. There she studied law and political economy, receiving her doctorate in 1898; during these years she also established herself as a leading socialist theoretician, studying the development of imperialism, which MARX had neglected.

In 1898 Luxemburg married a fellow socialist, Gustav Luebeck, in order to obtain German citizenship. She thereupon moved to Berlin and joined the leadership of the German Social Democratic party, which at that time was the strongest and best organized of its kind anywhere. She soon became involved in a debate that was tearing the party apart: namely, whether it was by reformist or revolutionary methods that the working class would come to power and socialism realized. Along with Franz Mehring and KARL LIEBKNECHT, Luxemburg found herself on the party's left (revolutionary) wing. When the RUSSIAN REVOLUTION OF 1905 broke out, she left for Warsaw to participate in it. Arrested by the czar's police, she used her time in prison to write her pathbreaking theoretical work, *The Mass Strike, the Political Party and the Trade Unions*.

Released from prison in 1907, Luxemburg went back to Berlin, where she taught at the Social Democratic party school and also continued her theoretical studies. When World War I broke out, she and Liebknecht disagreed with their party's decision to support the war effort, left the party, and set up their own SPARTAKUSBUND. Arrested once again—this time by the German government—she went on writing and publishing from her cell;

opposing LENIN, she took the line that the revolution would be carried out by a spontaneous workers uprising rather than by a disciplined movement or party.

Released in November 1918, Luxemburg at once resumed her revolutionary activities and tried to organized an uprising in Berlin. In January 1919 the socialist government called upon units of the imperial army to suppress the Bund; its leaders—Liebknecht and Luxemburg—were arrested and shot. Luxemburg's body was thrown into a canal and only found months later, a morbid scene that BERTOLT BRECHT was to compare to the death of Ophelia. Her remaining supporters formed the German Communist party which, joining the COMINTERN, soon found itself an instrument in the hands first of Lenin and then of STALIN. However, Luxemburg's legacy refused to die. It was revived in Germany during the 1960s, when novelist Heinrich Boell de-scribed it as "a page in the German book of socialism which was closed before people were able to read it."

LVOV, PRINCE GEORGI YEVGENYEVICH   (1861–1925) Russian liberal revolutionary. A liberal who had taken part in the attempt to establish a system of local (*Zemstvo*) government in czarist Russia, Lvov became head of the provisional government after the February RUSSIAN REVOLUTION OF 1917. An idealist and nationalist who tried to organize a parliamentary system of government while at the same time going on with the war against Germany, he was unable to cope with anarchy and the growing power of the Soviets that were being organized by the various left-wing revolutionary movements. In July, he successfully put down a BOLSHEVIK uprising in Petrograd, but then resigned in favor of KERENSKY and emigrated to Paris.

M

MACHEL, SAMORA (1933–1986) Born into a poor peasant family in Mozambique, Machel worked as a male nurse before joining FRELIMO. He was sent with the first group of guerrilla leaders to train in Algeria in 1963. On his return, he set up the first FRELIMO training camp in Tanzania. A student of strategy, Machel was well-versed in the military ideas of CHE GUEVARA and MAO ZEDONG. He specialized in the development of hit-and-run tactics. He always denied that FRELIMO was Communist, claiming that it was nationalist.

Following the assassination of EDUARDO MONDLANE on February 3, 1969, Machel became the head of FRELIMO. When the country gained its independence from Portugal on June 25, 1975, Machel became its first president. As president, Machel exercised his diplomatic skills in pursuit of both national goals and regional stability. He balanced relations with the Soviet Bloc with contacts with western powers. In 1984, Mozambique joined the World Bank and the IMF and a new liberal foreign investment code was announced.

Machel was killed in a plane crash in October 1986, under suspicious circumstances.

MADERO, FRANCISCO INDALÉCIO (1873–1913) Mexican revolutionary and president. The son of a northern landowner, Madero was educated both in Mexico and the United States. In 1905, he founded the Independent Democratic Party (*Partido Democratico Independiente*) and in 1910, he published the much acclaimed book *The Presidential Succession of 1910*, in which he directly opposed PORFIRIO DIAZ's eighth run for the Mexican presidency. Madero demanded greater popular participation in Mexico's political system, to put an end to the 30-year dictatorship of Diaz. In 1909, Madero formed the Anti-Reelection Center of Mexico. In 1910, Madero was chosen as the presidential candidate by the National Democratic alliance. Nevertheless, in September 1910, Diaz announced that he had once again won the Mexican presidency. Finding himself under persecution, Madero fled Mexico to the US, where he authored the Plan of San Luis Potosi. In it, Madero refused to recognize the Diaz presidency and delineated electoral irregularities. As a result, several Madero supporters rose against Diaz in various parts of Mexico. In 1911, after attempts at a negotiated peace, attacks by Madero himself led to success. In May 1911, Diaz was forced to resign and Madero became president of Mexico at the head of the Progressive Constitutionalist Party. Madero faced opposition from various factions, among them the Zapatistas, who believed that he was too conservative, and, con-versely, those who felt that he was too radical. In 1913, various forces rose simultaneously against Madero, bringing Mexico City under siege. Led by HUERTA and with the cooperation of the US ambassador, Henry Lane Wilson, the opposition forces succeeded in capturing Madero. In February 1913, Madero and his vice-president, Pino Suarez, were assassinated.

MAGSAYSAY, RAMON (1907–1957) Philippine politician. A Malay of lower-middle class origins, Magsaysay worked for the Manila Transport Company during the 1930s, before leading guerrilla forces against the Japanese on Luzon. After entering politics in 1946, he was made minister of defense in 1950 by President Elpidio Quirino, and successfully repressed the Huk rebellion in the south. In 1953 he ran for president and won. A liberal who would have liked to reform all aspects of Philippine life, his attempts to carry out land reforms were unsuccessful.

MAHDAVI-KANI, MUHAMMAD REZA (1931–) Iranian Islamic cleric and politician, prime minister September to October 1981. Born in the village of Kan to a religious family, Mahdavi-Kani began studying theology in Tehran. He moved to Qom in 1947, where he studied under AYATOLLAH KHOMEINI and other clergymen until 1961. In 1949 he cooperated with NAVAB SAFAVI, the founder of the FEDAYAN ISLAM. In 1953, during a revolt against the nationalist government of MUHAMMAD MOSSADDEQ, he was arrested in Isfahan.

In 1962 he returned to Tehran and resumed his political activities. In addition, he taught theology and led public prayers in mosques. Mahdavi-Kani was one of the founders of the Tehran Militant Clergy Association, which promoted the anti-shah protest movement in 1978. Arrested several times prior to the Islamic Revolution of 1979 (see IRAN, REVOLTS AND REVOLUTIONS), Mahdavi-Kani has since held prominent positions in the Iranian government.

AL-MAHDI, AL-SADEQ (1936–) Sudanese nationalist, a member of the Mahdiyya sect; the son of its Imam Siddiq Mahdi, grandson of the *Imam* Sir 'Abd-ul-Rahman Mahdi, and great-grandson of the Mahdi, Muhammad Ahmad ibn 'Abdullah, himself. Mahdi, an Oxford graduate, held no position in the religious establishment of the order, but became a leader of its political arm, the *Umma* Party, which advocated independence rather than union with Egypt and was considered anti-Egyptian. He became prime minister in July 1966, heading a coalition government, but was forced out in May 1967 by a split in his

Umma party, his uncle the Imam Hadi Mahdi sponsoring the semi-succession of a more conservative faction. NUMEIRI's coup of May 1969 put an end to his legal political activities, and he was in and out of prison or under house arrest. After the alleged MAHDIYYA rebellion of March 1970, he was deported to Egypt. He returned in 1972, was again arrested, and in May 1973 went into exile in England, Saudi Arabia and Libya. He was one of the leaders of a National Front, semi-clandestine in Sudan and mainly in exile, and was in the forefront of the fight against Numeiri, culminating in July 1976 in an attempt to overthrow him. After a reconciliation with Numeiri, he returned to Sudan in August 1977 and cooperated with the régime for a while, but soon fell out with Numeiri and resigned his position on the ruling single-party's Politburo. In September 1983 he publicly denounced Numeiri's decrees imposing the Islamic law (*Shari'a*) code of punishments. He was again arrested and kept in detention until January 1985.

In April 1985, Mahdi was among the leaders of the coup that overthrew Numeiri. A year later he led his *Umma* Party to victory in the April 1986 elections and formed a coalition government. He sought a rapprochement and a normalization of relations with Libya, while somewhat cooling down those with Egypt. He did not devise a formula to end the rebellion of the African tribes of South Sudan. Mahdi's moderate approach and willingness to compromise made him exceptional among Sudanese politicians.

Mahdi was overthrown in April 1989 by a military coup under General OMAR HASSAN AL-BASHIR. He has since been detained or kept under house arrest and surveillance.

MAHDIYYA An Islamic fundamentalist movement in Sudan which established a short-lived independence from Britain in the 19th century. It was founded in 1881 by Muhammad Ahmad ibn 'Abdullah, who claimed to be the Mahdiyya (the Muslim messiah). His fanatical followers, whom Europeans incorrectly call "Dervishes," defeated the Egyptian troops sent against them and conquered the provinces of Kordofan, Darfur and Bahr al-Ghazzal.

The British advised the Egyptians to evacuate these territories and sent General Gordon, former governor-general of Sudan, to organize the evacuation. The movement, however, besieged Gordon in Khartoum, took the town in January 1885, killed Gordon in the process and ruled over Khartoum and most of Sudan. The movement's leader died in 1885 and was succeeded by 'Abdullah ibn Muhammad, the *Khalifa* (Successor). The group lost much of its vigor and failed to establish a well-ordered state. An Anglo-Egyptian force commanded by General Kitchener reconquered Sudan, 1896–1898, and the Khalifa was killed in battle. Continuing resistance was quelled at the beginning of the 20th century.

The *Mahdiyya* gradually changed from a fanatic-military revolutionary force into an ordinary sect which, in time, gained great political influence. It later became generally pro-British and anti-Egyptian and was in favor of Sudanese independence (as opposed to union with Egypt). From the 1950s it was a focus of opposition to the military-revolutionary régimes controlling Sudan. It played an important role in the overthrow of NUMEIRI in April 1985 and in the new régime established after the elections of April 1986 (see AL-SADEQ AL-MAHDI).

MA HUALONG (Ma Hua-lung) (d. 1871) Chinese Muslim rebel. A native of Gansu, Ma was a leader of the New Teaching, a militant Muslim sect related to Sufism that had been founded in Gansu in the 18th century (see MUSLIM REBELLIONS). Ma was the chief leader of the rebellion that broke out in southern Shaanxi, near Xian, in 1862, and spread westward into Gansu. Muslim resentment of discriminatory practices by Chinese local officials and the influence of the fanatical New Teaching sparked the rebellion and sustained its momentum. At that time the Qing (Manchu) dynasty (1644–1912) was occupied trying to quell the TAIPING and other rebellions. It was only in 1868 that Chinese forces under Zuo Zongtang could give full attention to the rebellion in the northwest. Ma, looked upon as a Mahdi ("messiah"), was captured and executed by "slicing" in 1871. Without him, the rebellion was deprived of a centralized command. Reduced to scattered local resistance, it was systematically and mercilessly suppressed by 1873. The mutual slaughter of Chinese and Muslims left Gansu and Shaanxi with heavily reduced populations.

MAJI MAJI REBELLION A Tanganyikan guerrilla rebellion against German colonial domination, beginning in 1905. Provoked by misguided German attempts to force the population to grow cotton, taxation and the brutal methods by which it was often collected, the rebels based their hopes for success on the belief that the sprinkling of water—*Maji* in Swahili—would make them impregnable to German bullets. The rebellion lasted two years, claiming 75,000 lives and was quelled largely by famine. It did, however, bring about a revision in German colonial policy.

MAKARIOS III (1913–1977) Archbishop and first president of Cyprus. Archbishop Makarios III was born to a family of Greek shepherds in Ano Panayia, Cyprus, where he was christened Mikhail Khristodolou Mouskos. At age 13 he entered a monastery of the Orthodox Church of Cyprus; it was there that he adopted the name *Makarios*, meaning "blessed." After his ordination, he studied law and theology at the University of Athens and then traveled to the United States in 1946 to study at the Boston University School of Theology. He returned to Cyprus in 1948 to assume the position of bishop of Kition.

Upon the death of Archbishop Makarios II in 1950, Makarios was chosen to succeed him as archbishop of Cyprus, a position both political and religious. Cyprus was then ruled by the British; the majority Greek population favored *enosis*, a political union of the island with Greece, which the Turkish minority opposed. As temporal and religious leader of the Greek population, Makarios led the resistance to British rule and the struggle for *enosis*. The island erupted into violence and in 1956 Makarios, considered by the British authorities to be the principal agitator, was exiled to the Seychelles Islands. He was released a year later and settled in Athens. Increasing acts of terrorism prompted the British to agree to independence for the island, provided that Makarios and the Greeks abandoned their goal of *enosis*.

An agreement on independence was reached in 1959 and Makarios was elected president; independence was declared in 1960. Except for a few months during a 1974 coup, Makarios ruled Cyprus until his death.

MAKHARADZE, PHILIPE (1868–1941) Georgian revolutionary and statesman. In 1891, Makharadze joined Marxist groups during his studies at the veterinary institute in Warsaw. In 1893, he was arrested and returned to Georgia only in 1895. Between 1901 and 1907 he was arrested a number of times by the police for revolutionary propaganda. In 1908 he was transferred to Astrakhan. From 1911 Makharadze lived in Donbas, where he participated in the creation of various BOLSHEVIK organizations. At the beginning of World War I he was arrested and exiled, but escaped and went on to lead illegal revolutionary activity. From October 1917 he was a member of the Russian Social Democratic Workers Party (RSDWP) Caucasian regional committee and a member of the Terek Soviet. In 1919, Makharadze returned illegally to Georgia and was arrested. After the establishment of Soviet rule in Georgia, he held various top posts. Makharadze was also a literary critic who opposed and actually fought, on class grounds, the great late 19th-century writer and leader of the national movement in Georgia, Ilya Chavchavadze.

MAKHNO, NESTOR (1889–1934) Ukrainian peasant anarchist leader. Makhno's anarchist beliefs grew out of the RUSSIAN REVOLUTION OF 1905 and the subsequent reaction. Sentenced to death in 1910, his sentence was commuted and he was jailed in Moscow. During this imprisonment he contracted tuberculosis, which eventually caused his death.

Released in 1917, he returned to his home village of Gulyay Pole, where he became chairman of the Free Peasant Soviet. In 1918 he temporarily fled the German occupation, visiting Moscow. In July he formed the Revolutionary Insurgent army of the Ukraine in support of the Bolsheviks (see BOLSHEVIK PARTY). Fighting first the Germans and Austro-Hungarians and then, through 1919, Denikin's White Volunteer army as well as the Ukrainian national forces of Hetman Skoropadsky and of Petliura, Makhno contributed significantly to clearing the way for Bolshevik control of Ukraine. Wherever his forces went, Makhno urged the establishment of Free Soviets of workers and peasants. Together with his anarchist comrades, Volin and Arshinov and a staff of other Ukrainian anarchist intellectuals, Makhno tried to establish a new society but was unable to control all of his peasant anarchist recruits. Thus, despite his instructions, some of his units took part in pogroms against Jewish communities in the areas Makhno conquered. As was the case with other anarchists, Makhno's support of the Bolsheviks earned him no leeway for independence and LENIN's régime soon turned against its erstwhile ally. Makhno fled first to Romania, then to Poland and France. He wrote and published three volumes of memoirs before succumbing to poverty and tuberculosis.

MALAPARTE, CURZIO (1898–1957) Italian Fascist (see FASCISM) intellectual, publicist and writer. Born Kurt Eric Suckert but better known as Curzio Malaparte, Malaparte joined the Fascist party (PNF) in 1921, after having volunteered for military service and having been awarded a decoration in World War I. As a member of a Fascist squad, he participated in the MARCH ON ROME. In 1924 he founded the weekly *La Conquista dello Stato* (The conquest of the state), in which he expressed intransigent and revolutionary Fascist views opposed to MUSSOLINI's governmental practice. The glorification of *squadrismo*

("combativeness") by Malaparte resulted in the banning of his publication, a fact that caused him to voice greater moderation when it reopened. Deeply nationalist, Malaparte, as a leading Fascist intellectual, adopted revolutionary, syndicalist, corporatist and populist ideals and created a cultural movement in this spirit. He was the editor of *La Stampa* (the main newspaper in Turin and one of the most important in Italy) from 1929 to 1931. Later, he lived in Paris and wrote *Tecnica del Colpo di Stato* (The Technique of the coup d'etat) and attacked the Fascist establishment. Back in Italy, he was prosecuted and sentenced to one year of internal exile but was soon released. In World War II, Malaparte was a military correspondent in Africa and Russia. Arrested as a Fascist after Mussolini's fall, he was released and served as a liasion officer between the Allied forces and the Italian Liberation army. After the war he worked again as a journalist and died in 1957.

MALATESTA, ENRICO (1853–1932) Italian anarchist. Originally an advocate of MICHAEL BAKUNIN's peasant collectivism, Malatesta was converted to the anarchist communism of PETER KROPOTKIN in the 1870s and to "propaganda by the deed"—the belief that the most effective propaganda for revolution was the very act of insurrection. Together with Carlo Cafiero, Malatesta used these positions to dominate the anarchist conference held in Florence in 1876. The following year he helped organize a peasant's insurrection in Benevento; when the rebellion failed he went into exile. Malatesta returned to Italy in 1913 and founded the anarchist journal *Volontà*, but was soon forced back into exile for his role in the Red Week general strike that rocked Italy on June 6–13, 1914. During the strike, he allied himself with socialist agitator BENITO MUSSOLINI in calling for a revolution to overthrow Italy's government. He returned to Italy in 1919 and re-established the anarchist newspaper *Umanità Nova*. Malatesta died under house arrest, imposed by his former ally Mussolini.

Malatesta's revolutionary philosophy is expounded in his book, *L'Anarchia* (1921). In it he describes the belief that people share a basic instinct of mutual cooperation, upon which all human development is based. Since arbitrary laws only interfere with this instinct, government actually hinders humanity from attaining its true greatness.

MALCOLM X (1925–1965) US black leader, one of the founders of the Nation of Islam and voice of black discontent with white society. He was born Malcolm Little in Omaha, Nebraska; his mother was West Indian, and his father, Earl Little, a preacher devoted both to baptism as well as to the secularist nationalist teachings of MARCUS GARVEY.

The Little family was driven out of Omaha by a group of white vigilantes, who complained about Earl Little's "spreading trouble" by teaching the "back to Africa" message of Garvey to the "good Negroes" of Omaha. The family moved to Milwaukee and then to Lansing, Michigan, but their troubles were not over, and the Black Legion, a local antiblack group, caught up with Malcolm's father. Beating him senseless, they left him to die under the wheels of a streetcar. Malcolm was only six. The low wages their mother and older brother earned were not enough to feed the family and the children often went hungry.

Dropping out of school in eighth grade, Malcolm held a series of menial jobs before he began dealing in and using drugs, burglarizing homes and stores and steering white customers to black brothels. He was eventually given an 8–10-year sentence by the State of Massachusetts for burglary. While in prison he began to read the teachings of Elijah Muhammad, the founder of the Nation of Islam, who maintained that the white race was the race of devils created to torment the black sons and daughters of Allah.

When he was released from prison in 1952 Malcolm made his way to Detroit, where he met Elijah Muhammad and began to recruit young blacks to the fold. He soon received his "X" from the Muslims, which symbolized the true African family name he would never know. "For me," he wrote in his *Autobiography*, "my 'X' replaced the white slave-master name of 'Little' which some blue-eyed devil named Little had imposed on my paternal forebears."

Over the next few years, Malcolm X concentrated on recruiting young blacks from the streets, trying to bring Allah and Elijah Muhammad into their lives. Beginning in 1953, the minister of Malcolm X's temple in Detroit, recognizing his gift for oratory, urged him to speak. His passionate speeches inspired countless people. The central object of his life became to rid blacks of their shame of the past and to give them self-esteem. He began to see that rage could provoke people to action and he toured the country speaking, opening new mosques and starting a newspaper called *Muhammad Speaks.* Soon the media caught up and he was invited to appear on several talk shows.

His new found fame, however, precipitated tension with Elijah Muhammad. Malcolm's reaction to the assassination of President Kennedy provided enough reason to have him dismissed from the ministry and from the Nation of Islam in 1963.

Forming his own group, Muslim Mosques, Inc., Malcolm X began taking tutorials in orthodox Islam. He made a pilgrimage to Mecca where, for the first time, he came in contact with white Muslims. He embraced Sunni Islam, adopted the name El-Haj Malik el-Shabbaz and returned to the United States a changed man. He denounced his former guru as a racist and

Malcolm X and black anger, in 1963, when second in command to Elijah Muhammad, two years before he was murdered

> ### *MALCOLM X*
>
> • I can capsulize how I feel—I'm for the freedom of the twenty-two million Afro-Americans by any means necessary. By any means necessary. I'm for a society in which our people are recognized and respected as human beings, and I believe that we have the right to resort to any means necessary to bring that about. So when you ask me where I'm headed, what can I say? Isn't anything wrong with that.
>
> • Sitting at the table doesn't make you a diner, unless you eat some of what's on that plate. Being born here in America doesn't make you an American.
>
> • You show me a capitalist and I'll show you a bloodsucker.
>
> • Power never takes a backstep—only in the face of more power.
>
> • Be peaceful, be courteous, obey the law, respect everyone; but if someone puts his hands on you, send him to the cemetery.

changed his own theories on white people, saying he would now judge them on their behavior and not by the color of their skin.

By 1965, Malcolm X had begun to receive death threats from his former Nation of Islam followers. His house was firebombed and on February 21 of that year, while addressing a crowd of the Organization of Afro-American Unity at the Audubon Ballroom in Harlem, he was shot and killed by a group of BLACK MUSLIMS. Yet Malcolm X's message of black power and pride continues to influence thousands of black Americans today.

MALCOM-KHAN NEZAM-OD-DOWLE (1833–1908) Iranian statesman, the founder of the enlightenment-political modernization of Iran. Born in Tabriz, west Iran, Malcom-Khan was educated in France. He was a diplomat for many years, as Iranian ambassador to Britain and Italy, and was a leader of various enlightenment societies. In 1899, he founded one of the most radical Iranian newspapers, *Qanon*, and was also its editor. The paper printed anti-feudal and anti-shah slogans. He set up the first Iranian Freemasons' lodge. The social and political activities of Malcom-Khan favored the foundation and dissemination of Iran's national liberation movement ideology. In his works, *Principles of Civilization, Unarranged Iran, Country Policy* and *Voice of Justice*, he raised the need for power and law reforms, including setting up a National Assembly; the division of the legislative from the executive powers; a guarantee for personal immunity, honor and dignity; and freedom of speech of the press and of public organizations.

MALI, COUP OF 1968 The Republic of Mali became independent from France on September 22, 1960. It was led by

Modibo Keita and his *Union soudanaise* party. Keita declared a one-party state and pursued socialist policies, severing links with France and developing close ties with the Soviet Bloc in 1967–1968. This caused concern in the army, especially after the arrest of several officers.

On November 19, 1968, a group of young officers staged a successful coup d'état. Their leader was Lieutenant (later General) MOUSSA TRAORE. The constitution was abrogated and all political parties were banned. A 14 member *Comité militaire pour la libération nationale* (CMLN) was formed with Moussa Traoré as president and Captain Yoro Diakité as head of government.

MALINOVSKY, ROMAN   (1878–1918) BOLSHEVIK activist turned police agent. After a brief criminal career and jail sentence, Malinovsky settled in St. Petersburg. From 1905 on, Malinovsky, who was from a worker family, was active in organizing trade unions, enjoying the confidence of the workers. Arrested in 1909, he turned into a police agent. He joined the Bolsheviks in 1911 on police instructions, contributing to dissension between the Social Democratic factions. In 1912, he was elected to the Bolshevik central committee and the editorial board of *Pravda*. In the Fourth Duma he served as leader of the Bolshevik faction. Accused publicly of being a police spy, Malinovsky resigned his Duma seat early in 1914 and travelled to Cracow, where LENIN defended him vigorously. Malinovsky, however, continued on to Germany, where he was active during the war propagandizing Russian prisoners of war on behalf of the Bolsheviks at the behest of the German government. Following the 1917 revolutions (see RUSSIAN REVOLUTION OF 1917) he returned to Soviet Russia, where he was arrested, tried in camera and shot.

MANDELA, NELSON ROLIHLAHLA   (1918–) Mandela was born into a royal family of the Themba tribe, a Xhosa people, in the Transkei section of South Africa. After his father's death, he was raised by an important chief. It was in the chief's village, Mandela claims, that he absorbed the ability to lead.

Mandela became a lawyer and a political revolutionary, challenging the apartheid system in South Africa. He helped radicalize the AFRICAN NATIONAL CONGRESS (ANC) in the 1950s, pushing its leadership toward an alliance with the Communist party, and eventually into active violence against the state. In 1961, together with JOE SLOVO, Mandela founded the military wing of the ANC, *Umkhonto We Sizwe* (Spear of the Nation).

In 1960, after the Sharpeville shootings, the ANC was banned, and Mandela went underground. In 1961, he was tried and acquitted of treason. In 1962, he was captured and charged with incitement and with leaving South Africa without a passport. In June 1964, Mandela was tried again, convicted of conspiracy and sentenced to life imprisonment. He spent the next 27 years in prison, 18 of these on Robben Island, under very harsh conditions. Then, in 1988, he was moved to a luxury house, with a swimming pool and his own personal chef.

In February 1990, the ANC was unbanned by the South African president, Frederik de Klerk, and Mandela was set free. In 1994, Nelson Mandela was elected president of South Africa, as a result of South Africa's first multiracial elections in which the ANC won a majority. Mandela, who firmly believes in a democratic South Africa, has followed a moderate, cautious approach, pushing for reform, while trying to conciliate the white population. This policy has been criticized by more radical elements in South Africa, including Mandela's estranged wife, WINNIE MANDELA.

Mandela's life and philosophy are set out in his monumental autobiography, *Long Walk to Freedom,* published in 1994.

The price of revolt: after 29 years in prison Mandela emerged as leader of South Africa

MANDELA, WINNIFRED (WINNIE) NOMZANO ZANIEWE (1934–) Born in Pondoland, South Africa, Winnie Mandela studied social work and became the first black medical social worker in the Soweto hospital.

In 1957, she met NELSON MANDELA and they married in 1958. Three months later she was arrested for her role in a campaign against the passes that blacks were required to carry. Winnie Mandela served on the national executives of both the AFRICAN NATIONAL CONGRESS (ANC) Women's League and the Federation of South African Women.

In 1962, Winnie Mandela was banned under the terms of the Suppression of Communism Act and restricted to Orlando, Soweto. More stringent banning orders were served on her in 1965 and 1966 and she remained under banning orders almost continuously during her husband's 27-year-imprisonment. Winnie Mandela also served several spells in prison, including 17 months in solitary confinement. She was not cowed, however, and rose to international fame as an anti-apartheid campaigner in the 1970s and 1980s, being nicknamed "Mother of the Nation."

Winnie Mandela caused considerable controversy when, in a 1986 speech, she supported "necklace" killings of suspected government collaborators (killing by means of placing a burning tire around the victim's neck). Mandela also gained notoriety when members of the so-called "Mandela United Football Club," who guarded her, were accused of abducting four youths, one of whom—14 year old Stompie Seipei—was subsequently found murdered. Winnie Mandela was urged by the ANC president OLIVER TAMBO, and by her husband to disband the club.

Winnie Mandela's chief bodyguard was convicted of Stompie's murder. She herself was initially sentenced to six years in jail for kidnapping and assault, but the assault conviction was quashed on appeal and the sentence reduced to a fine.

On Nelson Mandela's release from prison in February 1990, Winnie Mandela became increasingly prominent and was appointed head of the ANC's welfare division. Then, in April 1992, Nelson Mandela announced that he and his wife were separating for personal reasons. She subsequently resigned from her post on the ANC. But in December 1993 she returned to center stage, winning election as president of the ANC Women's League. In South Africa's first multiracial election in April 1994, Winnie won a seat in parliament and was appointed deputy minister of arts, culture, science and technology. She has been the only prominent ANC member to voice discontent at the government's gradualist approach to social reform. There have also been more scandals—Winnie Mandela has been accused of mismanagement of funds under her control and of taking bribes.

Finally, in March 1995, Nelson Mandela fired her from the cabinet, but she remains a force to be reckoned with and has considerable support among ANC militants and among the poorest sections of the community.

MANIN, DANIELE (1804–1857) Italian revolutionary leader. Born in Venice to a father who was a Jew who had converted to Christianity, Manin studied law in Padua before joining the movement that sought to liberate Italy from the Austrian rule to which it had been subjected for some centuries. In January 1848, he and a number of fellow-nationalists petitioned the government for the establishment of home rule; for this he was imprisoned, only to be freed when Venice revolted the following March. Having been appointed provisional president of the Venetian republic, Manin led the defense of the city and was able to hold out for five months before it was captured by the Austrians. He was banished to Paris where, for the remaining eight years of his life, he did his best to rekindle the flames of revolution. In 1868, his remains were transported back to his native Venice where he was given a state funeral.

MANUILSKII, DMITRII (1883–1959) Born in a Ukrainian peasant family, Manuilskii joined the Bolsheviks (see BOLSHEVIK PARTY) in 1903 while a university student in St. Petersburg. His part in the RUSSIAN REVOLUTION OF 1905 earned him a five-year exile in Siberia from which he escaped, briefly joining a Bolshevik group in Kiev before emigrating in 1907 to Paris. There he combined revolutionary activity with a degree in law from the Sorbonne. In Paris, he advocated direct revolutionary action against the autocracy, opposing those such as BOGDANOV who advocated education and cultural or economic activities with the workers as a path toward political development.

In 1917, Manuilskii returned to Russia, joining TROTSKY's "In-

ter-District" group. He worked with the Communist party of the Ukraine and in December 1921 became First Secretary, drawing the Communists of the Ukraine toward autonomy in a centralized Soviet state rather than federal sovereignty. He was also active in the Third INTERNATIONAL and with BUKHARIN's removal in 1928 and MOLOTOV's promotion to chair the Council of People's Commissars in 1930, succeeded to the leadership of the COMINTERN. In 1933, he headed the purge of "bourgeois nationalists" from the Communist party of Ukraine.

Manuilskii led the Ukrainian delegation at the founding of the United Nations in 1945 and at the Paris peace conference the following year. As foreign minister of the Ukrainian Soviet Republic, he was Ukraine's representative at the first assemblies of the UN and from 1948 to 1952 was Permanent Representative of Ukraine to that body. In 1952 he was recalled to the USSR, fell ill and lived in seclusion until his death.

MAOISM Chinese Communist adaptation of Marxism-Leninism. Usually called MAO ZEDONG Thought, Maoism represents Mao's theoretical ideas as well as his revolutionary strategy. It became part of CHINESE COMMUNIST PARTY (CCP) doctrine at the 7th party congress (1945). Still linked with Marxism-Leninism as the official CCP ideology, it is virtually ignored in current practice. Less deterministic than orthodox MARXISM but affirming the Marxist faith in the inevitability of a socialist future, Maoism emphasizes voluntarism and subjective factors. According to Mao's teaching, a proletarian consciousness is not determined by class but by constant struggle and revolutionary activity. In its broadest sense, Maoism promises the triumph of the human will over objective conditions. Based upon his own experience, Mao saw the peasantry as the greatest potential force for revolution and made a virtue of rural backwardness and illiteracy. Intensely nationalistic and anti-imperialist, Maoism accorded China primacy in the world revolution. The Maoist strategy of encircling the cities with villages appealed to revolutionaries in underdeveloped countries.

MAO-TSE TUNG see MAO ZEDONG.

Mao Zedong (left), the leader of the Chinese Communist Party, being interviewed by an American reporter, 1937

MAO ZEDONG (1893–1976) Chinese Communist leader and founder of the People's Republic of China (see also CHINESE COMMUNIST REVOLUTION). Born in the Hunan village of Shaoshan into a poor peasant family that gradually improved its status, Mao began helping with farm work at age six. Two years later he entered the village school and began studying the Confucian classics. On his own he read popular novels glorifying bandit heroes and peasant revolts. At age 13 he had to leave school for full-time work on the land. Mao continued to read, not only novels, but political writings on contemporary issues. Defying his father, he enrolled in 1909 in a higher primary school in a nearby town. The first taste of modern learning aroused him intellectually and politically. He learned about world history and heroic figures like WASHINGTON, Napoleon and Peter the Great. Reformist writings made him more aware of China's plight. In early 1911, the search for further learning took him to the provincial capital, Changsha, a hotbed of modern intellectual and political activity. He attended middle school, read his first newspaper and learned about SUN YAT-SEN's revolutionary movement. When the CHINESE REPUBLICAN REVOLUTION OF 1911 reached Changsha, he joined the rebel army and served for six months as a water carrier and cook.

In early 1913, Mao enrolled in the Hunan 4th Provincial Normal School, later merged into the 1st Normal School, a breeding ground for Hunanese radicals (see LIU SHAOQI and LI LISAN). He formed a close relationship with his ethics teacher and future father-in-law, Yang Changji. A Kantian, Yang stressed idealism and self-discipline. His influence on Mao was lasting. Like Yang, Mao became an enthusiastic supporter of CHEN DUXIU's radical monthly, *New Youth*. In 1917, the magazine published Mao's first literary effort, an article advocating physical education and bemoaning China's lack of a military spirit. Mao was active in the Changsha student movement, and in 1918 his friend and classmate, Cai Hesen, helped him organize the "New People's Study Society," which aimed to stimulate patriotism and train students to become "new citizens." Graduating in 1918, Mao left for Beijing and thought of joining the work study program in France that was attracting many fellow students. He abandoned the idea, perhaps because he was a poor language student. LI DAZHAO, chief librarian at Beijing University, gave him a job as a library assistant, and he also audited classes at the university, the most prestigious in China and the fountainhead of the new culture movement. Li, an ardent nationalist and future co-founder of the CHINESE COMMUNIST PARTY (CCP), helped shape Mao's political thought.

Returning to Changsha in the spring of 1919 to care for his sick mother, Mao was swept into the MAY FOURTH MOVEMENT, the nationalist upsurge that activated students throughout the country. He was a leader of the movement in Hunan. He organized students, founded a weekly dedicated to "democracy and new culture," and led protests against the provincial warlord. In Beijing and Shanghai for brief stays in 1920, he moved with the leftward trend initiated by his mentors, Li Dazhao and Chen Duxiu. He read the Communist Manifesto and some other translations of Marxist and socialist works. In Shanghai, where he worked as a laundryman, talks with Chen Duxiu, future head of the CCP, made a deep impression on him. When he returned to Hunan in the summer, he considered himself a Marxist. Thanks to the new political climate in Hunan, he also gained a re-

spectable status, being appointed to the faculty of the First Normal School. His first real job, it gave him security and standing that enhanced his political activities, now directed toward the propagation of socialism. His improved circumstances also enabled him to marry Yang Changji's daughter, Yang Kaihui, in the autumn.

Mao played an active role in the formation and development of the CCP. In December, he helped organize the Changsha branch of the Socialist Youth Corps—the CCP's precursor. In July 1921, he was one of 12 delegates to the CCP's inaugural conference in Shanghai. He returned to Hunan as secretary of the provincial CCP and demonstrated a flair for organization and indoctrination. In 1923, he was elected to the Central Committee (CC) at the 3rd CCP congress, made head of the organization department and gave enthusiastic support to the united front with the GUOMINDANG (GMD). Mao attended the 1st congress of the reorganized GMD in Canton in 1924 and assumed high positions in the senior party. Returning to Hunan at the end of the year to convalesce from an illness, he discovered the revolutionary potential of the peasantry. In June 1925 he began organizing peasant associations, a task better suited to his background and temperament than the urban-oriented labor agitation emphasized by CCP policy. The CCP had not neglected the peasants (see PENG PAI), but considered them less important than the proletariat. Mao, however, was beginning to attach primary importance to the countryside. He missed the 4th CCP congress (January 1925) and was not reelected to the CC. Returning to Canton in the autumn, he directed the GMD's Peasant Movement Training Institute and headed the CCP's peasant department in Shanghai, established in July 1926. Peasants rose in support of the NATIONAL REVOLUTIONARY ARMY as it fought its way north.

Back in Hunan at the end of the year, Mao declared that the peasant problem was the national revolution's central issue. In early 1927, he wrote his famous "Report of an Investigation into the Peasant Movement in Hunan," which emphasized the primacy of the peasants and was a landmark in his adaptation of Marxism-Leninism to Chinese conditions. It was by omitting

China's Mao Zedong with the Soviet Union's Nikita Khrushchev, 1958; behind the smiles, they detested each other

the leading role of the proletariat that Mao departed from the orthodox line advocated by the CCP and Moscow.

The rupture of the united front later in the year forced the CCP to practice, but still not formally acknowledge, Mao's rural-based strategy. Driven underground in the cities, where GMD terror claimed thousands of victims, the CCP began a slow and agonizing process of recovery in the countryside. The NANCHANG UPRISING of August l, 1927, which marked the birth of the RED ARMY, and the AUTUMN HARVEST UPRISINGS of September, led by Mao, all ended in defeat, but by the end of the year, after leading a retreat to Jinggangshan in southern Jiangxi, Mao was firmly committed to the strategy that would eventually bring victory: a concentration on the peasants, the establishment of rural bases and a peasant-based army. Elected in absentia to the CC at the 6th CCP congress held in Moscow in 1928, Mao, backed by Zhu De's forces, built Communist power in south-central China while the official CCP leadership functioned underground in Shanghai. In 1929, GMD pressure forced Mao and Zhu to move to Ruijin in southern Jiangxi, which was to remain their main base for the next five years. In 1930, Mao ruthlessly suppressed a rebellion against his authority. In what was essentially a power struggle, he ordered several thousand opponents to be tied up and executed. The Futian "Incident," or "Massacre," was one of the bloodiest purges in CCP history, and one of the rare occasions Mao had party rivals killed in Stalinist fashion. That year too, Mao's wife, who had remained in Hunan, was executed by a warlord ally of the GMD. In 1928 Mao had begun living with an 18 year-old girl, whom he now presumably married.

Establishing guerrilla bases—called soviets—in Jiangxi and other provinces in south-central China, Mao's peasant-oriented strategy expanded Communist power. Land reform was the key to rural mobilization. The Communists not only confiscated and redistributed large holdings but indoctrinated peasants with the concept of class struggle. However, in 1931, the central CCP command moved to Jiangxi from Shanghai, where its position had become untenable. Moscow-trained leaders reduced Mao's authority, especially in the military sphere. ZHOU ENLAI, who sided with Mao's opponents, became political commissar of the Red Army. Mao, however, was elected chairman of the Chinese Soviet Republic established in November. Although the Red Army withstood four GMD encirclement campaigns (1930–1933), the fifth, launched in October 1933, forced the Communists to evacuate the Jiangxi base and embark upon the LONG MARCH to Shaanxi in the northwest (1934-1935). On the way, the Zunyi conference (January 1935) elected Mao chairman of the Politburo. He was now the CCP's supreme leader, the first not to have received Moscow's prior endorsement. In late December he led the Communists to Yan'an, their new capital.

The Yan'an decade (1937–1947) was crucial. Mao established monolithic authority, soon to bloom into a personality cult, and forged the tools required for final victory. Surviving the ordeal of the Long March had endowed him with a personal sense of destiny and unlimited faith in what could be accomplished by human will. This strong voluntarist belief distinguished Mao's ideology—MAOISM or Mao Zedong Thought—that became CCP orthodoxy during this period, and energized the build up of Red power in Yan'an. External events also helped. The kidnapping of Chiang Kai-shek by recalcitrant nationalist forces in Xi'an in December 1936 and the Japanese invasion of July 1937 induced the GMD to form a second united front with the CCP. The CCP gained legal status and several years' respite from GMD forces as well as from the Japanese invaders, who first concentrated on the nationalists. Mao had the opportunity to bring old party foes into line and indoctrinate new members through "thought reform" campaigns. Above all, he could have his way in turning the Communist revolution into a peasant revolution. Combining anti-Japanese and nationalist sentiments with a moderate land reform program, Mao brought hundreds of thousands into the Communist fold. He built a powerful, peasant-based Red Army using his own strategy of mobile warfare that withstood the Japanese after 1939 and the GMD after 1945. He also created an administrative system that could compete successfully with the GMD national government for the hearts and minds of China. In recognition of his supreme leadership, a new post, chairman of the CC, in essence chairman of the party, was created for him in 1943. His personal life had earlier evoked some criticism from comrades when he took up with JIANG QING, a glamorous actress, even before he had divorced his second wife (who had accompanied him on the Long March). As Mao's third wife, Jiang would symbolize the worst excesses of the Cultural Revolution (see GREAT PROLETARIAN CULTURAL REVOLUTION).

The 7th CCP congress, in May 1945, convened a few months before the end of the Sino-Japanese war of 1937–1945, found the CCP poised for the final struggle with the GMD. The new party constitution acknowledged Mao's ideological authority by taking Mao Zedong Thought as its guideline. Though Mao went through the motions of negotiating with Chiang Kai-shek, whom he met in Chongqing a few weeks after Japan's surrender on August 14, 1945, he prepared for a military showdown and was confident of victory. During three years of fighting, from 1946–1949, Communist forces, renamed the PEOPLE'S LBERATION ARMY (PLA), drove GMD forces from the mainland, leaving Taiwan as their sole remaining bastion. On October 1, 1949 Mao proclaimed the establishment of the People's Republic of China (PRC) with its capital in Beijing (formerly Beiping), and with himself as chairman of the central government.

One of the first items on Mao's agenda was to make arrangements with STALIN, who had been surprised by, and had contributed little to, the CCP triumph. Mao's visit to Moscow in December was his first trip outside China and resulted in a compromise treaty that gave the PRC protection against the US, along with loans and technical assistance, and allowed the Russians to retain rights temporarily in southern Manchuria. In the Korean War of 1950–1953, the PLA fought United Nations forces to a standstill, and relations with the US hardened. But Sino-Soviet relations also deteriorated in the late 1950s and ruptured completely in 1960. Attacking Soviet "revisionism," Mao challenged Moscow's leadership in the international anti-imperialist camp. In 1971, the UN voted to admit the PRC and expel Taiwan. Relations with the US had in the meantime improved, and President Nixon's visit to the PRC (1972) symbolized the end of mutual hostility. Thus Mao lived to see China regain national dignity and international recognition as a major power.

China under Mao made rapid strides toward modernization and industrialization and achieved greater social equality, especially through land-reform, in which at least a million landlords were killed. Concerned with maintaining revolutionary vigor—permanent revolution—Mao periodically convulsed China with struggles and mass campaigns. About one million counterrevolutionaries were killed in the 1950s. The "Hundred Flowers" campaign (1956–1957), ostensibly designed to win support of intellectuals, exposed the régime to unexpected criticism and resulted in the suppression of intellectuals. THE GREAT LEAP FORWARD (1958–1959), a frantic drive to increase production, was an unmitigated disaster, costing millions of lives. Comrades became disenchanted and tried to restore rationality to economic planning. Liu Shaoqi replaced Mao as chief of state in 1959. While resigning all executive authority, Mao began plotting against revisionism. The Cultural Revolution (1966–1976) was the last and most turbulent of his mass campaigns. Millions again suffered and died, including heroes of the revolution. Official history blames Lin Biao and Jiang Qing, Mao's wife, for Cultural Revolution atrocities, but that painful chapter in PRC history did not end completely until Mao died in September 1976.

The CCP has acknowledged Mao's errors, but claims that his "merits are primary and his errors secondary," which is how Mao evaluated Stalin. Mao and Mao Zedong Thought cannot be delegitimized without risking delegitimization of the party and the revolution. His memory, therefore, is officially honored in the PRC. In practice there is little left of his legacy. Yet if post-Mao economic development creates acute disparities in wealth, his utopian vision could become a rallying point for the discontented.

In retrospect, Mao can be seen as the product of the two forces that shaped modern Chinese history. The first was the intellectual awakening that began in the late 19th century, when he was born, and which by 1919 had turned into a real cultural revolution. The second was peasant violence, the force that throughout Chinese history had catalyzed dynastic upheavals. Mao's great achievement was in fusing the two. Applying Leninist technique to the countryside, he led modern intellectuals in the mass mobilization of peasants, whose grievances he had understood since childhood. The strategy worked in making a revolution. It was less successful in reaping its fruits. The calamities Mao's policies inflicted upon China can be attributed to aspects of traditional peasant culture as well as personal idiosyncrasies. In later years, scorn for intellectuals led him to scorn learning and science in general. Even Marxism, he felt, could be spoiled by too much study. He admired LI ZICHENG, the bandit who toppled the Ming dynasty (1368–1644), and illiterates who became Chinese emperors. Ironically, the man who started out to modernize China came to emulate the arrogance and disregard for human life that characterized the most despotic of traditional emperors.

MARAGEI, ZAIN AL-ABEDIN (1837–1910) Iranian statesman and ideologue for the modernization of Iranian society. Born in Maraga, Northern Iran, into a merchant family, Maragei emigrated to Caucasus (Russia) in 1855. He made a significant contribution to the development of nationalist writing and sociopolitical ideas in Iran. His long stay in Russia and repeated trips to European countries had an important influence on the formation of Maragei's world outlook. His works advocated the establishment of a parliamentary system in Iran. He was the author of

the first projected Iranian constitution. He was sharply opposed to official religion and religious fanaticism. At the same time, though, Maragei was an opponent of any pro-western orientation. He fought to renew the traditional institutions of the feudal society and to bring religious dogmas into line with the necessities of modern development.

MARAT, JEAN-PAUL (1743–1793) French physician, journalist and politician, leader of the Montagnard faction during the FRENCH REVOLUTION of 1789. Born to poor parents in Boudry, Switzerland, Marat settled in England in 1765. He studied medicine, acquired some repute as a doctor in London and Paris and published books on both scientific and philosophical subjects. His most famous work, *Philosophical Essay on Man* (1773), was attacked by the French philosopher Voltaire for its extreme materialism.

Marat returned to France in 1774 and secured an appointment as physician to the personal guards of the Comte d'Artois, Louis

The Death of Marat, *by Andrei Dimitrievich Goncharov, 1927*

XVI's youngest brother (later Charles X). Despite an increasingly lucrative practice among the wealthy aristocracy, Marat was obsessed with obtaining a reputation for himself as a scientist and philosopher. However, when he submitted a book of theory and experiments claiming to have toppled Isaac Newton's sacrosanct science of optics, the French Academy of Sciences categorically denounced it as a sham. Marat, thoroughly convinced that powerful enemies had conspired to persecute him and prevent his election to the academy, nursed his grievances and later had his revenge when, in 1793, he was instrumental in bringing about the abolition of France's corporate academies.

At the beginning of the French Revolution, Marat published a pamphlet entitled *Offering to Our Country*, in which he expressed the view that the monarchy was still capable of solving France's social and economic problems. However, the experiences of the early months of the revolution soon transformed him into one of the most radical of revolutionaries. In September 1789 he became the editor of the propagandist paper *L'Ami du Peuple* (Friend of the people), which he used to vent his bitter hatred and suspicion of those in power. He denounced those he suspected of treason and demanded that repressive measures be taken against counterrevolutionaries. "Blood must flow," he proclaimed.

From October 1789 to the fall of the monarchy on August 19, 1792, Marat was frequently arrested. Outlawed, he twice fled to England, in 1790 and in the summer of 1791, and during the interval between these two flights he hid in the sewers of Paris. During this difficult period he continued to publish his journal in secret and to attack Jacques Necker, the king's finance minister, and such moderate revolutionary figures as the MARQUIS DE LAFAYETTE, COMTE DE MIRABEAU, and Jean Sylvain Bailly, mayor of Paris.

He also continued to warn against the emigrés who were urging foreign powers to restore the monarchy. These inflammatory articles helped to foment the August 10, 1792 uprising and the September massacres.

Entering public life again in August 1792, his popularity ensured him a seat in the National CONVENTION, which was empowered to draft a new constitution. In the Convention, as a member of the JACOBINS and in his journal, Marat continued to call for the execution of counterrevolutionaries. Popular with the Parisians, Marat soon became one of the most influential members of the Convention. When, in the spring of 1793, France suffered further defeats in the war against Austria and internal rebellion brewed, Marat blamed the crisis on the GIRONDINS, the dominant political group in the Convention. His constant attacks against the Girondins made him a symbol of the radical Montagnard faction and in April the Girondins had him arraigned before the revolutionary tribunal of Paris for sedition. However, his popularity among the Parisans assured his acquittal and guaranteed the beginning of the fall from power of the Girondins.

His triumph, however, was short-lived. On July 13, 1793, seriously ill, he was at work preparing the Bastille Day issue of his newspaper when CHARLOTTE CORDAY, a 24-year-old Girondin supporter from Normandy, gained admission and stabbed him to death with a six-inch butcher knife. Marat's violent murder had a profound impact on the political scene. The Girondins were immediately hunted down and executed and his death served to consolidate and intensify the Terror. Marat was exalted to the

position of martyr and became the object of a revolutionary cult. The Enragés, a radical group that Marat had attacked during his lifetime, claimed to continue Marat's tradition and founded their own newspaper with the same title as Marat's journal. 21 French towns were named after him, and until the reaction of 1795 Marat was considered the "friend of the people and martyr for liberty." He was initially buried in the Panthéon, but when the moderate counteraction gained the upper hand, the body was removed.

MARATHA REVOLT The Marathas are a certain caste grouping in the region of India bounded by Bombay to the north, Goa to the south and the region around the town of Nagpur to the east. More generally, they are the leaders and warriors of the Maratha kingdom originally founded by SIVAJI in the 17th century and expanded by his successors (of many castes) during the 18th century. The Marathas are famed as martial champions of Hinduism, which they sought to defend first against the encroachments of Islam and later against British sovereignty. Traditionally, just 96 clans have the right to call themselves Marathas, but which clans actually constitute this elect group is the subject of considerable dispute.

The Maratha decline after Sivaji's death was arrested after the death of the Mughal emperor Aurangzeb in 1707, at which time Shahu, Sivaji's grandson, established a governmental system for the Maratha kingdom based on the rule of six peshwas, or governors, of leading Maratha families. Led by these peshwas, the Marathas enjoyed significant military successes against the Mughals to the north and managed to extend their kingdom up into modern-day Gujarat and beyond. However, factional infighting always dogged the Maratha hierarchy.

The control of the peshwas effectively ended with military defeats in 1772, to be replaced by a Maratha confederacy of five chieftains under the nominal leadership of the Peshwa of Poona. However, internecine quarrels continued to bitterly divide the confederation. It nonetheless managed to maintain its independence from the Mughals and other Muslim powers in India until the British achieved effective control of the subcontinent. Thereafter, through the Maratha wars of 1772–1782, 1803–1805 and 1817–1818, the Marathas put up sufficient resistance to these new invaders to enable their chieftains to negotiate agreements that allowed for Maratha rule (under British suzerainty) of significant areas of central and southern India.

MARCH ON ROME The coup d'état that took place on October 28, 1922, marking the rise to power of the Fascist party (see FASCISM) in Italy. Following the congress of the Fascist party held at Naples on October 24, tens of thousands of blackshirts began gathering in four towns surrounding Rome. They were largely unorganized and unarmed, yet King Emanuel II refused to allow the Italian army to act against them. Instead, he chose to summon BENITO MUSSOLINI from Milan to appoint him prime minister. Mussolini arrived in Rome on October 30 to take over the reins of government. This episode was later magnified by Fascist propaganda and turned into the organization's heroic "March on Rome."

MARCOS A Mexican young man who gave himself the pseudonymic title "Subcomandante Marcos" and who first appeared during the two-day takeover of San Cristobal de las Casas, Chiapas, southern Mexico, in January 1994. The name Marcos has since become almost synonymous with the EZLN (see ZAPATISTA NATIONAL LIBERATION ARMY), the indigenous armed revolutionary force which has since controlled the Lacandon forest and, at times, surrounding areas of extreme southern Mexico. During 1994, Marcos, whose face, like those of other EZLN members, has always been concealed behind a ski mask, captured the imagination of much of Mexico and, to a surprising extent, the media and informed public of the west, with his vehement eloquence and flamboyant gift for language. Several editions of his sometimes lengthy communiques on behalf of the EZLN have been published in the USA, France and Germany, among other countries, as well as throughout Latin America. Their contents range from relatively standard left-wing revolutionary rhetoric to powerful renderings of traditional Mayan mythology, from short stories and poetry to children's tales, liberally laced with quotes and footnotes ranging from Shakespeare and Cervantes to pop music. The communiques almost invariably have been published full-length in at least one and often three or more of Mexico City's most influential daily newspapers, sometimes occupying two or three tabloid-size pages.

It is these communiques of Subcomandante Marcos and others issued by the EZLN's general command, known as the Indigenous Clandestine Revolutionary Committee (CCRI), which have sounded the rallying cries for Mexico's mass democratic and peace movements. The key sections of these movements include the center-left Party of the Democratic Revolution (PRD), the nexus of the forces which supported Cuauhtemoc Cardenas in his independent bid for the presidency in 1988 (and as PRD candidate again in 1994); the National Democratic Coalition (CND), bringing together the democratic and pro-peace forces which mobilized in the wake of the EZLN uprising and which look to it for leadership; and the growing independent citizens' movements, joined in part into coalitions of such non-governmental organizations as *Alianza Civica*, which coordinated a

massive citizens' observer effort during the 1994 elections. To an extent, these alternative movements owe their visibility to the charisma of the man who calls himself Subcomandante Marcos.

MARCUSE, HERBERT (1898–1979) Left-wing philosopher and social theorist, considered the ideologue of the New Left. His family, of Jewish origin, had fairly well assimilated into the German middle class. Two years into World War I, Marcuse was drafted into the army. The war awakened him, for the first time, to political consciousness. Set on the road to radicalization, he joined the German Social Democratic Party and participated in the abortive German Revolution of 1918.

With the end of the war, Marcuse began to study, first in Berlin and later at Freiburg University. With a comfortable stipend from home, he was able to devote himself fully to the study of German literature and philosophy. Influenced at this stage by Hegel, he completed a doctoral dissertation on German literature that incorporated Hegelian dialectics. Returning to Berlin in 1922, he began a thorough study of KARL MARX, although the interpretation of Marx in the Soviet Union troubled him. It was also at this period that he became immersed in the works of Schiller, publishing *Schiller Bibliographie* in 1925.

In 1927, the publication of Martin Heidegger's *Being and Time* imprinted itself on Marcuse as a turning point in the history of philosophy, and he returned to Freiburg for further studies. The philosophy he himself eventually evolved, of "critical theory," was a blend of Schiller, existentialism, utopianism, MARXISM and Hegelian dialectical method—which analyzed and criticized prevailing social, political and cultural institutions.

In 1933, the specter of Nazism helped convince Marcuse to accept a position at the Frankfurt Institute for Social Research, which moved its center of activity from Germany to Geneva and, in the following year, to New York.

In the early 1940s, Marcuse accepted an invitation from Washington, where, over the next 10 years he served as an intelligence analyst in various agencies of the US government. In

Mussolini organizing the Blackshirts for the March on Rome, Milan, which took place on October 28, 1922; note the white spats

1951, after the onset of the cold war, he left government service to return to academic life. He was a fellow of Russian research centers at Columbia and Harvard and was appointed professor of philosophy and politics at Brandeis University in 1954. In 1965, he became a professor of philosophy at the university of California in San Diego.

Becoming increasingly radical and eventually a hero to the New Left, in all his writings Marcuse retained the idea of the fragmentation of human life in modern society. Challenging conventional American social thought, he sought to apply a Marxian analysis to society with the hope of eventually changing it. However, he rejected the versions of Marxian orthodoxy expounded by any particular nation or group. His concept of "one-dimensional man" exposes a society based on the domination of capitalism, regarding capitalist society as repressive by nature, satisfying those material needs it generates while suppressing human needs, including love and sex. In this society, which is totalitarian by virtue of its economic organization, man becomes tied to the commodity market. However, western man has the potentiality to move beyond violence and anarchy to construct a revolutionary new society based on a combination of Marxist and Freudian ideas.

His best writings include *Reason and Revolution: Hegel and the Rise of Social Theory* (1941, 1954), *Eros and Civilization: A Philosophical Inquiry into Freud* (1955), *One-Dimensional Man: Studies in the Ideology of Advanced Industrial Society* (1964) and *An Essay on Liberation* (1969).

MARSEILLAISE, LA

The French national anthem, written and composed in Strasbourg on April 15, 1792 on the eve of a turning point in the fortunes of the FRENCH REVOLUTION, by Rouget de Lisle, a young officer in the French Army of the Rhine stationed in Alsace across from the German frontier.

News of the French revolutionary government's declaration of war against the emperor of Austria had reached Strasbourg, where the mayor was giving a reception for a group of French officers, including the patriotic Rouget de Lisle, on their way to the front. The mayor deplored the lack of a revolutionary anthem on the eve of a war to be launched against the old régimes of the rest of Europe and asked the young officer to compose one.

Rouget de Lisle is said to have written both the lyrics and music in an upsurge of creative passion in the course of a single sleepless night, although his authorship of the words has sometimes been disputed.

First published in Strasbourg under the title *Le Chant de Guerre pour l'Armée du Rhin,* it spread like wildfire, all the way down the Rhône to the southern provinces of the Bouches du Rhône. It was immediately adopted as a marching song by the *fédérés* (or local militia) units marching from Marseilles to Paris, who sang it as they assembled at the Place de la Bastille to mark the anniversary of July 14, 1789 before launching the insurrection of August 10 which resulted in the sack of the Tuileries and the collapse of the monarchy in the name of the republic. Adopted in turn by the working class of Paris to replace their old revolutionary chant, *Ça Ira* (or "Things will get Better") and then gradually by the rest of the French provinces as the republic's national song, the *Marseillaise* became world-famous following the republic's great victory over the Austrians at the battle of Valmy on September 20, 1792. The German poet Goethe, who heard it for the first time as it was sung by an official order on the field of battle, hailed Valmy as the turning point in world history. It was banned for a time by Napoleon as too revolutionary for his taste and again during the Bourbon Restoration of Louis XVIII and Charles X from 1815 to 1830, as well as throughout most of the Second Empire (1852–1870) under Napoleon III. The *Marseillaise* did not become France's official national anthem until the Third Republic and the suppression of the PARIS COMMUNE in 1871. The Commune marked the introduction of a rival and even more stirring revolutionary anthem, the Communist *Internationale,* also composed by a talented Frenchman from the north.

MARTÍ, JOSÊ JULIAN

(1853–1895) One of the fathers of Cuban nationalism; founder of the Modernist movement in Spanish literature. The son of a Spanish colonial soldier, Martí was born in Havana, Cuba. An impressionable, bookish child, he later recalled that among his earliest memories was the sight of black slaves beaten for some minor infraction. Like his fellow students, Martí engaged in anticolonial activities, which gained impetus following RAFAEL MARLA DE MENDIVE's arrest in 1869. The next day, Martí's first underground newspaper, *La Patria Libre*, was published. One day, however, Martí and his friends jeered at a parade of Spanish soldiers from a window. That night the soldiers returned, bursting into the house and arresting Martí's friends. A search revealed several copies of *La Patria Libre* and a letter that Martí had sent to a schoolmate, castigating him for enlisting in the colonial army. Although only 15, Martí was charged with treason and sentenced to six years' imprisonment with hard labor. With the support of the local governor, he was granted permission to travel to Spain in 1871, since it was believed that this would prevent him from fomenting trouble on the island.

Martí impressed the Cuban expatriate community in Spain by his moving account of prison life. While a student in Madrid and Saragossa, he produced several nationalist pamphlets which received wide circulation; the atmosphere in Spain was charged with a revolutionary spirit. Although the short-lived first Spanish republic (1873–1874) offered considerable social changes in Spain, little was done to improve the lot of the colonies.

Martí supported the republicans in the civil war. After their defeat, he hastily completed his studies and traveled via France to Mexico, where he won renown as a journalist and playwright, celebrated for his *Amor Con Amor se Page* (Love is repaid with love).

Martí spent his last 15 years in New York, where he published some of his most memorable poetry; including *Ismaelilo* and *Guantanamero.* Much of the time he journeyed through Latin America seeking support for an independent Cuba. His activities resulted in the formation of the Cuban Revolutionary Party, opposition to any concessions to the Spanish as envisioned by the failed Peace of Zanjón, and advocating armed revolt as the sole feasible means of attaining independence. Encouraged by the Montecristi uprising, he sailed for Cuba to take part in the revolt.

Martí and his companions reached Cuba on April 11, 1895. The apostle of Cuban nationalism was named a major general in the rebel army. For one month he and his troops wandered the mountainous countryside, attempting to join the main rebel army but he was not successful; Martí was killed in his first skirmish. His collected writings, comprising 74 volumes, were published between 1936 and 1953.

MARSHAL REBELLION (1233–1234) Richard Marshal, the earl of Pembroke, led a rebellion against King Henry III of England and his advisers, the Poitevins, Peter des Roches, bishop of Winchester, and Peter de Rivaux. He allied himself with the Welsh, including Llywelyn the Great of Gwynedd. In essence, the rebellion was based on dislike of foreign influence and the diminishing of the influence at court of those who revolted. The actual fighting did not last long in Wales and Ireland, where Pembroke was wounded and then murdered by the English on April 1, 1234. Instead of a policy of repression, Henry III opted for reconciliation: he sacked the Poitevins and replaced their English allies with Pembroke's brother Gilbert and a number of others who had actually taken part in the rebellion.

MARTOV, YULY OSIPOVICH (1873–1923) Russian socialist politician. Born to a Jewish family named Tsederbaum, Martov was a revolutionary from an early age. In 1900, he helped found the newspaper *Iskra*, which he edited together with LENIN. He split with the latter, however, during the 1903 Congress of the Russian Social Democratic Party, from this point on becoming the leader of the party's reformist wing, the MENSHEVIKS. At the outbreak of World War I, he assumed leadership of an "Internationalist" group of Mensheviks that opposed the war, and took part in the Zimmerwald peace conference of 1917. After the October RUSSIAN REVOLUTION OF 1917, he was allowed to leave the country and spent his last years in Germany editing a socialist newspaper.

MARX, KARL (1818–1883) German social and political philosopher, founder and chief ideologist of many 19th and 20th century revolutionary movements including MARXISM, SOCIALISM, and COMMUNISM.

Marx was born in Trier to a Jewish family; his ancestors on both sides were distinguished rabbis. His father, a lawyer, had converted to Protestantism so as to continue working in his profession when the Prussians occupied the Rhineland in 1815. Marx himself was baptized in 1824; religion, however, never meant anything to him. Much later he was to dismiss it in his famous remark that "religion is the opium of the masses," meaning that it was used by the powers that were in control to make the people forget their economic plight.

At first, Marx studied at the University of Bonn—where, during the only period in his life, he got into wine, women and song—and then at Berlin. In Berlin he became a member of the Young Hegelian Circle, a loose group of students of philosophy who wished to extend the theories of Georg Friedrich Hegel in all directions, both probable and improbable. In 1842 he received his doctorate, his dissertation being on the ancient Greek philosopher Heraclitus. The next year he married the daughter of an aristocratic Trier family, Jenny von Westphalen, to whom he had been engaged for years.

A born rebel, Marx moved to Cologne, where he edited a liberal newspaper. He used his position to attack the conservative Prussian government of the day, even calling on the citizens to resist tax collectors, arms in hand. Within the year his paper was suppressed and he himself was forced to leave for Paris. There he met FRIEDRICH ENGELS, another young revolutionary of a good family, who was to become a lifelong friend and collaborator. The first fruit of their meeting, a work known as *The German Ideology*, was written in 1844, but remained unknown for almost a century before it was rediscovered.

In 1845, the Prussian government pressured France to expel Marx and he moved to Brussels. A short visit to the north of England, which was the world's manufacturing center and where Engels was serving an apprenticeship in his family's textile business, brought him face to face with the industrial revolution and the misery it had brought to the working classes. From this time on he was not just a rebel but something much more dangerous, a rebel with a cause. Over the next two years he was active in founding the German Workers' Party in Paris and also helped set up the COMMUNIST LEAGUE in London. It was for the latter that, in 1848, he and Engels wrote the *Communist Manifesto*—the most famous revolutionary tract of all time which, over the next century, was to be translated into over 100 languages and to sell 14 million copies.

In 1848, it was the turn of the Belgian government to expel Marx. The outbreak of the REVOLUTIONS OF 1848 enabled him to go back to Cologne, where he edited the *Neue Rheinische Zeitung* (New Rhinish Paper). Several months of fiery pro-worker journalism ensued; only to be broken off as Prussian troops restored order. Marx returned to France but, expelled once again, went to London in August 1849. There he and his family remained to the end of his life.

A frustrated revolutionary journalist, Marx's first London writings were *The Class Struggle in France* and *The Eighteenth of Brumaire of Louis Bonaparte*, masterly tracts in which he analyzed the events of 1848–1852. He dabbled in working-class politics but, too much of an intellectual to be an effective popular speaker, settled down to create a serious "scientific" basis for the revolutionary theories first proclaimed in *The German Ideology* and *The Communist Manifesto*. The result was *A Contribution to the Critique of Political Economy* (1859), possibly the best work he ever wrote.

The end of glory; Karl Marx and Vladimir Lenin after the failed Communist uprising, Moscow, August 1991

By this time Marx was 41 years old, a rather swarthy man (he was nicknamed "Moor") with a beard and huge mane of black hair that was later to turn a most impressive white. He, his wife, two daughters and young son lived in Soho, near the center of London. From time to time their material situation was such that Marx had to pawn his coat. He even tried to take on a job as a clerk, only to be dismissed for his illegible handwriting. He survived by drawing on friends, anticipating his own and his wife's inheritance, and making occasional contributions to American newspapers. In 1864, he helped found the First INTERNATIONAL, a working class organization for which he wrote a declaration of faith as well as provisional rules. Over the next few years he did a great deal of work for the organization, whose membership, at its peak, reached 180,000.

Meanwhile, his main occupation was to research what was to become his chef d'oeuvre, *Das Kapital* (Capital). Working in the reading room of the British Museum where his chair is still shown, he dedicated himself to this work for which, in his own words, he sacrificed health and family, though not enough to avoid fathering an illegitimate son with the Marx family's housekeeper, Helen Demuth. Despite his immense experience as a journalist, Marx was never a fluent writer or even a particularly well organized one. When the first volume of *Capital* (the other three were never finished and had to be published by Engels after Marx's death) appeared in 1867, it contained an outstanding historical account of the origin of capitalism as well as thundering pro-working class rhetoric, but also plenty of abstruse, barely readable, economic analysis. The book, which he had wanted to dedicate to Charles Darwin (who, however, refused the honor) sold poorly. Only in the last years of Marx's life did sales of the Russian translation pick up, which made him think that the revolution might come to that backward country before it visited the more highly industrialized west.

By this time, Marx was a recognized leader of the international working class movement, attending congresses and corresponding with other socialist leaders all over Europe. His financial situation was eased somewhat as Engels regularly sent him sums of money. Yet fame came only in 1871 when, after the crushing of the PARIS COMMUNE, he wrote a pamphlet entitled *The Civil War in France*, in praise of what he saw as the first experiment in the dictatorship of the proletariat. This made his name synonymous with revolution; yet he retained his sense of humor, describing himself as a "bookworm" and remarking that "I at any rate, am no Marxist."

The *Critique of the Gothe Program*, which he wrote in 1875 to counter the platform of the newly formed German Social Democratic Party, was Marx's last great effort. His (legitimate) son was dead, his wife ill, and the marriage of one of his daughters on the rocks. To top it all his health deteriorated. In another outburst of self-depreciating humor, he once said he would "yet make the capitalists pay for my boils." He was shattered by the deaths of his wife in December 1881 and of one of his daughters in January 1883. Two months later he, too, died of lung trouble and was buried in Highgate cemetery, not too far from the Hampstead home where he had spent his last years.

By that time, his system of revolutionary thought, known as Marxism and branching off into socialism on the one hand and communism on the other, was set to become the most important of its kind in history. Spreading into virtually every country, by 1917 it had taken over one large state. In 1950–1975, one third of the globe's population swore by Marx's name and much of the rest was busily trying to find antidotes to his influence. Though out of fashion just at present, the last word on him has certainly not been said. Nor is there any doubt that, as long as the problems of social classes and contrasts between wealth and poverty persist, Marx will be remembered as the man who made the greatest, most sustained and most impressive attempt to find a solution.

FROM THE WRITINGS OF KARL MARX

• A specter is haunting Europe—the specter of Communism.

• This history of all hitherto existing society is the history of class struggle.

• Hegel says somewhere that all great events and personalities in world history reappear in one fashion or another. He forgot to add: the first time as tragedy, the second as farce.

• Capitalist production begets, with the inexorability of a law of nature, its own negation.

• In proportion, as the antagonism between the classes vanishes, the hostility of one nation to another will come to an end.

• The proletariat have nothing to lose but their chains. They have a world to win. Workers of the world, unite!

The Communist Manifesto—written with Friedrich Engels

• From each according to his abilities, to each according to his needs.

Critique of the Gothe Program

MARXISM

Marxist Ideology. FRIEDRICH ENGELS eulogized KARL MARX by saying, "Just as Darwin discovered the law of evolution in organic nature, so Marx discovered the law of evolution in human history." Marx's evolutionary approach to history led to revolutionary ideologies. Until Marx, philosophers had seen their role as merely interpreting history; the Marxists took on the role of revolutionizing it. What the Marxists took from their intellectual predecessors was not only a philosophy of history but also the practical conclusion of avoiding collaboration between the classes. This separated Marxism from SOCIALISM.

In their book, *The German Ideology* (1845–1846), Marx and Engels claimed that revolutions are cataclysmic leaps from one means of production to another. A historical period is distinguished from the preceding one by the development of a new mode of production, which leads to a struggle between the class that represents the old order of the forces of production and the one that represents the new order. Engels wrote that "the final causes of all social changes and political revolutions are to be sought... in changes in the modes of production and exchange." The outcome of the "socialist revolution" will be equality between the old exploitative class and the new dominant class—that is, a classless society. Until then there will only be "bourgeois revolutions"—such as the British, American and French ones—which are motivated by the need for expansion of the new capitalist forces of production.

Revolutionary France in the 18th and 19th centuries was a laboratory of historical materialism. However, in contrast to Engels's interpretation, Marx did not consider France an arena for a socialist revolution. Rather, France's history served for him as a proof by reductio ad absurdum of the lack of class consciousness. The FRENCH REVOLUTION OF 1789 and the REVOLUTIONS OF 1848 as well as the PARIS COMMUNE, were a historical lesson and warning that economic conditions were not ripe for a socialist revolution.

Around 1848, Marx, as editor of the *Neue Rheinische Zeitung*, wrote more about democratic radicalism than about proletarian revolutions. His conclusion—that the workers' movement must undergo a bourgeois revolution—was adopted by Russian Marxists in the early 20th century. Nevertheless, Marx's and Engels's political activities were clearly revolutionary: They joined the First INTERNATIONAL as "Bund der Kommunisten" and even wrote the *Communist Manifesto* for it, describing the proletariat as "the only revolutionary class."

Historical Necessity Versus Philosophy of Action. Around 1900, a crisis occurred among the European Marxists, with far-reaching implications for the first quarter of the 20th century. The growing awareness that Marxist predictions were not being fulfilled in practice led to the conclusion that there was some serious flaw in Marxist analysis in the guise of scientific socialism. The revolution had not yet arrived, in spite of the economic, political and sociological processes that were supposed to bring it about. The agents of modernization, such as progressive education, the universal right to vote and compulsory army service, which had been expected to lead to class consciousness and motivate revolutionary action among the proletariat, served instead as a means for national and cultural integration and as catalysts for the growth of patriotism and a retreat from antimilitarism. The non-arrival of the expected proletarian revolution, combined with the growing nationalist trends, were a severe shock to the Marxists. This led to two revisions in Marxism, whose common denominator was the goal of forming an egalitarian, classless society: EDUARD BERNSTEIN pointed out the possibility of realizing socialism by playing the rules of the parliamentary game, without a social revolution, while VLADIMIR LENIN strove to bring about the revolution through a revolutionary elite organized into party cadres. The view associated with Bernstein, known as revisionism, cast doubt on the inevitability of the socialist revolution.

KARL KAUTSKY and GEORGI PLEKHANOV further developed the Marxist view of the proletariat as a universal revolutionary class. They claimed that objective historical necessity requires

stages of developed capitalism and polarization of the classes. At a certain point in human evolution, due to the relations between the classes, the forces of production are faced with the decreasing absorptive capability of their products. This socioeconomic contradiction creates social forces which are united in their revolutionary ideology, which brings down the old order and substitutes a new system of production. The revolutionary social order creates the social forces that will later bring it down; every revolution expands the base of the régime it sets up. The anti-feudal bourgeois revolution created the proletariat, which is the last revolutionary class.

If the economy is not yet ready for a revolution, no takeover of political power, such as that of Blanquism, will lead to the destruction of capitalism. There is no connection between objective economic laws and spontaneous violence, as illustrated by the JACOBIN dictatorship and the Paris commune. Revolutions, in Kautsky's view, are not one-shot aggressive acts, violent rebellions or civil wars, but the conscious takeover of political power by an organized proletariat when capitalism has reached a certain level of development. Here one can find the seeds of Kautsky's disagreement with Lenin. In contrast to Kautsky, who claimed that a Communist society would spring up as soon as the capitalist structure collapsed, the Bolsheviks believed that Russian Communism was a revolutionary transition stage and that the Russia of 1919 was in one stage of this transformation.

Kautsky opposed the October RUSSIAN REVOLUTION OF 1917, rejecting Lenin's idea of the dictatorship of the proletariat. He based his view on Marx's opposition to the Bakunists' (see MICHAEL BAKUNIN) attempt to foment a Communist rebellion in 1873 in Spain, as well as Marx's attitude to the Paris Commune. Kautsky claimed that the Bolsheviks (see BOLSHEVIK PARTY), like the Jacobins, were trying to solve economic problems by mass terror, which they wrongly called the dictatorship of the proletariat. In 1875, Marx announced in the Gotha Program that between the capitalist and Communist society lies a period of revolutionary transformation from one to the other. Corresponding to this is a political transition period during which the state can be nothing other than the revolutionary dictatorship of the proletariat. In 1919, Kautsky wrote that if the dictatorship of the revolution was to continue in Russia it would end up in militarization, bureaucratization and totalitarian rule. Lenin, on the other hand, accused Kautsky and the leaders of the Second INTERNATIONAL of being revolutionaries in language but reformists in practice.

The activists, whose spokesmen were Labriola, Goldmann and GRAMSCI, held a "philosophy of action," rejecting the Plekhanovist view of historical inevitability. They believed that the combination of the historical situation and social consciousness could lead to changes in the world. Following Marx, they claimed that the motivating force of the socialist revolution is the alliance of the suffering proletariat and the intellectuals. Thus Gramsci called the Communist party "the intellectual collective." Revolutionary ideologies turn sociological explanations into political forces: Marxism tried to make a revolutionary class out of the suffering of individuals.

Lenin developed a new view of revolutionary Marxism that did not wait for economic conditions to be ripe. He claimed that the party must take advantage of revolutionary situations and direct revolutions. The failure of the RUSSIAN REVOLUTION OF 1905

Marx's Das Kapital, *"second improved edition," 1877*

repeated the failure of the REVOLUTIONS OF 1848 in Western Europe, leading to the conclusion that a strategy of "PERMANENT REVOLUTION" must be adopted: there must be a continual thrust from bourgeois revolutions to socialist ones.

LEON TROTSKY, who after 1917 became the People's Commissar for War, believed that the democratic revolution in Russia would lead to a social-democratic régime which would necessarily continue the revolutionary trend toward socialism. Since the bourgeoisie was weak, the revolution would have to be led by the proletariat and therefore it would not stop at the bourgeois stage. Russia's economic situation would cause the bourgeois revolution to turn into a socialist one immediately and the revolutionary trend would spread from Russia to all of Europe, and from there to the entire world. If this did not happen and socialism would remain confined to one country, the revolution would not be maintainable. In 1924, STALIN formulated the expression, "SOCIALISM IN ONE COUNTRY," which was directed against Trotsky and the idea of the "permanent revolution." However, when Russian Communism failed to expand the revolution, it did indeed become a static power.

Bolshevism represented an attempt to change an evolutionary theory into a revolutionary practice. It combined the revolutionary elements in Marxism with the unique conditions in Russia:

forced industrialization, Russification of the population, a party dictatorship and class terror as a transition stage between capitalism and socialism, state socialism, the collectivization of the peasants, the exile and destruction of the Kulaks and the adoption of Taylor's methods of "scientific" management. The Communist end was supposed to justify all the revolutionary means.

While Marxist ideology was mainly theoretical, the revolutionary Bolshevik doctrine became a political practice carried out by a military and police organization. The revolutionary effort was concentrated on destroying the remnants of the bourgeois class and constructing the foundations of a Communist society. However, the revolutionary transition stage turned into a totalitarian reality for 70 years of Bolshevism. Kautsky accused Lenin and the Bolsheviks of maintaining their own rule through terror. The dictatorship of the proletariat, which Marx had considered a postrevolutionary transition stage, had become a dictatorship of the party. The great danger of using revolutionary means was the establishment of the revolutionary force to the point of centralizing bureaucratic power, violence, terror and the army.

Trotsky and ROSA LUXEMBURG both believed that a hierarchical, centralist party of professional revolutionaries contradicted the fundamental Marxist principle that the working class can liberate itself without outside help. Luxemburg's uncompromising revolutionary activity and her criticism of the socialists' defection in 1914 turned her into the principal opponent of both the revisionists and the bureaucratic establishment of Russian Marxism. In the "reformism vs. revolution" debate, she took the position that there is no contradiction between reform, which is a means, and the struggle for political power, which is an end in itself. The essence of reform is different from that of revolution; reform is not a stage of revolution. Luxemburg's blind faith that workers are naturally revolutionaries led her to place revolutionary spontaneity above organized party activity.

Marxism, Nationalism and Revolution. The Soviet Union, which considered itself the spearhead of the international revolution, was actually a disguise for Russian nationalism. Marxism, as well as the Marxism-Leninism that followed it, examined nationalism from the viewpoint of historical relativism: an independent national state is a structural part of the bourgeois revolution and a precondition for the victory of democracy. The fundamental economic assumption of the two doctrines is that the bourgeoisie, in order to achieve full control of production, dominates the local market by uniting territories into a state. The two consider the formation of "bourgeois nations" to be a historically progressive step. However, modern developments have shown that imperialism cannot exist with colonialist exploitation.

The Austrian Marxists, especially OTTO BAUER and Karl Ranner, devoted a great deal of thought to the problem of nationalism from the viewpoint of the Communist revolution. The Bolsheviks claimed that internationalism is the continuation of nationalism. The demand for national and racial equality played a more crucial role than the struggle for Communism in worldwide Communist propaganda.

Lenin advocated expanding the revolutionary movement to the colonial world. The Soviet Union inflamed nationalist struggles, moving them from Europe to the Third World. The fact that rightist military regimes supported by the west were in control of most of the countries of Asia and Africa left the revolutionary arena for the Russian Communists, who described themselves as the only effective alternative. After World War II, there was wide acceptance of the Soviet theory that socialism could spread throughout the world even during peacetime. This thesis was adopted at the same time as the competition with MAOISM for the leadership of the world socialist revolution.

The Revolution after Leninism—the Revolutionary Phase of Soviet Marxism. Many Marxists began to investigate postrevolutionary cultural, psychological and sociological issues, beginning in the 1930s. For example, the Frankfurt school, which combined the methods of Marx and Freud, used the Marxist view of the revolution as a starting point for diagnosing cultural and social conditions in which people lost their humanity in capitalism's "industrial culture." They aspired to formulate a critical theory that would expose the false consciousness of the proletariat. According to HERBERT MARCUSE, the proletariat has become part of the "one-dimensional society," which has lost its revolutionary imagination: the workers have become an inseparable part of the capitalist consciousness, which has neutralized the revolutionary option.

Maoism—the peasant's Marxism—is an ideological revolutionary branch that was adapted to the historical circumstances prevailing in China. The Maoists disagreed with the "orthodox" Chinese Marxists, who advocated the COMINTERN's conservative line and remained loyal to the Soviet strategy in which the revolution relies mainly on workers' strikes and rebellions in large industrial areas. In his 1940 article, "On New Democracy," Mao wrote that the Chinese revolution was essentially a peasant revolution relying on the peasants' demands, but the culture of the new democracy would develop under the leadership of the proletariat. At that time Mao's plan was similar to the first stage of Leninism: a peasantry led by the Communist party and a dictatorship of the proletariat. But soon, on the basis of the same internal logic that had prevailed in the Soviet revolution, the Chinese revolution as well turned into the totalitarian structure of a centralist, bureaucratic political power. In the Cultural Revolution (see GREAT PROLETARIAN CULTURAL REVOLUTION) of 1965 the radicals, led by Mao, tried to suppress the conservatives, who represented bourgeois ideology, especially in the universities.

The proletarian revolution is not only political but also cultural. When ANTONIO GRAMSCI, the leader of the COMMUNIST PARTY OF ITALY, analyzed the revolutions of the 19th century, he distinguished between "active rebellions," such as that of MAZZINI and "passive revolutions," such as that of Cavour, but claimed that both of them were necessary for post-1848 Europe. Gramsci did not consider a revolution to be a technical matter of taking over power.

The revolution is not proletarian and communistic because it destroys the institutions of the old régime, or because it calls its activists Communists, but because it liberates the existing productive forces and leads to the development of a society in which class distinction disappears. Forces must be found to transform the productive class from an instrument of suppression to an instrument of liberation. The role of the Communist party is to help liberate the proletariat, thus bringing the revolution closer.

György Lukács concentrated on explaining the revolutionary principle in theory and practice. For this purpose, he used the word *totalität* to describe the facts of the world as a "concrete whole." In this view, the truth of the parts is to be found in the whole: the whole is the motor of the revolutionary principle. According to Lukács, Lenin's greatness was that he understood this at the time of the Bolshevik revolution. Lenin identified the revolutionary moment in all the events of his time, uniting all the details into a revolutionary socialist perspective.

In the 1950s and 1960s, the Soviets suppressed national and civil liberties in the countries under the "protection" of the "revolutionary homeland." Rebellions broke out in Hungary and Czechoslovakia and there was a renaissance of the concept and topic of revolution. It was no longer an issue for the proletariat but became the province of suppressed minorities such as students, blacks and the countries of the Third World. The NEW LEFT tried to renew "true communism"; for this purpose, Maoists, Trotskyites and others made use of the jargon of the universal anti-capitalist revolution in the style of the Third World. They claimed that the idea of a society's "ripeness for revolution" was a bourgeois invention and that a well-organized group could radically change social conditions in a "revolution here and now." They adopted the notion of Lukács, Marcuse and the Frankfurt school that the capitalist society is an indivisible whole and can only change as such. The idea of a total revolution that requires destroying all the existing institutions and ruling elites came from their dynamist, nihilist orientation to the present as detached from the past and the future.

The Post Cold-War World. The 1990s are witness to the postrevolutionary age of Marxism. The Soviet Union had disintegrated, giving up its revolutionary Communist ideology, its nationalist imperialism and its Eastern European satellites. The creator of this counterrevolution was Gorbachev, who did not learn the lesson taught by Alexis de Tocqueville in the 19th century—that a totalitarian revolution which begins to conduct reforms presages its own downfall. The idea of the revolution in Marxism thus returns to its starting point—from practice to theory.

MASARYK, TOMÁS GARRIGUE (1850–1937) Founder of Czechoslovakia. The son of a Slovak coachman and a Czech domestic servant, Masaryk was born in a small town close to the present Czech-Hungarian border. After a short period working as a blacksmith's apprentice, Masaryk was enrolled in the local German high school in 1865. He graduated in 1876 with a doctorate in philosophy from the University of Vienna. That same year he married Charlotte Garrigue, an American music student he met while studying in Leipzig. In honor of her American family, he added their surname to his own, hence Garrigue Masaryk.

By 1881, Masaryk was a lecturer in philosophy at Vienna University; in 1882 he became a professor of philosophy at the Czech University in Prague. A strong interest in the revival of Czech culture provided the subject for some of his earliest works. He achieved a measure of fame in his unmasking of two literary forgeries. As in other parts of the Austro–Hungarian empire, cultural nationalism began to find political expression in the late 19th century, and Masaryk soon entered politics. As a democrat and a nationalist, Masaryk was first elected to the Austrian parliament in 1891, at which time he associated with the Young Czech movement.

In 1900 he founded his own Realist Party; it won only a few seats in the new parliament but its leader's influence far exceeded the number of votes at this time. Masaryk was a powerful advocate of minority rights within the empire and spoke out against the imperialist policies that paved the way for World War I. While a member of the imperial parliament, he again achieved renown through the discovery of forgeries—this time documents manufactured by the government to discredit the leaders of the Slavic minorities.

During World War I Masaryk went into voluntary exile in London, where he chaired the Czech National Council, a pressure group campaigning for an independent, democratic Czech-Slovak state. Viewing the war as a struggle between western liberal values and German totalitarian ones, he and others like him understood its implications for the minorities within the Austro-Hungarian empire who sought an opportunity to break free of rule from Vienna.

In June 1918, Czechoslovakia was recognized as an Allied power in the war against Germany, with frontiers as proposed by Masaryk.

Masaryk returned to his homeland and was elected president in November 1918, an office from which he worked tirelessly to mold the new state into an outpost of democracy within a Central Europe that had come to be dominated by totalitarian régimes. During 40 years of Communist rule that followed World War II, the name Masaryk was officially reviled and his works became unavailable. With the reestablishment of democracy in 1989, he again became a national hero.

MAU MAU   In Kenya, a Kikuyu tribe resistance movement which, from 1952 to 1955, fought both British rule and European planters. Relying on magic and extremely primitive weapons, the Mau Mau butchered 95 whites in all, before being crushed by the British with 11,000 casualties. The movement did, however, make necessary the imposition of martial law until 1959 and helped pave the way for Kenyan independence. The extreme cruelty of the methods it used have made its name into something of a byword for barbarity.

MAURRAS, CHARLES   (1868–1952) French writer, polemicist and anti-democratic activist. Maurras's proto-Fascist *Ligue d'Action Française*, both an extra-parliamentary league and a weekly, then a daily, newspaper by the same name which Maurras launched in 1908, played a major part in vilifying the Third Republic and contributed mightily to bringing about its fall in the summer of 1940.

Born north of Marseilles in the quaint Provençal village of Martigues, Maurras started his literary career by championing the Provençal literary revival known as the Félibrige. On his first voyage outside his country to attend the first Olympic games in Athens, he was abruptly struck by the decadence of the Latin race and the vigor displayed by the Anglo-Saxon athletes. His political interests were dramatically aroused by the outbreak of the Dreyfus affair, a judicial scandal involving the miscarriage of justice in a case of espionage, which turned into a national crisis of unique intensity with the publication of Émile Zola's *J'accuse* in Clemenceau's radical paper *l'Aurore*, in January 1898. A rabid anti-Dreyfusard and anti-Semite from the very outset of the affair, Maurras became the leader of a party of ultra-nationalist intellectuals dedicated to rescuing the country from the democratic and godless Third Republic, which he associated with the occult powers of Jews, FREEMASONS, Protestants and *métèques* (or metic foreigners). During a lifetime of relentless vituperation against these four "confederated powers" accused of corrupting France and debasing its values, Maurras' *Action Française* succeeded in undermining the moral basis of the republic and exposing its parliamentary system to ridicule and abuse.

The impact of *Action Française*, throughout its long existence until it was finally dissolved in the liberation of Paris in 1944, was far out of proportion to its size and exclusive character as a party restricted to a handful of intellectuals. The very word "Intellectual," defined as political engagement, was born in the intellectual ferment of the Dreyfus revolution: it was simply appropriated by Maurras and turned against the republic, condemned as the symbol of a Dreyfusard "betrayal of the Intellectuals." The influence of the *Action Française* extended well beyond such notable intellectuals as Maurice Barrès, Jacques Bainville, Léon Daudet, Paul Gaxotte, Pierre Bourget and virtually all the intellectual right, to make inroads in the petty and middling bourgeoisie, the civil service, the liberal professions, the army and the Church.

The young colonel Charles de Gaulle was an early sympathizer, so were André Gide, François Mauriac and, as revealed in 1994, even the Fifth Republic's two-time Socialist president, François Mitterand, gave it his support until he switched sides by joining the resistance in 1943.

Although the movement foreshadowed in may ways the French Fascist (see FASCISM) parties that emerged in the 1920s and 1930s, its doctrine as defined by Maurras was strictly rationalist and positivist, harking back to the Catholic and royalist traditions of the *ancien régime* and hostile to the romantic mysticism glorified by the rival leagues of Fascists led by Jacques Doriot or Marcel Déat on the eve of World War II. But despite the strict doctrines and royalist ideology espoused by the *Action Française* and the disclaimers of its champions, it is clear that the effect of its agitation was to strengthen fascism by the outbreak of World War II.

In 1940, Maurras hailed the defeat of the Third Republic as a "divine surprise" and gave his enthusiastic support to the "national revolution" carried out by the régime of Marshal Pétain. When stripped of his seat at the French Academy (where he had been elected in 1938 against Paul Claudel) and found guilty of collaboration with the Germans at his trial in 1945, the old man exclaimed, "Oh! This is the vengeance of Dreyfus."

MAYAKOVSKY, VLADIMIR VLADIMIROVICH (1893–1930) Russian poet. A revolutionary from youth, Mayakovsky started writing poetry in 1909 while sitting in solitary confinement. Between 1914 and 1916 he wrote plays noted for their stylistic innovations, such as the use of crude language, neologisms and staccato diction, all designed to be recited in front of mass audiences.

During and after the October RUSSIAN REVOLUTION OF 1917, he supported the Bolsheviks (see BOLSHEVIK PARTY) for whom he turned out a stream of highly effective propaganda in both written form and cartoons. In the later 1920s, however, he returned to a more personal and lyrical form of writing, mainly concerned, as in the 1916 days, with disappointed love. This led him into conflict with the authorities, and he finally committed suicide.

MAY FOURTH MOVEMENT (1917–1921) Chinese nationalist and new culture movement. The movement derived its name from the May 4, 1919 incident, when Beijing University students demonstrated to protest the decision of the Paris Peace Conference to award former German holdings in Shandong to Japan. Later it came to include the intellectual excitement that, from around 1915 to the early 1920s, evoked a critical appraisal of traditional culture and a demand for individual rights and democracy. CHEN DUXIU, in his monthly, *New Youth*, launched the attack on tradition in 1915, and it gathered momentum in the following years, especially at Beijing University under the chancellorship of CAI YUANPEI. In 1917, Cai named Chen Dean of Letters and also appointed Hu Shi, an American-trained scholar, to the faculty. Hu became famous for promoting use of the spoken language, *baihua*, as the written medium in place of literary Chinese. The literary language, replete with classical allusions, required years of study and could be fully mastered only by a tiny elite. Its replacement by *baihua*, like that of Latin by the national vernaculars of Europe, was an essential step toward the spread of literacy and greater popular involvement in the political and cultural life of the country. This was one of the lasting achievements of the May Fourth Movement. By 1920 most periodicals were written in the vernacular.

Though the pre-1919 intellectual ferment was not overtly political in the beginning, it could not long remain confined to the cultural domain. The CHINESE REPUBLICAN REVOLUTION OF 1911 had toppled the Qing (Manchu) dynasty, but the sham republic, dominated by warlords, made a mockery of parliamentary government and proved incapable of protecting national interests. The Shandong issue ignited mass political action, targeting both foreign imperialism and native warlordism. Started by a few thousand student demonstrators at the famous Tiananmen and lacking political party sponsorship, the movement, though spontaneous, soon spread and evoked responses from workers and merchants as well. Changes in Chinese society facilitated the movement's rapid growth. Since the turn of the century, modern education had been producing a new, more politically conscious student class, and industrialization, accelerated by World War I, enlarged the native entrepreneurial and working classes. These were the elements that engaged in demonstrations, strikes and anti-Japanese boycotts in the major cities of China, while the countryside remained largely unaffected. The unprecedented demonstration of nationalist sentiments stopped the Beijing government from signing the Paris peace treaty and forced the dismissal of pro-Japanese officials.

By 1920, students and intellectuals had become deeply involved in politics, infusing new life into the GUOMINDANG (GMD) and providing the nucleus for the formation of the CHINESE COMMUNIST PARTY (CCP) in 1921 (see LI DAZHAO). Some leaders of the movement, like Hu Shi, the disciple of John Dewey, eschewed monolithic ideologies and advocated a liberal, pragmatic approach to politics. But the nationalist mood was militant, and liberalism an inadequate response to warlordism and imperialism. The powerful appeal of nationalism also muted the original appeal of individualism and democracy.

As an intellectual phenomenon, the May Fourth Movement marked the erosion of traditional Confucian societal values, and in that sense was more revolutionary than the 1911 revolution. It also marked the politicization of Chinese students and intellectuals and their first sustained effort to reach the masses. In retrospect, the repudiation of tradition, as often happens in such cases, may have been too iconoclastic, too quick to discard traditional values in wholesale fashion. Its original message calling for democracy and individual rights is once more meaningful for Chinese intellectuals.

MAY REVOLUTION (1968) This student rising in France was sparked off by the refusal of the university authorities in Paris and Nanterre to allow women students to entertain men in their dormitories overnight. Deeper underlying causes were dissatisfaction with antiquated, overcrowded university facilities and with General Charles de Gaulle's conservative right-wing régime in general. Under the leadership of DANIEL COHN-BENEDIT ("Red Danny"), the students occupied the Latin Quarter and for two weeks fought pitched battles against the police. Though the students did enlist some support among the French workers, particularly those of the government-owned Renault automobile factory, this was not sufficient and the French government, led by Prime Minister Pompidou, succeeded in weathering the storm with the support of the police, the army and the middle classes. The immediate consequences of the revolution were a strong Gaullist backlash in the elections in 1969 and a round of inflation caused by the wage rises given to France's workers in order to keep them contented. Another result was the drastic lowering of academic standards in most French universities. Though defeated, the May Revolution shook the French establishment and helped spawn new movements in such fields as ecology and women's liberation.

MAY 30TH MOVEMENT (1925) Chinese Communist-influenced anti-imperialist movement. As a result of a labor dispute in a Japanese-owned factory in Shanghai, a Chinese worker was killed on May 15, 1925. On May 30, demonstrators protesting the incident were fired upon by British-led police in Shanghai's International Settlement. Thirteen demonstrators were killed, leading to extensive anti-British agitation in major cities, especially Canton. The situation was further aggravated on June 23 when Anglo-French forces, defending foreign consulates in Canton, killed 52 Chinese demonstrators. The ensuing 15-month Canton-Hong Kong strike and boycott against Hong Kong virtually paralyzed Britain's south China trade. The Communist-led Canton-Hong Kong strike committee established a quasi-government with its own armed picket corps, executive, legislative and judicial bureaus, hospitals, jails, etc. The movement enhanced the prestige and strength of the CHINESE COMMUNIST PARTY (CCP), especially in the growing labor movement (see also CHINESE COMMUNIST REVOLUTION; DENG ZHONGXIA).

MAZZINI, GIUSEPPE (1805–1872) Italian nationalist leader. His father, a professor of anatomy, supported the democratic ideals of the FRENCH REVOLUTION, and Mazzini was to inherit many of his political sensibilities from him. A sickly and stubborn child, he could not speak until the age of five but could already read at four. He was taught by Jansenist priests who inspired in him an abiding love of religion. As a young man,

Mazzini saw refugees fleeing from the failed Piedmontese revolution of 1821. This event moved him to put on a black suit in mourning for Italy's misfortunes, and he dressed in such somber hues for the rest of his life. He studied law at the University of Genoa.

In 1827 Mazzini, committed to the unification of Italy, joined the clandestine CARBONARI revolutionary society and was imprisoned for three months for his involvement with it. It was in prison that he decided to found his own organization, dedicated to attaining national independence through education and insurrection. Upon his release, Mazzini went into exile in France where he established YOUNG ITALY, based on belief in the existence of God, the unity of humanity and the necessity of progress. His principle of association stressed the duties of men to each other and society. Forced to leave France, he went to Switzerland, where he tried to instigate a mutiny in the Piedmontese army. He remained in Switzerland until he was expelled, whereupon he eventually found a home in liberal England in 1837.

Mazzini remained in London for more than a decade. In London he lived in poverty, while occasionally working as a journalist. Between 1840 and 1844 he published a journal called *Apostolato Popolare* and opened a school for Italian exiles. During this time he stayed in a dilapidated one-room apartment, where his many canaries flew about free. Despite the personal difficulties he faced, he was quickly becoming an important spokesman for nationalism and its expression through the modern nation-state.

In 1848 Mazzini returned to Italy, in order to participate in the Italian insurrections (see REVOLUTIONS OF 1848). He fought alongside GIUSEPPE GARIBALDI to take Rome from the Austrians and was elected a member of the triumvirate of the Roman Republic after the flight of the pope. Ruling Rome for just over three months, he was tolerant and enlightened. A man of integrity, he did not receive a salary and lived a modest life. He abolished the death sentence, granted clemency to imprisoned French priests and employed prostitutes as nurses, attempting to reconcile freedom, order, and justice with effective rule. Eventually, the short-lived republic was defeated by the French, in spite of Mazzini's concerted defense. With the help of the US consul, he escaped to London once again.

Mazzini was not one to compromise his political ideals. His friends now began to desert him as he attempted two more unsuccessful rebellions in Mantua (1852) and Milar (1853). During this period, he displayed his religious fervor by couching nationalist propaganda in spiritual rhetoric. He claimed that God spoke through the people, and that the only way to achieve national unification was through popular initiative. He continued to organize uprisings throughout the 1850s, but was not directly involved in Italy's declaration of statehood in 1861.

The unification of the country through its annexation to Piedmont, under a monarchist government and at the initiative of foreign forces, was unacceptable to him. Upon the final capture of Rome by Italian forces in 1870, Mazzini asserted: "I had thought to revive the soul of Italy, but all I find before me is its corpse."

Mazzini was elected to the new parliament as a representative of Messina, Sicily. However, he was not allowed to fill his position due to a political dispute. Being a republican, he never accepted united Italy in the monarchist form which it had assumed, but frequently traveled there from his exile. On one visit, as he set out for Sicily, he was imprisoned for several months for violating his exile. He died at Pisa, disguised as an English doctor, a stranger in the country he had helped to build.

MEDEM, VLADIMIR (1879–1923) Theoretician and activist of the Jewish BUND. Medem began his political activities as a student at Kiev University. Expelled from the university, he returned to his native Minsk and in the late 1890s was active in socialist circles. Though his father had converted to Christianity and Medem himself was baptized, he entered the Jewish Bund and became its foremost theoretician on problems of national minorities. At the second congress of the Social Democratic Workers party of Russia in 1903, he defended the Bund's position regarding revolutionary organization among Jewish workers. From 1906 he was a member of the Bund's central committee, formulating its program for national cultural autonomy. Forced into exile, he lived abroad from 1908 to 1913 and wrote profusely for both Bundist and general publications. From 1913 to 1921 he lived in Russian Poland before finally settling in the US, writing for the socialist Yiddish language *Forverts* until his death. He opposed the BOLSHEVIK seizure of power and the Bund's cooperation with the Soviet régime.

MEIJI RESTORATION The name given to a political and social revolution that shook Japan between about 1860 and 1889, breaking the country's traditional political system and leading to its emergence as a modern state.

The background to the revolution was formed by Japan's penetration by foreigners, beginning with the visit of the American commander Perry and his "black ships" in 1858. At the same time tension between town and country mounted. The latter was the base of the feudal lords (*daimyo*) who, coming under the shogun, had ruled Japan for some two and a half centuries, whereas the former were rapidly turning themselves into centers of banking, trade and industry (albeit backward by European standards) but did not possess influence over the country's political system.

Things were brought to a head when the reigning shogun, Ii Naosuke, ratified the Harris Treaty in 1858, thus opening Japan to foreign trade. This gave rise to opposition on the part of the younger *daimyo,* who felt their position in society threatened; in 1860 Ii was assassinated, an event that opened the way to several years of violence as various factions of *daimyo* fought each other for control and also sought to resist the ever-growing foreign presence. Antiforeign acts, such as assassinations, provoked harsh retaliation: the town of Kagoshima was bombarded in 1863, that of Shimonoseki a year later. From now on it was clear that, given their military superiority, the foreigners had come to stay and that Japan had to adapt its social and political system if it was to avoid the fate that, during those very years, was overtaking China.

From 1864 on, the various Japanese factions could be seen to coalesce into two camps. On the one hand were a group of *daimyo* centering around Shogun Iemochi Ii who, although forced to come to terms with the foreigners, desperately sought to save what they could of the old feudal system. On the other was the court nobility which, encouraged by the French and British ambassadors, sought to get rid of the shogun altogether and thereby restore imperial (Meiji) rule. In 1866 the two sides fought an open battle at Chosu; the shogun's forces were defeated and he himself died shortly thereafter. The new shogun, Yoshinobu, found himself confronted by a coalition whose leaders were Chosu and Satsuma, two court nobles claiming to act in the name of the emperor. In the brief civil war that followed, Yoshinobu's armies advanced on Kyoto but were defeated. In January 1868, the principal *daimyo* were summoned to Kyoto to be told officially that young Emperor Meiji had taken over from the shogun and that the latter's office had been abolished. In the summer of the next year, the last rebel forces who were still holding out in the north were defeated.

Next, and still claiming to act in the name of Emperor Meiji, the victors launched a social and political revolution. Antiforeign agitation came to an end; instead Japanese leaders went abroad and Japan began to import foreign technology and foreign advisers as fast as it could get them. In 1871 the *daimyo* were persuaded to return their land to the throne, whereupon the approximately 300 feudal fiefs into which the country had been divided were abolished and a new centralized system consisting of 72 prefectures and three metropolitan districts was set up. In 1873 conscription, modeled on the German system, was introduced and a start made on the registration of all land so as to transfer it from feudal to private ownership. In 1889, compulsory universal education was instituted and a constitution, centering around a bicameral legislature and universal male suffrage, introduced as a "gift" from the emperor. With that, the revolutionary period known as the Meiji Restoration can be said to have come to an end, and the history of modern Japan got under way.

MENDIVE, RAFAEL MARLA DE Poet and vociferous advocate of Cuban independence. Mendive was principal of the Havana Municipal School for Boys when his arrest for sedition in 1869 provoked a wave of nationalist protest.

MENGISTU, HAILE MARIAM (1937–) Ruler of Ethiopia in the years 1977–1991 and the main figure in the revolution of 1974 (see ETHIOPIA, 1974 REVOLUTION). Mengistu was born in 1937 to an Amharic father and a mother who belonged to one of the peoples of southwest Ethiopia, which were despised by the Amharians. Because of his mother's origin, his opponents gave him the name "*baria*" (slave). As a soldier he served in the army's third division, attaining the rank of major. He participated in Ethiopia's struggle for independence from Italy in 1961 and returned a military hero from the 1964 war with Somalia. In the years following the war, Mengistu became an outspoken opponent of the Ethiopian emperor. He studied in the military college of Holeta in Ethiopia and in the United States. Mengistu was one of the officers who was included in the coordinating committee called the Derg that led the Ethiopian Revolution of 1974. Very little is known of his private life and of his political views before the revolution. However, from the beginning of the revolution he was the main representative of the radical wing within the Derg. This was revealed in two main issues: his demand to execute all the old régime members and his determination not to negotiate with the rebel fronts in Eritrea. On February 2, 1977, Mengistu and his supporters broke into a Derg meeting and murdered all the participants, including the Derg leader TEFERI BANTI. From that date on, Mengistu led the

Derg and became the sole ruler of Ethiopia. This was a victory for the radical wing that had significant implications on the outcome of the revolution. By 1978, Mengistu had brutally eliminated all his opponents within and outside the Derg, in what later was known as the "red terror campaign."

Before the Ethiopia-Somalia war of 1978, Mengistu presented the new régime's ideology as Ethiopian Socialism. A comprehensive agrarian reform and large-scale nationalization were implemented in the name of this ideology. After winning the war with Somalia with massive help from the Soviets and under certain pressure from the eastern bloc, Mengistu declared his régime Marxist-Leninist and gave the party that was created in 1976 wider power. The decision of the Americans not to support Ethiopia in the war against Somalia also contributed to this act.

During the next 10 years, Mengistu's régime had to deal with the growing discontent of different ethnic groups in Ethiopia whose hopes had been raised by the revolution. Several ethnic fronts that fought the central government were created and by 1988 the military situation in Ethiopia had deteriorated. The Eritrean fronts gained massive military successes and the economic situation was worse than ever.

In 1990, Mengistu abandoned Ethiopian Socialism, opposition groups were invited to participate in a unity party, and free market principles replaced economic planning. This was, however, too little and too late. The collapse of the Soviet Union left the Ethiopian régime without any external support and, as the guerrilla forces approached Addis Ababa, Mengistu fled to Zimbabwe on May 21, 1991.

MENSHEVIKS In Russian history, the non-Leninist wing of the Social Democratic Party. The split in the latter occurred during its congress of 1903 when a group, led by YULY MARTOV, opposed LENIN's demand that the party be built as a disciplined revolutionary army rather than as a mass organization on the West European model. Due to the secession from the party of the BUND, a Jewish socialist organization, Lenin's supporters obtained a temporary majority and were henceforward known as BOLSHEVIKS (i.e., "the majority"). The Mensheviks (the "minority"), however, continued as an organized party, advocating cooperation with the left wing of the bourgeoisie and playing a leading part in the RUSSIAN REVOLUTION OF 1905. After World War I began in 1914, the Mensheviks were divided over the question whether to support the war. After the October RUSSIAN REVOLUTION OF 1917 they tried to act as a formal opposition to the Bolsheviks but were gradually expelled from all important positions and finally suppressed in 1922. This led to many Menshevik leaders, including Martov himself, going into exile.

MENZHINSKY, VYACHESLAV (1874–1934) Soviet police and intelligence official. Born in St. Petersburg, Menzhinsky earned a law degree at its university and joined the Social Democrats in 1902. After taking part in the RUSSIAN REVOLUTION OF 1905, he emigrated to Europe until 1917.

Returning to Russia, he served briefly as commissar for finance and from April to November 1918 as Soviet consul in Berlin. From 1919 his activities centered around the political police—the *Cheka*—in Ukraine, and around his position as head of the RED ARMY's security branch. In September 1923, Menzhinsky became deputy director of the political police. When the director, FELIX DZERZHINSKY, was appointed head of the Supreme Economic Council in 1924, Menzhinsky served for all practical purposes as head of the OGPU (secret police), a post to which he was formally appointed after Dzerzhinsky's death in mid-1926, serving until his own death in May 1934. From 1927 to February 1934 he was a member of the Bolshevik central committee. During his term of office, the OGPU supervised the collectivization of agriculture and extended the system of forced labor based on prison camps. Menzhinsky's successor, Yagoda, was later accused of poisoning him.

MESSALI HAJJ, AHMAD   (1898–1974) The most prominent leader of Algerian nationalism from the later 1920s to the early 1950s. Born in Tlemcen, Algeria, into a working-class family, Messali served with the French army in World War I and stayed in France after the war, marrying a Frenchwoman. He became an Algerian nationalist, rejecting the conception then prevailing of Algeria's integration in France. In 1924–1925 he co-founded an organization called L'ETOILE NORD-AFRICAINE (North African Star), which was at first linked to the Communists. Messali himself was reportedly for some time to be a member of the Communist party; he later severed these links and increasingly adopted Islamic tendencies, also maintaining ties with Fascist and extreme right-wing groups. *L'Etoile* was banned in 1929 and Messali was arrested again. In 1936–1937 he founded the *Parti du Peuple Algerien* (PPA—the PARTY OF THE ALGERIAN PEOPLE), which soon had to go underground. Messali was arrested in 1939 and sentenced in 1941 to 16 years in prison. However, he was released and exiled in 1943 after the Allied landing in North Africa. His temporary alliance with his more moderate rival, FERHAT ABBAS, materalized in the AMIS DU MANIFESTE ET DE LA LIBERTÉ but was disrupted by the Setif uprising of 1945, for which the PPA was purportedly responsble. In 1946 Messali founded a new party, the MOUVEMENT POUR LE TRI-OMPHE DES LIBERTÉS DÉMOCRATIQUES (MTLD), advocating full independence for Algeria. Electoral fraud deprived the MTLD of parliamentary influence in the 1947 elections. In the early 1950s it thus sponsored a new, more militant *Mouvement National Al-gerien* (MNA—Algerian National Movement) and Messali himself, in and out of prison (he reportedly spent 30 years of his life in jail), was again imprisoned in 1952. From the late 1940s he was increasingly out of touch with a younger generation of more radical nationalist leaders, including AHMAD BEN-BELLA, BELKACEM KRIM, HUSSEIN AIT-AHMAD and MUHAMMAD KHIDR, who broke away from the MTLD and set up organizations for armed struggle—against Messali's wishes or without his knowledge, even though Messali was still respected as the grand old man of Algerian nationalism. When they established the FRONT DE LIBÉRATION NATIONALE (FLN) in 1954 and launched an armed revolt on November 1, 1954, the break was complete. Messali denounced the revolt and the new leaders and was denounced by them. From the 1950s on he was completely alienated from what had become the mainstream of Algerian nationalism. Though still imprisoned as a nationalist, he had no part in the final struggle, including the negotiations of 1961–1962 that led to Algeria's independence and the establishment of the new state. Released in 1962, he remained in France as an exile. Though he had feeble links with attempts to organize groups in opposition to the Algerian régime, mainly in France, Ahmad Messali Hajj

played no major role in them and died after a decade of isolation and alienation, a relic of earlier times.

MESSENIAN REVOLT   see HELOTS.

MÉTIS REBELLION   The Métis Rebellion of Canada, which occurred in 1869, was led by LOUIS RIEL. The Métis, who were persons of mixed European (primarily French) and Indian descent, were alarmed by the transfer of the Hudson Bay Company's substantial land holdings in western Canada to the dominion. They feared being overrun by the English-speaking population. A temporary government was established at Fort Gary, now Winnipeg, which was headed by Riel. The Canadian government, in the Manitoba Act of 1870, established the province of Manitoba and promised the Métis amnesty. The Métis's government, however, tried and put to death an English–speaking Canadian, whereupon the amnesty was revoked, Fort Gary was captured and the Métis's government was overturned.

MEXICAN REVOLUTIONS
Revolution of 1810. See HIDALGO Y COSTILLA, MIGUEL.
Revolution of Reform. (1857–1860) The reform movement in Mexico resulted from the negative socioeconomic and political legacies bequeathed to Mexico by its colonial past. In the post-independence period, two opposing forces developed in the country. One represented conservative, traditional politicians and intellectuals, who favored the status quo. The other was made up of progressive-minded liberals, who were often influenced by anticlerical views. The principles underlying the liberal movement included the abolition of special privileges enjoyed by both the clergy and the military; the expropriation of the large land tracts owned by the Catholic church which, according to liberals, would help the circulation of wealth; the abolition of the church's monopoly on education; and the establishment of equal rights before the law of all citizens. The attacks launched against the clergy were based on socioeconomic and political considerations and were not antireligious in most cases. However, the Church immediately felt threatened by liberal ideals. The Church was held responsible for many of Mexico's economic ills, while the military was blamed for Mexico's political instability.

Mexico's defeat in its war with the United States in 1847 and the subsequent loss of more than half of its territory led to a tremendous question of "what was wrong with Mexico." Liberals always reached the same conclusion—that the Church and the military had to be blamed, while conservatives began to believe that Mexico was ungovernable by Mexicans. Conservatives also believed that Mexico had forged institutions which were simply not appropriate for Mexico and were an inadequate imitation of institutions existing in countries such as the United States. The conservatives represented class hierarchy and inequality, while liberals promoted equality and freedom for all. To many liberals and conservatives alike, however, conservative President Santa Anna had to be ousted for Mexico to stabilize and progress in any way.

In 1853, a number of liberals, among them IGNACIO COMONFORT, Melchor Ocampo and BENITO JUAREZ united under JUAN ALVAREZ against Santa Anna. Successful in their coup, these liberals set out to eliminate the Church's power over the state. Between 1855 and 1857, Mexican liberals instituted a variety of reforms which had a direct impact on the Church. The first and far-reaching one, which has been called the root cause for the Revolution of Reform, was proposed by Benito Juarez in 1855. In what has been called the Juarez Law, all special privileges enjoyed by the military and the clergy were eliminated. The law was implemented in 1856. Both the military and the Church reacted negatively to the law. Two other significant decrees implemented were the Lerdo Law and the Iglesias Law. The former freed all property held by the Church from mortmain (literally, "dead hand"—the perpetual holding of land). The latter reduced the Church's power of acquisition. Other laws passed included the suppression of Jesuit activities, limitations placed on ecclesiastic jurisdiction in civil and criminal matters and the implementation of a civil registry for births, marriages and deaths.

The laws were meant to restrict the Church's temporal and not spiritual powers, since liberals believed that the Church was not complying with its proclaimed duties by being too involved in political and economic issues. Threatened by liberal activities, the Church joined forces with Mexican conservatives and in 1857, the Reform war, one of Mexico's bloodiest civil wars, broke out. Felix Zuloaga was accepted by the conservatives as president, residing in Mexico City, while the liberals established their government on the run in Veracruz. In Veracruz, several other anticlerical laws were passed, among them one proclaiming freedom of religion. These laws were eventually compiled as the 1874 reform Laws.

The conservative and liberal forces fought one another in all areas of Mexico. However, by 1860 the liberals emerged victorious and Juarez entered Mexico City triumphantly at the head of a liberal, constitutionalist government. Although 1860 marked the end of the Revolution of Reform and the 1857 constitution remained in place with changes, the post-1860 consequences of the War of Reform were dire. The main ones of these were that the conservatives and the church refused to accept liberal rule and that, as a result of the civil war, Mexico's coffers were empty. Thus the Revolution of Reform laid the foundation for the War of French Intervention and Mexican imperial rule.

Revolution of 1910–1917. The Mexican revolution began on November 20, 1910, when a group of Mexicans rose against the more than 30 year dictatorship (1876–1911) of PORFIRIO DIAZ. The revolution was led by FRANCISCO MADERO. In 1908, Diaz had declared that he would not run for the 1910 presidential elections, thus inspiring hope for political renewal and change among young Mexicans. Soon Diaz reneged on his promise. As a result, Madero published *The Presidential Elections of 1910*, in which he called for truly democratic elections and an end to the Diaz dictatorship. Madero was imprisoned and Diaz claimed to have won all the presidential votes in 1910. Madero, though, escaped from prison and from his US exile proclaimed his Plan of San Luis Potosi.

The plan's main points were that the presidential and vice-presidential electoral results were to be annulled, the principles of "free suffrage and no reelection" were to be implemented, Madero was to become provisional president and all Mexicans were encouraged to rise up in arms against the Diaz government on November 20, 1910.

In the meantime, opposition to Diaz was growing in Mexico

from a variety of sectors. Unable to withstand the opposition, Diaz was exiled on May 25, 1911. With Diaz's ouster, Madero forged the Constitutionalist Progressive party. Other parties were also formed. Although all parties named different vice-presidential candidates, all agreed to nominate Madero to the presidency.

During Madero's uprisings, FRANCISCO (PANCHO) VILLA launched anti-government attacks in northern Mexico, while Emiliano Zapata rose against the government in the State of Morelos. Both demanded socioeconomic reforms. Even after Madero became president, Zapata and Villa continued to demand change from the government. Zapata announced his Plan of Ayala, in which he described his dissatisfaction with Madero's government, stating that Madero had betrayed revolutionary principles by "adhering to the demands of large landowners and caciques (rural bosses) who enslave us (the peasants)." In 1913, an opposition group, which termed Madero too radical and was led by VICTORIANO HUERTA and Felix Diaz, nephew of the deposed dictator, with the help of US Ambassador Henry Lane Wilson, overthrew Madero. Both Madero and his vice-president, Pino Suarez, were brutally assassinated. Mexicans were outraged. VENUSTIANO CARRANZA, governor of Coahuila, declared that Huerta was an usurper and refused to recognize his government. Carranza organized the Constitutionalist army. Many military figures, such as Villa and ALVARO OBREGON, joined the Carranza uprising. Zapata continued his struggle against the Huerta régime. Despite the support from Wilson, the Huerta government failed to achieve official US recognition.

In his efforts to maintain power, Huerta opted for assassination and repression against opposition forces. He had congressional representatives killed or imprisoned and when these methods proved ineffective he disbanded the legislature. The legislature fled from Mexico City and joined the constitutionalist forces. Carranza wooed Zapata by redistributing land, but Zapata distrusted him. Although successful in ousting Huerta by June 1914, Carranza alienated Villa and other revolutionaries. Only when the US invaded the port of Veracruz did the various factions briefly unite. The US supported Carranza.

While Villa openly declared his rupture with Carranza, Zapata continued fighting the régime. Both saw Carranza as a pro-US ruler who would continue to "sell out the country." In late 1914, Carranza called together a convention at Aguascalientes, choosing that location as neutral ground. Thus, representatives of Villa and Zapata were also present. Eulalio Gutierrez was declared president by the convention and Carranza in reaction moved to Veracruz and invalidated the convention results, at the same time declaring himself president. Gutierrez was forced to abandon the capital, which Obregon soon recaptured for Carranza. The so-called conventionists tried to establish their government out of Toluca but were soon dispersed.

In 1916, Carranza, now officially recognized by the US as the new president of Mexico, established his rule from Queretaro. US troops led by General Pershing pursued Villa with Carranza's permission, after Villa had raided a US border town. US troops remained in Mexico until 1917, although they were unable to capture Villa. In 1917, Carranza called for a constitutional assembly to discuss proposed reforms to the 1857 constitution. Despite Carranza's hesitations, various representatives at the assembly demanded and obtained modifications to the constitution, which had definite socioeconomic ramifications. Both the proposals of RICARDO FLORES MAGON and Zapata's Plan of Ayala were essential to this process. The most revolutionary articles incorporated into the 1917 constitution were Article 3—which referred to socialized, public education; Article 27—which dealt with land reform; Article 123—which established protective labor laws and Article 130—which reaffirmed freedom of religion. Although Mexico continued to face upheavals, the creation of the 1917 constitution officially marked the end of the revolution.

MEXICAN STUDENT MOVEMENT The 1968 student movement in Mexico unfolded more as a series of mass demonstrations than as an active revolution. In some ways, it was both ignited and extinguished by the 1968 Olympic Games scheduled for Mexico City. Students, protesting that the government of the Mexican Revolutionary party (PRI) was becoming more and more like the dictatorship that the revolution of 1910–1917 had overthrown and that the so-called Mexican economic miracle was a hoax, began demonstrating in increasing numbers on the campuses of officially autonomous public universities. The massive expenditures in preparation for the Olympics became symbolic, by contrast, of the governmental failure to allocate adequate funds to social programs needed to alleviate poverty. The demonstrations, first emanating from the Universidad Nacional Autonoma de Mexico (UNAM), were further fueled by internal academic disputes.

It was when these students expanded their protests from the campuses to the streets, recruiting ordinary citizens to their ranks, that then-President Gustavo Diaz Ordaz became alarmed. He was very concerned that the image of Mexico as a bastion of stability, central to the success of the Olympics, not be disturbed by visible evidence of dissent.

The first, relatively minor, incident of violent confrontation occurred when sporadic street fights unrelated to the student protests erupted in Mexico City on July 22, 1968. Many participants were working-class secondary school students. On July 23, the mayor overreacted by calling out a special force of police, who once again earned their reputation for harsh riot control methods by beating demonstrators.

In response, students of the Politecnico, many from the same socioeconomic class as those beaten on July 23, marched in sympathetic protest to the center of Mexico City on July 26, joining with UNAM students holding a rally to celebrate the 15th anniversary of the start of FIDEL CASTRO's Cuban insurrection. Once again they were met by riot police who countered peaceful protest with violence. The students called for a general university strike two days later: the government reacted by closing down all public schools in Mexico City. Further demonstrations resulted in scores of student casualties and more than 1,600 arrests.

UNAM, officially off-limits to the army and police but invaded by both by mid-September, launched a peaceful march of 80,000 students led by the rector. Among the slogans used and displayed by demonstrators were many insulting to the president. This, in a country where reverence for the president had been the norm for four decades, was unacceptable to President Ordaz, who was accosted by 400,000 demonstrators in front of

the National Palace on August 27. Student leaders demanded that the president address them directly on September 1, instead of delivering the sacrosanct state of the union address always presented on that date. The president resisted, voicing in his traditional address a hard-line policy and threatening to meet further protests with "all the elements that people have placed in our hands." He made good his threat on October 2.

On that date, with the official opening of the Olympics just 10 days away, a crowd assembled in the Plaza of the Three Cultures in the public-housing project of Tlalteloco. At 6:00 P.M., military and police began firing on the crowd from inside the plaza, killing students, parents and children indiscriminately. Escape routes were blocked and even those who attempted to surrender were gunned down, although many of the corpses mysteriously disappeared. It is estimated that several hundred met with violent death.

What was to became internationally famous as the Tlalteloco Massacre ended the 1968 student movement. On the next day, October 3, the rubber-stamp chamber of deputies resolved that all the marches and demonstrations that had transpired since July were in the nature of "subversive action...perpetrated by foreign elements." Protest had indeed been crushed—but so to a considerable extent had the faith of Mexicans in their national government. Relations between Mexican citizens and their government were to be marred by an air of cynicism from that point on.

MIAO REBELLIONS Uprisings of the Miao people in southwest China. The Miao are the original, non-Chinese inhabitants of southwest China. First conquered by China in the 3rd century B.C., Miao tribesmen resisted Chinese efforts to assimilate them. During the Qing (Manchu) dynasty (1664–1912), large uprisings occurred in Hunan (1795–1806) and in Guizhou (1850–1873). During this latter period, Chinese officials tried to sinicize the Miao by providing more schools and benefits. In practice, Miao land was confiscated for the resettlement of Chinese. The Miao either became tenants or retreated to the mountains.

MICHEL, LOUISE (1830–1905) French anarchist and revolutionary leader, credited as one of her country's first feminist activists, fondly remembered as the greatest heroine of the PARIS COMMUNE by her anarchist sympathizers and known under the designation of La Vierge Rouge or "The Red Virgin" by her more numerous bourgeois detractors.

The illegitimate child of a chambermaid from the Paris suburb of Vroncout in the Marne, Michel was brought up by her grandfather and dedicated herself to a career in education. She served heroically in the ambulance auxiliary service during the Prussian siege of Paris in 1870, where she was given the sobriquet of 'Florence Nightingale,' and then rallied to the Paris Commune, being one of the first women to wear the uniform of the revolutionary National Guard which resisted in vain the crushing onslaught launched by the Versailles government of Adolphe Thiers against the Paris insurrection. Deported for a life sentence as a Communard to New Caledonia, she was unable to live down her reputation as the "Red Virgin" of the Commune, which the public associated with the even more sinister "Pétroleuses," bloodthirsty bands of Communard women who had set fire to the Tuileries with petrol cans, thereby discrediting both their sex and the Commune. In New Caledonia, she befriended the Kanaka natives and later published an account of their language and culture, *Légendes et Chants de Guerre Canaques* (1895). After she had returned to France following a general amnesty for all exiled Communards, she lived up to her legendary fame by leading a women's raid on a Paris bakery. She was therefore exiled again, this time to London.

The London phase of her life, between 1886 and 1895, was the most productive in her career. She won fame as a pedagogue, teaching anarchist and syndicalist ideas to her students in her international language school and continuing her feminist and revolutionary propaganda when she was allowed to return to Paris in 1895.

A living symbol of feminism and revolution, she was venerated by the old Communards and wrote a variety of books, in addition to her memoirs and popular children's fairy tales. Her funeral cortége to the Père Lachaise, France's national shrine, drew the largest crowds ever assembled for a French woman, outnumbering by far the numbers recorded at Josephine Baker's, Edith Piaf's or Simone de Beauvoir's funerals.

MICHNIK, ADAM (1946–) Polish historian, political scientist, leading dissident and activist in the Workers' Self-Defense (KOR) and Solidarity movements. Engaged in dissident activities, Michnik was expelled from Warsaw University in 1968. In the mid-1970s he defined his ideas as "democratic-socialism" and promoted the ideals of a civil society. Frequently detained, he played a leading role among intellectuals in Solidarity and was jailed several times following the December 1981 army coup. Amnestied in 1986, he returned to activities leading to the collapse of the régime.

With the split of Solidarity and Walesa's presidency, Michnik became a leading critic of the new trends in Polish society and a keen analyst of the changes in Eastern Europe. For years he has played a leading role in the intellectual debates and contacts on the fate of Central Europe.

MIKOYAN, ANASTAS IVANOVICH (1895–1978) Soviet politician. An Armenian by nationality, Mikoyan received training for the priesthood but joined the BOLSHEVIKS in 1915, rising to become chief of the revolutionary organization in the Caucasus. After World War I, he supported STALIN and then Krushchev, and held ministerial posts during the 1930s. He was appointed a member of the State Defense Committee in 1942 and deputy prime minister in 1957, and remained a member of the Party's central committee until 1976.

MILYUKOV, PAVEL NIKOLAYEVICH (1859–1943) Russian historian and politician. A liberal who organized the Constitutional Democratic party in 1905, Milyukov sat in the Duma and, after the February RUSSIAN REVOLUTION OF 1917, became foreign minister in the provisional government of PRINCE LVOV. He wanted to continue the war at the side of the Allies, but was forced to resign in May 1917. An opponent of Bolshevism (see BOLSHEVIK PARTY), he left Russia in 1918 after an attempt to overthrow LENIN had misfired. He spent the rest of his life in Paris.

MINUTEMEN Units of the Massachusetts militia, organized on the eve of the American revolutionary war, who were to be prepared to go into active service "at a minute's notice." Regiments of Minutemen were first formed in central Massachusetts in September 1774 by order of the Worcester convention. With the escalation of the conflict between the American colonists and their English mother country, the revolutionary leaders found it necessary to purge the militia of pro-British Tories and to improve its readiness. Officers of the established militia were ordered to resign and the new officers elected were required to enlist one-third of their men in special regiments, which could be called on to face any emergency at a short notice. This process of reorganizing the militia and dividing its units by degrees of readiness into Minutemen regiments and regulars soon spread through the colony. Late in October, this differentiation was ordered to be completed throughout the colony by the provincial congress.

In the first clash of the revolutionary war, British troops advancing on Concord were challenged at Lexington by Minutemen and a number of the challengers fell in battle. Minutemen also led the march to block the British troops at Concord Bridge. However, as the skirmish progressed, Minutemen and regular militia acted together.

While in Massachusetts the distinction between Minutemen and other militia forces faded rapidly, the Continental Congress recommended, in July 1775, that the other colonies organize regiments of Minutemen. Maryland, New Hampshire and Connecticut accepted the recommendation.

MIRABEAU, COMTE DE (Honoré-Gabriel Riqueti) (1749–1791) French revolutionary and political leader; eldest son of the economist Victor Riqueti, Marquis de Mirabeau. His early years were characterized by wild excesses that ruined his health and caused him to be repeatedly jailed—several times at the request of his father, with whom he carried on a public feud. On returning home from cavalry service in Corsica, he was reconciled with his father and in 1772 married Emilie de Marignane, a Provençal heiress. Family harmony was short-lived and, following an adulterous involvement with the Marquise de Monnier, Mirabeau, arrested and disgraced, was forced to renounce the aristocratic society into which he had been born.

Following his release from jail, Mirabeau lived the life of an adventurer. While in London, he moved in influential Whig circles and in 1786 was sent on a secret mission to Prussia. However, he betrayed his government's trust by publishing unedited reports containing accounts of scandal and intrigue in the Prussian court.

In May 1789 the Estates-General, an assembly of three estates (the clergy, the nobility and the commons) was summoned in the hope of introducing much needed reforms into French society. As the author of numerous pamphlets violently denouncing abuses of the *ancien régime*, Mirabeau was elected in 1789 as a delegate of the Third Estate for Aix-en-Provence. With his fiery eloquence, his clear and practical ideas and his imposing appearance, Mirabeau became the spokesman of the Third Estate. When on June 23 Louis XVI ordered the Estates-General to leave the hall after the day's session had been declared closed, Mirabeau declared (his words have been variously reported): "Return to those who have sent you and tell them that we shall not stir from our places save at the point of the bayonet." His historic reply strengthened the resolve of the deputies to disobey and to establish the National Assembly. In the heady days of

July 1789, Mirabeau's speeches inspired the assembly to demand the removal of the troops concentrated around Paris.

However, despite such revolutionary outpourings, Mirabeau's overriding political objective was to create a strong constitutional monarchy modeled on that of Great Britain, which would permit him to play a decisive role as a minister. His political ideal was free but limited monarchy. To this end he opposed the assumption of national sovereignty by the Third Estate, criticized the expediency of drawing up a declaration of rights and vigorously advocated granting the king an absolute veto over legislation.

In October, after the Parisians marched on Versailles and took the king back to Paris, Mirabeau, concerned about rumors that he was plotting against the king, cast himself in the role of savior of the monarchy. Yet in December 1790 he held office as president of the Jacobin club, at the end of January 1791 was elected a member of the administration of the Department of Paris and acted, with great personal success, as president of the Constituent Assembly. Constantly troubled by reports in newspapers accusing him of treason, he was increasingly criticized in the Assembly, particularly by the JACOBINS, who opposed his moderation. His political position gradually became untenable.

Plagued by ill health ever since his ascendancy to the presidency of the Assembly, Mirabeau died on April 2, 1791, amid impressive manifestations of public sorrow and respect, for he had never lost his popularity with the masses. In his honor the new church of St. Genevieve was converted into the Pantheon for the burial of outstanding Frenchmen. His body was later removed, when papers proving his dealings with the court were found in an iron chest in the Tuileries palace.

Although he failed to achieve his political objective, Mirabeau is renowned as one of the greatest political minds in the National Assembly which governed France in the early phases of the FRENCH REVOLUTION.

MIXTON WAR The Mixton War of 1541 was the first attempt of the Mexican Indians to revolt against Spanish rule, just two decades after the final defeat of the Aztecs at Tenochtitlan. Had this rebellion succeeded, Spanish rule of the Americas might have been terminated. However, with the aid of warriors recruited from among the Indian tribes themselves, a force of Spanish cavalry led by Antonio de Mendoza, first viceroy of New Spain, managed to defeat the rebels.

MOBUTU, SESE SEKO (1930–) Mobutu Sese Seko Kuku Ngbendu Waza Banga was born in what was then the Belgian Congo as Joseph-Désiré Mobutu. He was educated in mission schools and then joined the Congolese army (1950–1956). From 1956–1958 he worked as a reporter, and later editor, of *L'Avenir,* a newspaper in the capital Kinshasa (then Leopoldville). In 1958 he took a course in journalism and social studies in Brussels.

Mobutu was a supporter of PATRICE LUMUMBA and had been a member of Lumumba's *Mouvement National Congolais* since 1957. As Zaire became independent with Lumumba as prime minister (1960), Colonel Mobutu was appointed chief of staff. Later that same year Mobutu and the army seized power to resolve the political conflict which had erupted, but Mobutu then restored power to the civilian president, Joseph Kasuvubu.

In November 1965, Mobutu, now a lietenant-general, seized power again, but this time he declared himself head of state and suspended parliament. In 1967, he founded the MOUVEMENT POPULAIRE DE LA REVOLUTION (MPR) to rule the country. It was the only legal political party until November 1990, when a multiparty political system was introduced.

Mobutu's anti-communism attracted Western support during the cold war. Despite his nationalization of the country's copper mines (1966), Mobutu has never been an economic socialist and has relied heavily on foreign investment, particularly from the USA.

Mobutu's intense nationalism, which found expression in his crusade for African authenticity. Mobutu adopted his present name in 1972 as part of this policy of "authenticity." He also renamed the Congo as Zaire, renamed cities and streets, and finally made private individuals adopt authentic African names. Mobutu's name, Sese Seko Kuku Ngbendu Waza Banga, means "the all-powerful warrior who, because of his endurance and inflexible will, will go from conquest to conquest, leaving fire in his wake."

MOCZAR, MIECZYLAW (1913–) Polish Communist politician. Moczar joined the Party in 1937 and, from 1944–1948, was responsible for the activities of the secret police that ended in the Communist takeover and the complete disappearance of all other parties. He suffered a political eclipse between 1948–1956, but then returned to the Party's central committee to be made deputy minister of internal affairs and minister of the interior. In charge also of the political police, he played a prominent part in the campaign of 1967–1969, when he came to symbolize the Stalinist tradition in Polish government.

He led the Partisans, a hard line, nationalist faction, with a strong base in the military and security police. He was dismissed from both his ministry and the Politburo and other top functions in June 1971, after EDUARD GIEREK had replaced GOMULKA as secretary-general of the party, and given the obscure job as chairman of the Supreme Chamber of Control. In a surprise comeback, Moczar published an article in November 1978 about administrative corruption and fraudulent statistical reports on the economy and called for "decisive purges" of "dishonest, incapable" officials who had no moral right to hold power. His attack on the Gierek leadership again called attention to the authoritarian-nationalist faction that Moczar represented in an era of continuing political-economic and moral crisis of the country and the ruling party. His services were further required when, in December 1980, as the régime attempted to cope with the challenge of Solidarity and the Communist party was crumbling, he was elected as a full Politburo member, representing a "law and order" line, whose main cards were evidence on the corruption of top officials. His faction was very active in the crisis of 1980–1981. General Jaruzelski's appointment as prime minister was a step toward blocking Moczar's way to power. Moczar's last stand was during 1981, when his authoritarian-populist-nationalist line was gradually neutralized and removed following bitter factional fights within the party, where Mozcar represented everything that the reformists had been warning about.

MOHTASHEMI, HOJATUL-ISLAM 'ALI AKBAR (1946–) Iranian Islamic cleric. Born in Tehran, Mohtashemi studied theology in Qom under AYATOLLAH KHOMEINI. In 1966, he moved to

Najaf, Iraq, where he continued his education. Mohtashemi was among the founders of the Council of Tehran Militant Clerics and of Militant Clergy Abroad. He worked in Khomeini's offices in Paris, Tehran and Qom, managed the delegation in the Foundation of the Oppressed (*Mustazafan*), an anti-shah group, in the name of Khomeini and served as his representative on the national radio.

During the 1970s, Mohtashemi received military training from Palestinian terror/guerrilla organizations and helped to establish *Hizbullah* in Lebanon. After the Islamic Revolution of 1979 (see IRAN, REVOLTS AND REVOLUTIONS) he returned home and was later appointed ambassador to Syria (1981–1985). He lost an arm and an ear in an explosion in Damascus. From 1985–1989 he was minister of the interior. He has been a member of the *majlis* (parliament) since December 1989. Mohtashemi is a leading radical hard-liner.

MOLOTOV, VYACHESLAV MIKHAYLOVICH (1890–)

Soviet politician. Born V.M. Skryabin, he took the name Molotov in 1906. Molotov was twice imprisoned for revolutionary activity, in 1909–1911 and 1915–1916; on this last occasion, he was deported to Irkutsk province but escaped. He rose through the Communist Party hierarchy after the October 1917 revolution (see RUSSIAN REVOLUTION OF 1917), becoming a secretary of the central committee in 1921. He held various posts in the Communist Party from 1925–1957, supporting and active in supporting Stalin in the struggle against TROTSKY and in the anti-party group against KHRUSHCHEV. Molotov was prime minister in 1930–1940 and foreign minister in 1939–1949 and 1953–1957.

Molotov with best friends: Stalin (left) and Kalinin (right)

MONDLANE, EDUARDO CHIVAMBO (1920–1966)

Mondlane was born in 1920 in Mozambique. As a young man, he was interrogated by the colonial police for his activities in a secondary school pupils' association. He completed his studies in the United States, where he obtained a B.A. and a Ph.D. While teaching at Syracuse University in the US, he wrote articles and spoke out against conditions in Mozambique and against the Portuguese colonial policy.

Mondlane took part in the creation of FRELIMO in Dar-es-Salaam in 1962 and was elected its first president. In FRELIMO's struggle, he sought to forge as wide a coalition of nations against Portugal as possible, and sought aid and diplomatic support from both east and west. Opponents of Mondlane within FRELIMO accused him of being pro-American and too moderate.

As the conflict intensified, Mondlane's ideas radicalized. He identified with other liberation movements around the world. He was as opposed to the exploitation of which the traditional chiefs were guilty as he was of the exploitation by the Portuguese concession companies. He wanted Mozambique to be free from exploitation but he also advocated multiracialism and war against Portuguese colonialism, not against the Portuguese people. For this, he was criticized by the radicals in FRELIMO.

Mondlane was killed on February 3, 1969 by a parcel bomb. It is still not clear who was responsible.

MONMOUTH'S REBELLION (1685) James Scott, Duke of Monmouth (1649–1685) and the illegitimate son of the English king, Charles II, attempted to rally the anti-Catholicism inside the country against King James II, who, although of legitimate birth, was of the Roman Catholic faith. Monmouth's rebellion was the last-ditch attempt by the duke to seize power. He landed at Lyme Regis on June 11, 1685 with about 150 men, denounced James II as a usurper and, with support from Wiltshire, Devon and Somerset, gathered about 4,000 country people who proclaimed him king. He failed to rally Bristol and Bath and was eventually defeated at Sedgemoor on July 6, 1685, in a decisive battle. Monmouth himself was caught and executed on July 15, 1685. His followers were massacred by the infamous Judge Jeffreys at the so-called Bloody Assizes.

MONTAZERI, AYATOLLAH HUSSEIN 'ALI (1922–)

Iranian Islamic cleric and revolutionary. In the early 1960s, Montazeri joined the Islamic resistance and took part in demonstrations against the arrest of AYATOLLAH KHOMEINI. In 1964 he visited Khomeini in his exile in Najaf, Iraq. He was arrested in 1966, along with other clergymen, and sentenced to 18 months in prison. After his release, he secretly went to Iraq and resumed contacts with Khomeini. Upon his return he was arrested once again and exiled into forced residence. In 1975, he was again arrested and sentenced to 10 years' imprisonment for conspiring against the shah. He was released in November 1978 when the escalating Islamic resistance erupted in riots.

Before the Islamic Revolution of 1979 (see IRAN, REVOLTS AND REVOLUTIONS), Montazeri concentrated on teaching philosophy, theology and science at the Islamic Seminary in Qom.

He also wrote several books on Islam. He was considered Khomeini's representative in Iran and Khomeini appointed him to the Council of the Islamic Revolution before the revolution began. After the victory of the revolution, he figured prominently in the Iranian government.

Montazeri gradually took moderate positions dissenting from the régime's leadership. He criticized the régime's harsh attitude toward political prisoners and advocated the return of exiles. He was willing to allow a measure of opposition and recommended a more liberal economy. He reportedly opposed the war against Iraq, but did not express this opinion publicly.

In March 1989, Montazeri resigned from his public posts in response to a letter from Khomeini advising him to stay out of politics and to concentrate on religious subjects. Since then he has kept a low profile and refrained from intervening in political and government affairs. When Khomeini died in June 1990, Montazeri was not even considered to serve as his successor and as the new spiritual leader of the country.

MORAZÁN, FRANCISCO   (1792–1842) Advocate of Central American unity; president of the Federation of Central America. Morazán was born in Tegucigalpa, Honduras, and received little formal education. A self-taught lawyer, he worked for the local municipal government, where he advocated liberal policies opposed by the aristocracy and the Church. He also resisted incorporating the Central American States (Costa Rica, Guatemala, Honduras, El Salvador and Nicaragua) into AGUSTIN DE ITURBIDE's Mexican empire, and commanded the local militia in a failed attack on the Honduran capital of Comayagua.

Iturbide was toppled in 1823 and the Central American States seceded soon after. Like most States of the new Central America Federation, Honduras elected a liberal government, with Morazán as secretary-general and as president of the State legislature. The federal government and Guatemala, however, continued to be dominated by conservatives. To institute more like-minded local administrations, the federal government did not hesitate to use its army. Morazán recruited his own small band of supporters in Tegucigalpa, but, lacking ammunition, it was no match for the well-equipped federal troops. Morazán was undeterred and, after a brief spell in prison, began recruiting a new army.

Morazán's new army originally consisted of only 500 men, but by routing the federal army at La Trinidad, its cause was adopted by thousands more. Tegucigalpa fell in 1827 and Morazán was declared chief of state of Honduras. His first act was the official establishment of the Protector of the Laws Army, dedicated to overthrowing the conservatives in neighboring States. El Salvador fell in 1828; Guatemala in 1829.

Morazán remained the president of Central America until 1840, when conservative rebels overthrew his régime. Still, he refused to relinquish his dream of a united Central America. He returned to Costa Rica in 1842 and invaded El Salvador before even asserting control over Costa Rica. His own army deposed him shortly afterwards and planned his execution.

Tied to a post in the main square of San Jose, Morazán was informed that, in deference to his position as head of state, he would be allowed to command his own firing squad. He gazed at the troops and sighed, "Very well, then... Fire!" They did and he was hit. Slowly raising his head, he called out, "I am still alive!" A second volley ended his life. 150 years later, Central American intellectuals still cherish the dream of unity espoused by the man many call the "GEORGE WASHINGTON of Central America."

MORELOS Y PAVON, JOSE MARIA   (1765–1815) Mexican independence fighter. Of Spanish origin, Morelos was a disciple of HIDALGO and was ordained as a priest. When Hidalgo initiated the independence movement in Mexico, Morelos voluntarily offered his services and distinguished himself with his tremendous military prowess. Morelos provided input into many issues regarding independence, long before its actual implementation in 1821. In 1815, Morelos was captured and executed by royalist forces. In his honor, the State of Morelos was named after him.

MOROCCO, REVOLT AGAINST FRANCE   A French protectorate from the beginning of the 20th century, Morocco witnessed its first anticolonialist stirrings during the 1930s. The initiative was taken by young students of Muslim theology. Also involved were other youngsters who had received a French education, such as Abd al-Aziz al Thalabi. In this way the movement was split between the traditionalists, who opposed the French in the name of Islam, and the modernists whose aim, on the contrary, was to turn Morocco into a modern country.

On the eve of World War II, the Moroccan *Istiqlal* (Independence) movement is said to have numbered approximately 5,000 members, almost all of them of an urban background. The disintegration of French authority during the war itself allowed it to grow almost unhindered, the lead being taken by King Muhammad V himself. The showdown between the two sides came in 1952 when the French, in a vain attempt to restore their much eroded authority, tried to force the king to ban the *Istiqlal* party but were met by a refusal. Thereupon the French mobilized the nomadic tribes which lived in the interior of the country and incited them to revolt against the king in his palace. The latter finally gave in to their demands, but let it be known to his own people that he was doing so under duress.

In 1953 the French, despairing of bending the king to their will, deposed him and exiled him to Madagascar. Another member of the royal family, Muhammad Ibn Arafa, was put on the throne; however, the change of government only made the *Istiqlal* Party more popular. Though most of the party's leadership had been imprisoned and the rest driven into exile, local organizations continued the struggle and committed numerous acts of terrorism against the French and their collaborators. Finally, in 1955, the French gave in. Muhammad V was brought back from Madagascar and restored to the throne and Morocco's 50 year history as a French protectorate came to an end.

MOSLEY, SIR OSWALD   (1896–1980) British Fascist. With an aristocratic and military upbringing, Mosley was elected as a member of parliament for the Conservative Party in 1918 and became an advocate of the rights of the unemployed. His outspokenness and opposition to Conservative Party policy caused him to quit the party in 1922, although he retained his seat as an Independent Conservative. He joined the Labour Party in 1924, was defeated in that year's election, but was returned to parliament in a by-election in 1926. Mosley won considerable esteem as a parliamentarian. He continued to pursue the rights of the underdog and was even taunted with the epithet Philippe Egalité by his critics, who were wary of the aristocrat who toiled unceasingly on behalf of the working class.

In 1929, as Chancellor for the Duchy of Lancaster, Mosley

submitted a memorandum to the Labour government on means of alleviating unemployment by adopting his policy of "national reconstruction." When the cabinet rejected his proposals, Mosley resigned his post. In 1931, he founded the New Party, with a platform of clearing out the slums, the "abolition of unemployment," the "rehabilitation of agriculture" and parliamentary reform. The party failed to win any seats in the 1931 election, leaving Mosley disillusioned with the efficiency of parliamentary democracy. Looking to Continental Europe for inspiration, he founded the British Union, modelled on the Fascist (see FASCISM) parties of Italy, Spain and Germany. The British Union's black-shirted cadres called for the establishment of a single-party state and were rabidly anti-Semitic. They opposed Britain's declaration of war on Germany in 1939 and called for the acceptance of ADOLF HITLER's peace proposals in 1940. For some time Mosley's group was a conspicuous element in non-parliamentary British politics. Despite its brutal attacks on immigrants and Jews in London's East End, it was tolerated by the authorities until the invasion of France. With Mosley's detention that year as a subversive element, the group practically disappeared.

Mosley was released from prison in 1943. Even after World War II he continued to advocate the implementation of fascism in Britain, but he was considered by the public to be little more than a curiosity. After failing to win reelection to parliament in the 1959 elections, he retired to France, where he continued to write prolifically in defense of fascism. Among his many books are *The Greater Britain* (1932), *Europe: Faith and Plan* (1958) and *300 Questions Answered* (1961). He died in France in 1980.

MOSSADDEQ, MUHAMMAD (1881–1967) Iranian politician, prime minister 1951–1953. Educated in Paris and Switzerland, Mossaddeq was elected to the *majlis* (parliament) in 1944. He served as minister of justice and as foreign minister, and was the governor of a province. In 1949, he became the leader of a national front of opposition parties, which gained power in 1951. In May 1951 he became prime minister. The same month he nationalized the Iranian oil fields, which led to a grave crisis and an international embargo by oil importers. The effectiveness of the embargo resulted in decreased public support for Mossaddeq and the loss of his majority in parliament.

As he was determined to continue his nationalist policies and rid Iran of the conservative shah, Mossaddeq dissolved the *majlis* in July 1953. But his Islamic allies deserted him and popular unrest erupted. The following month, the shah ordered Mossaddeq's removal from his post and appointed General Fazlullah Zahedi as prime minister. Mossaddeq refused to accept his dismissal, rebelled and the shah fled Iran. The revolt failed, however, when the army continued to support the shah. General Zahedi arrested Mossaddeq, suppressed the unrest and enabled the shah, supported by the American CIA—which feared a leftist revolution—to return to Iran. Accused of treason, Mossaddeq was jailed (1953–1956) and banned from participation in political activities. However, he enjoyed widespread popularity, and government attempts to silence him actually increased his political status. Mossaddeq died while under house arrest in Ahmadabad.

MOST, JOHANN JOSEPH (1846–1906) German anarchist.

According to many, the tragedies of Most's childhood seem to lie behind his extremist political philosophy. Raised in abject poverty (his parents could only afford to marry when he was two years old), Most lost his mother when he was 10, was an invalid for five years (his illness left him permanently disfigured) and was mistreated by a cruel stepmother. As a teen, he trained as a bookbinder but aspired to be an actor; he succeeded in neither profession. He wandered throughout Europe for several years, seeking work and absorbing socialist rhetoric. Finally, in Zurich, he joined the International Workingman's Association.

Most lived in Austria and Germany from 1868 to 1878, editing socialist newspapers and writing revolutionary pamphlets. He was elected to the German Reichstag twice but also spent two years in prison in Germany and three years in Austria and was expelled from both countries. He resettled in England, where he founded *Die Freiheit,* a German-language socialist newspaper.

While in England, Most was drawn to the anarchist movement and through his newspaper became a vocal spokesperson of the movement's platform and objectives. He was increasingly critical of KARL MARX and FRIEDRICH ENGELS from an anarchist perspective, and was expelled from the German Socialist party for his tirades against them. He was also an outspoken advocate of violence against governments and capitalists: in 1881 he was imprisoned for 16 months for praising the Russian nihilists' assassination of the Russian Czar Alexander II. Upon his release he moved to New York, where he continued to publish *Die Freiheit.* To American radicals, Most was a hero; he was instrumental in drafting the 1883 Pittsburgh Platform, the so-called "bible of Communist anarchism."

In America, Most continued to agitate for the violent overthrow of the existing order. He was sentenced to one year in prison in 1886, but was arrested shortly after his release and sentenced to another year for producing a pamphlet entitled *The Scientific Art of Revolutionary Warfare*, in which he described how to build bombs. Some time after this second incarceration he began to moderate his views on violence, losing him the support of many eager young radicals. He was jailed one last time in 1901, after the assassination of President William McKinley by Leon Czolgosz. Most died in 1906; he had spent many years in prison for advocating violence to further the anarchist cause, earning himself the title of the "apostle of propaganda by deed." Ironically, Most never participated in the violence he advocated.

MOTILAL see NEHRU MOTILAL.

MOUKANNA (?–783) The leader of an anti-Arab and anti-feudal people's movement in the 8th century in the territory of what are now Uzbekistan, Turkmenistan and Tajikistan. Moukanna (Arabic: "covered by veil") was born in Marv (in what is now Turkmenistan) into a craftsman's family. Due to his activities against the Arab conquerors of the region, he was imprisoned for a total of 15 years. After escaping from prison, he joined the peoples' revolt which began in Marv and soon became its leader. The revolt had a religious character. Moukanna, declaring that he was the personification of the Divinity, claimed to be showing the people the way to their liberation. The main aim of the revolt was to liberate central Asia and Khorasan from the Abbasite occupation. Arab troops eventually crushed the revolt, but with great difficulty. As a result of his tragic defeat, Moukanna committed suicide.

MOUVEMENT POPULAIRE DE LA RÉVOLUTION

(MPR) Colonel (later Marshal) JOSEPH-DÉSIRÉ MOBUTU became head of state of what was then called the Democratic Republic of the Congo (later renamed Zaire) in November 1965. He announced himself head of the "Second Republic." Parliament was suspended and Mobutu was empowered to rule by decree.

Upon becoming head of state, Mobutu imposed a five-year ban on party politics. In 1966, he founded the *Mouvement Populaire de la Révolution* (MPR), whose organization was imposed on the existing administrative structure. The MPR political bureau was responsible for policy formulation and political guidance. In fact, power was progressively concentrated in the office of the president.

The MPR, which advocated national unity and "African socialism" and was opposed to tribalism, was the sole legal party until 1990. In the 1980s there was strong opposition to Zaire's one-party system and, in October 1990, Mobutu announced the introduction of a multi-party system. In November, legislation was adopted to provide for the organization of such a system.

As part of Mobutu's and the MPR's policy of "authenticity," European place names were changed to African ones and the capital Léopoldville became Kinshasa. The country was renamed Zaire in October 1971 and, in 1972 Mobutu took the name of Mobutu Sese Seko Kuku Ngbendu Wa Za Banga as part of this policy of "authenticity."

MOUVEMENT POUR LE TRIOMPHE DES LIBERTÉS DÉMOCRATIQUES (MTLD—Movement for the Triumph of Democratic Liberties)

An Algerian nationalist organization restructured from the banned PARTY OF THE ALGERIAN PEOPLE and led by AHMAD MESSALI HAJJ. As a political party, the MTLD would have won considerable power in the Algerian Assembly in 1948 had the French conducted free elections. In the late 1940s, young radicals such as AHMAD BEN-BELLA and HUSSEIN AIT-AHMAD broke away from the MTLD to form the ORGANISATION SPECIALE (Special Organization), for the first time challenging Messali as the primary and most radical leader of the nationalist movement. The MTLD reformed as the National Algerian Movement (MNA), taking on a more aggressive stance toward the French in an abortive attempt to prevent the younger, more radical generation from splitting off and joining the FRONT DE LIBÉRATION NATIONALE.

MUGABE, ROBERT GABRIEL

(1924–) Robert Mugabe is a member of the Shona ethnic group (the largest in Zimbabwe). He was educated at mission schools and at Fort Hare University, South Africa, and worked as a teacher before entering politics.

Mugabe turned to politics in 1960 and joined the fight against white supremacy in what was then Southern Rhodesia. He was arrested several times. He escaped and went into exile in Tanzania where, in 1963, he helped found the ZIMBABWE AFRICAN NATIONAL UNION (ZANU)—of which he became president in 1964.

In September 1979, Mugabe led the ZANU delegation to the historic Lancaster House conference in London and then supervised ZANU's successful election campaign. In 1980, he became prime minister of his newly independent country, now called Zimbabwe. On December 31, 1987, Mugabe became Zimbabwe's first executive president (incorporating the post of prime minister). He is the leader of the ruling ZANU-PF (Zimbabwe African National Union-Patriotic Front) party, formed in 1989 following a merger between ZANU and the ZIMBABWE AFRICAN PEOPLE'S UNION (ZAPU), led by JOSHUA NKOMO.

During the pre-independence struggle, Mugabe was regarded as a radical Marxist and was expected to pursue extreme left-wing policies. Since achieving power, however, he has followed a policy of reconciliation. Marxism-Leninism has been replaced by economic liberalism, although there is an echo of the former in the use of "comrade" as a form of address for all party members, including Mugabe himself.

MUHAMMAD, ALI

(1769–1849) Ottoman governor of Egypt who revolted against the Porte and established his own and his descendants' right to govern Egypt as a semi-autonomous province of the Ottoman empire. The son of a minor Ottoman official in Macedonia, after his father's death he was brought up by the provincial governor, whose daughter eventually became his wife and the mother of 5 of his 95 known children.

In 1798, Ali joined the Ottoman army then being sent to Egypt in order to fight Napoleon Bonaparte. Even though the Turks were soundly beaten in the Battle of the Pyramids, Ali remained in Egypt and, after the French were evacuated in 1801, succeeded in rising in the Ottoman service until he was appointed governor in 1805. As governor he carried out various reforms, converting all land into state land, increasing revenue and replacing the slave-army of Mamelukes by one which consisted of Egyptian conscripts.

Having assisted the sultan in suppressing the GREEK REVOLT of 1825–1826, Ali felt strong enough in 1831 to revolt against the sultan. That year he declared war on the sultan and soon overran Palestine and Syria. However, Ali's successes—culminating in the defection of the Ottoman fleet (1810) which joined him—gave rise to concern in England and France, which feared that Ali's success would cause the Ottoman Empire to collapse and leave the Mediterranean exposed to Russian power. They therefore forced him to give up his conquests, but his revolt was nevertheless a success in so far as Ali and his family were recognized as hereditary rulers of Egypt. Furthermore, his rule marked Egypt's first attempt to reenter the modern world.

MUHAMMAD, 'ALI NASSER

(1939? 1940?–) South Yemeni politician, prime minister (1971–1985), president (1980–1986). Of tribal background, Muhammad was trained as a teacher in Aden, graduating in 1959, and became a school principal in his Dathina tribal area. In the 1960s he was one of the founders and leaders of the NATIONAL LIBERATION FRONT (NLF), the nationalist faction considered most anti-British and extreme, and especially of its fighting squads. During the decisive struggle of 1967, he commanded the NLF's guerrilla formations in the Beihan area. After South Yemen became independent under the NLF, late in 1967, he gradually rose to power by siding with the extremist-leftist faction, retaining the defense ministry post for some time.

As prime minister and president, Muhammad gradually tended to pragmatic leftist policies, aspiring to a measure of reintegration in the Arab mainstream and an improvement in South Yemen's relations with its Arab neighbors, particularly Saudi Arabia.

In December 1986, after the final showdown of his struggle with the more extreme Moscow loyalists led by ABDUL-FATTAH ISMA'IL, he was put on trial in absentia, with about 140 others; no verdict was reported. In 1992, Muhammad and five members of his faction were pardoned.

MUHYI-UL-DIN (MOHIEDDIN), KHALED   (1922–)
Egyptian officer and left–wing political leader. Born into a middle-class landowning family with medium-sized holdings, Muhyi-ul-din studied at the military academy and became a professional officer, attaining the rank of major. He also received a B.A. in economics at the University of Cairo. He was a member of the FREE OFFICERS group that staged the Egyptian Revolution of 1952 (see EGYPT, REBELLIONS, REVOLTS AND REVOLUTIONS), and of the Revolutionary Command Council established after the coup.

Since the 1950s, Muhyi has been the leader of the Egyptian Communist-leaning left (some maintain that he was a member of the Communist Party for some time) but remained inside GAMAL ABDUL NASSER's establishment despite "leftist" heresy. He received the Lenin Peace Prize in 1970. When in 1975–1977 various trends or platforms were allowed to crystallize within Egypt's ruling Arab Socialist Union (ASU) and finally to become separate, independent parties in 1976–1977, Muhyi headed the leftist "platform" that became the National Progressive-Unionist Rally (NPUR). In 1978 he founded the NPUR's organ, the weekly al-Ahali, and has remained its editor. The NPUR has not, however, developed into a strong organization and seems to have little influence.

MUHYI-UL-DIN, ZAKARIYYA   (1918–) Egyptian officer
and politician. Born into a middle-class landowning family with medium-sized holdings in the Dakahhiyya province. Muhyi became a professional officer, graduating from the military academy in 1938 (together with GAMAL ABDUL NASSER and ANWAR AL-SADAT). He was a senior member of the FREE OFFICERS group and joined them on the eve of the Egyptian Revolution of 1952 (see EGYPT, REBELLIONS, REVOLTS AND REVOLUTIONS), becoming a member of the Revolutionary Command Council (RCC) when the government was overturned. He figured prominently in Egyptian politics between 1953 and 1968, as interior minister (1953–1960, 1965–1967), vice president (1961, 1965–1967), deputy prime minister (1964–1965), prime minister and interior minister (1965). He was also a member of the National Defense Committee from 1962–1969. He often opposed Nasser's economic policies and Egypt's increasing dependency on the Soviet Union instead of ties with the United States. Nevertheless, Nasser and many others considered him a central figure who could be of great assistance. Nasser, following his defeat in the June 1967 war, declared that he was resigning from his post as president and elected Muhyi as his successor. Although Nasser cancelled his resignation the next day (June 10, 1967), Muhyi's nomination was evidence of his seniority and influence in the Egyptian leadership. A year later Muhyi resigned from all public activity.

MUJAHEDIN   Term derived from the Arabic mujahadah,
"striving," which may be applied either to man's struggle to control his own carnal desires or to the holy war against unbelievers (the word jihad, "holy war," is related to mujahadah). In the early 1980s, the tittle mujahedin, "fighters," was assumed by the Afghanistani rebels who resisted the Soviet-imposed government of their country. Consisting of a loose alliance of several groups—some more fundamentalist, some less so, but all based on various tribes—the Mujahedin, though they never learned how to operate in units larger than a battalion, waged an extremely effective guerrilla war against the Soviet army which, at that time, was considered the world's most powerful.

In 1988 the Soviets, having lost 13,000 men to death alone and despairing of obtaining victory, left Afghanistan. Their retreat gave the signal to the disintegration of the USSR, which soon followed. Meanwhile in Afghanistan itself the Mujahedin, now deprived of a common enemy, fell upon each other, and as of mid-1995 were still fighting with the greatest ferocity and with no end to the struggle in sight.

MUJAHIDIN KHALQ ORGANIZATION (MKO)   Founded
in Iran in 1965, the Mujahedin is a left-wing organization. Describing themselves as Islamic Marxists, the MKO members have tried to combine Islam and socialist theory. Its members are students, intelligetsia, clergy and workers. Its leader, ALI SHARI'ATI, was a progressive journalist and translator and was very popular among progressive youth as an interpreter of Islam as the revolutionary doctrine of the working people oppressed by the despotic shah's régime.

The MKO is the largest and best organized movement in opposition to the Islamic régime in contemporary Iran. Before switching to underground activities in 1981, the MKO had more then 500,000 members, with branches throughout Iran. Its detachments played the decisive role in the 1979 armed revolt.

As early as the revolutionary upsurge in 1978–1979, the MKO became aware of the attempts of the Shiite clergy, headed by KHOMEINI, to establish a clerical dictatorship. In 1979–1980, the Islamic authorities began doing everything possible to reduce MKO activities. All MKO branches and the movement's Tehran headquarters were closed. MKO members were subjected to beatings and arrests. Ever since June 1981, the MKO has been engaged in an armed struggle against the clerical Iranian régime. As its terroristic activities were not supported by the people, its endeavors to turn terrorism into a revolt were not successful. An extended campaign against the MKO, sometimes waged with savage ferocity, eventually achieved some success for the Iranian government and in February 1982 the Mojahedin leader in Iran, Musa Khiabani, was killed.

In 1983, the Islamic régime took strong repressive actions against the MKO. As a result, the most active MKO members were killed or imprisoned. At present, the MKO supports overthrowing the theocratic régime, the further development of the Iranian revolution and fundamental social and economical changes.

At present, Masoud Rajavi is the head of the MKO. Ever since 1986, the MKO headquarters have been located in Baghdad. At present the MKO represents a known threat to security inside Iran. Despite the government's intensified campaign against it, especially the bombing of MKO bases inside Iraq, the MKO has maintained its campaign of attacks against the régime with a series of bombings targeted against the internal security forces. At present, MKO activities inside Iran are mostly limited to actions against industrial and security installations, in order to avoid large numbers of casualties among the people.

MUJIBUR, RAHMAN (1920–1975) Bengali politician. The son of a middle-class landowner, Mujibur studied Islamic law in Calcutta and Dacca. From his student days he was involved in the struggle to make Bengali an official language in addition to Urdu. He was elected to the East Pakistan Assembly in 1954 and served as minister for trade and industry from 1955–1958. Under the régime of Ayub Khan, he was arrested three times between 1958 and 1966. In 1970 his party, the AWAMI LEAGUE, won a majority in the Pakistani National Assembly, which was therefore closed down by the rulers of West Pakistan. He thereupon proclaimed independence. Arrested in August 1971, he was released, despite his conviction for treason, after Indian intervention had helped clear East Pakistan of Pakistani groups and set up the State of Bangladesh. He became that country's first prime minister (January 1972) and tried to set up a democratic, socialist and neutralist state. All these good intentions, however, did not save him from being murdered together with his entire family in August 1975.

Rahman Mujibur

MÜNZER, THOMAS (c. 1490–1525) German religious leader and revolutionary. A priest who had studied at Leipzig and Frankfurt, Münzer joined the Reformation very early and in 1520 became a preacher at Zwickau. There he enunciated radical religious and social ideas, which led to his expulsion after a brief and stormy ministry. Münzer then tried to settle in Bohemia and, when he failed, went to the small town of Allstedt (1523), where his bold liturgical innovations attracted large crowd of worshipers.

By this time he had become a fierce opponent of LUTHER, whom he accused of moral opportunism, and it was at the latter's instigation that he had to leave (July 1524). Finding shelter in Mühlhausen, Münzer reached the climax of his career when he led the rebellious peasants in Thuringia. Preaching the imminent coming of the Kingdom of God and the destruction of all earthly rulers, he also spoke of equality and a kind of Communistic social order. On 15 May 1525, he and his peasant followers were defeated and dispersed in a battle near Frankenhausen. Captured in his hiding place, he was tortured and executed.

MURAVIEV, NIKITA MIKHAILOVICH (1796–1843) Russian DECEMBRIST leader. Son and heir of a wealthy senator

Thomas Münzer in the Battle of Mühlhausen

and officer in a Guards regiment, Muraviev became one of the triumvirate leading the Northern Society of the Decembrists. He was the author of *The Free Man's Catechism,* quoting Biblical passages in support of representative government and against the autocracy; and later of a draft constitution for Russia as a federal parliamentary monarchy, with a property-limited franchise but civil liberties for all. His death sentence for participation in the Decembrist revolt was commuted to 20 years at hard labor and he died in exile in Siberia.

MURAVIEV-APOSTOL, SERGEI IVANOVICH   (1796–1826) DECEMBRIST leader in southern Russia. A veteran of the Napoleonic wars, Muraviev-Apostol was the commander of the Chernigov regiment of the imperial army. Dissatisfied with the autocratic style of government, he became a cofounder of the Union of Salvation, which promoted the establishment of a democratic republic in place of the Romanov dynasty in Russia. He is known to have participated in a number of plots to overthrow Czar Alexander I and even called for his assassination.

Upon the death of Alexander, Muraviev-Apostol was one of a group of army officers that refused to take the traditional oath of allegiance to the new monarch, Nicholas I. When their call for the establishment of a constitutional assembly was rejected, the officers launched the failed Decembrist Revolt. Convicted of treason, Muraviev-Apostol was hanged in St. Petersburg.

MUSAVI, KHO'EINIHA MUHAMMAD   (1941–) Attorney-General of Iran. Born in Qazvin, Musavi studied theology in Qom under AYATOLLAH MONTAZERI and in the late 1960s in Iraq under AYATOLLAH KHOMEINI. He returned to Qom in 1967, participated in the struggle against the shah and was arrested. Musavi did not hold an official position during the initial period following the Islamic Revolution of 1979 (see IRAN, REVOLTS AND REVOLUTIONS), but later was appointed Khomeini's representative in the national radio and television. As the students' political leader and their liaison to Khomeini, Musavi played a major role during the occupation of the American Embassy in Tehran in November 1979 and the seizure of American hostages. In 1980 he was elected to the parliament (*majlis*), for Tehran, and appointed to the Second Assembly of Experts; he did not stand for a second parliamentary term in 1984. In 1986, Khomeini appointed him attorney-general.

MUSAVI, MIR HUSSEIN   (1941–) Iranian politician, prime minister 1981–1989. Born in Khamaneh near Tabriz (Azerbaijan), graduated in architecture (1969). Mussavi worked in private companies and was politically active in the Islamic Movement against the shah's régime. He was arrested in 1973. After the Islamic Revolution of 1979 (see IRAN, REVOLTS AND REVOLUTIONS) he was for some time a member of the Council of the Islamic Revolution and formed close ties to the Ayatollahs Beheshti and KHAMENEI. He became a member of the Central Council of Beheshti's Islamic Republic Party and editor of the party's organ, *Jumhuri Islami.*

After the fall of MEHDI BAZARGAN's provisional government (1979), Musavi was named foreign minister by the new prime minister, Raja'i, but was rejected by President Bani-Sadr. After Bani-Sadr's dismissal, 1981, Musavi became minister of foreign affairs, and in October 1981 was appointed prime minister. In his eight-year term he was under pressure from various factions, but with Khamenei's support, he won three votes of confidence.

AL-MUSAWI, HUSAYN   The only leader of Lebanon's Hizbullah Shiite movement who is not a cleric. A former teacher who later served as an official in the Shiite *Amal* movement, Husayn originally served as a liaison for *Amal* in Iran. Following the deterioration of relations between *Amal* and Iran in 1982 due to *Amal*'s unspoken support of the invasion of the Israeli army in Lebanon, Iran decided to develop an alternative Shiite movement to *Amal* in Lebanon that would act as the exporter of the Islamic revolution in the country. In order to achieve this, Iran caused *Amal* to split and established a faction named Islamic *Amal,* headed by al-Musawi. Later this faction was subsumed as an organization into *Hizbullah* but al-Musawi continued to hold the title of the leader of Islamic *Amal.*

In October 1989, the *Hizbullah* leadership went public. An executive council was founded with the founders of the movement, among them al-Musawi, as its members. These changes reflected the institutionalization of the movement and a new openness to other operational factors in Lebanon.

Al-Musawi sees Israel as the Islamic world's major enemy. In October 1991, it was he who announced the change in *Hizbullah*'s tactics in its struggle against Israel, extending its attacks into Israeli territory rather than just the security zone bordering Israel, created in south Lebanon in 1985. Al-Musawi also approved the kidnapping of western foreigners and the suicide attacks against the multinational forces in Beirut in October 1983.

Al-Musawi supported the presence of Iranian soldiers in Lebanon to promote the spread of Islam in Lebanon and to assist in the struggle against Israel. From the split in *Amal* in 1982 to the present, he follows the Iranian line on *Hizbullah* even at the price of disloyalty to the Lebanese state.

MUSAZI, KANGAYE IGNATIUS   (1905–) Born in Kampala, Uganda, Musazi was educated in Uganda and in England, where he obtained a diploma of education at St. Augustine's College, Canterbury, in 1930. In 1934 was appointed inspector of schools. In 1937, he founded the Peasant Farmers' Voluntary Organization, which demanded the improvement of farmers' conditions and the granting to them of title deeds to land.

In 1952, he founded the country's first nationalist party the Uganda National Congress (UNC), which demanded immediate self-rule and independence. It played an active part in the political upheavals in Uganda and organized riots and demonstrations against British government policies. The UNC was fundamentally radical in outlook and attracted radical elements from all over the country. Its demands were typical of nationalist movements. In 1959, Musazi was deported to northern Uganda by the protectorate government. After Uganda became independent, Musazi became president of the Uganda-Soviet Friendship and Cultural Society.

MUSEVENI, YOWERI   (1944–) Born in Uganda, Museveni was educated in Uganda and at the University of Dar-es-Salaam, Tanzania. In exile in Tanzania, he formed the Front for National Salvation (FRONSA). He led the FRONSA attack that, backed by Tanzanian troops, invaded Uganda from Tanzania in 1979 to topple IDI AMIN. That same year, when Yususu Lule was elected president of Uganda, Museveni became minister of defense.

The following year, when ousted President Milton Obote came to power again, Museveni founded the National Resistance Movement (NRM) to oppose Obote's government, and he himself led the NRM's military wing, the National Resistance Army (NRA).

Museveni also opposed the military government in power from July 1985 to January 1986. Claiming that law and order had broken down throughout Uganda, NRA troops surrounded Uganda's capital, Kampala, and took control on January 26, 1986. Three days' later, Museveni was sworn in as president. He is also minister of defense.

Museveni established the National Resistance Council (NRC) to rule the country and suspended political parties. Efforts have been made to restore law and order and Museveni has tried to reconcile the country's various factions while still not allowing any opposition parties.

A constitutional council was elected by universal suffrage and Museveni set up a constitutional committee to draw up a new constitution for a unitary non-party state. The draft constitution was approved by the constitutional council in June 1995 and elections for president and parliament are due to be held in December 1995.

MUSLIM BROTHERHOOD (al-Ikhwan al-Muslimun) An ultra-conservative, fundamentalist religious and political organization founded in Egypt in 1929 by Sheikh HASSAN AL-BANNA, who became its Supreme Guide (*al-Murshid al-'Aam*), a title taken from the vocabulary of the Muslim mystics, *Sufis* and the Dervish orders—though the organization was strictly orthodox and its teachings had no *Sufi* or Dervish tendencies. The aim of the Muslim Brotherhood is to impose the laws of Islam (the *Shari'a*) upon the social, political and constitutional life of Muslim nations. Though it displays certain conservative-reformist tendencies, its conception of Islam is orthodox-fundamentalist, with Pan-Islamic aspirations and strong xenophobic, anti-Christian and anti-Jewish sentiments.

The Muslim Brotherhood has become, over the years, a strong, semi-clandestine popular organization, rooted mainly in the lower classes and strong among university students. In the 1940s, its strength was variously estimated between 100,000 and 1 million members. It also maintained a paramilitary youth organization and underground hit squads. The organization has generally been in extreme opposition to all Egyptian governments: its power and influence have been extra-parliamentary and have been manifested through agitation and demonstrations. Its hit squads were held responsible for the wave of political assassinations that engulfed Egypt in 1945–1948. In 1948, the Muslim Brotherhood recruited volunteers to fight the Jews in Palestine. It saw action in southern Palestine and on the outskirts of Jerusalem. After the May 1948 invasion of Israel by the regular Egyptian forces, it was partly incorporated in those forces and lost impact.

In view of its violent, terroristic activities, the Muslim Brotherhood was banned in December 1948 by Premier Nuqrashi. It was in retaliation for this ban that Nuqrashi was assassinated. Measures to suppress the organization were now tightened, and the movement went underground. Al-Banna himself was murdered in February 1949—it was assumed by agents of the régime—and replaced by Sheikh Hassan Isma'il al-Hudeibi.

In April 1951, the Muslim Brotherhood was permitted to resume activity—on condition that it would limit its functions to spiritual, cultural and social matters and neither engage in political activities nor maintain any paramilitary formations. The Muslim Brotherhood does not seem to have regained, under its new Supreme Guide, its previous strength and impact. Some of the FREE OFFICERS who staged the revolution of July 1952 were considered close to the Muslim Brotherhood,; and when the new régime in 1953 banned all political parties, it accepted the Muslim Brotherhood's claim that the movement was not a party, and did not apply the decree to the movement. However, in October 1954 an attempt to assassinate NASSER was ascribed to the Muslim Brotherhood, and the régime took strong action. Thousands of Muslim Brothers were arrested, and their 19 top leaders were put on trial in December (a show trial in which the accused did not appear with much dignity). Some were sentenced to death, some to imprisonment and some to execution.

The Muslim Brotherhood—now reportedly under a collective leadership without a Supreme Guide—was not completely broken and continued operating underground. A revival of its activities was reported especially in the mid-1960s, including a plot on Nasser's life, and in 1965 and 1966 thousands were again arrested and hundreds were tried. The sentences in August–September 1966 included several death verdicts and three members were executed (including the Muslim Brotherhood's most prominent ideologue and writer, Sayyid Qutb). Hudeibi, who had been released in 1956 on compassionate and health grounds, was rearrested and sentenced to prison, with two of his sons. Yet, student unrest in 1968 was again ascribed to the Muslim Brotherhood.

Under SADAT from 1970, and since 1981 under Mubarak, the organization was treated more leniently and some observers saw a certain affinity between it and the new leadership (Sadat himself had reportedly been close to it in the 1940s and 1950s). As the Muslim Brotherhood was thought to have considerably moderated its stance—under the leadership of 'Umar Talmassani (without the title of Supreme Guide)—there was even talk of a sort of alliance between it and the régime against the left and against more extreme Islamic groups. In any case, it was allowed to acquire increasing influence, even a large measure of control, in lower-class quarters of the cities and especially at the universities.

But the Muslim Brotherhood was not permitted to establish a political organization or openly put up candidates for public office, such as the National Assembly. In the National Assembly elections of 1984, the Muslim Brotherhood made an informal alliance with the Wafd party and eight Muslim Brothers entered the Assembly on the Wafd ticket. In the 1987 elections, the organization ran in coalition with the Socialist Labor and Socialist Liberal parties, and among that list's 60 elected members, some 35 were reportedly Muslim Brothers.

The Muslim Brotherhood has never been the only Islamic organization in Egypt, but has usually been the most extremist one. Since the 1970s, however, the Muslim Brotherhood has been outflanked by more extremist underground Islamic organizations, using violent and terrorist means (which the Muslim Brotherhood had gradually abandoned)—such as the "Islamic Liberation" (*al-Tahrir al-Islam, al-Takif wa'l-Hijra, al-Jihad*) groups. The Muslim Brotherhood, though, has its own extremist wing; there are underground links, and there may be clandestine double membership.

The home and center of the Muslim Brotherhood is Egypt. Attempts to create branches in other African countries have been only partially successful, and no all-African or inter-African association for "Muslim Brotherhood" groups has been founded. Groups calling themselves Muslim Brotherhood were established, from about 1945, in Palestine, Jordan, Syria, Lebanon and later Sudan; some of them were short-lived, and the association of those surviving was rather loose with the Egyptian movement. The Muslim Brotherhood in Sudan, under Hassan Turbai, has mostly remained within the establishment and sometimes even participated in the government; under régimes that permitted multiparty elections, it did not field candidates under its own name but it was reported to be behind Islamic Front candidates who won a few seats in the elections of 1965 and 1968 and a larger representation (51 of 264) in 1986. In Jordan, too (including until 1967 the Palestinian West Bank), the Muslim Brotherhood—led by 'Abd-ul-Rahman al-Khalifa—was for most of the time a legal organization within the establishment, though often in opposition; it contested elections (though its candidates usually appeared, formally, as "Independents") and several times won seats in parliament.

The country outside Egypt where the Muslim Brotherhood had the strongest impact was Syria. The Syrian Muslim Brotherhood was founded in the late 1930s and became really active from 1945–1946. Until the early 1960s, the Syrian Muslim Brotherhood, though often dissenting from the mainstream (and linked to, or even clandestinely funding, more extreme groups of different names, such as an Islamic Liberation Party), was a legal part of the establishment and presented candidates for parliament, usually as independents. In the House elected in 1961, for instance, 7–12 deputies—according to different versions—were considered Muslim Brotherhood men. It even had ministers in the government, and its leader, Siba'i, was for some time deputy president of parliament. After the *Ba'ath* party came to power in the coup of 1963, the antagonism between the Muslim Brotherhood and the ruling leftist-revolutionary nationalist trends erupted into open mutual hostility—aggravated by the ever-increasing role played in the ruling establishment by members of the Alawi sect, whom the Sunni-fundamentalist Muslim Brotherhood could not but consider heretics or non-believers. The Muslim Brotherhood, now led by 'Issam al-'Attar (who soon went into exile), was outlawed in 1963 and went underground. In the 1970s it began stepping up acts of sabotage and violence, which escalated particularly from 1978–1979, including, for instance, a June 1979 attack on officer-cadets, most of them Alawis, in Aleppo, amounting to a massacre. Counteraction by the régime and its efforts to suppress the Muslim Brotherhood were equally brutal, leading in June 1980 to a massacre of Muslim Brotherhood detainees in Palmyra prison. In February 1982, a veritable insurrection in Hama and full-fledged army and special forces action against it left Hama nearly destroyed by artillery shelling and thousands killed (in the official version: c. 1,200; in other reports: 10–30,000). After these battles, Muslim Brotherhood violence and sabotage seem to have abated; but it was by no means clear that the Muslim Brotherhood had really been decisively suppressed.

MUSLIM LEAGUE   Founded in 1906 at the prompting of Nawab Salim-ul-lah of Dacca (now the capital of Bangladesh, but at that time part of East Bengal), the league sought to protect the interests of the minority Muslim community in British-ruled India in the light of what it regarded as growing Hindu influence. Its efforts bore fruit in the clause of the 1909 Indian Councils Act that granted separate communal representation for Muslims, on the grounds that the relative poverty of the Muslim population would prevent its enjoying influence in proportion to its size in general constituencies where a property franchise was in force.

The league joined with the INDIAN NATIONAL CONGRESS in issuing the Lucknow pact, a 1916 agreement wherein it agreed to work with the congress to secure self-government for India on the basis of separate electorates and a fair distribution of offices between the two communities, but, apart from this agreement, its relationship with the congress was marked by considerable mutual suspicion rather than wholehearted cooperation. The league enjoyed a considerable growth in power and influence during World War II, as the en masse resignation of the congress from provincial ministries in protest against Britain's not consulting with Indian representatives during the war period left the way open for the league to gain control of these ministries and to push its agenda with the British administration.

Early in 1940, MUHAMMAD ALI JINNAH, the league's leader, took the significant step of declaring an independent Muslim state of Pakistan to be the organization's goal. He had developed considerable support among the Muslim community at large, warning of the dangers of Hinduization and evoking a two nations theory to promote the notion that Indian Islam could never accept Hindu rule.

As the date for the subcontinent's independence drew nearer, communal violence and sustained league petitioning for a separate state for Muslims led to the British acceding to the league's demands, and August 14, 1947 saw two new independent nations come into being, despite the opposition of the congress leaders. Partition resulted in a massive movement of refugees from both sides of the new border, and communal atrocities claimed a number of lives that has been estimated as well in excess of one million. Jinnah, as president of the league, was president of Pakistan until his death (he had been terminally ill for some time) less than a year later. Relations between the nations of India and Pakistan have been poor since independence, and have declined on several occasions into armed conflict.

MUSLIM REBELLIONS (IN CHINA)   Muslims (Arabs and Persians) had lived in China since the Tang dynasty (618–907), generally following trade routes—by sea to China's southeastern coast and by land to the northwest. The largest influx came with the Mongol conquest of China and the establishment of the Yuan dynasty (1279–1368). The Mongols employed Muslims from western and central Asia as officials and advisors, utilizing their superior scientific and technical knowledge, including their ballistic expertise. The Chinese remembrance of the Muslims' role in the Mongol Yuan dynasty contributed to the underlying antagonism between them. Though Islam spread throughout China during this period, the communities that were to remain important were in the southwest (Yunnan) and in the northwest (Shaanxi, Gansu and Xinjiang). The Chinese call Muslims Hui, but the definition is based more on religion than ethnicity. Some, like the Uighurs in Xinjiang, form a distinct ethnic minority. Muslim clashes with Chinese, fanned by religious and cultural differences, and even minor rebellions, took place in earlier dynasties, but no major uprisings occurred until the 18th and 19th centuries during the Qing (Manchu) dynasty (1644–1912). The first (1781–1784) erupted in Gansu and was led by Ma Mingxin, founder of the fanatical, Sufi-influenced sect, the New Teaching. Muslim opponents of the sect joined in suppressing the rebellion. More serious Muslim rebellions occurred in the latter half of the 19th century (see DU WENXIU, MA HUALONG, YAKUB BEG). In recent years there have been reports of Uighur uprisings and Islamic fundamentalist influences in Xinjiang (1993, 1994).

MUSSAVI-ARDELBILI, AYATOLLAH 'ABDUL-KARIM (1926–) Iranian cleric, chief justice and head of the Supreme Judicial Council, 1981–1989. Born in Ardebil, eastern Azerbaijan, Mussavi-Ardelbili studied theology in Qom under the AYATOLLAH KHOMEINI and from 1948–1950 in Najaf, Iraq.

In 1960, Mussavi-Ardelbili and other clergymen in Qom published an Islamic newspaper, *Maktab-E Islam* (Islamic School). Between 1962 and 1971 he founded religious centers in his hometown, spreading Islamic revolutionary ideas and maintaining close ties with Khomeini. He moved to Tehran in 1971, becoming a prayer leader and preacher (Imam) in the Amir al-Mu'min Mosque and founded the Amir al-Mu'minin school. His close ties with Iranian youth and his forceful preaching earned him high praise from Tehran's religious leaders.

Following the Islamic Revolution of 1979 (see IRAN, REVOLTS AND REVOLUTIONS), he was one of the founders of the Islamic Republic party. He was one of Khomeini's closest advisers and was appointed to numerous prominent government positions. In the factional struggles of Islamic Iran, he has generally been considered a moderate.

MUSSOLINI, BENITO (1883–1945) Italian prime minister, first of Europe's Fascist (see FASCISM) dictators, who called himself *Il Duce* ("the Leader"). Mussolini would often exaggerate the degree of poverty he had to suffer as a child; in fact he grew up in a middle-class home in his birthplace of Romagna, where his father was a blacksmith and socialist journalist and his mother a schoolteacher. Nonetheless, his father's drinking and extravagant spending on his mistresses often caused the family hardship.

An aggressive and unruly child who was twice expelled from schools for knifing fellow pupils, Mussolini was also very intelligent; he easily passed his final examinations and qualified as a schoolteacher. He soon, however, realized that he was wholly unsuited for such a career and left for Switzerland, where he spent several months living a hand-to-mouth existence financed by a succession of temporary jobs.

Mussolini had inherited his father's socialist tendencies, and while in Switzerland sought to further his own political education through voracious, albeit superficial, reading of a wide variety of philosophers and political scientists. While he was particularly influenced by the vitalist philosophy of Henri Bergson, he turned toward an eccentric mélange of sources to buttress a radical socialist philosophy that advocated violent change. His

magnetism and charisma, allied with his burgeoning rhetorical talents, made him an arresting speaker and journalist. He was already well known (and marked as a troublemaker by the authorities) by the time he returned to Italy in 1904.

Mussolini's trade union activism and political extremism led to his arrest and imprisonment in his native country, but also earned him considerable credit among his political peers. As early as 1908 he was calling for the amalgamation of the working classes "in one formidable bundle [*fascio*]." His journal, *La Lotta di Classe* (The class struggle) was so successful that he was soon called to edit *Avanti*, the flagship broadsheet of Italian socialism.

When World War I broke out he opposed Italian involvement, in line with socialist policy. However, he broke with the mainstream of the socialist movement and came to advocate and support Italy's entry into the war. Undeterred by his expulsion from the Italian Socialist Party, he launched the paper *Il Popolo d'Italia* and went on to serve in the Italian army. Wounded in action, he became vehemently anti-socialist.

By now, Mussolini was openly advocating the emergence of a dictator, "a man who is ruthless and energetic enough to make a clean sweep." In 1919 he founded the organization of *Fasci de Combattimento*—squads of roughnecks who were dedicated to breaking strikes and beating political opponents, above all so-

Vote yes: Mussolini on a Fascist campaign-poster

MUSSOLINI'S PHILOSOPHY

• Blood alone moves the wheels of history.

• The Italian proletariat needs a bloodbath for its force to be renewed.

• The truth is that men are tired of liberty.

• You cannot govern nations without a mailed fist and an iron will.

• Let us have a dagger between our teeth, a bomb in our hands and an infinite scorn in our hearts.

• War alone brings up to their highest tension all human energies and imposes the stamp of nobility upon the peoples who have the courage to make it.

• Statesmen only talk of Fate when they have blundered.

cialists. Taking as its symbol the *fascinae* of the lictors, the ancient Roman symbol of authority—the Fascist movement was born. Mussolini's superb oratory and macho bombasticism and the regimented militarism of the Fascist blackshirts (Mussolini took the idea for their uniform from the dress of anarchists) attracted many supporters in an Italy traumatized by postwar economic depression. In 1922, a Fascist-organized MARCH ON ROME

to protest the calling of a general strike led to the fall of the government and King Victor Emmanuel III's call on Mussolini to head a new government. He was soon installed as Italy's youngest prime minister.

The Italian elections of 1924 confirmed Mussolini in power. The Fascists used ballot-box fraud to make sure of the result, but Mussolini and his movement were genuinely popular in Italy. He successfully tackled widespread unemployment by initiating a series of massive public works (such as the draining of the Pontine marshes), while also managing to improve the conditions of workers, attracting many admirers both at home and abroad. Between 1925 and 1929, Mussolini transformed Italy into a "corporative state" enjoying relative economic prosperity. However, during the 1930s his desire for foreign conquest led him into an alliance with ADOLF HITLER, forcing Italy into World War II.

From 1940 on, with Italy's military power wholly eclipsed by that of Germany, Mussolini became the latter's puppet and faced opposition and unpopularity at home; the July 1943 Allied invasion of Sicily heralded his doom. Mussolini was dismissed by the king and imprisoned on Gran Sasso in the Abruzzi mountains. The Germans managed to rescue him and set him up as head of their puppet administration headquartered in Salo in northern Italy, where he became increasingly estranged from reality and belatedly returned to his earlier socialist and collectivist ideals.

As the Axis forces crumbled, Mussolini and his mistress were captured and shot to death by Italian Communist partisans as he tried in vain to head for the Valtellina mountains as a last defense. The man who had been a popular hero in his homeland died unmourned by a nation he had led into a most costly and unnecessary war.

N

NABIS In Greek history, son of Damaratus, last king of Sparta (207–192 B.C.). Seizing the throne by force after the death of the young king Pelops, Nabis maintained power through mercenary troops and set out to carry through a revolutionary social program modeled on that of his predecessors, AGIS IV and CLEOMENES III.

He executed many members of the upper classes, redistributed their lands, and liberated serfs (Helots) in an effort to increase the number of Spartan citizens. Nabis eventually became involved in a war against the neighboring Achaean League, was defeated and subsequently murdered. Considered a bloody tyrant by some, he was regarded by others a revolutionary whose aim was to restore Sparta to its ancient greatness.

NABU-NAID Last of the kings of the new Babylonian kingdom (556–539 B.C.). Nabu-Naid was an army general who revolted against the Babylonian king Labashi-Marduk and overthrew him. When he came to power, he had to face two major issues: the perilous economical situation of the empire and the situation of the ancient Babylonian religion. The wars and building enterprises of Nebuchadnezzar and Neriglissar had caused a very high inflation rate in the years 560–550 B.C. Inflation caused hunger and the sale of children to temples for slavery. The fertility of the land decreased, and trade with the east and the north became problematic. Nabu-Naid reacted by leaving his capital Babylon in 556 B.C. and transferring the center of the empire to the west, thus securing trade with south Arabia. After nominating his son Bel-Shar-Usus (the Biblical Belteshazzar) regent, Nabu-Naid led his army to Teima, in northeastern Arabia, where he killed the local king and turned the oasis there into his base for the next 10 years. Later he turned to the south and reached the city of Yatrib (modern Medina). In Media and in Babylon, new ideas had been emerging concerning religion and morals, and these involved the forsaking of polytheism. That was the background of Nabu-Naid's attempt to establish the moon god, Sin, as the supreme god of the empire. He replaced the high priests in the major Babylonian temples, interfered with the economical management of the temples and reduced their incomes. He reduced the privileges of the major temple cities, especially Babylon and Sipar.

This revolution should not be understood as meaning that monotheism was adopted. It was an attempt to create a central force that would bind the empire. Marduk, the chief god of the Babylonian pantheon, could not serve this goal, because he was not accepted in the Aramean and Arabian pantheon. As opposed to this, Sin, the moon god, was admired in different forms by the Babylonians, Arameans and Arabs.

Nabu-Naid started his reforms by restoring Sin's temple which had been destroyed by the Medes in 610 B.C., using forced labor for the reconstruction. He also reconstructed the ziggurat of Ur. The city of Haran had been under the Medes's control ever since 610 B.C. In order to get rid of the Medes, Nabu-Naid asked the help of Cyrus, king of Persia. This act caused revolts of the population of the big cities of Babylon, led by the priesthood of the temples. Babylon was struck by a famine which was caused by economical reasons, but was attributed by Nabu-Naid to the lack of piety of the population.

The absence of Nabu-Naid for 10 years from his capital may have been the basis for the story of seven years of insanity that were attributed to Nebuchadnezzar, as mentioned in the book of Daniel (4:28–33). Nabu-Naid eventually returned to his capital to take command on the defense of Babylon against the invasion of the Persians led by Cyrus. The capital city, Babylon, was finally conquered by Cyrus almost without fighting in 539 B.C. The inhabitants of Babylon welcomed Cyrus, who claimed the supremacy of Marduk as the chief god. The Persian general Gobrias caught Nabu-Naid and exiled him to the city Carmania. The end of Nabu-Naid is unclear. According to Josephus Flavius (*Contra Apion*, 1:154) Cyrus expelled Nabu-Naid to central Iran and Nabu-Naid lived the rest of his life there in comfort.

NAGIB, MUHAMMAD (1901–1984) Egyptian officer and politician, president of Egypt 1953–1954. Born in Khartoum, the son of an Egyptian army officer, Nagib graduated from the University of Cairo (law) and from the military academy in 1921. He joined the regular army and slowly rose in rank, becoming a colonel in 1948. Later he became commander of the Frontier Forces and, in 1951, of the Land Army.

Among army officers, Nagib was admired for his integrity; he frequently voiced demands for army reforms and the elimination of corruption. He apparently was not a member of the FREE OFFICERS, but was in touch with them through his operations officer, 'ABDUL HAKIM 'AMER. In 1952, he was the Free Officers' candidate for the presidency of the Officers' Club and his election, against the wishes of the Egyptian king and the senior establishment, caused a minor crisis. Nagib himself claimed that he had joined the Free Officers from the start, in 1949–1950, and was their leader in the Egyptian Revolution of July 1952 (see EGYPT, REBELLIONS, REVOLTS AND REVOLUTIONS). However, according to the later official, generally accepted version, he did not take an active part in the coup but was asked by the young revolutionaries to represent them as a sort of figurehead, while GAMAL ABDUL NASSER was the real leader.

After the revolution of July 1952, Nagib was made commander in chief of the armed forces and chairman of the Revolutionary Command Council. When the civilian government formed after the coup resigned in September 1952, Nagib became prime minister and minister of war and, upon the proclamation of the republic in June 1953, president. He was ousted from power, however, in November by Nasser and placed under house arrest from 1956–1971. He had no political influence under ANWAR AL-SADAT's régime but was accorded the respect due to an elderly statesman.

NAGY, IMRE (1896–1958) Hungarian Communist politician. Taken prisoner by the Romanians during World War I, Nagy became a Communist, was released and became a Soviet citizen. In 1919, he took a minor part in BELA KUN's Soviet régime. After illegal activity on behalf of the Communist party during the 1920s, he went back to the USSR in 1930. Returning to Hungary with the RED ARMY in 1945, he became minister of agriculture that same year, then minister of the interior (1945–1946), and later prime minister (1953–1955). Ousted for being too independent of Moscow, he was returned to power in October 1956, just prior to the Hungarian revolution (see HUNGARY, 1956 UPRISING), and tried to quell the disturbances by abolishing one-party rule. This, together with his liberalizing reforms during his first term as premier, made him willy-nilly into the leader of the revolution. After it was suppressed, he found refuge in the Yugoslav embassy which, under false promises, induced him to leave. He was subsequently kidnapped by Soviet troops, tried and shot.

NANCHANG UPRISING (August 1927) Chinese Communist uprising. After the GUOMINDANG (GMD)-CHINESE COMMUNIST PARTY (CCP) rupture earlier in the year, CCP leaders, including MAO ZEDONG and ZHOU ENLAI, planned a series of uprisings (see AUTUMN HARVEST UPRISINGS). Some 10,000 troops, including Communist and pro-Communist soldiers of the NATIONAL REVOLUTIONARY ARMY, launched the attack on Nanchang in Jiangxi on August 1. This marked the opening of the first GMD-CCP civil war (1927–1937) and the birth of the RED ARMY. Though Nanchang was captured, it was retaken by GMD forces on August 5. Ill-planned and badly executed, the uprising lacked popular support, since no effort had been made to organize peasants or carry out land reform.

NARIMANOV, NARIMAN NADZHAF OGLI (1870–1925) The foremost social and political leader of Azerbaijan, a BOLSHEVIK revolutionary, a writer and popular literary figure. Narimanov was born in Tiflis to a poor family. During the time of his studies at the Goriysky seminary, he was involved in literature. In 1891 Narimanov moved to Baku, where he taught at a high school. During this period Narimarov devoted a lot of time to educational activities, wrote novels and plays, was involved in newspaper publications, conducted talks and lectures, performed with an amateur theater group, wrote textbooks and translated texts. Narimanov's literary and dramatic works raised Azerbaijani prose and its entire literature of that time to new heights.

Narimarov was one of the founders of the educational society *Nidzhat* (Deliverance), which was created in March 1906. This society played a significant role in awakening the feeling of national awareness and strengthening the struggle in Azerbaijan for national liberation.

At the same time Narimanov also began to be involved in revolutionary activities. He played a major role in the creation of the Social Democratic organization *Gummet* (Energy) in 1904, in which he played a leading role, along with MESHADI AZIZBEKOV. In 1917, Narimanov was part of the leadership core of the Baku Communist party together with SHAUMYAN and Azizbekov, and was the leader of the *Gummet* group. Under the supervision of the Baku Committee of the Russian Social Democratic Workers party (RSDRP), this group conducted important revolutionary work among the Azerbaijani workers. Starting July 3, 1917, the newspaper *Gummet* was published in the Azerbaijani language. Narimanov was its editor.

Narimanov was a member of the Committee for Revolutionary Defense of Baku, created at the end of March 1918, in the power struggle against the Musavat party. When the Soviet (council) of the People's Commissars of the Baku region was created on April 25, 1918, he was named commissar of the city's property and supervision. In 1919, after the fall of the Soviet control in Baku and the creation of the Azerbaijani Democratic Republic (1918–1920), he was the head of the Near East department of the People's Commissariat for Foreign Affairs of the RSFSR, and later he was assigned to the post of vice-principal people's commissar for ethnic affairs. He actively participated in addressing the issue of education in the Azerbaijani Soviet Republic. He was a member of he Azerbaijani Temporary Revolutionary Committee (Azrevcom) created on April 26, 1920, at the special meeting of the central committee of the Azerbaijani Communist party for the purpose of gaining control of Baku by the Communists.

NARODNAYA VOLYA see PEOPLE'S WILL.

NASSER, GAMAL ABDUL (1918–1970) Egyptian officer and statesman, president of Egypt (1956–1970). Born in Bani Mor, Asyut district, son of a postal clerk, Nasser graduated from secondary school in Cairo in 1936 and from the Royal Military Academy in 1938. He served in Sudan, and from 1941 was an instructor at the military academy. In the Arab-Israel 1948 war, he commanded a battalion and was besieged in the Faluja Pocket. In 1951 he was promoted to the rank of colonel and appointed a lecturer at the military college.

Nasser, like other cadets in the academy, came from the lower middle class which had become greatly disillusioned with the corruption of King Farouk's government and its dependence on western powers. In 1945 he became the most prominent founder of a clandestine group, the FREE OFFICERS, which conspired to remove Egypt's old leadership, whom they held responsible for both the humiliating defeat of 1948 and all the rest of Egypt's ills. On July 22, 1952, they mounted a successful coup, overthrowing King Farouk, who abdicated in favor of his infant son. The Egyptian republic was formally declared in June 1953.

Nasser quickly eliminated political opposition, placing General MUHAMMAD NAGIB under house arrest and severely repressing the MUSLIM BROTHERHOOD. While appearing moderate and quite pragmatic in his first years of power, by the mid-1950s Nasser turned against the west. He opposed the Baghdad Pact, a plan for a Middle East defense alliance linked to the west, led the neutralist block at the 1955 Bandung Conference, and in 1955 concluded an arms deal with Czechoslovakia. The US and the World Bank reciprocated by cutting off aid for the Aswan Dam, Nasser's pet project. Allying himself with the USSR, Nasser announced the nationalization of the Suez Canal, which triggered the Suez war. Emerging triumphant from the crisis of 1956 as the leader of a newly independent nation that had successfully withstood imperialist aggression, Nasser's standing within the Third World was greatly enhanced.

Having developed his doctrine of "Arab Socialism" in his booklet *The Philosophy of the Revolution* in 1954 and having strongly promoted Pan-Arabism, Nasser became the central driving force behind the regional coalition of Arab states. He engineered the merger of Egypt and Syria in February 1958 in the United Arab Republic and intervened in Yemen's 1962 civil war on behalf of the republican camp. He also strongly supported African unity, holding the 1964 congress of the Organization for African Unity in Cairo.

In 1967, Nasser precipitated the Six-Day war against Israel by closing the Straits of Tiran and expelling the UN peacekeeping force which had been stationed in Sinai since 1957. When the

Billboard celebrating Nasser's construction of the Aswan Dam

war turned into a stunning defeat, Nasser, taking personal responsibility, resigned, but stormy mass demonstrations—seemingly spontaneous but in fact carefully staged—"forced" him to retract the resignation. Thus he turned even that day of bitter defeat into a personal victory.

Nasser died suddenly in September 1970 of a heart attack, and his image dimmed somewhat after his death. His successors kept their distance from him, allowing previously hidden aspects of his rule to be revealed. The failure of his economic policies, particularly various state enterprises, the all-pervading corruption, and especially the police state he had created through suppression of freedom of speech, association and press and through the unlawful detention and torture of adversaries, were all made public. There is no doubt, however, that Nasser was endowed with unusual charisma and wielded immense, if controversial influence throughout the Arab world.

NATANSON, MARK (1850–1919) Populist revolutionary educator. As a medical student in St. Petersburg, Natanson joined student demonstrations in 1869, leading to his first arrest. Two years later he organized self-education circles of radical youth and distributed copies of radical literature. This became the nucleus for the CHAIKOVSKY CIRCLE. After Natanson's return from another period of exile in 1876, the circle was the basis for the LAND AND LIBERTY movement. Natanson was arrested again in 1877 and after two years in prison was exiled for 11 years to Siberia. Settling in Saratov in 1890, he resumed his political activity, attempting to organize a union of all liberal and socialist elements. He was re-arrested in 1894, remaining in exile for nine more years.

By this time, he had become a founder and central committee member of the SOCIAL REVOLUTIONARY PARTY (SR). During World War I he identified with the left wing of his party, opposing the war. After the February RUSSIAN REVOLUTION OF 1917 he returned to Russia as a leader of the left faction of the SR and, following the BOLSHEVIK seizure of power in October, helped negotiate the participation of the Left SR in the Bolshevik government. In 1918, splitting with the Bolsheviks, he helped found the Revolutionary Communist group. He emigrated to Switzerland, where he died soon afterwards.

NATIONAL CHRISTIAN ANTI-SEMITIC LEAGUE (LANC) Romanian Fascist student organization. Founded in 1923 by CORNELIU ZELEA CODREANU and a group of fellow students at the University of Iasi, the LANC incited riots which led to the closing of the university. Suspected of plotting the murder of Jews and enemies of the group, the leadership was arrested but acquitted by a sympathetic jury. Following differences with ALEXANDER CUZA, Codreanu broke away from the group to found the LEGION OF THE ARCHANGEL MICHAEL.

NATIONAL FRONT OF IRAN A movement founded in 1949 by a group of progressive statesmen and journalists headed by Dr. MUHAMMAD MOSSADDEQ. As a leading power in the Iranian democratic movement, the National Front played a major role in organizing the struggle for the nationalization of Iranian oil (1951). The National Front government of 1951–1955 rescinded the foreign oil concessions and worked toward attaining political and economical independence. In 1953, Iran underwent a coup, thereby bringing the activities of the National Front to a halt. In 1960, after receiving official permission from the Iranian government, the activities of the National Front were resumed. In 1963, the National Front was banned because of its anti-government activities, but it continued to be active among Iranian students studying in the United States and Eastern Europe. In 1977, the National Front was restored as a coalition of three political groups. At the beginning of the Islamic Revolution (see IRAN, REVOLTS AND REVOLUTIONS), a union was formed between the National Front and the Muslim clergy. Subsequently, political power was concentrated in the hands of the clergy, who halted the activities of the National Front.

NATIONAL LIBERATION FRONT FOR OCCUPIED SOUTH YEMEN (NFL)

A nationalist underground organization in Aden and South Arabia (later South Yemen). Founded in 1963 under the leadership of QAHTAN AL-SHA'BI, the organization was considered the strongest group in the nationalist rebellion which broke out in October 1963 and continued intermittently until the achievement of independence in 1967. In 1966, the NFL joined a roof organization, the Front for the Liberation of Occupied South Yemen (FLOSY), but seceded the same year. In a violent struggle between the two groups, the National Liberation Front won out. In 1967, it gained control of the South Arabian principalities one after the other, until the British had to transfer authority to it (and not to the princes or to FLOSY). The National Liberation Front formed the ruling group of the new People's Republic of South Yemen, where it was the only party and ran the government. Although at first sometimes supported by Egypt, the National Liberation Front was always associated with the extremist ARAB NATIONALIST MOVEMENT (*Harakat al-Qawmiyyin al-'Arab*) and influenced by Leninist-Maoist ideas. From 1967 it veered further to the left, amidst internal struggles and purges. Sha'bi was removed in 1969 and the leadership transferred to MUHAMMAD 'ALI HAITHAM as prime minister and 'ABDUL FATTAH ISMA'IL as party secretary.

NATIONAL REVOLUTIONARY ARMY

(1925–1928) Chinese nationalist (GUOMINDANG-GMD) army. Having formed a united front with the CHINESE COMMUNIST PARTY (CCP) in 1923, the GMD enhanced its strength in Guangdong and in June 1925, after securing Canton, reorganized its forces into the NATIONAL REVOLUTIONARY ARMY (NRA). Russian advisors (see BLÜECHER, VASILY) helped train the NRA and give the GMD a more effective force for unifying China. Following the Soviet example, party representatives, equivalent to Soviet political commissars, were attached to all units. CHIANG KAI-SHEK became the NRA commander in chief in June 1926, on the eve of the NORTHERN EXPEDITION. Regional forces, less subject to Chiang's direct control, were integrated into the NRA. Of the NRA's eight army corps, the First Corps, building upon cadets from the GMD's WHAMPOA MILITARY ACADEMY, was the best equipped and most loyal to the GMD. A Communist officer, YE TING, headed an independent regiment in the Fourth Corps. When the NORTHERN EXPEDITION was officially launched on July 9, 1926, NRA strength was close to 150,000, but only 100,000 were available for the drive north, the rest remaining to guard the southern base. By integrating warlord armies, the NRA ranks were swollen to over 2 million when the Northern Expedition was

completed in 1928. Of its five regional groupings, only one was controlled directly by Chiang's nationalist government, based in Nanjing.

NATIONAL SOCIALIST PARTY (National Socialist German Workers' Party; also known as the Nazi Party)

In German history, a political organization founded in 1919 by a blacksmith by the name of Anton Drexler and disbanded by the Allies in 1945. Originally known as the German Workers Party, it did not become famous until ADOLF HITLER assumed leadership in 1920–1921. Based in Bavaria, it attracted and engulfed many similar right-wing, racist, anti-Semitic movements, organizing its own uniformed army, the SA (*Sturmabteilung*, known as the Brownshirts).

In November 1923, the party attempted to carry out a coup in Munich; when this failed, it reverted to legal methods, without, however, giving up the use of terror against individual opponents, and finally came to power 10 years later. Rabidly nationalist and anti-Semitic, the party adopted a kind of sham socialism in order to seduce workers away from the officially recognized socialist parties. The Nazis were not very successful until the Great Depression of 1929 resulted in the various middle-of-the-road parties losing all standing in the eyes of the public at large. As a result, after the elections of 1930, National Socialism became Germany's second largest party. By 1932 it had become number one, although it never succeeded in obtaining an absolute majority in anything that resembled free elections.

Called to power in January 1933 by President Paul von Hindenburg, the party proceeded to remodel Germany into a totalitarian state, abolish all opposition, set up a system of terror and launch World War II. A vast organization with its own affiliated labor organization (after 1933, the only one permitted), publishing empire, youth movements and political army, the party permeated every field of German life between 1939–1945—when it was abolished by the victorious Allies, following which, all of sudden, not a single Nazi was to be found in the country. Since then, however, there have been several attempts to revive it under a variety of different names.

NAXALITES

In India, a movement which attempted to use violence in order to set up a Maoist-style Communist dictatorship. Founded in April 1969 by a group of extremists who had been expelled from the Indian Communist party, the movement, under Charu Mazumadar, advocated forcible seizure of land for redistribution to landless farm laborers and waged an intensive campaign of terror in nine Indian states between 1969–1970. In 1970 it even staged a Chinese style "Cultural Revolution" in Calcutta, where it went on a rampage burning books, destroying movie houses and murdering members of the university faculty. The movement was finally brought under control in 1974 by Prime Minister Indira Ghandi, but not before direct rule from New Delhi had been imposed on the states and a few tens of thousands of Naxilites thrown into prison.

Mazumdar died in imprisonment in 1972. Similar movements subsequently developed throughout India, often urging purges of the ruling classes; they are collectively known as Naxalites.

NECHAEV, SERGEI

(1847–1882) Russian nihilist and founder of PEOPLE'S RETRIBUTION. Born in Ivanovo, northeast of

Moscow, in 1847, Nechaev was the son of a former serf. While he liked to brag that he had only learned to read and write at the age of 16, by 1859 he was studying under a young teacher who introduced him into the circle of Ivanovo's INTELLIGENTSIA. In 1859, he participated in the Russian Sunday School Movement, which was the first large-scale effort on the part of the radical intelligentsia to educate the working class. In April 1866, after a few months' stay in Moscow, he arrived in St. Petersburg where he taught religion at a primary school. He became active in both the mainstream revolutionary student movement of 1868–1869 and in the more radical underground.

During disruptions which had broken out, Nechaev convinced nearly 100 students to sign a petition agreeing to take part in a future demonstration. Those who later refused to meet his demands he threatened to expose to the authorities. This act was the first in a series that would bring disrepute upon all those who became involved with him. In March 1869, he arrived in Switzerland and, telling tall tales about his arrest and escape from the infamous Peter-Paul fortress, gained enough prestige to engineer a meeting with NIKOLAI OGAREV and MICHAEL BAKUNIN. Exaggerating the strength of the revolutionary underground, Nechaev convinced Bakunin to cooperate with him in writing various pamphlets and to grant him a certificate of membership in Bakunin's European Alliance Revolutionary, an organization which seems to have been by and large a figment of Bakunin's imagination.

In September 1869, Nechaev returned to Russia. The arrest of numerous leaders of the underground and his association with Bakunin put him in a position to organize his own conspiratorial society, PEOPLE'S RETRIBUTION.

Nechaev's name has retained infamy primarily due to the structure of his group and its principles, as explicated in Nechaev's pamphlet, *The Catechism of a Revolutionary*. The group was organized into a hierarchy of cells, such that each member was acquainted only with the four or five individuals in his cell. This structure ensured utmost secrecy and an absolute authority of command.

Nechaev's ideas shocked even the most radical socialists, and transformed nihilism from a theory based on the rationalist principles of the Enlightenment to an advocacy of destruction. The self-sacrificing revolutionary had a single aim, "the all-shattering revolution." The ends justified all means, and Nechaev did not limit himself to theft, blackmail and murder. Relatively unconcerned with the future order, Nechaev argued that energies should not be wasted on such discussions. "The revolutionary despises any kind of doctrinairism," Nechaev wrote in the *Catechism*. "He knows only one science—the science of destruction."

In November, Nechaev engineered the murder of a fellow conspirator who had refused to carry out an order. After the arrest of many members of his group, Nechaev fled to Switzerland, where his flagrant misconduct, including theft and blackmail, eventually ostracized him from the emigré community. In October 1872, he was extradited and sentenced to 20 years in the Peter-Paul fortress.

Nechaev's powers of persuasion, however, were nowhere greater than in prison, where he eventually managed to recruit large numbers of prison guards into a secret society. He used them to reestablish contact in January 1881 with the PEOPLE'S WILL, the terrorist branch of the populist movement which assassinated Czar Alexander II in March of that year. Nechaev smuggled recommendations and information about the fortress to the executive committee. In the last months of 1881, however, 69 guards were arrested and Nechaev placed in total solitary confinement. In November 1882 he died of edema and scurvy.

NEHRU, JAWAHARLAL   (1889–1964) Indian statesman, first prime minister of independent India. Nehru was born in Allahabad, north India, where his father was a high court advocate and an influential member of Anglo-Indian society, mixing easily and familiarly with the country's British rulers. Nehru was educated by a succession of English tutors and sent to complete his studies in England, where he received an education befitting an English gentleman; he studied successively at Harrow, Trinity College, Cambridge, and the Inns of Court in London, where he qualified as a lawyer.

On his return to India in 1912, Nehru discovered the limits of his de-Indianization when he was refused entry to the local all-white British club. Despite his Anglicization, he was drawn to the growing Indian independence movement and joined the Congress party, where his activism in the NON-COOPERATION MOVEMENT led by GANDHI soon landed him in jail. In all, Nehru was to spend almost nine years in prison between 1921 and 1945. He described prison as "the best of universities"; the maturation of his political philosophy and much of his best writing can be credited to the periods of enforced inactivity and reflection he endured there. His travels among the common people in India in 1920 and 1921, later documented in his *Discovery of India*, had already given him a deep respect and sympathy toward them, although he always remained opposed to the centrality of religion in India, believing that it impeded the country's progress.

In 1926, while based in Geneva—where he sought treatment for his wife's poor health—Nehru traveled extensively in Europe and the USSR. He came into contact with socialist and anti-imperialist groups there and returned to India in 1927 a confirmed socialist and a believer in the necessity of industrialization in the country. Although never a Communist, his economic yardstick was consistently socialistic thereafter, and he always remained a supporter of the USSR.

He was elected to succeed his father as president of the INDIAN NATIONAL CONGRESS in 1929 and was the obvious candidate for the premiership when India became an independent nation on August 14, 1947. A superb orator, he commemorated that moment in his speech to the nation: "Long years ago we made a tryst with destiny, and now the time comes when we shall redeem our pledge, not wholly or in full measure, but very substantially. At the stroke of the midnight hour, while the world sleeps, India will awake to life and freedom. A moment comes which comes but rarely in history, when we step out from the old to the new, when an age ends and when the soul of a nation long suppressed finds utterance." He remained the unchallenged leader of both the party and the government until his death in 1964.

There followed a difficult period as Nehru faced a succession of problems at home and abroad, beginning with the refugee problem and bloodshed in the aftermath of partition. The attempted Pakistani invasion of the predominantly Muslim state of Kashmir in October 1947 marked the onset of a territorial dispute that persists to this day. Gandhi's assassination in January 1948 seemed to mark the end of an era, and Nehru's grief at the loss of his mentor was tangible in his words: "The light has gone out of our lives and there is darkness everywhere."

Nehru's personality and style of leadership profoundly influenced the functioning of the Indian political system. He was able to bring out the primacy of the prime minister's office and warded off any challenges from the Congress and the office of the president of India. He was convinced that the Indian National Congress should rule the country and establish its power not only in Delhi but in all the Indian states. Toward achieving this goal, Nehru used political manipulation and the power of the central government to undermine the positions of opposition parties and dissident Congress factions. However, after consolidating the Congress's position of power, Nehru acted generously toward most opposition parties and their leaders.

Nehru and his cabinet exercised firm control over both the civilian and military bureaucracies. This has ensured to the present day the supremacy of civilian control over the military. He also set forth a clear set of ideological and policy objectives which are most famously remembered for their commitment to a nondogmatic form of socialism, to secularism, to economic development through the state-directed planning, and to nonalignment in international affairs. After ruling India for 18 years, during which he tried to build up a socialist state at home and adopted a neutralist stance abroad, Nehru died in May 1964. In accordance with his wishes, his ashes were scattered from an aircraft "over the fields where the peasants of India toil so that they might mingle with the dust of the soil of India and become an indistinguishable part of her."

The evening of a revolutionary: Nehru, as prime minister of India, during a visit to London

NEHRU, MOTILAL (1861–1931) Father of JAWAHARLAL NEHRU (independent India's first and longest-serving prime minister), and an important Indian nationalist movement leader in his own right. A highly successful lawyer, Nehru joined the INDIAN NATIONAL CONGRESS in the late 1910s and gave up his extremely lucrative legal practice and his membership of the Indian legislative assembly in order to join the NON-COOPERATION MOVEMENT in 1920. Three years later he was to re-enter the legislature as a member of the Swarajist party, a subsidiary of the Indian National Congress.

As author of the Nehru Report of 1928, he recommended the immediate granting of dominion status to India. When this was rejected by the British government in India, he joined the Civil Disobedience movement. Arrest and imprisonment as a leader of the movement broke his health and he died soon thereafter.

NENNI, PIETRO (1891–1981) An Italian socialist leader. Nenni began his political career in the ranks of the Italian Republican party. He opposed the Italian invasion of Libya (1911) and with another prominent socialist at that time, BENITO MUSSOLINI, he organized the September 1911 general strike that tried to stop Italy's entry into a war against Turkey. These activities cost him some months in jail; as a result of these experiences, he moved to the left wing of the republicans. He actively participated in the 1914 "Red Week" of strikes and was again sent to jail. When World War I broke out Nenni sided with the interventionists, believing his stand to be true to the theory of revolutionary war, and collaborated in Mussolini's newspaper *Il Popolo d'Italia*. After serving in the army during the war, Nenni returned to politics. He left the Republicans and was one of the founders of the Bolognese *Fasci di Combattimento* (Combat Fasces). Later, though, he abandoned Mussolini and fascism and again drew closer to socialism. Involved in anti-Fascist activities, Nenni also took an anti-Communist stance. In 1922, he became the editor of the socialist newspaper, *Avanti*, a position he utilized to try to create an anti-Fascist bloc of democratic forces after the murder of the socialist leader Mateotti in 1924. Exiled to France, Nenni was active in the anti-Fascist ranks. Later he fought in the SPANISH CIVIL WAR within the framework of the International Brigades and was a member of the anti-Nazi resistance in France during World War II. After 1945, he emerged as secretary of the Italian Socialist party and vice-prime minister to Alcide De Gasperi. In the 1950s and 1960s, he was the undisputed leader of the Italian Socialist party. He steered it to moderate positions which allowed for its incorporation into Christian Democrat-led governments beginning in 1960, when he became vice-prime minister and foreign affairs minister. Nenni gradually retired from politics and died in 1981.

NEO DESTOUR In Tunisia, a nationalist party founded in 1934. In 1937, it came under the leadership of HABIB BOURGUIBA. From 1953–1956 it waged a guerrilla campaign against the French and, when independence was achieved, became the ruling party. Since 1961 it is the only legal party. So far it has succeeded in keeping control, though public disorders in 1977 showed the existence of considerable opposition.

NETHERLANDS, REVOLT OF THE A revolt, persistently and vigorously pursued by the Protestant leaders of the northern provinces of the Spanish Netherlands against the Habsburg monarchy from 1568 to 1648—when the Treaty of Westphalia finally acknowledged the secession of the republic from the United Spanish crown. It constitutes a major chapter in the progress of religious toleration and national independence against religious oppression and foreign tyranny. It also stands out as one of the earliest triumphs of the doctrine of popular sovereignty against the theory of royal absolutism and marks the most decisive setback suffered by the forces of the Counter-Reformation in its efforts to crush the ideas of the Protestant Reformation.

Originally known as the Burgundian circle on the lower Rhine, the Netherlands were the richest jewel in the Spanish crown inherited by Philip II. Following the abdication of his father, the Holy Roman Emperor Charles V, in 1556, the latter was resolved to stamp out heresy by means of the Inquisition launched throughout his realm; instead he found himself confronted by what amounted to a national Dutch rebellion against his authority. The rebellion was led by William of Orange (nicknamed the Silent because of his reputed refusal to be provoked into anger), the hereditary Stadtholder (local governor) of the province of Holland, and carried on after his assassination by his son, Maurice of Nassau, in the name of preserving regional and provincial liberties against the tyranny of a foreign despot of a different faith. The formidable Spanish armies, first under the command of the Duke of Alba and then under the leadership of Alexander Farnese, Duke of Parma, found it difficult to subdue an enemy which retired behind town walls and flooded the surrounding countryside by opening the dikes. As Spanish overland communications to the Netherlands by way of the Burgundian province of Franche-Comte were stretched to the outmost, the Dutch resorted to the sea in order to cripple the naval forces of their Catholic enemy. Soon they were able to rely on the help of their Protestant English allies, who in 1588 succeeded in repelling the great Spanish Armada launched by Philip II against the British Isles.

By then the Low Countries had become divided along their present lines: the 10 Catholic provinces of the south centered on the great port of Antwerp and the city of Brussels chose to come to terms with Spain. They became the nucleus of what in the course of time emerged as the modern state of Belgium, which gained its independence from Holland as a result of revolution in 1830. The seven northern provinces, however, predominantly Protestant and more attuned to the capitalist spirit of the age, consisting of Holland, Zeeland, Guelders, Utrecht, Overyssel, Friesland and Groningen, were far easier to defend and less accessible to the Spanish armies. By the beginning of the 17th century they succeeded in breaking away from Spanish rule to become the United Provinces of the Dutch Republic. In the course of the war, the Dutch had, in effect, pooled their resources by setting up a federation of regional oligarchies in which local liberties counted for more than national centralization.

The Dutch Revolution deserves to be singled out as a spectacular vindication of religious toleration in the Age of Absolutism and religious conformity. This was achieved more by accident than by design. The absence of any effective central government among the provinces of the northern Netherlands at war with Spain made enforcement of religious uniformity out of the question. This, in turn, had the effect of attracting to Holland such religious minorities as the English Puritans and the Jews from Spain and Portugal, who made a notable contribution to fostering the commercial prosperity of a country which, despite its small size and limited natural resources, was thereby able to achieve the status of a great power by the early 17th century.

NEW FOURTH ARMY Chinese Communist army. After the outbreak of the Sino-Japanese war of 1937–1945 and the formation of the second united front, the Nationalist (GUOMINDANG—GMD) government gave the CHINESE COMMUNIST PARTY (CCP) permission to create the New Fourth Army (N4A) in addition to the main CCP force, the EIGHTH ROUTE ARMY (8RA). Formally established in January 1938, the N4A was based upon scattered CCP bands that had survived in Jiangxi when the main force left on the LONG MARCH in 1934. The name alluded to the original Fourth Army that had been part of the NATIONAL REVOLUTIONARY ARMY during the joint GMD-CCP campaign to unify China of 1926–1927. Though its authorized strength was only 12,000, the N4A expanded rapidly but remained smaller than the 8RA. Assigned to the Yangtze area, it conducted guerrilla operations, mounting raids against Japanese-held railway lines. In late 1940, GMD forces clashed with the N4A, claiming it was operating out of bounds. In January 1941, a major conflict ensued when GMD forces defeated the outnumbered N4A in southern Anhui. The N4A commander, Ye Ting, was captured and imprisoned for five years. Called the New Fourth Army Incident, it was the worst GMD-CCP conflict during the war with Japan. CHIANG KAI-SHEK ordered the N4A's dissolution and strengthened his northwest blockade of the CCP. The CCP, however, reorganized the N4A, naming Chen Yi commander and LIU SHAOQI political commissar. The N4A built base areas in Jiangsu, Anhui and Henan. By 1945, it had reached a strength of 296,000 and occupied coastal areas from Zhejiang to Shandong. In late 1945, N4A detachments joined CCP forces in Manchuria. The N4A became the East China People's Liberation Army in 1947.

NEW LEFT American society and the American identity are unique in that they are not based on a common ethnicity, religion or past. Rather, they are based on an ideology: on adherence to a common set of ideas and on loyalty to a set of social and political institutions which embody them. In such a society, ideological convictions which are outside the consensus constitute a threat to social coherence, even to national existence itself.

American society, therefore, has very low tolerance for extremist ideology. In such an environment, reformers have traditionally done best by sacrificing the purity of their ideas and assimilating them into mainstream ideology. The alternative to the adaptation of revolutionary tenets to the dominant ideology was the marginalization of radicalism. The history of communism and socialism in America, or rather, their non-history, illustrates this dynamic.

Beginning in the late 1950s and throughout the 1960s and early 1970s, traditional western society was assaulted by a barrage of new and radical ideas which challenged the status quo and the traditionally dominant ideology. In Europe, neo-Marxist ideas, radical existentialism and GRAMSCI-inspired attacks on hegemonic ideology permeated the protest movement. In the old world, their political effect was to dramatically strengthen socialist and Communist parties.

In the United States, however, the new left characteristically advocated change in terms consonant with the American way. Its overall platform echoed the American declaration of independence, Jeffersonian liberalism and republican abolitionism. One focus of the movement was the civil rights campaign. Led by moderates such as MARTIN LUTHER KING JR., it was rapidly assimilated into the mainstream of American politics, legislation and law, through civil rights acts and liberal supreme court decisions.

Another focus of the movement was opposition to American military involvement in Vietnam. On this issue, a generation gap complicated the assimilation of protest into mainstream consciousness. Americans who had lived through the period of the Fascist (see FASCISM) assault on world peace, liberty and the rights of man, were conditioned to viewing foreign authoritarian régimes as a potential threat to the free world. They could be easily convinced that the containment of its spread was a legitimate cause. A younger generation, however, faced the Vietnam war without all this contextual baggage. Its members took it for what it was—a senseless blood bath of innocent civilians and young American soldiers. The distant local war, they believed, was none of America's business.

Opposition to the Vietnam war was considered by many conservatives an incendiary act. Law enforcement agencies occasionally responded to protests with inappropriate force. In the most notorious confrontation between protesters and law enforcement agencies, a national guard unit opened fire, on May 4, 1970, on protesters in Ohio's Kent State University, killing four students. In Mississippi 10 days later, police opened fire on a student dormitory in Jackson State University, killing two students. Yet essentially, opposition to the war in Vietnam held little that was ideologically controversial and the antiwar movement could easily resort to arguments which incorporated traditional American values. Indeed, as the war escalated and the chances of winning it diminished, opposition to the war managed to close the generation gap and spread to large segments of American society.

At the same time that the new left ideology was being diluted and assimilated into the framework of traditional and legitimate American values, the parallel process of marginalization of radicalism was taking place. On the civil rights front, radical thinkers such as MALCOLM X and Stokely Carmichael inspired extremist movements discontented with the perceived timidity of mainstream protest orchestrated by organizations such as the National Association for the Advancement of Colored People (NAACP) and the Southern Christian Leadership Conference (SCLC). But while the movements they inspired—such as the Nation of Islam and the BLACK PANTHERS—endorsed provocative revolutionary polemics, their actual activities seldom reflected them.

The antiwar protest developed its own cluster of radical splinter groups and most of these represented a fusion of peace protest with civil rights activism. Many of these radical revolutionary groups grew out of what was the most dominant organizational framework for new left activism—Students for a Democratic Society (SDS). The SDS called for radical changes in the American system, breaking up representative institutions and transferring their power to the people. It tagged its welfare policy "the new insurgency." Yet there was little in SDS activities that resembled insurgence, nor were its positions as revolutionary as the rhetoric would occasionally imply.

The activities of groups such as the WEATHERMEN or protests of the nature prescribed by the Chicago Seven could have represented real danger to the status quo. However, none of these revolutionary groups transcended the status of insignificant oddities.

NIAN REBELLION   (1853–1868) Chinese peasant rebellion. Bearing affinity to the WHITE LOTUS secret society, the Nian were first mentioned in imperial sources in the late 18th century. The exact meaning of the name "Nian" is not clear but it may simply mean "bands," the basic military units of the society. It was active in the southern region of the north China plain, encompassing Jiangsu, Anhui, Henan and Shandong, where secret societies had long proliferated. This was open country, suited to Nian cavalry. With few large cities, the area was relatively remote from official control. Nian bands had operated individually and sporadically, taking over villages and winning peasant support. The movement expanded in scope when the already declining Qing (Manchu) dynasty became preoccupied with the TAIPING REBELLION (1850–1864). Famine resulting from the flooding of the Yellow River in 1853 brought new recruits. In 1853, the emergence of ZHANG LUOXING as leader provided greater coordination of Nian activity. Though peasant-based, the Nian leadership came from various elements at odds with the authorities, e.g., salt smugglers, army deserters and, later, former Taiping veterans. They also included some disgruntled, ambitious, local scholars. Zhang Luoxing himself was a smuggler who originally came from a wealthy family. By 1856 the Nian had an effective army. Learning from the Taipings, they avoided positional warfare and emphasized high mobility. After taking over and fortifying villages, their cavalry would conduct raids, targeting wealthy merchants and landowners as well as governmental offices, prisons and granaries. Under Zhang's leadership, they acquired a solid territorial base by 1858, though they remained loosely organized.

Not much is known of Nian ideology, but the participation of scholars helped give them a political orientation. While their slogans called for the overthrow of the "barbarian" Manchus, the Nian never attempted to establish a new dynasty, nor did they threaten major cities. Their ritual resembled that of traditional secret societies, e.g., secret symbols and terminology and blood oaths. In wearing their hair long and in some other respects they imitated the Taipings, with whom they sometimes coordinated activities. North China peasants may have found their rule preferable to that of the government that was trying to exact higher taxes to pay for the anti-Taiping campaign and war with the western powers (1856–1860). Even official sources admitted that the people of north China feared imperial troops more than they feared the rebels.

Zhang Luoxing was captured and killed in 1863. Losing their firmly held base, the Nian became roaming bands again while retaining and even augmenting their military potency. The high point of Nian strength came in 1865, when they inflicted a heavy defeat on imperial forces in Shandong. Qing officials who had quelled the Taipings by combining shrewd military tactics with administrative measures to restore popular allegiance then used the same strategy against the Nian. The rebellion was finally subdued in 1868.

NIETZSCHE, FRIEDRICH WILHELM (1844–1900) German philosopher. Nietzsche revolutionized German philosophy during the second half of the 19th century and had a profound influence over intellectuals and others in Germany and abroad until World War II, especially when his original work was distorted and falsified by his sister, an admirer of HITLER. Nietzsche was very much influenced by Arthur Schopenhauer, who declared reality to be meaningless except for the power of the will. This power is only granted to the very few, such as artists and creative persons, who sometimes shine in the general darkness. Yet Nietzsche rejected Schopenhauer's pessimism and passive quietism, leaning toward Far-Eastern belief systems, and tried to develop the idea of the will as creator of reality. He became a major critic of traditional morality, especially of Christianity, as the "morality of the weak," which, he claimed, had invented a non-existent God to negotiate forgiveness with him for people's constant sins. Sensing the role of the subconscious in humans before Freud had done so, Nietzsche developed a theory of the "superman" (*Übermensch*), who was capable—unlike regular people who adopt traditional morality without question—to create a higher, genuine, morality of his own through contemplation and experience. Such experience may lead the "super-man," among other things, even to crime. Nietzsche was a troubled, individualistic, anti-Christian and anti-German thinker of great poetic talent, whose teachings were rationalized by many intellectuals as justification for a new, "genuinely" moral, anti-de-

Friedrich Nietzsche with his mother

mocratic elite, which would be allowed—under various circumstances—to use its will, i.e., force, to correct the maladies of the decaying European middle class and traditional-authoritarian societies. Nietzsche himself was totally disinterested in such broad-based attempts, arguing that in any event history repeats itself in circles. He aimed at the very few individuals who were capable of becoming "supermen" and possibly influencing mankind as such, or the other few who would understand them. However his vulgarized thought was widely accepted and used by a variety of radicals and even thinkers at the time, from George Bernard Shaw on the one hand, to conservative revolutionaries in Germany. Some supported Hitler at first. Indirectly, Nietzsche has had some influence among American radicals today.

NIGER, 1974 COUP Following independence from France in 1960, Niger was led by the conservative Hamani Diori. The catastrophic economic situation at the time of the 1969–1974 Sahelian drought was aggravated by falling world market prices for groundnuts, Niger's major export. There were also accusations of corruption and food-hoarding at the highest government levels.

On April 15, 1974, the army chief of staff, Lieutenant Colonel SEYNI KOUNTCHÉ, took power in a coup that met with little resistance.

NIGERIA, COUPS Nigeria was ruled by a civilian government from 1960 until January 15, 1966, when the government of Prime Minister Abubakar Tafawa Balewa was overthrown by a group of junior army officers, mainly of the Ibo ethnic group. Tafalwa was killed, as were the prime ministers of the northern and western regions of Nigeria. The federal minister of finance, Major General Johnson Aguiyi-Ironsi, an Ibo and commander-in-chief of the armed forces, took over and formed a Supreme Military Council (SMC) to govern the country.

On July 29, 1966, Aguiyi-Ironsi was killed in a countercoup, and Lieutenant Colonel (later General) Yakubu Gowon, a Christian from the Middle Belt of Nigeria, took over. It was during Gowon's tenure that the country was embroiled in the bloody Biafran war (1967–1971).

On July 29, 1975, while he was attending an OAU (Organization of African Unity) summit in Uganda, Gowon was removed by senior army officers and replaced by Brigadier (later General) Murtala Ramat Muhammad, the federal commissioner for communication. Murtala Muhammad undertook a radical and popular purge of the civil service. He also announced that the country would be returned to civilian rule by October 1979.

The charismatic Muhammad was assassinated in February 1976 by a disaffected army officer. Power was assumed by his deputy, Lieutenant General Olusegun Obasango, chief of staff of the armed forces.

Elections went ahead as planned in 1979 and were won by Alhaji Shehu Shagari and his National Party of Nigeria (NPN). Shagari became president of Nigeria's Second Republic (1979-1983).

On December 31, 1983, however, Shagari was deposed in a bloodless military coup led by Major General Muhammadu Buhari, a former military governor and federal commissioner for petroleum. All political parties were banned and a Supreme Military Council (SMC) was again established.

On August 27, 1985, while Buhari was in his home village

celebrating the Muslim feast of Id-el-Kabir, his régime was deposed in a bloodless coup led by Major General (later General) Ibrahim Babangida, who became Nigeria's new head of state, with the SMC being replaced by the Armed Forces Ruling Council (AFC) which, unlike the SMC, was composed solely of military personnel.

In January 1986, Babangida announced that the armed forces would transfer power to a civilian government on October 1, 1990. Elections were postponed more than once and were finally won by Babangida. Many Nigerians, though, believed that the winner of the elections was Bashorun Abiola, a wealthy publisher.

Babangida established an "interim government" in August 1993. The secretary of defense was General Sani Abacha. On November 17, 1994, Abacha seized power and became Nigeria's seventh military head of state.

NIHILISM Only in the revolutions of the 20th century were the concepts of nihilism as a philosophical category and as a political category joined. Whereas the original Greek concept of *nihil* (nothing, zero) was purely philosophical, modern nihilism has aesthetic, technological and totalitarian ramifications. Modern nihilism was formulated in 1799 by Friedrich Heinrich Jacobi, who considered nihilism a radical form of idealism. The Romantics turned it into an aesthetic category and during the course of the 19th century it was considered one of the social and political ramifications of atheism.

FRIEDRICH NIETZSCHE represents a crossroads: nihilism is no longer identified with a philosophical approach, a literary movement or a political demand. Instead, it characterizes a whole civilization or a moment in its (modern) history—specifically, the death of God. At this modern consciousness, the "new Man" was born and he creates his world ex nihilo. Nietzsche's basic assumption that the world is an aesthetic phenomenon places his aesthetics at the center of his revolutionary philosophy. One basic element of Nietzsche's revolution is his philosophic style of exposure as formulated by the genealogy of morals, which sought to destroy all the norms and conventions accepted in the Judeo-Christian world and the classical heritage of the west. Another is his historicist nihilist method, which becomes the starting-point for the reorientation of philosophy. Nietzsche's affirmative claims—the will to power, the superman, self-overcoming and the eternal recurrence—are necessary counterpoints to his nihilism.

Both the Janus-like nihilism and the will to power profoundly influenced cultural criticism at the beginning of the 20th century and provided a model for the "new Man."

When the "new Man" rebelled against history and the traditional criteria of good and evil, truth and falsehood, he became the midwife of his own world. Modern Man attempted paradoxically to change himself. The FRENCH REVOLUTION in the 18th century, the ideologies of the 19th century and the political myths of the 20th century constituted a revolutionary proclamation that human beings were ready to recreate their own humanity, which means to annihilate the "historic man." The criticism of European culture at the end of the 19th century was transformed, sometimes directly and sometimes indirectly, into radical political criticism that questioned the basic assumptions of European democracy. In the end it contributed to the undermining of democracy and the rise of totalitarian powers. The ideological development and political history of Europe in the early 20th century included a unique intellectual trend that characterized its revolutionary state of mind and reflected a nihilist-totalitarian syndrome.

Russian Nihilism. Russian nihilism was born out of the stagnation in governmental reform that followed the emancipation of the serfs in 1861. As the Russian INTELLIGENTSIA despaired of a victory for constitutionalism, its younger generation turned more and more to a conspiratorial POPULISM, the combination of a small elite of free-thinking leaders at the head of a massive, axe-wielding peasant revolt. The aim of this revolt would be the destruction not only of the autocracy but of all institutions of society—religion, the family, property—all to be replaced by free and critically thinking individuals coming together on the basis of equality and mutual aid inspired by the example of the Russian village commune. In this sense, nihilism was a Slavophile reaction against the western-style constitutionalism that underlay the thinking of ALEXANDER HERZEN and NIKOLAI OGAREV—a reaction of the "sons" of the 1860s against the "fathers" of the 1840s and 1850s.

The term "nihilism" was first applied to the attitudes of the young intelligentsia by Turgenev, who used it as a pejorative in his novel, *Fathers and Sons*. For some of its advocates, nihilism was indeed a truly Russian expression of "the passion of the Russian mind; which goes to extremes in all its conclusions.... Carrying things to extremes is the characteristic element of our history." Russian nihilism, however, was not a belief in nothing, an apathy to existing order, as exemplified by the character of Raskolnikov in Dostoevsky's *Crime and Punishment*. On the contrary, it was a passionate hatred of the existing order and a determination to substitute for it a freer and more universally just society. In the eyes of nihilists, it was Chernyshevsky's *What Is to be Done?* that portrayed their Rousseauan outlook that humans were meant to be free and equal but are shackled by the imperfections of society. The peculiarly Russian element in nihilism was perhaps its turn to conspiratorial organization and mass political violence as an integral element of its ideology—the only way, in their eyes, of achieving total social reform.

While Chernyshevsky's writings, and in particular their advocation of independent social organizations: student communes, artisan associations, peasant unions, etc., provided an inspiration for the practical activities of the younger intelligentsia, it was the focus on the individual advocated by DMITRI PISAREV and by the editors of the *Russkoe slovo* that captured their imaginations. The nihilists were focused on the strong, uninhibited and independent thinker. Their ideal was the person capable of survival in the Darwinian survival of the fittest.

Although nihilism was much discussed in the literary criticism of the 1860s and after, it did not give direct birth to any influential organizations. Its emphasis on individualism was too strong for this. Nevertheless, there is a clear root of intellect that leads from the rebellious all-criticizing individualism of the nihilist writers of *Russkoe slovo* to the anarchism of BAKUNIN's followers and successors. At the same time, nihilism nourished the concept of a revolutionary elite leading the "benighted masses" and thus was one of the cornerstones of Russian Jacobinism as personified in NECHAEV, TKACHEV and ultimately LENIN.

Totalitarian Nihilism. Over and above "nihilism" and "totalitarianism" as such, is an additional dialectical phenomenon: the nihilist mentality, whether from inner compulsion or immanent logic, is driven to accept totalitarian patterns of behavior which are characterized by extreme dynamism. The philosophy of activism, violence and dynamism thus typifies cultural protest and at the same time gives content to political revolts: dynamic nihilism is anchored in the aesthetic absolute of the totalitarian mentality.

GEORGES SOREL, Filippo Tommaso Marinetti, VLADIMIR MAYAKOVSKY, Wyndham Lewis and Ernst Jünger initiated this nihilist-totalitarian revolution. As cultural critics, they brought about an "intellectual revolution" according to the concept of Stuart Hughes. These "anti-intellectual" intellectuals revolted against the Enlightenment and gave political myth absolute primacy. Glorification of conflict as the structure of reality shaped the new type of authentic man. Modern technology, which they admired, provided the means of making revolutionary order out of chaos and gave them a new Romantic myth serving the politics of violence. This nihilist style was shaped by radical nationalism or mythical socialism, or a combination of the two in the form of National Socialism.

In his early book, *The Revolution of Nihilism* (1939), Herman Rauschning examined National Socialism as a dynamist philosophy without a doctrine. Nazism, in his view, is absolute liberation from the past, action for its own sake, a process of destruction which must develop, according to its own internal logic, into totalitarian tyranny. Thus, by a necessary paradox, "political nihilism" turned into a political religion in three totalitarian régimes—FASCISM, National Socialism and Bolshevism (see BOLSHEVIK PARTY). Ernst Bloch, the philosopher of the utopia in the 20th century, claimed in his book, *The Principle of Hope,* that the nihilistic inspiration common to the totalitarian mentalities of both the radical right and left is "action for its own sake, which can simultaneously lead to the affirmation of LENIN and pave the way for MUSSOLINI." Twelve years after Rauschning's book was published, Albert Camus further developed his thesis in *L'Homme Revolte*: unlimited freedom leads to unlimited despotism. The shortest way to negating everything is affirming everything. The year Camus's book was published, 1951, also saw the publication of J.L. Talmon's *The Rise of Totalitarian Democracy*, which claimed that it is not far from perfection-seeking anarchism to revolutionary centralism. The association between nihilism, totalitarianism and technology is one of the key issues of the 20th century. The most extreme manifestation of this association was the Holocaust, when 6 million Jews were annihilated by the Nazi machine.

In spite of the clear distinction which must be made between Nazi Germany and the Soviet Union, we have witnessed the major role played by engineers in these two revolutionary régimes. In both régimes, the engineers were attracted not by ideological content but by the totalitarian patterns in the nihilization of the old society and the construction of a new one.

NKOMO, JOSHUA MQABUKO (1917–) Born in what was then Southern Rhodesia, Joshua Nkomo graduated from university in South Africa and worked as a lay preacher before entering politics. He was president of the ANC (AFRICAN NATIONAL CONGRESS), Rhodesia, from 1952 until it was banned in 1959. He then toured the world trying to arouse public opposition against conditions in Rhodesia. He was imprisoned several times. Until the independence of Zimbabwe (1980), Joshua Nkomo was the leading black political figure in the country and a symbol of the struggle for independence. He became known as the "Father of Zimbabwean Independence."

From 1961, Nkomo was the leader of the ZIMBABWE AFRICAN PEOPLE'S UNION (ZAPU). ZAPU was mainly active in the Ndebele-speaking areas of the country (Nkomo is a member of the Ndebele tribe). In 1976, ZAPU formed a alliance with ZANU (ZIMBABWE AFRICAN NATIONAL UNION), led by ROBERT MUGABE, and the alliance was named the Patriotic Front (PF). In the 1980 elections, which ZANU and ZAPU contested separately, ZANU won and Nkomo became leader of the opposition. In 1988, the two parties merged and Nkomo became minister of home affairs and later one of the two vice-presidents of Zimbabwe.

Nkomo strikes a pose at an ANC meeting; on his right, Mugabe

NKRUMAH, KWAME (1909–1972) African nationalist; first president of Ghana. Kwame Nkrumah was born in the town of Nkroful in the Gold Coast (now Ghana). He was named Francis Nwia Kofi at birth. He attended the local Catholic mission school and continued on to the Government Training College in Accra, the first college on the continent specifically geared for native students. After graduating in 1930, he worked as a teacher.

As educational opportunities for Africans were limited at that time, as many of his compatriots Krumah was forced to travel abroad to further his education. He sailed to America in 1935 to study at Lincoln University, from which he graduated in 1939. He then did graduate work at the University of Pennsylvania but returned to Lincoln to lecture in political science. Nkrumah was also active in various African-American causes. He was president of the African American Student Organization of the United States and Canada and helped the famed black scholar William Edward Du Bois found the National Association for the Advancement of Colored People. Moving to England in 1945, Nkrumah continued his studies, and while there helped to organize the fifth Pan-African Conference.

His reputation as an ardent African nationalist and competent organizer reached his native Gold Coast, and in 1947 he agreed to return to the territory as general secretary of the United Gold Coast Convention. Nkrumah's demand that the Gold Coast receive immediate independence led to a rift between himself and the more established party leaders. He quit the party in 1949 to form his own CONVENTION PEOPLE'S PARTY (CPP). The CPP was a Pan-Africanist party that regarded Ghanian independence as a prerequisite for Pan-African independence and the emergence of a United States of Africa.

Nkrumah's platform called for "positive action" to attain independence. Other leaders heeded his call, sparking a year-long boycott of European and Syrian businesses, along with increased protests and violence. In order to quash the growing unrest, the British authorities arrested Nkrumah in 1950, but this action did not diminish his increasing popularity. Despite his detention, the CPP won the 1951 elections for self-government; Nkrumah was released from prison to assume the role of prime minister of the Gold Coast and used his position to further his demands for total independence.

In 1957 the Gold Coast, renamed Ghana, became the first black African state to achieve independence. Upon Ghana's becoming a republic in 1960, Nkrumah was appointed president for life. He continued to pursue a radical Pan-African policy which envisioned his country as the foundation for a United States of Africa. Believing that the political integration of the emerging States must take priority over economic integration, Nkrumah attempted to unite his State with other African countries. In 1958 Ghana nominally united with Guinea and in 1960 Mali joined the union. To show his personal commitment to African unity, Nkrumah married an Egyptian woman, Fahtia—only to neglect her in favor of his many mistresses.

At a conference of African States held in Casablanca, Morocco, in 1961, it was Nkrumah who presented the ideas which were to form the underlying beliefs of the Organization of African States. A socialist at home, he adopted a neutralist policy in international affairs, drawing accusations from the west that he was a Communist. His reply was: "It is very unfair to be accused of being a Communist on the basis of anti-colonialism."

Nkrumah was a flamboyant leader who stifled dissent and jailed his opponents. Two assassination attempts, in 1962 and 1964, were made on the man who styled himself *Osagyefo* (Victor). Other names and titles used to describe Nkrumah ranged from showboy to Messiah. Although his popularity waned at home, world leaders thought of him favorably. He traveled extensively, preaching his message of anticolonialism and pan-Africanism, for which he was awarded the Lenin Peace Prize in 1962.

FROM NKRUMAH'S ADDRESS TO THE FIRST PAN-AFRICAN CONGRESS, MANCHESTER, ENGLAND, 1945

We believe in the rights of all peoples to govern themselves. We affirm the right of all colonial peoples to control their destiny. All colonies must be given the right to elect their own government, a government without restrictions from a foreign power. We say to the peoples of the colonies that they must strive for these ends by all means at their disposal.

While Nkrumah was visiting China in 1966, his government was overthrown in a coordinated police and military coup. Unable to return to Ghana, he was granted asylum by his old friend and fellow pan-Africanist, SÉKOU TOURÉ, president of neighboring Guinea. Nkrumah died in Romania in 1972 while undergoing cancer treatment; his body was returned to Ghana for burial.

NONCOOPERATION MOVEMENT   The policy adopted by Indonesian nationalists by which they refused to cooperate with the Dutch colonial authorities during the 1930s. Based on the protest movements of colonial India and Ottoman Turkey, the objective of "the noncooperation tactic was to draw a line between them [the colonial authorities] and us, to awaken the people's spirit so that they can establish their own society."

According to the principles of noncooperation, even participation in the autonomous government provided by the Dutch was forbidden. MOHAMMUAD HATTA, a staunch advocate of noncooperation, explained: "Cooperation is only possible between two groups that have the same rights and obligations and furthermore, common interests." Under colonialism, however, "The stronger party bullies the weaker, using the latter as an instrument to support its own interests."

NORTH AFRICAN STAR   see L'ETOILE NORDE AFRICAINE..

NORTHERN EXPEDITION   (1926–1928) Chinese nationalist campaign to unify the country. In July 1926 the NATIONAL REVOLUTIONARY ARMY, led by CHIANG KAI-SHEK, launched the northern drive to eliminate regional militarists and restore national unity under the Nationalist Party (GUOMINDANG; GMD), which then included the CHINESE COMMUNIST PARTY (CCP). The first stage of the expedition was concluded in early 1927 with the capture of Nanjing and Shanghai, and coincided with the rupture of the GMD-CCP coalition. The second stage, without CCP participation, began in March 1928 and was completed in June with the capture of Beijing.

NORTHERN REBELLION   (1569–1570) Thomas Howard, the 4th Duke of Norfolk in England, objected to the all-pervasive influence of the Cecil family at the court of Elizabeth I. He had a plan to release Mary, queen of Scots, with Spanish help, but almost immediately withdrew and confessed to Elizabeth. The revolt had by that time acquired a certain momentum under the great northern families—the Percys of Northumberland and the Nevilles of Westmorland—which were now demanding the restoration of Catholicism and of Mary to the throne. Elizabeth's forces easily subdued them and peacefully imposed order on the north. A later rising by Leonard Dacre in January 1570 was the excuse for harsh reprisals, during which about 800 rebels were executed.

NORTHERN UNION OF RUSSIAN WORKERS   An illegal working people's union founded in 1878 by Viktor Obnorsky, a member of the LAND AND LIBERTY group, and by Stepan Khalturin, a radical who later turned terrorist and was executed in 1882 for the assassination of the Odessa military prosecutor. Membership in the union was limited to persons actually engaged in manual labor. The ultimate object of the union was to overthrow the autocracy, but it focused its immediate activities around achieving civil and personal rights and bettering the economic conditions of workers. At its peak, the group numbered some 200 members, mainly metal workers. Its activities in publishing revolutionary leaflets and organizing strikes led the government to suppress the union completely in 1881–1882.

NOVOTNY, ANTONIN (1904–1975) Czechoslovak Communist politician. Coming from a proletarian background, Novotny himself was a blacksmith by trade. In 1927 he became a founding member of the Czechoslovak Communist party. He spent World War II in a German prison because of this affiliation. In 1946, he was elected to the Czechoslovak party's central committee and in February 1948 played a leading part in the Communist coup in that country. In 1951 he joined the Politburo, becoming prominent during the SLANSKY trial of 1952, a purge in which 11 high-ranking party officials were tried and subsequently executed.

In 1953, he became the party's First Secretary and in 1957 took over also as president. A Stalinist who pursued harshly repressive policies, he was forced out of office in 1967 in favor of the liberal ALEXANDER DUBCEK. After the invasion of Czechoslovakia in 1967, however, the Soviets were wise enough not to allow him to return.

NUJOMA, SAMUEL DAVID CHAFISHUNA (1929–) Nujoma was born in what was then South-West Africa. He began his working life as a sweeper on the railway and then rose to clerk. His political activities led to him being arrested in 1959. In 1960, together with Herman Toivo ja Toivo, he founded the SOUTH-WEST AFRICAN PEOPLE'S ORGANIZATION (SWAPO). Nujoma then went into exile and turned his energies into presenting SWAPO's case to the world. In 1960, he appeared before the UN Special Committee on Apartheid.

Nujoma returned to the capital of South-West Africa, Windhoek, was arrested and ordered out of the country (1966). In that same year, SWAPO turned to armed struggle after the rejection by the International Court of Justice of its complaints against South Africa. When South-West Africa finally became independent as Namibia, on March 21, 1990, Sam Nujoma became its first president. Nujoma believes in democracy and has established a democratic form of government in Namibia.

NUMEIRI, (MUHAMMAD) JA'FAR (1930–) Sudanese officer and politician, ruler of Sudan 1969–1985. After graduating from the pre-independence Military College of Khartoum in 1952, Numeiri served in infantry and armor units. He was suspected of participating in antigovernment instigation and heading subversive cells, and was suspended and arrested several times (1957, 1959, 1965). After he was reinstated in 1966, he completed a course at an American military collage and later attained the rank of brigadier-general.

In May 1969, heading a FREE OFFICERS group, Numeiri seized power in a military coup. He dismissed the Presidential Council and the government, dissolved parliament, banned all political parties and formed a Revolutionary Council as the supreme state organ, with himself at its head. Ideologically a man of many faces, Numeiri chose to balance between Islamic and conservative groups and the Communists. After an abortive coup by leftist officers in 1971, he savagely repressed the Communists. In 1972 he founded a single party state on the Egyptian pattern, the Sudan Socialist Union, and headed its Politburo.

His régime, however, did not attain real stability. Numeiri gradually cultivated an alliance with fundamentalist Islamic groups, chiefly the MUSLIM BROTHERHOOD. In September 1983 he decreed the full implementation of the code of punishment of Islamic law, the *Shari'a*—a measure that aroused strong opposition. A new rebellion of the south Sudanese Africans also erupted. These two developments hastened Numeiri's fall. He was overthrown in April 1985 in a coup mounted by the army in collaboration with his political foes. Numeiri escaped to Egypt and received political asylum there—despite the new régime's repeated demands for his extradition.

Ja'far Numeiri

O

OBREGON, ALVARO (1880–1928) Mexican soldier and politician. Obregon took a prominent part in the confused civil wars of the period between 1910–1920, occupying Mexico City for the liberals under VENUSTIANO CARRANZA in 1914. In December 1920 he led an uprising that overthrew Carranza, was elected president, and stayed in office until 1924, initiating an era of liberal reforms. From 1924–1928 he had no official function; in 1928, however, he stood again for president and was elected. Immediately after this he was shot and killed by a religious fanatic. His memoirs were published in Spanish in 1957.

O'CONNELL, DANIEL (1775–1847) Irish politician known as "the Great Liberator." O'Connell was born in the family mansion of Derrynane Abbey in County Kerry in southwest Ireland. Income from the ancient O'Connell lands, supplemented by the proceeds of smuggling, supported a comfortable upbringing and schooling in Saint-Malo, France, at a school in fashion with Irish Catholic gentry. O'Connell was influenced by the libertarian ideas of the late 18th century and supported the IRISH REBELLION OF 1798. The violence of the revolt made a deep impression on him; he decided that violent protest was no solution to Ireland's woes and that the struggle should be confined to the political arena, with the threat of force used only as a last resort.

Catholics did not enjoy the same civil liberties available to Protestant citizens. This was especially irksome to men of O'Connell's class, who felt their social position entitled them to a share in the political power. Only in 1793 were Catholics in Ireland first allowed to serve as jurors, army officers or lawyers; it was the latter profession that O'Connell chose. He possessed a natural talent with words; ambitious and determined, he became very wealthy from his legal practice.

In pursuit of Catholic emancipation, O'Connell sought to galvanize the Irish masses in one of the first examples of a popular political campaign. In 1823 O'Connell formed the Catholic Association, which attracted mass support for its program of removing Irish political disabilities. Its low subscription rate of a penny a month allowed it to develop into a popular political organization. O'Connell was quick in realizing the potential of a body that could raise £20,000 in less than a year and draw the support of the Catholic church and peasantry. The association became a powerful force in Irish politics, registering supporters and electing candidates favorable to emancipation. The struggle culminated in the election of O'Connell as a member of parliament for Clare in 1828. He could not take his seat since it involved making an oath objectionable to Catholics, but the gov-

ernment, aware of his strong following, decided concession was the safest course. In 1829 the Act of Catholic Emancipation was passed by the British Parliament.

O'Connell became a key figure in Westminister politics, entering into alliance with the Whigs, whom he considered most likely to favor Irish advancement. In the 1840s, O'Connell initiated a campaign of "Monster Meetings" to press for the repeal of the 1800 union between Ireland and England; pageantry and quasi-military discipline was brought to bear. At the most famous of the meetings at Tara (a location associated with early Irish kings) he addressed some 750,000 people (almost 10% of the country's population) and told them that "the strength and majority of the national movement was never exhibited so imposingly." His forecast of the closeness of repeal of the Union was premature. The government viewed the price of concession as too high; a later meeting was banned and O'Connell arrested, and his goal took another 82 years to achieve.

O'Connell died in Genoa in 1847 while on his way to an audience with the pope. He asked for his heart to be buried in Rome and the rest of his embalmed body to be returned to Ireland. In his lifetime he had become a popular legend, who had brought to fruition of the potential political power of the Irish masses, paving the way for the birth of modern Ireland.

O'CONNOR, FEARGUS (1796–1855) British advocate of chartism. Born in Ireland, O'Connor was first elected to the House of Commons in 1832 on a platform calling for the repeal of the Act of Union between Britain and Ireland, universal suffrage and the secret ballot. He was reelected in 1834 but lost his seat one year later for failing to meet the parliamentary property qualification. Soon after, he founded the Marylebone Radical Association and in 1836 joined the London Working Men's Association, the forerunner of the Chartist movement.

At first, O'Connor was a welcome member of the movement: his newspaper, *The Northern Star,* quickly became Chartism's most important mouthpiece. By 1838, however, other Chartist leaders were distrustful of his support for the "physical-force wing" of the movement and his clamorous rhetoric. It is likely that he was linked to JOHN FROST's attempted uprising (1839), though both he and Frost later denied this. Found guilty of libel in 1840, O'Connor spent 18 months in prison. Upon his release he launched a series of virulent attacks on more moderate Chartist leaders and engaged in polemics with the Anti-Corn Law League and Irish nationalist DANIEL O'CONNELL. With the failure of the Chartist general strike in 1842, O'Connor publicly condemned the action as part of an anti-Chartist conspiracy.

Perhaps his most unusual contribution to Chartism was O'Connor's proposal of the Chartist land plan. According to the plan, workers would make small loans to a land bank and the money would be used to purchase estates and create rural working class communities. Despite some initial successes, the plan was a failure. Only two estates were ever purchased and settled and in 1848 the land bank was found to be bankrupt.

O'Connor was reelected to the House of Commons in 1848, but his erratic, sometimes violent, behavior led even his closest allies to question his sanity. In 1852, O'Connor was removed from the House of Commons and placed in an insane asylum.

OCTOBRISTS   In Russian history, a liberal party supported by businessmen, academics and bureaucrats that called for the fulfillment of an imperial manifesto issued by Czar Nicholas II during the RUSSIAN REVOLUTION OF 1905. The party formed a majority in the 3rd and 4th Dumas (1909–1917) and, after initially supporting the government's demand that it maintain sole executive authority, gradually moved to oppose it after 1915. The party disappeared after the October RUSSIAN REVOLUTION OF 1917.

ODINGA, AJUMA OGINGA   (1911–1994) Born in October 1911 in Central Nyanza, Kenya, Odinga was educated at Makerere University, Uganda, where he obtained a teacher's diploma. He worked as a teacher and headmaster before helping to found the Luo Thrift and Trading Corporation and becoming its managing director (1947–1962). After the 1963 general elections in Kenya, Odinga was appointed minister for home affairs. When Kenya became a republic in 1964, Odinga was appointed vice-president and minister without portfolio. He was also vice-president of the KENYA AFRICAN UNION (KANU) between 1960 and 1966. Always a rebel, Odinga's socialist beliefs brought him into conflict with the government and in 1966 he resigned as vice-president of Kenya and left KANU to lead an opposition party, the Kenya People's Union (KPU). In 1969, he was arrested and detained and his party proscribed. He was released toward the end of 1971, after which he rejoined KANU. In 1967, he had published his book, *Not Yet Uhuru* ("freedom" in Swahili).

In November 1979, Odinga was appointed chairman of the Cotton Seed and Marketing Board. In 1981, he resigned this post and soon after started to campaign for a multiparty system in Kenya. He attacked the government, especially "land-gabbers," in which group he included KENYATTA. He also attacked the US military presence in Kenya and claimed that Kenya's resources had been systematically plundered.

In August 1991, Odinga launched the Forum for the Restoration of Democracy party (FORD). After the multiparty elections in December 1992, FORD was one of the main opposition parties.

OGAREV, NIKOLAI   (1813–1877) Son of a wealthy landowner, Ogarev attended Moscow University where, under the influence of radical ideas and of the DECEMBRIST rebels, he first took part in radical activity, swearing together with ALEXANDER HERZEN to dedicate his entire life to the struggle the Decembrists had begun. Expelled from the university, he was confined to his father's estate, which he soon inherited. There he engaged in the study of medicine and economics and conducted social experiments, including freeing his serfs, establishing technical training schools in his villages and, out of belief that industry promised a better future, building a factory staffed with paid workers, which the workers themselves later burned to the ground.

Discouraged, Ogarev left Russia in 1856, never to return. He joined Herzen in London, where he helped found and coedited the journal *Kolokol* and engaged in organizing the populist circles, thinking and writing about the life of the peasantry. Both he and Herzen were bitterly critical of the form in which the serfs were freed in 1861. Gradually, under the frustration of his remoteness from the scene of political struggle, Ogarev formulated the idea that the radical intellectuals must go "to the people" if their ideas were to have any effect.

The first form in which this was suggested was a petition to the czar, written by Ogarev, to be signed by persons of all strata: nobles, peasants and intellectuals, entreating the czar to convene elected people's assemblies to correct the shortcomings of the emancipation which, Ogarev claimed, left the nobles as well as the peasants economically unable to live and work. He later called upon Russia's university students to leave their learning and devote themselves to enlightening the people. This call, taken up by BAKUNIN as well, began the agitation among Russian youth that was to culminate in the TO THE PEOPLE movement during the summer of 1874.

But overly-long exile and advancing age lessened Ogarev's effectiveness. His moderate ideas were out of contact with the radicalization that was growing in various INTELLIGENTSIA circles. Ogarev died just as revolutionary terror began to come into vogue among his erstwhile disciples.

O'HIGGINS, BERNARDO   (1778–1842) Chilean statesman and general, friend and student of Francisco Miranda in England. After completing his education in England, O'Higgins returned to Chile imbued with ideas of freedom. With JOSÉ DESAN MARTIN he organized a well-drilled, well-equipped army in Argentina which defeated the royalist army in the battle of Chacabuco—near Santiago—on February 12, 1817. One year later, on February 12, 1818, the independence of Chile was publicly proclaimed and O'Higgins named supreme Director. He created an army which was under the command of the British adventurer Lord Thomas Alexander Cochrane. Later O'Higgins became unpopular because of his dictatorial tendencies, his disregard for the Catholic church and his vindictive attitude toward his political enemies. In 1822 he called a constituent assembly, which drafted a constitution granting broad powers to the executive and extending his authority for 10 years. After several uprisings, O'Higgins resigned and transferred the executive powers to a junta on January 28, 1823. He moved to Peru, where he died in 1842.

OJUKWU, CHUKWUEMEKA ODUMEGWU   (1933–) Ojukwu was educated in Lagos, Nigeria, and at Oxford University, England. Members of the Ibo ethnic group dominated the Nigerian army and Ojukwu, himself an Ibo, embarked on a military career.

During 1966–1967, Ojukwu—now a lieutenant colonel—was military governor of the eastern region of Nigeria. He was urged by senior Ibo civil servants, who had fled from the capital Lagos because of violent anti-Ibo riots, to declare an independent Ibo state. Finally, in May 1967, the charismatic Ojukwu announced the secession of the eastern region of Nigeria and proclaimed its independence as the Republic of Biafra.

The Ibo achieved a series of initial successes but, by late 1967, the war had degenerated into a violent campaign of attrition. The war's military casualties were about 100,000, but between 500,000–2,000,000 Biafran citizens died, mainly from starvation as a result of the blockade imposed by the federal government. In January 1970, the Biafran forces surrendered. Ojukwu went into exile in the Ivory Coast (Côte d'Ivoire), where he was granted political asylum.

O'NEILL'S REVOLT   (1594–1603) Hugh O'Neill, the Earl of Tyrone in Ireland, led a rebellion of the northern Irish against English rule, in alliance with Hugh Roe O'Donnell. Their victory at Yellow Ford in August 1598 encouraged many Irishmen to join their cause, and the entire English situation in Ireland appeared to be in doubt. The revolt was largely suppressed by Charles Blount, Lord Mountjoy, in 1600, but a Spanish relief force landed in County Cork in September 1601 and gave the rebels new hope. Although the Spanish and the Irish were defeated at the end of the year, Tyrone himself only surrendered in March 1603, when he was pardoned by the new king, James I.

ORAKHELASHVILI, IVANE (MAMIA)   (1881–1937) Georgian revolutionary and statesman. Having been involved in revolutionary movements from adolescence, Orakhelashvili joined the BOLSHEVIK PARTY in 1903. After graduating from the St. Petersburg Military-Medical Academy, he engaged in various party tasks. In 1917–1918 he was the chairman of the Vladikavkaz Committee and Soviet of the Russian Social-Democratic Workers party and a member of the Caucasian Regional Committee. Following the secession of Georgia from Russia, Orakhelashvili returned to his homeland and began fighting against the MENSHEVIK government. In 1920 he became the chairman of the Central Committee of the Georgian Communist party and after the establishment of the Soviet rule became chairman of the revolutionary committee. Following the creation of the Transcaucasian Federation, he was appointed the chairman of the People's Commissars—i.e., the government.

In 1923–1925, Orakhelashvili held the post of deputy chairman of the Soviet of the People's Commissars. In 1926–1929 he became the first secretary of the Transcaucasian Regional Committee of the Communist Party. In 1930–1937 he held various party posts in Moscow and Tbilisi, being elected several times to the central committee of the Communist party. In 1937 Orakhelashvili was announced a public enemy and executed. Later he was exonerated.

ORDZHONIKIDZE, GRIGORY (SERGO)   (1886–1937) Georgian revolutionary and statesman. From 1901, Ordzhonikidze participated in a Social Democratic group and joined the BOLSHEVIK PARTY in 1903. He played a very active role in the RUSSIAN REVOLUTION OF 1905. In December 1905 he was arrested while transporting arms for revolutionary purposes. In 1907 he became a member of the Baku committee of the Russian Social Democratic Workers Party (Bolsheviks)—RSDWP(B),

was arrested for his activities and in 1909 transferred to Siberia. In 1911, Ordzhonikidze studied at the party school in France and later returned to Russia. In 1912, he was elected a member of the Russian Bureau of the Central Committee of the RSDWP(B). In April he was arrested once again and after three years of penal servitude was transferred to Yakutia. Freed by the first RUSSIAN REVOLUTION OF 1917, Ordzhonikidze became the special commissar for the Ukraine in December 1917. In 1918–1920, he was one of the political leaders of the RED ARMY. During that time, he organized the establishment of Soviet rule in Azerbaijan, Armenia and Georgia. In 1922–1926 he held the posts of the first secretary of the Transcaucasian and North Caucasian regional committees of the party. In 1926–1930 he was chairman of the Peoples' Commissars Soviet of the Soviet Union and in 1930 was elected to the Politburo of the party.

In the last years of his life, Ordzhonikidze voiced moderate criticism of Stalin for the latter's excessive demands for growth. The cause of his death is still a mystery. Some argue that he committed suicide.

ORGANISATION SPECIALE (OS—Special Organization) A militant Algerian nationalist organization, predecessor of the FRONT DE LIBÉRATION NATIONALE. A splinter group of the MOUVEMENT POUR LE TRIOMPHE DES LIBERTÉS DEMOCRATIQUES, the OS became the first group to advocate armed struggle for Algerian independence. Led by AHMAD BEN-BELLA and HUSSEIN AIT-AHMAD, the OS possessed a greater appeal to the younger, more radical generation of Algerian nationalists. In 1954, the OS initiated the formation of the COMITÉ RÉVOLUTIONNAIRE D'UNITE ET D'ACTION.

ORLÉANS, PHILIPPE, DUKE OF   (1747–1793) The Orléans were a branch of the reigning Bourbons and Philippe, a prince of the blood, was the immediate cousin, or *cousin germain*, of Louis XVI and the next in line of succession to the throne after Louis's son, the young and childless Dauphin.

Under the *ancien régime*, the Duke of Orléans had courted popular support by espousing the cause of the Parlement in its famous duel with the Crown during the dramatic Revolution of the Nobles in the 1780s. He sought public sympathy by such dramatic gestures as being inducted into the Masonic Order in a much publicized though secret ritual and rose to become Grand Master of the FREEMASONS of France in 1786.

With the outbreak of the FRENCH REVOLUTION, his Paris residence, the Palais Royal located near the Tuileries Palace, was transformed into a political salon where a secret committee, the Committee of Thirty headed by the MARQUIS DE LAFAYETTE, openly promoted the cause of the Third Estate in its struggle against Louis XVI's absolutist régime. The committee has been accused of plotting the overthrow of the king to assure the succession of the duke as heir to the throne, but modern research reveals that Orléans was only fishing in troubled waters during a period of sudden and abrupt revolutionary change. It was also from the gardens of the Palais Royal, a meeting place favored by mob orators and revolutionaries even before 1789, that the armed column which attacked the Bastille on July 14, 1789 was assembled, harangued and given its marching orders by CAMILLE DESMOULINS, allegedly in the committee's pay and reportedly also a Mason.

Elected as a member of the aristocrats' First Estate, the duc d'Orléans had openly sided with the revolution by defecting to the bourgeois Third Estate, abandoned his titles and privileges even before the session of the famous night of August 4 abolished the feudal order of the *ancien régime* and revealed his true colors by supporting Lafayette and the moderates in their campaign to establish a constitutional monarchy according to the principles of 1789.

After the fall of the monarchy in September 1792, the duc d'Orléans revealed his radical sentiments by rallying to the JA-COBIN Club. He had already given his blessing to the petition calling for a republic which had provoked the CHAMPS DE MARS massacre in July 1792. Now he sat with the Jacobins as a deputy in the convention, where in a dramatic gesture he voted for the abolition of the monarchy, the execution of Louis XVI and the creation of the revolutionary tribunal in March 1793 in order, as he said, to expedite the terror which the revolution had to reluctantly but vigorously endorse. It was at this time that the PARIS COMMUNE renamed the Duke "Philippe Égalité," in recognition of his services to the republic, but these were soon brought into question by his association with the GIRONDINS. Discredited, along with his Girondin political allies, by the defection of General DUMOURIEZ to the Austrians in April 1793, he paid the price for all his past opportunism and vague idealism and was arrested for treachery, imprisoned in the notorious fortress Notre Dame de la Garde in Marseilles, then brought to Paris to be guillotined on November 6, 1793.

His son, Louis Philippe, who had also cast his lot with the revolution but chose to exile himself to America during the terror, was later to become king of France and founded the Orléans monarchy after the July Revolution in 1830, following the abdication of Charles X, the last of the Bourbons. A patron of the arts with modest literary ambitions of his own, the duc d'Orléans also advanced the career of such writers as Sillery and Choderlos de Laclos, author of *Les Liaisons Dangereuses*. With commendable tact and discrimination, he also shared his remarkable mistress, Mme. de Genlis, with his son, Louis Philippe.

ORTEGA SAAVEDRA, DANIEL AND HUMBERTO

Humberto and Daniel Ortega Saavedra were brothers centrally involved in the Nicaraguan revolution of 1979. Following the victory of the Revolutionary Sandinista forces over the US-supported repressive régime of Anastasio Somosa, a new govern-ment was formed, consisting of the Sandinista army, the FSLN (*Frente Sandinista de Liberacion Nacional*), the Sandinista movement itself, a council of state, a governing (largely symbolic) junta and a cabinet. Real power, however, was vested in the FSLN and the army. Humberto Ortega, as chairman of the junta but also as a key figure in the FSLN directorate, and Daniel Ortega, as commander in chief of the Sandinista army, together formed what Latin American political scientist Martin Needler calls a "potent combination," largely determining the direction of Nicaragua's revolutionary government for a decade.

OTIS, JAMES

(1725–1783) A Massachusetts lawyer, publicist and politician who distinguished himself as a revolutionary in leading the colony's opposition to the Stamp Act of 1765, Otis was born in Barnstable, Massachusetts in 1725 and graduated from Harvard College in 1743. He went on to a distinguished legal career, specializing in legal theory and in admiralty law. His appointment as advocate general of the vice-admiralty court in Boston placed Otis in what would become a center of contention between the colonists and the British imperial administration. Vice-admiralty courts exercised ministerial discretionary power, and their jurisdiction represented to the colonists a subversion of the traditions of common law. Ministerial control, as applied in the jurisdiction of these courts and in their power to issue writs of assistance, were considered by the colonists to infringe on their rights under the English constitution.

In 1760, Otis resigned as advocate general and joined the opposition in contesting the constitutionality of the writs and the powers of the admiralty courts. His eloquence, coupled with the force of his legal arguments, made his orations and pamphlets highly effective in arousing public opinion and political action against the tightening of imperial control over the colonies. Consequently, his influence in Massachusetts politics increased rapidly. The convening of the Stamp Act Congress in 1765 marked Otis's rise to pan-colonial leadership. Notwithstanding his prominence in revolutionary circles, Otis was opposed, throughout the 1760s, to violent acts of resistance.

A head injury suffered in a 1769 fight with a crown official not only ended Otis's political career, it also seriously handicapped his intellectual capabilities. There is thus no clue to how his views would have developed with the escalation of the conflict. In 1783, he was struck by lightning and died.

P

PAINE, THOMAS (1727–1809) Political writer and analyst; advocate of democratic principles. Thomas Paine was born in Thetford, Norfolk, England, the son of a Quaker corset maker. He lived a rather unsettled life, trying a great variety of occupations for brief periods. These included attempts as a sailor, teacher, tobacconist, grocer and even customs inspector. In 1774 he decided, at the suggestion of Benjamin Franklin, to try his fortune in America. Soon thereafter he found his vocation as a writer and editor of the *Pennsylvania Magazine*.

In 1776 he published his *Common Sense*, the single most influential pamphlet inspiring Americans to fight for their inde-

Thomas Paine penning the Rights of Man

pendence from England. Declaring that "government is but a necessary evil," Paine argued convincingly for representative government. This work sold 120,000 copies within three months and total sales reached half a million, including four editions that were published in Europe. During the period of the revolutionary war (1776–1783), Paine not only served in the Continental army but published 16 *Crisis* papers as well. The opening passage of the first *Crisis* paper published in 1776 was so stirring that General GEORGE WASHINGTON ordered it to be read to the troops at all revolutionary encampments. The simple eloquent patriotism of this work allayed the fears and hesitation of many in, and even outside, the army.

From 1777 to 1779 Paine served as secretary of the Committee for Foreign Affairs and in 1779 was clerk of the Pennsylvania Assembly. Apparently looking for new challenges after the revolutionary war, Paine left the United States and lived in Europe from 1787 to 1802. In 1791, while in England, he wrote and published his *Rights of Man* as his answer to Edmund Burke's *Reflections on the French Revolution*, only to have the work suppressed for containing seditious passages. The English authorities then tried him for treason, but he managed to escape to France. Once in France, he was elected to the revolutionary National Convention, in appreciation of his *Rights of Man*. However, his French triumph was short-lived due to the advent of MAXIMILIEN ROBESPIERRE to power. In 1793, Paine was arrested, imprisoned and stripped of his French citizenship.

In November 1794, through the efforts of the US minister to France, James Monroe, Paine was released from prison, after a year of incarceration. While in prison, he wrote his famous work, *Age of Reason*, advocating moderate deism. In 1796, probably after considerable thought but without proper investigation of the circumstances, he wrote a letter to President George Washington, accusing him and Gouveneur Morris, Monroe's predecessor as minister to France, of deliberately plotting to keep him in jail in France. His letter only alienated the American public.

In 1797 he published his *Agrarian Justice*, a proposal for a broad government welfare program, to benefit youth as well as old age. By 1802, upon his return to the United States, he found no welcome—he had become a forgotten man due to his radical free thinking which upset people of all parties. He spent the last seven years of his life in poverty, ill-health and obscurity. An obituary gave the assessment: "He lived long, did some good, and much harm." In 1819, English essayist William Cobbett removed his remains to England, intending to give him an appropriate burial, but the bones were lost and never found.

These are the times that try men's souls. The Summer soldier and the sunshine patriot will, in this crisis, shrink from the service of their country, but he that stands it now deserves the love and thanks of man and woman. Tyranny, like Hell, is not easily conquered; yet we have this consolation with us, that the harder the conflict the more glorious the triumph. What we obtain too cheaply we esteem too lightly; it is darkness only that gives everything its value. Heaven knows how to put a proper price upon its goods; and it would be strange indeed if so celestial an article as freedom should not be highly rated.

The Crisis (first paper), 1776

● Character is much easier kept than recovered.

● My own mind is my own church.

● Where there are no distinctions there can be no superiority; perfect equality affords no temptation.

● Society is produced by our wants and government by our wickedness.

● He that would make his own freedom secure must guard even his enemy from oppression.

Thomas Paine

PALESTINE LIBERATION ORGANIZATION (PLO) The Palestine Liberation Organization (PLO) was officially created by a decision of the Arab League in 1964. President GAMAL ABDUL NASSER of Egypt backed the idea in order to co-opt the new organization into the League, thus providing a means of control over any Palestinian action. The PLO was headed by Ahmad al-Shuqeiri, a colorful and flamboyant Acre-born lawyer, known for his close relationship with Nasser. The Palestinian Army (PLA) was directly under the Arab Unified Command headed by an Egyptian.

Shuqeiri succeeded in calling a Palestinian conference in Jerusalem. The conference drew up a National Covenant, which is still in force. It also decided to create an executive arm—the Palestinian Liberation Organization (PLO)—and a Political agency—The Palestine National Council (PNC). Shuqeiri acted as the council's chairman until late in 1967. The PLO was designated to serve not only as an organization but also as a "Palestinian entity."

At first, the PLO was largely under Egyptian control and its activities were governed by the Arab League. This situation changed after *al-Fath* (see FATAH), led by YASIR ARAFAT, took over control of the PLO. Syria supported both *al-Fath* and the Palestine Liberation Front (PLF) of AHMAD JIBRIL.

The 1967 war was a disaster for the Palestinians as well as the Arab States, making it difficult for the PLO to build an organizational structure. By using persuasion rather than sheer force,

the large guerrilla groups contrived to co-opt small organizations and groups. A tolerance of division and diversity therefore characterized the PLO, but by February 1967 *al-Fath* had succeeded in getting it under its control and in uniting the fragmented guerrilla movement to a considerable degree.

Among the various groups, *al-Fath* attracted mainly the nationalists and Muslim activists who were not motivated by ideology. The Popular Front for the Liberation of Palestine (PFLP), headed by GEORGE HABASH, established in 1967, adopted a Marxist-Leninist ideology. While *al-Fath* stressed Palestinian interests first and Arabism second, the PFLP reversed the priorities. Ahmad Jibril broke with the PFLP in October 1968, establishing the Popular Front for the Liberation of Palestine—General Command (PFLP-GC), and taking a pro-Syrian line.

The left wing of the PFLP led by NA'IF HAWATMAH broke away from the PFLP in February 1969, establishing the Popular Democratic Front for the Liberation of Palestine (PDFLP) and adopting an extreme Marxist-Leninist ideology. Various Arab States also established their own Palestinian organizations. Syria established the *al-Sa'iqa* (Lightening), and Iraq the Arab Liberation Front.

In February 1969, Yasir Arafat was elected chairman of the PLO Executive Committee. A unity agreement between all Palestinian organizations was signed in May 1970, in which all the groups recognized the PLO as the umbrella structure of national unity. But each organization still retained a broad measure of autonomy. During the events of September 1970 (BLACK SEPTEMBER) in Jordan, the PFLP and the PDFLP dragged the whole of the resistance into a confrontation that the majority had been seeking to avoid. The period of 1968–1970 saw the emergence of the PLO as the institutional framework which the Palestinians and their organizations gradually came to see as their own, and which increasingly asserted itself as an autonomous factor in the politics of the Middle East.

The fundamental properties of the ideology of the PLO are encapsulated in the Palestinian National Covenant. Since the mutual recognition between Israel and the PLO and the agreement signed with the Palestinians in 1994, Arafat has kept promising to change some of the covenant's articles, which call for armed struggle against Israel. The covenant lays particular stress on Palestine's indivisibility and on restoring the rights of the Palestinians.

In signing the covenant, all the constituent organizations in the PLO agreed on three fundamental operational principles:

(a) The phase in which the Palestinians are living is that of the national struggle for the liberation of Palestine;

(b) the need for FEDAYEEN (guerrilla) action for the nucleus of the popular Palestine war of liberation;

(c) the liberation of Palestine is a national duty.

The PFLP and the PDFLP were rivals inside the framework of the PLO. According to the PFLP, the Palestinian struggle against Israel ought to be perceived, first not as a national struggle, but as part of an all Arab revolution, and it argued that there can be no cooperation between the PLO and reactionary Arab régimes. The PDFLP demonstrated a somewhat dogmatic ideological perfectionism.

The slogan of a "secular democratic state" was first introduced in January 1969 by the PDFLP. The proposal caused a debate within the PLO. Most organizations saw the slogan as a tactical one, while only the PDFLP was ready to see it as a strategic aim. It was reaffirmed by resolutions at the eighth PNC in 1971: "The future state in Palestine liberated from Zionist colonization will be a democratic state, where all enjoy the same rights."

The term "democratic state" was much used by the PLO, but the term "secular" did not appear at all in PLO resolutions, as the PLO often tries to emphasize its Muslim character. The PLO also introduced the notion of "the legitimate rights of the Palestinian people." The PNC of 1977 defined them as the rights of "return, self determination and establishing their national state on their national soil."

Since the October 1973 war, PLO strategy toward Israel has gradually evolved toward an increasingly sophisticated "strategy of phases" for the liberation of Palestine—an establishment of a Palestinian state on every part of Palestinian land that is to be liberated.

After the PLO's failure to establish cells in the occupied West Bank, Jordan became the center of PLO activities. These came to an end in September 1970. Several of the Palestinian organizations countered by declaring the northern part of Jordan a "liberated Palestinian area." King Hussein decided to crush the Palestinians by force. In the aftermath of this episode, he closed all PLO institutions and expelled the organization's leaders. For the next 15years relations between the PLO and Jordan were very poor. The Amman Agreement of 1985 envisioned a confederation between Jordan and a future Palestinian state, but a year later the agreement dissolved. Relations warmed again in 1990 and 1991, when Jordan and the PLO supported SADDAM HUSSEIN in the Gulf War.

With the uprooting from Jordan came the development of a state within a state in Lebanon. Arafat set up his headquarters in Beirut. Service and administrative organizations quickly followed. By the early 1980s, the Palestinian Red Crescent had built hospitals. The General Union of Palestine workers and the General Union of Palestine Women also gained most of their strength in Lebanon. In addition, the PLO set up a radio network and several newspapers. The organization had grown from a loosely organized collection of *Fedayeen* to a vast bureaucratic network. In addition, it had gained diplomatic recognition from over 50 states, established more than 100 foreign missions and won observer status in the United Nations.

The PLO control in Lebanon went far beyond the Palestinian refugee camps. The guerrillas had nearly free reign in a wide swathe of Lebanese territory. However, by 1976, the PLO was directly involved in the civil war which had started a year earlier. The result was the Syrian invasion of Lebanon, threatening the PLO, which stood to lose its last territorial base. The pro-Syrians, the Sa'iqa, PFLP-GC and parts of the PLA preferred to fight alongside Syria against their Palestinian brothers. The PLO organization then entered southern Lebanon, there being no Lebanese authority in the area. South Lebanon emerged as the PLO's last territorial base.

For the PLO, the civil war would bring previously unimagined brutality and disasters. It would end up facing two Israeli invasions, i.e., a limited incursion in 1978 and a full-scale attack in 1982. Moreover, in 1983, several groups, including Sa'iqa and PDFLP-GC, withdrew from the PLO, and an *al-Fath* colonel, Abu Musa, led a mutiny against Arafat. Palestinian mil-

itary, administrative and political forces were evacuated from Lebanon. Reestablished in Tunis, the PLO moved some of its branches to Iraq—paving the way for Arafat's support of Saddam Hussein in the 1991 Gulf War.

By the late 1980s, the PLO was again engaging in international initiatives. Arafat engineered a short-lived dialogue with the United States, denouncing the use of terrorism and publicly recognizing the right of Israel to exist. In November 1988, the PNC declared an independent Palestinian state that would rule in the West Bank and the Gaza Strip. Without defining its borders or establishing a government, the PNC authorized a declaration of independence. However, the PLO could not create enough autonomy to shape Palestinian society and to confront Israel, and could not even protect the Palestinian population in Lebanon.

Despite all the difficulties the PLO encountered in establishing control in the occupied territories, an uprising finally did materialize in the West Bank and the Gaza Strip. It was a massive act of resistance which erupted in December 1987. The events soon acquired the name *Intifada* (shaking off). Territory-wide leaflets which appeared by the end of December carried the signature of the PLO.

The *Intifada* leadership, consisting of second-rank local activists from various guerrilla organizations, mirrored the heavier influence of leftist groups inside the territories, compared to those on the outside, where *al-Fath*'s dominance was much more pronounced. The "Pamphlet Leadership" of the *Intifada* could not develop the autonomy that the *al-Fath*-dominated PLO feared, but it did develop independent political and operational views that the PLO on the "outside" had to take into account, and it is not surprising that after the first six months the *Intifada* lost some of its spontaneity and autonomy. The original unified leadership was decimated and the Arafat-led PLO exercised firmer control over those who replaced it. But things changed. The "outside" PLO based in Tunis had to combat local leaders of the "inside" PLO in the territories. Strain between the organization's top echelons and the unified leadership emerged during the *Intifada*, but there is disagreement about the level of overt conflict. Some argue that there was complete harmony between the outside and inside leadership—that the unified leadership sees itself as the local political activist arm of the PLO. Others see a continuation of the battle for local autonomy. But the more important point is that the *Intifada* enabled residents in the territories to influence the PLO's political positions. The local leadership pushed the PLO toward acceptance of Israel, a two-state solution to the conflict and participation in US-sponsored peace talks. It pushed the PLO to abandon armed struggle within the context of the *Intifada*. The PLO, for its part, projected the unified leadership into a more prominent national role.

The PLO's cause grew stronger, reaching its apogee in 1988 when the *Intifada* and Arafat's statement earned it a dialogue with the US, but less than two years later the PLO situation was harmed by the crisis in the Gulf which paralyzed the Arab world. The PLO was now face to face with "self-government" as the best it would get.

At the Madrid Conference of October 1991, the Palestinians and Israel agreed that there must be a transitional period preceding a final settlement which will be the focus of the first stage of negotiations. Next came the Declaration of Principles on Interim Self-Government Arrangements (DOP) for Palestinians in the Gaza Strip and Jericho, which was signed on September 13, 1993. Based on the PNC peace initiative of November 1988, which called for establishment of a Palestinian state on the basis of the concept of partition in the West Bank and Gaza Strip, this was a major shift in PLO political and ideological attitudes and thoughts. The DOP marked the most major of all breakthroughs in the century-old conflict between Arabs and Jews.

The PLO has been of vital importance in enhancing the growth of Palestinian nationalism and in bringing the Palestinians to their current achievements. The PLO and its front organizations have been active in all social, economic and cultural developments. In this sense they have contributed to the nation-building and to the development of a national institutional infrastructure, infusing it with a secular and modern orientation.

PALMYRA, REVOLT OF

Palmyra, a caravan city, rose to prominence thanks to its control of the trade between Mesopotamia and Syria. In 260 A.D. the Palmyrene Odaenathus defeated the Persian king Sapor, who had captured the Roman emperor Valerianus. Odaenathus assumed the royal title and was appointed by Gallienus, Valerianus's son, as commander of the Roman army in the east, in which capacity he reconquered Mesopotamia.

After the murder of Odaenathus in 267, his widow Zenobia took control of Palmyra. She revolted against the Roman emperor and attacked the Roman provinces in the east. Her armies occupied Syria, Egypt and most of Asia Minor (270) and in 271 she proclaimed her son emperor. The reigning emperor, Aurelian, embarked on a campaign against her, defeated her armies and captured Palmyra and Zenobia herself (273). The city was sacked and Zenobia and her son were led by Aurelian in triumph in Rome, but their lives were spared.

PANKHURST, EMMELINE

(1858–1928) Born as Emmeline Goulden, Pankhurst led the movement for women's voting rights in Britain. In 1879, she married the lawyer Richard Marsend Pankhurst, who was her associate in the fight for women's equality. In 1889, along with others, she founded the Women's Franchise League, which helped win the right for women to vote in local elections. The law was finally passed in 1894. In 1903, she founded the Women's Social and Political Union, which became important when she moved its center of operations to London and held public meetings and protest marches. Between 1908 and 1913 she was arrested and sentenced to jail several times and used hunger strikes as her way of protesting. When World War I began, she and her organization shifted their efforts to support for the war. Women were given full voting rights in England in May 1928 and she died shortly afterwards, on June 14, 1928.

PANNONIAN REVOLT

The Pannonii, a group of Illerian peoples with Celtic elements, inhabited the region south of the Danube extending to the Save valley, roughly in what is now western Hungary and part of Yugoslavia. The Roman conquest of their country began in 35 B.C. From 16 B.C. on, the generals of Caesar Augustus conducted a series of campaigns which extended Roman rule to the Danube by 8 B.C. For some time the Pannonii seemed to acquiesce in this turn in their fortunes. However, they rose in rebellion in 6 B.C., under two leaders by the name of Bato, taking advantage of the fact that Roman armies were busy attempting to subdue Maroboduus, king of the German Marcomanni who inhabited Bothemia. It took the Roman armies almost three years to subdue the revolt; no sooner had they done so when ARMINIUS revolted in Germany. The Pannonian revolt saved Maroboduus and indirectly brought about the halt of the Roman advance in Germany. Pannonia, however, remained a Roman province until the downfall of the Roman empire in the 4th century A.D.

PAN-RUSSIAN SOCIAL REVOLUTIONARY ORGANIZATION

A revolutionary movement founded in Zurich in 1875 by a heterogenous group of students from the Caucasus and Russian women students, including VERA FIGNER's sister, Lydia. After studying all the currents of European socialism, the group decided to form a commune (obshchina), based on direct democracy, economic equality and asceticism. The various communes of the organization, linked by an administrative center established in Moscow, were to maintain the principles of conspiratory secrecy.

Influenced by MARX as well as by BAKUNIN, this organization aimed its propaganda at the urban working class that was then growing relatively rapidly in Russia. The commune members sought employment among the workers and carried on propaganda among them through public readings, discussions, the founding of workers' libraries and, ultimately, workers' communes. They also aimed at organizing the workers to direct revolutionary action, strikes, demonstrations and even violent riots.

In their propaganda, the groups used all the populist and anarchist literature available, as well as publishing their own brochures and a newspaper, *Rabotnik* (The Worker), the first newspaper for workers in the Russian language. Members of the organization read this newspaper to groups of workers in the factory dormitories after work and in the taverns on their rest days.

However, the public activity undertaken by the young revolutionaries exposed them to the police. In April 1875, the Moscow center was arrested and little by little the other Russian communes in the textile city of Ivanovo and the metal-working center of Tula were rounded up. This left the emigrés, who published *Rabotnik* in Switzerland, cut off from their news sources and in April 1876, after 13 monthly and bi-monthly issues, its publication was terminated. The "Trial of the Fifty" in February and March 1877, in which Sophia Bardina, Alexander Tsitsianov, the worker Peter Alexeev and the other activists received heavy sentences of jail and exile, marked the organization's demise.

PAOLI, PASCAL

(1725–1807) A Corsican revolutionary officer who welcomed the liberation of his island from Genoa and was proclaimed national leader of his people in 1755. After Corsica was ceded to Louis XV in 1769, in alliance with the local clan of the Pozzo de Borgos and in opposition to the Francophile Carlo Bonaparte, Pascal led a sporadic vendetta against the French occupation. Carlo's son, Napoleon, born in Ajaccio on Ascencion Day 1769, was born a French subject and was even admitted to a military academy in Burgundy for the sons of the nobility on the grounds that he belonged to the Corsican aristocracy.

Paoli waged war against all nobles and therefore rallied enthusiastically to the FRENCH REVOLUTION. He was appointed military governor of Bastia in 1790. Breaking with the CONVENTION in 1793, he evicted all the French from Corsica and proclaimed the union of the island with Great Britain, with himself as viceroy. Disowned by his own people and faced with the animosity of General Napoleon Bonaparte, he and his clan were forced to seek exile in England. His name became a byword for Republican idealism. Indeed, he was idolized by the American revolutionaries, who named the Paoli line outside Philadelphia in his honor. He also made a strong impression on such intellectuals as Samuel Johnson, Boswell and Jean-Jacques Rousseau. The latter was even asked to draft a constitution for an independent Corsica.

PAPADOUPOLOS, GEORGE (1918–) Greek soldier and politician. In April 1967 he masterminded a coup that overthrew the Greek democracy and eventually drove the king into exile. He then emerged as the strongman of the new régime, becoming prime minister and minister of defense and in 1972 abolishing the monarchy. His right-wing, quasi-Fascist dictatorship, relying on torture and the power of the police, made Greece into something of an international pariah, though it did achieve some years of economic prosperity. In 1974, following the coup against President MAKARIOS of Cyprus and the subsequent Turkish invasion of that island, his government was overthrown and he was sent to prison.

PARIS COMMUNE The name adopted by the revolutionary government of the city of Paris in 1871 in emulation of the great insurrectionary Commune of September 1792 which, in alliance with the revolutionary CONVENTION, had radicalized the FRENCH REVOLUTION in the climactic years of 1792 to 1794. More specifically, the term "Commune" is used to refer to the bloody civil war which pitted the Parisian revolutionaries against the duly elected central government of France's provisional republic responsible for signing peace with Bismarck. The episode of the Commune took place in the aftermath of the fall of the Second Empire and the capture of the emperor in Sedan during the Franco-Prussian war.

Encouraged by other revolutionary communes which had also seized power in Lyons and Marseilles, the Commune's leaders formed a central committee, consisting of a motley coalition made up of neo-JACOBINS, socialists of all kinds, anarchists and even feminists, but including only one member of the First INTERNATIONAL, a foreigner by the name of Fraenkel. The committee immediately defied the authority of the bourgeois republic headed by Adolphe Thiers, which sat first in Bordeaux and then moved to the royal palace of Versailles, on the outskirts of the capital. The Commune tried to carry out its revolutionary program by means of a federation of autonomous self-governing communes to be spontaneously created throughout the land. Hailed at first by KARL MARX as the first step to the Communist revolution, it was violently resisted by armed forces recruited by Thiers from the provinces and aroused a wave of hysteria among the French bourgeois classes. The Commune and all it stood for were vigorously discredited by a convenient semantic

play on the name, associating the Communism preached by Marx with the French word *Commune*, which signifies municipal government. The course of events however, revealed that the central committee elected on March 16, 1871 was burdened by memories of the past rather than any desire to pave the way for a proletarian future and sought to recreate the achievements of the great Commune of 1792 rather than implement the Communist Manifesto of 1848.

As in September 1792, the Paris Commune was precipitated by war. After enduring a four-month siege at the hands of the Prussians, the capital was subjected to the humiliation of a Prussian victory parade and the forcible surrender of the guns which dominated the city from the heights of Montmartre to Thiers. Despite the intervention of Montmartre's mayor, Georges Clemenceau, rioters seized and hanged the two generals sent to remove the guns. The Commune was forced to devote its energies to defending the city from the Versailles army led by General Gallifet, which fought its way into the capital street by street, culminating in the summary execution of the last handful of Communards in the cemetery of Père Lachaise. The site of that butchery of the martyrs of the Commune, the *Mur des Fédéres,* has long been a shrine to the Communists of the world. Hostages were shot by both sides, the Tuileries and the City Hall destroyed by fire and more casualties suffered than during the Great Terror. The suppression of the Commune slowed down the growth of revolutionary socialism in France and marked the last act of defiance of the red capital against the rest of the country.

PARK CHUNG HEE (1917–1979) Born in what is now South Korea, Park Chung Hee served as an officer in the Japanese Kwantung army in Manchuria during World War II. Returning to South Korea, he was graduated from the Korean military academy and rose to the rank of brigadier general during the Korean war. Following the 1960 April Revolution, General Park became leader of the coup of 1961 (see KOREA, SOUTH, COUP OF 1960–1961) against the government of Premier Chang Myun. He was elected president of South Korea in 1963 and reelected in 1967. In 1968, a North Korean commando team sent to assassinate him in Seoul failed in the attempt. Park's wife was killed in an assassination attempt on him in 1974. He was killed in 1979 by the head of the South Korean Central Intelligence Agency.

PARNELL, CHARLES STUART (1846–1891) Irish leader. A surprising figure to emerge as leader of the predominantly Catholic Nationalist movement, Charles Parnell was a wealthy Protestant landowner. His family had links with the ruling Protestant landed elite. Parnell attended Cambridge University but was arrested after four years for involvement in a nasty street fight; a judge also fined him 20 pounds for participating in this affray and he returned to Ireland.

1875 Parnell stood for parliament on a platform supporting home rule for Ireland and was elected member for Heath. He did not take long to make his reputation as a fiery exponent of Irish autonomy and land reform, becoming the leader of the Irish members in the House of Commons in London. In 1879 he became president of the Land League, an organization campaigning for reform in the relationship between landlord and tenant in Ireland and an end to the widespread evictions that had caused bitter distress in many rural areas.

Aware that the leading officials of the Land League had backgrounds in the Fenian Brotherhood, a violent organization (forerunner of the IRISH REPUBLICAN ARMY—IRA), Parnell also advocated violent struggle for independence. His inflammatory speeches further aroused the passions of his supporters, encouraging the very actions which this astute politician thought prudent to condemn.

Parnell also encouraged the boycotting of particularly unpopular landlords or those who took over land from evicted tenants. Indeed, the word "boycott" dates from this period, for Captain Boycott was one of the unlucky Anglo-Irish landlords to whom the policy was applied, "isolating him from the rest of mankind as if he was a leper of old," in Parnell's words.

The Liberal government was moving toward reform of the Irish land laws, if only to remove a major cause of unrest, but its first priority was to quieten the country through the application of the appropriately named Coercion of Ireland Bill. Parnell and his colleagues tried to block the bill's passage but were suspended from the House of Commons.

When Parnell undertook a tour of America, he made no pretence about the ultimate aim of his crusade: "None of us will be satisfied until we have destroyed the last link which keeps Ireland bound to England." On his return he was viewed as too dangerous an agitator to be at large. Prison, however, only raised him to the status of martyr for the Irish cause and he emerged from custody an even more powerful force to be reckoned with.

The father of Irish Independence, Charles Parnell

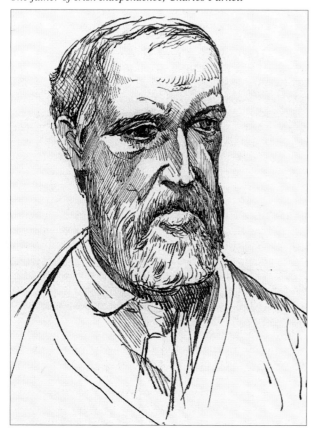

The Liberal government needed the support of Irish Members of Parliament and so, even while Parnell was still in prison, it entered negotiations with him. Thus, by the mid-1880s the majority of the Liberal Party was committed to home rule for the Irish. Although Parnell aroused English suspicions with his famous statement that "no man has a right to fix the boundary to the march of a nation," his support for the more limited Home Rule Bill was seen as genuine.

When he was at the height of his political power, Parnell's career collapsed around him. In 1889 he was cited in the divorce proceedings of a fellow Irish Member of Parliament, Captain William O'Shea, against his wife Katherine. This case produced a wave of anti-Parnell sentiment among his Irish Catholic supporters and among the non-conformists, who formed a major block in the Liberal Party's constituency. Parnell's colleagues deposed him from leadership, splitting the Irish Party in the process. Election results in Ireland showed him his power base had been undermined and his health broke under the strain. Within four months of his marriage to Katherine O'Shea, Parnell took ill and soon died.

PARTIDO AFRICANO DA INDEPENDÊNCIA DA GUINÉ E CABO VERDE (PAIGC) West African independence movement. The PAIGC was organized in Bissau, Portuguese Guinea, in 1956 from an earlier nationalist organization, MING (*Movimento da Independência Nacional da Guiné*), founded in 1954 by Henri Labery and AMILCAR CABRAL. It differed from MING in that it also supported independence for the Cape Verde Islands. Originally the PAIGC was a small movement—it had only about 50 members by 1958—but by organizing successful strikes it succeeding in mobilizing sympathy for its objectives and in provoking the Portuguese authorities. Troops sent to break up the Pijiguito dockworkers' strike in 1959 fired upon the strikers, killing fifty and wounding 100. The PAIGC leadership fled to Conakry, capital of neighboring Guinea, but continued to advocate peaceful resistance to Portuguese rule for another two years.

At a meeting in Casablanca, Morocco, in 1961, PAIGC leaders met with representatives of the nationalist movements in Angola (MPLA) and Mozambique (FRELIMO) to coordinate their struggles for independence. That same year it was decided to engage in armed struggle against Portugal. By 1964, the PAIGC was able to hold its first party conference in the "liberated zone" of Cassaca. By 1965, over half the countryside was under PAIGC rule.

The dominant figure in the PAIGC during this period was AMILCAR CABRAL, a Portuguese-trained agronomist and revolutionary nationalist. His ideas regarding African nationalism and MARXISM forged the PAIGC into a revolutionary movement, concerned with education and economics no less than with the cessation of Portuguese rule. In the liberated areas, Cabral organized *Armazens do Povo*, or Peoples' Stores, in which civilians could barter for the basic necessities at set values: for example, 3 kg. of rice could be exchanged for a pair of trousers.

Nevertheless, Cabral was not a Marxist dogmatist. He believed that traditional Marxism could be "amended or discarded as necessary," and wrote: "Never do we want to see a group or class of people exploiting or dominating the work of our people. That's our basis. If you want to call it Marxism, you may call it

Marxism." In fact, the basis of his ideology was nationalist: he demanded the "right of every people to have its own history" and defined national liberation as "the phenomenon in which a socioeconomic whole rejects the denial of its historical process." Socialism was to Cabral a means of improving the lot of the masses, but in his revolution the leadership would be provided by the petite bourgeoisie, who possessed the necessary education and means.

Cabral won the PAIGC widespread international support. The party adopted a nonaligned stance in its foreign relations, receiving military aid from the eastern bloc and economic assistance from western countries and Arab states. Although several other independence movements were functioning simultaneously in Portuguese Guinea and Cape Verde, among them the FLING (*Frente de Luta Pela Independência Nacional da Guiné*) movement of Henri Labery, in 1967 the PAIGC won the sole support of the Organization of African Unity and, in 1972, Cabral and the leaders of the MPLA and FRELIMO were granted an audience with the pope. In 1972, members of the United Nations Decolonization Committee visited the liberated areas of Portuguese Guinea and recognized the PAIGC as "the only effective movement" capable of leading Portuguese Guinea to independence.

The PAIGC military and diplomatic successes were jolted by the assassination of Cabral in 1973 by a cabal of PAIGC dissidents, FLING and the Portuguese authorities. At the second PAIGC party conference, held shortly thereafter, Aristides Pereira was elected secretary-general with Luís Cabral, the slain leader's brother, as his deputy. In September 1974, the PAIGC unilaterally declared the independence of Guinea-Bissau. Over 60 countries rushed to recognize the new state, but it was only one year later, after the Portuguese régime was overthrown in a military coup, that Portugal granted de jure recognition to its former colony.

Cape Verde became independent in 1975, eliminating any hopes of political union between the two former colonies. In the following years, economic obstacles and the preponderance of Cape Verdeans in the higher echelons of power (Cabral's father was from Cape Verde) lost the PAIGC support among the inhabitants of Guinea-Bissau. In 1980, the post-independence government of Guinea-Bissau was deposed in a coup. The PAIGC congress in 1981 reaffirmed the régime's commitment to socialism and rebuked the previous régime for deviating from the policies of Amilcar Cabral.

PARTY OF THE ALGERIAN PEOPLE (PPA—Parti Populaire Algérien) Algerian nationalist organization, formed from elements supporting the banned North African Star (L'ETOILE NORD AFRICAINE) and led by AHMAD MESSALI HAJJ. The PPA was purportedly responsible for organizing the demonstration which precipitated the SETIF UPRISING of 1945. After the uprising, the PPA was banned and reorganized under the name MOUVEMENT POUR LE TRIOMPHE DES LIBERTÉS DÉMOCRATIQUES (Movement for the Triumph of Democratic Liberties).

PASIONARIA, LA (1895–1977) Spanish Communist leader. Born to a poor peasant family under her original name of Delores Ibarrusi, she was a co-founder of the Spanish Communist Party, becoming a member of its central committee. During the

Austrian rebellion of 1934, and again during the SPANISH CIVIL WAR of 1936–1939, she became famous for her impassioned oratory in the Communist cause and for the slogan (borrowed from Pétain), "they shall not pass." From 1939 on, she lived in Moscow; shortly before her death, however, she was allowed to return to Spain. She wrote *They Shall Not Pass* (1967).

PAUKER, ANA (1890–1960) Romanian Communist leader and deputy premier. Born Hannah Rabinsohn, she was the daughter of an Orthodox kosher butcher, received a traditional upbringing and taught Hebrew in a Bucharest Jewish primary school. Jilted by her fiancé, she left home for Paris where she met (and later married) a zealous Communist, Marcel Pauker, who induced her to join the party in 1920. After covertly returning to Romania, she organized an underground Communist cell and began to win prominence in the Third International (COMINTERN).

Ana was, however, eventually arrested and sentenced, in 1936, to a long term of imprisonment. Her husband, while visiting the Soviet Union, fell victim to STALIN's purge of veteran BOLSHEVIKS. His execution as a "western spy" did not shake Ana's faith in the Russian dictator or in Soviet justice. Following the Soviet occupation of Bessarabia (1940), she was exchanged for Romanian political detainees and welcomed by Stalin in Moscow, remaining there until 1944, when her country was invaded and occupied by the USSR.

After World War II, Pauker became one of the most powerful and effective Communist leaders in Romania. She set up a coalition government, the Democratic Front, under Petru Groza (1944–1947), was secretary of the Communist Party's central committee and, following the Communist takeover in 1947, served as minister of foreign affairs and first deputy prime minister in President Groza's cabinet. Only fear of an anti-Semitic backlash deterred party colleagues from electing her to the premiership, but as foreign minister she wielded vast authority.

In June 1952, not long after the arrest of RUDOLF SLANSKY in Czechoslovakia, Pauker was also arrested on various trumped-up charges. These included "right-wing deviationism," pro-Zionist activity and the encouragement of Romanian emigration to Israel. Though expelled from the Communist Party and stripped of all her government posts, she never figured in a show trial, thanks to Stalin's death and the subsequent execution of KGB chief Lavrenti Beria (who had concocted the charges). Instead, she remained under house arrest for some years after her fall from power before finally going into retirement.

PAVELIC, ANTE (1889–1959) Croat nationalist leader. A lawyer who represented Croatia in the Yugoslav parliament during the 1920s, Pavelic opposed Serbian attempts to centralize the government. Driven into exile by King Alexander, who established a royal dictatorship in 1929, he founded the USTASHA terrorist group which assassinated the king in 1934. In 1941, after the German occupation of Yugoslavia, the state that emerged was nothing but a satellite of Germany, and Pavelic became its head. Under his leadership, it developed one of the most brutal régimes in all Europe and was responsible for the murder of several hundreds of thousands of people, mainly Serbs and Jews. After 1945, Pavelic lived in hiding, first in Argentina and then in Spain.

PAZ ESTENSSORO, VICTOR   (1907–) Bolivian politician. An economist who served in the Chaco war against Paraguay (1932–1935), he was elected to parliament as an independent in 1940. In 1941 he was a founding member of the Revolutionary National Movement (MNR) which favored economic nationalization, especially the expropriation of the American-owned tin-mining companies. He became minister of finance after a coup mounted by the MNR. Although exiled in 1951, he became president after another MNR rising overthrew the ruling junta in 1952. Retaining office until 1956, he carried out a program of nationalization and granted the vote to illiterate Indians. In 1960 he was again elected president, but when the election of 1964 resulted in a nomination for a third term, the Bolivian army rose and deposed him. He went into exile, returned, took part in the elections of 1972, failed to be elected and was exiled again in 1974. He was finally returned to Bolivia and reelected for his third term of presidency in 1985, a position he held until 1989 and during which Bolivia was to see economic advancement and domestic solidity.

PEASANTS' WAR   (1524–1525) A series of uprisings in southwest and central Germany, inspired by the religious zeal and defiance of authority of the leaders of the Reformation, and aimed at restoring the traditional rights of the peasants and ameliorating their lot. The revolt broke out at Stühlingen in the Black Forest in June 1524, and quickly spread into the Rhineland, Swabia, Franconia and Thuringia. The demands of the peasants, best expressed in the Twelve Articles of Memmingen, were concerned with forest, grazing and fishing rights; with tithes and feudal exactions; and with the lay election of the clergy. These were all presented as customary rights that had been abused and abrogated by the nobility. In certain areas, the peasants received support from the town and from the lesser nobility. Bands of peasants pillaged the countryside and destroyed abbeys and manor houses.

The revolt failed for lack of a united leadership; in the battle of Frankenhausen, on May 15, 1525, the peasants suffered a decisive defeat at the hands of the forces of the Protestant Philip of Hesse and the Catholic Duke George of Saxony. Their leader, THOMAS MÜNZER, was executed and the rebels crushed. Thereafter the peasantry of southern Germany ceased to have political significance.

LUTHER's reaction to the revolt received a great deal of attention from his contemporaries and historians. The peasants cited Luther's plea for the liberty of Christian men, and his enemies laid the blame for all religious and civil disobedience at his door. Luther, though, disassociated himself from the rebels. In May 1525 he wrote *Admonition to Peace*, a mild tract which recognized the justice of some of the peasants' claims. But the threat to order and the excesses of the peasants alarmed him, and he published the violently-phrased leaflet *Against the Murdering, Thieving Hordes of Peasants*—calling on the princes to punish the rebels with all severity. This tract alienated many of Luther's radical followers and placed him on the side of established authority.

P'ENG CHEN see PENG ZHEN.

PENG DEHUAI (P'eng Te-huai)   (1898–1974) Born in Hu-

nan, Peng endured hardship during his childhood, supporting himself with various jobs, including work in a coal mine. He joined the Hunan army in 1916, studied at the provincial military academy (1922–1923) and rose to the rank of regimental commander. As an officer in the NATIONAL REVOLUTIONARY ARMY, he participated in the first phase of the NORTHERN EXPEDITION to unify China (1926–1927). At that time he came into contact with the Communists and opposed the GUOMINDANG (GMD) after its anti-left purge in 1927. He joined the CHINESE COMMUNIST PARTY (CCP) in 1928 and commanded the RED ARMY's Fifth Army, which in December joined MAO ZEDONG and Zhu at Jinggangshan in southern Jiangxi. Peng played an important role in resisting CHIANG KAI-SHEK's first four extermination campaigns (1930–1933) and was elected an alternate member of the CCP central committee (CC) in January 1934. When Chiang's fifth encirclement campaign forced the CCP to evacuate the Jiangxi base in October and embark upon the LONG MARCH to the northwest, Peng led the First Front Army, along with Mao Zedong and LIN BIAO. On the way, he supported Mao at the Zunyi conference (January 1935) which made Mao leader of the CCP. In February 1936, Peng was appointed commander of the Red Army vanguard resisting Japan. During the Sino-Japanese war of 1937–1945 and the resumption of the GMD-CCP united front, Peng became deputy commander of the EIGHTH ROUTE ARMY (8RA), the main CCP military force. While the 8RA commander, ZHU DE, remained for most of the time in the CCP capital of Yan'an in northern Shaanxi, Peng was field commander and led the Communists to victory in the greatest battle they fought and won during the entire Sino-Japanese war, the "Hundred Regiments" campaign of August–December 1940.

The "Hundred Regiments" battle subsequently became a subject of controversy and was included in charges leveled at Peng during the Cultural Revolution (see GREAT PROLETARIAN CULTURAL REVOLUTION). What is apparently true is that Peng undertook the campaign without prior authorization from Yan'an. Various reasons for the 8RA offensive include increased Japanese pressure on CCP bases, fears that Chiang Kai-shek would capitulate to the enemy, and an effort to counter GMD charges that the CCP was using the war to augment its strength while avoiding the Japanese and leaving the GMD to bear the brunt of the war of resistance. Whatever the reasons, on August 20, 1940, the 8RA launched its greatest sustained offensive against the Japanese. Exploiting the element of surprise, 22 regiments (about 40,000 men) attacked Japanese-held railway lines in north China. Later the 8RA committed more forces, bringing the total to 104 regiments, constituting a large part of the 8RA (which at that time had about 400,000 men). By October, the Japanese had brought reinforcements, regained the initiative and inflicted heavy losses on the 8RA, which suffered from inadequate arms and supplies. In December the battle ended. According to Japanese sources, over 20,000 of their soldiers had been killed. If Mao Zedong had any reservations about the offensive, it did not stop him from sending a radio message congratulating Peng. Though the CCP glorified the victory, the Japanese retaliated vigorously. Backed by heavy reinforcements, the Japanese army's "three-all" policy (kill all, burn all, loot all) subjected soldiers and civilians in CCP territory to unrestrained terror. By 1942, CCP-held territory and its army were reduced considerably, but growth resumed in 1944.

In recognition of Peng's military achievements, the 7th CCP congress in 1945 awarded him full membership in the CC and Politburo. He commanded CCP forces in the northwest during the postwar struggle with the GMD in 1946–1949. After the establishment of the People's Republic of China (PRC) in October 1949, he held high military and civilian posts. In October 1950 he led the Chinese "volunteer" army that joined the Korean war (1950–1953), signed the Panmunjom armistice agreement in July 1953, and returned to a triumphal reception in Beijing. In 1954, he became minister of defense, a vice-premier and a vice-chairman of the National Defense Council. In 1955 he was one of the 10 military heroes honored with the rank of marshal of the PRC.

Peng's troubles began in 1959. He criticized Mao Zedong's GREAT LEAP FORWARD (1958–1959), which had caused famine and millions of deaths in the countryside. He also urged greater attention to military modernization. Having incurred Mao's disfavor, Peng lost his post as defense minister and was replaced by Lin Biao. In 1965, when Mao feared an American attack, Peng enjoyed a brief reprieve and was sent to the southwest as deputy chief of military construction. The following year, however, he became a principal target and victim of the Cultural Revolution. Used as a symbol of Chinese "revisionism," he was accused of conspiring with the Soviet Union as well as other alleged crimes and errors.

Beaten and kicked while under numerous interrogations, his ribs broken and lungs perforated, paraded through the streets on public display, Peng finally collapsed and died in November 1974. In December 1978 the post-Mao leadership rehabilitated him posthumously and restored his good name.

PENG PAI (P'eng P'ai)   (1896–1929) Chinese Communist, pioneer peasant organizer. Born to a wealthy landowning family in eastern Guangdong, Peng went to Japan in 1917 after completing high school. He studied political economy at Tokyo's Waseda University (1918–1921) and participated in anti-Japanese activities of overseas Chinese students who responded to the MAY FOURTH MOVEMENT at home. Influenced by socialist ideas prevalent at Waseda, after graduating and returning to China Peng joined the Socialist Youth Corps, precursor to the CHINESE COMMUNIST PARTY (CCP), in Canton in 1921. He returned to his native district, Haifeng, organized a socialist study society and led students in a May 1 demonstration. In 1922 he began working among peasants in Haifeng, which, like its neighboring district, Lufeng, had an unusually high rate of tenancy. Much of the land was owned by large lineages, in which poorer members were exploited by clan managers. In 1923, with 20,000 people attending, Peng founded the Haifeng District Federation of Peasant Associations and was elected chairman. This was the first district peasant association in the history of the modern Chinese revolution. He also headed a similar organization in Lufeng. Idealistic and sincere in his humanitarian beliefs, Peng burned the title deeds to his own property and identified completely with the peasants. His organization resisted landlord abuses and was innovative in providing practical education for peasant children. His influence expanding rapidly, he became chairman of Guangdong's provincial peasant association. After joining the CCP in 1924, Peng became secretary of the Peasant Bureau established by the GUOMINDANG (GMD), then united in a coalition with the CCP, and headed the bureau in 1925. He was in charge of sessions at the GMD's Peasant Movement Training Institute and influenced MAO ZEDONG, who was a staff member. Peng also directed the Guangdong peasant self-defense army, a precedent for the future peasant-based RED ARMY.

In early 1925, his Haifeng peasant movement was savagely suppressed by anti-GMD forces. In October, Peng returned in the wake of GMD military victories and rebuilt the peasant organizations. Despite GMD and CCP directives urging moderation, violence escalated as peasants took revenge. Peng had land confiscated and landlords executed.

Peng's report on Haifeng peasant activities, in January 1926, was the first document in CCP history that elaborated on the importance of the peasant movement. In 1927, the 5th CCP congress elected him to the central committee. After the GMD-CCP split he participated in the abortive NANCHANG UPRISING (August 1, 1927) and in November returned to Guangdong's East River area (Haifeng, Lufeng) and established a soviet government. This was actually the first of its kind, though CCP historians give precedence to Mao's soviet in Jiangxi.

Under his peasant soviet régime, policies were further radicalized. Traditional religious as well as Christian practices were attacked. Children were indoctrinated to the extent that some denounced their mothers as counterrevolutionaries. Declaring the destruction of the private property system, Peng tried to distribute land equally and achieve complete economic equality. His dictatorial régime also tried to outlaw opium, concubinage, brothels, gambling and other traditional vices. At the same time, he could not prevent a resurgence of primitive sadism and barbarism, fueled by old clan and secret society vendettas. Severed heads of slain enemies were publicly displayed, and their hearts and livers eaten at banquets. Thousands, and not all of them landowners, fled from the reign of terror. In February 1928, GMD forces attacked, occupied Haifeng and during the next few months subdued attempted uprisings.

At the 6th CCP congress, held in Moscow in July, Peng was reelected in absentia to the CC and to the Politburo as an alternate member. In November he went to Shanghai where he assumed leading positions in the party's underground apparatus. Betrayed by a party comrade, he was arrested in August 1929 and executed by GMD authorities. His wife later shared a similar fate. Though Peng had started as a selfless, idealistic, humanitarian, he became brutalized by revolutionary and counter-revolutionary violence, turning him into a merciless killer. The CCP honors him as a revolutionary martyr.

PENG SHUZHI (P'eng Shu-chih)   (1895–1984) Chinese Trotskyist leader. Born in Hunan to a relatively well-off peasant family, Peng participated in the patriotic MAY FOURTH MOVEMENT (1919) while studying at Beijing University. In 1920 he enrolled in the Shanghai foreign language school established by GREGORY VOITINSKY, a Russian COMINTERN agent, and joined the Socialist Youth Corps, precursor of the CHINESE COMMUNIST PARTY (CCP). He joined the CCP in 1921 and was in the first group of young party members sent to study at Moscow's Communist University of the Toilers of the East. Returning to China in 1923, he worked in the CCP propaganda department and in 1924 was a delegate to the 5th COMINTERN congress in Moscow. Peng was close to the CCP head, CHEN DUXIU, and was considered a rising star in the party. The 4th CCP congress elected him to the central committee (CC) and Politburo, and he became head of the party's propaganda department and edited CCP organs.

Favoring a proletarian revolution, Peng opposed continued collaboration with the GUOMINDANG (GMD) when relations worsened in 1926–1927. After Chen Duxiu was dismissed from CCP leadership in August 1927, Peng lost his party posts and in 1929 both he and Chen were expelled from the party. They organized a Trotskyist opposition group which was soon rent by internal quarrels. In 1932, Peng and Chen were arrested in Shanghai by GMD authorities, imprisoned after a lengthy trial and released in 1937 when a general amnesty was declared after the outbreak of the Sino-Japanese war (1937–1945).

Though Chen had left the movement, Peng remained faithful to Trotskyism. When the Sino-Japanese war ended, he published various journals in the name of the Chinese Communist Party Left Opposition, later called the Chinese Revolutionary Communist Party. He fled Shanghai on the eve of the CCP triumph in 1949 and in 1950 went to Paris where he worked for the Fourth (Trotskyist) INTERNATIONAL and published articles attacking the CCP. He later moved to the United States.

P'ENG TE-HUAI see PENG DEHUAI.

PENG ZHEN (P'eng Chen) (1902–) Chinese Communist leader. Born into a poor peasant family in Shanxi, Peng managed to study while working and was influenced by CHEN DUXIU's radical periodical, *New Youth*, and Communist literature. In 1923 he joined the Socialist Youth Corps and that same year also joined the CHINESE COMMUNIST PARTY (CCP). He was one of the founders of the Shanxi provincial CCP and later was assigned to organize workers and students in the Tianjin area. Betrayed by a comrade, he was arrested and imprisoned in Tianjin and led prisoners' hunger strikes. He was released in 1935, became head of the CCP's north China organization department and led the party's clandestine activities. In 1936–1937 he worked with LIU SHAOQI in capitalizing upon student agitation for a united front against Japan. At the outbreak of the Sino-Japanese war (1937–1945), he was sent to help establish the Shanxi-Chahar-Hebei base area. In 1941 he was called to Yan'an, the CCP capital, where he became educational director of the Central Party School. In 1943 he served as the school's assistant director and was active in the rectification campaign against unorthodox thinking. In 1944 he became head of the CCP organization department and was elected to the CCP central committee and the Politburo in 1945.

During the GMD-CCP civil war (1946–1949) Peng filled important political posts in the northeast and continued to head the party's organization department. With the establishment of the People's Republic of China in October 1949, Peng served in the government, specializing in political and legal work, and was Beijing's mayor from 1951–1966. The 8th CCP congress in 1956 confirmed his high party posts, ranking him just below DENG XIAOPING. Starting in 1956, he led several CCP delegations on overseas visits. He went to Moscow several times in the 1960s in futile attempts to settle the Sino-Soviet dispute.

Peng was one of the earliest victims of the Cultural Revolution (see GREAT PROLETARIAN CULTURAL REVOLUTION). Considered at the time one of China's most powerful political figures and a possible successor to MAO ZEDONG, Peng came under attack in May 1966 for protecting subordinates who had criticized Mao. In June he was dismissed from all posts and in December was subjected to humiliating criticism at a mass rally in Beijing.

Peng was one of the last targets of the Cultural Revolution to be rehabilitated. In February 1979 the CC cleared him of all charges and his high party positions were subsequently restored. In 1983 he was elected chairman of the National People's Congress, China's legislature. Though he opposed Maoist extremism, Peng is part of the old guard conservative faction that feels that Deng Xiaoping's reforms have been taken too far in the other direction.

PENRUDDOCK'S RISING (March 1655) A rebellion of English royalists under Colonel John Penruddock (1619–1655), who seized Salisbury and proclaimed Charles II king. The 200 rebels were easily defeated by CROMWELL's forces. The leaders were executed and many of the others were sent to Barbados. The Cromwellians used the rebellion as the excuse to put the entire country under military rule, with major-generals in charge of particular districts.

PEOPLE'S LIBERATION ARMY The present-day Chinese Communist armed forces. Originally called the RED ARMY when it was formed in 1927, the CHINESE COMMUNIST PARTY (CCP) army was renamed the EIGHTH ROUTE ARMY (8RA) when it was incorporated into the nationalist army during the Sino-Japanese war (1937–1945). In July 1946, at the onset of the CCP-GUOMINDANG (GMD) civil war (1946–1949), the 8RA and the other CCP force, the NEW FOURTH ARMY, were redesignated the People's Liberation Army (PLA). During the civil war, the PLA grew rapidly and reached a strength of several million when the CCP achieved final victory in October 1949. Comprising the army, navy and air force of the People's Republic of China (PRC), the PLA had a strength of 4 million until 1985, when it began to be reduced and modernized. It is now down to 3 million. The CCP, through its military commission, now headed by party leader and PRC chairman Jiang Zemin, exerts ultimate control over the PLA. However, under the pressure of increased professionalization and modernization, the PLA has developed its own separate institutional identity.

PEOPLE'S RETRIBUTION (Narodnaya Rasprava) A short-lived, conspiratorial organization established among Russian students in August 1869 by SERGEI NECHAEV in keeping with his belief in dictatorial centralism, conspiracy and strict hierarchical discipline. The object of the organization was to do away with "enemies of the revolution." When a member protested Nechaev's methods, he was murdered by Nechaev and a number of others. Nechaev fled abroad but was extradited to Russia and tried. Meanwhile, in December 1869, all the members of the organization were arrested by the police and 84 persons convicted of connection to it were jailed.

PEOPLE'S WILL (Narodnaya Volya) Formed in 1879, *Narodnaya Volya* was an expression of the divergence in the populist movement (see POPULISM) between those influenced by JACOBIN ideas—who believed in personal terror against officials as a means of inspiring the nation to overthrow autocracy and establish a democratic republic—and those influenced by European social democracy, who regarded mass organization, strikes and demonstrations as the key to organizing eventual mass political revolution.

The People's Will adopted organizational forms and ideas that had already taken root among the populists and had led to the assassination of several officials and an attempt on the life of the czar. Political assassination was seen not only as an instrument of vengeance against the cruelties of individual officials, but also as a blow aimed at the very heart of autocracy, "so as to make the entire system tremble." The innovation involved was the transformation of a random series of assassinations into an organized policy of political terror aimed at the highest officials of the State—first and foremost the czar—with the ultimate aim of having the heroic example of the individual's deed against the State galvanize the people into an uprising.

The heart of the People's Will movement was the executive committee, first proposed by a group of ten professional revolutionaries at a meeting in Lipetsk in June 1879 and adopted by a general meeting of populist groups at Voronezh at the end of June. It issued a journal and leaflets that publicized its ideas, and quickly created an impression of great size and activity, playing on the themes of "now or never," and "our cause is not that of a party, but of Russia itself," and emphasizing the total interdependence of the political and economic revolutions advocated by the populists. The executive committee also orchestrated the formation of military groups that played a leading role in the later history of the People's Will, and of urban workers' groups to be propagandized to the values of socialism through the *Rabochaya gazeta* (The workers' gazette).

The assassination of Czar Alexander II on March 1, 1881, after several unsuccessful attempts, was followed closely by the arrest or emigration of the entire executive committee except for VERA FIGNER. Those activists who remained at liberty in Russia were hunted down and jailed by the police in the following three years, and the People's Will was ended as an effective political force. Its outlook and tactics were revived when the Socialist Revolutionary party established its separate conspiratory Battle Group, assassinating hundreds of czarist officials, including members of the royal family and government ministers, in the first decade and a half of the 20th century.

PÉREZ JIMÉNEZ MARCOS   (1914–) Venezuelan dictator, who after not recognizing the election of Jóvito Villalba, launched a coup and was named president in 1952. He remained in power until 1958. His six-year rule can be characterized as a period of the complete suppression of political rights, citizen guarantees and democratic freedom, along with brutal repression, torture and a complete disregard of human rights. He granted new concessions to oil companies to an estimated value of 1,000 million dollars. The urbanization of Caracas took place during his dictatorship.

PERMANENT REVOLUTION   A school of Communist theory, usually associated with the name of LEON TROTSKY, that can be reduced in essence to two propositions, namely (a) that it was possible, in early 20th-century Russia, to pass directly from a feudal to a socialist order (that is, without first passing through a capitalist "bourgeois" period), and (b) that this was possible

only with the cooperation of proletarian revolutions all over Europe, the encouragement of which was therefore BOLSHEVIK Russia's first task. The first part of the theory was accepted by VLADIMIR LENIN; the second was rejected by JOSEPH STALIN, who preferred SOCIALISM IN ONE COUNTRY and finally used Trotsky's ideas as a battering ram to eliminate him from all his party posts.

PERON, JUAN   (1895–1974) and **EVA**   (1919–1952) Argentinian rulers. Juan Peron was raised on the expansive, treeless plains of the Argentinian pampas. As a youth, he lived the life of a gaucho (South American cowboy) on his family's small ranch. Sent off to military college at 16, he proved to be a poor student, but was a tough soldier and a brilliant sportsman. Tall and handsome, he was also witty and charming, with a compelling, persuasive personality and the gift of winning the support of people of diverse political beliefs by convincing them that he shared their convictions and goals.

A military attaché to Fascist Italy in the 1930s, Peron came to idolize BENITO MUSSOLINI. In 1940 he convinced his fellow officers in a rural Argentinian garrison to form a military political organization, the *Grupo de Oficiales Unidos* (GOU) dedicated to reducing government corruption by increasing the military's role in political affairs. Almost all of Argentina's army officers had become members of the GOU by 1943 when it came to power in a military coup, with Peron becoming head of the newly created secretariat of labor and welfare.

Evita (as she became known) Peron also came from the pampas, where her mother, Juana Ibarguren, was the mistress of a married man, Juan Duarte. Duarte rented her a one-room house where she brought up their five children (Evita was the youngest). Ostracized as bastards by their neighbors, the children were even refused permission to attend their father's funeral. Juana supported them after Duante's death by cooking for rich ranchers. Their kitchens provided Evita with her first glimpse of the life-style of the rich, which contrasted starkly with her own. Evita was 13 when her mother found a new protector, who moved them to a bigger house and town, 14 when participation in a school play fired her ambition to become a famous actress, and 15 when she ran away to Buenos Aires with a young tango singer.

Evita had the will to work, learn and suffer deprivation in her search for fame, but was neither talented nor especially attractive. She owed her acting jobs to her stubborn tenacity and a series of carefully chosen lovers in the theatrical business. When she was 23, a wealthy lover's sponsorship started her career in radio. Featured first in radio soap operas, then on magazine covers, she became a well-known figure throughout Argentina. She became Peron's mistress in 1944.

Peron was taking steps to secure his hold on the government. He quelled union leaders who opposed him with jail or threats; countered the attempts of the president (who had been installed as a puppet) to acquire real power by replacing him with someone more amenable and making himself vice-president; and seized control of the military establishment after some generals sought to restore civilian rule.

Peron had announced that the government's goal was to "strengthen national unity by securing greater social justice and an improvement in the standard of living of Argentina." Evita had the idea of broadening Peron's power base to include Argentina's working class. Declaring that, "the unrestricted ambitions of the conservative classes to keep everything for themselves has blinded them to the evidence; whoever wishes to keep everything will lose everything," Peron ignored the objections of employers, and passed laws providing workers with decent living accommodations, guaranteed minimum wages, paid holidays, sick leave, protection from arbitrary dismissal and a salary bonus at Christmas. For the first time, Argentinian workers also benefited from Argentina's prosperity. He united all the trade unions into a single, giant and vociferously pro-Peron organization.

A military coup forced Peron to resign as vice-president in 1945. Fired from the radio station, Evita refused to let Peron give up. She called on her contacts and Peron's supporters in the army, police, ministry of communications and unions. Anti-Peron newspapers were closed down, pro-Peron street demonstrations broke out, and radio stations broadcast Peron's farewell speech live, but these activities only resulted in his arrest. Ordered to arrest Evita too, the police had to leave her behind, unable to cope with her hysterical screaming, tears and threats to attack them. She immediately began organizing massive worker demonstrations that frightened the military into releasing Peron.

Taken from jail, Peron addressed a crowd of 300,000 from the balcony of the presidential palace with a speech resigning from the army and dedicating himself to the cause of Argentina's poor, "the shirtless ones (*descamisados*)." He married Evita the next day.

Juan Peron, in full splendor, with his wife, Evita

Peron won the 1946 election for president with the help of promises to the *descamisados* and dirty tricks which sabotaged his opponents' campaign. However, opposition to Peron's rule grew as Argentina's economy suffered from inflation and declining foreign reserves. Deprived of Evita's energy, guidance and ruthlessness by her death from cancer in 1952, Peron cut back his working hours drastically, preferring to spend time with his 13-year-old mistress. His attacks on the Catholic church and increasing dependence on force rather than reforms to silence criticism alienated many of his supporters. In 1955 he was overthrown by a military coup that revoked most of the economic benefits that his rule had brought to the *descamisados*.

In 1972, Argentina's military government invited Peron to return from exile in Spain. He was elected president, with his second wife Isabel as vice-president, but his ineffective leadership failed to solve Argentina's problems. When he died, the military tried to keep the Peronists' support by making Isabel president and bringing Evita's body back to Argentina, but after annual inflation approached 1000% and civil war almost broke out, Isabel was deposed by a coup and Evita was quietly buried.

PEROVSKAYA, SOFIA (1854–1881) The daughter of the governor of St. Petersburg, Perovskaya had a life-long dislike of her despotic father. Raised and largely self-educated on her mother's estate after her father lost his gubernatorial post in 1866, she soon returned to St. Petersburg to study in the women's courses opened at that time. Her discussions there converted her from a feminist to a political radical.

Eventually, Perovskaya joined the CHAIKOVSKY CIRCLE, becoming one of its central figures and delving deeply into the study of political economy. Her participation in the 1874 TO THE PEOPLE movement led to her first arrest. Acquitted in 1878, she went underground. After another arrest and escape, she returned to revolutionary action, briefly attempting to bridge between those advocating terror and those devoted to mass politics.

Perovskaya's urge for immediate action brought her into the PEOPLE'S WILL and a central role in attempts on the czar's life. When her lover, Zhelyabov, was arrested in February 1881, she took command of the ultimately successful March 1 assassination of Alexander II. She personally carried bombs to a hideout near the assassination site and signalled the assassins. For this she was tried and hanged a month later, becoming the first woman in Russia to be executed for a political offense.

PERU, REVOLUTIONS At the beginning of the 16th century the Spanish invaders, led by Pizarro, had defeated the Inca rulers of Peru and had set up a colonial régime there. Spanish rule was implemented by Spanish soldiers, civil servants and other envoys from Spain. It was generally corrupt and repressive. Opposition came from two widely different sectors of the population.

Great Uprising of 1737. The native Indian population, which included the descendants of Inca rulers, was kept in a situation barely better than slavery. Men were rounded up for forced labor in the mines and in agricultural work. Children aged five worked in the mines for starvation wages. The long-simmering Indian revolt came to a boil with the Great Uprising of 1737, which swept through 16 provinces. However, the Indians lacked weapons; they were easily defeated. Brutal repression followed.

Tupac-Amaru II Uprising. (1789) A number of local revolts kept erupting, fostered by continuing grievances and tales of the former greatness of the Inca empire. In 1789, Tupac-Amaru II, a self-styled descendant of the last Inca emperor, led a new revolt. It was defeated after atrocities had been committed by both sides. There were nearly a 100,000 casualties, of an estimated total population at the time of just over a million.

Creole Population. The other pole of opposition came from the Creole population, that is the descendants of the original Spanish settlers. These were for the most part prosperous and were made increasingly unhappy by the prominent role played in their country by Spanish envoys. Trade restrictions imposed by these envoys and the deeply corrupt nature of the régime hampered economic growth as well as upward mobility for the Creoles. The latter found themselves growing richer and richer while being denied any influence on the political or economic fields.

The members of the Creole society had various goals. There were those who sought greater freedom from Spain while remaining loyal to the Spanish monarchy, while others stressed the need to grant greater freedom and more humane conditions to the Indian population. The liberal fringe of Creole society was also the most articulate. Thinkers and doers such as José Baquijany y Carillo, Toribo Rogriguez de Mendoza and Hipolito Unanue left their marks on the generation of students who were to lead Peru to independence. A gradual economic decline, which had started by the middle of the 18th century, made matters worse. The great silver mines, for so long the mainstay of the country, were nearly exhausted.

1821 Independence Proclamation. Against this background of social and economic unrest, the political upheavals in the old and new worlds at the end of the 18th century and the beginning of the 19th had a devastating effect. The American colonies successfully rebelled against England; the FRENCH REVOLUTION swept throughout Europe. France conquered Spain and Napoleon's brother Joseph sat on the throne of Castille. Throughout the other Spanish colonies of South America, the fight for independence began, led by SIMON BOLIVAR and JOSÉ DE SAN MARTIN. Venezuela, Colombia and Ecuador broke free. San Martin crossed into Peru to take the lead of an uneasy coalition: liberals who wanted independence for ideological reasons, a prosperous middle class wanting to be free of restrictions and diehard conservatives unhappy about the changes which were taking place in Spain.

Independence was proclaimed in 1821 in the newly liberated capital of Peru, Lima. The first congress was convened but could not make up its mind as to the future régime: monarchy or republic, strong central government or federal régime. A weak constitution was voted in, solving nothing. The first of what was going to be a long list of military coups took place. After three years of instability and renewed attempts by the Spanish troops—who even briefly took over Lima—newly independent Peru would find a period of stability under the rule of General La Mar.

The country's problems, however, were far from solved. The economic situation was steadily worsening, the mines having been abandoned and the principal ports destroyed. More important perhaps, the Indians were no better off and their fight for better living conditions would carry into the 20th century.

PESTEL, PAVEL IVANOVICH (1793–1826) A leader of the DECEMBRIST movement. The son of a high-ranking czarist official, Pestel was educated at the exclusive Pages' School, and became an army officer who served throughout the Napoleonic War, rising to the rank of colonel.

Pestel, leader of the Southern Union in the Decembrist movement, was essentially an ideologue rather than an organizer. He composed the Russian Truth (*Russkaia pravda*) as a program for political reconstruction after the abolition of czarism. The régime he proposed was a mixture of republican egalitarianism based on equality before the law and universal suffrage; a mixed economy with both free enterprise and half the land socially owned and periodically redistributed to assure equality; and authoritarian control over the life of citizens, with a ban on all private organizations, prohibition of alcohol and card-playing, and close surveillance of private conduct. Regarding the national minorities, Pestel advocated their assimilation into Russian society, except for the Poles, who would be granted independence, and the Jews, who, if unwilling to assimilate, would be encouraged to emigrate en masse and establish their own state outside the empire.

On December 14, 1825, the day that the uprising was scheduled in St. Petersburg, Pestel was arrested by the czar's police. Despite a complete confession and recantation, Pestel was one of five Decembrists hanged for the uprising on July 13, 1826.

PETERLOO MASSACRE (August 16, 1819) This name was given to the violent suppression of a mass meeting in Manchester, England. When perhaps 80,000 gathered to hear Henry "Orator" Hunt speak of the economic distress of the Lancashire handloom weavers, the local magistrates panicked and attempted to arrest him. Troops fought their way through the crowd, killing 11 people and wounding perhaps another 400. The massacre became a symbol of repressive government in Britain, made worse by the passing of new legislation, the Six Acts, designed to prevent further meetings of this kind.

PETERS, YAKOV (1886–1938) Latvian revolutionary and Soviet police official. An early recruit (1904) to revolution, Peters spent two years in prison before emigrating to London in 1909. Coopted to the central committee of the Social Democratic party of Latvia in early 1917, his activities after October centered on Petrograd and Central Asia, as a leading official of the political police. He helped put down the Left Social Revolutionary rebellion in July 1918, led the investigations against foreign diplomats suspected of fomenting counterrevolution and in 1920–1922 organized the suppression of political opposition in Central Asia. He was prominent in the Moscow organization of the Communist Party when he was arrested in December 1937, at the height of the STALIN purges. He was executed some months later.

PETLYURA, SYMON (1879–1926) Ukrainian socialist and nationalist leader. Joining the socialist movement in the Ukraine while still a youth, Petlyura was expelled from the church seminary in which he was studying. His socialist activities focused on journalism and took him to various parts of the Russian empire. In 1911, he settled in Moscow and later in St. Petersburg. He wrote for a newspaper entitled *Ukrainian Life*. During World

War I, Petlyura organized aid for soldiers.

In April 1917, when the First All-Ukrainian national congress confirmed the Central Rada, Petlyura was elected one of two vice-presidents and he was active in attempting to establish a national army. He was also involved in negotiations for Ukraine's autonomy, first with the Provisional Government and then with the BOLSHEVIKS.

Under arrest during the German-sponsored rule of Pavlo Skoropadsky, Petlyura was part of the Directory led by VOLODYMYR VYNNYCHENKO that took power following the surrender of Germany in November 1918. He headed the Ukrainian forces that captured Kiev in December 1918. Within the new Directory, Petlyura led the faction opposed to any compromise with the BOLSHEVIKS and was a supporter of Ukraine's declaration of war against Soviet Russia in January 1919.

Divided within itself and unable to command sufficient resources, the Directory lost both authority and territory and was unable to maintain public order or field an effective fighting force. In April 1919, Petlyura formed a new Directory, but once again was thwarted by internal division and weakness, which continued despite his assuming the title in November of Supreme Ataman, with sweeping powers. A Polish-Ukrainian treaty of April 1920, negotiated between Petlyura and Pilsudski, brought temporary success against the Bolsheviks, but the Ukrainian government was forced into exile in mid-1921 and Petlyura eventually settled in Paris. He was assassinated there, allegedly for his guilt in regard to the brutal pogroms against Ukraine's Jews in 1918–1921.

PETRASHEVSKY CIRCLE   Between 1845 and 1849, a minor clerk in the Russian ministry of foreign affairs was host to a cultural salon that evolved into a discussion group embracing Fourierist socialism. Mikhail Butashevich-Petrashevsky, a small landowner, was a devotee of rationalism and scientific progress and saw himself destined to elevate humanity. Never an established writer, he published a dictionary of foreign words and phrases in which he succeeded in expounding many of his ideas of social reform.

Each week for four years, invited guests exchanged philosophical ideas, political gossip, world news and social criticism. His guests included such figures as Dostoevsky and the Slavophile publicist, Nikolai Danilevsky, as well as army officers, dilettante intelligentsia and government officials. Petrashevsky used his salon to advance the ideas of the French socialist Fourier against laissez-faire liberalism and communism, as well as for encouraging criticism of Russia's existing politics, society and religion. Petrashevsky adhered strictly to concepts of non-violent democratic persuasion in formulating his socialist outlook.

In April 1849, at a banquet in honor of Fourier's birthday, Petrashevsky noted that the creation of a socialist society was particularly difficult in Russia as it was "an ignorant country," on whose "savage soil" existed hardships of which Western European socialists could not conceive. Two weeks later, Petrashevsky and 30 of those who frequented his weekly gatherings were arrested and 100 more were under investigation for their "conspiracy of ideas." In the atmosphere of political fear created in Russia by the REVOLUTIONS OF 1848, Petrashevsky and 20 others were condemned to death. The death sentences were com-

muted to life-long exile, and Petrashevsky died in Siberia in 1866, at the age of 45.

PHILIPPINE NATIONAL MOVEMENT   The Philippine movement for independence from Spain had its roots in the second half of the 19th century, starting by way of student protests against Spanish corruption and greed. In 1896, a movement known as Katipunan emerged, headed by a self-educated warehouseman named Andres Bonifacio. In August 1896, the movement launched a revolt against Spain, but after initial successes was met by savage repression and forced to take to the hills. The rebel commander, EMILIO AGUINALDO, concluded a truce with the Spaniards and, having received a large sum of money, was permitted to go into exile in Hong Kong.

Next, war broke out between Spain and the United States, and the latter's armed forces invaded the Philippines. Though the Spaniards were quickly beaten by the United States forces, defeating the Malay insurgents, now again commanded by Aguinaldo—who had returned from exile—proved more difficult. Finally, in March 1901 Aguinaldo himself was captured by the United States army and was instrumental in signing a treaty that brought the insurgency to an end; however, this merely shifted the struggle for Philippine independence from the military to the political sphere. Already in 1901, a civilian government was established. In 1907, a bicameral Philippine legislature elected by the Filipinos themselves was created and in 1913 its powers were extended. In 1933, the Filipino revolutionaries were so far successful that the US Congress, in the Hare-Hawes-Cutting Act, was forced to set a date for Philippine independence; in 1935 a commonwealth was declared.

The Japanese invasion of December 1941 split the Philippine revolutionary movement. While one wing collaborated with the Japanese and formed a government under Jose Laurel, other members turned to guerrilla warfare. Most of the participants in the various guerrilla groups were of middle-class, urban origin and pro-American in their views; some, however, were of a rural background and represented a left-wing, Communist, approach. The Americans under General MacArthur, who returned to the Philippines in late 1944, naturally favored their own partisans and made one of these, Manuel A. Roxas, their candidate for the presidency. Elections were held, Roxas won, and on July 4, 1946, the Philippine republic was proclaimed. With that, the great Philippine national revolution arrived at its triumphant conclusion.

PHOENICIA REBELLION   see SATRAPS, REVOLTS OF.

PIJADE, MOSA   (1890–1957) Yugoslav revolutionary and Communist leader. Born in Belgrade to Jewish parents, Pijade originally studied painting abroad and then earned his livelihood as an art teacher, but was jailed in 1921, a year after joining the banned Yugoslav Communist Party. During his second and much longer term of imprisonment for revolutionary agitation (1925–1939), Pijade made his name by translating KARL MARX's *Das Kapital* into Serbian. The German-led invasion and occupation of Yugoslavia in April 1941 transformed him into a national hero: serving under JOSIP BROZ TITO, he became an outstanding organizer of the Communist partisans and Yugoslavia's most prominent Jewish resistance fighter.

Mosa Pijade, a Communist leader of Yugoslavia

When Tito assumed the premiership after the liberation (1945), Pijade was already one of his closest associates. Apart from safeguarding Yugoslav interests at postwar allied conferences, he helped draft Yugoslavia's new constitution and, as president of the Serbian republic, became one of the nation's four vice-presidents (with Tito as federal head of state). It was Pijade, the ranking Communist theoretician, who played a major role in distancing Yugoslavia from Moscow and the Cominform (1948), bringing it closer to the west. He also served as a key figure in the Politburo and as chairman of Yugoslavia's National Assembly, the federal parliament.

PILSUDSKI, JOZEF KLEMENS (1867–1935) Polish revolutionary and dictator. Pilsudski came from an old Polish-Lithuanian family. Although the once-powerful kingdom of Poland and Lithuania had disappeared—partitioned among Austria, Prussia and Russia in the 18th century—the desire for an independent Poland was still alive in the years Pilsudski grew up. Having suppressed a revolt in Polish Lithuania in 1864, Russia attempted to prevent further uprisings by prohibiting the teaching of the Polish language, literature and history. Nonetheless, Pilsudski's mother, like many others, continued to teach her children their Polish heritage in secret.

The Pilsudski family manor burned down and the family moved to Wilno (Vilnius). Life in cosmopolitan Wilno was the source of Pilsudski's tolerance and his firmly-held convictions that different peoples can live together. The contempt and ridicule for Polish culture expressed by the teachers at the Russian high school he attended deepened his feelings of patriotism toward Poland and resentment toward Russia.

Pilsudski's medical studies were permanently interrupted in 1886 when he was charged with participating in a plot to assassinate the czar. His trial made it clear that he was innocent but, as a known Polish nationalist with socialist sympathies, he was considered potentially dangerous and sentenced to five years in Siberia. His Siberian exile gave him the leisure to study history and socialism, experience the Russian empire from within and meet with other exiled revolutionaries. In 1892 he returned to Wilno with his socialism confirmed.

Poland had two socialist parties, one seeking to incorporate Poland into Russia for economic reasons, and the other, the Polish Socialist Party, wanting an independent Poland. Pilsudski joined the latter, becoming one of its leaders and the editor of its newspaper. Imprisoned in February 1902 for his activities, he faked insanity and escaped from a Russian military hospital. During the 1904 Russo-Japanese war he was in Tokyo, where he tried to persuade Japan that supporting revolution among Russia's subject nationalities was the best way to weaken Russia. His efforts failed because a rival from Poland's pro-Russian socialist party convinced Japan that Pilsudski's plan would only waste their time and money. Pilsudski returned to Poland to take an active part in the RUSSIAN REVOLUTION OF 1905. However his time in Japan had aroused his interest in military matters.

A European war was clearly on the horizon. Pilsudski studied military strategy, organized a secret Union of Military Action in 1908 (paid for with money he had stolen from a Russian mail train), and by 1914 had over 10,000 trained Polish soldiers. World War I found Poland divided over which side to join. Convinced that only the collapse of the Russian empire would give independent Poland a chance to be reborn, Pilsudski commanded a brigade in the volunteer Poland Legion fighting for the Central Powers (the Austrian and German empires) against Russia.

In 1916, Germany, hoping that a Polish army would solve its manpower shortage, proclaimed the creation of a Polish protectorate and appointed Pilsudski head of its Military Commission. Courageous, stubborn and with a gift for influencing people, Pilsudski refused to make the Polish troops swear a special oath of allegiance to the Central Powers. He was imprisoned and the Polish legions were dissolved, but his prestige and popularity in Poland increased as a result of his stand.

In 1918, when Germany's defeat freed him, Pilsudski was a national hero. He returned to Poland and became provisional head of state and commander in chief. Poland was in chaos: war devastation, starvation and lawlessness were widespread; Poles had become accustomed to resisting authority; prolonged unemployment and inflation had radicalized the working class; after the RUSSIAN REVOLUTION OF 1917 socialist leftists had formed a strong Communist Party advocating union with Russia; and the Russian RED ARMY was advancing into lands that were vacated by the Germans.

Pilsudski attempted to solve Poland's problems with domestic reforms while fighting the Red Army with mixed success. In

1921, Poland adopted a democratic constitution and held elections. Pilsudski became chief of the general staff, but resigned when a right-wing government came to power in 1923. His retirement lasted only three years before conditions in Poland led him to topple the government with a military coup; although he refused the presidency, his position as minister of defense left him as Poland's real ruler.

As dictator, Pilsudski mercilessly suppressed a 1930 center-left plot to overthrow his government. He wanted to take military action against Germany when Hitler came to power, but France (with which Poland had a defense treaty) refused. Although Pilsudski signed a 10-year non-aggression pact with Germany in 1934, he refused to meet HITLER or form a Polish-German anti-Soviet alliance. He died in 1936, was buried in the church that also contains the remains of Poland's kings and, after undergoing an eclipse during the period of Nazi and Communist rules, is now once again revered as the founder of the modern Polish state.

PISACANE, CARLO   (1818–1857) Italian revolutionary.

Forced to leave a promising military career because of a romantic affair, Pisacane went into self-imposed exile in 1847 and became attracted to the Italian nationalist cause as espoused by GIUSEPPE MAZZINI. He returned to Italy in 1849 to assist the Milanese revolutionary government against the Austrians and the Roman Republic in its war with France, serving as chief of staff in the latter conflict. He later described these events in *Guerra combattuta in Italia negli anni 1848–1849* (The war fought in Italy 1848–1849).

Soon after, Pisacane was converted to the socialist nationalism espoused by Carlo Branco. He argued that a bourgeoise nationalist victory might free Italy, but it could not free the lower classes from poverty and exploitation. This would require radical social reforms, including the expropriation of the possessions of the upper classes and the collectivization of agriculture and industry, leading to a new "social contract" uniting the people of Italy. The true liberation of Italy, he argued, would come about through a peasant revolution.

Pisacane was killed on a military expedition which went out to assist in a peasant revolt in the Kingdom of Naples. His political magnum opus, *Saggi storici-, politici-, militari-sull'Italia* (*Historical, Political, and Military Essays on Italy*), was published posthumously between 1858 and 1860.

PISAREV, DMITRI IVANOVICH   (1840–1868) Radical

Russian literary critic. Unlike most of his predecessors, Pisarev extolled the idea of the individual rather than that of society. He advanced concepts of egoism and self-interest as the keys to human progress, though he wrote that it was only natural that an enlightened person would work for the betterment of humanity in general, since the majority, who were either poor because they were ignorant, or ignorant because they were poor, stood in need of the leadership of an educated elite. While still in his early 20s, Pisarev became the idol of the radical youth he called Nihilists. His thoughts on the family, the role of women and all social conventions and authority helped form his generation. In 1862, he was sentenced to four and a half years' imprisonment for a scathing attack on the ruling dynasty and its bureaucracy, but continued to publish his writings even from prison.

Pisarev was a devotee of science. He regarded literature as useful only if it advanced the cause of rationality and material welfare in society, and once stated that there was more good in a pair of boots than in all of Shakespeare. His ideal was a society of modern, technologically-inclined entrepreneurs, whose enterprises would be managed by cultured and enlightened people considerate of the interests of those who labored in them. Two years after his release from prison, Pisarev drowned during an outing to the Baltic coast.

PISONIAN CONSPIRACY   The maltreatment of the Roman

aristocracy by the emperor Nero and his frivolous behavior induced several prominent senators and many Roman equites (cavalrymen) to form a conspiracy against him in 65 A.D. They agreed to kill the despotic emperor and chose as their leader Gaius Calpurnius Piso, a scion of an old noble family and a popular figure in Rome. Some of the conspirators may have wished to restore the republican régime. The conspiracy was betrayed, however. Piso, the poet Lucan and the senior statesman Seneca, whose participation on the conspiracy is doubtful, were forced to commit suicide. Nero had 20 conspirators executed and others exiled.

PKK (Workers Party of Kurdistan)   A Kurdish organization,

founded in the mid 1970s by Abdallah Ocalan, a Kurdish student in Ankara (see KURDISH REVOLT).

PLEBEIANS, REVOLT OF THE   The society of ancient

Rome consisted of two classes of people: patricians and plebeians. By the early 5th century B.C., the patricians had monopolized the position of magistrates and the priestly colleges. They were the only ones who had the knowledge of the law and intermarriage between the classes was not allowed. The patricians were well-to-do, while the plebeians included poor and indebted people and those dependent, legally or economically, on the wealthy patricians. The origins of this differentiation, however, are obscure.

The internal history of Rome until the early 3rd century B.C. is largely the struggle of the plebeians to acquire equal rights with the patricians and to solve their economic grievances. To some extent, this struggle justifies the declaration of MARX in the Manifest of the Communist Party (1848), that the history of human society is that of class war, referring specifically to the confrontation between patricians and plebeians. However, in Rome the struggle never evolved into open war and did not end in a revolutionary change, contrary to the axiomatic declaration of the Manifest. Whenever the plebeians felt that they could not tolerate their conditions any longer, they embarked on a *secessio* (withdrawal), that is, they retired from Rome to a nearby site. The patricians were wise enough to yield to their demands, thus precluding violent clashes. Five such secessions are recorded (in the years 494, 449, 445, 342 and 287 B.C.), but whether all indeed occurred is doubtful. In the course of this struggle, the plebeians formed their own assembly and officials (tribunes and aediles), the Roman law was published, public land was distributed to poor citizens, the laws of debts were relaxed, the position of magistrate was opened to the plebeians and finally even the priestly colleges became open to them. The long struggle finally ended in 287 B.C., when a law was enacted that resolutions of the assembly of the plebeians (*plebiscitum*) would have the force of regular laws.

PLEKHANOV, GEORGI VALENTINOVICH (1857–1918)

Russian revolutionary. Living abroad from 1880, Plekhanov created the Russian Social Democratic Labor Party in 1883. After the party split into BOLSHEVIKS and MENSHEVIKS (1903), he joined neither faction but took an independent stand. After the February RUSSIAN REVOLUTION OF 1917 he returned to Russia, where he tried to raise support for the continuation of the war, a position which cost him all his influence when VLADIMIR LENIN and the Bolsheviks took over.

PLO see PALESTINE LIBERATION ORGANIZATION.

POKROVSKY, MIKHAIL NIKOLAYEVICH (1868–1932)

Russian Bolshevik revolutionary and historian. Pokrovsky graduated in history from Moscow University in 1891, a student of V.O. Kliuchevsky. He was first active in liberal circles, joining the BOLSHEVIKS in 1905 and taking part in the abortive December RUSSIAN REVOLUTION OF 1905 in Moscow.

In 1909, Kliuchevsky was among the founders of the left-Bolshevik *Vpered* group, and taught at the Bolshevik party school organized by Gorky in Capri. He later returned to historical research and revolutionary journalism in Paris.

In August 1917 he returned to Russia as a Bolshevik. He became chairman of the Moscow Soviet, serving on its military-revolutionary committee. Although a member of the Russian delegation to the Brest-Litovsk peace negotiations, Pokrovsky joined BUKHARIN's left Communist faction in opposing acceptance of the draconian terms of peace with Germany.

In May 1918 he became deputy minister of education, a post he held until his death. He instituted major educational reforms, incorporating history into departments of social sciences in the universities, and instituting "workers' faculties" (the *rabfak*) for preparing adult workers for higher education. During the 1920s he wrote several major historical works that offered a Marxist interpretation of Russian history.

Throughout the 1920s he held a succession of administrative posts, supervising the institutionalization of Marxist historiography. He directed the Central Archive Administration and the Association of Marxist Historians, and headed the history sections both of the Communist Academy and of the Institute of Red Professors. From 1928, Pokrovsky was active in the purge and arrest of non-Marxist historians. Despite his dogged devotion to writing and teaching history according to the needs of the Communist Party, Pokrovsky was attacked for insufficient party-mindedness, but died before he could be disgraced. In mid-1934, ideological decisions of the Communist Party, authored by Andrei Zhdanov and Sergei Kirov, condemned the "mechanistic economism" of Pokrovsky's work and called for more emphasis on the importance of the leaders of any historical change. His work was removed from school use and only appeared again in 1957 following his rehabilitation.

POLAND, REVOLTS AND REVOLUTIONS

Liberal Revolution of 1794. Russia invaded Poland in 1792 in order to thwart the liberal reforms that had gone into effect in Poland following the first partition. The second and third partitions of 1793 and 1795 between Russia, Prussia and Austria put an end to the Polish state until 1918. In 1794, a popular insurrection against the Russians broke out under the leadership of TADEUZ KOSCIUSKO. This combined national and social aims. A partial liberalization in the rights of the peasants and the mass mobilization of 150,000 men were the main achievements of the insurrectionists. There were elements of Jacobinism and terror in the policies of the rebels.

The Polaniec Manifesto promised personal freedom for the serfs if they would join Kosciusko's forces, which many did. The insurgents' defeat by Russian troops and the capitulation of Warsaw at the end of 1794 ended all attempts by the Polish to free themselves, both socially and nationally. The influence of the FRENCH REVOLUTION was nevertheless evident and after the defeat the JACOBIN-oriented Society of Polish Republicans continued subversive activities. The Polish legions fighting in France's revolutionary wars were yet another legacy of the Polish struggle for independence.

Insurrection of 1830. This insurrection took place in Congress Poland under Russian rule. Nationalist stirrings were organized by secret societies that emerged under Czar Alexander I's rule and intensified after 1825 under the reign of Czar Nicholas I. As the Russian czar planned to send a Polish army against France and Belgium following the 1830 revolutions there, a republican insurrection with a romantic nationalist spirit broke out in Congress Poland. The army and most of the politicians joined in military and constitutional opposition to the Russian autocracy as a formal war was waged between Russia and breakaway Poland from January to September 1831. The aim was full Polish indepedendence. Historians note the "ineptitude" of the original leaders of the insurrection, which made the formulation of clear political aims slow and even unclear. From a moderate stance at the beginning of the insurrection, the leadership was taken over by more radical elements supported by the Warsaw mob. A military clique held power until superior czarist forces crushed the insurrection. Thousands of its leaders were jailed or exiled. Harsh Russian steps were taken to break Polish nationalism; in 1832, an Organic Statute replaced the previous liberal constitution. The army and Polish lands were subject to direct Russian rule, although a few autonomous rights still remained.

Insurrection of January 1863. Another manifestation of Polish nationalism was sparked off by a clash between patriotic youth and pro-Russian elements among the Polish leadership. It was led by the Polish aristocrat Count Alexander Wielopolski, the head of the Civil Administration of the Kingdom of Poland (Congress Poland). The Polish revolutionaries relied on French and Austrian support, which failed to arrive. The Polish revolutionary government was crushed in April 1864, followed by widespread Russian terror, executions and deportations. Hopes for a free and united Polish state faded and did not materialize until the end of World War I.

Nationalist Movement. In World War I, the Polish national movement was divided as to what the best path was to achieve complete independence. The country's division between three warring powers—Germany, Austria-Hungary and Russia—left some place for maneuvering. Roman Dmowski, the father of modern Polish nationalism, was convinced that Germany was Poland's greatest foe and promoted Polish support of the Russian-French alliance. Russian promises for a Polish entity under the Russian system should Czarist Russia emerge victorious raised hopes among Dmowski's camp. The Polish left, led by PILSUDSKI, believed that Russia posed the greatest danger to Poland and that full independence could be reached only with the collapse of the three partitioning powers. Polish troops under Pilsudski fought for a time with the Central Powers in what was seen as a tactical alliance by the Polish side. After the RUSSIAN REVOLUTION OF 1917, the mainstream Polish nationalist movement turned against the Central Powers, as the Polish National Committee laid the diplomatic groundwork for the emergence of a free and independent Poland. With the collapse of the Central Powers and given the participation of a Polish army composed of volunteers in France and a Polish Legion led by Pilsudski and numbering some 20,000 against the Central Powers, a new Poland emerged as an outcome of both the Polish nation's determination and of the war and the principles of Wilson's Fourteen Points. With its borders in flux and the rival factions of Pilsudski and Dmowski quarrelling over the political system, orientation and borders, a new independent, yet shaky Polish state was reborn. Its emergence was perceived by Polish nationalists less as a result of the war's outcome than of the success of the Polish nation, which had never accepted the partition of the country.

Communist Takeover 1947. The Communist takeover, which was completed in 1947–1948, followed a clear pattern. The Communist-dominated Polish Committee of National Liberation, or the Lublin Committee, was formed in July 1944 as an executive body, a nucleus of a government that included two former members of the Polish government in exile, which gradually took control of the devastated country. The Communists held the most important positions and were in effective control of main government agencies and ministries, as interior, justice, information and the armed forces. Redistribution of land, including areas which had been inhabited by Germans on the former German territories, assured widespread peasant support for the Communists. Supported by STALIN's drive to communize Eastern Europe, they continued their campaign of removing their opponents. Land reforms and the nationalization of major enterprises at the end of 1945 removed the landed gentry and much of the middle class from economic influence. The formula agreed upon at the Yalta conference on "free and unfettered elections" was never implemented. In the first elections held in January 1947, the government front controlled by the Communists won 80.1% of the votes whereas the Polish Peasants Party won only 10% after a long psychological and terror campaign against the leadership of party leader Stanislaw Mikolajczyk, who fled the country. In December 1948, the Polish United Workers party was formed, with the Communists, by means of "unification," eliminating the left after having acted to delegitimize and remove the peasant opposition. By the end of 1948, the party leaders BOLESLAW BIERUT and WLADYSLAW GOMULKA were in total control of the country.

Communist Collapse 1989. The collapse of the Communist régime took place against the background of Poland's continuing crisis following the imposition of martial law in 1981 and the clampdown on Solidarity, the demise of Communist authority, the emergence of reform wings within the party and the trends influenced by Gorbachev's reforms in the Soviet Union. Opposition to the régime intensified as the underground Solidarity reemerged legally as a partner for negotiations with the

régime in April 1989. Roundtable discussions between the opposition and the Communist Party divided the party on the nature of concessions. The deteriorating political and economic situation placed Solidarity in a better bargaining position, with the opposition more united than the Communists, the latter having split into several factions. General Jaruzelski handed over party leadership to Communist party reformers, who in turn tried to save the régime by more concessions. This in turn weakened and ultimately destroyed party rule. The Polish Communists, rapidly losing ground as well as party members in large numbers, were too weak to mount an "offensive" as conservative elements demanded. Attempts to gain some public confidence and legitimation by introducing reforms failed, as the Solidarity-led opposition made clear that the aim was not the introduction of liberal reforms but the dismantling of the Communist system.

Jaruzelski, as the new premier, tried to enlist the Church's support and attempted to overhaul the party. However, the party lost even more of its control and went through an identity crisis. In the June 1989 elections, Solidarity won a spectacular victory and only pre-election arrangements assured a solid Communist representation in the parliament. Power was transferred to the Solidarity-led coalition, as the Communist Party dissolved itself at its last congress in January 1990. The collapse of the Communist system was symbolised by LECH WALESA's election as president in December 1990. Once in power, Solidarity gradually split between rival factions, its previous moral message became somewhat tarnished and, after four Solidarity-led governments, the left returned in the 1993 elections. Solidarity focused its appeal against the government's economic policies and warned that Poland was being "re-communized." Walesa's campaign in the 1995 presidential elections was perhaps Solidarity's last great effort.

POLISARIO (Frente Popular Para la Liberacion de Saguia el-Hamra y Rio de Oro) A national liberation movement in the former Spanish Sahara which, supported by neighboring Algeria, fought a guerrilla war against Moroccan and Mauritanian troops who invaded the country after the Spaniards withdraw in 1976. In February 1976, the Polisario proclaimed the Sahrawi Arab Democratic Republic (SADR), which has since been recognized by 30 member states of the OAU (Organization of African Unity)—to which it was admitted in February 1982 as the 51st member—and by more than 70 countries worldwide. In 1978, following a change in the régime, Mauritania decided to withdrew from the struggle. Morocco, however, under King Hassan II, persisted and has been fighting the rebels ever since. By constructing a sand-berm around the area that contains the Saharan phosphate deposits, the Moroccan army has been able to take charge of the country's main source of wealth and secure it tolerably well against rebel attack. The outlying desert, however, is still being fought over and much of it is in rebel hands.

POL POT (1928–) The name adopted by Saloth Sar, who became leader of the new Kampuchean KHMER ROUGE, the renaissance of the Khmer Rouge which had been disbanded in 1954. After Lon Nol's government replaced that of Norodom Sihanouk (see CAMBODIA, 1970 COUP), the US action in Kampuchea helped to fuel a civil war, which in 1979 resulted in a takeover by Pol Pot's Khmer Rouge. The horrors and atrocities of the resulting Pol Pot "social experiment," which emptied the cities, shut down all major establishments and institutions and effectively closed Kampuchea to the world, have been well documented elsewhere.

POPIELUSZKO, JERZY (1947–1984) Polish pro-Solidarity priest, murdered by elements of the Polish secret police. A popular vicar of a Warsaw neighborhood, Popieluszko was an outspoken opponent of the Jeruzelski régime. His assassination by security service agents resulted in mass demonstrations against the régime, which felt compelled to arrest, bring to justice and convict the agents involved. As the assassination took place in a period of repressive steps against opposition activists on the one hand and attempts to conduct some sort of dialogue with them on the other, it is possible that his murder was a step in a complicated struggle between hard-liners and reformers.

POPISH PLOT   (1678) An imaginary Jesuit conspiracy to murder King Charles II of England, kill Protestants, set fire to London and put the Duke of York (the future James II) on the English throne with the help of Spanish and French troops. The inventors of the calumny were Titus Oates and Israel Tonge, who sparked off a panic which revealed at least one traitor, the duke's secretary, who had indeed been in questionable correspondence with the French. By the time the plot was revealed to be fictitious, about 35 people had been executed, including the unfortunate Roman Catholic primate of Ireland. The Popish Plot also led to the Test Act of 1678, which excluded Roman Catholics from parliament. Oates was convicted of perjury by King James II when the latter ascended to the throne.

POPULISM, RUSSIAN   A revolutionary movement based on the building of socialism in an agrarian society. Although strict interpretations limit the term populism to the period 1860–1890 (some limit it even further—to the years 1874–1878), it is widely applied to the entire pre-Marxist Russian agrarian socialist movement, beginning with ALEXANDER HERZEN.

Populism was the result of the contradictions sensed by those Russian intellectuals who had absorbed the social thought of 18th and 19th-century Europe and were shocked by its variance from the realities of Russian peasant life under the system of autocracy and serfdom. The populists were essentially romantics who attributed the virtues of simplicity, mutual aid and natural wisdom to the Russian peasant. The village commune, based on the democracy of the village meeting and often practicing redistribution of the land to maintain equality, was understood by populists to be a traditional institution of an essentially socialist nature. In addition, the peasants' negation of the concept of private property in land and the mutual aid that typified peasant life were interpreted as elements that showed a natural inclination to collectivism.

The populist movement gathered strength in the wake of Czar Alexander II's freeing of the serfs and the institution of local rural self-government in the form of the *zemstvo* in 1864. However, the limited redistribution of the land and the burden of debt placed on the peasants aroused disappointment and opposition among the INTELLIGENTSIA. The movement for agrarian reform became, among students, a general denial of the morals and

mores of Russian society, leading to a general radicalization marked by atheism, progress-oriented utilitarianism, a redefining of gender and class relations and in the end, political terror. While segments of the population were in sympathy with the radical movement and with the ideas of Nikolay Chernyshevsky, the support of the populists for the 1863 Polish uprising (see POLAND, REVOLTS AND REVOLUTIONS) turned public opinion against them.

Numerous trends of cultural, philosophical and political populism developed in Russia. The terrorism of MICHAEL BAKUNIN and SERGEI NECHAEV, the intellectual dedication to social justice of PETER LAVROV, the intellectual curiosity of MARK NATANSON and Nikolay Chernyshevsky and their followers—all of these contributed to populism. All these trends came together in the summer of 1874 in the TO THE PEOPLE movement, in which some 3,000 young radicals went to the villages to learn about peasant life; serve the peasants as teachers, medical personnel and artisans; and awaken the peasantry to SOCIALISM. About one-quarter of these were arrested and tried, many of them based on accusations from the peasants who rejected the radicals' atheism and opposition to the czar.

The failure of 1874 gave rise to an effort to organize urban workers and artisans as well as to active terrorism as a political weapon against the régime rather than as simple retribution for official cruelties. This led to the PEOPLE'S WILL movement and its assassination of the czar on March 1, 1881. The subsequent reaction blocked all attempts at liberal reform until the RUSSIAN REVOLUTION OF 1905 and the collapse of the autocratic régime in 1917.

Populism was essentially an outgrowth of the rationalist secular enlightenment of Western Europe. In this sense it was foreign to the Orthodox Russian religion and the conservative traditionalism of Russian peasant society. The populist movement, despite its devotion to improving the life of the peasants, never evoked a mass following. It thus moved almost inevitably into the path of revolutionary terror, sealing its own fate as a fringe movement until it evolved into a political party, the Party of Socialist Revolutionaries, which worked on both the mass political and terrorist planes simultaneously.

PO QU   see QIN BANGXIAN.

PORTUGAL, REVOLTS AND REVOLUTIONS
Republican Revolution. (1910) Despite attempts to suppress it, republicanism had been an important feature of Portuguese politics throughout the 19th century. During most of this time it was discussed and debated by upper and middle-class intellectuals, but by the end of the century republicanism and trade unionism had become hallmarks of the working classes, which sought to benefit from the country's rapid industrialization. At the same time, the anticlerical political philosophy of the Italian CARBONARI was making inroads among the working classes and the navy.

The first attempt to overthrow the royal house of the Braganzas was made on October 4, 1910, by a coalition of the navy, low ranking army officers and workers. King Manuel II was at home playing cards that night when the naval ship *Admastor* fired its cannon, signalling the start of the revolution. To everyone's surprise the king simply left his game, boarded a ship and sailed to England. No attempts were to made to stop the rebels and in just a few hours Portugal became Europe's second republic (the first was France). Republican politicians were long prepared to accept office and the transition to democracy proceeded smoothly.

Nevertheless, the new government had several faults, which eventually led to its downfall. Essentially an urban revolution, in many ways the government showed preference to factory workers over the sizeable agricultural community. A currency scam undermined confidence in the economy and corruption gradually entered the civil service. Perhaps most important, however, was the rabid anticlericalism of the government, which pitted the right and left against each other. By the early 1920s, the country was divided into two camps. One, identified with the *Seara Nova* (New Harvest) movement, had a socialist world view; the other, identified with the *Integralismo Lusitano* (Portuguese Fundamentalism) movement, was influenced by European Fascist trends and advocated the abrogation of all the civil liberties attained since the 1910 revolution.

1926 Coup. The country was on the brink of a civil war when, in 1926, a group of conservative Catholic army officers seized power and installed an authoritarian régime. Although the benefits of the republican revolution were suddenly lost, most Portuguese sighed in relief that a sense of stability had been restored to their country.

Officers' Coup (1974). During the final years of António Salazar's dictatorship, Portugal was undergoing dramatic changes. Industry was growing at an unprecedented pace and a nascent labor movement was emerging. The country enjoyed an influx of foreign tourists, who brought with them both hard currency and liberal convictions. Finally, Portugal remained the only major European colonial power in Africa, with all the attendant wealth that this entailed. By the time Salazar retired in 1968, the country seemed ready to catch up with the other states of Western Europe financially, if not politically. However, Salazar's successor, Marcello Caetano, was unable to preserve the momentum of the late 1960s. The unjust distribution of industry in the country (10 families controlled over half the nation's wealth) spurred a revival of socialism and MARXISM, while the army was unhappy with its inability to quell the nationalist uprisings taking place throughout Portuguese Africa.

In early 1973, General ANTONIO SPINOLA returned from Portuguese Guinea, convinced of his country's inability to maintain its colonial empire. In *Portugal and the Future*, published in February 1974, he expressed his belief that the colonial system should be replaced by a free association of independent Portuguese-speaking nations in a commonwealth. The book was particularly popular among Portugal's younger generation of officers, many of whom were generally dissatisfied with the Caetano régime and flirted with socialism. However, the book also earned the contempt of the army's high command: on March 14, Spínola was dismissed from the General Staff. Two days later there was a military uprising in Caldas da Reinha. The uprising was suppressed, but it was an indication of the direction the army was taking.

In the next weeks, the dissatisfied officers organized picnics and other social events in which they discussed the turn of events and planned their coup. The date chosen was April 25. On that day, tanks rolled through the streets of Lisbon while the national radio station played a popular patriotic song, "Land of the Free," repeatedly. Caetano fled to Brazil and in just 12 hours the *Junta de Salvação o Nacional* (Junta of National Salvation) assumed control of the country. Spínola, who was a hero to the young officers, was declared Portugal's new president.

The new government quickly began undoing almost 50 years of Fascist dictatorship. The army and civil service were purged of sympathizers with the old régime, the secret police and the Fascist youth movement were disbanded, censorship of the press was abolished and the colonies were promised independence. But the officers were politically inexperienced and did not know how to carry out their leftist ideology. In the course of just two years, they experimented with "Soviet-style communism," government by committee and rule by triumvirate. Meanwhile, the country was being overwhelmed by an influx of Portuguese settlers from the colonies. The population increased by 10% in just two years and attempts at nationalization and mass expropriations of land could not resolve the economic crisis facing the country. The officers also had to contend with an attempted countercoup by right-wing forces loyal to the old régime and the threat of an extreme left-wing putsch by some of their own ranks, who felt that change was not proceeding at a sufficient pace.

In autumn 1975, a group of moderate right-wing soldiers staged a successful countercoup to ensure that the democratic process was not stopped. They appointed General António Eanes as "keeper of the constitution" and began preparing for the country's first democratic elections in half a century. In 1976, Mario Soares, a socialist, was elected as the first prime minister of a democratic Portugal.

POTEMKIN RISING (June 1905) In a famous incident in the RUSSIAN REVOLUTION OF 1905, the sailors aboard the battleship *Potemkin* mutinied against their officers, complaining of rotten food and harsh regulations. Supported by the people of Odessa, the sailors were able to seize control of the town for a few days but were then driven out, with much loss of life, by the czar's troops. The ship then sailed to Romania, where it was interned. The incident formed the topic of a film by Eisenstein (1925), which is considered one of the greatest cinematic masterpieces of all time.

POTRESOV (STAROVER), ALEXANDER (1869–1934) Russian MENSHEVIK activist. The son of a senior judicial official, Potresov was one of the organizers in 1895 of the St. Petersburg Marxist Union of Struggle for Working Class Emancipation, together with YULY MARTOV and VLADIMIR LENIN. After being arrested and spending two years in prison, Potresov emigrated from Russia in 1900 and joined Martov and Lenin in establishing the Social Democratic newspaper, *Iskra* (the Spark). He left the newspaper's editorial board out of opposition to Lenin and his Bolshevism. For the rest of his life he maintained an active opposition to Bolshevism, which he regarded as a fundamentally corrupt movement.

Following the RUSSIAN REVOLUTION OF 1905, Potresov became active among the Mensheviks and in 1917 was a leader of its "defencist" faction. In March 1917, he attempted to form a broad political grouping of moderate socialists and liberals, the Union of Renaissance (*Soyuz vozrozhdeniia*). He was an outspoken opponent of the BOLSHEVIK seizure of power in the October RUSSIAN REVOLUTION OF 1917 and formed ties with French and English diplomats to gain military assistance against the Bolsheviks.

In 1924 he emigrated to Paris, where he wrote for the emigré socialist press and published his memoirs, entitled *Notes of a Social Democrat.*

POTTIER, EUGÈNE (1816–1887) French *chansonnier*, writer of popular songs, ditties and ballads; chiefly remembered as the author of the *Internationale*. This song, originally written to celebrate the PARIS COMMUNE of 1871, was later adopted as the revolutionary hymn of the Communists and the official anthem of the USSR.

Born of a provincial working-class family, Pottier began earning a modest living as a fabric designer and minor school official, but showed an early talent for writing lyrics and composing music. He published his first song, *Vive la Liberté*, at the tender age of 14. An ardent revolutionary, atheist and, above all, a fanatical opponent of militarism, he remained loyal to his proletarian roots despite his success as an entertainer, and contributed to disseminating revolutionary ideas at the popular level of Parisian cabarets and music halls. He played an active part in the June Revolution of 1848 (see REVOLUTIONS OF 1848), barely escaping with his life after its suppression, joined the First INTERNATIONAL at its inception and ended his turbulent political career as a member of the central committee of the Paris Commune in 1871. After the revolution was crushed, he managed to evade capture by fleeing, first to England, then to the United States, but returned to France in 1880, along with other amnestied *Communards*, to a triumphant welcome among his many fans and admirers.

Two of the most famous verses he wrote for the *Internationale* are the one containing a tribute to the memory of the legendary revolutionary LOUIS AUGUSTE BLANQUI and another calling on soldiers to turn their rifles against their own officers in order to bring war to an end. The *Internationale* was first performed in 1888 at a workers' congress in the industrial city of Lille to the music of a local delegate, Pierre de Geyter, who composed his score in a single night.

POZAN RIOTS (June 1956) Following the death of JOSEPH STALIN in 1953, the Polish Communist leadership felt it could afford to relax its control by setting free 100,000 political prisoners and abolishing the hateful ministry of the interior. These reforms, however, merely served to whet public expectations. In June 1956 a general strike broke out in the important industrial town of Poznan and riots followed. These were finally suppressed by the (Russian) minister of defense, Rokossovsky, but not before 53 people had been killed and over 200 wounded. Poland thus became the second Eastern European country (after East Germany) to attempt some kind of rebellion against Soviet-imposed Communist rule; it was followed by Hungary, which rose (unsuccessfully) in October of that year.

PRAGUE, SPRING OF 1968 The period of liberal reforms in Czechoslovakia from ALEXANDER DUBCEK's appointment as Communist Party (CP) leader in January 1968 to August 20, 1968, when a Soviet invasion brutally ended the unique attempt to reform the régime. In April of that year, the CP's Action Program

proclaimed far-reaching economic reforms, such as decentralization of planning and management, competition and elements of a free market. These same proposals later appeared in Gorbachev's reforms in the Soviet Union after 1985. The program was formulated by Ota Sik, the driving force behind the radical economic reforms, and envisaged a New Economic Model with far reaching political and social consequences. This was in fact never implemented, due to the Soviet invasion. The emerging "socialism with a human face" in the Prague Spring assured human rights and sought to reform the system by popular participation and internal democratization, through a complete overhaul of the system and a genuine restructuring of the Czechoslovakian federal structure. In June 1968, the *Manifesto of 2000 Words*, written by a group of intellectuals led by Ludvik Vaculik, brought an explosion of intellectual and artistic creativity and assured the support of the intellectuals for the party reforms. The reforms were accompanied by internal debates within the party between the hardliners and reformers, as the Spring of Prague became a topic of public debate in which free public opinion played a crucial role. The emergence of a genuine civil society and the impact of the media were, in the eyes of a foreign observer "intoxicating," as the country became one great debating society.

The Soviet-led invasion in August was preceded by strong pressures and warnings to stop the democratization process which, in Soviet eyes, endangered the "socialist camp." With the collapse of the Communist régime in 1989, the ideals of the Prague Spring lost their appeal, as any attempts to reform the Communist system were seen as futile. Leaders of the Prague Spring briefly came to the forefront of the Velvet Revolution (see CZECHOSLOVAKIA, COUPS) in 1989, but were gradually pushed to the fringes and lost their brief popularity as the first intitatiors of reforms.

PRESTES, LUIZ CARLOS Leader and general secretary, in the 1930s, of the Brazilian Communist Party which, until 1935, received the most fervent and determined support from the army, the intellectuals and the bourgeoisie but had little sympathy from the workers and the peasants. He was made a member of the COMINTERN Executive in Moscow. Upon his return to Brazil in 1935, Prestes gave the order to revolt in November. He formed the National Liberation Alliance, part of the Communist Party, which wanted the suspension of debts to "imperialist" countries, the nationalization of industry and the distribution of land. The Communist coup proved abortive, lasting only one night, mostly because by then the economy had been strengthened and the bourgeoisie was no longer interested in an alliance with this party. A month later President VARGAS banned the Communist party.

PRIMO DE RIVERA, MIGUEL (1870–1930) Spanish general and dictator, who at the start of his career fought in vain for the defense of the Philippines during the Spanish-American War of 1898. Primo de Rivera later fought in the Spanish colony of Morocco against the uprising led by ABDEL KRIM in the Rif mountains, which ended in the Spanish disaster at the battle of Anual in 1922. As the spread of anarchism and the revolt of the Catalans further weakened the authority and prestige of the Spanish Bourbon monarchy at home, Primo de Rivera seized power as a result of a military coup on September 13, 1923, carried out, oddly enough, with the blessing and encouragement of the reigning sovereign, Alfonso XIII, who himself still cherished anachronistic ideas on the possibility of preserving an absolute monarchy in the 20th century. The Cortes, or Spanish parliament, was dissolved; the press censored; due process in the courts suspended; opposition leaders imprisoned, tortured or forced into exile; and the country placed under martial law.

But Primo de Rivera never had any clear idea of what he intended to accomplish, except to align his country with MUSSOLINI's Italy and establish a Fascist-type dictatorship under the slogan of "Country, Religion and Monarchy." Confronted by growing agitation from workers, anarchists and students, Primo de Rivera was forced to step down as prime minister in January 1930, after the formal end of his dictatorship in December 1925, and died in Paris two months later.

The importance of Primo de Rivera's meteoric career—which paved the way to FRANCO's Spain—lies in his astonishing resemblance to other "strong men" who also came to the fore in the 1920s as part of a reactionary resistance to parliamentary democracy, and who likewise justified their authority in the name of a Fascist (see FASCISM) ideology based on a common faith in the corporatist state as the last remaining bulwark for preserving the old European order from its enemies and detractors. Not unlike Marshal PILSUDSKI in Poland, Oliveira de Salazar in Portugal and especially MUSSOLINI in Italy, these Fascist or proto-Fascist dictators set a pattern which serves to illustrate the decay of European liberalism when faced with the greater threat of international communism.

PRINCIP, GAVRILO   (1894–1918) Serb assassin. Coming from peasant stock, Princip joined the nationalist BLACK HAND terrorist organization which aimed at establishing Serb rule over those provinces of Austro-Hungary that were inhabited by southern (Yugo) slavs. In June 1914 he threw a bomb that killed the Austrian-Hungarian heir to the throne, Francis Ferdinand, and his wife Sophie, though Princip later stated he had meant to kill somebody else. Sentenced to life imprisonment, he died in prison of tuberculosis. His action sparked off World War I.

PROKOPOVICH, SERGEI   (1871–1955) Russian economist and political activist. Born of a noble family, Prokopovich was a populist (see POPULISM, RUSSIAN) in his youth but became a Marxist in the mid-1890s. He emigrated from Russia and was active in the League of Russian Social Democrats in Exile. Later, he became one of the ideologues of the so-called "Economist" movement in Social Democracy, arguing that by being involved in economic questions that personally affected them the workers would gain the organizational experience and consciousness necessary for a political revolution.

Returning to Russia in 1899, he published studies of the Russian and European workers' movements (1900) and *A Critique of Marx* (1901). Prokopovich took part in organizing the Union of Unions before the RUSSIAN REVOLUTION OF 1905 and was briefly a member of the Party of Constitutional Democrats. Moving to Moscow in 1910, he became active in the cooperative movement.

In August 1917 he served as minister of trade and industry in the provisional government and in September–October as minister of food and supply. After the BOLSHEVIK seizure of power he left politics for scholarship and work in the cooperative movement, serving on the Public Committee for Famine Relief in 1921. Exiled from Russia in 1922, he lived in Europe until his death. In 1924, he published *The Economic Conditions of Soviet Russia* and in 1952, *The National Economy of the USSR.*

PROMETHEUS   In Greek mythology, the wisest among a race of giants known as Titans, who rebelled against the rule of Zeus. Prometheus refused to join the rebellion of his brothers, who were sent to Tartaros (hell). Instead, he secretly taught the arts to men and stole fire from heaven to give to them. On yet another occasion, he tricked Zeus into accepting the worst portions of sacrificial animals, leaving the best for man to consume. For this Zeus had him chained to a rock and sent an eagle to tear out his liver every day as it grew back by night.

Already in classical times Prometheus was regarded as a rebel who, rising against the tyranny of the gods, sought to aid man and alleviate his lot. He became the subject of many literary productions, of which Aeschylus' *Prometheus Bound* is the most famous extant. To this day his name, which originally meant "forethought" or "foresight," has remained synonymous with the desire to tear loose and reach for the heavens.

PROTESTANT ASSOCIATION   An organization of settlers in Maryland's Calvert County, United States, that seized control of the colony in 1689. As early as 1676 the nucleus of this group of Protestant colonists attempted a rebellion against county authorities who represented Maryland's proprietors, the Catholic Calvert family.

When news of England's GLORIOUS REVOLUTION OF 1688 reached the colony, the same insurgents, now styling themselves the Protestant Association, rounded up some 250 settlers and seized the colony's government. They then successfully petitioned the new régime in England to take over control of Maryland, accusing the Calverts of disloyalty to the crown and misrule of the colony. Control over the colony was ultimately returned to the Calverts in 1715, by which time the proprietary family had become Protestant.

PROUDHON, PIERRE-JOSEPH   (1809–1865) Founder of French socialism and anarchist ideology known as "Mutualism." The son of a craftsman and a cook, Proudhon was born in Besancon, France, and raised in the country, where he gained great respect for the simple but independent life of the peasant. He attended college at Besancon after winning a scholarship, but was apprenticed as a printer when his father's bankruptcy left his family destitute. While learning the trade, however, Proudhon managed to learn Hebrew, Greek and Latin, study religion and philosophy and form his own theories on etymology. While an apprentice, his workshop printed Charles' Fourier's *Le Nouveau Monde Industriel et Societaire*, a piece which made a great impact on him at the time. In 1838, an essay of his on philology gained him the Besancon Academy's Suard Pension, which allowed him to travel to Paris and acquaint himself with the social conditions of the growing working class. In 1840, with the publication of his pamphlet *What Is Property?*, his name became renowned among radical groups throughout Europe. Declaring that "property is theft," Proudhon renounced both capitalism and government. His Suard Pension, however, was withdrawn after Proudhon again vocalized his radical beliefs in *A Warning to Property Owners* in 1842.

In 1843, Proudhon obtained a post as the managing clerk of a water transport company in Lyon, where he attended the revolutionary circles of factory workers influenced by the utopian ideas of Etienne Cabet, Henri de Saint-Simon and Fourier. He adopted the name of one of the groups, the Mutualists, to describe his own political thought. Proudhon's stronghold in Lyon lasted long after his death. His post also brought him to Paris on occasion, where he became involved with the German Left Hegelians, befriended the Russians ALEXANDER HERZEN and MICHAEL BAKUNIN, and increased his influence among the radical thinkers. In 1846 he published *Economic Contradictions* and *The Philosophy of Poverty*, a work important not only for its contribution to Proudhonian thought but also because it drew harsh criticism from KARL MARX and signaled the ideological break of anarchism from mainstream socialism.

Although Proudhon did not whole-heartedly support the French Revolution of 1848 (see REVOLUTIONS OF 1848), believing it lacking in ideological direction, he did participate actively in it. In 1848, Proudhon was back in Paris to pursue a career as a free-lance journalist. In February, he set up the first regularly published anarchist journal, *Le Representant du peuple.* As an independent voice, the paper soon attracted a wide reading audience among the working class, stirring up public opinion during the revolution. In June, Proudhon was elected to the Constituent Assembly and set up the foundations for a People's Bank to provide credit to the working class, a venture which never advanced past the planning stages due to Proudhon's arrest.

Proudhon's support for the June rebellion and his radical views led to the suppression of his paper. In the fall, Proudhon defied the authorities by coming out with a second journal entitled *Le peuple* (the People). After denouncing the new president, Louis-Napoleon, Proudhon was sentenced to three years imprisonment in early 1849.

His attitude toward Napoleon was hardly one-sided. In 1852, his *The Social Revolution Proved by the Coup d'État* called on Louis-Napoleon to join forces with the revolutionaries and to lead the movement. It was Napoleon's pardon which later allowed Proudhon to return from Belgium and Napoleon's courtship of the working class in the 1860s which fostered the rise of Proudhonism. Proudhon's condemnation of liberal democracy and universal suffrage as a false remedy in and of themselves to the social condition has enabled some to view him as a forerunner of the radical right of the early 20th century.

In prison, under the lenient conditions at the time, Proudhon continued to pursue his revolutionary activities. He set up yet another journal, *La Voix du Peuple* (The voice of the people), which folded like his earlier attempts due to government-imposed fines or outright suppression. He also completed two books of great significance: *The Confessions of a Revolutionary,* which reviewed the events of 1848 from his anarchist perspective, and *The General Idea of the Revolution*, which elaborated his ideas of a new non-political order of society based on federalism, decentralism and worker control of the means of production.

In prison, Proudhon also married Euphrasia Piegard, a young Parisian worker. Upon his release in 1852, he returned to Besan-

con to find employment to support his growing family. After struggling to find publishers not frightened by his radical reputation, his 1858 publication of *Of Justice in the Revolution and in the Church* earned him another three-year sentence.

He fled to Brussels, where he applied himself to a wide range of projects—most of which remained unfinished. In 1861, however, he authored *War and Peace*, a critique of nationalism and militarism. Napoleon's pardon returned him to Paris, where he published *Of the Federal Principle* in 1863 and *On the Political Capacity of the Proletariat* in 1864, just before his death in 1865.

Between the 1840s and the 1860s, Proudhon's writings reached a wide audience, inspiring the rise of anarchist associations throughout Europe. Within France, anarchist associations were founded for the explicit purpose of spreading propaganda and the economic organization of the working class. By the mid-1860s, Proudhonism had become the basis of working-class movements in France. Napoleon's decision to court the working class in the 1860s led to a vast increase in the number of workingmens' associations and Proudhonian Mutualist ideas pervaded in these organizations. In 1864, Proudhonian labor leaders arrived in England to help found the First INTERNATIONAL. By the time of his death, Proudhon had planted the seeds for the rise of an anarchist movement which was to shake Europe and the world for almost a century to come.

PRONUNCIAMIENTO (Spanish for "coup") In Spanish and Latin American history, the collective name given to the endless number of revolts, rebellions and coups that have taken place in those countries. The term, originally meaning simply "Proclamation" (so named for the proclamations issued by the rebels in each case) seems to have originated during the struggle for independence against Spain that broke out in Latin America during the early 1800s. Later it was applied indiscriminately whenever the military, the right or the left wing attempted to gain power by force. Made possible by the failure of civil society to develop, *Pronunciamientos* were long the normal way by which Latin American régimes were toppled and tin-pot dictators succeeded each other. Since 1980 or so they have become somewhat less frequent, but the possibility of one taking place still has to be taken into account in much of Latin America.

PUEBLO REBELLION The name given to the revolt of the Pueblo Indians against Spanish colonial rule. It began in 1680 and succeeded in terminating Spanish domination of what is now the state of New Mexico for a period of 12 years. The traditionally peaceful Pueblos had been cruelly oppressed in various ways by the Spanish from the time New Mexico was colonized in 1598, including enslavement, religious repression and cruel and arbitrary punishments.

Brief revolts beginning in 1645 were met with reprisals against the Pueblo religious leaders, the so-called "medicine men." In the latter half of 1680, the Pueblos united behind a once-imprisoned "medicine man" to expel the Spaniards and their Catholic priests. Leaving 400 dead, the Spaniards retreated for 12 years to El Paso. The Pueblo union was short-lived however, and the Spaniards, under Pedro de Vargas, took advantage of the resulting fragmentation to reconquer Santa Fe in 1692, thereby restoring Spanish rule.

PUGACHEV REBELLION Yemelyan Ivanovich Pugachev (1742–1775) was born to an illiterate family of Don Cossacks. Conscripted into the Russian army, he participated in the final battles of the Seven Years' war (1756–1763) as well as in Russia's subsequent wars against Poland and Turkey. In 1770 he was invalided out of the army and subsequently spent some time with the so-called Old Believers. This was a group of dissenters within the Russian Orthodox church which had resisted the imposition of Greek liturgical forms that had taken place during the previous century; subsequently they developed into opponents of the czar's absolute rule.

The year 1772 found Pugachev at Yaitsky Gorodok (present-day Uralsi) where a rebellion of Cossacks, directed against the growing power of the Russian state which was taking away their traditional way of life, was just getting under way. He himself was arrested for desertion and imprisoned; escaping, he crossed the Volga to the east and made an appearance claiming to be Emperor Peter III, who had been deposed by his German-born wife, the Empress Catherine II the Great. Decreeing the abolition of serfdom—the system that made the vast majority of Russia's population into the private property of the czar, landlords and the Church—Pugachev was able to gather a substantial following, particularly among peasants and Cossacks as well as the indentured workers of the Ural arms factories.

In the fall of 1773, Pugachev was able to besiege and occupy the town of Orenburg; that, however, marked the peak of the rebels' success, as Catherine sent an army commanded by General A.I. Bibikov against them. Operations against Pugachev nevertheless lasted throughout the spring and summer of 1774 and it was only in September of that year that, having once again crossed the Volga, his forces were pinned down and defeated at Tasaritsin (formerly called Stalingrad, the present-day Volgograd).

Pugachev himself managed to escape but was betrayed to the army by some Cossacks, brought to Moscow and executed. His demise marked the end of the greatest single uprising in Russian history between the time of troubles in the early 17th century and the RUSSIAN REVOLUTION OF 1905.

THE PURITAN REVOLUTION (1642–1660) A political and religious revolution that resulted in the overthrow of the English monarchy. The rise of Protestantism in the 16th century gained endorsement from the decision of Henry VIII of England to establish a national Anglican Church as the official state religion (1533). Yet, while his successors wavered between Protestantism and Catholicism, the masses often favored Puritanism, a reform movement within English Protestantism that demanded that the established Church of England be purified of elements they perceived as Catholic, superstitious or lacking in a scriptural basis.

Essentially Calvinists, the Puritans differed from other Christian sects in their description of the process of salvation. They held that a limited number of people could, by undergoing religious conversion, be "elected" by God for salvation. Those sharing this experience should be grouped together in democratic "communities of saints," aloof from temporal affairs.

At the same time, Kings James I and Charles I advanced the notion of the "divine right of kings," claiming that since kings received their authority from God, they were answerable only to God. Their refusal to recognize Parliament, the clergy and the law, won them the enmity of Parliament, which reciprocated by refusing to grant them adequate revenues. In 1629 Charles I, frustrated by his difficulties with Parliament, attempted to rule without it. For 11 years he refused to summon Parliament, raising funds for the navy without popular consent and antagonizing the Puritans by supporting the High Anglicans. In 1637 Scotland rebelled against attempts to impose Anglicanism there.

Forced to reconvene Parliament in 1640 to muster financial support for his campaigns in the north, Charles was infuriated when Parliament refused to grant him this support. He called new elections but, to his chagrin, the same members were returned and continued to frustrate his plans by using the Scottish rebellion to further their own demands, including calls to impeach and execute royal advisors. Known as the Long Parliament, it sat from 1640 to 1660, during which time no new elections were held.

The most extreme Calvinist elements, the "radicals" succeeded in passing a bill abolishing bishops, thereby revolutionizing the Anglican church. In 1642 Parliament and the monarch were at war, with Charles drawing support from the conservative counties of the north and west, and Parliament from the affluent south and east. To obtain Scottish support, Parliament adopted the Solemn League and Covenant, establishing Presbyterianism as the legal religion of England, Scotland and Ireland.

Parliamentary forces, known as Roundheads after the close haircuts favored by Puritans, gradually defeated the royalists, also known as Cavaliers. OLIVER CROMWELL, a devout Puritan, organized a new and more effective military force, the Ironsides, in which extreme Protestantism provided the basis for morale, discipline and the will to fight. Cromwell decided that a counterrevolution was a constant danger unless the defeated king, Charles I, was put to death. Parliament hesitated and Cromwell, backed by the army, broke it up, leaving a rump of 50 or 60 members loyal to him. This rump parliament put King Charles to death on the scaffold in 1649.

The British Isles were now declared a republic, the Commonwealth, with Cromwell as head of state and government. He governed to the best of his ability and decreed religious tolerance for all except Unitarians, atheists, Roman Catholics and extreme High Anglicans. But even Cromwell; however, had to subdue both Scotland and Ireland by force. In Scotland, the death of Charles, a scion of the ancient Scottish national monarchy of Stuart, had swung the nation back into the royalist camp; Cromwell crushed the Scots in 1650.

In 1641, newly arrived Protestant settlers had been massacred in Ireland. These deaths were now avenged as thousands of Catholics were put to the sword. Protestant landlords replaced Catholic landlords and retained the Catholic peasantry as their tenants. The native religion and clergy were driven underground and Anglicanism became the established religion.

In England itself, Cromwell ruled with great difficulty. He was constantly urged to make greater democratic reforms by the extreme democrats, variously known as LEVELLERS, DIGGERS and FIFTH MONARCHY MEN. Some of these elements, particularly in the army, even voiced demands for a written constitution and for democratic suffrage.

Cromwell was unable to conciliate between landed and Anglican, or even Presbyterian interests. In 1653, he dissolved the rump parliament and tried to govern as Lord Protector through representatives he and his followers appointed. A written constitution, the Instrument of Government, was composed. In fact, England was under military rule, the régime of the "major-generals." These officials repressed malcontents, vagabonds and criminals, closed ale houses and prohibited pursuits such as cock-fighting, in a combination of moral puritanism and political dictatorship. Cromwell died in 1658, and his son, Richard, was unable to maintain the Protectorate. In 1660, with almost universal consent, the monarchy was restored and Charles II, son of Charles I, became king of England and Scotland.

In the 1640s and 1650s, the Puritan emphasis on preaching, observance of the Sabbath, moral strictness and abstinence from pleasure prevailed. There was iconoclasm in the churches, and Puritan modes of worship and of ecclesiastical organization replaced Anglican liturgy and episcopacy. After the Restoration, however, there was a moral and political backlash against the Puritans and they lost influence and were persecuted.

Q

QADHDHAFI, MU'AMMAR (1938? 1935? 1942?–) Libyan officer and since his coup of 1969 Libya's top leader. Born in the Sirte desert, Libya, into a poor family of the Qadhadhifa tribe originating in the Fezzan region of southern Libya and adhering to the Sanussi sect, Qadhdhafi was imbued with a fighting tradition: his grandfather was reportedly killed in 1911 while resisting the Italian conquest, while his father and uncle fought in the resistance and were imprisoned. Qadhdhafi was sent to a secondary school in Sabha, Fezzan, but was expelled for organizing a demonstration. He continued his secondary studies in Tripoli and Misurata. He enrolled in the University of Benghazi to study history and geography, but transferred in 1963 to the military academy, from which he graduated in 1965. In 1966 the army sent him for further officer training in Britain.

A fervent revolutionary nationalist, deeply influenced by GAMAL ABDUL NASSER, Qadhdhafi agitated and organized revolutionary cells within the army and was reportedly imprisoned but reinstated. In September 1969 he took a leading part in a military coup d'état which overthrew the monarchy. He was promoted to commander in chief of the armed forces and chairman of the Revolutionary Council that headed the new régime. In March 1977, he declared Libya a *Jamahiriyya*—a new term he coined to mean "Republic of the Masses"—changing the structure, but mainly the terminology, of government institutions. He made himself chairman of the "General Secretariat" that replaced the Revolutionary Council as the supreme institution of the state. In March 1979 he gave up this post of head of state and retained only that of commander in chief. However, Qadhdhafi has remained the sole and supreme leader. In 1973, Qadhdhafi proclaimed a "Popular Revolution" and began building a network of People's Committees topped by a general local People's Congress.

Internationally, Qadhdhafi is violently anti-west and Pan-Arabist. In an attempt to establish a direct democracy in line with his doctrine of Islamic socialism, Qadhdhafi has granted every citizen the right to own a home or land and has encouraged the takeover of hundreds of companies by these people's committees.

Qadhdhafi has relentlessly pursued Libya's mergers with other Arab countries (Egypt 1969–1970 and 1972–1973; Sudan 1969–1970; Syria 1970–1971 and since 1980; Tunisia 1974; Morocco 1984). He has formulated his ideology, the Third Universal Theory, in the *Green Book* published in three volumes. These consist of: *The Solution of the Problem of Democracy* (1976), calling for direct democracy over representative democ-

racy and for the natural laws of society and the people's customs to prevail over written constitutions which allow for man's and not Allah's dictatorial rule; *The Solution of the Economic Problem* (1978) which accepts both public ownership and non-exploitive private ownership, while encouraging the formation of "corporations"; and *The Social Basis of the Third Universal Theory* (1979) in which he celebrates the role of heroes in history and solidarity among nations. These works reveal a strange mixture of European socialist and Fascist ideology with an Islamic humanism. Since that time, however, he has become most noted on the world arena as an instigator of international terrorism, directed, above all, against Israel and the United States. The most spectacular incident in which he was apparently involved occurred in December 1988, when a Pan Am jet was brought down over Lockerbie, Scotland, resulting in the deaths of several hundred people. When Qadhdhafi refused to surrender two of those alleged to have been involved in the bombing for trial, an embargo was placed on the country, one of which is still in effect at the time of writing.

QASSEM, ABDUL KARIM (1914–1963) Iraqi officer and politician, ruler of Iraq 1958–1963. Born in Baghdad to a Sunni-Muslim lower middle-class family, Qassem was commissioned in 1938 and became a professional army officer. He served as a battalion commander with the Iraqi expeditionary forces in the Arab-Israeli war of 1948 and, in 1956, by then a brigade commander, became head of a group of FREE OFFICERS plotting to overthrow the monarch and end Iraq's special relationship with Britain. On July 14, 1958, the group carried out its revolution, led by Qassem and his confederate Colonel ABDUL SALAM 'AREF, and proclaimed a republic. Contrary to his fellow-conspirators' plans and expectations, Qassem declined to form a Revolutionary Command Council, but appointed himself commander in chief, prime minister and acting minister of defense. He did not assume the title of president but in effect became dictator and "Sole Leader" (which was for some time his semi-official title).

In September 1958, Qassem enacted a major land reform law and attempted to revive political parties. However he became increasingly erratic—to the extent that he was nicknamed "the Mad Dictator." A combination of civilian *Ba'ath* activists and nationalist anti-Communist officers toppled Qassem on February 8–9, 1963. Qassem and his closest collaborators were shot.

AL-QAWUQJI, FAWZI (1890–1976) Syrian-Lebanese soldier, guerrilla leader and nationalist. Born in Tripoli, Lebanon,

Qawuqji served in the Ottoman Turkish army. His early life has remained obscure, but he took part in the Syrian-Druse revolt of 1925–1927, and escaped to Iraq. There he taught at the military academy. In August 1936, he recruited several hundred volunteers, mainly from Iraq and Syria, to assist the Arab rebels in Palestine, and entered the country at their head without being hindered by government troops or the police. His force, centered in the Arab-populated areas, mounted a number of attacks on Jewish settlements and communications, but had no major military impact or successes, and his efforts to organize a revolutionary army under his own centralized command failed. The Husseini-led command of the rebellion suspected him of being close to rival factions. When the first stage of the rebellion ended in the fall of 1936 through the British-arranged mediation of the Arab rulers, the Palestine government permitted Qawuqji to escape across the border with his troops. In 1941, he took part in the RASHID'ALI KILANI rebellion in Iraq and when it was quelled he fled to Germany, where he headed an Arab Office for Propaganda, along with the recruitment of volunteers and secret services. After World War II, he returned to Syria.

Qawuqji retired and took no further part in public affairs after the war. Some of his officers later became prominent in Syria's army and politics, particularly in its numerous military coups.

QIN BANGXIAN (Ch'in Pang-hsien) (Bo Gu, Po Ku) (1907–1946) Chinese Communist leader. Born to a Jiangsu gentry family, Qin received a modern education in the provincial technical school in Suzhou, became a student leader, and in 1925 enrolled in the English department of the Communist-influenced Shanghai University. In October he joined the CHINESE COMMUNIST PARTY (CCP). In 1926 he participated in the first armed uprising of Shanghai workers in support of the NATIONAL REVOLUTIONARY ARMY'S NORTHERN EXPEDITION and shortly afterward was sent to Moscow for study at the Sun Yat-sen University. Established in 1925, this was set up exclusively for Chinese students who had previously attended the Communist University of the Toilers of the East. Since the CCP-GUOMINDANG (GMD) coalition was still in effect, GMD students, including CHIANG KAI-SHEK's 15-year-old son, Chiang Ching-kuo, also attended. At the university, Qin became well-versed in Marxist-Leninist doctrine. Qin and WANG MING were among the Chinese students who strongly supported STALIN's China policies and became known as the "28 Bolsheviks."

Returning to China in 1930, Qin was active in CCP propaganda work and supported Wang Ming's opposition to LI LISAN in the struggle for party leadership. In 1931 he was elected to the temporary Politburo and the following year became CCP general secretary when Wang went to Moscow. The Wang Ming "leftist" line that Qin pursued was blamed for CCP disasters in "white" (non-Communist) areas. After the Shanghai CCP leadership was forced to move to the Jiangxi soviet base, Qin and the COMINTERN adviser, OTTO BRAUN, were held responsible for CCP strategic errors that forced the CCP to embark on the LONG MARCH in October 1934. Qin was dismissed from leadership at the Zunyi conference of January 1935 that enthroned MAO ZEDONG. For the remainder of the Long March, Qin directed the RED ARMY political department.

At Yan'an, the new CCP capital, Qin was active in CCP external affairs. In December 1936, he accompanied ZHOU ENLAI in the CCP delegation to Xi'an that negotiated the release of CHIANG KAI-SHEK, who had been kidnapped by Manchurian nationalist forces. At the outbreak of the Sino-Japanese war (1937–1945), he participated in the negotiations that led to the second united front with the GMD and the legalization of the CCP. In 1938 he represented the CCP's EIGHTH ROUTE ARMY in Chongqing, the nationalists' wartime capital. In 1940 he returned to Yan'an, where he managed the *Liberation Daily* and the Xinhua (New China) news agency. He acquitted himself well during the "rectification" (thought reform) campaigns launched in 1942 to "correct unorthodox tendencies," and in 1945 the 7th CCP congress elected him to the central committee. In early 1946 he was in the delegation that went to Chongqing for postwar negotiations with the GMD. In April, while flying back to Yan'an, the plane ran into bad weather and crashed in Shanxi. Qin and YE TING were among those killed.

QIU JIN (Ch'iu Chin) (1875–1907) Chinese woman revolutionary. Born in Amoy to a Zhejiang scholarly family, Qiu was tutored in the classics. Fond of reading novels, she pictured herself as a knight-errant and became skillful in using a sword and in horseback-riding. Obeying her parents, she married the son of a wealthy Hunan merchant and soon gave birth to a son and later a daughter. In 1903 the couple moved to Beijing, where her

Qiu Jin in a revolutionary pose

husband had purchased an official post. Though life in the capital and her enjoyment of writing poetry offered some relief from the boredom of an unhappy marriage, she remained dissatisfied. In 1904, Qiu left her family to study in Japan. Her mother was the only family member who supported her. While attending the Aoyama vocational girls school in Tokyo, she became involved with various revolutionary groups, including a Yokohama branch of the TRIAD SOCIETY, consisting mainly of student revolutionaries. She contributed articles to radical student journals, returned to China in 1905 and joined the GUANG FU HUI (Restoration Society), which plotted the overthrow of the Qing (Manchu) dynasty (1644–1912). Returning to Tokyo in 1906, she joined SUN YAT-SEN's TONGMENGHUI (Revolutionary Alliance), but soon left Japan after the Japanese imposed more serious restrictions on Chinese students. Though female revolutionaries were rare, she was accepted into the leadership echelon. Famous revolutionaries, like the Russian SOPHIA PEROVSKAYA, and daring rebels of traditional China inspired her to seek heroic action. Dissatisfied with Sun Yat-sen's focus on Guangdong, she and other revolutionaries in the lower Yangtze Valley planned independent action. In 1907, she helped prepare a revolt in Hangchou and enlisted Triad support. With the premature disclosure of the plot, Qiu was arrested at the girls school where she was teaching. She was beheaded in July. The protest aroused by her execution caused the suicide of a provincial magistrate, who had been wrongly accused of responsibility for her death. As a result of her martyrdom, anti-dynastic feelings intensified and Qiu became famous as one of the heroines of modern China.

AL-QUDSI, NAZEM (1906–) Syrian nationalist and political figure. Born in Aleppo to a wealthy, landholding family, al-Qudsi studied law in Lebanon, Syria and Switzerland. He served as Syrian ambassador to the United States between 1944 and 1946, and he was elected to Parliament shortly after his return to Syria. In Parliament, he cooperated with Rushdi al-Kikhya in forming the People's Party, an Aleppo-based nationalist bloc opposed to sectarianism and the communal distribution of power.

Syria was then in the midst of a political struggle between the Nationalist Party and the *Hizb al-Ahrar* (Liberal Party). Al-Qudsi affiliated himself with *Hizb al-Ahrar* and brought about its merger with other, like-minded parties to form the *Hizb al-Sha'ab* (Populist Party). He attained national prominence as leader of the *Hizb al-Sha'ab*, but he was not included in any cabinet, since his party constituted the Nationalists' main opposition. He supported Brigadier General HUSNI ZA'IM's coup in March 1949 and Colonel SAMI HINNAWI's coup in August of that year, serving on the committee to restore civilian government and as foreign minister following the election of HASHEM ATASSI.

In December 1949, Colonel ADIB SHISHAKLI overthrew al-Atassi's government in a third coup. Al-Qudsi was appointed premier and asked to form a cabinet, but he relinquished the post after only one day to protest Shishakli's interference in his decisions. Khaled al-Azm was then asked to form a government, but when his coalition collapsed, al-Qudsi was called back to the premiership. This time he succeeded in forming a transitional government, based mainly on the *Hizb al-Sha'ab*. In a public address, al-Qudsi described his government's main objective as providing Syria with a constitution, but he also warned that he "could not work miracles." The speech was gen-

erally treated with skepticism. In it, al-Qudsi failed to pay due homage to the republican (i.e., nationalist) cause, leading many to believe that he favored union with Iraq. At the same time, the Islamic Socialist and Syrian Social National Parties challenged his failure to take a firm stand on the Palestine issue. In 1951, his government narrowly survived a no-confidence motion in Parliament, but al-Qudsi's problems were not over. His deputy, Munir al-Ajlani, was arrested by the military for supposed collusion with King Abdullah of Jordan to annex Syria to his kingdom. After 18 months in power, al-Qudsi was forced to hand the premiership to al-Azm. Later that year Shishakli again staged a coup, ousting al-Azm from the premiership. In the new political climate, al-Qudsi was elected President of Parliament, a position he held until 1953, and again from 1954 to 1957, when Syria and Egypt merged to form the United Arab Republic.

In 1955, Shukri al-Quwwatli, Syria's first president, was reelected to the presidency. This signaled the political decline of al-Qudsi, despite his position as President of Parliament. While al-Quwwatli initiated Syrian ties with the Soviet Union, the *Hizb al-Sha'ab* favored a more pro-western and pro-Iraqi foreign policy. Therefore, although the *Hizb al-Sha'ab* was the largest party in Parliament, none of its members served in the government. Nevertheless, al-Qudsi was the first major Syrian political figure to speak in favor of union with Egypt, and he gradually adopted an increasingly left-wing orientation, which eventually led to the break-up of the *Hizb al-Sha'ab*.

Throughout the period of the United Arab Republic, al-Qudsi refrained from political activity and lived in semi-retirement. When Syria regained its independence in 1961, he was elected president, but he was deposed one year later following a military coup. However, Syria's new rulers were unable to form a government, and al-Qudsi was invited to return to power. After being deposed in the *Ba'athist* coup of 1963, al-Qudsi retired from public life and settled in Lebanon.

QUEZON Y MOLINA, MANUEL LUIS (1878–1944) Nationalist leader and first president of the Philippines. Born in Baler, Tayabas province, Quezon participated in EMILIO AGUINALDO's uprising against American colonial rule which was defeated in 1901. After six months in jail for his role in the rebellion, Quezon returned to law school, convinced that the cause of independence was best served by negotiating with the American authorities.

After completing his degree in 1903, Quezon was appointed prosecuting attorney for the provinces of Minaro and his native Tayabas. In 1905 he was elected governor of Tayabas and in 1909 one of the two resident commissioners for the Philippines in Washington. There, the "Patrick Henry of the Philippines" became a vociferous champion of independence. As a nonvoting member of Congress, he questioned whether the Jones Act (1916), enabling the formation of a local legislature for the Philippines, went far enough in ensuring self-rule. He, nonetheless, returned to the islands and was elected speaker of the newly formed Senate, the most prestigious post open to native Filipinos.

Similar reservations led Quezon to oppose deferred independence as proposed in the Here-Hawes-Cutting Bill of 1933. In 1934, however, Quezon accepted the Tydings-McDuffie Act assuring complete Philippine independence by July 4, 1946. In view of Japanese expansionism in the Pacific, he recognized that only the American military was capable of defending the islands, while the proposed transitional Commonwealth of the Philippines would allow him to formulate an independent policy to tackle the pressing problems of the islands. The following year, Quezon was elected president of the new commonwealth.

In 1941, with a Japanese invasion well underway, Quezon was elected to a second term as president by a seven to one margin. A heavy air raid shook Manila during the inauguration ceremonies, forcing the president and his entourage to flee to the US garrison of Corregidor. In 1942, Quezon reached the United States to organize his government in exile. Although he had earlier decided to retire from politics in 1943, President Franklin D. Roosevelt urged him to postpone his resignation until the Philippines were liberated, in return for a promise of immediate independence. Quezon, however, died of tuberculosis in August 1944. The American invasion began in October of that year and only succeeded in liberating Manila in February 1945. Although Quezon never lived to see the Philippines liberated, he is considered the father and first president of his country. A new city built near Manila was named Quezon City in his honor.

QU QIUBAI (Ch'ü Ch'iu-pai) (1899–1935) Chinese Communist leader and writer. Qu was born into a Jiangsu gentry family, soon driven to bankruptcy by his opium-smoking father. Before beginning his formal education, Qu received classical training at home and later retained his interest in classical poetry. The family's dire circumstances forced him to leave high school in 1915 and take a teaching post. Poverty and clan jealousies drove his mother to suicide. Deeply affected by the tragedy, Qu would later write bitterly of the cruelties inflicted by traditional society behind the "mask of Confucianism." He spent time writing classical Chinese poetry and delved into Buddhist thought. In 1916, Qu attended classes at Beijing University and then studied Russian and French at the tuition-free Russian language institute affiliated with the Chinese foreign ministry. The MAY FOURTH MOVEMENT (1919) aroused within him nationalist sentiments and resentment of social and economic grievances that soon took precedence over his poetic and metaphysical meditation. In *The New Society*, a journal he edited with friends, Qu's articles reflected strong socialist sympathies. He joined LI DAZHAO's Marxist study group in 1920 and went to Moscow as a correspondent for a Beijing newspaper. During the next two years he wrote candid reports of conditions in the Soviet Union. In 1921 he joined the Chinese section of the newly-

established Communist University of the Toilers of the East in Moscow, serving as an interpreter and assistant teacher. In 1922, while being treated for tuberculosis, he joined the Moscow branch of the CHINESE COMMUNIST PARTY (CCP), and impressed the CCP leader, CHEN DUXIU, for whom he interpreted when Chen attended the 4th COMINTERN congress. Qu returned to China in 1923, attended the 3rd CCP congress and took charge of drafting the party's program. He also became head of educational administration and of the sociology department at the Communist-influenced Shanghai University and edited CCP organs. After the formation of the CCP united front with the GUOMINDANG (GMD) in 1923, Qu became active in the GMD and was one of the Communists elected to its central executive committee in 1924. In 1925, he was elected to the CCP Central Committee.

In 1927, Qu joined CCP critics of Chen Duxiu's collaboration with the GMD, which had in fact been dictated by Moscow. When the GMD purged the CCP, Chen was denounced for "rightist capitulationism." Qu, as head of the Politburo, replaced him as CCP leader in August. But less than a year later Qu himself was criticized for "leftist putschism" at the 6th CCP congress, held in Moscow in July 1928. Encouraged by the Comintern, Qu had supported the CANTON UPRISING of December 1927. Since Stalin's infallibility could not be challenged, Qu was held responsible for the failure and removed from CCP leadership, but retained membership in the CC and Politburo. He stayed in Moscow as head of the CCP delegation to the Comintern and also worked with Russian scholars in devising a latinized writing system for Chinese. He returned to China in 1930 and opposed LI LISAN's leftist line. Dismissed from key party positions in 1931, Qu resumed literary work in Shanghai, where he was closely associated with the famous writer, Lu Xun. In 1934, he joined the Chinese Soviet in Ruijin, became commissar of education, and stayed in Jiangxi as propaganda chief when the main CCP force embarked upon the LONG MARCH in October. Falling ill during the winter, he was heading for Shanghai, carried on a stretcher, when GMD forces intercepted him in Fujian in February 1935. He sang the *Internationale* in Russian while on the way to face the firing squad that executed him in June.

A gifted writer, poet and translator, given to introspective, metaphysical, meditation, in the end Qu acknowledged his distaste and unfitness for political work. That he was nevertheless drawn into the vortex of revolutionary politics testifies to the crisis mood that gripped his generation of Chinese intellectuals.

R

RADCHENKO, STEPAN (1869–1911) As a student in St. Petersburg, Radchenko founded a Marxist study group in 1893. He developed expertise in conspiratorial organization and evolved an elitist party theory. His group recruited skilled workers but avoided mass public activity that might attract police attention. From 1894, he worked together with LENIN and was a co-founder of the League for Struggle for Emancipation of the Working Class. Arrested in 1896, he was briefly imprisoned and later restricted himself to consulting with the active Marxist organizers. He attended the first congress of the Social Democratic Workers Party of Russia in Minsk in 1898. Arrested in 1901, he spent five years in exile. Returning in poor health, he abstained from further involvement in revolutionary politics.

RADEK, KARL (1885–1939?) Russian revolutionary and publicist. Radek was born Karl Sobelsohn in the Polish town of Lemberg (today Lvov). Despite a well-rounded education in Jewish and classical sources, he rejected these at an early age in favor of revolutionary socialism and Polish nationalism. He assumed the Polish name of Radek after the revolutionary hero of a Polish novel. In 1901 he joined the Polish Social Democratic Party. He was arrested for his involvement in a Polish revolution in 1905, and upon his release served as a publicist for the left wing of the German Social Democratic Party. Noted for his pacifist opposition to the war, he attended the Zimmerwald and Kintel Pacifist congresses.

Radek settled in Switzerland, where he befriended VLADIMIR LENIN. Upon the outbreak of the February RUSSIAN REVOLUTION OF 1917, he accompanied Lenin in the historic sealed train carriage from Switzerland through Germany to Sweden, remaining in Sweden as representative of the BOLSHEVIK PARTY. He returned to Russia in the aftermath of the October Revolution and was appointed head of the central European section of the Foreign Affairs Commissariat, utilizing this position to promote revolutionary activity in the West.

Radek organized the first congress of the German Communist Party in 1918 and was elected to the Third INTERNATIONAL in 1922. He was particularly interested in promoting the revolution among the Jewish masses, lobbying fervently for the inclusion of the *Poalei Zion* ("Workers of Zion"), a Zionist movement, in the Third International.

Radek joined the growing Trotskyite opposition to STALIN, and as his reward was expelled from the party and exiled to the Urals in 1927. Following his recantation in 1930, he was read-mitted to the party. Radek served as editor of both *Pravda* and *Izvestia*. *Portraits and Pamphlets*, a collection of his writings, was published in 1935. He was also coauthor of the initial draft of Stalin's constitution, but Stalin had never fully forgiven Radek for his earlier support for TROTSKY. He was arrested in the great purges of 1936–1937. At a show trial, he was denounced as an enemy of the people, and sentenced to 10 years' hard labor. Radek disappeared in 1939 and died or was murdered in a prison camp.

RAFSANJANI, 'ALI AKBAR HASHEMI (1934–) Iranian politician, president of Iran since 1989. Born in Behraman in the province of Kerman, Iran, Rafsanjani studied Islamic theology in Qom. In the 1950s he joined in MUHAMMAD MOSSADDEQ'S struggle against the shah. Later he became a militant activist in the AYATOLLAH KHOMEINI's Islamic resistance. When Khomeini was exiled to Iraq in 1964–1965, Rafsanjani became one of his contacts in Iran. He was arrested and tortured by the *Savak* (secret police).

Rafsanjani was one of the founders of the Tehran Association of Militant Clergy. In the 1978–1979 revolutionary struggle, he was appointed to the Council of the Islamic Revolution (see IRAN, REVOLTS AND REVOLUTIONS); he co-founded the new régime's Islamic Republic Party (IRP) and was a member of its central committee. He served as president of the *majlis* (parliament) from 1980 to 1989.

In July 1989, Rafsanjani was elected president. While completely devoted to the principles and ideals of the Iranian Revolution of 1979, Rafsanjani was considered a realist and a pragmatist. Reportedly it was he who persuaded Khomeini to agree to an armistice with Iraq in August 1988. Extremist-radical factions tried to weaken his position by denouncing his pragmatism in foreign affairs (i.e., by leaking reports on his part in secret arms deals with the USA and Israel). So far he has kept them in check. Rafsanjani's writings (in Persian) include *The Story of Palestine*, *Revolution or a New Resurrection* and *Champion of the Struggle Against Colonialism*.

RAHMAN, MUJIBUR (1920–1975) Bengali leader in the struggle against Pakistan. The scion of a middle-class family, Mujibur studied law and political science and, while still a teenager, was arrested by the British for agitating in favor of Indian independence. His real political activity, though, began after Bengal became West Pakistan in 1947; two years later he founded the AWAMI LEAGUE, which demanded greater autonomy from eastern Pakistan. The League continued its activities throughout the 1950s and 1960s, until the Pakistani government finally arrested Mujibur.

In the elections of December 1970, the Awami League emerged victorious. Riots and civil war ensued. After Bangladesh proclaimed its independence, Mujibur was released from prison (January 1972) and became its first prime minister and then president. In January 1975, he and most of his family were assassinated in a coup.

RAJA'I, 'ALI (1934–1981) Iranian prime minister 1980–1981, president July–August 1981. Born in Qasvin, Iran, to a family of poor shopkeepers, Raja'i left school at the age of 16 and worked as a bricklayer. A few years later he enlisted in the Iranian air force as an orderly. Raja'i resumed his studies in the evenings and in 1960 received a degree in mathematics from Tehran Teachers College. In 1963 he joined MEHDI BAZARGAN'S IRAN LIBERATION MOVEMENT and was arrested for anti-shah activities. In 1973 he was again arrested after planting a bomb outside the Tehran offices of El Al, Israel's national airline; he was lamed by secret police and tortured in prison.

Raja'i was released from prison in 1978 and returned to teaching, joining the Council of the Islamic Teachers' Association, a fundamentalist Islamic group. During the Iranian Revolution of 1979 (see IRAN, REVOLTS AND REVOLUTIONS), he led demonstrations in Tehran. When the Islamic Republic's first government, headed by Mehdi Bazargan, was joined by the Revolutionary Council in July 1979, Raja'i was named minister of education. In this position, which he held for 10 months, he instituted a program of Islamization in Iran's educational system, banned the teaching of English and other subjects he deemed "non-Islamic," dismissed teachers found unsuited to the Islamic régime and closed universities.

When Iraq invaded Iran in September 1980, Raja'i presented Iran's case to the UN Security Council, claiming the invasion was due to the instigation of the USA. During the session, he removed his shoes, baring his feet to show the members of the Council the scars he had acquired as a political prisoner of the shah. A month after his election to presidency, he was killed in an explosion in the prime minister's office, together with Prime Minister Javad Bahonar.

RAJAVI, MAS'UD (1948–) Iranian politician; leader of the MUJAHIDIN KHALQ (MKh). Born in Tabas, Khorassan, Rajavi joined the MKh, an extreme Islamic reformist revolutionary organization, upon its foundation in the mid-1960s. He was a member of its central committee from 1970 and reportedly was sent for military training with the PALESTINE LIBERATION ORGANIZATION. In 1971, Rajavi was arrested by the shah's police and sentenced to death, but his sentence was commuted and he was released in 1978. After the Iranian Revolution of 1979 (see IRAN, REVOLTS AND REVOLUTIONS), the AYATOLLAH KHOMEINI disqualified him from running for president of the Islamic Republic of Iran, because Rajavi and the MKh had not supported the new Islamic constitution.

Rajavi, now the main leader of the MKh, went into exile in Paris and, together with former president ABDOLHASSAN BANISADR, founded a National Resistance Council. Meanwhile, in Iran, the MKh was suppressed and driven underground, and many of its leaders were killed or arrested. In 1986, Iran prevailed upon France to expel Rajavi and he moved his headquarters to Iraq.

RAJPUTS The collective designation for a group, consisting of some 36 clans, that claimed descent from the mythical dynasties whose deeds are related in the two great Indian epics, the *Ramayana* and the *Mahabharata*. The term (meaning "son of a king") represents a generic term for a warrior caste rather than referring to a particular physical race.

Ancestral myths notwithstanding, epigraphic evidence suggests that the Rajputs were in fact descendants of various tribal groups that entered India from the northwest during the 5th and 6th centuries A.D. and were subsequently assimilated into the preexisting Hindu caste structure. They came to prominence during the first half of the 7th century A.D., from which time they were the major force and ruling power in the region of northern India now known as Rajasthan but then denominated Rajputana.

A proud and martial people, the Rajputs were the only group to offer any real opposition to the Muslim expansion into northern India from Persia and Afghanistan. Their history comprises an assortment of tales of unlikely victories and heroic defeats against the encroaching forces of Islam. However, inter-clan rivalry mitigated their effectiveness against the invaders; the defeat by Babur (subsequently the first Mughal emperor of India) of the forces of the Rajput leader Rana Sanga at Kanwaha, on March 16, 1527, signaled the triumph of the Mughals and the end of Rajput efforts at hegemony in northern India.

The Rajputs' military prowess was subsequently exploited by the Mughals and later by the British, both of whom drafted them into their armed services, where they were to serve faithfully. Rajputana retained its independence throughout the colonial era, its princely states eventually ceding authority to the government of independent India established in 1947.

RAKOSI, MATYAS (1892–1971) Hungarian Communist politician and dictator. Born to Jewish parents, he left his native Ada (now in Yugoslavia) and moved to Budapest, where he studied and worked as a bank clerk. He joined the socialist movement while living for a time in England. After the outbreak of World War I, Rakosi served in the Austro-Hungarian army but was captured by the Russians, spent two years in a prisoner of war camp, and secured his release when he allied himself with the BOLSHEVIK PARTY following the short-lived Hungarian Soviet Republic of BELA KUN. After the counterrevolution of August 1919, he took refuge in the USSR, but smuggled himself back into Hungary five years later to reactivate the banned COMMUNIST PARTY OF HUNGARY. Arrested and condemned to death, Rakosi was fortunate to have his sentence commuted to life imprisonment when prominent European intellectuals raised an outcry on his behalf.

Released from prison in 1940, Rakosi went to Moscow and stayed there until 1944, orchestrating the Hungarian Communist propaganda campaign. After the Soviet occupation of Hungary, it was Rakosi who reorganized the Workers Party. He served as deputy leader of a coalition government from which the non-Communist partners were gradually excluded and, by May 1949, had converted Hungary into a "people's democracy" subservient to Moscow. Within the next few months, even dissident leaders of the Communist national wing faced execution or imprisonment on trumped-up charges. As Hungary's prime minister from 1952 on, Rakosi assumed dictatorial powers and obeyed STALIN's orders to the letter.

As a firm anti-Zionist, Rakosi—unlike other Jewish Politburo leaders such as ANA PAUKER—remained in power during the anti-Jewish frenzy of 1952–1953. However, after Stalin's death, he was harshly criticized by the new Soviet leadership and, in July 1953, the more liberal IMRE NAGY replaced him. Rakosi remained party secretary and was reinstated as prime minister in 1955, but was compelled to resign in disgrace shortly before the outbreak of the Hungarian Uprising of 1956 (see HUNGARY, REVOLTS AND REVOLUTIONS). Exiled to the USSR, Rakosi was expelled from the Communist Party in 1962. It was only toward the end of his life that he returned to Hungary.

RAKOVSKY, CHRISTIAN GEORGIYEVICH (1873–1941) Born to a wealthy Bulgarian family, Rakovsky became a doctor but devoted himself to Marxist revolution, traveling throughout Europe. He represented Romania, Serbia and Bulgaria at the 1904 congress of the Second INTERNATIONAL and devoted himself particularly to the idea of a union of Balkan socialist states.

In 1917, he aligned himself with LENIN's BOLSHEVIKS, after Russian soldiers freed him from a Romanian prison. After the Germans blocked an attempt by Rakovsky to organize a pro-BOLSHEVIK revolution in Bessarabia (now part of Moldava), he was active through the summer of 1918 in negotiating Russian-Ukrainian relations. In January 1919, he was appointed head of the Bolshevik government in Ukraine, where remained until 1923. From 1925 he was Soviet ambassador to France but was recalled and expelled from the central committee and from the Communist Party in 1927 as a supporter of TROTSKY. Although readmitted to the party in 1934, he was arrested and tried in 1938, sentenced to 20 years in prison, but executed in 1941 with a group of other political prisoners.

RANADE, MADAHEV GOVIND (1842–1901) Born to a Brahmin family in Maharashtra, western India, Ranade rose to the position of judge in the Bombay high court. An avid proponent of social reform, he also supported the foundation of the INDIAN NATIONAL CONGRESS in 1885, and was one of its most important figures and theoreticians in its early days, emphasizing the interdependence of social, economic, political and religious developments and propounding a comprehensive reform movement that could address all these spheres.

RASHID ALI see KILANI, RASHID ALI.

RASKOLNIKOV, FYODOR (1892–1939) Revolutionary sailor and Soviet diplomat. Raskolnikov began his revolutionary activity as a student at the polytechnical institute in his native St. Petersburg. In 1910, he was already a BOLSHEVIK and writing for the party press. Arrested in 1912, he was held in solitary confinement for four months and suffered a nervous breakdown.

In World War I, he served in the Russian navy and became a Bolshevik leader of the soviet in the Kronstadt naval base, bringing the soviet under Bolshevik influence and keeping control of the ultra-radical anarchist elements among the sailors.

During the civil war of 1918–1921, Raskolnikov commanded land units as well as Bolshevik naval forces and became deputy people's commissar of naval affairs.

During 1921–1923, he was Soviet representative in Afghanistan and in the mid-1930s served as envoy to Estonia, Denmark and Bulgaria. In April 1938, in the midst of the purges, he was recalled to Moscow but chose to defect to Belgium. In mid-1939, he wrote an open letter denouncing STALIN's purges as a betrayal of socialism. Two months later he died in unexplained circumstances in the south of France.

RASULZADE, MAMED EMIN (1884–1955) One of the foremost social and political leaders of Azerbaijan who stood at the cradle of Azerbaijani nationhood at the beginning of the 20th century. Rasulzade was born in the village of Novchani near Baku. He attended the Baku Trade School, where he first became acquainted with various political movements of that time, including MARXISM. In 1904 he became one of the founders of *Gummet* (Energy), the Azberbaijani Social Democratic Organization, whose members from 1905 included NARIMANOV and AZIZBEKOV.

In 1908, Rasulzade moved to Iran in order to participate in the national liberation struggle of the Azerbaijanis of Iran against the shah's rule. While also being deeply involved in southern Azerbaijan, he edited the newspaper *Iran Nou* (New Iran). In 1910, with his direct involvement, the Democratic Party of Iran was created.

The Czarist government became upset by Rasulzade's revolutionary activities in Iran and demanded his arrest by the Irani rulers. This forced him to emigrate to Turkey.

In 1913, taking advantage of the amnesty instituted to mark the 300th year of the Romanov dynasty's rule, Rasulzade returned to Azerbaijan. Starting in 1915, he edited the newspaper *Atch'ig Sez* (The honest word). In October 1917, Rasulzade was elected the party chairman. After the October RUSSIAN REVOLUTION OF 1917 and after the Transcaucasian Sejm had disbanded itself, the National Soviet of Azerbaijan became the government. Rasulzade was elected its chairman on May 28, 1918. At its first meeting, the National Council ratified "The Azerbaijan Independence Act" and announced the creation of the Azerbaijani Democratic Republic.

After the 11th RED ARMY entered Azerbaijan in April of 1918, Rasulzade was arrested but afterwards released and sent to Moscow, where he worked at the Comissariat of Nationalities of the Russian Soviet Federated Socialist Republic (RSFSR). In 1922 he succeeded in emigrating to Finland, from where he moved to Turkey for the second time. In 1931 Rasulzade was forced to leave Turkey for political reasons and moved first to Poland and then to Romania. He returned to Turkey only after World War II, in 1947, where he died. He was buried in Ankara.

RAWLINGS, JERRY JOHN (1947–) Ghanaian revolutionary. Rawlings was born in 1947 and educated in Ghana. He joined the air force and became a pilot, being promoted to flight lieutenant in 1978. In May 1979, he led the junior officers who staged an unsuccessful coup attempt against Ghana's ruling supreme military council. He was arrested, charged with mutiny and imprisoned, but subsequently released. On June 4, 1979, he and his associates seized power, amid great popular acclaim.

Rawlings and his fellow officers established an Armed Forces Revolutionary Council (AFRC) and initiated a campaign to eradicate corruption. The AFRC made clear that its assumption of power was temporary. General elections in June 1979 were won by the People's National Party (PNP) headed by Dr. Hilla Limann, who became president.

On December 31, 1981, Rawlings seized power for the second time, in a coup that was widely anticipated. The constitution was abolished, parliament dissolved and political parties banned. Rawlings assumed chairmanship of a Provisional National Defense Council (PNDC). This time he expressed no intention of restoring power to civilian politicians.

The PNDC decided to implement measures to "democratize" political decision-making and to decentralize power. It set up People's Defense Committees (PDCs) in an attempt to create mass participation at local level. These PDCs were to form the basic structure of the new government.

However, there was dissatisfaction among students, trade unions and some army members, which was encouraged by poor economic conditions. From 1990, the demand for increased democracy grew, both from within Ghana and from western donor countries. In September 1992, Rawlings retired from the armed forces and was nominated as the presidential candidate of the NDC (National Democratic Congress). He and his party were successful in the elections and Rawlings became president of Ghana's Fourth Republic. The PNDC was officially dissolved and a new parliament inaugurated.

REBEYNE In Lyons in 1426, this was a popular revolt against the French king. The town of Lyons, situated near the border between the kingdom of France and the duchy of Burgundy, had long suffered from the war between the two; at the same time it was able to play off the one against the other in order to avoid a variety of duties and taxes. When, in 1435, the Treaty of Arras put an end to the war, the town saw its independence threatened. Attempts at negotiation were to no avail; King Charles VII seemed determined to reimpose all the old taxes, including the hated *taille* (land tax) and *gabelle* (salt tax), and to levy them even without consent. Accordingly, the people of Lyons rose and drove out the royal officials, though in fact no one was killed. For two months (April–May 1536) the town remained in the rebels' hands until the king arrived "with many soldiers" and put an end to the revolt. In the reprisals that followed, a few of the ringleaders were decapitated and 120 citizens banished. The suppression of the Rebeyne marks a critical step in the reestablishment of royal control over the provinces of France during the later stages of the Hundred Years' War.

RED ARMY (China) The original Chinese Communist military force (1927–1937). After the GUOMINDANG (GMD) purged the CHINESE COMMUNIST PARTY (CCP) in 1927, the CCP resorted to armed struggle. Its NANCHANG UPRISING of August 1 is celebrated as the anniversary of the founding of the Red Army. Led by MAO ZEDONG and ZHU DE, the peasant-based Red Army grew in the CCP stronghold in Jiangxi until forced to embark upon the LONG MARCH in October 1934. Its strength radically depleted, the Red Army regrouped in northern Shaanxi. After the outbreak of the Sino-Japanese war (1937–1945) and renewal of the coalition with the GMD, the Red Army was renamed the EIGHTH ROUTE ARMY, and was subsequently redesignated the PEOPLE'S LIBERATION ARMY (see also AUTUMN HARVEST UPRISINGS, CANTON UPRISING, CHINESE SOVIET REPUBLIC).

RED ARMY A decree of the Council of People's Commissars in Russia, dated January 28, 1918, established a volunteer military force to be called The Workers' and Peasants' Red Army to replace the Imperial Russian Army that, demoralized by defeat and debilitated by desertion, had been officially disbanded. Only workers and toiling peasants were to bear arms, with non-proletarians called to serve in labor battalions.

As civil war intensified in the summer of 1918, compulsory service was introduced and the Red Army grew by 1920 to over 5 million soldiers. As a revolutionary force, the Red Army adopted democratic forms. Signs of rank were abolished and officers were addressed as "comrade commander." At the same time, the lack of experienced leadership brought the commissar for war, LEON TROTSKY, to conscript former czarist officers. These were balanced by political commissars, who, in addition to supervising the political education of the troops, countersigned every operational order before it was implemented.

Between 1921, when the civil war ended, and 1938, the Red Army underwent consolidation and modernization of its armaments and equipment. Military service became a universal obligation without distinction of class background. A sweeping reform in 1935 reintroduced officers' ranks.

Like all parts of Soviet society, the Red Army was hit by Stalin's purges. Three of five marshals, virtually all generals of armies and commanders of military districts, and about one-third of all other officers down to the rank of company commander, were dismissed, and many were jailed and executed.

World War II produced a new generation of skilled, professional Red Army commanders. From 1942, the political commissar was demoted from co-commander to deputy for political affairs, though he still maintained considerable authority. The Red Army also re-adopted titles, awards and traditions of the former Imperial Army: epaulettes, saluting, officers' privileges, etc. In 1946 the army's name was changed to the Soviet Army.

RED BRIGADES (Brigade Rosse) Italian terrorist-revolutionary group. Reputedly, its founder was Renato Curcio, (1945–) who, together with his wife and fellow radical Margherita Cagol, studied MARXISM and revolutionary theory during their years at the University of Trento. The Red Brigades took as their ideological starting point the notion that both the Italian Socialist Party and the Communist one had failed to do much for the country's working classes; hence the time for direct action had arrived.

The existence of the Red Brigades was proclaimed in November 1970 and marked by the firebombing of various factories and warehouses. From 1971 on their terrorist campaign intensified, culminating in the kidnapping and subsequent murder of former Italian prime minister Aldo Moro, which took place in 1978. In 1981, a senior American officer with NATO, Brigadier General James Dozier, was also kidnapped but was later rescued by Italian police. The group at its height probably counted fewer than 400 active members. Another 1,000 or so were active part time, and the Brigades also had several thousand supporters who provided funds, shelter and communications services.

However, from the mid-1970s on, the Italian police began to gain the upper hand as Curcio himself was captured (1974), was enabled to escape (1975) and captured again (1976). Since the late 1980s, little has been heard of the group.

RED EYEBROWS (18 A.D.) Chinese peasant rebels. Originating from a Daoist-influenced secret society, peasant bands with painted eyebrows started a revolt in Shandong that spread rapidly. The general administrative breakdown during WANG MANG's reign (9–23 A.D.), famines caused by bad harvests and the flooding of the Yellow river were main contributory factors. Devastating the land, the peasants lacked the political and administrative experience to create a new dynasty, but their rebellion hastened Wang Mang's downfall.

REICHSBANNER SCHWARZ-ROT-GOLD (1924–1933) During the years of the Weimar Republic, a paramilitary organization formed by the German left. Established in 1924, the Reichsbanner was supposed to supply an operative answer to the paramilitary organizations of the right and far-right, such as Hitler's SA and the Stalhelm. In theory it was apolitical; in practice, most of the 3 million members which it had during its heyday were members of the Social Democratic Party.

In theory, the Reichsbanner was a formidable organization, especially when joined by other left-wing forces with which it created the *Eiserne front* (Iron front). In fact, it turned out to be little more than a hestitant, loose and weak showcase of traditional social democratic policies. In 1931, it failed to react when chancellor Franz von Papen illegally deposed the Social Democratic government of Prussia, thereby breaking one of the party's principal power bases and greatly facilitating Hitler's final takeover. In 1933, after Hitler came to power, the organization was outlawed and disbanded without resistance.

RENAMO (RESISTÊNCIA NACIONAL MOÇAMBIQUE) (MNR) A guerilla group set up by the Rhodesian government intelligence organization during the undeclared war between Rhodesia and Mozambique (1976–1979). It was recruited from the disaffected, including some former members of FRELIMO.

By 1981, the collapse of the white régime in Rhodesia and internal dissension had substantially reduced Renamo's size and effectiveness. However, it received considerable sums of aid from South Africa and carried out acts of economic destruction, particularly against Mozambique's transportation infrastructure.

RENAMO's armed conflict with the FRELIMO government of Mozambique continued until FRELIMO announced multiparty elections and RENAMO became one of the newly-established political parties (1991–1992). In October 1992, a peace agreement was signed between the government and RENAMO, but it has not yet been fully implemented and serious violations have been reported. RENAMO's president is Afonso Dlakama.

REPUBLIC OF SALO see ITALIAN SOCIAL REPUBLIC.

RESTORATION SOCIETY see GUANG FU HUI.

REVERE, PAUL (1734–1818) American revolutionary. On the night of April 18, 1775, British troops sent by General Thomas Gage marched through Massachusetts to seize colonial military stores. "One if by land, two if by sea," was the signal for Paul Revere to gallop through Boston's surrounding towns and warn of their approach. His alarm enabled the MINUTEMEN in Lexington and Concord to confront them with the "shot that sounded around the world," launching the AMERICAN REVOLUTION. Revere became a legend in American history; his name evokes a "take charge" attitude of courage and patriotism. In *Tales of a Wayside Inn* (1863), Henry Wadsworth Longfellow included the ballad, "Paul Revere's Ride," to rally northern pride during the Civil War. Yet, Revere's contributions to America's struggle for independence went far beyond his famous ride.

While a boy in Boston, Revere learned silversmithing. As an adept craftsman, he became a prominent member of the SONS OF LIBERTY, a local group of merchants, intellectuals, and political leaders that discussed and organized responses to oppressive British policies in the colonies. These usually involved a passive boycott of British goods but there were several notable exceptions, among them the BOSTON TEA PARTY (1773). This strengthened the resolve of radicals in New York and Philadelphia to boycott British tea. In the fall of 1774, Revere presented the decisions of a group of Boston radicals, the Suffolk Resolves, at a meeting in Philadelphia of delegates from 12 of the colonies. They were adopted unanimously by the conference. Other important contributions by him to the revolution included the copper printing plates he produced, containing scathing political cartoons attacking the British. His Boston Massacre depicted a British platoon firing upon command at unarmed and helpless civilians. His jabs were a popular feature of *The Royal American Magazine* (published between January 1774 and March 1775) and did much to promote the colonists' cause among the masses.

Revere later served as a colonel in the American Revolution. His military career, however, was undistinguished. He commanded American troops at Castle William, Boston Harbor's primary defense, and artillery positions in several unsuccessful field campaigns. He also manufactured military equipment such as cannons and built a gun powder mill.

Despite his contributions to the revolutionary cause, Revere preferred the image later immortalized in a portrait by J. S. Copley: a simple silversmith seated at his workbench in a short-sleeved shirt. In fact, Revere was among the foremost American artists of his period. Not only had he contributed to the downfall of British rule; he had, with his art, helped forge an independent American identity.

REVOLT OF THE NETHERLANDS see NETHERLANDS, REVOLT OF.

REVOLT OF THE THREE FEUDATORIES see SAN FAN REBELLION.

REVOLUTIONARY ALLIANCE see TONGMENGHUI.

REVOLUTIONARY COMMITTEE OF UNITY AND ACTION see COMITÉ RÉVOLUTIONNAIRE D'UNITÉ ET D'ACTION.

REVOLUTION FROM ABOVE In German history, an attempt by Chancellor Otto von Bismarck (1815–1898) to weaken the Social Democratic Party by introducing reforms that would steal its thunder. A stern opponent of the socialists—he once described them as "rats" and tried to prevent them from participating in parliament—Bismarck was forced to stand by as they increased their power from one election campaign to the next. Accordingly, in the early 1880s, he changed tack: in a series of measures that were unprecedented for any country, he introduced old age, health and unemployment insurance schemes that were a model of their kind and which were later widely imitated. Though the so-called "revolution from above" was not a success—the workers took the benefits they were offered and continued to vote socialist—the term has entered the language, and many others have since followed in Bismarck's footsteps.

REVOLUTIONS OF 1830   The years 1780–1815 had been a period of war and turmoil during which the French Revolutionary and Napoleonic troops spread the message of *"liberté, egalite, fraternite"* far and wide. However, the settlement made by the Congress of Vienna left things much as they had been during the *ancien régime*. Countries such as France, Spain and Naples, whose monarchical régimes had been overthrown, saw them restored. To prevent a recurrence of the revolutionary movement everywhere, basic liberties such as the people's right to participate in government, freedom of assembly and freedom of the press were suppressed.

The period between 1815 and 1830 was also the one in which the industrial revolution, having been stimulated by the British blockade and Napoleon's *systeme continentale* during the years 1803–1815, began to conquer the continent. With the former French example in front of their eyes, the rapidly rising middle classes would not acquiesce in the superiority of the aristocracy nor have their right to participate in government denied. This was all the more so because it was precisely the sons of these classes who had formed the backbone of the officer corps of the French *grande armee*; and, consequently, of its opponents.

France. In the event, the first country to raise the standard of revolt against the régime imposed by Count Metternich at Vienna was France. Ruled by a brother of Louis XVI—the same who had lost his head to the guillotine in 1792—France since 1815 had retained some of the Revolutionary gains: including a constitution, a bicameral legislature (the upper house was hereditary, the lower one elected), a limited franchise, and basic liberties such as freedom of religion and of the press. In July 1830, King Charles X, having "forgotten nothing and learnt nothing" (as Louis-Napoleon put it), thought the time had come to undo these innovations. The occasion was formed by his attempt to raise money for the conquest of Algeria, which though successful was highly unpopular at the time. Led by the fanatical Polignac, his government arbitrarily lowered the interest-rates that it paid on its bonds. When that move led to a storm of protest, Charles also abolished freedom of the press; modified the constitution so as to cut the number of those entitled to vote by three quarters; and, to top it all, introduced a law which prescribed capital punishment for sacrilegious acts committed in churches.

The revolution, which broke out spontaneously on 27 July, succeeded almost without fighting. Having at first tried to compromise by dismissing Polignac, after a mere three days Charles was forced to give up and flee to England. A new liberal régime was set up under King Louis Philippe, grandson of the Duke D'ORLEANS who had supported the original FRENCH REVOLUTION

and lost his life as a result. Under the so-called July Monarchy, the electorate was extended by lowering the voting age and the minimum property-qualification; the Upper Chamber was transformed from a hereditary into a nominated house; censorship was abolished; Roman Catholicism ceased to be the state religion (the new constitution described it simply as "the religion of the majority of Frenchmen"); and the revolutionary *tricouleur* again became France's national flag.

German, Poland, Italy and Belgium.   As France was able to get rid of its king and régime, revolutionaries in other countries sought to follow its example. In particular, there were revolutionary outbursts in Germany, Poland and Italy; unlike their French colleagues, however, their aims were not only liberal but national as well. In Germany, which since 1815 had been divided into 39 states (instead of the 300 that existed until 1806) the uprisings were aimed at putting an end to the absolutist régimes imposed by the Congress of Vienna and achieving national unification. In Poland, they were aimed against the Russian czar, and in Italy they sought to expel the Austrians and achieve national independence (see RISORGIMENTO). However, the uprisings which broke out in many towns at once suffered from a lack of central direction and coordination. Consequently the revolutionaries proved unable to withstand the dragoons sent against them by the authorities, and were suppressed quite easily; the more so since Louis Philippe, once he had ascended to the French throne, chose the side of caution and refused to send support. The one exception to the rule was Belgium, where the uprising led to the country's separation from the Netherlands, of which it had formed part since 1815. The result was the establishment of Belgium as an independent state that has survived to the present day.

REVOLUTIONS OF 1848   Like the REVOLUTIONS OF 1830, the series of revolutions that broke out all over Europe in 1848 were partly liberal and partly nationalist in character. Likewise, they were really successful in only one country, i.e., France. The historical importance of the revolutions of 1848 was much greater, however, since they proved the last of their kind. When the next revolutions took place early in the 20th century, they were led by the Communist Party rather than by the middle classes. Accordingly, their goal was not to establish a liberal régime but a Soviet one supposedly dominated by the working class.

The first revolutions of 1848 took place in Sicily, a country which since 1815 had formed part of the kingdom of Naples; it was ruled by a reactionary Bourbon king and was one of the most backward regions of Europe. In the event, the revolutionaries—mostly urban residents belonging to the middle classes—achieved nothing. However, the fire which they ignited spread, first to France and then to other countries. By March most of Europe, except Spain (which had already gone through *its* revolutions by way of the series of conflicts known as the Carlist Wars), Russia and Scandinavia, was in flames. Even in normally placid Britain the revolutionary stirrings made themselves felt, albeit that they only took the relatively harmless form of Chartist demonstrations and (in Ireland) republican agitation that was quickly suppressed.

France. In France, the revolution of February 1848 was quickly successful. Initially both King Louis Philippe and his chief minister, Guizot, had underestimated the seriousness of the unrest;

The tricolor being adopted as the flag of the French Republic during the French Revolution of 1848

A revolutionary barricade in Vienna, a center of the Austrian nationalist revolution that took place in 1848

after just one day of clashes they fled, and a Second Republic embodying many of the principles of the First—including universal suffrage—was established. However, by this time the middle classes who made the revolution no longer possessed a monopoly over revolutionary fervor. At their side there had risen a numerous, politically conscious working class, for whom the establishment of a liberal republic did not go far enough. When the new régime, led by LAMARTINE, proved unwilling or unable to meet the demands of the left for far-reaching social and economic reforms, a second and much more violent revolution broke out in Paris in June 1848. Its was brutally suppressed by the army under the command of General Cabignac, whose reputation as a butcher had been made in Algeria; the number of those who died is estimated at 1,500, whereas 12,000 more were arrested. Now thoroughly frightened, the middle classes as well as the peasantry gave their votes to an adventurer, Louis Napoleon. Gaining an enormous majority at the polls, he was elected president of the republic and later (1851) made himself emperor by means of a coup d'état.

Germany and Austria. Meanwhile, the revolution had spread to Germany, where the most important outbursts took place in Berlin, Frankfurt am Main and Vienna. In March, the citizens of Berlin took to the barricades; after brief fighting, they succeeded in forcing King Frederik William IV and his army to leave the city for the nearby garrison town of Potsdam. This, as well as

the simultaneous uprising in Vienna which compelled prime minister Metternich to flee and temporarily paralyzed the power of Austria, encouraged nationalists from all over Germany to convene in Frankfurt. Here they made endless speeches and agitated in favor of national unification.

The Frankfurt Congress was, however, anything but united. Some of those present—they included a remarkably large percentage of professors—wanted a liberal republic modeled on the one which had just been established in France. Others wanted a "small" German monarchy under the king of Prussia, whereas others still looked to a "large" German empire ruled from Vienna and including also the non-German parts of the Austrian monarchy, i.e., what are now Czechoslovakia, Croatia, Northern Italy and parts of Romania. In the event, the congress decided to offer the crown to Prussia's Frederick William IV. The latter hesitated and in the end declined the offer because, coming from a democratic assembly, it was incompatible with his standing as the absolute king of Prussia. His refusal delayed the unification of Germany by another two decades. When it finally came, it was carried out by the Prussian military rather than by liberal professors.

Meanwhile in Vienna, the place of Metternich had been taken by Prince Felix zu Schwarzenberg. Using the army, he started by crushing the nationalist uprisings that had broken out in the outlying parts of the monarchy, i.e., Bohemia and Italy; in the latter General Radetzsky also took the opportunity to defeat Sardinia, which had sought to profit from the disorder in Vienna in order to try and take over Lombardy. By September, imperial forces, made up largely of "wild" men from the Croat frontier provinces and commanded by General Windischgraetz, were besieging Vienna itself. As had happened in Paris, the Viennese revolution was becoming radicalized and its leadership was passing out of the hands of the middle classes and into those of the workers; the former wanted order, the latter, bread. It took several days of brutal fighting, accompanied by massacres, to subdue the city.

Encouraged by these events, Frederick William of Prussia took heart. In December 1848 the Prussian army was able to re-enter Berlin, which surrendered without fighting; subsequently Prussian army contingents were sent to dispatch what remained of the revolution in Western Germany, a task that they achieved without undue difficulty.

Italy and Hungary. By this time, the only parts of Europe still in rebel hands were Rome, where MAZZINI had proclaimed a republic, and Hungary, where anti-Habsburg nationalists had taken over the country (see also HUNGARY, REVOLTS AND REVOLUTIONS). In the event it took a French army, sent by Louis Napoleon, to put down the Roman Republic and restore papal government, which was thereby granted another 22 years of life (see RISORGIMENTO). The Hungarian uprising was finally crushed by a Russian army which, acting on the invitation of Emperor Francis Joseph, invaded the country and occupied Budapest.

An observer surveying Europe at the end of 1849 might have concluded that, except in France, the revolutions had failed, but such an impression was misleading. In neither Prussia nor Austria were the hopes of the liberals realized; however, the former adopted a constitution (the same which was to last until 1918) whereas, in the latter, the last remains of serfdom were abolished. Equally important, the aspirations of nationalists in Germany, Italy, Hungary and Bohemia were suppressed but not broken. By 1871 the first two had gained unification and independence; the third had become an equal partner with Austria under Habsburg rule, whereas the fourth was continuing its agitation until success was eventually achieved in 1918. For all these reasons the revolutions of 1848 marked a decisive step in the historical development of modern Europe, putting some countries on the way to liberalism and others on the route that eventually led to national unity. Though the rebels' immediate goals were brought to nought by cannon-fire, the results of their actions are still with us today.

RIDOLFI PLOT (1571) A plan to kill Queen Elizabeth I and place Mary, Queen of Scots on the throne in her place. Mary was the wife of Thomas Howard, the Duke of Norfolk. The plot was devised by an Italian banker named Roberto Ridolfi (1531–1612) and had the support of King Philip II of Spain. It was uncovered in September 1571 when Ridolfi was abroad and thereby escaped, leaving the unfortunate Norfolk to pay for the plot with his life.

RIEL, LOUIS DAVID (1844–1885) Leader of the MÉTIS REBELLION. Born in Manitoba, Canada, on October 23, 1844, Riel is considered a real Canadian hero who supported and fought for the country's indigenous people. He was of Indian, French and Irish blood and was the leader of the Métis, people of mixed European (especially French) and Indian descent. He studied law and, when in 1869 the Hudson Bay Company sold a large tract of land to the Canadian government, he led the Métis rebellion. The Métis were afraid the Canadian government would override their interest and they would lose their rights. They also feared the influx of English-speaking people. They seized Fort Gary—the area that is now Winnipeg—which was the headquarters of the Hudson Bay Company at the time. There Riel established an interim government with himself as president and began negotiations on satisfactory conditions for joining Canada.

In May 1870, Canada established the province of Manitoba and guaranteed that the insurgents would not be prosecuted. However, Riel's government tried and executed an English-speaking Canadian. This led to the revocation of the amnesty and Canadian military forces were sent against the Riel government. Fort Gary was captured by the Canadian forces and Riel escaped. In 1871, he urged his followers to stave off an attack by Irish troops. He was elected to the dominion parliament in 1873 but he never attended. In 1874, he was dismissed but rapidly reelected. In 1875, the Canadian government exiled Riel for five years. He grew increasingly mentally unstable and spent a year in a mental institution and five relatively peaceful years in Montana in the United States, where he became a citizen in 1883. While in the United States, he began a movement to organize the Métis of America.

In 1884, he was approached by the Saskatchewan Métis to represent them in their land dispute with the Canadian government. He first proceeded legally but later, in 1885, established a temporary government, followed by an insurgency. When it was quelled, he gave up. He was tried, found guilty of treason and hanged. His execution caused large disturbances in Ontario and Quebec.

RIENZO, COLA DI (1313–1354) Roman demagogue and leader. Cola di Rienzo was the son of a poor publican and ever since childhood aspired toward a better career. An autodidact, he attained the position of notary and became involved in public affairs. In 1343, he was sent on a diplomatic mission to Pope Clement VI at Avignon. Impressed by the young man, the pope appointed him notary of the Apostolic Chamber at Rome, one of the most influential positions of the city. After his return to Rome, Rienzo began to dream about ways of restoring Rome's greatness under his own leadership. In 1347 he proclaimed himself tribune of the people, according to the ancient Roman tradition. Within a few months he succeeded in heading a popular movement and, styling himself master of the city, proclaimed the unity of Italy. He won wide support, especially in central Italy, where cities sent him armies to realize his dream. At the height of his ambitions, he proclaimed himself "August" and summoned the pope to Rome. A counterrevolution led by the aristocracy forced him to flee. He fled to Avignon, where he was imprisoned. He was freed in 1353 by Pope Innocent VI, who sent him to Italy with the army led by Cardinal Albornoz, in an attempt to reconquer the states which had been lost by the papacy. Appointed senator, Rienzo succeeded in imposing his rule on Rome in 1354. To secure his position, he repressed the population, which in turn revolted, causing his final defeat and death.

RISORGIMENTO   Also known as *rivoluzione Italiana,* the term refers to the political and cultural events between the years 1796 (the conquest of Italy by Napoleon) and 1861 (the establishment of the kingdom of Italy) that led to the unification of Italy. The term, which literally means rebirth or re-creation, was borrowed from the title of a newspaper founded in 1847 by Camillo Benso di Cavour, a newspaper which advocated the creation of a united Italy.

During the time of the Risorgimento, Italy was divided into a patchwork of small kingdoms, many under Austrian hegemony. Liberal and socialist intellectuals, enlightened aristocrats and even the Catholic church supported the concept of Italian reunification as a means of ending the foreign occupation of the country and of improving the lot of the impoverished peasantry: many believed that political change would necessarily lead to economic development.

Throughout this period, various ideologues of the Risorgimento proposed many different means of resolving the "Italian Question." Some advocated diplomatic and military ventures to create a federation of Italian states. Others, such as GIUSEPPE MAZZINI and the *Giovine Italia* (YOUNG ITALY) movement, were influenced by the FRENCH REVOLUTION and called for the establishment of a democratic republic. The latter believed that popular insurrections throughout the country would force the Habsburgs of Austria to stop interfering in Italian affairs. Vincenzo Gioberti won the support of Pope Pius IX for a united Italy under papal dominion (the idea was abandoned over disputes concerning the extent of the pope's temporal powers), while CARLO PISACANE believed that the political unification of the country should lead to far-reaching changes in the established social order and to secularization. There were also secret societies such as the CARBONARI, which united Freemasons and democrats in various schemes to overthrow local governments.

The Risorgimento was a time of numerous insurrections and revolutions throughout Italy. Particularly noteworthy were the revolutions of the early 1830s and those of 1848–1849, which paralleled the general state of revolutionary unrest that shook Europe (see REVOLUTIONS OF 1830 and REVOLUTIONS OF 1848). Yet, although much of the credit for Italian unity can be attributed to the sense of purpose that these revolutions elicited, it was actually the political and military machinations of King Victor Emmanuel II of Savoy, his minister Cavour and GIUSEPPE GARIBALDI that eventually led to the establishment of the Kingdom of Italy between 1861 and 1870.

RIZHINASHVILI, ABRAM (YITZKA)   (1886–1906) Georgian Jewish professional revolutionary. Rizhinashvili joined the revolutionary movement while still at school. In 1903, he began studying at the Leipzig University, where he continued his involvement in revolutionary activities in a BOLSHEVIK group. At the very beginning of the RUSSIAN REVOLUTION OF 1905 he returned to his homeland to lead the revolutionary struggle in Kutaisi—a major city in western Georgia—in the name of the Russian Social Democratic Workers Party. While involved in this task, Rizhinashvili arranged theoretical discussions with the MENSHEVIKS. Police agents killed him in 1906.

ROBESPIERRE, MAXIMILIEN-FRANÇOIS-MARIE-ISIDORE DE   (1758–1794) Leader of the FRENCH REVOLUTION

of 1789. Of Robespierre it was said that, "There are two Robespierres, the one a genuine patriot and man of principle up to 31 May [1794], and since then a man of ambition, the tyrant and the deepest of villains." It was in this former role, as a man who could galvanize support with a speech on any subject and with a fanatic determination to implement his beliefs, that Robespierre rose to rule Paris.

Born in Arras, France, Robespierre served as a criminal judge there until forced to resign to avoid giving a death sentence. He became a successful lawyer and entered the intellectual circles. Particularly drawn by Jean-Jacques Rousseau's eloquent denouncements of modern society's evils, he came to believe that human discord stemmed from the unequal distribution of wealth and the size and complexities of society, and that it could be remedied by the establishment of an egalitarian state united by fundamental beliefs and just laws. Going beyond Rousseau, he concluded that only by deposing existing régimes could such a society be forged. He advocated a religion of revolution with himself as its foremost prophet.

In 1789 Robespierre was elected to the Estates-General, the French parliament consisting of representatives from three different "estates" or classes. Soon after, his own Third Estate—comprising the middle class—seceded from the body to form the National Constituent Assembly. The bulk of his supporters came from the Society of Friends of the Constitution, better known as JACOBINS, the most radical of the groups advocating change. He had clashed with the more conservative GIRONDINS over the role of the monarchy and nobility in a reconstituted France, demanding that power be given to the majority lower classes; the Girondins believed that the bourgeoisie and upper classes should hold the bulk of power.

As his influence increased so did the Girondins' acerbic attacks on him. To counter these he started a journal, *The Defense of the Constitution*, in 1792. He also took a seat on the PARIS COMMUNE to try and foil the Girondins who held power in that group. But his biggest help came from the French losses in the war it had declared against the rest of Europe. This "Revolutionary War" was strongly supported by the Girondins, who wished to spread revolution to the rest of Europe. The military losses helped Robespierre raise counterrevolutionary suspicions against the Girondins, claiming that the war's true goal was to reinstate the power of the monarchy. Fired by these fears, the legislative convention met, abolished the monarchy and officially declared the new Republic of France. The overthrow of Louis XVI was completed with his trial in December. Robespierre "the Incorruptible," as he was popularly known, galvanized support for executing the king with these famous words: "It is with regret that I pronounce that fatal truth: Louis ought to perish rather than a hundred thousand virtuous citizens; Louis must die, that the country may live."

After the king was executed on January 21, 1793, Robespierre faced a tremendous task—that of instituting social change in France. The Montagnards' strongest support came from the SANS-CULOTTES, the lower-class mix of shopkeepers, workers, craftsmaen and farmers. The social changes Robespierre supported benefited them the most: higher taxes on the rich, a freeze on prices, free education and more assistance to the poor and disabled.

On the one hand, these changes were Robespierre's greatest

success, but on the other hand, his method of implementing them was ruthless and eventually caused his downfall. Robespierre attempted to eliminate all opposition, even if it also supported social change. He destroyed the Girondin Party in the Commune of Paris in the late spring of 1793. He was then elected to the COMMITTEE OF PUBLIC SAFETY on July 27. Because of his popularity and power, this practically put him in charge of the "terror" and the revolutionary tribunal. The terror eventually lost all connection to law; enemies of the revolution were denounced and executed without witnesses or a trial. In total, over 300,000 people were arrested and over 17,000 killed. Yet Robespierre saw this as an integral part of a revolution that was, "not just for man alive today but for all those who will live later."

The spring of 1794 marked the beginning of the end. Robespierre was ill and absent from his public posts for several weeks. In that time, he was severely attacked by the more moderate groups, led by GEORGES DANTON and JACQUES-RENÉ HÉBERT. Hébert, who was in favor of a much more decentralized rule, re-

So goes the woe of France; Robespierre as executioner

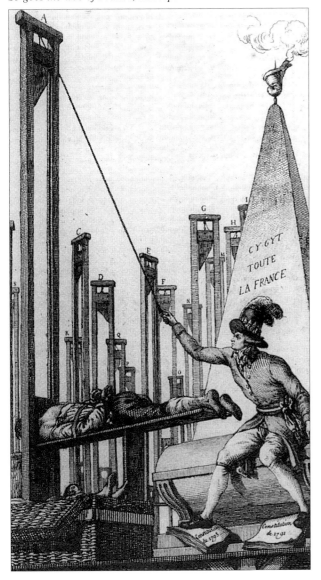

ferred to Robespierre in one speech as "the ambitious" and in another as "a man led astray, no doubt." On his return, Robespierre angrily denounced the "traitors" saying, "Would to God that my physical strength were equal to my moral strength." Danton and Hébert along with their supporters were soon arrested and executed.

In the last six weeks of his life, Robespierre further intensified the terror in Paris—no fewer than 1,285 people were guillotined in that time. His downfall came when he tried to further centralize power around himself. In his final speech at the CONVENTION he was constantly interrupted with shouts of "Down with the tyrant!" Isolated from the support of his colleagues and a defeated man, Robespierre was arrested on July 27, 1794—the 9th of Thermidor (according to the revolutionary calendar). He attempted to commit suicide, but only shot himself in the jaw and was executed the following day.

ROCCO, ALFREDO   (1875–1935) One of the main theorists of Italian nationalism, Rocco dealt with matters of socioeconomic and political organization and became one of the founders of the Fascist (see FASCISM) corporative State. Before World War I, Rocco was active in the ranks of the Italian Nationalist Association (ANI), where he presented his authoritarian ideals of economic nationalism as a response to socialist and liberal thought. Pursuing an academic legal career, Rocco moved into politics after the war. In 1918, he began publishing *Politica* with a fellow nationalist, Francesco Coppola, and became a member of the Fascist Party when the ANI joined the Fascists in February 1923. After serving in parliament and as undersecretary of the treasury and later of war pensions, Rocco was appointed minister of justice by MUSSOLINI in January 1925, at the beginning of the Fascist dictatorship. Rocco's alternative to the Italian liberal democratic state was a Fascist corporative totalitarian state. His basic economic vision was one of productionism leading to national economic self-sufficiency and imperialism. In order to strengthen the economy and carry out these plans, in 1926 Rocco drafted a series of syndical laws allowing for state intervention and control of the labor market, outlawing strikes and lockouts, and imposing state mediation in the case of conflicts. A further step was taken in 1927, with the publication of the *Carta del lavoro*, an ideological document based on Rocco's principles. In 1928, Rocco played a major role in the corporativist reform of parliament and in drafting the law that regulated the Fascist Grand Council. In 1931 he influenced the drafting of the new penal code. Removed from the ministry of justice in 1932 as part of Mussolini's personal changes in government, Rocco was appointed director of the University of Rome and a senator in 1934. He died in 1935.

ROCHAMBEAU, COMTE DE   (1725–1802) Jean-Baptiste-Donatien de Vineur. A general who, along with MARQUIS DE LAFAYETTE and the Comte de Segur, helped the American revolutionaries win the battle of Yorktown in Virginia. This helped guarantee American independence.

RÖHM ERNST   (1887–1934) German military and Nazi leader. Born to a family of officials, Röhm became a career army officer and served in World War I. In 1920 Röhm found himself on the army's staff in Bavaria, in charge of controlling paramilitary organizations to defy Allied and domestic German rules imposed after the defeat. One of the bodies which he tried to control was ADOLF HITLER's NATIONAL SOCIALIST PARTY; in 1923 they joined forces in the abortive revolt, or putsch, (see BEER-HALL PUTSCH) whose objective was to make the Bavarian leadership and the army overthrow the Weimar government.

Forced to resign from the army in 1924, Röhm was elected to parliament where he represented the right-wing Freedom Party. More social revolutionary-oriented than Hitler, he broke with him and tried to organize his own paramilitary force, the *Frontbanner*; however, Germany's return to economic prosperity thwarted his revolutionary plans and caused him to leave the country in disgust. He spent two years in Bolivia, training its army, before responding to Hitler's call to return home and assume command as chief of staff of the SA.

In his new post, Röhm was a great success. He reorganized the SA, built it up until it numbered a million members, and turned it into a serious threat to the republic and one which played a crucial role in its demise. When the Nazis took power, Röhm became a minister without portfolio in Hitler's cabinet, a position that seemed to him to maintain the SA's role as a middle power standing between the Nazi Party and the State; it also helped him cover up the illegal atrocities which were committed by his organization in the newly-established concentration camps.

Röhm, who was less anti-Semitic than Hitler but more inclined towards left-wing ideas, hoped to turn his SA into the armed force of the new German State. In this way he found himself caught between Hitler, the Party's racial ideologists, the army and the traditional institutions of the state. Declared to be a rebel and a traitor, Röhm, along with the rest of the SA's top leadership, was arrested and executed by the SS on June 30, 1934.

ROLAND, MANON (1754–1793) The wife of Roland de la Platière, a leading GIRONDIN politician during the FRENCH REVOLUTION. Roland held a salon in Paris frequented by such people as ROBESPIERRE, BRISSOT and other notable revolutionary leaders. It was thanks to her influence that her husband entered the royal cabinet during the Legislative Assembly, but her personal loathing for DANTON earned her the hatred of the JACOBIN majority in the CONVENTION, after she denounced the September massacres in 1792 and expressed her revulsion against the Terror. Along with other GIRONDINS, she was executed in November 1793, and is said to have exclaimed the celebrated words as she stepped up to the guillotine, "Oh liberty, what crimes are committed in thy name!"

ROMANIA, REVOLUTIONS
Communist Takeover (1947). Following Romania's royal coup d'état on August 23, 1944, the small Communist Party was in an excellent position to open its struggle for power. It had a leading position within the front organizations and political formations with non-Communists, especially in the National Democratic front with the National Liberals and National Peasants. Leading Communist activists, such as ANA PAUKER, returned with the Soviet forces, while local jailed leaders, especially GHEORGHIU-DEJ and Lucretiu Patrascanu, organized and built up the party structure. In the first cabinets, the Communists, pro-Communists and

Social Democrats held several important posts, with Gheorghiu-Dej, the party leader, serving as minister of communications. As a major test of the Yalta agreements, or rather of their Soviet interpretation, in March 1945 the first stage in the Communist takeover was introduced, with the imposition on King Michael of a government led by Petru Groza. Backed by Soviet political and military support and "spontaneous" demonstrations of Communist-manipulated masses, Dej and Pauker, who had conferred with STALIN in January 1945, acted with clear Soviet support for speeding up the country's "democratization," i.e., the agrarian reform which provided peasant support.

The return of northern Transylvania from Hungarian occupation to Romanian administration and later its reincorporation into Romania gave the Communists further popular support. From 1945, the Communists proceeded with tactics similar to those which they used in other East European states: working to cause rifts between the major opposition parties, deligitimizing those factions which did not succumb to Communist appeals for more "progressive" policies and successful attempts to act through front organizations, national minority organizations and trade unions. The "free" elections that were supposed to be held according to the Yalta agreements were postponed time after time. When they were finally held in November 1946, the National Democratic Front, "purified" of "bourgeois" elements, won a large majority. The Communists intensified their "divide and conquer" activities against the Social Democratic leaders who refused to unite with them. The unification finally took place in spring 1948—after dissident socialist leaders had been arrested for conspiracy. In 1947, the major dissident leaders of the National Peasants and National Liberals—the two "historical" Romanian parties—were discredited and some were arrested for ties with foreign agents. In late December 1947 came the turn of King Michael, who had been hailed in August 1944 by the Soviets and the Communists. Michael left the country and Romania was proclaimed a People's Republic. The process of Communist takeover was completed by March 1948, when new elections brought about the victory of the progressive forces and the new national assembly approved a Stalinist type of constitution. Tiny groups of peasants and liberals were left in the parliament, a poor shadow of their former power. By that time, the communization of the economy, educational system and the organizations of the national minorities—Hungarians, Germans, Jews—had been completed. The final stage in the Communist takeover coincided with the beginning of a bitter power struggle within the Communist Party, renamed the Romanian Workers' Party, as Lucretiu Patrascanu was accused and purged for "nationalist" leanings. He was executed in 1954.

Collapse of the Communist Régime (1989). The last years of the Ceausescu régime saw the height of the personality cult and megalomania of the dictator who, along with his wife and members of his family, brought Romania's Nationalist-Communist régime to almost complete isolation from the west and from the other bloc states. Its human rights record was absolutely atrocious, with grandiose plans of social engineering to be achieved by erasing hundreds of villages; the economy in a grave crisis, although foreign debts were repaid; the nation demoralized and ostracized by the world. The crisis was thus inevitable. Romania presented a "one man rejection front" against the Gorbachev type of reforms, as Ceausescu continued his policies regardless of the changing world around him. Dissidence was slow to emerge; several workers' disturbances were oppressed violently and there were isolated cases of dissident intellectuals who were gravely harassed and threatened by one of the most efficient security services of the Stalinist type of police state. In February 1989, several top veteran Communist leaders addressed the first known protest letter to Ceausescu, in which they warned of the dire consequences that would follow from the régime's policies and demanded immediate change, reforms and the resignation of the leader and his cronies.

The exact events of December 1989 are still shrouded in myths and conflicting versions. In early December 1989, the last congress of the Romanian Communist Party acclaimed the leader's policies, while some officials were blamed for problems in the economic situation. Even as the world crumbled around Romania, Ceausescu was promised the continuing loyalty of some 4 million party members. However, a well-orchestrated palace coup, along with popular resentment that was sparked in the Timisoara around the rough repression of the popular Hungarian Reverend Laszlo Tokes, developed into a wave of mass demonstrations in Bucharest and other major centers. The emerging National Salvation Front, which according to later versions was well organized underground and in which some former members of the *nomenklatura* (i.e., the party apparatus), including its leader, Ion Iliescu, took part, was supported by the armed forces. It engaged elements of the security service in a series of clashes. The violent clashes were later portrayed as either provocations or as myths created by the victors. Ceausescu and his wife were arrested and executed on Christmas Day following a summary trial. The charges against them focused more on the usurpation of rights, misuse of the people's trust and orders to open fire on demonstrators and not so much on the nature of the system itself. Due to the difficulties in transition to a stable democratic system and a market economy, the Romanian Revolution of 1989 was seen later by democratic and liberal elements as having been "kidnapped" by members of the former Communist *nomenklatura* and, as such, an uncompleted one. Thus, though it had discarded the elements of the "one-family" dynastic rule and removed the ideological framework, it had nevertheless kept intact some features of the previous power structures. On the other hand, powerful elements of the former *nomenklatura* adhered to Ceausescu's legacy and claimed that the revolution was the result of a coup engineered from outside—by foreign intelligence elements interested in destabilizing Romania, such as the Hungarian, the CIA, KGB and the Israeli Mossad.

ROME, ANCIENT, REVOLT OF THE PLEBEIANS   see PLEBEIAN REVOLT.

ROME, COMMUNE OF   Following the papal schism between Pope Innocent II and the antipopes Anacletus II and Victor IV in the 1130s, the great families of Rome initiated the *renovatio senatus* (renewal of the senate), a coup d'état aimed at setting up a civic régime, i.e., a commune (the medieval name for towns with a charter of liberties from an overlord, to which all residents had to swear allegiance). The heretic ARNOLD OF BRESCIA arrived two years later. He attacked the worldliness of the Church and maintained that confession should be made not to a priest but by one Christian to another. He also claimed that a priest's sinfulness destroys the value of the sacraments he administers. Arnold also asserted that the Church should not possess worldly goods or exercise temporal authority. He attempted to strengthen the civic régime by putting the government in the hands of rich laymen, whom he called the "equestrian order" after the ancient Roman model. After the accession of Frederick Barbarossa, a German king, to the Holy Roman Empire, the commune was crushed in 1155 and the power of the papacy in Rome strengthened.

ROSENBERG, ALFRED   (1893–1946) Nazi ideologue and politician. Rosenberg was born to a lower-middle-class family in Tallinn, Estonia, and studied architecture in Riga. Following the German defeat in World War I and the October RUSSIAN REVOLUTION OF 1917, which undermined German influence in his native Baltic world, he adopted a typically "border German" sense of decline and doom. All would come crashing down unless a revolutionary effort would be undertaken to save and revive the main German body and the German diaspora.

In Germany itself, Rosenberg called for a new sociopolitical and economic régime to save the country from the domestic disintegration and liberal atomization which he believed were caused by the combination of democracy and industrial capitalism. He blamed the Jews for much of these ills, and in an early book (*Jewish Influence over the Ages*, 1920) demanded their removal from German culture and for German culture to return to its "original, creative, fighting 'Germandom'." Rosenberg then came under the influence of the most violent anti-Semitic ideologue and HITLER's own sponsor, Dietrich Eckart, succeeding him as editor of the Nazi Party's paper, *Voelkischer Beobachter,* (*Popular Spectator*). This paper published typical admixtures of anti-Semitic, anti-BOLSHEVIK and anti-Slavonic diatribes, calling for the establishment of a Third Reich that would enforce the rule of the Aryan race over Europe by force. The proper release of the "manly instinct" and of the "cry of the blood" was a primitive transformation by Rosenberg of the crisis of traditional western rationalism and religion in Germany into a modern myth, which he tried to formulate in his *Mythus des 20. Jahrhunderts* (*The Myth of the 20th Century*) (1930). The book, although acknowledged as a major Nazi manifesto, was never officially recognized as such, due to Hitler's insistence on his own primacy and freedom of action. Rosenberg was a strong dogmatist but only a weak politician. He was granted several high offices after Hitler's ascendancy, including that of minister for the occupied Eastern territories—in which he tried to separate Jews and Russians (as mortal enemies) from the other Slavs. However, he failed to follow his master's decisions at the right moments and to successfully compete with Hitler's closer aides. His ministry was actively involved in the mass killings of the Jews and in the persecution of others in Eastern Europe to the very end. In 1946 he was convicted by the International Military Tribunal at Nuremberg as the "spiritual father of racial hate" and then hanged.

ROY, MANABENDRA NATH   (1887–1954) COMINTERN delegate to the CHINESE COMMUNIST PARTY (CCP). An Indian nationalist, Roy participated during World War I in a German-financed plot to overthrow the British in India. Arrested in New York on

the eve of the United States entry into the war, he escaped to Mexico, where he met the Russian Communist, MICHAEL BORODIN. During an all-night session playing checkers, Borodin converted Roy to MARXISM. He attended the 2nd Comintern congress in Moscow and became its leading Asian theoretician on Communist revolution for Asia. In April 1927, he was sent to China, where he served under Borodin as an adviser to the Chinese Communist Party in Wuhan, where it held its 5th party congress (April–May). CHIANG KAI-SHEK, leading the right-GUO-MINDANG (GMD), had purged the CCP earlier in the month, but the Communists were still allied with the left-GMD. Though ignorant of local conditions, Roy followed Stalin's instructions in calling for the CCP to take over the left-GMD. With the disclosure of STALIN's directive, the Wuhan GMD broke with the CCP in July and Roy returned to Moscow. Charged with deviations and expelled from the Comintern, Roy returned to India, where he led an anti-Stalinist Communist movement. He was captured and imprisoned by the British in 1931. Released in 1937, Roy moved away from Marxism and became an exponent of radical humanism.

ROY, RAM MOHUN (1772–1833) Often characterized as the "father of modern India," Roy was born into an affluent Bengali Brahmin family. He went on to work for the British East India Company and amassed considerable wealth before his retirement in 1815. Thereafter he devoted his time and efforts to developing and elucidating those ideas that were to have such a significant impact upon the evolution of Indian national and cultural consciousness. His activities were to include founding the first Indian newspaper, advocating the abolition of the practice of *sati* (whereby widows were forced or encouraged to immolate themselves upon their husband's funeral pyre), promoting civil and political rights for Indians, founding the *Brahmo Samaj* (Divine Society) and the publication of numerous books detailing his belief system.

A talented linguist, Roy learnt Persian, Arabic and Sanskrit during his childhood and later went on to master English, Greek and Latin. Knowledge of these put him in a position to grapple with the texts of Islam, Christianity and, of course, Hinduism. His studies led him to preach the unity of God and to argue that since reason and human rights underlay the philosophy of the *Upanishads* (the great elucidatory Hindu religio-philosophical texts) in the same way that they underlay western thought, Indians could claim the same rights as Europeans.

While asserting the rights of Indians and the value of Hindu thought and culture (which were commonly regarded by the British occupiers as little more than evidence of a debased, idol-worshiping and superstitious society), Roy was profoundly influenced by what he saw as the positive elements of exposure to western culture. He therefore supported the study of English, a western-style education system open to both sexes and the repudiation of the caste system.

These views, along with his denunciation of idolatry and his adoption of the Christian ethic (as expressed in his book, *The Precepts of Jesus*) meant that he fell foul of traditionalist Hindus. More importantly, however, these same views and the *Brahmo Samaj* that he founded (and which substituted theism for classical Hindu monism) had a significant influence upon the educated middle class that was then emerging and that went on

to form the backbone of the nationalist leadership in India. Roy was instrumental in giving educated Indians a sense of pride in their own cultural heritage, while at the same time utilizing western concepts of human dignity and freedom to argue the case for Indian emancipation. He also presented a blueprint for political agitation by constitutional means (presenting petitions against a number of items of British legislation that he opposed) that would later be adopted by the INDIAN NATIONAL CONGRESS.

RUSSIAN REVOLUTION OF 1905 On Sunday, January 9 (January 22 according to the Gregorian calendar), 1905, a procession of Russian citizens, holding icons and singing hymns and headed by a priest, Father GEORGES GAPONE, converged on the czar's Winter Palace in St. Petersburg, bearing a petition for economic and social reforms. Refusing to disperse, they were fired upon by the palace guards. Throughout the day, skirmishes with the police and army continued in various parts of the capital, leaving perhaps as many as 800 civilians dead. This was BLOODY SUNDAY, the beginning of Russia's 1905 revolution.

There were several causes for this outbreak. Russia had been industrializing, and the 1890s had seen extremely rapid growth. The recession of 1899–1905 had caused mass unemployment and hardship among the new urban workers. Peasants, pressed by land hunger and backward agriculture, also suffered widespread poverty.

In addition, Russia had become embroiled in a war against Japan, suffering humiliating defeats that undermined public support for the régime and for the war. This opposition was articulated by the growing INTELLIGENTSIA, which was forming new illegal political parties and movements. Typical of this was the formation in Switzerland in 1903 of the Union of Liberation as a party uniting various liberal and so-called "legal Marxist" figures into a movement demanding political reform. In May 1905, the Union of Liberation formed an alliance with a part of the socialist movement to work for a constitution and representative government. At the same time, the Socialist Revolutionary campaign of terror, typified by the assassination of the minister of the interior, V.K. Plehve, in July 1904, intensified the atmosphere of conflict in the country. The régime's offer of a consultative representative body, elected on a limited franchise, and made as a conciliatory gesture after Bloody Sunday, was rejected by the Russian society as "too little, too late."

Throughout the summer of 1905, industrial strikes, peasant unrest and opposition by the intelligentsia intensified, pressing the government for more reform. Even the signing of a peace agreement with the Japanese in August 1905 and the successful negotiation of a large development loan did not turn the tide.

In October 1905, a general strike of the railways, supported by many of the workers throughout the country, threatened Russia with collapse. The strikers in St. Petersburg, Moscow and other industrial centers, formed representative strike committees that in some centers began to debate and decree not only matters of industrial work conditions, but also general social and administrative matters.

Military units became more and more restive. In the face of growing economic and social chaos, the czar turned to Count Sergius Witte, architect of Russia's industrialization and negotiator of the Portsmouth Peace with the Japanese, appointing him prime minister. Witte presented the czar with two choices: a military dictatorship or a program of political reform. Unable to find a reliable and talented candidate to serve as a dictator, the czar chose reform.

Under the Manifesto of October 17, the czar granted a representative Duma to consider all government legislation; an end to press censorship; freedom of association, including trade unions; and other civil rights. The manifesto did not put an end to the social violence and turmoil. Reactionary circles instigated a wave of violence against Jews, intellectuals and revolutionary socialists. Disgruntled peasants and military units returning from the war revolted. But the manifesto split the opposition, with many moderate liberals and socialists turning to their newly legal opportunities for party, professional and trade union association as their main arenas of activity. At the beginning of December, the St. Petersburg soviet had been dispersed by the police and its leaders arrested. During December, attempts at armed uprising in Moscow and on the Ekaterinin Railroad in the south were put down by units of the army. Under the leadership of P.A. Stolypin, who became minister of the interior in February 1906 and prime minister in July, government authority was reestablished.

A Soviet poster commemorating the Russian Revolution of 1905; Vladimir Lenin was not even present at the time

RUSSIAN REVOLUTION OF 1917   On March 7 (this and all subsequent dates in this article are according to the Gregorian calendar) 1917 workers of the Putilov factory, Petrograd's largest industrial plant, producing munitions and metal products for the war effort, went on strike for better pay and working conditions. Their employers, faced with shortages of fuel and raw materials, closed the plant, locking the strikers out. The following day, International Women's Day, the idled workers joined Petrograd's women in protesting food shortages and high prices. The demonstrations grew more radical and more violent over the next two days as the police and units of the Petrograd garrison (reserve draftees who had replaced the elite Guards' Regiments that had been sent to the front) failed to curb the demonstrators.

On Monday, March 12, the garrison was in revolt against orders to fire on demonstrators. Parliament (the Duma) had formed a Provisional Committee that requested the czar's abdication as a necessary precondition for the restoration of order, and an ad hoc group of socialist leaders had formed a temporary executive to reconvene the Petrograd Workers' Soviet that had functioned in the RUSSIAN REVOLUTION OF 1905. All of the weaknesses of Russia's polity, society and economy found expression here in a week that brought to an end the dynasty that had ruled the Russian empire for three centuries, and launched Russia into 75 years of social experimentation.

On Thursday, March 15, Czar Nicholas II, having been refused the support of the generals of the Supreme Command of the Russian Imperial army, abdicated his, and his hemophiliac son Alexei's, right to the throne, in favor of his brother, the Grand Duke Michael Alexandrovich Romanoff. When the brother declined to accept the throne, the Duma provisional committee, in consultation with the executive of the Petrograd Soviet, decreed the formation of a provisional government dominated by members of the Progressive Bloc of the Duma: the liberal Constitutional Democratic Party (Kadets), headed by Professor PAVEL MILYUKOV, who became foreign minister, and the more conservative Octobrist Party headed by Alexander Guchkov, who assumed the post of war minister. The prime minister was PRINCE GEORGI LVOV, head of the Union of Zemstvo and Town Governments, a reform-minded liberal with more of a reputation for administrative skills than for political experience. Representatives of the Petrograd Soviet were invited to take portfolios in the new cabinet, but the dominant ideology of the socialist parties was that they should remain in opposition at this stage of the revolution.

Only ALEXANDER KERENSKY, a Socialist Revolutionary, accepted the post of minister of justice, having received permission from a reluctant Soviet Executive Committee. This period was known as the "dual power," with formal authority vested in the provisional government but the Petrograd Soviet enjoying the support of the majority of the population, and—more important—of the military garrison.

The central policy goal of the first provisional government was the successful prosecution of the war. Other questions, such as the political future of Russia, its relations with its imperial possessions and agrarian reform, were to be put off pending the convocation of a constituent assembly "as soon as stability is achieved." Among the first decisions of the provisional government was the abolition of all civic disabilities based on nationality or religion. This was the forerunner of a democratic election law guaranteeing universal, equal and direct suffrage by secret ballot.

The first provisional government dissolved in the wake of a crisis over war aims. The government had agreed at its formation to a statement of war aims defined by the Petrograd Soviet. This coupled defense of Russia with the desire for a swift and democratic peace without annexations or reparations. Such a statement was clearly at odds with Russia's agreements with the Entente, which coupled victory with the stripping of Germany, Austria-Hungary and Turkey of extensive territories, and the payment of punitive reparations to the Entente countries. In particular, Russia had been promised the possession of the Turkish Straits in the event of a victory in the war.

On May 1, Foreign Minister Milyukov forwarded the government's formal statement of war aims to the governments of the Entente, accompanied by a note stating that nothing in the statement was to be construed as contradicting Russia's determination to live up to all its agreements, and the expectation of reciprocity on the part of Russia's allies. When this note became public, there were demonstrations of soldiers and workers, leading to the resignation of Milyukov and Guchkov on May 5 and the adding of six ministers representing the MENSHEVIK, Trudovik, Popular Socialist and Socialist Revolutionary parties. Lvov remained prime minister, while Kerensky became minister of war.

Three factors brought this coalition government to an end at the beginning of July. Under pressure from the Entente powers and from his non-socialist colleagues, Kerensky began preparations for an offensive that would raise the morale of the army and the public, and reassure the Entente that the revolution in Russia, and particularly the inclusion of socialists in the cabinet, did not mean an abandonment of the war. The offensive, launched against the tottering Austro-Hungarian army in Galicia on July 1, enjoyed 10 days of spectacular advances. When the German army struck at the Russian flank, the offensive collapsed, turning into a demoralized rout that saw the Germans advancing into new Russian territories. At the same time, the Kadets in the government were outraged by a cabinet discussion granting autonomy to Ukraine within a federalized Russian empire and resigned from the government. All of this took place within the environment of a steady radicalization of the public mood in all of Russia, but particularly in Petrograd, which served as the sounding board for public debate. Representatives of 400 soviets that had been formed throughout Russia, and which in many places were already performing the functions of government, held their first all-Russian congress in Petrograd in early June. A debate developed around the demand that all state power be given over to the soviets. This view was promoted particularly by LENIN and his BOLSHEVIK PARTY. When the Kadets resigned from the first coalition government, Bolshevik and Anarchist supporters rioted for two days in the center of Petrograd, calling for the All-Russian Central Executive Committee of the Soviets to replace the defunct government. Lack of organization by the insurgents, and a combination of a few loyal troops and a whispering campaign accusing Lenin and the Bolsheviks of being German agents, were sufficient to render the "July Days" uprising abortive.

On August 7, Kerensky announced the formation of a second coalition made up of 10 socialist ministers and seven non-socialists. The radicalization of both public opinion and policy, evidenced by the July riots and by the socialist majority in the new government, caused anxiety in all the center and right-wing circles that had been politically quiescent since the czar's abdication. When Kerensky called for a state conference to convene in Moscow, in hopes of broadening the government's base of support, the conference turned into a call for a "strong man" to save Russia from the revolution. The candidate was General Lavr Kornilov, recently appointed commander in chief of the Russian armed forces.

At the end of August, Kornilov sent army units toward Petrograd, ostensibly to defend the government against possible uprisings, but apparently with the aim of arresting Kerensky and his ministers and setting up a military dictatorship. The move failed when socialist railwaymen refused to move the troops and their supplies, and when agitators from the Petrograd Soviet convinced Kornilov's soldiers not to attack "their brothers," the troops mobilized by the soviet for the defense of the capital. Bolshevik activists, ostracized since the July Days, were now re-legitimized by their loyal willingness to take up arms on behalf of the soviet. Suspicions that Kerensky, along with representatives of the Kadets, had somehow been involved in the Kornilov mutiny, completed the radicalization of the Russian public. Kerensky, who had demanded the resignation of his ministers during the Kornilov mutiny, was now ruling as a dictator with a four-member Directory, two of them senior military people, supervising matters of war, foreign affairs, posts and telegraphs, and marine affairs. A "Democratic Conference," called by the representatives of the Soviets to discuss a new government, failed to agree on terms for inclusion or exclusion of the Kadets from a new government.

On October 10, Kerensky set up a final coalition that called for the long-awaited elections to the Constituent Assembly to be held in November. There was little more that such a government could do, for both power and authority were lacking, while difficulties were multiplying daily. Throughout the summer of 1917, Russia had been disintegrating. Industrial production was falling as transport failed and supplies of fuel and raw materials grew scarce. Hunger spread and intensified across the entire country, and as winter approached the prospect of full-blown famine loomed large. In the countryside, a virtual revolt boiled over as the peasants, disillusioned by the provisional government's delay in giving the peasants more land, began to seize lands from private estates, looting and burning manor houses and farm buildings. After the abortive June offensive, desertion from the army reached epidemic proportions, partially as the soldiers "voted with their feet" against continuation of the war and against the unbearable conditions at the front, partially as drafted peasants hurried home to be sure that they received their fair share of the land that was being seized. On the periphery of the empire, national minorities took advantage of Russia's weakness to claim independence. The Caucasus, the Baltics, Ukraine, Poland and Finland all saw the possibility of escaping from "The Prison-House of Nations" as the Russian empire had been known in Europe. The life of Kerensky's last government was cut short by the Bolshevik seizure of power, timed to coincide with the Second All-Russian Congress of Soviets that convened on November 7, 1917. Central authority was already crumbling fast when the Bolsheviks completed Russia's transition from the autocratic czarist régime to a dictatorship of the proletariat, as represented by Lenin and his party of professional revolutionaries.

RUTENBERG, PINHAS (1879–1942) Socialist-revolutionary terrorist and Zionist electrical engineer. A youthful adherent of POPULISM, Rutenberg became part of the Party of Socialist Revolutionaries, eventually joining its underground fighting organization. In this capacity, he was the party's liaison with father GAPONE and his police-sponsored workers' organization. After BLOODY SUNDAY, when Gapone was suspected of betraying the revolutionaries, Rutenberg was detailed to lure him back from abroad and execute him. This he did and subsequently himself sought refuge in Italy.

In 1917, Rutenberg returned to Russia and was active in the SOCIAL REVOLUTIONARY PARTY. He opposed the BOLSHEVIK seizure of power and was jailed by the Soviet régime. Upon his release, he emigrated to Palestine, where he founded the Palestine electric company and built the country's first hydroelectric station at the confluence of the Jordan and Yarmuk rivers. In 1929, he was elected chairman of the National Council, the representative body of the Jewish population of Palestine under the British mandatory government.

RWANDA, 1973 COUP On July 5, 1973, Rwanda's minister of defense and head of the national guard, Major General JUVÉNAL HABYARIMANA, seized power in a bloodless army coup. The ruling Hutu Party, *Parmehutu,* which had begun as a fairly cohesive organization, had become dominated by elements from the central region. The ensuing rift—between Northerners and politicians from the central and southern regions—led to the coup. Habyarimana, himself a northern Hutu, proclaimed a second republic.

RYKOV, ALEXEI IVANOVICH (1881–1938) Soviet Communist politician. A revolutionary from an early age, Rykov was arrested for the first time in 1902 and played a prominent part in the RUSSIAN REVOLUTION OF 1905. From then until 1917 he lived abroad, becoming one of LENIN's principal collaborators. After the RUSSIAN REVOLUTION OF 1917, he specialized in economic affairs, directing the Supreme Council for the National Economy from 1919 and succeeding Lenin in 1924 as chairman of the Council of People's Commissars. He was chiefly responsible for the economic policy of those years, the New Economic Policy (NEP). In 1930 he opposed collectivization and in 1931 was forced by STALIN to retract his "rightist deviationism." He eventually lost all influence, until finally he was implicated during the purge trials and executed.

S

SA—STURMABTEILUNG HITLER's street fighting arm during his campaign for power in Germany. Combined with his propaganda machine, these became his most important tools at that time. The SA played a decisive role in bringing Hitler to power, but it soon imposed on him a choice between its loose, social-revolutionary ambition and his own priorities. On June 30, 1934, the SA was purged and lost its standing when compared to the SS, the regular army and party agencies under Hitler's direct command.

From the beginning, the command issue was one of the SA's main problems. The idea and the first actual experiment in raising a revolutionary street army seems to have been born in the mind of Captain ERNST RÖHM, a former imperial army officer who joined forces with Hitler's NAZI PARTY as a rather independent, nationalist-revolutionary leader still serving in the Bavarian army. Both Röhm and Hitler tried to mobilize young, former World War I veterans, elder victims of Germany's deteriorating economy and members of the industrial proletariat. The quasi-military character of the SA was blended with traditional forms such as Catholic-like (but basically anti-Christian) processions to suggest an old-new, restorative-revolutionary armed youth movement with a significant South German accent. Hitler's BEER HALL PUTSCH of 1923 was based, to a large extent, upon his use of the SA and Röhm's own "*Reichskriegsflagge*" as a direct threat to the conservative Bavarian government, in order to subordinate it to his will and to march on Berlin. The direct clash with the state's armed forces which followed this failed experiment taught Hitler never again to try an open revolt. Instead, he would use the SA as a threat, blackmailing the conservatives into giving him access to power when the opportunity would present itself. For this to succeed, he would need an all-German SA organization, even if it was small in numbers.

A former army officer, Captain Franz v. Pfeffer, created this national base but failed to discipline the different, sometimes impatient, SA leaders and units. Early in the 1930s, the SA gave rise to strong, locally entrenched leaders such as Edmund Heines in Breslau, who adopted an open social revolutionary spirit in competition with other left parties. While the SA assumed an urban character, it also mobilized many farmers and lower-middle-class members unwanted by both the left and the traditional right, with the economic crisis of that time contributing to the SA's appeal. Jobless youngsters were recruited in large numbers and an esprit de corps soon emerged in their various semi-military quarters. The SA gave them a routine to follow, street fights to be engaged in and dead heroes to worship.

Many SA men were members of the organization with the sheer and simple aim of gaining a material reward once the Weimar system collapsed. At that time, they believed, they would be repaid in the form of police or other jobs, army commissions, and access to the property of the rich and the Jews. The million-member SA was notably impatient, and several of its members proved it by moving to and from the Communist semi-military organizations as the winds shifted. In Berlin in April 1931, a group under former army Captain Walter Stennes revolted against the party's local leadership. As a result SA leader v. Pfeffer was removed and Hitler made himself "Oberster SA-Fuehrer," the supreme commander of the SA.

Ernst Röhm returned as "chief of staff" of the SA and soon reorganized it under various former generals, civilian managers who had risen from the ranks, and local leaders. To aid in Hitler's drive to power, modern, more disciplined SA motor car units (NSKK), were created. Together with other mass movement and propaganda tools, they helped transform Germany's cities into the chaotic scene for which Hitler blamed the "system" and which he promised to overcome.

The regular army hesitated between a policy of prohibiting the SA totally as a threat to the state's traditional norms—a step which it indeed took for a short while—and the view of the SA as a military reservoir for the Reichswehr itself. In any case, the SA's activities intensified toward Hitler's appointment as Reich chancellor on January 30, 1933. The conservatives, who had supported Hitler in the hope of controlling him, were soon faced with an SA-led takeover, justified by the (baseless) fear of a Communist revolt following the Reichstag fire. The SA joined the regular police in fighting Communists—and also its own political and social enemies, by virtue of emergency decrees signed by President von Hindenburg. The last free elections in Germany early in March 1933 were subjected to SA terror, and illegal "concentration" camps erected by local SA units mushroomed all over Germany. SA commander Ernst Röhm, hoping to increase his power, maneuvered the SA, as the "guarantor of the revolution," between the Nazi Party itself and the state apparatus. By so doing he sealed its fate. Hitler was not interested in a social but in a racial revolution. Nor was Hitler ready to allow Röhm and his locally entrenched leaders to threaten the army, the bureaucracy and the party itself. In the Night of the Long Knives (June 30, 1934), Röhm and most of the regional SA leadership were accused of treachery and murdered by the SS.

SA'ADEH, ANTOUN (1902–1949) Lebanese politician. Son

of a Greek Orthodox doctor who emigrated to Brazil, Sa'adeh was brought up there. He returned to Lebanon in 1930 and taught German at the American University of Beirut. In the 1930s he advocated Syrian nationalism, as opposed to Pan-Arab aspirations for all-Arab unity and the separate Lebanese national entity propounded by one wing of Christian-Lebanese mainstream opinion. He proposed the creation of a "Greater Syria" which was to include Lebanon. He was strongly influenced by German fascism. Sa'adeh called for the immediate independence of Syria-Lebanon and the eviction of the French. In 1932, he founded the SYRIAN NATIONALIST PARTY (*al-Hizb al-Suri al-Qawmi*). His party was banned and Sa'adeh was harassed by the authorities, until he left in the late 1930s—reportedly first to Italy and Germany and then to South America. In 1947 he returned to now independent Lebanon and resumed his political activity, adding the word "Social" (*al-Ijtima'i*) to the name of his party; but he was kept under surveillance and arrested on several occasions. In June 1949, clashes erupted between his party and the Christian Phalange in what was described as a coup attempt by Sa'adeh. He escaped to Syria but was extradited to Lebanon, sentenced to death by a summary military court and executed in July of that year.

AL-SADAT, MUHAMMAD ANWAR (1918–1981) Egyptian officer and statesman, president of Egypt 1970–1981. Born in Mit Abu'l-Kom in the Delta province of Minufiyya into a peasant family (his father was a clerk with the army, his mother a black Sudanese), Sadat graduated from the military academy in 1938 and became a professional officer. A keen nationalist of conservative Islamic tendency, he was close to, and for some time a member of the MUSLIM BROTHERHOOD and the right-wing, pro-Fascist *Misr al-Fata* (Young Egypt) Party. In 1941–1942 he was active in a pro-German underground group and in October 1942 he was expelled from the army. He was detained for about two years; in 1944 he escaped and went underground until the detention order was lifted in 1945. He was again arrested in 1946 and charged with complicity in the murder of the former finance minister, Amin Osman ('Uthman), and also suspected of involvement in an attempt to assassinate ex-Premier al-Nahhas. In prison for over two years during the trial, he was acquitted in December 1948. He then worked as a journalist, but in January 1950 was readmitted to the army.

Restored to his officer's rank and position, Sadat soon joined the secret group of FREE OFFICERS headed by GAMAL ABDUL NASSER and took part—he was then a lieutenant-colonel—in that group's coup of July 1952. He became a member of the 12-man Revolutionary Council heading the new régime and remained, in various capacities, one of the leaders of the new team throughout the years of its rule.

In December 1969 Sadat was appointed vice-president of Egypt, as Nasser's only deputy—an appointment seen as a step to balance rightist and leftist tendencies within the ruling team and particularly to check the advance of the left, led by the power-hungry 'Ali Sabri. On Nasser's death in September 1970, Sadat was chosen as president of Egypt and also of the single party, the Arab Socialist Union (ASU). Firmly in power, Sadat began changing Egypt's régime and policies. Gradually, and mainly from 1973, he introduced a liberalization of the economic régime. Intentionally, Sadat launched the October 1973 war against Israel, and in its wake initiated a significant rapprochement with the US and preached moderation in inter-Arab affairs.

In 1978, following the Camp David Agreements, Sadat received the Nobel Peace Prize jointly with MENAHEM BEGIN. The next year he became the first Arab leader to sign a peace treaty with Israel. He was murdered by Islamic extremists in October 1981, during a parade on the anniversary of the October War of 1973, and there were few signs of genuine mourning in the country. His memory as a leader and a statesman who had shaped Egypt's history seems to have been dimmed and not very actively cultivated.

Sadat wrote a book on the revolution of 1952, with autobiographical features (*Revolt on the Nile*, 1957), and an autobiography (*In Search of Identity*, 1977– 1978).

SAFAVI, SAYYID NAVAB (Sayyid Mujtaba Mirlavhi) (1919–1956) Iranian Islamic revolutionary. As a theological student in the turbulent years following the abdication of Reza Shah in 1941, Safavi was wary of secular Iranian nationalism and organized a small group of followers, the FEDAYAN ISLAM, to fight against "all forms of irreligion" in the country. Under his guidance this group, composed mainly of religious students and members of the urban poor, initiated a wave of assassinations disproportionate to the movement's true size. Among its victims were the secular writer and jurist Ahmad Kasravi (1946), government minister Abdul-Husayn Hazhir (1949) and prime minister General Ali Ramzara (1950), the latter for supporting the American-Iranian Oil Corporation (AIOC).

To his opponents, Safavi was a "half-educated fanatic," but he was also a competent spokesman for the religious and nationalist interests of Iran. In his manifesto, *Rahnama-y Haqa'iq* (*Guide to truths*), Safavi outlined his plans for an Islamic state. Alcohol, tobacco, opium, films, gambling and foreign clothing would all be banned. The educational curriculum would be purged of foreign subjects such as music, women would be forced to wear the veil, and the *Shari'a*—Muslim religious law—would be enforced. The shah himself would be subject to Islamic law, or else, according to Safavi, would be dismissed. But Safavi also expressed concern for the poor, who formed the bulk of his supporters. According to him, "The legitimate rights of the poor must be given to them, in accordance with the criteria of Islam." Among his proposed reforms were low-cost housing, free health care and the redistribution of all uncultivated land. Finally, there was a nationalist element to his ideology. Safavi attempted to purify the Persian language of foreign loan words and called for the reunification of all Shiite lands with Iran.

Although Safavi received no official support from the country's clerics, many expressed sympathy with his objectives. For instance, although there was overwhelming evidence against Kasravi's assassins, the clerics successfully lobbied for their acquittal. There is also evidence that the government was interested in fostering the *Fedayan Islam* as a weapon against the socialist TUDEH PARTY. However, as Muhammad Reza Shah consolidated his control over the country, the *Fedayan Islam* and its supporters were subdued. The movement was disbanded in 1952 and Safavi was later taken into custody. Official reports claim that he was shot while trying to escape, but it is generally believed that he was executed after undergoing harsh torture. In modern Iran, Safavi is considered a martyr of the Iranian Revolution of 1979 (see IRAN, REVOLTS AND REVOLUTIONS).

SAINT JOHN, VINCENT (1877–1929) Militant leader of the Western Federation of Miners and the Industrial Workers of the World, also known as "the Saint." As president of the miners' union in Telluride, Colorado, Saint John instigated the first sit-down strike in the United States in which the miners took possession of the mine. After an armed battle resulted in the death of a company manager, Saint John was arrested for murder and later acquitted. Modest and mild-mannered, he carried a handgun at all times, often entering the company towns incognito to unionize the workers.

SALLAL, 'ABDULLAH (1917? 1920?–) Yemeni officer, leader of the Yemen Revolution of 1962, president of the Yemen Republic (1962–1967). Son of a lower-class Zeidi family, Sallal was sent in the 1930s to the Baghdad Military Academy, from which he graduated in 1938. Upon his return, he was suspected of anti-régime activities and detained for some time, but was then allowed to resume his army career. He took part in the abortive al-Wazir coup of 1948 and was sentenced to death; the sentence was commuted to seven years' imprisonment. Sallal was close to Prince al-Badr, who made him commander of his guard in the mid-1950s and of the newly established military academy in 1959. When al-Badr became Imam (king) in September 1962, Sallal, then a major, became commander of the Royal Guard and, according to some reports, commander in chief of the army. In September 1962 he toppled the monarchy, became president of the republic and led the republican camp in the civil war that erupted between it and the royalists. He was prime minister from 1962 to 1963 and again in 1966, relying heavily on Egyptian support.

When Egypt withdrew its expeditionary force in 1967, after the Six-Day War, Sallal was overthrown in a bloodless coup in November of that year. He went into exile to Baghdad and lost all influence on Yemeni affairs. Late in 1981, apparently no longer considered a dangerous rival, he was allowed to return to Yemen.

SALO, REPUBLIC OF see ITALIAN SOCIAL REPUBLIC.

SAN DIAN HUI see TRIAD SOCIETY.

SANDINO, AUGUSTO (1895–1934) A Nicaraguan guerrilla leader and son of a well-to-do peasant, Sandino received very little education. Even so, he headed the guerrilla warfare against José Maria Moncada and the United States occupation of Nicaragua from 1927 to his death in 1934. He was an anticolonialist in the sense that he fought not only against the occupation of the American armed forces of Nicaragua but also against the direct imposition by that country of the "political personnel" of Nicaragua. He was assassinated by Anastasio Samoza Gracía in 1934.

SAN FAN REBELLION (1673–1681) A revolt against the Qing (Manchu) dynasty in China. WU SANGUI, the Chinese commander who had assisted the Manchus in their conquest of

China (1644), subsequently built up his own satrapy (feudatory) in the southwestern provinces. Two other such satrapies had been established in the southeast. Amassing wealth through trade and mining monopolies in Yunnan and Guizhou, Wu made his own official appointments, bypassing the imperial bureaucracy in Beijing. Yet the imperial treasury paid millions to subsidize his huge army. In 1673, the Qing court decided to abolish the satrapies, whose power rivalled its own. Wu responded by rebelling and establishing a new dynasty, which he called Zhou. The Fujian and Guangdong satraps also rebelled in 1674 and 1676 respectively. Though Wu declared himself emperor of his new dynasty in 1678, the tide had turned against the rebels. Wu died of dysentery in 1678 and was succeeded by his eldest grandson. With the suppression of what was called the Revolt of the Three Feudatories in 1681 and the conquest of Taiwan two years later, the Manchus consolidated their rule in China.

SAN HE HUI see TRIAD SOCIETY.

SANJABI, KARIM (1904–) Iranian politician. First foreign minister of Iran following the Iranian Revolution of 1979 (see IRAN, REVOLTS AND REVOLUTIONS). Born in Kermanshah (now Bakhtaran), Iran, Sanjabi graduated in political science and law from the University of Tehran (1928) and received his doctorate in Paris.

Sanjabi held a variety of ministerial posts while working as a professor of law and deputy dean of the law school in the 1930s. During World War II, Sanjabi was arrested several times by the British. Together with other intellectuals, he founded the leftist *Mihan* Party in the 1940s, and later joined the IRAN PARTY (allied with the Communist TUDEH PARTY), becoming a member of its central committee. In 1949 he was a founding member of the NATIONAL FRONT coalition. In 1951 he served briefly as minister of education under Prime Minister MOSSADDEQ. He was active in the National Resistance Movement reforms in the 1950s and was a leader of the second National Front in the 1960s. After the unrest of 1961 he was arrested.

In 1977, together with other leaders of the National Front (e.g., DARIUS FORUHAR and SHAHPUR BAKHTIAR), Sanjabi publicly denounced the rule of the shah. In 1978 he became secretary-general of the National Front. In December 1978, he was among the opposition leaders who negotiated with the shah on ways to save his rule by a program of liberal reform. The talks failed. Shortly afterwards, Sanjabi met with the exiled AYATOLLAH KHOMEINI in Paris and agreed to join his camp. In February 1979 he became foreign minister in MEHDI BAZARGAN's interim Islamic revolutionary government, but he was critical of the Revolutionary Council and resigned in April 1979. Disassociating himself from the Islamic régime, Sanjabi migrated to the United States.

SANJAR MALIK (?–1207) Leader of the People's Movement in Bokhara (Uzbekistan) in 1206–1207; born into a craftsman's family. After uniting Bokhara's craftsmen, who then rose up in arms against the arbitrary rule and despotism of the local governor, Muhammad ibn-Ahmad ibn-Abd-al-Azia, Sanjar Malik conquered Bokhara. He proceeded to confiscate the local rich men's property and divided it among poor persons. The army of Muhammad Shah of Khorezm finally captured Bokhara and crushed the revolt. Sanjar Malik drowned in the Sir-Darya River.

SANKARA, THOMAS (?–1987) Rebel in Burkina Faso (Upper Volta). Since August 1960, when it became independent of France, Burkina Faso has alternated between military and civilian government. During the early 1980s Sankara, originally an army captain and later a populist leader with a considerable following, served in several governments. In August 1983, he led a coup against the military government of Sergeant-Major Jean Baptiste Ouedraogo and seized power.

As the new head of government, Sankara set up a *Conseil National de la Revolution* (Revolutionary Council) with a membership consisting of army officers who had supported the coup. He purged the army, established "revolutionary tribunals" to try former public officials charged with corruption, reformed the judiciary and educational systems and restructured the government along centralist lines that greatly reduced the power of tribal chieftains. However, his régime met with opposition from within the trade unions as well as the Revolutionary Council itself. On October 15, 1987, a commando unit opened fire on him and killed him along with several of his associates.

SAN MARTIN, JOSÉ DE (1778–1850) Argentinian soldier and liberator. Born in Yapeyu in northern Argentina, where his father was a prominent official in the Spanish colonial administration, San Martin received a military education in Madrid, Spain, to which his family had returned when he was six years old. In 1793 he was commissioned as a second lieutenant, rising to the rank of lieutenant colonel by 1808. During this period he saw action on the Portuguese frontier against the British.

In 1812 San Martin resigned his commission and, after receiving permission to travel to the Peruvian city of Lima—which was the center of Spanish power in South America—went instead to Buenos Aires. There he offered his services to the revolutionary government in Argentina, then threatened by Spanish royalist forces. His sudden switch to opposition to Spain, which he had served loyally for nearly 20 years was precipitated, he claimed, by a conviction that he could no longer be indifferent to the call of his native land.

San Martin decided that the only way to liberate Argentina from the Spanish threat was in the context of a continental liberation plan which involved attacking Spain in its Peruvian stronghold. To this end, he took his forces north, defeating the Spanish at San Lorenzo on the Parana River in 1813. The following year he was promoted to the rank of general and appointed commander of the army of Upper Peru, which had suffered a series of defeats at the hands of the Spanish on the Bolivian plateau.

Instead of continuing with the abortive campaign in Peru, San Martin had himself elected military governor of Cuyo, a district of northern Argentina. There he spent three years developing an audacious and original plan to invade Chile and advance north toward Lima by sea, and drilled his solders into a force capable of such an ambitious venture. His task was made harder by the rout of the nationalist forces in Chile, with whom he had hoped to link up, and his army had to fight its way across the Andes. Its victory at the Maipo river in 1817 signaled the end of Spanish power in Chile.

Declining the Chilean presidency in favor of his lieutenant, Bernardo O'Higgins, San Martin set about creating the navy he needed to approach close enough to Lima for the final land-based attack. In 1820, his motley fleet of armed merchant ships set sail from Valparaiso with 4,500 solders on board. Disembarking at Arasian, his forces soon occupied the coast to within 150 miles south of Lima and roundly defeated the royalists at the Battle of Pisco, capturing the Spanish general and most of his artillery. San Martin rejected any terms that did not concede absolute independence and, when the royalists in Lima finally despaired of assistance from the Spanish king, was able to occupy the city virtually unopposed. Peruvian independence was declared on July 22, 1821, and San Martin was installed as "Protector." In this capacity, he expelled the majority of Spaniards and introduced a number of liberal reforms, which included ending the exploitation of native Indian labor, abolishing slavery and creating a system of annual redemptions of quotas of living slaves.

San Martin's political career ended abruptly after a secret meeting with SIMON BOLIVAR, the liberator of northern Latin America, in 1822. The substance of their discussion remains the subject of speculation, but shortly thereafter San Martin resigned his protectorship and military command and returned to Argentina. First and foremost a military man, he had been unprepared for handling such problems as his own officers' suspicions that he had dictatorial or even monarchical ambitions, or his uncertainty that the Peruvian people would remain loyal to the new order. In 1824 he sailed for Europe, thereby distancing himself from the chaos that followed Latin American independence; he remained in self-imposed exile until his death in Boulogne, France. In 1880, his remains were removed and reinterred in the cathedral in Buenos Aires.

Widely revered in the land of his birth, where he is hailed as the "Liberator of the South," San Martin evinced a dedication to continent-wide independence, and was in favor of a centralized constitutional monarchy for Latin America. As a military leader, he exhibited outstanding ability in training and motivating his forces, while his feat in leading his men across the Andes has led to comparisons with Hannibal and Napoleon.

SANMIN ZHUYI see THREE PRINCIPLES OF THE PEOPLE.

SANS-CULOTTES The name given to the masses in the FRENCH REVOLUTION, notably during the first phase of the decade of revolution after 1789, until they were finally neutralized by Napoleon following his seizure of power from the First Republic in November 1799. *Sans-culottisme* refers more specifically to the popular character of the political and social agitation carried out by the Paris crowd—or mob, as a conservative would refer to it—representing the sectional interests of the urban masses, made up of artisans and journeymen, shopkeepers and other urban workers acting in defiance of both the left and right, whether in the succession of revolutionary national assemblies from 1789 to 1799 or the capital's city government (the independent PARIS COMMUNE).

The *sans-culottes* played a decisive role in putting pressure on the GIRONDINS, JACOBINS and other left-wing political parties to put into practice more radical social reforms, such as guaranteeing cheap bread and imposing price controls, thereby propelling the revolution ever leftwards. At the same time, they also led a vigorous popular resistance against the growing forces of reaction within the entrenched bourgeoisie—increasingly divided into left and right factions—as well as against the royalist counterrevolutionary elements, the *aristos,* as they called the despised aristocratic classes; and above all the Church, now allied with the conservative provinces as a pillar of the old order. Such events as the spectacular capture of the Bastille on July 14, 1789, the sack of the Tuileries Palace in August 1792, followed by the September massacres and the two revolutionary *journées* which resulted in the overthrow of the Bourbon monarchy and the proclamation of the Jacobin republic, serve to illustrate the enormous impact of their revolutionary violence in determining the course of the French Revolution. As the revolution became increasingly radicalized, advancing from constitutional monarchy to the Jacobin dictatorship of 1793 and 1794—which for the first time in world history ushered in a constitution extending suffrage to the masses—the *sans-culottes* were perceived as an independent political force. Thus they often resorted to revolutionary violence and terror in alliance with the Jacobins, Girondins, Hébertistes or *Enragés* (the wild ones) and later—but less effectively—in support of the BABEUF conspiracy launched against the DIRECTORATE. The *sans-culottes* are sometimes called *sectionnaires,* due to the permanent sessions they convened in the 48 electoral wards or sections (corresponding to today's Paris *arrondissments*), into which the city of Paris was broken down for electoral, fiscal and administrative purposes.

But what really set them apart from the rest of the revolutionary citizenry was that they and they alone made a virtue of their plain and unadorned dress, since *sans-culottes* literally means "without knee breeches," the latter being a form of attire regarded as a sign of privilege associated with the *ancien régime.* In their speech and revolutionary argot they also dropped such "aristocratic" forms of address as "*monsieur*" in favor of the more egalitarian "*citoyen,*" substituted *tu* instead of the formal *vous* in addressing each other and took part in demonstrations or revolutionary *journées,* armed with symbolic pikes in lieu of the swords still in use in the bourgeois National Guard. They also wore the red Phyrigian cap (often decorated with the tricolor cockade) which they never doffed before their social betters. Nineteenth-century revolutionary historiography has applauded their revolutionary self-assertion as a precursor of all subsequent European national awakenings. Jules Michelet, for instance, idolized them as standing for all that is noble and virtuous in people up in arms. They also earned the admiration of Marxists as an embryonic form of the industrial proletariat, but have also been condemned for having so often been led astray by unscrupulous mob orators and bourgeois political agitators.

SARDAROV, BUNIAT MADAT OGLI (1889–1919) An activist of the revolutionary struggle for the victory of the Soviet government in Azerbaijan, Sardarov was a member of the Communist Party from 1906. He was born Ibragimov, in the village

A family of sans-culottes *taking its evening meal: a contemporary print*

of Kargabazar in the Karyagin area, to a family of poor farm workers. During the years of the first RUSSIAN REVOLUTION OF 1905, he actively participated in the revolutionary struggle, for which he was arrested and sent to the Bailov prison in Baku. After the liberation in 1908–1912, he conducted revolutionary work among the farm workers. In 1914, during the all-Baku political strike, he was the organizer of a major demonstration of the workers of the Balahan-Sabuntchi oil region. Sardarov was one of the leaders of the Central Bureau of Communist Muslims. In May of 1919 he was captured and killed by the English while crossing the Caspian Sea from Astrahan to Baku.

SATRAPS: REVOLTS OF, IN ASIA MINOR, AND REBELLION IN PHOENICIA (367–344 B.C.) By the mid-4th century B.C. some signs of disintegration of the Persian empire began to appear. For the first time it was not peoples subject to the Persians, but Persian governors—the so-called satraps—who revolted against the central authority.

Datamas, son of a Carian and of a Scythian woman, began his career as a commander of the king's bodyguard. In 378 B.C. he became the satrap of Cappadocia. By an astute policy and successful wars against local rebels, he enlarged his satrapy, which included territories from the Taurus mountains to the Black Sea. From 373 B.C. he began to issue his own coins and in 367 B.C. openly rebelled against the authority of the king. The satrap of neighboring Phrygia, Ariobarzanus, joined him, and the Carian ruler Mausolus secretly supported them. The rebels asked for support from Athens and Sparta and the Spartan king Agesilaus and the Athenian general Timotheus arrived with 8,000 Greek mercenaries and 30 ships. Phoenician cities also joined the rebellion. The satrap of Lydia, Autophradates, who had received orders to fight the rebels, became completely isolated and joined the rebels himself. Even the king's son-in-law, the satrap of Ionia, Orontes, supported the rebellion. Rebellious satraps concluded an alliance with Egypt, which had been independent since 404 B.C. Thus, the whole eastern Mediterranean entered into a state of war with Persia.

However, the rebels lacked unity and did not trust each other. In 363 B.C. Orontes, who commanded the army of invasion into Syria, crossed over to the king's side. Autophradates soon followed his example. In 360 B.C., Ariobarzanus was betrayed by his own son, Mitridates, and was executed. Finally, in 359 B.C. the army of Datamas revolted against him and he was killed. With his death, the great revolt of satraps came to an end. Only Mausolus remained unpunished since he had not officially participated in any rebellion.

In December 359 B.C. Artaxerxes II died, and his son Artaxerxes III Ochus became king. In 356 B.C. he ordered all satraps in Asia Minor to dissolve their mercenary forces. Artabazus, satrap of Phrygia, refused and revolted. The satrap of Mysia, Orontes, joined the rebellion. With the help of their mercenaries from Athens and Thebes, they defeated the king's army. However, in 352 B.C. Orontes capitulated and Artabazus fled to Philipp, king of Macedonia.

By 350 B.C. Artaxerxes III was ready to invade Egypt, but in 349 B.C. the Phoenician cities Tripolis and Sidon rebelled under the leadership of Tennes, king of Sidon. In 346 B.C. Pharaoh Nectanebes II sent 4,000 Greek mercenaries to Sidon under the command of Mentor of Rhodos. With their help the rebels defeated the two Persian armies led by Belesius (Bel-shunu), satrap of Trans-Euphrates, and Mazaeus, satrap of Cilicia. Cilicia, Judea and Cyprus supported the rebels.

In 345 B.C., Artaxerxes III himself assumed command and led a large army and navy to enforce a siege of Sidon. Tennes, the king of Sidon, decided to betray his subjects, and mercenaries of Mentor allowed the Persians to enter the city. Sidon was plundered, its inhabitants massacred and the survivors deported to Babylon and Susae. Tennes himself was nevertheless executed, but Mentor and his mercenaries remained in Persian service. In 344 B.C., the other Phoenician cities surrendered and rebellions in Judah and Cyprus were suppressed. The Jewish rebels were deported to Hyrcania on the banks of the Caspian Sea.

SATTAR-KHAN (1867–1914) Born to a peasant's family in Iran's Azerbaijan, Sattar-Khan rose to be an outstanding figure of Iran's democratic movement. In his youth, he was arrested repeatedly for participating in revolutionary activities. After the beginning of the Iranian Revolution of 1905–1911 (see IRAN, REVOLTS AND REVOLUTIONS), Sattar-Khan took an active part in the revolutionary events in Tabriz, Iran's Azerbaijan. In 1908–1909, he led the Tabriz people's revolt against the shah's absolutism, which caused a new upsurge of the revolutionary movement in Iran. Sattar-Khan remains very popular among Iranians.

SAVIMBI, JONAS MALHEIRO (1934–) Savimbi was born in Angola, the son of a preacher. After obtaining a law degree at Lausanne University, Switzerland, he returned to Angola (1966), where he founded UNITA (the National Union for the Total Independence of Angola) to win independence from the Portuguese.

However, when the Portuguese left Angola in 1975, a rival guerrilla movement—the MPLA (Popular Movement for the Liberation of Angola) seized power, with Soviet and Cuban support. Savimbi decided to fight on. Over the years, he built UNITA into a strong fighting force and conducted a guerrilla campaign against the MPLA government. With his anti-Communist rhetoric, Savimbi received aid from some western countries, especially the USA under President Ronald Reagan. In January 1986, when he visited the US, Savimbi was received like a head of state. UNITA was also backed by South Africa.

A flamboyant figure in his trademark red beret, Savimbi has presented himself as a champion of the poor and oppressed. However, he rules UNITA with an iron fist and there have been reports of human rights violations within the organization.

In 1991, Savimbi signed a peace agreement with the government and he then campaigned in the presidential elections. When he lost the elections in September 1992, however, he returned to guerrilla warfare, having threatened before the elections to win "or else."

SAVINKOV, BORIS VIKTOROVICH (1879–1925) Populist (see POPULISM) terrorist and literary figure. Son of a military prosecutor, Savinkov studied law in St. Petersburg but in 1899 was expelled for political activity. Originally influenced by MARXISM, he joined the populist movement during the exile that followed his university expulsion.

In 1903, Savinkov joined the Socialist Revolutionary Fighting Organization, participating in the assassinations of the minister of the interior, Plehve, and Grand Duke Sergei Alexandrovich in 1904 and 1905 respectively. He became head of the Fighting Organization after the exposure of its former chief, Evno Azef, as a police agent. He soon turned to literature, publishing fiction and poetry under the nom de plume of V. Ropshin. His best known works are *The Pale Horse* (1909), *What Never Happened* (1913) and his autobiographical *Memoirs of a Terrorist* (English translation, New York, 1931).

In 1914, Savinkov, then an emigrant in Paris, actively supported participation in the war and joined the French army. Returning to Russia in 1917, he became a political commissar and later deputy war minister under KERENSKY. Because of his duplicitous role in the August 1917 rebellion of General Kornilov, Savinkov was fired from the war ministry and expelled from the SOCIAL REVOLUTIONARY PARTY. During the civil war (1918–1921), Savinkov was active against the BOLSHEVIKS, organizing anti-Bolshevik uprisings along the Volga, recruiting anti-Bolshevik Russian forces in Poland and advocating the establishment of a democratic federal Russian state with independence for Finland and autonomy for Ukraine. With the support of Western European governments, he continued his anti-Bolshevik activities in exile after the end of the civil war.

In 1924, he was caught attempting to enter the Soviet Union. Tried and sentenced to death, he wrote a contrite article for the Soviet press and had his sentence commuted to 10 years. His death in prison the following year was attributed to suicide.

SAVONAROLA, GIROLAMO (1452–1498) Dominican friar and reformer, who dominated the political scene in Florence between 1494–1498. Born in Ferrara, Savonarola entered the Dominican order of Bologna in 1475. In 1482 he was sent to Florence as a preacher in the convent of San Marco. There he began his prophetic sermons, preaching about necessary reforms in the Church. He left Florence in 1487 but was recalled in 1490, at the request of Lorenzo de Medici, and became the prior of San Marco (1491). In his fiery sermons, which drew large crowds, he attacked corruption and criticized the Medici government. He predicted the invasion of Italy by Charles VIII of France, and called for repentance for the sake of a better future. When Piero de Medici was driven out of Florence (1494), Savonarola became the virtual leader of the city. He supervised the establishment of a popular theocratic government, based on a great council consisting of 3,200 citizens, and carried out social and moral reforms which were widely popular. He objected to the alliance of the Italian cities against France, which Florence therefore did not join.

His rigorous campaign against immorality, though, made him many enemies. Opposition formed in the city, and this was supported from the outside by the Medicis, who sought to return to power. Savonarola was also opposed by Pope Alexander VI, who wanted Florence to join the Italian alliance, and who saw him as a threat to his own authority. In a series of measures, the Pope tried to eliminate the friar's power. First he invited him to Rome to explain his revelations but Savonarola rejected the invitation. He then ordered him to abstain from preaching. Savonarola stopped preaching for a while, but in 1496 launched a new series of sermons directed against the corruption of Rome itself. In 1497 Savonarola was excommunicated by the pope and, when he continued his sermons, Florence was threatened

with an interdict. Famine, war, plague and the fear of excommunication reduced Savonarola's popularity and the tide finally turned against him. Savonarola was challenged to an ordeal by fire by Franciscan friars, an event which ended in turmoil and confusion. The next day a mob attacked San Marco and Savonarola was arrested. He was tortured and sentenced to death as a heretic. He was hanged on May 23, 1498 with two of his disciples, and their bodies were subsequently burned.

Savonarola *by Fra Bartolommeo*

SCHMITT, CARL (1888–1975) German jurist. Schmitt was a professor of law in Bonn, Berlin, Cologne and again Berlin during the rule of the Nazis. Although not an ardent Nazi himself, Schmitt was a major contributor to HITLER's rise and supplied arguments in favor of the régime's atrocities. Schmitt's teaching revolutionized German jurisprudence by introducing sociological and philosophical elements into it in the 1920s and early 1930s. He drew universal conclusions from Weimar's partisan politics, by arguing that the splintering of the Weimar parliament into multiple parties exposed the unbridgeable gap between constitutional liberal norms and reality. Parliamentarism thus allows for no social reform and institutional change but contributes to the decline and fall of the liberal "system" itself. Schmitt suggested the strong, powerful state as the only alternative to the declining parliamentary régime. The use of emergency rules, as well as domestic and foreign warfare, would eliminate the normative limitations on such a state—a process that Schmitt called "Decisionism" (*Dezisionismus*). Schmitt's understanding of "politics" was thus focused on the distinction created by him between "friend and foe" (*Freund-Feind Theorie*), which was later interpreted to mean fighting the liberals and the left inside Germany and to justify Hitler's foreign wars. Schmitt did in fact justify Hitler's Night of the Long Knives of June 30, 1934, and his atrocities against the Jews without being a racist ideologue himself.

SDS see STUDENTS FOR A DEMOCRATIC SOCIETY.

SECESSIO see PLEBEIAN REVOLT.

SECOND INTERNATIONAL see INTERNATIONAL.

SECRET SOCIETIES Illegal Chinese organizations. Dating back to the Han dynasty (206 B.C.–220 A.D.), when the RED EYE-BROWS appeared, secret societies, originating either as religious or faith-healing sects or fraternal associations, provided havens for various elements in the lower fringes of Chinese society who wished to escape bureaucratic controls, e.g., impoverished peasants, disbanded soldiers or deserters, bandits, salt smugglers, itinerant merchants and craftsmen and boatmen. Intellectuals or pseudo-intellectuals, semi-literate fortune-tellers, jobless lower-degree holders and failed examination candidates often filled leadership posts in these societies. Initiation into the secret societies created putative kinship ties, offering solidarity and protection when family or lineage support was either lacking or vulnerable to bureaucratic reprisals.

Normally, the sects and societies were not in open rebellion, but in times of disorder and acute distress their clandestine networks, esoteric symbols and secret passwords served as ready-made vehicles for rebellion. Under alien conquerors such as the Mongols (Yuan dynasty, 1279–1367) and the Manchus (Qing dynasty, 1644–1912), major secret societies like the WHITE LOTUS and TRIADS rebelled in the name of the ethnic Chinese. While attacking the established order, rebellious secret societies usually did not offer a counter-ideology. All they could invoke was the traditional Confucian "right to rebel" against tyrannical rule. Lacking sufficient support from the literate elite, they could help ignite and accelerate anti-dynastic movements but could not on their own establish new dynasties. During the 19th century, when the Qing dynasty was in decline, secret societies proliferated, though the White Lotus and Triads were the only ones specifically mentioned in the Qing code. Many of the others were off-shoots of these two main groups.

The TAIPING movement (1850–1864) does not fit into the secret society category, but it evoked responsive risings by secret orders. The other major 19th-century rebel society, the NIAN (1853–1868), may have stemmed from the White Lotus. The imperialist invasion of China exacerbated anti-foreign feelings among secret societies like the Boxers (1898–1900). In Southeast Asia and other regions where Chinese emigrated at this time, secret societies helped maintain group solidarity, providing protection in hostile environments, but they could also cloak criminal activities. Modern revolutionaries, from SUN YAT-SEN to MAO ZEDONG, tried to harness secret society support. Though proscribed, faith-healing sects are acknowledged as still existing in the People's Republic of China (see also GE LAO HUI, SMALL SWORD SOCIETY, 1911 REVOLUTION).

SECTIONS see SANS-CULOTTES.

SERBEDARS The participants of a political movement that appeared in the first half of the 14th century in Khorasan (northern Iran). The movement was directed against the oppression by the Mongol conquerors. From 1337 to 1381, a united power was founded in Khorasan with its center in Sabzevar. In 1365–1366, Serbedars (Persian for "hanged") headed the anti-Mongol movement in Samarkand. Eventually, the Serbedar movement grew weak because of the internal struggle between different social strata, with the movement eventually ceasing to exist in 1381.

SERGE (KIBALCHICH), VICTOR (1890–1947) Russian revolutionary, the son of emigré radical intellectuals. In Paris, Serge evolved from a revolutionary populist (see POPULISM) to anarchism. He edited the French *L'Anarchie,* simultaneously taking part in anarchist violence, for which he received a five-year jail sentence in 1910.

In August 1917, he decided to go to "liberated Russia," arriving only near the end of 1918. Joining the BOLSHEVIKS, he became part of the executive of the COMINTERN, where his international connections and knowledge of languages proved valuable. His anarchist attitudes to power brought him into conflict with the Soviet régime, and as part of TROTSKY's Left Opposition he was excluded from the Communist Party in 1928 and exiled to Siberia in 1933. In 1936, he left the USSR for France and later for Mexico, where he remained until his death. His best known writings are *Memoirs of a Revolutionary* (1901–1941) and *Year One of the Russian Revolution.*

SERTORIUS, QUINTUS Roman general who led a Spanish national rebellion against Rome. Born in 132 B.C., he served in various military and political positions until appointed governor of Spain in 82 B.C. However, in the next year he lost his position to another governor sent out by Sulla, the consul who had just established a régime based on Senatorial terror.

Fearing for his life, Sertorius escaped to Mauretania but returned to Spain at the request of the Lusitanian people. Accompanied by a white fawn—which was interpreted as a sign of divine protection—he led them and other Spanish peoples in a revolt against Rome, conquering a large part of the peninsula. He welcomed refugees fleeing from Sulla, all the while posing as the lawful Roman governor. At one point he even set up a senate of his own. Though he was able to withstand Roman assaults, his popularity diminished after 74 B.C., when his military fortunes declined and he was forced to take harsh measures against his remaining supporters. Finally, in 72 B.C., he was murdered by one of his own lieutenants, precipitating to the collapse of the revolt.

SETIF UPRISING An Algerian nationalist revolt in 1945. On May 8, a demonstration of approximately 8,000 Muslims was organized, apparently by the PARTY OF THE ALGERIAN PEOPLE, calling for independence and the release of its leader, AHMAD MESSALI HAJJ. The protest, however, erupted into violence when French gendarmes and Muslim demonstrators fired on each other. As the uprising spread from Setif to Guelma as well as other Algerian cities, over 100 European settlers were murdered during its first five days. France responded with a massacre: while French reports claimed only a few thousand deaths, Algerian nationalists held the figure to be closer to 45,000. The revolt temporarily split the Algerian nationalist movement, but induced the French government to institute a 1947 law introducing the first popularly elected Algerian Assembly.

AL-SHA'BI, QAHTAN MUHAMMAD   (1920–1981) South Yemeni politician, president of South Yemen 1967–1969. Born in Lahej Sultanate in the Aden Protectorates, Sha'bi worked for several years in the Lahej Land Development and became its director in 1955. He left the government service in 1958 to work for the nationalist insurgents and joined the South Arabian League. In 1960 he fled to Yemen. Around 1963, while still in exile in Yemen, he co-founded the NATIONAL LIBERATION FRONT FOR THE LIBERATION OF SOUTH YEMEN (NLF) and became one of its main leaders. He proclaimed an armed rebellion in October 1963 and led a guerrilla war against the British and the South Arabian federal authorities, as well as against rival nationalist groups, chiefly the Front for the Liberation of South Yemen. In 1967 he overcame these rival factions, and the NLF emerged as the only organization with which the transfer of power was to be negotiated. Sha'bi headed the NLF delegation to the November 1967 Geneva talks on independence. With independence achieved the same month, he became South Yemen's first president, prime minister and commander in chief. He was, however, soon involved in factional struggles within the NLF and the government, and in June 1969 he was deposed. He was expelled from the ruling party, detained, and, from April 1970, imprisoned. He was also ailing, and did not return to active public and political life before his death in 1981.

SHAMIL   (1797–1871) Religious, military and nationalist leader of the Caucasus Muslims in their fight against Russian expansionism. Shamil was the son of a Dagestan landowner from the town of Ghimri. As a child he proved an adept student in the Qur'an, Arabic, grammar, logic and rhetoric. Much of his education was undertaken by the Mullah Djemal ud-Din, an advocate of Muridism, a fundamentalist Muslim doctrine that called for *jihad* (holy war) against the Russians. Already recognized as a scholar, Shamil soon became an outspoken and acclaimed proponent of the doctrine.

The Muridist movement was under attack from without and within. The Russians perceived it as a threat to their territorial ambitions in the Caucasus, while local leaders often disapproved of the rigid implementation of Islamic law it demanded. In 1832 the first Muridist Imam of Dagestan was killed by the Russians; the second was assassinated by his own supporters in 1834. Shamil's uncompromising attitude led to his election that year as the third Imam.

Shamil set several goals for himself, including the unification of the warring Caucasus tribes, the establishment of the *Shari'a* (Muslim religious law) as the law of his territory, and universal recognition of his role not only as leader but as prophet. In all he proved successful—the fierce Chechen tribesmen submitted to him and all opposition was annihilated. In his wars against the Russians, Shamil proved an able tactician who preferred and mastered guerrilla warfare. Initially the Russians were terrified

of Shamil, especially as the Crimean war limited the number of troops available to the Russians. Shamil's fighters believed fervently in their mission, fighting to their last gasp and sometimes, it seemed, beyond that. The Russian novelist Mikhail Y. Lermontov commented in a novel about the war, "They don't seem to know when they ought to die!"

Shamil himself was a ruthless leader, willing to sacrifice even those most dear to him for his cause. He was intolerant of cowardice; any man suspected of shirking his duty in combat was instantly excommunicated until he proved himself. In one instance, the Chechens were overcome by Russian troops; surrender seemed their only option, but no one had the courage to ask Shamil for permission to do so. Finally, it was decided to send Shamil's mother to plead with her son to allow the Chechens to submit. Shamil sat with his mother determining what to do. After three days he came out of the mosque and addressed the crowd: "After much prayer and supplication, God has told me how to respond to the Chechens' foul request. One hundred lashes will be given to the first person to speak to me of surrender—my mother." Despite everyone's pleas, his mother was taken out to be beaten. After five strokes, the old woman fainted. Shamil promptly demanded that he receive the remaining 95 lashes himself, vowing to kill his soldiers if they did not beat him vigorously. After the beating, he sent the Chechens back to the front, ordering them to tell their companions all that they had seen.

Shamil led a precarious existence, often just barely eluding capture. The one time he was captured he managed to escape but lost his wife and infant son to Russian bullets. Another son was captured and brought to St. Petersburg. The czar raised the child, hoping he would one day succeed his father and prove a capable ally.

Shamil was finally defeated in 1859. The Russian army sent 200,000 troops, led by General A.I. Bariatinsky, to surround the Murid rebels. Shamil was no match for the overwhelming number of troops, nor could his poorly armed men compete with the 200 heavy guns the Russians had brought; after several fierce battles he was captured and taken to St. Petersburg and then to Kaluga for imprisonment. The terms of his imprisonment were, however, somewhat lax, since even the Russians respected the man who had fought against them so bravely. Shamil died on a pilgrimage to Mecca.

It was said: "Muhammad is Allah's first prophet; Shamil is his second."

SHARI'ATI, ALI   (1933–1977) Iranian thinker, next to the AYATOLLAH KHOMEINI, the most influential ideologist of the Iranian Revolution of 1979 (see IRAN, REVOLTS AND REVOLUTIONS). Born in Mazinan, a village near Mashhad, Shari'ati was the son of a well-known preacher and commentator of Islamic law who had a great deal of influence on him. In the early 1950s, as a student at Mashhad University, he was active in groups linked with MUHAMMAD MOSSADDEQ and was arrested. In 1960, he went to Paris to continue his studies and in 1964 received a Ph.D. in sociology and theology. In Paris, he met writers, philosophers and Islamologists. He was much influenced by the ALGERIAN REVOLUTION, which achieved success during his stay in Paris.

Upon his return to Iran, he taught at Mashhad University but was soon dismissed and went to Tehran. There he became a popular lecturer, and in 1967 co-founded *Husseiniya Arashad*, a progressive religious and social institution. The *Savak* (secret police) soon closed that institute and arrested Shari'ati. He was jailed for a year and a half and endured house arrest for an additional two years. In June 1977 he was permitted to travel to London.

Shari'ati's ideas were similar to those of the Ayatollah Khomeini in many ways. They both opposed the shah's régime and any influence from the west. They both led the masses toward an Islamic revolution. They opposed imperialism (especially cultural imperialism, i.e., alienating the people from its heritage), liberalism, capitalism, MARXISM and SOCIALISM. Yet Shari'ati hoped to realize his vision without an institutionalized religious establishment. He preached an Islamic humanism and rejected the determinist fatalism widespread in the Islamic establishment, because it deprived the individual of responsibility for his fate and that of society. According to Shari'ati, Muslims should not wait for Shiite Islam's secret Imam, but should act here and now, and an important precondition for action was preparing the soul and making an ideological change. He believed the ultimate goal was a society based on equality. Shari'ati's death under mysterious conditions led his followers to suspect *Savak* involvement, heightening their revolutionary fervor. By 1978, his writings were translated into slogans used in sermons in mosques across the country. Shari'ati's tenets, however, were not in accord with the official doctrine of Shiite Islam and Khomeini's régime. Following the revolution, an organization calling itself *Forqan* claimed into carry on Shari'ati's legacy.

SHARIATMADARI, AYATOLLAH SEIED (1905–1986) Iranian clergyman and revolutionary leader. Born in Azerbaijan, he studied theology at Tabriz and Qom where he met KHOMEINI and became his disciple. During his adult life as a teacher of religion, he alternated between Tabriz and Qom, keeping in touch with Khomeini. In 1962–1963 he played an important part in the antigovernment riots and on one occasion saved Khomeini's life; during the 1970s he became one of Iran's most important religious leaders.

During the years immediately before the Iranian Revolution of 1979 (see IRAN, REVOLTS AND REVOLUTIONS), Shariatmadari was a relative moderate. He called on the shah to observe Muslim laws and demanded that Iran adopt the *Shari'a* (Islamic law) as its constitution while appointing five Shiite clergymen to oversee all legislation. Once the shah had been deposed and the Khomeini régime was installed, however, Shariatmadari fell out with him, calling the first postrevolutionary elections (summer 1979) "a lie and a falsification." This brought him into disgrace and in 1982 he was put under house arrest.

SHAUMYAN, STEPAN GEORGIEVICH (1878–1918) (party code names: Suren, Surenin, Ayax) Famous revolutionary and an activist of the Communist Party. Shaumyan was born in Tiflis (Tbilisi). In 1898 he graduated from the Tiflis Trade College, where he actively participated in the work of illegal Marxist youth clubs. In 1899 he organized the first Marxist club in Armenia. In 1900 he joined the Russian Socialist Democratic Workers Party (RSDWP). In the same year he began his studies at the Riga Polytechnical Institute, from which he was expelled

for revolutionary activities and was then exiled to the Caucasus.

At the end of 1902 Shaumyan emigrated to Germany and enrolled in the Berlin University to study philosophy. In 1904 he returned to Tiflis. Together with STALIN and M. Tzchakaya, he was one of the leaders of the Caucasian Union Committee of the RSDWP.

During the RUSSIAN REVOLUTION OF 1905 he was actively involved in the struggle against the MENSHEVIKS and for the BOLSHEVIK strategy and tactics in the revolution. The Communist Party sent him to Baku, where he was one of the leaders in the Baku party. In 1911 he was arrested and exiled to Astrahan, where he continued to be actively involved in the local party organization. At a conference in Prague, he was elected by absentee ballot to be a candidate for the membership in the Central committee of the RSDWP.

When he returned from exile in 1914, Shaumyan headed the Baku Bolshevik organization and led an all-Baku political strike of the oil production workers, which had great political ramifications for all of Russia. In 1916, Shaumyan was arrested once again and exiled to Saratov, where the first RUSSIAN REVOLUTION OF 1917 found him. Shaumyan was elected by absentee ballot to be chairman of the Baku Soviet ("council") of Worker Deputies. After the October RUSSIAN REVOLUTION OF 1917, on November 2 the Baku Soviet decided, upon Shaumyan's report, to ratify the program of transferring the government control in Baku into the hands of the Soviet government and of spreading its control throughout all of the Caucasus. On December 16, 1917, the Soviet People's Committee (Sovnarcom) of the Russian Soviet Federated Socialist Republic (RSFSR) appointed Shaumyan special commissar for the affairs of the Caucasus. In April 1918, the Soviet of Worker Deputies took control of the entire Baku region. The Baku Sovnarcom was created with Shaumyan at the head and its work started with nationalizing banks and the oil industry, issuing a decree about confiscating the property of the landowners and transferring it to the farm workers, instituting a reform in the schools and the judicial system, and organizing the Baku Commune military force. After the fall of the Baku Commune, Shaumyan was among the 26 Baku commissars who were taken by the English to Krasnovodsk and executed on the night of September 20, 1918. Later his remains were transported and buried in Baku.

SHAYS'S REBELLION A violent uprising of 1786–1787, confined to central and western Massachusetts, in the United States. While Shays's rebellion was a distinctly local affair, it would have a resounding effect on the development of popular government in the American states, and ultimately, even on the framing of the American constitution.

The uprising was triggered by the deteriorating conditions of the small farmers and artisans of rural Massachusetts in a period of economic depression. Monetary contraction in the aftermath of the revolutionary war, coupled with the decisive influence of the commercial and financial sector over the young State's legislation and legal system, threatened many farmers with the danger of farm foreclosure and artisans with imprisonment for debt.

Captain Daniel Shays, a veteran of the revolutionary war, was among the leaders who channeled the swelling popular distress into a direct, and increasingly violent, challenge to the authority of the courts and oppressive local officers. Resistance gradually escalating into attacks on institutions of law enforcement, the government of Massachusetts called on its militia to reestablish law and order. In the summer of 1786, a violent clash with the militia was avoided though a negotiated agreement between the two sides. In January of the next year, however, an attack by more than 1,000 rebels on the federal arsenal in Springfield was met head-on by the militia. The rebels were dispersed and their leaders found refuge in neighboring states.

In the aftermath of Shays's rebellion, Massachusetts voters elected a more liberal state government that issued relief legislation. Beyond Massachusetts, the event demonstrated to leaders nationwide the internal weakness of the individual states, of their legislatures and their militias. This demonstration helped promote the idea of a more perfect union of the states under a federal constitution.

SHI DAKAI (Shih T'a-k'ai) (1831–1863) One of the leaders of the TAIPING REBELLION in China. Born in Guangxi to a landowning family and relatively well-educated, Shi, like other Taiping leaders was a Hakka, a sublinguistic community that had migrated from northern China centuries earlier. The Hakka were often at odds with the original inhabitants, including aboriginal Miao tribes. Like the Taiping leader, HONG XIUQUAN, Shi had failed in the civil service examinations. He joined the God Worshippers Society, the original Taiping religious organization, formed in 1847. In January 1851, when Hong declared the establishment of the Taiping Tianguo (Heavenly Kingdom of Great Peace), Shi was appointed "Assistant King." While Hong claimed to be Jesus' younger brother, secondary leaders were also ranked as sons of God. Shi, named 7th son, became the Taipings' foremost military leader during their spectacular drive north that in 1853 led to the capture of Nanjing, where they established their capital.

In 1856, dissension and intrigue led to bloody strife among the Taiping leaders. Fearful of Hong's megalomanic, jealous behavior, Shi left Nanjing, intending to establish a separate kingdom in Sichuan. While another brilliant commander, LI XIUCHENG, stayed to maintain the Taiping threat in the east, Shi led his followers, numbering more than 200,000, in a remarkable expedition through south and southwest China. His route was similar to that later taken by the Chinese Communists in their LONG MARCH of 1934–1935, but Shi had less success trying to cross Sichuan's treacherous terrain. In 1863, when surrounded by imperial troops, he surrendered and was executed.

SHINING PATH (Sendero Luminoso) The Shining Path guerrilla movement of Peru burst onto the continental stage on May 17, 1980, when it launched a revolutionary war against the country's recently reestablished civilian government headed by Fernando Be Laude Terry (who had been president previously between 1963 and 1968).

Sendero Luminoso is formally known as the Communist Party of Peru on the Shining Path of Jose Carlos Mariategui (PCP-*Sendero Luminoso*), named for the revolutionary intellectual who in 1928, founded the Peruvian Socialist Party, forerunner of the country's modern Communist movement. *Sendero* itself grew out of the divisions within the Peruvian left, engendered by the schism within the international Communist movement between Moscow and Beijing in the early 1960s. By 1965, the

Peruvian Communist Party—like many throughout the world—had split between pro-Moscow and pro-Beijing factions. The latter strongly supported an armed revolutionary path to taking power rather than the electoral struggle that was favored by those closest ideologically to Moscow and its politics of "peaceful coexistence."

Sendero is the direct descendant of the pro-Beijing faction in this split, known first as *Bandera Roja* (Red Flag) and then after 1970 as the PCP-*Sendero Luminoso*. The organization's key leader from the beginning was a bookish university professor named Abimael Guzman of the provincial city of Ayacucho—cradle of Peruvian independence from Spain in 1824—in the most impoverished Andean region of the country.

Guzman's aim was to successfully transfer the revolutionary strategy pursued by MAO ZEDONG in China to the conditions of Peru. He traveled to China at least twice during that country's most chaotic period since Mao's triumph in 1949, the GREAT PROLETARIAN CULTURAL REVOLUTION, between 1966 and 1970. From Mao and from ERNESTO CHE GUEVARA—who had described the Andes, hopefully, as the "Sierra Maestra of the Americas"—Guzman devised his own strategy for a Peruvian revolution that would comply with his dogmatic interpretation of the Maoist variant of Marxist-Leninist theory.

In his view, the three stages for taking power in Peru included a prolonged stage of "strategic self-defense" in regions where the movement was especially strong (among the most marginalized indigenous peasantry). This would eventually lead to a strategic equilibrium between the revolutionary forces and state power and culminate in the transformation of hit and run guerrilla struggles into a full-fledged "war of movement" capable of unleashing a climactic "strategic offensive," ending finally with the seizure of power. Much of this ideology was premised on a revolutionary countryside first surrounding the bourgeois cities and then obtaining their submission. This theory brought together elements from the classical Chinese philosopher of war, Sun Tzu; Mao himself; his then–anointed successor, LIN BIAO; Che Guevara and the writings of Italian Communist philosopher ANTONIO GRAMSCI.

The objective was a "people's democratic revolution" as the first step in the forging of a new state power that would lay the basis for the transition to socialism and ultimately communism. According to Guzman, given Peru's "semi-feudal" and "semi-colonial" society, where the indigenous peasantry was the largest potentially revolutionary bloc, and with a relatively small working class whose growth, consciousness and power had been stunted by the penetration of foreign imperialist interests, a two-stage revolution was necessary. *Sendero* has become notable as the only Latin American Maoist movement to become a serious contender for power in the last 30 years, for its willingness to employ terrorist tactics (including both assassinations and massacres) systematically rather than as aberrations, and for its complex fusion of the imported orthodoxies of Maoist-style Marxism-Leninism with deeply rooted indigenous traditions and symbolic vocabularies of resistance.

In a manner reminiscent of Argentina's Peronist Montoneros movement and Revolutionary Army of the People (ERP) and Uruguay's TUPAMAROS, *Sendero* became strong enough to help spark Peruvian President Alberto Fujimori's military-backed "coup from within," which shut down congress and suspended civil liberties in April 1992, but not strong enough to take power itself. It was further isolated by the arrest of Guzman, after Colombian drug-lord Pablo Escobar perhaps the continent's "most wanted man," in September 1992. Since then, *Sendero* has apparently split into several factions divided by Guzman's absence and by his increasingly mixed signals from his specially designed naval prison as to whether a dialogue is possible with the Fujimori régime. Meanwhile, after some 15,000 civilian deaths due to political violence since 1980, Fujimori consolidated his hold on power with a decisive victory in his race for a previously prohibited reelection in 1995, in a pattern similar to that of Argentina's Carlos Saul Menem, with parallel pitches combining a kind of personality cult with support for neo-liberal economic policies and a gift for populist demagoguery.

SHISHAKLI, ADIB (1909–1964) Syrian officer and nationalist, president of Syria, 1953–1954. Born in Hama, Shishakli served in the Special Troops set up by the French mandatory régime. In 1948 he was a senior officer in AL-QAWUQJI's Army of Deliverance which fought the Jews in Palestine. He is said to have been a member of the Syrian Nationalist Party of ANTOUN SA'ADEH.

Shishakli played a major part in HUSNI ZA'IM's coup in 1949, but was suspected by Za'im of disloyalty and dismissed from the army. He was reinstated by SAMI HINNAWI, after his coup, in August 1949. On December 19, 1949, Shishakli led a military coup which overthrew Hinnawi. At first, Shishakli permitted the formal parliamentary régime established by Hinnawi to continue and himself assumed only the title of deputy chief of staff, though in fact he ruled behind the scenes. He opposed the pro-Iraqi bent of the People's Party then in power and, on November 29, 1951, carried out a second coup. His rule now became more openly dictatorial, although he appointed as a figurehead president and prime minister Marshal Fawzi Selo, one of his supporters. He assumed formal power in June 1953.

On February 25, 1954, a coup forced Shishakli to resign. He left Syria and lived in Lebanon, Saudi Arabia and France. In 1957 he was charged with plotting a coup with the support of Iraq and the west, and was tried in absentia several times. In 1960 he emigrated to Brazil. There he was assassinated in 1964 by a Druse in revenge for the bombing of the Druse Mountain during his rule.

SHISHKO, LEONID (1852–1920) (pseudonyms: P.B., P. Batin, Blagoveshtchensky, etc.) Russian revolutionary. From 1871, Shishko studied at the St. Petersburg Technological Institute. In 1872 he joined the CHAIKOVSKY CIRCLE and propagandized among the workers. In 1874, he was arrested, condemned to nine years of penalty servitude and afterwards exiled. In 1890 he escaped. He became one of the founders of the Fund for a Free Russian Press. In 1900–1901, Shishko was one of the leaders of the AGRARIAN SOCIALIST LEAGUE. In 1902 he joined the SOCIAL REVOLUTIONARY PARTY and became one of the heads of its foreign committee.

Shishko wrote articles on the history of social movement in Russia and on agricultural matters. In those articles he laid down the basic postulates of the Social Revolutionary Party.

SHI T'A-K'AI see SHI DAKAI.

SHLIAPNIKOV, ALEXANDER GAVRILOVICH (1884–1943) Russian revolutionary. Born in the metalworking town of Murom, Shliapnikov helped support his widowed mother and siblings by becoming a skilled metal worker. A revolutionary from the 1890s, he was one of the early BOLSHEVIKS, organizing strikes in the metallurgy works of St. Petersburg and in the Donbas. From 1908 to 1914, after emigrating from Russia he wandered through Europe, working in metal factories and preaching revolution. After a brief return to Russia, he was sent to Scandinavia to organize the smuggling of Bolshevik correspondence and literature between the party's emigré centers and Russia.

In February 1917, he was one of the editors of the Bolshevik *Pravda* and later head of the metal workers' union. After the Bolshevik seizure of power in October 1917, he became people's commissar for labor. In 1919–1921, he headed the Workers' Opposition, advocating a leading role for autonomous, worker-led trade unions in the building of a Socialist state. Defeated and denounced at the 10th Communist party congress in 1921, Shliapnikov served briefly as a diplomat in France but was expelled from the Communist Party in 1933, arrested in 1935 and died in prison. He was the author of two books of memoirs: *On the Eve of 1917* and *The Year 1917*.

SIDON AND SOUTHEAST ANATOLIA, REVOLTS OF (678–676 B.C.) The Assyrian king Sennacherib was killed by his own sons in 681 B.C. His death was followed by civil war in Assyria. Egypt took advantage of the situation and occupied Philistia. The Phoenician city of Sidon rebelled, in alliance with Sanduari, the king of Kundu and Sissu, of southeast Anatolia. The latter is identified by Hawkins with Azatiwada, the author of the Phoenician-Luwian bilingual inscription at Kara-tepe in the plain of Adana.

After consolidating his power in Assyria, the new king, Esarchaddon, began the restoration of Assyrian rule in Philistia. In 678 B.C. he reached Arza in Wadi-el-Arish and captured its king, Asu-khili. In 677 B.C., Sidon was besieged and conquered with the help of its commercial rival, Tyre. The city was destroyed and an Assyrian colony, Kar-Ashur-aha-iddina (Port-Esarchaddon), was founded in its place. Its territory was handed over to Ba'al, king of Tyre. In 676 B.C., Sanduari was captured and beheaded, together with Abdi-milkutti, king of Sidon. The heads of both kings were displayed in triumph in Nineveh, hanging on the necks of nobles of both countries.

SIERRA GORDA REBELLION The Sierra Gorda rebellion of 1847–1850 occurred in a remote area where the Mexican states of Guanajuato, Queretaro and San Luis Potosi come together, and was precipitated directly by the war with the United States. The war encouraged arms trading, much of it illegal. To meet the cost of the war, a law was enacted allowing the government of Queretaro to sell Indian communal lands. The indigenous Otomis, Nahuas and Totonacos, rejecting the necessity of selling land from under them to pay for a war they little understood, protested vigorously. Tomas Mejia, an army officer executed much later at the side of Maximilian, and some peasants joined the Indian cause.

Many rebels ended up fighting both the US invaders and their own governmental forces; a few even rose up in favor of the invaders. By 1849, most of the prisoners captured by federal forces were being deported, preventing the movement from re-organizing. As an additional pacification measure, the government initially supported redistribution of land among the peasants; in the end, however, most new agricultural and forest legislation was directed at protecting the interests of the rural and urban property owners. Many peasants later found no other economic alternative than banditry, and no other political alternative in the continuation of their struggle than the formation of even more radical political groups.

SIEYÈS, EMMANUEL JOSEPH (1748–1836) More commonly known as the Abbé Sieyès, referred to as "the man of 1789." Sieyès was the most influential single revolutionary leader during the first phase of the FRENCH REVOLUTION, stretching from the fall of the Bastille on July 14, 1789 to the September massacres of 1792, which brought about the collapse of the constitutional monarchy under Louis XVI and the proclamation of France's first republic under the JACOBIN CONVENTION. Born in the Mediterranean port of Fréjus, he took up the priesthood with little conviction but with a strong determination to promote the right of the common man and the citizen against the tyranny of Throne and Altar.

Sieyès's moment of triumph came in January 1789 with the publication of his celebrated 20,000-word pamphlet entitled *What is the Third Estate?* published on the eve of the convocation of the Estates General in the royal palace of Versailles in May of that turbulent year. Its impact was immediate and electrifying. It has been accurately described as the most important catalyst to the upheaval that brought down the *ancien régime* in the summer of 1789. A revolutionary elite, groping to find an answer to the question of how to define the source of legitimate and representative government at a time of crisis, was relieved to find that Sieyès's ideas provided them with an admirable justification for the usurpation of power and a convenient pretext for condoning the necessity of revolutionary violence to bring about the triumph of the nation, one and indivisible.

Echoing the opening words of Jean-Jacques Rousseau in *The Social Contract*, Sieyès put forward the argument that national sovereignty rested with the people and no one else within the State and that, therefore, the people alone, manifesting the "general will" of the nation through the voice of their duly elected representatives, had the sole and indisputable right to overthrow the monarchy and replace the illegitimate despotism of the *ancien régime*, with its checks and balances on the functioning of their representatives, with a new constitution.

It was as a result of Sieyès's resolution, redrafted in the form of a decree adopted on June 17 over the opposition of moderates fearful of taking such a revolutionary step, that the Estates General arrogated to itself the title of the National Assembly, re-designated soon thereafter as the Constituent Assembly. It thereby abolished the very idea of any privileged body entitled to check its absolute authority and opened the way to a revolution squarely based on the principle of national sovereignty and self-determination, an article of faith that has since become the universal and sacrosanct dogma of democratic doctrine throughout the world. Thus an ideology far more extensive and inclusive, both in theory and practice, than anything ever claimed by the *ancien régime* was let loose upon the world, to shape the thinking of many other European and Third World revolutions, all of

which could trace their legitimacy to "the principles of 1789."

Although Sieyès's name is also associated with the legislation of a key committee of the National Assembly which redrew the *ancien régime*'s archaic patchwork of royal provinces, *pays d'états, pays d'élections* and more than 100 bishoprics, into today's more rational and Cartesian map of *départements* and *sous-départements*, he found it more prudent to withdraw from public life during the Jacobin Terror, only to reappear as a conspirator during the DIRECTORATE in 1798 that brought Bonaparte to power, first as consul, then as emperor. It was Sieyès who drafted the constitution of the consulate, only to have it scuttled by Napoleon, just as ROBESPIERRE and the Jacobins had scuttled his first experiment in constitutional monarchy. Elevated by Napoleon to the imperial peerage with the title of count, Sieyès was forced to go into exile during the first Restoration, remaining in Belgium during the reigns of Louis XVIII and Charles X and only returned to Paris to die under the July monarchy. When asked at the end of his life what he had done during Robespierre's Reign of Terror, he replied, *"J'ai survécu"*—"I remained alive."

SIKH REBELLION (1984–) The Sikhs, whose religion is an amalgam of the Muslim and Hindu faiths, mostly inhabit India's Punjab province. During the 1960s, their economic success—the Punjab is known as the breadbasket of India—encouraged them to seek autonomy from India; some even contemplated secession and the establishment of a separate Sikh state. When the government in New Delhi refused the Sikh demands, a terrorist campaign centering around the Golden Temple in Amritsar broke out. As part of what is now a 21-year-old conflict, the Indian army invaded the Golden Temple in June 1984 and four months later Sikh extremists assassinated Prime Minister Indira Gandhi. At the time of this writing in 1995, the revolt, which so far has claimed thousands of lives, is still going on in a disorganized way. Atrocities have been committed by both sides.

SIMA, HORIA (1903–1993) "The Commander," who in 1938 became the leader of the IRON GUARD, the Romanian Fascist movement, following the murder of CODREANU. Sima joined the movement at an early stage while at the Bucharest Polytechnic. In 1939, he led a campaign of political assassinations and between September 1940 and January 1941 served as deputy prime minister in the uneasy coalition with Marshal ION ANTONESCU. Following the Iron Guard's attempt to seize power in January 1941, he fled to Germany and with his followers was at the mercy of the Germans, who in late 1944 helped him form a Romanian Fascist government in exile in Vienna. After the end of World War II he attempted to revive the Romanian Fascist (see FASCISM) movement from Spain, where he edited and published Fascist literature. The small Fascist movement split in 1954, one section following Codreanu's "original" teachings while the other remained loyal to Sima. Sima died in Augsburg, Germany. He eluded publicity and details of his personal life were scarce. At present, the "Simist" legacy is being revived by extremists in post-Communist Romania. One publication, *Gazeta de Vest,* is loyal to Sima, and has published his memoirs and his book, *The Mission of Nationalism*, in which he attempts to prove the adaptability of nationalism and political extremism to the realities of the late century.

SINN FEIN A revolutionary, violently nationalist party committed to achieving Irish independence from Britain. Tracing its origins to a variety of 19th-century organizations, *Sinn Fein* (Irish: "We Ourselves" or "We Alone") became significant in 1902 when, under the leadership of ARTHUR GRIFFITH, it started a campaign of passive resistance to the British government. The party's members refused to pay taxes and attempted to set up an alternative system of justice that would bypass the official British courts; however, it was only after the abortive EASTER UPRISING of 1916 that it became the central pillar of Irish nationalism, winning 73 out of 105 seats in an election held in December 1918. In January 1919, the party, now led by EAMON DE VALERA, met and declared Irish independence from Britain.

In the event, it took another two years and a terrorism campaign before independence was achieved. As many members refused to accept the settlement—which excluded Ulster—or even to recognize the new Irish parliament, *Sinn Fein* split and its leader broke away and founded his own party, the *Fianna Fail.* In 1927, *Fianna Fail* gained an overwhelming victory in the polls, reducing *Sinn Fein* to electoral insignificance from which it has failed to emerge since. It does, however, continue to exist and its members have provided political backing for the IRISH REPUBLICAN ARMY during its various terrorist campaigns.

SIVAJI (c.1630–1680) Founder of the independent Maratha kingdom in central India. Born to a family of prominent Hindu nobles in the city of Poona, south of modern Bombay (then part of the Sultanate of Bijapur, now in the state of Maharashtra), Sivaji experienced at first hand the oppression of the Hindu population at the hands of its Muslim rulers. Early convinced that he had been divinely appointed to secure Hindu freedom, he gathered a force of followers from among the local hill peoples and engaged in a process of seizing the sultanate's military outposts. This process culminated in his defeating a force of some 20,000 men sent against him by the sultan in 1659.

By now a hero to the local Hindu population, Sivaji successfully repulsed the attacks launched against him by the Mughal emperor, Aurangzeb, even after the latter's forces had occupied Sivaji's headquarters of Poona. Under the pressure of continued aggression by Aurangzeb's armies Sivaji was, however, forced to make peace with them in 1665, surrendering 23 of the 35 forts that he had captured (this just a year after he had plundered the city of Surat). He was then taken to the Mughal court at Agra, where he was kept under close surveillance.

In December 1666, Sivaji, disguised as a wandering holy man, succeeded in escaping Agra and in returning to his own territories. There, he devoted himself to developing and strengthening the organizational structure of the government of his nascent kingdom. The Mughals were forced to recognize the status quo by conferring the title of Rajah (king) upon Sivaji, but this did not prevent him from extorting revenues from local Mughal officers or from plundering Surat once again. By 1674 he was powerful enough to have himself crowned independent king of Maharashtra; by the time of his death six years later his dominions extended over a considerable swathe of the western coastal region.

The Maratha kingdom that Sivaji founded, ably served by the guerrilla-war oriented military organization that he had developed, was to maintain its independence from the Mughals and

lesser Muslim powers until the early 19th century, at which time its chieftains were able to negotiate agreements with the British that gave them the right to rule large parts of central and southern India under the suzerainty of the Indo-British government.

Sivaji has become an important symbol for modern anti-Muslim Hindu fundamentalists and nationalists, as evidenced by the success of the *Shiv Sena,* the party named after him that achieved considerable success in Bombay, capital of Maharashtra, in the most recent municipal elections.

SKANDERBEG (George Kastrioti) (1405–1468) Albanian national hero. The son of an Albanian nobleman, George Kastrioti was taken hostage by the Ottoman overlords of Albania to ensure his father's submission to Istanbul. He was given the name Iskander (Alexander) and the title *bey;* Skanderbeg is an Albanian corruption of his Turkish name, Iskander Bey. The Ottomans trained Skanderbeg as a soldier and he took part in battles against the Venetians, Serbs and Hungarians. In 1443, news reached Skanderbeg that Albania had risen in revolt against the Ottomans. With 300 troops, he returned to his homeland and captured the fortress of Kruje. Realizing that the Turks would soon attempt to retake the fortress, he convened a conference of Albanian dignitaries at Lezhe the following year, in order to raise a rebel army from throughout the country.

Skanderbeg's first responsibility was to repulse the Venetians, who had taken advantage of the mayhem in Albania to seize strategic areas along the coast. Realizing he could not defeat them alone, he entered alliances with the Hungarians and Serbs, forcing Venice to reach a peace accord with him. Meanwhile, the Ottomans attempted to retake Kruje; they were finally repulsed after a costly five-month battle.

The Ottomans tried again to retake Kruje in 1455. They were only repulsed in 1458 and by 1462 were forced out of the entire country. For a short time it seemed that Skanderbeg's victory would be the turning point in Christian Europe's war against the Ottomans, but, in 1466, 60,000 Turkish troops again invaded Albania, this time under the leadership of Emperor Muhammad II himself. Fearing defeat, Skanderbeg traveled to Rome to win support of the pope. He returned to Albania the following year and again repulsed the Turks, but he died in 1468, before he could secure his victories. By 1475, all of Albania was again in Turkish hands.

SKVORTSOV-STEPANOV, IVAN (1870–1928) Russian BOLSHEVIK journalist and political economist. Trained as a teacher in Moscow, Skvortsov-Stepanov was implicated in a populist (see POPULISM) attempt to murder Czar Nicholas II and exiled. In Siberia (1896–1902) he became a Marxist (see MARXISM) and after emigrating to Switzerland joined the BOLSHEVIKS in 1904. Returning to Moscow, he was active in the Bolshevik press and in the campaigns for elections to the second and third Dumas, remaining independent of quarrels between Bolshevik factions.

In February 1917, he edited *Izvestia,* the newspaper of the Moscow soviet, and from June led the Bolshevik faction in the soviet. After LENIN's death in 1924, he supported STALIN against the Left Opposition and United Opposition of TROTSKY, ZINOVIEV and KAMENEV. As director of the Lenin Institute, he supervised the rewriting of Communist Party history. He published works on political economy and philosophy and was on the editorial boards of *Pravda* and *Izvestia* until his death from typhoid.

SLANSKY, RUDOLF (1901–1952) Secretary-general of the Czech Communist Party, executed for high treason after what was known as the Slansky Trial. Born Rudolf Schlesinger, Slansky rose in the ranks of the Communist Party. In 1939, when the Nazis entered Czechoslovakia, Slansky went into exile in the USSR, along with the other Communist leaders. During World War II Slansky was responsible for the recruitment of party members for the Czech army units formed in the Soviet Union and for contacts with the partisan units that parachuted into Slovakia when the Slovaks rose against the Nazis in August 1944. He himself fought in the Slovakian mountains and, as a tribute to his heroism in battle, many factories, quarries and other enterprises were named after him.

In 1945, Slansky was appointed secretary-general of the Czech Communist Party, second in command to the chairman and later president, KLEMENT GOTTWALD. Following suspicions in Moscow that Slansky was leading a Trotskyist conspiracy, he was arrested on November 24, 1951. Two weeks later, the party's central committee revoked his membership and removed him from all party posts.

After nine months of tortuous interrogation, Slansky broke down and pleaded guilty of espionage, high treason and sabotage. He admitted to having collaborated with the Zionist movement. Slansky and 10 others were sentenced to death, and he was executed on December 4, 1952. In 1968, the Pillar Commission appointed by the Czech government to investigate the trial vindicated Slansky.

SLAVE REVOLTS, SICILY Slavery was widespread in Sicily in the 2nd century B.C., under Roman rule. Many of the slaves originated from the eastern countries of the Mediterranean, notably from what is today Syria. Some were herdsmen while others were agricultural slaves. Their owners, partly Greek and partly rich Roman citizens, treated them harshly and many worked in chain gangs. The first revolt started at Henna, where the slaves of one particularly cruel landlord rose to kill him, his wife and the people of the city in c. 136 B.C. This soon became a general uprising under the leadership of Eunus, a Syrian who was proclaimed King Antiochus. Another revolt took place in Agrigentun under the leadership of Kleon, a slave from Cilicia.

The rebels defeated troops sent against them, took vengeance on the landlords and for a while controlled much of Sicily, obtaining support from the poor free population. Several Roman commanders were sent against them, but it was only in 132 B.C. that the rebels were finally subdued.

A second revolt broke out in 104 B.C. in particular circumstances. The Roman senate had instructed the governor to release citizens of allied communities who had been captured and sold into slavery by pirates. When the landowners induced the governor not to release these people, a major uprising took place. The rebels were organized in two bands, each with its own leader-king. As in the first revolt, poor Sicilians joined in, but this time the rebels did not capture cities. Nonetheless, several Roman generals had to fight the rebels and it was only in 100 B.C. that law and order were completely restored.

SLOVO, JOE (1926–1994) Born in Lithuania to a Jewish family which fled Lithuania for Argentina and then came to South Africa, Slovo was educated at the University of Witwatersrand, South Africa (1946–1951), and then at the London School of Economics and Political Science. He met NELSON MANDELA when they were both law students at Witwatersrand. In 1949, Slovo married Ruth First, a political activist and writer, who was killed by a parcel bomb in 1981.

Slovo was a founding member in 1953 of the reconstituted South African Communist Party and later became its leader. Together with Nelson Mandela, he founded the AFRICAN NATIONAL CONGRESS's military wing, *Umkhonto We Sizwe*, in 1961. From 1961–1987, he headed this military wing.

In 1963, Joe Slovo left South Africa and spent the next 27 years in exile. In February 1990, the South African Communist Party was unbanned by the government and he returned home. When Nelson Mandela became president of South Africa, he appointed Joe Slovo as housing minister. Although already sick with cancer, Slovo was an active minister. In spite of his Marxist–Leninist credentials, he followed a pragmatic policy and tried to encourage private initiative and free market policies in his efforts to promote massive building activity. He died on January 6, 1994 and was buried in Soweto's Avalon cemetery, only the second white person to be buried there, after the Liberal member of parliament, Helen Joseph.

SMALL SWORD SOCIETY Chinese secret society. Around 1850, lodges of the TRIAD secret society in Shanghai and Amoy became known as the Small Sword Society. Led by a Cantonese faith healer who had formerly interpreted for westerners and a Fukienese sugar broker, and supported by boatmen, the society seized the walled city of Shanghai in late 1853. This was several months after the TAIPING rebels had captured Nanjing. Sounding anti-Manchu slogans, the rebels called for the restoration of the fallen Ming dynasty (1368–1644). In the adjacent foreign settlement of Shanghai, western merchants made preparations for defense and organized a volunteer corps. Foreign gunboats were ready to intervene. In February 1855, government troops, assisted by the western naval blockade of the city, recaptured Shanghai. Meanwhile, the rebel threat had forced the Chinese government into making sweeping concessions that intensified the imperialist penetration of China. The British, French and American consuls obtained Chinese permission to establish local government organs, forming the basis for expansion of Shanghai's International Settlement and French concession. Foreigners gained further power in 1854, when it was agreed that their nominees were to serve as customs collectors for the Chinese government.

SNEEVLIET, HENDRIK (Maring) (1883–1942) COMINTERN representative in China. Born in Rotterdam, Sneevliet joined the Dutch Social Democratic Party in 1902. In 1913, the party sent him to the Dutch colony of Java, where in 1914 he was instrumental in the establishment of the East Indies Social Democratic Association, which later became the Indonesian Communist Party. In 1916 he expedited the party's cooperation with the Muslim nationalist organization, *Sarekat Islam*. The Dutch authorities expelled him in 1918. He attended the second Comintern congress in Moscow in 1920 and was appointed secretary of the Comintern's bureau dealing with national and colonial issues. At Lenin's recommendation, he was sent to China in 1921 to attend the founding congress of the CHINESE COMMUNIST PARTY (CCP). Known in China by his pseudonym, Maring, he met SUN YAT-SEN in December. Reporting in Moscow in July 1922, he urged cooperation with Sun's GUOMINDANG (GMD). Further talks with Sun in Shanghai in August helped negotiate the GMD-CCP coalition that required CCP members to join the GMD as individuals. Despite the CCP leaders' objections, the Comintern backed Sneevliet, whose experience in Java had showed that such an arrangement could benefit the Communists. Sneevliet left China in 1923 after attending the 3rd CCP congress, in which he emphasized working within the GMD. After a brief stay in Moscow, he returned to Holland in 1924 and was active in the Dutch Communist Party. He left the party and the Comintern in 1927. Two years later he established the Revolutionary Socialist Party. Active in the Dutch underground during the World War II German occupation, he was caught by German security police and executed in 1942.

SOCIALISM

The Varieties of Socialism. The different varieties of socialism can be classified according to their attitude to revolution—from Social Democracy, which seeks to improve the social conditions of life within the existing capitalist order, through reforms, legislation and education, to Communist socialism, which seeks to destroy capitalism by revolutionary means. When MARX and ENGELS formulated their party's manifesto in 1848, they intentionally chose the word "communism"—which expresses the idea of the revolutionary struggle—in order to distinguish their views from "socialism." There is a schematic distinction between modern socialism, which is "scientific," and the earlier socialism, which was "utopian": the distinction should be between revolutionary and evolutionary socialism. Communist or Marxist socialism is the revolutionary branch of 19th- and 20th-century socialism. Before that socialism was liberal, reformist, utopian, constitutional, experimental or parliamentary.

Socialism is a social ideology which seeks human justice, social solidarity and a decrease in the inequality between people. The word "socialism" reflects the emphasis on social relations, as opposed to "liberalism," which emphasizes the individual. Socialism is a constant striving for a more just society—that is, a society in which people's social tendency has more weight than their individualist tendency. Socialism's point of departure is thus revolutionary with respect to human nature.

The heralds of socialism were many and varied, and scholars tend to list them in an order which reflects their interpretive perspective. Some scholars note that the first modern use of the word "socialism" occurred in 1826, in Robert Owen's *Cooperative Magazine*, while others claim that the word was first used in 1832 by a Saint-Simonist in the French journal *Le Globe*. But movements with a socialist flavor existed at least since the Peasants' Rebellion in 1525 under the leadership of THOMAS MÜNZER, the ANABAPTIST rebellions, such as that in Münster in 1534, and the civil wars in England in 1642–1652, which produced the DIGGERS under the leadership of Gerrard Winstanley. Radical movements of the CROMWELL revolution, such as the LEVELLERS, were more rebellious than revolutionary.

The socialist utopias of the Renaissance were essentially rev-

olutionary texts, calling for the radical construction of an ideal society with new human beings. Such a revolutionary change in human nature is a condition for a perfect socialist society in which all the details of people's lives are shaped in a total manner. Thomas More's *Utopia* (1516) is a social critique of property differences and the eviction of the farmers from their land; More advocates democratic socialism. Tommaso Campanella's *Civitas Solis* (1623) describes a Communist sort of life. In Francis Bacon's *The New Atlantis* (1627), on the other hand, it is science that solves social problems. The utopia as a literary genre considered itself a microcosm of human society as a whole.

The idea of revolution had not yet arisen in the millennarist movements and the utopian literature. Their notions were sentimental, and they maintained the model of early Christianity, which advocated a poor man's socialism. Not until the 18th century was there a development of capitalism, an accumulation of wealth and an organization of the working class with a revolutionary consciousness. It was only the combination of the political consciousness of the FRENCH REVOLUTION and the social change initiated by the industrial revolution that created modern socialism with its revolutionary branches—namely MARXISM and ANARCHISM.

Socialism and the French Revolution. At the time of the FRENCH REVOLUTION the "social problem" arose as an ideological issue, not a moral one. Previously 18th-century Enlightenment thinkers had discussed the philosophical and ethical aspects of the problem: Mably and Morelly wrote about utopian socialism, while Jean-Jacques Rousseau, in his *Discourse on the Origin and Foundations of Inequality among Men* (1755), claimed that the growth of property rights was responsible for the decline of civilization. In Rousseau's view, the egalitarian natural situation of Man was replaced by a political situation in which the excess privileges of the rich were established by law. The laws protecting property and allowing economic exploitation made the rich a strong political force. This revolutionary social analysis of Rousseau's was not adopted by the initiators of the French Revolution, who chose to make their revolution bourgeois rather than socialist.

The Marxist interpretation is that the French Revolution was a political one, which established subjective will rather than a socioeconomic revolution, because France's pre-industrial character prevented the development of a working class. In the absence of the appropriate economic conditions, political terror was the only means available to the revolution. Marx believed that the French Revolution was a bourgeois political revolution of the civil society, which had separated itself from the political state. The French Revolution's contribution to socialism was thus the fact that it constituted a structural and mental stage which paved the way for the next stage—the socialist revolution.

The French constitution of 1793, which was the most socialist of the revolution's constitutions, was never actualized. GRACCHUS BABEUF aspired to bring it about, and for this purpose he sought to establish a dictatorship of the Parisian workers. The "*Conspiration des Equax*" of 1793 was accomplished through organized revolutionary means. It was the first to reveal the radical socialism at the margins of the revolution, although this was not its central trend. Babeuf was the originator of the concept of the proletariat as a revolutionary force. The French Revolution did not actualize socialism as a systematic social movement, but it developed the opposition between the rich and the poor into a political struggle for the first time. This was the first time that maximum prices were established, food hoarding limited, and exorbitant prices forbidden. But the revolutionaries who were busy abolishing the feudal order considered their goal to be the expansion of property rights. Babeuf's movement did not become a popular revolution, because the urban proletariat was weak and small in numbers. Nevertheless, the revolution paved the way for the prolonged social struggles in 19th-century Europe out of which modern socialism developed.

In the manifesto *On the Middle Class and the Nation* which Alexis de Tocqueville wrote in 1847 for the French Parliament, he predicted a revolutionary change which would lead to a demand for abolishing excess property rights. The right to property was the last barricade of the old political world: "There is reason to believe that the struggle among political parties will soon become a struggle between the haves and the have nots. The arena will be property." At the same time that de Tocqueville was writing about socialism as a modern "slave rebellion," Marx was reading the final proofs of the *Communist Manifesto*.

The Industrial Revolution as a Turning Point. The intensive social changes brought about by the industrial revolution—such as urbanization, modernization and the growth of the proletariat—led to a hatred of technology, which was reflected in such acts as the destruction of machines by the Luddites in the 1810s; the growth of a utopian socialist literature; and an increase in the revolutionary consciousness of the working class, which was accompanied by the development of revolutionary socialism, otherwise known as Marxism.

The new social problems associated with urbanization and industrialization were attributed to the acquisitive character of private ownership. This encouraged 19th-century socialist thinkers to move from the political to the economic realm. The French Revolution's failure to reshape human relations by political means led to a renewed interest in society, shifting the emphasis from event to process, and from making political revolutions to understanding economic systems, which are non-revolutionary by nature. Postrevolutionary disappointment led people to turn their backs on the political side of reforms and to concentrate on the problems of inequality, poverty, ignorance, education and social conditions such as health, pensions, working hours and unemployment. These were the problems that made it necessary to maintain a stubborn socialist struggle, far from the spotlights of revolution.

Utopian socialism claimed that changing from private to collective ownership and organizing the community into voluntary unions could solve a considerable number of social problems. In contrast with 18th-century socialism, which was based on the understanding of natural laws, utopian socialism relied on intellectual understanding, moral values, interclass fraternity and practical economic experiments in the form of socialist communities. The utopias were not programs for a general reorganization of society, nor did they associate themselves with any popular or proletarian movement for the realization of their visions. The social principles shared by Saint-Simon, Fourier and Owen were opposition to competition, suspicion of politics and belief in communitarianism and creativity. All three supported socialization in education, economic planning and cooperation in behavior, while attacking inequality and demanding restrictions on property rights. They did not, however, believe in a proletarian revolution against the bourgeois state. The economist Jerome Blanqui, in his description of the beginnings of political economics (1839), was the first to call them "utopian socialists," a name which was quickly adopted by Marx and Engels.

Revolution of the Intellectuals. Shades of the French Revolution could be detected in the REVOLUTIONS OF 1848 in Europe—the "revolution of the intellectuals," as it was called by the historian L.B. Namier. The utopias of the mid-19th century, which sought to construct the Heavenly City, added a collectivist element to the individualism which characterized 18th-century thought, and they transmitted this new element to the nationalist and socialist movements of their time. An important revolutionary in the 1848 events was AUGUSTE BLANQUI, who gave his name to the radical revolutionary trend of Blanquism. This trend, which involved great humanistic fervor, extended from the radical revolutionary groups—the *Enragés*, the Hébertistes and Babeuf—and the secret societies of the CARBONARI, through the neo-Jacobean movements—such as Young Europe, the *Amis de la Verite*, and the *Amis de Peuple*—to the early republican movement, the ideology of revolutionary SYNDICALISM, and the Social-Democratic and Communist parties.

Socialism developed differently in 19th-century England—more practically than ideologically. An empirical social trend developed gradually, from Locke's theory of natural rights, Ricardo's *Homo Oeconomicus*, Charles Hall's nationalization of agrarian socialism, theories of surplus value and class struggle, Thomas Hodgkin's labor theory of values, John Gray's circulation theory and William Thompson's iron law of wages, to the utopian socialist ideas of Robert Owen, the greatest figure of English socialism.

From 1830 to 1848, for the first time in the history of English socialism, the CHARTIST movement combined political action, class consciousness, legislative change and social work. At the same time the first socialist international organization was founded—the Society of Fraternal Democrats. In 1884, Sidney Webb and George Bernard Shaw in London founded the Fabian Society, which rejected the revolutionary paradigm of the class war. They fought poverty and want, as well as the exploitation and selfishness that stem from acquisitiveness. They believed that the historical necessity of the transition to socialism was not solely the responsibility of the working class, and that it was important to persuade all the political parties to join the struggle for gradual socialist reform. Consequently, they emphasized activity on the municipal level and in the trade unions, and they played an important role in forming the Labour Party and developing the idea of the welfare state.

In Germany, socialism was more abstract and theoretical than in France and England, due to the conservative structure of German society and the lack of an organized working class. LASSALLE, a socialist and nationalist, demanded cooperation between the proletariat and the state. In 1863 he succeeded in founding the first independent labor party, the *Allgemeiner Deutscher Arbeiterverein*. German socialism became a powerful revolutionary force in the Second INTERNATIONAL, which was established in 1889. Nevertheless, the German socialist movement was severely persecuted, and Bismarck's *socialistengesets* of 1878–1890 prevented it from growing. Later, German democratization and economic growth made the Social-Democratic

Party one of the strongest forces in the country. The most serious threat to Marx's revolutionary system was the democratic evolutionism proclaimed by EDUARD BERNSTEIN in 1889. This reformist socialism combined Fabian and Marxist ideas, claiming that the situation of the working class could be improved gradually without a social or economic revolution. Although the party remained loyal to KAUTSKY's conservative revolutionary line, its practical policies became more and more revisionistic.

In France and Italy, the development of socialism in the late 19th century led to the formation of the Syndicalist movement, while in England it led to trade-unionism. Whereas the English trade unions were primarily interested in improving the laborers' wages and working conditions, the Syndicalists had revolutionary educational aspirations. Syndicalism was a special sort of revolutionary socialism which was not based on historical determinism or economic mechanism, as Marxism was, but rather on the direct action of the workers, as well as political general strikes. Militant streams in French and Italian revolutionary Syndicalism also led to the beginnings of FASCISM.

The socialist movement in 19th-century Russia formed the basis for a wave of revolutionary anti-czarist activity. It began with the liberal socialism of thinkers such as HERZEN and LAVROV, which later divided into various streams. The Social-Democratic Party, which was founded by PLEKHANOV in 1898, was Marxist, while the SOCIAL REVOLUTIONARY PARTY, despite its name, opposed revolution of the Marxist variety. A hybrid of socialism and Jacobinism was first tried in the 20th century, during the BOLSHEVIK Revolution. According to LENIN's definition, a Social-Democrat is a Jacobean who has adopted socialism. Lenin claimed that in the 20th century it was impossible to attain a just régime, as the Jacobeans had sought in their time, without public ownership of the means of production and direction of the economy. Seventy years of Communism in Russia proved that there is still a wide gap between the enlightened, universal ideas of 19th- and 20th-century socialism and the distortion of these ideas in a totalitarian, bureaucratic, nationalistic historical experiment.

Universalism versus Particularism. World War I was a historic crossroads for the encounter between socialism and nationalism. The Social-Democratic parties had to choose between the party and the state, between the fraternity of the international proletariat and patriotism. They chose the nation rather than the proletariat. Lenin refused to play by the rules of the imperialist war: the socialist parties of the Allies believed that the war would free Russia from czarism, while the socialist parties of the Entente considered the war a struggle for the right to self-definition. One of the most important results of the war in the socialist camp was the outbreak of the Bolshevik Revolution. The German version of the revolution, the SPARTAKIST movement, was quickly suppressed, and the German counterrevolution executed KARL LIEBKNECHT and ROSA LUXEMBURG. The decline of the Second International's importance was evidence of the victory of nationalism over socialism.

Between the two world wars, at the same time as the rise of European fascism, there was also a growth of "humanist socialism," which stressed the moral aspect of social reforms. In 1951, the Socialist International endorsed "democratic socialism," an ideological platform of humanist principles for the European socialist parties. The United States lacked the conditions for the growth of socialism because of its unique history—the absence of feudalism, the class structure including a broad middle class, the idealization of individualism, and the American way of life, in which capitalism enjoyed wide national acceptance. The national liberation movements of the Third World flirted briefly with socialism, mainly during the 1960s, but a developed socialism that is conscious of its power requires a minimal level of industrial, urban and technological development.

In the past few years European socialism has moved its struggle to the parliamentary arena and the trade unions. The Marxist notion of nationalization has been superseded by the concept of a mixed economy; the advocacy of a dictatorship of the proletariat by support for parliamentary democracy; the classless society by the welfare state; and the concept of revolution by a continuous, democratic struggle for emending the distortions of an acquisitive consumer society.

SOCIALISM IN ONE COUNTRY In Soviet history, a slogan associated with JOSEPH STALIN and opposed to LEON TROTSKY's concept of the PERMANENT REVOLUTION. According to Stalin, it was necessary to build up socialism in the USSR first of all, and to postpone the world revolution to some unspecified future date. During the late 1920s, the doctrine of Socialism in One Country became a weapon in Stalin's hands against Trotsky and played a major role in the latter's defeat.

SOCIAL REVOLUTIONARY PARTY (RUSSIA) In Russian history, a non-Marxist revolutionary party with populist traditions. The party advocated direct action and took a major part in the RUSSIAN REVOLUTION OF 1905; in 1908, however, it split between those who advocated the nationalization of industry (the Maximalists) and those who opposed it. The party played a prominent role in the February RUSSIAN REVOLUTION OF 1917 and actually gained a majority in the Constituent Assembly of January 1918. Subsequently, however, it found itself thrust aside by the BOLSHEVIKS and became bitterly hostile to them; in August 1918 a Social Revolutionary shot and wounded LENIN, whereupon the party was suppressed.

SOCIAL REVOLUTIONS IN THE HELLENISTIC WORLD Some 60 social revolutions and cases of civil strife (*stasis*) are reported to have taken place in mainland Greece and the Greek diaspora from c. 370 B.C. to the late 2nd century B.C. These social-revolutionary revolts took place in many regions of the old Greek world but did not extend to the countries conquered by Alexander the Great, that is, to the Greek cities founded by the great Macedonian conqueror and his successors. The revolutions were sometimes carried out by legitimate rulers of states (e.g., CLEOMENES III), tyrants (NABIS), the democratic assembly of a city-state (SYRACUSE) or a frenzied mob (ARGOS). In some cases, the rebellions were associated with national resistance to the expansion of the Roman empire (e.g., ARISTONICUS). The fundamental socioeconomic conditions that formed the background to these social revolutionary movements had been in existence ever since the first half of the 4th century B.C.: the growth of both a rural and urban proletariat, the rise of unemployment in villages and towns alike with the expansion of slavery, the concentration of much wealth in the hands of relatively few and the growing number of those who had lost their properties, the dissatisfaction of the indebted and those who possessed but little. The conquests of Alexander did not change these basic conditions. The revolutionary measures implemented, aimed at or professed in these revolts included the abolition of debts and redistribution of land and other forms of real property. Sometimes, the expropriation of property and the manumission of slaves were added to the revolutionary program. A basic feature of many of the revolutions was the demand for socioeconomic equality and the stress on the polarity between poverty and riches as the motivation to end this anomalous situation. The revolutionaries aimed at establishing economic equality as the basis of a new social and political order, for to them equality meant freedom from poverty and servitude. In this respect, the social revolutions of the Hellenistic age differed from the revolutions of the classical period, which aimed only at gaining political freedom.

SOCIETY OF ELDERS AND BROTHERS   see GE LAO HUI.

SOCIETY OF THE PANTHEON   see BAYBARS.

SONG CH'ING-LING   see SONG QINGLING.

SONG JIAOREN (Sung Chiao-ren)   (1882–1913) Chinese nationalist revolutionary. Born in Hunan into a small landowning family, Song passed the first stage in the traditional examination system in 1901. In 1902 he entered the Wuchang Civil High School, which provided both modern and traditional studies. Hunan in particular was infected by the nationalist fever pervading student circles, aroused by Russia's refusal to withdraw from Manchuria. In 1904, Song joined the revolutionary organization HUA XING HUI. After its plot to seize Changsha failed at the end of the year, Song left for Japan, where he studied at the Kobun Institute and then enrolled in Tokyo's College of Law and Government. Meanwhile, he was active among Chinese student radicals and in 1905 founded the revolutionary journal, *Twentieth Century China*. In August 1905, Hua Xing Hui and another revolutionary organization, GUANG FU HUI, merged with SUN YAT-SEN's followers to form the TONGMENGHUI (TMH), which attracted overseas Chinese students and became the leading anti-Manchu organization. Song served in the TMH judicial department and managed the TMH monthly, *Min Bao (People's report)*. In 1906 he studied briefly at Tokyo's Waseda University under an assumed name, thereby receiving a stipend from the Chinese government. Interested in law and government, Song translated constitutions of various foreign countries and became the TMH's leading expert on constitutional government. In 1907 he went to southern Manchuria in an attempt to draw the "mounted bandits" (also known as the Red Beards) into the revolutionary fold. As a result of his interest in Manchuria, he prepared a study defending China's right to a border region disputed by Korea, then a protectorate of Japan. Written under a pseudonym, Song's pamphlet was published in Shanghai and is said to have helped the Chinese negotiators.

Song did not participate in the TMH uprisings of 1907–1908, which he felt lacked sufficient preparation and planning. In 1908 he was among those who disputed Sun Yat-sen's leadership and preferred HUANG XING. Despondent over continued revolutionary failures, Song is said to have taken to alcohol and opium. In late 1910 he went to Shanghai to become chief editor of *Min Li Bao*. In April 1911 he was in Hong Kong to participate in preparations for the abortive Canton revolt. He then became active in shifting TMH strategy to the middle Yangtze region. After the outbreak of the CHINESE REPUBLICAN REVOLUTION OF 1911 in October, he joined Huang Xing in Wuchang. As a Hunanese delegate, he participated in the election of Sun Yat-sen as provisional president of the republic in Nanjing in December.

After the establishment of the republic and Sun Yat-sen's assumption of an "elder statesman"'s role, Song led the struggle for true parliamentary government and a strong cabinet system to curb the authoritarian tendencies of Yuan Shikai, Sun's successor as provisional president. Appointed minister of agriculture in Yuan's cabinet in March 1912, Song and other TMH members resigned in July in protest of Yuan's abuse of presidential powers. In August, Song was instrumental in securing the TMH's merger with several minor parties and its conversion into an open political party, the GUOMINDANG (GMD). Taking Sun's place as de facto party leader, Song led the GMD to victory in elections held in the winter of 1912–1913. Results announced in February 1913 gave the GMD large pluralities of both houses of parliament. Although the electorate had been limited to the small minority possessing property or educational qualifications, it was one of the few instances of free elections in modern China. Song was expected to become the new premier and enforce constitutional rule. On March 20, 1913, when he was about to entrain for Beijing, Song was shot by a hired gunman. He died two days later, just two weeks before his 31st birthday. Incriminating evidence led to Yuan's office, but conclusive proof of his personal involvement in the assassination was not found.

Song's murder sharpened the GMD-Yuan conflict that would precipitate the CHINESE REVOLUTION OF 1913 ("second revolution") in July. The assassination also delivered a heavy blow to the cause of democratic government in China.

SONS OF LIBERTY   A coalition of activist groups which organized the resistance of the North American colonists to British colonial government. The designation "Sons of Liberty" connotes both the local organizations of American patriots which resisted the tightening of ministerial control over the British North American colonies in the 1760s and the New York-centered pan-colonial coalition of such groups which was organized in 1765.

Local Sons of Liberty groups, which were organized in the aftermath of the STAMP ACT crisis, worked to foster social cohesion in resistance to the acts of government and to turn the opposition to British colonial administration into a mass movement. The organizations were active in propaganda campaigns and political agitation within the provinces and in organizing crowd action. At first, however, they rejected any acts of violent resistance to government and denied a rebellious intention. Indeed, with the repeal of the Stamp Act in 1766, the Sons of Liberty organizations practically dissolved. They were revived, however, in 1768, after the issue of the oppressive Townsend Acts. From then until the outbreak of the AMERICAN REVOLUTION, the local Sons were characteristically the focus of organized group action in resistance to crown authority in the colonies.

The intercolonial Sons of Liberty organization, which was successfully maintained throughout the conflict, mainly by means of correspondence, ultimately served as a model for subsequent intercolonial institutions in the early national period.

SOONG QINGLING (Sung Ch'ing-ling; Soong Ch'ing-ling) (1892–1981) Left-wing Chinese nationalist; widow of SUN YAT-SEN, Soong was born in Shanghai into what became one of the most influential families in the republican period (1912–1949). Her father, Charles Jones Soong (1866–1918), had risen from obscure origins to become a wealthy businessman and was closely associated with SUN YAT-SEN. Her younger brother, T.V. Soong (Sung Ziwen) (1894–1971), served in various high positions during the GUOMINDANG (GMD) rule in China (1928–1949) and was particularly important in financial administration. Her younger sister, Soong Meiling, married CHIANG KAI-SHEK in 1927. Soong Qingling received her higher education in the United States (1908–1913). After returning to China in 1913, she and her family joined Sun Yat-sen in Japan, where she replaced her elder sister as Sun's English-language secretary. In 1915 she married Sun, who was 26 years older than she. She was constantly with him, serving as secretary and confidante until his death in 1925, after which she emerged as a political personality in her own right. Unlike other members of the Soong family, she identified with the left-wing opposition to Chiang Kai-shek. After Chiang broke with the CHINESE COMMUNIST PARTY (CCP), she felt he had betrayed Sun Yat-sen's principles. In August 1927 she left China and stayed in the Soviet Union for almost two years. After a brief return to China in 1929 to attend to the removal of Sun's remains to the mausoleum erected for him in Nanjing, she toured Europe for two years. She lived in Shanghai from 1932–1937. After the outbreak of the Sino-Japanese war (1937–1945), she became reconciled with her family and joined her sisters in relief work, first from Hong Kong and later from the wartime capital, Chongqing. In 1946, she resumed opposition to Chiang Kai-shek, and with the establishment of the People's Republic of China (PRC) in 1949, she was foremost among the non-Communist supporters of, and participants in, the new régime. She was a vice-chairman of the government and headed various social welfare organizations. In 1951 she was awarded the Stalin Peace Prize and met STALIN in 1953.

In 1966, at the height of the Cultural Revolution (see GREAT PROLETARIAN CULTURAL REVOLUTION), Red Guards criticized Soong's "bourgeois" life style and ransacked her home in Shanghai. Premier ZHOU ENLAI later apologized and in 1967 she received foreign dignitaries, taking the place of LIU SHAOQI, then still formal head of state.

Symbolically, Soong Qingling was important for the CCP. As Sun Yat-sen's widow, she reinforced the CCP's claim to his legacy and, like other non-Communist figureheads, could be used to help represent the PRC government as a "democratic coalition." It was only when close to death in May 1981 that she became a formal member of the CCP. At that time she was made honorary chairperson of the PRC.

SOREL, GEORGES (1847–1922) French political philosopher. A professional engineer, from 1892 he devoted himself exclusively to writing. He is known mainly for his work *Reflections on Violence* (1908), which is regarded as the textbook of SYNDICALISM; in it Sorel extols violence as both cathartic and as a politically useful tool in the hands of the working class to bring down capitalism. A somewhat lyrical and inconsistent thinker who was capable of supporting both the restoration of the French monarchy and the BOLSHEVIK Revolution as alternatives to the existing order, Sorel is perhaps best remembered for his influence on BENITO MUSSOLINI.

SOUPHANOUVONG (1902–) Following the Laotian Assembly's declaration of independence in 1945, the Free Lao (Lao Issarak) movement—including nearly the entire western-educated elite of the country—rose against the French. A provisional government was formed under the leadership of Souvanna Phouma and Souphanouvong. Sisavang Vong, who continued to support a Laotian protectorate under the French, was deposed. The French recaptured Laos in 1946 and by 1949 Souphanouvong had built ties with the Viet Minh. Traveling to North Vietnam, he announced, in August 1950, the formation of a new guerrilla organization called the *Pathet Lao*. In 1952, the Laotian Communist Party was established and control of the two northeastern provinces of Sam Neua and Phong Saly by Souphanouvong's Viet Minh-trained *Pathet Lao* was subsequently acknowledged at the Geneva conference of 1954. In 1975, Souphanouvong became head of state of the Lao People's Democratic Republic. He retired in 1986.

SOUTH KOREA, COUP OF 1960–1961 see KOREA, SOUTH, COUP OF 1960–1961.

SOUTH RUSSIAN UNION Founded in Odessa in 1874 by E.O. Zaslavsky, a follower of PETER LAVROV. This group was the result of disillusionment with the peasants' rejection of TO THE PEOPLE. The South Russian Union attempted to organize urban workers, taught them revolutionary socialism and managed to recruit some 200 members. In late 1874 and early 1875, the South Russian Union organized a number of industrial strikes before the police arrested its organizers, putting an end to the union's existence.

SOUTH-WEST AFRICAN PEOPLE'S ORGANIZATION (SWAPO) Namibia (formerly South-West Africa) was a German colony from 1884 until the end of World War I, when it was handed to South Africa as a League of Nations mandate. In 1951, the Ovamboland People's Congress (subsequently renamed the Ovamboland People's Organization) was founded to resist South African rule. Its main objective was to abolish the contract labor system. In 1960, it was renamed the South-West African People's Organization (SWAPO).

In 1966, the United Nations General Assembly revoked the mandate it had given South Africa, but South Africa refused to accept this. In the same year, SWAPO's military wing, the People's Liberation Army of Namibia (PLAN) began an armed struggle against South African rule in Namibia. In December 1973, the UN recognized SWAPO as the "sole and authentic representative of the Namibian people."

In the November 1989 election for the constituent assembly, SWAPO obtained a majority of seats and formed a government following Namibian independence in March 1990. SAMUEL NUJOMA, head of SWAPO, became president and commander in chief of the Namibian defense forces.

SOWETO RIOTS (March 1976) Riots that resulted from an attempt by the South African authorities to force Afrikaans, rather than English, upon African high school students; the resulting disturbances ended in the killing of some 20 people. The authorities were ultimately forced to retreat from their original position. At the time, the riots were widely regarded as the beginning of the end of South Africa's system of apartheid.

SPAIN, REVOLTS AND REVOLUTIONS

Coup of 1820. The 19th and early 20th centuries in Spain were characterized by revolutionary movement, swaying between liberal, republican and nationalist ideals, between monarchy, authoritarianism and dictatorship. After resuming his reign on Spain in 1814, King Ferdinand VII refused to support the liberal constitution that had been drawn up in 1812. At the same time, he oppressed liberals. His unproductive rule also led to increasing disquiet among the public and military sectors of Spain. Consequently, in January 1820, troops from Cadiz in southern Spain, under the guidance of Colonel Rafael Riego, marched to Madrid to bring down Ferdinand's rule. They succeeded in doing so and held him prisoner until 1823, even though he had agreed to restore the constitution of 1812. France then intervened in the affairs of Spain and forced the revolutionaries back, although Ferdinand remained with them and was held in Cadiz. It was at the Battle of Trocadero (August 31, 1823) that the revolutionaries were finally defeated and Ferdinand was restored to his former position as king. Once reinstated, even though the French encouraged him to shape a middle-of-the-road constitutional régime, he formed a repressive rule.

Revolutions of 1836–1868. Maria Cristina, Ferdinand's wife, succeeded him as queen regent of Spain in 1833 (Ferdinand's infant daughter, Isabella, became queen). She leaned toward the liberal cause and in 1834 produced the *Estatuto Real*—the royal constitution—which was less liberal than the 1812 constitution. This caused disharmony among the liberals and their division into two parties: those who accepted the royal constitution and those who still held that the constitution of 1812 should be maintained.

At that time, Don Carlos, Ferdinand's brother, held claims to the throne and against the 1834 constitution. His supporters, known as the Carlists, were defeated in 1836–1837, and he himself was exiled to France in 1839. In August 1836, further unrest had grown in several regions in northern and central Spain, forcing Cristina to adopt the 1812 constitution, although in a less liberal form. In October 1840, a revolt broke out under the guidance of General Espartero, who opposed this latest constitution in favor of the original version of 1812. Espartero was partially successful; Cristina was exiled and Espartero became regent of Spain. In October 1841, however, a year after his own victory, he was confronted by an insurrection in support of the exiled queen regent. General Espartero nevertheless succeeded in subduing the upheaval at Pampeluna. A year later, Espartero was up against another upheaval, this time republican. In November 1842, revolutionaries proclaimed a republic in Spain; following much bloodshed, Espartero once again succeeded in suppressing the revolution. Only in June 1843 was Espartero defeated as the combined forces of Spain's various factions, led by General Narvaez, entered Madrid and caused him to leave Spain for foreign shores. Ruling as lieutenant-general, Narvaez re-

mained in office until 1851, when Queen Cristina assumed personal control. As her rule became increasingly dictatorial, another coup began to be prepared—this time under General Espartero (who had returned from exile) and O'Donnell. Once again Queen Cristina had to flee Spain. O'Donnell thereupon set up a liberal régime.

In 1864, General Narvaez returned to power, formed an absolutist government and invited the queen back to Madrid. Liberal discontent was not slow to develop and in 1868 the various republican parties united once again and again forced Cristina to leave the country. A provisional government, led by Generals Juan Prim and Francisco Serrano, was formed.

The First Republic and the Coup of 1874. In 1873, the First Spanish Republic came into being as the result of a general election held that year. The various republican factions which formed the government soon started squabbling with each other, particularly over the question of centralization versus decentralization. The absence of a decisive government helped fan the trouble, as many regions represented by the ministries became restless and proclaimed their autonomy as cantons. Meanwhile, the Carlist movement continued to be active. What was to become known as the Ten Years' war had begun in Cuba and the government was up against monarchist hostility. A military coup ensued, motivated by the army's resentment of the republican program to take it out of politics. General Serrano once again took the leading position, this time as head of a provisional government. This situation was to last until December 1874, when the Bourbon monarchy was reinstated and the government was taken over by the liberals. In August 1883, the republicans staged an abortive revolt which finally led to their representatives being included in the government in 1894.

Revolution of 1909. In 1909, as the Spanish military, under the conservative rule of Antonio Maura, prepared to land in Morocco to put down rebellious native tribesmen, extremists protested the inequality of the conscription system, which weighed disproportionally on the poorer classes. Large-scale strikes broke out in many Spanish cities, organized by revolutionaries belonging to various movements. These strikes led to violent insurgencies and subsequent repression. From July to September 1909, martial law was imposed on Spain. Finally, the king was driven to proclaim a liberal administration in October, followed by the resignation of Prime Minister Maura.

Coup of 1923 and Spain's Fascist Involvement. The liberal movement continued to govern Spain through World War I and the years following it. However, in March 1922, Maura, who had been recalled to deal with the burning Morocco issue, was driven out of his post by several juntas that had collaborated against the government, holding it accountable for the deteriorating situation in Morocco. In September 1923, General MIGUEL PRIMO DE RIVERA, with the backing of the absent king, Alfonso, led a military coup against the government. He instituted a dictatorship, forced martial law and abolished the freedom of the press. Opposition to this rule on part of the liberals was reduced by numerous expulsions and imprisonments. A year later Primo de Rivera, accompanied by the king, visited Italy and developed ties with that country, beginning Spain's Fascist (see FASCISM) involvement.

Revolutions of 1926–1931. Although the dictatorship itself was terminated in late 1925, Rivera became prime minister of Spain, still controlling a military government. However, dissension was rife; in 1926 alone there were three would-be military coups and in 1929 another one had to be suppressed. A year later, physically run down, Rivera resigned from his position and General Damaso Berenguer inaugurated a more nationalist government. Student demonstrations and criticism by the intellectuals nevertheless continued to condemn the Spanish monarchy, holding it accountable for the country's oppression under a dictatorship. A revolutionary organization was set up, aiming at forming a Second Republic. In February 1931, following a failed military uprising, the government surrendered its position once again.

The Second Republic and the Revolts of 1932–1933. In April 1931, municipal and constitutional assembly elections returned the republicans to power under Alcalá Zamora, ousting King Alfonso from his throne and drawing up a new constitution. Thus, the Second Spanish Republic was founded by the provisional government of the revolutionary committee. This too, however, met with conservative opposition in the revolt led by General José Sanjurjo on August 10, 1932. The revolt was quickly put down and the new government continued vigorously. Another uprising occurred five months later as the result of dissatisfaction among the lower classes regarding the republic's social reform system. This too was efficiently suppressed, only to resume a year later and be put down by government forces (see also SPANISH CIVIL WAR).

SPANISH CIVIL WAR (1936–1939) The background to the Spanish civil war was the growing polarization between right and left that had been tearing Spain apart ever since the end of World War I. It worsened during the economic crisis of the early 1930s and culminated in February 1936, when the left won a narrow electoral victory. The left promptly found itself confronted by the right wing FALANGE, a Fascist organization which had been founded by JOSE PRIMO DE RIVERA some years earlier.

By the summer of 1936, the socialist-led government in Madrid, pressed by the Communists, was drifting steadily to the left. The murder of Jose Calvo Sotelo, the leader of the extreme right—with the connivance of the security forces—provided the final spark as Generals Emilio Mola and FRANCISCO FRANCO raised the standard of revolt in Spanish Morocco. German and Italian transport aircraft flew Franco's troops across from Africa to Spain; however, a right-wing attempt at a general uprising was defeated by government forces and armed workers.

Following these events, Spain was split. Old Castile, Navarre and—of the larger towns—Sargossa, Seville, Cordova, Valladolid and Cadiz, went over to the nationalist rebels and gave them control over most food-producing areas. Most of the remaining provinces, including Catalonia and the industrialized Basque country, remained loyal, as did Madrid, where power increasingly passed out of the hands of the elected government and into those of the trade unions and workers' committees. In the loyalist provinces a social revolution, albeit confused and unsystematic, was carried out. Factories were taken away from their owners and nationalized, the Church plundered, monasteries disbanded and priests as well as monks and nuns maltreated, subjected to all kinds of outrages and occasionally executed.

The scene was now set for the outbreak of full-scale civil war. On one side were the loyalists, consisting of a coalition between socialists and Communists which never worked well; on the other, the army led by Franco, which in April 1937 amalgamated with the Falange. Both sides drew on outside support. The loyalists received Soviet arms as well as foreign volunteers: the latter flocked to Spain from all over the west (mainly England, France and the USA) and were known as the International Brigades. On the other side, the Germans and Italians supplied Franco with arms as well as Fascist "volunteers."

Having started as an insurrection, the war increasingly turned into a regular one and some of its larger battles have been compared to that of Verdun in World War I. Franco's forces enjoyed unity of command as well as the support of a German-supplied air detachment (the Legion Condor with approximately 100 aircraft and 5,000 men), which in April 1937 showed what it could do by demolishing the town of Guernica. Two attempts by Franco in the winter of 1937 to take Madrid nevertheless failed. A struggle of attrition resulted, focusing in the northwest. It was only when Soviet support dried up in the summer of 1938 that the balance swung decisively to the insurgents' side. Catalonia fell and, in March 1939, Madrid as well. The nationalists thereupon took harsh reprisals against their opponents, executing and jailing thousands. Thousands more became refugees and remained in exile for decades on end. Spain itself was subjected to a régime which combined FASCISM with clericalism and which lasted until Franco's death in 1975.

SPARTACUS (?–71 B.C.) Roman gladiator who led the GLADIATORIAL REVOLT against Rome in 73–71 B.C. Very little is known about his life before the war began, except that he was originally from Thrace, had been captured in war and sold into slavery. Spartacus—according to Plutarch—was "a man not only of high spirit and bravery, but also in understanding and gentleness superior to his condition." He issued a call to all the slaves of Italy to rise up in revolt and soon had a following of 70,000 men, with whom he won astonishing victories against the Romans. In the third year he was overwhelmed by Crassus's army reinforced by Pompey's Legion. Struck down and unable to rise, he continued fighting on his knees. He was so badly wounded that his body could not later be identified. While the Romans mercilessly tortured and massacred the rebels, after Spartacus's death 3,000 Roman prisoners were discovered unharmed in his camp.

SPARTAKISTS (Spartakusbund) German revolutionary leftist organization. The Spartakusbund was named after the so-called *Spartakus Briefe* (*Spartacus letters*) circulated by the illegal, anti-World War I *Internationale Gruppe* founded by ROSA LUXEMBURG and Franz Mehring. In 1917, the Spartakusbund joined the Independent Social Democratic Party of Germany (USPD) for about a year, but following the November 1918 collapse of imperial Germany it regained its independence as a radical revolutionary body. Its pressure was responsible for forcing the ruling moderate SPD to declare Germany a republic, against its own wishes to transform the country into a constitutional monarchy.

In December 1918, the Spartakusbund joined with some north German workers to create the Communist Party of Germany (KPD) which, however, rejected LENIN's terrorist methods and minority dictatorship. On January 5–6, 1919, the Spartakusbund's agitation brought about the spontaneous, ill-coordinated rebellion, which led to the SPD's decision to use the old army to crush it. The Spartakusbund's leaders, Rosa Luxemburg and KARL LIEBKNECHT, were murdered by the army, and the ensuing rift between the German Communist and Socialist parties has never been healed.

SPECIAL ORGANIZATION   see ORGANISATION SPECIALE.

SPENGLER, OSWALD   (1880–1936) German philosopher of history. Spengler studied mathematics and natural sciences at Munich, Halle and Berlin, taught in a high school and later became an independent scholar. His master work, *Der Untergang des Abendlandes* (*The Decline of the West*, two volumes, 1918–1922) won much popular attention following Germany's defeat in World War I, in spite of devastating scholarly criticism. Even major professional historians such as Arnold Toynbee adopted Spengler's radical-revolutionary views of history in various respects, including his virulent—but not purely racist-grounded—criticism of Judaism.

Spengler claimed to be a follower of Goethe's and NIETZSCHE's thought, but in fact he carried some of the latter's ideas to the extreme by arguing that human history develops in circles, without any higher or objective reason leading to any purpose. Spengler then moved on to discuss "cultures" and their "morphology," as if these were spiritual reflections of their time and age, adopted as such by groups of peoples and manifested in their sense of space. According to his view, the classic ancient sense of space was local and limited whereas the westerner was trying to fill and give meaning to an unlimited space, as manifested, in Spengler's view, among other things in Gothic architecture and in colonial expansion later on. Spengler then argued that all cultures develop in a similar way: they are young and vital at first, develop further and mature, and then decline and fall due to materialism, greediness and a lust for sheer power leading to expansion and war.

Spengler's influence was enormous in his time—due to contemporary history which seemed to have proved his theories. Indeed, a common sense of spiritual decay in the west was manifested in the works of writers at the beginning of the century (see, for example, Anatole France in his *L'Ile des Pingouins*, 1908). At the same time, Spengler argued that members of a certain culture could not grasp other cultures. This effectively made any historical, and especially comparative, research, impossible. Spengler used this theory to explain what he regarded as an unbridgeable gap between cosmopolitan, dying, rootless Judaism and the younger German culture, rooted in the soil. Spengler's hysterical sense of decay was transformed by primitive revolutionaries of the right, including the NAZI leaders, into an aggressive campaign to save German culture. Spengler himself supported this by praising the culture of Prussian heroism and the Prussian will to fight. As Spengler regarded HITLER as an illiterate product of the mob, the Nazis used his teachings, but not the man himself, for their own purpose.

SPÍNOLA, ANTÓNIO   (1911–) Portuguese military officer. As a cavalry general in the ongoing colonial war in Portuguese Guinea, Spínola was introduced to the socialist teachings of his rival, AMILCAR CABRAL of the PARTIDO AFRICANO DA INDEPENDENCIA DA GUINÉ E CABO VERDE. He had already expressed sympathy with the Portuguese trade union movement and although he was not converted to Cabral's brand of MARXISM, he nevertheless became convinced of the futility of pursuing colonial wars in Africa. Upon his return to Portugal, he published a book, *Portugal and the Future* (1974), describing his belief that Portugal should grant its colonies their independence and instead pursue the formation of a Portuguese commonwealth of sorts. The book quickly made waves among other military officers, many of whom secretly held similar beliefs but were afraid to express them in the repressive atmosphere of post-Salazar Portugal. Within just two months, these military leaders, led by Spínola, organized the Officers' Coup (see PORTUGAL, REVOLTS AND REVOLUTIONS) which toppled the government of Marcello Caetano and initiated Portugal's return to democracy after a hiatus of almost 50 years. Since the election of Mario Soares as prime minister in 1976, Spínola has lived in retirement.

SPIRIDONOVA, MARIA   (1885–1941) Russian Left Socialist Revolutionary leader. Born in Tambov province and trained as a nurse, Spiridonova joined the Party of Socialist Revolutionaries (SR) in 1904, participating in the unrest that accompanied the RUSSIAN REVOLUTION OF 1905. Peasant uprisings in the region were brutally repressed and she volunteered to assassinate the vice-governor and head of gendarmes in the province, Luzhenovsky. She did so in January 1906, during one of his punitive expeditions in the countryside. Arrested and brutally tortured, Spiridonova became a folk heroine and internationally famous.

With the February RUSSIAN REVOLUTION OF 1917, Spiridonova was released from jail and was promptly elected head of the town soviet in the Siberian town of Chita, where one of her first municipal acts was to dynamite the local prison. Returning to St. Petersburg, she quickly became leader of the radical wing of the SR and in October led it in splitting from its party and into a coalition with LENIN's BOLSHEVIKS. In protest against the Bolsheviks' making a separate peace with the Germans, she led the July 6, 1918 rebellion against Lenin. As a result she was held in jail and Siberian exile by the Bolsheviks until 1941, when she was shot.

SPITAMEN   (?–328 B.C.) Famous Sogdian military leader who in 329 B.C. organized and led the Sogdians' armed revolt against Alexander the Great's occupation. Relying upon the Sogdian people and using the assistance of Khorezm and nomadic tribes of the Saka, Spitamen's military operations posed a threat to the Greek occupation of Sogd. In the autumn of 328, Spitamen was killed by the leader of one of the nomadic tribes. The struggle of Sogdians against Greco-Macedonian invasions continued after his death, and was finally suppressed in 327 B.C.

SPRING OF PRAGUE   see PRAGUE, SPRING OF.

SS—SCHUTZSTAFFEL   Defense Squad of the Nazi Party; the organization responsible for the Nazi régime's security and destruction policy against its so-called enemies.

The SS was established in the early 1920s, at first as *Stosstrup Hitler*—a small bodyguard, which was supposed to be an elite unit and absolutely reliable. The name and its notorious emblem—the death head—were copied from traditional elite units of the German army during World War I, the black uniform from the revolutionary Italian Fascists. Combining tradition and revolutionary zeal, the small SS adopted an elitist view of itself in comparison with the mass army of street fighters—the SA, which was the main carrier of Hitler's campaign to gain power but remained rather loose ideologically and less devoted to Hitler personally.

In March 1927, Erhard Heiden took over the SS and tried to make it "look like active soldiers in terms of discipline and order," while for the first time giving it the functions of a semi-secret police force of the party. This function was later institutionalized and further developed to become the secret police of Germany and of occupied Europe as a whole by HEINRICH HIMMLER.

Himmler was appointed *Reichesfuehrer SS* by Hitler's order of January 6, 1929. His concept of the still rather small organization was a combination of racist fanaticism and Germanic romanticism, and of semi-feudal personal relationships between himself and Hitler and between his own subordinates and himself. Himmler managed to use this as protection vis-á-vis third parties and at the same time to free himself from the SA's control. He created the SS's own race department under RICHARD WALTHER DARRE and a nucleus of the SS's own security service (SD) under Reinhard Heydrich, along with a general SS (*allegemeine SS*), regionally organized all over Germany. He tried to institutionalize his romantic fanatical racism by recruiting blonde, blue-eyed, tall "true" Aryans, but was also keen to attract organizational and managerial talent. Meanwhile the organization's functions were broadened to include looking after the Fuehrer's personal security, planning future responsibility for the domestic security and some aspects of the foreign security of a Germanic superpower.

Upon Hitler's ascendancy as chancellor of Germany, Himmler took aim at one target: the German domestic security services and their various, rather decentralized, police services. He centralized them, which took several years to accomplish, and amalgamated them with the SS. This, plus the actual transfer of the traditional powers of the juridical system to various sometimes deliberately competing branches of the SS, made the latter into police, judge and executioner at the same time. Himmler thus revolutionized the traditional German "*Rechtsstaat*" in vital spheres, capitalizing upon the German quest for the undemocratic, strong powerful state. However, the SS also gave its policing agencies a racist, future-oriented "modern" appearance.

The SS created its own master concentration camp at Dachau and soon took over the other camps of that kind which had mushroomed under the SA. The "power of the revolutionary right," as formulated by Theodor Eicke, the first head of Dachau, controlled the entire German concentration camp system, allowing it to establish its own internal camp rules, which deviated sharply from the still existent German law. Its aim was to break, "reeducate" or liquidate the Third Reich's "enemies." These enemies were at first political opponents, but by 1939 the "other planet," the SS's own judiciary—fully separated from traditional law, allowed the murder of any racial, "subhuman," homosexual or other "enemy" as defined by Hitler, or the use of their labor to enhance the SS's own financial needs or economic ambition of a "state within a state." The SS was removed from the juridical system of the state and given its own system.

In 1939, the SS command was divided into several "main offices" or branches, deliberately competing with and supplementing each other. The most important among them were the so-

called security branch (*Reichssicherheitshauptamt*, or RSHA), which combined the functions of the secret police (*Gestapo*) with those of the SS secret service (SD) and those of the criminal police and the border police; the uniformed police branch; the race and settlement branch (aimed at settling Germans in occupied territories and selecting those among foreign nations fit to be raised as Germans); the fighting SS branch; Himmler's own staff; the economic and organization branch (*Wirtschafts- und Verwaltungshauptamt*—WVHA)—in fact the command of the concentration and death camp system; and the SS's own "judiciary" branch. The territorial organization was broadened to encompass occupied Europe as a whole under regional "*Hoehere SS und Polizei Fuehrer*" (HSSPFs) and commanders of the combined SS-Police and SD operations; special killing units (*Einsatzgruppen*) were created to pursue immediate mass murder actions in collaboration with the regular army once a territory was occupied in Eastern Europe. Finally, the SS recruited foreigners, including Muslim volunteers and grew to a million men in a fighting and killing machine—still aiming at establishing itself as the true future elite of the Third Reich at the expense of more traditional or less race-oriented organizations.

The use of concentration and killing camp inmates for labor in collaboration with German firms on an enormous scale was partially given up due to the approaching collapse of Nazi Germany, and a campaign was launched to disguise and hide the mass murders. Himmler even hoped to offer himself and his organization to the western Allies as a new ally against the Soviet Union. The machine itself however, functioned, loyal to Hitler personally, largely without change to the very end.

STALIN, JOSEPH VISSARIONOVICH (1879–1953) Bolshevik revolutionary and leader of the USSR. Born in Gori, Georgia, son of an impoverished cobbler, young Joseph Djugashvili was sent to a Russian Orthodox seminary, but was expelled before graduation for violent political activity. Having already joined the Russian Social Democratic Workers Party, he devoted himself to revolutionary activity. Stalin attended the BOLSHEVIK PARTY congresses in Finland in 1905 and in Stockholm and London in the two following years, and was granted membership in the central committee in 1912, becoming one of the editors of *Pravda*, the party's leading newspaper. In 1913, at the request of LENIN, Stalin produced his first major theoretical work, "Marxism and the National and Colonial Question."

From February 1913 until the February RUSSIAN REVOLUTION OF 1917, Stalin was in exile in Siberia. Upon his return to Petrograd on March 25, he and KAMENEV displaced the editors of *Pravda*, and adopted a "revolutionary defensist" editorial policy, including support for the provisional government, in keeping with the policy adopted by the Petrograd Soviet. This policy was changed only with Lenin's return to Russia in mid-April. For the remainder of 1917, Stalin adhered closely to the policies advocated by Lenin, and remained an editor of *Pravda*. With the Bolshevik seizure of power, Stalin was named people's commissar for nationalities.

During the civil war, while still retaining his portfolio as commissar for nationalities, Stalin was appointed a senior military commissar, organizing the defense of Czaritsyn (later Stalingrad, today Volgograd) in mid-1918, and providing political-military leadership in the north Caucasus and in the war against

The private family life of a dictator; Stalin poses with his son Vasili and his daughter Svetlana

Poland. Here he not only worked with some of those who, like VOROSHILOV, became his closest associates, but also clashed with the commissar of war, TROTSKY, beginning their fateful enmity. From 1919 to 1923 Stalin also headed *Rabkrin*, the workers' and peasants' inspectorate, auditing the activities of all government offices. With the reorganization of the Communist Party in March 1919, Stalin was appointed to the Politburo and the Orgburo, gaining dominance in the appointment of party officials in the provinces. In April 1922, he was chosen for the newly-created post of secretary-general of the Communist Party.

In the planning for the political structure of the Union of Soviet Socialist Republics during 1921–1922, Stalin suggested a centralized state in which the national minorities would have cultural, but not territorial autonomy. Lenin insisted on an ethnic federalism that would give each minority the sense and symbolism of national identity. Differences between the two found expression in Lenin's political testament, written in January 1923, in which he critically assessed all the leading figures of the party. Regarding Stalin, he suggested finding a general secretary who would differ only in that he should be more patient and polite in his relations with the other party members.

Following Lenin's death in January 1924, Stalin initiated the "Lenin Enrolment" into the Communist Party of the Soviet Union. Party membership grew from 470,000 at the beginning of 1924 to over one million two years later. Stalin recruited

these Communists primarily from the growing numbers of new factory workers, swamping the politically experienced core of pre-revolutionary "Old Bolsheviks." With this mass as his base of support, and deftly shifting alliances and policies, Stalin built himself a position of power. Between 1927 and 1934, Stalin defeated all his leading rivals, first Trotsky, then ZINOVIEV and Kamenev, and finally BUKHARIN. During this same period he actively formulated and supervised the REVOLUTION FROM ABOVE, the first Five Year Plan for the industrialization of the Soviet Union, and the collectivization of agriculture.

By 1934, the Soviet Union had stabilized somewhat, the second Five Year Plan was being implemented and large-scale active resistance to collectivization had ceased. Stalin, as general secretary, convened the 17th Communist Party congress, dubbing it "the Congress of Victors." In the 10-member Politburo chosen at the end of the congress, only Stalin remained of those who had been included in the first post-Lenin Politburo a decade earlier.

On December 1, 1934, Sergei Kirov, First Secretary of the Leningrad Communist organization and a member of the Politburo, was assassinated. Today it is accepted that the murder was ordered by Stalin. At the time, it was blamed on opposition groups, headed by Zinoviev, Kamenev and Trotsky. The wave of arrests and executions that followed was bolstered by draconian emergency laws proposed by Stalin. The blood purges lasted until Stalin's death, interrupted only by World War II, and in the end struck virtually every pre-existing institution in the Soviet Union: the Communist Party (98 of 135 central committee members were shot and 1,108 of the 1,966 delegates to the 17th Congress of the Communist Party were arrested and tried); the RED ARMY (3 of 5 marshals were executed, as were almost all the commanders of armies, and about one-third of the officer corps was arrested); the political police (two of its heads were purged); the governmental apparatus and cultural organizations. All were reduced to a defenseless state before the totally arbitrary wave of accusations and the mass public hysteria of suspicion. This was the essence of the terror, by which, more than anything else, most of the world, including the population of the former Soviet Union, remembers Stalin. No satisfactory comprehensive explanation has yet been suggested for this phenomenon, much of which appears to have been based on Stalin's own mistrustful personality.

At the end of the 1930s, Stalin's foreign policy was based on trying to avoid being drawn into the European war that was clearly approaching. This brought him to the Molotov-Ribbentrop pact of non-aggression between the Soviet Union and Nazi Germany, with its secret appendix delineating spheres of influence between Germany and the USSR in Eastern Europe. The Soviet Union not only gained control of the Baltic coast, annexing Lithuania, Latvia and Estonia, but also pushed its borders westward, deep into Poland and Romania. Stalin did everything possible to live up to his side of the pact, and to gain time for the USSR to rearm and reorganize its armed forces. He apparently believed that Hitler, in keeping with German military doctrine, would not open an eastern front until he had conquered England. In this he erred, and the Nazi invasion of June 22, 1941 came as a shock.

Stalin took personal command of the army and government and was involved in almost every detail of the war effort. Stalin also managed the relations with the other anti-Nazi powers, Great Britain, headed by Prime Minister Winston Churchill, and the United States of America, headed by President Franklin D. Roosevelt. In the meetings of the Big Three at Tehran in 1943 and Yalta in 1945, Stalin established the place of the USSR as a power of equal status to the other two in the postwar world. Memoirs of these meetings show him as a compelling personality as well as a tough and skilled negotiator.

The final eight years of Stalin's life indicated a reversion to prewar patterns of purge and terror. Communist Party organizations in Leningrad, Georgia and the Ukraine, were purged, with various accusations proffered. A thinly-disguised campaign against "cosmopolitans" in Soviet culture resulted in the removal of Jews from numerous Soviet institutions and the closing of all Jewish cultural institutions. This campaign culminated in January 1953, when nine doctors, six of whom were Jewish, were accused of actual and intended murders of Soviet leaders through misdiagnosis and wrong treatment. Later testimony indicates that this was to have been accompanied by the deportation of all Jews from central areas of the Soviet Union, as had been done with various nationalities, particularly from the north Caucasus, during the war. Purges of political leaders also took place during these years in all the Soviet-controlled countries of Eastern Europe.

At the same time, what was later called "the cult of Stalin's personality" was assiduously cultivated, particularly around his 70th birthday in December 1949. In 1950, Stalin published an essay entitled "Marxism and Problems of Linguistics," determining which schools of linguistics were "proletarian" and which "bourgeois." In 1952, his "Economic Problems of Socialism in the USSR" set the stage for a resumption of economic teaching and research that had been largely suspended for over a decade. Stalin's pronouncements against cybernetics, and in support of Lysenko's theories of heredity, shaped an entire generation of Soviet scientific effort.

Stalin's death, on March 5, 1953, saw the Soviet Union in far different condition from that he had inherited after Lenin's death. Industry had largely been reconstructed and had passed the 1940 levels. The Soviet Union was a nuclear power. It had regained territories lost by Russia in wars throughout the century and added new territories. In addition, the Soviet régime controlled a security belt of Eastern European Communist states. From an embattled régime threatened by "capitalist encirclement," Stalin had led the Soviet Union to the status of leader of a worldwide camp of régimes and movements that was bidding for dominance of the globe.

STALINISM   A phenomenon in the USSR intertwining supremacy of state interests over the citizen; mobilization of all economic, social and cultural resources in service to state interests; and destruction of all political and social institutions through arbitrary terror; with STALIN as the sole ultimate focus and arbiter of all policy and practice. While some aspects of Stalinism may be traced back to roots in Russian history or in Leninist political theory, fully developed Stalinism, as exemplified in Stalin's régime between 1937 and 1953, was unique in its comprehensive and violent extremism.

Stalinism involved the ubiquitous politicization of life in the Soviet Union. The drive for total mobilization meant that all facets of personal and social behavior were scrutinized from the point of view of their contribution to the Stalinist state. All economic, cultural or professional activity was viewed through the prism of politics.

Born in part out of Russia's backwardness and in part out of political anxiety and insecurity, Stalinism was characterized by REVOLUTION FROM ABOVE—the attempt to forcibly remold reality so as to conform more closely to Stalin's perception of the Marxist ideal of society. Achieving this transformation meant that all sectors of life had to be subordinated to advancement of the heavy-industry sector of the economy. Not only natural resources, labor and capital, but also culture and politics were mobilized to serve the goal of production. The magnitude of this transformation was a source of genuine social enthusiasm generating support for the régime.

The Stalinist revolution from above caused a complete reordering of the Soviet social structure. Former elites and influential groups in all parts of society were dismantled or destroyed. Totally new elites were advanced and installed. This process was repeated during the blood purges of the 1930s, during which a postrevolutionary generation of leaders rose in almost every sector of Soviet society. The loyalty of these elites, whose status, power and social privileges flowed from the practices of Stalinism, provided the Stalinist régime with a powerfully placed base of support.

Stalinism also involved the using of Russian nationalism as a mobilizational tool. Raising the self-confidence of Russians by reference to their historic achievements in science, culture and international politics was mixed with warnings against foreign "class enemies." Suspicion and rejection of all things foreign eventually turned Stalinism into a xenophobic creed.

STAMBOLISKY, ALEXANDER   (1879–1923) Bulgarian agrarian politician. Of humble peasant origin and self-taught, Stambolisky finished agricultural high school in Halle. By 1911 he was the leader of the emerging Bulgarian Agrarian Union, later renamed the Peasant Union. In his militancy, he was outstanding among his generation's other peasant leaders. Indeed, he was characterized by historians as "intensely ideological and emotional." During World War I he attempted to plot against King Ferdinand and was sentenced to life in prison. Following Bulgaria's collapse and the ensuing peace process, he entered the government and became prime minister of a cabinet ruled by the Agrarians. He was deeply committed to bring about the rule of the village and the peasants, the "pure" element of society, against the "sinning" urban culture of the cities, the "Sodoms." His paramilitary units, the Orange Guards, served as shock troops of the Agrarians, breaking up internal opposition during Stambolisky's rise to dictatorial powers and in his attempts to create a peasant-based egalitarian society.

The Green International of peasant movements and the forming of an alliance of agrarian states in the Balkans was envisaged as an alternative to capitalism and Communism. Bulgarian nationalists—including the military, the Macedonian terrorist organization (IMRO) and other opposition forces—launched a violent coup in June 1923, during which Stambolisky was murdered and his body mutilated. The utopian peasant vision practiced by the Bulgarian agrarians did not survive his death. The strong post-World War II agrarian movement defeated by the

Communists was a milder version of Stambolisky's ideology.

STAMP ACT This act, which was ratified by the British parliament in 1765, extended to the American colonies a tax—the stamp duties—which already existed in Great Britain. Immediately in October 1765, a group that represented nine of the thirteen American colonies convened the Stamp Act Congress in New York to protest against and defy the tax. The congress petitioned the king and the British parliament, but they refused to consider the colonists' grievances. Among the colonists, there was fierce opposition from the SONS OF LIBERTY, whose members, among other things, attacked British stamp agents.

Colonial businesses then placed an embargo on the importation of British goods. The Stamp Act was indeed repealed about six months later, on March 4, 1766, but by then the damage had been done. The congress had declared many principles of independence, and the cry of "no taxation without representation" was used by leaders of the AMERICAN REVOLUTION. These principles were incorporated into the American declaration of independence. The Stamp Act is cited by many historians as one of the principal causes of the American Revolution.

STANTON, ELIZABETH CADY (1815–1902) A leader of social reform movements in the US, who advocated a revolutionary change in the status of enslaved Afro-Americans and in the legal and social status of women. Elizabeth Cady was born in Johnstown, New York in 1815. She was educated at the prestigious Emma Willard's Academy. At the home of her cousin, Gerrit Smith, a leading abolitionist, she was exposed to the tenets of radical social reform. In 1840 she married Henry B. Stanton, a veteran romantic reformer. In the marriage ceremony she insisted on omitting the word "obey," and for their honeymoon the couple traveled to London to attend the World Anti-Slavery Convention.

Until the end of the US civil war Stanton advocated both the cause of the slaves and of women. In 1848, a mother of seven, she and her close associate, Lucretia Mott, organized the world's first convention to advocate women's rights, in Seneca Falls, New York. Stanton insisted, against opposition, that the convention's resolutions—which paraphrased the declaration of independence—include a demand for women's suffrage.

During the civil war, Stanton campaigned for the constitutional abolition of slavery in the context of the National Woman's Loyal League, an organization she had founded with Susan Anthony. After the war, however, Stanton opposed the radical 14th and 15th amendments, even though they granted civil and political rights to Afro-Americans, because they did not grant the same rights to women. In 1869, Stanton and Anthony established the National Woman Suffrage Association to fight for equal political rights for women.

Stanton's campaign to free women from oppressive social norms and traditions was at least as revolutionary as her campaign for women's political equality. She advised women to prefer divorce to unsuccessful marriages, to take prophylactic measures to avoid unwanted pregnancy and advocated greater sexual freedom for women.

STASOVA, YELENA (1873–1966) BOLSHEVIK PARTY administrator. Born in a St. Petersburg INTELLIGENTSIA family in which her father was a lawyer known for his defense of arrested revolutionaries and her aunt a pioneer of the Russian feminist movement, Stasova's first social involvement was as a teacher in Sunday adult education schools for workers. She joined the Social Democratic Party at its inception in 1898 and two years later became a full-time party worker. From 1904, she became the organizational secretary of the Bolshevik faction of the party. In 1912, she was elected a candidate to its central committee and served as the central committee's secretary after the RUSSIAN REVOLUTION OF 1917.

Following her resignation as secretary of the central committee in 1920, Stasova served in a number of administrative posts in Soviet institutions, as an agent of the COMINTERN, as head of the International Red Workers' Aid Organization (MOPR) and in 1938–1946 as editor of *International Literature,* a journal.

STAUFFENBERG, COUNT CLAUS SCHENK VON (1907–1944) German army officer, one of the conspirators involved in the July 20, 1944 rebellion against HITLER's dictatorship in Germany. Stauffenberg was descended from an ancient South German noble family which was also close to the Prussian nobility that fought Napoleon I. As such, he developed a sense of mission and responsibility at a very early age. At first he welcomed Hitler's rise to power as the first step toward Germany's recovery from the defeat of World War I. Later he tried to have himself—he was then a young army captain—appointed governor of France, a position he felt he would fill benevolently. Stauffenberg fought in the Western Desert, was very badly wounded, and during his recovery realized that Hitler was not only destroying the old Prussian-German General Staff tradition—that of allowing the military their own professional judgment within the general direction given by the political level—

Count Claus Schenk Von Stauffenberg

but was losing the war itself. A man of determination and exceptional courage, Stauffenberg, by then chief of the German Home Replacement army, planned Operation Valkyre. As the practical man of action among a heterogeneous group of conservative, liberal and social-democrat rebels, including generals, civil servants, diplomats and trade union leaders torn by doubt and far from the actual centers of decision, Stauffenberg tried to smuggle a bomb into Hitler's quarters and to declare military rule in Germany once the Fuehrer was dead.

One such attempt failed, but on July 20, 1944 he believed he had succeeded and that Hitler was indeed dead. Upon his return to Berlin from Hitler's headquarters in East Prussia, Stauffenberg immediately tried a "revolution by telex," ordering the arrest of all Gestapo and ss police officials and a military takeover from the Nazi Party. The plot collapsed when Hitler proved to be alive, and Stauffenberg was executed the same evening. His motives and plans for the future remain debatable and obscure, and his legacy has also remained debatable in postwar Germany. Today, Stauffenberg is an official German hero.

STEINBERG, ISAAC NAHMAN (1888–1957) Leader of the SOCIAL REVOLUTIONARY PARTY in Russia, born in Dvinsk, Russia (now Daugavpils, Latvia). Due to the influence of an enlightened but religiously traditionalist upbringing, Steinberg remained an observant Orthodox Jew throughout his life. As a newly enrolled law student at Moscow University, he became active in the Social Revolutionary Party and was expelled from the university for his revolutionary activities. He continued his studies in Heidelberg, publishing his doctoral thesis, "Penal Law in the Talmud" (1910). Returning to Moscow, he embarked on a legal career. After the RUSSIAN REVOLUTION OF 1917, he joined the left-wing Social Revolutionaries who, in alliance with the BOLSHEVIK PARTY, called for an end to the "imperialist war" and for peace talks with Germany. He served briefly as minister of justice in VLADIMIR LENIN's first government (1917–1918), and it was rumored at the time that no cabinet meetings took place on Saturdays in deference to Commissar Steinberg's religious practices.

By 1923, however, Lenin had disposed of his non-Communist allies, and Steinberg had taken refuge in Berlin. There, for the next 10 years, he was the leading Social Revolutionary spokesman, championing the cause of parliamentary freedom, contributing to the left-wing press in many countries, and publishing works such as *The Moral Aspect of the Revolution* (1925) and *Memories of a People's Commissar* (1929). ADOLF HITLER's rise to power drove Steinberg to London in 1933 and from there he emigrated to New York a decade later.

Steinberg became a wholehearted advocate of Jewish territorialism, established the Freeland League, and advocated an autonomous Jewish settlement in Australia, but this proposition was rejected by the Australian government. His book, *Australia—The Unpromised Land*, records his bitter disappointment. In his last years, Steinberg, the one-time revolutionary, preached a kind of spiritual Zionism that would make Jerusalem the spiritual—as opposed to temporal—center of the Jewish people.

STRASSER, GREGOR (1892–1934) Nazi leader. A pharmacist by trade, Strasser became politically active after World War I when he joined the Nazi Party. He took part in ADOLF HITLER's BEER HALL PUTSCH of 1923 and later occupied leading positions in the party. However, instead of his leader's anti-Semitism and vague promises aimed at all segments of the public, he advocated a concrete social revolutionary program.

During the period of 1926–1932, Strasser was in charge of party propaganda and organization. Displaying great ability, he transformed it from a mob party into a relatively acceptable outfit that was made up of various organizations aimed at professionals, the young (including the youngest), women and the unemployed. Unlike his brother Otto, Gregor Strasser was not a doctrinaire socialist revolutionary; on the other hand, he abhorred his former aide, Goebbels, for his opportunism and lust for power.

In 1932, following the party's decline in the polls and its financial bankruptcy, Strasser suggested that it join a conservative coalition as a junior partner. Hitler refused, whereupon Strasser left the party. The party's fortunes were reversed at the last moment by the conservatives' fear that the Nazi voters would desert them in favor of the Communists, and by their belief that Hitler had been entrusted with the position of chancellor only as part of a coalition government. Denounced as a traitor, Strasser ended up by being murdered by the ss on June 30, 1934.

STRASSER, OTTO (1897–1974) German Nazi leader and dissident. As GREGOR STRASSER's younger brother, Otto Strasser joined the Nazi Party in the mid-1920s. He belonged to the party's left-wing; as such, he helped bring it the support of the lower middle classes as well as elements of the proletariat. However, toward the end of the 1920s Otto Strasser became disillusioned with the Nazi Party which, he felt, was relying too much on the conservative right for financial support and had deviated from its earlier revolutionary and socialist course. Accordingly, in 1930 he left to found his own political organization, the Black Front, which considered itself a true workers' party. The new organization's success was only moderate; when Hitler settled accounts with his political opponents in the so-called Night of the Long Knives of July 1934, Strasser managed to escape to Czechoslovakia, where he reestablished the Black Front and tried to subvert the Nazi régime. In 1938, just before Hitler invaded Czechoslovakia, he again escaped, this time to Canada. There he remained until 1955, when he returned to Germany and tried to reenter politics, but without success.

STUCHKA, PETER (1865–1932) Latvian BOLSHEVIK legal theorist. Born of a peasant family in Latvia, Stuchka graduated in law at St. Petersburg University in 1888. He worked both in a law office and as editor of left-wing newspapers, until arrested and exiled to the Vitebsk region in Byelorussia.

In 1903, he became a Bolshevik and founded what was later to be the Bolshevik Party of Latvia. As a lawyer, he defended a number of those tried for their activity in the RUSSIAN REVOLUTION OF 1905. His activities in 1917 centered around Petrograd, where he was a member of the Bolshevik Party committee, a delegate to the Petrograd Soviet and on the editorial board of *Pravda*. After the Bolshevik seizure of power in October 1917, he was twice briefly people's commissar for justice during 1917–1918 and active in judicial affairs, dismantling the legal system inherited from the czars and formulating the first Soviet statutes on court structures and practice. From the end of 1918 to 1920, he headed the Soviet government in Latvia.

During the 1920s, Stuchka published many volumes on questions of revolutionary socialist law, the Soviet constitution and MARXISM. He founded the law department in the Communist Academy and the Soviet Institute of Law and was appointed professor of law at Moscow State University. He also chaired the supreme court of the Russian Republic and authored a volume on the judicial practice of the supreme court. Although posthumously attacked for "harmful theories" during the STALIN era, Stuchka was fully rehabilitated and his teachings were again published and studied in the post-Stalinist Soviet Union.

STUDENT MOVEMENTS During the late 1960s, a series of radical movements which shook the establishment all over the western world. The most important among them were the Student Nonviolent Coordinating Committee (SNCC) and STUDENTS FOR A DEMOCRATIC SOCIETY (SDS) in the USA; the Provos in the Netherlands; and the Jasos in West Germany. In France an unnamed student movement actually started a full-scale uprising in May 1968, at the time threatening to bring down de Gaulle and the Fifth Republic (see FRENCH STUDENT REVOLUTION); in the US, where the movement was strongly associated with protest against the Vietnam war, the most important outbursts occurred in 1964 (Berkeley), 1968 (Columbia), 1970 (200 universities, among them Kent State University in Ohio, where several students were killed by National Guards). Intimately connected with the NEW LEFT and brandishing the gospel of HERBERT MARCUSE, the student movements of the period 1965–1972 are still not completely understood. They have, however, tended to die down in recent years, especially since 1973—a fact which may not be unconnected with the change in the world's economic climate.

STUDENTS FOR A DEMOCRATIC SOCIETY (SDS) The most important of the many student movements that were created in the United States in the 1960s. Founded in 1962, it worked for civil rights, sometimes putting on violent demonstrations against the Vietnam war and the draft. The movement probably reached the peak of its activity in 1971; after the end of the Vietnam war in 1973 its influence rapidly declined.

SUDAN, COUPS Since independence in 1956, Sudan has experienced four military coups, interspersed with periods of civilian rule.
Coup of 1958. The first military coup, on November 17, 1958, was led by a group of officers headed by General IBRAHIM 'ABBUD. It won the support of civilian politicians with assurances that the army had taken over with the aim of restoring stability and would not stay in power longer than necessary. It had some successes in the economic sphere, but the military's involvement in government and the internal corruption within the government created growing discontent. In addition, the government's military solution to the problem of the south created thousands of refugees. In 1964, the campaign for the restoration of civilian government gained momentum and 'Abbud was forced to surrender power to a civilian committee.
Coup of 1969. The ensuing civilian government was overthrown in 1969 by Colonel JA'FAR MUHAMMAD NUMEIRI. During

his first years, Numeiri followed radical policies. He modeled himself on NASSER of Egypt and adopted socialist polices, forging an alliance between the new military government and the formerly-banned Sudanese Communist Party (SCP). Numeiri's régime was a period of unprecedented repression in Sudan. In September 1983, Numeiri imposed Islamic *Shari'a* law on Sudan. The stringent application of Islamic law led to an armed insurrection in the south.
Coup of 1985. In April 1985, Numeiri was deposed in a bloodless coup led by Lieutenant General Swar al-Dahab, minister of defense and commander in chief of the army. Swar Al-Dahab established a Transitional Military Council (TMC) to govern the country. General elections were held in 1986 and the country returned to civilian rule, with AL-SADEQ AL-MAHDI's *Umma* Party winning the largest number of votes.
Coup of 1989. On June 30, 1989, al-Mahdi's government was deposed in Sudan's fourth military coup, led by Brigadier (later Lieutenant General) OMAR HASSAN AL-BASHIR. Since then, all political organizations have been banned.

SUDAN PEOPLE'S LIBERATION MOVEMENT (SPLM) The Sudan People's Liberation Movement (SPLM) and its military wing, the Sudan People's Liberation Army (SPLA) were founded in 1983 in protest against the régime of Sudanese President Colonel JA'FAR MUHAMMAD NUMEIRI (see SUDAN, COUPS). Numeiri's policy of Islamization and Arabization in the south and his decision to impose the Islamic *Shari'a* legal code on the whole population of Sudan led to armed insurrection by the Christians and animists, who form the majority in southern Sudan. The SPLM and its leader, JOHN GARANG, demanded that the government abrogate Islamic law and declare Sudan a united, secular country.

Since 1983, international efforts to achieve a peace settlement have failed, as successive Sudanese governments have insisted that Islamic law be imposed on the whole country. In recent years, there has been a split in the SPLM and a splinter group formed demanding complete independence for southern Sudan. This weakened the rebel movement and enabled the government forces to reconquer many of their strongholds. In addition, a change of régime in Ethiopia meant that the SPLA could no longer operate from within its borders, seriously undermining the movement. In 1993–1994, the SPLA lost many of the towns it controlled in the south to the Sudanese army.

In the early 1990s, the Organization of African Unity (OAU) set up a committee to try and find a solution to the conflict. This group (called IGAD) consists of Kenya, Uganda, Ethiopia and Eritrea, and is headed by Kenyan president Daniel Moi. There have been several meetings, in which IGAD has tried to bring the southern splinter groups together and to arrange a meeting with the Sudanese government, but so far without success.

SUFFRAGETTES A movement which was active in various countries between about 1850 and 1920, demanding that women be given the right to vote alongside men. The best-known leaders of the movement were: in the US—Lucy Stone and Susan Anthony; and in Britain, the three Pankhurst sisters—Sylvia, Emmeline (see EMMELINE PANKHURST) and Christabel. Their campaigns, which in both countries were coordinated on a national scale, proceeded through various means. Prominent among them were journalism, public meetings and demonstrations, some of which brought the suffragettes into conflict with the law and led to their leaders being arrested (see also ELIZABETH CADY STANTON).

In the US, the suffragettes first began making headway via the individual states. When Wyoming entered the Union in 1890, it became the first state to grant women the vote. Other states, pressed through vigorous propaganda campaigns, followed. By 1918, 15 states had awarded women the vote. However, attempts to revise the Federal Constitution failed in 1876 and in 1914. It was only in 1920, following the very important role that women had played in the mobilization for World War I, that the aims of the movement were attained and American women were finally enfranchised by an amendment (Article XIX) to the Federal Constitution.

Meanwhile, in Britain, developments took a different course. Though the suffragette movement had become very active from the 1890s on, no fewer than seven bills aimed at the enfranchisement of women were defeated during the years of Liberal government from 1906 on. Thereupon the movement turned militant. Demonstrations were held, leaders were imprisoned and hunger strikes ensued. The outbreak of World War I, far from assisting the movement, probably delayed its victory, as people turned their attention to other issues considered more vital to national life. By 1918, however, the battle had been won and in Britain, too, the suffragette movement gained its victory.

SÜHBAATAR, DAMDINY (Sukhe Bator) (1893–1923)
Mongolian revolutionary leader. After serving as a machine gunner in the Mongolian army, in 1919 Sühbaatar worked as a typesetter in Urga (present-day Ulaanbaatar) and organized a small group of revolutionaries into the *Dzüünhara* circle. This group merged with another revolutionary group in an attempt to end the Chinese occupation of Mongolia, after China achieved nominal independence in 1911. In 1920, Sühbaatar and six others visited Irkutsk in the newly constituted Soviet Union to garner support for their movement and conceded to most Soviet demands regarding the Marxist ideology that was to be imposed once they gained control of the country. While some members of the group continued on to Moscow, Sühbaatar returned to Mongolia to engage in political agitation and to organize, in 1921, the People's Army. With Soviet RED ARMY backing, the People's Army fought against both the Chinese and the forces of Baron Ungern von Sternberg, a renegade White Russian general who was wreaking havoc on the local population. That same year Sühbaatar was elected to the central committee of the Mongolian People's Party at its first congress, and with the establishment of a provisional government in Kyakhta (present-day Altanbulag) in March, was appointed minister of war. In July 1921, the People's Army and the Red Army entered Urga and established the world's second Communist régime (after the Soviet Union).

Sühbaatar died prematurely in 1923. There is no evidence supporting the claim that he was poisoned by enemies of the revolution. Although Mongolia only became a People's Republic officially in 1924, after the death of the last monarch, Sühbaatar is considered the guiding force behind modern Mongolia. A near-legendary account of his life has been enshrined in the annals of the revolution.

SUKARNO, AHMED (1901–1970) Indonesian nationalist; first president of Indonesia. Sukarno was born in east Java to a Japanese Muslim father and a Balinese Hindu mother. He graduated in 1925 from the Bandung Technical Institute, where he had studied civil engineering, and found work as an architect. Racist jibes at the institute and at work aroused Sukarno's nationalist sentiments and in 1928 he helped found the INDONESIAN NATIONALIST PARTY, dedicated to the liberation of the archipelago from Dutch colonial rule. Sukarno was a skilled orator who often found himself at odds with the colonial government. He was arrested in 1929. Upon his release in 1933, he was exiled to the remote eastern island of Endeh, where he remained until World War II.

The Japanese occupation of Indonesia (1942–1945) encouraged the nationalists to cooperate with the occupying army in return for self-government, and Sukarno was allowed to leave his exile as the president of a nominally independent Indonesia. This period is one of the most controversial in Sukarno's life. Although he did manage to negotiate a degree of autonomy for the islands, in return he was responsible for supplying thousands of Indonesians for forced labor in Japanese factories. Yet Sukarno maintained his popularity among the masses, and upon the collapse of Japan declared himself president of the independent United States of Indonesia. The Dutch were unwilling to forgo their colonial empire and a bloody insurgency ensued. For four years Sukarno and his vice president, MOHAMMAD HATTA, fought the Dutch and their British allies. Negotiations over the formation of a Dutch and Indonesian union began in 1946, but it was only on November 2, 1949 that the Netherlands recognized the independence of Indonesia. Sukarno was elected by unanimous acclamation as president. He preserved the terms of the treaty of union forged with the Netherlands until 1956, when he unilaterally abrogated it and repudiated Indonesia's debt to the Netherlands.

The early years of Indonesian independence were fraught with ethnic, religious, regional and political strains. Western Java, Sumatra and Celebes all sought various degrees of autonomy and the South Moluccas declared their independence. Muslims, composing 90% of the population, attempted to establish a theocratic state, and Sukarno himself was not a democrat. He favored Marhaemism, his own brand of SOCIALISM that included the principle of a "guided democracy" of economic and social reforms. This advocacy cost him much of his popularity. Sukarno was also a committed socialist despite his traditional Muslim life-style, and this led to a breach between himself and Vice-President Hatta.

Regarding himself as a world leader, Sukarno sought to unite the newly independent states of the Third World into a bloc independent of the United States and the USSR, aspiring to lead the non-aligned states himself. His own political position grew increasingly closer to the Indonesian Communist Party, and efforts were made to forge close bonds with China. It was Sukarno's flirtation with communism that led to his downfall. An attempted coup in 1965 (see INDONESIAN COUP) by Communist-leaning officers was suspected of being orchestrated by Sukarno; many leading generals were killed in the bungled coup attempt, and the majority Muslim population felt threatened. Sukarno was unable to prevent a massacre of suspected Communist sympathizers; the estimated death toll ranges between

300,000 and one million. In response to the failed coup attempt, Sukarno's supporters were pushed out of office. Sukarno himself was stripped of his titles and all powers in 1967; he died three years later in Jakarta.

SUKHANOV (GIMMER), NIKOLAI (1882–1939) MENSHE-VIK internationalist journalist and economist. Sukhanov's first revolutionary activities were as a populist (see POPULISM) while he was still a Moscow high school student, and his first writings as an economist were on agricultural economics and in populist journals. He served a year in prison in 1904 and 1905 for distributing populist revolutionary literature. By 1907, he had become a Menshevik Social-Democrat, though he continued publishing in the populist press as well as in Marxist publications. After a three-year exile in the Archangelsk region, he returned to St. Petersburg in 1913 and edited two radical journals, beginning a long journalistic association with Maxim Gorky.

In 1917, Sukhanov was a central figure in the executive of the Petrograd Soviet from its founding, writing proclamations and conducting negotiations aimed at setting the relations between the provisional government and the soviet. He opposed the socialist parties' joining the provisional government as a minority and was highly critical of the foreign and military policies of the "defencist" socialists who dominated the Petrograd soviet after April 1917. He was violently critical of both left and right in the political negotiations that followed the BOLSHEVIK seizure of power in October 1917. In June 1918, he was expelled from his post in the executive of the All-Russian Congress of Soviets and his newspaper, *Novaya zhizn* (*New life*) was closed down. He then wrote his *Notes on Revolution* (abridged English translation by Joel Carmichael, *The Russian Revolution of 1917: A Personal Record*. Oxford Press, 1955).

Sukhanov formally left the Menshevik Party in 1920 and worked as an agricultural economist in a number of Soviet institutions. In 1930, he was expelled from his position in the economics section of the Communist Academy for views that contradicted régime policy. A year later he was arrested and tried in the "Menshevik Trial." Sentenced to 10 years in prison, he was shot in August 1939.

SUKHE BATOR see SÜHBAATAR, DAMDINY.

SULTANGALIEV, MIRSAID (1880–1939?) Tatar revolutionary theorist and journalist. Trained in education at a Kazan school for teachers, Sultangaliev advocated the establishing of Tatar national schools and libraries. In 1911 he embarked on a career of journalism, writing under various names in both Russian and Tatar publications. In 1917, he became one of the leaders of the Islamic socialist movement in Russia, attending the two Islamic congresses held during the summer. In November 1917, he joined the BOLSHEVIKS and was active in the people's commissariat for nationalities headed by STALIN. He edited the newspaper of the commissariat, *Zhizn natsionalnostei* (*Life of nationalities*).

Sultangaliev advocated a Pan-Turkic Muslim socialism, combining religious and national features with the MARXISM advocated by the BOLSHEVIKS. He envisioned a Muslim state within Soviet Russia, uniting all the Turkic Islamic minorities and affiliated to a Colonial International of Islamic socialism.

Following the discussions on nationalism at the 12th Soviet Communist Party conference in 1923, Sultangaliev was arrested and expelled from the party. Released shortly after, he worked outside the Muslim areas of the USSR for another five years. In 1929, it was announced that he had been arrested once more, for conspiring with nationalist and anti-Communist movements. This time he was sentenced to 10 years at hard labor in the far north, where he died.

SUNAY, CEVDET (1899–1982) Turkish general and coup leader. General Sunay was born in Trabzon, northeastern Turkey, in 1899. During World War I he fought in Palestine and in 1918 was taken prisoner by the British. After his return to Istanbul in 1920, he joined the nationalist army. Sunay became chief of the general staff after a 1960 coup and was active in military circles until 1966. Although not doing so officially, he led the Armed Forces Union (*Silahli Kuvvetler Birligi*), a military organization which repeatedly interfered in politics between 1961 and 1962. This union, which was comprised of some 200 officers, including the heads of the navy and the air force, was primarily responsible for the execution of Prime Minister Adnan Menderes. Sunay was appointed to the senate in 1966 and in March 1966 became the fifth president (1966–1973) of the republic after Gursel resigned.

SUN CHIAO-JEN see SONG JIAOREN.

SUNG CH'ING-LING see SONG QINGLING.

SUN WEN see SUN YAT-SEN.

SUN YAT-SEN (Sun Wen; Sun Yixian; Sun I-hsien; Sun Zhongshan) (1866–1925) Chinese revolutionary leader. Born to a poor peasant family in southern Guangdong, where remnants of the TAIPING REBELLION (1850–1864) had just been eliminated when he was born, Sun was influenced by the anti-Manchu (Qing) dynasty (1644–1912) tradition from early childhood. His village teacher was a Taiping veteran. Close to Portuguese-held Macao and an early link to the west, his home district, Xiangshan, provided numerous missionary disciples, agents for foreign firms (*compradors*) and emigrants. In 1879, Sun joined his elder brother in Hawaii and received a western, Christian education that proved incompatible with local customs when he returned to his native village four years later. He continued studying in foreign institutions in Hong Kong, was baptized by an American missionary in 1884, was given the name Yat-sen by his Chinese Christian pastor, by which he became famous, and returned home to marry the bride chosen by his parents. He began medical studies in a Canton missionary college and finished in the Hong Kong College of Medicine for Chinese (1887–1892). Thus, except for a few years in a village school and private classical studies in Canton, Sun was educated in foreign, mainly missionary, institutions, making him the most westernized Chinese political leader of his time. Foreign modernizing influences and the native anti-Manchu tradition combined to mold his political personality. Yet, despite admiration of the Taiping leader, HONG XIUQUAN, and TRIAD secret society contacts, while in medical school he sought patrons in official circles. Though Sun did very well in medical school, neither

British nor Portuguese authorities recognized his credentials in Hong Kong and Macao respectively. In 1893, he opened an "East-West Apothecary" in Canton, combining herbalism with modern medicine, but closed shop in 1894 for a final try to impress officials with his western learning. He went to Tianjin with a reformist proposal for the empire's leading bureaucrat, Li Hongzhang (1823–1901). His attention riveted upon the Korean crisis and impending war with Japan (1894–1895), Li did not grant Sun an audience. Rejected by the traditional elite, Sun gave vent to the revolutionary inclinations he had already nurtured. He left for Hawaii and would devote himself to revolution for the rest of his life. As modern China's first professional revolutionary, Sun added modern ingredients to traditional patterns of rebellion. Drawing upon his wealthy brother's influence and his previous connections with immigrants from his home district, in November 1894 he enrolled some 20-odd members into his first revolutionary organization, XING ZHONG HUI (XZH—Society to Restore China's Prosperity). In February 1895, he and other western-educated young men of lower-class, non-literati origins formed the Hong Kong XZH. Their slogan called for the expulsion of the Manchus, restoration of China and the establishment of a republic. Recruiting fighters from Triads and other dissidents, and soliciting funds from overseas Chinese (huaqiao), they planned to seize Canton. The plot was aborted in October, and Sun fled with a price on his head and the Chinese authorities on his trail. After brief stays in Hong Kong and Japan, he went to Hawaii, where his wife, two children and widowed mother had taken refuge from Manchu retaliation. Finally, he sailed for England after canvassing for the support of American huaqiao communities.

On October 11, 1896, only 10 days after arriving in London, Sun was taken prisoner in the Chinese legation and held for 12 days, during which the Chinese authorities planned to ship him home for execution. The intervention of Sir James Cantlie, his former teacher in the Hong Kong medical school, secured his release. Widely publicized, the episode turned him into a celebrity and strengthened his conviction that he was China's man of destiny. His personal account, Kidnapped in London, published in England in 1897, did more than anything else before the CHINESE REPUBLICAN REVOLUTION OF 1911 to spread his name abroad. Months of intensive reading in the British Museum Library, where he met exiled Russian revolutionaries, broadened Sun's knowledge of world affairs and currents of thought. He concluded that Europe's unplanned Industrial Revolution had left an explosive legacy of social injustice and class conflict. He learned about SOCIALISM, Henry George's single-tax doctrine, and other remedies that, applied before China's full industrialization, could avoid the social revolution that seemed inevitable in the west. This was the origin of Sun's "principle of people's livelihood," which is the third of his THREE PRINCIPLES OF THE PEOPLE.

Leaving England in July 1897, and having been banished from British colonies in the East, Sun found refuge in Japan, where Pan-Asian nationalists, including some genuine idealists, were impressed by his qualifications for renovating China and joining the struggle against western imperialism. Japanese subsidization enabled Sun to revive revolutionary activity, which had come to a standstill after the 1895 failure in Canton. Pan-Asianism appealed to him. His first cooperative venture with Japanese comrades was an aborted attempt to help Filipino rebels, led by EMILIO AGUINALDO (1869–1964), resist the Americans in 1898. The BOXER REBELLION, which flared up in 1898 and embroiled the Beijing government in a war with the foreign powers in June 1900, prompted Sun into trying a multi-pronged approach for overthrowing the dynasty. However, the invading foreigners refused to cooperate. Neither did Li Hongzhang who, as governor-general of Guangdong-Guangxi, was withholding support from Beijing. Nevertheless, in October the XZH enlisted Triads and dissident peasants to stage a surprisingly strong campaign in Huizhou (Waichow) in eastern Guangdong. Anticipated Japanese aid, which Sun waited for in Taiwan, failed to materialize. After several weeks, the uprising was crushed.

Though the XZH was practically defunct, new opportunities arose as the government's post-Boxer reforms included education, which exposed students to radical influences at home and abroad, especially in Japan. Probably because of his lower-class, non-literati origins, students were not initially attracted to Sun. Meanwhile, he canvassed French support in Indochina, even offering to detach Guangdong and Guangxi from Beijing's control and to give France preferential rights. In 1904, while raising funds in the US, he appealed to Americans in a little pamphlet, The True Solution of the Chinese Question. Ignored by foreigners, Sun turned to the overseas students, first in Europe in early 1905 and then in Japan later in the summer. Non-Cantonese student radicals had meanwhile failed in their own revolutionary plots (see HUA XING HUI; GUANG FU HUI) and were open to a new approach. Endorsed by Japanese sympathizers, and known as an activist with ties to huaqiao money abroad and Triad fighters at home, Sun was chosen as leader of the new, multi-provincial revolutionary vehicle, the TONGMENGHUI (TMH). His purported ability to win foreign support or at least prevent pro-Manchu intervention was an important consideration. The TMH program, drafted in 1906, included ideas Sun had been developing for several years: the three principles of nationalism, democracy and socialism or people's livelihood (later called the Three Principles of the People); a nine-year period for the gradual attainment of constitutional government; and the "five-power constitution," which added two traditional Chinese institutions—the censorate for supervision and impeachment of officials, and an examination agency for testing the qualifications of all candidates for elective and appointive positions—to the American three-fold separation of powers (executive, legislative and judicial). Not all Sun's comrades subscribed fully to his platform, but it was largely his instrumental function, as a revolutionary conspirator rather than ideological authority, that earned him leadership status. While Sun was mainly abroad, soliciting huaqiao money and still pursuing foreign support, his colleagues, led by HUANG XING, staged six unsuccessful uprisings in southern China from Hanoi (1907–1908) and two from Hong Kong aimed at Canton (1910, 1911). The first six relied upon Triad fighters; the last two incorporated defecting soldiers. As a result of these successive defeats, by 1911 TMH leadership had been slipping from Sun's hands. During a visit to London, the Manchu embassy attempted to kidnap Sun and managed to hold him in the embassy for several days, awaiting orders to ship him back to China for execution. Although contact with the outside world was denied him, Sun managed to smuggle out a letter and was freed immediately. The Manchu government was greatly discredited in the resulting scandal. When the revolution finally erupted, unexpectedly and not directly instigated by the TMH, Sun was in the United States. Upon learning of the October 10, 1911 uprising in Wuchang, he returned by way of Europe in a vain attempt to harness foreign help. In late November he wired colleagues from Paris that either LI YUANHONG, the reluctant revolutionary leader in Hubei, or Yuan Shikai, a last-minute Manchu appointee as premier, would be acceptable for presidency of the republic. Aware that he lacked wide popular support and fearing that prolonged civil strife could provoke foreign intervention, he chose not to wage an all-out struggle for power when he returned to China in December.

On December 29, Sun was elected president of the provisional republican government in Nanjing, after delegates favoring either Huang Xing or Li Yuanhong were stalemated. However, he immediately notified Yuan Shikai, Britain's choice, that he could replace Sun if he declared allegiance to the republic. In February, Yuan secured the abdication of the Manchus and was inaugurated as provisional president in March. Acting as an elder statesman, Sun retained nominal leadership of the GUOMINDANG (GMD), successor to the TMH, though it had scrapped much of his program. Under its active leader, SONG JIAOREN, the GMD won the republic's first elections (1912–1913). His assassination in March intensified suspicions of Yuan that led to the unsuccessful 1913 Revolution. In Japan for the next three years, Sun focused on anti-Yuan plotting and on building a more disciplined organization. While Chinese patriots responded furiously to Japan's imperialist designs (21 Demands of 1915), Sun solicited and received Japanese help against Yuan. In order to ensure personal obedience, he created the CHINESE REVOLUTIONARY PARTY in Japan in 1914. Even veteran comrades balked. The only bright spot during this low period was his marriage in 1915 to SOONG QINGLING. A beautiful, 23-year-old woman, she would be Sun's trusted confidante during the last decade of his life.

After Yuan Shikai's demise in 1916, Sun took to lecturing and writing in Shanghai. While warlords held power in Beijing, in September 1917 Sun was elected "Grand Marshal" of a military government in Canton that attracted several hundred members of the former parliament who responded to his call for "protecting the constitution." Since local militarists made his position untenable, he left in May 1918. A renewed overture to the Japanese was no more successful than courtship of the wartime adversaries, Germany and the United States. But the recent RUSSIAN REVOLUTION OF 1917 began to interest him, and he had indirect contact with BOLSHEVIK leaders. After the European armistice in November, Sun began writing one of his major works, *The International Development of China*. A grandiose and impractical scheme for developing Chinese railroads, highways, mines, etc. with massive foreign loans, Sun's plan, broached to foreign officials in 1919 and published as a book in 1920, nevertheless exhibited presience in its basic thrust. World War I, he argued, had proved the obsolescence and futility of imperialism. In particular, he warned Japan of the folly of aggressive militarism. Calling for a new international order based on cooperation, he stressed that Chinese modernization would also benefit the industrialized nations. He wanted "to make capitalism create socialism in China." Meanwhile, he lacked a power base to enhance his credibility. Then, the 1919 MAY

FOURTH MOVEMENT, which galvanized opposition to imperialism and warlordism, infused new life into his political movement, and Lenin's awareness of the revolutionary potential in Asian nationalism gave Sun the foreign assistance he had been seeking.

In 1919, Sun began revamping the GMD, which replaced the CRP. Wielding supreme power, Sun injected the platform with his ideas: the Three Principles, including nationalism, now redefined as the attainment of equal international status; the five-power constitution; and a period of party-tutelage before the full establishment of democratic government. But a return to Canton proved premature. In July 1922 his militarist collaborator, CHEN JIONGMING, dislodged him from Canton. Now the Russian option seemed more inviting, both for invigorating the GMD and for material assistance. Previous contacts with COMINTERN agents—VOITINSKY in 1920, SNEEVLIET in 1921, Serge Dalin in 1922—had been inconclusive, but he was more receptive to Sneevliet's proposal for collaboration when they met again in Shanghai in September. The agreement that was eventually reached called for members of the CHINESE COMMUNIST PARTY (CCP) to join the GMD as individuals while retaining their separate organization. Subordinating Communists to bourgeois nationalists in the first revolutionary stage conformed to Lenin's formula for Asian anti-imperialist revolutions. For Sun, the arrangement meant he would be the chief recipient of Soviet aid. Moreover, he felt the CCP was too small to threaten him. Collaboration was formalized at Sun's meeting with the Soviet diplomat, ADOLF JOFFE, in Shanghai. Their joint statement, issued on January 26, 1923, finally gave Sun recognition by a foreign power. In the text, Joffe endorsed Sun's view that communism was unsuited for China and assured him of Soviet support for the achievement of Chinese unification and full independence. He also confirmed Russian intentions to renounce czarist treaties with China. In return, Sun backed Russian railway rights in Manchuria, and while accepting Joffe's denial of imperialist aims in Outer Mongolia, he recognized the inadvisability of an immediate withdrawal of Soviet troops.

Sun returned to Canton, where Chen Jiongming had been defeated. He still kept the door open to the west, but the Soviet connection served as an additional excuse for ignoring him. Western policy-makers, in their search for stability in China, preferred working with warlord régimes in Beijing. Moscow in the meantime decided to allocate a million dollars to Sun's Canton régime. In August Sun sent his trusted aide, CHIANG KAI-SHEK, on a three-month study mission to the Soviet Union. In October the Russian aid program gained momentum with the arrival of MICHAEL BORODIN (Gruzenberg). An experienced Bolshevik organizer with wide overseas experience and close to Lenin and other Soviet leaders, Borodin impressed Sun with his practical approach to revolution. Appointed adviser to the GMD's provisional central executive committee, he introduced a Bolshevik organizational format (democratic centralism), and specific appeals to peasants and workers in the GMD program. For the next few years Borodin's tutelary role in the Nationalist Revolution would make him one of the most influential men in China. On the other hand, Sun's relations with the western powers deteriorated almost to the point of armed conflict. In December they sent a fleet of gunboats in response to Sun's threat to seize the Canton customhouse, where foreign tax administrators were forwarding tax receipts to Beijing without giving a share to Canton. Sun backed down, but his militant anti-imperialism made him the spokesman for the rising tide of Chinese nationalism. Never in his entire career had he enjoyed such popular support. Borodin's influence and the strong anti-imperialist line were clearly evident in the January 20, 1924 1st national congress of the GMD which endorsed alignment with the Soviet Union, collaboration with the CCP and support of workers and peasants. Similar sentiments informed the hastily prepared lectures (January–August) in which Sun expounded on his Three Principles of the People, which later became the GMD bible. In April, Sun published a concise outline of his political program, "Fundamentals of National Reconstruction for the National Government of China," which bore few signs of Soviet influence. Though less stridently anti-imperialist, it demanded revision of unequal treaties and restoration of international equality and independence.

Soviet aid enabled the GMD to build the party-army Sun required. What he had learned about the Bolshevik revolution impressed him with the role the RED ARMY had played in securing the fruits of revolution. The WHAMPOA MILITARY ACADEMY, funded by the Russians, who also sent instructors, was the centerpiece of the Russian aid program. In October, a Russian ship brought the first load of Soviet arms. That month too, a high Russian officer, General VASILY BLÜCHER, arrived to head the Soviet military mission that would include dozens of officers and other personnel. With refurbished military forces, Sun consolidated the southern base and planned a drive north, though his health was failing. Meanwhile, a new warlord combination seized control of Beijing and invited him for discussions. On the slight chance that militarists would accept his political proposals and foreigners the demand for treaty revision, Sun traveled north in November by way of Shanghai and Kobe, where he delivered the famous speech on "Pan-Asianism." Urging the Japanese to renounce western-style imperialism, he called for Asian solidarity. His condition deteriorating when he reached Tianjin in December, he negotiated fruitlessly with the warlords. An ambulance took him to Beijing, where exploratory surgery confirmed that his illness, cancer of the liver, was incurable. On March 11, 1925 he signed a testament, drafted by the left-wing GMD leader, WANG JINGWEI, that enjoined his followers to complete the revolution according to his major works. He also signed a document, drafted by EUGENE CH'EN after consultation with Borodin, that was addressed to the Soviet Union and expressed the hope that the two nations would cooperate "for the liberation of the oppressed peoples of the world." He died the next day.

Sun left a disputed legacy. After its 1927 split with the CCP, the GMD canonized him, and in 1940 decreed that he henceforth be known as "father of the republic" (guofu). By stressing Sun's final leftist orientation, the CCP hailed him as the "pioneer of the revolution." Despite Sun's convoluted, improvised political style, his life-long struggle to build a modern and more humane society at home and attain equal status abroad continues to evoke admiration from Chinese of all political persuasions. During one of the darkest periods in Chinese history, he never doubted that China would be restored to greatness, and that once unified, could easily shake off demeaning concessions to foreigners. Implemented in Taiwan, his ideas have proved less impracticable than often thought, while in Communist China the demystification of MAO ZEDONG has invited a new look at Sun. The common celebration of his memory can bring the two closer together.

SUN ZHONGSHAN   see SUN YAT-SEN.

SVERDLOV, YAKOV MIKHAILOVICH   (1885–1919) Russian Communist, first head of the Soviet Union. Sverdlov was born Yakov Solomon in the Russian town of Nizhnii Norgorod (present-day Gorky). In 1901 he founded the RUSSIAN SOCIAL DEMOCRATIC PARTY, siding with the BOLSHEVIK PARTY. He established the Nizhnii Norgorod Revisionary Committee, probably at the instigation of his brother Zinovy, adopted son of the noted Russian author Maxim Gorky. In 1909, he was sent to Moscow by the Central Committee of the Bolshevik Party with the task of reestablishing the shattered party in that city.

Sverdlov's activities soon brought him into conflict with the authorities; he was arrested and exiled, but managed to escape to St. Petersburg, where he worked with the party's faction in the Duma, the Russian parliament. Following a demonstration, he was again arrested and exiled to the remote prison camp of Maksimkinlar near the Arctic Circle, accessible by boat only twice yearly. Sverdlov made five unsuccessful attempts to escape, in the last of which he fell ill. Taken to medical facilities at Narya, he tried to escape in a small boat. A storm rose and Sverdlov was nearly drowned. He was eventually picked up by a passing boat and returned to prison, where he remained until the outbreak of the revolution. While in prison he met JOSEPH STALIN, who had also been exiled to Siberia.

Despite his lengthy exile, Sverdlov's organizational skills in the party were well remembered. Much of his rise to power was the result of his organizational ability, and Stalin once called him "an organizer to the bones of his brains." In 1912, he was co-opted to the Communist Party central committee in absentia. After his release, he was elected secretary of the All-Russian Executive Committee of the party, making him the titular head of state of the Soviet Union on November 8, 1917.

Sverdlov was often ruthless. He used his skills in manipulating the Central Executive Committee, even barring the MENSHEVIK Party from attending meetings, thereby assuring total control by the Bolshevik faction. He cooperated closely with LENIN, and most policy decisions were made privately by the two. However, even he was unsettled by the magnitude of the order to execute the entire imperial family; when informing the central committee of the act, he only mentioned the execution of the czar.

Sverdlov died suddenly on his way to a party conference in Kharkov. In his honor, the city of Yekaterinburg was renamed Sverdlovsk.

SWAPO   see SOUTH-WEST AFRICAN PEOPLE'S ORGANIZATION.

SWISS REVOLT   In November 1847, the Federal Army of Switzerland, in a swift and almost bloodless campaign, defeated the forces of the "separate alliance" set up by the Catholic cantons of the country. Coming after nearly 50 years of revolts and counterrevolts, it was a victory of the liberal forces over the forces of reaction as well as of the predominantly Protestant cantons over the Catholic ones.

The Swiss régime at the time was based on the federal pact of

1815. Concluded with the help of the foreign powers which had just defeated Napoleon, that pact was both repressive and reactionary. Political power was in the hands of the cantons; regardless of the size of the population, each sent an equal number of representatives to the Diet where decisions were taken by majority vote. There was no provision for the amendment of the constitution, religious freedom was curtailed and local alliances between cantons were prohibited.

In 1823 Metternich, chancellor of Austria, together with Prussia and Russia, forced the Swiss government to agree to a number of restrictions. Switzerland was to curb its own liberal press, and was to deny asylum to liberals from other countries. These measures were opposed by students who took the lead in a liberal, nationalist movement. The Bund (Confederation) took fright; in 1829 it agreed to repeal all the restrictions imposed six years earlier. Encouraged by that first success, the liberals demanded more, including freedom of education and greater democracy by weighting the number of representatives each canton sent to the Diet in accordance with the number of the canton's inhabitants.

Things came to a head in 1845. Protesting against the Diet's decision to expel the Jesuits—which would have completed the process of secularization in education—the six Catholic cantons of Uri, Schwyz, Zug, Fribourg, Valais and Unterwalden concluded a secret alliance, or *Sonderbund,* that was directed against the Bund. In July 1847 the six cantons raised the standard of revolt and prepared for war; in November, though, they were overwhelmed by the army of the confederacy under General Defour, during a campaign that lasted 25 days. The suppression of the revolt led to the adoption of a new constitution modeled upon that of the US and, with it, the founding of the modern Swiss state.

SYNDICALISM A turn of the 20th century working-class movement which set out to promote the real and authentic interests of the oppressed masses. The syndicalist theory of social progress was designed to improve the lot of all mankind through a campaign of revolutionary terror and violence. More specifically, syndicalism was dedicated to wiping out every single vestige of capitalism, along with all its parliamentary and other civil institutions, by acting outside the political arena—this being perceived as a snare and an illusion. This was to be accomplished by the forcible seizure of industry and all other means of production and exchange on behalf of the trade unions and other labor organizations and cooperatives, mobilized for action by a working-class elite. According to the theory, which made a powerful impression on many intellectuals and free-lance journalists disillusioned with the hypocrisy and futility of political compromise, a vanguard of the laboring poor was to be entrusted with the task of carrying out an abrupt and sweeping victory over a decadent bourgeois order—but only after (and this was of crucial importance in the theory as expounded by its proponents) those involved had been thoroughly and systematically indoctrinated by a heightened awareness of their own self-consciousness and made fully aware of their role as the instrument for the creation of a more humane social order that would improve the quality of life for all members of society. It was this cataclysmic violence that was to be unleashed through the dissemination of the concept of "the myth of the general strike"

among wage-earners, tenant farmers and small shop owners.

The founding father and most articulate propagandist of revolutionary syndicalism was the French social theorist and writer, GEORGES SOREL (1847–1922). His celebrated *Reflections on Violence*, published in 1908 with the benefit of the editorial labors of a gifted disciple, the essayist and historian Daniel Halévy, put forward the idea that the revolution could be accomplished by proclaiming a universal "general strike"—which he conceived as a violent upsurge of proletarian fury and frustration aimed at the total eradication of all the shackles of bourgeois exploitation, thereby bringing about a complete and radical expropriation of the capitalist class and the reconstruction of society along truly socialist lines. This cluster of revolutionary ideas, whose name is a literal translation of the French word for "trade-union," was especially widespread among isolated groups of non-union workers and independent revolutionary activists mostly scattered in Latin-speaking countries, notably in France, Spain and Italy. Sorel's social theory served as a major catalyst in reviving a pre-existing and recurring strain in socialist thought derived from such famous anarchist militants and thinkers as PIERRE-JOSEPH PROUDHON and MIKHAIL BAKUNIN—hence the generic and all-inclusive label "anarcho-syndicalism," more commonly applied to designate the idiosyncratic ideas espoused by the movement as a whole, in order to distinguish the main thrust of its ideology and its program for action from the traditional doctrines promulgated by Marxists, whether of the "Utopian" or "Scientific" persuasion.

Syndicalists did not reject the orthodox Marxist theory of the class struggle and the importance of social revolution as their ultimate objective; what they added to the doctrine was an important corollary designed to modify the praxis contained in the corpus of Marxist writings, by introducing the argument that the state would not simply wither away, as predicted in *The Communist Manifesto* and *Das Kapital*, but should instead be seized by a "direct" and frontal assault and then brought to its knees and abolished altogether, to be supplanted by a federation of autonomous and self-governing units, known as the *syndicats*, owned, operated and managed by the workers themselves. The theory also postulated that the proletariat, driven by the "myth of the general strike" to act in accordance with an exalted sense of working class solidarity, would be stimulated to perform heroic deeds for the benefit of all mankind. Syndicalism proved to be a divisive element within the ranks of French SOCIALISM. It contributed to disrupting even further the fragile unity achieved—after much dissension and debate—following the defeat of the PARIS COMMUNE and the consolidation of the bourgeois Third Republic in the 1870s and 1880s as a result of an unholy alliance between royalists and moderate republicans united by a common resolve to keep the workers in their place.

In 1906, syndicalism was adopted by the so-called Charter of Amiens as the guiding principle of the *Confédération Générale du Travail* or CGT, France's mainstream trade union congress. The Amiens Charter rejected parliamentary socialism in favor of working-class insurrectionism, which triggered off a wave of sporadic industrial unrest, spreading from postal workers, school teachers and a general railway strike to include even the police force as well as destitute wine growers and peasants from the south, until the disturbances were forcefully repressed by Georges Clemenceau, the Radical prime minister of the Third

Republic from 1906 to 1909, and his successor, Aristide Briand. The latter, himself a former member of the Socialist Party, resorted to the ingenious device of breaking the back of the agitation by conscripting the striking workers into military service. Syndicalism survived even longer in one form or another in Spain until its main political wing, POUM (the *Partido Obrero de Unificacion Marxista*), consisting of a motley coalition of Trotskyites, Anarchists and anti-Stalinists, replenished by a steady flow of fellow travellers from abroad, was ruthlessly suppressed by FRANCO in the course of the SPANISH CIVIL WAR. Its most celebrated adherent, however, was MUSSOLINI, an early and constant admirer of Sorel, who was directly influenced by the master's syndicalist gospel of direct action in laying the basis of his own Fascist ideology. Although much less pervasive in the English-speaking world, syndicalist ideas were of paramount importance in shaping the thinking of a strikingly original federation of American workers which, at its peak in 1915, could boast of a membership in excess of 100,000: this was the Industrial Workers of the World (IWW) popularly known as "the Wobblies" or "the Bummery," founded at a congress held in Chicago in 1905, where it affirmed its resolution of overthrowing capitalism by violent means. The Wobblies, restricted in their activities to the US and among the loggers and forest workers of western Canada, are chiefly remembered today for their rich legacy of revolutionary marching songs.

SYRACUSE, REVOLUTION

(357–356 B.C.) Syracuse had been ruled by the tyrants Dionysius I (from 406 B.C.) and his son and successor Dionysius II (from 367 B.C.) for close to 50 years. The exiled Dion, a relative of the tyrants and an admirer of Plato, started military preparations in 360 B.C. to liberate the state from the tyrant's rule, basing himself in Corinth and helped by his friend Heracleides, another exile. Dion landed in Sicily in August 357 B.C., leading mercenary troops and taking advantage of Dionysius II's sojourn in a colony in Italy. As he approached the city, the populace rose up in rebellion and the tyrant's commander lost control of the city, though a strong garrison continued to hold the citadel of Ortygia for Dionysius II. On entering the city, Dion declared the liberation of Syracusans and other Sicelots from tyranny and was elected to head the new executive of the state. He was soon joined by Heracleides, who came with a fleet and a contingent of mercenaries, necessary for the war against the tyrant and his forces. However, Dion soon lost the support of the masses through his opposition to the radical democracy and socioeconomic revolutionary measures they demanded—demands which were backed by Heracleides. The latter won a decisive naval victory against the fleet of Dionysius II in the spring of 356 B.C., which gave the upper hand to the classes opposing Dion. The Assembly of the people then voted to stop paying Dion's mercenaries, to elect a new executive and to carry out redistribution of land and houses. The third resolution concerned the entire territory of Syracuse and was aimed at bringing about equality in landed and real property among the members of the citizen body. Dion and his mercenaries left Syracuse, but the revolutionary government did not last long. Defeated by the troops of Dionysius II, the Syracusans recalled Dion, who again saved them. However, his quarrel with Heracleides revived and he had Heracleides killed. Virtually sole master of Syracuse, he was suspected of an attempt at tyranny

and was then murdered in 354 B.C. by another disciple of Plato.

SYRIA, COUPS

Coups of 1949. The three coups in Syria in 1949 were the first in a long series taking place in that country for over 15 years. They were an outcome of a lack of internal stability and security that had developed into a severe deterioration in the status of the parliamentary régime and the national leadership. The defeat in the 1948 war against Israel added to the atmosphere of general political discontent in the country. The only sociopolitical group that could bring about change in the society and the ruling system were the army officers. Most of them came from the lower-middle stratum of society and shared the disappointment and discontent of the civil leadership.

The first coup was organized by Colonel HUSNI ZA'IM (1889–1949), the chief of staff. He removed President Quwatli and took the presidential power into his own hands. Assembling a government mainly with unknown figures, the new régime turned quickly into an open dictatorship of the army headed by Za'im. He was, however, the first of the Arab army politicians to have plans for social reform. For the first time in the Arab world, women were given the right to vote. However, the despotic way in which he conducted the state led to his fall in August 1949.

A second coup, led by Colonel SAMI HINNAWI (1898–1950), took place and Za'im was executed. Hinnawi, who enjoyed the support of veteran politicians, introduced an innovation in the system of military coups in the Arab world. He established a committee of officers that became the legislative, executive and judicial authority of the state. Unlike Za'im, he did not come up with a reform plan. His régime was pro-British and identified with the world view of the SYRIAN PEOPLE'S PARTY. Hinnawi's unification plan with Iraq, opposed by the army, was the excuse used to overthrow him on December 19, 1949.

This third coup was led by Colonel ADIB SHISHAKLI (1909–1964). Shishakli took the position of vice-chief of staff and ruled the state from behind the scenes. In September 1950, a new constitution was introduced and a government officially formed, although in fact the authority remained in Shishakli's hands and in the hands of the officers around him. As Syria could not reach a state of stable government, the country knew extreme social and political unrest that eventually led to a fourth military coup in December 1951, also engineered by Shishakli.

Coup of 1951. In December 1951, Colonel Adib Shishakli put an end to the parliamentary régime that he himself had created following his previous coup in December 1949. He dismissed the president of the republic and the parliament and established a military dictatorship. At first he remained behind the scenes as the chief of staff but in the summer of 1952 he joined the government as vice-prime minister and later as minister of the interior. Before that, in the spring of 1952, all political parties were dissolved and banned. Shishakli then established the Arab Liberation movement as the one and only political party. Although one-party rule existed, Shishakli wanted to give his régime a constitutional and democratic facade. Therefore, in June of 1953, he proclaimed a new constitution which left a wide range of authority in his hands although it again permitted the existence of political parties.

Many of Syria's old political activists, headed by the former president, HASHEM AL-ATASSI, saw the new moves as an effort to mislead the public and condemned them. In October, new elections were held and Shishakli, as the only presidential candidate, ascended to the president's seat. When Shishakli appeared on the political map in December 1949 he had stopped the rightist pro-Hashemite tendencies of Hinnawi, his predecessor. However, he himself moved to the right during his rule and established connections with Amman, Baghdad and the west. It was during his rule, it should be noted, that for the first time in the history of modern Syria wide-range agrarian reforms were introduced. In his reformist policy he was helped by Akram Hawrani, the leader of the Arab Socialist Party (and one of the leaders of the *Ba'ath* Party since 1953) and by leaders of the SYRIAN NATIONALIST PARTY. However, he never identified himself with these parties publicly.

In his reforms, Shishakli reduced the ownership of large estates and distributed state land to poor peasants. He also tried to weaken any autonomous rule of minorities and succeeded in making the previously autonomous Druze community subordinate to the central government. His deeds contributed to shaking up the status quo of the old sociopolitical order but also led to his fall. All parties in Syria, old and new, signed a "national pact" in 1953 against him and in February 1954 he was removed from office in a coup headed by army officers (many of them Druze) and civil leaders.

Coup of 1970. The coup that raised HAFEZ AL-ASAD to power as the ruler of Syria. The coup's roots lay in a power struggle between Asad and SALAH JADID, the strongmen in Syria ever since the 1966 coup. The 1966 coup split the SYRIAN BA'ATH PARTY into two factions and brought to power the leftist neo-Ba'athist faction in Syria. In brief, the world view of the neo-*Ba'ath* Party was socialist and radical-secularist. These characteristics were objected to by the conservative elements of the Syrian population, who represented the majority of the country. On top of that, an additional source of discontent was the fact that the 'Alawites and Druze played an increasingly important role in the ruling circles and, with the ascent of Jadid, he had nominated almost only 'Alawites to civil and military positions, thus effectively blocking out the majority Sunnites.

From the beginning of 1968 until November 1970, the date on which Asad executed his coup, his influence and power grew by using the authority and strength he enjoyed as minister of defense. With the help of his chief of staff, his right-hand man, Mustafa Tlas, Asad conducted a semi-coup in February 1968 when he removed Jadid's supporters from key positions in the army, the government and the party and instead nominated his own people. In November of 1970 he completed the process and removed Jadid and Atasi, the president and prime minister, from their posts. Asad made himself prime minister and continued to hold the position of minister of defense. He assembled a new leadership for the rest of the *Ba'ath* Party.

Aware of the tension and socioeconomic agitation caused to a large extent by the dogmatic ideology of the ruling circles, Asad named his régime the Reform Movement and took measures to suspend the tension and agitation among the different groups and religious communities. He worked for reconciliation with the commercial circles of the traditional middle class—mainly Sunnite Muslims and Christians. He softened the dogmatic socioeconomic policy of his predecessor and encouraged private

entrepreneurship. His main efforts of reconciliation were addressed to the majority group—the Sunnites. He restored to the constitution its Islamic color and made an effort to emphasize his image as a faithful Muslim.

SYRIAN BA'ATH PARTY A political party, founded in Syria in 1940 by MICHEL 'AFLAQ and SALAH-UL-DIN BITAR, two young intellectuals who studied in France and were influenced by MARXISM. In 1953, it merged with the Arab Socialist Party to form the Arab Socialist Resurrection Party. This party aspired to enhance national independence, carry out socioeconomic reforms, ensure the secularization of public life and foster Arab unity. It used the socioeconomic unrest among workers and peasants and the political aspirations of the middle class in order to extend its power in and out of the parliament. After the elections of 1954, it became the third largest party in parliament. Its influence extended beyond Syria, and branches of the party were founded in Jordan, Iraq and Lebanon.

The party drew its power from the support of army officers of the lower and middle classes, who found its ideology appropriate to their world view. An alliance between civilian leaders of the party and these army officers led to unification with Egypt in 1958. This move fitted the anti-imperialist, anti-capitalist and progressive ideology of the *Ba'ath*.

The unification with Egypt brought social and economic changes. The old and conservative elite lost its power in favor of improvements in the socioeconomic conditions of the lower and middle strata. An agrarian reform was introduced and social services were extended to urban workers. However, NASSER's banning of political parties, including the *Ba'ath*, which had played an instrumental role in the unification, along with his centralization efforts, brought about the separation of Syria from Egypt.

The *Ba'ath* regained its power after the Egyptian episode. In March 1963, due to the return of power in parliament of the old conservative politicians, pro-*Ba'ath* officers launched a coup that brought their party to power. The main principles of the socioeconomic policy of the new régime were set forth in the constitution of 1964. Syria was declared a socialist popular democratic state and a socialist system was formally adopted. This meant limiting private ownership, nationalization of the means of production, the extension of public services and the secularization of the state.

Young officers, many of them Druze and 'Alawites, were the backbone of the *Ba'ath* coup of 1963. In 1964, they removed the old leadership from the political life in Syria. Now a cruel struggle for power began inside the party among the new leadership. It was characterized by a communal struggle between 'Alawites and Druze, mainly army officers, on the one side and Sunnis, mainly civilians, on the other side, but the division was also characterized by ideological differences. The 'Alawites and Druze were considered more leftist and doctrinal, while the Sunnis were more rightist and flexible. In February 1966, the 'Alawite-Druze faction launched a coup and took over power in Syria. The coup also marked the end of the 'Alawite-Druze alliance, as the 'Alawite leaders of the new Syrian régime removed their Druze partners and embarked on an 'Alawite rule which has lasted until the present. However, a new confrontation was introduced between the two strongmen of the new régime, namely SALAH JADID and HAFEZ AL-ASAD. This struggle ended in November 1970 with the victory of Hafez al-Asad.

The *Ba'ath* Party under Asad's rule tried to achieve three main goals. It worked to consolidate its régime by recruiting support not only from the 'Alawite sect, to which Asad belonged, but also from other groups in the Syrian population—mainly Sunnis, the majority group. In order to do that, it gave the régime a more Muslim face. In the 1973 constitution, a paragraph was added stating that the president of the state must be Muslim. Sunni personalities and officers were posted in key positions in the state bureaucracy. The constitution also preserved the leading role of the *Ba'ath* Party in the political system and gave Asad almost unlimited power.

The second goal of the party was to break Syria's isolation from the rest of the Arab world after years of alienation, ever since Salah Jadid's rise to power in 1966. The 1973 war against Israel marked the return of Syria to the bosom of the Arab world. The war also rallied Syrians behind their government and the *Ba'ath* régime gained national legitimacy.

The third goal was to make Syria a regional power by establishing its status through military strength and hegemony in the Arab world—primarily against Lebanon, Jordan and the Palestinians. After the peace agreement with Israel and Egypt, the Syrian *Ba'ath* Party assumed the role of the guardian of Arab values. It pressured both Jordan and the PLO to prevent them from following Egypt and supported Iran in the Iran-Iraq war (1979–1989).

The Gulf war, in 1991, enabled Asad to demonstrate Syria's regional strength and to embark on a careful integration into the pro-western new world order that began to materialize in the Middle East, including initial peace talks with Israel.

SYRIAN NATIONALIST PARTY A political party, founded in 1932 in Lebanon by ANTOUN SA'ADEH (1902–1949), a member of the Greek Orthodox church. Sa'adeh argued for the existence of an exclusively Syrian nationalism as opposed to the Arab nationalism or Pan-Arabism expressed in those days. He saw Lebanon not as a nation by itself but rather as part of the Syrian nation, and preached for the establishment of Greater Syria.

The party itself began as a secret organization and soon after, due to its anti-Mandatory tendencies, was persecuted by the authorities of the French mandate and outlawed. Sa'adeh fled to Europe and then South America, returning to independent Lebanon in 1947. He immediately renewed his political activity and added the word "Socialist" to his party's name. He launched campaigns against the Arab and Lebanese nationalists, whom he accused of betraying the national interests of Syria. The activity of the party was based primarily on violent and Fascist tendencies. The political leaders in Lebanon were concerned with the party's activities and again its members were persecuted, the party outlawed and this time Sa'adeh was executed.

From that point, the headquarters of the party were moved to Damascus and its main political activity was conducted by its Syrian members. The party, never having been too strong, became even weaker due to internal conflicts and divisions. From 1949, violence became the major method by which it hoped to create favorable conditions for the realization of its objectives. It regained legal recognition in 1958 in Lebanon while supporting President Camile Chamoun against the Nasserists. However, at the end of 1961, the party was accused of instigating an at-

tempted military coup and once again it was outlawed. It was legalized once again in Lebanon in 1970, but never gained enough power to play an important role in the politics of Syria or Lebanon, which, for more than 40 continuous years, rejected its ideologies and its leaders.

SYRIAN PEOPLE'S PARTY A Syrian political party founded in 1947. Its origins were in the national bloc, a group of veteran nationalists who led the struggle for Syria's independence against the French mandate between the two world wars. Due to disagreements with the leadership of the national bloc, some activists from Aleppo and north Syria quit the bloc and established the People's Party. Its two leading figures were Nazim al-Kudsi and Rushdi al-Kihiyeh. Despite the support of the party for a unification with Iraq, it did not have pro-Hashemite or monarchical tendencies but rather continued to support the republican institutions of Syria.

The first time the party gained significant political strength was in the short period of SAMI HINNAWI's régime, beginning in August 1949. Hinawi supported open relations with Iraq and gave key positions to the heads of the party. The victory of the party in the November 1949 elections led to an expectation of unification with Iraq. However, SHISHAKLI's anti-Iraqi coup in December 1949 shook the status of the party. It still ruled parliament but had to fight the army, which paid little attention to parliamentary procedure.

New elections were held in September 1954, and the party lost half of its power at the expense of the rise of the new left wing headed by the *Ba'ath* Party. This was the first sign of the slow but sure death of the party. It kept playing an important role in Syrian political life, but the continuing rise of the anti-Iraqi, pro-Egyptian left in Syria reduced the party's role. During 1958–1961, the years of the unification of Egypt and Syria, the party—like other conservative parties—stopped its political activity. It regained its power in the parliament for a short period (1961–1963), until the coup by the *Ba'ath*, which put an end to all the old parties in Syria.

SZALASI, FERENC (1897–1946) Leader of the ARROW CROSS, the Hungarian extreme right-wing pro-Nazi party and leader of Hungary between October 1944 and the liberation of the country in early April 1945. Of mixed Magyar, Slovak and Armenian origin, Szalasi graduated from a military academy in 1915. During the 1930s he became active in a variety of radical, nationalist political movements. In 1933, he published his *Plan for the Construction of the Hungarian State,* in which he combined Fascist (*see* FASCISM) ideology with "Hungarist" ideas on the superiority of the Hungarians in the Danube basin. He also adopted Nazi ideas such as the "leadership principle." As to the Jews, he demanded their mass deportation.

Having founded the Arrow Cross movement, Szalasi saw his military career terminated in 1937 when he was arrested and jailed. During the war years, his movement gained momentum riding on the wave of extremism, but he was only able to seize power through a German-engineered coup in October 1944. He introduced a reign of terror against his opponents and against the Jews and remained loyal to his Nazi masters until the very end. After Hungary's occupation by the RED ARMY, he was tried and executed in March 1946.

T

TAIPING REBELLION (T'ai P'ing) (1850–1864) Chinese anti-dynastic rebellion. Claiming 20 to 40 million lives, the Taiping Rebellion was one of the most destructive conflicts in world history and almost toppled the already declining Manchu (Qing) dynasty (1644–1912). The contributing factors were both internal and external (see CHINESE REPUBLICAN REVOLUTION OF 1911). While over-population and administrative weakness had fueled rural turbulence and secret society activity since the end of the last century, the Opium war (1840–1842) signaled the invasion of the industrialized west, which not only damaged dynastic prestige but challenged the efficacy of the Confucian order which the Manchus had scrupulously maintained. The southern province of Guangdong, where the anti-Manchu tradition was strongest, suffered economic loss as a result of the post-Opium war settlement (Treaty of Nanjing, 1842) which opened Shanghai and other ports and deprived Canton of its predominance in foreign trade.

The rebellion started among the Hakka, a sublinguistic Chinese community that had moved from the north centuries earlier and had since been in conflict with the original Cantonese inhabitants. Led by the visionary HONG XIUQUAN (1814–1864), a frustrated examination candidate who suffered from mental illness, the movement began as a religious cult. Armed with a smattering of Christian Biblical knowledge and claiming to be God's second son, Hong blended Judeo-Christian and ancient Chinese themes to fashion a blueprint for the kingdom of God. First organized as the God Worshippers Society in Guangxi in the late 1840s, Hong's followers, mostly fellow-Hakka, clashed with imperial troops in 1850 and in 1851 broke into open revolt. Hong declared himself Heavenly King (*Tian Wang*) of the Kingdom of Heavenly Peace (*Taiping Tianguo*), a term he had started using earlier. Manchus were foremost among the "demons" marked for extermination by God's command. Departing from traditional secret society rebellions, the Taiping movement posed a counter-ideology that challenged traditional Confucian tenets. The Taipings preached but failed to implement completely a combination of primitive communism and totalitarian rule. Subscribing to economic and social egalitarianism, they called for equal distribution of land and wealth and equality of the sexes. Moral precepts were based on the Ten Commandments. Proscription of foot-binding, adultery, opium, alcohol, tobacco and other vices were part of the puritanical creed imposed upon the rank-and-file but these prohibitions were not followed by all the leaders. Hong himself is said to have selected women for his harem at the very outset of the movement. Despite the egalitarian ethos, followers were organized hierarchically by status and occupation, while Hong Xiuquan and regional and assistant kings held top authority. It is doubtful whether they ever attempted to implement their utopian scheme, except perhaps in the movement's initial stages in the south.

Rural distress and forced conscription swelled the Taiping army, and an innovative strategy of mobile warfare turned it into a formidable fighting force. Armed with primitive weapons but infused with religious zeal, farmer-soldiers swept through southern China, bypassed major cities and reached the Yangtze river in January 1853. Men and women were now organized in separate camps. Having captured several thousand boats, they improvised a flotilla that descended the Yangtze. In March, just two years after starting north from Guangxi, they seized Nanjing, which became the Taiping capital. On the way, their number had risen to at least 500,000.

Besides preaching his messianic message, Hong had little to do with the Taiping military success. As Taiping prime minister and commander in chief, YANG XIUQING provided the administrative and military talent to give the movement its initial coherence and momentum. Other leaders, notably SHI DAKAI and LI XIUCHENG, were naturally gifted strategists who for years outmaneuvered imperial troops.

After capturing Nanjing, the Taipings still remained a serious military threat, but lacked the political talent to consolidate their conquests with an effective administration. Dissension and jealousy led to internecine strife that weakened the top leadership in 1856. Yang, who also claimed to speak in God's name, tried to usurp Hong's authority and was murdered. Shi Dakai led part of the Taiping forces in an epic southwestern trek, while Li Xiucheng defended the capital in Nanjing. By 1860, efficient Confucian leaders began pacifying the countryside and turning the tide in favor of imperial forces. The ending of the Anglo-French war (1856–1860) enabled them to benefit from western arms and western mercenaries, including " Chinese" Gordon (General Charles George Gordon [1833–1885]). In 1864, the rebellion ended with the death of Hong Xiuquan and the capture of Nanjing. Three days of slaughter took thousands of rebel lives, but none surrendered. In 1866, Taiping remnants were annihilated in Guangdong.

The main reason for the Taipings' failure was their ineffective leaders, who, despite claims to the moral high ground, were ultimately rife with corruption and decadence. Having antagonized the gentry-literati with their heretical beliefs, they lacked the bureaucratic talent to capitalize upon the amazing military strength that had threatened 16 of China's 18 provinces. Religious fanaticism also prevented full cooperation with secret society and other traditional rebels. Moreover, in the end they faced an array of opponents who, in the best Confucian tradition, won popular support and prolonged the life of the Manchu dynasty. Nevertheless, the Taiping phenomenon revealed the potential for revolution in the Chinese countryside. It also marked a new phenomenon: the mixture, albeit crude, of western and indigenous beliefs. Having rocked the foundations of the empire and sounding a message of utopian egalitarianism, the Taipings left a legacy that inspired revolutionaries of the next generation.

TAIWAN REBELLIONS Chinese revolts in Taiwan (Formosa). Neglected by the Beijing government, Chinese settlers in Taiwan staged numerous uprisings against the Manchu (Qing) dynasty (1644–1912) after it had reasserted control of the island in 1683. In 1722, rebels whose leader claimed descent from the fallen Ming dynasty (1368–1644) occupied the entire territory. Dissension in rebel ranks and Qing reinforcements from Fujian brought the insurgency to an end in 1723. The next major uprising occurred in 1786. As a result of a quarrel among Fujianese settlers, who constituted the majority of the population, one faction, which belonged to the TRIAD secret society, started a rebellion that spread to most of the island. It was finally suppressed in 1788. The rebel leaders were taken to Beijing for execution.

TAIWAN REPUBLIC Chinese opposition to Japanese occupation. In April 1895, the Shimonoseki Treaty, ending the first Sino-Japanese war (1894–1895), ceded the island of Taiwan to Japan. In an effort to resist, Chinese patriots established an independent Republic of Taiwan (Republic of Formosa) and organized a volunteer corps in May, but failed to gain wide support. Plans to secure foreign recognition also failed. The republic fell in late June after the Japanese landed, though armed resistance continued until October. The Japanese suffered only 200 deaths in combat, while several thousand died of disease.

TALAT PASHA, MEHMED (1874–1921) One of the leaders of the revolution of the YOUNG TURKS, prime minister of Turkey 1917–1918. Born into a poor family in Adrianople (Edirne), Talat studied at local schools and became chief secretary of posts and telegraphs in Salonika. Talat was active in the Young Turks movement, and after its revolt became a member of parliament for Edirne and soon minister of the interior. Together with ENVER PASHA and KEMAL PASHA, he seized the government in a coup in 1913, forming a triumvirate that governed Turkey during World War I. In 1917, he became prime minister (grand vizier). When the Ottoman Empire fell, Talat escaped to Europe. He was assassinated in 1921 in Berlin by an Armenian, as he was considered by the Armenians to be responsible for the massacre of approximately 600,000 of their number during the war.

TALEGHANI, AYATOLLAH MAHMUD (1910–1979) Iranian religious leader. Born in Taleghan near Qazvin, Taleghani studied Islamic law and theology in Qom. Considered a rather progressive and liberal cleric, he joined the struggle against the shah and was first arrested in 1939. In the early 1950s he supported MUHAMMAD MOSSADDEQ, and after the shah's and Zahedi's countercoup in 1953 he was arrested again.

In 1961, he and MEHDI BAZARGAN founded the left-of-center IRAN LIBERATION MOVEMENT, which tried to revive Mossaddeq's NATIONAL FRONT coalition in the 1960s. He was again arrested and in 1971 was exiled to southeast Iran. In 1977 he was again arrested, accused of supporting the leftist-Islamic MUJAHIDIN KHALQ militants. Released in November 1978, when Islamic resistance neared its peak, he used his contacts with the various resistance factions—Islamic-clerical, right and left, including groups like the *Mujahedin* (one of his sons was a leader of the *Mujahedin* and another reportedly was with the Marxist FEDAYAN-E KHALQ)—to forge a united revolutionary camp in anticipation of the Iranian Revolution of 1979 (see IRAN, REVOLTS AND REVOLUTIONS). Taleghani was thus instrumental in the Islamic revolution, accepting AYATOLLAH KHOMEINI's supreme leadership. He was popular among intellectuals and students, who referred to him as the "intellectuals' Ayatollah"; when Iran's Kurds rebelled, they accepted only his mediation; and because of his contacts with leftists, he was sometimes called the "Red Mullah." But he soon found himself in growing conflict with the leaders of the new Islamic Republic. He believed that it was forbidden to force the government on the people and said so. He upheld the rights of political and religious minorities, including the Communist TUDEH PARTY. While he agreed that the heads of the shah's régime should be brought to trial, he warned against taking revenge against the innocent.

He refused to sit on the Islamic court trying members of the former régime and to become a member of the Council of the Revolution. In his writings and lectures he laid down guidelines for a just Islamic order, rejecting both capitalism and communism, because they valued material gains over the individual's freedom, and seeing freedom as the most important aspect of life. Taking a moderate position between Ayatollah Khomeini and SHARIATMADARI, he accepted some intervention by the clergy in government affairs, but opposed the concentration of power in their hands.

In April 1979, after two of his sons had been arrested and tortured for their left-wing activities, Taleghani left Tehran, threatening to leave Iran altogether in protest against the return of despotism and dictatorship. After a few days he met with Khomeini and accepted a reconciliation, expressing his loyalty to him (thereby disappointing many radicals). One month before his death, he also accepted a seat in the Council of Experts, the body guiding the régime.

TALIBOV, ABDOR-RAKHIM (1834–1911) Iranian statesman, writer and revolutionary democracy ideologist. Born in Tabriz (Iranian Azerbaijan) to a craftsman's family, Talibov emigrated to Russia in 1850, where he spent most of his life. In Russia he befriended a number of members of the liberal INTELLIGENTSIA, and these exerted a great influence on the formation of his world outlook. In his books (*Akhmad's Book, Life's Problems, The Ways of the Righteous Person, Freedom's Notes*, etc.) he familiarized his Iranian readers with the scientific and sociopolitical achievements of the west. For the first time in Iran, a view was heard that despotic monarchy had become an anachronism in the era of socioeconomic development. Talibov elucidated the main principles of constitutional government and showed the necessity of the transformation of the Iranian reality in the spheres of law and parliamentary democracy.

TALLEYRAND, CHARLES MAURICE DE COMTE DE (Prince de Bébévento)

(1754–1838) "His life," declares a biographical dictionary published during the FRENCH REVOLUTION, "would be the secret history of our epoch." Born into the aristocratic Talleyrand-Pérlgord family, Talleyrand was crippled as a child, thereby forfeiting the right of inheritance. Instead he secured an office in the Church, becoming bishop of Autun in Burgundy in March 1787, a diocese he hardly ever bothered to visit. He espoused the cause of the revolution as a member of the clergy elected to the Estates General of 1789, joined hands with MIRABEAU as a champion of constitutional monarchy, celebrated mass at the notorious festival held at the CHAMP DE MARS on July 14, 1790 to mark the anniversary of the storming of the Bastille and did not resign his see until January 1791.

His major achievement during this phase of his life was to draft and assure the passage in the National Assembly of the Civil Constitution of the Clergy, which nationalized Church property and required all members of the clergy, along with all other civil servants, to swear an oath of loyalty to the revolution.

Forced into exile during the Reign of Terror, first to London and then to Philadelphia, he eventually made his way back to France in 1797, to be appointed minister of foreign affairs in the government of the DIRECTORATE. He was largely responsible for assuring JACOBIN enthusiasm for Napoleon Bonaparte's invasion of Egypt in 1798. His relations with Bonaparte were of enormous importance to both of them. Talleyrand took part in the conspiracy which brought Bonaparte to power as a result of the coup d'état of 18 Brumaire, 1799, and then served as his foreign minister under the Consulate and the Empire, until the Peace of Tilsit with Alexander of Russia in August 1807 persuaded him of the dangers of French domination of all of Europe. It was at this time that Talleyrand was alleged to have entered into secret negotiations with the czar to restrain Napoleon's ambitions and restore the balance of power in Europe.

Talleyrand played a major role in bringing about the Bourbon restoration in 1814 and represented Louis XVIII as France's foreign minister at the Congress of Vienna in 1815. There, along with Metternich and Castlereagh, he helped in his own masterful way to redraw the map of Europe according to the principle of legitimacy and the restoration of a European equilibrium, following the enormous upheavals produced by the Revolutionary and Napoleonic wars. His diplomatic skill in persuading the other European powers to accept France as an equal partner illustrates his genius as the most astute statesman of his age and has earned him the accolades of all practitioners of the art of diplomacy.

His career was by no means over, however. He was to play a prominent part in bringing Louis Philippe to the throne in the revolution of July 1830. He turned down the offer to be the July Monarchy's foreign minister. Instead, he returned to London as the French ambassador from 1830–1834, playing a major role in bringing about the independence of Belgium in 1831.

In his memoirs, Talleyrand noted that the July Monarchy was the thirteenth French government he had served in his lifetime, and he argued that he had never really conspired against any of them, since the majority of Frenchmen were in every single case his accomplices. On his deathbed in Paris on May 17, 1838, he held out both hands for the anointing, and whispered, "Do not forget that I am a bishop."

TALLIEN, JEAN LAMBERT

(1767–1820) French revolutionary leader, orator and publicist. Tallien began his career as a journalist with the FRENCH REVOLUTION's premier official newspaper, *Le Moniteur.* He was elected secretary-general of the PARIS COMMUNE, which adopted the name of "Insurrectionary Commune" as a challenge to the duly elected Paris Commune, after the latter joined hands with the capital's SANS-CULOTTES in overthrowing the monarchy following the attack on the Tuileries palace in August 1792. As a JACOBIN deputy in the Convention of 1792, Tallien distinguished himself as one of the most persistent and eloquent opponents of the GIRONDINS, leading the Jacobin-inspired purge—with the aid of the *sans-culottes*—of 50 Girondin deputies in the CONVENTION in June 1793. A grateful Convention delegated him to root out the Girondins' provincial allies in Bordeaux, the party's major stronghold in the department of the Gironde (whence their name). It was in Bordeaux that Tallien fell in love with an outlandish beauty, Mme. Térèse Cabbarus, the daughter of a rich Spanish banker. Tallien intervened to save her from the guillotine and was to save her life once again following the coup d'état of Thermidor (July) 1794.

Tallien's chief claim to fame as a revolutionary—or counter-revolutionary, depending on one's political bias—was to have struck the first blow against the Jacobin dictatorship in the coup of Thermidor. It was he who led the parliamentary attack against ROBESPIERRE in a famous debate in the Convention of 9th of Thermidor, an attack concocted the previous night at the Jacobin Club headquarters on the Rue Saint-Honoré. This led to the fall of the COMMITTEE OF PUBLIC SAFETY and the execution of Robespierre and his two accolytrés, COUTHON and Saint-Just, on the following day, thus paving the way to what is known as the Thermidorian Reaction. Along with Barère, Vadier, Fréron and other opportunist members of the Convention who feared for their lives if Robespierre was allowed to remain in power, Tallien not only succeeded in saving his neck but also went out of his way to rescue Térèse Cabbarus—incarcerated by Robespierre because of her campaign in favor of releasing political prisoners—from being sentenced to the guillotine a second time. She then decided to marry him. The demimondaine or *merveilleuse Térèse,* who presided over a notorious salon under the Directorate, earned the sobriquet, Notre-Dame de Thermidor, promoted new fashions in dress and hair styles, notably a stunning hair-do called *à la victime,* and assisted her husband in a variety of ways to emerge as a figure of national importance—the leading spokesman for the Thermidorian reaction and the editor of its major newspaper, *L'Ami des Citoyens.* Térèse became the mistress of BARRAS, the perennial Director during the four years of the Directorate and was involved in many promiscuous liaisons, including a flirtation with General Bonaparte before he impulsively proposed to Joséphine de Beauharnais on the eve of leaving for his Italian command. She divorced her husband in 1802 and finally married the Comte de Caraman and Prince de Chimay in 1805. Napoleon forbade Joséphine from visiting her.

Crippled by debt and abandoned by his wife, Tallien, although elected to the Council of the Five Hundred and still active in the inner circles of the government, decided to accompany Bonaparte to Egypt in 1798, where he was appointed editor of *La Décade egyptienne,* the first journal ever published in the Arab world on the first printing press set up in that region.

He was also appointed French commissioner to the Cairo divan, the first parliament ever elected in Islam. Expelled from Egypt by General Abdullah Menou, in 1804 he secured the sinecure of the French consulate in Alicante through the good offices of his friend TALLEYRAND, Napoleon's minister of foreign affairs. He first rallied to Louis XVIII in 1814, then to Napoleon during the Hundred Days and died in obscurity in 1820.

TAMBO, OLIVER (1917–1993) South African nationalist leader, acting president-general of the AFRICAN NATIONAL CONGRESS (1967–1991). Tambo was born into a peasant household in the Transkei. He was educated in Anglican mission schools and attended St. Peter's secondary school in Johannesburg; his missionary education was to play a role in his political life later on, particularly in his initial rejection of communism. He was awarded a scholarship to study science at Fort Hare University College, a training-ground for African leaders in South Africa and other countries. There he became involved in student politics and first met NELSON MANDELA. Tambo was expelled during a student strike in 1942 and went back to Johannesburg to teach at St. Peter's. He renewed his friendship with Mandela, who was in Johannesburg studying law; the two opened a legal partnership in 1952. Their political collaboration would turn out to be extremely fruitful, Tambo's more reflective and deliberate personality complementing Mandela's passionate approach.

Walter Sisulu encouraged Tambo, Mandela and others to become involved in the African National Congress; in 1944 they became the founding members of the ANC's youth league. So began Tambo's lifelong commitment to the ANC as an organization of revolutionary political change in South Africa. The election of Tambo and seven other youth leaguers to the ANC's national executive in 1949 saw a change in the philosophy and direction of the ANC, which then adopted the youth league's program of action calling for civil disobedience. Impressed by the popular support given to a 1950 May Day strike organized by an ad hoc group of Communists, the Indian Congress and the Transvaal ANC, Tambo's own approach expanded from a narrow African nationalism, which resisted collaboration with the South African Communist Party—at least in part because it was anti-Christian—to a broader view of uniting all oppressed peoples against the apartheid system.

Tambo became acting secretary-general of the ANC in 1954 when Sisulu was banned by the South African government and forced to resign, even though Tambo himself was restricted to two magisterial districts and prohibited from attending gatherings. He was formally elected to the post in 1955 and became deputy president-general in 1958. In 1959, his banning order expired and he and ALBERT LUTHULI, the then president-general, attempted to revitalize ANC activity. Tambo was re-banned from gatherings for an additional five years. In 1960, he left South Africa via Botswana to rouse international protest against the Sharpeville Massacre—in which 69 people were killed by government forces during an anti-pass action—and to set up external ANC offices. His departure was timely; he was in Accra, Ghana, when he heard that the ANC and a rival organization, the Pan-Africanist Congress (PAC), had both been banned.

Tambo spent the next 30 years in exile, establishing the ANC's foreign mission and engaging in fund-raising and diplomatic representations around the world. In June 1960, he organized the South African United Front, with the South African Indian Congress, the PAC and the South West African National Union, but it collapsed in 1962 because of the PAC's unwillingness to cooperate with the ANC. He also arranged training facilities in Algeria for recruits to *Umkhonto we Sizwe* (MK—Spear of the Nation), the ANC's newly-created guerrilla force. He appeared before the United Nations Special Political Committee in 1963 and the UN Security Council responded by appointing a group to examine the situation in South Africa. Also in 1963, Tanzania became the main supporter of the ANC and the center of its external organization and there Tambo began the task of rebuilding the organization from the new ANC headquarters in Morogoro.

Tambo became acting president-general of the ANC in 1967 when Luthuli died in South Africa. The next few years saw a number of policy changes, in particular the decision to allow non-Africans to join the external ANC as individuals so as to establish more formal ties with South African whites, Indians and Coloreds whose congress bodies were not in exile. Through the 1970s and 1980s, Tambo continued traveling to obtain support for the ANC and to urge foreign governments to impose economic sanctions. He was continually called upon to explain ANC policy and plans for a post-apartheid South Africa, particularly after MK stepped up its internal campaign of sabotage and began to resort to car bombings. In June 1985, the ANC called a consultative conference in Lusaka, Zambia, at which Tambo issued his famous call: "Let us act together to make all of South Africa ungovernable." He called upon MK to strengthen its links to the people, so that all could work together to inflict the maximum amount of damage. He also acknowledged the working class as the "ideological lodestar" of the liberation movement. The increased radical activity within South Africa resulted in the government declaring a state of emergency to facilitate a repressive counterattack. As the internal situation deteriorated, Tambo targeted Britain and the United States, two of the main holdouts in his ongoing campaign for international sanctions. Officials in the Reagan administration, impressed with Tambo's presentation, conceded that any viable solution to South Africa's crisis would have to involve the ANC.

Tambo and Mandela were reunited in Stockholm, Sweden, after Mandela's release from prison in 1990. At this point Tambo, who had suffered a stroke the year before, was clearly ailing and asked Mandela to assume leadership of the ANC. Mandela refused, however, and became deputy president instead. Tambo was enthusiastically welcomed back to South Africa in December 1990 and participated in the formalities of the ANC's first national conference inside South Africa in 30 years, held in Durban in 1991, in which Mandela was elected president-general of the ANC. Though Tambo lived through the beginning of the end of the apartheid system, he died before the election of the transition government took place.

TAMIL SEPARATIST MOVEMENT Movement set up in Sri Lanka in 1972 as the Tamil United Liberation Front. The Tamils, who originate from the mainland of India, constitute the largest minority in Sri Lanka (formerly Ceylon; the name of the island was changed officially in 1972). Totalling more than 3 million people, they make up 21.6% of the population. They are, however, divided fairly equally into two very distinct groups: 1) the so-called Sri Lanka Tamils, settled on the island for centuries and enjoying full citizenship; they are to be found mainly on the coastal belt; 2) the Estate Tamils, living in the center of the island on the large tea estates were they work. The latter were brought from India in the late 19th and early 20th centuries to work on these large estates. Many are still Indian nationals or stateless. This group is at the root of much of the political activity. Tension between Tamils and the Sinhalese majority grew after the island became independent in 1948. The Sinhalese blame Tamil separatism while Tamils point out an increasingly nationalist trend in Sinhalese politics. Despite efforts by the government to find a solution (granting more rights to the stateless; recognizing Tamil as a "national language" alongside Sinhalese, the official language) violence flared up in the early 1980s amidst tales of mutual atrocities. The Indian army was called in to restore peace. It remained in the island from 1987 to 1990 but no solution was found. The island is still torn by periodic terrorist attacks and reprisal raids which perpetuate the situation. In 1993, President Premadasa was assassinated by the Tamil separatists.

TANGANYIKA AFRICAN NATIONAL UNION (TANU)

(1954–1977) Nationalist movement in colonial Tanganyika, and the first political party of independent Tanzania. The Tanganyika African National Union had its early roots in the African Association, one of the earliest proponents of African unity founded in Dar es Salaam in 1929. Whereas the African Association's program had been concerned chiefly with social and economic issues, a 1946 conference in Dar es Salaam formulated the first coherent demand that Tanganyika become an independent nation, marking the introduction of national consciousness into its program.

In 1954, a new Association constitution, based on those of Britain's Labor Party and Ghana's CONVENTION PEOPLE'S PARTY, was passed under Julius Nyerere, the organization's president. The name of the organization was changed to the Tanganyika African National Union (TANU) and its aims explicitly stated. These included preparing the people of Tanganyika for independence, building a united nationalism that would cross ethnic boundaries and cooperating with other national movements for Africa's liberation. In the same year, the UN accepted the feasibility of Tanganyikan self-government and recognized TANU as a national movement.

Tanganyikan nationalism developed in the shadow of MAU MAU in Kenya and MAJI MAJI, HEHE and other rebellions in Tanganyika which had been put down so brutally that they were still very much in people's minds. The goal of Nyerere and his colleagues was to convince Tanganyikan Africans that independence could be gained non-violently; the examples of India and Nigeria were often evoked in TANU speeches. While dominated by petty-bourgeois interests, TANU successfully crossed religious, ethnic and language boundaries. The nationalist cause also benefited from the phenomenal success of the labor union movement in Tanganyika, which had organized over 40% of the wage laborers by the 1950s. At the same time, the TANU movement grew as a mass rural movement in the 1950s largely because its actions, and Julius Nyerere's increasingly populist message became more appealing to the peasants. Diversity of leadership was also a strength.

The overwhelming success of TANU in local elections led to Tanganyikan independence in December 1961, much earlier than had been expected. In 1962 Tanganyika was declared a republic and Nyerere was elected president. Nyerere's first cabinet consisted of six factions, including educated men, rural activists, urban labor chiefs and conservatives, immigrants and TANU's professionals.

In 1960, TANU's National Executive Council had already asserted its opposition to capitalism and its support for an African democratic socialism. In 1967, Nyerere's ARUSHA DECLARATION, calling for the nationalization of financial, manufacturing and trade institutions, was adopted by TANU's National Executive Committee. The declaration also advocated the adoption of the concept of "*ujamaa*," a program which gave priority to rural development in the form of communal village production units similar to those of MAO's China. Parallel to this, the party guidelines issued in 1971 attempted to eliminate capitalist management by involving workers in management decisions.

In 1977, TANU and the AFRO-SHIRAZI PARTY, the ruling party of Zanzibar, were reorganized into the *Chama Cha Mapinduzi* (the Revolutionary Party). By the 1980s, many foreign investors and international agencies had responded to the policy of nationalization by shifting their investments to Kenya and Uganda, creating an economic crisis in Tanzania that was answered by a change in policy to denationalization.

TANIA LA GUERRILLERA   see BUNKE, TAMARA.

TANU   see TANGANYIKA AFRICAN NATIONAL UNION.

TARABI, MAKHMOUD   (?–1238) The leader of the peasants' and craftsmen's revolt against the Mongol rulers and local feuds in Boukhara (Uzbekistan). Born to a craftsman's family in Tarab village near Boukhara, Tarabi's activities as a preacher who exposed and revealed the tyranny of the Mongol administration and local feuds enjoyed success among the local peasants and craftsmen. His appeals for armed struggle resulted in a widespread people's revolt. The Boukharan ruler was overthrown and Tarabi was proclaimed sultan and caliph. The Mongols, with local feudal support, came out against the rebels. Makhmoud Tarabi was killed in battle and the revolt was cruelly suppressed. Fear of a repetition of such actions resulted in a decrease in the tyranny against the peasants and craftsmen.

TCHAIKOVSKY CIRCLE   see CHAIKOVSKY CIRCLE.

TCHERNOV, VIKTOR   see CHERNOV, VIKTOR.

TCHKHEIDZE, NIKOLAY (Karlo)   (1864–1926) One of the leaders of the Georgian and Russian MENSHEVIK group, Tchkheidze participated in the constituent assembly of the first Social Democratic group in Georgia—Mesame Dasi. This organization sent him to study abroad. In 1899–1900, he headed workers' groups in Batumi (a city on the Black Sea coast of Georgia) and wrote for Georgian Menshevik newspapers. From 1907, Tchkheidze was a member of the 3rd and 4th Russian Dumas (parliaments), representing the Tbilisi province, and led the Menshevik faction in the 5th Duma. During the February RUSSIAN REVOLUTION OF 1917 he was a member of the Provisional

William Tell's bow, arrow and apple, on a Swiss postage stamp

The legendary William Tell, depicted on a Swiss postage stamp

Committee of the Duma. From February to August he served as chairman of the Petrograd Soviet of Workers' and Soldiers' Representatives. Before the October revolution, Tchkheidze returned to Georgia and the Transcaucasian Sejm elected him to be its chairman (1918). He was also the chairman of the Constituent Assembly of Georgia between 1918 and 1921. Following the establishment of Soviet rule in Georgia, Tchkheidze emigrated to France and later committed suicide.

TELL, WILLIAM (Wilhelm)   In Swiss mythology, a peasant leader who is supposed to have lived some time during the late 13th and early 14th centuries. In November 1307 he supposedly defied the Austrian governor of his native Uri and, by way of punishment, was forced to shoot an apple off his son's head; next he was arrested for threatening the governor's life, saved the life of the same governor while en route to prison, escaped and finally killed the governor. The governor's death gave the signal for a general uprising by the Swiss. Though the legend probably does not have a foundation in historical fact, it circulated widely throughout Europe before being given its final form during the first half of the 18th century. In 1804 it became the subject of a famous play, *Wilhelm Tell,* by the great German romantic author Friedrich von Schiller.

TENG CHUNG-HSIA   see DENG ZHONGXIA.

TENG HSIAO-P'ING   see DENG XIAOPING.

TENG YEN-TA   see DENG YANDA.

TEN-YEAR WAR, CUBA   (1868–1878) Attempts to overthrow the Spanish régime in Cuba were made several times prior to 1868 but they were all unsuccessful. A new revolution began on October 10, 1868, in Yara, led by Carlos Manuel Céspedes and joined by Francisco Vicente Aguilera, Máximo Gómez and Vicente García. This time the revolution spread to many sections of the country and was aided by the United States. In 1869, a new constitution providing for a republican government was adopted by a popular assembly which met in Camagüey. Céspedes was elected as the first president of Cuba. However, the revolutionists were defeated on May 11, 1873. Spanish authorities boarded the *Virginius* and arrested and killed a large group of revolutionists who had sailed from the United States to help the independence movement. In 1873, Céspedes was replaced as president by Salvador Cisneros y Betancourt. Soon after, Céspedes was killed by the Spaniards. Cisneros y Betancourt resigned because his leadership was not recognized by Vicente García. The presidency was assumed by Juan Bautista Sportono, who was soon after replaced by Tomás Estrada Palma.

The rebellion was partly eliminated by the signing of the pact of Zanjón, on February 12, 1878, but a few revolutionaries led by Antonio Maceo refused to recognize the pact and continued the fight. They were compelled to leave the island and a short-lived peace was restored. Full independence in Cuba was not obtained until 1901.

THAKIN SOE   In Burma in the 1930s, the most important native party was *Thakin*, which had sprung from an organization launched in 1929 by students at the University of Rangoon. *Thakin* split into three groups during World War II, of which two, *Thakin Soe* and *Thein Pe*, were Communist-oriented. In early 1944, a small group of *Thakin Soe* Communists joined *Thakin* nationalists to oppose the Japanese. By August, *Thakin Soe* and other resistance groups had effectively been absorbed into the Anti-Fascist People's Freedom League (AFPFL), which revolted against the Japanese occupation on March 28, 1945. The Japanese withdrawal began on May 7, 1945, leaving the AFPFL in effective control of Burma. While the AFPFL demanded immediate independence, the British insisted upon a postwar transition period, finally announcing elections in January 1947. Elected almost unanimously, the AFPFL declared complete independence on January 4, 1948.

THEBES, REVOLT AGAINST ALEXANDER THE GREAT Thebes won a short-lived hegemony in Greece after its defeat of Sparta at Leuctra in 371 B.C. Along with Athens, it played a major role in the Greek opposition to the aggrandizement of Philip II, king of Macedonia, but both were decisively defeated at Chaeroneia in 338 B.C. When, in 336 B.C., news spread that Philip had been assassinated, Thebes and several other city-states announced their intention of regaining their liberty and the repudiation of their recognition of the Macedonian hegemony.

Alexander, Philip's heir, reacted swiftly. In a very short time he took Thessaly and pitched camp near Thebes, which surrendered at once. Alexander was elected hegemon of the Greek League against Persia and refrained from taking punitive actions against Thebes. However, in 335 B.C., rumors spread that Alexander had been killed in his campaigns in the Balkans. Thebes rose once again in rebellion, supported by Persian money, and laid siege to the Cadmea, the Theban citadel which was garrisoned by Macedonian troops. Athens decided to send military help but failed to do so. When the news reached Alexander, he made his way to Thebes by forced marches. This time the Thebans did not capitulate and made the mistake of engaging the Macedonian army outside the city walls. They were routed and the city was captured. The revolt was considered an act of treachery and the Greek League decided to raze the city to the ground and to sell the entire population into slavery. Its decision was executed by Alexander.

THIRD ESTATE The bourgeois who represented their class at the convocation of the Estates General in Versailles on May 5, 1789 (the First and Second Estates represented the Church and the nobility respectively). The decision by the Third Estate to speak for the whole nation on the ground that it was the source of national sovereignty, thereby challenging the right of the two privileged estates to exist, was the starting point of the FRENCH REVOLUTION.

THIRD INTERNATIONAL see COMINTERN; INTERNATIONAL.

THREE PRINCIPLES OF THE PEOPLE (Sanmin Zhuyi) SUN YAT-SEN's political philosophy and the basis of the Chinese Nationalist Party's (GUOMINDANG—GMD) ideology. In 1924, Sun Yat-sen delivered a series of lectures expounding ideas and policies he had advocated during previous decades. His interpre-

tation of nationalism, democracy and people's livelihood (SOCIALISM) had been incorporated in the TONGMENGHUI program in 1906, but was neglected by the Guomindang after the CHINESE REPUBLICAN REVOLUTION OF 1911. According to Sun, the principles, which he equated with the French revolutionary slogan—"liberty, equality and fraternity"—and Abraham Lincoln's "of the people, by the people and for the people," represented the latest achievements of western thought and government, to which he tried to add the spirit and some of the substance of traditional Chinese institutions. A voracious reader, Sun often culled ideas from the newest literature. Changed circumstances also induced modifications, e.g., the original anti-Manchu emphasis in nationalism was replaced by anti-imperialism in 1919. Yet the essential doctrine remained intact.

While building his Canton base in 1924, when the GMD was aligned with the CHINESE COMMUNIST PARTY (CCP), Sun undertook a definitive clarification of the Three Principles under difficult circumstances. Preoccupied with political and military crises and weakened by illness, he could not devote full time to prepare and revise a coherent, systematic, exposition of his political philosophy and policies. Inconsistencies, reflecting changes in mood, would enable rival claimants to his mantle to latch onto different parts of the lectures.

The first six lectures, delivered to an audience of several thousand GMD officials, members and students at weekly meetings (January–March), were devoted to nationalism. At this time, Sun's patience with the west was wearing thin. It had consistently rejected him, and foreign gunboats were still prowling Canton waters in the aftermath of a conflict over customs receipts. Moreover, the Soviet agent, BORODIN, had been with him for several months, orchestrating a Russian aid program. The lectures thus resonated with strong anti-imperialist and pro-Soviet tones. Raising the fear of imperialist conquest, Sun warned that unless rejuvenated, the Chinese would share the fate of the Poles and Jews. However, while these other victims of conquest had at least retained the spirit of nationalism, China, he claimed, had lost it. He described China's condition as that of a "hypo-colony," victimized by all the powers rather than one. He exhorted his countrymen to awaken to the danger and revive the national spirit. By adopting western technology, as Japan had done, he was certain that China would restore its greatness. Seeing the world divided into two camps and girded for a Darwinian struggle for survival, Sun asserted that China and Russia stood together, espousing the cause of peace. After their revolution, the Russian people had "broken with the other white races" and had joined the oppressed people of Asia. Sun promised that the new China, too, would not forget its obligations to its smaller neighbors and would protect them from imperialism.

The six lectures on democracy (March–April) combined traditional Chinese elitism with specific western political devices. Comparing the Chinese to a "sheet of sand," Sun claimed that, unlike Europeans, the Chinese had too much personal liberty. He was unimpressed by the record of the western parliamentary democracies, for they had "progressed less rapidly than autocratic states like Germany and Japan." Sovereignty, he asserted, belonged to all the people, but the government should be managed by specialists—"men of ability and skill." His solution was to guarantee the people power through the rights of suffrage, recall, initiative and referendum—as practiced in Switzerland and some American municipalities—and to organize government according to the "five-power" constitution, which combined the American three-fold separation of powers with two traditional Chinese institutions—the censorate and an examination authority (see SUN YAT-SEN).

In August, Sun resumed lecturing, but military affairs distracted him from completing the series on people's livelihood (a translation of the classical term, "*minsheng*," which he often equated with socialism). The four lectures he delivered were sufficient to dispel the notion that Sun had been converted to MARXISM. Responding to the growing appeal of Marxism to Chinese students, he not only argued that Marxism was inapplicable in China, but repudiated Marxist theory. A book he had recently read, *The Social Interpretation of History*, by Dr. Maurice William, a New York dentist, supplied arguments against the class struggle and surplus value concepts. William's thesis, that social rather than economic forces supplied the driving force of history, meshed with his own ideas, which stressed reconciliation, not struggle, and voluntarism, not determinism. Sun advocated a moderate form of socialism. Expressing concern over the problems of rural tenancy, he hoped that "each tiller of the soil will possess his own field." He believed that pre-industrialized China did not suffer from extreme inequality and proposed preventive measures that would obviate the need for social revolution later. What he called "equalization of land rights" was inspired by the ideas of Henry George (single tax) and John Stuart Mill. The government, according to this plan, would tax what Mill had termed the "future unearned increment increase" of land values, i.e., increases not resulting from landowners' efforts, but from the general growth and development of society. This was designed to prevent the land speculation that had earned easy fortunes in the west. In addition, Sun advocated public ownership of utilities and large industries. Despite his earlier strictures against imperialism, Sun had no fear of foreign capital as long as it was borrowed on terms negotiated by a united and sovereign China. He wanted investment capital and technical expertise from the industrialized west, according to the plan advanced in his *International Development of China*. He repeated the hope expressed in that plan, that foreign capital would build a "future Communist society in China." In this context, communism owed more to the Confucian vision of the Great Commonwealth or Great Harmony than Marxism-Leninism.

Though hastily prepared and marred by inconsistencies and needless digressions, the lectures gave a substantially accurate view of Sun's ideas, especially during the time they were delivered. The Three Principles—nationalism, democracy, socialism—reflect his overriding concern for China's modernization. As the GMD bible, it has served it well in Taiwan since 1949.

THROCKMORTON PLOT   (1583) The Roman Catholic Francis Throckmorton (1554–1584) was the go-between for Mary, Queen of Scots and her agent, and under torture revealed that a plot was afoot to place her on the throne of England. The plan was for the French Duke of Guise to command an invasion force sent from the Netherlands, aided by English Catholics when they arrived ashore. Throckmorton was executed and the Spanish ambassador, Mendoza, was deported.

TIAN DI HUI   see TRIAD SOCIETY.

TIBERIUS SEMPRONIUS   see GRACCHUS, TIBERIUS.

TIBETAN REBELLION   (1959) Disintegrating as an organized state in the 9th century, Tibet came under nominal Chinese control in the early 18th century but broke away after the CHINESE REPUBLICAN REVOLUTION OF 1911 overthrew the Manchu (Qing) dynasty (1644–1912). In October 1950, the PEOPLE'S LIBERATION ARMY (PLA) of the People's Republic of China (PRC) invaded Tibet and reasserted Chinese control in a year-long campaign of subjugation. The Tibetans, who have the strongest separatist tradition and best claim to national independence among non-Chinese minorities, staged armed uprisings in the 1950s against Chinese authority, especially after 1956 when the PRC stepped up its socialist revolution. The Tibetans feared that their way of life, dominated by Lamaism (Tibetan Buddhism), was threatened by Sinicization. Revolts among the warlike Khambas and Goloks in eastern Tibet were followed in March 1959 by an uprising in the capital city of Lhasa. The 14th Dalai Lama, the Tibetan temporal and spiritual leader, fled to India. Chinese repression was harsh and led to Tibetan charges of genocide. Tibet was granted autonomy in 1965, but suffered during the Cultural Revolution of 1966–1976 (see GREAT PROLETARIAN CULTURAL REVOLUTION), when most Buddhist monasteries were destroyed and monks were returned to lay life. Because of its contiguity with India, China considers Tibet a particularly sensitive region.

The Dalai Lama (sixth from left) with Tibetan guerrillas, 1959

TIGRE PEOPLE'S LIBERATION FRONT (TPLF) Founded in 1975 as a Marxist organization calling for self-determination for the province of Tigre, just south of Eritrea, the TPLF came to prominence in 1977 when the ERITREAN PEOPLE'S LIBERATION FRONT (EPLF) decided to arm and train it.

The TPLF became increasingly left-wing, setting up the Marxist-Leninist League of Tigre in the mid-1980s. It engaged in guerrilla warfare against the government and by 1989 had succeeded in taking control of Tigre province. The TPLF also founded the Ethiopian People's Revolutionary Democratic Front (EPRDF) as an alliance of insurgent groups seeking regional autonomy, and engaged in armed struggle against the Ethiopian Democratic Unity Party (EDUP) government of President MENGISTU.

The alliance comprised: 1) The Ethiopian People's Democratic Movement (EPDM) representing the interests of the Amhara people; 2) the Oromo People's Democratic Organization, founded by the TPLF to promote its cause in Oromo areas; and 3) the TPLF itself, the dominant organization within the alliance. Its original demands for self-determination were replaced by a demand for the removal of Mengistu and the establishment of a democratic government in Addis Ababa.

In May 1991, the TPLF under its leader, Meles Zenawi, took control of Ethiopia's capital, Addis Ababa, and formed a transitional government with the other organizations. In January 1991, following the revolutionary changes in Eastern Europe, the EPRDF produced a new political program which did not mention MARXISM and was moderate and democratic. The EPRDF advocated national self-determination for Ethiopia's different ethnic groups and a federal form of government. It won a majority in elections held in 1993.

TIKHOMIROV, LEV   (1852–1923) Russian populist (see POPULISM) turned conservative. An early member of the populist INTELLIGENTSIA, Tikhomirov participated in the CHAIKOVSKY CIRCLE and in 1873 was arrested and tried with the "193" in 1877–1878. He later collaborated with PETER LAVROV and was among those who set up the PEOPLE'S WILL movement.

In the aftermath of the assassination of Czar Alexander II, Tikhomirov underwent a crisis of conscience. He first wrote the czar a letter of allegiance promising that his movement would abstain from terror in return for a constitutional régime and then became an ideologist of conservative monarchism, seeking to integrate the teachings of the Russian Orthodox church into social and political reform in a Russian Christian Democratic theory. In 1905, he published his treatise *Monarchical Statehood* (*Monarkhicheskaia gosudarstvennost*). He advocated support for the "police socialism" of the Zubatov movement, supported the legitimacy of trade unions and later offered counsel to Prime Minister Stolypin on social reform. After the BOLSHEVIK seizure of power in October 1917, he took no part in politics but remained in Russia, dying in the monastery town of Zagorsk.

TIMOLEON   (?–c. 341 B.C.) Corinthian statesman and general who sought to overthrow the tyrants of the Greek cities of Sicily and to fight against the rule of Carthage in the island. In 344 B.C., Timoleon liberated Syracuse and sent the tyrant Dionysius II away to Corinth. Thereafter he succeeded in abolishing the rule of tyrants in other cities and won a decisive victory over the Carthaginians in 341 B.C. He also carried out successful measures of reconstruction, thus reviving the prosperity of the old Greek cities in Sicily. He spent his last years in Syracuse, where he died c. 334 B.C.

TITO (Josip Broz)   (1892–1980) Yugoslav leader, born Josip Broz. Broz was one of 15 children of peasants living near Zagreb in Croatia. Living conditions were harsh and food was frequently in short supply, although the family was in fact well off

in relation to many other peasants, since it owned a garden as well as 10 acres of land.

At 14 Broz left home to work as a waiter but was then offered an apprenticeship by a locksmith and quickly learned the trade. He found employment in several German cities as well as within the Austro-Hungarian Empire. From an early age he was a firm believer in SOCIALISM and was actively involved in promoting metal workers' trade unions and the Social Democratic Party.

In 1915, Broz overcame his ideological objections to World War I and served on the Russian front, winning a medal. Badly wounded, he was taken prisoner and held in Russia until 1920. Thus he was present during the heady days of the revolution and returned to Yugoslavia with a Russian wife and a strong Communist commitment.

During the 1920s and 1930s, Broz lived in straitened circumstances; two of his children died as he struggled to make a livelihood. He reached a high position in the Yugoslav Communist Party and became a constant irritant to the authorities. In 1928, after one dramatic escape from the police, he was caught red-handed with bomb-making equipment.

Deprived of sleep and beaten under police interrogation, he nonetheless made a defiant stand in court, refusing to acknowledge any authority apart from the Communist Party. His belligerence brought him to public attention but also earned him a six-year prison sentence.

Upon his release, Broz resumed promoting the growth of Yugoslavian communism. He traveled abroad frequently, and from 1935 to 1937 lived in Moscow, receiving training in Communist theory and leadership. The illegal nature of his activities within Yugoslavia led to him adopting a variety of disguises and false names—"Tito" was the name by which he became best known.

By the time of the German invasion in 1941, Tito had been chosen as Communist Party general secretary. He organized and led a ferocious partisan war against the German invaders and their Yugoslav collaborators. The struggle was bitter and merciless; several times Tito and his men were surrounded and fought their way out of German encirclement. By 1942, Tito's partisans were down to three bullets per man. As they waited for Russian supplies that never materialized, they were forced to eat their horses for food and Tito fled to an island off the Yugoslav coast.

Winston Churchill, however, concluded that Tito was an effective ally against the Nazis and was willing to set aside political differences to help him. Supplies sent to Tito's men by Allied forces gave them the means to carry on fighting, and they succeeded in liberating the country without the aid of foreign troops, founding a new Communist state in the process.

Tito had the distinction of being one of the few postwar European Communist leaders with a strong popular power base. This was confirmed by his victory in elections in 1946 and the deposing of the country's King Peter II.

The shooting down of two US planes by Yugoslav planes and support for Communist subversion in Greece led to the withdrawal of American aid in 1947. Tito turned to his natural ally, the Soviet Union, for assistance, but here also there were strings attached. JOSEPH STALIN wanted Tito to follow other East European leaders by making his country subservient to Russia's strategic needs, but Tito's independent nationalistic spirit led him to seek to develop the Yugoslav industry and to provide leadership in the Communist world himself. This was intolerable to Stalin, and in 1948 Yugoslavia was expelled from Cominform (the International Communist Organization) for "capitalist leanings." Despite a Russian trade boycott and threats of force, Tito remained resolute.

In 1955, the Soviet leader NIKITA KHRUSHCHEV visited Yugoslavia and a reconciliation of sorts was affected, but it was short-lived; Tito's criticism of Soviet actions in Hungary in 1956 and of Czechoslovakia in 1968 embittered relations once again. Now the Yugoslav president, Tito oversaw increasing liberalization within the state-planned economy. His 1959 tour of African and Asian countries marked his emergence as a leader of the non-aligned nations.

With his reputation as a womanizer, his liking for fine food and drink, expensive clothes and gaudy diamond rings, Tito remained until his death in 1980 the most non-conformist of Communist heads of state. His strong personality dominated Yugoslav politics to the exclusion of a viable alternative leadership, and the Yugoslav state did not long survive his demise.

TKACHEV, PETER   (1844–1885) Russian populist JACOBIN. Tkachev's first arrest came in 1861 when, as a newly enrolled student in St. Petersburg University, he was active in student protests. Many years later he earned a law degree extramurally. As a journalist, he contributed to populist (see POPULISM) publications, gaining something of a reputation in this field. At the same time he collaborated with SERGEI NECHAEV in leading St. Petersburg student protests. For this, he was rearrested in 1869 and only freed from prison in 1873.

Emigrating to Switzerland, he collaborated with PETER LAVROV, quickly quarrelled with the latter's preaching of political gradualism and joined a group of Russian and Polish Jacobins espousing the theories of LOUIS AUGUSTE BLANQUI regarding revolution by a tightly-organized clique of conspirators who would lead society in the seizure of power and then transform it by REVOLUTION FROM ABOVE. During this period (1875–1878), characterized in the revolutionary movement by disappointment with the failure of the TO THE PEOPLE movement, he publicized his theories in *Nabat* (*The alarm bell*), evoking counter-polemics written by leading European socialists such as FRIEDRICH ENGELS as well as by Russian populist ideologists. Both groups of critics objected to Tkachev's rejection of a class-based revolution. His theories of destroying autocratic power by "a single bold stroke at the center" influenced the PEOPLE'S WILL and other populist terrorists. Tkachev remained in exile, collaborating with Blanqui in publication of his newspaper. He was stricken by insanity in 1882 and spent his final years in a Paris asylum.

TOGLIATTI, PALMIRO   (1893–1964) Italian Communist leader. A lawyer who helped found the Communist Party in Italy in 1921, Togliatti spent most of the interwar period in Moscow and during the SPANISH CIVIL WAR served as head of the COMINTERN. In 1944 he returned to Italy and resumed leadership of the party, joining the government in 1944–1945 but later leading the opposition. After the death of STALIN in 1953, he began to diverge from the Soviet line and after KHRUSHCHEV's secret speech (1956) declared the right of Communist parties to pursue their own paths to SOCIALISM.

TONGMENGHUI (TMH—Revolutionary Alliance)   Chinese revolutionary organization. Founded in Tokyo in 1905 through a merger of XING ZHONG HUI, HUA XING HUI and GUANG FU HUI, the TMH became a major vehicle for subversive activity that helped precipitate the CHINESE REPUBLICAN REVOLUTION OF 1911. In terms of structure, ideology and geographical scope, it was the first Chinese organization to resemble a modern-type political party. It was formed after the three separate organizations, based in different regions of China, had failed in attempted plots against the Manchu (Qing) dynasty (1644–1912). Tokyo, hosting thousands of Chinese students as well as a number of leading anti-Manchu dissidents, was a convenient venue for launching a multi-provincial anti-dynastic movement. SUN YAT-SEN was chosen as leader (*zongli*). He was the senior and most famous anti-Manchu revolutionary, experienced in activating secret society fighters and in raising funds among the overseas Chinese (*huaqiao*). Endorsement by Japanese revolutionary sympathizers enhanced his prestige and he was able to allay fears that foreigners would intervene on behalf of the Manchu dynasty.

In 1905–1906, the TMH enlisted about 1,000 members, mostly students in Tokyo. On the eve of the 1911 Revolution it had close to 10,000 members, including 3,000 intellectuals, of whom several hundred constituted the party's activist nucleus. Eight Japanese also joined, among them Sun's confidant, Miyazaki Torazo (1870–1922). Formally organized into executive, legislative and judicial departments (paralleling the three branches of the American government), the TMH had its headquarters in Tokyo. Branches were later established among *huaqiao* and other overseas student communities in Hong Kong, Saigon, Singapore, Kuala Lumpur, Penang, Hanoi, Rangoon, Bangkok, the United States, Canada, Hawaii, Paris, Berlin, Brussels and Manila. Hong Kong, the regional center for south China, was the site of the most important branch until the summer of 1911, when Shanghai became the central China regional headquarters. The formal, hierarchical format was never fully enforced, and regional loyalties persisted. On the eve of the 1911 Revolution, Sun's leadership was eclipsed by Hunan-Hubei activists who resented his focus on Guangdong.

Palmiro Togliatti after an attempt on his life, 1948

During 1905–1907, the TMH organ, *Min Bao* (*People's report*), engaged in a propaganda battle with *Xin Min Cong Bao* (*New people's miscellany*) edited by Liang Qichao, modern China's foremost publicist. Liang and his mentor, Kang Youwei, led the *Bao Huang Hui* (Protect the Emperor Association), which advocated a constitutional monarchy under the Manchu dynasty. Despite their differences, both journals were instrumental in infusing modern ideas among students and intellectuals, though *Min Bao* was more in tune with prevailing radical sentiments. Largely Sun's handiwork, the TMH program, as formulated in 1906, was based upon his THREE PRINCIPLES OF THE PEOPLE (nationalism, democracy and SOCIALISM), but was not fully endorsed by all his comrades. Anti-Manchuism and fear of imperialism provided the broadest common themes. Sun's other contributions included the "five-power" constitution (the American three-fold separation of governmental powers plus censorial and examination institutions adapted from traditional China) and the three-stage plan for attainment of constitutional government (three years of military rule after the revolution; six years of martial law under a provisional constitution that would encourage development of self-governing institutions; and finally, promulgation of a constitution and popular elections).

Chosen more for his reputed conspiratorial skills than his ideological authority, Sun's leadership was weakened when his various anti-dynastic plots failed. After Sun was forced to leave Japan in 1907, the TMH made six attempts (1907–1908) from Hanoi, and two based in Hong Kong and aimed at Canton (1910, 1911). HUANG XING, the most prominent TMH leader after Sun, led the actual fighting while Sun concentrated on fund-raising and tried to enlist foreign support. The Wuchang uprising of October 10, which erupted into a nationwide revolution, was not started by the TMH, but its various activities during the previous six years had accelerated the erosion of governmental authority. Yet, the TMH lacked sufficient cohesiveness to assume power on its own. Above all, Sun and his colleagues preferred a negotiated surrender of the Manchu dynasty through the mediation of Yuan Shikai rather than the prospect of a prolonged civil war that could invite foreign intervention. Having achieved its immediate aim—the overthrow of the dynasty— and having ostensibly replaced the monarchical with a republican system of government, the TMH became an open political party, the GUOMINDANG (Nationalist Party), in August 1912.

TO THE PEOPLE (Khozhdenie k Narodu)   (1874) A populist movement of students and young INTELLIGENTSIA who participated in radical study groups, read and discussed SOCIALISM

The hanging of To The People's terrorists after their assassination of Czar Alexander II in 1881

and anarchism and, in the summer of 1874, went to the villages of Russia in an attempt to waken the Russian peasants to socialist revolution. Some 2,000 to 3,000 young people participated in this operation and some 700 were arrested, many of them denounced by the peasants they had come to "liberate." The arrests eventually led to the "Trial of the 193," in which severe sentences of prison and exile were handed out to the defendants who had been in detention for three years while the trial was prepared. The brutality of the régime, in contrast to the naive youth of the defendants, aroused tremendous public opinion against the trial, both in Russia and internationally. Among those tried were many of the subsequent leaders of both the populist and Marxist revolutionary groups in Russia.

The expedition of these young radical idealists was based on a dual concept. On the one hand, they were going to assist the peasant in bettering his life, by working in the villages as medical personnel, teachers, skilled artisans, etc. At the same time, they hoped to study and invigorate the communal and cooperative elements of Russian village life and to evolve a practical agrarian socialist society. The background of these urban radicals was so far removed from the peasants that little understanding was achieved. The students' attacks on the autocracy and on religion evoked rejection not only by the village clergy, whose values and status were threatened by the young rebels, but by many of the peasants, who were devout believers and loyal subjects of the czar.

In the populist movement, the failure of To The People led to a radicalization in the direction of terror, as well as to a new interest in seeking the social core of revolution among urban workers rather than in the villages.

TOULON, SIEGE OF   The recapture of the Mediterranean port of Toulon from an Anglo-Spanish force in December 1793 by a young Corsican artillery captain named Napoleon Bonaparte changed the military fortunes of the FRENCH REVOLUTION and marked the beginning of Napoleon's meteoric career. The great naval base of Toulon had revolted against the JACOBIN dictatorship of Paris and its royalist citizens had handed it over to the English on April 27, 1793. The revolt was part of large-scale federalist and GIRONDIN insurrection spreading all the way from Brittany and the Vendee to Lyons and Marseilles, which undermined the national war effort against the First Coalition. Although a British landing at Quiberon in Brittany had been repelled, the British had succeeded in establishing a firm hold in Toulon and made it seemingly impregnable by fortifying Le Fort Carre from the sea. The recapture of this fort, nicknamed "Little Gibraltar" by Bonaparte, who had conceived and executed the plan of attack, put the British squadron to flight and earned him a promotion to brigadier general following the death of his commanding officer, General Dugommier. His military career under the revolution was henceforth assured and reached a blaze of glory in the Italian campaign that he concluded with the triumphant Peace of Campo Formio in 1797. It was from Toulon that Napoleon sailed on his Egyptian expedition in May 1798.

TOURÉ, SÉKOU AHMED   (1922–1984) Politically active trade unionist before GUINEAN INDEPENDENCE in 1958, strongly influenced by KWAME NKRUMAH. Touré persuaded Guineans of the

need to follow Kwame Nkrumah's example of immediate and assertive African independence. As a result, in the 1958 referendum organized by the French President de Gaulle, Guinea was the only French colony to vote *non* to the proposal to associate with the French community. On Guinea's abrupt accession to independence on October 2, 1958, Touré became president.

Touré was secretary-general and later vice-president of the *Parti Démocratique de Guinée* (PDG), which was constitutionally established on November 10, 1958 as the country's only political party.

On independence, Guinea became one of the most militant countries in Africa and had an important influence on African unity movements. Touré pursued a policy of socialist revolution and any opposition was ruthlessly suppressed. Under him, Guinea's human rights record was very poor and thousands of Guineans went into exile abroad. Toure remained president of Guinea (and the PDG the sole political party permitted to operate), until his sudden death on March 26, 1984 of heart failure.

TOUSSAINT-L'OUVERTURE, FRANÇOIS-DOMINIQUE (1743–1803) Leader of the slave revolt in Haiti. Born to an African slave in Haiti, as a boy Toussaint showed remarkable intellect, learning some French and Latin (although he preferred to speak the local patois, Creole), and mathematics. Unlike other slaves, who adhered to mystic voodoo rites, Toussaint was an ardent Catholic. His fellow slaves revered him for his ability as a leader, but his true fascination was with military history, which he read as a child. His owner, the aristocratic de Noe family, recognized the young slave's potential and appointed him steward, and he was granted his freedom in 1777.

When the Haitian revolt broke out in 1791, Toussaint expressed his gratitude to the de Noes by helping the family escape to America. He then joined the slaves in their struggle for emancipation, convincing them of this own belief that he had been chosen by God to liberate the black and mulatto slaves of Haiti. An opportunity to prove himself came in 1794 when Spain, in possession of the eastern half of the island of Hispaniola (today Haiti and the Dominican Republic), invaded the French section. Toussaint led 9,000 of his followers in support of the Spanish and engaged in several successful encounters with the French. His remarkable victories earned him the epithet *L'Ouverture* (The Opening), as he was always able to break through French positions. Toussaint was not, however, an advocate of Spanish hegemony; the condition of black slaves in Spanish Santo Domingo was no better than on the French half of the island. Toussaint supported Spain for military motives; the ill-trained Haitian forces had a better chance to defeat reduced French forces. Once the French were sufficiently disabled, Toussaint abandoned the Spanish troops and their invasion collapsed.

Following the FRENCH REVOLUTION of 1789, slavery was abolished by the local French republicans (1793), of whom Toussaint was the acknowledged leader. The British attempted to take advantage of the uncertain turn of events by invading the island. Toussaint, now promoted to the rank of brigadier general, attacked the British and forced their withdrawal in 1798. He was promoted to the rank of major general and appointed lieutenant governor of the island for his supposed victory; in fact, a yellow fever epidemic had forced the British evacuation.

With foreign threats suppressed, racial tensions on the island flared. Léger Félicité Sonthonax, a Frenchman and radical republican stationed on the island, urged Toussaint to massacre the white inhabitants, but Toussaint recognized the value of the whites to the future development of the island and encouraged emigrés to return. The true focus of hostilities was between blacks, led by Toussaint, and mulattoes, led by André Rigaud. Toussaint appealed successfully for American military and economic aid to fight the French-backed mulattoes and defeated them in 1800. Toussaint was now recognized as the most powerful individual in the colony. The "First of the Blacks," as Toussaint was now called, received a lifetime appointment as governor general.

In 1801 Toussaint invaded Spanish Santo Domingo to liberate the slaves, and his successful campaign made him the de facto ruler of the entire island. He was a fair and competent leader who encouraged economic growth and hindered any attempts at dividing the inhabitants along racial lines. He abhorred atrocities, such as those committed during the island's lengthy wars, and had all perpetrators executed.

While Haiti flourished, France was coming under the influence of Napoleon Bonaparte, who wanted to reintroduce slavery. Troops, commanded by Napoleon's brother-in-law General Charles Leclerc, were sent to restore French rule on the island. Even as competent a general as Leclerc, however, was unable to defeat the wily rebel leader, while a yellow fever epidemic threatened Leclerc's own men.

Forgoing a military victory, Leclerc invited Toussaint to discuss the island's future, promising to renounce slavery if the rebels would lay down their arms. Toussaint agreed to attend the meeting, not suspecting that it was a trap, and was arrested, imprisoned and shipped to the French Alps. He died in captivity in 1803, but the revolutionary fervor he had ignited did not die. His legacy was carried on by his former partners-in-arms, Jean-Jacques Dessalines and HENRI CHRISTOPHE. Haiti achieved independence in 1804.

TPLF see TIGRE PEOPLE'S LIBERATION FRONT.

TRAORE, MOUSSA (1936–) Mali officer, politician and revolutionary leader. Traore received his military training in France and joined the army, being commissioned a lieutenant in 1964. On November 19, 1968, he led a group of young officers who staged a successful coup against the socialist government of Modibo Keita (see MALI, COUP).

As president, Traore abrogated the constitution and banned all political parties. In the elections of June 1979 he, as the sole candidate, received 99% of the vote. This led to the establishment of a Military Committee of National Liberation as the country's government. During the 1980s, his régime sought to dismantle Mali's socialist structure and strove to encourage foreign investment.

During the same period though, the pro-democracy forces gathered momentum. Pro-democracy demonstrations in March 1991 were harshly suppressed, but on March 26, 1991 Traore was ousted by an army coup. Arrested and put on trial along with 32 of his associates, he was condemned to death in February 1993 for "premeditated murder, battery and voluntary manslaughter," as well as for "economic crimes" such as embez-

zlement. At the time of writing, the sentence had not yet be carried out and Traore was still in jail.

TRIAD SOCIETY Chinese secret society. Under various names, e.g., (San Dian Hui—Three Dot Society; Hong Men—Hong Gate; Tian Di Hui—Heaven and Earth Society), the Triad society was influential in southern China, especially in the Guangdong and Fujian provinces. According to the traditional, but unsubstantiated, account, it originated in the Buddhist monastery of Shaolin in Fujian in 1674. It is known that the society became active in the late 17th century and was originally dedicated to the overthrowing of the Qing (Manchu) dynasty (1644–1912) and the restoration of the Ming dynasty (1368–1644). However, despite ritualistic fidelity to Ming restorationism, the Triads usually engaged in the fraternal, sometimes illegal, activities that characterized other secret societies. In the 19th century they drew the attention of Dutch and British colonial officials in Southeast Asia, where many Chinese from Guangdong and Fujian had settled. As a blood-brotherhood whose members were sworn to secrecy, the Triads became vehicles for revolt when the Qing dynasty began to decline. They were responsible for the TAIWAN REBELLION in the 1780s and were increasingly active in the 19th century. Organized as separate lodges, the Triads lacked a centralized organization and could not sustain a nationwide revolt. One such lodge, known as the SMALL SWORD SOCIETY, took over the Chinese city of Shanghai during the TAIPING REBELLION. SUN YAT-SEN, who worked with Triads in his early career, joined the Hawaiian lodge in 1904. In recent years, Triads have engaged in criminal activities abroad.

TROTSKY, LEON (Lev Davidovich Bronstein) (1879–1940) Russian revolutionary. Trotsky was born to a wealthy Jewish farming family in the village of Yanovka, near Bobrinetz in southern Ukraine, and at the age of nine was sent to school in Odessa. An excellent student, he became involved with revolutionary groups and interested in MARXISM. In the revolutionary fervor that erupted in 1896, he helped form the South Russian Workers Union. Arrested in 1898, Trotsky was imprisoned for two years until his trial and sentenced to four years of exile in Siberia. In 1902 he managed to escape and made his way to London, where he joined VLADIMIR LENIN in editing the Social Democratic journal, Iskra. He moved to Geneva the following year when the journal's offices were transferred there.

After the split in the Russian Social Democratic Labor Party in 1903, Trotsky for a time supported the MENSHEVIK Party and then wavered between the Mensheviks and the BOLSHEVIK PARTY. BLOODY SUNDAY, the St. Petersburg workers' march in 1905, brought Trotsky back to Russia. He helped to form the city's soviet (Council of Workers' Deputies), shaping most of its decisions. He also founded a revolutionary organ, entitled Nachalo (Beginning).

In 1907, after the abortive RUSSIAN REVOLUTION OF 1905, he was sentenced again to Siberian exile for an unspecified period of time. However, on the way there he managed to escape. Making part of the return journey on deer-back through blizzards, he doubled back to St. Petersburg, where he, his wife Sedova and their two sons took the train for Finland. He then traveled to London for the party congress that was being held there that year, and on to Berlin. As a journalist and by writing a book on

The most brilliant of the Soviet Communist revolutionaries, Trotsky ended up murdered by Stalin

---

TROTSKY'S TESTAMENT

● For forty-three years of my conscious life I have remained a revolutionary; for forty-two of them I have fought under the banner of Marxism. If I had to begin all over again I would of course try to avoid this or that mistake, but the main course of my life would remain unchanged. I shall die a proletarian revolutionary, a Marxist, a dialectical materialist, and consequently, an irreconcilable atheist. My faith in the communist future of mankind is not less ardent, indeed it is firmer today, than it was in the days of my youth.

● Natasha has just come up to the window from the courtyard and opened it wider so that the air may enter more freely into my room. I can see the bright green strip of grass beneath the wall, and the clear blue sky above the wall, and sunlight everywhere. Life is beautiful. Let the future generations cleanse it of all evil, oppression, and violence and enjoy it to the full.

German social democracy, he was able to support himself while continuing to formulate his theories and to attend socialist congresses throughout Europe. In 1908 he also began publishing a Russian language paper, *Pravda.*

In 1912, Trotsky was sent by a radical Kiev paper to cover the Balkan war, eventually traveling to the United States in January 1917. News of the Bolshevik revolution soon broke out and Trotsky sailed for Russia; the family was feted on arrival in Petrograd (the new name given to St. Petersburg in 1914).

After a tumultuous few months, Trotsky was arrested by ALEKSANDER KERENSKY, leader of the Russian Liberal government, only to be made head of the Petrograd Soviet after his release. Trotsky abandoned his theories to become one of Lenin's "lieutenants," playing a key supporting role in directing the armed uprising in the October Russian Revolution of 1917 and its aftermath—the civil war.

Lenin offered him a central position in his new government, but Trotsky's sensitivity to his Jewish origins led him to take the post of minister for foreign affairs. Sent to Brest-Litovsk, he signed an ignominious treaty of peace with the Germans at Lenin's insistence. He was next appointed commissar for military affairs in 1918, organizing the RED ARMY and steering it to victory.

In the following years, he came into frequent conflict with another close lieutenant of Lenin, JOSEPH STALIN. After Lenin's death in 1924, Stalin maneuvered Trotsky out of a central role, while he himself eventually became sole ruler. Trotsky continued to advocate world revolution; Stalin's policy, on the other hand, was to concentrate on establishing SOCIALISM IN ONE COUNTRY. Subsequently, in 1927, Trotsky was forced out of the party.

Expelled from the USSR in 1929 after a year of exile in Turkistan, Trotsky began another period of wandering in Turkey, France and Norway. In 1936, he and his wife sailed to Mexico, where he had been offered asylum.

In Mexico City, Trotsky resumed writing, including an unfinished work on Stalin and a treatise on revolutionary art with André Breton and Diego Rivera. He founded the Fourth INTERNATIONAL, a group devoted to pure communism, and continued to be a vociferous opponent of Stalin. Several Stalin-directed attacks were made on his life before a Spanish Communist armed with an ice pick succeeded in killing him in his home. Among the writings that Trotsky published over the years are *The Defense of Terrorism* (1921), *Literature and Revolution* (1925) and *My Life* (1930).

TS'AI AO   see CAI AO.

TS'AI HO-SEN   see CAI HESEN.

TS'AI T'ING-K'AI   see CAI TINGKAI.

TS'AI YUAN-P'EI   see CAI YUANPEI.

TSERETELI, IRAKLI   (1882–1959) One of the leaders of the Georgian and Russian MENSHEVIKS. In 1902, Tsereteli was exiled to eastern Siberia for participation in the movement of Russian students. After returning from exile, he edited the Menshevik journal, *Kvali,* and was the leader of the Social Democratic fraction in the 2nd Duma (parliament). Following the 1907 crackdown on the Duma, Tsereteli was sentenced to a prison term. The February RUSSIAN REVOLUTION OF 1917 brought about his release. Tsereteli returned to Petrograd and regained his leading position in the Menshevik Party. He held the post of the minister of post and telegraphs and later became minister of internal affairs in the provisional government. After the October Russian Revolution of 1917, Tsereteli led the anti-BOLSHEVIK fraction in the Constituent Assembly, but soon returned to Georgia to be elected to the Constituent Assembly of independent Georgia (1918–1921). Following the establishment of Soviet rule in Georgia, Tsereteli emigrated to France and later moved to the USA, where he continued his anti-Bolshevik struggle.

TSKHAKAIA, MIKHAIL   (1865–1950) Georgian revolutionary and statesman. Tskhakaia joined the revolutionary movement in 1886. He was one of the founders of the first Marxist organization—*Mesame Dasi*—in Georgia. In 1898–1900 he participated in the formation of the Ekaterinoslav (now Dnepropetrovsk) Committee of the Russian Social Democratic Workers Party (RSDWP). As a result of his activities, he spent 1900–1902 in prison. After his release, Tskhakaia was one of the leaders of the RSDWP Caucasian Union. In 1905, he opened the 3rd congress of the RSDWP and delivered a speech along with LENIN. During the RUSSIAN REVOLUTION OF 1905, he was involved in organizational activities in the St. Petersburg, Tbilisi and Baku committees. In 1907, he was forced to emigrate. In 1917, Tskhakaia returned from exile with Lenin. In 1917–1920 he led the RSDWP Caucasian Regional Committee. In 1919, the government of independent Georgia arrested him for his anti-national activity. In 1920, Tskhakaia became a member of the executive committee of the Communist International (see COMINTERN). After the establishment of Soviet rule in Georgia, he held various posts in Tbilisi and Moscow.

TSOU JUNG   see ZOU RONG.

TUDEH PARTY   An Iranian revolutionary party founded in September 1941, in the period of the upsurge of the democratic movement. The party program, adopted at its first congress, proclaimed its main aims: the liquidation of foreign monopolies; the realization of democratic reforms; freedom of speech, meetings and the press; an eight-hour work day; and adoption of a law in connection with handing over the land for the free use of peasants. Late in World War II the Tudeh Party became a popular political organization, with more than 100,000 members. In 1949, Shah Pahlavi's régime declared its activities unlawful. The Tudeh newspapers were closed and the party was compelled to go underground.

In the mid-1960s, the Tudeh split into two factions, one pro-Russian and the other pro-Chinese. The pro-Russian faction was the more moderate toward the government, mainly because of improved Iranian-Russian relations. Although it accused the shah of an anti-democratic approach, it opposed extremist movements and all terrorist and guerrilla activities. Later the party entered into an alliance with the Iraqi Communists, and in November 1973 the two parties issued a joint proclamation in Baghdad, in which they opposed China and Iran and praised Russia.

The pro-Chinese faction further splintered into the Tudeh

Party Revolutionary organization on the one hand and the Marxist-Leninist Storm organization on the other. The former, which was the more important one, took an active part in the revolution that overthrew the shah. On March 11, 1979, the Tudeh Party central committee announced the resumption of its legal activities and proclaimed that it was ready to support all the decisions of the new power directed to satisfy the people's desires.

The Islamic leadership, though, ignored the Tudeh Party and did not accept its appeals for cooperation. In spite of persecution on the part of Muslim organizations, the Tudeh Party tried to take part in all the activities of the Islamic political forces. However, its party position was not acceptable to the other left forces, and the other parties regarded the Tudeh political line as a betrayal and as flirting with the theocratic régime.

From February 1983, the Islamic authorities began attacks on all the leftist political forces. The Tudeh Party's secretary-general, Nured-din Kianuri, was arrested on charges of spying for the USSR. He was the first member of the party to publicly confess on television his crimes against the Islamic state. The majority of the leaders and activists of the Tudeh Party were imprisoned on such charges as "high treason" and espionage. The Tudeh Party was banned in May 1983 and many of the heads of the party and active participants in it were executed. According to non-official data, more than 10,000 members of the Tudeh Party were arrested, and more than 500 of those were executed. At present, the Tudeh Party functions as an underground. The Tudeh Party newspaper is *Na-me-ye-mardtom* (*The People's Herald*) and the party headquarters are located in Berlin.

TUKHACHEVSKY, MIKHAIL NIKOLAYEVICH   (1893–1937) BOLSHEVIK military leader. Born of a noble family, Tukhachevsky was given a military education in elite academies and entered the Russian army in 1914 as a junior officer of the Imperial Guards. Captured by the Germans, he spent two years in captivity, escaping on his sixth attempt and then returning to Russia.

He became a member of the Bolshevik Party in April 1918 and rose rapidly from company commander to army command, distinguishing himself for his military skill throughout the civil war (1918–1920). His attack on Warsaw failed for lack of support from the First Cavalry army commanded by STALIN, VOROSHILOV and Budenny, creating bad relations between him and the three future Soviet leaders. In March 1921, Tukhachevsky commanded the bloody suppression of the Kronstadt sailors' revolt. As deputy commissar for military and naval affairs and chief of staff of the RED ARMY, he was responsible for numerous innovations, particularly in armored warfare and in the formation of parachute divisions. In 1935, when the rank of marshal of the Red Army was introduced, Tukhachevsky was among the five officers promoted to this rank.

In 1937, he was stripped of his positions, tried in camera on charges of espionage and executed on the basis of documents alleging connections to German military intelligence. This was the beginning of mass purges in the Red Army. In 1956, he was posthumously rehabilitated.

T'UNG MENG HUI   see TONG MENG HUI.

TUNG PI-WU   see DONG BIWU.

TUNISIA, REVOLT AGAINST FRANCE   Tunisia became a French protectorate in 1881 as part of an agreement with the British. The first nationalist stirrings, mostly among young urban Tunisians who had received a western-style education, began to make themselves felt on the eve of World War I. Political activity, however, was driven underground by the French and it was only in 1920 that the *Destour* (Constitution) Party was founded. While the party was very popular and succeeded in setting up branch organizations throughout Tunisia, it proved too moderate for many youngsters who had reached adulthood after the World War and who, led by AL-HABIB BOURGUIBA, seceded from the party in 1934 and set up the NEO DESTOUR.

Originally, the *Neo Destour*—which was destined to lead Tunisia toward independence—was made up mainly of young liberals from Tunisia's cities (other then Tunis itself). Later, the party was able to change its tactics, emphasizing social justice and attracting members of the trade unions as well as the youth movements. In 1939, the party was said to have 30,000 members who recognized their *zaim* (leader), al-Habib Bourguiba. With the collapse of French authority following the defeat of 1940, the party was able to expand its activity almost without resistance.

In late 1942, Tunisia was occupied by German and Italian forces. Early in 1943 it was turned into a battlefield and in May 1943 it was liberated by American and British troops. Two months later the French, seeking to restore their status, replaced the bey with a very old relative, el Amin, who they considered as their tool. The outcome was a drastic drop in the prestige of the bey, whose government, run on his behalf by French policemen, was unable to prevent numerous acts of terrorism committed by members of the *Neo Destour*.

In 1949, faced with growing resistance and no prospect of victory in the conflict, the French allowed Bourguiba and his *Neo Destour* comrades to return from exile. The struggle between the two sides continued; in 1952 a low point was reached when the French murdered Ferhat Hashed, one of the principal leaders of the Tunisian trade unions. In 1954 France, under Prime Minister Mendes-France, finally recognized Tunisia's right to self-determination and effective independence was achieved in 1956.

TUPAC AMARU   An indigenous Peruvian of Inca ancestry who led the only effective challenge to Spanish rule in the central Andes between the time of the execution of Francisco Pizarro in 1548 and the beginning of sporadic revolts by Indians and Criollos in 1808. Tupac Amaru's insurrection, lasting from 1780 through 1783, experienced some initial successes but was later harshly repressed.

TUPAMAROS   In Uruguay, a Marxist group of urban guerrillas founded in 1963; since then similar groups have appeared in Guatemala, Argentina and Brazil. The name stems from an 18th-century Peruvian guerrilla leader (Inca), TUPAC AMARU, who fought the Spaniards. The Tupamaros were most active during the late 1960s and early 1970s, when they murdered several ministers and kidnapped foreign representatives. In 1972, however, their leader, Raul Sendic, was captured, and since then less has been heard of them. Their reign of terror can by no means be regarded as finished.

TÜRKES, ALPARSLAN   (1917–) Turkish officer and Fascist political leader. Born in Nicosia, Cyprus, Türkes moved with his family to Istanbul in 1932, graduated from the military academy there in 1938 and became a professional officer. He had strong pro-German sympathies and claimed that Nazism and the German principles of strong government were quite similar to Turkish Kemalism. He took part in an anti-Communist demonstration in 1944, was arrested and put on trial, but was released. He participated in the military coup of May 1960, and became a member of the National Unity Committee, the junta that ruled Turkey in 1960–1961, and a chief aide to General Gursel, its head. He advocated the extension of military rule and speedy radical reforms that would implement ATATÜRK's principles. Due to his radical views and his opposition to the return to civilian-political rule, he was expelled from the National Unity Committee and was sent as a military attache to India.

In 1963, after returning from India, he was accused of conspiring against the government, but was found not guilty. He resigned from the army and joined the right-wing Republican Peasants' National Party. In 1965 he became leader of the party, eventually exercising dictatorial power and appointing his supporters to key posts (causing the old founder-leaders of the party to leave it and reestablish their own party). He also changed the name of the party—which was widely considered to be Fascist—to the Nationalist Action Movement Party. In the elections of 1969 his party lost heavily, and he remained its only representative in parliament. He now increasingly fostered Pan-Turkish ideas, stressing Turkey's ties to all peoples of Turkish origin or speaking the Turkish language outside Turkey, e.g., in Soviet Central Asia, and its willingness to help them and reestablish the "Greater Turkish" nation and state.

In 1975–1976 and again in 1977–1978, Türkes was named deputy prime minister in Demirel's right-wing government. Türkes used his position to put his supporters in key military, police and government posts. He was accused of using extreme means to achieve and maintain his power, including the murder of political opponents, and of stepping up his extreme-rightist propaganda, even translating and distributing Nazi propaganda.

After the military coup of 1980 he went into hiding, but eventually gave himself up. He was put on trial in 1981, with several hundred of his men, but after a heart attack he was hospitalized in 1983 and provisionally released in 1985. In April 1987 he was sentenced to 11 years' imprisonment, but remained free for health reasons. The days of his political activity and influence, however, ended in 1980.

TURKEY, REVOLTS AND REVOLUTIONS
Revolts and Revolutions of 1906 and 1913. See YOUNG TURKS.
31 Mart Revolt. This revolt started among soldiers situated in the center of Istanbul, on April 13, 1909 (31 Mart 1325 in the Muslim calendar). The revolt sought the reimplementation of the *Shari'a*, the Islamic law. It was made possible due the involvement of different elements of society, including liberal journalists who felt disturbed by the YOUNG TURKS' absolutist régime and bureaucrats and military officers who had been discharged from government service as part of the "white revolution" of the Young Turks. In addition to the internal social unrest and dissatisfaction, there were external reasons for this protest—general disappointment in and a feeling of the failure

of the constitutional régime, after Crete announced *enosis* (union) with Greece and Bulgaria proclaimed its independence. The rebels' demands were mainly the discharge of the senior civil servants such as the grand vizier and the head of the parliament, new appointments and a full implementation of the *Shari'a*. The revolt ended on April 27, when Sultan Abd ul-Hamid II, who was accused of involvement in fermenting the rebels, was deposed.

Revolution of 1919. See KEMAL ATATÜRK.

Coup of 1980. On September 12, 1980, Turkey underwent its third coup d'état in 20 years. General Kenan Evren, the Turkish chief of staff, headed the coup, which deposed the government then headed by Suleiman Demirel. The coup was the result of a large number of factors. Turkey's trade deficit had grown continuously over the years and inflation was as high as 127% in September 1980. The economic difficulties and the chronic lack of housing exacerbated the social tension that was especially evident in the large cities. In the eastern districts, beset by religious and ethnic conflict, the feeling of social deprivation led to unrest, with relations between the Shiite minority and the Sunni majority becoming more and more strained. The result of this polarization on all sides was an outbreak of violent underground activity. From 1978 to the coup of September 1980, the situation had steadily deteriorated into a state of anarchy. In those two years, over 5,000 persons had been killed and another 14,000 injured. In this difficult time, a series of short-lived governments had arisen and no party had succeeded in obtaining a majority in order to establish a government without a coalition. This led to a generally dysfunctional state of affairs.

During this period, when there was no close governmental supervision and both leftist and rightist organizations enjoyed a relatively great degree of freedom, various religious groups became more active as well. This activity reached its peak in a mass demonstration in Konya. Whereas the original purpose of this demonstration had been anti-Israeli, it soon became a protest against the secular nature of the Turkish republic.

Finally, internal military moves may also have constituted an important factor in the coup. The general staff officers may have wished to neutralize a group of young officers with a neutralist-populist orientation, whom they considered as threatening the stability of the army. The military also desired to act as a body, in order to prevent any attempts by individual officers or groups to launch a coup of their own. Another motive may have had to do with the fact that the army had too often been forced to play policeman and keep the peace on the domestic front—a role which interfered with its regular military training and the effective guarding of the country's borders.

On September 12, the army took control of the country and martial law was imposed in all 67 Turkish provinces. Armed forces took over the headquarters of the political parties; various leaders were arrested and sent to remote military bases. Thanks to the imposition of a national emergency and the paralysis of political life, the committee for national security, established in order to lead the country during the period of military rule, succeeded in implementing most of the tasks which it had undertaken. In the area of legislation, the military régime under Bulent Ulusoy, which remained in power until the end of 1983, managed to complete the procedure for enacting most of the bills which had piled up over the years and whose stagnation

had paralyzed many aspects of state life. The advisory council prepared a new constitution. This constitution strongly emphasized closer state control of political activity and limited personal freedom and the freedom to organize. The government achieved a series of successes in the economic field and was able to reduce political violence by a wave of arrests and trials. In the wake of severe domestic pressure as well as economic and political pressure applied by western states, general elections were held in Turkey on November 6, 1993 and control of the state was restored to the hands of the citizens.

TU WEN-HSIU see DU WENXIU.

TYLER, WAT (?–1381) English rebel. Influenced by JOHN BALL, Tyler left his work in Kent and organized a peasants' revolt in Kent and Essex against the king, nobility and Church establishment. In the spring and summer of 1381 he led the revolt and seized London. At first, the revolt was granted certain concessions, but in a later meeting with the king, Tyler was killed in the king's presence. That ended the revolt and all the concessions were revoked.

TZELTAL REVOLT The Tzeltal revolt, which occurred in Chiapas, Mexico, in 1712, had its roots in religious dissension beginning in 1708. In 1712, Mayan inhabitants of the village of Cancuc erected a shrine at the location where a 13-year-old girl claimed to have seen the Virgin Mary. The Dominicans, however, who were the dominant religious force in Chiapas, refused to recognize the shrine's legitimacy and tried to destroy it. A new cult of the Virgin then arose under the leadership of Sebastian Gomez, and challenged both the secular and religious authorities. The rebellion spread to Ocosingo and 20 other towns, where priests and tax collectors were slaughtered. The rebel army of more than 6,000 men was defeated two months later by combined Mexican and Guatemalan forces, and the leaders were executed.

TZU LI HUI see ZILIHUI.

TZULUKIDZE, ALEXANDRE (Sasha) (1876–1905) Georgian professional revolutionary, one of the founders of the Leninist-Iskra organization in Georgia and Transcaucasian ideologist of MARXISM. In 1896, Tzulukidze joined the revolutionary wing of the Social Democratic organization, *Mesame Dasi*. He led revolutionary activities in Tbilisi and Baku. In 1897–1899, he was a member of the students' Marxist group in Moscow and preached its ideas widely. In 1900–1901, Tzulukidze was the leader of workers' strikes in Tbilisi and in the Batumi workers' circle. In 1902–1903, he participated in a number of Russian Social Democratic Workers Party (RSDWP) local committees in Kutaisi (a major city in western Georgia), Guria and Samegrelo (large provinces in western Georgia), and in the Transcaucasian Committee. Meanwhile, he edited and wrote for various BOLSHEVIK papers. In 1905, Tzulukidze was arrested, but he continued his revolutionary activity in prison as well. He died of disease while still in prison.

In his theoretical works, Tzulukidze criticized the so-called Legal Marxists, nationalists and MENSHEVIKS, and defended the Leninist trend in the revolutionary struggle.

U

UGANDA, 1971 COUP   In January 1971, while President Milton Obote was out of the country at a Commonwealth Heads of State meeting in Singapore, the head of the armed forces, General IDI AMIN, seized power in a military coup. In February 1971, Amin declared himself head of state, promising return to civilian rule within five years. He dissolved the national assembly and ruled by decree. He banned all non-government newspapers and many religious organizations.

Amin's brutal régime, which led to the expulsion of the Asian community of 70,000 and the deaths of hundreds of thousands of Ugandans, including political and religious leaders, was ended in April 1979, when anti-Amin forces invaded from Tanzania and captured Kampala. Amin fled to Libya and then to Saudi Arabia.

UGANDA PEOPLE'S CONGRESS (UPC)   Founded in 1960 with a socialist philosophy, its founder and leader was Apolo Milton Obote. The UPC was the ruling party in Uganda from 1962–1971 and from 1980–1985, and the sole legal political party from 1969–1971.

The UPC was founded as a splinter party which broke away from the Uganda National Congress (UNC). It opposed the federal government set up after the British left and wanted a unitary state. Its leftist ideology, known as the Common Man's Charter, was influenced by Julius Nyerere's *Ujamaa* policy (see ARUSHA DECLARATION).

In 1969, after an attempt on Obote's life in which he was seriously injured, other political parties were abolished.

Since 1985, the UPC has been out of power but it still exists, although organized political activity has been banned by President MUSEVENI.

ULBRICHT, WALTER   (1893–1973) East German Communist leader. Born in Leipzig to a working class family and later trained as a cabinetmaker, Ulbricht joined the Social Democratic Party in 1912 and served in the German army in World War I, deserting twice. In 1919 he joined the Communist Party, leading its Berlin organization from 1929 on. The accession of HITLER to power in January 1933 forced Ulbricht to escape Germany. He worked for the COMINTERN in Spain (1936–1939) and then moved to the USSR. There he distinguished himself as STALIN's henchman by persecuting Trotskyites and other Communists who had fallen out of favor with the Soviet dictator. After the German defeat at Stalingrad (1942), he founded and led the National Committee for a Free Germany. In 1945 he re-turned to Germany and helped reorganize the Communist Party, becoming its general secretary in 1950. From then until 1971, when he retired in favor of Erich Honnecker, he was virtually the dictator of East Germany.

ULYANOV, ALEXANDER   (1866–1887) Elder brother of VLADIMIR LENIN. Alexander was a brilliant student, winning gold medals at his secondary school graduation and for his studies in zoology at St. Petersburg University. At the beginning of 1887, depressed by his father's early death and outraged by police repression of student activities, he helped form a fringe group known as the PEOPLE'S WILL, writing a program for it that combined Marxist influence and terrorist activity. The group began planning the assassination of Czar Alexander III, but was quickly arrested and tried. Ulyanov was hanged on May 5, 1887. In Soviet historiography, Lenin's turn to Marxist revolutionary politics is attributed largely to the trauma of his brother's execution.

UNSHLICHT, IOSIF   (1879–1938) BOLSHEVIK police and military official. Of Polish origins, Unshlicht joined the Social Democratic Party of Poland and Lithuania in 1900 and quickly rose to membership in its national committee. His activities brought about his arrest and being jailed several times in the years 1902–1909 and a four-year sentence of Siberian exile in 1913–1916.

Released from exile, he was active in the Bolshevik Party and in the October RUSSIAN REVOLUTION OF 1917. He then became one of FELIKS DZERZHINSKY's deputies in the *Cheka,* the political police. In 1919, he was organizer of a Bolshevik government of Lithuania and Byelorussia and in the summer of 1920 became part of the Bolshevik revolutionary committee for Poland.

He later held a series of posts in the political police and in the army, rising to deputy commissar for military affairs in 1925–1930. From December 1925, he was a candidate member of the central committee of the Communist Party. After serving as director of civil aviation (1933–1935), he was appointed secretary of the central executive committee of the Congress of Soviets of the USSR. He served in this capacity until arrested in June 1937. A year later he was executed for suspected connections with the political opposition to STALIN. He was posthumously rehabilitated.

URUGUAYAN INDEPENDENCE   The liberation of the Banda Oriental (present-day Uruguay) from Spanish colonial rule was first proposed in 1811, one year after Argentina's declaration of independence. That year, Jose Gervasio Artigas (1764–1850) won several important victories over the Spanish but failed to take Montevideo, the colony's major city. Ironically, Artigas, who is now considered the "Father of Uruguay," never intended Uruguay to become independent. He envisioned its incorporation into Argentina. Despite that country's concession of Spanish sovereignty over the territory, Argentina too was interested in expanding across the Rio de la Plata. In 1814, Argentina took Montevideo and annexed the Banda Oriental. This victory, however, was short-lived; one year later Portuguese troops swept down from Brazil and captured the city from the Argentineans. Upon independence, Brazil declared Uruguay to be the Cisplatine province.

Three years later, in 1824, the Battle of Ayacucho brought an end to Spanish rule in South America. In Buenos Aires, the Uruguayan emigré community was encouraged by this and by reports of several small rebellions across the province to make a second attempt at liberating the country, this time from Brazilian control. Led by Juan Antonio Lavalleja, a group of 33 patriots (not all of them originally Uruguayan) crossed the Rio de la Plata and began amassing supporters for their bid for independence. By the summer of 1825 the group, now known as the *Treinte y Tres* (Thirty-three Immortals), had made considerable headway in its fight against the Brazilian authorities and had conquered the Sarandi and Rincónde las Gallinas regions. On August 25, 1825, the group declared the liberated areas of Uruguay to be an independent republic.

Throughout this period Argentina provided considerable support to the rebels, hoping that it would then be able to annex Uruguay itself. Brazil was finally defeated at the Battle of Ituzaingo in February 1827, but in the final peace treaty, brokered by Britain in 1828, it was decided that Uruguay would remain an independent buffer state between the two South American powers. In 1830, Jose Rivera, one of the original *Treinte y Tres,* was elected as Uruguay's first president.

USTASHA (USTASA) A name used by Croatian rebel bands since the 1920s. Between the years 1941–1945 of World War II, an extremist Croatian nationalist movement by the same name ruled the "Croatian Independent State," a Nazi puppet state whose forces participated in the Axis war effort. Founded by Zagreb lawyer ANTE PAVELIC in Italy in January 1927, the movement acted against the Yugoslav state from Italy, Austria and Hungary and participated in the assassination of King Alexander in 1934. From the beginning a tightly knit organization, its ideology was Fascist (see FASCISM) on the Italian model, devoutly Catholic, anti-Serb, anti-Orthodox and racist. Socially, it attracted the lower urban stratum. In the late 1930s it also attracted members of the clergy, students and intellectuals. Before the dismemberment of Yugoslavia in 1941, its membership numbered about 40,000.

Under its régime, hundreds of thousands of Serbs, Jews, Gypsies and anti-Fascists were murdered. The TITO régime, established after 1945, stamped out any signs of Croatian extremism associated with the Ustasha but the organization kept up its activities against Yugoslav targets in the west. Following the declaration of Croatia's independence in 1991, the Ustasha legacy crept—through various symbols and values—into the Croat nationalism which opposed the Serbs and the rump Yugoslav state. By 1995, there were several cases of rehabilitation of known war-time Ustasha leaders.

V

VARGAS, GETULIO (1883–1954) Brazilian statesman who, after losing the presidential seat in a fraudulent election, initiated with Góis Monteiro the 1930 Brazilian revolution. As a result of the coup, Vargas assumed executive power as a dictator in October 1930. The following year he declared a moratorium on the service of Brazil's foreign debt and the destruction of sugar and coffee crop surpluses because of the world market crisis. He developed a political ideal which corresponded to the interests of the industrial section of the population. It was during his rule that the working class obtained job stability, social welfare and the right to form unions. However, the peasantry was completely ignored by Vargas.

In 1932, a revolution was initiated because of the delay in the return to constitutional government in the province of Sao Paulo. Although the uprising was subdued in 83 days, a strongly nationalistic constitution was promulgated by a constituent congress in July 1934, as a direct result of the uprising. Vargas was then elected under this new constitution. In 1937 he set aside the constitution because of general unrest and resumed his dictatorship. He created the *Estado Novo* and proposed a strong democratic government. One year later the *integralistas,* a Fascist organization, revolted, but the revolt was quickly suppressed. Vargas severed diplomatic relations with the Axis powers during the 1942 conference of foreign ministers of the American States of Rio de Janeiro. Brazil declared war on Germany and Italy on August 22, 1945. On October 30, 1945, Vargas's 15-year dictatorship came to an end in a bloodless coup headed by general Góis Monteiro. However, in the 1950 election Vargas won by a plurality. On August 24, 1954 he committed suicide following a political crisis. His suicide letter declared: "To the hatred of my enemies I bequeath my death. I regret I was unable to do for the humble all I wanted."

VELVET REVOLUTION see CZECHOSLOVAKIA, COUPS.

VENDÉE UPRISING The Vendée is a rugged rural region in the lower part of Brittany, lying to the south of the Loire, where the Catholic and royalist Chouans rose up in arms against successive Paris governments during the first decade of the FRENCH REVOLUTION, and thereby served as a model and inspiration to other provinces caught up in the movement of the federalist (*les Fédérés*) and GIRONDIN counterrevolution against the JACOBIN dictatorship of the capital. The Vendée revolt was not finally crushed until Bonaparte pacified it during the CONSULATE by signing his concordat with the pope in April 1802. The Vendée

remained relatively quiescent during the Empire, but rose up again during Napoleon's Hundred Days in 1815, which ended with the battle of Waterloo. Napoleon was in fact so terrified of Vendéen vengeance that he decided to escape to England by a different route.

The Vendéens, priding themselves as the most loyal of monarchists and the most devout of Christians dating back to the *ancien régime*, from the outset vigorously manifested their defiance against the revolution's anticlericalist policies. However, it was not until the execution of Louis XVI on January 21, 1793 and the Jacobin government's attempt to enforce military conscription that the Vendée took up arms against the "Godless Republic." Sporadic revolts, beginning with CHARETTE's insurrection in Marchecoul, spread throughout Brittany, north and south of the Loire and served as a catalyst for similar outbreaks in the neighboring provinces of Anjou, Poitou and even Normandy, where the port of Granville joined the revolt against Paris in November. Such leaders as Lescure, Bonchamps and above all Stofflet, arousing the passions of what was virtually a peasant revolt against the urban revolution, associated with such cities as the Vendée capital, Nantes. They were able to keep in check no less than three successive Jacobin armies through their guerrilla tactics (later to be emulated by the Catholic Spaniards against Napoleon's armies) until General Moreau was forced to resort to a scorched earth policy, ruthlessly carried out by special units of regulars known as the *colonnes infernales* (infernal columns).

The enforcement of the anticlerical policies of the COMMITTEE OF PUBLIC SAFETY served to further envenom passions on both sides until Moreau's successor, General Lazare Hoche, succeeded in pacifying the region by signing the Convention of La Jaunaye with Charette and Stofflet on February 17, 1795, which guaranteed freedom of religion and a general amnesty, although this was in fact ignored. An aborted British landing at Quilberon of an expeditionary force of French royalist reinforcements—led by the youngest brother of Louis XVI, the Comte d'Artois—encouraged many Vendéens to take up arms again, but they were slaughtered in droves by the revolutionary forces. The repression continued unabated during the Thermidorian reaction and under the Consulate.

At the commemoration of the bicentennial of the French Revolution in 1989, right-wing French historians provoked an outcry by accusing the revolution of having carried out a policy of genocide and ethnic cleansing against a region that was perceived by revolutionaries as a bastion of Throne and Altar, and whose very existence posed such a challenge to the anticlerical and antimonarchist principles of 1789 that the revolution had no choice but to wipe out the Brittany peasantry, root and branch. Much of the flavor of the heroic struggle of the Vendée resistance is recaptured in Victor Hugo's *Les Chouans*.

VENEZUELA, COUPS

1945 Coup. The government of President Isaías Medina, from 1941 to 1945, was one of moderate and sporadic political repression. Important reforms took place regarding public administration, and the state intervened significantly in the country's economic growth. These economic policies were not welcomed by a certain portion of the population because they tended to favor new activities—mainly in the industrial sphere—modern agriculture, construction and services. Especially unwelcome were the president's control over imports and foreign currency, his land reform and income taxes. In 1944, the worker's national convention was dissolved, which caused general unrest.

The 1945 presidential election encountered problems because of the untimely sickness of the most popular candidate, Dr. Diógenes Escalante. The Venezuelan Democratic Party declared Dr. Angel Biaggini its official candidate, but he was not backed by other parties. The Democratic Action Party requested the congress to elect a provisional president and, when this was not accepted, a military rebellion exploded in Caracas and Maracay, amongst others, on October 19, 1945. Three days later, Medina and his cabinet were imprisoned. The leader of the revolutionary junta, Rómulo Gallegos, became the new head of the executive office. A constitution was adopted in July 1947, guaranteeing individual rights relating to property ownership, employment, education and health. The president's term was changed from five to four years and he was forbidden to succeed himself more than once. Rómulo Gallegos was elected president in 1947.

1948 Coup. The novelist Rómulo Gallegos was elected president in 1947 and inaugurated in February 1948, His cabinet consisted mainly of members of the Democratic Action Party. During his régime, the petroleum tax was modified to a "fifty-fifty" formula, meaning that half of the profits obtained would go to the government via taxes and contributions and the other half would remain with the oil companies.

The government also declared, in the name of the State, that it would not modify the taxation system of the petroleum companies in the future without first reaching an agreement with these companies. In November 1948 a coup, headed by Defense Minister Carlos Delgad, deposed Rómulo Gallegos only nine months after his inauguration.

A communique from the rebels indicated that they accused the Democratic Action Party of sectarianism, electoral abuse, the intention of dividing the armed forces and preparation for an abusive use of power. The main reason behind the coup was probably the fear that Gallegos and his cabinet might harm the businessmen's privileges through the promotion of political and union liberties, a populist orientation and socioeconomic benefits for the majority. Rómulo Gallegos fled to Cuba and in his farewell message he implied that the interests of the US were behind the coup. He also declared that the Venezuelan history of 1948 would reflect the confrontation between law and force and between the civilian and military forces.

1952 Coup. The 1948 coup against Rómulo Gallegos resulted in a military dictatorship in Venezuela. Although some political parties were allowed to continue their work, the Democratic Action Party was immediately banned. However the members of this party continued an underground battle in search of the restoration of democracy.

Within the military government there existed two main currents of thought, one which hoped for an electoral way out to the political crisis and the other strongly in favor of absolute dictatorship. During the first stage of the military government, between 1948 and 1952, repression was only mildly brutal. On November 13, 1950, Carlos Delgado Chalbaud, president of the junta and a believer in the electoral solution, was assassinated. On November 10, 1952 elections took place, and although the military powers used all the means in their power to win the election, the opposition won. Jóvito Villalba was now the new president-elect. On December 2, 1952—barely three weeks after the election—the military government dismissed the popular victory, a new coup took place and Colonel Marcos Pérez Jiménez was designated the new Venezuelan president.

1958 Coup. The military government which took over executive power in 1952 was one of brutal and absolute dictatorship. All political rights, citizen guarantees, democratic liberties and human rights were suppressed. Torture in all its forms, the exploitation of workers and the unlimited enrichment of government officials were all prevalent. On the other hand, it was during this time that Venezuela saw a vast economical bonanza and Caracas became a modern city. The banking business expanded and the government received enormous revenues from petroleum exports. The government was evidently interested in establishing the basis for a state-controlled capitalism that would allow the political and military forces to increase their economical power in the country. However, as the economic solvency of the government increased (in reality this was but illusory, as it was later discovered that the government had a miscellaneous debt of more than 4 billion bolivars), as did that of those engaged in foreign enterprise and of a few Venezuelan families, the popular unrest due to the lack of democratic as well as human rights also increased.

On January 21, 1958, a revolution broke out in Caracas, the nation's capital, and President Pérez Jiménez had to flee the country. Rear Admiral Wolfgang Larrazábal, head of the junta that had initiated the uprising, restored democratic rights and promised an election for that same year. Presidential elections were held on December 7, 1958 and ROMULO BETANCOURT won by a majority. He was inaugurated on February 13, 1959.

VEQUILHARXHI, NAUM (1797–1854) One of the early founders of Albanian nationalism. Vequilharxhi was among the hundreds of Albanians who fought in the Romanian revolution against the Ottoman Empire in 1821. Hoping to spread nationalist sentiment by encouraging a revival of the Albanian language, in 1844 he published a manual, *Eveta*, encouraging the use of an Albanian alphabet. This manual was secretly circulated in the country's schools. In 1850, in exile, he founded the Albanian Cultural Association. His subsequent murder at the hands of the Turks precipitated the transformation, in the late 19th century, of the cultural revival of the Albanian language into a significant and influential political movement.

VIET CONG The military arm of the Vietnamese National Liberation Front which, with North Vietnamese support, fought against the government of South Vietnam between 1955–1975. An extremely effective guerrilla organization known for the black pajama-like dress worn by its regular combatants, it succeeded, although with considerable aid from the North Vietnamese—in holding its own against the million-man army of South Vietnam and against American forces which in 1969 numbered 550,000 men. After the conclusion of a cease-fire in 1973, the Viet Cong quietly and effectively continued its work of building an alternative government in South Vietnam, so that, in 1975, only a small push was needed to topple the Saigon régime.

VIET MINH (Vietnam League for Independence) A national liberation movement founded in 1941 by HO CHI MINH. From 1943, the Viet Minh (official name, *Viet Nam Dec Lap Dong Minh Hoi*), waged a guerrilla war against the Japanese in which it was at first supported by the US. After the Japanese collapse, the Viet Minh took control of Hanoi, the capital of Vietnam, and proclaimed an independent republic (August 1945). It was, however, expelled by the French and, from 1946–1954, fought an extremely effective war of national liberation against the latter, culminating in a great military victory at Dien Bien Phu. After 1955, the Viet Minh was absorbed into the Lap Don, or Workers (Communist) Party of North Vietnam.

VILBUSHEVICH (SHOHAT), MANYA (1880–1961) Jewish revolutionary and Zionist. The daughter of a merchant, Vilbushevich first became involved in populist (see POPULISM) activity and then in Social Democratic circles. By 1900, she was one of the activists of the BUND in Minsk. She saw in Sergei Zubatov's police socialism a possibility of broadening the workers' movement and became an ardent convert. At the same time, she became acquainted with Zionist ideas and found in the *Poalei Zion* movement the synthesis of SOCIALISM and Zionism that fulfilled all her intellectual and emotional leanings. Shocked by the 1903 Kishinev pogrom against the Jews, she departed for Palestine, beginning a career of public activism that embraced both Jewish self-defense in Russia and the strengthening of Zionist settlement in Palestine. After marrying Israel Shohat, she helped found *Hashomer* (The Watchman), a self-defense group guarding the Jewish settlements in Palestine. Deported to Syria by the Ottoman authorities during World War I, she returned after the end of the war and settled in Galilee. Her activities included working with the *Histadrut* (the General Labor Federation), a society for Jewish-Arab coexistence set up after the 1929 disturbances in Palestine and raising funds abroad for Jewish self-defense in Palestine and for the illegal immigration of Jews to Palestine.

VILLA, PANCHO (1878–1923) Mexican revolutionary. Born Doroteo Arango, Villa was the orphan son of a poor farm laborer. Becoming a revolutionary when he was very young (he was forced to flee after killing a landowner who had molested his sister) his gifts of leadership enabled him to raise an irregular force of several thousand men; from 1909 he took a leading part in the civil war, first against dictator PORFIRIO DIAZ and then against VENUSTIANO CARRANZA, whom he, together with the leg-

endary Emiliano Zapata, fought. In 1916, in an effort to show that Carranza did not control the north, Villa executed 16 American citizens. This led to an American punitive expedition under the command of Pershing which, however, failed to capture him. In 1920 he made his peace with Carranza; in 1923 he was assassinated. The English version of his memoirs was published in 1965.

Bandit or revolutionary, Francisco (Pancho) Villa

VIMEUR, JEAN-BAPTISTE-DONATIEN see ROCHAMBEAU, COMTE DE.

VOITINSKY, GREGORY (1893–1953) Leader of the first COMINTERN mission to China. Born in Russia, Voitinsky (whose real name was Zarkhin) was a laborer with only four years of formal schooling. After living in the US (1913–1918), he returned to Russia, joined the Communist Party and participated in the civil war in Siberia.

As the head of a Comintern mission, he arrived in China in March 1920. He met LI DAZHAO and CHEN DUXIU and rendered financial and other assistance to Chinese Marxists who formed the CHINESE COMMUNIST PARTY (CCP) in 1921. In October 1920, he held discussions with SUN YAT-SEN in Shanghai. As a leading Comintern expert on China, he drafted instructions to the CCP and worked with its central committee in Shanghai. His last stay in China was in 1926–1927. Well-liked by his Chinese colleagues, Gregory Voitinsky was one of the few Soviet emissaries to survive STALIN's purges.

VOLIN (EIKHENBAUM), VSEVOLOD (1882–1945) Russian anarchist leader. As a student at the St. Petersburg University, Volin joined the Socialist Revolutionaries. Arrested and exiled to Siberia in 1905, he escaped from Russia and in 1911 became active in the anarchist (see ANARCHISM) movement in the United States.

In 1917, he returned to Russia and helped organize the anarcho-syndicalists of Petrograd. Under BOLSHEVIK pressure, he moved to the Ukraine where he created a theory of "united anarchism," uniting Communism and individualism, merging the thought of PETER KROPOTKIN with the village-based guerrilla movement of NESTOR MAKHNO.

The *Nabat (*Alarm Bell*)* United Anarchist movement lasted only until Bolshevik control of the Ukraine was firmly established in the spring of 1920. In 1921 Volin emigrated, settling in Paris, where he wrote a libertarian history of the RUSSIAN REVOLUTION OF 1917 (*The Unknown Revolution*, Chicago: Solidarity Press, 1974).

VOLKHOVSKY (Volkhovskoy) (1846–1914) Russian revolutionary and poet (pseudonym—Ivan Brut). Volkhovsky belonged to the nobility and studied at the Moscow University. In 1867, he founded the Roblevoe society for researching the peasants' lives and for distributing books among them. In the early 1870s, Volkhovsky was arrested several times. In 1873, he headed the Odessa branch of the CHAIKOVSKY CIRCLE. In 1874 he was arrested and exiled. In 1889 he escaped and lived in London from 1890 on, where he became one of the leaders of the Society of the Friends of Russian Freedom and of the Fund for Freedom of the Russian Press. In 1900–1901, Volkhovsky was one of the leaders of the Agrarian-Socialist League. He later joined the Socialist Revolutionaries.

VOROSHILOV, KLEMENT YEFRMEVICH (1881–1969) Soviet soldier and politician. Voroshilov joined the BOLSHEVIK PARTY in 1903, and during the Russian civil war became closely associated with STALIN, with whom he worked in the city of Tsaritsyn (also known as Stalingrad and as Volgograd). In 1925 he became minister of defense and in 1926 entered the Politburo. In 1935 he was created a field marshal.

Voroshilov's lackluster performance during the Finnish-Russian war (1939–1940) did not prevent him from being put in charge of the Northwestern Front defending Leningrad against the Germans. He continued to serve on the committee for state defense through the war. From 1953 until 1957 he served as chairman of the Presidium of the Supreme Soviet, i.e., as a figurehead of state. In 1957 he was implicated with an anti-party group but was nevertheless allowed to retire peacefully in 1960.

VYNNYCHENKO, VOLODYMYR (1880–1951) Ukrainian nationalist revolutionary and writer. An early Ukrainian Social Democrat, Vynnychenko participated in the RUSSIAN REVOLUTION OF 1905 and then spent the years until 1914 abroad. In 1917, he was elected deputy chair of the Central Rada of Ukraine, formulating its policy statements. He conducted negotiations regarding the autonomy of Ukraine with the provisional government of KERENSKY. With the formation of the *Skoropadsky Hetmanate* under German auspices, Vynnychenko became a central figure in the opposition Ukrainian National Union. With the fall of *Skoropadsky* and the German withdrawal from Ukraine, Vynnychenko became a member of the five-member Directory that ruled Ukraine. After resigning and a brief stay in Vienna, Vynnychenko made another effort to negotiate Ukrainian autonomy with the BOLSHEVIKS. In 1921 he moved to France, where he remained until his death in 1951.

WAFD (Delegation) Egypt's principal nationalist party from the 1920s to 1952–1953. The party evolved from a delegation sent in 1919 by nationalist leaders to the British to negotiate Egypt's independence. The delegation was led by AHMAD SA'D ZAGHLUL, as was the party until Zaghlul's death in 1927, when Mustafa al-Nahhas became its leader. The *Wafd* Party, with nationalism and the completion of Egypt's independence as its main planks, was modernistic and liberal-democratic in internal matters, and for many years fought the Egyptian king and his court because of their attempts to reduce the parliament's power. While the *Wafd* was a school and transition stage for most Egyptian politicians, many left it in the early 1920s to found rival, mostly more conservative parties. The *Wafd* won the elections of 1924, 1925 (a partial win), 1926, 1929, 1936, 1942 and 1950—usually when a *Wafd* or neutral government held the elections. But it was in power for only short periods in 1924, 1928 and 1930—with the king and his court finding ways to dissolve parliament or end the *Wafd*'s rule by other means—and was later in power in 1936–1937, 1942–1944 and 1950 to January 1952. It split in 1937 when it expelled a group of younger leaders headed by M.F. Nuqrashi and Ahmad Maher, who founded the Saadist Party, and in 1942 when it expelled the Coptic *Wafd* leader Makram Ubaid ('Obeid), who founded an "Independent *Wafdist* Block." In the 1940s, a reformist, moderately leftist faction grew inside the *Wafd*. The party also set up para-military formations (the "Blue Shirts"), but they had little impact.

Initially considered extremist and anti-British, the *Wafd* came to be regarded by the British as the group most representative of Egyptian nationalism, the one with which an agreement should, and could, be reached. Indeed, the Anglo-Egyptian Treaty of 1936 was concluded while Egypt was led by the *Wafd*. In February 1942, the British compelled King Farouq to dismiss his government and appoint Nahhas prime minister, hoping a *Wafd* government would cooperate with the British war effort more willingly than the king's men. Farouq dismissed Nahhas in October 1944, after the British toned down their interference in Egyptian politics.

Eventually, it was a *Wafd* government which in 1951 precipitated a severe crisis in Anglo-Egyptian relations; it had to resign in January 1952.

Following the 1952 FREE OFFICERS coup that brought GAMAL ABDUL NASSER to power, the *Wafd*, along with all other parties, was banned. It was allowed to reform itself in 1975–1977, but by then it was no longer revolutionary in any sense.

WAGNER, RICHARD (1813–1883) German composer, dramatist and writer. Wagner was born in Leipzig and raised in Dresden, where he later joined the 1848 revolutionaries following the government's refusal to adopt his ideas for musical reform in opera productions. This mixture of a modern, artistic quest for change and actual revolutionary activity transformed Wagner in many western eyes to a hero of freedom while in fact he was much more complex, sophisticated and duplicitous than his image. Wagner was a true revolutionary artist in the sense that he rejected classicism and tradition as dead wood and as separating the text, song and action from each other in music. Yet he suggested myth, especially ancient and medieval German myths, as the text of the modern "combined, or overall work of musical art" (*Gesamtkunstwerk*) and indeed blended them together in his giant opera circle, *Der Ring des Nibelungen*. Wagner was very much influenced by Schopenhauer, regarding himself as one of the few giants who could give meaning to a meaningless reality by invoking Christian, nationalistic and quasiracist elements in his artistic work, especially in his last opera, *Parcival*. His dramatic life, full of ups and downs, and his final triumph also inspired many young Germans, HITLER among them. Hitler, however rejected the Christian content of his works. Wagner's contribution to the "spirit of his time" was enormous, in establishing pre-Christian myths and myth per se as a kind of artistic reality that sometimes—especially in times of crisis—penetrated reality itself. His ardent pre-Christian mythology, his German nationalism and his pronounced, operational anti-Semitism alienated NIETZSCHE from him, but served as a revolutionary inspiration both for the Nazi movement and for Hitler personally.

WALESA, LECH (1943–) Polish labor leader and president of Poland from 1990. Trained as an electrician, Walesa emerged as a labor leader and founder of the Solidarity movement at the Lenin shipyards in Gdansk. Solidarity became an independent trade union in 1980. Walesa was its chairman until he was jailed in 1981 with the imposition of the martial law. Released a year later, he conducted Solidarity activities underground and led the organization until its legal reemergence in 1989. He played a leading role in the talks with the régime in early 1989, which led to the transfer of power to a Solidarity-led government. During his presidency, he saw Solidarity's demise and final decline. He has been criticized for his authoritarian style and for his frequent quarrels with former comrades and with various political factions within the executive and legislative branches over his presidential prerogatives and limits of power. His charisma somewhat tarnished, he was battling in 1995 for his reelection.

WALKER, WILLIAM (1824–1860) Born in Tennessee, USA, in 1824, Walker was an itinerant revolutionary best remembered as the only North American ever to become president of a Latin American nation. Walker's first colonization attempt involved Mexican territory. He landed at La Paz in 1853 and proclaimed Baja, California and Sonora an independent republic. He was forced by Mexican resistance to return to the USA in 1854. In 1855, he was invited to Nicaragua by local revolutionaries. Taking virtual control of the nation, he reigned as president from mid-1856 until early 1857. Walker returned to the USA to avoid capture by a coalition of Central American countries, but returned in November. This time, he was arrested and forcibly repatriated. His third expedition to Nicaragua, in 1860, was his undoing. He was again arrested—this time by the British Navy—and turned over to the Honduran authorities, who ultimately executed him.

WANG CHING-WEI see WANG JINGWEI.

WANG JINGWEI (Wang Ching-wei) (1883–1944) Chinese nationalist revolutionary. Born in Canton into a family that had moved from Zhejiang, Wang received a classical education, passed the provincial examinations in 1903 and won a government scholarship to study in Japan, earning a degree at the Tokyo Law College in 1906. He joined SUN YAT-SEN's revolutionary organization, TONGMENGHUI (TMH), in 1905. A persuasive political writer and inspiring orator, Wang became one of Sun's favorite disciples. He and Sun's other stalwart supporter, HU HANMIN, defended their leader's THREE PRINCIPLES OF THE PEOPLE in the TMH organ, *Min Bao* (People's Report) against the attacks of the constitutional monarchists, led by Liang Qichao (see CHINESE REPUBLICAN REVOLUTION OF 1911). Using his legal background, Wang became the leading expositor of Sun's principle of nationalism. After accompanying Sun to southeast Asia in 1907, Wang returned to Tokyo in 1909 to edit a clandestine edition of *Min Bao*. Despondent over the failure of revolutionary plots, Wang attempted in 1910 to assassinate the Manchu prince regent in Beijing. The plan was disclosed and Wang was imprisoned, but was released after the Chinese Revolution of 1911 overthrew the Manchu (Qing) dynasty (1644–1912). Influenced by the anarchist thinking then in vogue in intellectual circles, Wang disdained politics. Marriage in 1912 to the daughter of a wealthy overseas Chinese family enabled him to spend several years traveling abroad. He returned to China in 1917 and subsequently played a leading role in Sun's effort to revive the GUOMINDANG (GMD). As Sun's confidential secretary, he was the senior GMD official present at Sun's deathbed in March 1925 and drafted the leader's final testament. Wang then became leader of the GMD left wing and was in a favored position to inherit party leadership. Though elected chairman of the national government established in Canton in July 1925, he was out-maneuvered by CHIANG KAI-SHEK, forced to resign and went abroad in 1926. Returning in April 1927, he cooperated with the CHINESE COMMUNIST PARTY (CCP) in Wuhan, while Chiang, who purged the CCP, led the rival GMD right wing in Nanjing. In July, Wang's left-wing faction also broke with the CCP. Now staunchly anti-Communist and suspicious of Russian intentions, Wang nevertheless opposed Chiang Kai-shek's growing domination of the GMD. Lacking military support, Wang was never able to replace Chiang. A shaky period of collaboration enabled him to assume an executive position in the Nanjing government in the early 1930s, and he is credited with having inaugurated various administrative reforms. After the Japanese invasion of Manchuria in September 1931, Wang, as acting foreign minister, faced the difficult task of negotiating with the Japanese, who kept up the pressure on north China. Though Chiang Kai-shek was behind the policy of appeasement, it was Wang who drew the ire of public opinion, despite his attempts to defend Chinese sovereignty. In 1935 he was shot by a would-be assassin and in December left for medical treatment in Europe.

After the outbreak of the Sino-Japanese war in July 1937, Wang was named Chiang Kai-shek's deputy, but the position was purely nominal since Chiang was virtually party dictator. Pessimistic over China's prospects in the war, Wang favored a negotiated solution. In December 1938 he flew to Hanoi (Indochina) from southwestern China and at the end of the month issued a public declaration calling for a peaceful settlement with Japan. In March he was the target of another assassination attempt. Though Wang was uninjured, one of his close friends was killed. This apparently convinced him to make the fateful step of collaborating with the Japanese. He flew to Japanese-held Shanghai in early 1939, visited Tokyo twice, and at the end of the year signed a secret agreement on "new relations between China and Japan." In March 1940, he and a number of other disaffected GMD members established a new government in Nanjing modeled after the original GMD design. Tokyo accorded formal recognition to his régime in November.

Considering himself Sun Yat-sen's rightful heir, who acted in accord with Sun's dream of true Sino-Japanese cooperation, Wang found that the Japanese were only willing to give him nominal administrative responsibilities while maintaining their economic and military stranglehold on occupied territories. A new treaty, negotiated in 1943, gave Wang's régime more responsibilities as Tokyo sought to induce defections from the GMD government in Chongqing. Meanwhile, Japanese brutalities hardened Chinese resistance in unoccupied China and collaboration with the invaders became less attractive. Still suffering from bullet wounds inflicted earlier, Wang's condition deteriorated in 1944, and he went to Japan for medical treatment. He died in Nagoya in November.

In an era when Chinese politics became increasingly militarized, Wang had no army to support his claim to leadership. Frustrated, he finally felt he could do his best for China by seeking an accommodation with Japan, both against foreign imperialism and the Communist threat at home. Sincere in his intentions, he had not expected to become a puppet, and his régime did give the Chinese a measure of protection against a repetition of Japanese atrocities like the 1937 rape of Nanjing.

WANG MANG (?–23 A.D.) A minister under the Han dynasty who, by virtue of his popular support among the higher echelons of Chinese society, usurped the throne and established the Hsin (New) dynasty (9 A.D.–23 A.D.). Wang Mang instituted reforms in an attempt to restore centralized administration and to initiate economic reforms. At that time, China's population, concentrated mainly in the north, was about 60 million. Peasants had been suffering from a shortage of cultivable land, monopolized by large landowners, and the central government was being deprived of revenue. Wang's reforms were based upon a idealized version of ancient Chinese institutions. He widened the ranks of the nobility, heavily taxed city dwellers and redistributed the excess property of the wealthy in order to improve the peasants' lot, outlawed slave trade and centralized the economy under state control. The resistance of powerful families made his plan unenforceable. In addition, the general breakdown of administrative controls had made the country more vulnerable to floods, causing bad harvests and famines. Peasant rebellions, like that of the RED EYEBROWS, and invasions by northern nomads (Xiongnu—possibly the same nomads known in the west as Huns) accelerated Wang's downfall. He was killed by rebels in 23 A.D., and two years later a descendant of the Han restored the dynasty (later Han dynasty, 25–220).

WANG MING (Chen Shaoyu)   (1904–1974) Chinese Communist leader. Born Chen Shaoyu in Anhui to a well-to-do farming family, Wang studied in provincial schools and in 1925, while studying at the Wuchang commercial college, joined the Communist youth corps. That year he also joined the CHINESE COMMUNIST PARTY (CCP) and was selected by the Hubei CCP organization to study in Moscow's SUN YAT-SEN University, which had been established for training Chinese cadres. After studying Russian and Marxism-Leninism, he returned to China, acting as interpreter for Pavel Mif (1901–1938), vice-rector of the university, who specialized in China. Sent to China by the COMINTERN to head a propaganda mission, Mif attended the 5th CCP Congress, held in May. Soon after the CCP's split with the Wuhan GUOMINDANG (GMD), Wang and his mentor returned to Moscow, where Wang served as interpreter for the 6th CCP congress and the 6th Comintern congress in 1928.

At Sun Yat-sen University, where he replaced KARL RADEK as rector, Mif cultivated a group of students, including Wang and QIN BANGXIAN, known as the "28 Bolsheviks," who were firmly committed to STALIN's China policy.

In 1930, Mif was appointed Comintern representative to the CCP and his disciples, led by Wang (who may have returned to China the previous year), conducted an intra-party struggle against LI LISAN, scapegoat for the disastrous policy of urban insurrection. In January 1931, several months after Li's dismissal, Mif's proteges, the "Returned students," took control of the CCP. This has been considered the last instance of direct Soviet interference in CCP internal affairs. In 1931, when the nominal party leader, XIANG ZHONGFA, was executed by the GMD, the 24-year-old Wang, who had little revolutionary experience, directed the party from its underground headquarters in Shanghai. During this time, MAO ZEDONG was building Red power in Jiangxi. In September, Wang went to Moscow as the CCP representative to the Comintern and Qin Bangxian, likewise Moscow-trained, became CCP general secretary.

Returning to China in 1937, Wang, who had acquired a reputation as a Marxist theoretician bearing STALIN's endorsement, clashed with MAO ZEDONG by advocating closer collaboration with the GMD. Though still a member of the CCP central committee (CC), he could not effectively challenge Mao's authority, confirmed during the Yan'an "rectification" (thought reform) campaign in 1942. Though severely criticized, Wang and other "deviationists" benefitted from Mao's relatively lenient treatment of party opponents at that time. He was reelected to the CC at the 7th CCP congress (1945), next to the lowest on the list, and at the 8th (1956), when he was ranked the very lowest among 97 CC members. He did not hold any substantive governmental or party positions. In 1956, he travelled to the Soviet Union for medical treatment. Under various pseudonyms he later wrote scathing attacks against the CCP. He died in Moscow in 1974.

WASHINGTON, GEORGE   (1732–1799) Commander in chief of the Army of Independence and first president of the United States (1789–1797). Of British ancestry, the eldest of five children of his father's second wife, Washington was born in a modest farmhouse near Fredericksburg, Virginia. His education was limited—he was the only one of the first six United States presidents who did not go to college. The marriage of his beloved elder half-brother Lawrence into an aristocratic English family, the Fairfaxes, provided the young Washington with his first experience as a land surveyor.

In the early 1750s Britain and France both laid claim to the upper Ohio Valley. The Fairfax family recommended Washington to head a small expedition representing English interests, but tragedy resulted when Washington attacked a small French encampment, thinking its members were spies. Ten men, including the diplomatic commander, were killed; the French claimed they were on a peace mission. The event exacerbated tensions that led to the French and Indian war in 1755. Washington served as an aide to British general Edward Braddock in his campaign to capture Fort Duquesne at the Forks of the Ohio. The campaign ended in catastrophic defeat for the British, although Washington drew praise from the British commanders for his "courage and resolution."

At 22, Washington was elected commander of all Virginia forces, his main task that of protecting the Virginia borders from Indian attacks. After the retreat of the French from Fort Duquesne the war ended, having engaged Washington from 1753 to 1759. Resigning from military life, he turned his energies to Mount Vernon, the plantation home he had rented from the widow of his half-brother, which would later become his permanent estate in Virginia. In 1759 he married Martha Dandridge Curtis, a wealthy widow with two small children. The Washingtons were charitable landowners, believing that no needy person should be turned away from Mount Vernon "lest the deserving suffer." Though he employed slaves, Washington was greatly troubled by the institution of slavery all his life. In his will he granted all his slaves their freedom, the only Virginia founding father to do so.

In the mid-1760s, Britain's policy of taxing its colonies precipitated the AMERICAN REVOLUTION. At first Washington hoped that armed rebellion could be avoided. As a member of Virginia's House of Burgesses he protested the STAMP ACT, which imposed taxes on the colonies to support the British army, and the Townsend Revenue Act, a tax on tea and other staples. In 1774 Washington was a delegate to the First Continental Congress in Philadelphia, which agreed to ban all British goods. It was not until after the battles of Lexington and Concord and the subsequent convening of the Second Continental Congress, in

May 1775, that it become clear to Washington that the colonies would in fact have to take up arms.

In the year preceding the signing of the declaration of independence on July 4, 1776, Washington created a navy of six ships that were ordered to capture British vessels; initiated a campaign to arrest and detain British Tories; and encouraged leaders of the colonies to adopt independence.

With the exception of Washington's stunning success at Trenton on December 25–26, 1776, when he recrossed the Delaware and surprised the Hessian mercenaries, his army had suffered several defeats in New York, culminating in the misery of the hard winter at Valley Forge. The battle of Monmouth (June 28, 1778), when Washington took the initiative boldly and drove the British back to their strongholds in New York, was the critical breakthrough for the Continental army. In September 1781 Washington's army, assisted by able French troops, defeated the British garrison at Yorktown, Virginia, thereby inducing Britain's war-weary withdrawal. Washington was lauded for his outstanding conduct of the war, personal courage and his concern for the underfed and ill-equipped men of his army. His suffering with them in their harshest trials, and his leadership and organizational ability were later recognized by Congress as indisputably qualifying him for the presidency. He was already being called "the father of his country."

A period of longed-for retirement from 1783 to 1787 ended when Washington was called on to attend the Philadelphia Convention in May 1787. Lack of foreign markets for American goods and Britain's prohibition of trade with the British West Indies had led to a shortage of money and mounting debts. Following a mass insurgency in Massachusetts in 1786 called SHAYS'S REBELLION, in which farmers had demanded liquidation of their debts, fears of anarchy led to the growing conviction that a strong federal government was necessary. Washington used his influence with all the delegates to draft the constitution, which would establish a strong centralized federal government. By 1788, 10 of the 13 states had ratified the constitution and on April 30, 1789, after unanimous election by the electoral college, Washington took the oath in New York City as first president of the United States.

The judicial system and the executive departments (the latter later known as the cabinet) established by Washington during his presidency have remained American institutions to the present time. Washington's foreign policy emphasized avoiding involvement in a European war, seeking treaties with Britain and Spain to open up the Ohio valley to American settlement, and promoting the nation's import trade. In 1796, he retired to his Mount Vernon plantation, where he spent his final days.

AL-WAZIR, KHALIL (Abu Jihad) (1936–1988) Palestinian Arab guerrilla/terrorist organizer. Born in Ramla, Palestine, Wazir left his home with the Palestinian refugees in 1948, after Israel became independent. In the 1960s he was among the founders of the guerrilla/terrorist organization FATAH (which in 1969 became dominant in the PALESTINE LIBERATION ORGANIZATION (PLO) and its "military" arm, *al-Asifa).* In the 1970s al-Wazir emerged as *Fatah's* chief "military" leader and was thus co-responsible for most of its guerrilla/terrorist operations. A loyal associate of PLO chairman YASIR ARAFAT, he stood by Arafat in his efforts to impose PLO discipline and a centralized military

command on the various dissent factions. He was a member of the executive council of *Fatah,* but not of the PLO executive (as a "military" man, not a political leader). Wazir was killed at his home in Tunis in April 1988—reportedly carried out by an Israeli commando.

WEATHERMEN A small splinter group that broke off from the STUDENTS FOR A DEMOCRATIC SOCIETY (SDS) in June, 1969. The SDS had been chiefly an American university movement that sought to have Reserve Officer Training Centers (ROTC) removed from college campuses during the Vietnam war. In 1968, the SDS succeeded in terminating the program at Columbia and in getting the university to terminate a number of defense-related contracts undertaken for the US Department of Defense.

The Weathermen took their struggle off the campuses. More importantly, they advocated domestic terrorism, including bombing buildings. While the SDS organized openly on college campuses, the Weathermen went underground. The core group of the Weathermen included the famous SDS leader of the 1969 Columbia University riots, Mark Rudd, and Bernadine Dohrn. This faction took its name from a line in the Bob Dylan song, "Subterranean Homesick Blues": "You don't need a weatherman to know which way the wind blows."

The Weathermen had 200–400 followers and took a fiercely antiestablishment line, supporting violence against any target that represented the "ruling class." The Weathermen also adopted many prevalent aspects of the 1960s counter-culture, including drugs, long hair and free sexual relationships. They were inspired by the revolutionary tactics of CHE GUEVARA. They attempted to bring their activities to high schools in the American midwest as well as to cities like Chicago and Flint. Not long after the break-off from SDS, three men died in an accidental bomb blast in a bomb factory located in a Greenwich Village townhouse in New York City.

WHAMPOA MILITARY ACADEMY Chinese nationalist military academy. Founded in May 1924 on an island near Canton, Whampoa was a major beneficiary of Soviet material assistance to the GUOMINDANG (GMD), headed by SUN YAT-SEN, who had long felt the need for a party army. CHIANG KAI-SHEK was the commandant and LAO ZHONGKAI the chief administrator. Staffed by Russian advisers, including General VASILY BLÜCHER and Chinese officers trained either in Japan or modern academies at home, Whampoa's six-month course followed principles established by TROTSKY for the Soviet RED ARMY after the October RUSSIAN REVOLUTION OF 1917. The academy's curriculum combined military training and political indoctrination and provided the National Revolutionary army with a dedicated corps of junior officers.

Infected by the rising tide of nationalism, 3,000 young men, both GMD and CHINESE COMMUNIST PARTY (CCP) sympathizers, applied for admission; 499 were accepted for the first class. Some Vietnamese Communists also trained at Whampoa. LIN BIAO, soon to become a brilliant Chinese Red Army commander, enrolled in 1926. Adopting the Soviet Red Army political commissar system, Whampoa produced highly disciplined and heroic officers. Of the 5,000 graduates who joined the NORTHERN EXPEDITION in 1926, over half were killed during the campaign.

Survivors belonging to the GMD became Chiang's most loyal followers and were known as the "Whampoa clique." Moved to the GMD government's new capital, Nanjing, in 1927, the academy became the Central Military Academy.

WHISKEY REBELLION A 1794 uprising in western Pennsylvania, the United States, that expressed popular resistance to the federal excise on whiskey, and more generally, the mounting opposition to Federalist economic policies.

The 1791 excise on whiskey taxed the chief exportable staple of extensive agricultural areas in western counties and the attempts at its enforcement caused considerable irritation to citizens of the affected regions. Pent-up discontents broke into a series of organized, violent attacks on federal marshals and tax inspectors in the summer of 1794. These attacks culminated in a march of hundreds of disaffected westerners on Pittsburgh. In the meantime, President WASHINGTON had been mustering militia units from the mid-Atlantic states. After the failure of negotiations with the insurgents, the militia forces moved in and by November they had succeeded in controlling and pacifying the western counties.

The Whiskey Rebellion reflected the uneasy subordination of rural interests and local powers to centralized national authority during the formative, critical years of the American republic.

WHITE LOTUS SOCIETY (Bailian jiao) Chinese secret society. Originating in the first half of 12th century, during the Southern Song dynasty (1127–1279), the White Lotus was one of the oldest Chinese secret societies. Based mainly in north China, it was more religious in character than the TRIADS, the major southern secret order. During this period there was a proliferation of religious cults that burned incense and chanted the Buddha's name. The White Lotus was founded by a Buddhist monk as a branch of Tiantai Buddhism. Belief in the Bodhisattva Maitreya—the Buddha of the Future ("Messiah")—sanctioned anti-dynastic uprisings in the Yuan (Mongol) (1280–1368), Ming (1368–1644) and Qing (Manchu) (1644–1912) periods. Elements of Daoism and Manichaeism, the latter introduced from the Near East during the Tang dynasty (618–907), may also have influenced White Lotus beliefs and practices. While promising the advent of the Buddha, White Lotus rebels sounded egalitarian themes and, when opposing foreign rulers (Mongols and Manchus), added ethnocentric, racist motifs. Proscribed as a heterodox cult, the White Lotus inspired rebellions fueled by deteriorating economic conditions. Starting in 1351, White Lotus rebels, also called "Red Turbans" because of the red cloths on their heads, rose in north China proclaiming their messianic message. ZHU YUANZHANG, eventual winner in the contest to replace the Mongols, may have originally been a White Lotus member. In 1774, the sect staged an anti-Qing uprising in Shandong, the first rebellion in a century. The White Lutus Society's next rebellion (1796–1804), in the mountainous Hubei-Sichuan-Shaanxi border region, signaled the beginning of serious dynastic decline.

WHITE REVOLUTION (1963–1978) A number of socioeconomic reforms, with the aid of which Iran's monarchical régime tried to transform the country, which until then utilized semi-feudal modes of production, into a modern one with intensive capitalist development. The shah, Muhammad-Reza Pahlavi, was the ideologist behind the so-called White Revolution. His program was submitted to a referendum on January 26, 1963, and was supported by 99.3% of the population. During the first 10 years of the White Revolution, a favorable economic situation increased Iran's oil revenues 40–50 fold. During that time, Iran's economic growth was second only to that of Japan in all of Asia. At the beginning of the 1970s, the annual growth rate of industrial production was between 20% and 30%. Iran entered new industrial areas, such as metallurgy, mechanical engineering, oil chemistry and atomic energy.

The pace of economical development in agriculture was, however, much lower. The White Revolution fostered a policy of separation of religion and state and placed limits on clerical influence in education and legal proceedings. For the first time, the agricultural reforms in Iran encroached upon the land belonging to the clergy—the base of the Muslim clergy's prosperity. In the field of social reform, women were given the vote and there was increased success in combating illiteracy, etc. However, the financial-economic crisis of the mid-1970s, caused by the grandiose plans of the shah's régime and the rapid militarization of the country, revealed all the contradictions of the régime and its reformist policy.

The dissatisfaction of an overwhelming majority of the country's population, caused by economic and political conditions, was added to protests against the régime's repressive domestic policy and its pro-western orientation. As a result, the 1979 Islamic revolution (see IRAN, REVOLTS AND REVOLUTIONS) took place, with the Muslim clergy playing the role of the element which united the antimonarchical opposition.

WILLIAM THE SILENT (William of Orange) (1533–1584) French-German-Dutch nobleman, first leader of the REVOLT OF THE NETHERLANDS against Spain. Born Prince of Orange and Count of Nassau, he was brought up in Breda, not far from Brussels, and entered the service of Emperor Charles V of the Holy Roman Empire, who at that time ruled the Netherlands (as well as Spain, southern Italy, the German Empire and America) as part of his Burgundian inheritance. He carried on his service under Charles's son and heir, Philip II of Spain; however, the latter's preference for Spaniards in the government as well as his absolutist, centralizing tendencies caused William to go into opposition from 1561 on.

A Lutheran himself, William also resisted the efforts of Philip II to impose religious conformity on his subjects and, in a speech of 1565, argued that it was not right for princes to rule consciences. The king's religious policy led to increasing friction; it peaked in August 1566, when Calvinist mobs stormed churches all over the country, stripping them of their plate and breaking their images. Now convinced that only armed force would impress the Protestants, Philip replaced his half-sister, Margaret, with the Duke of Alba as governor. The duke was one of the foremost military commanders of the age and, taking up his post in December 1566, set up the "Council of Blood" which executed over 1,000 Protestants and other opponents of the king. William himself was a moderate who did not support the Calvinists, and, indeed, quarreled with them because of his wish to remain loyal to the king. However, in 1568 his principal associates, fellow-noblemen by the name of LAMORAAL EGMOND and

FILIPS VAN MONTMORENCY HOORNE, were executed by the Spaniards. Fearing for his own life as well, William fled the country and, back in his native Dillingen (west Germany), organized an armed force with which he tried to invade the Netherlands. However, as a general he proved no match for Alba and was defeated at Gembloux in 1568. He then set out to patch up his differences with the Calvinists. From 1569 they recognized him as their leader and he, in turn, used his international connections to help organize and finance their continuing uprising against Spain.

In April 1572 his supporters, known as *geuzen* (beggars), captured the port of Brille in southern Holland, and this success was followed by a series of successful uprisings all over the northern Netherlands. In July 1572 the rebel representatives met and officially recognized William as *stadholder* or governor of the Netherlands, nominally on behalf of Philip II but in fact laying the foundation for an independent country.

As William tried to build up a new government and—which was unprecedented for his day—laid the basis for a policy of religious toleration, desperate fighting took place between the king's forces and those of the Dutch. By 1576 it looked as if Alba would win; however, at the decisive point the Spanish armies, unpaid for months, rebelled and, instead of continuing the war, turned back and sacked the great commercial city of Antwerp. As living proof of what would happen to those who submitted to Spanish rule, this event played into William's

William of Orange, nicknamed the Silent

hands. He was able to bring about a closer union of the northern provinces, acting as their de facto leader; meanwhile the search went on for some foreign prince who could be nominated to rule over them and bring much needed military aid. Negotiations with various European princes lasted for years, but brought no success.

Meanwhile, the Spaniards recovered. Alba having been recalled by Philip II, his third successor was Alessandro Farnese, another great commander who reorganized the Spanish army of Flanders and started reconquering the southern provinces in particular. In 1585 he took Antwerp, his greatest success; by that time, however, William was dead, having been murdered in 1584 by one of his opponents' agents. Though William did not live to see his country's independence from Spanish rule, his son Maurice continued the struggle and his descendants of the House of Orange ended up as kings of the Netherlands. William himself lies buried in the New Church at Delft, where his memory is revered as the father of the Dutch nation.

WORKERS PARTY OF KURDISTAN   see PKK.

WU GUANG (Wu Kuang)   (?–209 B.C.) Chinese rebel. In 209 B.C., a year after the death of Shi Huang-di, founder of the Qin dynasty (221–206 B.C.), CHEN SHENG and Wu led a revolt of frontier guards in north China in response to the harshness of Qin rule. Quelled within a month, this was one of the first recorded peasant revolts in Chinese history.

WU KUANG   see WU GUANG.

WU SANGUI (Wu San-kuei)   (1612–1678) Chinese rebel. Born in Liaodong (southern Manchuria), Wu followed his father in serving the Ming dynasty (1568–1644) as a military officer. Rising to the rank of general in 1640, he was summoned in 1644 to defend Beijing from the rebel armies of LI ZICHENG. Unable to arrive in time to save the capital, he withdrew to Shanhaiguan, the strategic pass guarding entry through the Great Wall from Manchuria. Wu preferred to surrender to the advancing Manchu armies rather than see the bandit, Li, occupy the throne. After joining the Manchu armies in routing Li's forces, Wu pursued the remnant Ming armies in the south, crossed into Burma in 1661 and captured the last Ming claimant to the throne near Mandalay. Wu brought the man to Yunnan and had him strangled. After the newly established Qing (Manchu) dynasty (1644–1912) rewarded Wu with a high title, he built up his own satrapy in the southwest. Amassing a huge fortune, he began defying Beijing's authority. In 1673, when threatened with the abolition of his feudatory, Wu revolted and established a new dynasty named Zhou. Two other Chinese satraps also rebelled. Wu died of dysentery in 1678, the year he declared himself emperor of his new dynasty, and was succeeded by his grandson. What became known as the SAN FAN REBELLION (Revolt of the Three Feudatories) was finally suppressed in 1681. The Manchu hold on the China mainland was now consolidated.

WU SAN-KUEI   see WU SANGUI.

WYATT'S REBELLION   (January–February 1554) Sir Thomas Wyatt the Younger of England, highly incensed at the

Sir Thomas Wyatt *by Holbein the Younger*

proposed marriage of Queen Mary to Philip II of Spain and the vision of a never-ending line of Roman Catholic offspring, led a rebellion of about 400 men in an attempt to replace the monarch with her Protestant sister Elizabeth. Wyatt and about 100 rebels actually managed to enter London, but they were soon routed and their leader executed.

WYCLIFFE, JOHN (c. 1328–1384) English theologian and reformer. The son of a wealthy rural family, Wycliffe studied at Oxford, where he became master of Balliol College in about 1360. During the next few years he vainly looked for a substantial ecclesiastical benefice until, in 1374, he was given the parish of Lutterworth, which he retained until the end of his life. Wycliffe lectured at Oxford and was employed by the crown in its negotiations with the papacy over the tribute owed to Rome by England. In 1375 and 1376 Wycliffe wrote two treatises, *De Dominio Divinio* (*On Divine Lordship*) and *De Civili Dominio* (*On Civil Lordship*). Arguing that only as long as he is in a state of grace can man have a rightful claim to property, he demanded the confiscation of the possessions of the Church, since it had lost its right to dominion because of moral decay. In a further work, *De Potestate Papae* (*On the Power of the Pope*), written in about 1379, he denied the divine origins of the papacy and referred to the pope as antichrist, and to his followers as "twelve daughters of a diabolical leech." Wycliffe also questioned the prevalent belief of transubstantiation and called for a return to primitive Christianity. Regarding the Bible as the only source of religious truth, he began to translate it into English, a work later continued by his followers.

Wycliffe's teachings, which became known outside England, were condemned by Pope Gregory XI in 1377. He himself, however, finding in John of Gaunt (1340–1399), Duke of Lancaster, a powerful protector, was not molested. While the higher clergy took steps to suppress his followers in Oxford, Wycliffe himself was only forbidden to lecture and allowed to die in his home parish. In 1415, however, the Council of Constance ordered his writings to be destroyed and his bones were disinterred and burned. Wycliffe's teachings were adopted by the LOLLARDS, a movement which gained adherents among the lower classes. His link with the 16th-century Reformation is demonstrated by the essential religious principle which he was the first to proclaim: the individual's right to seek salvation on his own, without the sacramental mediation of the established Church.

X

XIANG YU (Hsiang Yü) (232–202 B.C.) Chinese rebel. A native of present-day Jiangsu, Xiang was a general of aristocratic descent who overthrew the Qin dynasty (221–206 B.C.). In the ensuing struggle for control of the empire, he was defeated in 202 B.C. by his former associate, LIU BANG, who in 206 B.C. had established the Han dynasty.

XIANG ZHONGFA (Hsiang Chung-fa) (1880–1931) Chinese Communist leader. Born in Hubei and poorly educated, Xiang worked as miner, a laborer in a mint and a sailor and stevedore before joining the CHINESE COMMUNIST PARTY (CCP) in 1922. He was active in organizing workers and became vice-chairman of the Hanyeping general labor union. In 1926, he became a member of the CCP's Hubei regional committee and was elected to the central committee (CC) at the 5th CCP congress in 1927. He was elected to the temporary Politburo established at the emergency CC meeting in August that deposed CHEN DUXIU from party leadership. In 1928, he participated in a meeting of the COMINTERN executive committee in Moscow and was elected to its presidium.

At the CCP 6th congress, also held that year in Moscow, he was elected general secretary of the party. He wasthe only CCP general secretary during the pre-1949 period who came from a working-class background. The position, however, was purely nominal, since real power was held first by LI LISAN and then by WANG MING and the "Returned students." Betrayed by a comrade who had been arrested, Xiang was executed by the GUOMINDANG (GMD) in Shanghai in 1931. Though extremely popular and influential among Hubei workers, Xiang had had little influence on CCP policy.

XIAO DAO HUI see SMALL SWORD SOCIETY.

XINGZHONGHUI (XZH—Hsing Chung Hui, Society to Restore China's Prosperity) Chinese revolutionary organization. Formed in Hawaii in 1894 and then in Hong Kong in 1895, this was not so much a political party as an ad hoc conspiratorial group that plotted the downfall of the Manchu (Qing) dynasty (1644–1912). Without a well-defined program or organization, it nevertheless served as a vehicle for launching SUN YAT-SEN's political career. It marked the challenge to the traditional elite by non-literati, western-educated Chinese of lower-class origin who felt they were best equipped to neutralize the imperialist danger and preside over the modernization of China. The XZH constitution reflected strong nationalist convictions and republican sympathies. Members, mainly Hawaiian and Hong Kong Cantonese, swore an oath to "Expel the Manchus, Restore China and Establish a Republic." Its plots depended upon overseas Chinese funds and TRIAD secret society fighters. Beginning with some 20-odd members recruited in Hawaii, the total XZH membership may have reached 500 during its 11 years of existence. Sun and Yang Quyun (1861–1901), leader of an earlier Hong Kong group and Sun's rival for XZH leadership, were the organization's main activists. After its first plot, an elaborate plan to seize Canton and start a chain reaction for toppling the dynasty was aborted in October 1895, XZH remained inactive until 1900, when it instigated a surprisingly strong uprising at Huizhou (Waichow) in eastern Guangdong. It then became virtually moribund, and was supplanted in 1905 by the TONGMENGHUI. Yet, it had been innovative in trying to inject modern goals into the traditional pattern of secret society rebellions.

Y

YAKUB BEG (c. 1820–1877) Leader of a Muslim anti-Chinese rebellion. Born near Tashkent in the former KHANATE of Kokand (Khokand), Yakub established an independent Muslim state in Xinjiang (Chinese Turkistan) from 1865 to 1877, with its capital in Kashgar (Kashi). By 1873, his régime controlled the entire Tarim basin from the Pamirs to Lob Nor and had received semi-recognition from Britain and Russia. The sultan of Turkey conferred upon him the title of Emir of Kashgaria. Chinese forces, led by the able strategist, Zuo Zongtang, enlisted in a campaign to recover Xinjiang for the Qing (Manchu) dynasty (1644–1912). Yakub died in 1877 and with the capture of Khotan in 1878 the rebellion came to an end. (See also MUSLIM REBELLIONS.)

YANGA Yanga was one of the runaway black slaves, called "*cimarrones*," who in early 17th-century Mexico organized a slave revolt which lasted from 1607 until 1611. The revolt took place along the Veracruz-Puebla road, and the rebels defeated a heavily-armed force sent by the viceroy to subdue them. The government was forced to accept the status quo and to grant freedom and the right to settle in the mountains surrounding the city of Cordoba to Yanga and his followers. The rebels agreed to return all other runaways. As most of the rebels were male, they married local Indians. The communities they established have since, through continued intermarriage, lost all African identity.

YANG HSIU-CH'ING see YANG XIUQING.

YANG SHANG-K'UN see YANG SHANGKUN.

YANG SHANGKUN (Yang Shang-k'un) (1907–) Chinese Communist leader. Born in Sichuan, Yang joined the Communist youth league in 1925 and the CHINESE COMMUNIST PARTY (CCP) the following year. He was active in student and labor movements in Sichuan and Shanghai and in 1927 was sent to Moscow to attend SUN YAT-SEN University, an institution devoted to the training of Chinese Communist cadres. Returning in 1931, he belonged to the "Returned Student" faction that opposed MAO ZEDONG (see WANG MING), but subsequently made his peace with Mao. He was political commissar to the RED ARMY's 3rd Front Army in the LONG MARCH (1934–1935), during which he supported Mao Zedong at the Zunyi conference (January 1, 1935). During the Sino-Japanese war of 1937–1945, he was active behind enemy lines in the northwest and after 1945 he headed the secretariat of the military commission of the CCP's central committee (CC). With the establishment of the People's Republic of China (PRC) in 1949, Yang held important party posts and was elected to the CC in 1956. For a long period he headed the CCP's General Office, a post which made him the deputy of the CCP general secretary, DENG XIAOPING. In 1966, he was an early victim of the Cultural Revolution (see GREAT PROLETARIAN CULTURAL REVOLUTION). Rehabilitated in 1978, he was appointed vice-chairman of the Guangdong CCP. In 1981, he became secretary-general of the CCP military commission, working under its chairman, Deng Xiaoping, and in 1982 was elected to the Politburo. From 1988 to 1992 he served as chairman of the PRC as well as vice-chairman of the government's military commission.

YANG XIUQING (Yang Hsiu-ch' ing) (1820–1856) One of the leaders of the TAIPING REBELLION in China. A native of Guangxi and orphaned at an early age, Yang earned a living as a charcoal burner. In 1846, he joined the God Worshippers society, formed by followers of HONG XIUQUAN. While Hong claimed to be God's second son, Yang asserted he was God's mouthpiece. Like Hong, he fell into trances and purportedly received divine instructions. Hong was the Taiping prophet but Yang, an extremely capable yet ruthless organizer and administrator, led the movement to its most impressive gains. Within the leadership brotherhood, Yang was ranked God's third son, following Jesus and Hong. When the Taiping Rebellion erupted in 1850, Yang, as Eastern King, became commander-in-chief, supported by the Northern, Western, Southern and Assistant Kings. Imposing rigid discipline, Yang molded the Taiping bands into an imposing military force that in 1853 captured Nanjing, which became the capital of the Heavenly Kingdom. As God's alleged spokesman and Taiping prime minister, Yang claimed even greater authority in leadership councils than Hong, who could only claim to be God's son. In 1856, Hong responded to the challenge by ordering Yang's murder by the Northern King, who also had Yang's family and thousands of his followers assassinated. No less ambitious than Yang, the Northern King was in turn killed by order of Hong. Only the military genius of LI XIUCHENG kept the strife-ridden Taiping régime from an early demise (see also SHI DAKAI).

YAQUI REBELLIONS Rebellions by the Yaquis of the state of Sonora against the Spanish and later Mexican governments occurred sporadically from 1740 through the time of final reconciliation in 1920. The Yaquis, whose tribal territory now straddles the US-Mexican border, were, in the 1600s, under Jesuit missionary control. The 30,000 Yaquis constituted both the most numerous and most agriculturally advanced of the tribes of northwestern New Spain. Reorganized by the Jesuits into eight towns along the Yaqui river, their cultural identity was so strengthened thereby that their creation story came to begin with these eight communities.

For over a century the "showpiece" of the Jesuit missionary system, the Yaquis in 1740 led several neighboring tribes in what was to become the most significant revolt of the mission Indians. The revolt appears to have been triggered by three events: 1) the demands of mine owners and estate owners for a larger portion of Indian labor and agricultural produce; 2) attempts by the secular authorities to increase their control; and 3) the desire of the Yaquis for change in the mission system. The rebellion lasted six months, involving a combined rebel force of 12,00–14,000 men, in strike units numbering 300–400 individuals.

In 1828, shortly after Mexican independence, a decree was enacted awarding supervision of the Yaqui villages to a neighboring Mexican town, while another promoted the immigration of non-Yaqui Mexicans and the colonizing of Yaqui lands. Land was allotted to Yaquis in individual plots, to which they received title; a draft was enacted; and the Yaqui militia, created during the Spanish colonial period, was disbanded. The resulting rebellion, lasting from 1828 through 1833 and led by Yaqui Captain-General Juan Balderas, was aimed at quashing the above decrees. Some were rescinded by the government, but the revolt continued until Balderas was captured and executed in 1833.

During the 1870s, a new Yaqui leader, Cajeme, emerged. Under Cajeme, the Yaqui gained greater autonomy over all aspects of their lives, effectively becoming a "state within a state." This was unacceptable to the newly-elected Mexican president, PORFIRIO DIAZ, and his Sonoran representatives launched a military campaign to crush the Yaqui republic. With the pacification of the neighboring Apaches in the 1880s, the first railroads entered Sonora and the federal government for the first time assumed responsibility for pacifying the Yaquis, defeating Cajeme in 1887. Yaquis were encouraged to leave their homeland as wage laborers. Many did so, but a number of these became a more widely dispersed band of guerrillas. Under their new leader, Tetabiate, these began to conduct hit-and-run attacks. Government attempts to implement a resettlement policy resulted in the Yaqui villages taking up arms en masse once again in 1899, resulting in a massacre and the death of Tetabiate at Mazocoba in 1900.

The Yaquis now reverted to guerrilla attacks and the Diaz government responded with the massive, forced deportation of Yaqui men, women and children to central and southern Mexico, to be subjected to conditions of near-slavery, and to cruel and arbitrary punishments for the most minor offenses. The guerrillas in the north held out, however, until the US began patrolling the Arizona-Sonora border in 1909, thus cutting off an important avenue of escape.

What saved the Yaqui deportees from cultural extinction was the Mexican Revolution of 1910 (see MEXICO, REVOLUTIONS). When they learned that the Diaz dictatorship had been overthrown and Diaz himself forced into exile, most of the Yaquis returned to their Sonora homeland, where many joined the revolution. One guerrilla faction, however, under the leadership of Luis Espinsosa, continued to resist. Forces under the command of General OBREGON campaigned against this guerrilla band, but to no avail. Finally, in 1920, with the revolution essentially over, President Adolfo de la Huerta offered to acknowledge the heretofore unrecognized authority of the traditional leaders of the eight Yaqui communities of the 1600s; to negotiate with these leaders; to assist with Yaqui repatriation, resettlement and home reconstruction; and, finally, to relocate many neighboring non-Yaquis. 180 years of Yaqui struggle had ended: they had been recognized as a semi-autonomous entity, subject, however, to the higher authority of the nation-state.

YAZDI, AYATOLLAH MUHAMMAD (1931–) Iranian Islamic cleric, Member of the Council of the Islamic Revolution, 1979, member of the *majlis* (Iranian parliament).

Born in Qom, Yazdi studied and taught theology. In his struggle against the régime of Shah Muhammad Reza, he was jailed several times. After the Islamic Revolution of 1979 (see IRAN, REVOLTS AND REVOLUTIONS) he became president of the Islamic Revolutionary Court in Qom and director of the AYATOLLAH KHOMEINI's office, and held several prominent government positions. Despite his defeat in the 1988 parliamentary elections, Yazdi continued to fill public offices. The author of several religious books on Islamic government and jurisprudence, he sought to limit government involvement in small details of the citizen's life. Aligned with the conservative-moderate faction, he has frequently been attacked by hard-line radicals.

YAZDI, MORTEZA (1890–?) Iranian Communist leader. Born in 1890, Yazdi served as a physician in the ministry of health and professor at the University of Tehran. In 1936 he was arrested as a Communist. He was released in 1941 and was among the founders of the Communist TUDEH PARTY in 1942, and a member of its central committee. He became health minister in 1940–1941 and again in 1946. He was also involved with the Social Insurance Organization and social welfare groups. He was arrested again in 1954 and sentenced to death, but was pardoned by the shah and released later that year.

YEH CHIEN-YING see YE JIANYING.

YEH T'ING see YE TING.

YE JIANYING (Yeh Chien-ying) (1897–1986) Chinese Communist military leader. Born in Guangdong to a merchant family, Ye graduated from the Yunnan military academy in 1919 and joined the Guangdong army, which at that time supported SUN YAT-SEN. Ye was influenced by the nationalist, radical ideas promoted by the MAY FOURTH MOVEMENT and in 1922 remained loyal to Sun when CHEN JIONGMING revolted. In 1924, he was appointed deputy director of the instruction department of the WHAMPOA MILITARY ACADEMY. He served as a staff officer in the NATIONAL REVOLUTIONARY ARMY during the first phase of the NORTHERN EXPEDITION of 1926–1927 and joined the CHINESE COMMUNIST PARTY (CCP) in 1927. After the CCP split with the GUOMINDANG (GMD) in the summer of 1927, he was deputy commander of Communist forces that staged the CANTON UPRISING in December. In 1928, he went to Moscow for military training and in 1930 joined the CCP guerrilla base in Jiangxi, serving as a RED ARMY staff officer. During the LONG MARCH (1934–1935), he filled major command positions and in December 1936 assisted ZHOU ENLAI in securing CHIANG KAI-SHEK's release at Xi'an and in discussions leading to a revival of the CCP-GMD united front in September 1937. During the Sino-Japanese war of 1937–1945, he was chief of staff to ZHU DE, commander of the CCP's EIGHTH ROUTE ARMY. Elected to the CCP central committee in 1945, he remained chief of staff of CCP forces, redesignated the PEOPLE'S LIBERATION ARMY (PLA) in 1946. After the establishment of the People's Republic of China (PRC) in 1949, Ye became the principal CCP and government leader of his native province of Guangdong and the south China region. In 1955, he was among the 10 Communist officers awarded the rank of marshal of the PRC. In 1966, he was appointed vice-chairman of the CCP military commission, headed its secretariat and was elected to the Politburo. During the Cultural Revolution (see GREAT PROLETARIAN CULTURAL REVOLUTION), he opposed the radical LIN BIAO-JIANG QING clique and took charge of military affairs after Lin's demise in 1971. In 1973, he was elected to the Politburo's Standing Committee and became a CC vice-chairman. In 1975 he received the formal appointment as defense minister, a position he held until 1978. After the death of MAO ZEDONG in 1976, he was instrumental in the arrest of the "gang of four," accused of responsibility for Cultural Revolution atrocities. In 1978, he was elected chairman of the Standing Committee of the National People's Congress—equivalent to head of state—and in the following year delivered a major address rejecting Mao Zedong's definition of revisionism, thus undermining the ideological premise of the Cultural Revolution. His health seriously declining, Ye Jianying relinquished the National Congress chairmanship in 1983.

YELLOW TURBANS   Chinese rebels. Near the end of the 2nd century A.D., the Later Han dynasty (25–220 A.D.) started to decline. The imperial court was ridden with corruption and peasants were burdened with exorbitant taxes and victimized by floods and famine. It was in this period of general political and economic deterioration that the messianic message of popular Daoism exerted tremendous appeal. ZHANG JUE, leader of a faith-healing Daoist sect called Tai Ping Dao (Way of Great Peace), gathered converts and organized a church hierarchy. Growing rapidly in over 10 years of activity, the sect posed a challenge to imperial authority. In 184 A.D., while the government was preparing countermeasures, 360,000 members of the sect put on yellow kerchiefs and rose in revolt in eastern China. Thus the sect also came to be known as the Yellow Turbans. Though Zhang Jue was killed in that year, Yellow Turban bands continued to harass the government for a number of years. Meanwhile, another Daoist faith-healing cult, the FIVE PECKS OF RICE BAND, had revolted in the southwestern province of Sichuan. Both rebellions contributed to the dynasty's downfall.

YEMEN, REVOLUTIONS   After attaining independence in 1918, Yemen was ruled by a despotic, ultra-conservative royal house belonging to the Zeidi Muslim sect. Attempts by Imam Ahmad during his reign (1948–1962) to retain feudalism and isolate the country from all outside influences were overwhelmingly resented by many segments of the population. The Sunni Muslim majority suffered discrimination, merchants (mostly

Sunni) opposed strict trade restrictions, and even members of the Zeidi clan resented the monarchy for its nepotism and its autocratic, often whimsical, method of government. Opponents of the régime were generally executed; the execution of a Hashed tribal leader in 1959 sparked an uprising that was crushed ruthlessly. Another increasingly disgruntled segment of the population was the military: many of its officers had been trained in Egypt and Iran and were well aware of the benefits of modernization to the country.

When Imam Ahmad died in September 1962, the country poised itself for at least some degree of modernization. Although the new Imam, al-Badr, seemed to be inclined to follow his father's policies, he also surrounded himself with a group of military figures who had traveled abroad and were eager to implement their findings in Yemen. Chief among these was 'ABDULLAH SALLAL, whom al-Badr immediately appointed chief of the royal guard and, according to some reports, commander in chief of the army. Within days of al-Badr's ascending the throne, however, it became clear to Sallal that the Imam planned to preserve his father's legacy. One week later, Sallal seized Sana'a, the capital, and declared Yemen a republic, with himself as president and prime minister.

Al-Badr fled to the north, from where his family originated, and mustered a large group of supporters. Sallal was unable to quash this resistance to his régime, and within just one week of assuming power, Egyptian forces entered the country to defend the republican government. Meanwhile, Saudi Arabia, whose royal family was afraid that republican sentiment might reach it, gave its support to the royalists. Heavy fighting continued until 1963, when the Americans finally managed to broker a peace agreement, but the truce was soon violated and fighting resumed. A second, short-lived truce was arranged by President GAMAL ABDUL NASSER of Egypt in 1964, but it was only in 1965 that Nasser and King Faisal of Saudi Arabia arranged what seemed to be a lasting peace.

According to the terms of the agreement, Sallal would settle temporarily in Egypt, although he would still officially retain the presidency. True power, however, would be in the hands of Hassan al-Amri, a member of the Revolutionary Council and vice-president since 1963. Al-Amri was also opposed to the Zeidi monarchy, but he was more inclined to the conservative elements in the country and was, therefore, believed capable of bridging the gap between them and the liberal-minded republicans. By 1966, however, it became clear to Nasser that al-Amri was also anti-Egyptian. Sallal was returned to the country and reinstated as both president and prime minister. In response, the royalists escalated their attacks.

In 1967 Sallal was removed from power in a military coup and Qadi Abd al-Rahman al-Iryani, a Zeidi cleric, was appointed president. Despite dangerous royalist advances that were even threatening Sana'a, he succeeded in quashing them by 1969 and in bringing about a reconciliation between the Republic of Yemen and Saudi Arabia. Al-Iryani was deposed by a coup in 1974.

YE TING (Yeh T'ing)   (1896–1946) Chinese Communist military leader. Born to a Guangdong peasant family, Ye began studying sericulture but soon shifted to a military career. After studying in local military academies, he joined SUN YAT-SEN's

Guangdong army in 1919 and the GUOMINDANG (GMD). In 1924, LIAO ZHONGKAI, a GMD leader at the WHAMPOA MILITARY ACADEMY, sent him to Russia to study at the University of the Toilers of the East and the RED ARMY military academy. He soon joined the Moscow branch of the CHINESE COMMUNIST PARTY (CCP). During the first stage of the NORTHERN EXPEDITION of 1926–1927, he commanded an independent regiment that included Communist officers trained at Whampoa. After the CCP-GMD split, Ye, who had risen to the rank of division commander, participated in the CCP NANCHANG UPRISING of August 1, 1927. He was a leader in the December Canton uprising, after which he fled to Hong Kong.

In 1928, he was sent to Moscow for further study but subsequently broke contact with the CCP. After traveling in Europe, he returned to China in 1931 but was politically inactive until the outbreak of the Sino-Japanese war (1937–1945) and the resumption of the CCP-GMD united front. In 1938, he became commander of the CCP's NEW FOURTH ARMY and was captured by the GMD when its forces clashed with Ye's in January 1941. Imprisoned for five years, he was finally released in March 1946 and requested to be reinstated as a CCP member. MAO ZEDONG telegraphed his approval. In April of that year he and several other CCP leaders were killed in a plane crash while on the way to Yan'an, the CCP headquarters.

YHOMBI-OPANGO, JOACHIM Yhombi-Opango was born in the Congo and educated in France, where he also received his military training at the St. Cyr military academy. He served in the French army and then, in 1962, enlisted in the Congolese army. His jobs included military aide to President Massamba-Débat, military attaché at the Congolese embassy in Moscow and—finally—chief of staff of the armed forces.

Yhombi-Opango's politics are anti-left and he opposed the left-wing critics of the Congolese head of state, Marien Ngouabi, who had seized power in a military coup in 1968–1969 (see CONGO-BRAZZAVILLE, COUPS). When Ngouabi was assassinated in 1977, Yhombi-Opango was appointed head of state by the ruling party, the Marxist-Leninist *Congolais du Travail* (PCT). Colonel (later Brigadier General) Yhombi-Opango improved relations with the USA and France, but his régime inherited severe economic problems and he came into conflict with the party's left wing. In February 1979, he surrendered his powers to a provisional committee appointed by the PCT, and he himself was imprisoned. In 1984, he was released from detention and placed under house arrest.

On August 31, 1992, the new democratic government of Pascal Lissouba took office and in June 1993 Yhombi-Opango was appointed prime minister in this government, following elections in May. Yhombi-Opango is head of the *Rassemblement Pour la Démocratie et la Développement* (RDD) Party, founded in 1990, which advocates a mixed economy.

YOUNG ITALY Italian movement for independence and unification. Founded in 1831 by GIUSEPPE MAZZINI as a successor to the CARBONARI, whose terrorist methods had failed to bring down Austrian rule in the revolution of 1830, the movement was intended to rejuvenate the Italian people by means of moral influence, education and propaganda. Originally it had a mere 40 members. However, it spread rapidly and within two years was claimed by its leader to have no fewer than 50,000 adherents, mainly in Liguria, Piedmont and Lombardy.

Intended by its leader to be the model of similar movements elsewhere, Young Italy's finest hour came in 1848–1849. Its members led anti-Austrian and anti-papal revolts throughout Italy, and for a brief time they were even able to occupy Rome. However, Austrian and French troops put down the revolution, causing the influence of Young Italy to be largely taken over by the kingdom of Piedmont on the one hand and by GIUSEPPE GARIBALDI on the other.

YOUNG RUSSIA The title of a manifesto printed in the summer of 1862, the term came to signify the outlook of the radical, action-oriented Russian youth of the 1860s and early 1870s. It was modeled on the thinking of MAZZINI and YOUNG ITALY. The manifesto emphasized the need to destroy the existing institutions of political and social relations in Russia. It pointed out the advantages of close cooperation between the revolutionary INTELLIGENTSIA elite and the popular masses. In this sense, it was the epitome of populist (see POPULISM) thinking, with the addition of a clear JACOBIN tendency that was to become progressively stronger in Russian revolutionary theory as the decades passed. The core of the manifesto was the statement that there was no alternative to a total overthrowing of the existing régime, under which "everything is false, everything is foolish, from religion...to the family." This would be accomplished by "a revolution, a bloody and pitiless revolution...bringing about the ruin of all who support the existing order.... Remember that when this happens, all who are not with us are against us, are our enemy, and every means is used to destroy an enemy."

The writing and publication of the manifesto was almost entirely the work of Peter G. Zaichnevsky, a Moscow student of mathematics. An ardent socialist who had studied the writings of socialist theoreticians in Europe, Zaichnevsky was outraged by the limited nature of the 1861 emancipation of the serfs and urged the peasants to prepare themselves both ideologically and militarily for revolt against the autocracy. The Young Russians began a literacy campaign in the villages and towns that was quickly terminated by the police. They then turned to printing and peddling in the villages the works of HERZEN and OGAREV, along with translations of European socialists.

The aim of Young Russia was a democratic socialist federal republic based on the free initiative of the various regions making up the Russian empire. Each region was to be made up of rural communities, voluntarily formed. These would function much as did the traditional peasant community, redistributing the land periodically and adjusting the tax burden owed by each member. Other points were the emancipation of women, free education and the abolition of monasteries.

Herzen in particular was critical of the manifesto as "un-Russian." He felt that the West European concepts of democracy, SOCIALISM and even the idea of a republic were foreign to the understanding of the Russian peasant. Chernyshevsky, who was also against a Jacobin and elitist revolutionary movement, criticized the dictatorial and statist elements that he found in the manifesto.

YOUNG TURKS A group of Ottoman officers, officials and intellectuals who, in 1908, revolted against the régime of Sultan

Abdülhamid II and consequently, except for six months, ruled the empire until the end of World War I. The opposition movement dated back to 1889, when a secret society was formed by students of the military medical school to fight against the sultan's absolutist and tyrannical régime. Students from other institutes joined the society, but police began to crack down on the revolutionaries, and many of them had to escape abroad. In European capitals and in Cairo, the exiles, the most prominent of these being Ahmed Riza and Murad Bey, formed a number of societies and published periodicals which were smuggled into the Ottoman Empire. In 1899, they were joined by the sultan's own brother and two of his sons—one of whom, Sabahettin, later rose to a position of leadership. In the early 20th century, particularly after 1906, many new secret societies were organized by officers and officials within the empire itself. In 1907, a loose umbrella organization of these groups was established, called the Committee of Union and Progress (CUP).

Military unrest reached its peak in summer 1908, when several high-ranking officers in Macedonia defected. This led to revolution. The revolution itself was carried out by the strongest of the secret societies, which was located in Salonika. The Sultan failed to prevent the mutiny from spreading and, on July 24, he yielded to the officers' demands by reactivating the constitution of 1876 and reinstating parliamentary institutions. Until the end of World War I, the CUP was the dominant force in the government. Its power was further strengthened when a conservative counterrevolution failed in April 1909, leading to the sultan's deposition and his replacement by his compliant brother, Mehmed Resad.

The Young Turks' revolution gave rise to great hopes for brotherhood and equality among all the nations of the empire, but the CUP gradually became centralistic and authoritarian. It was committed to the preservation of the empire and tried to achieve this by enacting a harsh policy of Ottomanism, including the prohibition of nationalist organizations and the compulsory dissemination of the Turkish language. It was therefore opposed by more liberal groups and by non-Muslim and non-Turkish elements which supported decentralization.

In 1911, liberal opposition in parliament was consolidated in the Liberal Union; parliament was dissolved and new elections were won by the CUP. An officers' coup in 1912, however, ousted the party. In a countercoup in January 1913, led by ENVER PASHA, the CUP regained power, and until 1918 the state was in fact ruled by a military dictatorship headed by a triumvirate of Enver, KEMAL ATATÜRK and TALAT PASHA.

The Young Turks introduced important measures of modernization. They reorganized provincial administration (1913), passed new land laws and encouraged local industry and economic development. They reduced the influence of religion on state affairs, adopting, for example, a new liberal family law (1917). By maintaining at least the outward forms of parliamentarianism, elections and party life, they permeated the country with the principles of democratic procedure. Finally, the relative freedom of expression led to the crystallization of various ideologies, among which were secularism and Turkish nationalism—the latter founded by ZIYA GÖKALP. The Young Turks in effect provided the groundwork for the radical reforms of Atatürk.

In spite of their efforts, the Young Turks did not succeed in preserving the integrity of the empire. Not only did they lose territory during the Balkan wars, but their decision to join World War I on what became the losing side hastened the empire's final dissolution. The government was unable to prevent the ARAB REVOLT of Sharif Hussein of Mecca in 1916, and by the end of the war the Arab provinces were occupied by Allied and Arab troops. The Young Turk leaders fled the country and, though they later attempted to reestablish their rule, the new nationalist forces remained in power.

YUGOSLAVIA, COMMUNIST TAKEOVER   During World War II, Yugoslavia experienced the occupation and disintegration of the country and a bitter and painful political, ethnic, religious and ideological civil war. The takeover of the country by the victorious partisan forces led by TITO was in fact almost over by the time the country was liberated in autumn 1944. The main ingredients of power were already in Tito's hands, as the infrastructure of a reconstituted federal state from its prewar pieces had been set up during the partisans' victorious advances against the retreating Italians, Nazis and the local forces opposing the partisans.

The birth of postwar Communist Yugoslavia can be considered to have taken place in November 1943, when the Anti-Fascist Council of National Liberation (AVNOJ) declared itself as the supreme legislative body of the federal structure and prohibited the return of King Peter II. In agreements reached in 1944–1945 between Tito and the prime minister of the Yugoslav government in exile, Ivan Subasic, reinforced by the Yalta agreements, a regency council was appointed until a plebiscite would decide the fate of the monarchy and on the formation of a coalition government between Tito and the London-based government. The new government formed in March 1945 was short-lived, as the actual assumption of power by the Communists proceeded rapidly. In the 1945 elections, the Communists received some 90% of the votes, after a long campaign of intimidation and the resignation of non-Communist members of the government before the elections. The institution of monarchy was abolished and King Peter II discredited as having supported collaborators. The revival of the prewar Yugoslav political parties was bluntly opposed by the Communists, who had already built up strong power bases on the local and national levels and across all segments of society. The new Assembly proclaimed the Federal People's Republic of Yugoslavia and the new cabinet of early 1946 included eleven ministers who were Communists and 10 others who were fellow-travellers. The capture and execution of USTASHA leader Mihailovic in July 1946, along with wide-scale trials of real or alleged collaborators with the enemy during the war, ensured the removal of any possible opposition to Tito. Along with parallel steps in the social and economic fields, Yugoslavia was for all practical purposes a one-party Communist state by early 1946 and its constitution of 1946 was the replica of the 1936 Stalinist one in the Soviet Union.

Following the rift with JOSEPH STALIN that erupted in 1948, Tito could justly claim that he did not owe the takeover of the country either to a Soviet military presence or to Soviet pressure, unlike the case in the other bloc States.

Z

ZAGHLUL, AHMAD SA'D (1860–1927) Egyptian politician and major leader of Egyptian nationalism. Born to a prosperous land-owning family of farmers in Ibiana in the Nile delta, Zaghlul studied law after a traditional Islamic education. At the beginning of the century he was one of the young modernists close to the *Umma* Party who opposed the conservative-Islamic trend. He was thus regarded by some as collaborating with the British administrators, although he also remained close to the Islamic revivalist circles around Muhammad Abdul. In 1906, he was appointed minister of education and in 1910 minister of justice. He resigned in 1913 to head the opposition in the legislative assembly. At the end of World War I he emerged as a leader of the nationalists and headed a delegation (Arabic:*Wafd*) to the British which demanded full independence; from this delegation the WAFD evolved as a political party and the main proponent of the national struggle. In an effort to suppress nationalist ferment, the British exiled Zaghlul twice—in March 1919 to Malta (released in April), and in 1922 to Aden, the Seychelles and Gibraltar. In 1923–1924 Zaghlul led the *Wafd* Party to victory in nominally independent Egypt's first elections, and in January 1924 he became prime minister. However, when the British high commissioner, Lord Allenby, reacted to the murder of the governor-general of Sudan and commander of the Egyptian army, Sir Lee Stack, in November 1924, by presenting the government with an ultimatum and conditions considered extreme and humiliating, Zaghlul resigned. In new elections, in March 1925, the *Wafd* won a partial victory and Zaghlul was elected speaker of the House—whereupon the House was dissolved. In the elections of May 1926, Zaghlul again led the *Wafd* to victory, but declined to form a government and was reelected speaker. His death in September 1927 was a great blow to the nationalist movement and still today his memory as a great national leader has remained alive.

ZA'IM, HUSNI (1889? 1896? –1949) Syrian officer and nationalist, president of Syria in 1949. Born in Aleppo, reportedly of Kurdish origin, Za'im served as a professional officer in the Ottoman army and after World I in the "Special Troops" formed by the French authorities. During World War II he remained loyal to the Vichy-French authorities, and after the conquest of Syria by the British and Free French in 1941 he was detained, but returned to the army after his release. During the Arab-Israel war of 1948, he was chief of staff with the rank of brigadier. On March 30, 1949, Za'im mounted Syria's first military coup, deposed President al-Quwwatli and dissolved parliament. In June,

he held a referendum which endorsed him as president with wide powers. He dissolved all political parties and ruled without a legislative or parliamentary body. Za'im had ambitious plans for reforms inspired by those of KEMAL ATATÜRK. He was the first Arab leader to give women the franchise and tried to separate state and religion. He was pro-French and anti-Hashemite and strengthened relations with Egypt, Saudi Arabia and Turkey. He also tried to establish contacts with the leaders of Israel, indicating that he was interested in peace and the constructive settlement of the issues in dispute, such as the refugee problem.

Za'im did not have the time to implement any of his far-reaching plans. He was overthrown on August 14, 1949 by a pro-Hashemite coup stage by Colonel SAMI HINNAWI. A military court summarily sentenced him to death together with his prime minister, Mushin al-Barazi, and he was immediately executed.

ZAIRE, COUP OF 1965 On November 26, 1965, the Zairean army, led by Lieutenant General MOBUTU seized power in a military coup. It intervened because of the political conflict between the president and head of state, JOSEPH KASAVUBU, and the prime minister, Moise Tshombe.

All executive powers were transferred to Mobutu, who declared himself head of state of a "Second Republic." Parliament was suspended and Mobutu ruled by decree. In 1967, Mobutu founded a party, the MOUVEMENT POPULAIRE DE LA REVOLUTION (MPR), to rule the country.

ZANU see ZIMBABWE AFRICAN NATIONAL UNION.

ZAPATISTA NATIONAL LIBERATION ARMY (EZLN— Ejercito Zapatista de Liberacion Nacional) The latest expression of a long-standing history of revolutionary struggle in Mexico, dating back to the Spanish conquest initiated by Hernan Cortes between 1519 and 1521. Specifically, it embodies the confluence of deep-seated traditions of indigenous and peasant resistance to economic and cultural oppression with the legacy of the socialist-oriented guerrilla movements of the 1960s and 1970s. The Mexican state which is the principal bastion of the EZLN, Chiapas, borders Guatemala and has a long history of its own of indigenous and peasant rebellion.

The Zapatista movement is rooted in a complex fusion of indigenous and non-indigenous traditions of struggle, which trace their lineage both to centuries of resistance to Spanish colonial rule and to Emiliano Zapata and the most radical strains of the Mexican revolution. According to the EZLN's initial public communique and entitled the *First Declaration of the Lacandon Jungle,* issued on January 1, 1994, "We are the product of 500 years of struggle: first against slavery, in the war of independence against Spain...later in resistance against our threatened absorption by North American expansionism, and then...in order to expel the French empire from our soil. [Afterwards] we fought against the dictatorship of PORFIRIO DIAZ when the people rebelled under leaders forged by them such as VILLA and Zapata, poor men like ourselves.... [We] have nothing, absolutely nothing: without a dignified place, without work, without health care, food or education, deprived of the right to freely and democratically choose those who govern us, without independence from foreign control, without peace or justice for ourselves and for our children. But today we say, ENOUGH!"

The declaration was issued simultaneously with the EZLN's spectacular emergence into public life by seizing the seats of municipal government in seven heavily indigenous townships in the highlands region of Chiapas: San Cristobal de las Casas, Ocosingo, Las Margaritas, Altamirano, Oxchuc, Chanal and Huixtan, early on the first day of the year 1994.

Both the armed forces and the country's democratic opposition movements hesitated during the first few hours after the uprising became known throughout Mexico, seeking to take their bearings amid widespread confusion and disbelief. The EZLN was unknown until the uprising itself began, although clashes between army troops and the incipient guerrilla movement had been reported in the independent press as early as May 1993. The régime of then-President Carlos Salinas de Gortari apparently did its best to kill the story of these clashes, in order to prevent word of them further complicating the bitter debate over congressional approval of the North American Free Trade Agreement (NAFTA) in the US.

Once the armed forces began to respond to the EZLN's surprise offensive with Vietnam-style "search and destroy" missions and bombings of civilian settlements alleged to be EZLN strongholds, a peace movement began to mobilize in the capital and other major cities. The first mass demonstration against the war took place in Mexico City on January 12 and was, according to observers and the independent press, one of the largest such mobilizations since the 1968 student movement, with several hundred thousand people participating. The political pressures which this march generated even before it took place, together with widespread international media coverage of the uprising and of the indiscriminate military response, led President Salinas to announce a cease-fire the same day.

The EZLN's seizure of San Cristobal was of especially powerful symbolic value. The city is named in honor of the first Bishop of Chiapas, Fray Bartolome de las Casas, renowned as the defender of indigenous rights throughout the Spanish empire, a precursor of both liberation theology and the very notion of international human rights. Traditionally, in San Cristobal the sidewalks have been reserved for "*ladinos,*" with indigenous pedestrians being relegated to negotiating the traffic of its narrow cobbled streets regardless of the heavy loads on their backs.

The caste-like patterns of systematic discrimination against the indigenous people in Chiapas, like that prevalent in the rest of Mexico, transcends lines of race and skin color. Dark-skinned "*ladinos*" distinguish themselves from their brethren who are identified as and discriminated against as indigenous by their western dress and rejection of the use of the widely used indigenous languages. The discriminatory effects of language use are exacerbated by the close relationship between indigenous identity and illiteracy (either in Spanish or in the principal indigenous languages spoken—Tzotzil, Tzeltal, Tojolabal, Mam, Zoque), especially among indigenous women. In this way indigenous identity is automatically equivalent to second-class citizenship, in a manner similar to that of Afro-Americans in the US in the pre-civil rights movement in the south, or of blacks in pre-1994 South Africa. But the closest parallels are to the treatment of fellow indigenous peoples in neighboring Guatemala and in Andean countries such as Ecuador, Bolivia, Peru and the Amazonian region.

The EZLN is notable as the most successful attempt thus far in Latin America to blend a revolutionary strategy derived from the Cuban Revolution (see CUBA, REVOLTS AND REVOLUTIONS) itself and its multiple emulators throughout the region in the spirit of ERNESTO CHE GUEVARA, with home-grown elements, including a gift for tactics combing a mastery of traditional Mayan imagery, symbols and rhetoric together with mass media outreach skills. This has led observers to describe the EZLN's uprising as the First "post-Communist" revolution, as claimed by prominent Mexican writer Carlos Fuent, and as the first revolt "against the world market," according to Marc Cooper in the *Village Voice.* Mexican Interior Secretary Jose Angel Gurria has recently commented to a gathering of worried US investors that the war in Chiapas since January, 1994 has been more a "war of ink and Internet than of bullets" since the January 12, 1994 cease-fire. The revolt's alleged "post-modernist" qualities are highlighted by the fusion in its leadership and discourse between indigenous and non-indigenous elements, especially its charismatic spokesperson and chief military strategist, the masked leader known as Sub-commander MARCOS.

Marcos, who first appeared during the two-day takeover of San Cristobal de las Casas, has captured the imagination of much of Mexico and, to a surprising extent, of the media and informed public of the west, with his vehement eloquence and flamboyant gift for language. Several editions of his sometimes lengthy communiques on behalf of the EZLN have been published in the USA, France and Germany, among other countries, as well as throughout Latin America. Their content ranges from relatively standard revolutionary left rhetoric to powerful renderings of traditional Mayan mythology, from short stories and poetry to children's tales liberally laced with quotes and footnotes, ranging from Shakespeare and Cervantes to pop music. The communiques almost invariably have been published full-length in at least one and often three or more of Mexico City's most influential dailies, sometimes occupying two or three tabloid-size pages.

The Zedillo administration attempted to blame the EZLN for the precipitate devaluation of the peso in December. EZLN does indeed seem likely to play a key role as a catalyst for change, playing a similar kind of "revolutionary reformist" role to that of the April 19 (M-19) Movement based in Colombia and the Arabundo Marti National Liberation Front (FMLN) in El Salvador. In both countries, major steps toward fundamental reform would not have occurred without pressure from armed movements with widespread public backing. At the same time, however, these movements have been confronted with the dilemma of transition: how to disarm while still retaining their vanguard leadership roles. If Mexico's transition is violent—which, given its history, is indeed possible—the EZLN's role will be central, with the probability of armed uprisings along similar lines emerging in such other marginalized states such as Oaxaca, Tabasco, Veracruz, Guerrero, Hidalgo and Chihuahua, and of a geographically more broadly-based EZLN providing leadership and serving as a coordinating body.

In either case, the EZLN uprising of 1994– 1995 is likely to transform the Mexican social and political landscape in one or both of two fundamental ways: either precipitating a more accelerated transition to democracy or by forcing the hand of the most repressive sectors of the ruling class and sparking a right-wing militaristic crack-down.

ZAPU see ZIMBABWE AFRICAN PEOPLE'S UNION.

ZASULICH, VERA (1849–1918) Russian terrorist and later founder of Russian MARXISM. Zasulich was born to a noble family in Smolensk. At the age of three her father died and she was sent to live with a rich relative. In 1867, Zasulich arrived in Moscow, where she spent two years at a boarding school in preparation for the exam for governesses. Here, she came into contact with radical ideas. In 1869, she left for St. Petersburg to work in a bookbinding firm. She attended lectures at the University of St. Petersburg and participated in the revolutionary student movement of 1868–1869. Arrested for involvement with SERGEI NECHAEV, she was detained in prison for two years. Zasulich joined the underground *Narodniki* movement. She joined the Young Rebels in Kiev who, like great numbers of other populist youth, went to live among the peasants, in the hope of spreading socialist ideas.

Outraged by the arrest, conviction and mistreatment of other *Narodniki* members, she decided to take action. On January 24, 1878, she shot and wounded the governor of St. Petersburg, General Trepov. This act earned her worldwide attention and prestige among European radicals. Furthermore Zasulich's act had set a precedent, and during 1878 widespread attacks on police followed attempts to arrest *Narodniki* members. In the wake of massive public sympathy, Zasulich was acquitted and left for Switzerland where, in 1879, she reversed her support of terrorism, believing that it would ultimately lead to a rift between a revolutionary elite and the people.

In 1882, with three other radicals, Zasulich founded the Liberation of Labor, the first Russian Marxist organization. More an activist than a theorist, Zasulich secretly returned to her homeland in 1899 to resolve the split between the Social Democrats in Russia and those in Geneva. She met VLADIMIR LENIN in St. Petersburg and they agreed to set up the socialist journal, *Iskra*. In 1903, however, after Lenin broke away and formed the BOLSHEVIK PARTY, Zasulich ardently opposed him. She sharply criticized his elitist view of the Marxist revolution and remained with the MENSHEVIK Party. In 1905, after the revolution, she returned to Russia, where suffering from poor health, she refrained from political activity and earned her living by translating literature into Russian. In 1908, she led the liquidationists who believed that the socialists should come out of the underground. In 1918, shortly after the RUSSIAN REVOLUTION OF 1917, she died of tuberculosis.

ZENZINOV, VLADIMIR (1880–1953) Socialist Revolutionary leader and writer. The son of a Moscow-Siberian family of Old Believers, Zenzinov received an education in law, philosophy and history at the Heidelberg, Halle and Berlin universities. A member of the central committee of the Socialist Revolutionary Party from its founding, Zenzinov participated in the preparations for the RUSSIAN REVOLUTION OF 1905 but was arrested and banished to Siberia. He escaped to Geneva, returning only after October 1905. Re-arrested early in 1906, he walked 500 miles through Siberia to escape to Japan. His third arrest brought him six months in jail followed by exile to the Siberian north, where he wrote a book on the peoples of the Russian Arctic. Released in 1915, he returned to political activity, helping reorganize the SOCIAL REVOLUTIONARY PARTY.

From February 1917, he was chair of the party's Petrograd committee as well as filling other responsible elected posts, including membership in the short-lived Constituent Assembly of January 1918. Following the bolsheviks' seizure of power, he was active in organizing anti-Bolshevik groups in Siberia. He emigrated to France in 1919, where he was a central figure in the Russian emigre press and politics. With the coming of World War II he moved to New York, where he continued his activities until his death.

ZHANG BINGLIN (Chang Ping-lin; Zhang Taiyan, Chang T'ai-yen) (1869–1936) Chinese nationalist revolutionary. Born into a scholarly Zhejiang family, Zhang received an excellent classical education at home and in 1890 continued studies at the famous Hangchou academy, Gujing jingshe. China's defeat in the first Sino-Japanese war (1894–1895) and the intensified imperialist threat convinced him of the need for radical reform. He supported Kang Youwei and Liang Qichao (see CHINESE REPUBLICAN REVOLUTION OF 1911), but when their 1898 reformist program was aborted, Zhang took an increasingly radical stand against the Manchu (Qing) dynasty (1644–1912). After the BOXER REBELLION of 1900, he became overtly revolutionary. In 1902, he was close with the Shanghai intellectuals who later formed the revolutionary GUANGFUHUI (Restoration society). In 1903, Zhang's anti-Manchu insults, printed in the radical Shanghai newspaper *Su Bao*, led to his arrest in the International Settlement. He was tried and imprisoned along with his young friend, ZOU RONG, whose inflammatory pamphlet, *The Revolutionary Army*, became the most famous anti-dynastic tract. Zou died in prison, but Zhang survived. Upon his release in 1906 he traveled to Japan, joined SUN YAT-SEN'S TONGMENGHUI (TMH) and became an editor of its journal, *Min Bao (People's Report)*. Zhang then used his vitriolic pen, not only against the Manchus, but against the TMH's reformist rivals, who still clung to the hope of establishing a constitutional monarchy. He became the leading anti-Manchu publicist of the 1911 Revolution.

Influenced by elements from traditional Chinese thought, including Confucianism and Daoism, and by Buddhist and German, particularly Kantian, philosophy, Zhang was the most learned of the anti-Manchu revolutionaries and one of the greatest classical Chinese scholars in modern times. He was also attracted to SOCIALISM and ANARCHISM. Always difficult to get along with, he quarreled with Sun Yat-sen in 1907 and joined the opposition to his leadership. Though he agreed to serve as an advisor during Sun's brief presidency of the republic in Nanjing in

1912, he severed his ties with the Tongmenghui. He was briefly involved in politics during the early republican period, opposed Yuan Shikai in 1913 and worked with Sun again in Canton in 1917–1918. He then devoted most of his time to teaching and research, making important contributions to the study of Chinese philology and linguistics. Fervently devoted to the preservation of Chinese culture, he opposed the iconoclasm of the 1919 MAY FOURTH MOVEMENT.

His final political involvement was in urging resistance to Japanese aggression in the 1930s. On June 4, 1936, just 10 days before his death, Zhang wrote to CHIANG KAI-SHEK urging cooperation with the Chinese Communists against Japan. Though he distrusted the Communists and their Soviet connections, he was confident they would never collaborate with the Japanese.

ZHANG GUOTAO (CHANG KUO-T'AO) (1897–1979) Chinese Communist leader. Born into a Jiangxi landlord family, Zhang received a modern education and as a teenager helped GUOMINDANG (GMD) members in the CHINESE REVOLUTION OF 1913 against Yuan Shikai. In 1916, he enrolled in Beijing University, headed by the progressive chancellor CAI YUANPEI. Zhang soon came under the influence of CHEN DUXIU and LI DAZHAO, two faculty members who later founded the CHINESE COMMUNIST PARTY (CCP). Active in the 1919 MAY FOURTH MOVEMENT, in which students sparked a nationwide anti-imperialist campaign, Zhang became more radical and by 1920 was convinced that MARXISM held the solution for China's problems. He joined a Beijing Communist group, was active in the labor movement and in 1921 became one of the founding members of the CCP. Chosen to head the organization department of the CCP central committee, Zhang was also assigned to the labor field, and became head of the China trade union secretariat. Later in the year he was sent to Moscow to attend the first congress of the Toilers of the East and he met LENIN in the Kremlin. In early 1923, he and DENG ZHONGXIA were leaders of the Beijing-Hankou railway strike.

At this time the issue of the united front with the GMD found Zhang in a minority position. Though he favored cooperation, he opposed having CCP members join the GMD, a condition insisted upon by SUN YAT-SEN. Other CCP leaders, however, submitted to orders from HENDRIK SNEEVLIET, the COMINTERN representative, and agreed. Zhang was therefore not reelected to the CC at the 3rd party congress in 1923, but was reinstated at the 4th congress in 1925. He was active in the 1925 MAY 30TH MOVEMENT and as head of the CC's military department helped in the preparation of the NORTHERN EXPEDITION (see CHINESE NATIONALIST REVOLUTION) in 1926. At the 5th CCP congress in 1927, he was elected to the standing committee of the newly-created Politburo. He attended the 6th CCP congress in Moscow in 1928, had a long discussion with STALIN and did not return to China until 1930, when the CCP was rent by internal conflict (see LI LISAN, WANG MING). In 1931, Zhang was sent to administer the Hubei-Henan-Anhui soviet (guerrilla base). When the Chinese Soviet Republic was established at Ruijin in November under the chairmanship of MAO ZEDONG, Zhang was elected a vice-chairman in absentia.

Forced to retreat westward by GMD pressure, Zhang and the CCP 4th Front Army relocated in western Sichuan. Isolated from the central soviet in Jiangxi, Zhang's group acted independently, giving him an opportunity to build his own power base. In June 1935, the 4th Front Army met Mao Zedong's 1st Front Army, which had embarked on the LONG MARCH the previous October. The two leaders clashed. Zhang disputed the authority of the January Zunyi conference that had established Mao's leadership of the CCP and opposed the plan to relocate in northern Shaanxi. Instead, he favored moving further westward to the Sichuan-Xikang border area, largely inhabited by ethnic minorities. After arguing for several months, it was decided they would go their separate ways, thus splitting the CCP into two centers, one led by Mao and the other by Zhang. Zhang's strategy failed. After suffering military defeats, the rival party center was abolished and Zhang's forces joined the north Shaanxi base in late 1936, though some did not arrive until 1937. Though severely criticized in the Yan'an headquarters, Zhang benefitted from Mao's practice at that time of acting leniently toward party foes after they could no longer mount an effective challenge to his leadership. Zhang retained membership in the Politburo and after the outbreak of the Sino-Japanese war of 1937–1945 became acting chairman of the Shaanxi-Gansu-Ningxia border region. In April 1938, he left Yan'an, issued an anti-Communist statement in Wuhan and joined the GMD. Expelled from the CCP later in the month, Zhang stayed in Chongqing, the GMD's wartime capital, for the duration of the war. After the Communist victory in 1949, he remained in Taiwan for a brief period and then lived in Hong Kong. In 1968, he joined his son in Toronto, Canada, where he died.

ZHANG JUE (?–184 A.D.) Chinese rebel. Leader of a Daoist faith-healing sect, Zhang was born in present-day Hebei, in northeast China. His cult, called the *Taiping Dao* (Way of Great Peace), cured the sick in public confessional ceremonies. Around 175 A.D., Zhang sent missionaries to the central and eastern provinces, organized a church hierarchy and took for himself the title Celestial Master. Attracting numerous converts during a period of dynastic decline when thousands were homeless and destitute, the sect grew rapidly. In 184, the Later Han dynasty (25–220) government took countermeasures. In response Zhang staged a revolt and his followers, who put on yellow kerchiefs and were called the YELLOW TURBANS. Zhang was killed in 184 but Yellow Turban bands continued the rebellion for a number of years.

ZHANG LU (Chang Lu) (fl. 188–220) Chinese rebel. Zhang collaborated with ZHANG XIU, leader of the Daoist faith-healing sect, the FIVE PECKS OF RICE BAND, that revolted in Sichuan in 184 A.D. during the declining period of the Later Han dynasty (25–220 A.D.). After killing Zhang Xiu, Zhang Lu took over the sect. Calling himself Celestial Master, he established a theocratic state and ruled for 30 years. In 215, he surrendered to the Han general, Cao Cao, and received a princely fief.

ZHANG LUOXING (?–1863) Chinese rebel. Born into a large landowning family, Zhang became a salt smuggler when his family lost property. In 1852, he was made chief of a peasant band of marauders known as Nian (see NIAN REBELLION). An excellent organizer though said to be illiterate, Zhang coordinated the activities of scattered Nian bands and became their supreme leader in 1853, when the movement turned openly rebellious.

Styling himself Great Han Heavenly-Mandated King, he injected a racial theme in the rebellion against the Manchu (Qing) dynasty (1644–1912). The Nian ransacked towns and villages, cooperated with the Taiping rebels and expanded their territory. Zhang was captured in 1863. Asked at his trial why he had rebelled, he replied: "I am not fond of rebellion, but the government forced me to it." Zhang and his wife, son and daughter were executed. His second cousin (or nephew) succeeded him as commander in chief of the Nian Rebellion, which was finally suppressed in 1868.

ZHANG TAILYAN   see ZHANG BINGLIN.

ZHANG WENTIAN (Chang Wen-t'ien)   (1900–1976) Chinese Communist leader. Born into a wealthy farming family near Shanghai (Jiangsu province), Zhang studied engineering for three years in Nanjing. In 1919, the nationalist fervor generated by the MAY FOURTH MOVEMENT induced him to join the Young China association, a patriotic group opposing the pro-Japanese policies of the government. He traveled to the US in 1922 and worked as a translator for a Chinese-language newspaper in San Francisco. Returning to China in 1924, he engaged in literary work, translating works of western writers, e.g., Oscar Wilde, D'Annunzio, Tolstoy, Turgenev and Henri Bergson, into Chinese, and also wrote a novel and play. In 1925, he joined the CHINESE COMMUNIST PARTY (CCP) in Shanghai and was sent to the Soviet Union. As a student at Moscow's SUN YAT-SEN University, he became one of the proteges of the vice-rector and future rector, Pavel Mif (see WANG MING).

Returning to China in 1930, Zhang belonged to the so-called "28 Bolsheviks"—Mif's pro-Stalinist Chinese pupils. In 1931, Zhang took charge of the propaganda department of the central committee (CC) in Shanghai. In 1933, he joined the CCP guerrilla base in Jiangxi, was elected to the Politburo in 1934 and went on the LONG MARCH in October. At the Zunyi conference of January 1935, Zhang abandoned Wang Ming's "left-adventurist" line and supported MAO ZEDONG, who then assumed party leadership. Zhang replaced QING BANGXIAN as CCP general-secretary, assumed charge of routine party activities and supported Mao in his clash with ZHANG GUOTAO. At the Yan'an CCP headquarters during the Sino-Japanese war (1937–1945), Zhang engaged in propaganda work and headed the Marxist-Leninist Institute. At the 7th CCP congress in 1945, he was reelected to the CC and Politburo and served in Manchuria following the Japanese surrender in 1945.

After the establishment of the People's Republic of China (PRC) in 1949, Zhang was involved mainly with foreign affairs. He was head of the PRC delegation to the UN that bid unsuccessfully to replace Taiwan, was ambassador to Moscow (1951–1955) and vice-minister of foreign affairs (1955–1959). In 1956, he was demoted to alternate membership in the Politburo. Criticized in 1959 for past mistakes, he lost all political positions and engaged in economic research at the Chinese Academy of Sciences.

ZHANG XIANZHONG (Chang Hsien-chung)   (1605–1647) Chinese rebel. A native of Shaanxi, Zhang was a brigand who raised havoc in north China during the declining years of the Ming dynasty (1368–1644). After more than a decade of plundering, in 1644 he invaded Sichuan and enthroned himself as King of the Great Western Kingdom. He established a formal government according to the traditional format, but his terrorization of the bureaucratic-gentry elite gave him little chance of success. Sharing the fate of the other major anti-Ming rebel, LI ZICHENG, he could not match the superior organizational strength of the Manchu invaders, who had captured Beijing in 1644 and then consolidated their hold on north China. Indeed, in 1647, Zhang's forces were defeated by the Manchus in Sichuan province and he was executed.

ZHANG XIU (Chang Hsiu)   (?–188? 191? A.D.) Leader of the Daoist faith-healing cult, the FIVE PECKS OF RICE BAND, Zhang revolted against the Later Han dynasty (25–220 A.D.) in Sichuan in 184. He was subsequently killed by ZHANG LU, who succeeded him in the leadership of the cult and the rebellion.

ZHAO KUANGYIN (Chao K'uang-yin)   (618–907) Chinese rebel and future emperor. After the fall of the Tang dynasty, attempts to reestablish centralized imperial rule failed while nomadic invaders threatened the northern borders. Sent to fight the Qidan (Khitan) Mongols, Zhao, who was a Chinese military commander, usurped the throne and established the Song dynasty (960–1279). He became known as Song Taizu (Grand Progenitor of the Song).

ZHELYABOV, ANDREI   (1850–1881) Russian populist (see POPULISM) terrorist. Born to a family of former serfs in South Russia, Zhelyabov succeeded in enrolling in the University of Odessa but was expelled for his attitude toward the university authorities. Joining the Populists, he participated in the TO THE PEOPLE movement in the summer of 1874, was arrested, but was later freed for lack of proof.

Having joined the first LAND AND LIBERTY group, Zhelyabov took part in the debate on terror in 1879 and was among the founders of PEOPLE'S WILL. Between 1879 and 1881, he led a number of attempts to assassinate the czar. Two days before the successful attempt of March 1, 1881, Zhelyabov was captured by the police. Despite a full confession, he was executed in public in April 1881 for regicide, together with his colleague and life-partner, SOFIA PEROVSKAYA, who had taken command of the assassination plot after Zhelyabov had been captured, and three other participants.

ZHENG CHENGGONG (Cheng Ch'eng-kung; "Koxinga")   (1624–1662) Chinese rebel. Son of a former Chinese pirate and his Japanese wife, Zheng was born in Japan, near Nagasaki. After the Manchus captured Beijing and established the Qing dynasty (1644–1912), Zheng remained loyal to the Ming cause and fought the new régime. Based in Amoy, he controlled much of the coast of Fujian, his father's native province, from 1646 to 1658. Earlier, the refugee Ming court had given him the imperial surname of Zhu. Thus he became popularly known as Guoxingyeh (Lord of the Imperial Surname), from which the Dutch derived "Koxinga." Defeated in an attempt to seize Nanjing in 1659, he withdrew with a fleet of ships to Taiwan (Formosa) in 1661. In the following year he expelled the Dutch, who had established trading stations in the island. Zheng died in 1662, but the rebel régime, which absorbed mainland refugees, continued to exist and made an effort to support the SAN FAN REBELLION. Taiwan surrendered to the Qing in 1683.

ZHIVKOV, TODOR KHRISTOV (1911–) Bulgaria's Communist leader for 35 years and six months, i.e., most of the period after World War II, until his removal in November 1989. The longest ruler in Bulgarian history was born into a peasant family, studied at the High School of Drawing and Engraving and worked as a printer. He joined the Bulgarian Young Communist League in 1928 and in 1931 joined the Communist Party, rising in the ranks while still employed as a printer. During World War II he served in the Communist partisan underground (1941–1944) and was one of the leading organizers of the September 1944 coup. In 1948, he served as Sofia party boss, rising to the secretariat of the central committee in 1950. From 1945 on he was also member of the national assembly. After 1954, he was second in line in the party leadership under Vulko Chernenko, and in April 1956 he became First Secretary of the Party, in charge of de-Stalinization. This in effect marked the beginning of his long rule. In 1971 he became president. A master of survival and an excellent tactician, Zhivkov played various factions against others. Up to the mid-1980s his policy was manifested by its strong pro-Soviet line and characterized by stagnation in all fields, not unlike the Brezhnev rule in the Soviet Union. However, Zhivkov the masterful tactician failed to advance with the times, and his relations with Gorbachev after 1985 were rather sour. He rejected Soviet and internal pressure for a "Bulgarian *glasnost*" and the steps taken in Bulgaria were more verbal than practical.

In 1989, Zhivkov tried to play the born-again liberal, but it was to little and too late. An internal coup in the party leadership led by the foreign minister, Petur Mladenov, sent him home on November 10, 1989, with "heartful thanks" from the party and the nation. However, shortly after, accused of corruption and mismanagement, he was confined to house arrest. By 1995, still under house arrest and with the return of the former Communists as the Bulgarian Socialist Party, Zhivkov found himself in some ways more popular than during his decades of rule, a symbol of stability and order. His works, always carefully published by the party, do not present a first rate theoretical thinker and they bear titles such as *Agricultural Production* (1961) and *The XXII Congress of the CPSU and its lessons for the BCP.* His vanity was the target of grim jokes and, as one of them went, he was the only man who had written more books than he had read.

ZHORDANIA, NOE (1868–1953) (also known as Kostnov, Ani, Nari, Naridze, etc.) One of the leaders of the Georgian MENSHEVIKS, a member of the constituent assembly of the Social Democratic group, *Mesame Dasi,* a leader of the Opportunist Faction of this organization. Zhordania did not recognize the dictatorship of the proletariat and considered a parliamentary republic to be the best form of popular rule. He participated in the second conference of the Russian Social Democratic Workers Party (1903) and joined its MENSHEVIK wing. After returning to Georgia, Zhordania became a leader of the Georgian Mensheviks and began publishing Menshevik newspapers. During the RUSSIAN REVOLUTION OF 1905 he was against the armed uprising. Following the creation of the parliament—the Duma—Zhorda-

nia was elected to it and led the Social Democratic faction. At the 5th conference of the Russian Social Democratic Workers Party, he was elected to the central committee.

After the February RUSSIAN REVOLUTION OF 1917, Zhordania was the chairman of the Executive Committee of the Soviet of Workers' Representatives. After the October revolution that year, he supported the secession of Georgia from Russia and later became the head of the government of independent Georgia. The establishment of Soviet rule in Georgia following the Russian invasion in 1921 compelled Zhordania to emigrate to France, where he led a struggle to liberate Georgia and tried to organize a Menshevik uprising in Georgia in 1924 (see also GEORGIA, REVOLTS AND REVOLUTIONS).

ZHOU ENLAI (Chou En-lai) (1898–1976) Chinese Communist leader. Born in Jiangsu to an upper-class Zhejiang family that suffered financial difficulties when he was a child, Zhou lived for a while with his grandfather—who educated him in the Chinese classics—and then with an uncle in Shenyang (Mukden), where he attended primary school. In 1917, he graduated from Tianjin's Nankai Middle (high) school, an institution pioneering in liberal education. He then went to Japan, where he stayed for about a year and a half studying Japanese and preparing for college entrance examinations. During this short period he did not formally enroll in any university. Contemporary developments though, especially his own government's demeaning concessions to Japanese imperialism, aroused his political awareness. The 1918 Japanese Rice Riots, an unprecedented upsurge of popular discontent, revealed the ugly side of Japanese society. Now less inclined to consider Japan worthy of emulation, he became interested in the socialist alternative being promoted by writers like Kawakami Hajime. A professor of economics at Kyoto University, Kawakami had been converted to MARXISM and Zhou became an avid reader of his journal, *Research on Social Problems,* which began appearing in January 1919. The October RUSSIAN REVOLUTION OF 1917 also drew Zhou's attention and he read John Reed's *Ten Days That Shook the World.*

Though not yet committed to Marxism, Zhou saw it as a "ray of sunlight" when he returned to China in April 1919, planning to study at Tianjin's Nankai University, scheduled to open in the fall. Meanwhile, he became a student leader of the 1919 patriotic MAY FOURTH MOVEMENT. Among other activities, he participated in a small discussion group dealing with contemporary issues. LI DAZHAO, a future co-founder of the CHINESE COMMUNIST PARTY (CCP), was one of the lecturers. In January 1920, following an anti-Japanese demonstration, Zhou began a six-month term in prison which led him to more radical, revolutionary ideas. While in jail, he gave several lectures on Marxism to fellow-prisoners. In late 1920 he left China, intending to join the work-study program in France, but first spent five weeks in England, where he was impressed by the massive miners' strike of 1921. In Paris later that year (or 1922) he was inducted into the CCP by a member who had been delegated to organize overseas branches, and became an active Communist recruiter. In Berlin in 1922 he brought ZHU DE, the future RED ARMY commander, into the CCP. In 1923, after the CCP had formed a united front with the GUOMINDANG (GMD), Zhou joined the overseas GMD. He returned to China in 1924 and there took charge of the political department at WHAMPOA MILITARY ACADEMY, where he spread Communist doctrine among young cadets, one of whom was LIN BIAO. A loyal supporter of the United Front, Zhou contributed to the consolidation of the national revolutionary base in Guangdong. In 1925 he married Deng Yingchao, who had also been a student activist in Tianjin and had recently become a CCP leader there. They would continue to work as an ideal team.

In 1926, Zhou became secretary of the CCP military affairs committee in Shanghai and in 1927 led the workers' uprising that anticipated the arrival of the NATIONAL REVOLUTIONARY ARMY. When the GMD launched a bloody purge of the CCP in April, he was arrested but managed to escape. He was elected to the CCP central committee (CC) in May and to the Politburo in July, when it was reorganized. Credited with being one of the architects of the August 1 NANCHANG UPRISING that gave birth to the Red Army, he served in the CCP underground apparatus in Shanghai after attending the 6th party congress in Moscow in 1928. He returned to Moscow in 1930 to report to the COMINTERN and receive new instructions. Back in China after several months, he joined in the criticism of LI LISAN and in January 1931 acknowledged his own error in having been too lenient with Li. Retaining key political positions, including leadership of the CCP military committee, he joined the CCP guerrilla base in Jiangxi in 1931, fought against the GMD encirclement campaigns and went on the LONG MARCH (1934–1935). During these years, Zhou demonstrated the unique ability to shift with prevailing winds when the CCP was rent by intra-party conflict. As leaders were thrust aside, stigmatized as either "right capitulationists" or "left adventurists," Zhou was always ready to switch sides and remain in the top echelon. Though he had previously overruled MAO ZEDONG's military strategy (which turned out to be correct), he supported Mao at the January 1935 Zunyi conference which gave Mao supreme leadership. Zhou would remain loyal to Mao for the rest of his life. Zhou's flexibility was not merely opportunistic but was also realistic. During this arduous period of adjustment for the CCP, he was quick to realize when changing conditions required new strategies. What remained consistent in his behavior was the concern for party unity. Colleagues and former opponents came to recognize his indispensability for healing rifts and keeping the party intact. He was the only Politburo member elected in 1927 who retained his position at the 7th party congress in 1945. One reason for Zhou's survival capacity was that he never tried to build his own power-base and contend for top leadership. Hence he had few enemies who felt constrained to purge him. A persuasive speaker with a moderate, conciliatory style, at least on one occasion Zhou revealed a ruthless streak. In 1931, one of his trusted lieutenants was captured by the GMD and revealed information leading to the arrest and execution of as many as 800 party activists. In retaliation, Zhou had the traitor's entire family killed in Shanghai.

Zhou's negotiating skills proved vital to the CCP soon after the Long March had brought its shattered forces to north Shaanxi. In 1936, he convinced Zhang Xueliang, leader of the Manchurian troops assigned to combat the Communists, that resistance to Japan required a new united front. Zhang then stopped fighting the Red Army. When CHIANG KAI-SHEK flew to Xi'an to revitalize the anti-Communist campaign, he was taken captive by Zhang's forces and confronted with an ultimatum de-

manding a united front. A CCP delegation, headed by Zhou Enlai, arranged a compromise solution that probably saved Chiang's life and also facilitated the establishment of the second united front in September 1937, which Zhou also negotiated. As a result, the CCP gained legal status, its forces were integrated into the nationalist army, and the way opened for the phenomenal expansion of Communist power during the Sino-Japanese war of 1937–1945.

During the war, Zhou was chief CCP liaison officer to the GMD, working hard on behalf of the second united front but at the same projecting an image of Chinese COMMUNISM that won sympathy from non-Communist intellectuals as well as foreigners in GMD-held territory. With the end of the war in 1945 and the GMD-CCP civil war on the horizon, Zhou served as a vice-chairman of the CCP military council headed by Mao and as the chief negotiator with the GMD, buying time for the CCP. He worked with American mediators, including General George C. Marshall, who arrived in late December. Even after a cease-fire broke down and fighting resumed in mid-1946, Zhou stayed available for negotiations and remained for a while in Nanjing, where the GMD had reestablished the nationalist capital. Later in the year, when both sides assumed fixed positions, he moved to Yan'an and served on the staff of the PEOPLE'S LIBERATION ARMY (PLA). In March 1949, while the PLA was sweeping through the rest of China, Zhou was among the leaders who stayed in recently-captured Beijing (Beiping) to lay plans for

Zhou Enlai at the end of the Long March

the future government. With the establishment of the People's Republic of China (PRC) in October, Zhou became premier and foreign minister. In addition to his administrative functions, he did much to improve the CCP's image. He was the quintessential "outside" man, extending a hand to non-Communist intellectuals who were uncertain of their fate under the new régime and presenting an assuring, sympathetic face to foreigners. Handsome and sophisticated and with more overseas experience than other CCP leaders, Zhou invariably made a positive impression upon foreigners, including General Marshall, despite the failure of Marshall's mediation effort.

As foreign minister, Zhou played a critical role in steering China's course on the world scene. He participated in the negotiations that led to the signing of the 30-year alliance with the Soviet Union in February 1950 and acquitted himself well during the Korean war (1950–1953), advancing proposals that formed the basis of the armistice agreement. He emerged from the Geneva conference (1954) dealing with Indochina as a diplomat of international stature, more than holding his own with leaders like Anthony Eden and John Foster Dulles. After a successful debut performance for western leaders, Zhou spearheaded China's move into the non-western world, where he had been cultivating relations since 1952. He scored a personal triumph at the Bandung conference of Afro-Asian nations in 1955, the year he helped arrange talks with the US on an ambassadorial level. He made frequent overseas trips, including several to the Soviet Union, with whom relations began to deteriorate in the late 1950s and ruptured completely in the 1960s.

Though he had formally relinquished the foreign minister portfolio in 1958, he remained a key foreign policy strategist. After the Soviet invasion of Czechoslovakia in 1968 and the Sino-Soviet border clash of 1969, the opening to the west and Japan—which Zhou had long advocated—became more pertinent. In 1972, President Nixon's visit to China energized the Sino-US rapprochement process and Japan soon extended diplomatic recognition to the PRC, which had already replaced Taiwan at the UN in 1971.

As premier, a post he held until his death in January 1976, Zhou had the difficult task of trying to weather Chairman Mao's stormy mass campaigns that rocked the bureaucratic and economic structure. Whether he was willing or able to curb Mao's excesses is an open question. The cultural revolution of 1966-1976 (see GREAT PROLETARIAN CULTURAL REVOLUTION) was his most trying experience. As the situation was at times beyond even Mao's control, Zhou shifted right and left and tried to mediate between warring factions. Again, he was either unwilling or unable to protect old friends and comrades from Red Guard harassment. He denounced LIU SHAOQI in 1968. Yet, Zhou must be given major credit for preventing the complete breakdown of the Chinese State and society during this tumultuous period. In 1973, he succeeded in bringing back DENG XIAOPING, who helped him in restoring order. Both were targets of the "Anti-Confucius" campaign in 1974, the year Zhou was hospitalized suffering from cancer. Still holding office, in 1975 he revived the commitment to the "four modernizations" (in agriculture, industry, defense, and science and technology) which he had proposed in 1964. In April 1976, three months after his death, the removal of wreaths honoring him at Tiananmen Square precipitated riots and the second purging of Deng Xiaoping. In 1983, a

memorial room for Zhou was established in Mao's mausoleum. Preferring to absolve him of compliance with Maoist extremism, the Chinese continue to honor his memory.

ZHU DE (Chu Te) (1886–1976) Chinese Communist military leader. Born into a Sichuan tenant-peasant family, Zhu had both traditional and modern schooling. In 1909, he enrolled in the Yunnan military academy and joined SUN YAT-SEN's revolutionary organization, TONGMENGHUI. After the overthrow of the Qing (Manchu) dynasty (1644–1912), he returned to Yunnan in 1912, joined the GUOMINDANG (GMD) and distinguished himself in Cai's pro-republican, anti-Yuan Shikai campaign of 1915–1916. While serving as a brigade commander with the rank of major-general in the Yunnan army, which was stationed in Sichuan, Zhu was influenced by the October RUSSIAN REVOLUTION OF 1917 and the 1919 MAY FOURTH MOVEMENT. Though a Sichuan warlord offered him command of a division, Zhu turned down the offer and went to study in Germany in 1922. Later in the year, ZHOU ENLAI and other Communists enlisted him in the CHINESE COMMUNIST PARTY (CCP). After studying briefly at the University of Gottingen, Zhu returned to Berlin, where he was twice arrested for Communist activities and finally expelled in 1925. He traveled to Moscow for military studies at the Communist University of the Toilers of the East.

In 1926, the CCP called him back for political activity in Sichuan, where he served as party representative to the NATIONAL REVOLUTIONARY ARMY's (NRA) 20th army, joined the CCP's military committee in Chongqing and helped plan several campaigns. After the CCP-GMD split, he was one of the leaders of the CCP's NANCHANG UPRISING on August 1, 1927 that gave birth to the RED ARMY. He led CCP forces in the Guangdong, Jiangxi and Hunan border areas and in early 1928 joined MAO ZEDONG at the Jinggangshan base in southern Jiangxi, where he became commander of the Red Army's 4th Front Army. In 1930, after Mao's guerrilla fighters had established a new headquarters in Ruijin (1929), Zhu was appointed commander of the 1st Front Army and was elected to alternate membership in the CCP central committee (CC). In November 1931, when the Chinese Soviet Republic was established, he became head of the CC's military commission and commander in chief of the Red Army. Highly respected for his military talent and experience, he worked well with other professionally trained CCP army leaders and helped Mao Zedong win their support. Outsiders, who called the Red Army the "Zhu-Mao army," sometimes identified the duo as a single person. Under their leadership, the Red Army developed the strategy and combat effectiveness that turned it into a formidable fighting force.

In 1934, Zhu was elected to full membership in the CC and the Politburo. When the Red Army was forced to embark on the LONG MARCH in October 1934, he supervised the evacuation of the Jiangxi base. In January 1935, Zhu supported Mao Zedong's successful bid for CCP leadership at the Zunyi conference. However, when the marchers met up with ZHANG GUOTAO's forces in the summer and Mao and Zhang argued over strategy, Zhu and part of the 1st Front Army joined Zhang, who had opted for a retreat further west. Zhu's decision has been attributed to his concern for party unity and to the hope that he could convince Zhang to change his mind. In late 1936, Zhu's forces joined Mao's in northern Shaanxi and the two subsequently worked in tandem during the final stages of the CCP's rise to power. During the Sino-Japanese war of 1937–1945 he commanded the Red Army, now called the EIGHTH ROUTE ARMY, and continued to head the Communist forces, renamed the PEOPLE'S LIBERATION ARMY, in the civil war with the GMD (1946–1949).

After the establishment of the People's Republic of China (PRC) in 1949, Zhu held various high governmental and party posts. He was senior vice-chairman of the PRC government from 1950 to 1959, after which he was less active politically. Though he had been mentioned as a possible candidate to succeed Mao when in 1958 he announced his decision to relinquish the PRC chairmanship, Zhu, who was first and foremost a military man, showed little evidence of political ambitions. He received full recognition and honors for his contribution to the CCP's military successes. In 1955, he was the first of the CCP commanders to be awarded the rank of Marshal of the PRC and was given all the highest military designations. Nevertheless, this did not spare him defamation by the LIN BIAO-JIANG QING clique during the Cultural Revolution of 1966–1976 (see GREAT PROLETARIAN CULTURAL REVOLUTION). Zhu De died in July 1976 and in 1983 a memorial room for him was established in Mao Zedong's mausoleum.

ZHU YUANZHANG (Chu Yüan-chang)

ZHU YUANZHANG (Chu Yüan-chang) (1328–1399) Chinese rebel and later emperor. Born to a poor family in Anhui, Zhu was orphaned and entered a Buddhist monastery, where he became literate. In 1352, he joined a rebel band and probably also the WHITE LOTUS SOCIETY. Attracting his own following, he captured Nanjing in 1356. Rivalries among commanders of the ruling Mongol (Yuan) dynasty (1280–1368) facilitated his advance to the north and he took Beijing in 1368. Retaining Nanjing as his capital, he established the Ming dynasty (1368–1644). He and LIU BANG, founder of the Han, were the only commoners who established lasting dynasties in China. He is best known by his regal title, Hongwu.

ZHU ZHIXIN (CHU CHIH-HSIN)

ZHU ZHIXIN (CHU CHIH-HSIN) (1885–1920) Chinese revolutionary. Born in Guangdong to a scholarly Zhejiang family, Zhu received a traditional and modern education and at an early age demonstrated outstanding intellectual talent. In 1902, he organized a group for studying western learning and in 1904 qualified for entrance into Beijing University. Instead, he went to study in Japan, having achieved the first rank in the competitive examinations for scholarships from the Guangdong government. He studied at the Tokyo Law College's accelerated course for Chinese students. Among fellow-Cantonese students were his relative, WANG JINGWEI, and HU HANMIN. All three played pivotal roles in SUN YAT-SEN's revolutionary career, which began with the struggle to overthrow the Manchu (Qing) dynasty (1644–1912). In 1905, Zhu joined Sun's TONGMENGHUI and became a leading contributor to its monthly organ, *Min Bao*. His articles were the journal's first to call attention to MARXISM, about which he learned from Japanese translations of western works. Yet, he also found SOCIALISM compatible with elements of traditional Chinese thought and society and he considered the peasants a revolutionary force. He is credited with the first Chinese translation of the 10-point program of the *Communist Manifesto*. A great admirer of the German Social Democrats, he believed in a peaceful transition to socialism. Zhu was not only

a pioneer Chinese expositor of socialism, but a highly sophisticated and original thinker in adapting Marxist theory to Chinese conditions. In 1907, he returned to Canton as a schoolteacher while engaged in secret revolutionary work, including efforts to subvert imperial army troops. His activities contributed greatly to the TONGMENGHUI's success in Guangdong when the CHINESE REPUBLICAN REVOLUTION OF 1911 erupted. Always faithful to Sun Yat-sen and his teachings, Zhu followed him to Japan after the failure of the 1913 revolution against Yuan Shikai.

After joining Sun's CHINESE REVOLUTIONARY PARTY in 1914, Zhu wrote anti-Yuan articles and also led uprisings against him. In 1917–1918, he joined Sun's endeavor to gain a foothold in Canton. In 1917, at Sun's bidding, he wrote a lengthy treatise arguing against China's participation in World War I. Originally called *The Question of China's Survival,* it was translated into English under the title, *The Vital Problem of China.* Sun was listed as the author and Zhu also helped with Sun's other writings during this period. An ardent supporter of the new culture promoted by the 1919 MAY FOURTH MOVEMENT, Zhu was co-founder that year of *Jianshe* (Reconstruction) magazine, which introduced western ideas and institutions, including democracy and socialism. It was also the major organ for propagating Sun's doctrines. Zhu felt that the GUOMINDANG (GMD), which Sun revitalized in 1919, should give prime importance to ideology.

Sent by Sun on a military mission to Guangdong, Zhu was killed in 1920. His death at the early age of 35 deprived the Guomindang of one of its most brilliant thinkers and revolutionary activists.

ZILIHUI (ZLH—Tzu-li Hui, Independence Association)

ZILIHUI (ZLH—Tzu-li Hui, Independence Association) Chinese revolutionary organization. In the spring of 1900, while the Qing (Manchu) dynasty (1644–1912) was involved with the anti-foreign BOXER REBELLION, supporters of the reform movement organized students into the ZLH. Vacillating between reformism under the young emperor or revolutionary, anti-Manchu republicanism, the ZLH planned an uprising in Hankou in conjunction with the GE LAO HUI secret society. The ZLH "Independent Army" called for the preservation of Chinese sovereignty and the restoration of national independence. Though the plotters stated explicitly their intention of not harming foreigners, British officials cooperated with Chinese authorities in apprehending the conspirators in August. The execution of 20 of the leaders added to growing anti-dynastic sentiments.

ZIMBABWE AFRICAN NATIONAL UNION (ZANU)

ZIMBABWE AFRICAN NATIONAL UNION (ZANU) A movement founded in August 1963, when African nationalist opposition to Prime Minister Ian Smith's unilateral declaration of independence in what was then Southern Rhodesia split into two—ZANU and the ZIMBABWE AFRICAN PEOPLE'S UNION (ZAPU).

ZANU was led by the Reverend Ndabaningi Sithole and later by ROBERT MUGABE, formerly its secretary-general. ZANU espoused a socialist policy and maintained close links with FRELIMO, which was fighting the Portuguese in Mozambique, and with the People's Republic of China. ZANU was banned by the Rhodesian government between 1964–1979.

ZANU concentrated on infiltration and rural mobilization in the Shona-speaking areas in the northeast and, later, in the eastern and central areas of the country. In 1976, ZANU and ZAPU formed an alliance, the Patriotic Front (PF), but they contested the elections of February 1980 separately. These elections took place after the 1979 Lancaster House constitutional conference, chaired by Britain, which negotiated a cease-fire in the guerrilla war and made arrangements for the transition to majority rule. ZANU-PF, led by Mugabe, won 63% of the votes, in a turn-out estimated at 94%. In the July 1985 general elections, ZANU-PF again won a majority. In 1989, ZANU-PF merged with its former rival, ZAPU-PF.

The ZANU-PF government has committed itself to establishing an egalitarian and socialist state. One of the most important measures it has passed to this end is the Land Acquisition Bill of 1992, which aims to redistribute white-owned land to benefit black smallholders.

ZIMBABWE AFRICAN PEOPLE'S UNION (ZAPU) This movement was founded in 1961 in what was then Southern Rhodesia, as an African nationalist movement whose aim was to overthrow the white minority government of Prime Minister Ian Smith. In 1962, ZAPU was banned by the government.

ZAPU's leader was JOSHUA NKOMO and its secretary for information and publicity, as well as its acting secretary-general, was ROBERT MUGABE. A split in the ZAPU leadership in August 1963 led to the formation of the ZIMBABWE AFRICAN NATIONAL UNION (ZANU).

ZAPU was based mainly in Zambia and received training and weaponry from the USSR. Its operations within Zimbabwe were confined mainly to Ndebele-speaking areas (Zimbabwe's principal minority ethnic group, after the majority Shona). In 1976, ZAPU and ZANU formed an alliance, led by Nkomo and Mugabe and known as the Patriotic Front (PF). However, after the independence settlement of 1979, ZANU and ZAPU contested the February 1980 elections separately. ZAPU won 20 seats and became the junior partner in a coalition government formed by Mugabe. Nkomo originally rejected Mugabe's offer of the presidency and refused to accept a merger of ZANU and ZAPU.

Several years later, however, in December 1987, a unity agreement was finally signed between ZAPU and ZANU, leading to the merger of the two parties. This was ratified by both parties in April 1987, and Nkomo became one of Zimbabwe's two vice-presidents.

ZINOVIEV, GRIGORY YEVSEYEVICH (1883–1936) Russian Communist leader, one of the triumvirate that ruled the Soviet Union after LENIN's death, and first chairman of the COMINTERN. Zinoviev was born in Kirovograd (then Yelizavetgrad) to a Jewish bourgeois family whose name was Radomyslski. He joined the RUSSIAN SOCIAL DEMOCRATIC PARTY in Switzerland in 1901 and the BOLSHEVIK PARTY in 1903. He played an active role in the St. Petersburg uprising during the RUSSIAN REVOLUTION OF 1905 and was a delegate to the party's congress in Stockholm in 1906. Zinoviev was exiled in 1908 and became one of Vladimir Lenin's closest collaborators, editing various Bolshevik newspapers and journals. He was elected to the party's central committee in 1912. He and Lenin wrote *Against the Tide*, criticizing World War I and the social democratic leaders who supported it.

In April 1917, after the collapse of the czarist régime, Zinoviev and Lenin traveled in a sealed train across Europe to Russia. Together, after the July uprising against the provisional government, they went into hiding. In October, Zinoviev split with Lenin on the question of the seizure of power, believing that a Bolshevik coup in Russia at that time would lead to foreign intervention and a counterrevolutionary peasant uprising. After the revolution, he was opposed to the formation of a one-party government. He nevertheless remained a member of the party's central committee, becoming chairman of the Leningrad (then Petrograd) Soviet and Party and in 1922 was appointed to the Politburo.

In 1919 he was made head of the Comintern. Following Lenin's death in January 1924, Zinoviev joined with JOSEPH STALIN and LEV KAMENEV to form the triumvirate that drove LEON TROTSKY into political isolation and ruled the country. In 1925 he and Kamenev, however, became leaders of the "new opposition," which argued that SOCIALISM could not be created in Russia without the support of proletarian revolutions in the west, in contrast to Stalin's call for the creation of SOCIALISM IN ONE COUNTRY.

In 1927, Zinoviev joined with Trotsky in a last bid for political survival by organizing demonstrations in Moscow and Leningrad during celebrations to mark the 10th anniversary of the revolution. A week later, Zinoviev was expelled by the party and in January 1928 he was exiled to Siberia.

In 1936, during Stalin's purges, Zinoviev was arrested and charged, along with other former political leaders, with plotting to overthrow Stalin's government. After public admissions of guilt they were all executed.

ZIONISM Zionism is the movement of Jewish national revival calling for return of Jews to Zion and the restoration of Zion to the Jews, ultimately as a sovereign state. The yearning for Zion inheres in the prayers and rituals of Judaism, and the belief in the divine promise that Jews will ultimately return to the Land of Israel is a fundamental part of Judaism's messianic faith. However, the nationalist movement known as Zionism is a product of modernity, traceable to the last quarter of the 19th century. The term Zionism was coined and entered usage in the early 1890s, but nationalistically-motivated resettlement of Palestine by Jews was first set in motion by the loosely-organized *Hibbat Zion* (Lovers of Zion) movement that mushroomed in the 1880s. A worldwide Zionist Organization was founded at the First Zionist congress held in Basel in 1897. It formulated the aim of Zionism as being "to create for the Jewish people a home (Heimstatte) in Palestine secured by public law."

One may gauge the revolutionary character of Zionism by examining its effect on the status of the Jews in the world. After two millennia of dispersion as a vulnerable minority throughout the countries of Europe and the Arab world (and latterly also the New World), the Jews now have a national polity of their own in their traditional homeland—the State of Israel. This revolutionary transformation was accomplished by Zionism within a period of only about 50 years. Demographic projections indicate that early in the 21st century more than half of the world Jewish population will be domiciled in Israel.

For the major period of their dispersion amid Christian or Muslim majorities, Jews were, at best, tolerated. Their personal security and rights of occupational opportunities were precarious and, owing to the religious hostility of the Christian and Muslim majorities, they were often exposed to indignities and persecution. Modernity and the emergence of culturally homogenizing nation states based on the liberal principle of uniform citizenship paved the way, in the course of the 19th and early 20th centuries, for the dissolution of Jewish corporate autonomy and the civic emancipation of the Jews in the expectation that they would become wholly acculturated if not assimilated. However, their emancipation provoked a widespread reaction almost everywhere. The age-old hostility to the Jews assumed the racist form that came to be known as anti-Semitism. Escalation of this rabid hostility culminated in the ideologically motivated program of genocide perpetrated by the German Nazis during World War II—the Holocaust.

This tragic historical record attendant upon the totally diasporic situation of the Jews has been dramatically transformed by the Zionist revolution. Having successfully established an independent national state, serving both as a place of refuge for persecuted Jews and as a renascent cultural center, the Jews now constitute a relatively secure and prosperous ethnic-religious entity in the world. Part of that entity enjoys a full national existence in Israel while other parts enjoy civic rights and the freedom to cultivate their Jewish ethnic-religious identity in various diaspora communities.

The revolution wrought by Zionism was of a dialectical nature. Traditionalist theses of Judaism relating to messianic return to Zion were challenged, but the outcome was a synthesis comprising elements of continuity as well as transformation. Thus traditionalist resignation to diasporic existence as the divinely ordained fate of *Galut* (exile) was challenged by the secularized Zionist *intelligentsia* who regarded *Galut* as a condition of political homelessness and alien status. Whereas traditionalists believed that only profound religious learning, piety and ritual observance might advance the divinely promised redemption (*Geula*), Zionists vigorously advocated national self-emancipation. The secular diagnosis of the *Galut* condition inspired the creation of a nationalist movement aimed at a return to Zion and the restoration of Zion as a Jewish homeland. In Czarist Russia, which contained by far the larger part of the world Jewish population at the end of the 19th century, this diagnosis was articulated, among others, by Leon Pinsker in his *Autoemancipation: An Appeal to his People by a Russian Jew of 1882*. An even more consequential formulation of this sharp challenge to aspirations for integration into European societies was *Der Judenstaat (The State of the Jews)* published in 1896 by Theodor Herzl, who, abandoning his former belief in emancipated integration, became the founder of the Zionist Organization.

The major ideological proposition of the Zionist revolution was thus its rejection of the belief in emancipation and integration as the solution for the Jewish problem. Zionists argued that hostility to the Jews was endemic because Jews were regarded everywhere as unassimilable aliens; their upward economic mobility after the attainment of civic emancipation only served to exacerbate the hostility of the majority. Zionists rebelled against the prevalent view that emancipated Jews constituted a purely religious denomination. They affirmed that the Jews were an entity possessing national, not just religious attributes. Zionism therefore constituted an ideological revolt against the modernized leadership of the Jewish communal and philanthropic organizations and congregations of Reform Judaism that had emerged as a by-product of emancipation in the 19th century. However, liberal anti-Zionism was weakened as the Jewish

problem in Jewish interwar Europe was aggravated by the rise to power of Nazism and a concurrent closure of the gates of entry to the United States and other countries of the New World. In 1929, prominent non-Zionist personalities joined with the Zionist Organization to form an expanded Jewish Agency for Palestine and after the Holocaust there was a broad consensus of Jewish support for Zionist aspirations in Palestine.

Although the spark that created the Zionist movement was set off when highly European acculturated personalities such as Theodor Herzl rebounded to Jewish national consciousness, the main body of Zionists consisted of East European Jews who had neither experienced civic emancipation nor ever abandoned their ingrained ethnic identification as Jews. Theirs was an organic nationalism in search of a synthesis between modernity and the age-old Jewish cultural heritage. They produced a cultural school of Zionists who followed their leading intellect, Ahad Ha'am (pseudonym of Asher Ginzberg, 1856–1927), in arguing that not only anti-Semitism, but even more so Jewish cultural survival was the core problem that faced the Jews. Even if emancipation would be successful, the result would be a deplorable process of assimilation and loss of Jewish identity. Hence, irrespective of the problem of anti-Semitism, an autonomous national cultural center in the Land of Israel was an indispensable prerequisite for the survival of the Jews as a distinctive culture. They advocated revival of Hebrew as a living national language undergirding a thorough educational and cultural renaissance. This would produce a modern type of "national Jew."

SOCIALISM provided a universalist alternative for the liberal belief in emancipation and integration as a solution for the Jewish Problem. In the late 19th century, many Jews found their way individually into the ranks and also the leadership of revolutionary socialist parties in Europe. Moreover, in Eastern Europe a Jewish socialist workers party, known as the BUND, was founded. Yet, the crushing of the Bund by the BOLSHEVIK régime in Soviet Russia of the late 1920s and the destruction of most of European Jewry by the Nazi Germans ultimately vindicated the Zionist strategy of a revolution in the life of the Jews rather than the alternative socialist strategy of the Bund.

In the context of socialist ideals as a solution to the Jewish Problem, the Zionist revolution took the form of a spectrum of socialist Zionist syntheses, some Marxist and others non-Marxist. Socialist or Labor Zionists rejected the notion that the Jewish Problem could be solved by the abandonment of Jewish identity in favor of participation in a universal socialist revolution. They called for normalization of the Jewish people through the creation of a Jewish working class in its own national-territorial base and the building of a socialist society from the bottom upwards. Following this program, Labor Zionism in all its variety wrought a revolution in the socioeconomic profile of the Jews. It uniquely advocated and implemented a process of downward economic mobility, in reverse of the trend characteristic of diaspora Jews to aspire upwardly into the middle and professional classes of society. As well as generating a class of agricultural and industrial workers in Palestine, Labor Zionism created a form of commune known as the *kibbutz*, that has proved to be the most successful of its genre in the world. It also formed a powerful and comprehensive trade union and cooperative organization in Palestine, known as the *Histadrut*. By the early 1930s, Labor Zionism, led by DAVID BEN-GURION, democratically gained political hegemony over the world Zionist organization. The sharp contrast between the socioeconomic profile of diaspora Jews and the Jews of the State of Israel at its establishment in 1948 reflected the revolutionary transformation effected by Labor Zionism.

Although the secular nationalist challenge to traditionalist passivity as well as to the belief in integration into the host majority societies was the essence of the Zionist revolution, a subsidiary revolution was also wrought by part of the traditionalist or Orthodox religious body of Jewry. They reinterpreted traditional sources to prove that the Messiah's advent was dependent on a preliminary phase of human action involving resettlement of the Land of Israel by Jews who were both fully observant of religious precepts and economically productive. The segment of Orthodox religious Jewry that participated in the Zionist organization not only engaged the secular majority in an ongoing struggle over the desired character of the Zionist project but also wrought a revolution within the framework of Orthodox Jewry. Whereas most of Orthodox Jewry opposed the entire Zionist enterprise as a heretical interference with the divinely ordained order and a threat to the integrity of Judaism and rabbinical authority, the religious Zionists justified the principle of self-help in cooperation with secular Jews.

Neither the ideological ethos nor the strategies of the Zionist revolution were predicated on violent means. The Zionist program was based on international diplomacy, land purchases and various settlement strategies. Nevertheless, in the course of its progress in Palestine, Zionism clashed with the national aspirations of the Arab majority. The resistance mustered by the latter included resorting to violence. This necessitated the creation of a self-defense force by the Zionists (the HAGANAH) and also stimulated the growth of the Revisionist Zionist Party founded by Vladimir Jabotinsky in 1925 on a platform that emphasized military preparedness and a right-wing form of integral nationalism. Radical elements of Revisionist Zionism in turn went on to form dissident underground military organizations that resorted to violent actions in retaliation for Arab violence as well as terrorist actions against the British régime in Palestine. Ultimately, as the British withdrew from rule of Palestine, full-scale war broke out in 1947/8 between the Jews and the Arabs of Palestine and the surrounding Arab states. In the course of that war a major part of the Arab Palestinian population was displaced and rendered refugees. Thus, in the final analysis, the Zionist revolution that created the State of Israel was not accomplished without violence and the precipitation of a tragic conflict between Jews and Arabs that has not been resolved to this day.

ZIYA GÖKALP (MEHMED) (1875?–1924) Turkish poet and writer and the theorist of Turkish nationalism. Born in Diyarbekir (Eastern Anatolia), Gökalp made contact with the YOUNG TURKS at an early stage. After the revolution of 1908 he was elected to the council of the Committee of Union and Progress in Salonika. There, and later in Istanbul, where he became professor of sociology at the university, Gökalp wrote his main nationalist essays and became the spiritual leader of the Young Turks. After the proclamation of the republic in 1923, he

was elected to the National Assembly. Prior to the dissolution of the Ottoman Empire, Gökalp favored the preservation of the supernational state, but called for the revival and promotion of Turkish national culture, the acceptance of European scientific and technical knowledge and the relegation of Islam to an ethical and personal religion. For some time an advocate of Pan-Turkism, his thoughts later grew closer to those of ATATÜRK. His social and cultural ideas paved the way for many reforms during the republican period.

His only book, *The History of Turkish Civilization,* was written a short time before he died, and only one volume of that was completed.

ZOU RONG (1885–1905) Chinese revolutionary pamphleteer. Born into a Sichuan merchant family, Zou was a child prodigy who, at the age of 12, abandoned the idea of pursuing an official career and in 1898 began studying English and Japanese in Chongqing. He read reformist literature and was introduced to western ideas, including Social Darwinism. After preparation in a modern Shanghai school, he went to Japan for further study in 1902. He associated with radical Chinese students and returned to Shanghai the following year after an altercation with a Chinese official. In the meantime, his readings on the AMERICAN REVOLUTION and the FRENCH REVOLUTION and ideas inspired by Rousseau and other western thinkers had prompted him to start writing an inflammatory tract calling for the overthrow of the Manchu (Qing) dynasty (1644–1912) and the establishment of a republic. Resistance to foreign aggression, he charged, first required the purging of the "internal evil." Called *The Revolutionary Army,* the pamphlet was published in 1903 in Shanghai, where the anti-Manchu scholar, ZHANG BINGLIN, had taken Zou under his wing. Accused of seditious libel after Zhang had praised the pamphlet in the Shanghai newspaper, *Su Bao,* both were arrested in June in the International Settlement. In 1904, Zhang was sentenced to three years imprisonment and Zou to two. Only 20 years old, Zou died a few weeks before his scheduled release. Distributed in hundreds of thousands of copies, *The Revolutionary Army* became the most famous of anti-Manchu writings.

ZU'AYYIN, YUSSUF (1931–) Syrian politician. A Sunni Muslim born in Abu Kamal in the Euphrates region, Zu'ayyin studied medicine at Damascus University and practiced as a physician. He became a leading member of the SYRIAN BA'ATH PARTY. He first joined the government in 1963, after the *Ba'ath* coup and in 1964–1965 became prime minister. He was deposed late in December 1965 when SALAH-UL-DIN BITAR and his "moderate" *Ba'ath* faction tried to return to power. Zu'ayyin supported the extremist "military" wing of General SALAH JADID which deposed the civilian wing in a coup in February 1966, and became prime minister under the ruling junta of Generals Jadid and HAFEZ AL-ASAD. He included Communists in his government and advocated closer relations with the USSR. When al-Asad completed his takeover in November 1970, Zu'ayyin was detained, along with other leaders of the Jadid faction. He was released in 1983, but his liberty was limited as he was not allowed to resume any public-political activity.

BIBLIOGRAPHY

General

Communist and Marxist Parties of the World. London: Longman, 1991.

Andrein, Charles F. *Political Changes in the Third World*. Boston: Unwin Hyman, 1988.

Andreski, Stanislav. *Wars, Revolutions, Dictatorships: Studies of Historical and Contemporary Problems from a Comparative Viewpoint*. London: Frank Cass, 1992.

Appleby, Joyce Oldham. *Liberalism and Republicanism in the Historical Imagination*. New York: Oxford University Press, 1992.

Armstrong, James David. *Revolution and World Order: The Revolutionary State in International Society*. Oxford: Clarendon Press, 1993.

Calvert, Peter. *Revolution and International Politics*. London: F. Pinter, 1984.

Cassinelli, Charles William. *Total Revolution: A Comparative Study of Germany under Hitler, the Soviet Union under Stalin, and China under Mao*. Santa Barbara: Clio Books, 1976.

Goldstone, Jack A. *Revolution and Rebellion in the Early Modern World*. Berkeley: University of California Press, 1991.

Kimmel, Michael S., *Revolution, A Sociological Interpretation*. Cambridge, Mass.: Polity Press, 1990.

Mollat, Michel and Philippe Wolff. *The Popular Revolutions of the Late Middle Ages*. London: G. Allen and Unwin, 1973.

Sperber, Jonathan. *The European Revolution, 1848–1851*. Cambridge University Press, 1993.

Tilly, Charles. *European Revolutions, 1492–1992*. Oxford: Blackwell, 1993.

Venturi, Franco. *Roots of Revolution*. New York: Grosset and Dunlap, 1966.

Worrall, David. *Radical Culture: Discourse, Resistance and Surveillance, 1790–1820*. New York, 1992.

Yarmolinsky, Avraham. *Road to Revolution*. New York: Collier, 1962.

Zagorin, Perez. *Rebels and Rulers, 1500–1660*. Cambridge University Press, 1993.

Political Ideologies

Ali, Tariq. *Trotsky for Beginners*. New York: Pantheon Books, 1980.

Appighanesi, Richard. *Lenin for Beginners*. New York: Pantheon Books, 1978.

Avrich, Paul. *Anarchist Portraits*. Princeton: Princeton University Press, 1988.

Brooker, Paul. *The Faces of Fraternalism: Nazi Germany, Fascist Italy and Imperial Japan*. Oxford, United Kingdom: Clarendon Press, 1991.

Cahn, Caroline. *Kropotkin and the Rise of Revolutionary Anarchism 1872–1886*. Cambridge University Press, 1989.

Morton, Marian J. *Emma Goldman and the American Left: "Nowhere at Home"*. New York: Twayne Publishers, 1992.

Rius, Pseud. *Mao for Beginners*. New York: Pantheon Books, 1980.

Rius, Pseud. *Marx for Beginners*. New York: Pantheon Books, 1976.

Africa

Africa South of the Sahara. Vols. 1994, 1995. England: Europa Publications Ltd.

Political Leaders of Contemporary Africa South of the Sahara: A Biographical Dictionary. Westport, Conn.: Greenwood Press, 1992.

Adamolekun, Lapido. *Sekou Toure's Guinea: An Experiment in Nation Building*. London: Methuen, 1976.

Agyeman, Opoku. *Nkrumah's Ghana and East Africa: Pan–Africanism and African Interstate Relations*. Rutherford: Fairleif Disckinson University Press, 1992.

Bienen, Henry. *Armies and Parties in Africa*. New York: Africana Publishing Company, 1978.

Bienen, Henry. *Armed Forces Conflict and Change in Africa*. Boulder, Colo.: Westview Press, 1988.

Biko, Stephen. *I Write What I Like: A Selection of His Writings*. New York: Harper and Row, 1986.

Birmingham, David. *Frontline Nationalism in Angola and Mozambique*. London: J. Currey, 1992.

Braginsky, N. *A Short History of the National Liberation Movement in East Africa*. Moscow: Progress Press, N.D.

Cabral, Amilcar. *Unity and Struggle: Speeches and Writings*. London: Heinemann, 1980.

Chabal, Patrick. *Amilcar Cabral: Revolutionary Leadership and People's War*. Cambridge University Press, 1984.

Davis, Stephen M. *Apartheid's Rebels: Inside South Africa's Hidden War*. New Haven: Yale University Press, 1987.

De St. Jorre, John. *The Brothers' War: Biafra and Nigeria*. Boston: Houghton Mifflin Company, 1972.

Decalo, Samuel. *Coups and Army Rule in Africa: Studies in Military Style*. New Haven: Yale University Press, 1976.

Ellis, Stephen. *Comrades Against Apartheid: The African National Congress and the South African Communist Party in Exile*. London: J. Currey, 1992.

Fage, John Donelly. *A History of Africa*, 3d ed. London: Routledge, 1995.

First, Ruth. *The Barrrel of a Gun: Political Power in Africa and the Coup d'Etat*. London: Allen Lane, The Penguin Press, 1970.

Fredrikse, Julie. *South Africa: A Different Kind of War: From Soweto to Pretoria*. Johannesburg: Ravan Press, 1986.

Goldsworthy, David. *Tom Mboya: The Man Kenya Wanted to Forget*. Nairobi, Heinemann, 1982.

Grant, Stan. *The Call of Mother Africa*. Kingston, Jamaica: Courrier Press, 1973.

Hadjor, Kofi Buenor. *The Dilemma of Post-Colonial Power*. London: Kegan Paul, 1988.

Hargreaves, John Desmond. *Decolonization in Africa*. London: Longman, 1988.

Hooder-Williams, Richard. *An Introduction to the Politics of Tropical Africa*. London: G. Allen and Unwin, 1984.

Isaacman, Allen Frederick. *Mozambique: From Colonialism to Revolution, 1900–1982*. Boulder, Colo.: Westview Press, 1983.

Lamb, David. *The Africans*. New York: Vintage Books, 1984.

Langley, J. Ayodele. *Ideologies of Liberation in Black Africa, 1856–1970: Documents on Modern African Political Thought from Colonial Times to the Present*. London: R. Collins, 1979.

Liebenow, J. Gus. *African Politics: Crises and Challenges*. Bloomington, Ind.: Indiana University Press, 1986.

Lopes, Carlos. *Guinea-Bissau: From Liberation Struggle to Independent Statehood*. Boulder, Colo.: Westview Press, 1987.

Luthuli, Albert John. *Let My People Go*. London: Collins, 1962.

Mandela, Nelson. *Long Walk to Freedom*. Little Brown, 1994.

Manning, Patrick. *Francophone Sub-Saharan Africa, 1880–1985*. Cambridge: Cambridge University Press, 1988.

Marcum, John A. *The Angolan Revolution*. Cambridge, Mass.: The MIT Press, 1978.

Markakis, John. *National and Class Conflict in the Horn of Africa*. Cambridge University Press, 1987.

McCullough, Jack. *In the Twilight of the Revolution: The Political Theory of Amilcar Cabral*. London: Routledge and Kegan Paul, 1983.

Meer, Fatima. *Higher than Hope*. London: H. Hamilton, 1990.

Newitt, Mary Dudley Dunn. *A History of Mozambique*. Bloomington and Indianapolis: Indiana University Press, 1995.

Obasanjo, Olusegun. *My Command: An Account of the Nigerian Civil War, 1967–1970*. London: Heinemann, N.D.

Odetola, Theophilus Olatunde. *Militray Regimes and Development: A Comparative Analysis of African States*. London: G. Allen and Unwin, 1982.

Oliver, Roland Anthony. *The African Experience*. Icon Editions, 1992.

Omer-Cooper, John D. *History of Southern Africa*. London: J. Currey, 1987.

Ottaway, David. *Afrocommunism*. New York: Africana Publishing Company, 1981.

Senghor, Leopold Sedar. *Nationhood and the African Road to Socialism*. Paris: Presence Africaine, 1962.

Senghor, Leopold Sedar. *On African Socialism*. New York: F.A. Praeger, 1964.

Spikes, Daniel. *Angola and the Politics of Intervention: From Local Bush War to Chronic Crisis in Southern Africa*. Jefferson, N.C.: McFarland, 1993.

Strayer, Robert W. *Protest Movements in Colonial East Africa: Aspects of Early African Responses to European Rule*. Syracuse, N.Y.: Syracuse University Press, 1973.

Vambe, Lawrence. *From Rhodesia to Zimbabwe*. London: Heinemann, 1976.

Van Rensburg, Abraham Paul Janse. *Contemporary Leaders of Africa*. Capetown: Haum, 1975.

Vansina, Jan. *Paths in the Rainforest: Toward a History of Political Tradition in Equatorial Africa*. London: J. Currey, 1990.

Walshe, Peter. *The Rise of African Nationalism in South Africa: The African National Congress, 1912–1952*. London: C. Hurst, 1970.

Wiseman, John A. *Democracy in Black Africa: Survival and Revival*. New York: Paragon House Publishers, 1990.

Wiseman, John A. *Political Leaders in Black Africa: A Biographical Dictionary of the Major Politicians since Independence*. Aldershot, United Kingdom: E. Elgar, 1991.

Wolfers, Michael. *Angola in the Frontline*. London: Zed Press, 1983.

Woods, Donald. *Biko* (rev.). London: Penguin Books, 1987.

The Ancient World

Avi Yonah, Michael and Israel Shatzman. *Illustrated Encyclopedia of the Classical World*. Jerusalem: The Jerusalem Publishing House Ltd., 1976.

Boardman, J. et al., editors. *The Oxford History of the Classical World*. Oxford: Oxford University Press, 1986.

Brunt, P. A. *Social Conflicts in the Roman Republic*. London: Chatto & Windus, 1978.

Fuks, A. *Social Conflict in Ancient Greece*. Jerusalem: The Magnes Press, 1984.

Hammond, N. G. L. and H. H. Scullard, editors. *The Oxford Classical Dictionary*. (2d ed.). Oxford: Clarendon Press, 1970.

Raaflaub, K. A., editor. *Social Struggles in Archaic Rome: New Perspectives on the Conflict of the Orders*. Berkeley: University of California Press, 1986.

Ste Croix, G. E. M. de. *The Class Struggle in the Ancient Greek World from the Archaic Age to the Arab Conquests*. London: Duckworth, 1981.

Syme, Sir Ronald *The Roman Revolution*. Oxford: Clarendon Press, 1939.

Central America and the Caribbean

Everyday Forms of State Formation: Revolution and the Negotiation of Rule in Modern Mexico. Durham, N.C.: Duke University Press, 1994.

Mexico: From Independence to Revolution, 1810–1910. Lincoln, Neb.: University of Nebraska Press, 1982.

Nicaragua in Revolution. New York: Praeger, 1982.

Riot, Rebellion and Revolution: Rural Social Conflict in Mexico. Princeton, N.J.: Priceton University Press, 1988.

Sandino: The Testimony of a Nicaraguan Patriot, 1921–1934. Princeton, N.J.: Princeton University Press, 1990.

The Independence of Mexico and the Creation of a New Nation. Los Angeles: UCLA Latin American Center Publications, University of California, 1989.

The Mexican Revolution, 1910–1914: The Diplomacy of the Anglo-American Conflict. Cambridge: Cambridge University Press, 1968.

The Myth of the Revolution: Hero Cults and the Institutionalization of the Mexican State, 1920–1940. New York: Greenwood Press, 1986.

Ankerson, Dudley. *Agrarian Warlord: Saturnino Cedillo and the Mexican Revolution in San Luis Potosi.* Dekalb: Northern Illinois University Press, 1984.

Atkin, Ronald. *Revolution: Mexico 1910–1920.* London: Macmillan Press, 1969.

Bonsal, Peter G. *Fidel: A Biography of Fidel Castro.* New York: Dodd, Mead, 1986.

Bonsal, Philip Wilson. *Cuba, Castro and the United States.* Pittsburgh: University of Pittsburgh Press, 1971.

Brenner, Anita. *The Wind That Swept Mexico: The History of the Mexican Revolution 1910–1942.* Austin: University of Texas Press, 1984.

Bunck, Julie Marie. *Fidel Castro and the Quest for a Revolutionary Culture in Cuba.* University Park: Pensylvania State University, 1994.

Cline, Howard Francis. *Mexico: Revolution to Evolution, 1940–1960.* Oxford: Oxford University Press, 1962.

Cockcroft, James Donald. *Intellectual Precursors of the Mexican Revolution 1900–1913.* The Institute of Latin American Studies: Austin: University of Texas Press, 1968.

Dodson, Michael. *Nicaragua's Other Revolution: Religious Faith and Political Struggle.* Chape Hill, N.C.: University of North Carolina Press, 1990.

Draper, Theodore. *Castroism: Theory and Practice.* London: Pall Mall Press, 1965.

Dulles, John Watson Foster. *Yesterday in Mexico: A Chronicle of the Revolution, 1919–1936.* Austin: University of Texas Press, 1961.

Flores Caballero, Romeo. *Counterrevolution: The Role of the Spaniards in the Independence of Mexico, 1804–38.* Lincoln: University of Nebraska Press, 1974.

Halperin, Maurice. *The Taming of Fidel Castro.* Berkeley: University of California Press, 1981.

Hamill, Hugh M. *The Higaldo Revolt: Prelude to Mexican Independence.* Westview Conn.: Greenwood Press, 1981.

Henderson, Peter V. N. *Felix Diaz, The Porfirians, and the Mexican Revolution.* Lincoln: University of Nebraska Press, 1981.

Hodges, Donald Clark. *Mexico, 1910–1982: Reform or Revolution* (2d ed.). London: Zed Press, 1983.

Llerena, Mario. *The Unsuspected Revolution: The Birth and Rise of Castroism*. Ithaca, N.Y.: Cornell University Press, 1978.

Lockwood, Lee. *Castro's Cuba, Cuba's Fidel*. Boulder, Colo.: Westview Press, 1990.

Montaner, Carlos Alberto *Secret Report on the Cuban Revolution*. New Brunswick: Transaction Books, 1981.

Paterson, Thomas G. *Contesting Castro: The United States and the Triumph of the Cuban Revolution*. New York: Oxford University Press, 1994.

Raat, William Dirk. *Revoltosos: Mexico's Rebels in the United States, 1903–1923*. College Station: Texas A&M University Press, 1981.

Tannenbaum, Frank. *Peace by Revolution: Mexico after 1910*. New York: Columbia University Press, 1966.

Womack, John, Jr. *Zapata and the Mexican Revolution*. Harmondsworth: Penguin Books, 1972.

China

Zhongguo Geming Shi Renwu Cidian [Dictionary of personalities in Chinese revolutionary history]. Beijing: Beijing Chubanshe Chuban (Beijing Publishing House), 1991.

Bernal, M. *Chinese Socialism to 1907*. Ithaca and London: Cornell University Press, 1976.

Bodde, D. *China's First Unifier*. Leiden: E. J. Brill, 1938.

Boorman, H. L. and R. C. Howard, editors. *Biographical Dictionary of Republican China*. New York: Columbia University Press, 1967–71.

Ch'en, J. *Mao and the Chinese Revolution*. New York: Oxford University Press, 1967.

Chesneaux, J. *Secret Societies in China*. Ann Arbor, Mich.: University of Michigan Press, 1971.

Chu, W. D. *The Moslem Rebellions in Northwest China 1862–1878*. The Hague/Paris: Mouton & Co., 1966.

Esherick, J. W. *Reform and Revolution in China: The 1911 Revolution in Hunan and Hubei*. Berkeley: University of California Press, 1976.

Esherick, J. W. *The Origins of the Boxer Uprising*. Berkeley: University of California Press, 1987.

Fairbank, J. K. and A. Feuerwerker, editors. *The Cambridge History of China*. Vol. 13. *Republican China 1912–1949*. Part 2. Cambridge: Cambridge University Press, 1986.

Fairbank, J. K., and E. O. Reischauer and A. M. Craig. *East Asia: The Modern Transformation*. Boston: Houghton Mifflin, 1965.

Feuerwerker, Albert. *Rebellion in Nineteenth-Century China*. Ann Arbor, Mich.: Center for Chinese Studies, University of Michigan, 1975.

Giles, H. A. *A Chinese Biographical Dictionary*. Shanghai, 1898. Reprinted by Literature House, Taipei, 1964.

Ho Kan-chih. *A History of the Modern Chinese Revolution*. Peking: Foreign Languages Press, 1960.

Holubnychy, L. *Michael Borodin and the Chinese Revolution, 1923–1925*. Ann Arbor, Mich.: University Microfilms International, 1979.

Houn, F. W., *A Short History of Chinese Communism*. Englewood, N.J.: Prentice-Hall, 1967.

Hsiung, S. I. *The Life of Chiang Kai-shek*. London: Peter Davies, 1948.

Hsueh, C. T. *Huang Hsing and the Chinese Revolution*. Stanford: Stanford University Press, 1961.

Hsueh, C. T., editor. *Revolutionary Leaders of Modern China*. London: Oxford University Press, 1971.

Hummel, A. W., editor. *Eminent Chinese of the Ch'ing Period (1644–1912)*. Washington: United States Government Printing Office, 1943.

Jiang Yihua, *Zhang Taiyan Sixiang Yanjiu* [A Study of Zhang Taiyan's thought]. Shanghai: Renmin Chubanshe (People's Publishing House), 1985.

Jin Chongji, editor. *Zhou Enlai Zhuan, 1898–1949* [Biography of Zhou Enlai, 1898–1949]. Beijing: Renmin Chubanshe (People's Publishing House), 1989.

Klein, D. W. and A. B. Clark, editors. *Biographic Dictionary of Chinese Communism, 1921–1965*. Cambridge, Mass.: Harvard University Press, 1971.

Li, U. B. *Outlines of Chinese History*. Shanghai, 1914. Reprinted by Ch'eng-wen Publishing Company, Taipei, 1967.

Liew, K. S. *Struggle for Democracy: Sung Chiao-jen and the 1911 Chinese Revolution*. Berkeley: University of California Press, 1971.

Lo, J. P. *K'ang Yu-wei: A Biography and Symposium*. Tucson, Arizona: University of Arizona Press, 1967.

Michael, F. *The Taiping Rebellion*. Vol. 1. Seattle: University of Washington Press, 1966.

Muramatsu, Y. "Some Themes in Chinese Rebel Ideologies." In *The Confucian Persuasion*, edited by A. F. Wright. Stanford: Stanford University Press, 1960.

North, R. C. and X. J. Eudin. *M. N. Roy's Mission to China*. Berkeley: University of California Press, 1963.

Pulleyblank, E. G. *The Background of the Rebellion of An Lu-shan*. London: Oxford University Press, 1955.

Rankin, M. B. *Early Chinese Revolutionaries: Radical Intellectuals in Shanghai and Chekiang, 1902–1911*.

Cambridge, Mass.: University of Harvard Press, 1971.

Reischauer, E. O. and J. K. Fairbank. *East Asia: The Great Tradition*. Boston: Houghton Mifflin, 1958, 1960.

Salisbury, H. E. *The Long March*. New York: Harper & Row, 1985.

Scalapino, R. A. and G. T. Yu. *The Chinese Anarchist Movement*. Berkeley: Center for Chinese Studies, University of California, 1961.

Schiffrin, H. Z. *Sun Yat-sen and the Origins of the Chinese Revolution*. Berkeley: University of California Press, 1970.

Schiffrin, H. Z. *Sun Yat Sen: Reluctant Revolutionary*. Boston: Little Brown & Co., 1980.

Schram, S. *Mao Tse-tung*. Harmondsworth, England: Penguin, 1966.

Teng, S. Y. *The Nien Army and their Guerrilla Warfare 1851–1868*. Paris: Mouton & Co., 1961.

Welch, H. *The Parting of the Way: Lao Tzu and the Taoist Movement*. Boston: Beacon Press, 1957.

Wilbur, C. M. and J. How. *Missionaries of Revolution: Soviet Advisers and Nationalist China, 1920–1927*. Cambridge, Mass.: Harvard University Press,1989.

Wright, M. C. *The Last Stand of Chinese Conservatism, the T'ung-chih Restoration, 1862–1872* Stanford: Stanford University Press, 1957.

Wright, M. C., editor. *China in Revolution: The First Phase 1900–1913*. New Haven and London: Yale University Press, 1968.

Yu, G. T. *Party Politics in Republican China: The Kuomintang, 1912–1924*. Berkeley: University of California Press, 1966.

Eastern Europe

Bol'shaia Sovetskaia Entsiklopediia, 3d ed. Moscow: Sovetskaia Entsiklopediia, 1970–1978.

Abraham, Richard, *Alexander Kerensky: The First Love of the Revolution*. New York: Columbia University Press, 1987.

Ascher, Abraham. *The Revolution of 1905*. Stanford, Calif: Stanford University Press, 1988.

Basil, John D., *The Mensheviks in the Revolution of 1917*. Columbus: Slavica Publishers, 1983.

Beilharz, Peter. *Trotsky, Trotskyism, and the Transition to Socialism*. London: Croom Helm, 1987.

Benvenuti, Francesco. *The Bolsheviks and the Red Army, 1918–1980.* Cambridge University Press, 1988.

Berlin, Isaiah. *Russian Thinkers.* Harmondsworth, United Kingdom: Pelican Books, 1979.

Besancon, Alain. *The Intellectual Origins of Leninism.* Oxford: Basil Blackwell, 1981.

Boer, S.P. de. *Biographical Dictionary of Dissent in the Soviet Union, 1956–1975.* The Hague: M. Nijhoff, 1982.

Bronkin, Vladimir N. *Behind the Front Lines of the Civil War: Political Parties and Social Movements in Russia, 1918–1922.* Princeton: Princeton University Press, 1994.

Brown, J. F. *Surge to Freedom.* Durham, N.C.: Duke University Press, 1991.

Bruce, Allen. *Germany East: Dissent and Opposition.* Montreal: Black Rose, 1989.

Burdzhalov, Edward Nikolaevich. *Russia's Second Revolution: The February 1917 Uprising in Petrograd.* Bloomington: Indiana University Press, 1987.

Bushnell, John. *Mutiny and Repression: Russian Soldiers in the Revolution of 1905–06.* Bloomington: Indiana University Press, 1985.

Carrere d'Enacausse, Helene. *A History of the Soviet Union, 1917–1953.* London: Longman, 1982.

Clark, Ronald William. *Lenin.* New York: Harper and Row, 1988.

Daniels, Robert Vincent. *Trotsky, Stalin and Socialism.* Boulder, Colo.: Westview Press, 1991.

Dawisha, Karen. *The Kremlin and the Prague Spring.* Berkeley: University of California Press, 1984.

de Weydenthal, Jan B. *The Communists of Poland.* Stanford, 1987.

Djilas, Milovan. *Tito: The Story from Inside.* London: Weidenfeld and Nicolson, 1980.

Djordjevic, Dimitrije. *The Balkan Revolutionary Tradition.* New York: Columbia University Press, 1981.

Draper, Hal. *The "Dictatorship of the Proletariat" from Marx to Lenin.* New York: Monthly Review Press, 1987.

Ferro, Marc. *October 1917: A Social History of the Russian Revolution.* London: Routledge and Kegan Paul, 1980.

Figes, Orlando. *Peasant Russia, Civil War: The Volga Countryside in Revolution (1917–1921).* Oxford: Clarendon Press, 1989.

Fitzpatrick, Sheila. *The Russian Revolution.* New York: Oxford University Press, 1982.

Florinsky, Michael, Editor. *The Mc-Graw-Hill Encyclopedia of Russia and the Soviet Union.* New York: McGraw-Hill, 1961.

Freeze, Gregory L. *From Supplication to Revolution: A Documentary Social History of Imperial Russia.* New York: Oxford University Press, 1988.

Galili Y. Garcia, Ziva. *The Menshevik Leaders in the Russian Revolution: Social Realities and Political Strategies.* Princeton, N.J.: Princeton University Press, 1989.

Garton Ash, Timothy. *The Polish Revolution: Solidarity.* New York: Charles Scribner's Sons, 1983.

Hasegawey, Tsuyoshi. *The February Revolution: Petrograd, 1917.* Seattle: University of Washington Press, 1981.

Koenker, Diane. Strikes and Revolution in Russia, 1917. Princeton, NJ: Princeton University Press, 1989.

Leblanc, Paul. *Lenin and the Revolutionary Party.* Atlantic Highlands, N.J.: Humanities Press International, 1990.

Lincoln, William Bruce. *Passage through Armageddon: The Russians in War and Revolution.* New York: Simon and Schuster, 1986.

Longworth, Philip. *The Making of Eastern Europe.* New York: Macmillan, 1992.

Lovenduski, Joni and Jean Woodall. *Politics and Society in Eastern Europe.* New York: Macmillan, 1987.

Medvedev, Roy Aleksandrovich. *The October Revolution.* New York: Columbia University Press, 1979.

Melograni, Piero. *Lenin and the Myth of World Revolution: Ideology and Reasons of State, 1917–1920.* Atlantic Highlands, N.J.: Humanities Press International, 1989.

Modsley, Evan. *The Russian Civil War.* Boston: G. Allen and Unwin, 1987.

Molyneux, John. *Leon Trotsky's Theory of Revolution.* New York: St. Martin's Press, 1981.

Mylnar, Zednek. *Night Frost in Prague: The End of Humane Socialism.* London: C. Hurst, 1980.

O'Meara, Patrick. *K.F. Ryleev: A Political Biography of the Decembrist Poet.* Princeton, N. J.: Princeton University Press, 1984.

Pavlowitch, Stevan K. *Tito: Yugoslavia's Great Dictator: A Reassessment.* Columbus: Ohio University Press, 1992.

Philipsen, Dirk. *We Were the People: Voices from East Germany's Revolutionary Autumn of 1989.* Durham, N.C.: Duke University Press, 1993.

Pipes, Richard. *Revolutionary Russia.* Cambridge, Mass.: Harvard University Press, 1968.

Pipes, Richard. *The Russian Revolution.* New York: Alfred A. Knopf, 1991.

Reed, John. *Ten Days That Shook the World.* New York: Vintage Books, 1960.

Reichman, Henry, *Railwayman and Revolution: Russia, 1905.* Berkeley: University of California Press, 1987.

Rice, Christopher. *Russian Workers and the Socialist Revolutionary Party Through the Revolution of 1905–07.* Macmillan Press, 1988.

Salisbury, Harrison Evans. *Black Night, White Snow: Russia's Revolutions, 1905–1917.* 1978.

Schapiro, Leonard B. *The Communist Party of the Soviet Union.* New York: Random House, 1960.

Schapiro, Leonard B. *The Russian Revolutions of 1917: The Origins of Modern Communism.* New York: Basic Books, 1984.

Service, Robert. *Lenin, A Political Life.* Bloomington: Indiana University Press, 1985.

Shawcross, William. *Crime and Compromise: Janos Kadar and the Politics of Hungary since the Revolution.* New York: E.P. Dutton, 1974.

Shukman, Harold, Editor. *The Blackwell Encyclopedia of the Russian Revolution.* Oxford: Basil Blackwell, 1994.

Stites, Richard. *Revolutionary Dreams, Utopian Vision and Experimental Life in the Russian Revolution.* New York: Oxford University Press, 1989.

Stokes, Curtis. *The Evolution of Trotsky's Theory of Revolution.* Washington D.C.: United Press of America, 1982.

Stokes, Gale. *The Wall Came Tumbling Down.* Oxford, 1993.

Verner, Andrew M. *The Crisis of Russian Autocracy: Nicholas II and the 1905 Revolution.* Princeton, N.J.: Princeton University Press, 1992.

Volkogonov, Dmitrii Antonovich. *Lenin: A New Biography.* New York: Free Press, 1994.

Walicki, Andjei. *A History of Russian Thought from the Enlightenment to Marxism.* Oxford: Oxford University Press, 1980.

Warth, R. Douglas. *Leon Trotsky.* Boston: Twayne Publishers, 1977.

Williams, Robert Chadwell. *The Other Bolsheviks: Lenin and His Critics, 1904–1914.* Bloomington: Indiana University Press, 1985.

Wynn, Charles. *Workers, Strikes and Pogroms: The Dombass-Dneipr Bend in Late Imperial Russia, 1870–1905.* Princeton, N.J.: Princeton University Press, 1992.

The Middle East and North Africa

Abu Jaber, Kamel S. *The Arab Ba'th Socialist Party.* Syracuse, New York: Syracuse University Press, 1966.

Amos, John W. *Palestinian Resistance—Organization of a Nationalist Movement.* New York: Pergamon Press, 1978.

Baram, Amatzia and Barry Rubin, editors. *Iraq's Road to War*. New York: St. Martin's Press, 1994.

Baram, Amatzia. *Culture, History and Ideology in the Formation of Ba'thist Iraq*. Oxford, London, New York: Macmillan and St. Martin's, 1991.

Ben-Rafael, E. *Israel-Palestine—A Guerrilla Conflict in International Politics*. New York: Greenwood Press, 1987.

Cobban, H. *The Palestinian Liberation Organization—People, Power and Politics*. Cambridge: Cambridge University Press, 1984.

Danchev, Alex and Dan Keohane. *International Perspectives on the Gulf Conflict 1990–91*. Oxford, London, New York: St. Martin's Press, Macmillan, 1994.

Devlin, John F. *The Ba'th Party: A History from its Origins to 1966*. Stanford: Hoover Institute Press, 1979.

Farouq-Sluglett, Marion and Peter Sluglett. *Iraq Since 1958: From Revolution to Dictatorship*. London, New York: KPI, 1987.

Gerber, Haim. *Islam, Guerilla War and Revolution: A Study in Comparative Social History*. Boulder, Colo.: L. Rienner, 1988.

Hart, A. *Arafat—A Political Biography*. Bloomington and Indianapolis: India University Press, 1989.

Hart, Alan. *Arafat: A Political Biography*. Bloomington: Indiana University Press, 1989.

Israeli, R., editor. *PLO in Lebanon—Selected Documents*. London: Weidenfeld and Nicolson, 1983.

Jureidini, P. and William E. Hazen. *The Palestinian Movement in Politics*. Lexington, Mass.: Lexington Books, 1976.

Kazzhiha, Walid. *Palestine in the Arab Dilemma*. London: Croom Helm Ltd., 1979.

Khalil, Samir al-(Kanan Makiya). *Republic of Fear: The Politics of Modern Iraq*. London and New South Wales, Australia: Hutchinson Radius, 1989.

Kienle, Eberhard. Ba'th v. Ba'th: *The Conflict between Syria and Iraq 1968–1989*. London, New York: Tauris, 1990.

Kirisci, K. The PLO and World Politics—*A Study of the Mobilization and Support for the Palestinian Cause*. London: Frances Pinter, 1986.

Makiya, Kanan. *Cruelty and Silence*. New York, London: N. W. Norton, 1993.

Marr, Phoebe. *The Modern History of Iraq*. Boulder, Colo.: Westview Press, 1985.

O'Neill, Bard E. *Armed Struggle in Palestine: A Political-Military Analysis*. Boulder, Colo.: Westview Press, 1978.

Parsa, Misagh. *Social Origins of the Iranian Revolution*. New Brunswick: Rutgers University Press, 1989.

Sahliyeh, Emile F. *The PLO after the Lebanon War*. Boulder, Colo.: Westview Press, 1986.

Said, Edward W. *The Question of Palestine*. New York: Times Books, 1980.

Sayigh, R. *Palestinians: From Peasants to Revolutionaries*. London: Zed Press, 1979.

Sciolino, Elaine. *The Outlaw State: Saddam Hussein's Quest for Power and the Gulf Crisis*. New York: John Wiley, 1991.

Yaari, Ehud. Strike *Terror—The Story of Fatah*. New York: Sabra Books, 1970.

Yodfat, Aryeh Y. and Yuval Arnon-Ohanna. *PLO Strategy and Politics*. New York: St. Martin's Press, 1981.

North America

Beyond the American Revolution: Explorations in the History of American Radicalism. Dekalb, Ill: Northern Illinois University Press, 1992.

James Madison and the American Nation, 1751–1836: An Encyclopedia. New York: Simon and Schuster, 1994.

Major Problems in the Era of the American Revolution 1760–1791: Documents and Essays. Lexington, Mass.: Health and Co., 1992.

Patriots, Redcoats and Loyalists. New York: Garland Pub., 1991.

Perspectives on Revolution and Evolution. Durham, N.C.: Duke University Press, 1979.

The American Revolution: Its Characters and Limit. New York: New York University Press, 1987.

The Blackwell Encyclopedia of the American Revolution. Cambridge, Mass.: Basil Blackwell, 1991.

The Queen v. Louis Riel Toronto, Ont.: University of Toronto Press, 1974.

Bailyn, Bernard. *Faces of Revolution: Personalities and Themes in the Struggle for American Independence*. New York: A. A. Knopf, 1990.

Bailyn, Bernard. *The Ideological Origin of the American Revolution* (enl. ed.) Cambridge, Mass.: Belknap Press, 1992.

Barwick, Colin. *The American Revolution*. Charlottesville, VA.: University Press of Virginia, 1991.

Bishop, Jim. *The Birth of the United States*. New York: William Morrow, 1976.

Block, Ruth H. *Visionary Republic: Millennial Themes in American Thought, 1756–1800*. Cambridge: Cambridge University Press, 1985.

Brandt, Clare. *The Man in the Mirror: A Life of Benedict Arnold.* New York: Hill and Wang, 1985.

Brown, Wallace. *The King's Friends: The Composition and Motives of the American Loyalists Claimants.* Providence: Brown University Press, 1965.

Claeys, Gregory. *Thomas Paine: Social and Political Thought.* Boston: Unwin Hyman, 1989.

Countryman, Edward. *The American Revolution.* Hill and Wang, 1985.

Currey, Cecil B. *Road to Revolution: Benjamin Franklin in England, 1765 – 1775.* 2d ed. Gloucester, Mass.: P. Smith, 1978.

Dull, Jonathan R. *A Diplomatic History of the American Revolution.* New Haven: Yale University Press, 1985.

Egnal, Mark. *A Mighty Empire: The Origins of the American Revolution.* Ithaca: Cornell University Press, 1988.

Eidelberg, Paul. *On the Silence of the Declaration of Independence.* Amherst: University of Massachusetts Press, 1976.

Flanagan, Thomas. *Riel and the Rebellion: 1885 Reconsidered.* Saskatoon, Sask.: Western Producer Prairie Books, 1983.

Fliegelman, Jay. *Declaring Independence: Jefferson, Natural Language, and the Culture of Performance.* Stanford, Calif.: Stanford University Press, 1993.

Foner, Eric. *Tom Paine and Revolutionary America* . New York:

Hutson, James H. *John Adams and the Diplomacy of the American Revolution.* Lexington: University Press of Kentucky, 1980.

McConnell, Francis John. *Evangelicals, Revolutionists and Idealists: Six English Contributors to American Thought and Action.* New York: Kennikat Press, 1972.

McLean, Donald George. *1885: Metis Rebellion or Government Conspiracy?.* Winnipeg: Pemican Pub., 1985.

MiddleKuff, Robert. *The Glorious Cause: The American Revolution in Two Volumes.* Indianapolis: Liberty Classics, 1990.

Norman, K. *Thomas Jefferson*: Madison House, 1994.

Randall, Willard Sterne. *Thomas Jefferson: A Life.* Harper Collins, 1994.

Reid, John Phillip. *Constitutional History of the American Revolution: The Authority of Rights.* Madison: University of Wisconsin Press, 1986.

Siggins, Maggie. *Riel: A Life of Revolution.* Toronto: Harper Collins, 1983.

Stanley, George Francis Gillman. *The Birth of Western Canada: A History of the Riel Rebellion*. Toronto: The University of Toronto Press, 1992.

Tyler, John W. *Smugglers and Patriots: Boston Merchants and the Advent of the American Revolution*. Boston: Northeastern University Press, 1986.

Van Tyne, Claude Halstead. *The Loyalists in the American Revolution*. Gloucester, Mass.: P. Smith, 1959.

Washington, George. *The Making of an American Symbol*. New York: Free Press, 1987.

Yazrva, Melvin. *From Colonies to Commonwealth: Familial Ideology and the Beginnings of the American Republic*. Baltimore: John Hopkins University Press, 1985.

South America

Brazil: Empire and Republic, 1822–1930. Cambridge: Cambridge University Press, 1993, 1989.

Juan Peron and the Reshaping of Argentina. Pittsburgh, Penn.: University of Pittsburgh Press, 1983.

Adams, Jerome R. *Liberators and Patriots of Latin America: Biographies of 23 Leaders from Dona Marina to Bishop Romero*. Jefferson, N.C.: McFarland and Company, 1991.

Alexander, Robert Jackson. *Juan Domingo Peron: A History*. Boulder, Colo.: Westview Press, 1979.

Arriagada Herrera, Gerardo. *Pinochet: The Politics of Power*. Boston: Unwin Hyman, 1988.

Barager, Joseph R., Editor. *Why Peron Came to Power: The Background to Peroism in Argentina*. New York: Alfred A. Knopf, 1968.

Constable, Pamela. *A Nation of Enemies: Chile Under Pinochet*. New York: W.W. Norton, 1991.

Crassweller, Robert D. *Peron and the Enigma of Argentina*. New York: W.W. Norton, 1987.

Falcoff, Mark, Editor. *Prologue to Peron: Argentina in Depression and War, 1930–1943*. Berkeley: University of California Press, 1975.

Kelley, Jonathan. *Revolution and the Rebirth of Inequality: A Theory Applied to the National Revolution in Bolivia*. Berkeley: University of California Press, 1981.

Macaulay, Neill. *The Prestes Column: Revolution in Brazil*. New York: New Viewpoints, 1974.

Macaulay, Neill. *The Struggle for Liberty in Brazil and Portugal, 1798–1834*. Durham, N.C.: Duke University Press, 1986.

Malloy, James M. *Bolivia: The Uncompleted Revolution*. Pittsburgh: University of Pittsburgh Press, 1970.

Page, Joseph A. *Peron: A Biography*. New York: Random House, 1983.

Selbin, Eric. *Modern Latin American Revolutions*. Boulder, Colo.: Westview Press, 1993.

Sobel, Lester A., Editor. *Argentina and Peron: 1970–1975*. New York: Facts on File, 1975.

Spooner, Mary Helen. *Soldiers in a Narrow Land: The Pinochet Regime in Chile*. Berkeley: University of California Press, 1994.

Street, John. *Artigas and the Emancipation of Uruguay*. London: Cambridge University Press, 1959.

Timmerman, Jacobo. *Chile: Death in the South*. New York: Alfred A. Knopf, 1987.

Young, Jordan M. *The Brazilian Revolution of 1930 and the Aftermath*. New Brunswick: Rutgers University Press, 1967.

Zeitlin, Maurice. *The Civil War in Chile, or, The Bourgeois Revolutions that Never Were*. Princeton: Princeton University Press, 1988.

South and Southeast Asia

Bakshi, S.R. *Nehru and his Political Ideology*. New Delhi: Criterion Pub., 1988.

Baneri, Jayantanuja. *Mao Tse-Tung and Gandhi: Perspectives on Social Transformation*. Bombay: Allied Publishers, 1973.

Bhattacharyya, Sailendra Nath. *Mahatma Gandhi, the Journalist*. Westport, Conn.: Greenwood Press, 1984.

Brown, Judith Margaret. *Gandhi and Civil Disobedience: The Mahatma in Indian Politics, 1928–1934*. Cambridge: Cambridge University Press, 1977.

Brown, Judith Margeret. *Gandhi's Rise to Power: Indian Politics 1915–1922*. Cambridge: Cambridge University Press, 1972.

Buttinger, Joseph. *A Defiant Dragon: A Short History of Vietnam*. New York: Praeger Publishers, 1972.

Buttinger, Joseph. *Vietnam: A Dragon Embattled*. New York: F.A. Praeger, 1967.

Buttinger, Joseph. *Vietnam: A Politcal History*. New York: F.A. Praeger, 1968.

Chalapati Rau, M. *Builders of Modern India: Jawaharlal Nehru*. New Delhi: Publications Division, Ministry of Information and Broadcasting, Government of India, 1973.

Duiker, William J. *The Communist Road to Power in Vietnam*. Boulder, Colo.: Westview Press, 1981.

Duiker, William J. *The Rise of Nationalism in Vietnam: 1900–1941*. Ithaca, N.Y.: Cornell University Press, 1976.

Duiker, William J. *Vietnam: Nation in Revolution*. Boulder, Colo.: Westview Press, 1983.

Erikson, Erik Homburger. *Gandhi's Truth on the Origins of Militant Non-Violence.* New York: W.W. Norton, 1969.

Gordon, Leonard A. *Bengal: The Nationalist Movement 1876–1940.* London: Columbia University Press, 1974.

Green, Martin Burgess. *Tolstoy and Gandhi, Men of Peace: A Biography.* New York: Basic Books, 1983.

Halberstam, David. *Ho.* New York: Random House, 1971.

Horsburgh, H.J.N. *Nonviolence and Aggression: A Study of Gandhi's Moral Equivalent of War.* London: Oxford University Press, 1968.

Korejo, Muhammed Soaleh, *The Frontier Gandhi, His Place in History. Karachi:* Oxford University Press, 1994.

Kumar, Chardra. *Mahatma Gandhi: His Life and Influence.* London: Heinemann, 1982.

Macleavy, Henry. *Black Flags in Vietnam: The Story of a Chinese Intervention* London: G. Allen and Unwin, 1968.

McLane, John R. *Indian Nationalism and the Early Congress.* Princeton: Princeton University Press, 1977.

Post, Ken. *Revolution, Socialism and Nationalism in Vietnam.* Dartsmouth, United Kingdom: Aldershot, Harts, 1989–1994.

Reid, Anthony. *The Indonesian National Revolution, 1945–1950.* Victoria: Hawthorne, 1974.

Schofield, Victoria. *Bhutto: Trial and Execution.* London: Cassell, 1979.

Shaplen, Robert. *The Lost Revolution: Vietnam, 1946–1965.* London: A. Deutsch, 1966.

Taseer, Salmana. *Bhutto: A Political Biography.* London: Ithaca Press, 1979.

Truong, Nhu Tang. *A Vietcong Memoir.* New York: Vintage Books, 1986.

Wande, Bal Ram. *Gandhi and his Critics.* Delhi: Oxford University Press, 1993.

Wolpert, Stanley A. *Jinnah of Pakistan.* New York: Oxford University Press, 1989.

Western Europe

Aftalion, Florion. *The French Revolution: An Economic Interpretation.* Cambridge, Mass.: Cambridge University Press, 1990.

Agulhon, M. *Le cercle dans la France bourgeoise 1810–1848: Étude d'une mutation de sociabilité.* Paris, 1977.

Agulhon, M. *Pénitents et Franc-Maçons de l'ancienne provence: Éssai sur la sociabilité méridionale.* Paris, 1966; 1984.

Agulhon, M. "La Révolution française au rang des accusés." In *Histoire vagabonde*. Paris, 1988.

Aston, Nigel. *The End of an Elite: The French Bishops and the Coming of the Revolution, 1786–1790*. Oxford: Clarendon Press, 1992.

Auspitz, K. *The Radical Bourgeoisie, the Ligue de l'Enseignement and the Origins of the Third Republic, 1866–1885*. Cambridge, 1982.

Bell, John Bower. *The Secret Army: The Irish Republican Army, 1916–1979*. Dublin: Academy Press, 1979.

Bosher, J.F. *The French Revolution*. New York: W.W. Norton, 1988.

Brinton, Crane. *A Decade of Revolution, 1789–1799*. New York: Harper and Row, 1963.

Carr, Raymond. *Spain: From Dictatorship to Democracy*. London: G. Allen and Unwin, 1979.

Cobb, Richard Charles. *Reactions to the French Revolution*. London: Oxford University Press, 1972.

Combes, A. *Les trois siècles de la Franc-Maçonnerie Française*. Paris, 1987.

Coogan, Timothy Patrick. *The I.R.A.* London: Fontana, 1982.

Forrest, Alan. *Society and Politics in Revolutionary Bordeaux*. London: Oxford University Press, 1975.

Forrest, Alan. *The French Revolution*. Oxford: Blackwell, 1995.

Furet, François. *Revolutionary France 1770–1880*. Oxford, United Kingdom: Blackwell, 1992.

Gallagher, Tom. *Portugal: A Twentieth-Century Interpretation*. Dover, N.H.: Manchester University Press, 1983.

Garvin, Tom. *Nationalist Revolutionaries in Ireland, 1858–1928*. Oxford: Clarendon Press, 1988.

Hampton, Norman. *The First European Revolution, 1776–1815*. New York: Harcourt, Brace and World, 1969.

Harvey, Robert. *Portugal: Birth of a Democracy*. London: Macmillan Press, 1978.

Huard, R. *La préhistoire des partis: le mouvement républicain en Bas-Languedoc: 1848–1881*. Paris, 1982.

Joes, Anthony James. *Mussolini*. New York: F. Watts, 1982.

Johnson, Douglas W.J., Editor. *French Society and the Revolution*. Cambridge, Mass.: Cambridge University Press, 1976.

Kim, Kyung-Won. *Revolution and International System*. New York: New York University Press, 1970.

Kirchberger, Joe H. *The French Revolution and Napoleon: An Eyewitness History*. New York: Facts on File, 1989.

Lefebvre, George. *The Great Fear of 1789: Rival Panic in Revolutionary France*. London: NLB, 1973.

Lefebvre, G. *La Grande Peur.* Paris: Éditions Social, 1953.

Lefebvre, G. *La Révolution Française,* Paris: PUF, 1963.

Ligou, D. *Frédéric Desmons et la Franc-Maçonnerie sous la 3e République.* Paris, 1968.

Mack Smith, Dennis. *Mazzini.* New Haven: Yale University Press, 1994.

Mack Smith, Dennis. *Mussolini.* London: Weidenfeld and Nicolson, 1981.

Mathiez, Albert. *After Robiespierre: The Thermidorian Reaction.* New York: The Universal Library, Grosset and Dunlap, 1965.

Opello, Walter C. *Portugal: From Monarchy to Pluralist Democracy.* Boulder, Colo.: Westview Press, 1991.

Ozouf, Mona. *Festivals and the French Revolution.* Cambridge, Mass.: Harvard University Press, 1988.

Paxton, John. *Companion to the French Revolution.* New York: Facts on File, 1988.

Popkin, Jeremy D. *Revolutionary News: The Press in France, 1789–1799.* Durham, N.C.: Duke University Press, 1990.

Ritter, Joachim. *Hegel and the French Revolution: Essays on the Philosophy of Right.* Cambridge, Mass.: MIT Press, 1982.

Roberts, James. *The Counter-Revolution in France, 1787–1830.* New York: St Martin's Press, 1990.

Ross, Steven T. *The French Revolution: Conflict or Continuity?* New York: Holt, Rinehart and Winston, 1971.

Rudé, G., *la Foule dans la Révolution Française,* Paris, Maspero, 1982.

Rudé, George. *The French Revolution.* London: Weidenfeld and Nicholson, 1989.

Schama, Simon. *Citizens: A Chronicle of the French Revolution, 1789–1799.* New York: Alfred A. Knopf, 1989.

Soares, Mario. *Portugal's Struggle for Liberty* (trans. Mary Gawsworth). London: G. Allen and Unwin, 1975.

Soboul, Albert. *A Short Story of the French Revolution, 1789–1799.* Berkeley: University of California Press, 1977.

Soboul, Albert. *The French Revolution 1787–1799: From the Storming of the Bastille to Napolean.* New York: Vintage Books, 1975.

Sole, Jacques. *Questions of the French Revolution: A Historical Overview.* New York: Pantheon Books, 1989.

Sperber, Jonathan. *Rhineland Radicals: The Democratic Movement and the Revolution of 1848–1849.* Princeton: Princeton University Press, 1991.

Sutherland, Donald M.G. *France, 1789–1815: Revolution and Counterrevolution*. New York: Oxford University Press, 1986.

Sydenham, Michael John. *The First French Republic, 1792–1804*. London: B.T. Batsford, 1974.

Valiulis, Maryann Gialanella. *Portrait of a Revolutionary: General Richard Mulcahy and the Founding of the Irish Free State*. Dublin: Irish Academic Press, 1992.

Vovell, M., *la Chute de la monarchie 1787–1792,* Paris, Points-Histoire, Seuil, 1972.

Vovell, Michel. *The Fall of the French Monarchy, 1787–1792*. Cambridge University Press, 1983.

Wells, Roger. *Insurrection: The British Experience 1795–1803*. Gloucester, Mass.: Alan Sutton, 1986.

Wiarda, Howard John. *Corporatism and Development: The Portuguese Experience*. Amherst: University of Massachusetts Press, 1977.

Wright, David Gordon. *Revolution and Terror in France, 1789–1795*. Harlow, United Kingdom: Longman, 1981.

INDEX

A

Abacha, Sani → Nigeria, Coups

'Abdullah ibn Muhammad → Mahdiyya

Abramovich, Rafael → Bund

Abu Musa → Palestine Liberation Organization (PLO)

Abu Musa Revolt → Fatah

Acevedo, Maria Concepcion → Cristero Revolution

Achoris → Egypt, Rebellion, Revolts and Revolutions

Aden Trade Unions Congress (ATUC) → al-Asnaj, 'Abdullah

Aelianus → Bagaudae

Afghan Mellat → Afghanistan Revolutions

African Democratic Organization → Guinean Independence

African People's Organization → African National Congress (ANC)

Aguilera, Francisco Vicente → Ten-Year War, Cuba

Aguiyi-Ironsi, Johnson → Nigeria, Coups

Ahad Ha'am → Zionism

al-Ajlani, Munir → al-Qudsi, Nazem

Albanian Cultural Association → Vequilharxhi, Naum

d'Alema, Massimo → Communist Party of Italy (PCI)

Alexeev, Peter → Pan-Russian Social Revolutionary Organization

'Ali, Hussein ibn → Arab National Movement, Nationalism; Arab Revolt

Ali, Muhammad and Shaukat → Khilafat Movement

All African People's Conference → Lumumba, Patrice Hemery

All-China Congress of Soviets → Chinese Communist Revolution; Chinese Soviet Republic

All-China Federation of Trade Unions → Chinese Communist Revolution

All-Russian Central Executive Committee of the Soviets → Russian Revolution of 1917

Allgemeiner Deutscher Arbeiterverein (General Association of German Workers) → Lassalle, Ferdinand

Altamirano, Luis → Chile, Coups

Amandus → Bagaudae

Amin, Hafizullah → Afghanistan Revolutions

Amis de la Verité → Socialism

Amis de Peuple → Socialism

al-Amri, Hassan → Yemen, Revolutions

Amyrtaeus → Egypt, Rebellion, Revolts and Revolutions

Anderson, James → Freemasonry, French

Anthony, Susan → Suffragettes

Anti-Fascist Bloc → Anielewicz, Mordecai

Anti-Fascist Council of National Liberation (AVNOJ) → Yugoslavia, Communist Takeover

Anti-Fascist Democratic Bloc → German Democratic Republic (GDR)

Anti-Fascist Organization (AFO) → Aung San, Thakin

Anti-Fascist People's Freedom League (AFPFL) → Aung San, General Thakin; Thakin Soe

Anya Nya → Garang, John

Arab Club → al-Husseini, Hajj (Muhammad) Amin

Arab Liberation Movement → Syria, Coups

Arab Pact (al-'Ahd) → Arab National Movement, Nationalism

Arab Socialism → Nasser, Gamal Abdul

Arab Socialist Party → Syria, Coups

Arab Socialist Resurrection Party → Syrian Ba'ath Party

Arakha → Darius I, General Rebellion Against

Arango, Doroteo → Villa, Pancho

Arditi → Fascism

Ariobarzanus → Satraps: Revolts of

Aristagores → Ionia Revolt

Armed Forces Revolutionary Council (AFRC) → Rawlings, Jerry John

Armed Forces Union → Sunay, Cevdet

M

Macé, Jean → Freemasonry, French

Maceo, Antonio → Ten-Year War, Cuba

Magloire, Paul E. → Duvalier, François

Maher, Ahmad → WAFD

Makaresos, Nikolaos → Colonels' Coup

Makhaysky, Vatslav K. → Anarchism, Russian

Mamun, Abdul → Almohades

Manifesto of 2000 Words → Prague, Spring of 1968

Manuilski, Dmitri → Antonov-Ovseenko, Vladimir Alexandrovich

Mar, Earl of → Fifteen Rebellion

Marcel, Etienne → Jacquerie

Marchais, Georges → Communist Party of France (PCF)

Marduk-apla-iddina → Babylon, Revolt of 710–689 B.C.

Marduk-zakirshumi II → Babylon, Revolt of 710–689 B.C.

Mariategui, José Carlos → Shining Path

Martiya → Darius I, General Rebellion Against

Marylebone Radical Association O'Connor, Feargus

Marzel, Baruch → Kach

al-Masri, 'Aziz 'Ali → Arab Revolt

Maurice of Nassau → Netherlands, Revolt of the

Mazumadar, Charu → Naxalites

Medvedev, Roy → Dissent (Soviet Union)

Mehring, Franz → Luxemburg, Rosa; Spartakists

Mejia, Tomas → Sierra Gorda Rebellion

Melanchthon, Philipp → Luther, Martin

Mesame Dasi → Tzulukidze,

Alexandre; Tchkheidze, Nikolay (Karlo); Zhordania, Noe

Metla, P. → Byelorussian Peasants-Workers Gromada

Mif, Pavel → Wang Ming

Mihailovic, Draza → Chetniks

Mikhaylov, Alexander D. → Land and Liberty (Zemlya i Volya)

Militant Clergy Abroad → Mohtashemi, Hojatul-Islam 'Ali Akbar

Militant Clergy Association → Mahdavi-Kani, Muhammad Reza

Miranda, Francisco de → Bolívar, Simon

Mkwawa → Hehe Rebellion

Mohapi, Mapetla → Black Consciousness Movement

Moi, Daniel arap → Kenya African Union (KANU)

Montagnards → Jacobins

Monteiro, Góis → Vargas, Getulio

Montgomery Improvement Association → King, Martin Luther Jr.

Moplah Rebellion → Khilafat Movement

Moscow Society for Improving the Lot of Women → Armand, Inessa Fyodorovna

Mott, Lucretia → Stanton, Elizabeth Cady

Movimiento de Liberacion Nacional (MLN) → Castillo Armas, Carlos

Muhammad Ahmad ibn 'Abdullah → Mahdiyya

Muhammad, Elijah → Black Muslims; Malcolm X

Muhammad, Sinan ibn Salman ibn → Assassins

Muhammed, Murtula Ramat → Nigeria, Coups

al-Muntada al-Adabi → Arab National Movement, Nationalism

Murad Bey → Young Turks

Muridism → Shamil

Mushezib-Marduk → Babylon, Revolt of 710–689 B.C.

N

Nabu-bel-shumati → Babylon, Revolt of 652–648 B.C.

al-Nadi al-'Arabi → Al-Husseini, Hajj (Muhammad) Amin

Nadintu-Bel → Darius I, General Rebellion Against

Narváez, Ramón María → Spain, Revolts and Revolutions

Nassau, Maurice of → Netherlands, Revolt of the

Nation of Islam → Malcolm X

National Bloc → al-Atassi, Hashem

National Council of the Corporations → Fascism

National Front → Bakhtiar, Shahpur; Bani-Sadr, Abolhassan; Bazargan, Mehdi; al-Mahdi, al-Sadeq

National Guard → French Revolution

National Liberation Alliance → Prestes, Luiz Carlos

National Patriotic Front of Liberia (NPFL) → Liberian Civil War

National Progressive Front → Hourani, Akram

National Resistance Council → Bani-Sadr, Abolhassan; Rajavi, Mas'ud

National Union for the Total Independence of Angola (UNITA) → Savimbi, Jonas Malheiro

National Union of South African Students → Biko, Stephen; Black Consciousness Movement

National Woman Suffrage Association → Stanton, Elizabeth Cady

National Woman's Loyal League → Stanton, Elizabeth Cady

CHRONOLOGICAL INDEX

ACKNOWLEDGMENTS

The Publishers wish to express their appreciation to the following individuals and institutions for their help:

Illustrations:
p. 15 National Archives and Records Administration; p. 25 Reproduced from the collections of the Library of Congress; p. 31 State of Israel Government Press Office; p. 43 Popperfoto; p. 54 Popperfoto; p. 55 (top left) The Department of Antiquities, Israel Ministry of Education; p. 55 (bottom right) Musée Carnavalet, Paris; p. 57 Mansell Collection, London; p. 58 Popperfoto; p. 63 (top left) Popperfoto; p. 63 (bottom right) State of Israel Government Press Office; p. 71 The Jerusalem Publishing House; p. 73 Planet News Ltd.; pp. 74, 75, 76 Popperfoto; p. 84 University Library, Geneva; pp. 88, 94 Popperfoto; p. 118 John R. Freeman; pp. 129, 132, 136 Popperfoto; p. 142 Mansell Collection, London; p. 159 copyright photo: Erich Lessing—Musée Carnavalet, Paris; p. 166 copyright photo: Erich Lessing—Musée de la Publicite, Paris; p. 169 Popperfoto; p. 171 Scala; p. 183 copyright photo: Erich Lessing—Musée des Beaux-Arts, Bordeaux; p. 200 United States Holocaust Memorial Museum; p. 207 Popperfoto; p. 209 Elsevier Publishing Projects, Amsterdam; p. 213 John R. Freeman; p. 220 Magnum Photos Ltd.; p. 221 Popperfoto; p. 226 National Archives and Records Administration; p. 231 Mansell Collection, London; p. 235 Central Zionist Archives; pp. 236, 237, 240 Popperfoto; p. 243 Popperfoto; p. 256 Roger-Viollet, Paris; p. 265 Warsaw National Museum; p. 272 Gordon Parks; pp. 273, 274 Popperfoto; p. 275 Associated Press; p. 277 copyright photo: Erich Lessing—Tretyakov Gallery, Moscow; p. 279 Il Messaggero, Rome; p. 286 The Jerusalem Publishing House; p. 304 Foto Italia; p. 308 Magnum Photos Ltd.; p. 311 Popperfoto; p. 316 Popperfoto; p. 318 Associate Press; p. 323 Mansell Collection, London; p. 328 The Jerusalem Publishing House; p. 334 Popperfoto; p. 337 Jewish Historical Museum; p. 358 (left) Popperfoto; p. 361 Musée Carnavalet, Paris; p. 365 copyright photo: Erich Lessing—Lenin Library, Moscow; p. 372 British Museum, London; p. 374 Museo della Basilica di S. Francesco, Assisi; p. 413 Popperfoto; p. 415 Foto Italia; p. 416 Mansell Collection, London; p. 427 Popperfoto; p. 434 Mansell Collection, London; p. 435 British Royal Collection, Windsor Castle, Crown copyright.

Bibliographical Research: Avi Markus, Kevin Rosner.

Typesetting and Pagination: Devorah Sowalsky Meyer—The Jerusalem Publishing House.

Secretary: Shoshanna Lewis.

Films: Printone Ltd., Jerusalem.

Printing and Binding: Mandarin Offset Ltd., Hong Kong.